The Illustrated Bible Dictionary

George W. Knight
with Rayburn W. Ray

BARBOUR
PUBLISHING

© 2005 by George W. Knight and Rayburn W. Ray

ISBN 978-1-59789-852-2

Cover images © HIP/Art Resources, NY (top); Greg Schneider (bottom)

Published by Barbour Publishing, Inc., P.O. Box 719, Uhrichsville, Ohio 44683
www.barbourbooks.com

Our mission is to publish and distribute inspirational products offering exceptional value and biblical encouragement to the masses.

Member of the
Evangelical Christian
Publishers Association

Printed in Malaysia.

To all my Bible teachers and students,
past and present,
who have sparked my commitment
to a lifetime of study
of God's Word.

Acknowledgments

A book like this doesn't happen without the encouragement and support of many people. My special thanks to those who have played a major role in its creation.

Paul K. Muckley, senior editor for non-fiction at Barbour Publishing, served as cheerleader and problem-solver for the entire project. He worked under an impossible schedule to make sure all the pieces came together in the right order. My thanks to him for a job well done.

As an editor myself, I realize that behind-the-scenes book publishing professionals seldom get the recognition they deserve. So let me say a special "thank you" to those creative professionals on the production team who assisted Paul so capably: Steve Miller, photo researcher; Jason Rovenstine, design director; Robyn Martins, page designer; Lauren Schneider, proofreader; and others who played smaller but very important roles in the process.

I am also grateful to my friend and colleague, Rayburn Ray, who worked with me several years ago to cowrite *The Layman's Bible Dictionary*, on which this book is based. My thanks for Rayburn's contribution to this project, and his continuing friendship.

Finally, I express the warmest "thank you" of all to my wife, Dorothy. For more than forty years she has encouraged me in my writing efforts. She has tolerated my "creative moodiness," never complaining about the hours I spend at the typewriter or word processor. In recent years, she has even gone the second mile by helping me with some of the "grunt work" required for the creation of a reference book such as this—checking scripture references, doing proofreading, and compiling indexes. King Solomon, author of the book of Proverbs, described her well: "She openeth her mouth with wisdom; and in her tongue is the law of kindness. . . . Let her own works praise her in the gates" (Proverbs 31:26, 31).

Introduction

A s a regular, everyday student of the Bible, you deserve biblical study tools that are handy, affordable, and easy to understand. And that's exactly what you get in *The Illustrated Bible Dictionary*.

This book contains articles on the most important persons, places, objects, and doctrines mentioned in the Bible. Concordance entries of key Bible words and phrases are placed alphabetically among the dictionary articles.

Another handy feature is the maps section at the back of the book. Whenever a city, nation, or other biblical place name is mentioned, these locations are cross-referenced in the text to the appropriate maps. This valuable visual aid should give you a better understanding of biblical geography. The map icon, shown at left, includes the appropriate map number in the maroon circle and coordinates for identifying the location in the golden rectangle below. The map section begins on page 359.

Speaking of visual aids, your study and research will also be enhanced by the drawings and photographs—most of them in full color—of Bible places and personalities throughout the book. These art pieces were specifically selected to make the scriptures come alive for students of God's Word.

You will also enjoy the abundance of scripture references included. These are intended to encourage you to dig deeper in your study of the Bible. The copious cross-references to related subjects in the articles also serve this same practical purpose.

The translation on which this book is based is the familiar Authorized, or King James Version. But variant readings are cited from the New International Version and the New Revised Standard Version to clarify obscure words and phrases. Variant readings for a key word from the NIV and NRSV are included in parentheses immediately following that word. For example, **FIRMAMANT (EXPANSE, DOME).** The word *firmament,* the key word for this article, is from the KJV. *Expanse* and *Dome* are how the word firmament is rendered by the NIV and the NRSV in the account of creation in Genesis 1:6. This helpful format makes the book usable with these two modern translations, in addition to the King James Version.

Another helpful feature is the inclusion of all variant names for a person or place recorded in the King James Version itself. For example, the ancient kingdom of Babylonia is also referred to in the KJV as Sheshach, Shinar, and Chaldea. This is how the key word is listed in the entry on Babylonia: **BABYLONIA/SHESHACH/SHINAR/CHALDEA.** The slash marks between these words indicate these are variant names for Babylonia that occur at different places in the KJV. These variant names are also cross-referenced to Babylonia at the appropriate places in the dictionary text. Example: **SHESHACH:** See *Babylonia.* This helpful feature should clear up some of the confusion about variant biblical names in the King James Version for serious students of the scriptures.

My prayer is that *The Illustrated Bible Dictionary* will serve as a valuable source of information for all students who, like the citizens of Berea in the New Testament, are eager to learn more about the Bible, studying expectantly and "with all readiness of mind" (Acts 17:11).

GEORGE W. KNIGHT
NASHVILLE, TENNESSEE

Abbreviations for Books of the Bible

Biblical books noted in *The Illustrated Bible Dictionary* will be abbreviated as follows:

Old Testament

Gen.	Genesis
Exod.	Exodus
Lev.	Leviticus
Num.	Numbers
Deut.	Deuteronomy
Josh.	Joshua
Judg.	Judges
Ruth	Ruth
1 Sam.	1 Samuel
2 Sam.	2 Samuel
1 Kings	1 Kings
2 Kings	2 Kings
1 Chron.	1 Chronicles
2 Chron.	2 Chronicles
Ezra	Ezra
Neh.	Nehemiah
Esther	Esther
Job	Job
Ps./Pss.	Psalm/Psalms
Prov.	Proverbs
Eccles.	Ecclesiastes
Song of Sol.	Song of Solomon
Isa.	Isaiah
Jer.	Jeremiah
Lam.	Lamentations
Ezek.	Ezekiel
Dan.	Daniel
Hosea	Hosea
Joel	Joel
Amos	Amos
Obad.	Obadiah
Jon.	Jonah
Mic.	Micah
Nah.	Nahum
Hab.	Habakkuk
Zeph.	Zephaniah
Hag.	Haggai
Zech.	Zechariah
Mal.	Malachi

New Testament

Matt.	Matthew
Mark	Mark
Luke	Luke
John	John
Acts	Acts
Rom.	Romans
1 Cor.	1 Corinthians
2 Cor.	2 Corinthians
Gal.	Galatians
Eph.	Ephesians
Phil.	Philippians
Col.	Colossians
1 Thess.	1 Thessalonians
2 Thess.	2 Thessalonians
1 Tim.	1 Timothy
2 Tim.	2 Timothy
Titus	Titus
Philem.	Philemon
Heb.	Hebrews
James	James
1 Pet.	1 Peter
2 Pet.	2 Peter
1 John	1 John
2 John	2 John
3 John	3 John
Jude	Jude
Rev.	Revelation

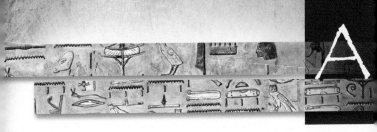

AARON. The first high priest of the Israelites (Exod. 28:1) and Moses' brother (Exod. 4:14). Designated by God as spokesman for Moses (Exod. 4:13–16), Aaron helped Moses lead the Hebrew slaves out of Egypt (Exod. 7:8–12). In the wilderness, he was consecrated by God as Israel's first high priest, and his sons inherited this position from their father (Num. 3:38). Like Moses, Aaron was not allowed to enter the Promised Land because of his act of unfaithfulness in the wilderness (Num. 20:6–12). His earthly priesthood is compared unfavorably to the eternal priesthood of Christ (Heb. 5:4; 7:11). See also *High Priest; Priest.*

AARONITES. Descendants of Aaron who were a part of the priestly tribe of Levi. A large force of Aaronites fought with David against King Saul (1 Chron. 12:23–27).

AB. The fifth month of the Jewish year, roughly equivalent to our modern August. This month is referred to, though not specifically by name, in Num. 33:38.

ABADDON/APOLLYON. A Hebrew word meaning "destruction," used to characterize the angel of the bottomless pit (Rev. 9:11). *Apollyon:* Greek form.

ABANA RIVER. A river of Syria that flowed through the

AARON. Aaron, older brother of Moses, became Israel's first high priest—starting a family dynasty of priests that lasted more than a millennium.

2
F
1

city of Damascus. It was mentioned by Naaman the leper as more favorable for bathing than the Jordan River (2 Kings 5:12). See also *Pharpar*.

ABARIM. A rugged mountain range east of the Jordan River in Moab from which Moses viewed the Promised Land before his death (Deut. 32:48–50).

ABASE [D]

Ezek. 21:26 exalt him that is low, and *a* him that is high
Luke 18:14 every one that exalteth himself shall be *a'd*
Phil. 4:12 I [Paul] know…how to be *a'd*…how to abound

ABBA. An Aramaic word meaning "father," used by Jesus while praying in Gethsemane (Mark 14:32, 36). It was also used by Paul to express the Christian's sonship with God the Father (Rom. 8:15).

ABDON. A minor judge of Israel who ruled for eight years (Judg. 12:13–15). See also *Judges of Israel*.

ABED-NEGO/AZARIAH. One of Daniel's three friends. Thrown into the fiery furnace by King Nebuchadnezzar of Babylonia (Dan. 3:13–27), he was later promoted by the king after his miraculous deliverance at the hand of God (Dan. 3:28–30). *Azariah:* Hebrew form (Dan. 1:7).

ABEL

1. Second son of Adam and Eve (Gen. 4:2). Abel's animal sacrifice was pleasing to God (Gen. 4:4). Abel was then killed by his brother Cain in a jealous rage (Gen. 4:5, 8). Jesus regarded "righteous Abel" as the first martyr (Matt. 23:35). Abel's works were called "righteous" (1 John 3:12), and his sacrifices were commended as a testimony of faith (Heb. 11:4).

2. A fortified city in northern Israel where Sheba sought refuge during his rebellion against David. The citizens of Abel killed Sheba to end the siege by the king's army (2 Sam. 20:14–22).

ABIA. See *Abijah*.

ABIAH. A son of Samuel and corrupt judge of Israel. Abiah's dishonesty, along with that of his brother Joel, led the people to ask Samuel to appoint a king to rule the nation (1 Sam. 8:2–5). See also *Joel*, No. 2.

ABIATHAR. A high priest under David who remained faithful to the king during Absalom's rebellion (2 Sam. 15:24–35). He was later banished from the royal court by Solomon for supporting Adonijah as king (1 Kings 1:7–25; 2:22–35).

ABIB/NISAN. The first month of the Hebrew year, the time when barley opened (Exod. 13:4). Roughly equivalent to our modern April, this month was known as *Nisan* after the Babylonian Exile (Esther 3:7).

ABIDE [ING, TH]

Ps. 91:1 *a* under the shadow of the Almighty
Luke 2:8 shepherds *a'ing* in the field
John 3:36 believeth not the Son…wrath…*a'th* on him
John 14:16 another Comforter…may *a* with you for ever
John 15:5 He that *a'th* in me [Jesus]…bringeth…fruit
1 Cor. 13:13 *a'th* faith, hope, charity
1 John 2:10 He that loveth his brother *a'th* in the light
1 John 2:17 he that doeth the will of God *a'th* for ever

ABIGAIL. A wife of David and the mother of Chileab (2 Sam. 3:3). While married to Nabal, Abigail appeased David's anger after Nabal rejected David's servants (1 Sam. 25:14–35). See also *Nabal*.

ABIHU. One of Aaron's four sons. Abihu and his brother Nadab offered "strange fire," or a forbidden sacrifice, to God—an act for which they were destroyed by fire from God (Lev. 10:1–7). See also *Nadab*, No. 1.

ABIJAH/ABIJAM/ABIA. The son and successor of Rehoboam as king of Judah (reigned about 913–911 B.C.; 2 Chron. 11:20–22). *Abijam:* 1 Kings 14:31; *Abia:* Jesus' ancestry (Matt. 1:7).

ABILENE. A province of Syria governed by the tetrarch Lysanias during the ministry of John the Baptist (Luke 3:1–2). See also *Lysanias.*

ABIMELECH
1. A Philistine king of Gerar in Abraham's time. He took Sarah, Abraham's wife, into his harem, then returned her to Abraham when he was informed in a dream that she was married (Gen. 20:1–18).
2. A rebellious son of Gideon who killed all his brothers after his father's death in an attempt to become king over all Israel (Judg. 9:5–22). He was killed by his armorbearer after a woman dropped a stone on his head from a city wall (Judg. 9:50–54).

ABINADAB
1. A man of Kirjath-jearim whose household kept the ark of the covenant for twenty years after it was returned by the Philistines (1 Sam. 7:1–2).
2. A son of King Saul killed at Gilboa, along with Jonathan (1 Chron. 10:1–6).

ABIRAM. A rebel against Moses in the wilderness who died in an earthquake because of his disobedience (Num. 16:1–33).

ABISHAG. A young woman who served as David's nurse in his old age (1 Kings 1:1–15).

David's son Adonijah was killed by Solomon for desiring to marry her after David's death (1 Kings 2:13–25).

ABISHAI. The deputy commander of David's army (2 Sam. 10:9–10). Loyal to David in Absalom's rebellion (2 Sam. 16:9–12), he also saved David's life by killing a giant (2 Sam. 21:16–17).

ABISHALOM. See *Absalom.*

ABLUTION. The ceremonial washing of a person's body or clothing to make him pure. Such washing was commanded in the O.T. Law (Exod. 40:12–13). True cleansing is found only in the blood of Christ (Rev. 1:5). See also *Clean.*

ABNER. The commander-in-chief of Saul's army. He introduced David to King Saul (1 Sam. 17:55–58) and established Saul's son Ish-bosheth as king after Saul's death (2 Sam. 2:8–10). Later he shifted his loyalty to David and persuaded all the tribes of Israel to follow David's leadership (2 Sam. 3:17–21).

ABOLISH [ED]
Isa. 2:18 the idols he [God] shall utterly *a*
Isa. 51:6 my [God's] righteousness shall not be *a'ed*
2 Tim. 1:10 Jesus Christ, who hath *a'ed* death

ABOMINATION. Something considered repulsive by the Hebrews. Examples of these despised practices are heathen idolatry (Deut. 7:25–26), blemished animal sacrifices (Deut. 17:1), sexual transgressions (Lev. 18), child sacrifice (Deut. 12:31), and the practice of witchcraft, magic, and spiritism (Deut. 18:9–12).

ABOMINATION OF DESOLATION. The action of Antiochus Epiphanes in sacrificing a pig in the Jewish temple about 165 B.C. This despised act of the Syrian ruler is considered fulfillment of Daniel's prophecy (Dan. 9:24–27; Matt. 24:15). See also *Antiochus IV Epiphanes; Maccabees.*

THINGS CONSIDERED ABOMINABLE BY THE LORD

1. Graven images, or idols (Deut. 7:26)
2. The froward, or wicked (Prov. 3:32)
3. Cheating with a false balance (Prov. 11:1)
4. Lying lips (Prov. 12:22)
5. Sacrifice of the wicked (Prov. 15:8)
6. Thoughts of the wicked (Prov. 15:26)
7. Vanity and pride (Prov. 16:5)

ABOUND [ED]

Rom. 5:15 grace of God… *a'ed* unto many
Rom. 5:20 grace did much more *a*
Rom. 6:1 continue in sin, that grace may *a*?
Rom. 15:13 *a* in hope, through the…Holy Ghost
Eph. 1:8 he [God] hath *a'ed* toward us in all wisdom
Phil. 4:12 I [Paul] know…how to be abased…how to *a*

ABOVE

Gen. 1:7 God…divided the waters… *a* the firmament
Deut. 7:6 chosen thee to be a special people… *a* all people
1 Chron. 16:25 great is the LORD…to be feared *a* all gods
Ps. 95:3 the LORD is…a great King *a* all gods
Prov. 31:10 a virtuous woman? For her price is far *a* rubies
Jer. 17:9 heart is deceitful *a* all things
Matt. 10:24 The disciple is not *a* his master
1 Cor. 10:13 God…not suffer you…tempted *a*…ye are able
Eph. 4:6 One God…who is *a* all, and through all
Phil. 2:9 given him [Jesus] a name… *a* every name
Col. 3:1 seek those things which are *a*
James 1:17 Every good…and…perfect gift is from *a*

ABRAHAM/ABRAM. The father of the nation of Israel (Ps. 105:6, 9). A native of Ur in southern Babylonia, he married Sarah and went to Haran (Gen. 11:26–31). Later he obeyed God's call to leave Haran for a "land that I will shew thee" (Gen. 12:1–5). God made a covenant with Abraham to bless all nations of the world through him (Gen. 12:2–3). The land of Canaan was also promised to Abraham's descendants (Gen. 12:7; 13:14–18).

Although Abraham and Sarah were childless at an advanced age, God promised Abraham a son (Gen. 15:1–4; 17:19). At Sarah's urging, Abraham fathered Ishmael by Sarah's servant Hagar (Gen. 16:1–4, 15). God changed the names of Abraham and Sarah from *Abram* and *Sarai* (Gen. 17:5, 15) and established circumcision as a covenant sign (Gen. 17:10–14). The covenant was to be fulfilled through Isaac rather than Ishmael (Gen. 17:20–21; Gal. 4:22–31). Isaac was born in the couple's old age (Gen. 21:1–7).

As a test of faith, God asked Abraham to sacrifice Isaac (Gen. 22:1–13). Then God Himself intervened to save Isaac and again promised to bless Abraham for his unwavering faith (Gen. 22:16–18). Abraham died at 175 years of age and was buried beside Sarah near Hebron (Gen. 25:7–10).

Abraham remains a model of righteousness and faith for all believers (Gen. 26:24; Ps. 47:9; Isa. 41:8). An ancestor of Christ, he is viewed as a spiritual father of all who share a like faith in Christ (Matt. 1:1; 3:9; Gal. 3:6–9). See also *Sarah.*

ABRAHAM'S BOSOM. A symbolic expression for the blissful state after death (Luke 16:22). The Jews believed they joined their forefathers, particularly "father Abraham," upon their death (Gen. 15:15).

ABSALOM/ABISHALOM. The vain, rebellious son of David (2 Sam. 3:3). He killed his brother Amnon for molesting their sister Tamar (2 Sam. 13:22–33). Absalom conspired against David and seized Jerusalem

(2 Sam. 15:1–29). Massing an army against David (2 Sam. 17:24–26), he was killed by David's commander Joab after his hair was tangled in a tree (2 Sam. 18:9–18). David mourned grievously at Absalom's death (2 Sam. 18:19–33). *Abishalom:* 1 Kings 15:2, 10. See also *David.*

ABSTINENCE. To refrain from eating or drinking harmful substances or participating in sinful acts. Priests and Nazirites abstained from strong drink (Num. 6:1–4). Gentile Christians were advised to abstain from fornication and idolatry (Acts 15:20). All believers are counseled by Paul to refrain from any practices that might offend a weak brother (Rom. 14:21). See also *Moderation; Temperance.*

ABUNDANCE
Ps. 37:11 meek shall…delight…in the *a* of peace
Eccles. 5:12 *a* of the rich will not suffer him to sleep
Matt. 12:34 out of the *a* of the heart the mouth speaketh
Luke 12:15 life consisteth not in the *a*…he possesseth

ABUNDANT
2 Cor. 4:15 *a* grace might…redound to the glory of God
2 Cor. 11:23 in labours more *a*, in stripes above measure
1 Tim. 1:14 grace of our Lord was exceeding *a* with faith

ABYSS/BOTTOMLESS PIT. A word translated literally as "bottomless pit" in the book of Revelation, indicating the place where Satan dwells (Rev. 9:1–2, 11).

ABRAHAM. In a test of faith, God asked Abraham to sacrifice his son Isaac. An angel stops Abraham at the last moment, and Isaac grows up to become one of the fathers of the Jewish nation.

ACACIA. See *Shittah*.

ACCAD (AKKAD). A fortified city built by Nimrod, a descendant of Noah (Gen. 10:8–10), in the land of Shinar—an ancient kingdom between the Tigris and Euphrates rivers. *Akkad:* NIV.

ACCEPT [ED]
Job 42:9 the LORD also *a'ed* Job
Jer. 37:20 my supplication...be *a'ed* before thee [God]
Amos 5:22 burnt offerings...I [God] will not *a* them
Luke 4:24 No prophet is *a'ed* in his own country
Acts 10:35 feareth him [God]...is *a'ed* with him

ACCEPTABLE
Ps. 19:14 meditation of my heart...*a* in thy [God's] sight
Prov. 21:3 To do justice...is more *a*...than sacrifice
Isa. 61:2 To proclaim the *a* year of the LORD
Rom. 12:1 bodies a living sacrifice...*a* unto God
Eph. 5:10 Proving what is *a* unto the Lord
1 Tim. 2:3 good and *a* in the sight of God
1 Pet. 2:5 spiritual sacrifices, *a* to God by Jesus Christ

ACCESS
Rom. 5:2 By whom [Jesus]...*a*...into this grace
Eph. 2:18 through him [Jesus]...*a*...unto the Father
Eph. 3:12 In whom [Jesus]...*a* with confidence

ACCHO/ACRE (ACCO).
A coastal city near Mount Carmel in the territory of Asher (Judg. 1:31). This is the same city as N.T. *Ptolemais* (Acts 21:7). It is known today as *Acre*. *Acco:* NIV, NRSV.

ACCOMPLISHED
Isa. 40:2 Jerusalem...her warfare is *a*
Luke 2:6 days were *a* that she [Mary] should be delivered
John 19:28 Jesus knowing that all things were now *a*

ACCORD
Acts 1:14 These all continued with one *a* in prayer
Acts 2:1 Pentecost was...come, they were all with one *a*
Acts 2:46 one *a*...and breaking bread from house to house
Phil. 2:2 having the same love, being of one *a*

ACCOUNT [ED]
Ps. 144:3 son of man, that thou makest *a* of him!
Matt. 12:36 idle word that men...speak, they shall give *a*
Luke 21:36 *a'ed* worthy to...stand before the Son of man
Rom. 14:12 every one...shall give *a* of himself to God
Gal. 3:6 Abraham believed God...*a'ed*...for righteousness
1 Pet. 4:5 give *a* to him...ready to judge...the dead

ACCOUNTABILITY. The biblical principle that each person is answerable to God and responsible for his or her actions (Rom. 14:12). Accountability also involves the obligation to act with love toward fellow believers (Rom. 14:15–19).

ACCURSED
Josh. 7:1 For Achan...took of the *a* thing
Rom. 9:3 myself [Paul] were *a* from Christ for...kinsmen
1 Cor. 12:3 no man speaking by the Spirit...calleth Jesus *a*

ACCUSATION
Matt. 27:37 his *a*...Jesus the King of the Jews
Luke 6:7 watched him [Jesus]...find an *a* against him
John 18:29 Pilate...said, What *a*...against this man [Jesus]

ACCUSE [D]
Matt. 12:10 heal...sabbath day...might *a* him [Jesus]
Matt. 27:12 *a'd* of the chief priests...he [Jesus] answered nothing
Luke 23:2 *a* him [Jesus]...perverting the nation

ACELDAMA (AKELDAMA, HAKEL-DAMA). A field near Jerusalem purchased with the money that Judas was paid to betray Jesus. The name means "field of blood" (Acts 1:15–19). *Akeldama:* NIV; *Hakeldama:* NRSV.

ACHAIA. A province of Greece visited by the apostle Paul (Acts 18:12). Christians at Achaia contributed to their impoverished brethren at Jerusalem (Rom. 15:26).

ACHAN/ACHAR. A warrior under Joshua who was stoned to death for withholding the spoils of war (Josh. 7:16–25). *Achar:* 1 Chron. 2:7.

ACHAZ. See *Ahaz.*

ACHISH. A Philistine king of the city of Gath who provided refuge to David when he fled from King Saul (1 Sam. 21:10–15; 27:5–7).

ACHMETHA (ECBATANA). The capital city of the empire of the Medes and later one of the capitals of the Persian Empire (Ezra 6:2). *Ecbatana:* NIV, NRSV.

ACKNOWLEDGE
Ps. 51:3 I *a* my transgressions...my sin is ever before me
Prov. 3:6 ways *a* him [God], and he shall direct thy paths
Jer. 14:20 *a*, O Lord, our wickedness...sinned against thee

ACRE. See *Accho.*

ACTS
Deut. 11:7 eyes have seen all the great *a* of the Lord
Ps. 103:7 his [God's] *a* unto the children of Israel
Ps. 150:2 Praise him [God] for his mighty *a*

ACTS OF THE APOSTLES. The one book of history in the N.T. that traces the expansion and development of the early church from the ascension of Jesus to Paul's imprisonment in Rome—a period of about thirty-five years. Written by Luke as a companion or sequel to his Gospel and addressed to Theophilus (see Luke 1:3–4; Acts 1:1–2), Acts shows clearly how the Christian witness spread in accordance with the Great Commission of Jesus (see Acts 1:8): (1) in Jerusalem (1:1–8:3), (2) throughout Judea and Samaria (8:4–12:25), and (3) to the entire world (12:26–28:31). See also *Luke.*

ADAM. The first man. Created in God's image (Gen. 1:26–27), Adam was an upright and intelligent being (Gen. 2:19–20)—the first worker (Gen. 2:8, 15) and the first husband (Gen. 2:18–25). He received God's law

(Gen. 2:16–17) and knowingly sinned, along with Eve (Gen. 3:6). Their sin resulted in broken fellowship with the Creator (Gen. 3:8) and brought God's curse (Gen. 3:14–19) and eviction from Eden (Gen. 3:22–24). Adam fathered Cain and Abel (Gen. 4:1–2), Seth (Gen. 4:25), and other children (Gen. 5:3–4). He died at age 930 (Gen. 5:5).

As head of the human race, Adam introduced sin into the world. He represents the lost and dying condition of all unrepentant sinners (Rom. 5:12–19; 1 Cor. 15:22). But Christ, referred to in the N.T. as the "second Adam," offers deliverance from the curse of sin and death (Rom. 5:14–19; 1 Cor. 15:22). See also *Eden, Garden of; Eve; Fall of Man.*

ADAR. The twelfth month of the Jewish year, roughly equivalent to parts of our modern February and March. Haman ordered the massacre of the Jews on the thirteenth day of this month (Esther 3:13).

ADAMANT. A precious stone, possibly corundum (Ezek. 3:9; Zech. 7:12).

ADDER. See *Asp.*

ADMAH. One of the five cities near the Dead Sea destroyed with Sodom and Gomorrah (Gen. 10:19; Deut. 29:23). See also *Cities of the Plain.*

ADMONISH [ING]
Rom. 15:14 ye also are...to a one another
Col. 3:16 *a'ing* one another in psalms and hymns
2 Thess. 3:15 not as an enemy, but a him as a brother

ADONAI. The Hebrew name for God, translated "Lord" (Ezek. 11:8). See also *God; Lord.*

ADONIJAH. David's fourth son and rival of Solomon for the throne (2 Sam. 3:4; 1 Kings

A

1:5, 30). Adonijah was executed by Solomon (1 Kings 2:19–25).

ADONI-ZEDEC. One of five Amorite kings who joined forces to oppose Joshua's army at Gibeon. He was defeated and killed by Joshua (Josh. 10:1–26).

ADOPTION. The legal act of giving status as a family member (Exod. 2:9–10; Esther 2:7). Paul spoke of adoption in symbolic, spiritual terms (Rom. 11:1–32; Gal. 4:4–7). Adoption as God's children is made possible by faith in Christ (Gal. 3:24–26). See also *Inheritance.*

Rom. 8:15 Spirit of *a,* whereby we cry, Abba
Rom. 8:23 waiting for the *a.*..redemption of our body
Eph. 1:5 predestinated us unto the *a* of children by Jesus

3 C 6 ADORAM. A city in southwest Judah rebuilt and fortified by King Rehoboam, son of Solomon (2 Chron. 11:5, 9). Now known as *Dura,* it is located five miles southwest of Hebron.

ADRAMMELECH. A pagan god worshiped by Assyrian colonists who settled in Samaria after the fall of the Northern Kingdom. Children were offered as sacrifices to this god (2 Kings 17:31).

ADRAMYTTIUM. An important seaport in the Roman province of Asia. Paul boarded a "ship of Adramyttium" to begin his voyage to Rome (Acts 27:2).

4 D 3 ADRIA/ADRIATIC SEA. A name for the central part of the Mediterranean Sea, south of modern Italy. Paul was shipwrecked here during his voyage to Rome (Acts 27:27). *Adriatic Sea:* NIV.

3 C 6 ADULLAM. A royal Canaanite city conquered by Joshua (Josh. 12:7, 15). In later

years David sought refuge in a cave near here (1 Sam. 22:1–2).

ADULTERY. Sexual intercourse with a person other than one's husband or wife. Adultery is specifically prohibited by the seventh of the Ten Commandments (Exod. 20:14). Jesus expanded the concept to prohibit the cultivation of lust and desire that leads to adultery (Matt. 5:28). See also *Fornication.*

Deut. 5:18 Neither shalt thou commit *a*
Prov. 6:32 committeth *a.*..destroyeth his own soul
Mark 10:11 put away his wife, and marry another, committeth *a*
John 8:3 brought unto him [Jesus] a woman taken in *a*
Gal. 5:19 works of the flesh are…*A,* fornication

ADVENT OF CHRIST, THE FIRST. The birth of Jesus Christ in human form to the virgin Mary. His coming was foretold in the O.T. (Isa. 7:14; 9:6). Joseph was reassured by an angel that Mary's pregnancy was supernatural (Matt. 1:20–21). The angel Gabriel announced His coming birth to Mary (Luke 1:26–35).

Jesus was born to Mary in Bethlehem (Matt. 1:25; 2:1). His birth was revealed to shepherds (Luke 2:8–16). Wise men from the East brought gifts to the Christ child (Matt. 2:1–11). His birth was defined as a redemptive mission (Matt. 1:21–23; Luke 2:10–11). It nullified the O.T. ceremonial law (Heb. 9) and introduced the gospel age (Acts 3:20–26). See also *Incarnation of Christ; Virgin Birth.*

ADVERSARY. An active opponent; a term descriptive of Satan (1 Pet. 5:8). God's wisdom is promised to believers when they face the adversary (Luke 21:15). God's judgment will ultimately fall on His enemies (Heb. 10:27).

ADVERSARY [IES]
Deut. 32:43 he [God] will…render vengeance to his *a'ies*
Ps. 69:19 mine *a'ies* are all before thee [God]
Ps. 109:29 Let mine *a'ies* be clothed with shame

ADVENT OF CHRIST, THE FIRST. Displayed on a wall in Bethlehem's Church of the Nativity is this reminder of why the world's oldest church exists. An angel tells shepherds to go into the village to see the newborn Christ. An ancient tradition says Jesus was born in a cave beneath this very church.

Nah. 1:2 Lord will take vengeance on his *a'ies*
Matt. 5:25 Agree with thine *a*...in the way with him
1 Cor. 16:9 great door...is opened...many *a'ies*

ADVERSITY. Difficult or unfavorable circumstances, perhaps caused by sin (Gen. 3:16–17) or disobedience toward God (Lev. 26:14–20). Adversity may also be used by God to test our faith (1 Pet. 1:6–7) or to chasten and correct (Heb. 12:5–11). See also *Suffering; Tribulation.*

Prov. 17:17 a brother is born for *a*
Prov. 24:10 faint in the day of *a*, thy strength is small
Isa. 30:20 bread of *a*, and the water of affliction

ADVOCATE. One who pleads the cause of another (1 John 2:1). As the advocate, the Holy Spirit provides power for worldwide evangelism (Acts 1:8) and will abide with believers forever (John 14:16). See also *Comforter; Counsellor; Holy Spirit; Paraclete.*

AENON. A place near Salim, exact location unknown, where John the Baptist baptized. It was probably near the Jordan River, "because there was much water there" (John 3:23).

AFFECTION

Rom. 1:31 Without understanding...without natural *a*
Col. 3:2 Set your *a* on things above
Col. 3:5 uncleanness, inordinate *a*
2 Tim. 3:3 Without natural *a*, trucebreakers

AFFLICT [ED]

Exod. 1:12 more they *a'ed* them [Israelites]...more they...grew
Job 34:28 he [God] heareth the cry of the *a'ed*
Ps. 88:15 I am *a'ed* and ready to die
Isa. 49:13 Lord...will have mercy upon his *a'ed*

Isa. 53:4 him [God's servant] stricken…smitten…**a'ed**
Lam. 3:33 he [God] doth not **a** willingly nor grieve
Matt. 24:9 **a'ed**, and shall kill you…for my [Jesus']…sake
James 4:9 Be **a'ed**…your laughter be turned to mourning
James 5:13 any **a'ed**? let him pray

AFFLICTION. Any condition that causes suffering or pain. Affliction may come as a result of God's judgment on sin (Rom. 2:9), or it may be an instrument of purification and perfection for believers (Rom. 5:3–5; 2 Thess. 1:4–7). See also *Anguish; Persecution; Suffering.*

AFFLICTION [S]
Exod. 3:7 I [God] have…seen the **a** of my people
Deut. 16:3 unleavened bread…the bread of **a**
Ps. 34:19 Many are the **a's** of the righteous
Isa. 30:20 bread of adversity, and the water of **a**
2 Cor. 4:17 light **a**…worketh for us…exceeding…glory

2 Tim. 4:5 endure **a's**…make full proof of thy ministry
Jas. 1:27 visit the fatherless and widows in their **a**

AFRAID
Gen. 3:10 I [Adam] was **a**…and I hid myself
Exod. 3:6 Moses…was **a** to look upon God
Josh. 1:9 be not **a**…for the LORD…is with thee
Job 5:21 neither shalt thou be **a** of destruction
Ps. 56:3 What time I am **a**, I will trust in thee [God]
Isa. 12:2 not be **a**…Jehovah is my strength
Jer. 2:12 Be astonished…be horribly **a**…saith the LORD
Matt. 14:27 Jesus spake…it is I; be not **a**
Luke 2:9 and they [shepherds] were sore **a**
John 14:27 Let not your heart be troubled, neither let it be **a**

AFRICA. See *Libya.*

AGABUS. A Christian prophet who warned Paul in Antioch of Syria of a worldwide famine

AFFLICTION. Jesus heals a man born blind. Famed for His healing miracles and His message of hope, Jesus seemed constantly surrounded by crowds of sick and disheartened people.

(Acts 11:28). At Caesarea, Agabus used a symbolic demonstration to predict Paul's impending arrest (Acts 21:10–11).

AGAG

1. A king of Amalek in Balaam's prophecy. Balaam predicted that Israel's king would be more powerful than Agag (Num. 24:7)

2. An Amalekite king spared by King Saul in disobedience of God's command. Saul's disobedience led to his rejection as king of Israel by the Lord (1 Sam. 15:8–23). This may be the same king as *Agag*, No. 1.

AGAPE. A Greek word for selfless love, the type of love that characterizes God (John 15:13; 1 John 3:16). Agape is primarily an act of the will rather than the emotions (John 3:16; Rom. 5:8). Agape love for others is a badge of discipleship (John 13:34–35). This love is the greatest and most enduring of all Christian virtues (1 Cor. 13). See also *Love*.

AGAR. See *Hagar*.

AGATE. A precious stone in the breastplate of the high priest (Exod. 28:19), probably a distinct variety of quartz. See also *Chalcedony*.

AGORA. See *Marketplace*.

AGREE [D]
Amos 3:3 two walk together, except they be *a'd*
Matt. 5:25 **A** with...adversary quickly
Matt. 20:13 not thou *a* with me for a penny?

AGRIPPA. See *Herod*, No. 5 and No. 6.

AGUE. See *Burning Ague*.

AGUR. The author of Proverbs 30. Nothing else is known about Agur.

AHAB. The wicked king of Israel (reigned about 874–853 B.C.) and husband of Jezebel. Ahab was known as an aggressive builder (1 Kings 22:39). Influenced by Jezebel, he introduced Baal worship into Israel (1 Kings 16:31–33). His pagan practices were denounced by the prophet Elijah (1 Kings 17:1). Ahab waged war against King Ben-hadad of Syria (1 Kings 20) and was killed in a battle at Ramoth-gilead (1 Kings 22:34–38). See also *Jezebel*.

AHASUERUS. A king of Persia who married Esther and listened to her counsel regarding the Jewish people. He ordered his aide Haman executed—an act that saved the Jewish people from destruction (Esther 7). Most scholars agree that this Ahasuerus is the same person as King Xerxes I of Persian history (reigned 485–464 B.C.). See also *Esther; Haman*.

AHAVA/IVAH (IVVAH). A town in Babylonia where the Jewish exiles gathered after their deportation to this pagan nation. Ezra camped near a stream with this name before leading a group of exiles back to Jerusalem (Ezra 8:15–31). *Ivah:* 2 Kings 18:34; *Ivvah:* NIV, NRSV.

AHAZ/ACHAZ. A king of Judah (reigned about 742–727 B.C.) who practiced idolatry. Ahaz defended Jerusalem against Rezin of Syria and Pekah of Israel (2 Kings 16:5–6), but he was eventually defeated and many citizens of Judah were taken captive (2 Chron. 28:5–8). He foolishly paid tribute to the king of Assyria (2 Kings 16:7–9). *Achaz:* Jesus' ancestry (Matt. 1:9).

AHAZIAH

1. A king of Israel (reigned about 853–852 B.C.) and son of Ahab. A Baal worshiper

(1 Kings 22:52–53), he was injured in a fall from the balcony of his palace. After consulting a pagan god for help, he died, in fulfillment of Elijah's prophecy (2 Kings 1:2–17).

2. A king of Judah (reigned about 850 B.C.). The son of Jehoram and Athaliah, he followed in their evil ways by practicing idol worship. He was eventually assassinated by Jehu (2 Kings 9:27–28). *Jehoahaz:* 2 Chron. 21:17; *Azariah:* 2 Chron. 22:6.

AHIJAH. A prophet who revealed to Jeroboam the forthcoming split of Solomon's united kingdom (1 Kings 11:29–31). Later, Ahijah foretold the death of Jeroboam's son and the elimination of his line from the kingship (1 Kings 14:1–11). See also *Jeroboam,* No. 1.

AHIKAM. A royal official who protected the prophet Jeremiah from the persecution of King Jehoiakim (Jer. 26:24).

AHIMAAZ. A son of Zadok the high priest (1 Chron. 6:8–9) who warned David of Absalom's plans for rebellion. Ahimaaz also reported Absalom's defeat and death to David (2 Sam. 18:19–30).

AHIMELECH. The high priest at Nob during the reign of Saul (1 Sam. 21:1). He befriended David during his flight from Saul (1 Sam. 21:2–9). Ahimelech was killed at Saul's command (1 Sam. 22:16–19).

AHITHOPHEL. One of David's aides who joined Absalom's rebellion (2 Sam. 15:12, 31). He committed suicide when he realized Absalom's plot was doomed (2 Sam. 17:23).

AI/AIATH/AIJA/HAI. A royal Canaanite city that first defied Joshua and then later was defeated and destroyed by the invading Israelites (Josh. 7:2–5; 8:18–21). *Aiath:* Isa. 10:28; *Aija:* Neh. 11:31; *Hai:* Gen. 12:8.

AIJALON/AJALON. A city in the territory of Dan (1 Sam. 14:31) where Joshua battled the five Amorite kings. During this battle the sun stood still (Josh. 10:12–13). *Ajalon:* Josh. 19:42.

AIJELETH SHAHAR. A musical term in the title of Ps. 22, probably indicating the melody to be sung.

AJALON. See *Aijalon.*

AKELDAMA. See *Aceldama.*

AKKAD. See *Accad.*

ALAMOTH. A musical term in the title of Ps. 46, perhaps referring to a choir of women's voices (1 Chron. 15:20).

ALEXANDER THE GREAT. Greek ruler and world conqueror. He took the throne in 336 B.C. and extended his empire from Greece around the Mediterranean Sea to Egypt and then to India. Although he is not mentioned by name in the Bible, Alexander is perhaps the "mighty king" of Dan. 11:3–4. (See also Dan. 7:6; 8:21.)

ALEXANDRIA. A city of Egypt founded by Alexander the Great that was a cultural center and capital city of Egypt in N.T. times. Citizens of Alexandria opposed Stephen (Acts 6:9). Apollos was a native of this city (Acts 18:24). Paul left Malta for Rome on a ship from Alexandria (Acts 28:11). Seventy Jewish scholars were commissioned in this city to translate the O.T. from Hebrew to Greek—the famed version of the Bible known as the Septuagint.

Alexandria was well known for its extensive library, which drew scholars from throughout the ancient world. See also *Septuagint*.

ALGUM/ALMUG. A tree imported from Lebanon (2 Chron. 2:8). Its wood was used in Solomon's temple in Jerusalem. *Almug:* 1 Kings 10:11–12.

ALIEN. A foreigner or stranger from a country other than Israel (Exod. 18:3). Regarded as Gentiles, aliens did not enjoy the rights of the citizens of Israel (Deut. 14:21; Job 19:15). See also *Foreigner*.

ALIVE
Gen. 7:23 Noah only remained *a*
Luke 15:24 my son was dead, and is *a* again
Acts 1:3 he [Jesus] showed himself *a*
1 Cor. 15:22 in Christ shall all be made *a*
Rev. 2:8 first and the last, which was dead, and is *a*

ALLEGORY. A story that communicates an important truth in symbolic fashion. Paul spoke of the births of Ishmael and Isaac in allegorical terms (Gal. 4:22–26).

ALLELUIA. The Greek form of the Hebrew word *Hallelujah*, meaning "praise ye the Lord" (Rev. 19:1–6).

ALLIANCE. A treaty between nations or individuals. Alliances with conquered Canaanite nations were forbidden (Exod. 23:32; Deut. 7:2–5). The prophets warned Israel against forming alliances that might replace their dependence on God (Jer. 2:18).

Nevertheless, alliances between O.T. personalities and foreigners were common. Examples are (1) Abraham with Abimelech of Gerar (Gen. 21:22–34); (2) King Solomon with Hiram of Tyre (1 Kings 5:1–12); and

ALMOND. *Bursting into springtime bloom, an orchard of almond trees awakens the colors of a small field in Israel.*

(3) Solomon's many marriage alliances (1 Kings 3:1; 11:1–3). See also *League*.

ALMIGHTY. A title of God that indicates His absolute power and majesty. God used this term to identify Himself as He talked to Abraham (Gen. 17:1). Ezekiel portrayed God in this light in his vision of God's glory (Ezek. 1:24; 10:5). "Almighty" is also used of Christ (Rev. 1:8; 19:15). See also *Sovereignty of God*.

ALMOND. A small tree known for its early spring blossoms. Jeremiah visualized an almond branch as a sign of God's rapidly approaching judgment against the nation of Judah (Jer. 1:11–12). See also *Hazel*.

ALMS. Voluntary gifts to the needy. The Israelites were commanded to be generous to the poor (Deut. 15:11; Luke 12:33). Jesus cautioned His disciples not to give alms for show or the praise of others (Matt. 6:2–4). See also *Beggar; Poor*.

ALMUG. See *Algum*.

ALOES. A spice for embalming the dead, used by Joseph of Arimathea and Nicodemus on the body of Jesus (John 19:38–39).

ALONE
Gen. 2:18 not good that the man should be *a*
Isa. 2:11 the LORD *a* shall be exalted
Luke 5:21 Who can forgive sins, but God *a*?
James 2:17 faith, if it hath not works, is dead, being *a*

ALPHA AND OMEGA. The first and last letters of the Greek alphabet. Symbolic of the eternity of Christ, this title is applied to God the Father and God the Son (Rev. 1:8; 21:6). The risen Christ described Himself in this fashion, indicating He is the Creator, Redeemer, and Final Judge of all humankind (Rev. 22:13).

ALTARS BUILT BY OLD TESTAMENT PERSONALITIES

1. Noah (Gen. 8:20)
2. Abraham (Gen. 12:7)
3. Isaac (Gen. 26:25)
4. Jacob at Shalem (Gen. 33:20)
5. Jacob at Bethel (Gen. 35:7)
6. Moses (Exod. 17:15)
7. Joshua (Josh. 8:30)
8. Gideon (Judg. 6:24)
9. Saul (1 Sam. 14:35)
10. David (2 Sam. 24:25)

ALTAR. A platform, table, or elevated structure on which sacrifices were placed as offerings. Altars were originally made of earth or rocks (Exod. 20:24–25), but they evolved into more sophisticated structures after the construction of the tabernacle (Lev. 9:24). Pagan Canaanite altars were often called "high places" because they were built on hills or high platforms (Num. 33:52). See also *High Place*.

ALTASCHITH. A word of uncertain meaning in the titles of Pss. 57, 58, 59, and 75.

ALWAYS
Gen. 6:3 My [God's] spirit shall not *a* strive with man
Prov. 5:19 be thou ravished *a* with her love
Mark 14:7 me [Jesus] ye have not *a*
Luke 18:1 men ought *a* to pray
Acts 7:51 ye do *a* resist the Holy Ghost
2 Cor. 4:10 *A* bearing about…the dying of the Lord

AMALEK. The son of Eliphaz, grandson of Esau, and ancestor of the Edomites (Gen. 36:9–12).

LTAR. A restored sacrificial altar in Beersheba where Abraham once lived. The altar's four corners, called horns, may have helped keep the burning wood and animal sacrifice from falling off.

his army, Amasa was killed by Joab (2 Sam. 20:9–12).

AMAZED

Matt. 12:23 people were *a*…Is not this the son of David?

Matt. 19:25 disciples heard it, they were exceedingly *a*

Mark 9:15 people…were…*a,* and…saluted him [Jesus]

Luke 9:43 they were all *a* at the…power of God

Acts 2:7 they were all *a*…are not all these…Galilaeans?

AMAZIAH. A king of Judah (reigned about 796–767 B.C.; 2 Kings 14:1–20). He assembled an army to attack Edom and embraced the false gods of Edom (2 Chron. 25:5–15). Amaziah was assassinated by his political enemies (2 Chron. 25:25–28).

AMBASSADOR. A messenger, spokesman, or representative of a ruler or king. Paul considered himself an ambassador for Christ (Eph. 6:20) and applied this term figuratively to all believers (2 Cor. 5:20).

AMALEKITES. A tribal enemy of the Israelites. Their animosity against the Hebrews apparently began during the years of wilderness wandering with an unprovoked attack (Exod. 17:8–16). Saul battled this tribe as well (1 Sam. 14:48), and they suffered a major defeat at the hands of David (1 Sam. 30).

AMASA. David's nephew and commander of Absalom's rebel army (2 Sam. 19:13). Later forgiven by David and appointed to command

AMBER. A gem or precious stone known for its yellowish-orange brilliance. The prophet Ezekiel compared God's glory to amber (Ezek. 1:4, 27; 8:2).

AMEN. A solemn word used to express approval (Neh. 8:6), confirm an oath (Neh. 5:13), or close a prayer (1 Cor. 14:16). Jesus is called "the Amen," meaning He is true and reliable (Rev. 3:14).

AMETHYST. Violet-colored amethyst was one of twelve precious stones worn on the breastplate of Israel's high priest. Each stone represented a tribe of Israel.

AMETHYST. A violet-colored precious stone in the breastplate of the high priest (Exod. 28:19), also used in the foundation of New Jerusalem (Rev. 21:20).

AMMONITES. A race or tribe descended from Ammon who became enemies of the Israelites during the Exodus (Deut. 23:3). Their chief pagan god was Chemosh (Judg. 11:24), and the Israelites often indulged in their idolatrous practices (Ezra 9:1). Tobiah, an Ammonite, tried to prevent Nehemiah from rebuilding the walls of Jerusalem (Neh. 2:10, 19).

AMNON. A son of David. Amnon assaulted his half sister Tamar—an act avenged with his death at the hand of her brother Absalom (2 Sam. 3:2; 13:1–29). See also *Tamar,* No. 2.

AMON. An evil and idolatrous king of Judah who reigned for only two years, about 643–641 B.C. Assassinated by his own servants, he was succeeded by his son Josiah after his assassins were killed by the people of Judah (2 Kings 21:18–26).

AMORITES. One of the tribal groups of Canaan defeated by the Israelites. Descendants of Ham through his son Canaan (Gen. 10:6), the Amorites were a formidable enemy, but Joshua broke their strength with victories over the armies of Sihon and Og (Josh. 12:1–6). Remnants of the Amorites were reduced to servitude under King Solomon (1 Kings 9:19–21). See also *Canaan,* No. 1.

AMOS. A herdsman from Tekoa in the Southern Kingdom (Judah) who prophesied against the Northern Kingdom (Israel) during the tenure of King Jeroboam II (Amos 1:1; 7:14–15). Known as the great "prophet of righteousness" of the O.T., he condemned the rich and indulgent for oppressing the poor (Amos 8:4–6) and foretold Israel's collapse and captivity by Assyria (Amos 7:17). Amos was a contemporary of the prophets Isaiah and Hosea.

AMOS, BOOK OF. A prophetic book of the Old Testament written by the prophet Amos about 760 B.C. to call the wayward people of the Northern Kingdom back to worship of the one true God.

A short book of only nine chapters, Amos falls naturally into three major divisions: (1) pronouncement of judgment on surrounding nations and Israel (1:3–2:16); (2) three sermons of judgment against the idolatry, corruption, and oppression of Israel (3:1–6:14); and (3) five visions of God's approaching judgment against the nation (7:1–9:10).

Perhaps the greatest contribution of the book is the concept that religion demands righteous behavior. True religion is not a matter of observing rituals and feast days, Amos declared. It consists of following God's commands and treating others with justice: "Let judgment run down as waters, and righteousness as a mighty stream" (Amos 5:24).

AMOS THE HERDSMAN AND FARMER

Amos insisted that he was not a prophet by profession but only "an herdman, and a gatherer of sycamore fruit" (Amos 7:14). The sycamore was a type of fig that grew in his native Judah. The "summer fruit" in Amos's vision (8:1–2) probably included figs.

ANAK. The son of Arba and ancestor of a tribe of giants (Deut. 9:2), or men of renown.

ANAKIMS (ANAKIM, ANAKITES). A tribe of giants, descended from Anak, who inhabited Canaan and were greatly feared in Joshua's time (Num. 13:28, 33; Deut. 9:2). The term may also refer to prominent people, or men of renown. Joshua divided their forces and captured their major walled city, Hebron, or Kirjath-arba (Josh. 14:12–15). The remnants of the Anakim may have been absorbed into

the Philistine people. *Anakim:* NRSV; *Anakites:* NIV. See also *Emims.*

ANAMMELECH. A false god worshiped at Samaria by foreigners who settled the land after the defeat of the Northern Kingdom by Assyria (2 Kings 17:24, 31).

ANANIAS

1. An early believer at Jerusalem struck dead for lying and withholding money he had pledged to the church's common treasury (Acts 5:1–11). See also *Sapphira.*

2. A believer at Damascus who ministered to Paul after the apostle's dramatic conversion (Acts 9:10–18).

ANATHEMA. The transliteration of a Greek word that means "accursed" or "separated." In 1 Cor. 16:22, anathema expresses the concept of excommunication, or a cutting off of the offending party from the church.

ANATHOTH. A village about three miles north of Jerusalem and the birthplace of the prophet Jeremiah (Jer. 1:1).

ANCIENT OF DAYS (ANCIENT ONE). A title for God used by the prophet Daniel to show His ruling authority over the world empires of his day (Dan. 7:9–22). *Ancient One:* NRSV.

ANDREW. One of the twelve disciples of Jesus and brother of Simon Peter. A fisherman from Bethsaida (John 1:44) on the shore of the Sea of Galilee, Andrew was a follower of John the Baptist before he became a disciple of Jesus (John 1:35–40). He was known as one who introduced others to Jesus, including his brother Simon (John 1:41–42), the boy with the loaves and fish (John 6:5–9), and certain Greek

ANGEL APPEARANCES

1. To Hagar during her pregnancy with Ishmael (Gen. 16:7–11)
2. To Lot (Gen. 19:1)
3. To Hagar and Ishmael in the wilderness (Gen. 21:17)
4. To Abraham (Gen. 22:11, 15)
5. To Jacob at Haran (Gen. 28:12; 31:11)
6. To Jacob at Mahanaim (Gen. 32:1)
7. To Moses (Exod. 3:2)
8. To Balaam (Num. 22:22–35)
9. To Gideon (Judg. 6:11–22)
10. To Samson's mother and father (Judg. 13:3–21)
11. To Elijah (1 Kings 19:5, 7; 2 Kings 1:3, 15)
12. To David (1 Chron. 21:16)
13. To Gad (1 Chron. 21:18)
14. To Ornan (1 Chron. 21:20, 27)
15. To Shadrach, Meshach, and Abed-nego (Dan. 3:24–28)
16. To Zechariah (Zech. 1:9)
17. To Joseph in Nazareth (Matt. 1:20)
18. To Joseph in Bethlehem (Matt. 2:13)
19. To Joseph in Egypt (Matt. 2:19)
20. To Zacharias (Luke 1:11–29)
21. To Mary (Luke 1:26–38)
22. To shepherds at Jesus' birth (Luke 2:9–13)
23. To Jesus in the Garden of Gethsemane (Luke 22:43)
24. To Jesus at the resurrection (Matt. 28:2)
25. To women at the tomb (Matt. 28:5)
26. To Mary Magdalene at the empty tomb (John 20:11–12)
27. To the apostles (Acts 5:19)
28. To Philip (Acts 8:26)
29. To Cornelius (Acts 10:3)
30. To Peter in prison (Acts 12:7–11)
31. To Paul (Acts 27:23–24)
32. To John on the isle of Patmos (Rev. 1:1)

citizens who came to talk with Jesus (John 12:20–22). See also *Twelve, The.*

ANGEL. A spiritual or heavenly being whom God sends as His special messenger or helper to human beings. Angels are not the same as God, since He created them (Ps. 148:2, 5). They serve under His direction and obey His commands (Ps. 103:20). Special functions of angels are delivering God's message to human beings (Luke 1:13), protecting God's people (Dan. 3:28), relieving human hunger and thirst (Gen. 21:17–19), and praising the name of the Lord (Ps. 103:20–21).

Before the creation of the world, certain angels revolted against God and were cast out of heaven. The ringleader of this revolt was Satan (Rev. 12:7–9). Another of these fallen angels is Abaddon or Apollyon, "the angel of the bottomless pit" (Rev. 9:11). See also *Angel of the Lord; Gabriel; Michael,* No. 2.

ANGEL OF THE LORD. A heavenly being sent by God to human beings as His personal agent or spokesman. This messenger appeared to Hagar in the wilderness (Gen. 16:7–12), to Moses (Exod. 3:2–3), and to Gideon (Judg. 6:11–12).

ANGELS
Ps. 8:5 thou [God] hast made him [man] a little lower than the *a*
Luke 15:10 joy in the presence of the *a*...over one sinner
1 Cor. 13:1 tongues of men and of *a*, and have not charity
Heb. 13:2 some have entertained *a* unawares

ANGER. A strong feeling of displeasure. God is sometimes pictured as slow to anger (Nah. 1:3). Jesus condemned anger without cause (Matt. 5:22). See also *Wrath.*

Ps. 6:1 LORD, rebuke me not in thine *a*
Ps. 30:5 his [God's] *a* endureth but a moment
Ps. 103:8 LORD is merciful...slow to *a*
Prov. 16:32 He that is slow to *a* is better than the mighty

ANOINT. As his older brothers watch, young David is anointed with oil by the prophet Samuel, marking David as Israel's future king—also known as the "anointed one."

Jer. 4:8 fierce *a* of the Lᴏʀᴅ is not turned back
Mark 3:5 he [Jesus] looked…with *a*…for the hardness of their hearts
Col. 3:8 put off all these; *a*, wrath, malice
Col. 3:21 Fathers, provoke not your children to *a*

ANGUISH. Mental or emotional stress caused by physical pain (2 Sam. 1:9), conflict of soul (Job 7:11), or physical hardships (Exod. 6:9). See also *Affliction; Suffering.*

ANISE (DILL). A common plant of little value used for seasoning food and for medicinal purposes. Jesus condemned those who tithed this insignificant plant but overlooked more important matters, such as judgment, mercy, and faith (Matt. 23:23). *Dill:* ɴɪᴠ, ɴʀsᴠ.

ANNA. An aged prophetess who praised God at Jesus' presentation as an infant in the temple at Jerusalem (Luke 2:36–38).

ANNAS. A Jewish high priest who presided at the trial of Jesus. He questioned Jesus about His disciples and His doctrine. After interrogation, Annas sent Jesus bound to Caiaphas (John 18:12–24). The apostles Peter and John also appeared before Annas (Acts 4:6–7).

ANOINT. To set a person apart for a specific work or task. In O.T. times kings, priests, and prophets were anointed by having oil poured on their heads (Exod. 29:7). Anointing for healing was practiced in N.T. times with the application of oil (Mark 6:13). See also *Oil*.

ANOINT [ED, EST, ING]

Exod. 30:30 a Aaron and his sons
Judg. 9:8 trees went forth...to *a* a king
2 Sam. 2:4 they *a'ed* David king over...Judah
Ps. 23:5 thou [God] *a'est* my head with oil
Isa. 61:1 LORD hath *a'ed* me [God's servant]...to proclaim liberty
Mark 14:8 come...to *a* my [Jesus'] body to...burying
John 12:3 Mary...*a'ed* the feet of Jesus
James 5:14 *a'ing* him with oil in the name of the Lord

ANOINTED ONE. See *Jesus Christ; Messiah*.

ANSWER

Ps. 27:7 have mercy...and *a* me
Prov. 15:1 a soft *a* turneth away wrath
Prov. 26:4 *A* not a fool according to his folly
Luke 21:14 not to meditate before what ye shall *a*
1 Pet. 3:15 give an *a* to every man that asketh you a reason

ANT. A small insect cited as an example of hard work (Prov. 6:6–8).

ANTEDILUVIANS. Persons who lived before the great flood. All except Noah were condemned for their wickedness (Gen. 6:5–8). See also *Flood, The*.

ANTHROPOMORPHISMS. Human attributes ascribed to God. For example, God is described as having an arm of deliverance (Exod. 6:6), eyes too pure to look upon evil (Hab. 1:13), and a nature that is provoked to anger and jealousy by idolatry (Ps. 78:58).

ANTICHRIST. The archenemy of Christ and all Christians who will be defeated in the end-time. Rooted in the prophecies of Daniel (Dan. 7:7–8), the Antichrist receives his authority and power from Satan (Rev. 13:4). He is lawless and deceitful (2 Thess. 2:3–12; 2 John 7).

APOCALYPSE. Four horsemen of the apocalypse stampede the earth with death and destruction, as envisioned by John in the book of Revelation.

Characterized as a "beast," the Antichrist will appear before the return of Christ to wage war against Christ and His people (Rev. 13:6–8). However, he will be defeated by Christ and cast into a lake of fire (Rev. 19:20; 20:10). See also *Dragon*.

ANTINOMIANISM. The concept that grace exempts a person from the moral law. According to Paul, this idea is based on an erroneous view of grace (Rom. 6:1–2). Inconsistent with life in the spirit, antinomianism may cause a weak brother to stumble (1 Cor. 8:9). Abuse of Christian liberty violates the spirit of brotherly love (Gal. 5:13–16).

ANTIOCH OF PISIDIA. A city of Pisidia, a district in Asia Minor. Paul preached in the synagogue in this city, where resistance to the gospel caused him to redirect his ministry to the Gentiles (Acts 13:14–51). See also *Pisidia*.

ANTIOCH OF SYRIA. A city in Syria and site of the first Gentile Christian church that sent Paul on his missionary journeys (Acts 13:1–4; 15:35–41). Believers were first called Christians in this city (Acts 11:26). The church at Antioch was troubled by Judaizers who insisted that Gentile believers be circumcised (Acts 15:1–4).

ANTIOCHUS IV EPIPHANES. The cruel ruler of the Seleucid dynasty in Syria (ruled about 175–164 B.C.) whose atrocities led the Jewish people to revolt. He is not mentioned by name in the Bible, but see *Abomination of Desolation; Maccabees*.

ANTIPATRIS. A city between Jerusalem and Caesarea where Paul was lodged as a prisoner while being transported to Caesarea (Acts 23:31).

ANVIL. A block of iron on which metal was shaped by a blacksmith (Isa. 41:7).

APE. A type of monkey, perhaps a baboon or chimpanzee, imported into Judah by King Solomon (1 Kings 10:22).

APOCALYPSE. A Greek word translated "revelation" that refers to an unveiling of the hidden things known only to God (Gal. 1:12). The book of Revelation depicts the end of the present age and the coming of God's future kingdom through symbols, visions, and numbers. This imagery was probably used to hide the message in a time of persecution.

Other examples of apocalyptic writing in the Bible are Dan. 7–12, Isa. 24–27, Ezek. 37–41, Zech. 9–12, Matt. 24, and Mark 13. See also *Revelation of John*.

APOCRYPHA. A group of sacred books written about 150 B.C. to A.D. 70 and included in the Bibles of some religious groups. These books are generally not considered authoritative in the same sense as the universally recognized books of the Bible.

The books of the Apocrypha are Baruch; Bel and the Dragon; the Wisdom of Jesus, the Son of Sirach; the First and Second Books of Esdras; Additions to the Book of Esther; Epistle of Jeremiah; Judith; First and Second Maccabees; Prayer of Azariah and the Song of the Three Young Men; Prayer of Manasseh; Susanna; Tobit; and Wisdom of Solomon.

APOLLOS. A Jewish believer from Alexandria in Egypt who worked with the church at Ephesus after it was founded by Paul. Eloquent and learned, Apollos was a disciple of John the Baptist (Acts 18:24–25). Aquila and Priscilla instructed him in the true doctrines of the faith, and he became an effective church leader, preaching also in Achaia and Corinth with great success (1 Cor. 3:4–6, 22). Paul mentioned Apollos as one whom a faction of the Corinthian church favored (1 Cor. 1:12). See also *Aquila*.

APOLLYON. See *Abaddon*.

APOSTASY. A falling away from the truth or renunciation of one's faith in Christ (Heb. 3:12). Apostasy is caused by Satan (Luke 22:31–32) and influenced by false teachers (2 Tim. 4:3–4). Professed believers may fall away because of persecution (Matt. 13:21) or love of worldly things (2 Tim. 4:10). Apostasy will not occur if believers are grounded in the truth (Eph. 4:13–16) and depend on God's protective armor (Eph. 6:10–18).

APOSTLE. A person personally commissioned by Christ to represent Him (Matt. 10:1–4). The original twelve apostles or disciples were chosen by Jesus after He had prayed all night (Luke 6:12–16). Apostles are persons sent with a special message or commission (John 15:16). Jesus empowered His apostles to cast out evil spirits and to heal (Matt. 10:1).

Paul regarded himself as an apostle because of his encounter with Christ on the Damascus Road and his personal call by Jesus to missionary work (1 Cor. 15:8–10). In Paul's letters, persons who saw the risen Christ and who were specially called by Him are regarded as apostles (1 Cor. 15:5–8). See also *Disciple; Twelve, The*.

APOSTLE [S]
Acts 2:43 wonders and signs were done by the *a's*
Acts 8:1 they [believers] were…scattered…except the *a's*
Rom. 11:13 I [Paul] am the *a* of the Gentiles
1 Cor. 12:29 Are all *a's*? are all prophets?
Eph. 2:20 built upon the foundation of the *a's*
Eph. 4:11 gave some, *a's*; and some, prophets
Heb. 3:1 *A* and High Priest of our profession, Christ Jesus

APOTHECARY (PERFUMER). A person who made perfumes, which were used in worship ceremonies or to anoint the bodies of the dead (Exod. 30:25–35). *Perfumer:* NIV, NRSV.

APPEAR [ED, ETH, ING]
Gen. 1:9 let the dry land *a*: and it was so
Ps. 42:2 when shall I come and *a* before God?
Ps. 102:16 the LORD…shall *a* in his glory
Matt. 17:3 *a'ed*…Moses and Elias talking with him [Jesus]
Mark 16:9 Jesus…*a'ed* first to Mary Magdalene
Mark 16:14 he [Jesus] *a'ed* unto…eleven
Luke 1:11 there *a'ed* unto him [Zacharias] an angel
2 Cor. 5:10 all *a* before the judgment seat of Christ
1 Tim. 6:14 keep this commandment…until the *a'ing* of our Lord
2 Tim. 4:1 judge the quick and the dead at his *a'ing*
James 4:14 It [life] is…a vapour, that *a'eth* for a little time

APPII FORUM (FORUM OF APPIUS). A station on the Roman road known as the Appian Way about forty miles south of Rome. Paul's friends traveled here to meet him as he approached the Roman Empire's capital city (Acts 28:15). *Forum of Appius:* NIV, NRSV.

APPOINT [ED]
Num. 1:50 *a* the Levites over the tabernacle
Ps. 104:19 He [God] *a'ed* the moon for seasons
Luke 10:1 Lord *a'ed* other…and sent them two and two
Acts 6:3 seven men…may *a* over this business
2 Tim. 1:11 I [Paul] am *a'ed* a preacher
Heb. 9:27 *a'ed*…once to die, but after this the judgment

AQUILA. A Christian believer who, with his wife, Priscilla, worked with Paul at Corinth (Acts 18:2) and continued Paul's work at Ephesus (Acts 18:24–26). They were also associated with the church at Rome (Rom. 16:3).

ARABAH. The valley on both sides of the Jordan River that stretches for about 240 miles from Mount Hermon in the north to the Red Sea in the south (Josh. 18:18).

ARABIA. A hot, dry, and sparsely inhabited desert area southeast of Palestine about 1,400 miles long by 800 miles wide. The queen of Sheba came from Arabia, bringing gold and precious jewels to King Solomon (1 Kings 10:2–15).

ARAM. See *Syria*.

ARARAT, MOUNT. A mountainous region where Noah's ark landed (Gen. 8:4). The location of this mountain is uncertain. Several unsuccessful expeditions to find the ark on Mount Urartu in eastern Armenia (modern Turkey) have been undertaken. See also *Ark, Noah's*.

ARAUNAH/ORNAN. A Jebusite from whom David bought a threshing floor as a place to build an altar (2 Sam. 24:16–24). This plot of ground was the site on which Solomon's temple was built in Jerusalem in later years (2 Chron. 3:1). *Ornan:* 1 Chron. 21:15; 2 Chron. 3:1.

ARBA. The father of Anak and ancestor of a tribe of giants known as the Anakims or Anakim (Josh. 14:15). See also *Anakims*.

ARCHAEOLOGY OF THE BIBLE. The study of remains of past civilizations in an attempt to understand the life and times of biblical peoples. Archaeology involves scientific excavations, examination, and publication by museums and laboratories. Fragments of ancient writings as well as bones, metal, stone, and wood are studied. The focus area for N.T. archaeology largely coincides with the ancient Roman Empire. For the O.T. period, the focus of archaeology includes Palestine (Canaan), Syria, Egypt, the Mesopotamian Valley, and Persia (modern Iran).

Major methods of establishing dates for archaeological finds are (1) examination of the layers of soil in mounds or "tells" (stratigraphy), (2) the study of pottery materials and designs (typology), and (3) measurement of the

ARARAT, MOUNT. Snow-topped Mount Ararat rises nearly seventeen thousand feet, higher than any other mountain in the Ararat range. Neighboring Little Ararat rises about thirteen thousand feet.

A

radioactivity of an object's carbon content (radiocarbon dating).

Archaeology helps us understand the Bible better by revealing what life in biblical times was like, throwing light on obscure passages of Scripture, and helping us appreciate the historical setting of the Bible. For example, exploration of the city of Ur revealed that the home of Abraham was a thriving city of industry and idolatry in O.T. times. The Dead Sea Scrolls, the greatest manuscript discovery of modern times, includes a complete scroll of the book of Isaiah and fragments of most of the other O.T. books. See also *Dead Sea Scrolls.*

ARCHANGEL. A chief angel or perhaps a spiritual being next in rank above an angel. In the end times Michael the archangel will contend with Satan (Jude 9) and proclaim the Lord's return (1 Thess. 4:16). See also *Angel; Michael,* No. 2.

ARCHELAUS. See *Herod,* No. 2.

ARCHEVITES. Foreign colonists who settled in Samaria after the Northern Kingdom fell to Assyria (Ezra 4:9–16). See also *Samaritan.*

ARCTURUS. A constellation of stars cited as evidence of God's sovereignty (Job 9:9).

AREOPAGUS. A council of Greek philosophers in Athens before whom Paul appeared to defend his claims about Jesus and His resurrection (Acts 17:19). The hill on which these philosophers met was apparently called *Mars' hill* (Acts 17:22). See also *Athens.*

ARGOB. A district of Bashan included in Solomon's kingdom. Argob contained sixty fortified cities (1 Kings 4:13).

ARIEL. A symbolic name for the city of Jerusalem, meaning "lion of God" (Isa. 29:1–2, 7). See also *Jerusalem.*

ARIMATHAEA (ARIMATHEA). A city in the Judean hills about five miles northwest of Jerusalem and home of the Joseph who buried the body of Jesus in his own tomb (John 19:38). *Arimathea:* NIV, NRSV. See also *Joseph,* No. 3.

ARISE

Josh. 1:2 now…*a*, go over this Jordan
Prov. 31:28 children *a up*, and call her blessed
Isa. 60:1 **A**, shine; for thy light is come
Mal. 4:2 Sun of righteousness *a* with healing in his wings
Matt. 24:24 shall *a* false Christs
Acts 11:7 **A**, Peter; slay and eat
Acts 20:30 men *a*, speaking perverse things

ARISTARCHUS. A Christian who accompanied Paul on the third missionary journey (Acts 20:4). Later he traveled with Paul to Rome (Acts 27:2).

ARK, NOAH'S. A large wooden ship in which Noah and his family and selected animals were delivered by the Lord. The ark was necessary because God wished to preserve righteous Noah and his family while destroying the rest of humankind because of their wickedness.

Noah built the ark according to God's directions (Gen. 6:14–16). Then he and his family entered the ark, along with a pair of all living creatures (Gen. 6:19–20). Rain fell for forty days (Gen. 7:17), and water covered the earth for 150 days (Gen. 7:24).

Finally, God sent a wind to restrain the water (Gen. 8:1–3) and the ark rested on a mountain in Ararat (Gen. 8:4). Noah and his passengers were delivered safely to dry land (Gen. 8:18–19). Upon leaving the ark, Noah built an altar and offered sacrifices to God for their deliverance. God promised Noah that the

ARK, NOAH'S. Noah's ark stretched longer than a football field, end zones included. Looking a bit like a floating warehouse, this covered barge—for about one wet year—became home to Noah's family and pairs of land animals.

earth would not be destroyed by water again (Gen. 8:20–22).

The ark is symbolic of baptism (1 Pet. 3:20–21) and God's preserving grace (Luke 17:26–27; Heb. 11:7). See also *Ararat, Mount; Noah.*

ARK OF THE COVENANT/ARK OF THE TESTIMONY.

A wooden chest containing two stone tablets on which the Ten Commandments were inscribed. The ark symbolized God's presence to the nation of Israel (Deut. 10:3–4). It was taken into battle by the Israelites (1 Sam. 4:4–5) and captured by the Philistines (1 Sam. 4:10–11).

After its return to Israel (1 Sam. 6:1–15), the ark was later placed in the temple in Jerusalem (1 Kings 8:1–9). It was probably carried away by King Nebuchadnezzar of Babylonia along with other treasures after the fall of Jerusalem in 587 B.C. (2 Chron. 36:7, 18). *Ark of the Testimony:* Exod. 25:22.

ARMAGEDDON.

A Greek word for the valley between Mount Carmel and the city of Jezreel. This valley was the site of many battles in Bible times due to its strategic location on two major trade routes. Because of its bloody history, this region became a symbol of the final conflict between God and the forces of evil, and of God's ultimate victory (Rev. 16:16). See also *Megiddo.*

ARMENIA.

A mountainous land north of Syria formerly known as Ararat (Isa. 37:38). See also *Ararat, Mount.*

ARMOUR.

Defensive covering used as protection during battle. The word is also symbolic of God's spiritual protection (Eph. 6:11).

ARMOURBEARER.

An aide or attendant who carried the armor and weapons of a military officer or warrior of high rank (Judg. 9:54).

ARNON.

A swift river that runs through the mountains east of the Jordan River and into the Dead Sea (Josh. 12:1).

AROMATIC CANE. See *Calamus.*

ARPHAXAD.

A son of Shem born after the great flood (Gen. 11:10–13).

ARROW.

A projectile shot from a bow. This word is also used symbolically to denote a calamity inflicted by God (Job 6:4) or to signify something injurious, such as false testimony (Prov. 25:18).

ARTAXERXES I.

The successor of Cyrus as king of Persia and the king in whose court Ezra and Nehemiah served (Ezra 7:1, 7). About 458 B.C. Artaxerxes authorized Ezra to lead a large group of Jews back to Jerusalem for resettlement (Ezra 7). About thirteen years later he allowed Nehemiah to return to rebuild the walls of Jerusalem (Neh. 2:1–10; 13:6). See also *Ezra; Nehemiah.*

ARTEMIS. See *Diana.*

ARTIFICER. A workman especially skilled in metalworking. Solomon hired craftsmen from Tyre with these skills to help build the temple in Jerusalem (2 Chron. 2:3, 7). See also *Smith.*

ASA. Third king of Judah (reigned about 911–869 B.C.) who led in a national religious revival. He destroyed the places of idol worship (2 Chron. 14:2–5) and fortified Judah to usher in a period of peace (2 Chron. 14:6–8). Reproved by Hanani the prophet for not relying on the Lord, he died from a foot disease (2 Chron. 16:7–14).

ASAHEL. David's nephew and a captain in his army (1 Chron. 27:7). Asahel was killed by Abner, commander in Saul's army (2 Sam. 2:17–23).

ASAPH. A Levite choir leader and writer of psalms mentioned in the titles of Pss. 50 and 73–83.

ASCEND [ED, ING]
Ps. 24:3 who shall *a* into the hill of the LORD
Ps. 68:18 hast *a'ed* on high…led captivity captive
John 1:51 angels of God *a'ing*…upon the Son of man
John 20:17 I [Jesus] am not yet *a'ed* to my Father

ASCENSION OF CHRIST. Jesus' return to His Father after His crucifixion and resurrection (Luke 24:50–51). Foretold in the O.T. (Ps. 68:18), the ascension occurred forty days after the Resurrection (Acts 1:2–11). Christ

will return to earth as surely as He ascended to heaven (Acts 1:11).

ASENATH. The Egyptian wife of Joseph and mother of Manasseh and Ephraim (Gen. 46:20). The pharaoh of Egypt approved this union and probably arranged the marriage (Gen. 41:45). See also *Joseph,* No. 1.

ASHAMED
Gen. 2:25 both [Adam and Eve] naked…and were not *a*
Mark 8:38 of him also shall the Son of man be *a*
Rom. 1:16 I [Paul] am not *a* of the gospel
2 Tim. 2:15 workman that needeth not to be *a*
1 John 2:28 not be *a* before him [Jesus] at his coming

ASHDOD. A major Philistine city (Josh. 13:3) and center of Dagon worship (1 Sam. 5:1–7). It was called Azotus in N.T. times (Acts 8:40). See also *Dagon; Philistines.*

ASHER/ASER. A son of Jacob by Zilpah (Gen. 30:12–13) and ancestor of one of the twelve tribes of Israel (Deut. 33:24). Asher's tribe settled in northern Canaan. *Aser:* Greek form (Luke 2:36). See also *Tribes of Israel.*

ASHES. Residue from burning. A symbol of mourning and repentance, ashes were also used for purification (Heb. 9:13).

ASHIMA. A false god worshiped by foreign colonists who settled in Samaria after the fall of the Northern Kingdom to Assyria (2 Kings 17:30).

ASHKELON/ASKELON. One of five major cities of the Philistines (Josh. 13:3) and a pagan center denounced by the prophet Amos (Amos 1:8). *Askelon:* Judg. 1:18. See also *Philistines.*

ASHTAROTH/ASHTORETH. A pagan fertility goddess worshiped by the Philistines and also by the Israelites soon after the death of

ASCENSION OF CHRIST. *Jesus ascended to heaven from this very spot on top of the Mount of Olives, according to an ancient tradition. In this tiny chapel—the Dome of the Ascension—rests a small rock with an indentation said to have been made by Christ's departure. Once a church, this memorial was captured by Muslims in the 1100s and remains in their control.*

Joshua (Judg. 2:13). Her symbol was an ever-green tree, a pole, or a pillar near a pagan altar. *Ashtaroth* and *Ashtoreth* are plural forms of her name (1 Sam. 7:4; 1 Kings 11:33). Her name in the singular form was *Asherah*.

ASIA. A Roman province in western Asia Minor that included the cities of Ephesus, Smyrna, and Pergamos—the first three cities mentioned in the book of Revelation (Rev. 1:11; 2:1–17). At first forbidden by a vision to enter Asia (Acts 16:6), Paul later did extensive evangelistic work in this province, and his message was well received (Acts 19:10).

ASK

Matt. 6:8 Father knoweth what…ye…need…before ye *a*
Matt. 21:22 shall *a*…believing, ye shall receive
Luke 11:13 Your…Father give the Holy Spirit to them that *a* him
John 16:24 *a*, and ye shall receive
Eph. 3:20 abundantly above all that we *a*
James 1:5 lack wisdom, let him *a* of God
James 4:2 ye have not, because ye *a* not

ASKELON. See *Ashkelon.*

ASNAPPER (ASHURBANIPAL, OSNAP-PAR). The last of the great kings of Assyria (reigned about 668–626 B.C.), called the "great and noble" (Ezra 4:10). Asnapper required King Manasseh of Judah to kiss his feet and pay trib-ute to him. This is probably the same king as the Ashurbanipal of Assyrian history. *Ashur-banipal:* NIV; *Osnappar:* NRSV. See also *Assyria.*

ASP. A deadly snake of the cobra variety that is symbolic of man's evil nature (Isa. 11:8). This is probably the same snake as the *adder* and *viper.*

ASS. A donkey; a common beast of burden in Bible times (Gen. 22:3). Jesus rode a young donkey rather than a prancing warhorse into Jerusalem to symbolize His humble servanthood

and the spiritual nature of His kingdom (Luke 19:30–35). See also *Foal.*

ASSEMBLY. A gathering or congregation of people for worship. God directed Moses to assemble the Israelites at the door of the tab-ernacle (Num. 10:2–3). The psalmist gathered with God's people for worship and praise (Ps. 111:1). Assembling for worship is enjoined for all Christians (Heb. 10:25). See also *Congrega-tion; Church.*

ASSHUR. A son of Shem and ancestor of the Assyrians (Gen. 10:22). See also *Assyria.*

ASSUR. See *Assyria.*

ASSURANCE. Complete confidence in God's promises. Our spiritual security is based on our adoption as God's children (Eph. 1:4–5). Be-lievers are secure in the grip of the Father and Son (John 10:28–30).

ASSYRIA/ASSHUR/ASSUR. An ancient kingdom between the Tigris and Euphrates rivers that became the dominant power in the ancient world from about 900 to 700 B.C. The aggressive and warlike Assyrians were known for their cruelty in warfare, often cutting off their victims' hands or heads and impaling them on stakes. For this cruelty and their pa-gan worship, they were soundly condemned by the O.T. prophets (Isa. 10:5; Ezek. 16:28; Hosea 8:9).

The region that developed into Assyria was originally settled by the hunter Nimrod, a de-scendant of Noah (Gen. 10:8–12). An early name for Assyria was *Asshur,* after a son of Shem who was connected with their early his-tory (Gen. 10:11).

About 722 B.C. King Shalmaneser of Assyria overthrew the Northern Kingdom of Israel, enslaved many of its inhabitants, and resettled the region with foreigners (2 Kings 18:10–11). Several years later Sennacherib invaded Judah (2 Kings 18:13) and exacted tribute from King Hezekiah (2 Kings 18:14–16). *Assur:* Ezra 4:2. See also *Asshur; Nineveh.*

ASTROLOGER. A person who studied the stars in an attempt to foretell the future—a practice especially popular among the pagan Babylonians (Isa. 47:13). See also *Wise Men.*

ASWAN. See *Sinim.*

ATHALIAH. The daughter of Ahab and Jezebel who murdered the royal heirs of Judah and claimed the throne (reigned as queen of Judah about 841–835 B.C.; 2 Kings 11).

ATHEISM. The denial of God's existence. This defiant attitude is illustrated by the Egyptian pharaoh's refusal to release the Hebrew slaves (Exod. 5:2). The psalmist declared that disbelief in God is a characteristic of the foolish (Ps. 14:1). God's clear revelation of His nature and His intent for humankind leaves unbelievers without excuse (Rom. 1:18–25). See also *Infidel; Unbelief.*

ATHENS. The capital city of ancient Greece where Paul debated with the philosophers about Christ and Christianity during the second missionary journey. Known as the center of Greek art, literature, and politics, Athens also struck Paul because of its idolatry, with shrines erected to numerous deities, including the "unknown god" (Acts 17:23). See also *Areopagus.*

ATONEMENT. Reconciliation of God and man through sacrifice (Rom. 5:11). In O.T.

ATHENS. A temple to the Greek goddess Athena towers above the Acropolis hilltop in Athens. This temple was more than four hundred years old by the time Paul arrived with his message about the "Unknown God."

times such reconciliation was accomplished through animal sacrifices symbolic of the people's repentance. But true reconciliation is made possible by Christ's atoning death and resurrection (Rom. 5:1; Eph. 1:7). Man's justification in God's sight is made possible by repentance and faith (Eph. 2:8).

God's righteousness is imparted through Christ's sacrifice (2 Cor. 5:21). His atonement is the foundation for genuine peace (Eph. 2:13–16). All who are redeemed through their acceptance by faith of the sacrifice of Christ are called as ministers of reconciliation (2 Cor. 5:18–21). See also *Atonement, Day of; Justification; Reconciliation.*

ATONEMENT, DAY OF. A Jewish holy day (Yom Kippur) on which atonement was made for all Israel (Lev. 16:29–30; 23:27–28). Preceded by special sabbaths (Lev. 23:24) and fasting, this event recognized man's inability to make atonement for himself. On this day the Jewish high priest made atonement first for himself and then for the sins of the people by sprinkling the blood of a sacrificial animal on the altar (Lev. 16:12–15). The scapegoat, representing the sins of the people, was released into the wilderness to symbolize pardon (Lev. 16:21–23). See also *Atonement; Scapegoat.*

A SUPERIOR ATONEMENT

The Day of Atonement was a time when all the people of Israel sought atonement for their sins (Lev. 16). The writer of Hebrews in the New Testament declared that this ritual is no longer necessary because Christ laid down His life as a permanent, once-for-all sacrifice to make atonement for our sins (Heb. 10:1–10).

ATTAIN [ED]
Ps. 139:6 knowledge is too wonderful…I cannot *a*…it
Phil. 3:12 as though I [Paul] had already *a'ed*
Phil. 3:16 already *a'ed*, let us walk by the same rule

AUGUSTUS. A title of honor, meaning "his reverence," bestowed upon the emperors of the Roman Empire (Luke 2:1). See also *Caesar; Roman Empire.*

AUL. See *Awl.*

AUTHORITY
Prov. 29:2 righteous are in *a*, the people rejoice
Matt. 8:9 a man under *a*, having soldiers under me
Mark 1:22 he [Jesus] taught them as one that had *a*
Luke 9:1 he [Jesus]…gave them…*a* over all devils

AUTUMN RAIN. See *Former Rain.*

AVA. An Assyrian city whose citizens settled in Samaria after the Northern Kingdom fell to Assyria (2 Kings 17:24–31). This is perhaps the same place as Ahava. See also *Ahava; Samaritan.*

AVEN. See *On*, No. 2.

AVENGER OF BLOOD. The closest of kin to a slain person who was expected to kill the slayer. Cain feared the avenging relatives of his brother after he murdered Abel (Gen. 4:14). Six cities of refuge were established throughout Israel to provide a haven for those who had accidentally taken a human life (Num. 35:12). Jesus counseled against such vengeance, calling for love of one's enemies and unlimited forgiveness instead (Matt. 5:43–44). See also *Cities of Refuge; Manslayer.*

AWL/AUL. A tool used by carpenters and leather workers to punch holes. *Aul:* Exod. 21:6; Deut. 15:17.

AXE. A tool for cutting wood (Deut. 19:5).

AZARIAH

1. Another name for Ahaziah, king of Judah. See *Ahaziah,* No. 2.

2. A prophet who encouraged King Asa of Judah to destroy all idols in the land (2 Chron. 15:1–8).

3. The Hebrew name of Abed-nego. See *Abed-nego.*

4. Another name for Uzziah, king of Judah. See *Uzziah.*

AZAZEL. See *Scapegoat.*

AZOTUS. See *Ashdod.*

AZZAH. See *Gaza.*

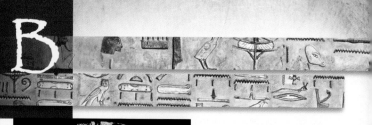

B

BAAL/BAALIM. The chief Canaanite god (Judg. 2:13) who, as the god of rain, was thought to provide fertility for crops and livestock. Baal worship was associated with immorality (Hosea 9:10) and child sacrifice (Jer. 19:5)—pagan rituals considered especially offensive to the one true God of the Israelites.

During their history, the Hebrew people often committed idolatry by worshiping this god of their Canaanite neighbors. The prophet Elijah denounced the prophets of Baal, and the God of Israel won a decisive victory over this pagan god on Mount Carmel (1 Kings 18:17–40). *Baalim:* plural form (1 Sam. 12:10).

BAALAH. See *Kirjath-jearim.*

BAAL-BERITH. A name under which the pagan Canaanite god Baal was worshiped at Shechem in the time of the judges (Judg. 9:4). See also *Baal.*

BAALIM. See *Baal.*

BAAL-PEOR. A local manifestation of the pagan Canaanite god Baal. Baal-peor was worshiped by the Moabites (Deut. 4:3). See also *Baal.*

BAAL-PERAZIM/PERAZIM. A place in central Palestine where David defeated the Philistines (2 Sam. 5:18–20). *Perazim:* Isa. 28:21.

BAAL-ZEBUB/BEELZEBUB. A name under which the pagan Canaanite god Baal was

BAAL. Baal, the Canaanite god of rain and fertile land, holds a spear that resembles lightning or a blossoming branch.

worshiped by the Philistines at Ekron (2 Kings 1:2). The N.T. form of this name was *Beelzebub*, used as a title for Satan, meaning "prince of devils" (Matt. 12:26–27).

BAASHA. A king of the Northern Kingdom (reigned about 909–886 B.C.) who gained the throne by killing King Jeroboam's heirs (1 Kings 15:16–30).

BABEL, TOWER OF. A tall structure known as a ziggurat built on the plain of Shinar in ancient Babylonia as a show of human pride and vanity. God confused the language of the builders so they could not communicate. After they abandoned the project, they were scattered abroad (Gen. 11:1–9). See also *Ziggurat.*

BABOON. See *Peacock.*

BABYLON. The capital city of the Babylonian Empire, built by Nimrod the hunter (Gen. 10:9–10). Site of the tower of Babel, Babylon was a magnificent city-state that attained its greatest power under Nebuchadnezzar (Dan. 4:1–3, 30). The Jewish people were taken to Babylon as captives after the fall of Jerusalem in 587 B.C. (2 Chron. 36:5–21).

BABYLONIA/SHESHACH/SHINAR/ CHALDEA. A powerful nation in Mesopotamia that carried the Jewish people into exile about 587 B.C. Also called *Sheshach* (Jer. 25:26), *Shinar* (Isa. 11:11), and the land of the *Chaldeans* (Ezek. 12:13), Babylonia reached the zenith of its power under Nebuchadnezzar (reigned about 605–560 B.C.). The nation was a center of idolatry dominated by worship of Merodach, the Babylonian god of war (Jer. 50:2).

After holding the Jewish people captive for many years, the Babylonians were defeated by the Persians about 539 B.C., fulfilling the prophecies of Isaiah and Jeremiah (Isa. 14:22; Jer. 50:9). See also *Mesopotamia; Sumer.*

BABYLONISH GARMENT. An expensive embroidered robe kept by Achan as part of the spoils of war after the battle of Jericho (Josh. 7:21).

BACKBITING. The act of reviling, slandering, or speaking spitefully of others—behavior considered unworthy of a Christian (2 Cor. 12:20).

BACKSLIDING. The act of turning from God after conversion. The causes of backsliding are spiritual blindness (2 Pet. 1:9), persecution (Matt. 13:20–21), or love of material things (1 Tim. 6:10). This sin separates the backslider from God's blessings (Isa. 59:2). But confession and repentance will bring God's forgiveness (1 John 1:9) and restoration (Ps. 51).

BACKSLIDING [S]
Jer. 3:14 Turn, O *b* children, saith the LORD
Jer. 14:7 our *b's* are many; we have sinned
Hosea 4:16 Israel slideth back as a *b* heifer
Hosea 14:4 I [God] will heal their *b*

BADGER (HIDES OF SEA COWS). An animal whose skins were used as the covering for the tabernacle (Exod. 25:5). *Hides of sea cows:* NIV. See also *Coney.*

BAG. See *Scrip.*

BALAAM. A soothsayer or magician hired by the king of Moab to curse the Israelites to drive them out of his territory. Prevented from doing so by an angel, Balaam blessed the Israelites instead (Num. 22–24). See also *Balak.*

BALAK/BALAC. The king of Moab who hired Balaam the soothsayer to curse the Hebrews as they crossed his territory. His scheme failed when God forced Balaam to bless them instead (Num. 22–24). *Balac:* Greek form (Rev. 2:14). See also *Balaam.*

BALANCE (SCALES). An instrument with matched weights, used by merchants to weigh money or food in business transactions (Prov. 11:1). *Scales:* NIV.

BALANCE [S]
Lev. 19:36 Just *b's,* just weights, a just ephah
Job 31:6 Let me be weighed in an even *b*
Dan. 5:27 Thou [Belshazzar] art weighed in the *b's*

BALM OF GILEAD. An aromatic gum or resin exported from Gilead in Arabia. It apparently was used as an incense and for medicinal purposes (Jer. 8:22).

BALSAM. See *Mulberry.*

BAND [S]
Jer. 2:20 I [God] have...burst thy *b's*
Hos. 11:4 I [God] drew them...with *b's* of love
John 18:12 the *b*...took Jesus, and bound him
Acts 10:1 Cornelius...of the *b* called...Italian *b*

BANNER. See *Standard.*

BANQUET. An elaborate and sumptuous meal, usually served on a special occasion. Esther exposed the plot of Haman to destroy the Jews during a banquet (Esther 7:1).

BAPTISM. A rite signifying a believer's cleansing from sin through Christ's atoning death. John the Baptist baptized converts to signify their repentance (Matt. 3:6–8). Jesus was baptized by John in the Jordan River to fulfill all righteousness and to set an example for us (Matt. 3:15).

In the N.T. church, Gentiles who received the Holy Spirit were promptly baptized (Acts 10:44–48). Christian baptism memorializes the death, burial, and resurrection of

BAPTISM. A minister visiting the Holy Land baptizes a fellow visitor in the Jordan River. Many Christian pilgrims follow the footsteps of Jesus by being baptized in the same river where he was baptized by John the Baptist.

Christ (Rom. 6:3–5). For the believer, baptism is a testimony of faith and a pledge to "walk in newness of life" with Jesus Christ (Rom. 6:4).

Matt. 20:22 the *b* that I [Jesus] am baptized with
Matt. 21:25 The *b* of John, whence was it
Mark 1:4 John did…preach the *b* of repentance
Eph. 4:5 One Lord, one faith, one *b*
Col. 2:12 Buried with him [Jesus] in *b*
1 Pet. 3:21 The like figure…*b* doth…save us

BAPTIZE [D, ING]
Matt. 3:11 he [Jesus] shall *b* you with the Holy Ghost
Matt. 3:13 Jesus… to be *b'd* of him [John]
Matt. 28:19 teach all nations, *b'ing* them
John 4:1 Jesus made and *b'ed* more disciples than John
Acts 2:38 Repent, and be *b'd*…in the name of Jesus
Acts 8:12 they [the Samaritans] were *b'd*
Acts 8:36 what doth hinder me [the eunuch] to be *b'd*
Acts 9:18 he [Paul] received sight…arose, and was *b'd*
Acts 16:15 she [Lydia] was *b'd*, and her household
Acts 16:33 he [Philippian jailer]…was *b'd*
Acts 22:16 arise, and be *b'd*, and wash away thy sins
Rom. 6:3 into Jesus Christ were *b'd* into his death
1 Cor. 12:13 by one Spirit are we all *b'd* into one body
Gal. 3:27 many of you as have been *b'd* into Christ

BARABBAS. A notorious prisoner, guilty of murder and insurrection, at the time when Jesus appeared before Pilate (John 18:40). Incited by Jewish leaders, the mob demanded that Barabbas be released instead of Jesus (Mark 15:9–11).

BARAK. A general under Deborah and judge of Israel. He and Deborah were victorious against the Canaanites (Judg. 4). See also *Deborah*.

BARBARIAN. A word meaning "uncivilized" and a title used by the Greeks to designate foreigners, or citizens of other nations besides Greece (Rom. 1:14).

BAR-JESUS/ELYMAS. A sorcerer and false prophet who opposed Paul and Silas at Paphos during the first missionary journey (Acts 13:6–12). *Elymas:* Acts 13:8.

BAR-JONA. The surname of the apostle Peter, meaning "son of Jonah" (Matt. 16:17). See *Simon*, No. 1.

BARLEY. A grain similar to oats, used as food for livestock (1 Kings 4:28) and also ground into bread by poor people (John 6:13).

BARNABAS/JOSES. A Jewish Christian who befriended Paul after Paul's conversion, introduced the apostle to the Jerusalem church (Acts 9:27), and traveled with Paul during the first missionary journey (Acts 11:22–26). *Joses:* Acts 4:36.

BARRACKS. See *Castle*.

BARREN. Unable to bear children. In the O.T., barrenness was seen as a sign of God's judgment (1 Sam. 1:5–7). Women in the Bible who had this problem—but who were eventually blessed with children—were Sarah (Gen. 11:30), Rachel (Gen. 29:31), Hannah (1 Sam. 1:5), and Elisabeth (Luke 1:7). See also *Children; Womb*.

BARRIER. See *Middle Wall of Partition*.

BARTHOLOMEW. One of the twelve apostles of Jesus (Mark 3:18). Some scholars believe he is the same person as Nathanael (John 1:45–49). See also *Twelve, The*.

BARTIMAEUS. A blind beggar healed by Jesus on the road to Jericho (Mark 10:46–52).

BARUCH. The friend and scribe of the prophet Jeremiah. Baruch recorded Jeremiah's messages warning of the impending defeat of the nation of Judah (Jer. 36:4–32). Like Jeremiah, he fled to Egypt after the fall of Jerusalem (Jer. 43:1–7). See also *Jeremiah*.

BARZILLAI. An aged friend of David who helped the king during his flight from Absalom (2 Sam. 17:27–29).

BASHAN. A fertile plain east of the Jordan River conquered by the Israelites (Num. 21:33) and allotted to the half-tribe of Manasseh (Josh. 13:29–30).

BASKET [S]
Jer. 24:2 One *b* had very good figs
Amos 8:1 behold a *b* of summer fruit
Matt. 14:20 fragments that remained twelve *b's* full
Acts 9:25 disciples…let him [Paul] down…in a *b*

BASON (BASIN, BOWL). A container used in the home (2 Sam. 17:28) and as a ceremonial vessel in the temple or tabernacle (Exod. 24:6). *Basin:* NRSV; *bowl:* NIV. See also *Bowl; Laver*.

BAT. A nocturnal flying mammal, considered unclean by the Hebrews (Lev. 11:19).

BATH. The standard Hebrew measure for liquids, equivalent to about six gallons (1 Kings 7:26).

BATHING. A washing of the body to make it ceremonially clean and pure (Lev. 15:5, 16). See also *Clean; Wash*.

BATH-SHEBA/BATH-SHUA. The wife of Uriah who committed adultery with David and became his wife (2 Sam. 11:2–27). Because of their sin, Bath-sheba's first child died. She later gave birth to four sons, including Solomon,

who succeeded David as king. *Bath-shua:* 1 Chron. 3:5. See also *David; Solomon*.

BATTLEMENT (PARAPET). A railing around the roof of a house, required by law to prevent falls (Deut. 22:8). *Parapet:* NIV, NRSV.

BDELLIUM. A word that probably refers to a fragrant gum resin (Num. 11:7) as well as a precious stone (Gen. 2:12).

BEAR. A large animal similar to our brown bear that was common in Palestine in Bible times. David killed a bear to protect his father's sheep (1 Sam. 17:34–37).

BEAR [ETH, ING]
Gen. 17:19 Sarah thy [Abraham's] wife shall *b*…a son
Exod. 20:16 not *b* false witness against thy neighbour
Deut. 32:11 eagle…*b'eth* them [her young] on her wings
Ps. 91:12 *b* thee up…lest thou dash thy foot against a stone
Isa. 7:14 virgin shall…*b* a son…Immanuel
Ezek. 18:20 father *b*…iniquity of the son
Matt. 3:11 whose [Jesus'] shoes I [John the Baptist] am not worthy to *b*
Mark 15:21 compel one Simon…to *b* his [Jesus'] cross
Luke 4:11 they [angels] shall *b* thee [Jesus] up
Luke 13:9 if it *b* fruit, well: and if not…cut it down
Luke 14:27 doth not *b* his cross…cannot be my disciple
John 1:7 came for a witness, to *b* witness of the Light
John 10:25 works that I [Jesus] do…*b* witness of me
John 16:12 many things to say…but ye cannot *b* them
Rom. 8:16 Spirit itself *b'eth* witness with our spirit
Rom. 15:1 strong…*b* the infirmities of the weak
1 Cor. 13:7 [charity] *b'eth* all things
Gal. 6:2 *B* ye one another's burdens
Gal. 6:17 I [Paul] *b* in my body the marks of the Lord Jesus
Heb. 9:28 Christ was once offered to *b* the sins of many
Heb. 13:13 Let us go forth…*b'ing* his [Jesus'] reproach

BEARD. Trimmed and groomed facial hair—a mark of pride among Jewish men. To shave one's beard or pull out the hair was a gesture of anguish and grief (Jer. 48:37–38).

BEAT [ETH]
Isa. 2:4 shall *b* their swords into plowshares
Isa. 3:15 ye *b* my [God's] people to pieces
Joel 3:10 *B* your plowshares into swords
Matt. 7:25 winds…*b* upon that house
Acts 16:22 commanded to *b* them [Paul and Silas]
1 Cor. 9:26 so fight I [Paul], not as one that *b'eth*
the air

BEATITUDES. Pronouncements of blessing at the beginning of Jesus' Sermon on the Mount. God's special reward is promised to those who recognize their spiritual need (Matt. 5:3); those who mourn (5:4); those who are humble (5:5), obedient (5:6), merciful (5:7), and pure in heart (5:8); those who practice peacemaking (5:9); and those who are persecuted for Jesus' sake (5:10–11). See also *Sermon on the Mount*.

BEAUTIFUL
1 Sam. 16:12 he [David] was…of a *b* countenance
2 Sam. 11:2 David…saw a woman…very *b*
Eccles. 3:11 He [God] hath made every thing *b*
Matt. 23:27 ye [scribes and Pharisees]…appear *b*
Rom. 10:15 as it is written, How *b* are the feet of them

BEATITUDES. From the Chapel of the Beatitudes near the Sea of Galilee, visitors can look down over a sloping hillside where tradition says Jesus preached his famous Sermon on the Mount.

BEAUTIFUL GATE. A gate that served as one of the main entrances into the temple area in Jerusalem in N.T. times (Acts 3:2).

BEDAN. A minor judge of Israel who served after Gideon and before Jephthah. His name is not recorded in the book of Judges (1 Sam. 12:11). See also *Judges of Israel*.

BEDCHAMBER (BEDROOM). The sleeping room in houses of Bible times (2 Sam. 4:7). *Bedroom:* NIV.

BEELZEBUB (BEELZEBUL). *Beelzebul:* NRSV; see *Baal-zebub*.

BEER-SHEBA. The name of a well in southern Judah that Abraham and Abimelech dug to seal their covenant of friendship (Gen. 21:31). The name was also applied to the surrounding wilderness (Gen. 21:14) and an important city that grew up around the well (Gen. 26:32–33; Judg. 20:1). See also *Well*.

B

BEGAN

Gen. 6:1 men *b* to multiply on…the earth
Matt. 4:17 Jesus *b* to preach, and to say, Repent
Mark 6:7 he [Jesus] called…the twelve…*b* to send them forth
Mark 8:31 he [Jesus] *b* to teach them…Son of man must suffer
Luke 14:18 they all with one consent *b* to make excuse
Luke 19:45 he [Jesus]…*b* to cast out them that sold
John 13:5 he [Jesus]…*b* to wash the disciples' feet

BEGGAR. One who lives by handouts (Luke 16:3). The Israelites were commanded by God to care for the poor (Deut. 15:7–11). See also *Alms; Poor.*

BEGINNING

Gen. 1:1 the *b* God created the heaven
Job 42:12 Lord blessed the latter end of Job more than his *b*
Ps. 111:10 The fear of the Lord is the *b* of wisdom
Eccles. 7:8 Better…end of a thing than the *b*
Matt. 20:8 give them their hire, *b* from the last
John 1:1 In the *b* was the Word
Col. 1:18 he [Jesus] is the *b*, the firstborn from the dead
2 Thess. 2:13 God hath from the *b* chosen you to salvation
Heb. 7:3 [Melchisedec] having neither *b* of days
2 Pet. 3:4 all things continue as they were from the *b*
1 John 1:1 That which was from the *b*…we have heard
Rev. 22:13 Alpha and Omega, the *b* and the end

BEGOTTEN. A word that describes Christ as the only and unique Son of His heavenly Father (John 3:16–18).

BEHAVE [D]

1 Sam. 18:14 David *b'd* himself wisely
1 Cor. 13:5 [charity] doth not *b* itself unseemly
2 Thess. 3:7 we *b'd* not ourselves disorderly

BEHEADING. To cut off a person's head; a form of execution or capital punishment. John the Baptist was put to death in this manner (Matt. 14:10).

BEHEMOTH. A large beast mentioned by Job (Job 40:15–24), probably referring to the elephant or the hippopotamus.

BEHIND

Matt. 16:23 he [Jesus]…said unto Peter, Get thee *b* me
Phil. 3:13 forgetting those things which are *b*
Col. 1:24 fill up that which is *b* of the afflictions of Christ
Rev. 1:10 I was in the Spirit…and heard *b* me a great voice

BEHOLD [EST, ING]

Ps. 119:18 *b* wondrous things out of thy [God's] law
Prov. 15:3 eyes of the Lord…*b'ing* the evil and the good
Isa. 7:14 *B*, a virgin shall conceive, and bear a son
Luke 1:38 Mary said, *B* the handmaid of the Lord
Luke 6:41 why *b'est* thou the mote…in thy brother's eye
John 1:36 [John the Baptist] saith, *B* the Lamb of God
2 Cor. 5:17 *b*, all things are become new

BEKAH. A Hebrew weight equal to one-half shekel, or about one-quarter ounce (Exod. 38:26).

BELA. See *Zoar.*

BELIAL. A word for wickedness or wicked people (1 Kings 21:10). The word also means wickedness personified—a reference to Satan (2 Cor. 6:15). See also *Satan.*

BELIEVE. To accept or trust fully. Belief or trust in Christ is necessary for salvation (Acts 16:31) and essential to righteousness (Gal. 3:6). See also *Faith; Trust.*

BELIEVE [D, TH]

Gen. 15:6 he [Abraham] *b'd* in the Lord
Mark 5:36 he [Jesus] saith…Be not afraid, only *b*
Mark 9:24 Lord, I *b;* help thou mine unbelief
John 3:36 He that *b'th* on the Son hath everlasting life
John 4:48 Except ye see signs and wonders, ye will not *b*
John 11:26 whosoever…*b'th* in me [Jesus] shall never die
John 14:1 ye *b* in God, *b* also in me [Jesus]
John 20:29 they that have not seen, and yet have *b'd*
Rom. 1:16 power of God…to every one that *b'th*
Rom. 4:3 Abraham *b'd* God…counted…for righteousness
Rom. 6:8 we *b* that we shall also live with him [Jesus]
Rom. 10:14 call on him in whom they have not *b'd*
Rom. 13:11 salvation nearer than when we *b'd*
1 Cor. 1:21 foolishness of preaching to save them that *b*

1 Cor. 13:7 [charity] beareth all things, *b'th* all things
1 John 3:23 we should *b* on the name of his Son Jesus
1 John 5:1 *b'th* that Jesus is the Christ is born of God

Dan. 9:9 to the Lord our God *b* mercies
1 Cor. 7:32 unmarried careth for the things that *b* to the Lord

BELIEVERS. A term for Christian converts (Acts 5:14). Paul encouraged Timothy to serve as an example for other believers (1 Tim. 4:12). See also *Brother*.

BELLOWS. A blacksmith's tool, used to force air onto a fire to make it hot enough to work metal (Jer. 6:29). See also *Smith*.

BELONG [ETH]
Ps. 3:8 Salvation *b'eth* unto the LORD
Ps. 94:1 LORD God, to whom vengeance *b'eth*

BELSHAZZAR. The son or grandson of Nebuchadnezzar and the last king of the Babylonian Empire (Dan. 5:1–2). Daniel interpreted a mysterious handwriting on the wall for Belshazzar as a prediction of doom for the Babylonians (Dan. 5:17). That night, Belshazzar was killed when the Persians captured Babylonia (Dan. 5:30–31). See also *Babylonia*.

BELT. See *Girdle*.

BELSHAZZAR. Babylonian ruler Belshazzar is terrified as he watches a disembodied hand write on the palace wall. The prophet Daniel interpreted the cryptic message, which revealed Belshazzar had reason to fear. Invaders killed him that same night.

BELTESHAZZAR. See *Daniel*, No. 1.

BENAIAH. A loyal supporter of David and Solomon. A commander of David's bodyguard (2 Sam. 20:23), he later became commander-in-chief of Solomon's army (1 Kings 2:35).

BEN-AMMI. Lot's son by his youngest daughter. Born in a cave near Zoar (Gen. 19:30–38), he was the ancestor of the Ammonites. See also *Ammonites; Lot.*

BENEDICTION. A prayer for God's blessings upon His people. The benediction that priests were to use was spoken by God to Aaron through Moses (Num. 6:22–26). See also *Blessing.*

BENEVOLENCE. Generosity toward others. Paul commended generosity toward the needy (Gal. 2:10). Christian benevolence should be shown toward God's servants (Phil. 4:14–17) and even our enemies (Prov. 25:21).

BEN-HADAD. A general title for the kings of Damascus, Syria. Three separate Ben-hadads are mentioned in the Bible:

1. Ben-hadad I (reigned about 950 B.C.). In league with Asa, king of Judah, he invaded the Northern Kingdom (1 Kings 15:18–21).

2. Ben-hadad II (reigned about 900 B.C.). He waged war against King Ahab of Israel. This Ben-hadad is probably the unnamed "king of Syria" whose officer Naaman was healed of leprosy by the prophet Elisha (2 Kings 5:1–19).

3. Ben-hadad III (reigned about 750 B.C.). He was defeated by the Assyrian army, as the prophet Amos predicted (Amos 1:4).

BENJAMIN. The youngest of Jacob's twelve sons and ancestor of the tribe of Benjamin. His mother, Rachel, died at his birth (Gen. 35:16–

SAVING BENJAMIN

At one point in Israel's history, the tribe of Benjamin was almost wiped out. Thousands of Benjaminite men were killed by the other tribes in retaliation for a heinous crime they committed (Judg. 20). To save the tribe from extinction, the other tribes provided women from the clan of Jabesh-gilead to marry the remaining Benjaminite men.

This paid off for the entire nation in future years. Israel's first king, Saul, was from the tribe of Benjamin (1 Sam. 9:1–2). The apostle Paul also traced his lineage through this tribe (Rom. 11:1).

20). Benjamin was greatly loved by his father, Jacob (Gen. 42:2–4), and by his brother Joseph (Gen. 43:29–34). See also *Tribes of Israel.*

BEREA (BEROEA). A city in southern Macedonia visited by Paul. The Bereans searched the Scriptures eagerly, and many became believers (Acts 17:10–12). *Beroea:* NRSV.

BERNICE. The sister of Herod Agrippa II, Roman governor of Palestine before whom Paul appeared. She was present when Paul made his defense (Acts 26).

BERODACH-BALADAN/MERODACH-BALADAN. A king of Babylonia (reigned about 721–704 B.C.) who sent ambassadors to visit King Hezekiah of Judah. Hezekiah showed them his vast wealth—an act condemned by the prophet Isaiah (2 Kings 20:12–19). *Merodach-baladan:* Isa. 39:1. See also *Babylonia.*

BEROEA. See *Berea.*

BERYL (CHRYSOLITE). A precious stone, probably similar to emerald, used in the breastplate of the high priest (Exod. 28:20) and in the foundation of New Jerusalem (Rev. 21:20). *Chrysolite:* NIV. See also *Carbuncle; Chrysolite.*

BESEECH. To request or ask earnestly (Rom. 12:1).

BESEECH [ING]
Matt. 8:5 came unto him [Jesus] a centurion, *b'ing* him
1 Cor. 4:16 I [Paul] *b* you, be ye followers of me
2 Cor. 2:8 I [Paul] *b* you...confirm your love toward him
2 Cor. 5:20 ambassadors for Christ...God did *b* you by us
Philem. 10 I [Paul] *b* thee for my son Onesimus
1 Pet. 2:11 I [Peter] *b* you...abstain from fleshly lusts

BESIEGE. To surround with armed forces (Deut. 20:12). This battle tactic was used against walled cities of Bible times to starve the inhabitants into submission. See also *Fenced City; Wall.*

BESTIALITY. Sex relations with an animal. The death penalty was imposed on those who were guilty of this offense (Exod. 22:19).

BESTOW [ED]
1 Cor. 13:3 though I [Paul] *b* all my goods to feed the poor
Gal. 4:11 lest I [Paul] have *b'ed* upon you labour in vain
1 John 3:1 love the Father hath *b'ed* upon us

BETHABARA. A place on the Jordan River where John the Baptist baptized believers (John 1:28). Jesus was also apparently baptized at this place (John 1:29–34).

BETHANY. A village near the Mount of Olives outside Jerusalem (Mark 11:1) and home of Lazarus, Mary, and Martha—friends of Jesus (John 11:1). Jesus ascended to heaven from Bethany (Luke 24:50).

BETHEL/LUZ/EL-BETHEL. A city north of Jerusalem where Jacob had a life-changing vision of angels going up and down a staircase (Gen. 28:10–19). Before it was renamed by Jacob, Bethel was known by its Canaanite name, *Luz* (Gen. 28:19). *El-bethel:* Gen. 35:7.

BETHESDA (BETH-ZATHA). A pool in Jerusalem believed to have miraculous healing powers. Jesus healed a lame man at this pool (John 5:2–8). *Beth-zatha:* NRSV. See also *Pool.*

BETH-HORON. Upper and Lower Beth-horon were twin towns in the territory of Ephraim that served as important military outposts in Bible times. They stood on the main pass through the mountains between the Mediterranean Sea and Jerusalem. Solomon fortified the cities to protect Jerusalem from invading armies (2 Chron. 8:5).

BETHLEHEM/BETHLEHEM-JUDAH/EPHRATH/EPHRATAH. A town in southern Palestine near Jerusalem, also called *Bethlehem-judah* (Judg. 19:18), where Jesus was born in fulfillment of prophecy (Mic. 5:2; Luke 2:4–7). It was called the "City of David" because King David grew up there centuries before (1 Sam. 16:1–13). David's ancestor Ruth gleaned grain in the fields of Boaz nearby (Ruth 2:4–8). Bethlehem was known in O.T. times as *Ephrath* (Gen. 35:19) and *Ephratah* (Ruth 4:11). See also *City of David.*

BETH-MILLO. See *Millo,* No. 1

BETH-PEOR. A town of Moab east of the Jordan River in the territory where Moses was buried (Deut. 34:6).

BETHPHAGE. A village near Bethany and the Mount of Olives just outside Jerusalem

B

mentioned in connection with Jesus' triumphant entry into the city (Matt. 21:1).

BETHSAIDA. A fishing village on the Sea of Galilee; the home of Andrew, Peter, and Philip—apostles of Jesus (John 1:44). Some scholars believe the Bethsaida where the 5,000 were fed (Luke 9:10–17) was a different city with the same name.

BETHSHAN/BETH-SHEAN. A Philistine city where King Saul's corpse was displayed (1 Sam. 31:10–13). In later years, Solomon stationed troops in this city (1 Kings 4:12). *Bethshan:* Josh. 17:11.

BETH-SHEMESH/IR-SHEMESH. A border town between the territories of Judah and Dan taken by the Philistines. Later the ark of the covenant was kept here (1 Sam. 6:1–7:2). *Irshemesh:* Josh. 19:41.

BETH-ZATHA. See *Bethesda.*

BETH-ZUR. A city in the mountains of Judah fortified by King Rehoboam as a defensive outpost along the road leading to Jerusalem (2 Chron. 11:7).

BETRAY [ED, EST, ETH]
Matt. 26:2 Son of man is *b*'ed to be crucified
Matt. 26:16 he [Judas] sought opportunity to *b* him [Jesus]
Mark 14:21 woe to that man by whom the Son of man is *b*'ed
Luke 22:21 hand of him that *b*'eth me [Jesus] is with me on the table
Luke 22:48 Judas, *b*'est thou the Son of man with a kiss?
John 6:64 Jesus knew...who should *b* him
1 Cor. 11:23 Lord Jesus the same night in which he was *b*'ed took bread

BETROTHAL. A marriage agreement, usually made by the groom with the parents of the bride. A betrothed woman was regarded as the lawful wife of her spouse. Joseph and Mary were betrothed before the birth of Jesus

(Matt. 1:18–19; *espoused:* KJV). See also *Dowry; Marriage.*

BETTER
1 Sam. 15:22 to obey is *b* than sacrifice
Ps. 84:10 day in thy [God's] courts is *b* than a thousand
Prov. 8:11 wisdom is *b* than rubies
Prov. 19:22 poor man is *b* than a liar
Prov. 27:5 rebuke is *b* than secret love
Eccles. 7:1 good name is *b* than precious ointment
Matt. 12:12 How much then is a man *b* than a sheep
1 Cor. 7:9 it is *b* to marry than to burn
Phil. 1:23 desire...to be with Christ; which is far *b*
Heb. 1:4 made so much *b* than the angels

BEULAH. A name for Israel after the Babylonian Exile when the nation would be in a fruitful relationship with God (Isa. 62:4).

BEZER. A fortified city in the territory of Reuben designated as one of the six cities of refuge (Josh. 20:8). See also *Cities of Refuge.*

BIBLE. God's written record of His revelation that is accepted by Christians as uniquely inspired and authoritative for faith and practice. The Bible's O.T. books chronicle the expectation of a messiah, while the N.T. books reveal the fulfillment of God's redemptive purpose through Jesus Christ and the church.

The Bible was written under God's inspiration during a period of more than 1,000 years from the time of Moses through the first century A.D. The N.T. was completed within about sixty years of Jesus' resurrection. Much of the N.T., including the Gospels, was recorded by eyewitnesses of the events about which they wrote. The O.T. was written originally in Hebrew and Aramaic, while the N.T. was recorded in the Greek language.

All copies of the Scripture were written by hand until the invention of printing in the fifteenth century A.D. The original writings have been translated into hundreds of languages

BETROTHAL. A Jewish bride and groom in Israel dress in the traditional wedding garments of their former homeland: Yemen, a small nation south of Saudi Arabia. Many Israelis today are Yemenite Jews.

BIBLE. A rabbi touches up fading letters in an old scroll, as scribes in ancient times did to preserve their sacred writings. When scrolls became too worn, scribes made fresh copies from the old ones, carefully preserving the message.

and dialects to make the Bible the world's best-loved and most accessible book. The Geneva Bible, published in 1560, was the first complete English Bible translated from the original languages. The popular King James Version appeared in 1611, and numerous English versions and revisions have followed.

Although written by many people over a long period, the Bible has a remarkable unity, explained only by the inspiration and oversight of the Holy Spirit to bring God's redemptive message to humankind.

BIER. A portable frame for carrying a body to its burial place (2 Sam. 3:31).

BILDAD. One of the three friends who comforted the sorrowing Job (Job 2:11). His speeches expressed the conviction that all suffering is the direct result of sin (Job 8, 18, 25). See also *Job, Book of.*

BILHAH. Rachel's maid and a wife of Jacob. She bore two of Jacob's twelve sons, Dan and Naphtali (Gen. 30:1–8). See also *Jacob.*

BIND [ETH]
Deut. 6:8 shalt *b* them for a sign upon thine hand
Ps. 147:3 He [God]…*b'eth* up their wounds
Prov. 3:3 *b* them [mercy and truth] about thy neck
Isa. 61:1 the Lord…hath sent me to *b* up the brokenhearted
Matt. 16:19 whatsoever…*b* on earth shall be bound in heaven
Mark 5:3 no man could *b* him [demon-possessed man]

BIRD OF PREY. See *Speckled Bird.*

BIRTHRIGHT. The inheritance rights of the firstborn son, who received a double portion of his father's assets (Deut. 21:17) plus the father's blessing and responsibility for family leadership. These inheritance rights could be taken away and conferred on another because of immoral acts or irresponsible behavior by the oldest son (Gen. 25:29–34). Esau sold his birthright to his brother, Jacob, for a bowl of stew (Gen. 25:31; Heb. 12:16). See also *Firstborn; Inheritance.*

BISHOP. An overseer, pastor, or elder who served as leader of a local church in N.T. times (Titus 1:5–9). See also *Deacon; Elder; Pastor.*

BISHOP [S]
Phil. 1:1 saints...at Philippi, with the *b's*
1 Tim. 3:1 man desire the office of a *b*...a good work
1 Tim. 3:2 A *b* then must be blameless...husband of one wife
1 Pet. 2:25 returned unto the Shepherd and *B* of your souls

BITHYNIA. A Roman province of Asia Minor that Paul was prevented from entering through the intervention of the Holy Spirit (Acts 16:7). The gospel did enter this province later (1 Pet. 1:1).

BITTER
Isa. 24:9 strong drink shall be *b* to them that drink it
Jer. 31:15 voice was heard in Ramah...*b* weeping
Hab. 1:6 I [God] raise up the Chaldeans, that *b*...nation
James 3:11 fountain send forth...sweet water and *b*

BITTER HERBS. Herbs eaten by the Hebrew people during their celebration of the Passover to help them remember their bitter affliction during their enslavement in Egypt (Exod. 12:8). See also *Passover.*

BITTER WATER. A test or trial to which a woman was subjected when her husband suspected her of being unfaithful (Num. 5:11–31). See also *Water of Jealousy; Water of Separation.*

BITTERN (SCREECH OWL). A bird noted for its melancholy cries and thus symbolic of the loneliness and despair that follow God's judgment (Zeph. 2:14). *Screech owl:* NIV, NRSV. See also *Screech Owl.*

BITTERNESS
Job 9:18 He [God]...filleth me [Job] with *b*
Acts 8:23 thou art in the gall of *b*
Rom. 3:14 mouth is full of cursing and *b*
Eph. 4:31 Let all *b*...be put away from you

BITUMEN. See *Slime.*

BLACK VULTURE. See *Ospray.*

BLAINS (BOILS). Infectious boils on the skin; one of the plagues brought upon the Egyptians for their refusal to release the Hebrew slaves (Exod. 9:8–11). *Boils:* NIV, NRSV.

BLAMELESS
1 Cor. 1:8 ye may be *b* in the day of our Lord
1 Tim. 3:2 bishop...must be *b*, the husband of one wife
1 Tim. 3:10 office of a deacon, being found *b*
Titus 1:7 bishop must be *b*, as the steward of God

BLASPHEME. To revile, curse, or show contempt toward God. This was considered a capital offense by the Jewish people, punishable by death. Jesus was accused of blasphemy by the Jewish leaders. They considered Him only a man, while He claimed to be God's Son (Matt. 9:3).

BLASPHEME [D]
Ps. 74:10 shall the enemy *b* thy [God's] name for ever
Ps. 74:18 foolish people have *b'd* thy [God's] name
Mark 3:29 shall *b* against the Holy Ghost hath never forgiveness

BLASPHEMY [IES]

Matt. 12:31 *b* against the Holy Ghost shall not be forgiven
Matt. 26:65 He [Jesus] hath spoken *b*
Mark 2:7 Why doth this man [Jesus] thus speak *b'ies*?
Col. 3:8 put off all these; anger, wrath, malice, *b*

BLASPHEMY AGAINST THE HOLY SPIRIT.

A sin that consists of attributing Christ's miracles to the work of Satan (Matt. 12:31–32). Jesus declared that such contempt for the work of God was an unforgivable sin (Mark 3:28–29). Paul regarded a person's bitter opposition to the gospel as a form of blasphemy against God (Rom. 2:24). See also *Unpardonable Sin*.

BLESS.

To invoke or declare God's goodness and favor upon others, as Jacob did with his twelve sons (Gen. 49:1–28). God also blesses His people by giving life (Gen. 1:22) and forgiving our sins (Rom. 4:7–8). See also *Benediction*.

BLESS [ED, ING]

Gen. 2:3 God *b'ed* the seventh day, and sanctified it
Gen. 9:1 God *b'ed* Noah and his sons
Gen. 12:2 I [God] will *b* thee [Abraham]
Num. 6:24 Lord *b* thee, and keep thee
Deut. 11:26 set before you…a *b'ing* and a curse
Job 1:21 Lord hath taken away; *b'ed* be the name of the Lord
Job 42:12 Lord *b'ed* the latter end of Job
Ps. 1:1 *B'ed*…walketh not in the counsel of the ungodly
Ps. 32:1 *B'ed*…whose transgression is forgiven
Ps. 41:13 *B'ed* be the Lord God…from everlasting
Ps. 67:1 God…*b* us; and cause his face to shine upon us
Ps. 96:2 Sing unto the Lord, *b* his name
Prov. 31:28 children arise up, and call her *b'ed*
Ezek. 34:26 there shall be showers of *b'ing*
Matt. 5:3 *B'ed* are the poor in spirit
Luke 1:28 *b'ed* art thou [Mary] among women
Luke 11:28 *b'ed*…that hear the word of God, and keep it
Rom. 12:14 *B* them which persecute you: b, and curse not
James 1:12 *B'ed* is the man that endureth temptation

BLIND.

Unable to see, in either a physical (Matt. 9:27) or spiritual (Eph. 4:18) sense. The Hebrews were enjoined to show compassion toward the blind (Deut. 27:18).

Ps. 146:8 The Lord openeth the eyes of the *b*
Isa. 35:5 the eyes of the *b* shall be opened
Matt. 11:5 The *b* receive their sight…lame walk
Matt. 23:24 Ye *b* guides [Pharisees]…strain at a gnat
Mark 10:46 *b* Bartimaeus…sat by the highway
Luke 6:39 Can the *b* lead the *b*?
Luke 7:22 tell John…the *b* see, the lame walk
John 9:2 who did sin…that he was born *b*

BLOOD.

Life-sustaining fluid of the body. In the O.T., the blood of a sacrificial animal represented the essence of life and symbolized repentance and atonement for sin (Lev. 17:11). In the N.T., the phrase "the blood of Christ" refers to the sacrificial death of Jesus on the cross (Heb. 9:12–14).

Jesus' sacrificial blood is the agent of redemption for believers (Heb. 9:12). Christ's shed blood is memorialized in the Lord's Supper (1 Cor. 10:16). Nothing perishable or material can save; only Christ's precious blood has the power to redeem (1 Pet. 1:18–19). See also *Atonement; Redeem*.

Gen. 9:6 sheddeth man's *b*, by man shall his *b* be shed
1 Kings 22:38 dogs licked up his [Ahab's] *b*
1 Chron. 22:8 thou [David] hast shed much *b*
Joel 2:31 sun…turned into darkness…moon into *b*
Matt. 16:17 flesh and *b* hath not revealed it unto thee [Peter]
Matt. 26:28 my [Jesus'] *b* of the new testament
Matt. 27:8 field was called, The field of *b*
Matt. 27:25 answered all the people…His [Jesus'] *b* be on us
Luke 22:44 his [Jesus'] sweat was as…great drops of *b*
Acts 17:26 made of one *b* all nations of men
Eph. 2:13 ye…far off are made nigh by the *b* of Christ
Eph. 6:12 wrestle not against flesh and *b*
Col. 1:14 redemption through his [Jesus'] *b*
Heb. 13:12 he [Jesus] might sanctify…with his own *b*
1 John 1:7 *b* of Jesus Christ…cleanseth us from all sin
Rev. 6:12 sun became black…moon became as *b*

BLOT [TED]
Exod. 32:33 him will I [God] *b* out of my book
Ps. 51:1 *b* out my transgressions
Acts 3:19 Repent…that your sins may be *b'ted* out

BOANERGES.
A name meaning "sons of thunder," given by Jesus to James and John, the sons of Zebedee (Mark 3:17). This was a reference to their fiery zeal. See also *James*, No. 1; *John the Apostle*.

BOAR.
A male wild hog, noted for its vicious nature (Ps. 80:13).

BOAST [ETH, ING]
Ps. 44:8 In God we *b* all the day long
Prov. 27:1 *B* not thyself of to morrow
2 Cor. 9:3 lest our *b'ing* of you should be in vain
Eph. 2:9 Not of works, lest any man should *b*
James 3:5 the tongue is a little member…*b'eth* great things

BOAZ/BOOZ.
The husband of Ruth and an ancestor of Christ. He married Ruth, who gave birth to Obed, grandfather of David (Ruth 4:17). *Booz:* Jesus' ancestry (Matt. 1:5). See also *Ruth*.

BODY
Matt. 26:26 Jesus took bread…Take, eat; this is my *b*
Mark 15:43 Joseph of Arimathaea…craved the *b* of Jesus
Luke 12:22 Take no thought…for the *b*, what ye…put on
Rom. 6:12 sin therefore reign in your mortal *b*
Rom. 7:24 deliver me from the *b* of this death
Rom. 12:5 we, being many, are one *b* in Christ
1 Cor. 6:18 fornication sinneth against his own *b*
1 Cor. 12:12 the *b* is one, and hath many members
1 Cor. 15:44 sown a natural *b*…raised a spiritual *b*
2 Cor. 5:8 absent from the *b*…present with the Lord
Gal. 6:17 I [Paul] bear in my *b* the marks of the Lord Jesus
Col. 1:18 he [Christ] is the head of the *b*, the church
James 3:6 it [the tongue] defileth the whole *b*

BODY OF CHRIST.
A symbolic expression for the church. Paul identified the church as Christ's body (Rom. 7:4; Col. 1:24). The risen Christ dwells in His body and presides over the church (Eph. 1:19–23). Christ assigns spiritual gifts to His body to accomplish His work and bring believers to maturity (Eph. 4:7–13). Members of the body are to care for one another (1 Cor. 12:25–27). See also *Church*.

BODY, SPIRITUAL.
The glorified or redeemed body of believers. Our hope of a glorified body is based on Christ's victory over the grave (Rom. 6:6). Believers will receive a glorified body, free of sin and death, at the return of Christ (1 Cor. 15:50–57). The redeemed body of a believer will be like that of Christ's glorified body (Phil. 3:21), immortal and incorruptible (1 Cor. 15:53–54).

Christians need not fear death, because we are provided a new spiritual body "eternal in the heavens" (2 Cor. 5).

BOILS.
See *Blains*.

BOLDLY
Acts 9:29 he [Paul] spake *b* in the name of the Lord Jesus
Acts 19:8 he [Paul] went into the synagogue, and spake *b*
Heb. 4:16 Let us…come *b* unto the throne of grace

BOLDNESS.
Courage and confidence. Boldness that honors God is aided by earnest prayer (Eph. 6:18–20).

Acts 4:13 they saw the *b* of Peter and John
Eph. 3:12 In whom [Jesus] we have *b*
1 John 4:17 that we may have *b* in the day of judgment

BOND [S]
Ps. 116:16 thou [God] hast loosed my *b's*
Gal. 3:28 neither Jew nor Greek…*b* nor free
Eph. 4:3 unity of the Spirit in the *b* of peace
Eph. 6:20 I [Paul] am an ambassador in *b's*
Col. 3:11 neither…*b* nor free: but Christ is all
Philem. 10 Onesimus, whom I [Paul] have begotten in my *b's*

BONDAGE. Jews once invited to Egypt to escape a drought in their homeland eventually became a slave race, forced to build cities for the king. Moses led them to freedom.

BONDAGE. To be held against one's will by an oppressor. The Israelites were enslaved by the Egyptians for more than 400 years. Sin also holds a person in spiritual bondage (Rom. 8:15). See also *Slave.*

Exod. 6:6 I [God] will rid you [the Israelites] out of their *b*
John 8:33 We be Abraham's seed…never in *b* to any man
Gal. 5:1 not entangled again with the yoke of *b*

BONDSERVANT. A slave; a person who serves another against his will and without wages (1 Kings 9:21). See also *Slave.*

BONE. The skeletal framework of humans. The phrase "bone of my bones" uttered by Adam (Gen. 2:23) showed that he was united to woman in the closest possible relationship.

BOOK. Pieces of animal skin or papyrus written on and then bound together (Job 19:23). See also *Roll; Scroll.*

BOOK OF JASHER. A lost book that apparently described great events in the life of Israel (Josh. 10:13).

BOOK OF LIFE. God's record of the names of the saved and deeds of the righteous (Mal. 3:16–18). This book will be used as the basis for God's final judgment (Rev. 3:5; 20:12–15). Inclusion in the book of life by virtue of one's salvation by God's grace provides reason for joy (Luke 10:20; Phil. 4:3) and hope of heaven (Rev. 21:27).

BOOK OF THE LAW. A term for the Law of Moses or the Pentateuch, the first five books of the O.T. After receiving and recording these instructions from God, Moses delivered the law to the priests for public reading (Deut. 31:9–11). In later years, the Book of the Law became the basis for King Josiah's religious reforms (2 Kings 23:1–25).

BOOK OF THE WARS OF THE LORD. A lost book that may have celebrated Israel's victories in battle under Moses (Num. 21:14).

BOOTH. A temporary shelter made of tree branches. During the Feast of Tabernacles, also called the Feast of Booths, the Israelites lived in such shelters as a reminder of their harsh life in the wilderness after their deliverance from Egyptian slavery (Neh. 8:13–18).

BOOTHS, FEAST OF. See *Tabernacles, Feast of.*

BOOTY. Anything of value taken in war, including livestock, slaves, gold and silver, clothing, and tools (Zeph. 1:13). See also *Spoil.*

BOOZ. See *Boaz.*

BORN

Gen. 17:17 child be **b** unto him [Abraham]…hundred years old
Job 14:1 Man that is **b** of a woman is of few days
Prov. 17:17 brother is **b** for adversity
Eccles. 3:2 time to be **b**, and a time to die
Isa. 9:6 unto us a child is **b**
Matt. 2:1 Jesus was **b** in Bethlehem of Judaea
Luke 1:35 holy thing…**b** of thee [Mary]…called the Son of God
Luke 2:11 unto you is **b** this day…a Saviour
Acts 22:28 Paul said, But I was free **b**
1 John 3:9 Whosoever is **b** of God doth not commit sin
1 John 4:7 every one that loveth is **b** of God

BORN AGAIN. See *New Birth.*

BOSOM. Another word for the human chest, or breast, used symbolically to imply closeness or intimacy (Isa. 40:11). See also *Abraham's Bosom; Breast.*

Prov. 5:20 thou…embrace the **b** of a stranger
Luke 16:22 beggar died…carried…into Abraham's **b**
John 1:18 only begotten Son…in the **b** of the Father
John 13:23 leaning on Jesus' **b** one of his disciples

BOTTLE (WINESKIN). A vessel made of animal skins (Josh. 9:4). Old wineskins became brittle and unable to hold new wine during the fermentation process. Thus, Jesus declared, "No man putteth new wine into old bottles; else the new wine will burst the bottles, and be spilled" (Luke 5:37). *Wineskin:* NIV, NRSV.

BOTTOMLESS PIT. See *Abyss.*

BOUGHT

Jer. 32:9 I [Jeremiah] **b** the field of Hanameel
Matt. 13:46 sold all…he had, and **b** it [pearl]
Mark 11:15 Jesus…cast out them that sold and **b**
1 Cor. 6:20 ye are **b** with a price…glorify God

BOUND

Matt. 18:18 ye shall bind on earth shall be **b** in heaven
John 11:44 he [Lazarus] came forth, **b**…with graveclothes
Acts 20:22 I [Paul] go **b** in the spirit unto Jerusalem
2 Tim. 2:9 but the word of God is not **b**

BOUNDARY MARKER, BOUNDARY STONE. See *Landmark.*

BOW. A weapon used in war and for hunting (Gen. 48:22). Soldiers of the tribe of Benjamin were especially skilled with the bow (1 Chron. 12:2).

BOW, BOWING. To show reverence or submission, performed by kneeling on one knee and bending the head forward. Bowing is considered appropriate for prayer and worship (Ps. 95:6). Jesus knelt or bowed to pray in Gethsemane (Matt. 26:36–39). See also *Kneel.*

BOWED

Ps. 38:6 troubled; I am **b** down greatly
Matt. 27:29 they **b** the knee before him [Jesus]…mocked him
John 19:30 Jesus…**b** his head, and gave up the ghost

BOWELS (INWARD PARTS). The internal digestive system of the human body. The bowels were considered the center of a person's feelings and emotions, expressive of compassion and tenderness (Job 30:27–28). *Inward parts:* NRSV.

BOWL. A vessel for holding food or liquids. Bowls were made of wood, clay, or silver. Large

B

bowls were used by priests in sacrificial rituals (Zech. 9:15). See also *Bason.*

BOX TREE (CYPRESS, PINE). An evergreen that produced a wood ideal for carving. Boxwood was used in the temple in Jerusalem (Isa. 60:13). *Cypress:* NIV; *pine:* NRSV.

**3
D
7**

BOZRAH. The ancient capital city of Edom. Isaiah spoke of this city in figurative terms to describe the Messiah's victory over the pagan nations (Isa. 63:1). See also *Edom,* No 2.

BRACELET. A piece of jewelry worn on the wrist (Isa. 3:19). The bracelet of King Saul (2 Sam. 1:10) was probably a military armband.

BRAMBLE (THORNBUSH). A bush of thistles. In Jotham's parable, the bramble bush, representing Abimelech, ruled over the trees of the forest, in spite of its lowly position (Judg. 9:7–15). *Thornbush:* NIV. See also *Brier.*

BRASEN SEA (BRONZE SEA). A large brass basin in the temple court that held water for purification rituals (2 Kings 25:13). *Bronze sea:* NIV, NRSV. See also *Molten Sea.*

BRASS. An alloy of copper with some other metal, perhaps zinc or tin (Num. 21:9). The word is also used as a symbol of stubbornness, insensibility, and rebellion toward God (Isa. 48:4).

BRASS SERPENT (BRONZE SNAKE). A serpent cast from metal and raised up by Moses in the wilderness on a pole as an instrument of healing for those who had been bitten by poisonous snakes (Num. 21:9). *Bronze snake:* NIV. See also *Fiery Serpents.*

BREAD. A word often used for food in general. Bread was made from flour or meal and baked in loaves. Jesus described Himself as the "bread of life" (John 6:35). See also *Corn; Wheat.*

BREAD OF THE PRESENCE. See *Shewbread.*

BREAK [ETH, ING]

Job 34:24 He [God] shall *b* in pieces mighty men

Ps. 89:34 My covenant will I [God] not *b*

Eccles. 3:3 a time to *b* down, and a time to build up

Jer. 23:29 my [God's] word like…a hammer that *b'eth* the rock

Hosea 1:5 I [God] will *b* the bow of Israel

Matt. 6:20 treasures…where thieves do not *b* through nor steal

Matt. 12:20 A bruised reed shall he [Jesus] not *b*

Luke 24:35 he [Jesus] was known of them in *b'ing* of bread

1 Cor. 10:16 bread which we *b*…communion of the body of Christ

BREAST. The chest of the human body. To strike or beat one's chest was to signify extreme sorrow (Luke 23:48).

BREASTPLATE (BREASTPIECE). The vestment worn by the Jewish high priest. It contained twelve precious stones and was engraved with the names of the tribes of Israel (Exod. 28:15–30). Paul spoke figuratively of the "breastplate of righteousness" for Christians (Eph. 6:14). *Breastpiece:* NIV.

BREASTS. See *Paps.*

A SAVING SERPENT

Jesus referred to the brass serpent raised up by Moses in the wilderness when He declared, "And I, if I be lifted up from the earth, will draw all men unto me" (John 12:32). He was predicting His atoning death on the cross.

BREATH OF GOD. A symbolic phrase that portrays God as the source of life (Job 33:4). His breath demonstrates His power and creative ability (2 Sam. 22:14–16). In the N.T., God "breathed" the Holy Spirit upon His disciples (John 20:22).

BREECHES (UNDERGARMENTS). Trousers or perhaps an undergarment worn by priests (Exod. 28:42). *Undergarments:* NIV, NRSV.

BRIBERY. The act of giving gifts or favors inappropriately to influence others—a practice condemned often in the Bible (Amos 5:12).

BRICK. A building block made of clay that was mixed with straw then baked in the sun or placed in a kiln for curing. The Israelites made bricks during their enslavement in Egypt (Exod. 1:14). See also *Tile.*

BRICK-KILN. An oven or furnace for curing bricks (2 Sam. 12:31). See also *Furnace.*

BRIDE. A newly married woman. In the N.T., the Church is spoken of figuratively as the bride of Christ (Eph. 5:25–33). See also *Church.*

BRIDEGROOM. A newly married man. The N.T. speaks figuratively of Christ as the Bridegroom (John 3:29) and of the Church as His bride (Eph. 5:25–33).

BRIER. A shrub or plant with thorns and thistles. The word is often used figuratively to describe man's sinful nature (Mic. 7:4).

BRIGANDINE (COAT OF MAIL). Flexible body armor, probably worn by kings and commanders (1 Sam. 17:38; Jer. 46:4). *Coat of mail:* NRSV.

BRIMSTONE (BURNING SULFUR). A bright yellow mineral that burns easily and gives off a strong odor. The cities of Sodom and Gomorrah were destroyed with burning brimstone (Gen. 19:24–25). *Burning sulfur:* NIV.

BRONZE SEA. See *Brasen Sea.*

BRONZE SNAKE. See *Brass Serpent.*

BROOM. See *Juniper.*

BROTHER. A male sibling. The word is also used figuratively for all Christian believers (Matt. 23:8). Christians are counseled not to offend a weak brother (Rom. 14:10–13). See also *Believers.*

BROTHERS OF CHRIST. The four earthly brothers, or half brothers, of Jesus—James, Joses (Joseph), Simon, and Juda (Jude)—who were born by natural conception to Joseph and Mary after the virgin birth of Christ (Mark 6:3). James was leader of the church in Jerusalem (Acts 15:13–21) and likely the author of the epistle of James (James 1:1). Jude wrote the N.T. epistle that bears his name (Jude 1).

BUCKLER (SHIELD). A small piece of protective armor worn on the arm by warriors (Song 4:4). *Shield:* NIV. See also *Shield.*

BUILDER [S]
Mark 12:10 stone which the *b's* rejected...head of the corner
Acts 4:11 This is the stone...set at nought of you *b's*
Heb. 11:10 he [Abraham] looked for a city...whose *b* and maker is God
1 Pet. 2:7 stone which the *b's* disallowed...head of the corner

BUILDING [S]
2 Chron. 3:3 Solomon was instructed for the *b* of the house of God
Mark 13:2 great *b's*? there shall not be left one stone
1 Cor. 3:9 God's husbandry, ye are God's *b*
2 Cor. 5:1 a *b* of God, an house not made with hands

BUL. The eighth month of the Hebrew year, roughly equivalent to parts of our October and November (1 Kings 6:38).

BULL. A general term for the male of the ox or cattle species (Job 21:10).

BULLOCK. A young bull used in animal sacrifices (Num. 15:24).

BULRUSH (PAPYRUS). A reedlike plant that grew in marshy areas of the Nile River and was used for making papyrus, an ancient writing material. The infant Moses was placed in a basket made of this plant (Exod. 2:3). *Papyrus:* NIV, NRSV. See also *Paper; Reed.*

BULWARK (RAMPARTS). A tower in a city's defensive wall that provided a better

BURIAL. On the Mount of Olives' western slope, stone burial boxes in an ancient cemetery stand guard over Jerusalem. Visitors to grave sites leave small rocks as a witness of their visit.

position for firing on the enemy below (Ps. 48:13). *Ramparts:* NIV, NRSV.

BURDEN [S]

Ps. 38:4 heavy *b* they [sins] are too heavy for me
Ps. 55:22 Cast thy *b* upon the LORD
Matt. 11:30 my [Jesus'] yoke is easy, and my *b* is light
Matt. 20:12 we have borne the *b* and heat of the day
Matt. 23:4 they [the Pharisees] bind heavy *b's*
Gal. 6:2 Bear ye one another's *b's*
Gal. 6:5 every man shall bear his own *b*

BURIAL. The ceremonial disposal of a body by placement in the ground or a tomb. In Bible times, burial usually took place as soon as possible because of the warm climate and because a body was considered ceremonially unclean (Deut. 21:23). Jesus' body was prepared for burial with aromatic oils and spices and wrapped in a linen cloth (John 19:39–40). See also *Funeral; Sepulchre.*

BURN [ED, ING]

Exod. 3:2 bush *b'ed* with fire…not consumed
Job 30:30 my [Job's] bones are *b'ed* with heat
Ps. 79:5 thy [God's] jealousy *b* like fire
Prov. 6:27 fire in his bosom, and his clothes not be *b'ed*
Dan. 3:17 our God…deliver us from the *b'ing* fiery furnace
Luke 24:32 Did not our heart *b* within us
Rom. 1:27 the men…*b'ed* in their lust one toward another
1 Cor. 7:9 it is better to marry than to *b*
2 Pet. 3:10 earth…shall be *b'ed* up

BURNING AGUE (FEVER). A severe fever, possibly a symptom of a serious illness, such as typhoid or malaria (Lev. 26:16). *Fever:* NIV, NRSV.

BURNING BUSH. The flaming shrub through which God spoke to Moses. As the bush burned, God expressed compassion for His captive people and called Moses to return to Egypt to deliver them from bondage (Exod. 3:9–10).

BURNING SULFUR. See *Brimstone.*

BURNT OFFERING. A meat sacrifice consisting of an unblemished animal that was totally consumed by fire, except for the hide (Lev. 7:8). Burnt sacrifices were made to atone for sin and to restore the broken relationship between man and God (Num. 6:10–11).

BUSHEL. A dry measure of about one peck (Matt. 5:15).

BUSYBODY (MEDDLER, MISCHIEF MAKER). A gossip and troublemaker. This type of behavior is inappropriate for believers (1 Pet. 4:15). *Meddler:* NIV; *mischief maker:* NRSV. See also *Gossip.*

BUTLER. See *Cupbearer.*

BUY [ETH]

Prov. 23:23 *B* the truth, and sell it not
Prov. 31:16 considereth a field, and *b'eth* it
Amos 8:6 *b* the poor for silver…needy for a pair of shoes
Matt. 13:44 man…selleth all…he hath, and *b'eth* that field
John 6:5 Whence shall we *b* bread, that these may eat

BUZZARD. See *Vulture.*

BYWORD. A degrading saying or remark, usually delivered in taunting fashion (1 Kings 9:7).

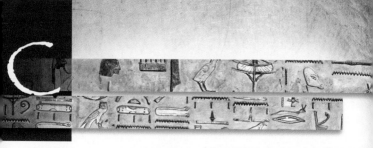

C

CAB (KAB). The smallest unit of measure for dry material, equal to about three pints (2 Kings 6:25). *Kab:* NRSV.

CAESAR. A formal title for several emperors of the Roman Empire. Four separate Caesars are mentioned in the N.T.:

1. Caesar Augustus (reigned about 27 B.C. to A.D. 14), who issued the taxation or census decree that required Joseph to go to Bethlehem, where Jesus was born (Luke 2:1).

2. Caesar Tiberius (reigned about A.D. 14–37), whose administration paralleled the public ministry of Jesus. Tiberius was known for his strict discipline of subject nations and his intolerance of potential rivals (John 19:12).

3. Caesar Claudius (reigned about A.D. 41–54), who sought to reduce strife throughout his empire. One of his tactics was to expel all the Jewish people living in Rome (Acts 18:2).

4. Caesar Nero (reigned about A.D. 54–68), the first emperor under whom the Christians were persecuted. As a Roman citizen, Paul appealed to him (Acts 25:8–12).

CAESAREA. A Roman coastal city, also known as Caesarea Maritima, named for the Roman

CAESAR. Caesar Augustus was the Roman ruler who ensured that Jesus would be born in Bethlehem. He ordered all Jews to return to their ancestral homes for a census. Joseph and pregnant Mary traveled to Bethlehem, hometown of Joseph's most famous descendant: King David.

emperor Caesar Augustus. As the political capital of Palestine during N.T. times, it was the city of residence for Roman rulers of the district, including Agrippa II, before whom Paul appeared (Acts 26:28–32).

CAESAREA PHILIPPI. A city at the foot of Mount Hermon in northern Palestine where Peter confessed Jesus as the Messiah (Matt. 16:13–16). Named for the Roman tetrarch Philip who rebuilt the city, it was called Caesarea Philippi to distinguish it from the city of Caesarea on the Mediterranean coast in central Palestine.

CAESAR'S HOUSEHOLD. A group of converts probably associated with the palace of the emperor in Rome. Paul sent greetings from this group to the church at Philippi (Phil. 4:22).

CAIAPHAS. The Jewish high priest who presided at the trial of Jesus and advised that He be put to death (Matt. 26:57–66; John 18:12–14). After Jesus' resurrection, the apostles John and Peter also appeared before Caiaphas (Acts 4:6).

CAIN. The oldest son of Adam and Eve who murdered his brother Abel. Exiled by God, he built a city that he named for his son (Gen. 4:1–17).

CAINAN. See *Kenan.*

CALAH. An ancient city of Assyria built by Nimrod (Gen. 10:8–12).

CALAMUS (FRAGRANT CANE, AROMATIC CANE). A reedlike plant known for its sweet fragrance (Song 4:14). It was used in anointing oil (Exod. 30:23). *Fragrant cane:* NIV; *aromatic cane:* NRSV.

CALDRON. A large kettle used by priests for boiling meats for sacrificial purposes (2 Chron. 35:13). See also *Kettle.*

CALEB'S DELAYED REWARD

Caleb must have been more than eighty years old when he was finally rewarded for his faithfulness with a tract of land in the Promised Land (Josh. 14:6–15). He was forty when he served on the scouting expedition into Canaan (Josh. 14:7), and another forty years had passed while the Israelites wandered in the wilderness (Num. 14:33).

God's promised reward may be slow in coming, but He always delivers!

CALEB. One of the twelve spies who scouted Canaan. Along with Joshua, he recommended that Israel attack the Canaanites immediately (Num. 13:30). He lived to enter the land forty years later (Josh. 14:6–14). See also *Spies.*

CALF. A young cow prized as a delicacy (Gen. 18:7) and often sacrificed as a burnt offering (Lev. 9:8). See also *Fatling.*

CALF, GOLDEN. An idol built and worshiped by the Israelites in the wilderness as they waited for Moses to come down from Mount Sinai (Exod. 32:1–4). It was probably an image of Apis, a sacred bull worshiped by the Egyptians. In later years, King Jeroboam of Israel set up pagan golden calves at Dan and Bethel (1 Kings 12:26–33). See also *Idol.*

CALL [ED]
Gen. 1:5 God *c'ed* the light Day...the darkness...Night
Gen. 35:10 name shall not be *c'ed...* Jacob
2 Chron. 7:14 my [God's] people...*c'ed* by my name, shall...pray

Ps. 18:6 In my distress I c'ed upon the Lord
Isa. 9:6 his [Messiah's] name...c'ed Wonderful
Isa. 65:24 before they c, I [God] will answer
Matt. 1:21 thou [Joseph] shalt c his name JESUS
Matt. 9:13 I [Jesus] am not come to c the righteous, but sinners
Matt. 20:16 many be c'ed, but few chosen
Luke 6:46 why c ye me, Lord, Lord
Acts 2:21 shall c on...the Lord shall be saved
Acts 11:26 disciples...c'ed Christians first in Antioch
Rom. 1:1 Paul, a servant...c'ed to be an apostle
Rom. 8:28 work together for good...to them...c'ed
Rom. 10:14 c on him in whom they have not believed
1 Cor. 1:26 not many mighty...are c'ed
Eph. 4:1 walk worthy of the vocation...ye are c'ed
Heb. 11:8 Abraham, when he was c'ed...obeyed
1 John 3:1 we should be c'ed the sons of God

CALLING. The special summons to service that all Christians receive as part of their salvation experience (1 Cor. 7:20). See also *Vocation.*

CALNEH/CALNO. An ancient city built in southern Mesopotamia by Nimrod (Gen. 10:9–10). This may be the same city as *Canneh* (Ezek. 27:23). *Calno:* Isa. 10:9.

CALVARY (THE SKULL). A hill just outside the city walls of Jerusalem where Jesus was crucified (Luke 23:33). The word comes from a Latin word meaning "skull," thus "place of the skull." The Aramaic form of this word is *Golgotha* (Mark 15:22). *The Skull:* niv, nrsv. See also *Cross.*

CAMEL. A hardy, humpbacked animal ideally suited to the desert climate of Palestine and used as a riding animal and beast of burden (Gen. 24:64).

CAMP. A place where tent dwellers and nomads pitch their tents. The Israelites camped in many different places during their years of wandering in the wilderness (Num. 33:1–49). See also *Wilderness Wanderings.*

CAMPHIRE (HENNA). A plant that produced a valuable red dye, used by women to adorn their lips and fingernails (Song 1:14). *Henna:* niv, nrsv.

CANA OF GALILEE. A village near Capernaum in the district of Galilee where Jesus performed His first miracle—the transformation of water into wine at a wedding feast (John 2:1–11).

CANAAN
1. A son of Ham whose descendants founded several tribal peoples in and around Palestine (Gen. 10:1, 6, 15–18).
2. The region between the Red Sea and the Jordan River where Canaan's descendants settled and the territory that God promised to Abraham and his descendants (Gen. 15:3–7). *Chanaan:* Greek form (Acts 7:11). See also *Land of Promise.*

CANAANITES
1. The original inhabitants of Canaan who settled the land before Abraham arrived about 2000 b.c. (Gen. 12:5–6). They were eventually forced out of the land by Israel at God's command because of their pagan religious practices. Intermarriage with Canaanites by the Israelites was distinctly prohibited by God (Deut. 7:3).
2. Members of a Jewish sect in N.T. times known for their fanatical opposition to the rule of Rome. Jesus' apostle Simon the Canaanite may have been a member of, or a sympathizer with, this sect (Matt. 10:4). They were also known as the *zelotes* or *zealots.*

CANDACE. A title of the queens of Ethiopia in N.T. times (Acts 8:27).

CANDLE (LAMP). A shallow clay bowl filled with oil and a burning wick, used for illumination (Matt. 5:15). *Lamp:* NIV, NRSV.

CANDLESTICK (LAMPSTAND). A stand that held several small oil-burning lamps (Mark 4:21). *Lampstand:* NIV, NRSV.

CANKER (GANGRENE). A disease that caused rapid deterioration of the flesh (2 Tim. 2:17). *Gangrene:* NIV, NRSV.

CANKERWORM (LOCUST). A locust or grasshopper in the caterpillar stage of its growth (Joel 1:4). *Locust:* NIV, NRSV. See also *Locust; Palmer Worm.*

CAPERNAUM. A city on the northwestern shore of the Sea of Galilee that served as the headquarters for Jesus during His Galilean ministry (Matt. 9:1; Mark 2:1). Capernaum was the home of His disciples Matthew (Matt. 9:9), Simon Peter, Andrew, James, and John (Mark 1:21–29).

CAPHTOR. The original home of the Philistines, probably the island of Crete (Jer. 47:4). See also *Crete; Philistines.*

CAPITALS. See *Pommels.*

CAPPADOCIA. A Roman province of Asia Minor. Christians of Cappadocia were addressed by Peter (1 Pet. 1:1).

CAPTAIN (AUTHOR, PIONEER). A title for a civil or military officer (Judg. 4:7). This is also a title for Christ (Heb. 2:10). *Author:* NIV; *pioneer:* NRSV.

CAPTIVE [S]

Isa. 61:1 anointed me [God's servant]...proclaim liberty to the *c's*

Ezek. 1:1 I [Ezekiel] was among the *c's* by the river

Luke 4:18 he [God] hath anointed me [Jesus]...to preach deliverance to the *c's*

Eph. 4:8 When he [Jesus] ascended...he led captivity *c*

CANDLE. A worshiper lights a candle in Bethlehem's Church of the Nativity, where an ancient tradition says Jesus was born. Candles or lamps have been used in the worship of God for more than three thousand years—since the Exodus, when Jews worshiped at a tent sanctuary.

CENTURION. Dressed for military success, this Roman soldier is suited in a metal vest and helmet. The figurine is from Roman times.

CAPTIVITY. The carrying away of the citizens of a country by a conquering nation. The nation of Israel (the Northern Kingdom) was carried into captivity by the Assyrians about 722 B.C. (2 Kings 15:29), while Judah (the Southern Kingdom) suffered the same fate at the hands of the Babylonians in 587 B.C. (2 Chron. 36:6–7). See also *Dispersion*.

CARBUNCLE (BERYL, EMERALD). A precious stone of deep red color in the breastplate of the high priest (Exod. 28:17). *Beryl:* NIV; *emerald:* NRSV. See also *Emerald*.

CARCHEMISH CHARCHEMISH. An ancient city near the Euphrates River in Mesopotamia (Jer. 46:2), where the Assyrian army was victorious over the Egyptians. *Charchemish:* 2 Chron. 35:20–24.

CARE [S, TH]
Mark 4:19 the *c's* of this world...choke the word
John 10:13 hireling, and *c'th* not for the sheep
1 Cor. 7:33 he that is married *c'th* for the things...of the world
1 Tim. 3:5 shall he take *c* of the church of God
1 Pet. 5:7 your *c* upon him [Jesus]; for he *c'th* for you

CARMEL, MOUNT. A prominent mountain in northern Palestine where the prophet Elijah demonstrated the power of God in a dramatic encounter with the priests of the pagan god Baal (1 Kings 18:17–39).

CARNAL (WORLDLY). To give in to the desires of the flesh. Following their natural desires led the Christians of Corinth into division and strife (1 Cor. 3:1–5). *Worldly:* NIV.

CARRION VULTURE. See *Gier Eagle*.

CART. A two-wheeled wagon, usually pulled by oxen (1 Sam. 6:7–8). See also *Wagon*.

CASLUHIM (CASLUHITES). An ancient people descended from Mizraim (the Hebrew word for Egypt), son of Ham (Gen. 10:14). *Casluhites:* NIV. See also *Egypt; Mizraim.*

CASSIA. The dried bark of a tree similar to the cinnamon that was prized for its pleasing fragrance. Cassia was used as an ingredient of holy oil (Exod. 30:24).

CAST [ING]
Job 8:20 God will not *c* away a perfect man
Ps. 42:11 Why art thou *c* down, O my soul?
Ps. 51:11 *C* me not away from thy [God's] presence
Ps. 71:9 *C* me not off in the time of old age
Ps. 94:14 the LORD will not *c* off his people
Eccles. 3:5 time to *c* away stones, and a time to gather
Eccles. 11:1 *C* thy bread upon the waters
Jer. 7:15 I [God] will *c* you out of my sight
Matt. 3:10 tree...bringeth not forth good fruit is...*c* into the fire
Matt. 21:12 Jesus...*c* out all them that sold and bought in the temple
Matt. 27:5 he [Judas] *c* down the pieces of silver
Mark 12:43 this poor widow hath *c* more in
John 8:7 without sin...let him first *c* a stone
1 Pet. 5:7 *C'ing* all your care upon him [Jesus]; for he careth for you
Rev. 12:9 great dragon was *c* out, that old serpent

CASTAWAY. A word for "worthlessness" or "rejection." Paul used this word to express the idea of "disqualified" or "rejected" (1 Cor. 9:27).

CASTLE (BARRACKS). A fortress or defense tower. The "castle" into which Paul was taken was the quarters of the Roman soldiers at Jerusalem in the fortress of Antonia near the temple (Acts 21:34). *Barracks:* NIV, NRSV.

CASTOR AND POLLUX (TWIN BROTHERS). The twin sons of Zeus in Greek and Roman mythology who were considered special protectors of sailors. Paul's ship to Rome featured a carving of these two pagan gods (Acts 28:11). *Twin Brothers:* NRSV.

CATHOLIC EPISTLES. See *General Epistles.*

CAVE. A natural passageway or cavern within the earth. Caves were used as residences (Gen. 19:30) and burial places (Gen. 49:29). See also *Sepulchre.*

CEASE [D, ING]
Gen. 8:22 earth remaineth...day and night shall not *c*
Ps. 37:8 *C* from anger, and forsake wrath
Ps. 85:4 God...cause thine anger toward us to *c*
Mark 4:39 wind *c'd*, and there was a great calm
Acts 5:42 they [the apostles] *c'd* not to...preach Jesus Christ
1 Cor. 13:8 whether there be tongues, they shall *c*
1 Thess. 5:17 Pray without *c'ing*

CEDAR. A cone-bearing evergreen tree that produces a reddish, fragrant wood. Lumber from the cedars of Lebanon was used in the temple in Jerusalem (1 Kings 5:1–10).

CEDRON. See *Kidron.*

CENCHREA (CENCHREAE). A harbor of Corinth through which Paul passed during the second missionary journey (Acts 18:18). This was the site of a church mentioned by Paul (Rom. 16:1), perhaps a branch of the church at Corinth. *Cenchreae:* NRSV.

CENSER. A small, portable container in which incense was burned (Num. 16:6–39). See also *Firepan; Incense.*

CENSUS. A count of the population of a country or region (2 Sam. 24:1–9; Luke 2:1–3).

CENTURION. A Roman military officer who commanded a force of one hundred soldiers (Acts 10:1, 22).

CHARIOT. *Storming across a field in his chariot, Ramses II, king of Egypt in the 1200s B.C., leads his army to victory over Hittite warriors.*

CEPHAS. See *Simon*, No. 1.

CHAFF. The leftover husks of threshed grain, separated when the grain was tossed into the air. The ungodly are compared to chaff (Ps. 1:4). See also *Winnowing.*

CHALCEDONY (AGATE). A precious stone cut from multicolored quartz and used in the foundation of the heavenly city, or New Jerusalem (Rev. 21:19). *Agate:* NRSV. See also *Agate.*

CHALDEA, CHALDEANS. See *Babylonia.*

CHALKSTONE. A soft and easily crushed rock, similar to limestone (Isa. 27:9).

CHAMBER. A word for a room or an enclosed place in a house or public building (2 Kings 23:12).

CHAMBERLAIN (EUNUCH). An officer in charge of the royal chambers or the king's lodgings and wardrobe, and perhaps his harem (Esther 2:3). *Eunuch:* NIV, NRSV. See also *Eunuch.*

CHAMELEON. See *Mole.*

CHAMOIS (MOUNTAIN SHEEP). A word that probably refers to a wild goat or a wild mountain sheep (Deut. 14:5). *Mountain sheep:* NIV, NRSV.

CHANAAN. See *Canaan.*

CHANCELLOR (COMMANDING OFFICER, ROYAL DEPUTY). A high official of the Persian kings whose exact duties are unknown (Ezra 4:8). *Commanding officer:* NIV; *royal deputy:* NRSV.

CHANGE [D, TH]
Jer. 2:11 Hath a nation *c'd* their gods
Jer. 13:23 Can the Ethiopian *c* his skin
Dan. 2:21 he [God] *c'th* the times and the seasons
Rom. 1:23 *c'd* the glory of the uncorruptible God
Rom. 1:26 women did *c* the natural use into that…against nature
1 Cor. 15:51 shall not all sleep, but we shall be *c'd*
Phil. 3:21 shall *c* our vile body…like…his glorious body

CHARCHEMISH. See *Carchemish.*

CHARGE [D]
Deut. 3:28 *c* Joshua, and encourage him
1 Kings 2:1 David…*c'd* Solomon his son
Ps. 91:11 he [God] shall give his angels *c* over thee
Luke 8:56 he [Jesus] *c'd* them…tell no man what was done
Acts 7:60 Lord, lay not this sin to their *c*

CHARGER (PLATTER). A dish or shallow basin used in sacrificial ceremonies (Num. 7:13, 79). The head of John the Baptist was placed on a charger (Matt. 14:11). *Platter:* NIV, NRSV. See also *Platter.*

CHARIOT. A two-wheeled carriage drawn by horses. High government officials rode in chariots, and chariots were also used as instruments of war (Judg. 4:15).

CHARIOT CITIES. The cities where Solomon stored or headquartered his chariots and chariot forces (1 Kings 9:19).

CHARIOT OF FIRE. The fiery chariot with blazing horses that came between Elijah and Elisha as Elijah was taken into heaven by a whirlwind (2 Kings 2:11). See also *Elijah.*

CHARIOTS OF THE SUN. Chariots dedicated to the sun—a popular custom among the Persians, who worshiped this heavenly body. All chariots devoted to this practice among the Israelites were burned by King Josiah of Judah (2 Kings 23:11). See also *Sun.*

CHARITY. An Old English word for "love" (1 Cor. 13). See *Love.*

Col. 3:14 above all these things put on *c*
1 Tim. 4:12 an example…in conversation, in *c*
1 Pet. 4:8 *c* shall cover the multitude of sins
Rev. 2:19 I [Jesus] know thy works, and *c*, and service

CHARMERS. Magicians who claimed to be able to commune with the dead (Isa. 19:3). See also *Divination; Magic; Medium; Necromancer.*

CHARRAN. See *Haran.*

CHASTE. A term indicating inward cleanliness, generally referring to sexual purity (2 Cor. 11:2). See also *Clean.*

CHASTEN [ED, EST, ETH, ING]
Ps. 73:14 the day long have I been…*c'ed* every morning
Ps. 94:12 Blessed is the man whom thou *c'est*, O LORD
Prov. 3:11 My son, despise not the *c'ing* of the LORD
Heb. 12:6 whom the Lord loveth he *c'eth*
Rev. 3:19 As many as I love, I rebuke and *c*

CHASTISEMENT (DISCIPLINE). Punishment or discipline inflicted by God for guiding and correcting His children (Heb. 12:8). *Discipline:* NIV, NRSV. See also *Discipline.*

CHEBAR. A river or canal of Babylonia where Jewish captives settled during the Exile. Ezekiel's visions came to him at Chebar (Ezek. 1:3; 10:15, 20).

CHEDORLAOMER. A king of Elam who invaded Canaan in Abraham's time (Gen. 14:1–16).

CHEEK. To strike a person on the cheek was considered a grave insult (Job 16:10). Jesus taught believers to react to such acts with kindness (Luke 6:29).

CHEER
Matt. 9:2 Son [man with palsy], be of good *c*
John 16:33 be of good *c*, I [Jesus] have overcome the world
Acts 23:11 Be of good *c*, Paul...thou bear witness also at Rome

CHEERFUL
Prov. 15:13 merry heart maketh a *c* countenance
Zech. 9:17 corn shall make the young men *c*
2 Cor. 9:7 let him give...for God loveth a *c* giver

CHEMOSH. The chief pagan god of the Moabites and Ammonites to which children were sacrificed (Judg. 11:24; 2 Kings 23:13). See also *Human Sacrifice*.

CHERETHITES/CHERETHIMS. A tribe of the Philistines in southwest Palestine (1 Sam. 30:14). *Cherethims:* Ezek. 25:16.

CHERITH. A brook where the prophet Elijah hid and where he was fed by ravens during a famine (1 Kings 17:3–5).

CHERUBIMS. An order of angelic, winged creatures (Gen. 3:24). Their function was to praise God and glorify His name (Ezek. 10:18–20).

CHIEF. Head of a tribe or family (Num. 3:24, 30, 32, 35). See also *Duke*.

CHIEF SEATS. Places of honor sought by the scribes and Pharisees. Jesus taught His followers that the highest honor is to serve others (Mark 12:38–39).

CHILD
Gen. 17:17 a *c* be born unto him...an hundred years old
Prov. 22:6 Train up a *c* in the way he should go

Isa. 9:6 unto us a *c* is born
Jer. 1:6 behold, I [Jeremiah] cannot speak: for I am a *c*
Hosea 11:1 When Israel was a *c*, then I [God] loved him
Matt. 1:23 a virgin shall be with *c*
Matt. 18:4 humble himself as this little *c*...is greatest
Luke 2:40 the *c* [Jesus] grew, and waxed strong in spirit
1 Cor. 13:11 When I [Paul] was a *c*, I spake as a *c*

CHILD SACRIFICE. See *Human Sacrifice*.

CHILDREN. Children were looked upon as blessings from God (Ps. 127:3), and childlessness was considered a curse (Deut. 7:14). The word is also used symbolically of those who belong to Christ (Rom. 8:16–17). See also *Parents*.

Gen. 3:16 in sorrow thou [Eve] shalt bring forth *c*
Exod. 1:7 *c* of Israel were fruitful, and increased
Exod. 20:5 iniquity of the fathers upon the *c*
Josh. 4:6 your *c*...What mean ye by these stones
Ps. 103:13 father pitieth his *c*, so the LORD pitieth them that fear him
Ps. 127:3 *c* are an heritage of the LORD
Prov. 20:7 *c* are blessed after him [the just man]
Prov. 31:28 *c* arise up, and call her blessed
Jer. 31:15 Rahel weeping for her *c*
Matt. 7:11 give good gifts unto your *c*
Matt. 18:3 become as little *c*, ye shall not enter into the kingdom
Mark 10:13 they brought young *c* to him [Jesus]
John 12:36 that ye may be the *c* of light
Eph. 6:1 *c*, obey your parents in the Lord
Eph. 6:4 fathers, provoke not your *c* to wrath

CHINNEROTH. See *Galilee, Sea of*.

CHISLEU (KISLEV, CHISLEV). The ninth month of the Hebrew year, roughly equivalent to parts of our November and December (Neh. 1:1). *Kislev:* NIV; *Chislev:* NRSV.

CHITTIM. See *Cyprus*.

CHLOE. A Christian disciple at the place from which Paul sent his first epistle to the Corinthians—probably Philippi (1 Cor. 1:11).

CHOOSE [ING]

Deut. 7:7 Lord did not... c you, because ye were more in number
Deut. 30:19 c life, that both thou and thy seed may live
Josh. 24:15 c you this day whom ye will serve
Phil. 1:22 yet what I [Paul] shall c I wot not
Heb. 11:25 C'ing rather to suffer affliction

CHORAZIN. A city north of the Sea of Galilee where Jesus did many works. He pronounced a woe on this city because of its unbelief (Matt. 11:21).

CHOSEN

Deut. 7:6 God hath c thee to be a special people
Prov. 22:1 good name is rather to be c than great riches
Isa. 43:10 Ye are...my [God's] servant whom I have c
Matt. 12:18 Behold my [God's] servant, whom I have c
Matt. 20:16 many be called, but few c
Luke 10:42 Mary hath c that good part
John 15:16 Ye have not c me [Jesus], but I have c you
Acts 9:15 he [Paul] is a c vessel unto me [Jesus]
1 Cor. 1:27 God hath c the foolish things of the world to confound the wise
2 Thess. 2:13 God hath... c you to salvation
1 Pet. 2:9 ye are a c generation, a royal priesthood

CHOSEN LADY. See *Elect Lady.*

CHRIST. See *Jesus Christ.*

CHRISTIAN. A disciple or follower of Christ. The name apparently was first used of the believers in the church at Antioch (Acts 11:26). Other words that express the same idea are *saint* (Acts 9:13) and *brethren* (Acts 6:3). See also *Way, The.*

CHRONICLES, BOOKS OF FIRST AND SECOND. Two historical books of the O.T. that cover several centuries of history, beginning with a genealogy of Adam and his descendants (1 Chron. 1–9) and ending with the return of Jewish captives to their homeland about 538 B.C. following a period of exile among the Babylonians and Persians (2 Chron. 36).

Major events covered in the books include (1) the death of King Saul (1 Chron. 10); (2) the reign of King David (1 Chron. 10–29); (3) the reign of King Solomon (2 Chron. 1–9); and (4) the reigns of selected kings of Judah after the division of the kingdom into two nations following Solomon's death (2 Chron. 10–36).

CHRYSOLYTE (CHRYSOLITE). A precious stone, possibly yellow topaz, used in the foundation of the heavenly city, or New Jerusalem (Rev. 21:20). *Chrysolite:* NIV, NRSV. See also *Beryl.*

CHRYSOPRASUS (CHRYSOPRASE). A precious stone, green in color and similar to agate, used in the foundation of the heavenly city, or New Jerusalem (Rev. 21:20). *Chrysoprase:* NIV, NRSV. See also *Beryl.*

CHURCH. A local body of believers assembled for Christian worship (Acts 15:4; 1 Cor. 1:22) as well as all the redeemed of the ages who belong to Christ (Gal. 1:13; Eph. 5:27). The word *church* is a translation of a Greek term that means "an assembly."

Christ is head of His body, the Church, and His will is to be preeminent (Col. 1:18) by virtue of His redeeming work and lordship (Col. 1:14; 3:15–17). The Church's mission is to win the lost (Luke 4:18) and minister to others in the world. See also *Assembly; Congregation; People of God; Saint.*

CHURCH [ES]

Matt. 16:18 Peter, and upon this rock I [Jesus] will build my c
Matt. 18:17 neglect to hear them, tell it unto the c
Acts 2:47 added to the c daily such as should be saved
Acts 5:11 fear came upon all the c
Acts 8:3 Saul, he made havock of the c
Acts 14:23 they [Paul and Barnabas] had ordained them elders in every c
Acts 20:28 the Holy Ghost hath made you overseers, to feed the c of God

Rom. 16:16 The *c'es* of Christ salute you
1 Cor. 14:4 he that prophesieth edifieth the *c*
Gal. 1:13 I [Paul] persecuted the *c* of God
Eph. 3:21 be glory in the *c* by Christ Jesus
Eph. 5:25 Christ also loved the *c*, and gave himself for it
Col. 1:18 he [Christ] is the head of the body, the *c*
1 Tim. 3:5 how shall he take care of the *c* of God
1 Tim. 3:15 *c* of the living God...pillar and ground of...truth
James 5:14 elders of the *c*; and let them pray over him
Rev. 1:4 John to the seven *c'es* which are in Asia

CHUSHAN-RISHATHAIM (CUSHAN-RISHATHAIM). A king of Mesopotamia who oppressed the Israelites. He was defeated by the first judge, Othniel (Judg. 3:8–10). *Cushan-rishathaim:* NIV, NRSV.

CILICIA. A province of Asia Minor whose major city was Tarsus, Paul's hometown. Paul visited Cilicia after his conversion (Acts 15:40–41; Gal. 1:21).

CIRCUMCISE [D]
Gen. 17:11 shall *c* the flesh of your foreskin
Gen. 17:24 Abraham was ninety years old and nine, when he was *c'd*
Jer. 4:4 *C* yourselves to the LORD
Acts 15:1 certain men...said, Except ye be *c'd*...cannot be saved
Gal. 5:2 I if ye be *c'd*, Christ shall profit you nothing
Phil. 3:5 *C'd* the eighth day, of the stock of Israel

CIRCUMCISION. The removal of the foreskin of the male sex organ, a ritual performed generally on the eighth day after birth (Lev. 12:3). This practice, probably initiated with Abraham (Gen. 17:9–14), signified the covenant between God and His people, the Israelites. In the N.T., the word is often used symbolically for the casting off of sin or worldly desires (Col. 2:11).

Acts 10:45 they of the *c* which believed were astonished
Rom. 3:1 or what profit is there of *c*
Rom. 15:8 Christ was a minister of the *c* for the truth of God
1 Cor. 7:19 *C* is nothing, and uncircumcision is nothing
Col. 3:11 neither Greek nor Jew, *c* nor uncircumcision

CIRCUMSPECT. Prudent and holy. Paul charged the Ephesian Christians to live circumspectly (Eph. 5:15).

CISTERN. A large pit or hole in the ground that served as a water reservoir (2 Kings 18:31). Empty cisterns were sometimes used as dungeons or prisons (Gen. 37:24). See also *Pit; Prison.*

CITIES OF REFUGE. Six cities assigned to the Levites and set aside as sanctuaries for those who killed other persons by accident. These cities, scattered throughout Palestine, were Bezer, Golan, Hebron, Kedesh, Ramoth-gilead, and Shechem (Josh. 20:7–9). See also *Avenger of Blood; Manslayer.*

SAFETY IN THE CITIES

In the six cities of refuge (Josh. 20), Jewish citizens were protected from revenge by relatives of the deceased while a system of due process was put into motion. After investigating the matter, city officials issued the final judgment on whether a person was innocent or guilty of murder.

CITIES OF THE PLAIN. Five cities on the plain of Jordan destroyed in Abraham's time because of the great sin of their inhabitants. These cities were Admah, Bela or Zoar, Gomorrah, Sodom, and Zeboiim (Gen. 14:1–2).

CITRON WOOD. See *Thyine Wood.*

CITY. A population center where trade and commerce flourished. Many biblical cities were protected by massive defensive walls. The first city mentioned in the Bible was built by Cain (Gen. 4:17). See also *Fenced City.*

CITY CLERK. See *Town Clerk.*

CITY GATE. A massive wooden door in a city wall, often reinforced with brass or iron for greater strength. Goods were often bought and sold and legal matters were discussed just inside the gate (Ruth 4:11). Gates in the wall of Jerusalem mentioned by name in the Bible include the Beautiful Gate (Acts 3:10), Fish Gate (Neh. 3:3), Horse Gate (2 Chron. 23:15), and Water Gate (Neh. 3:26). See also *Fenced City.*

CITY OF DAVID. A title applied to Bethlehem and Jerusalem because of David's close association with these cities (Neh. 3:15; Luke 2:11). See also *Bethlehem; Jerusalem.*

CITY OF GOD. A name applied to the city of Jerusalem, religious capital of the nation of Israel (Ps. 46:4–5).

CLAUDIUS. See *Caesar, No. 3.*

CLAUDIUS LYSIAS. A Roman military officer who rescued Paul from an angry mob at Jerusalem (Acts 21:30–35; 23:22–30).

CLAY. Fine soil used for making bricks and pottery (Jer. 18:1–6). While still moist, squares of clay were also written on, then baked to produce a hard, permanent tablet.

CLAY TABLET. See *Tile.*

CITY OF DAVID. The City of David rested on a ridge in what is now just a small plug of ground in the urban sprawl of Jerusalem. David's capital sat in the outlined area below the dotted line. His son Solomon later expanded the city above by adding the temple complex.

CLEAN. A word used by the Hebrews to describe things that were ceremonially pure (Lev. 11). The word is also used symbolically to signify holiness or righteousness (Ps. 24:4). See also *Purification; Wash.*

CLEANSE [D, TH]
Lev. 16:30 priest make an atonement…to **c** you
Ps. 51:2 Wash me…**c** me from my sin
Matt. 11:5 lepers are **c'd**, and the deaf hear

Matt. 23:26 *c* first that which is within the cup
Luke 17:17 not ten *c'd?* but where are the nine
Acts 10:15 God hath *c'd,* that call not thou [Peter] common
2 Cor. 7:1 let us *c* ourselves from all filthiness
1 John 1:7 blood of Jesus Christ…*c'th* us from all sin
1 John 1:9 he [Jesus] is faithful…*c* us from all unrighteousness

CLEAVE.
To hold firmly to or to remain faithful. Husbands are instructed to cleave to their wives (Matt. 19:5).

Gen. 2:24 leave his father…mother…*c* unto his wife
Josh. 23:8 But *c* unto the Lord your God
Mark 10:7 leave his father…mother…*c* to his wife
Rom. 12:9 Abhor…evil; *c* to that which is good

CLEOPAS.
A Christian believer to whom Christ appeared on the road to Emmaus after His resurrection (Luke 24:18).

CLOKE/CLOAK.
A one-piece, sleeveless garment, similar to a short robe, worn by both men and women in Bible times (Matt. 5:40). *Cloak:* NIV, NRSV. See also *Mantle.*

CLOTH.
See *Handkerchief; Napkin.*

CLOTHED [ING]
2 Chron. 6:41 Lord God, be *c* with salvation
Ps. 93:1 The Lord…is *c* with majesty
Prov. 31:25 Strength and honour are her *c'ing*

Isa. 61:10 he [God] hath *c* me with the garments of salvation
Matt. 7:15 false prophets…in sheep's *c'ing*
Matt. 25:36 Naked, and ye *c* me
Mark 1:6 John was *c* with camel's hair
Mark 12:38 the scribes…love to go in long *c'ing*
Mark 15:17 they *c* him [Jesus] with purple
Luke 16:19 a certain rich man…*c* in purple

CLOTHES
Josh. 7:6 Joshua rent his *c,* and fell to the earth
Prov. 6:27 take fire in his bosom, and his *c* not be burned
Luke 2:7 wrapped him [Jesus] in swaddling *c*
John 19:40 wound it [Jesus' body] in linen *c*

CLOUD.
A mass of water vapor in the sky. Clouds are often associated with God's presence and protection (Exod. 16:10). At His second coming, Christ will come in "the clouds of heaven" (Matt. 24:30). See also *Pillar of Fire and Cloud.*

CLUB.
See *Maul.*

COAT OF MAIL.
See *Brigandine.*

COCK.
A rooster. The crowing of the cock in Mark 13:35 refers to the third watch of the night, just before daybreak.

COCKATRICE (ADDER, VIPER).
A poisonous snake (Isa. 11:8). *Adder:* NRSV; *viper:* NIV.

COCKLE (WEED).
A weed that grows in fields of grain (Job 31:40). *Weed:* NIV, NRSV.

COLOSSE (COLOSSAE).
A city about 100 miles east of Ephesus and the site of a church to which Paul wrote one of his epistles (Col. 1:2). Whether Paul visited this city is uncertain. *Colossae:* NRSV.

COLOSSIANS, EPISTLE TO THE.
A short epistle of the apostle Paul on the theme

CHRIST'S SUFFICIENCY IN COLOSSIANS

In his epistle to the Colossians, Paul presents Jesus Christ as the all-sufficient Savior. He is the Redeemer (Col. 1:14), the firstborn from the dead (1:18), the mystery of God (2:2), the victor over all principalities and powers (2:10), the exalted and glorified One (3:1), and the guarantee of our eternal inheritance (3:24).

8
D
3

of Christ's glory and majesty and His work of redemption (chaps. 1–2). Paul also challenged the Christians at Colosse to put on the character of Christ and to express His love in their relationships with others (chaps. 3–4).

COLT. A young donkey. Christ rode a colt into Jerusalem (Matt. 21:1–7). See also *Ass.*

COMFORT [ED]
Job 2:11 Job's three friends...came...to *c* him
Ps. 23:4 thy [God's] rod and thy staff they *c* me
Isa. 40:1 *C* ye, *c* ye my people, saith your God
Jer. 31:15 Rahel weeping...refused to be *c'ed* for her children
Matt. 5:4 Blessed are they that mourn...shall be *c'ed*
1 Thess. 4:18 *c* one another with these words

COMFORTER (COUNSELOR, ADVOCATE).
A title for the Holy Spirit that means "to strengthen" or "to bolster" (John 14:16, 26; 15:26; 16:7). *Counselor:* NIV; *Advocate:* NRSV. See also *Advocate; Helper; Holy Spirit; Paraclete.*

COMMAND [ED, ETH]
Gen. 7:5 Noah did...all that the LORD *c'ed* him
Matt. 28:20 observe all things whatsoever I [Jesus] have *c'ed* you
Mark 6:8 [Jesus] *c'ed* them...take nothing for their journey
Luke 4:3 this stone that it be made bread
Luke 8:25 he [Jesus] *c'eth* even the winds and water
John 15:17 These things I [Jesus] *c* you...love one another

COMMANDING OFFICER. See *Chancellor.*

COMMANDMENT. An order imposed by a person of rank or authority (Neh. 11:23). Jesus described the statute to love God and man as the greatest commandment (John 13:34). See also *Statute.*

COMMANDMENT [S]
Exod. 34:28 he [Moses] wrote...the ten *c's*
Ezra 9:10 we have forsaken thy [God's] *c's*
Ps. 111:7 his [God's] *c's* are sure
Prov. 10:8 wise in heart will receive *c's*
Amos 2:4 have...not kept his [God's] *c's*

Matt. 15:3 ye [Pharisees]...transgress the *c* of God
Mark 12:28 Which is the first *c* of all
John 14:15 love me [Jesus], keep my *c's*
John 15:10 keep my [Jesus'] *c's*, ye shall abide in my love
1 John 2:3 we know him [Jesus], if we keep his *c's*
2 John 6 this is love, that we walk after his [God's] *c's*

COMMANDMENTS, TEN. See *Ten Commandments.*

COMMEND [ED, ETH]
Prov. 12:8 man shall be *c'ed* according to his wisdom
Luke 16:8 the lord *c'ed* the unjust steward
Luke 23:46 into thy hands I [Jesus] *c* my spirit
Rom. 5:8 God *c'eth* his love toward us...Christ died for us

COMMISSION. A special assignment from a person of authority (Ezra 8:36). Jesus' Great Commission to all His followers is to make disciples of all people everywhere (Matt. 28:19–20).

COMMIT [TED, TETH]
Exod. 20:14 Thou shalt not *c* adultery
Ps. 31:5 Into thine [God's] hand I [Jesus] *c* my spirit
Prov. 16:3 *C* thy works unto the LORD
Matt. 5:28 looketh on a woman to lust...hath *c'ted* adultery
John 5:22 Father...hath *c'ted* all judgment unto the Son
John 8:34 Whosoever *c'teth* sin is the servant of sin
1 Cor. 6:18 he that *c'teth* fornication sinneth against his own body
2 Cor. 5:19 God...hath *c'ted* unto us the word of reconciliation
1 John 3:9 Whosoever is born of God doth not *c* sin

COMMUNICATION [S]
Matt. 5:37 let your *c* be, Yea, yea; Nay, nay
Luke 24:17 What manner of *c's* are these
Eph. 4:29 Let no corrupt *c* proceed out of your mouth

COMMUNION
1 Cor. 10:16 cup of blessing...*c* of the blood of Christ
2 Cor. 6:14 what *c* hath light with darkness
2 Cor. 13:14 *c* of the Holy Ghost, be with you all

COMPACT. See *League.*

COMPANION. See *Yokefellow*.

COMPASSION. An attitude of mercy and forgiveness. As the compassionate Savior (Matt. 15:32), Jesus expects His followers to show compassion toward others (Matt. 18:33). See also *Mercy*.

Ps. 145:8 The Lord is gracious, and full of *c*
Jer. 12:15 I [God] will return, and have *c* on them
Matt. 14:14 Jesus…was moved with *c* toward them
Mark 9:22 if thou canst do any thing, have *c* on us
Luke 10:33 a certain Samaritan…had *c* on him
Luke 15:20 his father…had *c*, and ran, and fell on his neck
1 Pet. 3:8 be ye all of one mind, having *c* one of another

CONCEIT. Vanity or pride; to have an exaggerated opinion of oneself. Paul warned Christians against such behavior (Rom. 11:25; 12:16). See also *Pride; Vanity*.

CONCEIVE [D]
Gen. 21:2 Sarah *c'd*, and bare Abraham a son
Ps. 51:5 in sin did my mother *c* me
Isa. 7:14 a virgin shall *c*, and bear a son
Matt. 1:20 that…*c'd* in her [Mary] is of the Holy Ghost
Heb. 11:11 Sara herself received strength to *c* seed

CONCUBINE. A female slave or mistress; a secondary or common-law wife. Concubines were common among the patriarchs of the O.T. (Gen. 35:22), but Jesus taught the concept of monogamy—marriage to one person only (Matt. 19:4–9). See also *Paramour*.

CONCUPISCENCE (EVIL DE-SIRES). Sinful desire or sexual lust. Paul warned Christians of the dangers of this sin (Col. 3:5). *Evil desires:* NIV, NRSV.

CONDEMN [ED, ETH]
Job 15:6 Thine own mouth *c'eth* thee
Prov. 12:2 man of wicked devices will he [God] *c*
Matt. 12:37 by thy words thou shalt be *c'ed*
Luke 6:37 *c* not, and ye shall not be *c'ed*
John 3:17 God sent not his Son…to *c* the world
John 8:11 Neither do I [Jesus] *c* thee: go…sin no more

CONDEMNATION. The act of declaring a sinner guilty and deserving of punishment

CONDUIT. Israel's most famous conduit is Hezekiah's Tunnel, chiseled through nearly six hundred yards of solid rock. King Hezekiah built the conduit to bring water from an underground spring outside Jerusalem's protective walls to a pool inside the city.

(Rom. 5:18). Jesus' mission was not to condemn but to save (John 3:17–18).

Rom. 8:1 no **c** to them which are in Christ Jesus
James 3:1 we shall receive the greater **c**
James 5:12 yea be yea…lest ye fall into **c**

CONDUIT. A pipe or aqueduct through which water was channeled. King Hezekiah of Judah cut a conduit through solid rock to pipe water into Jerusalem (2 Kings 20:20). See also *Hezekiah.*

CONEY (BADGER). A small, furry animal that lived among the rocky cliffs of Palestine—probably the rock badger (Prov. 30:26). *Badger:* NRSV.

CONFESS. To admit or acknowledge one's sin (Josh. 7:19) and to proclaim one's faith in a bold and forthright manner (Rom. 10:9–10).

CONFESS [ETH]

Ps. 32:5 I will **c** my transgressions unto the Lord
Luke 12:8 him shall the Son of man also **c**
Rom. 10:9 if thou shalt **c** with thy mouth the Lord Jesus
Phil. 2:11 tongue should **c** that Jesus Christ is Lord
James 5:16 **c** your faults one to another
1 John 1:9 we **c** our sins, he is faithful and just to forgive
1 John 4:2 every spirit that **c'eth** that Jesus Christ is come in the flesh is of God
Rev. 3:5 I [Jesus] will **c** his name before my Father

CONFIDENCE

Ps. 118:9 better to trust in the Lord…put **c** in princes
Prov. 14:26 In the fear of the Lord is strong **c**
Isa. 30:15 in quietness and in **c** shall be your strength
Eph. 3:12 In whom [Jesus] we have…access with **c**

CONFIDENT

Prov. 14:16 the fool rageth, and is **c**
2 Cor. 5:8 We are **c**…willing…to be absent from the body
Phil. 1:6 Being **c**…he which hath begun a good work…will perform it

CONGREGATION. A gathering of people for worship or religious instruction (Acts 13:43). See also *Assembly.*

CONIAH. See *Jehoiachin.*

CONSCIENCE

John 8:9 they [scribes and Pharisees]…convicted by their own **c**
Acts 23:1 I [Paul] have lived in all good **c** before God
1 Cor. 10:27 eat, asking no question for **c** sake
1 Tim. 3:9 mystery of the faith in a pure **c**

CONSECRATION. To dedicate or set apart for God's exclusive use. Believers are encouraged to consecrate or sanctify themselves to God's service (2 Tim. 2:21). See also *Ordain; Sanctification.*

CONSENT [ING]

Prov. 1:10 if sinners entice thee, **c** thou not
Luke 14:18 all with one **c** began to make excuse
Acts 8:1 Saul was **c'ing** unto his [Stephen's] death
1 Cor. 7:5 Defraud ye not…except it be with **c** for a time

CONSIDER [ING]

1 Sam. 12:24 **c** how great things he [God] hath done
Job 37:14 stand still, and **c** the wondrous works of God
Ps. 8:3 When I **c** thy [God's] heavens, the work of thy fingers
Prov. 6:6 Go to the ant, thou sluggard; **c** her ways
Isa. 43:18 neither…**c** the things of old
Hag. 1:5 thus saith the Lord of hosts; **C** your ways
Matt. 6:28 **C** the lilies of the field, how they grow
Gal. 6:1 **c'ing** thyself, lest thou also be tempted

CONSOLATION. A word that expresses the idea of comfort combined with encouragement. Believers find consolation in Jesus Christ and His Holy Spirit (Rom. 15:5).

Luke 2:25 man [Simeon]…waiting for the **c** of Israel
Acts 4:36 Barnabas…being interpreted, The son of **c**
Phil. 2:1 If there be therefore any **c** in Christ

CONTENTION (DISAGREEMENT). Severe disagreement that leads to sharp divisions among people, including Christian believers (Acts 15:39). Christians are encouraged to pursue peace with others (Rom. 12:18–21). *Disagreement:* NIV, NRSV. See also *Discord; Strife.*

CONTENTMENT. Satisfaction; freedom from worry and anxiety. This state of mind was modeled for all believers by Paul (Phil. 4:11; 1 Tim. 6:8).

CONTINUE [D, ING]
Luke 6:12 he [Jesus]…*c'd* all night in prayer
John 8:31 ye *c* in my [Jesus'] word…ye my disciples indeed
Acts 1:14 These all *c'd* with one accord in prayer
Acts 2:46 they [the believers], *c'ing* daily with one accord
Rom. 6:1 Shall we *c* in sin, that grace may abound
1 Tim. 4:16 Take heed…unto the doctrine; *c* in them
Heb. 13:1 Let brotherly love *c*
2 Pet. 3:4 all things *c* as they were from the beginning

CONTRITE. A meek or humble attitude (Ps. 51:17). A contrite person also shows genuine grief or sorrow over his or her sin (2 Cor. 7:10). See also *Humility; Meekness; Repentance.*

CONVERSATION. A word for behavior or lifestyle. Paul urged Christians to live in accordance with the gospel of Christ (Phil. 1:27).

Gal. 1:13 heard of my [Paul's] *c* in time past
1 Tim. 4:12 be thou an example…in *c*, in charity
Heb. 13:5 Let your *c* be without covetousness

CONVERSION. See *New Birth.*

CONVERTED [ING]
Ps. 19:7 The law of the LORD is perfect, *c'ing* the soul
Ps. 51:13 sinners shall be *c* unto thee [God]
Matt. 18:3 Except ye be *c*, and become as little children
Acts 3:19 Repent ye therefore, and be *c*

CONVICTION. An awareness of one's sin and guilt (John 8:9) that leads to confession and repentance. The Holy Spirit is the agent

of conviction (Heb. 3:7). See also *Holy Spirit; Repentance.*

CONVOCATION. A sacred assembly of the people of Israel for worship in connection with observance of the Sabbath or one of their major religious festivals, such as Passover or Pentecost (Lev. 23:2–8). See also *Assembly.*

COPPER. See *Brass.*

COR. The largest liquid measure used by the Hebrew people, possibly equivalent to fifty or more gallons (Ezek. 45:14).

CORAL. A precious substance formed in the sea from the bodies of tiny sea creatures (Ezek. 27:16). Coral was apparently used for making beads and other fine jewelry (Job 28:18). See also *Ruby.*

CORBAN. A Hebrew word meaning a sacred gift, or an offering devoted to God. Jesus condemned the Pharisees for encouraging people to make such gifts while neglecting to care for their own parents (Mark 7:11–13).

CORD. See *Line; Rope.*

CORE. See *Korah.*

CORIANDER. A plant whose seeds were used as a medicine and as a seasoning for food (Num. 11:7).

CORINTH. A major port city in Greece on the trade route between Rome and its eastern provinces where Paul lived for eighteen months, establishing a church (Acts 18:1–11). The city was known for its immorality, paganism, and corruption.

C

THE GOSPEL IN CORINTH

A thriving commercial city, Corinth had a population of about 500,000 people in Paul's time. It was an ideal location for a church, since it could bear a witness to the merchants who visited the city as well as the people in the smaller towns that surrounded the metropolitan area. In spite of its reputation as a pagan and immoral city, Corinth was open to Paul's proclamation of the saving grace of Jesus Christ.

CORINTHIANS, FIRST AND SECOND EPISTLES TO THE. Two letters of the apostle Paul to the church at Corinth, written to believers who were struggling to move beyond their pagan background and lifestyle.

First Corinthians deals mainly with problems in the church, including divisions (chaps. 1–4), sexual immorality (chaps. 5–6), and abuses of the Lord's Supper and spiritual gifts (chaps. 11–12; 14).

The themes of 2 Corinthians include Paul's view of ministry and reconciliation (chaps. 1–6), support of the impoverished Christians at Jerusalem (chaps. 8–9), and Paul's example of suffering and abuse and defense of his credentials as an apostle (chaps. 10–13).

CORMORANT (DESERT OWL, HAWK). A large bird cited by Isaiah as a symbol of desolation and destruction (Isa. 34:11). *Desert owl:* NIV; *hawk:* NRSV. See also *Pelican.*

CORN (GRAIN). A generic term for several different grains, including wheat, barley, and millet (Matt. 12:1). *Grain:* NIV, NRSV. See also *Wheat.*

CORNELIUS. A Roman soldier from Caesarea who sought out the apostle Peter at Joppa and became the first Gentile convert to Christianity (Acts 10). This event showed clearly that the Christian faith was meant for Gentiles as well as Jews (Acts 15:7–11).

CORNER STONE. A stone strategically placed to align two walls and tie the building together. This is also a title for Christ as the keystone of the church (Eph. 2:20). See also *Foundation.*

CORNET (HORN). A musical instrument similar to the horn or trumpet (Dan. 3:5–7). *Horn:* NIV, NRSV.

CORRUPT [ED]
Gen. 6:11 earth also was **c** before God
Job 17:1 My [Job's] breath is **c**
Matt. 6:20 treasures in heaven…moth nor rust doth **c**
Luke 6:43 good tree bringeth not forth **c** fruit
James 5:2 Your riches are **c'ed**…garments are motheaten

CORRUPTION
1 Cor. 15:42 It [the body] is sown in **c**…raised in incorruption
Gal. 6:8 he that soweth to his flesh shall of the flesh reap **c**

COULTER (PLOWSHARE). An agricultural instrument of metal, probably the tip of a plow (1 Sam. 13:21). *Plowshare:* NIV, NRSV. See also *Plowshare.*

COUNCIL/SANHEDRIN. The highest court of the Jewish nation in N.T. times, composed of seventy-one priests, scribes, and elders and presided over by the high priest. The Council accused Jesus of blasphemy against God, but it didn't have the power to put Jesus to death. It brought Him before Pilate, the Roman procurator, for sentencing (Matt. 26:65–66; John 18:31; 19:12). The Council also brought charges against Peter and John and the other

COURT OF THE GENTILES. The expansive Court of the Gentiles outside these walls was as close as non-Jews could get to the Jerusalem temple sanctuary inside. Jews, however, could go to interior courtyards. Only priests were allowed inside the sanctuary.

apostles (Acts 4:1–23; 5:17–41) and Paul (Acts 22–24). *Sanhedrin:* NIV.

COUNSELLOR (COUNSELOR). A person who gives wise counsel or imparts advice. Kings employed counselors (1 Chron. 27:33). This is also one of the messianic titles of Christ (Isa. 9:6). *Counselor:* NIV, NRSV. See also *Comforter; Holy Spirit; Paraclete.*

COUNT [ED, ETH]
Gen. 15:6 and he [God] *c'ed* it [Abraham's faith]…for righteousness
Ps. 44:22 we are *c'ed* as sheep for the slaughter
Luke 14:28 sitteth not down first, and *c'eth* the cost
Rom. 4:3 it was *c'ed* unto him [Abraham] for righteousness
Phil. 3:8 I [Paul] *c* all things but loss
Phil. 3:13 I [Paul] *c* not myself to have apprehended
2 Thess. 1:5 may be *c'ed* worthy of the kingdom of God
James 1:2 *c* it all joy when ye fall into…temptations

COUNTENANCE. A word for the face or the expression on a person's face (Dan. 5:6).

COURAGE. Fearlessness and bravery in the face of danger (Acts 28:15). Moses exhorted Joshua to have courage (Deut. 31:7–8).

COURIER. See *Post.*

COURT. An enclosed yard or patio attached to a house or public building. Both the tabernacle (Exod. 27:9) and the temple in Jerusalem had courts or courtyards (1 Kings 6:36).

COURT OF THE GENTILES. An outer court in the Jewish temple beyond which Gentile worshipers could not go. The splitting of the curtain between this court and the inner court at Jesus' death symbolized the

Gentiles' equal access to God (Matt. 27:51; Eph. 2:11–14). See also *Gentile; Middle Wall of Partition.*

COUSIN. A general term denoting any degree of relationship among blood relatives—cousin, nephew, aunt, uncle, etc. (Luke 1:36).

COVENANT. An agreement between two people or groups, particularly the agreement between God and His people that promised His blessings in return for their obedience and devotion (Gen. 15). Through His sacrificial death, Jesus became the mediator of a new covenant, bringing salvation and eternal life to all who trust in Him (Heb. 10:12–17). See also *Testament.*

COVENANT [S]
Gen. 9:9 I [God] establish my **c** with you [Noah]
Gen. 15:18 the Lord made a **c** with Abram
Deut. 4:23 Take heed…lest ye forget the **c** of the Lord
Deut. 29:9 Keep therefore the words of this **c**
1 Sam. 18:3 Jonathan and David made a **c**
Jer. 11:3 Cursed be the man that obeyeth not…this **c**
Jer. 31:31 I [God] will make a new **c** with…Israel
Eph. 2:12 aliens…and strangers from the **c's** of promise
Heb. 8:6 he [Jesus] is the mediator of a better **c**

COVERED COLONNADE. See *Portico.*

COVET [ED]
Exod. 20:17 Thou shalt not **c** thy neighbour's house
Acts 20:33 I [Paul] have **c'ed** no man's silver
1 Cor. 12:31 But **c** earnestly the best gifts

COVETOUSNESS. Greed, or a burning desire for what belongs to others. This sin is specifically prohibited by the Ten Commandments (Exod. 20:17), and Paul warned against its dangers (Col. 3:5). See also *Greed.*

Ps. 119:36 heart unto thy [God's] testimonies…not to **c**
Luke 12:15 Take heed, and beware of **c**
Heb. 13:5 Let your conversation be without **c**

COW. See *Kine.*

CREATE [D]
Gen. 1:1 God **c'd** the heaven and the earth
Gen. 1:27 God **c'd** man in his own image
Ps. 51:10 **C** in me a clean heart, O God
Jer. 31:22 the Lord hath **c'd** a new thing in the earth
1 Cor. 11:9 Neither was the man **c'd** for the woman
Eph. 2:10 we are his workmanship, **c'd** in Christ Jesus
Col. 1:16 all things were **c'd** by him [Jesus]
Rev. 4:11 for thou [God] hast **c'd** all things

CREATION. The actions of God through which He brought man and the physical world into existence. God existed before the world, and He produced the universe from nothing (Gen. 1:1–2). As the sovereign, self-existing God, He also rules over His creation (Ps. 47:7–9). See also *Creature.*

CREATOR. A title for God that emphasizes that He is the maker of all things and the sovereign ruler of His creation (Isa. 40:28; John 1:1–3; Col. 1:15–16). See also *Almighty; Sovereignty of God.*

CREATURE (CREATION). Any being created by God, including humans (Gen. 2:19). Through God's redemption, a believer becomes a new creature (2 Cor. 5:17). *Creation:* NIV, NRSV. See also *Creation.*

CRETE. A large island in the Mediterranean Sea by which Paul sailed during his voyage to Rome (Acts 27:1–13). Titus apparently served as leader of a church on Crete (Titus 1:4–5). See also *Titus.*

CRIMINAL. See *Malefactor.*

CRIMSON. See *Scarlet.*

CRISPING PIN (PURSE, HANDBAG). A purse or bag for carrying money (Isa. 3:22). *Purse:* NIV; *handbag:* NRSV. See also *Purse.*

CRISPUS. Chief ruler of the synagogue at Corinth who became a Christian believer (Acts 18:8) and was baptized by Paul (1 Cor. 1:14).

CROCUS. See *Rose.*

CROOKED
Deut. 32:5 a perverse and *c* generation
Isa. 40:4 the *c* shall be made straight
Phil. 2:15 sons of God…in the midst of a *c*…nation

CROSS. A wooden stake with a cross beam on which Jesus was put to death by the Roman authorities—a common form of capital punishment in N.T. times. Attached to the cross with nails or leather thongs, the victim generally suffered for two or three days before dying from exposure, exhaustion, and the loss of body fluids.

But Jesus died after only six hours on the cross (John 19:30–33). His sacrificial death freed believers from the power of sin (Rom. 6:6–11) and sealed their reconciliation to God (2 Cor. 5:19). See also *Atonement; Redeem; Savior.*

Matt. 27:32 they compelled [Simon] to bear his [Jesus'] *c*
Matt. 27:42 let him [Jesus] now come down from the *c*
Luke 9:23 take up his *c* daily, and follow me [Jesus]
John 19:17 he [Jesus] bearing his *c* went forth into…the place of a skull
1 Cor. 1:18 preaching of the *c* is to them that perish foolishness
Gal. 6:14 forbid that I [Paul] should glory, save in the *c*
Phil. 2:8 he [Jesus]…became obedient unto…death of the *c*
Heb. 12:2 who [Jesus] for the joy that was set before him endured the *c*

CROWN. An ornamental headdress worn by kings and queens as a symbol of power and authority (2 Kings 11:12). The word is also used symbolically for righteous behavior befitting a believer (2 Tim. 4:8) and God's gift of eternal life (James 1:12). See also *Diadem.*

CROWN [ED, EDST]
Ps. 8:5 thou [God]…hast *c'ed* [man] with…honour
Prov. 17:6 Children's children are the *c* of old men
Mark 15:17 a *c* of thorns, and put it about his [Jesus'] head
Phil. 4:1 joy and *c*, so stand fast in the Lord
2 Tim. 4:8 laid up for me [Paul] a *c* of righteousness
Heb. 2:7 thou *c'edst* him [Jesus] with glory and honour

CROWN OF GLORY/ CROWN OF LIFE
Prov. 16:31 The hoary head is a *c-o-g*
Isa. 62:3 shalt…be a *c-o-g* in the hand of the LORD
James 1:12 he is tried, he shall receive the *c-o-l*
1 Pet. 5:4 chief Shepherd…appear…receive a *c-o-g*
Rev. 2:10 faithful unto death…give thee a *c-o-l*

CRUCIBLE. See *Fining Pot.*

CRUCIFIXION. See *Cross.*

CRUSE (JUG). A small earthen jug or flask for holding liquids (1 Kings 17:14). *Jug:* NIV, NRSV. See also *Pitcher.*

CRYSTAL. A transparent, colorless rock, perhaps a form of quartz (Rev. 22:1).

CUBIT. The standard unit for measurement of length, equivalent to about eighteen inches (Gen. 6:15–16).

CUCKOW (SEA GULL). A bird considered unclean by the Hebrews, probably a type of sea bird (Lev. 11:16). *Sea gull:* NRSV.

CUCUMBER. A climbing vine that produced vegetables probably similar to our cucumbers (Num. 11:5).

C

CUP. *A pair of silver Roman cups from the first Christian century, when Jesus lived on earth.*

CUMMIN. A plant that produced seeds used for medicines and for seasoning food (Isa. 28:25, 27). Jesus criticized the Pharisees for their shallow legalism in tithing the seeds from this insignificant plant while ignoring more important matters, such as mercy and faith (Matt. 23:23).

CUP. A drinking utensil (Gen. 44:12). The cup is also symbolic of the blood of the new covenant established by Christ (Matt. 20:22; 1 Cor. 10:16).

CUPBEARER. A royal household servant who tasted wine before it was served to the king to make sure it had not been poisoned (Neh. 1:11). The butler imprisoned with Joseph was probably a cupbearer to the Egyptian pharaoh (Gen. 40:1–13).

CURSE. A call for evil or misfortune against another (Gen. 4:11). Jesus taught that Christians are to return kindness for such actions (Luke 6:28).

CURSE [D, ING, TH]
Gen. 3:14 thou [the serpent] art *c'd* above all cattle
Lev. 20:9 one that *c'th* his father…shall be…put to death
Deut. 27:15 *C'd* be the man that maketh any graven or molten image
Deut. 30:19 I [Moses] have set before you life and death, blessing and *c'ing*
Matt. 5:44 bless them that *c* you
Matt. 15:4 He that *c'th* father…let him die
Mark 14:71 he [Peter] began to *c*…I know not this man [Jesus]
Rom. 12:14 Bless them which persecute you: bless…*c* not
Gal. 3:13 Christ hath redeemed us from the *c* of the law
James 3:10 Out of the same mouth proceedeth blessing and *c'ing*

CURTAIN. See *Veil,* No. 1.

CUSH. Ham's oldest son and a grandson of Noah (1 Chron. 1:8–10).

CUSHAN-RISHATHAIM. See *Chushan-rishathaim*.

CUSTOM
Matt. 9:9 he [Jesus] saw…Matthew…at the receipt of *c*
John 18:39 a *c*, that I [Pilate] should release…one at the passover
Rom. 13:7 Render…to all their dues…*c* to whom *c*

CUTH/CUTHAH. A city or district of Babylonia that provided colonists who settled the Northern Kingdom after it fell to the Assyrians (2 Kings 17:30). *Cuthah:* 2 Kings 17:24.

CYMBALS. Curved metal plates used as musical instruments (1 Cor. 13:1).

CYPRESS. See *Box Tree; Fir; Gopher Wood*.

CYPRUS/CHITTIM/KITTIM. A large island in the Mediterranean Sea about 125 miles off the coast of Palestine that Paul and Barnabas visited during the first missionary journey (Acts 13:2–5). Barnabas was a native of Cyprus (Acts 4:36). *Chittim:* Jer. 2:10; *Kittim:* Gen. 10:4.

CYRENE. A Greek city in North Africa and home of Simon of Cyrene who carried the cross of Jesus (Matt. 27:32).

CYRENIUS (QUIRINIUS). The Roman governor of Syria at the time of Jesus' birth (Luke 2:1–4). *Quirinius:* NIV, NRSV.

CYRUS. The founding king of the Persian empire (reigned about 559–530 B.C.). After defeating the Babylonians, he allowed the Jewish captives to return to their homeland about 536 B.C. (2 Chron. 36:22–23; Ezra 1:1–4). See also *Persia*.

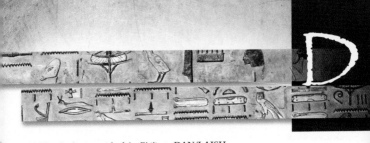

DAGON. The chief pagan god of the Philistines. It apparently had the head of a man and the tail of a fish. This idol fell before the ark of the covenant in the pagan temple at Ashdod (1 Sam. 5:1–5). See also *Philistines.*

DALMANUTHA. A place on the western shore of the Sea of Galilee visited by Jesus (Mark 8:10).

DALMATIA. A province on the eastern coast of the Adriatic Sea visited by Titus (2 Tim. 4:10).

DAMASCUS/SYRIA-DAMASCUS. The capital city of Syria, located north of Mount Hermon in northern Palestine. Paul was traveling to Damascus to persecute Christians when he met the risen Lord in a life-transforming vision (Acts 9:1–8). Damascus is considered the oldest continually inhabited city in the world. *Syria-damascus:* 1 Chron. 18:6. See also *Syria.*

DAMNATION. Judgment and consignment to everlasting punishment; the fate of the wicked or those who reject Christ (Mark 16:16). See also *Hell; Judgment, Last; Perdition.*

Mark 3:29 blaspheme…Holy Ghost…danger of eternal *d*
John 5:29 that have done evil, unto the resurrection of *d*
1 Cor. 11:29 eateth and drinketh *d* to himself

DAMSEL. A word for a young woman (Mark 5:39–42).

DAN/LAISH

1. Jacob's fifth son and ancestor of one of the tribes of Israel (Gen. 30:6; Num. 1:38–39). See also *Tribes of Israel.*

2. A village in the territory allotted to the tribe of Dan. It was located farther north than any other city of Palestine during most of the O.T. era. The phrase "from Dan even to Beersheba" (Judg. 20:1) described the entire territory of the Hebrew nation from north to south. *Laish:* Isa. 10:30.

DANCE. Rhythmic body movements, usually to musical accompaniment, to express joy and gratitude to God (Exod. 15:20–21). King David danced when the ark of the covenant was recovered and brought to Jerusalem (2 Sam. 6:14–16).

DANIEL (BELTESHAZZAR). A prophet of the O.T. known for his faithfulness to the God of Israel among the pagan Babylonians and Persians. Refusing to worship King Darius, he was thrown into a den of lions but was miraculously delivered by the Lord (Dan. 6:1–24). *Belteshazzar:* Babylonian form (Dan. 1:7).

DANIEL, BOOK OF. An apocalyptic book of the O.T. known for its images of horns and beasts that are similar to those described in the Revelation to John in the N.T. The two major sections of Daniel are (1) the trials and tribulations suffered by Daniel and his three friends as captives of the Babylonians and Persians (chaps.

1–7) and (2) Daniel's visions and dreams about the future (chaps. 8–12).

The prophet's famous "seventy weeks" prophecy has been interpreted as a period of 490 years (seventy weeks, representing seventy years, multiplied by seven) from Daniel's time until the coming of the Messiah (9:20–27). See also *Apocalypse*.

DARIUS AND DANIEL

King Darius (Darius the Mede) of Persia was a friend and supporter of Daniel, even though the prophet was thrown into a den of lions under an edict that Daniel's enemies had persuaded the king to pass (Dan. 6:1–28). Many scholars believe this king was actually Cyrus, the Persian king who allowed the Jewish exiles to return to their homeland after the Persians defeated the Babylonians (2 Chron. 36:22–23).

DARIC. See *Dram*.

DARIUS. A title for the kings of Persia. Four different kings with this title are mentioned in the O.T.:

1. Darius I or Darius the Great (reigned about 522–485 B.C.). Successor to Cyrus, he continued Cyrus's policy of restoring the Jewish people to their homeland (Ezra 6:1–12).

2. Darius II or Darius the Persian (Neh. 12:22), who reigned about 424–405 B.C.

3. Darius III or Darius Codomannus (reigned about 336–330 B.C.). He is probably the "fourth" king of Persia mentioned by the prophet Daniel (Dan. 11:2).

4. Darius the Mede, who had the prophet Daniel thrown into a den of lions. He eventually made Daniel a ruler over several provincial leaders (Dan. 6:1–2).

DARKENED

Isa. 24:11 joy is *d*, the mirth of the land is gone
Joel 3:15 sun and the moon shall be *d*
Mark 13:24 tribulation, the sun shall be *d*
Rom. 1:21 they (ungodly)…became vain…heart was *d*

DARKNESS. The absence of light. Darkness ruled the world before God's creation of light (Gen. 1:2). Thus, darkness is symbolic of humankind's sin, rebellion, and ignorance (Job 24:13–17). See also *Light*.

Exod. 10:22 thick *d* in…Egypt three days
2 Sam. 22:29 Lord will lighten my *d*
Job 34:22 no *d*, nor shadow of death
Isa. 5:20 Woe unto them that…put…light for *d*
Isa. 9:2 walked in *d* have seen a great light
Joel 2:31 sun shall be turned into *d*
Matt. 4:16 people…in *d* saw great light
Luke 23:44 a *d* over all the earth until the ninth hour
John 1:5 the *d* comprehended it [the light] not
John 3:19 men loved *d* rather than light
John 12:46 whosoever believeth…not abide in *d*
Acts 2:20 sun shall be turned into *d*
Acts 26:18 open their eyes, to turn them from *d* to light
Eph. 6:12 wrestle…against…of *d* of this world
1 John 1:5 God is light, and in him is no *d* at all
1 John 2:11 he that hateth his brother is in *d*

DART (JAVELIN, SPEAR). A javelin or short spear. Absalom was killed by darts (2 Sam. 18:14). *Javelin:* NIV; *spear:* NRSV. See also *Javelin; Spear*.

DATHAN. A leader of the rebellion against Moses in the wilderness. All the rebels were destroyed by an earthquake (Num. 16:1–33).

DAUGHTER. A word for female offspring of parents as well as a distant female relative, such as a granddaughter or niece (Gen. 20:12; 24:48).

DAUGHTER OF ZION. A symbolic expression for the city of Jerusalem and its inhabitants (Ps. 9:14). See also *Jerusalem*.

DAVID. The popular king of Judah described by the Lord as "a man after mine own heart" and an earthly ancestor of the promised Messiah, Jesus Christ (Luke 2:4–7). A descendant of the tribe of Judah (1 Chron. 28:4), he was a native of Bethlehem (1 Sam. 17:12). As a shepherd boy, he defeated the Philistine giant Goliath (1 Sam. 17:44–52).

David served as King Saul's musician and armorbearer (1 Sam. 16:14–21) and was anointed king after Saul's sin and disobedience (1 Sam. 16:11–13). Forced to flee from Saul's jealousy and wrath (1 Sam. 21:10), he was befriended by Saul's son Jonathan (1 Sam. 19:1–3). After he became king, he united the Hebrew tribes into one nation with Jerusalem as the capital city (2 Sam. 5:1–10) and defeated many enemy nations (2 Sam. 8:1–15).

In a moment of weakness, David committed adultery with Bath-sheba (2 Sam. 11:1–4), but he later repented (Pss. 32; 51). He was forgiven and restored, but the consequences of his sin remained (2 Sam. 12:13–14). He suffered family tragedies (2 Sam. 12:15–20; 18:31–33) and wrote many psalms (see Pss. 54; 59; 65). He was succeeded as king by his son Solomon (1 Kings 2:12). In the N.T., Jesus is called the "son of David" (Matt. 1:1; Mark 10:48). See also *Absalom; Bethlehem; Jerusalem*.

DAVID, TOWER OF. A fortress built by David at an unknown location (Song 4:4).

DAY. The twenty-four-hour period during which the earth rotates on its own axis. The Hebrews measured their day from sunset to sunset (Exod. 12:18). The twelve hours of daylight began with the first hour at sunup (about 6:00

A.M.). Midday or noon was the sixth hour, and the twelfth hour ended at sundown, or about 6:00 P.M.

Gen. 1:5 evening...morning were the first *d*
Josh. 24:15 choose you this *d* whom ye will serve
Job 3:3 the *d* perish wherein I [Job] was born
Ps. 1:2 in his [God's] law doth he meditate *d* and night
Ps. 50:15 call upon me [God] in the *d* of trouble
Ps. 84:10 a *d* in thy [God's] courts is better than a thousand
Ps. 118:24 This is the *d* which the LORD hath made
Isa. 60:19 sun shall be no more thy light by *d*
Joel 2:31 before...the terrible *d* of the LORD come
Mal. 3:2 who may abide the *d* of his [God's] coming
Matt. 6:11 Give us this *d* our daily bread
Matt. 25:13 neither the *d* nor the hour...Son of man cometh
Luke 2:11 born this *d* in the city of David a Saviour
Luke 19:9 This *d* is salvation come to this house
John 9:4 [Jesus] must work...while it is *d*
2 Cor. 6:2 behold, now is the *d* of salvation
Phil. 3:5 Circumcised the eighth *d*...stock of Israel
Heb. 13:8 Jesus Christ the same yesterday, and to *d*
2 Pet. 3:8 one *d* is with the Lord as a thousand years
Rev. 1:10 I [John] was in the Spirit on the Lord's *d*

DAY OF THE LORD. A phrase usually interpreted as a period in the end-time when God will bring His purpose for humans and the world to fulfillment. This will be a day of judgment for the rebellious and sinful (Jer. 46:10) and a time of deliverance for the godly (Joel 2:28–32). Any time—whether now or in the distant future—when the Lord acts, intervening in history for the purpose of deliverance and judgment, may also be described as the "day of the Lord" (Isa. 13:6). See also *Damnation; Judgment, Last; Punishment*.

Joel 1:15 Alas...for the *d-o-t-L* is at hand
Amos 5:20 Shall not the *d-o-t-L* be darkness
Mal. 4:5 Elijah...before the...dreadful *d-o-t-L*
Acts 2:20 darkness...before that great...*d-o-t-L*
1 Thess. 5:2 the *d-o-t-L*...cometh...thief in the night

DAY'S JOURNEY. The distance that could be traveled in one day on foot, probably about twenty-five miles (Jon. 3:3–4).

DAYSMAN (UMPIRE). A word for a mediator, umpire, or judge between contending parties (Job 9:33). *Umpire:* NRSV.

DAYSPRING. A word for dawn or daybreak (Job 38:12).

DAY STAR/LUCIFER (MORNING STAR). A star that appears just before daybreak, signaling the beginning of a new day (2 Pet. 1:19). The word for "day star" is also translated as *Lucifer* (Isa. 14:12) and used as a name for the king of Babylon. *Morning star:* NIV. See also *Morning Star.*

DEACON. An officer or servant of the church. The first "deacons" were probably the seven men of Greek background who were appointed by the church at Jerusalem to coordinate the distribution of food to the needy (Acts 6:1–7). The strict qualifications for deacons (1 Tim. 3:8–13) show this was an important office in the early church. Phoebe, a female believer, is called a "deacon" in the NRSV translation of Rom. 16:1 (*servant:* KJV).

DEAD

Eccles. 9:5 the **d** know not any thing
Matt. 10:8 Heal the sick…raise the **d**
Luke 15:24 son was **d**, and is alive again
Luke 24:46 Christ to suffer…rise from the **d**
John 11:25 though he were **d**, yet shall he live
Acts 17:32 resurrection of the **d**, some mocked
Rom. 6:4 Christ was raised up from the **d**
1 Cor. 15:13 no resurrection of the **d**…Christ not risen
Col. 1:18 who [Jesus] is…firstborn from the **d**
1 Thess. 4:16 **d** in Christ shall rise first
James 2:17 faith, if it hath not works, is **d**
Rev. 14:13 Blessed are the **d** which die in the Lord

DEAD SEA/SALT SEA/EAST SEA. A body of water (about fifty miles long by ten miles wide) into which the Jordan River empties at the lowest point on earth in southern Palestine.

DEAD SEA. The Dead Sea, photographed from the Space Shuttle. The lowest spot on earth, this super-salty sea is rich in minerals. The southern half is divided into shallow drying pools, making it easier to mine the minerals.

Because of the hot, dry climate, the water evaporates, leaving a high concentration of salt and other minerals. *Salt sea:* Josh. 3:16; *East sea:* Joel 2:20.

DEAD SEA SCROLLS. A group of scrolls or ancient manuscripts discovered since 1947 in caves around the Dead Sea. Written between 250 B.C. and A.D. 68 and placed in clay jars, the scrolls were preserved by the dry climate of the area. Among the scrolls was a complete manuscript of the book of Isaiah, written in Hebrew. See also *Qumran, Khirbet.*

DEAF. Unable to hear. The word is also used symbolically of spiritual coldness or apathy (Isa. 42:18–19).

Isa. 35:5 ears of the *d* shall be unstopped
Mark 7:32 bring unto him [Jesus] one that was *d*
Luke 7:22 tell John…lepers are cleansed…*d* hear

DEATH. The end of physical existence. Death is the price humans pay for their sin and rebellion against God, but God provides salvation and eternal life for believers through the atoning death of Jesus Christ (Rom. 6:23). "Second death" is eternal separation from God—the fate of unbelievers (Rev. 20:6).

Deut. 30:15 I [Moses]…set before thee…*d* and evil
Ps. 23:4 valley of the shadow of *d*
Ps. 116:15 sight of the LORD…*d* of his saints
Mark 14:34 My [Jesus'] soul is…sorrowful unto *d*
John 5:24 believeth…passed from *d* unto life
Acts 8:1 Saul was consenting unto his [Stephen's] *d*
Rom. 5:12 so *d* passed upon all men
Rom. 7:24 shall deliver me [Paul] from the body of…*d*
1 Cor. 11:26 show the Lord's *d* till he come
1 Cor. 15:55 O *d*, where is thy sting
Phil. 2:8 he [Jesus] humbled himself…obedient unto *d*
1 John 3:14 from *d* unto life…we love the brethren
Rev. 21:4 no more *d*, neither sorrow

DEBASED. See *Reprobate.*

DEBAUCHERY. See *Lasciviousness.*

DEBORAH. A prophetess and judge of Israel who, along with Barak, defeated the Canaanite forces of Sisera (Judg. 4:4–14). She celebrated the victory in a triumphant song (Judg. 5). See also *Sisera.*

DEBT. Borrowed property or money that must be repaid. The Hebrews were encouraged not to charge interest to their own countrymen (Lev. 25:35–38), but foreigners could be charged (Deut. 23:20). See also *Usury.*

DEBT [S]
Matt. 6:12 our *d's*, as we forgive our debtors
Matt. 18:27 lord of that servant…forgave him the *d*
Rom. 4:4 to him that worketh is the reward…of *d*

DECALOGUE. See *Ten Commandments.*

DECAPOLIS. A Roman province or district with a large Greek population that was situated mostly on the eastern side of the Jordan River in northern Palestine (Matt. 4:25).

DECEIT. See *Guile.*

DECEIVE [D,ING]
Deut. 11:16 Take heed…your heart be not *d'd*
Prov. 20:1 Wine is a mocker…whosoever is *d'd* thereby is not wise
Luke 21:8 be not *d'd*: for many shall come in my [Jesus'] name
Gal. 6:7 Be not *d'd*; God is not mocked
Eph. 5:6 Let no man *d* you with vain words
James 1:22 doers of the word, and not hearers only, *d'ing* your own selves
1 John 1:8 we say that we have no sin, we *d* ourselves

DECEIVER. A person who misleads another. Deception is one of the evil tricks used by Satan (2 John 7). See also *Satan.*

DECISION, VALLEY OF. See *Jehoshaphat, Valley of.*

DECLARE [D]

1 Chron. 16:24 *D* his [God's] glory among the heathen
Ps. 19:1 heavens *d* the glory of God
Isa. 12:4 Praise the LORD… *d* his doings among the people
John 1:18 only begotten Son…he hath *d'd* him [God]
Rom. 1:4 *d'd* to be the Son of God with power
1 Cor. 15:1 I [Paul] *d* unto you the gospel
1 John 1:3 which we have seen… *d* we unto you

DECREE. A command or official order issued by a king. Mary and Joseph were affected by the decree of the Roman emperor Caesar Augustus (Luke 2:1). See also *Statute*.

DEDICATION, FEAST OF. An eight-day festival commemorating the Jewish victories that restored the temple during the era of the Maccabees about 160 B.C. Jesus attended one of these festivals in Jerusalem (John 10:22–23). This feast was also known as the *Feast of Lights* or *Hanukkah*.

DEED [S]

1 Chron. 16:8 known his [God's] *d's* among the people
Luke 23:41 receive the due reward of our *d's*
John 3:19 loved darkness…their *d's* were evil
Rom. 2:6 to every man according to his *d's*
1 John 3:18 not love in word…but in *d* and in truth

DEER. A fleet-footed animal that could be eaten by the Hebrews (Deut. 14:5). See also *Hart; Hind*.

DEFILE [TH]

Ezek. 20:7 *d* not yourselves with the idols of Egypt
Dan. 1:8 Daniel…would not *d* himself
Matt. 15:20 eat with unwashen hands *d'th* not a man
Mark 7:18 from without…it cannot *d* him
1 Cor. 3:17 any man *d* the temple of God
James 3:6 tongue… *d'th* the whole body

DEFILEMENT. Contamination; the act of making something impure by acts of sin and rebellion. The O.T. law emphasized ceremonial cleanliness (Lev. 15:24; Num. 9:13), but Jesus emphasized the need for ethical living and moral purity (Mark 7:1–23).

DEGREES, SONGS OF. A title used in fifteen psalms of the book of Psalms (Pss. 120-134). The Hebrew word for "degrees" means "goings up." These songs of ascent may have been pilgrim psalms, sung by worshipers as they were "going up" to the temple at Jerusalem.

DEHAVITES. An Assyrian tribe that settled in Samaria after the defeat of the Northern Kingdom by the Assyrians. In later years the Dehavites opposed the rebuilding of the Jewish temple at Jerusalem (Ezra 4:9–16). See also *Samaritan*.

DELILAH. A woman, probably a Philistine who cut off Samson's long hair—the source of his strength—so he could be captured by his Philistine enemies (Judg. 16:13–21). See also *Samson*.

DELIVER [ED]

Job 16:11 God hath *d'ed* me [Job] to the ungodly
Ps. 17:13 LORD, *d* my soul from the wicked
Ps. 116:8 thou [God] hast *d'ed* my soul from death
Jer. 1:8 am with thee to *d* thee, saith the LORD
Dan. 3:17 God…is able to *d* us from the…furnace
Joel 2:32 call on…the LORD shall be *d'ed*
Matt. 6:13 not into temptation… *d* us from evil
Luke 2:6 that she [Mary] should be *d'ed*
Luke 9:44 Son of man… *d'ed* into the hands of men
Rom. 7:24 shall *d* me [Paul] from…this death
2 Tim. 4:18 Lord shall *d* me from every evil work

DEMAS. A fellow believer who deserted Paul (2 Tim. 4:10) after having worked with him on earlier occasions (Col. 4:14; Philem. 24).

DEMETRIUS. A silversmith at Ephesus who made replicas of the temple where the pagan goddess Diana was worshiped. When his livelihood was threatened by Paul's preaching

DELILAH. A freshly shorn Samson, attacked by Philistine soldiers, finds his superhuman strength gone. Delilah earned a treasure of silver by passing along the secret of Samson's power—that he never cut his hair.

Demetrius incited a riot against the apostle (Acts 19:24–31). See also *Diana.*

DEMON. An evil spirit with destructive power who opposes God. In His healing ministry, Jesus cast demons out of several people (Matt. 12:22–24; Luke 8:27–39).

DEMON POSSESSION. Invasion and control of a person by evil spirits. In N.T. times, these demons often caused disability (Mark 9:17–25), mental anguish (Matt. 8:28), and antisocial behavior (Luke 8:27–39). Jesus cast demons out of several people—an act that showed His power over the demonic forces of Satan (Mark 1:25; 9:29).

DEN OF LIONS. A deep cavern where lions were kept by the Persian kings, probably for the sport of lion hunting. Daniel was thrown into one of these pits, but he was delivered by God's hand (Dan. 6:16–24). See also *Daniel,* No. 1.

DENARIUS. See *Penny.*

DENY [IED, IETH]

Matt. 10:33 him will I also *d* before my Father
Mark 14:30 thou [Peter] shalt *d* me [Jesus] thrice
Luke 9:23 let him *d* himself, and take up his cross
1 Tim. 5:8 hath *d'ied* the faith...worse than an infidel
2 Tim. 2:12 if we *d* him [Jesus], he also will *d* us
1 John 2:23 Whosoever *d'ieth* the Son...hath not the Father

DEPOSIT. See *Earnest.*

DEPRAVED. See *Reprobate.*

DEPTH [S]

Ps. 106:9 he [God] led them through the *d's*
Ps. 130:1 Out of the *d's* have I cried unto thee, O LORD
Mic. 7:19 thou [God] wilt cast...their sins into...*d's* of the sea
Rom. 8:39 nor *d*...shall...separate us from...God

DEPUTY. A person empowered to act for another (1 Kings 22:47). See also *Proconsul.*

DERBE. A city or village of the province of Lycaonia visited by Paul and Barnabas during the first missionary journey (Acts 14:6, 20).

DESCEND [ED, ING]

Gen. 28:12 angels…ascending and *d'ing* on it [a ladder]
Matt. 7:27 rain *d'ed*, and the floods came
Mark 15:32 Let Christ… *d* now from the cross
Luke 3:22 Holy Ghost *d'ed*…like a dove
John 1:32 I [John] saw the Spirit *d'ing* from heaven like a dove
Rom. 10:7 Who shall *d* into the deep…to bring up Christ
1 Thess. 4:16 Lord himself shall *d* from heaven

DESERT. A dry, barren wilderness place (Isa. 48:21; Luke 1:80). See also *Wilderness*.

DESERT OWL. See *Cormorant; Hawk; Pelican*.

DESIRE [D, TH]

Gen. 3:16 *d* shall be to thy [Eve's] husband
Deut. 5:21 Neither shalt thou *d* thy neighbour's wife
Ps. 38:9 all my *d* is before thee [God]
Ps. 73:25 none…that I *d* beside thee [God]
Song 7:10 my beloved's, and his *d* is toward me
Isa. 26:9 my soul have I *d'd* thee [God]
Hosea 6:6 I [God] *d'd* mercy, and not sacrifice
Mark 9:35 man *d* to be first, the same shall be last
Rom. 10:1 my [Paul's] heart's *d*…for Israel…might be saved
Phil. 1:23 a *d* to depart, and to be with Christ
1 Tim. 3:1 office of a bishop, he *d'th* a good work
1 Pet. 2:2 newborn babes, *d* the sincere milk of the word

DESIRE OF ALL NATIONS (DESIRED OF ALL NATIONS, TREASURE OF ALL NATIONS). A title for the coming Messiah that emphasizes His universal rule and power (Hag. 2:6–7). *Desired of all nations:* NIV; *treasure of all nations:* NRSV.

DESTRUCTION [S]

Job 5:22 At *d* and famine thou shalt laugh
Ps. 90:3 Thou turnest man to *d*
Ps. 107:20 He [God]…delivered them from their *d's*
Prov. 16:18 Pride goeth before *d*…haughty spirit before a fall
Isa. 13:6 day of the LORD…as a *d* from the Almighty
Matt. 7:13 broad is the way, that leadeth to *d*

DEUTERONOMY, BOOK OF. A book of the O.T. containing a series of speeches that Moses delivered to the Hebrew people as they prepared to enter and conquer the land of Canaan. This book repeats many of the laws of God revealed to Moses on Mount Sinai about two generations earlier—thus its name Deuteronomy, which means "second law."

In these speeches (chaps. 1–33), Moses cautioned the people to remain faithful to God in the midst of the pagan Canaanite culture they were about to enter. The final chapter (34) recounts the death of Moses and the succession of Joshua as the leader of the Hebrew people. See also *Moses; Pentateuch*.

DEVIL. A title for Satan which emphasizes his work as a liar and deceiver (Luke 4:3). See also *Satan*.

DEW. Moisture that condenses on the earth during the night (Exod. 16:13–14; Judg. 6:37–40). The heavy dews of Palestine during the dry season from April to September provide moisture for the growing crops (Gen. 27:28).

DIADEM (CROWN). A headpiece decorated with precious stones and worn by a king (Isa. 28:5). *Crown:* NIV. See also *Crown*.

DIAMOND (EMERALD, MOONSTONE). A precious stone in the breastplate of the high priest (Exod. 28:18). *Emerald:* NIV; *moonstone:* NRSV.

DIANA (ARTEMIS). The Roman name for the pagan goddess of hunting and virginity. Paul's preaching at Ephesus, a center of Diana worship, caused an uproar among craftsmen who earned their living by making images of Diana (Acts 19:24–34). *Artemis:* NIV, NRSV. See also *Demetrius*, No. 1; *Ephesus*.

DIDYMUS. See *Thomas*.

DIE [D]

Gen. 2:17 eatest thereof [the forbidden tree]...surely *d*
2 Chron. 25:4 every man shall *d* for his own sin
Job 14:14 man *d*, shall he live again
Eccles. 3:2 time to be born...time to *d*
Jon. 4:3 better for me [Jonah] to *d* than to live
John 11:50 expedient...one man should *d* for the people
John 12:24 if it [grain of wheat] *d*, it bringeth forth much fruit
Rom. 5:8 yet sinners, Christ *d'd* for us
Rom. 14:8 live...or *d*, we are the Lord's
1 Cor. 15:22 Adam all *d*...in Christ...all be made alive
2 Cor. 5:14 one *d'd* for all, then were all dead
Phil. 1:21 to me [Paul] to live is Christ, and to *d* is gain
Heb. 9:27 appointed unto men once to *d*
Rev. 14:13 Blessed...dead which *d* in the Lord

DILL. See *Anise*.

DINAH. The daughter of Jacob who was assaulted by Shechem (Gen. 34).

DINAITES. An Assyrian tribe that populated Samaria after the Northern Kingdom fell to the Assyrians (Ezra 4:9). See also *Samaritan*.

DIONYSIUS. A member of the Areopagus of Athens who believed Paul's testimony about Jesus the Messiah (Acts 17:34). See also *Areopagus*.

DIOTREPHES. A church leader condemned by the apostle John for his false teachings (3 John 9–10).

DISAGREEMENT. See *Contention*.

DISCERN [ING] *d*

1 Kings 3:9 I [Solomon] may *d* between good and bad
Matt. 16:3 hypocrites, ye can *d* the face of the sky
1 Cor. 11:29 damnation to himself, not *d'ing* the Lord's body

DISCERNING OF SPIRITS (DISTINGUISHING BETWEEN SPIRITS). A spiritual gift that enables certain believers to tell the difference between true and false teachers and teachings (1 Cor. 12:10). *Distinguishing between spirits:* NIV.

DISCIPLE. A person who follows and learns from another person or group, especially a believer who observes the teachings of Jesus (Acts 6:1–7). See also *Apostle*.

Matt. 10:24 The *d* is not above his master
Luke 14:26 man...hate not his father...cannot be my [Jesus'] *d*
John 19:38 Joseph of Arimathaea, being a *d* of Jesus

DISCIPLINARIAN. See *Schoolmaster*.

DISCIPLINE. To train or teach, as parents impart important truths to a child (Prov. 22:6). A disciplined person also controls his impulses, speech, and actions (1 Pet. 3:10). God disciplines His children through corrective actions (Heb. 12:6). See also *Chastisement*.

DISCORD. Disagreement produced by a contentious spirit (Prov. 6:14). Discord is a sign of worldliness among believers (1 Cor. 3:3). See also *Contention*.

DISGRACE. See *Shame*.

DISH. See *Platter*.

DISOBEDIENT

Acts 26:19 I [Paul] was not *d* unto the heavenly vision
2 Tim. 3:2 boasters, proud...*d* to parents
Titus 1:16 deny him [God], being abominable, and *d*

DISPERSION. A word that refers to the scattering of the Jewish people among other nations. Jeremiah predicted such a scattering (Jer. 25:34), and this happened when the Babylonians overran Judah in 587 B.C. and carried its leading citizens into exile. See also *Captivity*.

DISPUTATION. Argument or dissension. Paul cautioned believers against such behavior (Phil. 2:14).

DISTAFF. The staff around which flax or wool was wound for spinning (Prov. 31:19). See also *Spinning; Warp; Weaver.*

DISTINGUISHING BETWEEN SPIRITS. See *Discerning of Spirits.*

DISTRESS [ED, ES]
Ps. 18:6 my *d* I called upon the LORD
Ps. 107:13 he [God] saved them out of their *d's*
Rom. 8:35 separate us…love of Christ? shall tribulation, or *d*
2 Cor. 4:8 troubled on every side, yet not *d'ed*
2 Cor. 12:10 I [Paul] take pleasure…in *d'es* for Christ's sake

DIVIDE [D, ING, TH]
Gen. 1:6 let it [the firmament] *d* the waters
Num. 33:54 shall *d* the land by lot
Judg. 7:16 he [Gideon] *d'd*…men into three companies
Job 26:12 he [God] *d'th* the sea with his power
Dan. 5:28 Thy [Belshazzar's] kingdom is *d'd*
Luke 11:17 kingdom *d'd* against itself is brought to desolation
Luke 12:53 father shall be *d'd* against the son
1 Cor. 1:13 Is Christ *d'd*? was Paul crucified for you?
2 Tim. 2:15 not…ashamed, rightly *d'ing* the word of truth

DIVIDING WALL. See *Middle Wall of Partition.*

DIVINATION. Foretelling the future or determining the unknown through performing acts of magic or reading signs (Jer. 14:14). See also *Magic; Soothsayer.*

DIVINER. See *Soothsayer.*

DIVISION [S]
John 9:16 a *d* among them [Pharisees]
Rom. 16:17 mark them which cause *d's* and offences
1 Cor. 3:3 among you envying, and strife, and *d's*

DIVORCE. A breaking of the ties of marriage. The divine ideal is for permanence in marriage (Matt. 19:3–6), and divorce violates the oneness that God intended (Gen. 2:24). Under the Mosaic Law, divorce was permitted in certain situations (Deut. 24:1–4), but this provision was greatly abused (Matt. 19:8).

Christ regarded adultery as the only permissible reason for divorce (Matt. 5:31–32; 19:9; Mark 10:11; Luke 16:18), and He reprimanded the Jews for their insensitive divorce practices (Matt. 19:3–9). Unfaithfulness to God was regarded as spiritual adultery (Hosea 2:2). See also *Marriage.*

DIVORCE [D]
Lev. 21:14 or a *d'd* woman…these shall he [a priest] not take
Jer. 3:8 I [God] had put her [Israel] away, and given her a bill of *d*

DOCTORS (TEACHERS). Teachers of the Law of Moses who were held in high esteem by the Jewish people. At the age of twelve, Jesus discussed the law with some of these teachers in Jerusalem (Luke 2:46). *Teachers:* NIV, NRSV. See also *Lawyer.*

NO BLACK MAGIC

The word *divination* may also be translated as "the occult." God made it clear that all forms of the occult are off-limits to His people (Deut. 18:9–14). These practices are "an abomination" (Deut. 18:12) to Him because they are a form of idolatry. Practitioners of black magic attempt to control the so-called "spirit world" to man's advantage, but there is only one supreme power in the universe—and He cannot be manipulated.

DOCTRINE. A system of religious beliefs that followers pass on to others. Paul impressed upon young Timothy the importance of sound doctrinal teachings (1 Tim. 4:6).

Mark 11:18 people was astonished at his [Jesus'] *d*
John 7:16 My [Jesus'] *d* is not mine, but his that sent me
Acts 2:42 continued stedfastly in the apostles' *d*
Eph. 4:14 carried about with every wind of *d*
2 Tim. 3:16 All scripture is…profitable for *d*
2 Tim. 4:3 time will come…not endure sound *d*

DOEG. An overseer of King Saul's herds who betrayed the high priest Ahimelech for assisting David and his soldiers (1 Sam. 22:9–10).

DOER [S]

Prov. 17:4 A wicked *d* giveth heed to false lips
Rom. 2:13 the *d's* of the law shall be justified
James 1:22 be ye *d's* of the word, and not hearers only

DOG. An unclean animal (Deut. 23:18) looked upon with contempt by the Jewish people. Gentiles were called "dogs" (Matt. 15:26). See also *Gentile.*

DOME. See *Firmament.*

DOMINION. Authority to govern or rule. After his creation by God, man was given dominion over God's creation (Gen. 1:26–28).

Job 25:2 *D* and fear are with him [God]
Ps. 8:6 him [man] to have *d* over the works of thy hands
Ps. 72:8 He [God] shall have *d* also from sea to sea
Dan. 4:3 his [God's] *d* is from generation to generation
Rom. 6:9 death hath no more *d* over him [Jesus]
1 Pet. 4:11 to whom [Jesus] be…*d* for ever and ever
Jude 25 To…God our Saviour, be…*d* and power

DOOR (GATE). An opening through which a house or public building is entered. Jesus spoke of Himself as the doorway to salvation and eternal life (John 10:7–10). *Gate:* NIV, NRSV. See also *Gate.*

DOORKEEPER. A person who stood guard at the entrance of a public building (Ps. 84:10). See also *Gate Keeper; Porter.*

DORCAS. See *Tabitha.*

DOTHAN. A city west of the Jordan River near Mount Gilboa. Dothan was the place where Joseph was sold into slavery by his brothers (Gen. 37:17–28).

DOUBT [ED, ING]

Matt. 14:31 thou of little faith, wherefore didst thou *d*
Matt. 28:17 worshipped him [Jesus]: but some *d'ed*
1 Tim. 2:8 lifting up holy hands, without…*d'ing*

DOVE. See *Pigeon; Turtledove.*

DOWRY. Compensation paid by the groom to the bride's family for loss of her services as a daughter (Gen. 24:47–58). See also *Betrothal; Marriage.*

DOXOLOGY. A brief hymn or declaration that proclaims God's power and glory (1 Chron. 29:11; Luke 2:14).

DRAGON. A mythical sea creature or winged lizard. The name is applied to Satan (Rev. 12:9) and the Antichrist (Rev. 12:3). See also *Antichrist.*

DRAM (DRACHMA, DARIC). A Persian coin of small value (Neh. 7:70). *Drachma:* NIV; *daric:* NRSV.

DRAWER OF WATER (WATER CARRIER). A person who carried water from the spring or well back to the household—a menial chore assigned to women, children, or slaves (Josh. 9:27). *Water carrier:* NIV.

DREAMS AND VISIONS. Mediums of revelation often used by God to make His will known. Joseph distinguished himself in Egypt by interpreting dreams for the pharaoh and his officers (Gen. 40–41). Daniel interpreted King Nebuchadnezzar's dream that he would fall from power (Dan. 4:18–27). Paul's missionary thrust into Europe began with his vision of a man from Macedonia appealing for help (Acts 16:9–10).

DREGS. Waste that settled to the bottom of the vat in the wine-making process (Ps. 75:8). The word is also used symbolically of God's wrath and judgment (Isa. 51:17). See also *Lees*.

DRINK [ETH]

Ps. 69:21 my thirst they gave me vinegar to *d*
Prov. 5:15 *D* waters out of thine own cistern
Prov. 20:1 Wine is a mocker, strong *d* is raging
Eccles. 9:7 *d* thy wine with a merry heart
Matt. 6:31 shall we eat? or, What shall we *d*
Matt. 25:42 thirsty, and ye gave me no *d*
Mark 2:16 he [Jesus]…*d'eth* with…sinners
Mark 10:38 *d* of the cup that I [Jesus] *d* of
Mark 15:23 gave him [Jesus] to *d* wine…with myrrh
John 6:53 *d* his [Jesus'] blood, ye have no life in you
Rom. 12:20 he [your enemy] thirst, give him *d*
Rom. 14:17 kingdom of God is not meat and *d*
1 Cor. 11:25 oft as ye *d* it, in remembrance of me [Jesus]
1 Cor. 11:29 eateth and *d'eth* damnation to himself

DRINK OFFERING. An offering of fine wine, usually given in connection with

DROMEDARY. Camels were still a main source of transportation in Egypt at the turn of the 1900s, as suggested by this colorized photo taken near the Great Pyramid at Giza.

another sacrifice, such as a burnt offering (Num. 29).

DROMEDARY (YOUNG CAMEL). A distinct species of camel with one hump and known for its swiftness (Jer. 2:23). *Young camel:* NRSV.

DROPSY. A disease that causes fluid buildup in the body. Jesus healed a man with this disease on the Sabbath (Luke 14:2).

DROSS. Impurities separated from ore or metal in the smelting process (Prov. 25:4). The word is used symbolically of God's judgment against the wicked (Ps. 119:119).

DROUGHT. Lack of rainfall for an extended time (Ps. 32:4). The prophet Jeremiah spoke symbolically of a spiritual drought throughout the land (Jer. 14:1–7). See also *Famine.*

DRUNKARD. See *Winebibber.*

DRUNKENNESS. A state of intoxication caused by consuming too much wine or strong drink. This vice is condemned in both the O.T. and the N.T. (Deut. 21:20; 1 Cor. 5:11).

DRUSILLA. The wife of Felix, Roman governor of Judea, who heard Paul's defense (Acts 24:24–25).

DUKE (CHIEF). A leader of a clan (Gen. 36:15–43). *Chief:* NIV. See also *Chief.*

DULCIMER (PIPES). A musical instrument used in Babylonia, probably similar to the bagpipe (Dan. 3:5). *Pipes:* NIV.

DUMB. Unable to speak, or the temporary loss of speech (Ezek. 33:22). The word is also used figuratively of submission (Isa. 53:7).

Mark 7:37 he [Jesus] maketh…the *d* to speak
Luke 1:20 thou [Zacharias] shalt be *d*, and not able to speak
1 Cor. 12:2 Gentiles, carried away unto these *d* idols

DUNG (RUBBISH). Excrement of humans or animals (2 Kings 9:37). Dried dung was used for fuel in Palestine (Ezek. 4:12–15). The word is also used figuratively to express worthlessness (Phil. 3:8). *Rubbish:* NIV, NRSV.

DUNGEON. An underground prison. Some of these were little more than cisterns with the water partially drained. Joseph and Jeremiah were imprisoned in dungeons (Gen. 39:20, 40:15; Jer. 37:15–16). See also *Cistern; Pit; Prison.*

DURA. A plain in Babylonia where the golden image of King Nebuchadnezzar of Babylonia was set up (Dan. 3:1). See also *Adoraim.*

DUST. Dried earth in powdered form. Sitting in the dust was a symbol of dejection and humiliation (Lam. 3:29). The word is also used symbolically of man's mortality (Gen. 3:19).

DWELLING. See *Pavilion.*

DYSENTERY. See *Flux.*

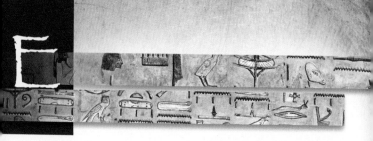

EAGLE. A large bird of prey, considered unclean by the Hebrews (Lev. 11:13). Many scholars believe the eagle of the Bible was actually the griffon vulture.

EAR. The ears of the unregenerate are called dull or unhearing (Matt. 13:15). The "ears of the LORD" (1 Sam. 8:21) signify that He hears prayers, in contrast to dumb idols (Ps. 115:6).

EARLY RAIN. See *Former Rain.*

EARNEST (DEPOSIT, FIRST INSTALL-MENT). A down payment given as a pledge toward full payment of the loan. The Holy Spirit is given as a pledge of the believer's in-heritance of eternal life (2 Cor. 1:22). *Deposit:* NIV; *first installment:* NRSV.

EARRING. A piece of jewelry worn suspended from the ear lobe (Gen. 35:4).

EARTH
Gen. 1:1 God created the heaven and the *e*
Gen. 9:1 Be fruitful…multiply…replenish the *e*
Ps. 8:1 how excellent is thy [God's] name in all the *e*
Ps. 24:1 The *e* is the LORD's, and the fulness thereof
Ps. 37:11 But the meek shall inherit the *e*
Ps. 96:1 sing unto the LORD, all the *e*
Isa. 6:3 the whole *e* is full of his [God's] glory
Hab. 2:20 all the *e* keep silence before him [God]
Matt. 5:13 Ye are…salt of the *e*
Matt. 16:19 loose on *e* shall be loosed in heaven
Luke 2:14 on *e* peace, good will toward men
John 12:32 if I [Jesus] be lifted up from the *e*
Acts 1:8 ye shall be witnesses…the uttermost part of the *e*
Rev. 21:1 I [John] saw a new heaven and a new *e*

EARTHQUAKE. A violent shaking of the earth (Ps. 77:18). These earth tremors are a token of God's wrath and judgment (Judg. 5:4).

EAST SEA. See *Dead Sea.*

EAST WIND. A violent, scorching desert wind, also known as the sirocco (Job 27:21). See also *Wind.*

EASTER. A word that refers to the Passover festival (Acts 12:4). Easter as a celebration of the resurrection of Jesus developed among Christians many years after the N.T. era.

EAT [ETH]
Gen. 2:17 tree of…good and evil, thou shalt not *e*
Exod. 16:35 children of Israel did *e* manna
Eccles. 2:24 nothing better… he should *e* and drink
Matt. 6:25 thought for your life, what ye shall *e*
Mark 14:18 One…which *e'eth* with me [Jesus] shall betray me
Luke 5:30 Why do ye *e* and drink with…sinners
Luke 15:23 bring…the fatted calf…let us *e*, and be merry
Acts 10:13 came a voice…Rise, Peter; kill, and *e*
1 Cor. 10:31 ye *e*, or drink…do all to the glory of God
2 Thess. 3:10 any would not work, neither should he *e*

EBAL. A rocky mountain in Samaria, or the territory of Ephraim, where Joshua built an altar after destroying the city of Ai (Josh. 8:30).

EBED-MELECH. An Ethiopian eunuch who rescued the prophet Jeremiah from a dungeon (Jer. 38:7–13).

EBENEZER. Site of Israel's defeat by the Philistines (1 Sam. 5:1). Years later, Samuel erected an altar on this site and called it Ebenezer, meaning "the stone of help," to commemorate Israel's eventual victory over the Philistines (1 Sam. 7:10–12).

EBER. A great-grandson of Shem (Gen. 10:21–25) and ancestor of the Hebrew race (Gen. 11:16–26).

EBONY. A hard, durable wood used for decorative carvings and musical instruments (Ezek. 27:15).

ECBATANA. See *Achmetha.*

ECCLESIASTES, BOOK OF. A wisdom book of the O.T., probably written by King Solomon, that declares that life derives joy and meaning not from riches, fame, or work but from reverence for God and obedience to His commandments. One of the book's most memorable passages is the poem on the proper time for all of life's events: "A time to be born, and a time to die...a time to weep, and a time to laugh...a time to keep silence, and a time to speak" (see 3:1–8).

EDEN, GARDEN OF. The fruitful garden created specifically by the Lord as the home for Adam and Eve. The four rivers of Eden, including the Euphrates, suggest that it may have been located in Mesopotamia. Because of their sin and rebellion against God, Adam and Eve were expelled from the garden (Gen. 2:8–3:24). See also *Adam; Eve.*

EDIFICATION. The process by which believers grow in holiness, wisdom, and

EDEN, GARDEN OF. Lush and peaceful—where even predators and prey get along. That's how the Garden of Eden is portrayed in this painting from the 1600s.

righteousness (1 Cor. 14:3; 1 Thess. 5:11). See also *Sanctification*.

EDOM

1. The name given to Esau, Jacob's brother, after he traded away his birthright (Gen. 25:30). See also *Esau*.

2. The land where the descendants of Esau settled. It was in extreme southern Palestine in the barren territory below the Dead Sea. Mount Seir was located in this territory (Gen. 36:8). Edom was referred to by the Greeks and Romans as *Idumaea* (Mark 3:8).

EDOMITES.
The descendants of Esau who were enemies of the Israelites. The king of Edom refused to allow the Israelites to pass through his territory after the Exodus (Num. 20:14–21). In later years, David conquered the Edomites (2 Sam. 8:14). But they apparently existed with a distinct territory and culture for several centuries (see Ps. 137:7). See also *Edom; Esau*.

EDREI.
A capital city of Bashan. King Og was defeated here by the Israelites (Num. 21:33–35).

EGYPT.
The ancient nation along the Nile River that held the Hebrew people in slavery for more than 400 years before their miraculous deliverance by the Lord at the hand of Moses. Egypt had flourished as a highly civilized culture for several centuries before the time of Abraham about 2000 B.C. Soon after entering Canaan in response to God's call, Abraham moved on to Egypt to escape a famine (Gen. 12:10).

This same circumstance led Jacob and his family to settle in Egypt after his son Joseph became a high official of the Egyptian pharaoh (Gen. 45–46). Ham's son Mizraim apparently was the ancestor of the Egyptians (1 Chron. 1:8). See also *Mizraim; Nile River; Pharaoh*.

EHUD.
The second judge of Israel who killed Eglon, king of Moab (Judg. 3:15). See also *Judges of Israel*.

EKRON.
One of the five chief Philistine cities. It was captured by Judah the judge and allotted to Dan (Judg. 1:18). See also *Philistines*.

ELAH

1. A valley in Judah where David killed the Philistine giant Goliath (1 Sam. 17:2, 49).

2. A king of Israel (reigned about 886–885 B.C.) who was assassinated and succeeded by Zimri (1 Kings 16:6–10).

ELAM.
A son of Shem and ancestor of the Elamites (Gen. 10:22).

ELAMITES.
Descendants of Elam who lived in Mesopotamia in the area later populated by the Medes and Persians (Jer. 25:25). See also *Persia*.

EL-BETHEL.
See *Bethel*.

ELDER

1. In the O.T., an older member of a tribe or clan who was a leader and official representative of the clan (Num. 22:7).

2. In the N.T., a local church leader who served as a pastor and teacher (1 Tim. 5:17).

ELDER [S]
Matt. 15:2 thy [Jesus'] disciples transgress the tradition of the *e's*
Acts 14:23 they [Paul and Barnabas] had ordained them *e's*
Acts 20:17 he [Paul] sent to Ephesus, and called the *e's*
1 Tim. 5:1 Rebuke not an *e*, but entreat him as a father
Rev. 4:10 four and twenty *e's* fall down before him [God]

ELEAZAR.
A son of Aaron who succeeded his father as high priest (Num. 20:25–28), serving under Moses and Joshua. He helped divide the land of Canaan among the twelve tribes of Israel (Josh. 14:1).

ELIJAH. On a hilltop in the Mount Carmel range stands this imposing statue of the prophet Elijah. After defeating Queen Jezebel's prophets of Baal in a spiritual battle by calling down fire from heaven to consume a sacrifice, Elijah ordered the false prophets executed.

ELECT LADY (CHOSEN LADY). The person, or perhaps a local church, to which the second epistle of John is addressed (2 John 1:1). *Chosen lady:* NIV.

ELECTION, DIVINE. The doctrine that deals with God's choice of persons who will be redeemed. Conflicts between God's electing grace and Christ's invitation that "whosoever will" may come to Him are not easily resolved. God's intentional will is for all to "come to repentance" and be saved (2 Pet. 3:9), but those who reject His Son will be lost (John 5:40).

God's grace is unmerited (Rom. 9:11–16), but it will be lavished on those who are committed to His truth and His will for their lives (2 Thess. 2:13). The elect are characterized by Christlikeness (Rom. 8:29), holiness (Eph. 1:4), good works (Eph. 2:10), and eternal hope (1 Pet. 1:2–5). See also *Foreknowledge; Predestination.*

EL-ELOHE-ISRAEL. A name, meaning "God, the God of Israel," given by Jacob to the altar that he built at Shechem after he was reconciled to his brother, Esau (Gen. 33:20).

ELEVATION OFFERING. See *Wave Offering.*

ELI. A high priest of Israel with whom the prophet Samuel lived during his boyhood years (1 Sam. 1–4). Eli's own two sons, Phinehas and Hophni, were unworthy of the priesthood (1 Sam. 2:12–17, 22–25). They were killed in a battle with the Philistines. Eli died upon learning of their death (1 Sam. 4:1–18).

ELIADA. See *Beeliada.*

ELIAKIM

1. A son of Hilkiah and overseer of the household of King Hezekiah of Judah. Eliakim was praised by the prophet Isaiah for his role in mediating peace with the invading Assyrian army (2 Kings 18:18; Isa. 22:20–25).

2. Another name for Jehoiakim, a king of Judah. See *Jehoiakim.*

ELIAS. See *Elijah.*

ELIHU. A friend who spoke to Job after Eliphaz, Bildad, and Zophar failed to answer Job's questions satisfactorily (Job 32:2–6).

ELIJAH/ELIAS. A courageous prophet who opposed King Ahab and his successor, Ahaziah, because of their encouragement of Baal worship throughout the Northern Kingdom. Because of Ahab's wickedness, Elijah predicted a drought would afflict the land (1 Kings 17). He wiped out the prophets of Baal after a dramatic demonstration of God's power on Mount Carmel (1 Kings 18:17–40).

After selecting Elisha as his successor, Elijah was carried into heaven in a whirlwind (2 Kings 2:1–11). The coming of the Messiah was often associated in Jewish thought with Elijah's return. Some people even thought Jesus was Elijah (Luke 9:8). *Elias:* Greek form (Matt. 17:4). See also *Elisha.*

ELIMELECH. The husband of Naomi and the father-in-law of Ruth. He died in Moab, leaving his family destitute (Ruth 1:1–3).

ELIPHAZ

1. A son of Esau (Gen. 36:2–4).

2. One of Job's friends or "comforters" (Job 2:11). In his speeches, Eliphaz defended the justice, purity, and holiness of God (Job 4; 15; 22; 42:7–9).

MERALD. *The green emerald was one of twelve precious stones worn on the ~astplate of Israel's high priest. The stones symbolized how precious Israel's twelve ~bes were to God.*

ELISABETH (ELIZABETH). The mother of John the Baptist and a relative of Mary, earthly mother of Jesus. Elisabeth rejoiced with Mary over the coming birth of the Messiah (Luke 1:36–45). *Elizabeth:* NIV, NRSV. See also *Mary,* No. 1.

ELISHA/ELISEUS. The prophet selected and anointed by Elijah as his successor (1 Kings 19:16–21). He followed Elijah for several years and was present at his ascension into heaven when the mantle of leadership fell upon him (2 Kings 2:9–14).

Elisha served as a counselor and adviser to four kings of the Northern Kingdom—Jehoram, Jehu, Jehoahaz, and Joash—across a period of about fifty years (850–800 B.C.). *Eliseus:* Greek form (Luke 4:27). See also *Elijah.*

ELISHEBA. The wife of Aaron and mother of Abihu, Eleazar, Nadab, and Ithamar (Exod. 6:23).

ELOTH. An Edomite seaport city on the Red Sea captured by David, then later turned into a station for trading ships by King Solomon (1 Kings 9:26).

EL-PARAN. See *Paran.*

ELUL. The sixth month of the Hebrew year, roughly equivalent to our September (Neh. 6:15).

ELYMAS. See *Bar-jesus.*

EMBALM. To prepare a body for burial to protect it from decay. This art was practiced by the Egyptians. Jacob and Joseph were embalmed for burial (Gen. 50:2–3, 26).

EMBROIDERY. The art of fancy needlework (Exod. 28:39).

EMERALD. A precious stone of pure green color used in the high priest's breastplate (Exod. 28:18) and the foundation of New Jerusalem (Rev. 21:19). See also *Diamond.*

EMERODS (TUMORS, ULCERS). A strange disease, exact nature unknown, that struck the Philistines when they placed the stolen ark of the covenant next to their false god Dagon (Deut. 28:27). *Tumors:* NIV; *ulcers:* NRSV.

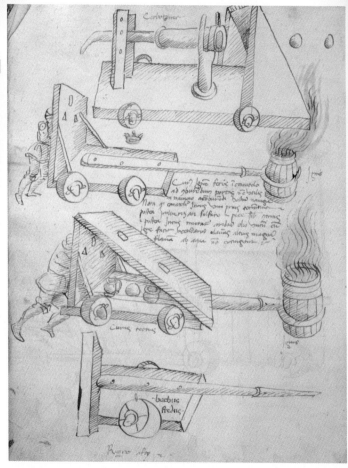

ENGINES. Catapults that could launch fire and stones were used in Bible times to help capture walled cities. This is a partial design for building a fire launcher from the 1400s, not Bible times. Still, it shows the basic workings of a catapult.

EMIMS (EMITES, EMIM). A race of giants east of the Dead Sea (Gen. 14:5). They were closely related to another race of giants known as the Anakims (Deut. 2:10–11). *Emites:* NIV; *Emim:* NRSV. See also *Anakims.*

EMMANUEL/IMMANUEL. The name given to the Christ child, meaning "God with us" (Matt. 1:23). The birth of a Savior bearing this name was foretold by the prophet Isaiah (Isa. 7:14; *Immanuel*). As this symbolic name suggests, God incarnate came in the person of Jesus Christ (1 John 4:2). See also *Jesus Christ; Messiah; Son of God; Son of Man.*

EMMAUS. A village near Jerusalem where Jesus revealed Himself to two of His followers shortly after His resurrection (Luke 24:13–31).

EMPTY. See *Void.*

ENCHANTER (MEDIUM, SOOTHSAYER). A person who used magical chants and rituals to drive away evil spirits (Jer. 27:9). *Medium:* NIV; *soothsayer:* NRSV. See also *Medium; Soothsayer.*

END [ED]

Gen. 2:2 seventh day God *e'ed* his work
Ps. 102:27 thy [God's] years shall have no *e*
Eccles. 7:8 Better...*e* of a thing than the beginning
Eccles. 12:12 making many books there is no *e*
Isa. 9:7 Of...his [the Messiah's]...peace...shall be no *e*
Dan. 12:9 words are...sealed...time of the *e*
Matt. 10:22 endureth to the *e* shall be saved
Matt. 24:6 things must come to pass...is not yet
Matt. 28:20 I [Jesus] am with you always...*e* of the world
Eph. 3:21 glory in the church...world without *e*
1 Pet. 4:7 the *e* of all things is at hand
Rev. 22:13 Alpha and Omega, the beginning and the *e*

ENDOR. A city in the territory of Issachar (Josh. 17:11). King Saul sought advice from a witch in this city (1 Sam. 28:7–10).

ENDURE [D, TH]

Exod. 18:23 thou [Moses] shalt be able to *e*
1 Chron. 16:34 his [God's] mercy *e'th* for ever
Ps. 9:7 Lord shall *e* for ever
Ps. 30:5 his [God's] anger *e'th* but a moment
Ps. 89:36 his [David's] seed shall *e* for ever
Matt. 10:22 that *e'th* to the end shall be saved
1 Cor. 13:7 [charity] hopeth all things, *e'th* all things
2 Tim. 2:3 hardness, as a good soldier of Jesus Christ
2 Tim. 4:5 watch thou in all things, *e* afflictions
Heb. 12:2 who [Jesus] for the joy...set before him *e'd* the cross
James 1:12 Blessed is the man that *e'th* temptation

ENEMY [IES]

Deut. 20:4 Lord...goeth...to fight...against your *e'ies*
Job 19:11 he [God] counteth me...as one of his *e'ies*
Ps. 9:3 *e'ies* are turned back, they shall fall
Ps. 18:17 He [God] delivered me from my strong *e*
Ps. 110:1 I [God] make thine *e'ies* thy footstool
Prov. 25:21 thine *e* be hungry, give him bread
Matt. 5:44 I [Jesus] say unto you, Love your *e'ies*
Rom. 12:20 Therefore if thine *e* hunger, feed him
1 Cor. 15:25 he [Jesus] must reign...put all *e'ies* under his feet
1 Cor. 15:26 last *e*...destroyed is death
Gal. 4:16 I [Paul]...your *e*, because I tell you the truth
2 Thess. 3:15 count him not as an *e*, but admonish him
James 4:4 friend of the world is the *e* of God

EN-GEDI. An oasis on the western shore of the Dead Sea where David hid from King Saul (1 Sam. 23:29–24:1).

ENGINES (MACHINES). A word that refers to the ingenuity of a machine or apparatus. The "engines" in 2 Chron. 26:15 (*machines:* NIV, NRSV) were used to hurl objects from the walls of besieged cities upon the enemy below. See also *Fenced City; Siege; Wall.*

ENGRAVER. A craftsman who engraved metals or carved wood and stone (Exod. 35:35).

ENMITY. Deep animosity toward another (Gen. 3:15). This sin is characteristic of unredeemed persons (Rom. 1:29–30; 8:7). See also *Hate.*

ENOCH/HENOCH

1. The firstborn son of Cain and the name of a city built by Cain and named after Enoch (Gen. 4:17).

2. The father of Methuselah who was taken into God's presence without experiencing physical death (Gen. 5:21–24). *Henoch:* 1 Chron. 1:3.

ENOS (ENOSH).

A son of Seth and a grandson of Adam (Gen. 5:6) who is listed in the N.T. ancestry of Jesus (Luke 3:38). *Enosh:* NIV, NRSV.

ENSIGN (BANNER).

A symbol on a long pole that identified an army or tribe (Num. 2:2). *Banner:* NIV. See also *Standard.*

ENTER [ED]

Ps. 100:4 *E* into his [God's] gates with thanksgiving
Matt. 6:6 when thou prayest, *e* into thy closet
Mark 14:38 pray, lest ye *e* into temptation
Luke 13:24 Strive to *e* in at the strait gate
Luke 18:25 easier for a camel...rich man to *e* into the kingdom
Luke 22:3 Then *e'ed* Satan into Judas
Rom. 5:12 by one man sin *e'ed* into the world
Heb. 9:12 he [Jesus] *e'ed* in once into the holy place

ENVY.

Resentment toward another person's good fortune (Prov. 27:4). Paul cautioned Christians against the dangers of this sin (Rom. 13:13). See also *Jealousy.*

ENVY [IETH, ING]

Prov. 3:31 *E* thou not the oppressor
1 Cor. 13:4 charity *e'ieth* not...vaunteth not itself
Gal. 5:26 not be desirous of...glory,...*e'ing* one another
Phil. 1:15 Some...preach Christ even of *e* and strife
James 3:16 where *e'ing* and strife is, there is confusion

EPAPHRAS.

A leader of the Colossian church (Col. 1:7–8) whom Paul called his "fellow prisoner" in Rome (Philem. 23).

EPAPHRODITUS.

A believer from Philippi who brought a gift to Paul while he was under house arrest in Rome (Phil. 4:18).

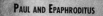

PAUL AND EPAPHRODITUS

Epaphroditus must have stayed in Rome for a while to offer comfort and encouragement to Paul. The apostle informed the Philippian believers that Epaphroditus had been sick but had recovered and would be returning to them soon (Phil. 2:27–28). Paul may have sent his letter to the Philippians by Epaphroditus (Phil. 2:29).

EPHAH.

A dry measure equal to about one bushel (Exod. 16:36).

EPHESIANS, EPISTLE TO THE.

A letter of the apostle Paul to the church at Ephesus on the theme of the risen Christ as Lord of creation and head of His body, the Church. The first three chapters of the epistle focus on the redemption made possible by the atoning death of Christ and His grace that is appropriated through faith—"not of works, lest any man should boast" (2:9). Chapters 4–6 call on the Ephesian Christians to model their lives after Christ's example and to remain faithful in turbulent times.

EPHESUS.

The chief city of Asia Minor and a center of worship of the pagan goddess Diana where Paul spent two to three years, establishing a church (Acts 18:19–21; 19:1–10). Archaeologists have uncovered the remains of the temple of Diana and a Roman theater on this site. See also *Diana.*

EPHOD. A sleeveless linen garment, similar to a vest, worn by the high priest while officiating at the sacrificial altar (2 Sam. 6:14).

EPHPHATHA. An Aramaic word, meaning "be opened," spoken by Jesus to heal a deaf man (Mark 7:34).

EPHRAIM
1. The second son of Joseph who became the founder of one of the twelve tribes of Israel (Gen. 48:8–20). Joshua was a member of this tribe. See also *Tribes of Israel.*
2. A name often used symbolically for the nation of Israel (Hosea 11:12; 12:1).
3. A city in the wilderness to which Jesus and His disciples retreated (John 11:54).
4. A forest where the forces of Absalom were defeated by David's army (2 Sam. 18:6).

EPHRATAH, EPHRATH. See *Bethlehem.*

EPHRON. A Hittite who sold the cave of Machpelah to Abraham as a burial site (Gen. 23:8–20). See also *Machpelah.*

EPICUREANS. Followers of the Greek philosopher Epicurus, who believed the highest goal of life was the pursuit of pleasure, tempered by morality and cultural refinement. Epicureans were among the crowd addressed by Paul in the city of Athens (Acts 17:18). See also *Athens; Stoicks.*

EPISTLE. A type of correspondence best described as a "formal letter." Twenty-two of the twenty-seven N.T. books were written as epistles.

EQUAL
John 5:18 God was his [Jesus'] Father…*e* with God
Phil. 2:6 Who [Jesus]…thought it not robbery to be *e* with God
Col. 4:1 give unto your servants…just and *e*

ERR [ED]
Job 6:24 understand wherein I [Job] have *e'ed*
Isa. 9:16 leaders of this people cause them to *e*
Matt. 22:29 Ye do *e*, not knowing the scriptures
1 Tim. 6:10 they have *e'ed* from the faith

ERROR
2 Sam. 6:7 God smote him [Uzzah]…for his *e*
Matt. 27:64 last *e*…worse than the first
2 Pet. 3:17 led away with the *e* of the wicked

ESAIAS. See *Isaiah.*

ESAR-HADDON. A son of Sennacherib who succeeded his father as king of Assyria (reigned about 681–669 B.C.; 2 Kings 19:37). Esar-haddon apparently was the king who resettled Samaria with foreigners after the fall of the Northern Kingdom (Ezra 4:1–2). See also *Samaritan.*

ESAU/EDOM. The oldest son of Isaac who sold his birthright to his twin brother, Jacob, for a bowl of stew (Gen. 25:25–34). Esau was the ancestor of the Edomites. *Edom:* Gen. 36:8. See also *Edom; Edomites.*

ESCAPE [D]
1 Sam. 22:1 David…*e'd* to the cave Adullam
Job 19:20 I [Job] am *e'd* with the skin of my teeth
Isa. 37:31 remnant that is *e'd* of the house of Judah
John 10:39 he [Jesus] *e'd* out of their hand
1 Cor. 10:13 with the temptation also make a way to *e*
Heb. 2:3 shall we *e*, if we neglect so great salvation

ESDRAELON. See *Jezreel,* No. 3.

ESEK. A well in the valley of Gerar over which the servants of Isaac and Abimelech quarreled (Gen. 26:20).

ESH-BAAL. See *Ish-bosheth.*

ESPOUSED. See *Betrothal.*

ESAU. In a foolish moment, red-haired Esau—hungry from hunting—trades his inheritance for a bowl of stew. As Isaac's oldest son, Esau would have gotten a double share of the rich inheritance. It's uncertain if he traded everything or just the rights of an elder brother. Either way, the stew was overpriced.

ESSENES. A religious group of N.T. times that practiced strict discipline, withdrawal from society, and communal living. Although they are not mentioned by name in the Bible, many scholars believe they are the group that preserved the Dead Sea Scrolls in caves at Qumran near the Dead Sea. See also *Dead Sea Scrolls; Qumran.*

ESTABLISH [ED]

Gen. 9:9 I [God] *e* my covenant with you [Noah]
Ps. 78:5 he [God] *e'ed* a testimony in Jacob
Ps. 90:17 *e* thou [God] the work of our hands
Ezek. 16:62 I [God] will *e* my covenant with thee
Matt. 18:16 mouth of...witnesses every word...be *e'ed*
Acts 16:5 so were the churches *e'ed* in the faith

ESTHER. A young Jewish woman who became queen under King Ahasuerus of Persia and used her influence to save her countrymen. Her Persian name was *Hadassah.* See also *Ahasuerus; Haman.*

ESTHER, BOOK OF. A historical book of the O.T. named for its major personality, Queen Esther of Persia, who saved her people, the Jews, from annihilation by the evil and scheming Haman—a high official of the Persian king. The book shows clearly that God protects and sustains His people.

ETERNAL

Deut. 33:27 The *e* God is thy refuge
John 17:3 life *e*, that they might know...God

2 Cor. 4:18 things which are not seen are *e*
2 Cor. 5:1 not made with hands, *e* in the heavens
1 Tim. 1:17 unto the King *e*, immortal, invisible
Heb. 5:9 he [Jesus] became the author of *e* salvation
Heb. 9:12 his [Jesus'] own blood...obtained *e* redemption

ETERNAL LIFE. Life without end, or everlasting existence. Eternal life was promised to believers at their conversion by Christ (John 11:25–26) and affirmed by the appearance of Moses and Elijah to Jesus and the three disciples (Matt. 17:1–9). Through His resurrection, Christ became the "firstfruits" of eternal life for all believers (1 Cor. 15:12–23). Life everlasting represents God's final victory over sin and death (Rev. 21:4).

Mark 10:17 I do that I may inherit *e-l*
John 3:15 believeth in him [Jesus]...have *e-l*
John 6:54 Whoso eateth my [Jesus'] flesh...hath *e-l*
John 6:68 thou [Jesus] hast the words of *e-l*
John 10:28 I [Jesus] give unto them *e-l*
Rom. 6:23 gift of God is *e-l* through Jesus Christ
1 Tim. 6:12 Fight the good fight...lay hold on *e-l*
1 John 3:15 no murderer hath *e-l* abiding in him
1 John 5:11 God hath given to us *e-l...*in his Son

ETHAN. See *Jeduthun.*

ETHANIM. The seventh month of the Hebrew year, corresponding roughly to our October (1 Kings 8:2).

ETHIOPIA. An ancient nation south of Egypt. Moses married an Ethiopian woman (Num. 12:1). Philip witnessed to a servant of the queen of Ethiopia (Acts 8:27).

EUNICE. The mother of Timothy. She was commended for her great faith by the apostle Paul (2 Tim. 1:5). See also *Timothy.*

EUNUCH. A male household servant of a king. These servants were often emasculated

to protect the king's harem (2 Kings 9:32). See also *Chamberlain.*

EUPHRATES. A major river in the territory of the ancient Babylonians and Persians in Mesopotamia that is also mentioned as one of the rivers of the Garden of Eden (Gen. 2:14). See also *Tigris.*

EUROCLYDON (NORTHEASTER). A violent wind that struck Paul's ship bound for Rome (Acts 27:14). *Northeaster:* NIV, NRSV.

EUTYCHUS. A young man who went to sleep and fell from a window during Paul's sermon at Troas. He was restored by Paul (Acts 20:9–12).

EVANGELIST. A person who traveled from place to place, preaching the gospel (Eph. 4:11; 2 Tim. 4:5). Philip was one of the zealous evangelists of the early churches (Acts 21:8).

EVE. The name given by Adam to his wife as the mother of the human race (Gen. 3:20). Fashioned from one of Adam's ribs, she was created to serve as his helpmate and companion (Gen. 2:18–23). Because of her sin and rebellion, Eve was to experience pain and sorrow, especially in connection with the birth of children (Gen. 3:16). See also *Adam; Fall of Man.*

EVERLASTING

Deut. 33:27 underneath are the *e* arms
Ps. 24:7 be ye lift up, ye *e* doors
Ps. 90:2 even from *e* to *e*, thou art God
Ps. 100:5 LORD is good; his mercy is *e*
Ps. 119:144 righteousness of thy [God's] testimonies is *e*
Isa. 9:6 his [Jesus'] name shall be called...*e* Father
Isa. 40:28 the *e* God...fainteth not
Isa. 60:19 LORD shall be unto thee an *e* light
Jer. 31:3 I [God] have loved thee with an *e* love
Dan. 7:14 his [God's] dominion is an *e* dominion
Matt. 25:41 Depart from me [Jesus]...into *e* fire

E

EVE. Eve holds unidentified fruit from the Tree of Knowledge, of which God told humanity's first couple not to eat. The fruit is often mistakenly called an apple.

EVERLASTING LIFE. See *Eternal Life.*

EVIL. A force that stands in opposition to God and righteousness. This evil force originates with Satan, the archenemy of good, truth, and honesty (Matt. 13:19). In the end-time, God will triumph over evil, and Satan will be thrown into a lake of fire (Rev. 20:10). See also *Iniquity; Sin; Wickedness.*

1 Sam. 16:14 an *e* spirit…troubled him [Saul]
Ps. 23:4 shadow of death…fear no *e*
Ps. 34:13 tongue from *e*, thy lips from…guile
Prov. 3:7 fear the LORD, and depart from *e*
Prov. 15:3 eyes of the LORD…beholding the *e*
Isa. 5:20 that call *e* good, and good evil
Matt. 6:13 not into temptation…deliver us from *e*
Luke 11:13 being *e*, know how to give good gifts
Rom. 7:19 the *e* which I [Paul] would not, that I do
Rom. 12:9 Abhor that which is *e*; cleave to…good
Eph. 5:16 Redeeming the time…days are *e*
1 Thess. 5:22 Abstain from all appearance of *e*
1 Tim. 6:10 love of money is the root of all *e*
James 3:8 tongue…is an unruly *e*

EVIL DESIRES. See *Concupiscence.*

EVILDOER [S]
Ps. 26:5 I have hated the congregation of *e's*
Ps. 119:115 Depart from me, ye *e's*
1 Pet. 4:15 none of you suffer…as an *e*

EVIL-MERODACH. A successor of Nebuchadnezzar II as king of Babylonia (reigned about 562–560 B.C.). He released King Jehoiachin of Judah from prison (2 Kings 25:27–30). See also *Babylonia.*

EWE LAMB. A female sheep (Gen. 21:30).

EXALT [ED, ETH]
1 Chron. 29:11 thou [God] art *e'ed*…above all
Ps. 57:11 Be thou *e'ed*, O God, above the heavens
Ps. 97:9 thou [God] art *e'ed* far above all gods
Prov. 14:34 Righteousness *e'eth* a nation
Isa. 25:1 LORD, thou art my God; I will *e* thee
Luke 14:11 he that humbleth himself shall be *e'ed*
Phil. 2:9 God also hath highly *e'ed* him [Jesus]

EXAMPLE
Matt. 1:19 Joseph…not willing to make her [Mary] a public *e*
John 13:15 I [Jesus] have given you an *e*
1 Tim. 4:12 be thou an *e* of the believers, in word

EXCEEDING
Matt. 2:10 they [the wise men] rejoiced with *e* great joy
Matt. 5:12 be *e* glad: for great is your reward

Matt. 26:38 My [Jesus'] soul is *e* sorrowful
Eph. 2:7 he [God] might show the *e* riches of his grace
Eph. 3:20 him [Jesus] that is able to do *e* abundantly

EXCELLENT
Ps. 8:9 how *e* is thy [God's] name in all the earth
Ps. 150:2 praise him [God] according to his *e* greatness
Isa. 12:5 he [God] hath done *e* things
1 Cor. 12:31 show I [Paul] unto you a more *e* way
Heb. 8:6 he [Jesus] obtained a more *e* ministry
Heb. 11:4 Abel offered…a more *e* sacrifice than Cain

EXCUSE
Luke 14:18 they all…began to make *e*
Rom. 1:20 they are without *e*

EXHORT [ED, ING]
1 Thess. 2:11 we *e'ed* and comforted…every one of you
2 Tim. 4:2 *e* with all longsuffering and doctrine
Titus 2:9 *E* servants to be obedient unto…masters
Heb. 10:25 Not forsaking the assembling of ourselves…but *e'ing* one another

EXHORTATION. A strong message of encouragement or warning (Heb. 12:5).

EXILE. See *Captivity.*

EXODUS, BOOK OF. A book of the O.T. that recounts the release of the Hebrew people from Egyptian enslavement and the early years of their history as a nation in the wilderness.

Important events covered in the book include (1) God's call of Moses to lead the people out of slavery (chaps. 3–4); (2) the plagues on the Egyptians (chaps. 7–12); (3) the release of the Israelites and the crossing of the Red Sea (chap. 14); (4) God's miraculous provision for His people in the wilderness (16:1–17:7); (5) Moses' reception of the Ten Commandments and other parts of the law (chaps. 20–23); and (6) the building of the tabernacle for worship at God's command (chaps. 36–40). See also *Moses.*

EXPANSE. See *Firmament*.

EXPEDIENT

John 11:50 *e*...one man should die for the people
John 16:7 *e* for you that I [Jesus] go away
1 Cor. 6:12 All things are lawful...all things are not *e*

EYE. An organ of sight (Matt. 6:22). The word is also used symbolically to portray sinful desire (1 John 2:16).

Exod. 21:24 *E* for *e*, tooth for tooth
Job 42:5 now mine [Job's] *e* seeth thee [God]
Ps. 6:7 Mine *e* is consumed because of grief
Ps. 17:8 Keep me as the apple of the *e*
Prov. 28:22 He that hasteth to be rich hath an evil *e*
Mark 9:47 thine *e* offend thee, pluck it out
Luke 6:41 mote that is in thy brother's *e*
1 Cor. 2:9 *E* hath not seen, nor ear heard
1 Cor. 12:21 the *e* cannot say unto the hand
1 Cor. 15:52 twinkling of an *e*, at the last trump
Rev. 1:7 he [Jesus] cometh...every *e* shall see him

EZEKIAS. See *Hezekiah*.

EZEKIEL. A prophet of Judah who was carried into exile by the Babylonians and who prophesied faithfully to his countrymen for more than twenty years. He is the author of the book of Ezekiel in the O.T.

APOCALYPTIC LANGUAGE IN EZEKIEL

Ezekiel is one of the few books in the Bible that contains apocalyptic literature. This was a distinctive type of writing that used visions, numbers, strange creatures, angels, and demons to express religious truths (Ezek. 10:1–17). The best-known example of apocalyptic literature in the Bible is the book of Revelation in the New Testament.

EZEKIEL, BOOK OF. A prophetic book of the O.T. addressed to the Jewish captives in Babylon about 585 B.C. and offering God's promise that His people would be restored to their homeland after their period of suffering and exile was over. This promise from God is exemplified by Ezekiel's vision of a valley of dry bones: "I...shall put my spirit in you, and ye shall live, and I shall place you in your own land" (37:13–14).

EZION-GABER/EZION-GEBER. A place on the coast of the Red Sea where the Israelites camped during their years of wandering in the wilderness (Num. 33:35). This settlement later became a town, serving as a harbor for Solomon's trading ships. *Ezion-geber:* 1 Kings 9:26.

EZRA. A scribe and priest who led an important reform movement among the Jewish people after the Babylonian Exile. He is the author of the book of Ezra. See also *Nehemiah*.

EZRA, BOOK OF. A historical book of the O.T. that describes events in Jerusalem after the Jewish captives began returning to their homeland about 500 B.C. following their period of exile in Babylonia and Persia. After the rebuilding of the temple (Ezra 6:14–15), the people under Ezra's leadership committed themselves to God's law, put away foreign wives (Ezra 10:1–17), and confessed their sins and renewed the covenant (Neh. 9–10).

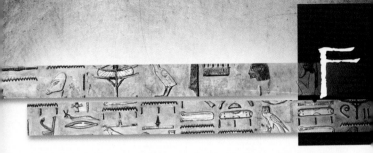

FABLE. A story in which inanimate things are personalized, as in Jotham's narrative of the trees and the bramble (Judg. 9:7–15).

FAIR HAVENS. A harbor on the southern side of the island of Crete where Paul's ship stopped during his voyage to Rome (Acts 27:8).

FAITH. Belief and confidence in the testimony of another, particularly God's promise of salvation and eternal life for all who place their trust in Jesus Christ (John 5:24). A gift of God, faith is essential to salvation (Eph. 2:8). The word also refers to the teachings of Scripture, or the "faith which was once delivered unto the saints" (Jude 3). See also *Trust*.

Hab. 2:4 the just shall live by his *f*
Matt. 17:20 *f* as a grain of mustard seed
Acts 6:8 Stephen, full of *f* and power
Rom. 3:28 justified by *f* without the deeds of the law
Rom. 10:17 So then *f* cometh by hearing
1 Cor. 13:13 abideth *f*, hope, charity
Gal. 2:20 I [Paul] live by the *f* of the Son of God

FAIR HAVENS. Sailing for Rome in a dangerous season, near the start of winter, Paul tried to convince the captain to winter at Crete's harbor in Fair Havens. But the captain sailed for a better harbor at Phoenix. On the short trip, a storm engulfed the ship and drove it some six hundred miles west before running it aground.

Gal. 3:24 unto Christ, that we might be justified by *f*
Gal. 5:22 fruit of the Spirit is love...goodness, *f*
Eph. 2:8 by grace are ye saved through *f*
Eph. 6:16 Above all, taking the shield of *f*
1 Tim. 5:8 denied the *f*, and is worse than an infidel
1 Tim. 6:12 Fight the good fight of *f*
2 Tim. 4:7 finished my course, I [Paul] have kept the *f*
Heb. 10:23 hold fast the profession of our *f*
Heb. 11:1 Now *f* is the substance of things hoped for
Heb. 12:2 Jesus the author and finisher of our *f*
James 2:17 *f*, if it hath not works, is dead
1 John 5:4 victory that overcometh the world, even our *f*

FAITHFUL [NESS]

Ps. 31:23 Lord preserveth the *f*
Ps. 119:90 Thy [God's] *f'ness* is unto all generations
Prov. 27:6 *F* are the wounds of a friend
Lam. 3:23 great is thy [God's] *f'ness*
Matt. 25:21 Well done...good and *f* servant
Luke 16:10 *f* in that which is least is *f* also in much
1 Cor. 4:2 required in stewards...man be found *f*
1 Cor. 10:13 God is *f*...not suffer you to be tempted
2 Thess. 3:3 Lord is *f*, who shall stablish you
1 John 1:9 he [Jesus] is *f*...to forgive us our sins
Rev. 2:10 be thou *f* unto death

FALL [EN, ING]

Ps. 145:14 Lord upholdeth all that *f*
Prov. 16:18 Pride goeth before destruction...haughty spirit before a *f*
Hos. 14:1 thou [Israel] hast *f'en* by thine iniquity
Luke 2:34 child [Jesus] is set for the *f*...of many
1 Cor. 10:12 thinketh he standeth take heed lest he *f*
Heb. 10:31 fearful thing to *f* into the hands of...God
James 1:2 joy when ye *f* into divers temptations
Jude 24 unto him [Jesus]...able to keep you from *f'ing*

FALL OF MAN. A phrase that refers to Adam and Eve's state of sorrow and misery that followed their sin and rebellion against God (Gen. 2–3). Their original sin has afflicted the human race ever since (Rom. 3:23)—a condition cured only by the atoning death of Christ (Rom. 5:6). See also *Adam; Eve; Man; Sin.*

FALLOW DEER. A distinct species of deer, common in Mesopotamia in Bible times, and a clean animal to the Hebrews (Deut. 14:4–5). See also *Deer.*

FALLOW GROUND (UNPLOWED GROUND). A field plowed and left idle for a short time before planting again (Jer. 4:3). *Unplowed ground:* NIV.

FALSE [LY]

Exod. 20:16 not bear *f* witness against thy neighbour
Lev. 19:11 shall not steal, neither deal *f'ly*
Prov. 11:1 A *f* balance is abomination to the Lord
Jer. 29:9 prophesy *f'ly* unto you in my [God's] name
Matt. 5:11 all manner of evil against you *f'ly*, for my [Jesus'] sake

JEREMIAH AND FALSE PROPHETS

False prophets have lived in every age, but the God-called prophet Jeremiah had more than his share of trouble from "yes-men" who told the officials of Judah what they wanted to hear. They denied Jeremiah's message of certain judgment for the nation unless the people changed their ways.

Hananiah was one of the worst of these misleading messengers (Jer. 28:1–17). Jeremiah declared that God would deal severely with Hananiah. He will do the same with anyone who speaks lies in His name and deliberately leads people astray.

FALSE PROPHET. A person who delivers a false or misleading message under the pretense that it comes from God. Believers are warned to beware of false prophets (Matt. 24:11, 24; 2 Pet. 2:1).

FALSE PROPHET [S]

Matt. 7:15 Beware of *f-p's*...in sheep's clothing
Mark 13:22 *f-p's* shall rise...signs and wonders
Acts 13:6 a *f-p*...whose name was Barjesus

1 John 4:1 many *f-p's* are gone out into the world
Rev. 19:20 beast was taken…with him the *f-p*

FALSE WEIGHTS. Deceptive measurements used in weighing merchandise—a practice condemned by the Lord (Deut. 25:13–14).

FALSE WITNESS (FALSE TESTIMONY). A person who gives false testimony or tells lies about others in an attempt to undermine their credibility or slander their character. Such testimony is specifically prohibited by the Ten Commandments (Exod. 20:16). *False testimony:* NIV.

FAMILIAR SPIRIT. The spirit of a dead person that a sorcerer "calls up" in order to communicate with that person (Deut. 18:11). The spirit of Samuel was called up by a witch at Endor (1 Sam. 28:3–20). Such sorcery was considered an abomination by God. See also *Sorcery; Witchcraft.*

FAMILY. A group of persons related to one another by blood kinship and the ties of marriage. The N.T. implies that all Christians are related to one another in a spiritual sense, since we are all members of the "household of faith" (Gal. 6:10). See also *Kindred.*

FAMILY RECORDS. See *Register.*

FAMINE. A time, often an extended period, when food or water is in short supply because of lack of rain and the failure of crops (Gen. 12:10). See also *Drought.*

FAN (FORK). A wooden pitchfork for winnowing grain (Isa. 30:24). The grain was thrown into the wind to separate it from the straw (Matt. 3:12). The fan is also spoken of as

a symbol of God's judgment (Jer. 15:7). *Fork:* NIV, NRSV. See also *Winnowing.*

FARMER. See *Husbandman.*

FARTHING (PENNY). A Roman coin of small value (Matt. 10:29). *Penny:* NIV, NRSV. See also *Penny.*

FAST. The practice of giving up eating and drinking for a specified time, generally as part of a religious ritual in times of peril. Elijah and Jesus each fasted for forty days (1 Kings 19:8; Matt. 4:2).

FAST [ING]
Ps. 109:24 knees are weak through *f'ing*
Matt. 17:21 this kind goeth not out but by prayer and *f'ing*
1 Cor. 6:13 Watch ye, stand *f* in the faith
1 Thess. 5:21 Prove all things; hold *f* that which is good
Heb. 10:23 hold *f* the profession of our faith

FAT CALF. See *Fatling.*

FATHER. The male head of a household who was the undisputed authority in the family. This word was also used by Jesus as a title for God (Matt. 11:25).

FATHOM. A nautical measure, equal to about seven feet. The term is mentioned in the account of Paul's shipwreck (Acts 27:28).

FATLING (FAT CALF). A young animal fattened for slaughter (Matt. 22:4). *Fat calf:* NRSV. See also *Calf.*

FAULT [LESS, S]
Luke 23:4 I [Pilate] find no *f* in this man [Jesus]
Gal. 6:1 if a man be overtaken in a *f*
James 5:16 Confess your *f's* one to another
Jude 24 present you *f'less*…presence of his [Jesus'] glory
Rev. 14:5 without *f* before the throne of God

FEAR. An emotion aroused by danger or risk to one's safety (1 Sam. 21:10). The word is also used for respect or reverence toward God (Deut. 10:20).

FEAR [ED, ETH]

Deut. 6:13 *f* the LORD thy God, and serve him
1 Chron. 16:25 he [God]...to be *f'ed* above all gods
Job 1:1 Job...was perfect...*f'ed* God
Job 28:28 the *f* of the Lord, that is wisdom
Ps. 19:9 *f* of the LORD is clean, enduring for ever
Ps. 27:1 LORD is my...salvation; whom shall I *f*
Ps. 111:10 *f* of the LORD is the beginning of wisdom
Ps. 112:1 Blessed is the man that *f'eth* the LORD
Eccles. 12:13 *F* God, and keep his commandments
Phil. 2:12 work out your own salvation with *f*
2 Tim. 1:7 God hath not given us the spirit of *f*
Heb. 13:6 I will not *f* what man shall do unto me
1 John 4:18 perfect love casteth out *f*

FEAR NOT

Gen. 15:1 *F-n*, Abram: I [God] am thy shield
Gen. 21:17 What aileth thee, Hagar? *F-n*
Dan. 10:12 *F-n*, Daniel...words were heard
Joel 2:21 *F-n*, O land; be glad and rejoice
Matt. 1:20 Joseph...*f-n* to take unto thee Mary
Matt. 28:5 *F-n*, ye [women at the tomb]...ye seek Jesus
Luke 1:13 *F-n*, Zacharias...thy prayer is heard
Luke 1:30 *F-n*, Mary...hast found favour with God
Luke 2:10 *F-n*...I [angel] bring you [shepherds] good tidings
Luke 12:32 *F-n*...it is your Father's good pleasure to give you the kingdom
Acts 27:24 Saying, *F-n*, Paul; thou must be brought before Caesar
Rev. 1:17 *F-n*; I [Jesus] am the first and the last

FEARFUL [LY, NESS]

Ps. 55:5 *F'ness* and trembling are come upon me
Ps. 139:14 I am *f'ly* and wonderfully made
Matt. 8:26 Why are ye *f*, O ye of little faith?
Heb. 10:31 a *f* thing to fall into the hands of the living God

FEAST. A festival or a major religious holiday that marked some great event in Jewish history. The Jews celebrated several major festivals.

FEAST OF BOOTHS. See *Tabernacles, Feast of.*

FEAST OF HARVEST. See *Pentecost.*

FEAST OF INGATHERING. See *Tabernacles, Feast of.*

FEAST OF LIGHTS. See *Dedication, Feast of.*

FEAST OF UNLEAVENED BREAD. See *Passover and Feast of Unleavened Bread.*

FEAST OF WEEKS. See *Pentecost.*

FEET. The removal of sandals and the washing of one's feet upon entering a house or a holy place was a token of respect, similar to our custom of taking off the hat (Exod. 3:5).

FELIX. The governor of Judea who heard Paul's defense at Caesarea (Acts 23:24; 24:10–27).

FELLOWSHIP. A mutual sharing or friendly association, particularly that between believers who have a common faith in Jesus Christ (1 Cor. 1:9).

Acts 2:42 continued stedfastly in the apostles' doctrine and *f*
2 Cor. 6:14 what *f* hath righteousness...unrighteousness
Eph. 5:11 no *f* with the...works of darkness
Phil. 3:10 I [Paul] may know him [Jesus]...*f* of his sufferings
1 John 1:7 we have *f* one with another

FENCED CITY (FORTIFIED CITY). A city with a strong defensive wall (2 Sam. 20:6). The wall was erected to provide protection against enemies in times of war. *Fortified city:* NIV, NRSV. See also *City; Siege; Wall.*

FERRET (GECKO). A burrowing animal considered unclean by the Hebrews (Lev. 11:30). *Gecko:* NIV, NRSV.

FESTUS. Successor of Felix as Roman governor of Judea. Paul made his defense before Festus (Acts 24:27).

FETTERS (SHACKLES). Metal bands for binding the wrists or ankles of prisoners (2 Kings 25:7). *Shackles:* NIV. See also *Stocks.*

FEVER. See *Burning Ague.*

FIELD OF BLOOD. See *Aceldama.*

FIERY SERPENTS (VENOMOUS SNAKES, POISONOUS SERPENTS). Snakes that attacked the Israelites in the wilderness. Moses erected a brass serpent on a pole as an antidote for those who were bitten (Num. 21:6–9). *Venomous snakes:* NIV; *poisonous serpents:* NRSV. See also *Brass Serpent.*

FIG. The pear-shaped fruit of the fig tree. The spies sent into Canaan brought back figs to show the bounty of the land (Deut. 8:8). Figs were pressed into cakes and also preserved by drying (1 Sam. 25:18). The fig tree was considered a symbol of prosperity (1 Kings 4:25).

FIGHTING MEN. See *Mighty Men.*

FILTH. See *Offscouring.*

FILTHY
Ps. 14:3 they are all together become *f*
Isa. 64:6 our righteousnesses are as *f* rags
1 Tim. 3:8 deacons be grave...not greedy of *f* lucre

FILTHY LUCRE. A phrase for money (1 Tim. 3:3), which is condemned as an unworthy motive for ministry (1 Pet. 5:2). See also *Money.*

FINER (SILVERSMITH, SMITH). A craftsman who refined or shaped precious metals (Prov. 25:4). *Silversmith:* NIV; *smith:* NRSV. See also *Smith.*

FINGER
1. A digit of the human hand. The word is also used symbolically of God's power (Exod. 8:19; 31:18; Luke 11:20).
2. A measure of length equal to about three-fourths of an inch (Jer. 52:21).

FINING POT (CRUCIBLE). A vessel for melting and purifying metal (Prov. 17:3). *Crucible:* NIV, NRSV.

FINISH [ED]
Gen. 2:1 heavens and the earth were *f*'ed
Luke 14:28 counteth the cost...sufficient to *f* it
John 17:4 *f*'ed the work which thou [God] gavest me [Jesus]
John 19:30 is *f*'ed: and he [Jesus]...gave up the ghost
2 Tim. 4:7 I [Paul] have *f*'ed my course

FIR (PINE, CYPRESS). An evergreen tree that grew on Mount Lebanon. Its lumber was used in the construction of Solomon's temple in Jerusalem (1 Kings 6:15, 34). *Pine:* NIV; *cypress:* NRSV.

FIRE. Burning material used for cooking and in religious ceremonies. Fire is often associated with the presence and power of God (Exod. 3:2), as well as the final punishment of the wicked (Matt. 13:49–50). See also *Pillar of Fire and Cloud.*

FIREPAN. A vessel in which incense was burned during worship ceremonies in the tabernacle (Exod. 27:3). See also *Censer.*

FIRKIN. A liquid measure equal to about five or six gallons (John 2:16).

FIRMAMENT (EXPANSE, DOME). A word for the heavens, or the sky above the earth (Gen. 1:6–8). *Expanse:* NIV; *dome:* NRSV.

FIRST DAY OF THE WEEK. Sunday, or the day of Christ's resurrection, which was adopted as the day of worship by the early church (Acts 20:7).

FIRST INSTALLMENT. See *Earnest.*

FIRSTBORN. The first child born into a family (Gen. 49:3). The firstborn son received a double portion of his father's property as his birthright and assumed leadership of the family. See also *Birthright; Inheritance.*

FIRSTFRUITS. The first or best of crops and livestock. According to Mosaic Law, these were to be presented as sacrifices and offerings to the Lord to express thanks for His provision (Exod. 23:19; Prov. 3:9).

JESUS AS THE FIRSTFRUITS

The apostle Paul described Jesus Christ as "the first fruits of them that slept" (1 Cor. 15:20). Just as the firstfruits promised the full harvest to come, the resurrection of Christ guarantees resurrection and eternal life for all who accept Him as Savior and Lord.

FISH GATE. A gate in the wall of Jerusalem, probably so named because fish from the Mediterranean Sea were brought into the city through this gate (Neh. 3:3).

FISHER, FISHERMAN. One who makes his living by fishing. Several of Jesus' disciples were fishermen, and He promised to make them "fishers of men" (Matt. 4:19).

FITCH (SPELT). A plant that produces grain similar to oats or rye (Ezek. 4:9). *Spelt:* NIV, NRSV. See also *Rie.*

FLAG (RUSH). A coarse grass that grows in marshes or wetlands (Isa. 19:6). *Rush:* NIV, NRSV.

FLAGON

1. A cake of dried grapes or raisins served as a delicacy or dessert (Song 2:5).

2. A flask or leather bottle for holding liquids (Isa. 22:24). See also *Spoon; Vial.*

FLASK. See *Vial.*

FLAX. A plant grown in Egypt and Palestine for its fiber, which was woven into linen cloth (Exod. 9:31). See also *Linen.*

FLEA. A tiny insect that sucks the blood of animals or humans. David used this word as a symbol of insignificance (1 Sam. 24:14).

FLEECE. Wool that grows on a sheep. Gideon used a fleece to test God's call (Judg. 6:36–40). See also *Sheep; Wool.*

FLESH. A word for the human body in contrast to the spirit (Matt. 26:41). The word is also used for unredeemed human nature and carnal appetites or desires that can lead to sin (Gal. 5:16–17). See also *Carnal.*

FLESH AND BLOOD
Matt. 16:17 **f-a-b** hath not revealed it unto thee [Peter]
1 Cor. 15:50 **f-a-b** cannot inherit the kingdom of God
Eph. 6:12 wrestle not against **f-a-b**, but…principalities

FLESHHOOK (MEAT FORKS). A large pronged fork used to handle meat for sacrificial purposes (2 Chron. 4:16). *Meat forks:* NIV.

FLINT. A very hard stone, perhaps a variety of quartz (Deut. 8:15). The word is also used symbolically to denote firmness (Ezek. 3:9).

FLOCK. A group of sheep or birds (Gen. 4:4). The word is also used to designate a Christian congregation under a pastor's leadership (1 Pet. 5:2).

FLOGGING. See *Scourging.*

FLOOD, THE. The covering of the earth by water in Noah's time; the instrument of God's judgment against a wicked world. This great deluge came after forty days of continuous rainfall, but Noah and his family and the animals in the ark were saved by the hand of God (Gen. 6–8). See also *Noah; Ark, Noah's.*

FLOUR. Wheat or barley ground into a fine powder and used for baking bread. Flour was often offered as a sin offering (Lev. 5:11). See also *Bread; Wheat.*

FLUTE (PIPE). A musical instrument, played by blowing, similar to the modern flute (Dan. 3:5). Flute players were hired for funerals during N.T. times (Matt. 9:23–24). *Pipe:* NRSV. See also *Organ; Pipe.*

FLUX (DYSENTERY). KJV word for dysentery, a common disease in the Mediterranean world. Paul healed Publius of this ailment (Acts 28:8). *Dysentery:* NIV, NRSV.

FOAL. A colt, or young donkey. Jesus rode a colt on His triumphant entry into Jerusalem (Matt. 21:5), an event foretold in the O.T. (Zech. 9:9). See also *Ass.*

FISHER. Fishermen in the Sea of Galilee at the turn of the 1900s. At least four of Jesus' disciples were fishermen who worked in this freshwater lake in northern Israel.

F

FOOD. Food served Middle Eastern family style—on the floor—becomes a banquet for a group of men in Saudi Arabia. In Bible times, people often ate food from a blanket or a low table that allowed them to sit on the ground.

FODDER. See *Provender.*

FOOD. Plants and animals eaten for nourishment. Specific foods mentioned in the Bible include lentils (Gen. 25:34), honey, nuts, and spices (Gen. 43:11). The meats of certain animals were considered unclean and unfit for eating (Lev. 11; Deut. 14).

FOOL. An absurd person; one who reasons wrongly (Prov. 29:11).

FOOLISH. A word characterizing actions that show a lack of wisdom or faulty and shallow reasoning (Prov. 26:11). Jesus described the five virgins who were unprepared for the wedding feast as foolish (Matt. 25:1–13).

FOOLISH [LY, NESS]
Ps. 5:5 The *f* shall not stand in thy [God's] sight
Ps. 69:5 God, thou knowest my *f'ness*
Prov. 12:23 heart of fools proclaimeth *f'ness*
Prov. 14:17 He that is soon angry dealeth *f'ly*
Prov. 15:20 a *f* man despiseth his mother
Matt. 7:26 a *f* man…built his house upon the sand
1 Cor. 1:23 Christ crucified…unto the Greeks *f'ness*
1 Cor. 1:27 chosen the *f* things…to confound the wise
1 Cor. 3:19 wisdom of this world is *f'ness* with God
Gal. 3:1 *f* Galatians, who hath bewitched you
Titus 3:9 avoid *f* questions, and genealogies

FOOT. See *Feet.*

FOOTMAN. A member of the infantry or walking unit of an army (Jer. 12:5); a swift runner who served as a messenger for a king (1 Sam. 22:17). See also *Post.*

FOOTSTOOL. A low stool upon which the feet are rested. The word is also used symbolically to describe the fate of God's enemies (Ps. 110:1).

FOOT-WASHING. An expression of hospitality bestowed upon guests in Bible times. Foot-washing was generally performed by lowly domestic servants, but Jesus washed His disciples' feet to teach them a lesson in humble ministry (John 13:4–15).

FORBEARANCE (TOLERANCE). Restraint and tolerance. God, in His forbearance or patience, gives people opportunity for repentance (Rom. 2:4). *Tolerance:* NIV. See also *Long-suffering; Patience.*

FORD. A crossing through shallow water across a brook or river (Gen. 32:22).

FOREHEAD. The part of the human face above the eyes. God's people were instructed to learn the law so well that it would be as if it were written on their foreheads (Deut. 6:8). See also *Frontlet.*

FOREIGNER (TEMPORARY RESIDENT). A word for an outsider or stranger—a person who was not of the same ethnic stock as the Hebrews and who had no loyalty to Israel's God (Exod. 12:45). *Temporary resident:* NIV. See also *Alien; Sojourner.*

FOREKNOWLEDGE. God's knowledge of events before they happen and His ability to influence the future by actually causing such events (Isa. 41:4). See also *Election, Divine; Predestination.*

FORERUNNER. One who goes before and makes preparations for others to follow (Heb. 6:20). John the Baptist was a forerunner of Christ.

FORESAIL. See *Mainsail.*

FORESKIN. The fold of skin that covers the male sex organ. This foreskin is removed in the rite of circumcision (Gen. 17:11). See also *Circumcision.*

FORGIVE [ING]

Num. 14:18 LORD is longsuffering…*f'ing* iniquity
2 Chron. 7:14 then will I [God] hear…*f* their sin
Ps. 86:5 Lord, art good, and ready to *f*
Matt. 6:14 heavenly Father will also *f* you
Matt. 18:21 oft shall my brother sin…and I [Peter] *f*
Mark 11:26 neither will your Father…*f* your trespasses
Luke 5:21 Who can *f* sins, but God alone
Luke 6:37 *f,* and ye shall be forgiven
Luke 23:34 *f* them; for they know not what they do
Eph. 4:32 be ye kind…*f'ing* one another
1 John 1:9 he [Jesus] is faithful…*f* us our sins

FORGIVEN

Ps. 32:1 Blessed is he whose transgression is *f*
Matt. 12:31 blasphemy against the Holy Ghost shall not be *f*
Luke 6:37 forgive, and ye shall be *f*
Rom. 4:7 Blessed are they whose iniquities are *f*
1 John 2:12 sins are *f*…for his [Jesus']…sake

FORGIVENESS. To pardon or overlook the wrongful acts of another person; God's free pardon of the sin and rebellion of humans. Our sin separates us from God, but He forgives us and reestablishes the broken relationship when we repent and turn to Him in faith (Acts 10:43; Col. 1:14). Just as God forgives believers, He expects us to practice forgiveness in our relationships with others (Matt. 5:43–48). See also *Pardon.*

FORK. See *Fan.*

FORMER RAIN (AUTUMN RAIN, EARLY RAIN). The first rain of the growing season, essential for the germination of seed and the growth of young plants (Joel 2:23). *Autumn rain:* NIV; *early rain:* NRSV.

FORNICATION (SEXUAL IMMORAL-ITY). Sexual relations between two persons who are not married to each other; any form of sexual immorality or unchastity. Paul cited fornication as a sin that believers should scrupulously avoid (1 Cor. 6:18). *Sexual immorality:* NIV. See also *Adultery; Chastity.*

Matt. 19:9 put away his wife, except it be for *f*
1 Cor. 5:1 reported…*f* among you
Gal. 5:19 works of the flesh are…Adultery, *f*
1 Thess. 4:3 will of God…abstain from *f*

FORT. A high wall or fortification built to provide protection against one's enemies in times of war (Isa. 25:12). See also *Fenced City; Wall.*

FORTIFIED CITY. See *Fenced City.*

FORUM OF APPIUS. See *Appii Forum.*

FOUNDATION. The strong base on which a building is erected. The apostle Paul described Christ as the sure foundation for believers (1 Cor. 3:11). See also *Corner Stone.*

FOUNDATION [S]
Matt. 25:34 kingdom prepared for you from the *f* of the world
Eph. 2:20 built upon the *f* of the apostles
Heb. 1:10 Thou, Lord…hast laid the *f* of the earth
Heb. 11:10 city which hath *f's*…builder…is God
Rev. 21:14 wall of the city [New Jerusalem] had twelve *f's*

FOUNTAIN. A source of fresh, flowing water; a spring (Deut. 8:7). The word is also used symbolically of God's blessings upon His people (Jer. 2:13).

FOUNTAIN GATE. A gate in the wall of Jerusalem, perhaps named for the fountain or pool of Siloam (Neh. 12:37).

FOWLER. A person who captures birds by nets, snares, or decoys (Hosea 9:8). The word is also used symbolically of temptations (Ps. 91:3). See also *Hunter.*

FRANKINCENSE. A block of frankincense recovered from a Red Sea shipwreck. Harvested as sap from a tree, hardened resin was burned as fragrant incense during worship services.

FOX. An animal of the dog family known for its cunning (Judg. 15:4). See also *Jackal*.

FRAGRANT CANE. See *Calamus*.

FRANKINCENSE (INCENSE). The yellowish gum of a tree, known for its pungent odor when burned as incense during sacrificial ceremonies (Neh. 13:9). Frankincense was one of the gifts presented to the infant Jesus by the wise men (Matt. 2:11). *Incense:* NIV. See also *Incense*.

FREE [LY]
Gen. 2:16 every tree of the garden thou mayest *f'ly* eat
Matt. 10:8 *f'ly* ye have received, *f'ly* give
John 8:32 truth shall make you *f*
Rom. 3:24 justified *f'ly* by his [God's] grace
Rom. 8:2 Jesus hath made me *f* from the law of sin
1 Cor. 9:19 though I [Paul] be *f* from all men
Gal. 3:28 neither bond nor *f*
Gal. 5:1 liberty…Christ hath made us *f*
Col. 3:11 neither Greek nor Jew…bond nor *f*
Rev. 22:17 take the water of life *f'ly*

FREEDMEN. See *Libertines*.

FREEWILL OFFERING. An offering given freely and willingly (Amos 4:5), in contrast to one made to atone for some misdeed (Num. 15:3).

FRINGE (TASSEL). An ornament worn on the edges of one's robe as a profession of piety and commitment to God (Deut. 22:12). *Tassel:* NIV, NRSV. See also *Hem*.

FROG. An amphibious animal sent by the Lord as the second plague upon Egypt (Exod. 8:2–14).

FRONTLET. A small leather case holding passages of Scripture, worn on the forehead as a literal obedience of Deut. 6:6–9. See also *Forehead; Phylactery*.

FRUITFULNESS. Productive; reproducing abundantly. Paul declared that believers should be fruitful in righteousness and goodness toward others (Col. 1:10).

FULLER (LAUNDERER). A laborer who treated or dyed clothes and also did ordinary laundry work (Mal. 3:2). *Launderer:* NIV.

FULLER'S FIELD (WASHERMAN'S FIELD). A place near the wall of Jerusalem where fullers worked and perhaps where they spread their laundry to dry (2 Kings 18:17). *Washerman's field:* NIV.

FUNERAL. A ceremony honoring the dead before burial. These ceremonies were sometimes accompanied by sad music and the loud wailing of friends and professional mourners (Eccles. 12:5; Matt. 9:23). See also *Burial; Minstrel*.

FURLONG. A Greek measure of length equal to about 650 feet or one-eighth of a mile (Luke 24:13).

FURNACE (SMOKING FIREPOT). An enclosed oven for baking (Gen. 15:17; *smoking firepot:* NIV, NRSV), smelting (Gen. 19:28), or drying and firing bricks (Dan. 3:15–17). See also *Brick-kiln*.

F

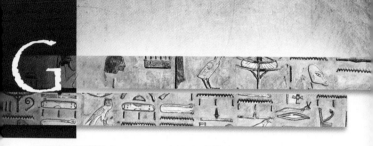

GAASH, MOUNT. A mountain in the hill country of Ephraim where Joshua was buried (Josh. 24:30).

GABBATHA. See *Pavement, The.*

GABRIEL. An archangel who appeared to Daniel (Dan. 8:16), Zacharias (Luke 1:18–19), and the Virgin Mary (Luke 1:26–38). See also *Archangel.*

GABRIEL. Gabriel tells the Virgin Mary that she will have a son. His name will be Jesus, "Son of the Most High."

GAD. The seventh son of Jacob, born of Zilpah (Gen. 30:10–11), and ancestor of one of the twelve tribes of Israel. Known as a fierce, warlike people, the Gadites settled east of the Jordan River (Josh. 13:24–28). See also *Tribes of Israel.*

GADARA. A Greek city about six miles southeast of the Sea of Galilee. In N.T. times, Gadara was the capital city of the Roman province of Perea.

GADARENES/GERGESENES. People from the area of Gadara in Perea. Jesus healed a wild, demon-possessed man in this area (Mark 5:1–20). *Gergesenes:* Matt. 8:28.

GAIN
Mark 8:36 profit a man...*g* the whole world
1 Cor. 9:20 I [Paul] became as a Jew...*g* the Jew
Phil. 1:21 me [Paul] to live is Christ...die is *g*
1 Tim. 6:6 godliness with contentment is great *g*

GAIUS
    1. A Macedonian and companion of Paul (Acts 19:29).
    2. A man of Derbe and companion of Paul (Acts 20:4).
    3. A Corinthian baptized under Paul's ministry (1 Cor. 1:14).
    4. The person to whom John addressed his third letter (3 John 1).

GALATIA. A territory of central Asia Minor that contained several cities visited by Paul during the first missionary journey—Antioch of Pisidia, Derbe, Iconium, and Lystra (Acts 13–14)—all located in southern Galatia. Paul's letter to the Galatians (Gal. 1:1–2) was apparently addressed to churches in and around these cities.

GALATIANS, EPISTLE TO THE. A short epistle of the apostle Paul to the churches of Galatia on the themes of Christian liberty and justification by faith alone.

The content of the epistle includes (1) a defense of Paul's apostleship and the gospel (chaps. 1–2); (2) his argument that salvation comes by God's grace through faith, not through obeying the law (chaps. 3–4); and (3) the practical dimension of one's faith—living in obedience to God and in harmony with others (chaps. 5–6).

GALBANUM. A gum from a plant used to produce sacred incense, which was burned at the altar (Exod. 30:34).

GALE. See *Whirlwind.*

GALILEAN. A native of the province of Galilee. All of Jesus' disciples except Judas were Galileans. Peter was recognized as a Galilean because of his distinct accent (Mark 14:70).

GALILEE (GALILEE OF THE GENTILES). A Roman province in northern Palestine during N.T. times and the area where Jesus spent most of His earthly ministry (Mark 3:7). Because of its far-north location, Galilee had a mixed population of Jews and Gentiles. The prophet Isaiah referred to it as "Galilee of the nations" (Isa. 9:1). *Galilee of the Gentiles:* NIV.

GALILEE, SEA OF/SEA OF CHINNEROTH/LAKE OF GENNESARET/SEA OF TIBERIAS. A freshwater lake about fourteen miles long and seven miles wide that took its name from the surrounding Roman province. Fed by the Jordan River, it provided the livelihood for many commercial fishermen, including several disciples of

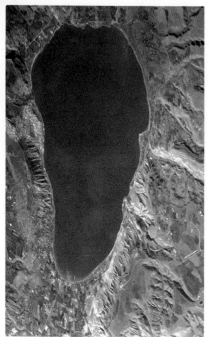

GALILEE, SEA OF. The Sea of Galilee, photographed here from a space shuttle, is actually a freshwater lake. It drains into the Jordan River at the south.

Jesus: James, John, Peter, and Andrew (Mark 1:16–20).

Jesus calmed the waters of this lake after He and His disciples were caught in a boat in a sudden storm (Mark 4:35–41). *Sea of Chinneroth:* Josh. 12:3; *Lake of Gennesaret:* Luke 5:1; *Sea of Tiberias:* John 21:1.

GALL. A bitter, poisonous herb used to make a painkilling substance. While on the cross, Jesus

was offered a drink containing gall (Matt. 27:34).

GALLIO. The Roman provincial ruler of Achaia who refused to get involved in the dispute between Paul and the Jewish leaders in Corinth (Acts 18:12–17).

GALLOWS. A structure used for executing people by hanging. The wicked Haman was hanged on the gallows that he had prepared for Mordecai (Esther 5:14; 7:10). See also *Haman.*

GAMALIEL. A teacher of the law under whom Paul studied (Acts 22:3). As a member of the Jewish Sanhedrin, he advised against persecution of the apostles and the early church (Acts 5:33–39). See also *Council.*

GAME. See *Venison.*

GANGRENE. See *Canker.*

GARDEN. A fenced plot generally outside the walls of a city where fruit trees or vegetables were grown. The most famous garden in the Bible is the Garden of Eden (Gen. 2:8–10). See also *Orchard.*

GARLAND (WREATH). A ceremonial wreath woven from flowers or leaves and worn on the head (Acts 14:13). *Wreath:* NIV.

GARLICK (GARLIC). A vegetable or herb similar to the onion that was used to flavor food. The Hebrews longed for this vegetable after leaving Egypt (Num. 11:5). *Garlic:* NIV, NRSV.

GASHMU. An influential Samaritan leader who opposed the Jewish people while they were rebuilding Jerusalem's walls under Nehemiah after the Exile (Neh. 6:6).

GATE. An entrance, door, or opening, particularly the strong gate in the walls of a fortified city (Judg. 16:3). The word is also used symbolically of salvation (Matt. 7:13) and heaven (Rev. 21:25). See also *Door.*

GATE KEEPER. A person who guarded the gate in a walled city (1 Chron. 9:19). See also *Doorkeeper; Porter.*

GATH. A royal Philistine city captured by David (1 Chron. 18:1) and home of the giant Goliath, whom David defeated (1 Sam. 17:4). See also *Philistines.*

GATH-HEPHER/GITTAH-HEPHER. A city in the territory of Zebulun and home of the prophet Jonah (2 Kings 14:25). *Gittah-hepher:* Josh. 19:13.

GAZA/AZZAH. A Philistine city where Samson was killed when he destroyed the temple of their pagan god Dagon (Judg. 16:21–30). *Azzah:* Jer. 25:20. See also *Philistines.*

GAZELLE. See *Roe.*

GAZER. See *Gezer.*

GECKO. See *Ferret.*

GEDALIAH. A friend of the prophet Jeremiah (Jer. 39:14; 40:5–6). After the fall of Jerusalem to the Babylonians in 587 B.C., Gedaliah was

made supervisor of the vinedressers left in the land (2 Kings 25:22–25).

GEDEON. See *Gideon.*

GEHAZI. A servant of the prophet Elisha who was struck with leprosy because of his dishonesty and greed (2 Kings 5).

GEHENNA. See *Hell; Hinnom, Valley of.*

GENEALOGY. A record of the descendants of a person or family (1 Chron. 1–8). These records were important to the Jewish people because they documented inheritance rights and the right of succession as a clan leader, king, or high priest. See also *Register.*

GENERAL EPISTLES. The epistles of Hebrews; James; 1 and 2 Peter; 1, 2, and 3 John; and Jude—so named because they are addressed to broad, general problems rather than to local, specific issues. They are also referred to as *Catholic Epistles.*

GENERATION. A single step or stage in the line of descent from one's ancestors (Gen. 5:1; Matt. 24:34). The word is used in a more general sense to designate a period or age (Gen. 7:1).

GENERATION [S]
Gen. 2:4 the *g's* of the heavens and of the earth
Ps. 90:1 thou [God]...dwelling place in all *g's*
Ps. 100:5 his [God's] truth endureth to all *g's*
Eccles. 1:4 One *g* passeth...another *g* cometh
Dan. 4:3 his [God's] dominion is from *g* to *g*
Luke 3:7 *g* of vipers, who hath warned you
Luke 16:8 their *g* wiser than the children of light
Col. 1:26 mystery...hath been hid...from *g's*
1 Pet. 2:9 ye are a chosen *g,* a royal priesthood

GENESIS, BOOK OF. The first book of the O.T., often referred to as "the book of

G

beginnings" because of its accounts of the world's creation and the early history of the Hebrew people. Major events and subjects covered in the book include:

1. God's creation of the physical world and Adam and Eve's life in the Garden of Eden; Adam and Eve's sin and introduction of sin to humankind (chaps. 1–3);

2. Adam's descendants and the great flood (chaps. 4–9);

3. The tower of Babel and the scattering of humankind (chap. 11); and

4. The life stories of the Hebrew patriarchs: Abraham and Isaac (chaps. 12–27), Jacob (chaps. 25–35), and Joseph (chaps. 37–50).

GENNESARET. See *Galilee, Sea of.*

GENTILE. A member of any ethnic group other than the Jewish race. The Jews looked down on other races as barbarous and unclean (Jer. 9:26). Jesus, however, abolished this distinction through His atoning death and His acceptance of all people through repentance and faith (Gal. 3:28). See also *Heathen.*

GENTILE [S]

Isa. 60:3 *G's* shall come to thy [God's] light
Jer. 16:19 *G's* shall come unto thee [God]
Mal. 1:11 my [God's] name...great among the *G's*
Matt. 12:18 my [God's] servant...judgment to the *G's*
Acts 9:15 he [Paul] is a chosen vessel...before the *G's*
Acts 13:46 we [Paul and Barnabas] turn to the *G's*
Acts 14:27 he [God]...opened the door of faith unto the *G's*
Acts 18:6 henceforth I [Paul] will go unto the *G's*
Rom. 2:9 Jew first, and also of the *G*
Rom. 3:29 God of the Jews only...also of the *G's*
1 Cor. 12:13 baptized into one body... Jews or *G's*
Eph. 3:6 *G's* should be...partakers of his [God's] promise

GERAH. A coin of small value, equal to one-twentieth of a shekel (Lev. 27:25). See also *Shekel.*

GERAR. An ancient city of southern Canaan, or Philistia, where Abraham was reprimanded by Abimelech for lying about his wife, Sarah's, identity. (Gen. 20).

GERGESENES. See *Gadarenes.*

GERIZIM, MOUNT. A mountain in central Canaan where Joshua pronounced God's blessings for keeping God's laws when the Hebrew people entered the land (Deut. 11:29; 28:1–14). In later years, this mountain was considered a sacred worship place by the Samaritans. See also *Samaritan.*

GESHEM. An Arabian who opposed the rebuilding of Jerusalem's walls under Nehemiah after the Exile (Neh. 2:19; 6:2).

GETHSEMANE. A garden near the Mount of Olives outside Jerusalem where Jesus prayed in great agony of soul on the night before He was betrayed and arrested (Mark 14:32–46). The garden was probably a grove of olive trees, since Gethsemane means "oil press."

GEZER/GAZER. A Canaanite city captured by Joshua (Josh. 10:33) and assigned to the Levites (Josh. 21:21). In later years, Solomon turned Gezer into an important military center (1 Kings 9:15–19). *Gazer:* 2 Sam. 5:25; 1 Chron. 14:16.

GHOST (SPIRIT). An Old English word for "spirit" (Matt. 27:50; 28:19). *Spirit:* NIV, NRSV.

GIANTS. People of unusually large size, such as the Philistine Goliath (2 Sam. 21:22). Races of giants mentioned in the Bible are the *Anakims* (Deut. 2:11), *Emims* (Deut. 2:10),

GETHSEMANE. The Garden of Gethsemane is now a church courtyard on the bottom toes of the Mount of Olives. Flowers and gnarled old olive trees line the paths.

the judges (Judg. 20:19–36). *Gibeath:* Josh. 18:28.

GIBEON. A royal Canaanite city whose inhabitants surrendered to Joshua to avoid the fate of Jericho and Ai (Josh. 9:3–15).

GIBEONITES. Inhabitants of Gibeon who were made slaves following their surrender to Joshua (Josh. 9:21).

GIDEON/GEDEON/JERUBBAAL. The famous judge of Israel who delivered the Israelites from oppression by defeating the mighty Midianite army with a force of only 300 warriors. Gideon came from an obscure family of the tribe of Manasseh, but he trusted God at every step of his military campaign and thus was successful (see Judg. 6–8). He is listed in the N.T. as one of the heroes of the faith (Heb. 11:32; *Gedeon*). *Jerubbaal:* Judg. 6:25–32. See also *Midianites*.

Rephaims (Gen. 14:5), and *Zamzummims* (Deut. 2:20).

GIBEAH/GIBEATH. The native city of King Saul and capital of his kingdom (1 Sam. 14:16; 15:34). This was apparently the same city destroyed by the Israelites during the period of

GIER EAGLE (OSPREY, CARRION VULTURE). A bird of prey considered unclean by the Hebrews (Lev. 11:18). *Osprey:* NIV; *carrion vulture:* NRSV. This is probably the same bird as the Egyptian vulture.

GIFT [S]

Prov. 19:6 every man is a friend to him that giveth **g's**
Matt. 2:11 they [wise men] presented...him [Jesus] **g's**
1 Cor. 12:4 diversities of **g's**...same Spirit
1 Cor. 12:31 covet earnestly the best **g's**
1 Cor. 13:2 though I [Paul] have the **g** of prophecy
2 Cor. 9:15 Thanks be unto God for his unspeakable **g**
1 Tim. 4:14 Neglect not the **g** that is in thee
James 1:17 good **g** and every perfect **g** is from above

GIFT OF GOD

John 4:10 If thou knewest the **g-o-G**
Rom. 6:23 **g-o-G** is eternal life through Jesus
Eph. 2:8 saved through faith...it is the **g-o-G**
2 Tim. 1:6 stir up the **g-o-G**

GIFTS, SPIRITUAL. See *Spiritual Gifts.*

GIHON

1. One of the four rivers of the Garden of Eden, associated with Ethiopia (Gen. 2:13). Some scholars believe this was either the Nile or the Ganges.

2. A place near Jerusalem where Solomon was anointed and proclaimed king (1 Kings 1:33).

GILBOA, MOUNT. A mountain range in the territory of Issachar where King Saul died after his defeat by the Philistines (1 Chron. 10:1–8).

GILEAD

1. A fertile, flat tableland east of the Jordan River (Judg. 20:1), known in N.T. times as the region of Perea.

2. A mountain or hill overlooking the plain of Jezreel where Gideon divided his army for battle against the Midianites (Josh. 7:2–5).

GILEAD, BALM OF. See *Balm of Gilead.*

GILGAL. A site between the Jordan River and the city of Jericho where the Hebrew people erected memorial stones to commemorate God's faithfulness in leading them into the Promised Land (Josh. 4:19–20). Gilgal apparently served as Joshua's headquarters in his campaign against the Canaanites (Josh. 10). In later years, Saul was crowned as Israel's first king at Gilgal (1 Sam. 11:15).

GIRDLE (BELT). A belt or sash made of cloth or leather and worn by men and women to hold their loose outer garments against the body (2 Kings 1:8). *Belt:* NIV, NRSV.

GIRGASITES/GIRGASHITES. Members of an ancient tribe, descendants of Canaan (Gen. 10:15–16), who inhabited part of the land of Canaan before the arrival of the Hebrew people. *Girgashites:* Deut. 7:1.

GITTAH-HEPHER. See *Gath-hepher.*

GITTITH. A musical instrument or tune associated with the city of Gath. The word is used in the titles of Pss. 8, 81, and 84.

GIVE

1 Chron. 16:34 **g** thanks unto the LORD; for he is good
Ps. 29:11 LORD will **g** strength unto his people
Prov. 25:21 thine enemy be hungry, **g** him bread
Matt. 6:11 **G** us this day our daily bread
Matt. 10:8 freely ye have received, freely **g**
Matt. 11:28 Come unto me [Jesus]...I will **g** you rest
Matt. 20:28 Son of man came...to **g** his life a ransom
Mark 8:37 a man **g** in exchange for his soul
Luke 12:32 Father's good pleasure to **g** you the kingdom
Luke 22:22 lawful for us to **g** tribute unto Caesar
John 14:16 he [God] shall **g** you another Comforter
Rom. 14:12 every one...shall **g** account...to God
2 Cor. 9:7 let him **g**; not grudgingly, or of necessity
1 Pet. 3:15 ready always to **g** an answer
Rev. 2:10 I [Jesus] will **g** thee a crown of life

GLAD [LY, NESS]

1 Chron. 16:31 heavens be **g**...earth rejoice
Ps. 9:2 be **g** and rejoice in thee [God]
Ps. 68:3 let the righteous be **g**

Ps. 100:2 Serve the LORD with *g'ness*
Joel 2:21 be *g* and rejoice...LORD will do great things
Matt. 5:12 be exceeding *g*: for great is your reward
Mark 12:37 common people heard him [Jesus] *g'ly*
John 20:20 disciples *g*, when they saw the Lord
Acts 13:48 Gentiles heard this, they were *g*
Rom. 10:15 beautiful...feet...that...bring *g* tidings

GLASS. A clear liquid mineral used to make utensils, ornaments, and vases. The "sea of glass" in John's vision probably represents God's purity or holiness (Rev. 4:6).

GLEANING. The gathering of grain left behind by the reapers—a courtesy offered to the needy (Lev. 19:9–10). Ruth gleaned in the fields of Boaz (Ruth 2).

GLEDE (RED KITE). A bird of prey, probably the kite or hawk (Deut. 14:13). *Red kite:* NIV.

GLORIFY [IED, ING]

Ps. 86:12 *g* thy [God's] name for evermore
Matt. 5:16 see your good works, and *g* your Father
Luke 2:20 shepherds returned, *g'ing*...God
Luke 23:47 centurion saw what was done, he *g'ied* God
John 12:23 hour is come...Son of man should be *g'ied*
John 17:1 thy Son also may *g* thee [God]
Rom. 8:30 whom he [Jesus] justified, them he also *g'ied*
1 Cor. 6:20 *g* God in your body
2 Thess. 1:12 name of our Lord...*g'ied* in you

GLORY. Splendor, honor, or perfection. The "glory of the Lord" signifies the supreme perfection of His nature (Exod. 16:7). Jesus also partook of the glory of His Father (John 2:11). He shares His divine glory with all believers (John 17:5–6). See also *Transfiguration of Jesus*.

1 Chron. 16:24 Declare his [God's] *g* among the heathen
1 Chron. 29:11 Thine, O LORD, is the greatness...and the *g*
Ps. 24:7 King of *g* shall come in
Ps. 29:2 Give unto the LORD the *g* due unto his name
Ps. 72:19 whole earth be filled with his [God's] *g*
Ps. 96:3 Declare his [God's] *g* among the heathen
Prov. 17:6 the *g* of children are their fathers

Jer. 13:16 Give *g* to the LORD your God
Matt. 6:13 kingdom, and the power, and the *g*
Mark 10:37 sit, one on thy [Jesus'] right hand...in thy *g*
Luke 21:27 Son of man coming...with...great *g*
John 1:14 we beheld his [Jesus'] *g*...full of grace

GLORY OF GOD/GLORY OF THE LORD

Exod. 24:16 the *g-o-t-L* abode upon mount Sinai
Ps. 19:1 The heavens declare the *g-o-G*
Luke 2:9 *g-o-t-L* shone round about them [shepherds]
John 11:4 sickness is not unto death, but for the *g-o-G*
Rom. 3:23 all have sinned...come short of the *g-o-G*
1 Cor. 10:31 whatsoever ye do, do all to the *g-o-G*
Phil. 2:11 Jesus Christ is Lord, to the *g-o-G* the Father

GLUTTONY. The act of eating or drinking to excess—a sin against which believers are warned (Prov. 23:1–8, 21).

GNASH. See *Tooth*.

GNAT. A small, stinging insect considered a great pest in the marshlands of Egypt and Palestine (Matt. 23:24). See also *Lice*.

GNOSTICISM. A heretical movement of N.T. times that taught that salvation came through superior knowledge. While gnosticism is not mentioned by name in the N.T., it was probably what Paul condemned when he declared that true knowledge comes from God and does not consist of idle speculation (Col. 2:8–23).

GOAD. A sharp, pointed stick or rod used in guiding oxen. Shamgar used a goad as a weapon against the Philistines (Judg. 3:31). See also *Ox*.

GOAT. A domesticated animal used for food (Gen. 27:9), clothing (Num. 31:20), and in religious sacrifices (Exod. 12:5). See also *Kid*.

GOAT DEMON. See *Satyr.*

GOD. The creator and ruler of the universe (Isa. 40:28–31); the first person of the triune Godhead—God the Father, God the Son, God the Spirit (Matt. 28:19; 2 Cor. 13:14)—who reveals Himself through the natural world, the Bible, and His Son, Jesus Christ (Col. 1:19). God is infinite in being and character: omnipresent (Jer. 23:23–24), all-powerful (Rev. 19:6), perfect in holiness (Lev. 11:44), and infinite in mercy (Ps. 136), wisdom (Col. 2:2–3), and truth (Titus 1:2).

God is active in salvation history. He covenanted with Abraham to "make of thee a great nation" and to make the Hebrew people a blessing to the rest of the world (Gen. 12:1–4). He called Moses to deliver the Israelites from Egyptian bondage (Exod. 3:9–10). He promised a Savior to rule Israel (Isa. 9:6–7). This promise was fulfilled in Jesus Christ (Matt. 1:18–21), God's love gift of salvation to the world (John 3:16, 36).

God's Spirit convicts unbelievers of sin and coming judgment (John 16:8–11). Humans can know God through faith in Christ (John 14:1, 6) and obedience to the Father's will (Matt. 7:21; Mark 3:35). God welcomes the worship and fellowship of His adopted children (John 4:23–24; Rom. 8:15–17). See also *I Am; Jehovah; Yahweh.*

THE ALL-KNOWING GOD KNOWS ALL ABOUT US

He knows our weaknesses (Ps. 103:14).
He knows our thoughts (Ps. 44:21).
He knows our words (Ps. 139:4).
He knows our actions (Ps. 139:2).
He knows our needs (Matt. 6:32).

GODDESS. A female deity or idol. Goddesses were prominent in the pagan cultures of Mesopotamia, Egypt, Canaan, Greece, and Rome. For example, Ashtaroth or Asherah was the wife of Baal in Canaanite mythology (1 Kings 11:33; *Ashtoreth:* plural form). Diana (or Artemis) was worshiped in the great temple at Ephesus (Acts 19:24–28). See also *Ashtaroth; Diana.*

GODLINESS. Holy living and righteous behavior that issue from devotion to God. Godliness also leads to love for others (1 Tim. 4:7–9). See also *Righteousness.*

GODLY [INESS]

2 Cor. 7:10 *g* sorrow worketh repentance
1 Tim. 6:6 *g'iness* with contentment is great gain
2 Tim. 3:5 form of *g'iness,* but denying the power
2 Tim. 3:12 live *g* in Christ Jesus...suffer persecution
Titus 2:12 live soberly, righteously, and *g*

GOG, PRINCE OF MAGOG. The leader of a tribal people, enemies of the Israelites, who was condemned by the prophet Ezekiel (Ezek. 38:2; 39:1). In the book of Revelation, Gog and Magog represent the forces of evil that oppose God and His people (Rev. 20:8).

GOLAN. A city in the territory of Manasseh designated as one of the six cities of refuge (Deut. 4:43). See also *Cities of Refuge.*

GOLD. A precious mineral used to make coins, jewelry, and utensils. Used extensively in Solomon's temple (1 Kings 7:48–50), gold also symbolized the splendor of the heavenly city, or New Jerusalem (Rev. 21:18).

GOLD FILIGREE SETTINGS. See *Ouches.*

GOLGOTHA. See *Calvary.*

GOLIATH. Philistine champion Goliath loses his head in mortal combat with a shepherd boy. Young David takes Goliath's head as a trophy to signal his victory to the Philistine and Israelite armies watching from a distance.

GOLIATH. A Philistine giant from the city of Gath who defied the entire army of King Saul. He was killed by David the shepherd boy with a single stone from his sling (1 Sam. 17:4–54).

GOMER. The unfaithful wife of the prophet Hosea. After her unfaithfulness, Gomer left Hosea and was sold into slavery, but the prophet restored her as his wife at God's command. His forgiveness of Gomer represented God's unconditional love for His wayward people (Hosea 3). See also *Hosea.*

GOMORRAH/GOMORRHA. A city near the Dead Sea destroyed by God with earthquake and fire because of the sin and wickedness of its inhabitants (Gen. 19:23–29). The city was cited in later years as an example of God's punishment (Isa. 1:9). *Gomorrha:* Matt. 10:15. See also *Cities of the Plain; Sodom.*

GOODMAN (LANDOWNER). A word for the head of a household, head of the house, or "master of the house," as rendered by some translations (Matt. 20:11). *Landowner:* NIV, NRSV.

GOODNESS. Purity and righteousness; a fruit of the Spirit that should characterize followers of Christ (Gal. 5:22). True goodness comes from God, who is holy, righteous, merciful, and loving (Ps. 31:19; Rom. 15:14). See also *Grace; Love; Righteousness.*

Ps. 23:6 Surely *g* and mercy shall follow me
Ps. 33:5 earth is full of the *g* of the LORD
Ps. 107:8 men would praise the Lord for his *g*

GOOD WORKS

Matt. 5:16 see your *g-w*...glorify your Father
Acts 9:36 Dorcas...full of *g-w*
Eph. 2:10 his [God's] workmanship...unto *g-w*
2 Tim. 3:17 man of God...furnished unto all *g-w*

GOPHER WOOD (CYPRESS). The wood used in building Noah's ark, probably cypress (Gen. 6:14). *Cypress:* NIV, NRSV.

GOSHEN. An Egyptian district where the Israelites settled and lived during their years in Egypt (Gen. 45:10).

GOSPEL. The "good news" that God has provided salvation for all people through the atoning death of His Son (Mark 1:1, 15). The word is also used of the teachings of Jesus and the apostles (Col. 1:5).

Matt. 24:14 *g* of the kingdom...preached in all the world
Mark 16:15 preach the *g* to every creature
Luke 4:18 he [God] hath anointed me [Jesus] to preach the *g* to the poor
Rom. 1:16 I [Paul] am not ashamed of the *g*
Rom. 10:15 beautiful...feet...preach the *g* of peace
1 Cor. 9:14 which preach the *g* should live of the *g*
Gal. 1:7 some...would pervert the *g* of Christ
Eph. 6:15 feet shod...*g* of peace
Phil. 1:12 things...fallen out...furtherance of the *g*
2 Tim. 1:8 partaker of the afflictions of the *g*
2 Tim. 2:8 Jesus...raised from the dead according to my [Paul's] *g*

GOSPELS, FOUR. The four books at the beginning of the N.T.—Matthew, Mark, Luke, and John—that describe the life and ministry of Jesus. Each Gospel tells the story from a slightly different perspective, giving us a fuller picture of the Savior than we would get from a single narrative. See also *Synoptic Gospels.*

GOSSIP. Idle talk, rumors, or fruitless tales. This type of speech is associated with the wicked and troublemakers (Prov. 16:28; 1 Tim. 5:13). See also *Busybody; Talebearer.*

GOURD. A poisonous plant that produces fruit similar to the common melon (2 Kings 4:39). Jonah sat under the shade of a gourd vine (Jon. 4:6–10).

GOVERNMENT. A system of power and authority through which stability and order are maintained in society. Governments have a vital function and should be supported by Christians, as long as they do not intrude into the role that belongs to God alone (Mark 12:13–17).

GOVERNOR (RULER). A general term for rulers or officials of differing rank or status (1 Kings 10:15). The chief in command of a Roman province was called a governor (Matt. 27:2; Acts 23:24). This title was applied to Christ (Matt. 2:6). *Ruler:* NIV, NRSV. See also *Lieutenant; Tirshatha.*

GOVERNOR'S HEADQUARTERS. See *Praetorium.*

GOZAN. A town, district, or river of Mesopotamia to which the people of the Northern Kingdom were deported after the fall of Samaria to the Assyrians (2 Kings 18:11).

GRACE. God's unmerited favor and love that lead Him to grant salvation to believers through the exercise of their faith in Jesus Christ (Titus 2:11; Acts 15:11). Salvation cannot be earned; it is a gift of God's grace (Eph. 2:8). See also *Mercy; Salvation.*

Gen. 6:8 Noah found *g* in the eyes of the Lord
Ps. 84:11 Lord will give *g* and glory
John 1:14 his [Jesus'] glory...full of *g* and truth
John 1:17 *g* and truth came by Jesus Christ
Rom. 3:24 justified freely by his [God's] *g*
Rom. 5:20 sin abounded, *g* did much more abound
Rom. 6:1 continue in sin, that *g* may abound
2 Cor. 8:9 ye know the *g* of our Lord Jesus Christ
2 Cor. 9:8 God is able to make all *g* abound
2 Cor. 12:9 My [God's] *g* is sufficient for thee
Eph. 4:7 *g* according to the measure of the gift of Christ
Col. 4:6 speech be alway with *g*, seasoned with salt
1 Tim. 1:14 *g* of our Lord was...abundant

G

GRAPE. *Vineyard workers prune the vines in early spring to improve the harvest in the summer.*

Heb. 4:16 come boldly unto the throne of **g**
James 4:6 God...giveth **g** unto the humble
2 Pet. 3:18 grow in **g**...knowledge of...Jesus
Rev. 22:21 **g** of our Lord...be with you all

GRACE OF GOD

Luke 2:40 child [Jesus] grew...**g-o-G** was upon him
1 Cor. 15:10 by the **g-o-G** I [Paul] am what I am
Eph. 3:7 I [Paul]...made a minister...gift of the **g-o-G**
Titus 2:11 the **g-o-G** that bringeth salvation
Heb. 2:9 he [Jesus] by the **g-o-G** should taste death
1 Pet. 4:10 as good stewards of the manifold **g-o-G**

GRACIOUS

Num. 6:25 Lord...be **g** unto thee
Ps. 77:9 Hath God forgotten to be **g**
Ps. 103:8 Lord is merciful and **g**, slow to anger
Isa. 33:2 Lord, be **g** unto us
Amos 5:15 God...will be **g** unto the remnant of Joseph

GRAIN. See *Corn; Wheat.*

GRAIN OFFERING. See *Oblation.*

GRAPE. A fruit used for food and wine-making. It was one of the most important agricultural crops of Palestine (Num. 13:23). See also *Wine.*

GRASS. A word for various types of common plants, such as that which livestock grazed. It is used symbolically for the brevity of life (Ps. 90:5–6). See also *Hay.*

GRASSHOPPER. An insect of the locust species that destroyed vegetation. Also eaten by the Hebrews (Lev. 11:22), the grasshopper was

GRAVE. Graves cover the southern ridge of the Mount of Olives, facing Jerusalem. Since ancient times, thousands of Jews, Christians, and Muslims have chosen to be buried near the Holy City. (Inset) The view from inside a Jerusalem tomb.

seen as a symbol of insignificance (Isa. 40:22). See also *Locust*.

GRATITUDE. See *Thanksgiving*.

GRAVE. A burial place for the dead. In Bible times, bodies were buried in pits (Gen. 35:8), caves (Gen. 25:9), and sepulchres hewn in rocks (Matt. 27:60). See also *Cave; Sepulchre*.

GRAVE [S]

Job 17:1 the *g's* are ready for me [Job]
Job 21:13 moment [the wicked] go down to the *g*
Ps. 30:3 thou [God] hast brought up my soul from the *g*
Ps. 88:3 my life draweth nigh unto the *g*
Eccles. 9:10 no work...nor wisdom, in the *g*
Isa. 53:9 he [God's servant] made his *g* with the wicked
Matt. 27:52 *g's* were opened...bodies of the saints...arose
John 5:28 all that are in the *g's* shall hear his [Jesus'] voice
John 11:17 he [Lazarus] had lain in the *g* four days
1 Cor. 15:55 O *g*, where is thy victory?
1 Tim. 3:8 deacons be *g*, not doubletongued

GRAVEN IMAGE (IDOL). An image of a false god made from wood or stone and set up in a prominent place as an object of worship (Exod. 20:4). The prophets warned God's people against such idolatry (Isa. 44:9–10; Hosea 11:2). *Idol:* NIV, NRSV. See also *Idol*.

GRAVING TOOL. An instrument or tool used for carving or engraving. Aaron used this tool to shape the golden calf (Exod. 32:4).

GREAT [ER]

Gen. 12:2 I [God] will make of thee [Abraham] a *g* nation
Ps. 48:1 *G* is the Lord, and greatly to be praised
Ps. 77:13 who is so *g* a God as our God
Prov. 22:1 good name...to be chosen than *g* riches
Isa. 9:2 people...in darkness have seen a *g* light
Matt. 5:12 Rejoice...for *g* is your reward in heaven
Matt. 20:26 *g* among you...your minister
Mark 12:31 none other commandment *g'er* than these
Luke 10:2 harvest truly is *g*...labourers are few
John 13:16 servant is not *g'er* than his lord

John 15:13 *G'er* love hath no man than this
Heb. 2:3 escape, if we neglect so *g* salvation
Heb. 4:14 Seeing then...we have a *g* high priest [Jesus]

GREAT LIZARD. See *Tortoise*.

GREAT OWL. A species of owl considered unclean by the Hebrews (Deut. 14:16).

GREAT SEA. See *Mediterranean Sea*.

GREAVES. Armor for the legs, covering the area from the knees to the ankles (1 Sam. 17:6).

GRECIAN JEWS, GRECIANS. See *Greeks*.

GREECE/JAVAN. An ancient world power that reached its greatest strength in the time between the testaments, about 400 B.C. to A.D. 1. The O.T. word for Greece was *Javan* (Gen. 10:2). See also *Athens*.

GREED. Excessive desire for material things. The Bible warns that this sin leads to disappointment and destruction (Luke 22:3–6; 1 Tim. 6:9). See also *Covetousness*.

GREEKS (GRECIAN JEWS, HELLENISTS). Natives of Greece or people of Greek heritage or descent. The N.T. often uses the word for people influenced by Greek traditions who were not Jews (John 12:20). The word *Grecians* is used of Greek-speaking Jews (Acts 6:1). *Grecian Jews:* NIV; *Hellenists:* NRSV.

GREYHOUND (STRUTTING ROOSTER). An animal cited as an example of gracefulness (Prov. 30:31). *Strutting rooster:* NIV, NRSV.

GRIDDLE. See *Pan*.

GRIEF

Job 2:13 saw that his [Job's] *g* was very great
Ps. 6:7 eye is consumed because of *g*
Prov. 17:25 foolish son is a *g* to his father
Isa. 53:3 man of sorrows [God's servant], and acquainted with *g*
Jer. 45:3 LORD hath added *g* to my [Jeremiah's] sorrow

GRIEVE [D]

Ps. 78:40 oft did they...*g* him [God] in the desert
Ps. 95:10 Forty years...was I [God] *g'd* with...generation
Mark 3:5 he [Jesus]...*g'd* for the hardness of their hearts
Mark 10:22 he [rich young ruler]...went away *g'd*
Eph. 4:30 *g* not the holy Spirit

GROVE. A wooden pole that represented the Canaanite fertility goddess Ashtoreth (2 Kings 21:7).

GROW

Ps. 104:14 He [God] causeth the grass to *g*
Matt. 6:28 Consider the lilies...how they *g*
1 Pet. 2:2 milk of the word, that ye may *g*
2 Pet. 3:18 *g* in grace, and in...our Lord

GUARANTEE. See *Surety*.

GUARD. A soldier who provided personal protection for a ruler; a bodyguard (2 Chron. 12:11).

GUIDE [S]

Ps. 48:14 God...will be our *g* even unto death
Isa. 58:11 LORD shall *g* thee continually
Matt. 23:24 Ye blind *g's*, which strain at a gnat
John 16:13 he [Holy Spirit] will *g* you into all truth

GUILE (DECEIT). Craftiness, cunning, or deception (Ps. 55:11). Nathanael was commended by Jesus as an Israelite without guile—a model of honesty and truthfulness (John 1:47). *Deceit:* NRSV.

GUILT. Remorse for sin and wrongdoing (Lev. 6:4). The guilt of sin is covered for believers by the sacrificial death of Christ (Rom. 5:1–2). See also *Conviction; Repentance.*

GUILT [Y]

Deut. 19:13 put away the *g* of innocent blood from Israel
Matt. 26:66 They...said, He [Jesus] is *g'y* of death
James 2:10 yet offend in one point, he is *g'y* of all

GUM RESIN. See *Stacte*.

GUTTER (WATERING TROUGH). A drinking trough for animals (Gen. 30:38). *Watering trough:* NIV.

G

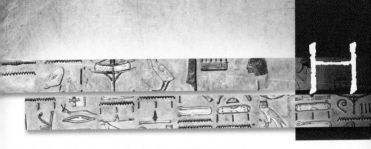

HABAKKUK. A prophet of Judah who was probably a contemporary of Jeremiah; the author of the book that bears his name (Hab. 1:1; 3:1).

HABAKKUK, BOOK OF. A short prophetic book of the O.T. that questions the coming suffering and humiliation of God's people at the hands of the pagan Babylonians (1:1–4; 1:12–2:1). God's response makes it clear that He is using the Babylonians as an instrument of judgment against His wayward people (1:5–11; 2:2–20). The book closes with a psalm of praise to God for His mercy and salvation (chap. 3).

HABERGEON. An Old English word for the priest's breastplate (Exod. 28:32; 39:23). See also *Breastplate.*

HABITATION. A place of residence (Num. 15:2; Acts 17:26).

HADAD. An Edomite prince or ruler who became an enemy of King Solomon (1 Kings 11:14–25).

HADADEZER/HADAREZER. A king of Zobah in Syria. He was defeated by David and Joab (2 Sam. 8:3–13; 10:6–19). *Hadarezer:* 1 Chron. 18:10.

HADASSAH. See *Esther.*

HADES. See *Hell.*

HAGAR/AGAR. Sarah's Egyptian slave who became the mother of Ishmael by Abraham (Gen. 16). She was driven into the wilderness with her son because of conflict with Sarah, but God intervened to save them (Gen. 21:9–21). *Agar:* Gal. 4:24. See also *Ishmael.*

HAGGAI. A prophet after the Babylonian Exile and author of the book that bears his name.

HAGGAI, BOOK OF. A short prophetic book of the O.T. written to encourage the Jewish captives who had returned to their homeland after three generations under the Babylonians and Persians. The people were encouraged to finish the task of rebuilding the temple in Jerusalem (1:1–2:9) and to remain faithful to God in difficult times (2:10–23).

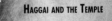

HAGGAI AND THE TEMPLE

The temple in Jerusalem was the central place of worship for the Jewish people, so Haggai declared that it should be rebuilt with all deliberate speed. But the prophet also reminded the people that the physical temple could not serve as a substitute for a living faith. Obeying the Lord was more important than temple sacrifices (Hag. 2:10–19).

HAI. See *Ai*.

HAIL. Frozen rain (Job 38:22). The word is also used as a symbol of God's judgment (Rev. 8:7).

HAIR. Fibers on the human body, especially the head. They are used as a symbol of God's special care of believers (Matt. 10:30).

HAKELDAMA. See *Aceldama*.

HALAH. A region in Assyria where captives from the Northern Kingdom were carried (2 Kings 17:6).

HALF-SHEKEL TAX. A temple tax, also called the two-drachma tax (Exod. 30:13–14; Matt. 17:24–27). See also *Tribute*.

HALF-TRIBE OF MANASSEH. A phrase that refers to the two distinct settlements of the tribe of Manasseh—one in central Palestine and the other east of the Jordan River (Num. 32:33; Josh. 22:10). See also *Manasseh*.

HALLELUJAH. See *Alleluia*.

HALLOW. To set apart for holy use; to make holy (Exod. 20:11; Luke 11:2). See also *Consecration*.

HAM. The youngest son of Noah. Ham's four sons are thought to be the ancestors of the people of several nations: Canaan (Canaanites), Cush and Phut (Africa and Ethiopia), and Mizraim (Egypt). See Gen. 10:6.

HAMAN. An aide to King Ahasuerus of Persia who plotted to kill the Jewish leader Mordecai and all the Jews, only to be hanged himself on the gallows that he had built for Mordecai's execution (Esther 3:1–9:25). See also *Esther; Mordecai*.

HAMATH/HEMATH (LEBO-HAMATH). A Hittite city north of Damascus (Josh. 13:5). *Hemath:* Amos 6:14. *Lebo-Hamath:* NIV, NRSV.

HAMMER. A driving tool (Judg. 4:21). It is used as a symbol of the power of God's Word (Jer. 23:29).

HAMMOTH-DOR/HAMMATH/HAMMON. A city of refuge in the territory of Naphtali (Josh. 21:32). This is probably the same city as *Hammath* (Josh. 19:35) and *Hammon* (1 Chron. 6:76).

HAMMURABI, CODE OF. An ancient and influential law code named for an early king of Babylonia. The code was discovered in 1901–1902 by an archaeologist at Susa.

HANAMEEL (HANAMEL). A cousin of Jeremiah the prophet (Jer. 32:7). Jeremiah bought a field from Hanameel during the siege of Jerusalem by the Babylonians to signify hope for the future for God's people (Jer. 32:8–12). *Hanamel:* NIV, NRSV.

HANANI. Nehemiah's brother, who became governor of Jerusalem (Neh. 7:2). Hanani brought news of the suffering citizens of Jerusalem to Nehemiah in Persia (Neh. 1:2–3).

HANANIAH. See *Shadrach*.

HANDBAG. See *Crisping Pin*.

HANDBREADTH. A measure of length (about four inches) based on the width of the palm of one's hand (Exod. 25:25). It is also symbolic of the frailty and brevity of life (Ps. 39:5).

HANDKERCHIEF (CLOTH). A small cloth for wiping the face or hands (Acts 19:12) and also a burial cloth placed over the face of corpses (John 20:7). *Cloth:* NIV, NRSV. See also *Napkin.*

HANDMAID (MAIDSERVANT). A female servant (Gen. 29:24). This word also signified humility, as in Ruth's conversation with Boaz (Ruth 2:13). *Maidservant:* NIV.

HANDS, LAYING ON OF. See *Laying on of Hands.*

HANGING. A form of capital punishment (2 Sam. 18:10). Haman, the enemy of the Jews, was hanged on the gallows that he had prepared for Mordecai (Esther 7:9–10). See also *Haman.*

HANNAH. The mother of Samuel the prophet. She prayed earnestly for Samuel to be born (1 Sam. 1:5–11), devoted him to God's service (1 Sam. 1:24–28), and offered a beautiful prayer of thanksgiving for God's blessings (1 Sam. 2:1–10). See also *Samuel.*

HANUKKAH. See *Dedication, Feast of.*

HARA. A site in Assyria where some of the captives from the Northern Kingdom were settled after the fall of their nation (1 Chron. 5:26).

HARAN/CHARRAN. A city of Mesopotamia known as a center of pagan worship (2 Kings 19:12). Abraham lived in Haran for a time before he left at God's command to settle in Canaan (Gen. 12:4–5). *Charran:* Acts 7:2, 4.

HARDNESS OF HEART. A symbolic expression for rebellion or a stubborn and unyielding spirit, such as that exemplified by the pharaoh of Egypt in refusing to free the Hebrew slaves (Exod. 9:35).

HARE (RABBIT). A rabbitlike animal with long ears and legs (Deut. 14:7). Hares were considered unclean by the Israelites (Lev. 11:6). *Rabbit:* NIV.

HAREM. A group of women married to one man, especially a king. Esther was a member of the harem of King Ahasuerus of Persia (Esther 2:8–14).

HARLOT (PROSTITUTE). Harlotry was forbidden among God's people (Lev. 19:29). Engaging in prostitution was often compared to the spiritual adultery of God's people (Isa. 57:7–9; Rev. 17). *Prostitute:* NIV.

HARP (LYRE). A stringed musical instrument frequently used in worship (2 Chron. 29:25). David calmed King Saul by playing his harp (1 Sam. 16:16, 23). *Lyre:* NRSV. See also *Psaltery.*

HARPIST. See *Minstrel.*

HARROW. An agricultural tool or implement, probably used to level a plowed field for planting (Job 39:10).

HART (DEER). A male deer. The word is used to illustrate spiritual thirst (Ps. 42:1) and conversion (Isa. 35:6). *Deer:* NIV, NRSV. See also *Deer.*

HARVEST. The gathering of mature crops (Lev. 23:10). This word is used to illustrate the ripe spiritual harvest (Matt. 9:37–38). See also *Reaper.*

HARVEST, FEAST OF. See *Pentecost.*

H

HARLOT. In the city of Jericho, a harlot named Rahab welcomes Israelite scouts sent by Joshua. Because she protected the men, Joshua spared her when the Israelites later destroyed the city.

HATE. Extreme dislike or animosity toward another. Jesus enjoined believers not to hate their enemies but to return love for malice (Luke 6:27). See also *Enmity; Malice.*

HATE [D, TH]
Lev. 19:17 shalt not *h* thy brother in thine heart
Ps. 119:163 I *h*...lying...thy [God's] law do I love
Prov. 8:13 fear of the Lord is to *h* evil
Prov. 14:20 poor is *h'd* even of his own neighbour
Eccles. 3:8 A time to love, and a time to *h*
Amos 5:21 I [God] *h*, I despise your feast days
Matt. 5:44 do good to them that *h* you
Matt. 6:24 will *h* the one, and love the other
Mark 13:13 *h'd* of all men for my [Jesus'] name's sake
Luke 14:26 and *h* not his father, and mother
John 12:25 he that *h'th* his life...shall keep it
John 15:23 He that *h'th* me [Jesus] *h'th* my Father also
1 John 4:20 man say, I love God, and *h'th* his brother, he is a liar

HAUGHTINESS. An arrogant spirit. God's Word indicates that haughty persons will be humbled (Prov. 16:18; Isa. 2:11, 17). See also *Conceit; Pride.*

HAWK. A bird of prey considered unclean by the Israelites (Deut. 14:15). See also *Cormorant.*

HAY (GRASS). A word for grass, which was cut and fed to livestock while fresh and green (Isa. 15:6). *Grass:* NIV, NRSV. See also *Grass.*

HAZAEL. A leader who was anointed king of Syria at God's command by the prophet Elijah (1 Kings 19:15). He murdered Ben-hadad in order to take the throne (2 Kings 8:7–15). Hazael conducted military campaigns against both Judah (2 Kings 12:17–18) and Israel (2 Kings 10:32). See also *Syria.*

HAZEL (ALMOND). A tree from which Jacob cut a rod or switch (Gen. 30:37). *Almond:* NIV, NRSV. See also *Almond.*

HAZOR. A royal Canaanite city destroyed by Joshua (Josh. 11:1–13). The rebuilt fortress city was later ravaged by Deborah and Barak during the period of the judges (Judg. 4:2–24). Hazor was ultimately destroyed by King Tiglath-pileser of Assyria (2 Kings 15:29).

HEAD [S]
Gen. 3:15 it shall bruise thy [the serpent's] *h*
1 Chron. 29:11 thou [God] art exalted as *h* above all
Ps. 23:5 thou [God] anointest my *h* with oil
Matt. 10:30 hairs of your *h* are all numbered
Matt. 21:42 stone...builders rejected...*h* of the corner
Luke 9:58 Son of man hath not where to lay his *h*
Acts 18:6 blood be upon your own *h's*
Rom. 12:20 coals of fire on his [your enemy's] *h*
1 Cor. 11:3 the *h* of the woman is the man
Col. 1:18 he [Jesus] is the *h* of the body, the church

HEAL. To restore a person to good health. Jesus' healing ministry showed His compassion and God's power over sickness and death (Mark 1:34). See also *Balm of Gilead; Medicine.*

HEAL [ING]
2 Chron. 7:14 I [God will] hear...*h* their land
Ps. 41:4 Lord, be merciful...*h* my soul
Eccles. 3:3 A time to kill, and a time to *h*
Jer. 3:22 I [God] will *h* your backslidings
Mal. 4:2 Sun of righteousness...*h'ing* in his wings
Matt. 4:23 Jesus went about...*h'ing*...sickness
Matt. 10:8 *H* the sick... raise the dead
Luke 4:18 he [Jesus] hath sent me [Jesus] to *h* the brokenhearted
Luke 9:2 he [Jesus] sent them [disciples]...to *h* the sick

HEAR [ETH, ING]
Deut. 6:4 *H*, O Israel...Lord our God is one
Job 42:5 heard of thee [God] by the *h'ing* of the ear
Ps. 4:3 Lord will *h* when I call unto him
Prov. 13:1 wise son *h'eth* his father's instruction
Isa. 59:1 neither his [God's] ear heavy, that it cannot *h*
Jer. 22:29 earth...*h* the word of the Lord
Ezek. 37:4 dry bones, *h* the word of the Lord
Matt. 13:9 Who hath ears to *h*, let him *h*
Mark 7:37 he [Jesus] maketh...the deaf to *h*
John 10:27 My [Jesus'] sheep *h* my voice
Acts 2:8 how *h* we every man in our own tongue

Rom. 10:14 how shall they *h* without a preacher

James 1:19 every man be swift to *h*, slow to speak

HEARD

Gen. 3:8 they [Adam and Eve] *h*...the Lord

Exod. 3:7 I [God] have surely...*h* their [Israel's] cry

Ps. 34:4 I sought the Lord, and he *h* me

Ps. 116:1 I love the Lord...he hath *h* my voice

Jer. 31:15 voice was *h* in Ramah...bitter weeping

Matt. 6:7 heathen...think...be *h*...much speaking

Mark 12:37 common people *h* him [Jesus] gladly

Luke 2:20 shepherds...praising God for all...they had *h*

Acts 4:20 speak the things...seen and *h*

Acts 17:32 *h* of the resurrection...some mocked

Rom. 10:14 believe in him [Jesus] of whom they have not *h*

1 Cor. 2:9 Eye hath not seen, nor ear *h*

Phil. 4:9 things, which ye have...*h*, and seen...do

1 John 3:11 message that ye *h* from the beginning

HEART.

To the Hebrews, the heart was the center of a person's existence, including emotions (Gen. 42:28), wisdom or skill (Exod. 35:35), and even physical life (Deut. 6:5). A person acts and speaks from the heart, so he or she should guard it carefully (Matt. 15:18–19).

HEART [S]

Deut. 6:5 love the Lord...with all thine *h*

Deut. 10:16 Circumcise...foreskin of your *h*

1 Sam. 12:24 serve him [God]...with all your *h*

Ps. 13:5 my *h* shall rejoice in thy [God's] salvation

Ps. 19:14 meditation of my *h*, be acceptable

Ps. 51:10 Create in me a clean *h*, O God

Ps. 119:11 Thy [God's] word have I hid in mine *h*

Prov. 3:5 Trust in the Lord with all thine *h*

Jer. 17:9 The *h* is deceitful above all things

Matt. 5:8 Blessed are the pure in *h*

Matt. 6:21 your treasure is...your *h* be also

Matt. 11:29 I [Jesus] am meek and lowly in *h*

Mark 12:30 love the Lord...with all thy *h*

John 14:1 Let not your *h* be troubled

2 Cor. 9:7 purposeth in his *h*, so let him give

2 Thess. 3:5 Lord direct your *h*'s into the love of God

Heb. 4:12 word of God is...a discerner...of the *h*

HEATH.

A dense shrub or bush that grew in the desert regions of Palestine (Jer. 17:6).

HEATHEN (NATIONS, GENTILES).

A word for ethnic groups besides the Jews (Ezek. 22:15). It was also used for unbelievers, pagans, or Gentiles (Gal. 1:16). *Nations:* NIV, NRSV. *Gentiles:* NIV, NRSV. See also *Gentile.*

HEAVE OFFERING/PEACE OFFERING.

An offering that consisted of the firstfruits of the harvest (Num. 15:17–21) and a tenth of all tithes (Num. 18:21–29). It was presented to God before being given to the priests. This was also known as a *peace offering* (Josh. 22:23).

HEAVEN.

A word for (1) the atmosphere or the sky (Ps. 146:6), (2) the place where God dwells (1 Kings 8:45), and (3) the future home of all believers (Col. 1:5), who will dwell with God eternally (Isa. 65:17). See also *Heavenly City; Paradise.*

HEAVEN [S]

Gen. 1:1 God created the *h* and the earth

2 Chron. 7:14 will I [God] hear from *h*...forgive their sin

Ps. 19:1 The *h*'s declare the glory of God

Ps. 139:8 ascend up into *h*, thou [God] art there

Eccles. 3:1 time to every purpose under the *h*

Matt. 5:3 poor in spirit...theirs is the kingdom of *h*

Matt. 6:20 lay up for yourselves treasures in *h*

Luke 24:51 he [Jesus] was parted...carried up into *h*

Acts 4:12 none other name under *h*...whereby we must be saved

1 Thess. 4:16 Lord...shall descend from *h* with a shout

2 Pet. 3:13 we...look for new *h*'s...new earth

Rev. 21:1 I [John] saw a new *h*...new earth

HEAVENLY

Matt. 6:14 your *h* Father will also forgive you

John 3:12 believe, if I [Jesus] tell you of *h* things

Acts 26:19 I [Paul] was not disobedient...*h* vision

HEAVENLY CITY.

The future city built by God as a dwelling place for those who belong to Him (Heb. 11:13–16). It will be known as "New Jerusalem," the place where God dwells eternally among the redeemed (Rev. 21:2–10). See also *Heaven; Paradise*.

HEBREWS, EPISTLE TO THE.
An epistle of the N.T., author unknown, written to a group of believers of Jewish background to show that Jesus had replaced the O.T. ceremonial law and sacrificial system. Hebrews declares that Jesus is superior to angels (1:1–2:18) and Moses (3:1–16) and that He is our great High Priest who offered Himself—rather than a sacrificial animal—as an atoning sacrifice for our sins (chaps. 4–10).

The book closes with an appeal to believers to remember the great heroes of the faith (chap. 11) and to remain steadfast and true in their commitment to Christ (chaps. 12–13).

HEBRON/KIRJATH-ARBA.
An ancient town in Canaan where Abraham lived and where Sarah died (Gen. 23:2–6). After the conquest of Canaan, it was designated as one of the six cities of refuge. *Kirjath-arba:* Josh. 14:15. See also *Cities of Refuge*.

HEED
Josh. 23:11 Take good *h*...love the Lord
Matt. 6:1 Take *h*...do not your alms before men
Mark 8:15 Take *h*, beware of the...Pharisees
1 Cor. 3:10 take *h* how he buildeth thereupon
1 Cor. 10:12 thinketh he standeth take *h* lest he fall
Heb. 3:12 Take *h*...lest there be in...you an evil heart

HEIFER. A young cow (Gen. 15:9). This word is sometimes used figuratively of contentment or complacency (Jer. 50:11).

HEIR [S]
Mark 12:7 This is the *h*; come, let us kill him
Gal. 3:29 Abraham's seed, and *h's* according to the promise
Gal. 4:7 if a son, then an *h* of God through Christ
Titus 3:7 justified by his [Jesus'] grace...be made *h's*
Heb. 1:2 whom he [God] hath appointed *h* [Jesus] of all things

HELI. Father of Joseph (husband of Mary) in the ancestry of Jesus (Luke 3:23).

HELL. The place of eternal torment reserved for unbelievers. *Sheol*, a Hebrew word rendered as "hell" in the O.T., corresponds to the Greek word *Hades*, which means "unseen underworld" or "place of the dead."

In the N.T. both *Hades* and *Gehenna* are rendered as "hell." *Gehenna* is derived from the Valley of Hinnom, a site for pagan worship that became a dumping ground near Jerusalem where filth and dead animals were burned; hence hell's association with the final state of lost souls in a place of eternal fire (Mark 9:47–48).

Hell is described as a "lake of fire" (Rev. 19:20), "everlasting destruction" (2 Thess. 1:9), and the "second death" (Rev. 20:14). See also *Damnation; Hinnom, Valley of; Lake of Fire*.

Job 26:6 *H* is naked before him, and destruction hath no covering
Ps. 18:5 sorrows of *h* compassed me about
Ps. 139:8 make my bed in *h*, behold, thou [God] art there
Prov. 27:20 *H* and destruction are never full
Jon. 2:2 out of the belly of *h* cried I [Jonah]
Matt. 5:22 say, Thou fool, shall be in danger of *h* fire
Matt. 10:28 fear him...able to destroy...soul and body in *h*
Matt. 16:18 gates of *h* shall not prevail against it [the church]
Luke 10:15 Capernaum...shalt be thrust down to *h*
Rev. 1:18 I [Jesus]...have the keys of *h* and of death

HELLENISTS. Greek-speaking Jews. See *Greeks*.

HELMET. An armored covering for the head to protect soldiers in combat. Paul spoke of the "helmet of salvation" that protects believers in spiritual warfare (Eph. 6:17).

HELPER. One who assists another. This word is used for the Holy Spirit's comfort and intercession on behalf of believers (Rom. 8:26). See also *Advocate; Comforter; Holy Spirit; Paraclete*.

H

HELL. The word hell *comes from the Valley of Hinnom, which was a dumping ground for ancient Jerusalem. In this painting of Jerusalem in the 1800s, the valley is to the left of the distant ridge where Jerusalem rests. The Kidron Valley and the Mount of Olives are to the right.*

HELP MEET (HELPER). A helper, companion, or mate. God created Eve as a help meet for Adam (Gen. 2:18). *Helper:* NIV, NRSV.

HEM. A decorative border or fringe on a piece of clothing, worn to remind the Jews of God's commandments (Exod. 28:33–34). See also *Fringe.*

HEMAN. A talented musician under David and a grandson of Saul (1 Chron. 6:33; 15:16–17). Heman was regarded as a person of spiritual insight (1 Chron. 25:5).

HEMETH. See *Hamath.*

HEMLOCK (WORMWOOD). A bitter and poisonous plant (Amos 6:12). *Wormwood:* NRSV.

HENNA. See *Camphire.*

HENOCH. See *Enoch*, No. 2.

HEPHZI-BAH. A symbolic name meaning "my delight is in her" that would be used for Jerusalem after her restoration to God's grace and favor (Isa. 62:4).

HERALD. A person sent by a high government official to deliver a formal and public message or to announce good news (Dan. 3:4)

HERB. A plant used to promote healing or to season food (Gen. 1:29). The Israelites used bitter herbs in their bread at the first Passover (Exod. 12:8). See also *Mallows.*

HERD. A group of cattle, sheep, or oxen (1 Sam. 11:5). In O.T. times, a person's wealth was measured by the size of his herd (2 Sam. 12:1–3).

HERDSMAN (SHEPHERD). A tender or keeper of livestock. The prophet Amos was a herdsman and farmer (Amos 7:14). *Shepherd:* NIV. See also *Shepherd.*

HERESY. False teachings that deny essential doctrines of the Christian faith—a serious problem condemned by Paul (1 Cor. 11:19). See also *Doctrine; Gnosticism; Judaizers.*

HERMES. See *Mercurius.*

HERMON, MOUNT/SIRION/ SHENIR/SENIR. The highest mountain in Syria, with an elevation of almost 10,000 feet (Josh. 12:1). It was also called *Sirion* and *Shenir* (Deut. 3:9) and *Senir* (Ezek. 27:5).

HEROD. The name of several Roman rulers in Palestine during N.T. times:

HERDSMAN. *A herdsman and his son tend sheep in the springtime fields along the Jordan River.*

1. Herod the Great (ruled 37 to 4 B.C.), in power when Jesus was born, who ordered the slaughter of innocent children (Matt. 2:3–16). Herod reconstructed the temple in Jerusalem and completed other ambitious building projects.

2. Herod Archelaus (ruled 4 B.C. to A.D. 6), the son and successor of Herod the Great as Roman ruler in Judea soon after the birth of Jesus (Matt. 2:22).

3. Herod Antipas (ruled 4 B.C. to A.D. 39), who granted his wife's request that John the Baptist be executed. This was the Herod who returned Jesus for sentencing by Pilate (Luke 23:6–12).

4. Herod Philip (ruled 4 B.C. to A.D. 33), ruler in extreme northern Galilee at the time when Jesus began His public ministry (Luke 3:1, 19–20).

5. Herod Agrippa I (ruled A.D. 37–44), who

persecuted the apostles and executed James, leader of the Jerusalem church (Acts 12:1–23).

6. Herod Agrippa II (ruled A.D. 50–100), before whom Paul made his defense at Caesarea (Acts 25:13–26:32).

HERODIANS. An influential Jewish group that favored Greek customs and Roman law in New Testament times. The Herodians joined forces with the Pharisees against Jesus (Mark 3:6).

HERODIAS. The wife or queen of Herod Antipas, the Roman provincial ruler of Palestine, who had John the Baptist executed. Herodias was angry with John because of his criticism of her immorality and illicit marriage (Matt. 14:1–11).

HERON. An unclean bird that lived in the lakes and marshes of Palestine (Deut. 14:18).

HETH. A son of Canaan and ancestor of the Hittites. Abraham dealt with the sons of Heth in securing a burial place for Sarah (Gen. 23:3–20).

HEWER (WOODCUTTER, STONE-CUTTER). A person who cut wood (Josh. 9:21; *woodcutter:* NIV) or stone (2 Kings 12:12; *stonecutter:* NIV, NRSV).

HEZEKIAH/EZEKIAS. The godly king of Judah (ruled about 716–686 B.C.) who implemented religious reforms by abolishing idol worship, restoring and reopening the temple in Jerusalem, and leading in celebration of major religious festivals, such as the Passover (2 Kings 18:4; 2 Chron. 29). Preparing for a siege against Jerusalem by the Assyrians, he cut a tunnel through solid rock to bring water from a spring outside the city wall into the city (2 Kings 20:20). *Ezekias:* Matt. 1:9.

HID

Gen. 3:8 Adam and his wife *h*...from...the LORD
Exod. 3:6 Moses *h* his face...afraid to look upon God
Ps. 38:9 groaning is not *h* from thee [God]
Ps. 119:11 Thy [God's] word have I *h* in mine heart
Matt. 5:14 A city...set on an hill cannot be *h*
Matt. 11:25 thou [God] hast *h* these things from the wise

HIDDEKEL. See *Tigris River.*

HIDE [ING, ST]

Job 14:13 thou [God] wouldest *h* me in the grave
Ps. 13:1 how long wilt thou [God] *h* thy face from me
Ps. 17:8 *h* me under the shadow of thy [God's] wings
Ps. 119:114 Thou [God] art my *h'ing* place and my shield
Isa. 45:15 thou art a God that *h'st* thyself

HIEL. A native of Bethel who rebuilt the city of Jericho in King Ahab's time (1 Kings 16:34). This was a fulfillment of Joshua's curse against the city (Josh. 6:26).

HIERAPOLIS. A city of the district of Phrygia in Asia Minor. This city was mentioned by Paul, implying that Christianity had been planted here (Col. 4:13).

HIGGAION. A musical term translated "meditation" in Ps. 19:14, perhaps signifying a soft, quiet sound.

HEZEKIAH AND ISAIAH

King Hezekiah of Judah was fortunate to reign during the time of Isaiah's prophetic ministry. The prophet advised Hezekiah on several matters, assured him of God's mercy when he was sick (Isa. 38:1–8), and even confronted him about his foolish judgment when the king showed off his royal treasures to a Babylonian official (Isa. 39:1–8).

HIGHWAY. The Appian Way was an ancient Italian road that led to Rome. Paul walked on this road when he was taken to Rome for trial.

HIGH PLACE. An elevated place where worship of false gods was conducted (2 Kings 12:3). These shrines of idolatry provoked God's wrath (Ps. 78:58). See also *Altar*.

HIGH PRIEST. The chief priest or head of the priesthood—an office filled by succession of the oldest son of each generation through the lineage of Aaron, Israel's first high priest (Exod. 28). Jesus is called our "great high priest" (Heb. 4:15) because He laid down His life as a "living sacrifice" on our behalf (Heb. 9:26). See also *Priest*.

HIGHWAY. The "highways" of the Bible were little more than paths or crude trails, and they generally connected large cities or major trading centers (Isa. 19:23). See also *Road*.

HILKIAH. A high priest during the reign of King Josiah of Judah who found the lost Book of the Law and used it to bring about religious reforms (2 Kings 22:8–23:4).

HILL. An elevated site. Pagan altars were often built on hills (1 Kings 14:23). See also *High Place*.

HILL COUNTRY (MOUNTAIN REGION). A region of low, rugged mountains in southern Lebanon and northern Judea (Josh. 13:6). *Mountain region:* NIV.

HIN. A unit of measure equal to about one and one-half gallons (Exod. 29:40).

HIND (DEER). A female deer. The word is used symbolically to show spiritual resilience (Hab. 3:19; Ps. 18:33). *Deer:* NIV, NRSV. See also *Deer*.

7
C
5

HINNOM, VALLEY OF. A deep, narrow ravine southwest of Jerusalem where pagan worship involving child sacrifice was conducted (2 Chron. 28:3; Jer. 19:2–4). Some scholars believe this site in N.T. times became a garbage dump for the city of Jerusalem known as *Gehenna*—a word translated "hell" (Matt. 5:22; Mark 9:43). See also *Hell.*

H

HIRAM/HURAM. The king of Tyre—or perhaps a son and his successor—who assisted David and Solomon with their building projects in Jerusalem by providing materials and skilled workmen (2 Sam. 5:11; 1 Kings 5:1–11). *Huram:* 2 Chron. 2:3–12. See also *Tyre.*

HIRELING (HIRED HAND, LABORER). A common laborer hired for a short time to do farm chores (Job 7:1–2). Unlike a hireling, Jesus as the Good Shepherd takes a personal interest in His sheep (John 10:12–13). *Hired hand:* NIV, NRSV. *Laborer:* NRSV. See also *Laborer.*

HISS. A sound made by forcing air between the tongue and the teeth to show scorn and contempt (Job 27:23; Isa. 5:25–26).

1
C
1

HITTITES. An ancient people who lived in Canaan apparently before Abraham's time, since he bought a burial cave from Ephron, who was probably a Hittite (Gen. 23:7–20). Hittites also served in David's army (2 Sam. 11:6, 15).

HIVITES. Descendants of Canaan (see Gen. 10:6) who lived in the Promised Land before and after the Hebrew people occupied their territory (Deut. 7:1). Some scholars believe these are the same people as the Horites. See also *Horites.*

HOBAB. See *Jethro.*

HOE. See *Mattock.*

HOLD [ING]
Exod. 20:7 Lord will not *h* him guiltless...taketh his name in vain
Ps. 83:1 Keep not thou silence, O God: *h* not thy peace
Jer. 2:13 have...hewed them out...cisterns, that can *h* no water
Phil. 2:16 *H'ing* forth the word of life...I [Paul] may rejoice
1 Tim. 3:9 *H'ing* the mystery of the faith
Heb. 10:23 *h* fast the profession of our faith

HOLINESS. Moral purity; to be set apart and sanctified for service to God. God is holy (Exod. 15:11), and He expects holiness of His people (Rom. 12:1). Since Jesus was the perfect example of holiness, He was called the "Holy One of God" (Mark 1:24). See also *Righteousness.*

HOLY [INESS]
Exod. 3:5 place...thou [Moses] standest is *h* ground
Exod. 20:8 Remember the sabbath day, to keep it *h*
Lev. 11:44 ye shall be *h*; for I [God] am *h*
Lev. 20:7 be ye *h*: for I am the Lord your God
Ps. 11:4 Lord is in his *h* temple
Ps. 24:3 who shall stand in his [God's] *h* place
Ps. 29:2 worship the Lord...beauty of *h'iness*
Ps. 51:11 take not thy [God's] *h* spirit from me
Ps. 103:1 all...within me, bless his [God's] *h* name
Hab. 2:20 Lord is in his *h* temple...earth keep silence
Rom. 16:16 Salute one another with an *h* kiss
1 Cor. 3:17 temple of God is *h*, which temple ye are
Eph. 5:27 it [the church] should be *h*
1 Thess. 4:7 God hath...called us unto...*h'iness*
1 Tim. 2:8 men pray every where, lifting up *h* hands
1 Pet. 2:5 Ye also...are built up...an *h* priesthood
1 Pet. 2:9 are a chosen generation...an *h* nation
Rev. 21:2 I John saw the *h* city, new Jerusalem

HOLY GHOST. An Old English phrase for "Holy Spirit" (Acts 5:3). See *Holy Spirit.*

Matt. 1:18 she [Mary] was found with child of the *H-G*
Matt. 3:11 he [Jesus] shall baptize you with the *H-G*
Matt. 12:31 blasphemy against the *H-G*...not be forgiven
Matt. 28:19 baptizing them in the name of the...*H-G*
Luke 1:35 The *H-G* shall come upon thee [Mary]
Luke 1:67 Zacharias was filled with the *H-G*
Luke 2:25 the *H-G* was upon him [Simeon]

Luke 3:22 *H-G* descended...upon him [Jesus]
John 14:26 the *H-G*...shall teach you all things
Acts 1:8 receive power...*H-G* is come upon you
Acts 6:3 look ye out...seven men...full of the *H-G*
Acts 13:2 *H-G* said, Separate me Barnabas and Saul
Rom. 14:17 kingdom of God is...joy in the *H-G*
1 Cor. 12:3 no man can say that Jesus is the Lord, but by the *H-G*
2 Pet. 1:21 holy men of God spake...by the *H-G*

HOLY OF HOLIES (HOLY PLACE).

The sacred innermost sanctuary of the temple and tabernacle, containing the ark of the covenant and the mercy seat, which only the high priest could enter. Even he could go in only one day a year on the Day of Atonement, when he made a special sacrifice for the sins of the people (Heb. 9:2–3, 7). *Holy Place:* NRSV. See also *Ark of the Covenant; Atonement, Day of; Mercy Seat.*

HOLY PLACE.

A KJV phrase for the section of the tabernacle just outside the Holy of Holies (Exod. 28:29). See also *Holy of Holies.*

HOLY SPIRIT.

The third person of the Trinity. The O.T. contains glimpses and promises of the Holy Spirit (Gen. 1:2, 6:3; Zech. 4:6), and the Spirit rested on Jesus from His birth (Luke 1:35), but the full manifestation of the Spirit's power occurred at Pentecost after Jesus' resurrection and ascension to the Father (Acts 2:1–21).

Jesus promised He would send the Holy Spirit as a comforter and advocate in His absence (John 14:16; 1 John 2:1). The Spirit would glorify the Son (John 15:16), empower believers (John 14:12–27), and convict unbelievers of sin and coming judgment (John 16:8–11).

Another function of the Holy Spirit is to inspire the Scriptures, thus providing guidance and direction to believers. See also *Advocate; Comforter; Helper; Paraclete.*

H

THE HOLY SPIRIT IN ROMANS 8

Romans 8 is one of the greatest chapters in the Bible on the nature and work of the Holy Spirit. A believer can count on God's indwelling presence to guide him or her through every experience of life. God's Spirit frees us from the law of sin and death (Rom. 8:2), gives us life (Rom. 8:10), makes us children of God (Rom. 8:14–15), and intercedes on our behalf with God the Father (Rom. 8:27).

HOMER.

The standard unit of dry measure, equal to about six bushels (Ezek. 45:11).

HOMOSEXUALITY.

The practice of sexual activity among persons of the same sex—a sin strictly forbidden by the O.T. Law (Lev. 18:22). Paul also condemned this practice (Rom. 1:26–27; 1 Cor. 6:9).

HONEST [LY]

Acts 6:3 seven men of *h* report
Rom. 13:13 Let us walk *h'ly*...not in rioting
Phil. 4:8 things are *h*, whatsoever things are just

HONESTY.

Speaking the truth and acting fairly and without deceit in human relationships. This is a virtue that all believers should practice (2 Cor. 13:7).

HONEY.

A sweet liquid substance produced naturally by bees and artificially from fruit. It was used to sweeten food (Exod. 16:31). The word is also used symbolically for abundance (Exod. 3:8, 17).

HONEYCOMB. The wax cells built by bees to hold their eggs and honey (1 Sam. 14:27).

HONOR. Respect and esteem toward God and other people. The Ten Commandments enjoins honor toward one's parents (Exod. 20:12). God and His Son, Jesus Christ, are worthy of our highest honor (John 5:23).

HONOUR [ETH]

1 Chron. 16:27 Glory and *h* are in his [God's] presence
Ps. 8:5 thou [God]...hast crowned him [man] with glory and *h*
Prov. 3:9 *H* the Lᴏʀᴅ with thy substance
Matt. 13:57 prophet...not without *h*...own country
Mark 7:6 *h'eth* me [Jesus] with their lips...heart...far from me
John 12:26 any...serve me [Jesus]...will my Father *h*
Rom. 12:10 in *h* preferring one another
Rev. 4:11 worthy, O Lord, to receive glory and *h*

HOOK. Wire twisted together forms a fishing hook, which was used during Roman times.

HOOK. A metal grasping tool. Different types of hooks mentioned in the Bible include flesh-hooks (Exod. 27:3), fish hooks (Matt. 17:27), pruning hooks (Isa. 18:5), and the hooks that supported the tabernacle curtains (Exod. 26:32).

HOOPOE. See *Lapwing*.

HOPE. A sure and steady faith in God's promises. The believer has hope in God's promise of salvation (1 Thess. 5:8), resurrection (Acts 26:6–7), and eternal life (1 Cor. 15:19–26). See also *Promise*.

HOPE [D]

Job 7:6 My [Job's] days...spent without *h*
Ps. 38:15 in thee, O Lᴏʀᴅ, do I *h*
Ps. 71:5 thou art my *h*, O Lord
Ps. 146:5 Happy is he...whose *h* is in the Lᴏʀᴅ
Lam. 3:24 Lᴏʀᴅ is my portion...I *h* in him
Rom. 12:12 Rejoicing in *h*; patient in tribulation
Rom. 15:13 God of *h* fill you with all joy
1 Cor. 13:13 now abideth faith, *h*, charity
Col. 1:27 Christ in you, the *h* of glory
1 Thess. 4:13 sorrow not...as others which have no *h*
Heb. 11:1 faith is the substance of things *h'd* for

HOPHNI. A sinful and immoral son of Eli the high priest who was not considered worthy of conducting priestly duties (1 Sam. 1:3; 2:22–25). Along with his evil brother Phinehas, he was killed by the Philistines (1 Sam. 4:1–11). See also *Phinehas*, No. 2.

HOPHRA. See *Pharaoh*, No. 5.

HOR, MOUNT. A mountain in the territory of the Edomites where Moses' brother Aaron died and was buried (Num. 20:22–29). A different mountain with the same name was located in northern Palestine (see Num. 34:7–8).

HOREB, MOUNT. See *Sinai*.

HORITES/HORIMS. Inhabitants of Mount Hermon who were driven out by Esau's descendants (Gen. 36:20). These may have been the same people as the Hivites of Joshua's time. *Horims:* Deut. 2:22. See also *Hivites.*

HORMAH. See *Zephath.*

HORN. A bonelike protrusion from an animal's head. The word is also used as a symbol of strength (Hab. 3:4; Rev. 13:1). See also *Cornet.*

HORNET. A wasplike insect with a painful sting, portrayed as a symbol of God's judgment against the enemies of His people (Exod. 23:28).

HORNS OF THE ALTAR. Projections at the four corners of an altar (Exod. 27:1–2). The blood of a sacrificial animal was sprinkled on these four projections (Exod. 29:12). See also *Altar.*

HORSE. An animal used for transportation (Gen. 47:17) as well as in warfare. God warned his people not to "multiply" horses for use in war (Deut. 17:16).

HORSE GATE. A gate in the old wall of Jerusalem, mentioned by Nehemiah as having been destroyed and then rebuilt under his supervision (Neh. 3:28).

HORSELEACH (LEECH). A parasite that attaches to humans and animals and sucks blood; probably a leech (Prov. 30:15). *Leech:* NIV, NRSV.

HOSANNA. A triumphal shout by the crowds as Jesus entered Jerusalem a few days before His crucifixion (Matt. 21:9, 15). The expression means "save us now."

HOSEA/OSEE. A prophet who delivered God's message of judgment to the Northern Kingdom in the years shortly before this nation fell to the Assyrians in 722 B.C. Author of the book of Hosea, he is best known for his marriage to a prostitute in obedience of God's command (Hosea 1:2–9). *Osee:* Rom. 9:25.

HOSEA, BOOK OF. A prophetic book of the O.T. that compares the spiritual adultery or idolatry of God's people with the physical adultery of the prophet's wife, Gomer (1:2–5; 2:2–5). Just as Hosea redeemed her from slavery and restored her as his mate, God promised that He would eventually restore His people as His own after a period of punishment at the hand of their enemies (chaps. 4–14).

This book is one of the greatest treatises in the Bible on the nature of God, emphasizing His demand for righteousness and impending punishment as well as His steadfast love. See also *Gomer.*

SOWING AND REAPING IN HOSEA

The prophet Hosea's metaphor of sowing the wind and reaping the whirlwind (Hosea 8:7) would have been well understood in the agricultural society of his day. A farmer expects a few planted seeds to grow into an abundant crop. Likewise, sin will yield a crop of wickedness.

The apostle Paul may have had this passage from Hosea in mind when he warned the Galatian believers, "Whatsoever a man soweth, that shall he also reap" (Gal. 6:7).

HOSEN (TROUSERS). An Old English word for trousers, possibly referring to the tunic or inner garment worn during Bible times (Dan. 3:21). *Trousers:* NIV, NRSV.

HOSHEA

1. The original name of Joshua (Deut. 32:44). See *Joshua*.

2. The last king of Israel, or the Northern Kingdom (reigned about 730–722 B.C.), who paid tribute to King Shalmaneser of Assyria. After Hoshea rebelled, Israel was defeated, and Hoshea was taken to Assyria as a captive (2 Kings 17:1–6).

HOSPITALITY. The gracious provision of food and lodging to strangers. Kindness toward travelers and strangers was encouraged in both O.T. and N.T. times (Lev. 19:33–34; 1 Tim. 3:2; 1 Pet. 4:9).

HOST. A hospitable person who entertained guests (Heb. 13:2), or a multitude or crowd of people (Gen. 2:1).

HOST OF HEAVEN. Heavenly beings created by God and associated with His rule of the universe. These beings ("a multitude of the heavenly host") praised God at the angels' announcement of the birth of Jesus (Luke 2:13).

HOUSEHOLD. A Bedouin household poses for a portrait at the turn of the 1900s. They lived in tents and traveled with their herd from one grazing pasture to another.

HOSTS, LORD OF (LORD ALMIGHTY). A title of God that emphasizes His sovereignty (Isa. 1:9; 10:23). *Lord Almighty:* NIV.

HOUR [S]

Matt. 24:42 know not what *h* your Lord doth come
Matt. 26:40 ye [Peter] not watch with me [Jesus] one *h*
Mark 13:32 that day and that *h* knoweth no man
Luke 12:40 Son of man cometh at an *h* when ye think not
John 11:9 Are there not twelve *h's* in the day
John 12:23 *h* is come...Son of man...glorified

HOUSE (TENT). A building or residence for a family (1 Sam. 9:18). The word is also used of a clan or all the descendants of a family (1 Sam. 20:16) as well as the believer's final dwelling place in heaven (2 Cor. 5:1). *Tent:* NIV, NRSV. See also *Tent.*

HOUSEHOLD. Members of a family who lived together in the same dwelling or a compound of dwellings, perhaps including several generations (2 Sam. 6:11). Believers are members of God's household (Gal. 6:10; Eph. 2:19).

HOUSEHOLD IDOLS. Images of pagan gods kept in the house in the belief that they protected the family (Gen. 31:19–35). See also *Teraphim.*

HOUSEHOLDER (OWNER). The head of a household or owner of a house (Matt. 13:27). *Owner:* NIV.

HULDAH. The wife of Shallum and a prophetess who foretold the collapse of Jerusalem (2 Kings 22:14–20).

HUMAN SACRIFICE. The practice of sacrificing children to a pagan god (2 Kings 3:26–27). This was common among the pagan religions of Bible times, but the custom was specifically prohibited by God (Lev. 20:2–5; Deut. 18:10). See also *Hinnom, Valley of; Jephthah.*

HUMBLE [D, TH]

Ps. 10:12 God...forget not the *h*
Isa. 5:15 mighty man shall be *h'd*
Matt. 18:4 shall *h* himself...little child...is greatest
Luke 18:14 he that *h'th* himself shall be exalted
Phil. 2:8 he [Jesus] *h'd* himself...obedient unto death
James 4:10 *H* yourselves...he [God] shall lift you up

HUMILITY. The opposite of arrogance and pride; an attitude that grows out of the recognition that all we are and everything we own are gifts from God (Rom. 12:3; 1 Pet. 5:5). See also *Meekness.*

HUNTER. A person who stalks and kills wild animals. Nimrod, a descendant of Noah, was a "mighty hunter" (Gen. 10:9). See also *Fowler.*

HUR. A man who helped Aaron hold up the arms of Moses to give the Israelites victory over the Amalekites (Exod. 24:14).

HURAM. See *Hiram.*

HUSBAND. The male partner in a marriage relationship. Husbands had total authority over their wives in Bible times, but Paul called on male believers to love their wives (Eph. 5:25).

HUSBAND [S]

Gen. 3:16 thy [Eve's] desire shall be to thy *h*
Prov. 12:4 virtuous woman is a crown to her *h*
Matt. 1:19 Joseph her [Mary's] *h,* being a just man
Mark 10:12 put away her *h*...committeth adultery
1 Cor. 7:3 *h* render unto the wife due benevolence
1 Cor. 7:14 unbelieving *h* is sanctified by the wife
Col. 3:19 *H's,* love your wives
1 Tim. 3:2 bishop...must be blameless...*h* of one wife
1 Tim. 3:12 deacons be the *h's* of one wife
1 Pet. 3:1 wives, be in subjection to your own *h's*
Rev. 21:2 new Jerusalem...as a bride adorned for her *h*

HUSBANDMAN (FARMER). A farmer or tiller of the soil (Gen. 9:20). In N.T. times, a husbandman, like a tenant farmer, often took a share of the crops as payment for his labor (2 Tim. 2:6). *Farmer:* NIV, NRSV.

HUSHAI. A friend and adviser of King David (2 Sam. 15:32–37). Hushai remained loyal to David during Absalom's revolt (2 Sam. 17:1–16).

HUSKS (PODS). The fruit of the carob tree, a type of locust. The prodigal son in Jesus' parable was reduced to eating this coarse and unappetizing food in order to survive (Luke 15:16). *Pods:* NIV, NRSV.

HYMENAEUS. An early Christian who denied the faith and was excommunicated by Paul (1 Tim. 1:19–20; 2 Tim. 2:16–17).

HYMN. A song of praise and thanksgiving to God (Eph. 5:19). Jesus and His disciples sang a hymn after they finished the Last Supper (Matt. 26:30).

HYPOCRITE. A person who pretends to be something he or she is not. Jesus called the Pharisees hypocrites because they did good deeds to gain the praise of others and pretended to be godly and righteous but were actually insensitive to God's truth (Matt. 23:13–29; Mark 12:15).

HYPOCRITE [S]

Job 20:5 joy of the *h* but for a moment
Matt. 6:2 do not sound a trumpet...as the *h's* do
Matt. 6:16 be not, as the *h's*, of a sad countenance
Matt. 7:5 *h*, first cast out the beam...thine own eye

HYSSOP. A plant used in purification ceremonies (Exod. 12:22). It was also symbolic of spiritual cleansing (Ps. 51:7). Hyssop was used to relieve Jesus' thirst on the cross (John 19:29).

I AM. The name by which God revealed Himself to Moses at the burning bush. It shows His eternity, self-existence, and unsearchableness (Exod. 3:14). In John's Gospel Jesus also used the phrase "I am" several times to reveal His identity as the divine Savior. See also *God; Jehovah; Yahweh.*

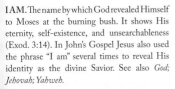

"I AM" STATEMENTS OF JESUS IN JOHN'S GOSPEL

1. Bread of life (John 6:35)
2. Light of the world (John 8:12)
3. Door of the sheep (John 10:7)
4. Good shepherd (John 10:11, 14)
5. Resurrection and the life (John 11:25)
6. Way, the truth, and the life (John 14:6)
7. True vine (John 15:1)

IBEX. See *Pygarg.*

IBZAN. A judge of Israel for seven years. A native of Bethlehem, he had thirty sons and thirty daughters (Judg. 12:8–10). See also *Judges of Israel.*

I-CHABOD. The son of Phinehas and grandson of Eli. He was given this symbolic name, meaning "inglorious," by his dying mother when she learned the ark of the covenant had been captured by the Philistines and that Eli and Phinehas were dead (1 Sam. 4:19–22).

ICONIUM. An ancient city in Asia Minor near Lystra and Lycaonia. Paul and Barnabas introduced Christianity here on the first missionary journey (Acts 13:51; 14:1, 21–22). Paul apparently also visited Iconium on the second journey (Acts 16:1–5).

IDLE. Inactive or lazy. This behavior is condemned in the Proverbs (Prov. 24:30–34) and by Paul (2 Thess. 3:10). See also *Sluggard.*

IDLE [NESS]
Prov. 19:15 an *i* soul shall suffer hunger
Prov. 31:27 She...eateth not the bread of *i'ness*
Matt. 12:36 every *i* word that men shall speak...give account
Luke 24:11 words seemed to them [the disciples] as *i* tales

IDOL, IDOLATRY. The worship of false gods or something created rather than the Creator (Rom. 1:25). Idolatry was prohibited by the first two of the Ten Commandments (Exod. 20:3–4). Abraham migrated to Canaan to escape idol worship (Josh. 24:2–3). Prominent idols mentioned in the Bible are the golden calves of Aaron (Exod. 32:4) and King Jeroboam (2 Chron. 11:15) and the grain god of the Philistines known as Dagon (Judg. 16:23).

The prophet Elijah helped overthrow Baal worship in Israel (1 Kings 18:17–40), and the prophet Isaiah described the folly of idolatry (Isa. 44:9–20). In the N.T., idolatry is anything that comes between the believer and God (Col. 3:5). See also *Graven Image.*

IDOL [S]

Lev. 19:4 Turn ye not unto *i's*

1 Chron. 16:26 gods of the people are *i's*

Ps. 135:15 The *i's* of the heathen are silver and gold

Ezek. 14:6 Repent, and turn...from your *i's*

1 Cor. 8:4 an *i* is nothing in the world

2 Cor. 6:16 what agreement hath...temple of God with *i's*

1 John 5:21 Little children, keep yourselves from *i's*

IDUMEA. See *Edom,* No. 2.

IGNORANCE. Lack of knowledge or understanding. While sins of ignorance are less grievous than premeditated sins (Lev. 4; Num. 15:30–31), they are still destructive (Hosea 4:6) and require repentance (Acts 17:30–31). At Pentecost, Peter declared Christ was crucified out of ignorance—a sin that required repentance (Acts 3:17, 19).

IGNORANT [LY]

Acts 4:13 they [the Sanhedrin]...perceived that they [Peter and John] were...*i* men

Acts 17:23 Whom...ye *i'ly* worship, him [Jesus] declare I [Paul] unto you

1 Cor. 12:1 concerning spiritual gifts...I [Paul] would not have you *i*

1 Thess. 4:13 not have you to be *i*...concerning them which are asleep

2 Pet. 3:8 be not *i* of this...one day is with the Lord as a thousand years

ILLYRICUM. A district on the eastern coast of the Adriatic Sea. Paul mentioned Illyricum as the farthermost point to which he had traveled (Rom. 15:19).

IMAGE. An exact likeness or representation of some object of idolatrous worship. God warned Israel to destroy such pagan images (Exod. 34:13, 17).

Exod. 20:4 not make unto thee any graven *i*

Mark 12:16 he [Jesus] saith...Whose is this *i*

Rom. 1:23 glory of...God into an *i*...corruptible man

Rom. 8:29 be conformed to the *i* of his [God's] Son

1 Cor. 15:49 we shall also bear the *i* of the heavenly

Col. 1:15 Who [Jesus] is the *i* of the invisible God

IMAGE OF GOD. Human beings were created to perfectly reflect God's image (Gen. 9:6), marred that image by sinning, but have the potential to be molded back into that image (Rom. 8:28–30). Jesus is the image of the "invisible God" (Col. 1:15), and humans express God's image when they are in right relation with their Creator and faithfully tend God's creation (Gen. 1:26–28). Human's unique attributes of reason, will, and personality are further evidences of divine image.

IMAGINATION [S]

Gen. 6:5 every *i* of the thoughts of his [man's] heart was only evil

Jer. 16:12 ye walk every one after the *i* of his evil heart

Luke 1:51 he [God]...scattered the proud in the *i* of their hearts

Rom. 1:21 they glorified him not as God...but became vain in their *i's*

IMMANUEL. See *Emmanuel.*

IMMORALITY. Behavior that violates established moral principles or laws. This word is used to condemn illicit sexual activity outside of marriage (Prov. 2:16; Rom. 1:26–27) and to describe Israel's worship of pagan gods (Ezek. 23:8, 17). See also *Adultery; Fornication.*

IMMORTALITY. See *Eternal Life.*

IMMUTABILITY. An attribute of God's nature that refers to His unchangeableness (Mal. 3:6). The unchangeable nature of Christ assures us that God's mercy is constant (Heb. 13:8). God, who cannot lie, offers an anchor of hope for all believers, who are the "heirs of promise" (Heb. 6:17–19). See also *God.*

IMPARTIALITY. Justness and fairness. God is impartial in His loving concern for all persons (2 Pet. 3:9) and in His command for repentance (Rom. 3:6). Peter learned that all persons who are cleansed by the Lord are brothers (Acts 10:15, 34–35).

IMPOSSIBLE

Matt. 17:20 nothing shall be *i* unto you

Mark 10:27 With men it is *i*, but not with God

Heb. 11:6 without faith it is *i* to please him [God]

IMPUTATION.

To transfer something to another person. Adam's sin was imputed to all persons (Rom. 5:12). Our iniquity was laid on Jesus (Isa. 53:5–6), and He bore our sins (John 1:29). Jesus, the "second Adam," imputed grace and righteousness to all who put their trust in Him (Rom. 5:17–19).

IN CHRIST

Rom. 8:1 no condemnation to them...*i-C*

Rom. 12:5 we...are one body *i-C*

1 Cor. 4:10 fools for Christ's sake...ye are wise *i-C*

1 Cor. 15:19 in this life only we have hope *i-C*

1 Cor. 15:22 in Adam all die...*i-C*...all be made alive

1 Cor. 5:17 any man be *i-C*...a new creature

2 Cor. 5:19 God was *i-C*, reconciling the world

Eph. 1:10 he [God] might gather...all things *i-C*

Phil. 2:5 this mind be in you, which was also *i-C*

Phil. 3:14 prize of the high calling of God *i-C*

1 Thess. 4:16 the dead *i-C* shall rise first

INCARNATION OF CHRIST.

The birth and existence of Christ in human form. This was foretold by the O.T. prophets (Isa. 7:14). When Jesus was born into the world, He was described as "the Word...made flesh" (John 1:14). Belief in the incarnation of Christ is a mark of the Christian (1 John 4:2–3). See also *Advent of Christ; Virgin Birth.*

INCENSE.

Sweet perfume extracted from spices or gums and used in worship ceremonies. Incense was burned on the altar of incense in the tabernacle by the priests (Exod. 30:7–8). See also *Censer; Frankincense.*

INCEST.

Sex relations with members of one's own family. Prohibited by the Levitical law (Lev. 18:6–12), incest was considered such a serious offense that it was punishable by death (Lev. 20:11–17). Lot committed incest with his two daughters (Gen. 19:30–38), and Reuben with his father's concubine (Gen. 35:22).

INCLINE [D]

Ps. 17:6 *i* thine [God's] ear unto me

Ps. 40:1 I waited patiently...and he [God] *i'd* unto me

Prov. 4:20 My son...*i* thine ear unto my sayings

INCREASE [D, TH]

Exod. 1:7 children of Israel...*i'd* abundantly

Lev. 26:4 land shall yield her *i*

Ps. 67:6 Then shall the earth yield her *i*

Prov. 1:5 wise man will hear...*i* learning

Prov. 24:5 man of knowledge *i'th* strength

Eccles. 1:18 he that *i'th* knowledge *i'th* sorrow

Luke 2:52 Jesus *i'd* in wisdom and stature

Luke 17:5 apostles said unto the Lord, *I* our faith

John 3:30 He [Jesus] must *i*, but I [John the Baptist] must decrease

Acts 6:7 word of God *i'd*...disciples multiplied

1 Cor. 3:7 neither is he that planteth any thing...but God that giveth the *i*

1 Thess. 3:12 Lord make you to *i* and abound in love

INDIA.

A region near the Indus River that served as the eastern limit of the Persian Empire (Esther 1:1; 8:9). Scholars believe this "India" covered essentially the same region as the modern nations of India and Pakistan.

INDIFFERENCE.

Lack of interest and concern—behavior characteristic of unbelievers and backsliders (Rev. 3:15–16). Indifference breeds moral callousness (Matt. 27:3–4; Acts 18:12–16).

INFIDEL (UNBELIEVER).

An unbeliever (1 Tim. 5:8). Infidelity is caused by an unregenerate heart (Rom. 2:5) and hatred of the light (John 3:20). An infidel will be punished by eternal separation from God (2 Thess. 1:8–9). *Unbeliever:* NIV, NRSV. See also *Atheism; Unbelief.*

INFIRMITY [IES]

Prov. 18:14 spirit of a man will sustain his *i*
Matt. 8:17 Himself [Jesus] took our *i'ies*
Rom. 8:26 Spirit also helpeth our *i'ies*
Rom. 15:1 strong...bear the *i'ies* of the weak
2 Cor. 12:9 gladly...will I [Paul]...glory in my *i'ies*

INGATHERING, FEAST OF. See *Tabernacles, Feast of.*

INHERIT [ED]

Ps. 37:9 those that wait upon the LORD...*i* the earth
Ps. 37:29 righteous shall *i* the land
Matt. 5:5 Blessed...meek...*i* the earth
Matt. 25:34 Come...*i* the kingdom prepared for you
Luke 18:18 what shall I [rich young ruler] do to *i* eternal life
1 Cor. 6:10 nor extortioners, shall *i* the kingdom of God
Rev. 21:7 He that overcometh shall *i* all things

INHERITANCE. A gift of property or rights passed from one generation to another. In ancient Israel, a father's possessions were passed on to his living sons, with the oldest receiving a double portion (Deut. 21:17). Reuben lost his inheritance because he committed incest with Bilhah (Gen. 35:22; 49:4). Esau traded his birthright as the oldest son to his brother, Jacob, for a bowl of stew (Gen. 25:29–34).

Christians enjoy a spiritual birthright (Eph. 1:13–14). All the redeemed, including Gentiles, become God's adopted children with full inheritance rights (Gal. 4:5–7). See also *Adoption; Birthright; Firstborn.*

Num. 18:23 among...Israel they [Levites] have no *i*
Deut. 32:9 Jacob is the lot of his [God's] *i*
Josh. 11:23 Joshua gave it [Canaan] for an *i* unto Israel
Ps. 2:8 I [God] shall give thee the heathen for thine *i*
Ps. 94:14 neither will he [God] forsake his *i*
Mark 12:7 kill him [the heir], and the *i* shall be ours
Eph. 1:11 In whom [Jesus] also we have obtained an *i*
Eph. 5:5 no...idolater, hath...*i* in the kingdom of Christ

INIQUITY (WICKEDNESS). Sin, wickedness, or evil. Jesus taught that evil or iniquity originates in the heart, or from within (Matt. 23:28). Christ redeems believers from their iniquity, purifies them, and sets them apart for His service (Titus 2:14). *Wickedness:* NIV. See also *Wickedness.*

INIQUITY [IES]

Num. 14:18 LORD is longsuffering...forgiving *i*
Ps. 25:11 LORD, pardon mine *i*; for it is great
Ps. 103:10 He [God] hath not...rewarded us according to our *i'ies*
Isa. 53:6 LORD...laid on him [God's servant]...*i* of us all
Jer. 31:30 every one shall die for his own *i*
Matt. 23:28 ye [Pharisees] are full of...*i*
Rom. 4:7 Blessed are they whose *i'ies* are forgiven
James 3:6 tongue is a fire, a world of *i*

INK. Writing fluid. The earliest ink was probably a mixture of water, charcoal or soot, and gum. The scribe Baruch used ink to write Jeremiah's prophecies (Jer. 36:18). See also *Paper; Writing.*

INKHORN. A carrying case for pens and ink, probably made from the horn of an animal and carried on a belt (Ezek. 9).

INN. A shelter that provided lodging for travelers. Inns were often crude stopping places with no indoor accommodations. Jesus was born in a stable of an inn, which provided shelter for people and their animals (Luke 2:7).

INSANE. See *Mad.*

INSCRIPTION. See *Superscription.*

INSPECTION GATE. See *Miphkad.*

INSPIRATION. Divine influence. God's inspiration is the source of human understanding (Job 32:8). Scripture is inspired by God for our correction and instruction (2 Tim. 3:16). The Holy Spirit moved holy men to prophesy and record God's message (2 Pet. 1:20–21). God has communicated with humans in various ways, including by spoken words (Rev. 1:10–11), dreams (Dan. 7:1), and visions (Ezek. 11:24–25).

INSTRUCT [ED]

Job 40:2 Shall he that contendeth with the Almighty *i* him?
Ps. 32:8 I [God] will *i* thee and teach thee
Prov. 21:11 the wise is *i'ed*, he receiveth knowledge

INTEGRITY

Job 2:9 Dost thou [Job] still retain thine *i*?
Ps. 25:21 Let *i* and uprightness preserve me
Prov. 19:1 Better...poor that walketh in his *i*, than...perverse
Prov. 20:7 just man walketh in his *i*

INTELLIGENT. See *Prudent.*

INTERCESSION. Prayer offered on behalf of others. Christ made intercession for those who were crucifying Him (Luke 23:34) and for His disciples (John 17:6–26). Elders of the early church were instructed to pray for the sick (James 5:14–16).

Paul prayed for Israel to be saved (Rom. 10:1) and for the Colossians to grow spiritually (Col. 1:9–12). Christ, our high priest, lives to make intercession for us (Rom. 8:34; Heb. 7:25–26). The Holy Spirit helps us intercede for others (Rom. 8:26; 1 Tim. 2:1). See also *Petition; Prayer.*

INTERCESSOR. An advocate for others (Isa. 59:16). Abraham interceded for Sodom to be spared (Gen. 18:23–26). Paul encouraged intercession for all people (1 Tim. 2:1–2). Christ is the Christian's advocate or intercessor (Heb. 7:25–26).

INN. *The Good Samaritan Inn isn't really a working inn. It's a monument built to look like an ancient inn. It commemorates Jesus' parable of the good Samaritan, and it's located along the route described in the parable—about halfway between Jericho and Jerusalem.*

INTEREST. See *Usury.*

INTERMARRIAGE. Marriage between members of different races or religions. Intermarriage of the Israelites with the idolatrous Canaanites was forbidden by God (Josh. 23:12–13). Paul counseled the Corinthian Christians not to marry unbelievers (2 Cor. 6:14–17). See also *Marriage.*

INTERMEDIATE STATE. The condition of believers between death and the resurrection. Paul characterized this state as being "absent from the body" (2 Cor. 5:8) while awaiting the resurrection (1 Thess. 4:13–18) and anticipating a glorified body like that of Jesus (Phil. 3:20–21). This condition is also characterized as a sleeplike state (John 11:11) that is enjoyable (Ps. 17:15) and unchangeable (2 Cor. 5:1).

INVISIBLE
Rom. 1:20 *i* things of him [God]...are clearly seen
Col. 1:15 Who [Jesus] is the image of the *i* God
1 Tim. 1:17 King eternal, immortal, *i.*.be honour

INWARD PARTS. See *Bowels.*

IRON

1. A fortified city in the territory of Naphtali (Josh. 19:38), also known as *Beth-shemesh* and *Yiron.*

2. An ancient metal first mentioned in Gen. 4:22. Iron was used to make weapons (Job 20:24) and tools (1 Kings 6:7).

IR-SHEMESH. See *Beth-shemesh.*

ISAAC. The son born to Abraham and Sarah in their old age (Gen. 21:1–3) and thus the person through whom God's chosen people, the Israelites, were descended (Gen. 21:9–13). He married Rebekah (Gen. 24:57–67)—a union to which twin sons Jacob and Esau were born (Gen. 25:19–26). Isaac was considered a man of faith (Heb. 11:9, 20), a patriarch of Israel (Exod. 32:13), and an ancestor of Christ (Luke 3:34). See also *Rebekah.*

ISAIAH/ESAIAS. A major prophet of Judah whose career spanned forty years (about 740–701 B.C.). The son of Amoz, he was married to a "prophetess" (Isa. 8:3). Working in the capital city of Jerusalem, Isaiah was the confidant of King Uzziah (Azariah) and his successors (Isa. 1:1). He warned that the city and nation would be destroyed by Assyria, but a righteous remnant would be saved (Isa. 1:2–9; 11:11). He gave his two sons symbolic names to underscore his message (Isa. 7:3; 8:1–4).

Isaiah encouraged King Hezekiah but foretold the king's death (2 Kings 20:1). He was the author of the book of Isaiah, which prophesied the coming of the Messiah (Isa. 7:14), His rejection (Isa. 53), and the conversion of the Gentiles (Isa. 61:10–11). *Esaias:* Greek form (Matt. 4:14).

ISAIAH, BOOK OF. A major prophetic book of the O.T. noted for its prediction of the coming Messiah (7:14; 9:7) and particularly its emphasis on the Messiah as God's "suffering servant" (42:1–9; 49:1–7; 50:4–9; 52:13–53:12). These messianic passages occur in the midst of the prophet's prediction that God would punish the nation of Judah because of its rebellion and idolatry (1:1–12:6). Other prophecies in the book are directed at the pagan nations surrounding Judah (13:1–23:18).

Many Bible students call Isaiah the "fifth Gospel" because it echoes the N.T. themes of salvation and redemption. Jesus began His public ministry by identifying with this book's promise of comfort and healing for God's people: "The Spirit of the Lord GOD is upon me; because the LORD hath anointed me to preach good tidings unto the meek; he hath sent me to bind up the brokenhearted, to proclaim liberty to the captives" (Isa. 61:1; see also Luke 4:18–19). See also *Messiah*.

ISCARIOT, JUDAS. The disciple who betrayed Jesus (John 13:2, 26; 18:1–8). The word *Iscariot* identifies Judas as a citizen of Kerioth, a city in southern Judah (Josh. 15:25), to distinguish him from Judas (or Jude), brother of James, who was also one of the Twelve (Luke 6:16).

Judas Iscariot apparently served as the treasurer for Jesus and His disciples (John 13:29). After realizing the gravity of his act of betrayal, Judas committed suicide (Matt. 27:3–5). See also *Twelve, The*.

ISH-BOSHETH/ESH-BAAL. The youngest son of Saul who became king of Israel for two years (2 Sam. 2:8–9). He was eventually defeated by David and assassinated in his bed (2 Sam. 4:8–12). *Esh-baal:* 1 Chron. 8:33.

ISHI. A symbolic name meaning "my husband" to be given to God when the Israelites returned to Him (Hosea 2:16–17). Ishi was to be used instead of Baali because the name Baal was associated with a pagan god.

ISHMAEL. Abraham's son born to Sarah's Egyptian maid Hagar (Gen. 16). After conflicts with Sarah, Hagar fled with Ishmael into the desert, where she was assured by angels that Ishmael would have many descendants (Gen. 21:9–

ISCARIOT, JUDAS. Judas betrays Jesus with a kiss—the prearranged code that let the temple officers know who to arrest.

18). Tradition holds that the Arab peoples are descendants of Ishmael. See also *Hagar*.

ISHMAELITES. Descendants of Ishmael, Abraham's son by Hagar (Gen. 16:15). God promised to bless the Ishmaelites, although Ishmael was not Abraham's covenant son (Gen. 21:12–13). Ishmael had twelve sons, whose descendants lived as nomads in the deserts of northern Arabia. Most modern-day Arabs claim descent from Ishmael. See also *Arabia*.

ISH-TOB. See *Tob*.

ISRAEL

1. Another name for Jacob. Jacob was renamed Israel by an angel at Penuel because of his influence with God and man (Gen. 32:28; 35:10). His name was extended to the nation of Israel (Exod. 3:16) and finally narrowed to designate the Northern Kingdom after the nation divided following Solomon's administration. See also *Jacob*.

2. The Northern Kingdom. This nation was formed in 931 B.C. when the ten northern tribes rebelled against the two southern tribes and established their own kingship under Rehoboam (1 Kings 12). Samaria was established as the capital city. After about two centuries, the Northern Kingdom was carried into captivity by Assyria in 722 B.C. and Samaria was populated by foreigners (2 Kings 17:23–24). See also *Samaritan*.

ISRAELITES. Descendants of Israel, or Jacob (Gen. 35:9–12), a nation that was designated by God as His special people. The Israelites were regarded as children of the covenant and heirs of the promises that God made to Abraham (Gen. 12:1–3; Rom. 9:4; 11:1). See also *Jews*.

ISSACHAR. Jacob's fifth son by Leah; father of one of the twelve tribes of Israel (Gen.

30:17–18). The tribe occupied fertile land bounded on the north by Zebulon and Naphtali, on the east by the Jordan River, and on the south and west by Manasseh. The judges Deborah and Barak are assumed to be Issacharites, since they came from this territory (see Judg. 4–5). See also *Tribes of Israel*.

ITALIAN BAND (ITALIAN COHORT, ITALIAN REGIMENT). A unit of the Roman army stationed in Caesarea. Cornelius, one of the first Gentile converts to Christianity, was attached to this unit (Acts 10:1). *Italian Regiment:* NIV; *Italian Cohort:* NRSV.

ITALY. The boot-shaped country between Greece and Spain that juts into the Mediterranean Sea (Acts 18:2). Its capital city, Rome, was the seat of the Roman Empire in N.T. times. Paul sailed to Rome as a prisoner (Acts 27:1–6; 28:14–16).

ITCH. See *Scall*.

ITHAMAR. The youngest son of Aaron who was consecrated as a priest (Exod. 6:23). He oversaw the tabernacle during the wilderness wanderings (Exod. 38:21).

ITUREA. A small province in Palestine at the base of Mount Hermon. This area was ruled by Herod Philip when John the Baptist began his ministry (Luke 3:1).

IVAH, IVVAH. See *Ahava*.

IVORY. Decorative trim from the tusks of elephants that was a symbol of luxury. King Ahab's house was known as the "ivory house" (1 Kings 22:39). See also *Ahab*.

IYYAR. See *Zif*.

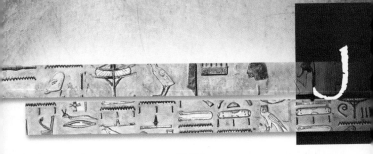

JAAZER. See *Jazer*.

JABBOK. A small stream that enters the Jordan River about twenty miles north of the Dead Sea (Num. 21:24). Beside this stream, at a point later called Peniel, Jacob wrestled with an angel (Gen. 32:24–31).

JABESH-GILEAD. A city of Gilead about twenty miles south of the Sea of Galilee. King Saul defended this city against Nahash, king of the Ammonites (1 Sam. 11:1–11).

JABIN

1. The Canaanite king of Hazor who was killed by Joshua at the Merom Brook (Josh. 11:1–14).

2. Another king of Hazor who was defeated by Deborah and Barak at the Kishon River (Judg. 4).

JACHIN (JAKIN) AND BOAZ. Two ornamental bronze pillars, constructed by Hiram of Tyre, that stood in front of Solomon's temple at Jerusalem (1 Kings 7:13–22). *Jakin:* NIV.

JACKAL. A jackal was a wild dog that often traveled in packs. This figurine is from Roman times.

JACINTH. A precious stone, perhaps the same as sapphire, used in the foundation of the heavenly city, or New Jerusalem (Rev. 21:20). See also *Ligure*.

JACKAL. A wild dog, or a scavenger that ran in packs. The "foxes" that Samson used to destroy crops of the Philistines may have been jackals (Judg. 15:4). See also *Fox*.

JACOB. The son of Isaac and Rebekah and father of several sons who became the ancestors of the twelve tribes of Israel. Jacob was the twin brother of Esau, who was the firstborn son and thus entitled to the birthright of his father, Isaac. But Jacob bought Esau's birthright for a pot of stew (Gen. 25:29–34). With his mother, Rebekah's, help, he deceived his father and received his blessing as well (Gen. 27:6–29).

While fleeing his brother's wrath, Jacob struggled with an angel and was given the name Israel, meaning "prince with God" (Gen. 32:22–30). His descendants were known as Israelites, or descendants of Israel.

In his later years, after the birth of many children to his wives, Rachel and Leah, and their handmaids, Jacob mourned his favorite son, Joseph, whom he presumed dead. But his joy was restored when Joseph was discovered alive and well in Egypt. Jacob died in Egypt after moving there at Joseph's initiative to escape a famine in Canaan. He was returned to his homeland for burial. See also *Israel; Israelites*.

JACOB'S WELL. The well dug by Jacob and the site where Jesus offered the Samaritan woman "living water" (John 4:1–26). Not mentioned in the O.T., the site today is associated with the ancient city of Shechem (Tell Balatah) near the highway from Jerusalem to Galilee.

JAEL. The wife of Heber the Kenite who killed Sisera, a commander of the forces of King Jabin of Hazor (Judg. 4:17–22). See also *Sisera*.

JAFFA. See *Joppa*.

JAH. See *Jehovah*.

JAIR. The eighth judge of Israel, a member of the tribe of Gilead, who led the nation for twenty-two years (Judg. 10:3–5). See also *Judges of Israel*.

JAIRUS. A ruler of the synagogue near Capernaum whose daughter was raised from the dead by Jesus (Mark 5:22–23).

JAKIN. See *Jachin*.

JAMBRES. A magician of the Egyptian pharaoh who opposed Moses. While he is not mentioned in the O.T., Jambres is cited by Paul as a person who resisted God's truth (2 Tim. 3:8).

JAMES
  1. A son of Zebedee and a disciple of Jesus. He and his brother John were called "sons of thunder" by Jesus because of their fiery temperament (Mark 3:17).
  2. A son of Alphaeus and a disciple of Jesus (Matt. 10:3).
  3. The half brother of Jesus who became a leader in the church at Jerusalem (Acts 21:17–18; Gal. 1:19). He was probably the author of the epistle of James. See also *Brothers of Christ*.

JAMES, EPISTLE OF. A short N.T. epistle—written probably by James, the half brother of Jesus—known for its plain language and practical application of the gospel to the believer's daily life. According to James, the true test of Christianity is in the living and doing of its truth rather than in the speaking, hearing, and even believing of its doctrines (1:22–27).

Authentic faith results in acts of ministry to others, or as James puts it, "Faith, if it hath not works, is dead" (2:17). Other emphases in James are equality of all people before God (2:1–10) and the power of the tongue (3:3–10).

JANNES. A magician of the Egyptian pharaoh who opposed Moses. While he is not mentioned in the O.T., Jannes is cited by Paul as a person who resisted God's truth (2 Tim. 3:8).

JAPHETH. A son of Noah who was saved in the ark (Gen. 5:32). Japheth is considered the father of the Indo-European races (Gen. 9:18–27; 10:2–5).

JAPHO. See *Joppa.*

JAR. See *Cruse; Pitcher.*

JASHER. See *Book of Jasher.*

JASHOBEAM. The chief of David's mighty men, or brave warriors, who helped him become king and kept his kingdom strong (1 Chron. 11:10–11). See also *Mighty Men.*

JASON. A citizen of Thessalonica who was persecuted because he provided lodging for Paul and Silas (Acts 17:5–9). This may be the same Jason whom Paul referred to as "my kinsman" (Rom. 16:21).

J

JAVELIN. Egyptian warriors carry javelins and shields, used in battle.

JASPER. A precious stone, probably a type of quartz, used in the breastplate of the high priest (Exod. 28:20) and in the foundation of the heavenly city, or New Jerusalem (Rev. 21:19).

JAVAN. A son of Japheth and grandson of Noah. Javan was the father of the Ionians, or Greeks (Gen. 10:2; Isa. 66:19). See also *Greece.*

JAVELIN (SPEAR). A short spear or dart. A javelin was used by King Saul (1 Sam. 19:9–10) and by the high priest Phinehas (Num. 25:7). *Spear:* NIV, NRSV. See also *Dart; Spear.*

JAZER/JAAZER. A fortified Amorite city east of the Jordan River (2 Sam. 24:5) noted for its fertile land (Num. 32:1) and occupied by the conquering Israelites (Josh. 13:24–25). *Jaazer:* Num. 21:32.

JEALOUSY. Ill feelings toward others because of their blessings or favored position. Jacob's sons were jealous of their brother Joseph because he was their father's favorite (Gen. 37:11). Christians are counseled not to participate in such behavior (Rom. 13:13). See also *Envy.*

JEBUS. See *Jerusalem.*

JEBUSITES. Tribal enemies of the Israelites who were descended from Canaan (Gen. 10:15–16). They controlled Jerusalem (known as Jebus at that time) before David conquered the city (2 Sam. 5:6–8) and turned it into his capital. Remnants of the Jebusites became bondservants during Solomon's reign (1 Kings 9:20–21). See also *Jerusalem.*

JECONIAH. See *Jehoiachin.*

JEDIDIAH. A name for Solomon, meaning "beloved of Jehovah," bestowed on him at birth

by Nathan the prophet (2 Sam. 12:25). This name suggested that David's sin of adultery had been forgiven.

JEDUTHUN/ETHAN. A Levite musician and writer of psalms (1 Chron. 9:16) who led in praise services when the ark of the covenant was returned to Jerusalem (1 Chron. 16:41–42). *Ethan:* 1 Chron. 6:44.

JEHOAHAZ/SHALLUM

1. The son and successor of Jehu as king of Israel (reigned 814–798 B.C.; 2 Kings 10:35). A wicked king, he led Israel into sin and idolatry (2 Kings 13:2).

2. The son and successor of Josiah as king of Judah about 610 B.C. A sinful monarch, he reigned only three months before being deposed by Pharaoh Nechoh of Egypt (2 Kings 23:31–34). *Shallum:* 1 Chron. 3:15.

3. Another name for Ahaziah, king of Judah about 850 B.C. See *Ahaziah, No. 2.*

JEHOASH. See *Joash, No. 1.*

JEHOIACHIN/CONIAH/JECONIAH/ JECHONIAS. The son and successor of Jehoiakim as king of Judah (reigned only three months, about 597 B.C.). Evil like his father, Jehoiachin was king when the nation was captured by Nebuchadnezzar and the people were deported to Babylonia (2 Kings 24:8–16). He was released after thirty-seven years in prison (Jer. 52:31–34). Jehoiachin is listed as an ancestor of Christ (Matt. 1:11–12). *Coniah:* Jer. 22:24; *Jeconiah:* 1 Chron. 3:16–17; *Jechonias:* Matt. 1:11–12.

JEHOIADA

1. A military leader at Hebron who apparently recruited 3,700 of his countrymen to serve in David's army (1 Chron. 12:27).

2. A high priest who protected young King Joash from Queen Athaliah until Joash was crowned king of Judah. Jehoiada also led in reducing Baal worship (2 Kings 11:4–21). See also *Joash,* No. 1.

JEHOIAKIM/ELIAKIM. The son and successor of Josiah as king of Judah (reigned about 609–597 B.C.). An evil ruler who exploited the people and led them into idolatry, Jehoiakim died while Jerusalem was under siege by the Babylonians (2 Chron. 36:6). The prophet Jeremiah foretold his defeat (Jer. 22:18–19). *Eliakim:* 2 Kings 23:34.

JEHORAM/JORAM

1. The wicked king of Judah (reigned about 848–841 B.C.) who murdered his own brothers (2 Chron. 21:1–4) in order to succeed his father, Jehoshaphat (1 Kings 22:50). Struck down by God, he died in disgrace, as predicted by the prophet Elijah, from a mysterious disease (2 Chron. 21:12–20). *Joram:* 2 Kings 8:21.

2. Ahab's son and successor as Israel's king (reigned about 852–841 B.C.; 2 Kings 1:17). He died in battle against the Syrians (2 Kings 8:28–29). *Joram:* 2 Kings 8:16.

JEHOSHABEATH/JEHOSHEBA. The daughter of King Jehoram of Judah who hid her nephew Joash from Queen Athaliah's wrath until Joash was crowned king (2 Chron. 22:11–12). *Jehosheba:* 2 Kings 11:2.

JEHOSHAPHAT/JOSAPHAT. The son and successor of Asa as king of Judah (reigned about 870–848 B.C.). A reformer like his father, Jehoshaphat attacked idolatry and sent teachers to help people learn about God (2 Chron. 17:3–9). He was rebuked by the prophet Jehu for forming an alliance with King Ahab of Israel (2 Chron. 19:1–3). *Josaphat:* Matt. 1:8.

JEHOSHAPHAT, VALLEY OF. A place where God will judge the nations in the end-time, according to the prophet Joel (Joel 3:2–14). This site is believed to be part of the Kidron Valley between Jerusalem and the Mount of Olives. The name may refer to a symbolic "valley of decision," where God will judge all nations.

JEHOSHEBA. See *Jehoshabeath.*

JEHOSHUA. See *Joshua.*

JEHOVAH/JAH. A translation of *Yahweh,* a Hebrew word for God in the O.T. that indicated his eternity and self-existence. This word is based on a Hebrew verb meaning "to be"; thus the name "I AM" by which God revealed Himself to Moses at the burning bush (Exod. 3:14).

Yahweh is rendered as "Lord" and printed in small capital letters (LORD) in most English versions of the Bible, although some translations use *Yahweh* or *Jehovah. Jah* is an abbreviated form of this name (Ps. 68:4). See also *I Am; Lord; Yahweh.*

JEHOVAH-JIREH. A name for God meaning "the Lord will provide." It was used by Abraham to commemorate God's provision of a ram in place of Isaac as a sacrifice (Gen. 22:14).

JEHOVAH-NISSI. A name for God meaning "the Lord is my banner." Moses used this name to show God's victory over the Amalekites (Exod. 17:15–16).

JEHOVAH-SHALOM. The name of an altar built by Gideon, meaning "the Lord is peace" (Judg. 6:24).

JEHOVAH-SHAMMAH. The name of a

city of the future envisioned by the prophet Ezekiel, indicating that "the Lord is there" (Ezek. 48:35).

JEHOVAH-TSIDKENNU. The name for the coming Messiah used by the prophet Jeremiah, meaning "the Lord our righteousness" (Jer. 23:6).

JEHU

1. A violent and deceitful king of Israel (reigned about 841–814 B.C.) who gained the throne by killing King Ahab's descendants (2 Kings 9–10).

2. A prophet who delivered a message of doom to King Baasha of Israel (1 Kings 16:1–2) and rebuked King Jehoshaphat of Judah for forming alliances with King Ahab (2 Chron. 19:1–3).

KING JEHU'S MISSION

Jehu was anointed king of Israel by the prophet Elisha (2 Kings 9:1–13) in order to end the dynasty of the wicked king Ahab, who had encouraged Baal worship among his subjects. Jehu seized the throne by assassinating Ahab's son and successor, King Jehoram/Joram. Then he murdered the other sons of Ahab as well as Ahab's wife, Queen Jezebel, to assure that no one connected with Ahab would ever rule over Israel.

JEPHTHAH/JEPHTHAE. A judge of Israel who delivered the nation from the Ammonites. After making a rash and foolish vow, Jephthah sacrificed his only child as an offering to God (Judg. 11). *Jephthae:* Heb. 11:32. See also *Judges of Israel.*

JEREMIAH/JEREMIAS/JEREMY. A major prophet of the O.T. who preached God's message of doom to the nation of Judah for about forty years during the reigns of the last five kings of the nation: Josiah, Jehoahaz, Jehoiakim, Jehoiachin, and Zedekiah (Jer. 1:2–3). Called to his prophetic ministry even before he was born (Jer. 1:4–10), he wept openly over the sins of Judah (Jer. 9:1) and declared that the nation would fall to a foreign enemy as punishment for its sin and idolatry (Jer. 16:1–13).

After Judah was overrun by the Babylonians, Jeremiah remained in Jerusalem while most of his countrymen were deported to Babylonia. Eventually he was taken to Egypt, where he continued to preach to a remnant of Jewish people (Jer. 43:5–13). *Jeremias:* Greek form (Matt. 16:14); *Jeremy:* Matt. 2:17; 27:9.

JEREMIAH, BOOK OF. A major prophetic book of the O.T. noted for its stern warnings to the nation of Judah that it was destined to fall to the Babylonians unless the people repented and turned back to God. After being called and assured of God's guidance and presence (chap. 1), Jeremiah pronounced prophecies of doom against Judah (chaps. 2–45) and then the surrounding pagan nations (chaps. 46–51). The book closes with a description of the destruction of Jerusalem (52:1–23) and the deportation of the influential people of Judah to Babylonia (52:24–30).

The concept of a new covenant (chap. 31) is unique to the book of Jeremiah. This new agreement between God and His people, based on grace and forgiveness, was needed because the old covenant of law had failed to keep the people on the path of righteousness and holiness. See also *Babylonia.*

JERICHO. A fortified Canaanite city near the Jordan River and the Dead Sea (Deut. 32:49)

JERUSALEM. Jerusalem, seen from the Mount of Olives in the east. (Inset) The crowded Damascus Gate serves as a marketplace as well as an entrance into the Old City of Jerusalem.

that was captured by Joshua when the Israelites entered the Promised Land (Josh. 6:1–22).

JEROBOAM

1. Jeroboam I. The first king of Israel (reigned about 931–910 B.C.) after the kingdom of Solomon split into two separate nations following Solomon's death. An official in Solomon's administration, Jeroboam led the ten northern tribes to rebel against the two southern tribes when Rehoboam succeeded his father, Solomon, as king (1 Kings 12:17–20). Jeroboam established idol worship in the cities of Bethel and Dan (1 Kings 12:26–30) and was ultimately defeated by King Abijah of Judah and struck down by the Lord (2 Chron. 13:19–20).

2. Jeroboam II. A wicked king of Israel (reigned about 782–753 B.C.) who succeeded his father, Jehoash (2 Kings 14:23–29). He was denounced by the prophet Amos for his evil deeds and encouragement of idol worship (Amos 7:7–9).

JERUBBAAL/JERUBBESHETH.

A name given to the judge Gideon by his father after he destroyed the altar of Baal at Ophrah (Judg. 6:32). It probably means "let Baal contend." Another name given to Gideon was Jerubbesheth (2 Sam. 11:21; Jerubbaal: NRSV), probably meaning "contender with the idol." See also Gideon.

JERUSALEM/JEBUS/SALEM.

The religious and political capital of the Jewish people. Situated forty-eight miles from the

Mediterranean Sea and eighteen miles west of the Jordan River, Jerusalem was known as *Salem* in Abraham's time (Gen. 14:18) and as *Jebus* when the people of Israel entered Canaan, or the Promised Land (Josh. 15:8).

David captured the city from the Jebusites, renamed it, and turned it into his capital (2 Sam. 5:6–9). It was often called the "city of David" (2 Chron. 32:5). Solomon built the magnificent temple in Jerusalem as the center of worship for the Jewish people about 950 B.C. (1 Kings 5:5–8). The city fell to the Babylonians in 587 B.C., and its leading citizens were taken away as captives (Jer. 39:1–8).

After the Persians defeated the Babylonians, King Cyrus of Persia allowed Jewish exiles to return to their homeland and rebuild Jerusalem, including the temple and the city wall (Ezra 1:1–4; Neh. 12:27–47; Zech. 4).

In N.T. times, Christ wept over the city because of its sin and spiritual indifference (Luke 19:41–42). He predicted its destruction (Luke 19:43–44), entered Jerusalem as a conquering spiritual leader (Matt. 21:9–10), and was crucified on a hill just outside the city wall (Luke 23:33). As Jesus predicted, Jerusalem was destroyed in A.D. 70 during a fierce battle between the Roman army and Jewish zealots.

The church was launched in Jerusalem, where it experienced spectacular growth (Acts 2). The apostle John described the future heavenly city as "new Jerusalem" (Rev. 21:2). See also *City of David; Jebusites; Zion*.

JERUSALEM COUNCIL. A conference held during the early days of the Christian movement to determine how Gentile believers would be received into the church. Participants representing the church at Antioch and the church in Jerusalem included Peter, Paul, Barnabas, and James.

The issue was whether Gentile converts first had to identify with Judaism by being circumcised before they could be baptized and received as full members of the church (Acts 15:6).

The council concluded that since Gentile and Jewish believers are saved by grace alone, circumcision was unnecessary (Acts 15:6–19). This solution averted a conflict that would have hampered missionary efforts and could have made Christianity a sect of Judaism. See also *Judaizers*.

JESHANAH GATE. See *Old Gate*.

JESHUA

1. A priest who returned to Jerusalem with Zerubbabel after the Babylonian Exile and helped rebuild the temple and reestablish worship (Ezra 2:2; 3:2–9).

2. Another name for Joshua (Neh. 8:17). See *Joshua*.

JESSE. The father of David and an ancestor of Christ. Jesse presented his eight sons to the prophet Samuel, who anointed David as the future king of Israel (1 Sam. 16:10–13). Jesse is mentioned in Scripture as the root or shoot that would produce the royal line of David (Isa. 11:1, 10; Rom. 15:12) and ultimately the Savior (Matt. 1:5–6).

JESUS CHRIST. The Son of God and Savior of the world. Jesus is the Greek form of the name *Joshua*, meaning "Savior." Christ means "the anointed one," identifying Him as the promised Messiah of O.T. prophecy (Gal. 4:4–5).

Jesus was born during the reign of Herod the Great, Roman ruler over Palestine, sometime before 4 B.C., the date of Herod's death (Matt. 2:1). After a public ministry of perhaps three years, He was crucified about A.D. 30. He

JESUS CHRIST. Astonished disciples watch as Jesus meets with Moses and Elijah on the Mount of Transfiguration.

preexisted as the eternal Word of God (John 1:1, 18; 8:58) and participated in the creation of the world (John 1:3). His advent in human form, including his virgin birth in Bethlehem (Isa. 7:14; Mic. 5:2), was foretold in the O.T. (Ps. 2:7–8; Isa. 9:6–7). As the God-man, Jesus was incarnated to reveal God in an understandable way (Matt. 1:23; John 1:14–18) and "to make reconciliation for the sins of the people" (Heb. 2:17–18).

As a boy, Jesus grew physically and advanced in knowledge (Luke 2:51–52). Yet He had a consciousness of His divine mission (Luke 2:49). He was baptized by John the Baptist to "fulfill all righteousness" and to identify with humanity (Matt. 3:15–17). In resisting Satan's temptations at the beginning of His public ministry, the sinless Savior refused to break dependence on the Father and to establish His kingdom in any fashion other than by suffering (Matt. 4:7–10).

Jesus' public ministry was short and revolutionary (John 17:4). He came preaching and healing (Mark 1:38–42), teaching (Luke 6:6), and seeking the lost (Luke 19:10). After an early campaign in Judea in southern Palestine, He began a major campaign in the region of Galilee in northern Palestine with Capernaum as His home base. His hometown synagogue in Nazareth rejected Him, but the common people heard Him gladly (Luke 4:16–32).

Jesus proclaimed a spiritual kingdom that required repentance and faith rather than blind and ritualistic obedience to the law and the legalistic demands of the Pharisees (Matt. 6:10, 33; Luke 13:3). His later ministry was devoted to training His disciples and preparing them for His death and their witness to others in the Holy Spirit's power (Luke 24:46–49).

Jesus' actions such as denouncing the Pharisees (Matt. 23), healing on the Sabbath (Matt. 12:8–14), and cleansing the temple angered the religious leaders among the Jews and disturbed Roman officials (Matt. 21:23). His triumphal entry into Jerusalem on a donkey disappointed His followers who wanted an earthly king (Luke 24:17–21). After observing the Passover with His disciples and instituting the Lord's Supper, He was betrayed into enemy hands (Luke 22:15–21).

In His trial before Pilate, Jesus acknowledged His kingship but declared His kingdom "not of this world" (John 18:36–37). Nevertheless, He was charged with treason and crucified between two thieves (Luke 23:33; John 19:14–16). On the third day He arose from the grave, conquering sin and death for believers (Acts 13:30; 1 Cor. 15:57). He ascended to the Father, where He "ever liveth to make intercession" (Heb. 7:25).

Christ will return for righteous judgment (Acts 17:31), to raise the dead (1 Thess. 4:14–17), and to usher in the time when everyone must confess that "Jesus Christ is Lord" (Phil. 2:9–11; Rev. 11:15). See also *Emmanuel; Messiah; Son of God; Son of Man.*

JETHRO/REUEL/HOBAB. The father-in-law of Moses who was a priest of Midian. Moses married his daughter Zipporah (Exod. 2:16–22; 4:18). Jethro visited Moses in the wilderness and advised him to select leaders to share the responsibility of dispensing justice and settling disputes among the Hebrews (Exod. 18:17–26). *Reuel:* Exod. 2:18; *Hobab:* Judg. 4:11.

JEWELS. Precious stones used as ornaments or jewelry. The breastplate of Aaron the high priest contained twelve jewels symbolizing the twelve tribes of Israel (Exod. 25:7).

JEWS. A word for the Israelites that came into general use during the period after the

Babylonian Exile. In the N.T., it designates Israelites as opposed to Gentiles. See also *Israelites.*

JEZEBEL. The scheming wife of King Ahab who promoted Baal worship in the nation of Israel (Northern Kingdom). She led Ahab to erect pagan altars (1 Kings 16:32–33), killed several prophets of the Lord (1 Kings 18:4–13), and plotted the death of the prophet Elijah (1 Kings 19:1–2), who prophesied her death (1 Kings 21:23). King Jehu had Jezebel assassinated when he came into power, in fulfillment of Elijah's prophecy (2 Kings 9:7–37). See also *Ahab.*

JEZREEL

1. A symbolic name given by the prophet Hosea to his son to show that King Jehu and his family would be punished for murdering King Ahab's family. The name means "God scatters" or "God sows" (Hosea 1:3–5).

2. A fortified city where King Ahab's palace was located (1 Kings 21:1) and where his family was assassinated by Jehu's forces (2 Kings 10:1–11).

3. The name of a valley in O.T. times that separated Samaria from Galilee. Many major battles have occurred here. Some scholars believe the battle of Armageddon in which Satan will be overthrown will be fought in this valley (Rev. 16:16; 20:1–10). The Greek word for this valley is *Esdraelon.*

JOAB. The commander of King David's army during most of David's reign (2 Sam. 8:15–16). He became commander because he was the first to launch an attack against the Jebusites in their fortified city known as Jebus (later called Jerusalem; see 1 Chron. 11:6). His military exploits included victories over the Edomites (1 Kings 11:15) and the Ammonites (2 Sam.

10:6–14). Joab carried out David's plan to have Uriah the Hittite killed in battle (2 Sam. 11:14). He was murdered on orders from the king when Solomon succeeded David as ruler of Judah (1 Kings 2:5–6, 31–34).

JOANNA. A woman who was a faithful follower of Jesus (Luke 8:1–3). She prepared spices for His burial and proclaimed His resurrection (Luke 23:55–56; 24:1–10).

JOASH/JEHOASH

1. The eighth king of Judah (reigned about 798–782 B.C.) who succeeded his father, Ahaziah (2 Kings 11:20), at age seven. He was hidden by his aunt from wicked Queen Athaliah to prevent his assassination (2 Kings 11:1–3). Jehoiada the priest served as his counselor (2 Kings 11:12, 17). Joash brought needed religious reforms to Judah (2 Kings 12:4–5), but he turned to idol worship after Jehoiada's death (2 Chron. 24:17–19). He was assassinated by his own officers (2 Chron. 24:24–25). *Jehoash:* 2 Kings 11:21.

2. The son and successor of Jehoahaz as king of Israel (reigned about 798–782 B.C.). He led the nation into sin through his idolatry (2 Kings 13:10–25).

JOATHAM. See *Jotham.*

JOB. A godly man of the O.T. whose faith sustained him through fierce trials and sufferings. Afflicted by Satan with God's permission (Job 1:6–19), Job refused to blame or curse God for his misfortune (1:20–22; 2:10), although he did complain to God, lamenting the day he was born (3:1).

Job and his three friends had long discussions about his misfortunes and what they meant. He eventually came to a greater understanding of God's ways of dealing with humans (42:3–6), and God restored his family and possessions (42:10–15). Job was praised by James in the N.T. for his patience and faith (James 5:11).

JOB OF UZ

The exact location of the land of Uz where Job lived (Job 1:1) is unknown. The best guess is that it was east of the Jordan River in the Arabian desert. This land is mentioned in only two other places in the Bible (Jer. 25:20; Lam. 4:21).

JOB, BOOK OF. A wisdom book of the O.T. that addresses the issue of human suffering, particularly the question of why the righteous suffer. The book is written in the form of a poetic drama revolving around the discussion of this problem by Job and his three friends: Eliphaz, Bildad, and Zophar.

After Job lost his children and earthly possessions (chaps. 1–2), his three friends arrived to "comfort" him and discuss the reason for Job's suffering (chaps. 3–37). God assured Job that He is the sovereign, almighty God who doesn't have to defend His actions (chaps. 38–41). Armed with a new understanding of God and His nature ("I have heard of thee by the hearing of the ear: but now mine eye seeth thee," 42:5), Job was rewarded by the Lord with the restoration of his family and possessions (42:10–15). See also *Wisdom Literature.*

JOCHEBED. The mother of Moses, Aaron, and Miriam (Exod. 6:20). She is listed as one of the heroes of the faith (Heb. 11:23).

JOEL

1. A prophet of Judah in the days of King Uzziah and author of the O.T. book that bears his name. He predicted the outpouring of God's Spirit at Pentecost (Joel 2:28–32; Acts 2:16–21), proclaimed salvation through Christ (Joel 2:32), sounded the note of God's universal judgment (Joel 3:1–16), and pictured the eternal age with blessings for God's people (3:17–21).

2. The son of Samuel and a corrupt judge of Israel. Joel's dishonesty, along with that of his brother Abiah, led the people to ask Samuel to appoint a king to rule the nation (1 Sam. 8:2–5).

JOEL, BOOK OF. A brief prophetic book of the O.T. that uses a devastating swarm of locusts (chap. 1) as an early warning sign of God's judgment in order to call His people to repentance. The prophet predicted the outpouring of God's Spirit (2:28–32), an event that happened on the day of Pentecost (Acts 2:16–21); proclaimed salvation through Christ (2:32); and pictured the eternal age with blessings for God's people (3:17–21). See also *Pentecost.*

JOHANAN. A supporter of Gedaliah, governor of Judah (2 Kings 25:22–23), who took a remnant of the Jews to Egypt, in spite of the prophet Jeremiah's warning (Jer. 41:16–18; 43:4–6).

JOHN THE APOSTLE. A fisherman from Galilee, the son of Zebedee and brother of James, who became one of the twelve apostles of Jesus (Matt. 4:21–22). He was described as the disciple "whom Jesus loved" and a member of Christ's inner circle of disciples, which included his brother James and Simon Peter (Mark 5:37; 9:2; 14:33). John was ambitious for position and prestige in Christ's kingdom

(Mark 10:35–37), but he showed a willingness to die for Jesus (Mark 10:38–39).

Associated with Peter in bold evangelism in Jerusalem after Jesus' ascension (Acts 4:13; 8:14–15), John left Jerusalem about A.D. 65 for Ephesus, where he wrote the Fourth Gospel and the three epistles of John. He wrote the book of Revelation while exiled as a political prisoner on the island of Patmos (Rev. 1:9–11).

JOHN THE BAPTIST. The prophet of righteousness and preacher of repentance who prepared the way for Christ. John's birth, Nazarite lifestyle, and unique role as the Messiah's forerunner were revealed to his father, Zechariah (Luke 1:13–17), and his mother, Elizabeth, a cousin of Mary—the mother of Jesus (Luke 1:5–7, 39–41).

John preached repentance and baptized converts in the Jordan River (Matt. 3:1–6), reluctantly agreeing to baptize Jesus after proclaiming Him as the "Lamb of God" (Matt. 3:13–17; John 1:29).

John denounced the hypocrisy of the Pharisees and the immorality and adultery of Herod Antipas, a Roman ruler in Palestine (Matt. 3:7–8; 14:4). He was executed by Herod at the request of his wife, Herodias's, dancing daughter (Matt. 14:3–12). John always magnified Jesus rather than himself (John 3:30), and Jesus commended him highly for his faithfulness (Luke 7:24–28).

JOHN, EPISTLES OF. Three short epistles of the N.T. written by John, one of the twelve disciples of Jesus.

First John, the longest of the three, focuses on such themes as the incarnation of Christ (1:1–5), Christian discipleship (1:6–10), false teachings about Christ (2:1–8), and the meaning of love and fellowship (2:15–5:3). Second John calls on believers to abide in the commandments of God (vv. 1–10) and reject false teachers (vv. 7–13). Third John commends the believers Gaius (vv. 1–8) and Demetrius (v. 12), while condemning Diotrephes (vv. 9–11).

The apostle John probably wrote these epistles from Ephesus about A.D. 95. See also *Demetrius, No. 2; Elect Lady; Gaius, No. 4; John the Apostle.*

JOHN THE BAPTIST. As the son of a priest, John the Baptist could have enjoyed the luxury of life in Jerusalem. Instead, he became a traveling prophet who dressed in camel hair clothing and ate locusts and wild honey.

J

JOHN, GOSPEL OF. One of the four Gospels of the N.T., written by the apostle John to show that "Jesus is the Christ, the Son of God" (20:31). John is unique among the Gospels in that it majors on the theological meaning of the events in Jesus' life rather than the events themselves. Many of the miracles of Jesus are interpreted as "signs" of His divine power and unique relationship to the Father (2:1–11; 5:1–18).

The "I am" sayings of Jesus, in which He reveals selected attributes or characteristics of His divine nature, are also unique to the Gospel of John. See also *John the Apostle; Synoptic Gospels.*

SEVEN SIGNS OF JESUS IN JOHN'S GOSPEL

1. Turning of water into wine (John 2:1–11)
2. Healing of a nobleman's son (John 4:46–54)
3. Healing of a paralyzed man (John 5:1–9)
4. Feeding of the five thousand (John 6:5–14)
5. Walking on the water (John 6:15–21)
6. Healing of a man born blind (John 9:1–7)
7. Raising of Lazarus from the dead (John 11:38–44)

JOKTAN. A son of Eber and descendant of Shem. He was an ancestor of several tribes in the Arabian desert (1 Chron. 1:19–27).

JONAH/JONAS. An O.T. prophet who was swallowed by a "great fish" while fleeing from God's call to preach to the pagan citizens of Nineveh in Assyria (Jon. 1:17). In predicting His death and resurrection, Jesus referred to Jonah's experience (Luke 11:30; *Jonas*). See also *Assyria; Nineveh.*

JONAH, BOOK OF. A short prophetic book of the O.T. that emphasizes God's universal love. Jonah, the "reluctant prophet" (1:1–2:10), finally preached to the citizens of Nineveh in Assyria, a pagan nation noted for its cruelty and opposition to Israel. To his surprise and disappointment, the pagans repented and turned to God (4:1–10). Through this experience, Jonah learned that God is concerned for all people, not just the citizens of his native land (4:1–11). See also *Assyria.*

JONATHAN

1. King Saul's oldest son (1 Sam. 14:49), who was a loyal friend of David, even while his father was trying to kill David (1 Sam. 20). David mourned Jonathan (2 Sam. 1:17–26) after he was killed by the Philistines (1 Sam. 31:2). See also *Mephibosheth.*

2. A supporter of David during Absalom's rebellion. Jonathan hid in a well to warn David of Absalom's plans (2 Sam. 17:17–21).

JONATHAN: A LOYAL FRIEND

The friendship between David and Jonathan is a model of rich and meaningful personal relationships. Jonathan was so committed to David that he risked his life to warn David that Jonathan's father, King Saul, was determined to kill him (1 Sam. 20).

Jonathan was eventually killed by the Philistines, but David never forgot his loyal friend. After David became king, he provided food and lodging for Jonathan's handicapped son, Mephibosheth, at the royal palace in Jerusalem (2 Sam. 9).

JOPPA/JAFFA/JAPHO. A coastal city on the Mediterranean Sea where Peter had his vision of full acceptance of the Gentiles (Acts 10:9–23). This area is known today as *Jaffa*, a part of the city of Tel Aviv. *Japho:* Josh. 19:46.

JORAM. See *Jehoram.*

JORDAN RIVER. The largest and most important river in Palestine. It runs the length of the country, from the Sea of Galilee in the north to the Dead Sea in the south. Jesus was baptized by John in the Jordan (Matt. 3:13).

JOSAPHAT. See *Jehoshaphat.*

JOSEPH

1. The son of Jacob by Rachel who was sold to a band of traders by his jealous brothers. Enslaved and imprisoned in Egypt, Joseph became an important official under the pharaoh. He was eventually reunited with his father and brothers when they came to Egypt to buy grain. A model of faith and forgiveness, Joseph saw God at work in human events (Gen. 37–50; Heb. 11:22). He was called *Zaphnath-paaneah* by the Egyptian pharaoh (Gen. 41:45).

2. The husband of Mary, Jesus' mother. A descendant of King David (Matt. 1:20), he was a carpenter (Matt. 13:55) and a righteous man (Matt. 1:19). Joseph took Mary as his wife after an angel explained Mary's condition (Matt. 1:19–25). He was with Mary when Jesus was born in Bethlehem (Luke 2:16). He took his family to Egypt to escape Herod's wrath, then returned later

to Nazareth, where the young Jesus was obedient to His earthly parents (Matt. 2:13–23; Luke 2:51). Since Joseph does not appear later in the Gospels, it is likely that he died before Jesus' public ministry.

3. A devout man from Arimathea (Luke 23:50–51) and secret disciple of Jesus (John 19:38) who prepared Jesus' body for burial and placed Him in his own tomb (Mark 15:43–46; Luke 23:53).

4. A half brother of Jesus. See *Brothers of Christ.*

JORDAN RIVER. Israel's largest river, the Jordan, flows out of the Sea of Galilee and winds its way seventy miles south, emptying into the Dead Sea.

J

JOSES

1. A half brother of Jesus (Mark 6:3). See *Brothers of Christ*.

2. Another name for Barnabas. See *Barnabas*.

JOSHUA/OSHEA/HOSHEA/JEHOSH-UAH/JESHUA.

Moses' successor who led the Israelites into the Promised Land and rallied the people to victory over the Canaanites. One of two spies who gave Moses a favorable report on Canaan (Num. 13:8), he was the Lord's choice as Moses' successor (Num. 27:18–20).

After his conquest of Canaan (Josh. 10–12), Joshua divided the land among the twelve tribes (Josh. 13–19). Before his death, he led the people to renew their covenant with God (Josh. 24:15–27). *Oshea:* Num. 13:8; *Hoshea:* Deut. 32:44; *Jehoshuah:* 1 Chron. 7:27; *Jeshua:* Neh. 8:17.

JOSHUA, BOOK OF.

A book of the O.T. that details the conquest and settlement of the land of Canaan by the Israelites under the leadership of Joshua.

Major events covered by the book include (1) Joshua's succession of Moses as leader of the people and their spiritual preparation for conquest (chaps. 1–5); (2) battles against the Canaanites and allied tribes (6:1–13:7), (3) division of the land among the tribes of Israel (13:8–19:51); (4) the cities of refuge and Levitical cities (chaps. 20–21); and (5) the farewell address and death of Joshua (chaps. 23–24). See also *Cities of Refuge; Joshua; Levitical Cities*.

JOSIAH/JOSIAS.

The son and successor of Amon as king of Judah (reigned 640–609 B.C.; 2 Kings 21:26). Crowned at age eight, he made a covenant to obey God (2 Kings 23:3) and led an important reform movement to reestablish God's law, repair the temple (2 Kings 22:3–9), and abolish idolatry (2 Kings 23:4–24). *Josias:* Jesus' ancestry (Matt. 1:10–11).

JOTHAM/JOATHAM.

The son and successor of Azariah (Uzziah) as king of Judah (reigned about 750–732 B.C.). A contemporary of the prophets Isaiah, Hosea, and Micah (Isa. 1:1; Mic. 1:1), he was a good king but failed to destroy places of pagan worship (2 Kings 15:34–35). Jotham improved the temple, strengthened the city wall, and fortified buildings throughout Judah (2 Chron. 27:3–4). *Joatham:* Matt. 1:9.

JOY.

Great delight or positive feelings. Joy attended Christ's birth (Luke 2:10) and resurrection (Matt. 28:8). A believer's spiritual joy is produced by the Holy Spirit (Luke 10:21; Phil. 4:4).

Ps. 16:11 in thy [God's] presence is fulness of *j*
Ps. 30:5 *j* cometh in the morning
Ps. 51:12 Restore...the *j* of thy [God's] salvation
Ps. 126:5 They that sow in tears shall reap in *j*
Hab. 3:18 I will *j* in the God of my salvation
Matt. 2:10 they [wise men]...rejoiced with...great *j*
Luke 15:10 *j*...over one sinner that repenteth
John 16:20 your sorrow shall be turned into *j*
Acts 20:24 I [Paul] might finish my course with *j*
Rom. 14:17 kingdom of God is...peace, and *j*
Gal. 5:22 fruit of the Spirit is love, *j*, peace
Heb. 12:2 who [Jesus] for the *j*...set before him
James 1:2 count it all *j* when ye fall into divers temptations
3 John 4 no greater *j*...children walk in truth

JOYFUL [LY]

Ps. 35:9 my soul shall be *j* in the LORD
Ps. 66:1 Make a *j* noise unto God, all ye lands
Ps. 149:5 Let the saints be *j* in glory
Eccles. 9:9 Live *j'ly* with the wife whom thou lovest
Isa. 49:13 Sing, O heavens; and be *j*, O earth

JUBAL.

A son of Lamech, descendant of Cain, and a skilled musician regarded as the ancestor of those who play the harp and the flute (Gen. 4:21).

JUBILE (JUBILEE). A year of celebration devoted to liberty and justice and observed every fifty years by the Israelites. During this year, Israelites serving as indentured servants were released from their debts and set free. All properties that had been given up because of indebtedness since the last Jubilee were returned to the original owners. Cropland was allowed to go unplanted as a conservation measure (Lev. 25:8–55). *Jubilee:* NIV, NRSV.

JUDAH/JUDA

1. A son of Jacob and Leah and ancestor of the tribe of Judah (Gen. 29:35). Judah interceded for his brother Joseph to be sold rather than killed (Gen. 37:26–27). He offered himself as a ransom for his brother Benjamin before Joseph in Egypt (Gen. 43:8–9; 44:32–34). His father, Jacob, predicted that Judah's descendants would become the royal line from which the Messiah would emerge (Gen. 49:10). He is listed as an ancestor of Christ (Matt. 1:2–3) and called *Juda* in Luke's ancestry (Luke 3:33). The tribe Judah is spelled *Juda* in the N.T. (Heb. 7:14). See also *Tribes of Israel.*

2. The Southern Kingdom, or nation of Judah. Founded after Solomon's death, the Southern Kingdom was composed largely of the tribes of Judah and Benjamin, while the rebellious ten northern tribes retained the name of Israel. Solomon's son Rehoboam was the first king of Judah, with the capital at Jerusalem (1 Kings 14:21).

The nation of Judah drifted into paganism and idolatry under a succession of kings, turning a deaf ear to great prophets such as Isaiah and Jeremiah, who tried to bring them back to worship of the one true God. Judah was overrun and taken into exile by the Babylonians about 587 B.C. A remnant returned to rebuild Jerusalem about 530 B.C. (2 Chron. 36:20–23).

JUDAIZERS. An early Christian sect that advocated that Gentiles must be circumcised before they could become Christians (Acts 15:1). They were denounced by Paul, who insisted that believers are justified by faith alone (Acts 15:12; Gal. 6:15). The Judaizers were also opposed by Peter and James at the Jerusalem Council (Acts 15:8–19). See also *Circumcision; Jerusalem Council.*

JUDAS. See *Iscariot, Judas; Jude.*

JUDAS, BROTHER OF JAMES/LEBBAEUS/THADDAEUS. One of the twelve disciples of Jesus, also called *Lebbaeus* (Matt. 10:3) and *Thaddaeus* (Mark 3:18). He was called "brother of James" to set him apart from the Judas who betrayed Jesus (Luke 6:16). See also *Twelve, The.*

JUDE/JUDAS. The half brother of Christ and author of the N.T. epistle that bears his name. He did not believe in Jesus in the beginning (John 7:5), but he apparently became a disciple after His resurrection (Acts 1:14). *Judas:* Matt. 13:55. See also *Brothers of Christ.*

JUDE, EPISTLE OF. A short N.T. letter written like a brief essay or tract and addressed to the problem of false teachings in the early church. Jude called on believers to root their faith in the true doctrine taught by the apostles (v. 17) as well as the love of Christ (v. 21).

JUDEA. A district in southern Palestine in N.T. times. The name was derived from *Jewish,* a word describing Jewish exiles who returned to southern Palestine from the Babylonian Exile about 530 B.C. Judea was a Roman province annexed to Syria when Jesus was born (Matt. 2:1).

JUPITER. Jupiter, better known by the Greeks as Zeus, was the chief god in Roman times. After people of one village saw Barnabas and Paul perform miracles, they thought the men were gods Jupiter and Hermes, arriving for a visit.

JUDGE [S]

Gen. 18:25 Shall not the **J** of all the earth do right?

1 Sam. 2:10 Lᴏʀᴅ shall **j** the ends of the earth

Ps. 7:8 **j** me, O Lᴏʀᴅ, according to my righteousness

Ps. 43:1 **J** me, O God, and plead my cause

Ps. 72:2 He [God] shall **j** thy people with righteousness

Prov. 31:9 **j** righteously, and plead the cause of the poor

Matt. 7:1 **J** not, that ye be not judged

John 7:24 **J** not according to the appearance

Rom. 14:10 why dost thou **j** thy brother

2 Tim. 4:1 Jesus Christ, who shall **j** the quick and the dead

James 2:4 ye...are become **j's** of evil thoughts

Rev. 19:11 in righteousness he [Jesus] doth **j**

JUDGES, BOOK OF. A historical book of the O.T. that records the exploits of several different judges, or military deliverers, in Israel's history. The key to understanding Judges is the phrase "The children of Israel again did evil in the sight of the Lᴏʀᴅ" (see 4:1), which occurs several times throughout the book.

After each period of sin against God, He would send enemy oppressors in judgment. The Israelites would repent and pray for a deliverer, and God would answer their prayer. After their deliverance at the hand of a judge, the cycle of sin/oppression/repentance/deliverance would start all over again. See also *Judges of Israel.*

JUDGES OF ISRAEL. Popular military leaders or deliverers who led Israel between the time of Joshua's death and the beginning of the kingship (about 1380–1050 ʙ.ᴄ.). Israel's judges served in times of disunity and spiritual decline among the twelve tribes (Judg. 17:6; 21:25) as well as times when all the tribes were oppressed by their enemies.

While some judges were weak or wicked, noteworthy exploits include Deborah and Barak's defeat of the Canaanite king Jabin (4:4–24), Gideon's 300 warriors who subdued the Midianites (7:1–8:21), and Samson's massacre of the Philistines (15:14–16).

JUDGMENT. Divine retribution against human activities. God's judgment is designed to punish evil (Exod. 20:5), to correct the misguided (2 Sam. 7:14–15), and to deter His people from wrongdoing (Luke 13:3–5). His judgment is an expression of His chastening love for the believer (Heb. 12:5–6). Jesus, God's resurrected Son, has authority to judge all humankind (John 5:27; Acts 17:31). Believers in Jesus will avoid condemnation and enter eternal life (John 9:39). See also *Punishment; Retribution.*

Exod. 12:12 against all the gods of Egypt I [God]...execute *j*
1 Chron. 18:14 David reigned...and executed *j*
Job 8:3 Doth God pervert *j*?
Ps. 72:2 He [God] shall judge...thy poor with *j*
Ps. 119:66 Teach me good *j* and knowledge
Prov. 29:26 every man's *j* cometh from the Lord
Eccles. 12:14 God shall bring every work into *j*
Jer. 9:24 I am the Lord which exercise...*j*
Jer. 33:15 he [Messiah] shall execute *j* and righteousness
Amos 5:24 let *j* run down as waters
John 5:30 as I [Jesus] hear, I judge: and my *j* is just
John 9:39 For *j* I [Jesus] am come into this world
Rom. 14:10 we shall all stand before the *j* seat of Christ
Heb. 9:27 unto men once to die, but after this the *j*
1 Pet. 4:17 *j* must begin at the house of God
1 John 4:17 may have boldness in the day of *j*
Rev. 14:7 Fear God...hour of his *j* is come

JUDGMENT, LAST. Final judgment of unbelievers of all ages. The final judgment is called a day of wrath for unbelievers (Rom. 2:5–8) but a day when believers will enter into eternal life (Rom. 2:7). The Lord will appear suddenly to gather His elect (Matt. 24:32, 42) and to separate unbelievers for judgment (Matt. 25:31–33). We should be prepared for this time (1 Thess. 5:1–11) and avoid self-deception regarding God's final judgment (Matt. 7:21–27). See also *Day of the Lord; Hell; Tribulation, Great.*

JUG. See *Cruse.*

JUNIPER (BROOM). A bush with dense twigs that was used for charcoal (Ps. 120:4). *Broom:* NIV, NRSV.

JUPITER (ZEUS). The chief god of Roman mythology and a name applied to Barnabas by the superstitious citizens of Lystra (Acts 14:12). The Greek name for this god was *Zeus* (NIV, NRSV).

JUST [LY]
Gen. 6:9 Noah was a *j* man
Job 4:17 Shall mortal man be more *j* than God?
Ps. 37:12 wicked plotteth against the *j*
Prov. 11:1 a *j* weight is his [God's] delight
Prov. 20:7 The *j* man walketh in his integrity
Mic. 6:8 doth the Lord require...but to do *j'ly*
Hab. 2:4 the *j* shall live by his faith
Matt. 1:19 Joseph her [Mary's] husband, being a *j* man
1 John 1:9 he [Jesus] is faithful and *j* to forgive us our sins

JUSTICE. Fair and impartial treatment; righteousness. Justice is characteristic of God's nature (Deut. 32:4) and descriptive of Christ (Acts 3:14) and believers (Heb. 12:14). Just dealings with others by God's people were demanded by the O.T. prophets (Mic. 6:8; Amos 5:24). God's justice is fair and merciful (Acts 17:31).

Job 8:3 doth the Almighty pervert *j*
Ps. 82:3 do *j* to the afflicted and needy
Prov. 21:3 To do *j*...is more acceptable...than sacrifice
Jer. 23:5 a King [Jesus] shall...execute...*j*

JUSTIFICATION. The act or event when God both declares and makes a person just or right with Him (Rom. 4:25; 5:9). Justification is not accomplished by personal merit or good works (Gal. 2:16) but by God's grace through personal faith in Christ (Rom. 5:18; Eph. 2:8–9). To be justified is to have peace with God and hope for eternity (Titus 3:5–7). See also *Atonement; Propitiation; Reconciliation.*

JUSTIFIED
Job 25:4 How then can man be *j* with God?
Matt. 12:37 by thy words thou shalt be *j*
Rom. 3:24 *j* freely by his [God's] grace
Rom. 3:28 *j* by faith without the deeds of the law
Rom. 5:1 being *j* by faith, we have peace with God
1 Cor. 6:11 ye are *j* in the name of the Lord
Gal. 2:16 man is not *j* by the works of the law
James 2:21 Was not Abraham our father *j* by works

K

KAB. See *Cab.*

KADESH/KADESH-BARNEA. A wilderness region between Canaan and Egypt that served as the southern boundary of the Promised Land (Num. 34:4). The Israelites camped in this area during the wilderness wandering years before they entered the Promised Land (Num. 32:8; 27:14). *Kadesh-barnea:* Josh. 14:7. See also *Wilderness Wanderings.*

KEDAR. A son of Ishmael, grandson of Abraham, and founder of an Arabic tribe that lived in the desert between Arabia and Babylonia (Gen. 25:12–13).

KEDESH/KEDER/KISHION/KISHON

1. One of the six cities of refuge, situated in the territory of Naphtali in northern Palestine (Josh. 20:1–7). This city is now called *Keder.* See also *Cities of Refuge.*

2. A Canaanite town captured by Joshua

KADESH. *Kadesh-barnea, an oasis along the Egyptian-Israeli border, is where Moses and the Israelites probably spent much of their forty years in the wilderness, waiting for God to allow them into the Promised Land.*

(Josh. 12:7, 22) and allotted to the tribe of Issachar (1 Chron. 6:72). *Kishion:* Josh. 19:20; *Kishon:* Josh. 21:28.

KEEP [ING]

Exod. 20:8 Remember the sabbath day, to *k* it holy
Ps. 91:11 he [God] shall...*k* thee in all thy ways
Prov. 4:23 *K* thy heart with all diligence
Eccles. 3:7 time to *k* silence...time to speak
Hab. 2:20 earth *k* silence before him [God]
Luke 2:8 shepherds...*k'ing* watch over their flock
John 14:15 love me [Jesus], *k* my commandments
Phil. 4:7 peace of God...*k* your hearts...through Christ
2 Tim. 1:12 he [Jesus] is able to *k* that...I [Paul] have committed
1 John 5:3 this is the love of God...*k* his commandments
Jude 24 unto him [Jesus]...able to *k* you from falling

KENAN/CAINAN. A son of Enoch and grandson of Adam who lived in the days before the great flood (1 Chron. 1:1–2). *Cainan:* Gen. 5:9.

KENITES. A nomadic Midianite tribe associated with the Amalekites (Gen. 15:19). Friendly toward the Israelites, this tribe was likely absorbed into Judah (1 Sam. 27:10).

KENIZZITES. A Canaanite tribe whose land was promised to Abraham's descendants (Gen. 15:18–19).

KENOSIS. Relating to the dual nature of Christ—His divinity and humanity. Citing Phil. 2:7, advocates of this theory claim that God's Son laid aside or "emptied himself" of certain divine attributes when He became human. Most scholars reject the notion that Jesus stopped being God or that He gave up any divine attributes. Rather, the phrase refers to Christ's voluntary servanthood (John 17:5).

KEPT

Ps. 18:21 For I have *k* the ways of the LORD
Ps. 32:3 When I *k* silence, my bones waxed old
Matt. 19:20 these things have I *k* from my youth

Luke 2:19 Mary *k* all these things...in her heart
Gal. 3:23 before faith came, we were *k* under the law
2 Tim. 4:7 I [Paul]...have fought a good fight...*k* the faith
1 Pet. 1:5 *k* by the power of God through faith

KERIOTH. A town in southern Judah (Josh. 15:25). This may have been the hometown of Judas Iscariot, Jesus' disciple and betrayer, since Iscariot means "man of Kerioth."

KETTLE. A vessel used for cooking and in worship rituals (1 Sam. 2:14). The Hebrew word for "kettle" is also translated "basket," "caldron," or "pot" (Jer. 24:2; Job 41:20). See also *Caldron.*

KETURAH. The wife of Abraham after Sarah's death (Gen. 25:1). The six sons born to their union were ancestors of six Arabian tribes in Palestine or Arabia (1 Chron. 1:33).

KEY. A tool used to unlock a door. In Bible times, keys were long rods with metal pins (Judg. 3:25). The word is also used figuratively as a symbol of authority (Isa. 22:22; Rev. 1:18).

KID. A young goat. Kids were used as sacrificial offerings or butchered for special occasions (Luke 15:29). See also *Goat.*

KIDNEY. See *Reins.*

KIDRON/CEDRON. A valley or ravine with a wet-weather stream near Jerusalem. David crossed the Kidron Brook while fleeing from his son Absalom (2 Sam. 15:13–23). Idols from pagan cults were burned in this valley (1 Kings 15:13). Jesus probably crossed this valley on the night of His arrest (John 18:1; *Cedron*).

KILL [ED, EST, ETH]

Exod. 20:13 Thou shalt not *k*
Ps. 44:22 for thy [God's] sake are we *k'ed* all the day long

KID. A boy in the Middle East cradles in his arms a kid—a young goat. Kids were among the animals offered as sacrifices in Bible times.

K

KING. The monarch or supreme ruler of a nation. Beginning with the first king, Saul, who was anointed with God's authority (1 Sam. 10:1), Judah and Israel had a succession of kings across several centuries until both nations were overrun by foreign powers.

The books of 1 and 2 Samuel, 1 and 2 Kings, and 1 and 2 Chronicles report on the reigns of many of these kings. A few were godly and kind rulers who honored God and followed His law, but most were evil and corrupt. They led God's people into sin and idolatry.

The believer should remember that God is our eternal King, worthy of all honor (1 Tim. 1:17). Christ, our ultimate ruler, is Lord of Lords and King of Kings (John 18:37; Rev. 17:14).

Eccles. 3:3 A time to *k*, and a time to heal
Matt. 23:37 Jerusalem...thou that *k'est* the prophets
Mark 8:31 Son of man must suffer...and be *k'ed*
Luke 12:4 Be not afraid of them that *k* the body
Luke 15:23 bring hither the fatted calf, and *k* it
Luke 22:2 sought how they might *k* him [Jesus]
John 16:2 whosoever *k'eth* you...think...doeth God service
Rom. 8:36 For thy sake we are *k'ed* all the day long
2 Cor. 3:6 letter *k'eth*...spirit giveth life

KINDRED. Relatives, or members of one's immediate or extended family. The clan or tribe was the basic family unit in early Hebrew history. Family members considered it their duty to protect one another (Gen. 34). See also *Family; Kinsman-Redeemer.*

KINE (COW). An archaic word for a cow or an ox (Gen. 32:15). The prophet Amos used this word for the oppressive, indulgent leaders of Israel (Amos 4:1–3). *Cow:* NIV, NRSV.

KINGDOM [S]
Exod. 19:6 unto me [God] a *k* of priests
2 Sam. 7:16 thine [David's]...*k*...established for ever
Ps. 68:32 Sing unto God, ye *k's* of the earth
Dan. 4:3 his [God's] *k* is an everlasting *k*
Matt. 6:10 Thy [God's] *k* come. Will be done
Matt. 24:7 nation...against nation...*k* against *k*
Mark 3:24 *k*...divided against itself...cannot stand
Luke 1:33 of his [Jesus'] *k* there shall be no end
Luke 12:32 Father's good pleasure to give you the *k*
John 18:36 My [Jesus'] *k* is not of this world
1 Thess. 2:12 God, who hath called you unto his *k*
Rev. 11:15 *k's* of this world are become the *k's* of our Lord

KINGDOM OF GOD. The spiritual reign of God in the hearts of believers (Luke 17:20–21). Partially attained in this life for those who seek God's will, God's kingdom will be fully established in the world to come (John 18:36). Jesus preached the "gospel of the kingdom" (Mark 1:14) and taught His disciples to seek His kingdom (Matt. 6:33) and to pray for its arrival on earth (Matt. 6:10).

Unrepentant sinners cannot inherit this kingdom (Eph. 5:5). It is reserved for those who repent (Matt. 3:2) and experience spiritual rebirth (John 3:3–5). Other phrases for this kingdom are "kingdom of heaven" (Matt. 4:17) and "kingdom of Christ" (Col. 1:13).

Rom. 14:17 *k-o-G* is not meat and drink; but righteousness

1 Cor. 6:9 the unrighteous shall not inherit the *k-o-G*

1 Cor. 15:50 flesh and blood cannot inherit the *k-o-G*

KINGDOM OF HEAVEN

Matt. 5:10 Blessed...[the] persecuted...theirs is the *k-o-h*

Matt. 5:20 shall in no case enter into the *k-o-h*

Matt. 7:21 Not every one...saith...Lord, Lord...enter...*k-o-h*

Matt. 16:19 I [Jesus] will give...thee...keys...*k-o-h*

Matt. 18:4 humble...little child...greatest in the *k-o-h*

Matt. 23:13 ye [scribes and Pharisees] shut up the *k-o-h*

KINGS, BOOKS OF. Two historical books of the O.T. that cover a period of roughly four centuries in Jewish history—from about 970 to 587 B.C. First Kings records the reign of Solomon as successor to David (1 Kings 1–11); the division of the kingdom into two separate nations, Judah and Israel (12–14); and the reigns of selected kings in both these nations until the time of Ahaziah of Israel (about 853–852 B.C.)

Second Kings continues the narrative of Ahaziah's reign (chap. 1) and reports on the reigns of selected kings in both nations up until the time of the fall of the Northern Kingdom under Hoshea (reigned about 730–722 B.C.; chap. 17). Chapters 18 through 25 cover the final years of the surviving nation of Judah, until it fell to the Babylonians in 587 B.C. See also *King*.

KING'S DALE/SHAVEH. The ancient name for a valley east of Jerusalem where Abraham met the king of Sodom and Melchizedek (Gen. 14:17–18). Also called *Shaveh*, this is perhaps the same place as the Valley of Jehoshaphat (Joel 3:2). See *Jehoshaphat, Valley of.*

KING'S HIGHWAY. An important road linking Damascus and Egypt that ran through Israel. While in the wilderness, the Israelites were denied passage on this road as they traveled toward Canaan (Num. 20:17–21).

KINSMAN-REDEEMER. A close relative who had first option to buy back or redeem personal freedom or property that had been forfeited by impoverished members of the clan (Lev. 25:48–49). Boaz, a near kinsman of Naomi, acted as a redeemer in his marriage to Ruth (Ruth 4). Jesus is our "elder brother" who redeems the believer (Heb. 2:11–17). See also *Kindred.*

KIRIOTH/KERIOTH. A fortified city in Moab and possibly its capital in the eighth century B.C., since the prophet Amos predicted its destruction (Amos 2:2). *Kerioth:* Jer. 48:24, 41.

KIRJATH-ARBA. See *Hebron.*

KIRJATH-JEARIM/BAALAH. A fortified city of the Gibeonites where the ark of the covenant was kept for twenty years before being taken to Jerusalem (1 Chron. 13–16). *Baalah:* Josh. 15:9.

KISHION/KISHON. See *Kedesh*, No. 2.

KISHON/KISON. A river in the valley of Jezreel in northern Palestine where Elijah killed the prophets of Baal (1 Kings 18:40). *Kison:* Ps. 83:9.

KISLEV. See *Chisleu.*

KISS. A sign of affection practiced by parents and children (Gen. 27:26). Jesus was betrayed by Judas with a kiss (Matt. 26:49).

KISS [ED]

Gen. 50:1 Joseph...wept upon him [Jacob], and *k'ed* him
Ps. 85:10 righteousness and peace have *k'ed* each other
Luke 15:20 his [prodigal son's] father...*k'ed* him
Luke 22:48 Judas, betrayest thou...with a *k*
2 Cor. 13:12 Greet one another with an holy *k*
1 Pet. 5:14 Greet ye one another with a *k* of charity

KITE. A bird of prey belonging to the hawk family and regarded as unclean by the Israelites (Deut. 14:12–13).

KITTIM. See *Cyprus.*

KNEADING TROUGH. A large bowl used to knead dough to prepare it for baking (Exod. 12:34).

KNEEL. A symbol of respect (Ps. 95:6) or subjection and surrender (2 Kings 1:13). Kneeling was also a customary stance in prayer, indicating reverence for God (Luke 22:41). See also *Bowing.*

KNIFE. A sharp-edged weapon or tool made of flint or bronze (Josh. 5:2).

KNIFE. A gold ceremonial knife from Babylon, in what is now Iraq. Most knives in Bible times were made of flint, bronze, or iron.

KNOCK [ED]

Luke 11:9 *k*, and it shall be opened unto you
Acts 12:13 as Peter *k'ed*...a damsel came
Rev. 3:20 I [Jesus] stand at the door, and *k*

KNOP. An Old English word for the ornamental cap on a column. The word is also used for a decoration on the golden candlesticks in the tabernacle (Exod. 25:31–36).

KNOWLEDGE. A body of facts or information gained through study and experience. The prophets of the O.T. lamented the Israelites' lack of knowledge (Isa. 5:13). Paul indicated that knowledge of God is to be desired above all else (Phil. 3:8). The verb "to know" was often used in the O.T. for sexual intimacy (Gen. 4:1).

Gen. 2:17 tree of the *k* of good and evil...not eat
1 Sam. 2:3 LORD is a God of *k*
Job 21:22 Shall any teach God *k*?
Job 35:16 he [Job] multiplieth words without *k*
Ps. 144:3 man, that thou [God] takest *k* of him
Prov. 1:7 fear of the LORD...beginning of *k*
Prov. 20:15 lips of *k* are a precious jewel
Prov. 24:5 man of *k* increaseth strength
Eccles. 1:18 he that increaseth *k* increaseth sorrow
Hab. 2:14 earth...filled with the *k* of...the LORD
1 Cor. 13:2 though I [Paul]...understand...all *k*
1 Tim. 2:4 all men...to come unto the *k* of the truth
2 Pet. 1:5 add to your faith virtue...to virtue *k*
2 Pet. 3:18 grow in grace, and in the *k* of our Lord

KOHATH. The second son of Levi (Gen. 46:8, 11) and founder of the Kohathites, priests who cared for the ark of the covenant and other accessories used in the tabernacle in the wilderness (Num. 3:30–31). Moses and Aaron were Kohathites (Exod. 6:18–20).

KORAH/CORE. A grandson of Kohath who incited a rebellion against Moses and Aaron in the wilderness. Korah and his followers were swallowed by the earth as punishment for their sin (Num. 16:28–33). *Core:* Greek form (Jude 11).

LABAN. A brother of Jacob's mother, Rebekah, and father of Leah and Rachel, who were given in marriage to Jacob. Jacob visited Laban to escape the wrath of his brother, Esau (Gen. 27:43). He worked seven years for Laban for the privilege of marrying Rachel, only to be tricked into marrying Leah instead. Then Jacob worked another seven years for Rachel (Gen. 29:18–30).

LABORER. An unskilled worker who performed such menial tasks as tilling the fields and gathering the crops in Bible times (Ruth 2:2; Ps. 90:10). See also *Hireling*.

LABOUR [ED]
Exod. 20:9 Six days shalt thou *l*, and do all thy work
Ps. 127:1 Except the LORD build...they *l* in vain that build it
Eccles. 3:13 man should...enjoy the good of all his *l*
Matt. 11:28 Come unto me [Jesus], all ye that *l*
1 Cor. 15:58 your *l* is not in vain in the Lord
Phil. 2:16 I [Paul] have not...*l'ed* in vain
Heb. 4:11 Let us *l* therefore to enter into that rest

LABOURER [S]
Matt. 9:37 harvest...is plenteous, but the *l's* are few
Luke 10:7 the *l* is worthy of his hire
1 Cor. 3:9 we are *l's* together with God

LACHISH. An Amorite city in southern Judah captured by Joshua (Josh. 10:31–35) and later besieged by King Sennacherib of Assyria (2 Kings 18:13–14). Lachish was reoccupied by the Israelites after the Babylonian Exile (Neh. 11:30).

LACK
Hosea 4:6 people are destroyed for *l* of knowledge
Matt. 19:20 things have I [rich young ruler] kept...what *l* I yet
James 1:5 any of you *l* wisdom, let him ask of God

LAISH. See *Dan*, No. 2.

LAKE OF FIRE. The place of final punishment. Filled with burning brimstone (Rev. 19:20), this place is described as the "second death" (Rev. 20:14). Those consigned to the lake of fire include Satan (Rev. 20:10), persons not named in the Book of Life (Rev. 20:15), and unbelieving sinners (Rev. 21:8). See also *Hell*.

LAKE OF GENNESARET. See *Galilee, Sea of*.

LAMB. A young sheep, used for food (2 Sam. 12:4), clothing (Prov. 27:26), and religious sacrifices (Exod. 12:5, 7). A lamb also symbolized the sufferings of Christ (Isa. 53:7) and the reign of the Messiah (Isa. 11:6). See also *Sheep*.

LAMB OF GOD. A title of Christ that emphasizes the sacrificial nature of His life and His atoning death. This aspect of His ministry was foretold by the prophet Isaiah (Isa. 53:7). John the Baptist greeted Jesus with this title (John 1:29, 36). As the Lamb of God, Jesus is worthy of eternal honor and praise (Rev. 5:12–13). See also *Atonement; Cross*.

LAME. Unable to walk due to an injury (2 Sam. 4:4) or a birth defect (Acts 3:2). Persons with this disability were healed by Jesus (Matt. 11:5) and Peter (Acts 3:2–7).

LAMECH. A son of Methuselah and a man of faith who found "comfort" in the birth of his son Noah (Gen. 5:25–31). Lamech is listed in the ancestry of Jesus (Luke 3:36).

LAMENTATIONS OF JEREMIAH. A short O.T. book that expresses in poetic form the prophet Jeremiah's deep grief and anguish at the destruction of Jerusalem and the Jewish temple by the pagan Babylonians. Chapter 4 paints a bleak picture of life in Jerusalem during the extended siege against the city. See also *Babylonia; Jeremiah.*

IMAGES OF DESPAIR IN LAMENTATIONS

The prophet Jeremiah used numerous images of despair in Lamentations to show his anguish over the fall of Jerusalem. He spoke of throwing dust on one's head (Lam. 2:10), a sign of mourning. He described people as hissing and shaking their heads (Lam. 2:15–16) to show their contempt for the fallen city. The phrase "The crown is fallen from our head" (Lam. 5:16) expresses the loss of Judah's position of honor.

LAMP. See *Candle.*

LAMPSTAND. See *Candlestick.*

LANCE. See *Spear.*

LAND OF PROMISE. Canaan, or the land inhabited by the Israelites. This land was promised by God to Abraham's descendants (Gen. 12:1–7). The promise was fulfilled centuries later when Joshua led the Israelites to take the land from the Canaanites (Josh. 10–12). See also *Canaan, No. 2; Palestine.*

LANDMARK (BOUNDARY STONE, MARKER). A marker, usually consisting of a pile of stones, that indicated property lines. Removal of a landmark was forbidden (Deut. 19:14). *Boundary stone:* NIV; *marker:* NRSV.

LANDOWNER. See *Goodman.*

LANTERN. A torch covered with skin or transparent horn for outdoor use. On the night before His crucifixion, Jesus was arrested by armed men with lanterns (John 18:3). See also *Torch.*

LAODICEA. A major city in Asia Minor, located on the Lycus River. One of the seven churches addressed in the book of Revelation was located in Laodicea (1:11). This church was rebuked because of its complacency (Rev. 3:14–18).

LAPIDOTH (LAPPIDOTH). The husband of Deborah the prophetess (Judg. 4:4). *Lappidoth:* NIV, NRSV. See also *Deborah.*

LAPWING (HOOPOE). A small European bird, considered unclean by the Hebrews, that wintered in Palestine (Lev. 11:19; Deut. 14:12, 18). *Hoopoe:* NIV, NRSV.

LASCIVIOUSNESS (DEBAUCHERY, LICENTIOUSNESS). Unbridled lust, a sin characteristic of life apart from Christ (1 Pet. 4:3), which believers are warned to avoid.

According to Paul, victory over lasciviousness requires repentance (2 Cor. 12:21) and living in the spirit of Christ (Gal. 5:19, 22–25). *Debauchery:* NIV; *licentiousness:* NRSV.

LAST

Isa. 44:6 I [God] am the first, and...the *l*
Mark 9:35 desire to be first...shall be *l*
Mark 10:31 many that are first shall be *l*
1 Cor. 15:26 The *l* enemy...destroyed is death
1 Cor. 15:45 the *l* Adam was made a quickening spirit
2 Tim. 3:1 in the *l* days perilous times shall come
Heb. 1:2 in these *l* days spoken...by his [God's] Son
Rev. 1:11 I [Jesus] am Alpha and Omega...first and the *l*

LAST SUPPER. See *Lord's Supper.*

LATCHET (THONGS). A strap that fastened a sandal to the foot (Gen. 14:23). John the Baptist declared he was unworthy to untie the latchet of Christ's sandals (Mark 1:7). *Thongs:* NIV, NRSV. See also *Sandal.*

LATTER RAIN (SPRING RAIN). The rain that fell late in the growing season, allowing crops to reach full maturity before the harvest (Jer. 3:3). *Spring rain:* NIV, NRSV. See also *Former Rain; Rain.*

LATTICE. A screened opening or porch on a house to provide privacy and let in night breezes (Judg. 5:28; 2 Kings 1:2).

LAUNDERER. See *Fuller.*

LAVER (BASIN). A container placed near the altar outside the tabernacle where priests could wash their hands and feet before offering animal sacrifices (Exod. 30:17–21). *Basin:* NIV, NRSV. See also *Bason.*

LAW, LAW OF MOSES. The authoritative rule of conduct spelled out in the Ten Commandments and the Pentateuch—the books of Genesis, Exodus, Leviticus, Numbers, and Deuteronomy. This code was revealed to Moses by the Lord on Mount Sinai (Deut. 5:1–2). While many of the regulations are ceremonial or procedural in nature, the moral law embodied in the Law of Moses is eternal and unchangeable (Rom. 7:7–12). It was fulfilled by the gospel and confirmed by Christ (Matt. 5:17–18). See also *Moses.*

LAWFUL [LY]

Matt. 19:3 Is it *l* for a man to put away his wife
Mark 3:4 Is it *l* to do good on the sabbath...or...to do evil?
Mark 12:14 Is it *l* to give tribute to Caesar
1 Tim. 1:8 law is good, if a man use it *l'ly*

LAWYER/SCRIBE. An interpreter or teacher of the law in the synagogues and schools of N.T. times (Matt. 22:34–40), also called a *scribe* (Luke 11:53). See also *Scribe.*

LAY [ING]

Prov. 10:14 Wise men *l* up knowledge
Matt. 6:20 *l* up...treasures in heaven
Luke 9:58 Son of man hath not where to *l* his head
John 10:15 I [Jesus] *l* down my life for the sheep
John 15:13 man *l* down his life for his friends
1 Tim. 5:22 *L* hands suddenly on no man
Heb. 12:1 *l* aside...sin which doth...beset us
1 Pet. 2:1 *l'ing* aside all malice, and all guile

LAYING ON OF HANDS. A ritual blessing or ordination for service. This ritual was used by the high priest on the Day of Atonement. By placing his hands on the scapegoat, he ritually transferred the sins of the people to the animal (Lev. 16:21).

The patriarchs placed their hands on their descendants to confirm birthright or convey special blessings (Gen. 48:14, 18). The church at Antioch laid hands on Paul and Barnabas to confirm their calling as missionaries and to set them apart for this service (Acts 13:2–3).

LAZARUS. A brother of Mary and Martha whom Jesus raised from the dead. This event impressed the common people (John 11:41–45) but provoked the Jewish leaders to seek the death of both Jesus and Lazarus (John 11:47–57; 12:10–11).

LEAD. A heavy metal cast into weights (Zech. 5:8). It was also a useful agent for refining gold and silver (Num. 31:22–23). The word is used figuratively for the cleansing of Israel (Jer. 6:29).

LEAD [ETH]
Ps. 23:2 he [God] *l'eth* me beside the still waters
Ps. 61:2 *l* me to the rock that is higher than I

Isa. 11:6 a little child shall *l* them
Isa. 40:11 He [God]...gently *l* those...with young
Matt. 6:13 *l* us not into temptation
Matt. 7:14 narrow is the way, which *l'eth* unto life

LEAGUE (COMPACT, TREATY). An alliance of nations for fostering common interests and providing protection against enemies (2 Sam. 5:3). Leagues with the Canaanites and other pagan nations were prohibited (Exod. 23:31–33). *Compact:* NIV (1 Kings 5:12). *Treaty:* NIV, NRSV. See also *Alliance.*

LEAH. Laban's oldest daughter and Jacob's first wife (Gen. 29:16–25). She bore seven children (Gen. 29:32–35; 30:17–21) and remained loyal

LAZARUS. Jesus calls Lazarus back from the dead—four days after Lazarus died.

to Jacob when he had to flee from Laban (Gen. 31:17–20). See also *Jacob*.

LEANNOTH. A musical term of uncertain meaning in the title of Ps. 88.

LEARN [ED, ING]
Prov. 1:5 A wise man...will increase *l'ing*
Matt. 11:29 Take my [Jesus'] yoke...and *l* of me
Phil. 4:11 I [Paul] have *l'ed*...therewith to be content
2 Tim. 3:7 *l'ing*, and never able to come to...truth
Heb. 5:8 he [Jesus] were a Son, yet *l'ed* he obedience

LEAST
Matt. 25:40 ye have done it unto one of the *l* of these
Luke 7:28 *l* in the kingdom...greater than he [John the Baptist]
Luke 9:48 *l* among you all...shall be great
Eph. 3:8 Unto me [Paul]...less than the *l* of all saints

LEATHER. Treated animal skins used for clothing (Lev. 13:48), tent coverings (Exod. 26:14), sandals (Ezek. 16:10), and water and wine containers (Matt. 9:17). See also *Tanner*.

LEAVEN (YEAST). A fermentation agent used in making bread or wine (Hosea 7:4; 1 Cor. 5:6). Jesus used the term to warn against the teachings of the Pharisees and Sadducees (Matt. 16:11–12; Luke 12:1). *Yeast:* NIV, NRSV.

LEBANON. A rugged mountainous region in northern Palestine. Cedar and fir trees from Lebanon were used in the construction of the temple in Jerusalem under Solomon (1 Kings 5:6–10; 7:2).

LEBBAEUS. See *Judas, Brother of James*.

LEBO-HAMATH. See *Hamath*.

LED
Luke 4:1 Jesus...*l* by the Spirit into the wilderness
Luke 24:50 he [Jesus] *l* them out as far as to Bethany
Acts 8:32 He [Jesus] was *l* as a sheep to the slaughter

Rom. 8:14 *l* by the Spirit of God...are the sons of God
Gal. 5:18 if ye be *l* of the Spirit...not under the law

LEECH. See *Horseleach*.

LEEK. An onionlike plant. In the wilderness, the Israelites longed for this vegetable that they had enjoyed in Egypt (Num. 11:5).

LEES (DREGS). The waste that settled to the bottom of the container in the process of wine making (Isa. 25:6). The term is used figuratively for indifference or laziness (Jer. 48:11; Zeph. 1:12). *Dregs:* NIV, NRSV. See also *Dregs*.

LEGION
  1. A Roman military division consisting of several thousand foot soldiers plus cavalrymen (John 18:3–12).
  2. Any large number, such as angels available to Jesus (Matt. 26:53) or demons inhabiting a demoniac (Luke 8:30).

LEMUEL. An unknown king mentioned in the book of Proverbs (Prov. 31:1). Some scholars identify Lemuel as Solomon.

LENTIL. A plant of the pea family used in Jacob's pottage, or stew. Esau sold his birthright to Jacob for a bowl of this stew (Gen. 25:29–34).

LEOPARD. A wild animal of the cat family noted for its speed and fierceness (Jer. 5:6). The reign of the Messiah is pictured as a time when leopards will lie down with goats (Isa. 11:6).

LEPER [S]
2 Kings 5:1 Naaman...a mighty man...but he was a *l*
2 Kings 15:5 king (Azariah)...was a *l* unto...his death
Matt. 8:2 came a *l* and worshipped him [Jesus]
Matt. 11:5 *l's* are cleansed, and the deaf hear
Mark 14:3 house of Simon the *l*...[Jesus] sat at meat
Luke 17:12 met him [Jesus] ten men that were *l's*

LEPROSY. A variety of dreaded skin diseases. The Mosaic Law required a leper to live in isolation from others and to cry, "Unclean," so people could avoid him (Lev. 13:45–46). Jesus healed ten lepers and sent them to the priest for verification and purification (Luke 17:11–14).

LETTER. See *Jot.*

LEVI

1. The third son of Jacob and Leah (Gen. 29:34) and ancestor of the Levites (Exod. 2:1; Num. 1:49). His three sons were ancestors of the three major branches of the Levitical priesthood: Kohathites, Gershonites, and Merarites (Gen. 46:11). See also *Levites; Tribes of Israel.*

2. Another name for Matthew. See *Matthew.*

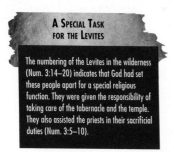

A SPECIAL TASK FOR THE LEVITES

The numbering of the Levites in the wilderness (Num. 3:14–20) indicates that God had set these people apart for a special religious function. They were given the responsibility of taking care of the tabernacle and the temple. They also assisted the priests in their sacrificial duties (Num. 3:5–10).

LEVIATHAN. A sea monster, believed by some scholars to be the crocodile (Job 41:1). The word is also used figuratively to describe one of Israel's enemies, probably Egypt (Isa. 27:1).

LEVIRATE MARRIAGE. The marriage of a man to the widow of a deceased relative if she had no male heir. The purpose of this law

was to provide an heir and an estate for the deceased relative and to provide for widows (Deut. 25:5–10). The union of Boaz and Ruth was a Levirate marriage (see Ruth 3–4). See also *Widow.*

LEVITES. Members of one of the twelve tribes of Israel who were descendants of Levi, third son of Jacob and Leah (Gen. 29:34). Moses and Aaron were Levites of the family of Kohath, Levi's son. When Canaan was divided, the Levites were assigned forty-eight towns in various tribal territories rather than a specific part of the land (Josh. 21:1–8). See also *Levitical Cities.*

LEVITICAL CITIES. Forty-eight cities assigned to the tribe of Levi instead of one specific territory (Num. 35:2–7). This arrangement gave the priestly class access to the spiritual needs of the other tribes. Six of these cities were designated as cities of refuge to protect those who accidentally killed persons from avenging relatives (Josh. 20:1–6). See also *Cities of Refuge.*

LEVITICUS, BOOK OF. An O.T. book filled with instructions about sanctification of the priests, regulations for worship and ceremonial offerings, and personal purification and dietary laws. The theme of the book is holiness. Because God is a holy God, He demands a holy and separated people who are totally committed to Him. This holiness is obtained through rituals of acceptable sacrifice, the emphasis of the first part of the book (chaps. 1–17); and rituals of sanctification, the theme of the book's second major section (chaps. 18–27).

These instructions in holiness and appropriate worship were revealed by the Lord to Moses during the Israelites' wandering years in the wilderness of Sinai. See also *Clean; Sacrifice; Unclean Animals.*

LIAR. One who tells untruths. Satan is the father of lies (John 8:44), and liars are his agents (Acts 5:3). Lying is associated with idolatry and perversion of truth (Rom. 1:18, 25).

LIAR [S]
Ps. 116:11 I said in my haste, All men are *l's*
Prov. 19:22 a poor man is better than a *l*
Rom. 3:4 let God be true, but every man a *l*
1 John 4:20 say, I love God...hateth his brother...a *l*

LIBERALITY. A generous spirit of helpfulness toward those in need. Ministering in such a spirit validates our faith (Gal. 6:10). Those who are generous will be treated with generosity (Luke 6:38).

LIBERTINES (FREEDMEN). Jews carried to Rome by Pompey as captives (63 B.C.) and later freed. Members of the Jerusalem synagogue who opposed Stephen were Libertines (Acts 6:9). *Freedmen:* NIV, NRSV.

LIBERTY
Lev. 25:10 hallow the fiftieth year, and proclaim *l*
Isa. 61:1 me [God's servant]...proclaim *l*
Luke 4:18 to set at *l* them that are bruised
Acts 26:32 This man [Paul] might have been set at *l*
1 Cor. 8:9 this *l* of yours become a stumblingblock
2 Cor. 3:17 where the Spirit of the Lord is, there is *l*
Gal. 5:1 the *l* wherewith Christ hath made us free

LIBYA/PHUT/LUBIM. The Greek name for the continent of Africa west of Egypt (Acts 2:10). Persons from Libya were in Jerusalem on the day of Pentecost (Acts 2:10). The man who carried Jesus' cross was from Cyrene, Libya's chief city (Matt. 27:32). In the O.T., Libya was also called *Phut* (Ezek. 27:10) and *Lubim* (Nah. 3:9). See also *Phut.*

LICE (GNATS). Small biting insects, perhaps sand ticks, gnats, or mosquitoes. An invasion of lice was the third plague sent by God to

persuade the pharaoh to allow the Israelites to leave Egypt (Exod. 8:16–18). *Gnats:* NIV, NRSV. See also *Gnat.*

LICENTIOUSNESS. See *Lasciviousness.*

LIE. See *Liar.*

LIEUTENANT (SATRAP). A military officer (Ezra 8:36). Also a general title for the governor of a Persian province (Esther 3:12). *Satrap:* NIV, NRSV. See also *Satrap.*

LIFE
Ps. 23:6 follow me all the days of my *l*
Ps. 31:10 *l* is spent with grief
Prov. 18:21 Death and *l* are in...tongue
Jer. 21:8 I [God] set before you...*l*, and...death
Matt. 6:25 thought for your *l*, what ye shall eat
Mark 8:35 will save his *l* shall lose it
John 1:4 him [Jesus] was *l*...light of men
John 3:36 believeth on the Son hath everlasting *l*
John 6:35 I [Jesus] am the bread of *l*
John 10:10 I [Jesus] am come that they might have *l*
John 11:25 I [Jesus] am the resurrection, and the *l*
John 15:13 man lay down his *l* for his friends
Rom. 6:23 gift of God is eternal *l* through Jesus Christ
1 John 5:12 He that hath the Son hath *l*
Rev. 22:17 take the water of *l* freely

LIFE, ETERNAL. See *Eternal Life.*

LIGHT. Illumination. God's first act of creation was to bring light into existence (Gen. 1:3–5). The word is used figuratively in the Bible to represent truth and goodness (Ps. 119:105), which dispel the darkness of ignorance and wickedness (Matt. 4:16; 5:15). See also *Darkness.*

LIGHT [S]
Gen. 1:16 the greater *l* to rule the day
Ps. 27:1 Lord is my *l* and my salvation
Isa. 9:2 people...in darkness have seen a great *l*
Isa. 60:1 Arise, shine; for thy *l* is come

L

LICE. A woman in the Middle East checks a child for lice in a photo from the turn of the 1900s.

Isa. 60:3 Gentiles shall come to thy [God's] *l*
Matt. 5:14 Ye are the *l* of the world
Matt. 11:30 my [Jesus'] yoke is easy...burden is *l*
Luke 2:32 A *l* to lighten the Gentiles
John 1:4 In him [Jesus] was life
John 1:9 That was the true *L* [Jesus]
John 8:12 I [Jesus] am the *l* of the world
Acts 13:47 set thee [Paul] to be a *l* of the Gentiles
Acts 26:18 turn them from darkness to *l*
Rom. 13:12 let us put on the armour of *l*
James 1:17 good gift...is...from the Father of *l's*
1 Pet. 2:9 [Jesus] hath called you...into his...*l*
1 John 1:5 God is *l*, and in him is no darkness
1 John 2:10 loveth his brother abideth in the *l*

LIGHTS, FEAST OF. See *Dedication, Feast of.*

LIGN ALOES. A tree from which perfume was made (Num. 24:6).

LIGURE (JACINTH). A precious stone in the breastplate of the high priest (Exod. 28:19). *Jacinth:* NIV, NRSV. See also *Jacinth.*

LILY. A general term for any flower resembling the lily (Song 5:13; Matt. 6:28).

LIME. Powdered limestone used for plaster and cement work (Isa. 33:12).

LINE (CORD). A method of measuring land with a cord (Josh. 2:18). Amos told Amaziah the priest that the Lord's punishment would include division of his land by line (Amos 7:17). *Cord:* NIV, NRSV. See also *Cord; Rope.*

LINEN. Cloth made from flax. The rich wore "fine linen" (1 Chron. 15:27), while the poor wore garments of unbleached flax. Linen was also used for curtains and veils in the tabernacle (Exod. 26:1). See also *Flax.*

LINTEL. A beam of wood over a door (Amos 9:1). In Egypt, the Hebrews were commanded to place blood from a sacrificial lamb over the lintels of their doors to avoid the angel of death (Exod. 12:22–23).

LION. A large catlike animal that preyed on sheep (1 Sam. 17:34–36). Those who offended the king of Persia were thrown into a den of lions (Dan. 6).

LIPS. A part of the human body associated with speaking. Moses described his poor speaking skills as "uncircumcised lips" (Exod. 6:12, 30). Covering the lips was a gesture of shame or mourning (Mic. 3:7). See also *Mouth; Throat; Tongue.*

LIQUOR. A fermented beverage associated with both festive occasions (Luke 15:23, 32) and drunkenness (Rom. 13:13). Paul counseled that believers should be "filled with the spirit" rather than strong drink (Eph. 5:18).

LITTER. A portable chair on poles upon which people were carried. A covering provided protection from the sun and rain (Isa. 66:20).

LIVE [ING, TH]
Gen. 2:7 man became a *l'ing* soul
Job 14:14 man die, shall he *l* again
Hab. 2:4 just shall *l* by his faith
Matt. 4:4 Man shall not *l* by bread alone
Mark 12:27 God of the dead, but...of the *l'ing*
Luke 24:5 Why seek...the *l'ing* among the dead
John 6:51 I [Jesus] am the *l'ing* bread
John 11:26 *l'th*...in me [Jesus] shall never die
Rom. 12:1 your bodies a *l'ing* sacrifice
Rom. 14:8 we *l*...or die, we are the Lord's
Phil. 1:21 to me [Paul] to *l* is Christ...die is gain
1 John 4:9 sent his...Son...we might *l* through him

LIVING GOD

Josh. 3:10 know that the *I-G* is among you
Matt. 16:16 Thou art the Christ...Son of the *I-G*
2 Cor. 6:16 for ye are the temple of the *I-G*
1 Tim. 3:15 church of the *I-G*...ground of the truth
Heb. 10:31 fearful...fall into the hands of the *I-G*

LIZARD. A reptile regarded as unclean by the Mosaic Law (Lev. 11:30). Numerous species of lizards are found in Palestine.

LOAF. See *Bread.*

LO-AMMI. A symbolic name meaning "not my people" given by Hosea to his second son to signify God's rejection of rebellious Israel (Hosea 1:8–9). See also *Hosea.*

LOAN. Borrowed money that had to be repaid with interest. To secure a loan, a debtor often pledged his children or himself (2 Kings 4:1; Amos 8:6). The Mosaic Law specified that loans to the poor were not to accrue interest (Exod. 22:25). See also *Debt; Usury.*

LOCUST. A migratory, plant-eating insect similar to the grasshopper. Swarms of locusts were sent as a plague on the Egyptians to convince the pharaoh to free the Israelite people (Exod. 10:1–4). See also *Cankerworm; Grasshopper; Palmerworm.*

LOD/LYDDA. A town near Joppa built by Shemed, a descendant of Benjamin (1 Chron. 8:12). Peter healed a lame man here (Acts 9:32–35; *Lydda*).

LOFT (UPPER ROOM, UPPER CHAMBER). The small room or upper story built on the flat roof of a house (1 Kings 17–19). *Upper room:* NIV; *upper chamber:* NRSV. See also *Upper Room.*

LOG. A unit of liquid measure equal to about one-twelfth of a hin (Lev. 14:10). See also *Hin.*

LOGOS. A Greek term that means both "the Word" and "reason." Jesus came into the world as the Logos, or the Word of God incarnate—in human form (John 1:1–3; Col. 1:15–17). See also *Word of God.*

LOINS. The midsection of the human body, just below the stomach. The Jewish people wrapped their loose garments around their loins when working or traveling to give greater freedom of movement (2 Kings 4:29). The word is used figuratively by Peter to advise his readers to be ready for Christ's return (1 Pet. 1:13).

LOIS. The grandmother of Timothy who was commended by Paul for her faith (2 Tim. 1:5). See also *Timothy.*

LONGSUFFERING (PATIENT). Forbearance or patience; an attribute of God's nature (Exod. 34:6; Ps. 86:15). His longsuffering is intended to bring people to repentance (2 Pet. 3:9). *Patient:* NIV, NRSV. See also *Forbearance; Patience.*

LORD. A rendering of various Hebrew words that refer to the God of Israel, Jesus, and persons in authority such as kings. The word is also used as a translation of the divine name *Yahweh*, which the Hebrews did not pronounce out of reverence (Gen. 12:8; Exod. 3:15–16). See also *Jehovah; Yahweh.*

LORD ALMIGHTY. See *Hosts, Lord of.*

LORD'S DAY. Sunday, the first day of the week and the Christian day of worship (Rev. 1:10). The Jewish day of rest and worship fell on Saturday, the last day of the week. But after

LORD'S PRAYER. *A priest leads tourists through Jerusalem's Church of the Lord's Prayer, which commemorates the prayer Jesus taught His disciples. Sixty-two panels of the prayer decorate the church walls—each panel in a different language.*

Christ's resurrection on the first day, Christians adopted this as their normal day of worship (Acts 20:7). The Christian custom of Sunday worship was already well established when the Roman emperor Constantine instituted the day as a Christian holiday in A.D. 321.

LORD'S PRAYER. Jesus' model prayer that He taught to His disciples in response to their request, "Lord, teach us to pray" (Luke 11:1). The prayer teaches us to approach God reverently (Matt. 6:9–10), to ask Him to meet our physical needs, and to seek His forgiveness and protection (Matt. 6:11–13). See also *Prayer; Sermon on the Mount.*

LORD'S SUPPER. Jesus' final meal with His disciples that He observed as a Passover

ritual to symbolize His approaching death (Luke 22:15–16). In this act, He established a memorial supper, symbolizing His broken body and shed blood (Matt. 26:26–28), which Christians are enjoined to observe until the Lord's return (1 Cor. 11:26). See also *Love Feast.*

LO-RUHAMAH. A symbolic name for the prophet Hosea's daughter, meaning "unloved." It expressed God's displeasure with rebellious Israel (Hosea 1:6).

LOSE [TH]
Eccles. 3:6 A time to get, and a time to *l*
Matt. 10:39 *l'th* his life for my [Jesus] sake shall find it
Mark 8:36 gain the whole world...*l* his own soul
Luke 17:33 Whosoever shall...save his life shall *l* it

LOSS

Acts 27:22 no *l* of any man's life...but of the ship
1 Cor. 3:15 man's work shall be burned, he shall suffer *l*
Phil. 3:7 things were gain to me [Paul]...I counted *l*

LOST

Ps. 119:176 I have gone astray like a *l* sheep
Luke 15:6 found my sheep which was *l*
Luke 19:10 Son of man is come to...save...*l*

LOT. Abraham's nephew. He accompanied Abraham to Canaan and traveled with him to Egypt to escape a famine (Gen. 12:5; 13:1). His uncle gave him first choice of Canaan's land on which to settle. He selected the fertile Jordan Valley (Gen. 13:10–11) and settled with his family near the pagan city of Sodom. Lot escaped the destruction of this city, but his wife looked back on their possessions and was turned into a pillar of salt (Gen. 19:15–26).

Lot was an ancestor of the Moabites and the Ammonites, tribes that became bitter enemies of the Israelites in later centuries (Gen. 19:37–38). See also *Ammonites; Lot's Wife; Moabites.*

LOTAN. See *Moab,* No. 2.

LOTS, CASTING OF. The practice of making decisions by casting small stones out of a container, similar to our modern practice of "drawing straws" (Josh. 18:6). It was believed that God made His will known through this method (Prov. 16:33). Matthias was chosen as an apostle to succeed Judas by the casting of lots (Acts 1:26).

LOT'S WIFE. The wife of Abraham's nephew who was turned into a pillar of salt as she looked back on Sodom (Gen. 19:26). Jesus used her experience to warn of the dangers of delay and disobedience (Luke 17:32).

LOVE. Unselfish, benevolent concern for other persons (1 Cor. 13:4–7; *charity:* KJV). To love

God supremely and to love others unselfishly are the two most important commands of Jesus (Matt. 22:37–40). Christ's sacrificial death was the supreme expression of love (John 13:1; 15:13). See also *Agape.*

THE TEST OF LOVE

The message that Jesus taught from the very beginning of His ministry was "that we should love one another" (1 John 3:11). This love principle is a simple test for believers. God's love for us empowers our lives and motivates us to love others. Genuine love is an action as well as an emotion: "Let us not love in word, neither in tongue; but in deed and in truth" (1 John 3:18).

LOVE [D, TH]

Lev. 19:18 *l* thy neighbour as thyself
Deut. 6:5 *l* the LORD thy God with all thine heart
Ps. 119:97 how *l* I thy [God's] law
Prov. 17:17 friend *l'th* at all times
Eccles. 3:8 A time to *l*, and a time to hate
Song 8:7 Many waters cannot quench *l*
Hosea 11:4 I [God] drew them with...bands of *l*
Matt. 5:44 *L* your enemies, bless them that curse you
Matt. 22:39 shalt *l* thy neighbour as thyself
John 13:34 *l* one another; as I [Jesus]...*l'd* you
Rom. 5:8 God commendeth his *l* toward us
Rom. 8:37 conquerors through him [Jesus] that *l'd* us
2 Cor. 9:7 God *l'th* a cheerful giver
Eph. 4:15 speaking the truth in *l*
Eph. 5:25 Husbands, *l* your wives
Phil. 1:9 your *l* may abound yet more
1 Tim. 6:10 *l* of money is the root of all evil
2 Tim. 1:7 not given us the spirit of fear; but *l*
Heb. 12:6 whom the Lord *l'th* he chasteneth
1 John 2:10 He that *l'th* his brother abideth in the light
1 John 4:7 every one that *l'th* is born of God
1 John 4:19 We *l* him [Jesus], because he first *l'd* us

LOVE FEAST. A meal observed by the early churches in connection with the Lord's Supper. The purpose of the meal was to promote Christian fellowship and brotherly love (Acts 2:42, 46; 1 Cor. 10:16–17). Paul condemned some of the Corinthian Christians for their sinful behavior and selfish indulgence at such love feasts (1 Cor. 11:20–22). See also *Lord's Supper.*

LOVE ONE ANOTHER
John 13:34 ye *l-o-a*; as I [Jesus] have loved you
Rom. 13:8 Owe no man any thing, but to *l-o-a*
1 John 3:11 message...ye heard...we should *l-o-a*
1 John 4:7 let us *l-o-a*: for love is of God

LOVE THY NEIGHBOUR
Matt. 19:19 Thou shalt *l-t-n* as thyself
Gal. 5:14 law is fulfilled in one word...*l-t-n* as thyself
James 2:8 fulfil the royal law...*l-t-n* as thyself

LOVER. See *Paramour.*

LOVINGKINDNESS. God's gentle and steadfast love and mercy that He extends freely to His people (Pss. 63:3; 69:16; 103:4–12; Jer. 9:24). See also *Mercy.*

LUBIM. See *Libya.*

LUCAS. See *Luke.*

LUCIFER (MORNING STAR, DAY STAR). A name for the pompous king of Babylonia used by the prophet Isaiah (14:12). Some scholars believe this passage describes the fall of Satan (see Luke 10:18). *Morning star:* NIV; *day star:* NRSV. See also *Devil; Satan.*

LUCIUS. A Jewish Christian and kinsman of Paul who greeted believers at Rome (Rom. 16:21). He may be the same person as Lucius of Antioch (Acts 13:1).

LUCRE (GAIN). Material wealth, represented by money or goods (1 Sam. 8:3; Titus 1:7, 11). *Gain:* NIV, NRSV. See also *Filthy Lucre; Money.*

SOLOMON ON WEALTH

Solomon was one of the wealthiest people of his time (1 Kings 4:21–24), but he concluded that great riches were actually a burden because they brought such worries that a rich person couldn't enjoy his possessions (Eccl. 6:1). Jesus taught us not to worry about accumulating earthly riches but to "lay up for yourselves treasures in heaven...where thieves do not break through nor steal" (Matt. 6:20).

LUDIM (LUDITES, LUD). A people descended from Mizraim, a son of Ham (Gen. 10:13, 22). *Ludites:* NIV; *Lud:* NRSV.

LUKE/LUCAS. A Christian of Gentile descent, apparently a physician by vocation (Col. 4:14), who accompanied Paul on some of his missionary journeys (Acts 16:10; 20:5; 28:30). Luke wrote the Gospel that bears his name as well as the book of Acts. Paul commended Luke for his loyalty and friendship (2 Tim. 4:11). *Lucas:* Philem. 24. See also *Acts of the Apostles.*

LUKE, GOSPEL OF. One of the four Gospels of the N.T., written by Luke—a physician of Gentile background—to portray Jesus as the Savior of all people, Gentiles as well as Jews. Luke shows that Jesus associated with all types of people, including sinners (5:30; 15:2), the poor and outcasts (6:20–23; 16:19–31), and the Samaritans (17:11–19).

This theme of Christ as the universal Savior is continued in the book of Acts, which Luke wrote as a sequel to his Gospel. Acts tells how the gospel eventually spread from Jerusalem, the center of Judaism, to Rome, the capital city and nerve center of the Roman Empire. See also *Acts of the Apostles; Luke; Roman Empire.*

LUKEWARM. Neither hot nor cold; a term for indifference or complacency. Members of the church at Laodicea were criticized for their tepid spirituality (Rev. 3:16).

LUST. Evil desire, usually associated with the sex drive. Unbridled lust leads to sin and produces death (Eph. 2:3; James 1:14–15). Believers are warned to flee worldly lust (Titus 2:12) and "follow righteousness" (Gal. 5:16; 2 Tim. 2:22).

LUST [S]

Matt. 5:28 looketh on a woman to *l* after her
Mark 4:19 the *l*'s...entering in, choke the word
James 4:3 that ye may consume it upon your *l*'s
1 John 2:16 the *l* of the eyes...pride of life

LUZ. See *Bethel.*

LYCAONIA. A Roman province in southern Asia Minor visited by Paul. Cities in this region where he preached included Derbe, Lystra, and Iconium (Acts 14:1–7).

LYCIA. A province of Asia Minor that juts into the Mediterranean Sea. Paul made stops in Patara (Acts 21:1) and Myra, Lycia's major cities.

LYDDA. See *Lod.*

LYDIA. A businesswoman of Thyatira, a dealer in purple cloth, who was apparently converted under Paul's ministry at Philippi. After her conversion, she invited Paul and his friends to spend time in her home (Acts 16:14–15). See also *Philippi.*

LYE. See *Nitre.*

LYRE. See *Harp; Psaltery; Sackbut; Viol.*

LYSANIAS. The governor of Abilene, a region in Syria, when Herod was ruler over Galilee and when John the Baptist began his ministry (Luke 3:1). See also *Abilene.*

LYSIAS, CLAUDIUS. See *Claudius Lysias.*

LYSTRA. A city in the province of Lycaonia in central Asia Minor. Paul preached and healed a lame man here and was stoned by unbelieving Jews (Acts 14:6–20).

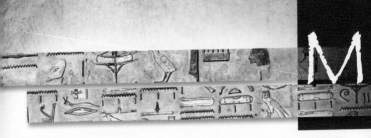

MACCABEES. A family of Jewish patriots who headed a religious revolt against the Syrians in Palestine from 167 to 63 B.C. See also *Antiochus IV Epiphanes.*

MACEDONIA. A mountainous country north of Greece and the first European territory visited by the apostle Paul. He planted churches in the cities of Philippi and Thessalonica (see Acts 16, 17, 20). Paul was beckoned to visit this region through his famous "Macedonian call"—a vision of a man pleading, "Come over into Macedonia, and help us" (Acts 16:9).

MACHINES. See *Engines.*

MACHIR (MAKIR). The oldest son of Manasseh (Josh. 17:1), a grandson of Joseph (Gen. 50:23), and a military hero who became the ancestor of the Macherites (1 Chron. 7:17–18). The Macherites won significant victories over the Amorites during the conquest of Canaan (Num. 32:39). *Makir:* NIV.

MACHPELAH. A field with a cave that Abraham bought as a burial ground (Gen. 23:7–18). Buried here were Abraham and Sarah, Isaac and Rebekah, and Jacob and Leah (Gen. 25:9–10; 49:29–33).

MAD (INSANE). A term for insanity, but it may also refer to anger or confusion (1 Cor. 14:23). David pretended to be insane in order to escape from Achish (1 Sam. 21:13–15). *Insane:* NIV.

MADAI. A son of Japheth and ancestor of the Medes (Gen. 10:2). See also *Medes.*

MADIAN. See *Midian,* No. 2.

MAGDALA. A city of Galilee near Capernaum, and probably the home of Mary Magdalene (Matt. 27:56).

MAGDALENE. See *Mary,* No. 2.

MAGI. See *Wise Men.*

MAGIC. The practice of illusion and sleight of hand to bring benefits or to deceive. The Israelites were forbidden to consult magicians or sorcerers (Lev. 19:31). See also *Sorcery; Witchcraft.*

MAGISTRATE. A civil authority or ruler. Magistrates in Philippi beat and imprisoned Paul and Silas for healing a demented slave girl (Acts 16:16–24).

MAGNIFICAT. The poem or song of the Virgin Mary upon learning she would give birth to the Messiah (Luke 1:46–55). Mary praised God for remembering "the lowliness of his servant" (NRSV) and for keeping His promise to bless Abraham and his descendants. See also *Mary,* No. 1.

MAGNIFY [IED]
Job 7:17 What is man, that thou [God] shouldest **m** him?
Ps. 40:16 The Lord be **m'ied**

203

M

MAGIC. In a moment beyond magic, the witch of Endor calls up the spirit of Samuel, at the request of King Saul. Famous as a medium, the woman is shocked and terrified when Samuel actually appears.

Luke 1:46 Mary said, My soul doth *m* the Lord
Phil. 1:20 Christ shall be *m'ied* in my [Paul's] body

MAGOG. See *Gog, Prince of Magog.*

MAHALATH, MAHALATH LEAN-NOTH. A phrase in the titles of Pss. 53 and 88 that probably refers to a musical instrument or a tune to be used in worship.

MAHANAIM. The name that Jacob gave to a site near the Jabbok River where he was visited by angels while waiting for his brother Esau (Gen. 32:1–2). The name means "two armies" or "two camps," perhaps referring to the meeting of his and Esau's forces or to the camps of Jacob and God. A city by the same name was established later on this site (Josh. 21:38).

MAHER-SHALAL-HASH-BAZ. The symbolic name given by the prophet Isaiah to his second son, meaning "hasten the booty" (Isa. 8:1–4). It signified that Assyria would conquer Israel and Syria.

MAHLON. Ruth's first husband and the elder son of Naomi. He died about ten years after his marriage to Ruth (Ruth 1:5).

MAID. A young unmarried woman, often of the servant class (Ruth 2:8). The word may also refer to a virgin or a female slave.

MAIDSERVANT. A female servant or handmaid (Ruth 3:9). Sometimes the word refers to a female slave. See also *Handmaid; Servant.*

MAIL, COAT OF. See *Brigandine.*

MAINSAIL (FORESAIL). The dominant or principal sail of a ship (Acts 27:40). *Foresail:* NIV, NRSV.

MAJESTY. A term referring to the dignity, power, and authority of a king or other high official (1 Chron. 29:24–25).

MAJOR PROPHETS. A term for the prophetic books that appear first in the O.T.—Isaiah, Jeremiah, Ezekiel, and Daniel—because of the longer length of their books. See also *Minor Prophets*.

MAKIR. See *Machir*.

MALACHI. An O.T. prophet and the author of the book that bears his name. His name means "my messenger" (Mal. 1:1). He lived after the Babylonian Exile and was probably a contemporary of the prophet Nehemiah.

MALACHI, BOOK OF. A short prophetic book of the O.T. written about 100 years after the Babylonian Exile and directed against shallow and meaningless worship practices. The prophet condemned the people of Israel for presenting defective animals as sacrifices (1:8) and withholding tithes and offerings (3:8–10). The book closes with a note of hope regarding the future Messiah (chap. 4).

MALCHI-SHUA/MELCHI-SHUA (MALKI-SHUA). A son of King Saul who was killed by the Philistines in the battle at Gilboa (1 Sam. 14:49). *Melchi-shua:* 1 Sam. 31:2; *Malki-shua:* NIV.

MALCHUS. A servant of the high priest whose ear was cut off by Peter. Jesus rebuked Peter and restored the severed ear (John 18:10–11).

MALE SLAVE. See *Manservant*.

MALEFACTOR (CRIMINAL). A rebel or criminal. Christ was crucified between two malefactors (Luke 23:32–33). *Criminal:* NIV, NRSV.

MALICE. A burning desire or intention to hurt others. Christians are urged to renounce malice (Eph. 4:31; 1 Pet. 2:1) and pray for those guilty of this sin (Matt. 5:44). See also *Hate*.

MALKI-SHUA. See *Malchi-shua*.

MALLOWS (HERB). A wild plant or shrub that thrived in the dry, salty regions near the Dead Sea. It was sometimes eaten by the poor (Job 30:3–4). *Herb:* NIV.

MALTA. See *Melita*.

MAMMON (MONEY, WEALTH). Material wealth or possessions. Christ warned that money or physical goods were false gods that should not be worshiped (Matt. 6:24). He urged believers to seek kingdom interests and promised that their material needs would be met (Matt. 6:33). *Money:* NIV; *wealth:* NRSV. See also *Filthy Lucre; Money*.

MAMRE
1. A town or district near Hebron where Abraham lived (Gen. 13:18; 18:1).
2. An Amorite chief and supporter of Abraham who gave his name to the plain where Abraham lived (Gen. 14:13).

MAN. The being created by God in His image and for His glory (Gen. 1:26–27; 9:6; Isa. 43:7). The crown of God's creation, man was given dominion over the natural world (Ps. 8:4–6). Man's sin has separated him from God (Rom. 3:23), but he may be redeemed by God's grace through faith in Christ (Rom. 3:22–24). See also *Fall of Man; Sin*.

MANASSEH/MANASSES
1. Joseph's firstborn son whose descendants became one of the tribes of Israel (Gen. 48:4–6) and occupied both sides of the Jordan

River (Josh. 16:4–9). *Manasses:* Rev. 7:6. See also *Tribes of Israel.*

2. The son and successor of Hezekiah as king of Judah (reigned about 687–642 B.C.; 2 Kings 20:21). A wicked ruler who encouraged pagan worship throughout Judah, Manasseh was captured and taken to Babylonia (2 Chron. 33:10–11). He later repented and was allowed to return to Jerusalem (2 Chron. 33:12–13). He was succeeded as king by his son Amon (2 Chron. 33:20).

MANDRAKE. A plant with an aromatic fragrance (Song 7:13). Its fruit was thought to generate fertility (Gen. 30:14–16).

MANEH (MINA). A Hebrew weight equal to fifty shekels, or about two pounds (Ezek. 45:12). *Mina:* NIV, NRSV.

MANGER. A feeding trough for livestock. The infant Jesus was laid in a manger after His birth (Luke 2:7–16).

MANIFEST [ED]
Mark 4:22 nothing hid, which shall not be *m'ed*
John 9:3 works of God...made *m* in him [Jesus]
1 Cor. 3:13 Every man's work shall be made *m*
1 John 3:8 this purpose the Son of God was *m'ed*
1 John 4:9 this [Jesus' death]...*m'ed* the love of God

MANNA. Food miraculously provided by the Lord for the Israelites in the wilderness (Num. 11:7–9). Called "bread from heaven" (Exod. 16:4), manna was provided daily except on the Sabbath for forty years. A different substance by this name drops from various trees, particularly the tamarisk, in the valleys near the Sinai wilderness. See also *Wilderness Wanderings.*

MANSERVANT (MALE SLAVE). A male domestic servant, often a slave (Exod. 21:32). *Male slave:* NIV, NRSV.

MANSLAYER (SLAYER). A person who accidentally killed another. This person could seek asylum from the avenging relatives of the victim in a city of refuge (Num. 35:6–12). *Slayer:* NRSV. See also *Avenger of Blood; Cities of Refuge.*

MANTLE (CLOAK). An outer garment, similar to a robe, made of coarse cloth or sheepskin. Elijah's mantle was placed on Elisha as a symbol of succession and blessing (1 Kings 19:19–21). *Cloak:* NIV. See also *Cloke.*

MARA. A name meaning "bitter" that was assumed by Naomi because it expressed her sorrow at the death of her husband and sons (Ruth 1:3–21).

MARANATHA. An Aramaic phrase meaning "come, O Lord" that expresses hope for the second coming of Jesus (1 Cor. 16:22). See also *Second Coming.*

MARBLE. Crystalline limestone noted for its beauty and durability as a building material. Marble was used in the building of the temple in Jerusalem (1 Chron. 29:2).

MARCUS. See *Mark.*

MARDUK. See *Merodach.*

MARESHAH. A town of Judah (Josh. 15:20, 44) built for defensive purposes by King Rehoboam (2 Chron. 11:5, 8). A battle between King Asa of Judah and King Zerah of Ethiopia was fought here (2 Chron. 14:9–10).

MARINER. A seaman or sailor. Paul reassured the mariners on his ship during a storm (Acts 27:31–36). See also *Ship.*

MARK, GOSPEL OF. One of the four Gospels of the N.T. and probably the first to be written, according to most scholars. A short Gospel of only sixteen chapters, Mark portrays Jesus as a person of action. He uses the words *immediately* (1:12; 2:8) and *straightway* (8:10) to show that Jesus was on an important mission for God and had no time to waste.

While Mark makes it clear that Jesus was the Son of God (15:39), he also emphasizes the humanity of Jesus more than the other Gospel writers, including incidents that reveal His disappointment (8:12), anger (11:15–17), sorrow (14:34), and fatigue (4:38). See also *Mark; Synoptic Gospels.*

MARK, JOHN/MARCUS. A relative of Barnabas who accompanied Paul and Barnabas on the first missionary journey as far as Perga and then returned to Jerusalem (Acts 13:3–5). After Paul's refusal to allow Mark to go with them on the second journey, Barnabas and Paul went their separate ways (Acts 15:36–41). In later years, Paul spoke of Mark with warmth and affection (Col. 4:10–11).

Most scholars believe Mark was the author of the Gospel of Mark, drawing perhaps on the reflections of Peter, who worked closely with Mark (1 Pet. 5:13; *Marcus*).

MARKER. See *Landmark.*

MARKET, MARKETPLACE. A large open area in a city where trade, public trials, and discussions were conducted (Acts 16:19–20). Children often played in this area (Luke 7:32). The Greek word for marketplace is *agora.*

MARRIAGE. The union of a man and a woman in commitment to each other as husband and wife. First instituted by God in the Garden of Eden (Gen. 2:18), marriage was also confirmed by Christ (Matt. 19:5). Love for and submission to one's mate were enjoined by Paul (Eph. 5:22–29). The love of a husband and wife for each other is symbolic of Christ's love for the Church (Eph. 5:23–25). See also *Betrothal; Dowry.*

Matt. 22:2 certain king...made a *m* for his son
Mark 12:25 neither marry, nor are given in *m*
John 2:1 there was a *m* in Cana of Galilee
Heb. 13:4 *M* is honourable in all...the bed undefiled
Rev. 19:9 called unto the *m* supper of the Lamb

MARROW. Tissue in the cavities of the bones. This word is used to illustrate the piercing power of God's Word (Heb. 4:12).

MARRY [IED]
Matt. 5:32 shall *m* her...divorced committeth adultery
Mark 10:11 put away his wife...*m* another, committeth adultery
Luke 14:20 *m'ied* a wife...I cannot come
1 Cor. 7:9 it is better to *m* than to burn
1 Cor. 7:33 that *m'ied* careth for...things...of...world
1 Tim. 5:14 the younger women *m*, bear children

MARS' HILL. See *Areopagus.*

MARTHA. The sister of Mary and Lazarus (John 11:1–2). Jesus rebuked Martha because of her unnecessary worry after she welcomed Him into her home (Luke 10:38–42). She grieved at the death of her brother, Lazarus, and sought Jesus' help (John 11:20–22).

MARVEL [LED]
Matt. 8:10 he [Jesus] *m'led*...not found so great faith
Mark 6:6 he [Jesus] *m'led*...their unbelief
Mark 15:44 Pilate *m'led* if he [Jesus]...already dead
John 3:7 *M* not that I [Jesus] said...Ye [Nicodemus] must be born again

MARVELLOUS
1 Chron. 16:24 Declare...his [God's] *m* works
Ps. 139:14 praise thee [God]...*m* are thy works
1 Pet. 2:9 called you out of darkness...*m* light
Rev. 15:3 Great and *m* are thy works, Lord

M

M

MARY

1. The earthly mother of Jesus (Matt. 1:16). A descendant of David from Bethlehem, Mary was engaged to Joseph (Luke 1:27). She was informed by an angel that she had been divinely chosen to give birth to the Messiah (Luke 1:28–33). She traveled with Joseph to Bethlehem (Luke 2:4–5) and gave birth to Jesus in fulfillment of prophecy (Isa. 7:14). She was forced to flee to Egypt with Joseph to escape Herod's slaughter of innocent children (Matt. 2:13–18). After she and Joseph returned to Nazareth, she gave birth to other children (Mark 6:3).

Mary visited Jerusalem during the Passover feast with Joseph and Jesus (Luke 2:41–46). She attended a marriage in Cana of Galilee, where Jesus worked His first miracle (John 2:3). She was present at the cross when Jesus commended her to John's care (John 19:25–27). Mary was also present with one of the praying groups in the upper room after the ascension of Jesus (Acts 1:14).

2. Mary Magdalene. A woman who witnessed the crucifixion and visited the tomb of Jesus (Matt. 27:55–61). She told the apostles of Jesus about the empty tomb (John 20:1–2) and was one of the first persons to see the risen Lord (Mark 16:9).

3. The sister of Martha and Lazarus. She was an eager listener at Jesus' feet while Martha performed household duties (Luke 10:38–41). She anointed the feet of Jesus and wiped them with her hair (John 12:1–3). Jesus defended her contemplative temperament (Luke 10:42).

4. The mother of the disciple James. This Mary is probably one of the women who provided food for Jesus and His disciples (Luke 8:2–3). She was also among those who went to the tomb to anoint Jesus' body and discovered He had been raised from the dead (Mark 16:1–8).

5. The mother of John Mark (Acts 12:12). Her house may have been a meeting place for the early Christians of Jerusalem.

6. A fellow believer at Rome greeted and commended by Paul in his letter to the Roman Christians (Rom. 16:6).

MARY OF MAGDALA

The name Magdalene probably indicates that Mary Magdalene was a resident of Magdala, a town on the southwestern coast of the Sea of Galilee. She became a follower of Jesus after He healed her by casting out seven demons (Luke 8:1–2).

MASCHIL. A Hebrew word that appears in the titles of thirteen psalms, apparently giving directions for the melody to be sung (Pss. 32, 42, 44–45, 52–55, 74, 78, 88–89, 142).

MASHAL. See *Misheal*.

MASON. A bricklayer or stoneworker. Phoenician masons were used by Solomon to build the temple in Jerusalem (1 Kings 5:17–18).

MASSAH AND MERIBAH. A site in the wilderness where the Israelites rebelled against Moses and Aaron (Exod. 17:4–7). Their complaints provoked the wrath of the Lord (Deut. 6:16). See also *Wilderness Wanderings*.

MAST. The rigging or wooden frame that held the sails on a ship (Ezek. 27:5). The word was used figuratively to show the strength of Israel's enemies (Isa. 33:23). See also *Ship*.

MASTER (TEACHER). A word meaning "teacher" that was often applied to Christ

(Matt. 22:16, 24). The word was also used in the O.T. as a term of respect for one's superiors (Gen. 24:48–49). *Teacher:* NIV, NRSV. See also *Teacher.*

MATHUSALA. See *Methuselah.*

MATTANIAH. See *Zedekiah.*

MATTHEW/LEVI. A tax collector who became a disciple of Jesus (Matt. 9:9) and writer of the Gospel that bears his name. He was also known as *Levi* (Mark 2:13–17; Luke 5:27–32). See also *Publican.*

MATTHEW, GOSPEL OF. One of the four Gospels of the N.T., written by a tax collector who became one of the twelve apostles of Jesus. This Gospel apparently was written to show the Jewish people that Jesus was the Messiah promised in the O.T., since many events in His life are interpreted as fulfillment of the Scriptures (1:22; 4:14; 12:17; 21:4; 27:35). In Matthew's genealogies, Jesus' ancestry through Joseph, His earthly father, is traced to two of the greatest personalities in Jewish history—Abraham (1:2) and David (1:6).

Matthew's Gospel also emphasizes the teaching ministry of Jesus, particularly His instructions to His disciples in the Sermon on the Mount (chaps. 5–7). Another prominent

M

MAST. With its sail rolled up and lashed to the mast, this fishing boat in 1938 is rowed ashore to Caesarea, on what is now Israel's Mediterranean coast.

theme of this Gospel is the kingdom of God or the kingdom of heaven (5:3; 6:33; 8:11; 12:28; 13:43–46; 19:23; 21:31; 25:34). See also *Beatitudes; Kingdom of God; Sermon on the Mount.*

MATTHIAS. The person who replaced Judas as an apostle. Matthias was chosen by the other apostles through the casting of lots (Acts 1:15–26). See also *Lots, Casting of; Twelve, The.*

MATTOCK (HOE). An agricultural tool, similar to a crude hoe, used to loosen the soil and remove roots (Isa. 7:25). *Hoe:* NIV, NRSV.

MATURITY. See *Perfection.*

MAUL (CLUB). A heavy club used as a weapon of war. The head was often studded with spikes (Prov. 25:18). *Club:* NIV, NRSV (Jer. 51:20).

MAW (STOMACH). The stomach of an animal that chews the cud. Considered a delicacy by the Hebrews, the maw, shoulders, and cheeks became the priests' portion of sacrificial animals (Deut. 18:3). *Stomach:* NRSV.

MAZZAROTH. A constellation of stars cited by Job as evidence of the power and sovereignty of God (Job 38:31–33).

MEAT FORK. See *Fleshhook.*

MEAT OFFERING. An offering of a sacrificial animal, made to atone for sin (1 Chron. 21:23).

MEDDLER. See *Busybody.*

MEDES, MEDIA. Descendants of Japheth (Gen. 10:2) and an ancient kingdom between the Tigris River and the Caspian Sea to which Sargon of Assyria brought Hebrew captives (2 Kings 17:6; 18:11).

MEDIATOR, CHRIST THE. A title of Christ that describes His work in reconciling us to God. His sacrificial death has made it possible for us to have peace with God and with one another (Eph. 2:13–16; 1 Tim. 2:5). As our mediator, He has made a full and final sacrifice for our salvation (Heb. 7:27; 9:15). See also *Atonement; Propitiation; Reconciliation.*

MEDICINE. A healing substance. In Bible times, medicine was made from herbs, fruits, and minerals. The balm of Gilead was probably made from the gum of an evergreen tree (Jer. 8:22). See also *Balm of Gilead; Healing.*

MEDITATE
Ps. 1:2 in his [God's] law doth he *m* day and night
Ps. 119:15 I will *m* in thy [God's] precepts
Luke 21:14 not to *m* before what ye shall answer

MEDITATION. Contemplation of spiritual truths (Ps. 119:148) that produces understanding (Ps. 49:3) and spiritual satisfaction (Ps. 63:5–6). Meditation on God's commands encourages obedience (Josh. 1:8).

MEDITERRANEAN SEA/GREAT SEA. The sea on Israel's western border that was also called the *Great Sea* (Josh. 9:1). Solomon used the Phoenicians to provide import/export services for Israel across this body of water (1 Kings 9:27). Paul often sailed the Mediterranean during his missionary journeys (Acts 9:30; 18:18; Acts 27).

MEDIUM. A communicator between humans and the spirit world. The Mosaic Law specified that professing mediums or wizards were to be stoned to death (Lev. 20:27). The prophet Isaiah warned against consulting the dead rather than listening to the Lord (Isa. 8:19–20; 19:3). See also *Enchanter; Familiar Spirit; Wizard.*

MEEK. Kind, gentle, and humble. The meek will find spiritual satisfaction (Ps. 22:26) and receive God's instruction (Ps. 25:9). Paul cited meekness as one of the fruits of the spirit (Gal. 5:22–23). Jesus declared that the meek will inherit the earth (Matt. 5:5). See also *Humility; Kindness.*

MEEK [NESS]
Num. 12:3 Moses was very *m*
Ps. 37:11 the *m* shall inherit the earth
Isa. 61:1 preach good tidings unto the *m*
Matt. 11:29 I [Jesus] am *m*...lowly in heart
Col. 3:12 Put on...kindness...*m'ness*

MEGIDDO/MEGIDDON. A fortified city west of the Jordan River in the plain of Jezreel associated with the great battle in the endtime. This city was the site of Barak's victory over Sisera (Judg. 4:14–16) and King Josiah's death in a battle with Pharaoh Necho of Egypt (2 Chron. 35:22–24). In this area the final battle between God and the forces of evil will occur (Zech. 12:11; Rev. 16:16). *Megiddon:* Zech. 12:11. See also *Armageddon.*

MELCHI-SHUA. See *Malchi-shua.*

MELCHIZEDEK/MELCHISEDEC. The king of Salem who received tithes from Abraham (Gen. 14:18–20) and who is depicted as a type of Christ because of his endless priesthood (Heb. 5:6–10; 7:15–17). The Messiah who is to come was also described as a priest "after the order of Melchizedek" (Ps. 110:4). *Melchisedec:* Heb. 7:11.

MELITA (MALTA). An island south of Sicily in the Mediterranean Sea where Paul was shipwrecked while sailing to Rome (Acts 28:1–8). *Malta:* NIV, NRSV.

MELON. A fruit, apparently grown in Egypt, for which the Israelites longed during their wilderness wanderings (Num. 11:5). Various melons are grown today in Palestine.

MEMBER [S]
Rom. 12:5 one body in Christ...*m's* one of another
1 Cor. 6:15 bodies are the *m's* of Christ
1 Cor. 12:26 one *m* suffer, all the *m's* suffer
James 3:5 tongue is a little *m*...boasteth great things

MEMPHIS. See *Noph.*

MENAHEM. A cruel and idolatrous king of Israel (ruled about 752–742 B.C.) who killed Shallum in order to assume the throne. He paid tribute to Tiglath-pileser III, king of Assyria, in order to maintain his power. He was succeeded by his son Pekahiah (2 Kings 15:16–22).

MEPHIBOSHETH/MERIB-BAAL. The crippled son of David's friend Jonathan and a grandson of King Saul. He was dropped by his nurse and crippled at age five when she received the news that Jonathan and Saul had been killed by the Philistines (2 Sam. 4:4). David sought out Mephibosheth,

MYSTERIOUS MELCHIZEDEK

This mysterious king of Salem (a shorter, older name for Jerusalem) was apparently a priest as well, and he worshiped the Lord just as Abraham did. He appears suddenly out of nowhere and disappears from the biblical record just as quickly (Gen. 14:18–20).

Centuries later, the writer of Hebrews in the New Testament declared that the priesthood of Jesus was far superior to that of Melchizedek, even though this strange priest of Abraham's time seemed supernatural in origin (see Heb. 7:1–17).

MERCY SEAT. Golden angelic images sit on the mercy seat, or cover, of the ark of the covenant—a chest containing the Ten Commandments. In this scene the Philistines have captured it and put it on display in their temple. But the statue of their god has toppled over in the presence of the ark.

M

restored his family's land, and gave him a place at the king's table. *Merib-baal:* 1 Chron. 8:34. See also *Jonathan*, No. 1.

MERARI. The third son of Levi and ancestor of the Merarites (Gen. 46:11; Exod. 6:19).

MERCIFUL
Deut. 21:8 Be *m*, O Lord, unto thy people
Ps. 103:8 Lord is *m*...slow to anger
Matt. 5:7 Blessed are...*m*...shall obtain mercy

MERCURIUS (HERMES). The Roman name for the pagan god Mercury—the god of commerce—and the name applied to Paul by the people of Lystra (Acts 14:12). *Hermes:* NIV, NRSV.

MERCY (COMPASSION). Compassion for others. God's mercies are abundant (1 Pet. 1:3) and fresh every morning (Lam. 3:22–

23). Paul described God as "the father of all mercies" (2 Cor. 1:3). Jesus commended the Samaritan who showed mercy for a wounded traveler (Luke 10:36–37). *Compassion:* NIV. See also *Compassion; Lovingkindness; Pity.*

Ps. 6:2 Have *m* upon me, O Lord; for I am weak
Ps. 23:6 *m* shall follow me all the days of my life
Ps. 103:17 *m* of the Lord is from everlasting
Hosea 6:6 For I [God] desired *m*...not sacrifice
Mic. 6:8 Lord require of thee, but to...love *m*
Eph. 2:4 God, who is rich in *m*...loved us
Titus 3:5 according to his [God's] *m* he saved us
1 Pet. 2:10 but now have obtained *m*

MERCY SEAT (COVER). The gold lid that covered the ark of the covenant. It was called the "mercy seat" because God was believed to be present to hear and answer prayers (Exod. 25:21–22). On the Day of Atonement, the high priest sprinkled blood of the sin offerings on the mercy seat as a propitiation for the people's sins (Lev. 16:11–16). *Cover:* NIV. See also *Ark of the Covenant; Atonement.*

MERIBAH. See *Massah* and *Meribah.*

MERIB-BAAL. See *Mephibosheth.*

MERODACH (MARDUK). The pagan Babylonian god of war whose overthrow was predicted by the prophet Jeremiah (Jer. 50:2). *Marduk:* NIV.

MERODACH-BALADAN. See *Berodach-baladan.*

MERRY
Prov. 15:13 A *m* heart maketh a cheerful countenance
Luke 15:23 bring...the fatted calf...eat, and be *m*
James 5:13 Is any *m*? let him sing psalms

MESHA. A king of Moab who led an unsuccessful invasion of Judah (2 Chron. 20). He offered his oldest son as a sacrifice to the pagan god Chemosh (2 Kings 3:4, 26–27).

MESHACH/MISHAEL. The Babylonian name for Daniel's friend who was thrown into the fiery furnace for refusing to worship an idol (Dan. 1:7). He was saved through God's miraculous intervention. His Hebrew name was *Mishael* (Dan. 1:6). See also *Daniel.*

MESOPOTAMIA/PADAN-ARAM. The territory between the Tigris and Euphrates rivers also known as *Padan-aram* (Gen. 25:20). Abraham and his family migrated from the city of Ur in this region (Gen. 11:31–32; Acts 7:2). The Babylonian Empire flourished in this general vicinity during O.T. times. Citizens of Mesopotamia were present in Jerusalem on the day of Pentecost (Acts 2:9). See also *Ur of the Chaldees.*

MESS. A portion of food served at a meal (2 Sam. 11:8). To receive a larger-than-usual mess or portion was considered an honor (Gen. 43:34).

MESSENGER. A person sent to deliver a special message. Jewish kings sent couriers to distant cities to proclaim laws and edicts (2 Chron. 36:22–23). John the Baptist was a messenger who prepared the people for the coming of Jesus (Matt. 11:10).

Prov. 13:17 A wicked *m* falleth into mischief
Mal. 3:1 I [God] will send my *m*
Luke 7:27 I send my [God's] *m* before thy face

MESSIAH/MESSIAS (ANOINTED ONE). The title given by the Jewish people to a future leader whom they expected to restore their honor and glory after delivering them from their oppressors (Dan. 9:25–26). Jesus fulfilled their longing but in an unexpected way by becoming a spiritual Savior who delivered believers from sin (Rom. 6:1–9). *Messias:* Greek form (John 1:41; 4:25). *Anointed one:* NIV. See also *Emmanuel; Jesus Christ; Son of God.*

METHUSELAH/MATHUSALA. A son of Enoch (Gen. 5:21) and the grandfather of Noah. Methuselah lived to the age of 969, the oldest recorded age in the Bible. *Mathusala:* Luke 3:37.

MICAH. A prophet of the O.T., a contemporary of Isaiah, whose ministry paralleled the reigns of kings Jotham, Ahaz, and Hezekiah from about 750 to 687 B.C. (Mic. 1:1). A stern prophet of judgment, he denounced the social injustices of his time (Mic. 2:1–3).

MICAH, BOOK OF. A short prophetic book of the O.T. known for its prediction that the Messiah would be born in Bethlehem (5:2). The prophet also condemned the rich for oppressing the poor (2:1–2; 6:7–13) and announced that God's judgment against the nations of Judah and Israel would be wrought by the conquering Assyrians (chaps. 1; 3; 7:10–13).

THE REMNANT IN MICAH

The prophet Micah declared that God would make a new beginning with "the remnant of Israel" (Mic. 2:12). The remnant was a small group of people who remained faithful to the Lord, even though the rest of the nation was rebellious and disobedient. This theme of the faithful few occurs throughout the Bible.

MICAIAH. An O.T. prophet who predicted that King Ahab of Israel would be killed in a battle at Ramoth-gilead, in contrast to false prophets who assured the king he would be victorious (1 Kings 22:8–28). Micaiah was imprisoned for his stinging message, but his prediction was correct (1 Kings 22:29–39).

MICHAEL

1. A son of Jehoshaphat, king of Judah. Michael was killed by his brother Jehoram, who became king (2 Chron. 21:2–4).

2. An archangel who was thought to serve as a prince and guardian over the nation of Israel (Dan. 10:21; 12:1). See also *Archangel.*

MICHAL. A daughter of King Saul presented to David as a wife after David killed 200 Philistine warriors (1 Sam. 14:49; 18:25–27). She died without children (2 Sam. 6:21–23).

MICHMAS/MICHMASH (MICMASH). A town near Jerusalem occupied by Saul's army (1 Sam. 13:2–4) and the site of Jonathan's victory over the Philistines (1 Sam. 14:6–18). Some Jewish citizens returned to this city after the Babylonian Exile (Ezra 2:27). *Michmash:* Isa. 10:28; *Micmash:* NIV.

MICHTAM. A word in the titles of Ps. 16 and Pss. 56–60, perhaps designating a particular type of psalm.

MIDDLE WALL OF PARTITION (BARRIER, DIVIDING WALL). The curtain or barrier in the Jewish temple at Jerusalem that separated Jews and Gentiles. Christ's atonement removed this partition and brought reconciliation and peace to people of all races and nationalities (Eph. 2:14–18). *Barrier:* NIV; *Dividing wall:* NRSV. See also *Court of the Gentiles.*

MIDIAN/MADIAN

1. A son of Abraham by Keturah and founder of the Midianites (Gen. 25:1–4; 1 Chron. 1:32–33).

2. A region in the Arabian desert east of the Jordan River, including Edom and the Sinai Peninsula, that was occupied by the Midianites (Exod. 2:15). *Madian:* Acts 7:29.

MIDIANITES. Nomadic traders who occupied the land of Midian. A band of Midianites probably bought Joseph and sold him as a slave in Egypt (Gen. 37:28). This tribe joined the Moabites in attacking Israel but failed (Num. 22). The Midianites were probably absorbed into the Moabites and the Arabs. See also *Gideon.*

MIDWIFE. A Hebrew woman who assisted other women in the process of childbirth. Many midwives refused the Egyptian pharaoh's orders to kill male children (Exod. 1:15–17).

MIGDOL. A place in northeastern Egypt where some citizens of Judah fled after their nation fell to the Babylonians about 587 B.C. (Jer. 44:1; 46:14).

MIGHT

Deut. 6:5 love the Lord...with all thy *m*
2 Sam. 6:14 David danced...all his *m*
Zech. 4:6 Not by *m*...but by my [God's] spirit
John 3:17 world through him [Jesus] *m* be saved
John 10:10 I [Jesus] am come that they *m* have life
John 20:31 ye *m* believe that Jesus is the Christ
Gal. 4:5 we *m* receive the adoption of sons
Eph. 6:10 be strong in the Lord...power of his *m*

MIGHTY

Exod. 1:7 children of Israel...waxed...*m*
2 Sam. 1:27 How are the *m* fallen
Job 12:19 He [God]...overthroweth the *m*
Job 36:5 Behold, God...is *m* in strength
Ps. 50:1 The *m* God...hath spoken
Isa. 9:6 his [Jesus'] name...called...*m* God
Acts 2:2 sound from heaven...rushing *m* wind
1 Cor. 1:26 not many *m*...are called
1 Cor. 1:27 weak things...confound the...*m*
1 Pet. 5:6 Humble yourselves...under the *m* hand of God

MIGHTY MEN (FIGHTING MEN, WARRIORS). The brave and loyal warriors who risked their lives for David before and after he became king (2 Sam. 23:8–39). Joshua also had the support of courageous warriors known as "mighty men of valor" (Josh. 1:14; 10:7). *Fighting men:* NIV; *warriors:* NRSV. See also *Jashobeam*.

MILCOM/MOLECH/MOLOCH. The supreme god of the Ammonites (1 Kings 11:5). Solomon built a sanctuary for worship of this pagan god, but it was destroyed during King Josiah's reforms (2 Kings 23:12–13). *Molech:*

Lev. 20:2; *Molech:* NIV; *Moloch:* Acts 7:43. See also *Ammonites*.

MILE. A Roman unit for measuring distance that equaled 1,000 paces, or 1,616 yards. Jesus used this term to teach His followers forgiveness and forbearance (Matt. 5:41).

MILETUS/MILETUM. A coastal city of Asia Minor about forty miles south of Ephesus. Paul met the leaders of the Ephesian church here and gave a moving farewell address (Acts 20:15–38). *Miletum:* 2 Tim. 4:20.

MILK. A liquid for drinking and cheese making taken from cows, goats, sheep, and camels (Gen. 32:14–15). The word is also used figuratively to indicate abundance (Exod. 3:8) and the diet of immature Christians (1 Cor. 3:1–2).

MILL. A device for grinding grain into flour, consisting of two stones that pulverized the grain between them (Exod. 11:5; Matt. 24:41).

MILLENNIUM. A term for the period of 1,000 years described in Rev. 20:1–8. Opinions vary on how to interpret this period. Premillennialists expect a literal reign of 1,000 years by Christ on earth after His return. Postmillennialists believe that 1,000 years of peace will precede Christ's second coming, during which time much of the world will be converted. While believing in the Lord's return, amillennialists view Christ's millennial reign in a spiritual sense.

MILLET. A plant that produced small heads of grain, used for making bread (Ezek. 4:9).

MILLO/BETH-MILLO

1. A stronghold or fortress at Shechem whose occupants proclaimed Abimelech as

MILK. *A Middle Eastern herder milks a camel. The milk is used as a drink and to make cheese, as is milk from goats and cows.*

their king (Judg. 9:6, 20). *Beth-millo:* NIV, NRSV.

2. A defensive fortress tower built by David near Jerusalem (2 Sam. 5:9) and improved by Solomon in anticipation of an Assyrian siege (1 Kings 9:15).

MINA. See *Maneh; Pound.*

MIND. The reasoning faculty of human beings. In the Bible, the word *heart* often means "mind" (see Ps. 19:14). Those who reject God have corrupt minds (Rom. 1:28), and the carnally minded are enemies of God (Rom. 8:5–7). Jesus urged His followers to love God with all their minds and hearts (Matt. 22:37). Paul encouraged the Christians at Rome to have their minds renewed so they would know and follow the will of God (Rom. 12:2).

MIND [S]

Neh. 4:6 people had a *m* to work
Prov. 29:11 fool uttereth all his *m*
Mark 12:30 love the Lord...with all thy *m*
Rom. 11:34 hath known the *m* of the Lord
Phil. 2:2 being of one accord, of one *m*
Phil. 2:5 this *m* be in you...also in Christ
Phil. 4:7 peace of God...keep your hearts and *m's*
2 Tim. 1:7 not given us the spirit of fear; but...of a sound *m*

MINE. A place where metals were extracted from the earth. Iron and copper were mined in the area around the Dead Sea, especially during Solomon's reign (1 Kings 9:26–28).

MINISTER. A term for a person who serves others, often used interchangeably with the word *servant.* In addition to the religious meaning of the word, it is also applied to court attendants (1 Kings 10:5) and civil rulers (Rom. 13:4–6). All Christians are instructed to "preach the word" and perform duty as God's servants (2 Tim. 4:2–5). See also *Deacon; Pastor; Priest; Shepherd.*

MINISTER [ED, S]

Ps. 9:8 he [God] shall *m* judgment to the people
Matt. 20:28 Son of man came not to be *m'ed* unto
Mark 10:43 great among you, shall be your *m*
Rom. 15:16 I [Paul] should be...*m* of Jesus
2 Cor. 11:23 Are they *m's*...I [Paul] am more
Eph. 3:7 I [Paul] was made a *m*

MINISTRY. Service in the name of God. Such service demands a spirit of sacrificial service after the example of Christ (Matt. 20:26–28). All Christians are called to be ambassadors for Christ in the work of reconciliation (2 Cor. 5:18–20), to be fishers of men (Mark 1:17), and to perfect believers (Eph. 4:11–12).

Acts 6:4 give ourselves...to the *m* of the word
2 Tim. 4:5 make full proof of thy *m*
Heb. 8:6 he [Jesus] obtained a more excellent *m*

MINOR PROPHETS. The twelve prophets of the O.T. whose books were placed last in the prophetic writings because of their shorter length—Hosea, Joel, Amos, Obadiah, Jonah, Micah, Nahum, Habakkuk, Zephaniah, Haggai, Zechariah, and Malachi. See also *Major Prophets.*

MINSTREL (HARPIST, MUSICIAN). A singer or musician (2 Kings 3:15); often employed at funerals or wakes, as in the case of the daughter of Jairus (Matt. 9:23). *Harpist:* NIV; *musician:* NRSV.

MINT. A common, inexpensive herb used in medicine and for seasoning foods. Jesus mentioned mint as an object scrupulously tithed by the scribes and Pharisees (Matt. 23:23).

MIPHKAD (INSPECTION GATE, MUSTER GATE). A gate in the walls of Jerusalem

or the temple rebuilt by Nehemiah (Neh. 3:31). *Inspection Gate:* NIV; *Muster Gate:* NRSV.

MIRACLE. God's intervention or suspension of the natural laws of the universe. Miracles are described in the N.T. as signs, wonders, mighty works, and powers. Most miracles in the Bible occurred during (1) the period of the Exodus (Exod. 7, 9, 10, 14), (2) Elijah's and Elisha's ministry (2 Kings 4:2–7), (3) the period of the Exile (Dan. 3:9–27), (4) the ministry of Jesus, when miracles attested to His divine power (Matt. 15:33–39), and (5) the ministry of the apostles, signifying their apostleship (Acts 3:6).

Jesus worked miracles to relieve suffering (Matt. 8:14–17), to raise the dead (Matt. 9:23–25), to calm nature (Luke 8:22–25), or to give an object lesson (Mark 11:12–14). See also *Sign.*

MIRACLES

John 2:11 beginning of *m* did Jesus in Cana
John 9:16 How can a man that is a sinner do such *m*?
Acts 6:8 Stephen...did great wonders and *m*
1 Cor. 12:10 To another the working of *m*

MIRIAM. The sister of Aaron and Moses (1 Chron. 6:3). Miriam protected her baby brother Moses by arranging for their mother, Jochebed, to care for him (Exod. 2:4–10). She led a triumphant song of praise and thanksgiving to God after the Israelites were delivered from the pursuing Egyptian army at the Red Sea (Exod. 15:2–21). She died and was buried in the wilderness at Kadesh (Num. 20:1). See also *Aaron; Jochebed; Moses.*

MISCHIEF MAKER. See *Busybody.*

MISHAEL. See *Meshach.*

MISHEAL (MISHAL). A city in the territory of Asher assigned to the Levites and designated as a city of refuge (Josh. 19:26). *Mishal:* NIV, NRSV. See also *Cities of Refuge.*

MISSIONS. The process of carrying out Jesus' Great Commission to disciple and teach all peoples. Even in the O.T., Abraham was called to be a blessing to all nations (Gen. 12:1–3), and Jonah was sent by the Lord to preach to the pagan citizens of Nineveh (Jon. 1:2). Missions is prompted by God's love (John 3:16) and humankind's lost condition (Rom. 3:9–31).

Believers are equipped for the task of missions by the Holy Spirit's presence (Acts 1:8), the Word of God (Rom. 10:14–15), and the power of prayer (Acts 13:1–4). Christ's followers are to evangelize all nations, baptize believers, and teach His commands (Matt. 28:19–20). See also *Commission.*

MIST. A vapor or fog. The earth was watered by a mist before the first rainfall (Gen. 2:6). Mist and darkness are used figuratively to describe spiritual blindness (Acts 13:11).

MISTRESS. A woman with power or authority (Gen. 16:4–9). The Queen of Sheba (1 Kings 10:1–3) and Queen Jezebel (1 Kings 21:7–11) were women of authority.

MITE. The coin of smallest value in N.T. times, worth less than a penny. Jesus commended a poor widow's sacrificial gift of two mites (Mark 12:42).

MITRE (TURBAN). A headdress worn by the high priest (Lev. 8:9). A gold plate inscribed with "holiness to the Lord" was attached to the mitre (Exod. 39:28–31). *Turban:* NIV, NRSV.

MIZPAH. A place where Jacob and his father-in-law, Laban, made a covenant and agreed to a friendly separation. They marked the site with a pile of stones (Gen. 31:44–53).

MIZRAIM

1. The second son of Ham and father of Ludim (Gen. 10:6–13). His descendants settled in Egypt (Gen. 45:20; 50:11).

2. The Hebrew name for Egypt (Gen. 50:11). See *Egypt.*

MNASON. A Christian from the island of Cyprus who accompanied Paul on his last visit to Jerusalem (Acts 21:16).

MOAB

1. A son of Lot and an ancestor of the Moabites (Gen. 19:33–37).

2. The country of the Moabites, lying east of the Jordan River and the Dead Sea and south of the Arnon River (Deut. 1:5–7). Its earliest name was *Lotan* or *Lot,* since the inhabitants were descended from Lot (Gen. 19:37).

MOABITE STONE. A black memorial stone that confirms a significant event of the O.T.— the rebellion of King Mesha of Moab against King Ahaziah of Israel (2 Kings 3:4–27).

MOABITES. Pagan inhabitants of Moab, worshipers of Chemosh (Num. 21:29), and enemies of the Israelites. The strength of the Moabites varied across several centuries of Israel's history. The tribes of Reuben and Gad settled in northern Moab before the conquest of Canaan (Num. 32:1–37). Ehud won a significant victory over their forces during the period of the judges (Judg. 3:15–30). David also fought and conquered the Moabites (2 Sam. 8:2). Ruth was a native of Moab (Ruth 1:22).

MOCK [ED, ETH]

Prov. 17:5 Whoso *m'eth* the poor reproacheth his Maker
Jer. 20:7 I am in derision daily, every one *m'eth* me
Mark 10:34 they shall *m* him [Jesus]...scourge him

MOABITE STONE. The Moabite Stone confirms the Bible's report [that] King Mesha of Moab drove off the Israelite army. The stone was [app]arently engraved at Mesha's command.

Luke 23:36 soldiers also *m'ed* him [Jesus]
Gal. 6:7 Be not deceived; God is not *m'ed*

MODERATION. Temperance and forbearance. Paul described moderation as a quality of gentleness to be practiced before others (Phil. 4:5). Christians are counseled to be moderate in all things (1 Cor. 9:25). See also *Temperance*.

MOLE (CHAMELEON). A KJV word that probably refers to a chameleon or lizard since no true moles are found in Palestine (Lev. 11:30). *Chameleon:* NIV, NRSV.

MOLECH, MOLOCH. See *Milcom.*

MOLTEN SEA. A large bronze vessel made by King Hiram of Tyre for ceremonial use by the priests in Solomon's temple at Jerusalem (1 Kings 7:23). See also *Brasen Sea.*

MONEY. A medium of exchange. In O.T. times before the Babylonian Exile, money was a specific weight of precious metal, such as silver or gold. The coins of N.T. times were issued by the Romans or Greeks (Matt. 17:27; Mark 12:42). The earliest coins used in Palestine before the N.T. era were Persian in origin. See also *Filthy Lucre; Mammon.*

MONEYCHANGERS. Independent agents, much like cashiers, who converted money into "shekels of the sanctuary," which could be used in the temple at Jerusalem. These "bankers" provided worshipers with the required temple tax, the half-shekel (Exod. 30:13–15). Jesus denounced these moneychangers who were charging excess fees for their services. He overturned their tables and drove them out of the temple (Matt. 21:12).

MONOGAMY. The marriage of a man to one woman only—the pattern established by God in the Garden of Eden (Gen. 2:18–24). Many of the O.T. patriarchs, such as Jacob, had more than one wife (Gen. 29:16–35). See also *Marriage; Polygamy.*

MONOTHEISM. The belief in one—and only one—supreme God, in contrast to polytheism, or the worship of several gods. The one true God is to be loved supremely and His commands taught to others (Deut. 6:4–7). God demands absolute loyalty, and He will not tolerate the worship of any other god by His people (Exod. 20:3–5). See also *Polytheism.*

MONTH. One of the twelve divisions of the year. The length of the Hebrew month was calculated from one new moon to the next (Num. 10:10; 28:11–14).

MOON. The heavenly body or satellite that revolves around the earth, referred to as the "lesser light" in the account of creation (Gen. 1:16). Each new moon marked the beginning of another Jewish month, and its arrival was celebrated with special sacrifices (Num. 28:11–15). The moon was worshiped under various names by pagan peoples, but God forbade this practice by the Hebrews (Deut. 4:19).

MOONSTONE. See *Diamond.*

MORDECAI. A Jewish exile in Persia who befriended Esther, helping her to become the king's favorite and assume the queenship (Esther 2:5–11). With Esther's help, Mordecai thwarted the plot of Haman to destroy the Jews (Esther 2:19–23). He was honored by the king and promoted (Esther 6:10–11; 8:1–2). See also *Ahasuerus; Esther; Haman.*

MORESHETH-GATH. The birthplace of Micah the prophet in the lowland plain of Judah (Mic. 1:14).

MORIAH. The mountainous area in Jerusalem where Abraham was commanded by God to sacrifice his son Isaac (Gen. 22:1–13). After God provided a sacrifice other than Isaac, Abraham renamed the site Jehovah-jireh, meaning "the Lord will provide" (Gen. 22:14).

MORNING STAR. The planet Venus as it appears at dawn and a figurative title for Christ (Rev. 22:16). Christ is described as the morning star, which outshines the light of prophetic witness (2 Pet. 1:19). See also *Day Star.*

MORTALITY. The human condition that leads eventually to physical death. Mortality is the common lot of all human beings, but it serves as the entrance to eternal life for believers (2 Cor. 5:4–6). For the Christian, bodily resurrection and eternal life are as certain as physical death (1 Cor. 15:21–23). See also *Eternal Life.*

MORTAR. A mixture of lime and sand used to build the tower of Babel (Gen. 11:3). The Israelites in Egypt worked with bricks and mortar (Exod. 1:14). See also *Untempered Mortar.*

MOSERA/MOSEROTH. A place in the wilderness where the Israelites camped on their way to Canaan. Aaron died and was buried here (Deut. 10:6). *Moseroth:* Num. 33:30–31.

MOSES. The great lawgiver and prophet of Israel who led the Hebrew people out of Egypt. His life is best understood in three forty-year periods.

Forty years in Egypt. Moses was born into slavery and hidden by his mother to escape the pharaoh's order that all male Hebrew babies should be killed (Exod. 1:22; 2:1–10). Discovered and "adopted" by the pharaoh's daughter, he was raised and schooled as an

MOSES. *Michelangelo's famous statue of Moses rests on display in Rome's Church of Saint Peter in Chains. The statue covers the tomb of Pope Julius II, a lover of art who lived at the time of Michelangelo. Julius died in 1513.*

Egyptian (Exod. 2:10). After killing an Egyptian who was abusing an Israelite slave, he became a fugitive in the desert (Exod. 2:14–15).

Forty years in Midian. Moses became a shepherd (Exod. 3:1) and married Zipporah, the daughter of a priest, and she bore two sons, Gershom and Eliezer (Exod. 18:3–4). Moses reluctantly answered God's call to lead His people out of slavery (Exod. 3:11–4:9) and returned to Egypt, where he enlisted his brother, Aaron, as his helper and spokesman (Exod. 4:27–31). After ten plagues sent by the Lord upon the Egyptians, the pharaoh finally released the Hebrews, who entered the wilderness area in the Sinai Peninsula under Moses' leadership.

Forty years in the wilderness. In the wilderness Moses received the Ten Commandments (Exod. 20:1–24) and other parts of the Mosaic Law, exhorted the people to remain faithful to God, built the tabernacle at God's command (Exod. 36–40), and sent spies to investigate Canaan (Num. 13). He impatiently struck a rock for water at Kadesh (Num. 20:1–13), a sin that led God to deny his entrance into the Promised Land. He died in Moab at Canaan's border at the age of 120 (Deut. 34:1–8). See also *Aaron; Law.*

MOST HIGH. A name for God signifying His majesty (Acts 7:48–49). The title was used by nonbelievers in both the O.T. (Num. 24:16) and the N.T. (Acts 16:17). See also *I AM; Jehovah; Yahweh.*

MOTE (SPECK). A small particle of anything. Jesus used this word to indicate the hypocrisy of those who found small flaws in others while ignoring major defects of their own (Matt. 7:3–5). *Speck:* NIV, NRSV.

MOTH. A destructive insect. Since wealthy Jews stored clothes that could be destroyed by moths, Jesus used the word to indicate the fleeting nature of earthly riches (Matt. 6:19–20).

MOTHER. A term for a female parent as well as a grandmother and other female relatives. Eve is regarded as the "mother of all living" (Gen. 3:20). Mothers are worthy of honor and obedience by those who desire long life (Exod. 20:12; Eph. 6:1–3). The prophets alluded to Israel as "mother" in denouncing the nation's shameful sins (Jer. 50:12–13; Ezek. 19).

MOUNT OLIVET. See *Olives, Mount of.*

MOUNT PARAN. See *Paran, Mount.*

MOUNTAIN REGION. See *Hill Country.*

MOUNTAIN SHEEP. See *Chamois.*

MOURN. To express grief or sorrow. The usual mourning period was seven days, but this was extended to thirty days for Moses and Aaron (Num. 20:29). Jesus mourned at the death of his friend Lazarus (John 11:33–36). See also *Sackcloth; Sorrow.*

MOURN [ETH, ING]

Job 2:11 Job's...friends...came...to **m** with him
Ps. 38:6 I am troubled...**m'ing** all the day long
Ps. 88:9 Mine eye **m'eth** by reason of affliction
Eccles. 3:4 a time to **m**, and a time to dance
Isa. 61:2 to comfort all that **m**
Matt. 5:4 Blessed are they that **m**...shall be comforted

MOUSE. A rodent (1 Sam. 6:5). Many species of these destructive animals are found in Palestine. They were "unclean" according to Mosaic Law (Lev. 11:29; Isa. 66:17).

MOUTH. The mouth has potential for good or evil. It may be used for praise and prayer (Ps.

34:1; 1 Sam. 1:12) or as an instrument of idolatry (1 Kings 19:18) and lying (1 Kings 22:13, 22). See also *Lips; Throat; Tongue.*

MOVE [D]

Gen. 1:2 Spirit of God *m'd* upon the...waters
Ps. 96:10 Lord reigneth...world...shall not be *m'd*
Mark 6:34 Jesus...was *m'd* with compassion
Acts 17:28 in him [God] we live...*m*...have our being
Heb. 12:28 kingdom which cannot be *m'd*

MUFFLER (VEIL, SCARF). A
veil or a long scarf worn about the head or chest (Isa. 3:19). *Veil:* NIV; *scarf:* NRSV.

MULBERRY (BALSAM). A
common tree of Palestine, probably the aspen, baca, or balsam (2 Sam. 5:23). *Balsam:* NIV, NRSV. See also *Sycamine.*

MULE. A beast of burden of
the horse family used extensively by the Hebrews. A runaway mule carried Absalom to his death (2 Sam. 18:9–15).

MULTITUDE [S]

Gen. 32:12 thy [Jacob's] seed...cannot be numbered for *m*
Matt. 5:1 seeing...*m's*, he [Jesus] went up into a mountain
Matt. 22:33 *m* heard this, they were astonished
Luke 2:13 with the angel a *m* of the heavenly host
John 6:2 great *m* followed him [Jesus]
Rev. 7:9 great *m*...no man could number

MURDER. The unlawful killing of a human
being, an act that was prohibited by Mosaic Law (Exod. 20:13). The Israelites exacted the death penalty for willful murder (Exod. 21:12; Lev. 24:17) but provided cities of refuge for persons guilty of manslaughter, or accidental

MUSIC. Listening to music from a small harp, called a lyre, was a popular form of relaxation in Bible times. David played a lyre to calm King Saul. This silver lyre is from Abraham's era and his hometown of Ur, in modern-day Iraq.

killing (Num. 35:11). Jesus warned of intense anger that could lead to murder (Matt. 5:20–25). See also *Avenger of Blood; Manslayer.*

MURMUR [ED, ING, INGS]

Exod. 15:24 people *m'ed* against Moses
Num. 14:27 I [God] have heard the *m'ings* of...Israel
Luke 5:30 Pharisees *m'ed* against his [Jesus'] disciples
John 7:12 much *m'ing*...concerning him [Jesus]

MURRAIN. A mysterious disease and the fifth
plague that God brought against the Egyptians, attacking their animals (Exod. 9:1–6). It may have been anthrax.

MUSIC. Vocal and instrumental music were prominent in temple choirs (2 Sam. 6:5). Musical instruments were invented by Jubal, son of Lamech (Gen. 4:21). The Hebrews used cymbals, harps, organs, pipes, psalteries, and trumpets in their worship (1 Chron. 15:16–22).

MUSICIAN. See *Minstrel.*

MUSTARD SEED. The tiny, almost microscopic seed from a common herb of Palestine. Jesus used this small seed to illustrate the power of faith in the believer's life (Luke 17:6). See also *Faith.*

MUSTER GATE. See *Miphkad.*

MUTH-LABBEN. A musical term in the title of Ps. 9, perhaps referring to the tune for the psalm.

MYRRH (RESIN). An aromatic gum resin found chiefly in Arabia (Gen. 37:25). It was one of the gifts presented to the infant Jesus (Matt. 2:11). Myrrh was used in incense, perfume, anointing oil, embalming fluid, and medicine (Exod. 30:23; John 19:39). *Resin:* NRSV.

MYRTLE. A common evergreen shrub of Palestine. Its branches were used at the Feast of Tabernacles (Neh. 8:15). A myrtle tree in the desert was symbolic of God's provision for His people (Isa. 41:19; 55:13).

MYSTERY (SECRET). Something unknown except through divine revelation (Rom. 16:25–26). The gospel is called a mystery (Eph. 3:8–9). Jesus taught in parables to reveal the mysteries of God's kingdom to His disciples (Luke 8:10). Paul reveals that Christ within us inspires our hope to share in His glory (1 Cor. 15:51; Col. 1:26–27). *Secret:* NIV, NRSV.

MYSTERY [IES]

Mark 4:11 you [the disciples]...know the *m* of the kingdom
1 Cor. 2:7 we speak the wisdom of God in a *m*
1 Cor. 4:1 stewards of the *m'ies* of God
1 Cor. 13:2 though I [Paul]...understand all *m'ies*
1 Tim. 3:9 the *m* of the faith in a pure conscience

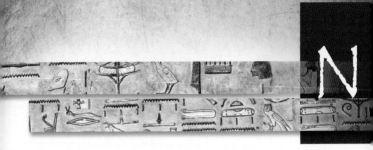

N

NAAMAN. A captain in the Syrian army who was healed of leprosy by the prophet Elisha. At first Naaman was reluctant to bathe in the Jordan River for healing, as commanded by Elisha. But he finally obeyed, received healing, and praised the God of Israel (2 Kings 5:1–15). Naaman was mentioned by Jesus (Luke 4:27).

NABAL. A wealthy herdsman who refused to provide food for the desperate David and his army in the wilderness. His wife, Abigail, secretly offered hospitality, and Nabal died ten days later (1 Sam. 25). See also *Abigail.*

NABOTH. An Israelite who was framed and killed by Jezebel so Ahab could take possession of Naboth's vineyard. God pronounced judgment against them for this despicable act (1 Kings 21:1–23).

NACHOR. See *Nahor.*

NADAB
  1. The oldest son of Aaron who was destroyed, along with his brother Abihu, for offering "strange fire" to God (Lev. 10:1–2). See also *Abihu.*
  2. A king of Israel (reigned about 910–909 B.C.), the son of Jeroboam I. Nadab was assassinated by Baasha, who succeeded him (1 Kings 15:25–31).

NAHASH. A king of Ammon who befriended David. David tried to return the favor to his son Hanun but was rejected (2 Sam. 10:1–4).

NAHOR/NACHOR. The grandfather of Abraham and father of Terah (Gen. 11:22–25). *Nachor:* Luke 3:34.

NAHUM. A prophet of Judah from Elkosh who prophesied against Nineveh before 612 B.C., probably during the reign of King Hezekiah (Nah. 1:1, 8, 13); author of the book of Nahum.

NAHUM, BOOK OF. A short prophetic book of the O.T. that predicted the downfall of the pagan nation of Assyria (3:7–19) because of the atrocities that it committed against God's people. The prophet portrays God as the sovereign Lord of history who has the final word in the conflict between good and evil (chap. 1). See also *Assyria.*

NAIN. A village south of Nazareth near the Sea of Galilee where Jesus raised a widow's son from the dead (Luke 7:11–17).

NAIOTH. A place in Ramah where David fled from King Saul and where Samuel lived and conducted his school for prophets (1 Sam. 19:18–20).

NAME. The word or title by which someone or something is known. Adam gave names to the animals (Gen. 2:20). Persons and places in the Bible often bore symbolic names, such as the children of the prophets Isaiah (Isa. 8:3) and Hosea (Hosea 1:4).

NAOMI. The mother-in-law of Ruth. After marrying Elimelech, Naomi moved to Moab to escape a famine. Her husband and two sons died, leaving Naomi and her two daughters-in-law alone. She returned to Bethlehem with Ruth and helped arrange Ruth's marriage to Boaz (see Ruth 1–4).

NAPHTALI

1. A son of Jacob by Bilhah, Rachel's maid (Gen. 30:1, 8). He received Jacob's blessing (Gen. 49:21–28), and his descendants became one of the twelve tribes of Israel.

2. The tribe consisting of Naphtali's descendants (Num. 1:42), who were assigned the fertile, mountainous territory in northern Palestine, including the cities of Hazor, Kedesh, and Ramah (Josh. 19:36–38; 20:7). Isaiah prophesied that Naphtali in "Galilee of the nations" would see a great light (Isa. 9:1–7). This was fulfilled in Jesus' Galilean ministry (Matt. 4:12–16). See also *Tribes of Israel.*

NAPHTUHIM (NAPTUHITES). The inhabitants of central Egypt who were descendants of Mizraim, son of Ham (Gen. 10:13). *Naptuhites:* NIV in 1 Chron. 1:11.

NAPKIN (CLOTH). A handkerchief or small piece of cloth (Luke 19:20) used for wiping perspiration and for other purposes (Acts 19:12). A similar cloth was used for binding the face and head of the dead for burial (John 11:44; 20:7). *Cloth:* NIV, NRSV. See also *Handkerchief.*

NARD. See *Spikenard.*

NATHAN

1. A son of David by Bath-sheba, born after David became king (1 Chron. 3:5). A brother of Solomon (2 Sam. 5:14), he is listed as an ancestor of Jesus (Luke 3:31).

2. The brave prophet who used an allegory to rebuke King David for his sin with Bath-sheba and his plot to kill Bath-sheba's husband, Uriah (2 Sam. 12:1–15). Nathan also assisted David when Adonijah attempted to seize the throne (1 Kings 1:8–45) and wrote histories of David's and Solomon's administrations (1 Chron. 29:29; 2 Chron. 9:29).

NATHAN THE BRAVE

The prophet Nathan dared to stand toe to toe with King David and tell him the unvarnished truth about his sin of adultery with Bath-sheba (2 Sam. 12:1–9). The prophets of the Old Testament were often called on by the Lord to deliver unpopular messages to those in authority (Jer. 36:27–32; Dan. 5:17–28).

NATHANAEL. See *Bartholomew.*

NATION. A word used in various ways in the Bible: (1) to describe all the inhabitants of a country or the country itself (Deut. 4:34); (2) to refer to natives of the same stock (Acts 26:4); (3) to denote the father or head of a tribe or clan; and (4) to refer to pagans or Gentiles (Isa. 9:2).

NATION [S]
Gen. 12:2 make of thee [Abraham] a great *n*
Exod. 19:6 ye [Israel] shall be...an holy *n*
Ps. 33:12 Blessed is the *n* whose God is the LORD
Ps. 72:11 all *n's* shall serve him [God]
Ps. 113:4 LORD is high above all *n's*
Prov. 14:34 Righteousness exalteth a *n*
Isa. 2:4 not lift up sword against *n*
Hag. 2:7 desire of all *n's* shall come
Matt. 25:32 before him [Jesus]...gathered all *n's*
Matt. 28:19 teach all *n's*, baptizing them
Luke 24:47 repentance...preached...among all *n's*
Acts 2:5 devout men, out of every *n*

נצרת

الناصرة

NAZARETH

ZARETH. Jesus' hometown of Nazareth sits on a hilltop above the ʾilean plains. Today, it's home to Jews, Christians, and Muslims.

Acts 17:26 [God] hath made of one blood all **n's**
1 Pet. 2:9 ye are a chosen generation...an holy **n**

NATURE. A word that refers to the physical universe as well as the essence or disposition of humans. God created the natural world and gave humans dominion over it (Gen. 1:1, 26–31). Adam and Eve's disobedience in the garden introduced sin and corrupted nature (Gen. 3:12–19).

The natural world is intended to draw humankind to the Creator (Ps. 8; Rom. 1:20), but the carnal nature of humans has worshiped the creature instead of the Creator (Rom. 1:25–26). Fallen humanity's faith in Christ appropriates God's divine nature (2 Pet. 1:3–4).

NAVE (RIM). The hub or rim of a wheel into which spokes were fitted (1 Kings 7:33). *Rim:* NIV, NRSV.

NAVEL. The umbilical connection of a newborn child with its mother. Ezekiel compared Jerusalem's unfaithfulness and neglect to an untended newborn child whose navel cord had not been cut (Ezek. 16:1–4).

NAZARENE (NAZOREAN). A native or inhabitant of the city of Nazareth. Since this was His hometown, Jesus was referred to as a "Nazarene" (Matt. 2:23). *Nazorean:* NRSV in Mark 1:23–24.

NAZARETH. An obscure town in Galilee that was the boyhood home of Jesus (Mark 1:24). Mary, Joseph, and Jesus returned to Nazareth after their flight into Egypt (Matt. 2:20–23). The town was located in the district of Galilee beside the plain of Esdraelon, fifteen miles southeast of Mount Carmel. Jesus was rejected by the townspeople of Nazareth at the beginning of His public ministry (Luke 4:16–30).

NAZARITE (NAZIRITE). A man or woman especially consecrated to God according to the law of the Nazarites (Num. 6:2). Voluntarily or because of a devout parent's promise, a Nazarite assumed strict

NAZARETH. A priest performs Mass in Nazareth's Church of the Annunciation. The church was built to commemorate the announcement that Gabriel made to the Virgin Mary—that Mary would have a son named Jesus.

religious vows, including abstaining from strong drink and not cutting his hair. The vow might be for life or a fixed period. Samson (Judg. 13:4–7), Samuel (1 Sam. 1:11, 28), and John the Baptist (Luke 1:15) were Nazarites. *Nazirite:* NIV, NRSV.

NEAPOLIS. A seaport at Philippi where Paul landed on the second missionary journey (Acts 16:11).

NEBO

1. The highest point of Mount Pisgah in Moab near Jericho where Moses died after viewing the Promised Land and where he was buried (Deut. 32:49; 34:5–6). See also *Pisgah, Mount.*

2. The Babylonian god of science and knowledge. Mount Nebo was possibly a center of Nebo worship. Isaiah declared the vanity of such idols (Isa. 46:1).

NEBUCHADNEZZAR/NEBU-CHADREZZAR. The king of Babylonia (reigned about 605–561 B.C.) who captured Jerusalem and carried Judah into exile about 587 B.C. (see Dan. 1–4). The only strong Babylonian king, he was the son of Nabopolassar, founder of the empire. After a revolt by King Zedekiah of Judah, Nebuchadnezzar destroyed Jerusalem, burned the temple, and carried the nation's leading citizens into exile (2 Kings 25:1–26). *Nebuchadrezzar:* Jer. 51:34. See also *Babylonia.*

NEBUZAR-ADAN. An officer in Nebuchadnezzar's army during the the Babylonian siege of Jerusalem (2 Kings 25:8–20). He looked after the prophet Jeremiah, who remained in Jerusalem after the siege (Jer. 39:11–14; 40:1–5).

NECHO. See *Pharaoh,* No. 4.

NECK. A word used figuratively for stubbornness ("stiffnecked," Deut. 9:6). It was also used to express the coming siege of Judah by Assyria (Isa. 8:8) and to represent the burden which circumcision would place on Gentile Christians (Acts 15:10).

NECKLACE. An ornament or jewelry worn around the neck. The pharaoh placed a gold chain around Joseph's neck, symbolizing his appointment as governor of Egypt (Gen. 41:41–43).

NECROMANCER. A person who communicated with the dead in an effort to foretell the future (1 Sam. 28:7–20). This practice was forbidden by the Mosaic Law (Deut. 18:11). See also *Familiar Spirit; Medium; Wizard.*

NEED [ETH]
Matt. 6:8 Father knoweth what...ye have *n* of
Luke 5:31 They that are whole *n* not a physician
1 Cor. 12:21 eye cannot say unto the hand...no *n* of thee
Phil. 4:19 my God shall supply all your *n*
2 Tim. 2:15 workman that *n'eth* not to be ashamed
Heb. 4:16 grace to help in time of *n*

NEEDLE. A tool for sewing. Jesus compared the difficulty of the wealthy reaching heaven with a camel passing through the eye of a needle (Matt. 19:24).

NEEDLEWORK. Embroidery or delicate sewing. Embroidered robes and curtains were used in the tabernacle (Exod. 28:39; 36:37).

NEEDY. See *Poor.*

NEGEV. See *South Country.*

NEGINAH/NEGINOTH. Phrases in the titles of several psalms that may refer to stringed instruments (Pss. 4, 6, 54, 55, 61, 67, 76).

NEHEMIAH. The governor of Jerusalem (445–433 B.C.) who helped rebuild the city wall after the Babylonian Exile; author of the book of Nehemiah. The son of Hathaliah, he was cupbearer to King Artaxerxes of Persia (Neh. 1:11; 2:1). He received permission from the king to return to Jerusalem to assist the returned exiles in their rebuilding efforts (Neh. 2:3–6).

In addition to rallying the people to rebuild the city wall, Nehemiah led a religious reform with the assistance of Ezra the priest (Neh. 8:1–13; 12:36). See also *Ezra*.

NEHEMIAH THE CUPBEARER

While they were in exile among the Babylonians and Persians, many of the Jewish citizens rose to responsible positions among their captors. For example, Nehemiah served as a cupbearer for King Artaxerxes of Persia (Neh. 1:11; 2:1). A cupbearer tasted the king's wine before he drank it to make sure it had not been poisoned by his enemies.

NEHEMIAH, BOOK OF. A historical book of the O.T. that records the rebuilding of Jerusalem's defensive wall after the Babylonian Exile under the leadership of Nehemiah (chaps. 1–7). The book also recounts the religious reforms undertaken by Nehemiah and Ezra. They led the people to renew the covenant and recommit themselves to God's law (chaps. 8–13). See also *Ezra*.

NEHILOTH. A musical term in the title of Ps. 5, probably denoting a wind instrument such as the flute.

NEIGHBOR. A fellow human being. Paul declared that Christians should love and speak truth to their neighbors (Rom. 13:9–10; Eph. 4:25). The Pharisees restricted the meaning of "neighbor" to people of their own nation, but Jesus' parable of the good Samaritan indicates that all people are neighbors and should help one another (Luke 10:25–37).

NEIGHBOUR
Exod. 20:16 not bear false witness against thy *n*
Lev. 19:18 thou shalt love thy *n* as thyself
Prov. 11:12 He that is void of wisdom despiseth his *n*
Prov. 24:28 Be not a witness against thy *n* without cause
Jer. 31:34 teach no more every man his *n*
Matt. 22:39 Thou shalt love thy *n* as thyself
James 2:8 fulfil the royal law...love thy *n* as thyself

NEPHEW. A term for a grandson (Judg. 12:14) or other male relative (Job 18:19). Lot, however, was a true nephew of Abraham (Gen. 11:27).

NERGAL. The Babylonian god of war that was worshiped by the men of Cuth (2 Kings 17:30). Images of Nergal were placed throughout Israel by King Shalmaneser of Assyria (2 Kings 17:24, 30).

NERGAL-SHAREZER. A Babylonian prince of King Nebuchadnezzar's court during the capture of Jerusalem (Jer. 39:1–3). He helped release Jeremiah from prison (Jer. 39:13–14).

NERO. The fifth emperor of Rome (reigned A.D. 54–68) who severely persecuted Christians. Although he is not named in the Bible, he is probably the emperor under whom Paul and Peter were martyred. Secular history confirms that Nero placed blame for Rome's great fire (A.D. 64) on the Christians and had many put to death during his administration. See also *Roman Empire*.

NERO. Roman Emperor Nero started the officially sanctioned persecution of Christians in A.D. 64, after accusing them of setting the fire that destroyed most of Rome. He committed suicide four years later.

NEST. The dwelling place of birds. The loftiness of the eagle's nest demonstrated the foolishness of man's pride (Jer. 49:16; Obad. 4).

NET. A meshed fabric used to capture birds or fish. The word is also used figuratively for entrapment of the innocent and for winning others to Christ (Matt. 4:18).

NETHANEEL (NETHANEL). A priest who helped transport the ark of the covenant to Jerusalem (1 Chron. 15:24). *Nethanel:* NIV, NRSV.

NETHER, NETHERMOST. The lower or lowest part. The children of Israel assembled on the nether part of Mount Sinai to receive a message from God (Exod. 19:17).

NETHINIM (TEMPLE SERVANTS). Persons assigned to do menial work as assistants to the priests in temple service. Many of the Nethinim were slaves or captives of war assigned to the Levites (Ezra 8:17–20). *Temple servants:* NIV, NRSV.

NETTLE. A shrub with prickly briars (Prov. 24:31), possibly a variety of acanthus that grew near the Mediterranean Sea (Isa. 34:13).

NEW
Exod. 1:8 arose a *n* king...knew not Joseph
Ps. 96:1 sing unto the LORD a *n* song
Eccles. 1:9 no *n* thing under the sun
Isa. 65:17 I [God] create *n* heavens...new earth
Lam. 3:23 they [God's mercies] are *n* every morning
Ezek. 36:26 a *n* spirit will I [God] put within you
Mark 2:22 no man putteth *n* wine into old bottles
Luke 22:20 cup is the *n* testament in my [Jesus'] blood
John 13:34 A *n* commandment I [Jesus] give unto you
2 Cor. 3:6 ministers of the *n* testament...of the spirit
2 Cor. 5:17 any man be in Christ, he is a *n* creature
2 Pet. 3:13 we...look for *n* heavens...new earth
Rev. 21:5 Behold, I [Jesus] make all things *n*

NEW BIRTH. A state of regeneration or resurrection from spiritual death (Rom. 6:4–8). The Holy Spirit brings regeneration (John 3:5–8) and produces a changed person. This comes about by God's grace through faith in Christ rather than through one's own efforts or good works (Eph. 2:8–9).

Regeneration helps the believer overcome the world and lead a victorious life (1 John 5:4–5). The new birth is required before a person can enter the kingdom of God (John 3:3–7). See also *Regeneration; Salvation.*

NEW COVENANT. God's final covenant with His people through which His grace is expressed to all believers. Prophesied by the prophet Jeremiah (Jer. 31:31–34), the new covenant was symbolized by Jesus at the Passover meal with His disciples. He called the cup the "new covenant in my blood" (Luke 22:20 NIV, NRSV). Christ, mediator of a new and better covenant, assures our eternal inheritance (Heb. 8:6–8, 13; 9:11–15; 12:24). See also *Covenant; Jeremiah, Book of; Testament.*

NEW JERUSALEM. See *Jerusalem.*

NEW MOON. See *Month; Moon.*

NEW TESTAMENT. The second major division of the Bible, composed of twenty-seven books, also known as the "new covenant" to magnify the coming of the Messiah and His redemptive ministry of grace (Jer. 31:31–34; Heb. 9:15). The complete N.T. in its current form was formally adopted by the Synod of Carthage in A.D. 397.

NIBHAZ. An idol of the Avites, a displaced Assyrian tribe that settled in Samaria (2 Kings 17:31). The name means "barker"; this pagan god was in the form of a dog-headed man.

NILE RIVER. *The Nile River cuts a fertile swath through the desert nation of Egypt. (Inset) A space shuttle photo shows the Nile flowing north into the Mediterranean Sea. Above and to the right is the Red Sea with its two rabbit ears, the Gulf of Suez and the Gulf of Aqaba. Between the two gulfs is the rugged Sinai Peninsula, where Moses led the Israelites.*

NICODEMUS. An influential Pharisee who talked with Jesus about the new birth. Jesus impressed upon him the necessity of being born of the Spirit (John 3:1–7). Later, Nicodemus cautioned the Jewish officials not to prejudge Jesus (John 7:50–51). He helped prepare Jesus' body for burial (John 19:39).

NICOLAITANES (NICOLAITANS). An early Christian sect whose origin is unknown. Their idolatrous practices were abhorrent to God, being compared to those of Balaam (Rev. 2:14). The church at Ephesus was commended

for not tolerating the Nicolaitanes (Rev. 2:6), while the church at Pergamos was rebuked for its openness to their teachings (Rev. 2:15). *Nicolaitans:* NIV, NRSV.

NIGER. See *Simeon,* No. 3.

NIGHT. The period of the day when darkness prevails. The Creator established night along with the daylight hours (Gen. 1:5). The word is used figuratively to denote death (John 9:4) or sin (1 Thess. 5:5).

233

NIGHT HAWK (SCREECH OWL). An unclean bird, probably an owl or other night creature (Lev. 11:13–16; Deut. 14:15). *Screech owl:* NIV.

NILE RIVER. The great river of Egypt that begins in Africa and runs for more than 4,000 miles across Africa and Egypt, emptying finally into the Mediterranean Sea. In Bible times, Egypt's fertility depended on the annual overflow of the Nile (Isa. 23:10). God's judgment on Egypt was often depicted as a drying up of the Nile (Zech. 10:11). The baby Moses was hidden in the tall grass at the edge of the river (Exod. 2:3). See also *Egypt.*

NIMROD. Ham's grandson and son of Cush. A skilled hunter and warrior, he became a powerful king and empire builder in Babylonia, or Shinar (Gen. 10:8–12; 1 Chron. 1:8–10).

NINEVEH/NINEVE. The capital of Assyria on the Tigris River where the prophet Jonah preached God's message of judgment. Founded by Asshur, a son of Shem, Nineveh reached the height of wealth and splendor during Jonah's time (Jon. 3:3). It was taken by the Medes about 750 B.C. and destroyed by the Medes and Babylonians about 606 B.C. *Nineve:* Luke 11:32. See also *Assyria.*

NISAN. See *Abib.*

NISROCH. An Assyrian god with a temple at Nineveh where King Sennacherib was killed about 698 B.C. It was believed to have a human body with an eagle's head (2 Kings 19:36–37).

NITRE (SODA, LYE). A mineral used as a cleaning agent; probably lye or sodium carbonate (Jer. 2:22). *Soda:* NIV; *lye:* NRSV.

NO (THEBES). A thriving Egyptian city on both sides of the Nile River that served as the capital of upper Egypt (Nah. 3:8). No was destroyed in 81 B.C., as predicted by the prophet Jeremiah (Jer. 46:25). *Thebes:* NIV, NRSV.

NOADIAH. A prophetess who tried to frighten Nehemiah and hinder his efforts to rebuild the wall of Jerusalem (Neh. 6:14).

NOAH/NOE. The person chosen by the Lord to preserve life on earth by building an ark to escape the great flood. Noah was the son of Lamech and the father of Shem, Ham, and Japheth. He "found grace in the eyes of the Lord" (Gen. 6:8) and was described in the N.T. as a preacher of righteousness (2 Pet. 2:5). After building the ark, he entered with his family and selected animals (Gen. 7:1–24). Upon leaving the ark after the flood ended, he built an altar for worship (Gen. 8:18–22).

God covenanted with Noah not to destroy the earth with water again (Gen. 9:1–19). After pronouncing blessings and curses on his sons, he died at the age of 950 (Gen. 9:29). *Noe:* Greek form (Luke 17:26). See also *Ark, Noah's.*

NOAH'S FAITHFULNESS

The account of Noah and the flood (Gen. 6:9–8:22) shows that God has never given up hope for the salvation of humankind. The world may be filled with sin, but He always preserves a remnant, or a tiny minority, who remain faithful to Him and His commandments. This concept of the faithful remnant appears throughout the Bible, particularly the prophets of the Old Testament.

NOSE JEWELS. Nose rings, popular in Bible times, are still among the jewelry favored by various tribal groups throughout the Middle East.

NOB. A Levitical city near Jerusalem (Isa. 10:32) where David fled to escape King Saul's wrath (1 Sam. 21:1–6). Saul ordered the slaughter of eighty-five priests here in retaliation for their kindness to David (1 Sam. 22:13–19).

NOBLEMAN (ROYAL OFFICIAL). A person of high rank or privileged position. A nobleman sought Jesus to heal his son who was seriously ill (John 4:46–54). *Royal official:* NIV, NRSV.

NOD. An unknown region east of Eden where Cain lived after murdering his brother Abel (Gen. 4:16–17). It may have been China, according to some scholars.

NOE. See *Noah.*

NOMADS. Tent dwellers or herdsmen who moved from one grazing ground to another with their flocks (Gen. 13:5–7). The children of Israel led a nomadic life in the wilderness for forty years (Num. 14:2). See also *Wilderness Wanderings.*

NOOSE. See *Snare.*

NOPH (MEMPHIS). An ancient royal city of the Egyptians (Jer. 46:19). Noph flourished about 3000 to 2200 B.C. on the west bank of the Nile River about thirteen miles south of modern Cairo. Many of the royal pyramids and the famous Spinx are located near the site of this ancient city. *Memphis:* NIV, NRSV.

NORTHEASTER. See *Euroclydon.*

NOSE JEWELS. Jeweled rings worn in the nose as ornaments (2 Kings 19:28).

NOSE, NOSTRILS. God created man and breathed life into his nostrils (Gen. 2:7). The word is figurative of God's power in parting the Red Sea for the Israelites (Exod. 15:8).

NOTHING

Isa. 40:17 nations before him [God] are as *n*
Jer. 32:17 there is *n* too hard for thee [God]
Matt. 5:13 salt...good for *n*, but to be cast out
Matt. 17:20 *n* shall be impossible unto you
Mark 7:15 *n* from without a man...can defile him
John 3:27 receive *n*, except...given...from heaven
John 5:19 The Son [Jesus] can do *n* of himself
John 15:5 without me [Jesus] ye can do *n*
1 Cor. 7:19 Circumcision is *n*...uncircumcision is *n*
1 Tim. 6:7 For we brought *n* into this world
Heb. 7:19 For the law made *n* perfect

NOVICE (RECENT CONVERT). An inexperienced or recent Christian convert. Paul instructed Timothy that a novice in the faith lacked the maturity to serve as a pastor or bishop (1 Tim. 3:1, 6). *Recent convert:* NIV, NRSV.

NUMBERS, BOOK OF. An O.T. book that focuses on the Israelites in the wilderness of Sinai—a period of more than forty years between their departure from Egypt and their occupation of Canaan. The book describes the "numbering" of the people in two separate censuses (chaps. 1, 26); their failure to trust God and fear of the Canaanites (chap. 13); their numerous rebellions and complaints in the wilderness (chaps. 15–25); and their final preparation for entering the Land of Promise (chaps. 26–36). See also *Wilderness Wanderings.*

NUN. The father of Joshua and an Ephraimite servant of Moses who helped lead the Israelites across the Jordan River into the Promised Land (Josh. 1:1–2).

NURSE. A woman servant who breast-fed an infant or helped rear the child. Deborah, Rebecca's nurse, accompanied the family to Canaan (Gen. 24:59; 35:8).

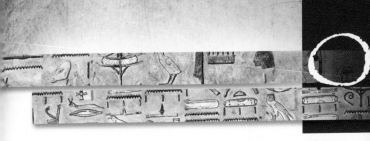

OAK. Several species of oak grew in Palestine. This word was often used to describe any strong tree or grove of trees (Gen. 35:8). Oak was used for carving idols (Isa. 44:9–15).

OAR. A paddle for pulling a ship through the water. Even large sailing vessels used oars when there was not enough wind to fill the sails (Isa. 33:21–23).

OATH. A solemn promise, often used to appeal to God to attest that a statement was true or to affirm a covenant (2 Sam. 21:7). The taking of an oath was accompanied by raising the hand or placing the hand under the thigh (Gen. 24:2–3). Jesus warned against careless oaths (Matt. 5:34–36).

Matt. 26:72 he [Peter] denied with an *o*
Heb. 7:20 not without an *o* he [Jesus] was made priest
James 5:12 neither by any other *o*: but let your yea be yea

OBADIAH
1. A prophet of Judah and author of the O.T. book that bears his name (Obad. 1). He probably lived after the destruction of Jerusalem in 587 B.C. Nothing more is known about him.
2. A godly servant of King Ahab who hid 100 prophets in a cave so they could escape Jezebel's wrath (1 Kings 18:3–16).

OBADIAH, BOOK OF. A prophetic book of only twenty-one verses—the shortest book in the O.T.—that pronounces judgment against the Edomites, the descendants of Esau (vv. 1,

6), because of their mistreatment of God's people, the Israelites (vv. 10–14). See also *Edomites; Esau.*

OBED-EDOM. A Philistine from the city of Gath. The ark of the covenant was left at his house for three months before its removal to Jerusalem (1 Chron. 13:13–14).

OBEDIENCE
Rom. 5:19 the *o* of one [Jesus]...many be made righteous
2 Cor. 10:5 captivity every thought to the *o* of Christ
Heb. 5:8 he [Jesus] were a Son, yet learned he *o*

OBEDIENT
Acts 6:7 company of the priests were *o* to the faith
Phil. 2:8 he [Jesus] humbled himself...*o* unto death
1 Pet. 1:14 As *o* children, not...according to the former lusts

OBEY. To submit to authority. Children are commanded to obey their parents (Exod. 20:12; Eph. 6:1–3). Jesus was obedient to Joseph and Mary (Luke 2:51). Jesus was perfectly obedient to the Father, and He requires obedience of His followers (Heb. 5:8–9).

OBEY [ED, ETH]
Gen. 22:18 thou [Abraham] hast *o'ed* my [God's] voice
Deut. 27:10 Thou shalt...*o* the voice of the LORD
1 Sam. 15:22 to *o* is better than sacrifice
Jer. 11:3 Cursed be the man...*o'eth* not...this covenant
Mark 4:41 the wind and the sea *o* him [Jesus]
Acts 5:29 We [the apostles]...*o* God rather than men
Col. 3:20 Children, *o* your parents
Heb. 11:8 he [Abraham]...*o'ed*...not knowing whither he went

OBLATION (GRAIN OFFERING). An offering sanctified to God, consisting usually of meat, meal, firstfruits of the harvest, or land (Lev. 2). *Grain offering:* NIV, NRSV.

OBSERVER OF TIMES. A person who was thought to be able to foretell the future through reading signs (Deut. 18:10–14). See also *Omen; Witchcraft.*

OFFENSE. A charge or accusation against another. Reconciling with an offended brother should take priority over making an offering (Matt. 5:24).

OFFER [ED, ING, INGS]
Gen. 4:4 Lord had respect unto Abel…his *o'ing*
Lev. 10:1 Nadab and Abihu…*o'ed* strange fire
Ps. 51:16 thou [God] delightest not in burnt *o'ing*
Ps. 96:8 bring an *o'ing,* and come into his [God's] courts
Mal. 3:8 have we robbed thee [God]? In tithes and *o'ings*
Matt. 5:24 be reconciled to thy brother…*o'* thy gift
Eph. 5:2 Christ…hath given himself for us an *o'ing*
2 Tim. 4:6 I [Paul] am now ready to be *o'ed*
Heb. 7:27 he [Jesus] did once…*o'ed* up himself
Heb. 13:15 let us *o* the sacrifice of praise to God

OFFERING. Something given to God as a confession, consecration, expiation, or thanksgiving, generally as a part of worship. Because of his sinfulness and frailty, man recognizes he cannot covenant with God without obedience and faith. Jesus offered Himself as a full and final sacrifice for sin (Heb. 7:25–27). See also *Sacrifice.*

OFFSCOURING (SCUM, FILTH). Refuse; something vile or despised (Lam. 3:45). Paul indicated that faithful Christians may be regarded as "the scum of the earth" by the world (1 Cor. 4:13). *Scum:* NIV; *filth:* NRSV.

OFFSPRING. Children or descendants (Job 5:25). The risen Lord declared He was the "offspring of David" (Rev. 22:16). All people are regarded as offspring of the Creator (Acts 17:28–29). See also *Posterity; Seed.*

OG. An Amorite king of Bashan who was defeated by the Israelites at Edrei (Num. 21:33–35). His territory was assigned to the tribe of Manasseh (Deut. 3:1–13).

OIL. A liquid extracted from olives that was burned in lamps (Matt. 25:3) and used for anointing (Ps. 23:5), food preparation (1 Kings 17:12), and medicine (Luke 10:34). Olive groves were numerous throughout Palestine. See also *Anointing; Olive.*

OIL TREE (OLIVE). The olive tree or the oleaster shrub (Isa. 41:19). The oleaster shrub resembled the wild olive, with its yellow flowers and olivelike fruit. *Olive:* NIV, NRSV.

OINTMENT (PERFUME). A salve or perfumed oil made of olive oil and spices and used in anointing ceremonies. Jesus was anointed by devoted followers (Mark 14:3). *Perfume:* NIV in John 12:3. See also *Perfume.*

OLD GATE (JESHANAH GATE). A gate in the walls of Jerusalem rebuilt by Nehemiah (Neh. 3:6; 12:39). *Jeshanah Gate:* NIV.

OLD TESTAMENT. The first major section of the Bible, containing thirty-nine books, also known as the "old covenant" because it points to the coming of the new covenant in Jesus Christ. The O.T. begins with God's creation of the world, contains the books of the law and wisdom, and ends with prophecies that point to the Messiah's coming (Isa. 53; Jer. 31:31–34).

OLIVE. Black and green olives along with a jar of pickled lemons—each a delicious fruit of the tree—decorate a dinner table.

OLIVE. The fruit of the olive tree that was used for food and olive oil. The branch of an olive tree was a symbol of peace (Gen. 8:11). See also *Oil.*

OLIVES, MOUNT OF/MOUNT OLIVET. A hill in eastern Jerusalem where Jesus was betrayed by Judas on the night before His crucifixion (Matt. 26:30, 47). The branches of olive trees from the Mount of Olives were used to make booths for the Feast of Tabernacles (Neh. 8:15). *Mount Olivet:* Acts 1:12.

OMEGA. See *Alpha and Omega.*

OMEN. A sign used to predict future events. Witchcraft and divination were forbidden by the Mosaic Law (Deut. 18:10). The Lord frustrates the efforts of fortune-tellers and astrologers (Isa. 44:25). See also *Observer of Times; Witchcraft.*

OMER. A dry measure of two to three quarts (Exod. 16:16).

OMNIPOTENCE. The unlimited and infinite power that belongs to God. This characteristic of God's nature is expressed by His names *almighty* (Gen. 17:1) and *omnipotent* (Rev. 19:6). God controls nature (Amos 4:13) and the destiny of nations (Amos 1–2). God's omnipotence is also expressed by the Holy Spirit's power to convict and save (Rom. 15:19). See also *God; Sovereignty of God.*

OMNIPRESENCE. The universal presence of God. No person can hide from God (Jer. 23:23–24). Christ is present with the multitudes or with two or three believers (Matt. 18:20). God's Spirit is our companion in all circumstances (John 14:3, 18). See also *God.*

OMNISCIENCE. The infinite knowledge of God. The all-wise and all-knowing God requires no counselor (Isa. 40:13–14). Christ is the key who opens all the hidden treasures of God's wisdom and knowledge (Col. 2:2–3). God's Spirit reveals the "deep things of God" to those who are spiritually receptive (1 Cor. 2:10–14). See also *God.*

OMRI. The king of Israel who built Samaria as the capital city of the Northern Kingdom (reigned about 885–874 B.C.; 1 Kings 16:23–28). He was a wicked king who led the nation into idolatry (1 Kings 16:26). Omri was the father of the wicked king Ahab, who succeeded him (1 Kings 16:29), and grandfather of the ruthless queen Athaliah of Judah (2 Kings 11:1–3). See also *Samaria.*

ON

1. A Reubenite leader who joined Korah and others in the rebellion against Moses and Aaron in the wilderness (Num. 16:1–14).

2. A city of lower Egypt noted for its learning and its prominence as a center of sun worship. Joseph's wife, Asenath, was from this city (Gen. 41:45). *Aven:* Amos 1:5.

ONAN. The second son of Judah who was killed because of his failure to consummate a marriage union with Tamar, wife of his slain brother (Gen. 38:8–10).

ONESIMUS. A slave who was converted under Paul. Onesimus escaped and fled to Rome, where he came under Paul's influence. After his conversion, he returned to his master Philemon with an epistle from Paul, who

ONESIMUS THE SLAVE

Slavery was a common practice in New Testament times. Slaves were used as agricultural workers and as household servants. Onesimus was probably a household slave (Philem. 16). Paul did not condemn the practice of slavery, but he did commend the principle of Christian love to Philemon, the owner of Onesimus. Christian love and brotherhood were two factors that eventually led to the decline of slavery throughout the world.

appealed for Onesimus to be treated with mercy (Col. 4:9; Philem. 10). See also *Philemon.*

ONESIPHORUS. A Christian from Ephesus who befriended Paul when he was a prisoner in Rome. Paul commended him for his service (2 Tim. 1:16–18; 4:19).

ONION. A popular vegetable in Egypt and Palestine (Num. 11:5).

ONYCHA. An ingredient in sacred incense that Moses was instructed to prepare (Exod. 30:34). It may have come from the mollusk shell. See also *Incense.*

ONYX. A precious stone in the breastplate of the high priest (Exod. 28:20). David collected onyx to decorate the temple in Jerusalem (1 Chron. 29:2). See also *Sardonyx.*

OPHEL. The southern side of ancient Jerusalem's eastern hill, perhaps a tower or other fortification. The Nethinims lived here after the Babylonian Exile (Neh. 3:26).

OPHIR

1. A son of Joktan and grandson of Eber (Gen. 10:26–29).

2. The territory, probably in Arabia, populated by Ophir's descendants (Gen. 10:29–30). A famous gold-producing region, Ophir was visited by the ships of Solomon and the Phoenicians (1 Kings 9:26–28).

OPHRAH. Gideon's hometown in Manasseh where an angel assured him of the Lord's guidance and protection (Judg. 6:11–14).

OPPRESSOR. One who defrauds and mistreats others. The Egyptians oppressed the Hebrews by making them slaves (Exod. 3:9). See also *Taskmasters.*

ORACLE. A revelation or wise saying given to a person for his or her guidance (Rom. 3:2). Ministers are charged to preach God's message (1 Pet. 4:11).

ORCHARD. A garden planted with trees (Eccles. 2:5), particularly fruit-bearing trees (Song 4:13). See also *Garden.*

ORDAIN. To set a person apart for special service. Paul and Silas ordained elders for the churches they established (Acts 14:23). Paul instructed Titus to ordain elders to serve as leaders in the churches he served (Titus 1:5). Christ ordained His disciples to bear enduring fruit (John 15:16). See also *Consecration.*

ORDAIN [ED]
1 Chron. 17:9 I [God] will *o* a place for my people
Mark 3:14 he [Jesus] *o'ed* twelve…they should be with him
Rom. 13:1 powers that be are *o'ed* of God

ORDINANCES. Baptism and the Lord's Supper, rituals or procedures intended to commemorate the great events of redemption.

The Lord's Supper memorializes the shed blood and broken body of Christ (1 Cor. 11:23–26). Baptism symbolizes the death, burial, and resurrection of Jesus and the believer's victory over sin and death (Rom. 6:3–6). See also *Baptism; Lord's Supper.*

ORGAN (FLUTE, PIPE). A wind instrument made of reeds of various lengths and played by blowing across their open ends (Gen. 4:21). *Flute:* NIV; *pipe:* NRSV. See also *Pipe.*

ORION. A constellation of stars cited as evidence of God's power (Job 9:9).

ORNAMENTS. Items of jewelry, such as rings on the fingers, ears, and nose (Isa. 3:18–23). Bracelets and earrings were presented to Rebekah by Abraham's servant (Gen. 24:22).

ORNAN. See *Araunah.*

ORONTES. The major river of Syria. The important cities of Kadesh, Riblah (2 Kings 23:33), and Hamath (1 Kings 8:65) were situated on the Orontes.

ORPAH. A Moabite woman who married Chilion, son of Naomi and Elimelech. She returned to her own people after the death of her husband (Ruth 1:4–15).

ORPHANS. Children whose parents have died. Kindness toward orphans was commanded by the Mosaic Law (Deut. 24:17). Visiting orphans and widows was considered a mark of true religion, or godliness (James 1:27). Jesus promised that believers would not be treated as orphans (John 14:18).

OSEE. See *Hosea.*

OSHEA. See *Joshua*.

OSNAPPAR. See *Asnapper*.

OSPRAY (BLACK VULTURE). An unclean bird, perhaps similar to the eagle or hawk (Lev. 11:13). *Black vulture:* NIV. See also *Gier Eagle*.

OSSIFRAGE (VULTURE). An unclean bird, probably similar to the eagle, or perhaps the vulture (Deut. 14:12). *Vulture:* NIV, NRSV. See also *Vulture*.

OSTRICH. A large, flightless bird noted for its speed (Job 39:13–18) and its mournful cry (Mic. 1:8, NRSV). It was listed as "unclean" in the Mosaic Law (Lev. 11:16, NRSV).

OTHNIEL. The first judge of Israel who defeated the king of Mesopotamia (Judg. 3:9–11). See also *Judges of Israel*.

OUCHES (GOLD FILIGREE SETTINGS). Sockets or mountings in which precious stones were set in the ephod of the high priest (Exod. 28:11–14). *Gold filigree settings:* NIV, NRSV.

OUGHT

Luke 18:1 men *o* always to pray, and not to faint
John 13:14 ye also *o* to wash one another's feet
Acts 5:29 We [the apostles]…*o* to obey God rather than men
Rom. 12:3 think of himself more highly…he *o* to think
Eph. 5:28 So *o* men to love…wives as their own bodies
Col. 4:6 ye may know how ye *o* to answer every man
1 John 4:11 Beloved…we *o* also to love one another

OVEN. Replica of a clay oven and stove used in Bible times. Hot coals burned inside, while food cooked on top. Bread was baked inside the oven, on top of the coals.

OUTCASTS. Dispossessed people. This word was used by the prophets to describe the Jews scattered among foreign nations (Isa. 11:12; Jer. 30:17). Jesus had compassion on lepers who were social outcasts (Luke 17:11–19). See also *Remnant*.

OVEN. A large earthenware container filled with hot coals and ashes. Utensils with food were placed over the opening for cooking (Hosea 7:7).

OVERCOME [TH]
Num. 13:30 we are well able to *o* it [Canaan]
John 16:33 I [Jesus] have *o* the world
Rom. 12:21 Be not *o* of evil, but *o* evil with good
1 John 5:4 the victory that *o'th* the world
Rev. 21:7 He that *o'th* shall inherit all things

OVERSEER. An elder, bishop, presbyter, or supervisor in charge of a congregation (Acts 20:28).

OWL. A bird of prey with large eyes and strong claws that hunts at night (Ps. 102:6). It was considered unclean by the Israelites (Lev. 11:13–17).

OWNER. See *Householder*.

OX. An animal of the cow family used for plowing (Deut. 22:10), for threshing grain (Deut. 25:4), and as a beast of burden (1 Chron. 12:40). Oxen also supplied milk and meat and were used as sacrifices (Lev. 17:3–4). See also *Bull; Bullock*.

OX GOAD. A spike used to drive oxen. Shamgar, judge and deliverer of Israel, killed 600 Philistines with an ox goad (Judg. 3:31).

OZIAS. See *Uzziah*.

O

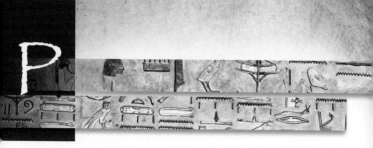

P

PACE (STEP). A measure of length, based on the step of a man (2 Sam. 6:13). *Step:* NIV.

PADAN-ARAM. See *Mesopotamia*.

PADDLE. A spadelike tool at the butt end of a spear for digging a hole in the ground to cover waste (Deut. 23:13).

PAINT. A cosmetic cover. Hebrew women painted around their eyes, but the practice was condemned (Jer. 4:30). Paint was also used to color walls and adorn pagan temples (Ezek. 23:14).

PALACE. A residence for a king or other high official. Solomon's palace on Mount Zion near the temple featured an ivory throne (1 Kings 7:1–12; 10:18). Jesus was tried in the hall of Herod's palace by Pilate (Mark 15:16) and in the palace of Caiaphas the high priest (Matt. 26:57–58).

PALESTINE/PALESTINA. The territory of the Canaanites that became known as the land of the people of Israel. The name *Palestine* referred originally to the territory of the Philistines, especially the coastal plain south of Mount Carmel. The name was extended during the Christian era to include all of the Holy Land, including both sides of the Jordan River and the Dead Sea region south to Egypt.

After the Canaanites were displaced, the country was called the land of Israel (1

Sam. 13:19) and the "land of promise" (Heb. 11:9). Three great world religions—Judaism, Christianity, and Islam—originated here. *Palestina:* Exod. 15:14. See also *Canaan*, No. 2; *Land of Promise*.

PALM. A tropical tree (Exod. 15:27), so named because its leaf resembles a human hand. Most biblical references are to the date palm, which grows sixty to eighty feet tall.

PALMERWORM (LOCUST). A caterpillar or a distinct species of locust that ate vegetation (Joel 1:4). This insect or worm was sent as a plague upon rebellious Israel (Amos 4:9–10). *Locust:* NIV, NRSV. See also *Locust*.

PALSY. A disease that caused paralysis and possible loss of feeling (Acts 8:7). Although it was regarded as incurable, Jesus healed many people with palsy (Matt. 4:24).

PAMPHYLIA. A coastal region in southern Asia Minor visited by Paul (Acts 13:13; 14:24). Perga was its capital and Attalia its main seaport (Acts 14:25). Residents of Pamphylia were present in Jerusalem on the day of Pentecost (Acts 2:1–10).

PAN (GRIDDLE). A utensil or cooking container (Lev. 6:21). *Griddle:* NIV, NRSV.

PANTHEISM. A doctrine that teaches that God and His universe are identical, or that

PALACE. *This is a model of the Jerusalem palace of Herod the Great—one of many elegant residences for this vicious king of the Jews appointed by Rome.*

physical things are merely attributes of an all-encompassing God. Jews and Christians reject this doctrine because God created the universe separate and apart from Himself (Gen. 1:1). He exists apart from, in addition to, and above the world (see Ps. 8). See also *Creation*.

PAPER. Papyrus, or an ancient writing material made from reeds that grew on the banks of the Nile River in Egypt (2 John 12). See also *Bulrush; Ink; Reed; Writing*.

PAPHOS. A city on the island of Cyprus where Paul blinded Elymas the magician. This led to the conversion of the Roman governor, Sergius Paulus (Acts 13:6–13).

PAPS (BREASTS). An Old English word for "breasts" (Luke 11:27). *Breasts:* NRSV.

PAPYRUS. See *Bulrush*.

PARABLE. A short story drawn from daily life that is used to convey an important truth; a favorite teaching device used by Jesus (Matt. 13:3). In the O.T., Nathan told a parable to convict King David of his sin of adultery (2 Sam. 12:1–7). Jesus used parables to present truth to His receptive hearers and to conceal the lesson from those who were critical or unreceptive (Matt. 13:10–16, 35). Drawn from daily life, His parables revealed lessons about salvation, the kingdom, and the future life (Luke 15).

PARACLETE (COUNSELOR, ADVOCATE). A Greek word for the Holy Spirit that expresses the idea of a helper called to one's side. It is translated as "Comforter" in the Gospels (John 14:16). *Counselor:* NIV; *Advocate:* NRSV. Also *advocate* in 1 John 2:1. See also *Advocate; Comforter; Helper; Holy Spirit*.

PARADISE. A word that describes the heavenly home of the redeemed (2 Cor. 12:4). Jesus used the term to comfort the repentant dying thief (Luke 23:43). See also *Heaven; Heavenly City*.

PARADOX. A contradictory statement that expresses a great truth; a favorite teaching device of Jesus. He declared that a person can find his or her life by losing it (Matt. 10:39) and that a person becomes great by serving others (Mark 10:43).

PARALYSIS. See *Palsy*.

PARALYTIC. A paralyzed person. Jesus honored the faith of a paralytic by offering forgiveness and healing (Matt. 9:1–7).

PARAMOUR (LOVER). A slave or concubine who provided sexual favors (Ezek. 23:20). *Lover:* NIV. See also *Concubine*.

PARAN/MOUNT PARAN/EL-PARAN. A mountainous wilderness region in the Sinai Peninsula, sometimes called *Mount Paran* (Hab. 3:3) or *El-paran* (Gen. 14:6). The Israelites camped here during their years in the wilderness (Num. 10:12; 12:16).

PARAPET. See *Battlement*.

PARCHED CORN (ROASTED GRAIN, PARCHED GRAIN). Roasted grains of wheat, barley, or millet (1 Sam. 25:18). *Roasted grain:* NIV; *parched grain:* NRSV.

PARCHMENT. Writing material made from the skin of sheep or goats. Paul asked Timothy to bring parchments to him in prison (2 Tim. 4:13).

PARDON. Forgiveness. God will pardon those who repent and turn to the Lord (Isa. 55:7). The loving father in Jesus' parable had compassion on his repentant son, extended pardon, and celebrated his return (Luke 15:18–24). God promised to pardon the iniquity of Judah and Israel that led to their captivity and exile (Jer. 33:8–9). See also *Forgiveness; Remission.*

PARDON [ED, ETH]

Neh. 9:17 a God ready to *p*, gracious and merciful
Ps. 25:11 O Lord, *p* mine iniquity; for it is great
Isa. 40:2 her [Jerusalem's] iniquity is *p'ed*
Jer. 33:8 I [God] will *p* all their iniquities
Mic. 7:18 Who is a God like unto thee, that *p'eth* iniquity

PARENTS. People who bear and rear children. The duty of parents is to train (Deut. 4:9; 6:6–7) and correct (Deut. 21:18–21) their children. They should avoid favoritism (Gen. 25:28) and anger (Eph. 6:4). God promised to bless parents who bring up their children in the nurture of the Lord (Prov. 22:6; Eph. 6:4). See also *Children.*

PARLOUR. A room in a house for entertaining guests (1 Sam. 9:22), a secret chamber for retreat (1 Chron. 28:11), or a room on the roof for enjoying cool breezes (Judg. 3:20–25).

PAROUSIA. A Greek word that refers to the second coming of Christ. See also *Second Coming.*

PARTHIANS. Inhabitants of Parthia, a country north of Media and Persia. Parthians were in Jerusalem on the day of Pentecost (Acts 2:1, 9).

PARTIALITY. To show favoritism or preference toward some people over others.

PARCHMENT. Before paper came along, Jews wrote on scrolls of parchment—made from the leather of animals, usually sheep or goats. The leather was cut into strips, stitched together, and rolled into scrolls.

God's wisdom is available to all and free of favoritism or hypocrisy (James 3:17).

PARTITION. See *Middle Wall of Partition.*

PARTRIDGE. A wild bird in Palestine prized for its meat and eggs. Jeremiah compared ill-gotten wealth to a partridge sitting on eggs that will not hatch (Jer. 17:11).

PARVAIM. An unidentified place that provided gold for Solomon's temple (2 Chron. 3:6). Some scholars believe this was the same place as Ophir (1 Kings 9:28).

PASCHAL LAMB. See *Passover.*

PASHUR. A priest who struck Jeremiah and had him imprisoned. Jeremiah predicted that Pashur and his household would die as captives in Babylonia (Jer. 20:1–6).

PASSOVER AND FEAST OF UNLEAVENED BREAD. A Jewish festival that commemorated the Exodus from Egypt (Josh. 5:10). The Passover celebrated how God "passed over" the Hebrew houses in Egypt that were sprinkled with blood while killing the firstborn of the Egyptians on the eve of the Exodus (Exod. 12). The seven-day Feast of Unleavened Bread recalled the haste with which the slaves left Egypt (Exod. 12:33–34).

PASTOR. One who leads and instructs a congregation. Jeremiah predicted the coming of faithful pastors who would lead Israel back to God (Jer. 3:15). Pastors are called of God to perfect the saints and build up the body of Christ (Eph. 4:11–13). See also *Bishop; Elder; Minister; Shepherd.*

PASTORAL EPISTLES. The three letters of Paul—1 and 2 Timothy and Titus—that deal with pastoral concerns, or practical matters involving the operation and government of a local church.

PASTURE. Grazing lands for livestock. The word is also used figuratively for the protection of God's people under the Good Shepherd (Ps. 23:1–2; Ezek. 45:15).

PASTURE LANDS. See *Suburbs.*

PATH. A crude road. The word is also used figuratively for the route of one's life. The righteous are warned not to walk the paths of darkness (Prov. 2:13–15).

PATHROS (UPPER EGYPT). A name for upper Egypt where Egyptian civilization likely began. Jewish people lived here during the Babylonian Exile (Jer. 44:1, 15). *Upper Egypt:* NIV.

A Permanent Passover

Of all the Jewish religious holidays and holy days specified in the Old Testament (Lev. 23), perhaps the annual Passover was the most important in terms of its significance for modern believers.

Centuries after the first Passover, Jesus was crucified when the Jewish people gathered in Jerusalem to celebrate this religious holiday. The apostle Paul declared that Christ is "our passover," or sacrificial lamb, who has been "sacrificed for us" (1 Cor. 5:7).

PAUL, THE
APOSTLE. *Paul is
beheaded—punishment
for preaching about
Jesus. The Bible doesn't
say how Paul died, but
church leaders later said
he was beheaded in
Rome.*

P

PATIENCE. Forbearance or restraint. God is the author of patience (Rom. 15:5), and Christ is its perfect model (2 Thess. 3:5). Believers are urged to labor with patience in the service of Christ (1 Thess. 5:14). See also *Forbearance; Longsuffering; Steadfastness.*

Rom. 5:3 tribulation worketh **p**

1 Tim. 6:11 follow after…faith, love, **p**, meekness

Heb. 12:1 run with **p** the race…set before us

James 1:3 the trying of your faith worketh **p**

PATIENT [LY]

Ps. 40:1 I waited **p'ly** for the Lord

Eccles. 7:8 the **p** in spirit is better than the proud in spirit

Rom. 12:12 Rejoicing in hope; **p** in tribulation

James 5:7 **p** therefore, brethren, unto the coming of the Lord

PATMOS. A desolate island in the Aegean Sea, used as a prison by the Romans, where the apostle John was exiled and where he wrote the book of Revelation. Christ revealed Himself to John and told him to send messages to the seven churches of Asia Minor (Rev. 1:9–20). See also *John the Apostle.*

PATRIARCH. The head of a tribe or clan in O.T. times who ruled by authority passed down from father to oldest son. Abraham, Isaac, and Jacob, along with the sons of Jacob and David, are notable examples of patriarchal rule (Acts 2:29; 7:8–9).

PAUL THE APOSTLE. The great apostle to the Gentiles; defender and advocate of the Christian faith in its early years through his thirteen N.T. letters. A complex personality, Paul demonstrated both toughness and tenderness in his devotion to Christ. His teachings are both profound and practical (Phil. 3:7–10).

Paul's Hebrew name as a Jew of Benjamite ancestry was Saul, but his Roman name was Paul (Acts 13:9). A Roman citizen born at Tarsus in Cilicia (Acts 22:3), he was a tentmaker by trade—a vocation by which he often supported himself as a minister to the churches that he established (Acts 18:3).

A strict Pharisee and member of the Jewish Sanhedrin, Paul opposed Christianity in its early years in Jerusalem. He consented to the death of Stephen, the first martyr of the church (Acts 7:58–8:1). He was on his way to persecute Christians at Damascus when he converted to Christianity in his famous "Damascus road" experience (Acts 9:1–19). From that point on, Paul was zealous for the cause of Christ.

Under the sponsorship of the church at Antioch in Syria, Paul undertook three great missionary journeys to the Roman world, extending westward through Cyprus and Asia Minor into Europe (Acts 13–21). His traveling companions on these tours included Barnabas, John Mark, Timothy, Silas, Titus, and Luke. Along with his successes in making disciples, healing, and planting churches, he suffered a "thorn in the flesh" (2 Cor. 12:7), was frequently arrested, was stoned, and was imprisoned (Acts 16:22–23).

Falsely accused by his enemies, he appealed to the Roman emperor for justice (Acts 25:10–12). After an arduous voyage by ship, he spent two years in Rome under house arrest. While guarded by Roman soldiers, he received friends and preached the gospel (Acts 28:16–31; Phil. 1:12–14).

Four of Paul's epistles—Ephesians, Colossians, Philippians, and Philemon—were written from Rome. Most scholars believe he was beheaded in Rome about A.D. 67 during Nero's reign (Phil. 2:17; 2 Tim. 4:6–8).

PAULUS, SERGIUS. The Roman proconsul of Cyprus who was converted under Paul's ministry (Acts 13:4–12). See also *Cyprus; Paphos.*

PAVEMENT, THE/GABBATHA. An area in Pilate's courtroom paved with stones where Jesus was judged, sentenced to crucifixion, and turned over to the mob (John 19:13–16). Its Aramaic name was *Gabbatha.*

PAVILION (DWELLING, SHELTER). A tent or booth for kings or other members of the royal family. The word is also used figuratively for the dwelling place of God (Ps. 27:5). *Dwelling:* NIV; *shelter:* NRSV.

PAY [ETH]

Ps. 37:21 wicked borroweth, and *p'eth* not again
Ps. 66:13 I will *p* thee [God] my vows
Matt. 18:34 delivered…tormentors, till he should *p* all

PEACE. Harmony and accord brought about by cordial relationships. Peace has its source in God (Phil. 4:7) through Christ (John 14:27) and the Holy Spirit (Gal. 5:22). Christians are urged to pursue peace and to live peaceably with all people (2 Cor. 13:11; 2 Tim. 2:22).

Ps. 4:8 lay me down in *p,* and sleep
Ps. 55:18 He [God] hath delivered my soul in *p*
Prov. 17:28 a fool…holdeth his *p,* is counted wise
Eccles. 3:8 a time of war, and a time of *p*
Isa. 9:6 his [Messiah's] name…Prince of **P**
Isa. 53:5 chastisement of our *p*…upon him [God's servant]
Matt. 10:34 I [Jesus] came not to send *p,* but a sword
Luke 2:14 on earth *p,* good will toward men
John 16:33 in me [Jesus] might have *p*
Rom. 5:1 we have *p* with God through…Jesus Christ
1 Cor. 14:33 God is not the author of confusion, but of *p*
Eph. 2:14 he [Jesus] is our *p*…made both one
Col. 3:15 the *p* of God rule in your hearts

PEACE OFFERING. See *Heave Offering; Wave Offering.*

PEACOCK (BABOON). An exotic animal imported by King Solomon, probably from Spain (2 Chron. 9:21). *Baboon:* NIV.

PEARL. A precious stone found in the shells of oysters. Jesus compared the kingdom of heaven to a merchant seeking valuable pearls (Matt. 13:45–46).

PEG. See *Pin.*

PEKAH. A king of Israel (reigned about 740–732 B.C.) who assassinated Pekahiah to gain the throne. He was killed by Hoshea in a conspiracy (2 Kings 15:23–31).

PEKAHIAH. An evil king of Israel (reigned about 742–740 B.C.) who was murdered and succeeded by Pekah, one of his military officers (2 Kings 15:23–26).

PELEG/PHALEC. A descendant of Shem (Gen. 10:25, 31). *Phalec:* Luke 3:35.

PELETHITES. A unit or division of David's soldiers who remained loyal to him during the rebellions of Absalom and Sheba (2 Sam. 15:14–18; 20:7).

PELICAN (DESERT OWL). A large bird, considered unclean by the Israelites (Lev. 11:13, 18), that was cited as a symbol of loneliness and desolation (Ps. 102:6). This may be the same bird as the *cormorant* (Isa. 34:11). *Desert owl:* NIV. See also *Cormorant.*

PEN. A word for various writing instruments, including those that wrote on scrolls (Jer. 8:8), skin or parchment, and stones (Job 19:24). See also *Ink; Writing.*

PENKNIFE (SCRIBE'S KNIFE). A small knife used for sharpening the writing pen, or reed pen (Jer. 36:23). *Scribe's knife:* NIV.

PENCE. See *Penny.*

PENIEL/PENUEL. A place east of the Jordan River near the Jabbok River where Jacob wrestled with an angel (Gen. 32:24–32). *Penuel:* Judg. 8:8. See also *Jacob.*

PENITENCE. See *Repentance.*

PENNY/PENCE (DENARIUS). A silver coin of small value (Matt. 20:1–13). It varied in value, but it generally equaled the daily wage of an unskilled worker. *Pence:* plural form (Luke 10:35). *Denarius:* NIV. See also *Farthing.*

PENTATEUCH. The Greek name for the first five books of the O.T.: Genesis, Exodus, Leviticus, Numbers, and Deuteronomy. It was called the Torah or the Law of Moses by the Hebrews (Ezra 7:6). Jesus recognized the value of the law and came to fulfill its spiritual requirements (Matt. 5:17–18; 12:5). See also *Law.*

PENTECOST/FEAST OF WEEKS/ FEAST OF HARVEST. An annual Jewish feast or holy period, commemorating the end of the harvest, that fell on the fiftieth day after the Passover. This was the holiday being observed in Jerusalem when the Holy Spirit came in power upon the early Christian believers (Acts 2). This feast was also known as the *Feast of Weeks* and the *Feast of Harvest* (Exod. 34:22).

PENUEL. See *Peniel.*

PEOPLE OF GOD. A phrase for the nation of Israel as well as the people of the new covenant, or the Church. The Israelites were called by God as His special people (Deut. 8:6–9), but all who have accepted Christ as Lord and Savior, including Gentiles, are also His people—members of God's "chosen generation, a royal priesthood" (1 Pet. 2:9–10). God's people include every kindred, tongue, and nation (Rev. 5:9; 7:9). See also *Church; Congregation; Saints.*

PEOR. A mountain of Moab across the Jordan River from Jericho. From Peor, Balak and Balaam observed the camp of the Israelites with the intention to curse them (Num. 23:28; 24:1–2).

PERAZIM. See *Baal-perazim.*

PERCEIVE [D, ING]
Job 38:18 Hast thou [Job] *p'd* the breadth of the earth?
Isa. 6:9 see ye indeed, but *p* not
Luke 8:46 I [Jesus] *p* that virtue is gone out of me
Luke 9:47 Jesus, *p'ing*…their heart, took a child
Acts 10:34 I [Peter] *p* that God is no respecter of persons

PERDITION. The state of the damned, or those who have rejected Christ. Jesus called Judas the "son of perdition" because of his betrayal of Christ (John 17:12). Perdition is the final destiny of the ungodly (2 Pet. 3:7) as well as the final abode of the Antichrist (Rev. 17:8, 11). See also *Damnation; Hell; Judgment, Last.*

PEREA. A word used by some translations of the Bible for the territory east of the Jordan River across from Judea and Samaria. Jews often traveled from Galilee to Judea through Perea to avoid going through the territory of the despised Samaritans (Matt. 4:15; 19:1). This region is called the land "beyond Jordan" in the KJV.

PEREZ. See *Pharez.*

PERFECT [ING]
Gen. 6:9 Noah was…just…*p* in his generations
Job 1:1 that man [Job] was *p* and upright
Ps. 19:7 law of the LORD is *p*, converting the soul
Matt. 5:48 Father which is in heaven is *p*
Rom. 12:2 prove what is that…*p*, will of God
2 Cor. 12:9 strength is made *p* in weakness

Eph. 4:12 **p'ing** of the saints...work of the ministry
2 Tim. 3:17 the man of God may be **p**
Heb. 5:9 made **p**, he [Jesus]...author of...salvation
James 1:17 good gift and every **p** gift is from above
1 John 4:18 but **p** love casteth out fear

PERFECTION (MATURITY).

A state of completion or fulfillment. Believers are urged to advance to mature teachings and "perfection" or fulfillment in good works (Heb. 6:1). While disclaiming perfection, Paul urged believers to keep striving for perfection by being like Christ (Phil. 3:12–15). *Maturity:* NIV.

Ps. 50:2 Out of Zion, the **p** of beauty, God hath shined
2 Cor. 13:9 this also we wish, even your **p**
Heb. 7:11 If...**p** were by the Levitical priesthood

PERFUME.

A sweet-smelling fragrance, usually an extract of spices used in ointments, incense, and oils (Prov. 27:9). See also *Oil; Ointment.*

PERFUMER. See *Apothecary.*

PERGA.

The capital of Pamphylia and a city visited by Paul. John Mark left Paul and Barnabas at Perga (Acts 13:13–14), and Paul preached here on the return to Antioch after the first missionary journey (Acts 14:25).

PERGAMOS (PERGAMUM).

A city where one of the seven churches of Asia Minor addressed by John in Revelation was located. The church was rebuked for its toleration of sexual immorality and false teachings. The phrase "where Satan's seat is" is probably a reference to a pagan temple in the city (Rev. 2:12–17). *Pergamum:* NIV, NRSV.

PERFUME. As Egyptian perfumers have done for thousands of years, they continue to gather a delicate harvest of scents from flowers and herbs that grow along the Nile River.

PERISH [ETH]

Ps. 1:6 way of the ungodly shall *p*
Ps. 68:2 wicked *p* at the presence of God
Prov. 19:9 he that speaketh lies shall *p*
Prov. 29:18 Where there is no vision, the people *p*
Mark 4:38 carest thou not that we [the disciples] *p*
John 3:16 whosoever believeth in him [Jesus] should not *p*
John 6:27 Labour not for the meat which *p'eth*
1 Cor. 1:18 preaching of the cross is to them that *p* foolishness

PERIZZITES. Descendants of Perez who were subdued by Joshua's forces. Natives of the hill country, they were associated with the Canaanites (Josh. 3:10).

PERSECUTE [D, ST]

Ps. 31:15 deliver me…from them that *p* me
Matt. 5:11 Blessed are ye when men shall…*p* you
Matt. 5:44 Love your enemies…pray for them…*p* you
Acts 9:4 Saul, Saul, why *p'st* thou me [Jesus]?
Rom. 12:14 Bless them which *p* you…curse not
2 Cor. 4:9 *P'd*, but not forsaken; cast down, but not destroyed

PERSECUTION. Oppression in matters of conscience or religious practice, or punishment because of one's convictions. Believers who are not well grounded in the faith cannot endure persecution (Matt. 13:21). Jesus declared that those who are persecuted because of their commitment to Him will inherit the kingdom of God (Matt. 5:10–12). See also *Affliction; Suffering; Tribulation.*

Lam. 5:5 necks are under *p*: we…have no rest
Acts 8:1 great *p* against the church…at Jerusalem
Rom. 8:35 separate us…love of Christ? shall…distress, or *p*

PERSEVERANCE. Persistence, or the ability to endure through difficult circumstances. Paul counseled steadfastness in the Lord's work because labor for Him is never in vain (1 Cor. 15:58). Endurance of God's chastening or discipline is a mark of God's sonship (Heb. 12:7–8). See also *Patience; Steadfastness.*

PERSIA. A great empire whose territory covered what is now western Asia and parts of Europe and Africa, reaching the height of its greatness around 486 B.C. under Cyrus. The Persians conquered Babylonia in 539 B.C. and allowed the Israelites to return to their native land (2 Chron. 36:20–23). The Persian king Artaxerxes allowed Nehemiah to return to Jerusalem to rebuild the city wall (Neh. 2:1–8). The Persians were defeated by the Greek military conqueror Alexander the Great in 330 B.C. (Ezek. 38:5). See also *Elam; Elamites.*

PERSUADE [D, ST]

Luke 16:31 be *p'd*, though one rose from the dead
Acts 26:28 thou [Paul] *p'st* me [Agrippa] to be a Christian
Rom. 8:38 I [Paul] am *p'd*…neither death, nor life
2 Tim. 1:12 I [Paul] have believed…am *p'd*…he [Jesus] is able

PESTILENCE. A plague or widespread fatal disease (Hab. 3:5), usually coming as a result of God's judgment against sin (Exod. 5:3; Ezek. 33:27). See also *Plague.*

PESTLE. A short, blunt tool used for grinding grain or crushing other material in a container known as a mortar (Prov. 27:22).

PETER. See *Simon,* No. 1.

PETER, EPISTLES OF. Two short N.T. epistles, probably from the apostle Peter, written to encourage Christians experiencing persecution and discouragement (1 Peter) and to warn them against false teachers (2 Peter).

In response to scoffers who doubted the second coming of Christ—since He had not yet returned—Peter declared, "The Lord is not slack concerning his promise, as some men count slackness; but is longsuffering to us-ward, not willing that any should perish, but that all should come to repentance" (2 Pet. 3:9).

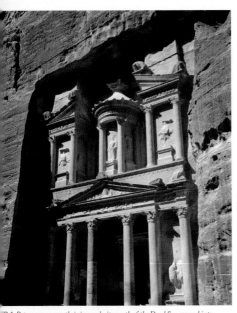

RA. Petra was once a thriving rock city south of the Dead Sea, carved into This temple-looking building, however, is just a façade. It's chiseled just a few deep.

PETHOR. A town in northern Mesopotamia near the Euphrates River; home of Balaam, who was sent to curse the Israelites (Num. 22:5–7).

PETITION. An earnest request. King Ahasuerus granted Esther's petition to save her people (Esther 7:2–5). Believers are confident their petitions will be answered (1 John 5:14–15). See also *Intercession; Prayer.*

PETRA. An ancient city located south of the Dead Sea. Named for its rocky terrain, Petra was once the capital of Edom and later of

Nabatea. Some scholars believe it was the same city as *Selah* (2 Kings 14:7).

PHALEC. See *Peleg.*

PHARAOH. The title of the king of Egypt. The pharaoh of Egypt, who is unnamed (Exod. 1:8–11), refused to release the Israelites from slavery until God killed the Egyptian firstborn throughout the land. The named pharaohs of the Bible are:

1. Shishak, who attacked Jerusalem and plundered the temple (1 Kings 14:25–26).

2. So, who made an alliance with King Hoshea of Israel (2 Kings 17:4).

3. Tirhakah, who aided King Hezekiah of Judah against Sennacherib of Assyria (2 Kings 19:9).

4. Necoh, whose archers mortally wounded King Josiah of Judah at Megiddo (2 Kings 23:29). *Necho:* Jer. 46:2.

5. Hophra, whom God declared would fall to his enemies (Jer. 44:30).

PHAREZ/PEREZ/PHARES. One of Judah's twin sons by Tamar (Gen. 38:24–30) and founder of the family or clan of Pharzites (Num. 26:20–21). *Perez:* Neh. 11:4; *Phares:* Matt. 1:3.

PHARISEES. Members of a Jewish sect pledged to uphold the oldest traditions of Israel. In Jesus' time the Pharisees were the most powerful party—political or religious—among the Jews. Jesus exposed the hypocrisy of the Pharisees, who emphasized minute details of the law while neglecting more important issues such as justice, mercy, and love (Matt. 23:1–7). Pharisees in the N.T. who were known for their generosity and noble spirit were the apostle Paul, Nicodemus, Gamaliel, and Joseph of Arimathea. See also *Sadducees*.

PHARPAR. One of two rivers of Damascus mentioned by the Assyrian commander Naaman. He was offended when told by Elisha to bathe in the Jordan River rather than the rivers of Damascus (2 Kings 5:9–12). See also *Abana River*.

PHEBE (PHOEBE). A believer at Cenchrae near Corinth who was commended by Paul for her support of him and others (Rom. 16:1–2). *Phoebe:* NIV, NRSV.

PHENICE/PHENICIA (PHOENICIA). A Mediterranean coastal region, including the cities of Ptolemais, Tyre, and Sidon. The inhabitants of Phoenicia, descended from the Canaanites, became a seafaring and colonizing people. King Hiram of Tyre furnished cedar timber and craftsmen for the construction of Solomon's temple in Jerusalem (2 Sam. 5:11; 1 Kings 5:1–10). Jesus ministered in this region (Matt. 15:21), and Christians fled here to escape persecution after Stephen's death (Acts 11:19). *Phenicia:* Acts 21:2. *Phoenicia:* NIV, NRSV. See also *Hiram; Tyre*.

PHILADELPHIA. A city of Lycia in Asia Minor and site of one of the seven churches of Asia Minor addressed in the book of Revelation (Rev. 1:11). This church was commended for its faithfulness (Rev. 3:7–9).

PHILEMON. A Christian at Colossae to whom Paul wrote on behalf of Philemon's slave Onesimus (Philem. 1). See also *Onesimus*.

PHILEMON, EPISTLE TO. A short N.T. book written by Paul to help a runaway slave Onesimus—a convert under Paul's ministry. Philemon, the owner of Onesimus and a fellow believer, was encouraged to welcome his slave back as a Christian brother (v. 16). Paul also hinted that Onesimus be given his freedom in the spirit of Christian love (v. 21).

PHILIP

1. One of the twelve apostles of Jesus. He responded to Jesus' invitation to discipleship and brought another disciple, Nathanael, to Jesus (John 1:43–51). He also brought a group of Greeks, or Gentiles, to see Jesus in Jerusalem (John 12:21). See also *Twelve, The.*

2. One of the seven men of Greek background chosen as "deacons" in the church at Jerusalem (Acts 6:5–6) and an evangelist in the early church. Philip preached extensively in Samaria and responded to God's call to the Gaza desert (Acts 8:25–27), where he led a eunuch to Christ and baptized him (Acts 8:28–38). He entertained Paul's group of missionaries (Acts 21:8) and was the father of four daughters who prophesied (Acts 21:9).

3. A Roman ruler in northern Palestine. See *Herod*, No. 4.

PHILIPPI. A city of Macedonia where Paul and Silas were imprisoned but miraculously rescued by God. This was the first city in Greece to receive the gospel, and Lydia became the first convert (Acts 16:12–15). While imprisoned in Rome, Paul wrote a letter to the Christians in the church at Philippi (Phil. 1:1). See also *Lydia*.

PHILIPPIANS, EPISTLE TO THE. A short N.T. epistle written by Paul to the church at Philippi—a group for whom the apostle expressed great appreciation, thanksgiving, and admiration (1:1–11). Paul appealed to these fellow believers to follow Christ's example of humility (chap. 2), to continue to grow toward maturity in Christian service (chap. 3), and to experience the peace and joy that Christ promises to all believers (chap. 4).

Philippians has been called Paul's "epistle of joy" because of his exhortation, "Rejoice in the Lord alway: and again I say, Rejoice" (4:4). See also *Kenosis; Philippi.*

PHILISTIA. A coastal region about forty miles long beside the Mediterranean Sea that served as the land of the Philistines in O.T. times (Gen. 21:32–34). The name *Palestine* was derived from *Philistia.* The chief cities of Philistia were Ashdod, Askelon, Ekron, Gath, and Gaza (Josh. 13:3). See also *Palestine.*

PHILISTINES/PHILISTIM. The people of Philistia who were enemies of the Israelites, especially during the days of Saul and David. After settling in Canaan, the Philistines often battled the Israelites (2 Sam. 5:17–25). Their chief pagan gods were Dagon (Judg.16:23) and Baalzebub (2 Kings 1:2–3).Their kingdom disappeared after the Babylonian Exile. *Philistim:* Gen. 10:14. See also *Caphtor.*

PHILOSOPHY. The study of truths regarding ultimate reality. The early Christians encountered Greek dualism and the teachings of the Stoics and Epicureans (Acts 17:18; Col. 2:8–10).

PHINEHAS

1. Aaron's grandson who became Israel's high priest and chief of the Korahite branch of the Levites (1 Chron. 9:19–20). He killed Zimri and Cozbi at God's command for allowing Israel to be corrupted with idolatry (Num. 25:6–15).

2. A priest who corrupted his office by immorality and corrupt leadership (1 Sam. 1:3; 2:22–24). Phinehas and his brother Hophni died in battle with the Philistines, as foretold by a prophet (1 Sam. 2:27, 34; 4:10–11). Phinehas's wife also died in childbirth (1 Sam. 4:19–20). See also *Hophni.*

PHOEBE. See *Phebe.*

PHOENICIA. See *Phenice.*

PHRYGIA. A region of central Asia Minor visited by Paul (Acts 16:6). Jews from Phrygia were in Jerusalem on the day of Pentecost (Acts 2:1–10).

PHUT/PUT. A son of Ham (Gen. 10:6). This reference may be to people related to the Egyptians, or possibly to the Libyans. *Put:* 1 Chron. 1:8. See also *Libya.*

PHYGELLUS (PHYGELUS). A believer condemned by Paul because he deserted the apostle Paul in the Roman province of Asia (2 Tim. 1:15). *Phygelus:* NIV, NRSV.

PHYLACTERY. A verse of Scripture worn on the forehead or near the heart (Exod. 13:11–16; Deut. 6:4–8). Jesus denounced the conspicuous wearing of phylacteries (Matt. 23:5). See also *Forehead; Frontlet.*

PHYSICIAN. A healer or person who practiced medicine. Medical studies were prominent in Egypt (Gen. 50:2), with midwives and physicians practicing among the Israelites (2 Chron. 16:12). Luke was described as a "beloved physician" (Col. 4:14).

PHYSICIAN [S]

Jer. 8:22 Is there no balm in Gilead…no *p* there?
Mark 5:26 [a certain woman]…suffered…of many *p's*
Luke 5:31 They that are whole need not a *p*

PIERCE [D]

Zech. 12:10 me [the Messiah] whom they have *p'd*
Luke 2:35 sword shall *p* through thy [Mary's]…soul
John 19:34 one of the soldiers…*p'd* his [Jesus'] side

PIG. See *Swine.*

PIGEON. A bird used for sacrifices, particularly by the poor. The word is used interchangeably with *dove* in most Bible passages. Mary and Joseph offered bird sacrifices when Jesus was dedicated to God in the temple (Luke 2:24). See also *Turtledove.*

PILATE. The procurator or Roman governor of Judea (ruled about A.D. 26–36) who presided at Jesus' trial. An opportunist, Pilate was unwilling to condemn Jesus as a criminal (John 18:28–38), so he sought to have him tried by Herod at the next judicial level (Luke 23:11). Then he proposed that Jesus be the prisoner customarily dismissed at Passover, but this move also failed (John 18:39–40). Finally he released Jesus to be crucified but tried to dodge responsibility for the decision (Matt. 27:24–25).

PILGRIMAGE. A stay in a foreign country (Exod. 6:4). The term is applied figuratively to the earthly life span (Heb. 11:13). See also *Alien; Foreigner.*

PILLAR OF FIRE AND CLOUD. Supernatural signs that guided the Israelites in the wilderness (Exod. 13:21). Given to protect the Hebrews, the signs represented God's presence with His people (Num. 14:13–14). These signs

PILGRIMAGE. Jews from around the world make a pilgrimage to Jerusalem to celebrate the springtime festival of Passover. This holiday commemorates Moses' leading the Israelites to freedom, out of Egypt. Jews not able to make the trip often add this phrase to their observance: "Next year in Jerusalem."

were repeated in the transfiguration of Christ (Matt. 17:5). See also *Cloud; Fire.*

PILLOW. A headrest for sleeping. The Hebrews used quilts, stones (Gen. 28:18), netting of goat hair (1 Sam. 19:13), or leather cushions (Mark 4:38).

PIN (PEG). A peg or stake. Copper or brass tent pins were used to hold the cords of the tabernacle (Exod. 27:19). The Hebrew word for "pin" is also rendered as *nail* (Judg. 4:21). *Peg:* NIV, NRSV.

PINE. See *Fir; Box Tree.*

PINNACLE (HIGHEST POINT). A wing of the temple, perhaps an elevated area over Solomon's porch. Satan tempted Jesus to impress the crowds with a spectacular leap from this high place (Matt. 4:5–7). *Highest point:* NIV.

PINT. See *Pound.*

PIPE (FLUTE). A musical instrument probably blown like a flute (Isa. 30:29). This may have been similar to the instrument called an organ in some passages. *Flute:* NIV, NRSV. See also *Flute; Organ.*

PIPES. See *Dulcimer.*

PISGAH, MOUNT. A mountain peak in Moab from which Moses viewed Canaan before his death (Deut. 34:1–6). Balaam built altars and offered sacrifices on this mountain. The highest point of Pisgah was called *Nebo.* See also *Nebo, No. 1.*

PISHON. See *Pison.*

PISIDIA. A large mountainous district in Asia Minor visited by Paul, who preached in the city

of Antioch (Acts 13:14–50). See also *Antioch of Pisidia.*

PISON (PISHON). One of four rivers that flowed out of the Garden of Eden (Gen. 2:10–14). *Pishon:* NIV, NRSV.

PIT (CISTERN). A hole in the ground. This word may refer to a deep hole lightly covered to trap animals (Jer. 18:22) as well as to an empty cistern like that into which Joseph was thrown (Gen. 37:24). Sometimes Sheol is referred to as a pit (Num. 16:30). *Cistern:* NIV. See also *Cistern; Prison.*

PITCH. A tarlike substance used on Noah's ark, probably asphalt or bitumen found in the Dead Sea area (Gen. 6:14). It was used like mortar and caulk. See also *Slime.*

PITCHER (JAR). An earthenware vessel used to carry water (Gen. 24:14). The word is also used symbolically of the human life span (Eccles. 12:6). *Jar:* NIV, NRSV. See also *Cruse.*

PITHOM. An Egyptian city built by Hebrew slaves (Exod. 1:11). It was located in Goshen east of the Nile River.

PITY. Compassion toward others. James described God as "very pitiful, and of tender mercy" (James 5:11). God showed pity on the pagan peoples of Nineveh (Jon. 4:10–11) as well as His people, the Israelites (Isa. 63:9). See also *Mercy.*

PLAGUE. A disastrous affliction or epidemic. Plagues were often interpreted as signs of God's judgment (Exod. 9:14). Ten plagues were sent upon the Egyptians for their failure to release the Hebrew slaves (Exod. 7–12). The children of Israel were plagued for their complaining in the wilderness (Num. 11:1, 31–33). See also *Pestilence*.

TEN PLAGUES AGAINST EGYPT

1. Water turned into blood (Exod. 7:15–25)
2. Frogs (Exod. 8:1–15)
3. Lice (Exod. 8:16–19)
4. Flies (Exod. 8:20–32)
5. Diseased livestock (Exod. 9:1–7)
6. Boils, or sores (Exod. 9:8–12)
7. Hail (Exod. 9:13–35)
8. Locusts (Exod. 10:1–20)
9. Darkness (Exod. 10:21–29)
10. Death of Egyptian firstborn (Exod. 12:29–36)

PLAIN. A meadow or rolling expanse of land (Judg. 11:33). Given a choice by Abraham, Lot chose the fertile plain near Sodom rather than Canaan's hill country (Gen. 13:10–12).

PLASTER. A thick paste used as a coating for walls and stones (Lev. 14:42).

PLATTER (DISH, PLATE). A dish or utensil for food. Jesus used the word figuratively to condemn the scribes and Pharisees for their hypocrisy (Matt. 23:25–26). *Dish:* NIV; *plate:* NRSV. See also *Charger*.

PLEASURE [S]
Ps. 147:11 Lord taketh *p* in them that fear him
Ezek. 33:11 I [God] have no *p*...death of the wicked
Luke 12:32 Father's good *p* to give you the kingdom
2 Tim. 3:4 lovers of *p's* more than lovers of God

PLEDGE. A vow or something given for security of a debt. Under the Mosaic Law, an outer garment pledged by a poor man had to be returned at sunset for his use as a bed covering (Exod. 22:26–27). A creditor was forbidden to enter his neighbor's house to take a pledged item (Deut. 24:10–11). See also *Surety*.

PLEIADES. A constellation of stars cited as evidence of God's sovereignty (Job 9:9). See also *Seven Stars*.

PLOWSHARE. A piece of iron at the end of a plow shaft, used to till the soil. The word is also used figuratively for a coming age of peace (Isa. 2:4). See also *Coulter*.

PLUMBLINE. A tool used by carpenters to determine precise uprightness of a wall. The word is also used figuratively for God's test for the uprightness of His people (Amos 7:7–9).

PLUNDER. See *Spoil*.

PODS. See *Husks*.

POETIC WRITINGS. The five books of the O.T. that are written almost entirely in poetic form—Job, Psalms, Proverbs, the Song of Solomon, and Lamentations—as well as those sections of other books that use this form. Sections of several of the prophetic books, for example, appear in poetry.

POETRY, HEBREW. A unique form of Hebrew writing that uses a repetition technique known as parallelism rather than rhyming or alliteration to express ideas. In parallelism, one line of poetry is advanced, contrasted, or repeated by the next line to convey thought. For example, "Have mercy upon me, O LORD; for I am weak: / O LORD, heal me; for my bones are vexed" (Ps. 6:2).

POISON. A deadly substance when swallowed or introduced into the bloodstream. Dipping

P

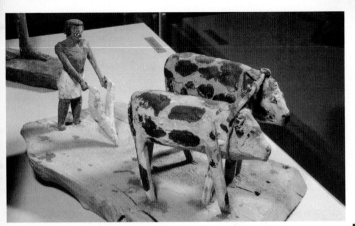

PLOWSHARE. In this ancient model, an Egyptian farmer breaks ground with a wooden plow pulled by oxen. The tips of such plows were often plated with metal and were called plowshares.

the tips of arrows into poison is probably referred to in Job 6:4. The word is also used figuratively for destructive speech (James 3:8). See also *Venom.*

POISONOUS SERPENTS. See *Fiery Serpents.*

POLLUX. See *Castor and Pollux.*

POLYGAMY. A family system under which a man is allowed to have more than one wife at the same time. The O.T. patriarchs practiced polygamy (for example, Abraham; Gen. 16:1–4), but it was contrary to God's original plan (Gen. 2:24) and divine ideal of marriage (Matt. 19:5). See also *Monogamy.*

POLYTHEISM. The practice of worshiping many gods, in contrast to monotheism, which emphasizes devotion to the one and only true God. The nations surrounding Israel worshiped multiple gods, a practice that led to immorality (Num. 25:1–9), prostitution (2 Kings 23:7), and child sacrifice (Jer. 7:29–34).

The first two of the Ten Commandments make it clear that devotion to the one and only supreme God was not to be mixed with worship of any other false or pagan god (Exod. 20:3–5). See also *Monotheism.*

POMEGRANATE. A small tree that bore apple-shaped fruit that was popular in Palestine. The spies who explored Canaan discovered this tree (Deut. 8:7–8).

POMMELS (CAPITALS). Round ornaments at the top of pillars or columns; an architectural feature used in Solomon's temple at Jerusalem (2 Chron. 4:11–13). *Capitals:* NIV, NRSV.

PONTIUS PILATE. See *Pilate.*

PONTUS. A coastal region along the Black Sea in northern Asia Minor where Priscilla and Aquila settled (Acts 18:2; 1 Pet. 1:1).

POOL. A water reservoir that supplied water for cities (John 5:2). King Hezekiah of Judah built a pool with an aqueduct to pipe water into Jerusalem (2 Kings 20:20). See also *Bethesda; Siloam; Solomon, Pools of.*

POOR. Needy or impoverished people. The Hebrews were instructed by the Lord to show compassion for the poor (Luke 14:13–14). Gleanings of the harvest were left for the poor (Lev. 19:9–10; Ruth 2). Jesus showed compassion for widows and other poor persons (Mark 12:42–44). The early church appointed "deacons" to serve the neglected poor (Acts 6:1–4). See also *Alms; Beggar.*

Deut. 15:11 the *p* shall never cease out of the land
Job 36:6 he [God]...giveth right to the *p*
Ps. 72:13 He [God] shall spare the *p* and needy
Prov. 22:2 rich and *p*...LORD...maker of them all
Isa. 25:4 thou [God] hast been a strength to the *p*
Amos 2:6 they [Israel] sold...*p* for a pair of shoes
Matt. 5:3 Blessed are the *p* in spirit
Mark 14:7 ye have the *p* with you always
Luke 4:18 anointed me [Jesus] to preach...to the *p*
Luke 19:8 half of my [Zacchaeus's] goods I give to the *p*
2 Cor. 8:9 he [Jesus] was rich, yet...became *p*
James 2:5 God chosen the *p* of this world rich in faith

POOL. *A young resident of Jerusalem washes in Siloam Pool. King Hezekiah built the pool inside the walled city of Jerusalem. Then he connected it to an underground spring outside the city—by chiseling through almost 600 yards of solid rock. The passageway became known as Hezekiah's Tunnel.*

POPLAR. A tree of the willow family. Jacob used poplar branches to produce speckled flocks (Gen. 30:37–39). See also *Willow*.

PORCH (PORTICO, VESTIBULE). A veranda or covered deck around a building. Solomon's porch was along the east side of the temple in Jerusalem (1 Kings 6:3). *Portico:* NIV; *vestibule:* NRSV. See also *Portico*.

PORCIUS FESTUS. See *Festus*.

PORK. The flesh of pigs, an unclean meat to the Jews (Lev. 11:7–8).

PORTER (GATEKEEPER, DOOR-KEEPER). A doorkeeper or watchman stationed at a city gate (2 Sam. 18:26) or private house (Mark 13:34). Porters were also assigned to guard duty in the temple at Jerusalem (1 Chron. 23:5). *Gatekeeper:* NIV; *doorkeeper:* NRSV. See also *Doorkeeper; Gatekeeper*.

PORTICO (COVERED COLONNADE). A porch. Jesus healed a paralytic lying on one of the porches of the Pool of Bethesda (John 5:2–9). *Covered colonnade:* NIV. See also *Porch*.

PORTION. See *Mess*.

POSSESSION [S]
Gen. 17:8 I [God] will give…Canaan, for an everlasting **p**
Mark 10:22 he [rich young ruler]…grieved…had great **p**'s
Acts 5:1 Ananias, with Sapphira his wife, sold a **p**

POSSIBLE
Matt. 19:26 with God all things are **p**
Matt. 26:39 if it be **p**, let this cup pass from me [Jesus]
Mark 9:23 all things are **p** to him that believeth
Luke 18:27 things…impossible with men are **p** with God
Rom. 12:18 If it be **p**…live peaceably with all men

POST (COURIER). A person who relayed messages for a king or other high official. King Hezekiah used posts to order the Israelites to keep the Passover (2 Chron. 30:6–10). *Courier:* NIV, NRSV. See also *Footman*.

POSTERITY. One's children and grandchildren. The prophet Jehu told King Baasha of Israel that his sinful leadership would destroy him and his family (1 Kings 16:1–4). See also *Seed*.

POT. A kitchen vessel usually made of clay (Isa. 29:16), but brass pots were used in the sanctuary (1 Kings 7:45).

POTENTATE (SOVEREIGN). A person of great power or authority. Jesus Christ will be recognized as the only true Potentate (1 Tim. 6:15). *Sovereign:* NRSV.

POTIPHAR. A high Egyptian officer who had Joseph imprisoned because his wife accused Joseph of trying to seduce her (Gen. 39:1–20).

POTSHERD. A fragment of pottery, often used by the poor as a drinking vessel or for carrying coals (Ps. 22:15). See also *Pottery*.

POTTAGE (STEW). A thick vegetable soup (Hag. 2:12); the price paid by Jacob for his brother, Esau's, birthright (Gen. 25:29–34). *Stew:* NIV, NRSV.

POTTER. A craftsman who made vessels from clay on a revolving wheel (Jer. 18:3). To Isaiah, the power of the potter over the clay was symbolic of the Creator's sovereignty (Isa. 45:9).

POTTER'S FIELD. A burial place for poor people outside Jerusalem. This field was bought with the betrayal silver returned by Judas to Jewish officials (Matt. 27:6–8).

POTTERY. Vessels made from clay. The broken piece of pottery cited by Jeremiah was a symbol of Judah's coming destruction (Jer. 19:1–11). See also *Potsherd.*

POUND (PINT, MINA). A dry measure of uncertain volume. Mary of Bethany anointed Jesus with a pound of costly ointment (John 12:3). *Pint:* NIV. This term was also used of money (Luke 19:13). *Mina:* NIV.

POWER

Job 37:23 he [God] is excellent in *p*
Prov. 18:21 Death and life are in the *p* of the tongue
Nah. 1:3 LORD is slow to anger, and great in *p*
Zech. 4:6 might, nor by *p*, but by my [God's] spirit
Matt. 6:13 thine [God's] is the kingdom, and the *p*
Matt. 28:18 All *p* is given unto me [Jesus]
John 1:12 gave he [Jesus] *p* to become the sons of God
Acts 6:8 Stephen, full of faith and *p*, did great wonders
1 Cor. 4:20 kingdom of God is not in word, but in *p*
Eph. 6:10 be strong in the Lord…*p* of his might
2 Tim. 1:7 God hath not given…spirit of fear; but of *p*

POWER OF GOD

Matt. 22:29 not knowing…scriptures, nor…*p-o-G*
Luke 22:69 Son of man sit…right hand of…*p-o-G*
Rom. 1:16 it [the gospel]…*p-o-G* unto salvation
1 Cor. 1:18 preaching of the cross…is the *p-o-G*
1 Cor. 2:5 faith should…stand…in the *p-o-G*

PRAETORIUM (GOVERNOR'S HEADQUARTERS). The Roman governor's official residence at Jerusalem. After being scourged by Pilate, Jesus was taken to Pilate's residence, where he was mocked by the soldiers (Mark 15:16). *Governor's headquarters:* NRSV.

PRAISE. Worship of God with honor and thanksgiving (Ps. 42:4). God is pleased and glorified with our praise (Ps. 50:23). Our praise of the Father is commanded in Jesus' model prayer (Matt. 6:9–13). See also *Thanksgiving.*

PRAISE [D, ING, S]

1 Chron. 16:25 great is the LORD…greatly to be *p'd*
Ps. 18:3 call upon the LORD…worthy to be *p'd*
Ps. 67:3 Let the people *p* thee, O God
Ps. 79:13 show forth thy [God's] *p* to all generations
Luke 2:20 shepherds returned, glorifying and *p'ing* God
Acts 16:25 Paul and Silas…sang *p's* unto God
Rev. 19:5 *P* our God, all…ye that fear him

PRAY [EST, ING]

2 Chron. 7:14 my [God's] people…humble…and *p*
Matt. 6:6 thou *p'est*, enter into thy closet
Mark 6:46 he [Jesus] departed into a mountain to *p*
Mark 11:25 when ye stand *p'ing*, forgive
Luke 6:28 *p* for them which despitefully use you
Luke 11:1 Lord, teach us [disciples] to *p*
John 14:16 I [Jesus] will *p*…Father…give…Comforter
Rom. 8:26 know not what we should *p* for as we ought
1 Thess. 5:17 *P* without ceasing
James 5:13 any among you afflicted? let him *p*

PRAYER. Communion with God. Elements of sincere prayer are adoration (Matt. 6:9–10), confession (1 John 1:9), supplication (1 Tim. 2:1–3), intercession (James 5:15), and thanksgiving (Phil. 4:6).

Jesus was a model for His followers in the practice of prayer. He arose early in the morning to pray (Mark 1:35), prayed all night before choosing the Twelve (Luke 6:12), prayed in Gethsemane on the night of His betrayal (Luke 22:44), and prayed on the cross for His enemies (Luke 23:34). He also gave His disciples a model prayer to follow in their communion with the Father (Matt. 6:9–13). See also *Intercession; Petition.*

2 Chron. 7:12 I [God] have heard thy [Solomon's] *p*
Ps. 66:20 God…hath not turned away my *p*
Matt. 21:22 ye…ask in *p*, believing, ye shall receive
Luke 19:46 My [God's] house is the house of *p*
Acts 6:4 we [the apostles] will give ourselves…to *p*
James 5:15 the *p* of faith shall save the sick
James 5:16 fervent *p* of a righteous man availeth much

PRAYER. An Orthodox Jew prays at Jerusalem's famous Western Wall, the most sacred place on earth for Jews. This wall is all that's left of their temple, destroyed by Romans 2,000 years ago. The wall once held up dirt for the mound on which the temple was built.

PREACH. To proclaim the truths of the gospel. Paul's preaching was motivated by the lost condition of His hearers (Rom. 10:1–3). The prophets were anointed by God to preach good tidings of His deliverance (Isa. 61:1–2). Jesus urged His disciples to preach the gospel to everyone (Mark 16:15).

PREACH [ED, ING]

Matt. 3:1 John the Baptist, *p'ing* in the wilderness
Matt. 4:17 Jesus began to *p*...to say, Repent
Matt. 24:14 gospel...shall be *p'ed* in all the world
Acts 5:42 they [the apostles] ceased not to...*p* Jesus Christ
Acts 8:4 they [believers]...went...*p'ing* the word
1 Cor. 1:18 the *p'ing* of the cross is...foolishness
1 Cor. 15:14 if Christ be not risen...our *p'ing* vain
2 Cor. 4:5 we *p* not ourselves, but Christ Jesus
Eph. 3:8 I [Paul] should *p* among the Gentiles
2 Tim. 4:2 *P* the word; be instant in season
1 Pet. 3:19 he [Jesus]...*p'ed*...spirits in prison

PREACHER

Eccles. 1:2 Vanity of vanities, saith the *P*...all is vanity
Rom. 10:14 how shall they hear without a *p*
2 Tim. 1:11 I [Paul] am appointed a *p*...of the Gentiles

PREACH THE GOSPEL

Mark 16:15 Go ye...and *p-t-g* to every creature
Luke 4:18 he [God]...anointed me [Jesus]...*p-t-g* to...poor
Rom. 1:15 I [Paul]...ready to *p-t-g* to you...at Rome
Rom. 10:15 beautiful...feet of them that *p-t-g*
1 Cor. 1:17 Christ sent me [Paul] not to baptize...*p-t-g*
1 Cor. 9:14 they which *p-t-g* should live of the gospel

PRECEPT. A command or directive. Vain worship results when human precepts rather than God's commands are given priority (Matt. 15:9).

PRECIOUS

Ps. 116:15 *P* in the sight of the Lᴏʀᴅ is the death of his saints
Eccles. 7:1 A good name is better than *p* ointment
1 Cor. 3:12 build upon this foundation gold, silver, *p* stones

PREDESTINATE [D]

Rom. 8:29 whom he [God] did foreknow, he also did *p*

Eph. 1:5 Having *p'd* us unto the adoption of children
Eph. 1:11 *p'd* according to the purpose of him [God]

PREDESTINATION. God's plan for the eternal salvation of those who choose Him. God has ordained good for those who love Him and are called within His purpose (Rom. 8:28). Those called to salvation will be justified and will share God's glory (Rom. 8:30). Those chosen before the foundation of the world will be adopted by God, redeemed, and given an eternal inheritance (Eph.1:4–11). See also *Election, Divine; Foreknowledge.*

PREPARATION DAY. The day before the Jewish Sabbath or the celebration of a religious festival (Matt. 27:62). Preparation for the Passover celebration involved cooking the Passover meal, baking unleavened bread, and choosing appropriate clothing for the occasion.

PRICE

Job 28:18 the *p* of wisdom is above rubies
Isa. 55:1 buy wine...without money and without *p*
Matt. 13:46 when he had found one pearl of great *p*
1 Cor. 6:20 ye are bought with a *p*: glorify God

PRIDE. Arrogance, vanity, or conceit. This sin results in self-righteousness (Luke 18:11–12) and self-deception (Jer. 49:16). Paul, however, expressed justifiable pride in his fellowship with the Philippians (Phil. 1:3–6). See also *Conceit; Haughtiness; Vanity.*

Lev. 26:19 I [God] will break the *p* of your power
Ps. 10:2 wicked in his *p* doth persecute the poor
Prov. 16:18 *P* goeth before destruction
1 John 2:16 the lust of the eyes...*p* of life

PRIEST. A religious leader who made sacrificial offerings. The priesthood originated with Aaron, and his descendants were sanctified to the office (Exod. 29:9, 44). Jesus, our faultless high priest, paid for our sins once and for all by sacrificing Himself (Heb. 7:26–28). See also *High Priest.*

PRIESTHOOD OF BELIEVERS. The doctrine that each believer has direct access to God. This was symbolized by the torn veil in the temple at Jerusalem when Jesus died on the cross, providing access to the Holy of Holies for all believers (Matt. 27:50–51). Christ is the only authorized mediator between God and man (Eph. 3:11–12). Therefore, we can come boldly and directly to Him (Heb. 4:15–16). As priests of God, believers should minister to others in a spirit of love (Gal. 5:13).

PRIESTHOOD OF CHRIST. One of Christ's offices as the Son of God, emphasizing His offering of Himself on our behalf. Christ obtained eternal redemption for believers by making a perfect sacrifice "by his own blood" (Heb. 9:11–12).

PRINCE (RULER). A leader or ruler; a title for tribal officials (Exod. 2:14). Also a title for Jesus, who is called the "Prince of life" (Acts 3:15) and the "prince of the kings of earth" (Rev. 1:5). The word is also applied to Satan as the ruler of evil (John 12:31). *Ruler:* NIV, NRSV.

PRINCESS. The daughter of a king. King Solomon had princesses among his hundreds of wives (1 Kings 11:3). Athaliah, daughter of King Ahab, killed all the royal descendants and usurped Judah's throne (2 Kings 11:1–3).

PRINCIPALITY. A powerful class of angels and demons. Christ is "far above" all earthly or cosmic powers (Rom. 8:38; Eph. 1:21; 3:10). Believers will share His victory over hostile principalities (Col. 2:10, 15).

PRISCILLA, PRISCA. See *Aquila.*

PRISON. A place of confinement for prisoners, often consisting of little more than a crude dungeon, cistern, or hole in the ground,

PRISON. This dungeon in Rome's Mamertinum Prison is where Peter and Paul were imprisoned, according to an ancient tradition. Prisoners were dropped in through the hole at the top and sealed in utter darkness.

P

particularly in O.T. times (Jer. 52:11). Paul wrote several epistles from prison and regarded his confinement as an opportunity to advance the gospel (2 Cor. 6:3–5; Phil. 1:12–14). See also *Cistern; Pit.*

PRIVY. Something kept private or secret. Solomon said Shimei's heart was privy to the wickedness plotted against King David (1 Kings 2:44).

PROCLAMATION. A reading or announcement of an official decree. King Cyrus of Persia proclaimed that the Jewish exiles could return to Jerusalem to rebuild the temple (Ezra 1:1–3).

PROCONSUL. An official of a Roman province, perhaps the second in command. Paul was brought before the proconsul Gallio at Corinth (Acts 18:12). See also *Deputy.*

PRODIGAL SON. The main character in Jesus' parable who spent his inheritance foolishly, fell into poverty, and finally returned to his father to ask forgiveness and reinstatement as a servant. His father, representing the love and forgiveness of God, welcomed him back as a son (Luke 15:11–32).

PROFANE [D]
Ezek. 23:38 they have…*p'd* my [God's] sabbaths
Mal. 2:11 Judah hath *p'd* the holiness of the LORD
1 Tim. 4:7 refuse *p* and old wives' fables
2 Tim. 2:16 shun *p* and vain babblings

PROFESS [ING]
Matt. 7:23 will I [Jesus] *p*…I never knew you
Rom. 1:22 *P'ing* themselves…wise…became fools
Titus 1:16 *p* that they know God; but…deny him

PROFESSION
1 Tim. 6:12 thou…hast professed a good *p*
Heb. 3:1 consider the High Priest of our *p*, Christ Jesus
Heb. 10:23 Let us hold fast the *p* of our faith

PROFIT [ETH]
Eccles. 1:3 what *p* hath a man of all his labour
Mark 8:36 *p* a man…gain the…world…lose his…soul
Rom. 3:1 what *p* is there of circumcision
1 Cor. 13:3 have not charity, it *p'eth* me nothing

PROGNOSTICATOR. A fortune-teller, or one who foretold the future by consulting the stars. The Lord promised to judge Babylonia, in spite of the power of these astrologers (Isa. 47:12–14). See also *Astrologer.*

PROMISE. A pledge or guarantee, particularly of some blessing from God. Israel's history included significant promises from God: (1) the promise of a son to Abraham (Gen. 18:10); (2) the land of Canaan promised to Israel (Exod. 6:4); and (3) a Savior promised from the house of David (Isa. 7:13–14; Matt. 1:20–23). See also *Hope.*

PROMISE [D]
Jer. 33:14 I [God] will perform…which I have *p'd*
Luke 24:49 I [Jesus] send the *p* of my Father
Gal. 3:29 Abraham's seed…heirs…to the *p*
Gal. 4:28 we, brethren…are the children of *p*
Eph. 3:6 Gentiles should be…partakers of his [God's] *p*
Heb. 11:9 he [Abraham] sojourned in the land of *p*
James 1:12 crown of life…Lord hath *p'd*
2 Pet. 3:4 Where is the *p* of his [Jesus'] coming

PROPHECY [IES]
1 Cor. 12:10 another *p*…another discerning of spirits
1 Cor. 13:2 though I [Paul] have the gift of *p*
1 Cor. 13:8 there be *p'ies*, they shall fail

PROPHESY [IED]
Joel 2:28 sons and your daughters shall *p*
Matt. 7:22 we not *p'ied* in thy [Jesus'] name
1 Cor. 13:9 know in part, and we *p* in part

PROPHET. An inspired messenger called by God to declare His will (Ezra 5:2). Prophets were described as God's servants (Zech. 1:6), watchmen (Ezek. 3:17), and holy men (2 Pet. 1:21). In the N.T., the prophets were cited as a noble example of patient suffering (James 5:10). Another word for prophet is *seer.*

SYMBOLIC ACTIONS OF THE PROPHETS

The prophet Isaiah walked around without his outer robe at the Lord's command (Isa. 20:2). This was a symbolic action designed to get the attention of the people and warn them to turn from their sinful ways, or they would be stripped by their enemies. The prophet also gave his sons symbolic names that predicted God's judgment (Isa. 7:3; 8:1–4).

The prophets Jeremiah and Ezekiel also declared God's message in dramatic fashion through symbolic actions (Jer. 13:1–11; Ezek. 4).

PROPHETESS. A female prophet or the wife of a prophet. Noted prophetesses include Miriam (Exod. 15:20), Deborah (Judg. 4:4), Hulda (2 Kings 22:14), and Anna (Luke 2:36). Four daughters of Philip were said to prophesy (Acts 21:8–9).

PROPITIATION. Atonement or expiation. Christ was appointed to be a propitiation for our sins "through faith in his blood" (Rom. 3:24–25). His sacrificial death is the supreme demonstration of love (1 John 2:2; 4:10). See also *Atonement; Mediator, Christ the; Reconciliation.*

PROSELYTE (CONVERT). A Gentile who converted to Judaism. Some of these converts renounced their pagan lifestyle but refused to accept such Jewish practices as circumcision. Well-known proselytes of the Bible include Cornelius, Lydia, and Nicolas of Antioch (Acts 6:5). *Convert:* NIV.

PROSTITUTE. See *Harlot.*

PROUD
Ps. 119:69 The *p* have forged a lie against me
Prov. 6:17 A *p* look, a lying tongue
Prov. 16:5 one that is *p* in heart...abomination
Eccles. 7:8 patient in spirit...better than...*p* in spirit
2 Tim. 3:2 men shall be...covetous, boasters, *p*
James 4:6 God resisteth the *p*...giveth grace unto the humble

PROVE
Ps. 26:2 Examine me, O LORD, and *p* me
Mal. 3:10 *p* me now...saith the LORD of hosts
Rom. 12:2 *p* what is that good, and...perfect, will of God
Gal. 6:4 let every man *p* his own work
1 Thess. 5:21 *P* all things; hold fast that which is good

PROVENDER (FODDER). Food for livestock, consisting of chopped straw mixed with barley, beans, or dates (Gen. 24:32). *Fodder:* NIV, NRSV.

PROVERBS, BOOK OF. A book of wisdom in the O.T. filled with short, pithy sayings on how to live with maturity and integrity under the watchful eye of God—the source of all wisdom. These wise sayings, written by Solomon as well as other sages of Israel, deal with such practical matters as strong drink (23:20–21), pride (16:18), work (6:6–11), child rearing (22:6), friendship (17:17), anger (19:11), speech (15:1–4), sexual temptation (chap. 5), and honesty in business (11:1–4). See also *Solomon; Wisdom Literature.*

PROVIDENCE. Divine guidance of human events (Neh. 9:6). This doctrine affirms God's absolute lordship over His creation and the activities by which He preserves and governs. God is constantly working in accord with His purpose (Eph. 1:11). He sustains the moral universe by operating within spiritual principles (Gal. 6:7–9).

PROVINCE. A district or section of a nation, often the outlying area of an extended world power such as the Persian and the Roman empires (Esther 3:12). In the N.T., this word refers to districts conquered and controlled by the Romans (Acts 25:1).

PROVISION. A supply or ration of some substance, such as food. Solomon's court required a large provision of food (1 Kings 4:22–23).

PROVOKE [D]
Deut. 32:16 They *p'd* him [God]...with strange gods
1 Cor. 10:22 Do we *p* the Lord to jealousy?
1 Cor. 13:5 [charity] is not easily *p'd*, thinketh no evil
Eph. 6:4 fathers, *p* not your children to wrath

PRUDENT (LEARNED, INTELLIGENT). To have discernment or understanding (Matt. 11:25). The prudent person foresees evil (Prov. 22:3) and is crowned with knowledge (Prov. 14:18). *Learned:* NIV; *intelligent:* NRSV.

PRUNINGHOOK. A tool for cutting shrubs and vines. To beat pruninghooks into spears was a sign of war (Joel 3:10). To do the opposite was a sign of peace (Isa. 2:4).

PSALMS, BOOK OF. A poetic book of the O.T. filled with hymns of praise and prayers of thanksgiving to God as well as laments against one's enemies and misfortune. Its title is derived from a Greek word that implies that these psalms were to be sung to the accompaniment of a musical instrument. King David of Judah wrote many of these psalms (see 54, 59, 65). But many other unknown writers contributed to this book, which was probably compiled across many centuries of Jewish history.

Generations of believers have found the psalms to be a rich source of devotional inspiration, with their emphasis on the goodness, stability, power, and faithfulness of God. See also *David; Poetic Writings; Poetry, Hebrew.*

MUSICAL TERMS IN THE PSALMS

Several musical terms appear throughout the Psalms, particularly in the titles of individual psalms. For example, the word *michtam* in the title of Psalm 16 probably indicated that this psalm was to be sung to a particular cadence or tune. The word *selah* (Ps. 44:8) may have marked the place for a pause in the singing. *Sheminith* (Ps. 12 title) probably indicated the instrument to be used when this particular hymn was sung.

PSALTERY (LYRE, HARP). A stringed musical instrument that was probably similar to the harp (1 Sam. 10:5). *Lyre:* NIV; *harp:* NRSV. See also *Harp.*

PTOLEMAIS. See *Accho.*

PTOLEMY. The title of Greek kings who ruled throughout Egypt and Palestine from about 323 to 30 B.C. These kings are possibly referred to in Daniel's visions (see Dan. 11:5–30). Their kingdom eventually fell to the Romans.

PUBLICAN (TAX COLLECTOR). A Jewish citizen who purchased the right to collect taxes in a specific area of his country for the Roman government. Publicans were hated and looked upon as traitors by their fellow citizens (Matt. 5:46). Matthew (Matt. 9:9–11) and Zacchaeus (Luke 19:1–10) were prominent publicans who followed Jesus. *Tax collector:* NIV, NRSV. See also *Matthew*.

PUBLIUS. A Roman official who entertained Paul on the island of Miletus after a shipwreck. Paul healed his father of a fever (Acts 28:7–8).

PUL. See *Tiglath-pileser*.

PULSE (VEGETABLES). Food made of vegetables, such as peas or beans; the food eaten by Daniel and his friends instead of the king's provisions (Dan. 1:12–16). *Vegetables:* NIV, NRSV.

PUNISHMENT. A penalty for wrongdoing. Cain reacted to God's penalties for murdering Abel by saying, "My punishment is greater than I can bear" (Gen. 4:13). Jesus urged forgiveness of offenders rather than the Mosaic tradition of "an eye for an eye" (Matt. 5:38–39). See also *Judgment; Retribution; Wrath*.

PURIFICATION. Ceremonial or spiritual cleansing. The Mosaic Law prescribed purification rites for those ceremonially defiled by touching a corpse, by contact with bodily discharges, by childbirth, and by leprosy (see Lev. 14–15). The mother of Jesus offered turtledoves and pigeons as a sacrifice in her ceremonial cleansing (Luke 2:21–24). See also *Clean; Wash*.

PURIFY [IED, IETH]
James 4:8 and **p** your hearts, ye double minded
1 Pet. 1:22 **p'ied** your souls in obeying the truth
1 John 3:3 man that hath this hope... **p'ieth** himself

PURIM, FEAST OF. A Jewish festival that celebrated the rescue of the Jews from Haman's oppression in Esther's time (Esther 9:20–32).

PURPLE. The color preferred by kings and other royal officials; a bright dye made from shellfish. Lydia was a businesswoman who sold purple cloth (Acts 16:14).

PURPOSE [TH]
Eccles. 3:1 a time to every **p** under the heaven
Rom. 8:28 to them...called according to his **p**
2 Cor. 9:7 as he **p'th** in his heart, so let him give

PURSE. A bag for carrying items (Luke 10:4), generally placed in the folds of the sash around the waist. The purse in Jesus' instructions to His disciples was probably a money bag (Mark 6:8). See also *Crisping Pin*.

PUT. See *Phut*.

PYGARG (IBEX). An animal of the deer family, perhaps the antelope or the addax. It was considered unclean by the Jews (Deut. 14:5). *Ibex:* NIV, NRSV.

QUAILS. Small game birds provided miraculously by the Lord as food for the Israelites in the wilderness (Exod. 16:12–13).

QUATERNION. A company of four soldiers who guarded prisoners during a night-watch assignment consisting of three hours (Acts 12:4).

QUEEN. A woman who exercised royal power, or the wife or mother of a king. Esther exercised great power as the wife of King Ahasuerus of Persia (Esther 5:2). Solomon provided a seat at his right hand for his mother, Bath-sheba (1 Kings 2:19).

QUEEN OF HEAVEN. A fertility goddess worshiped by the citizens of Jerusalem during the idolatrous days before the fall of the nation of Judah (Jer. 7:18; 44:17). This may have been the goddess Ashtaroth, or Asherah. See also *Ashtaroth*.

QUEEN OF SHEBA. See *Sabeans*.

QUAILS. Quail like these migrate between Africa and Europe each year. Not strong fliers, they sometimes stop to rest, too exhausted to move. These may have been the kinds of quail God provided for the Israelites during the Exodus.

QUENCH [ED]

Song 8:7 Many waters cannot *q* love
Jer. 7:20 mine [God's] anger…not be *q'ed*
Mark 9:44 worm dieth not…fire is not *q'ed*
Eph. 6:16 shall…*q*…fiery darts of the wicked
1 Thess. 5:19 *Q* not the Spirit

QUICKEN.

To preserve or give life. The psalmist praised God who will "quicken me again" (Ps. 71:20). The Father and Son have authority to raise the dead and give eternal life (John 5:21).

QUICK [EN, ENED, ENING]

Ps. 143:11 *Q'en* me, O Lord, for thy name's sake
1 Cor. 15:45 last Adam was made a *q'ening* spirit
Eph. 2:1 hath he *q'ened*…dead in trespasses and sins
2 Tim. 4:1 Jesus Christ…judge the *q* and the dead
Heb. 4:12 the word of God is *q*, and powerful

QUICKSANDS (SYRTIS).

Sandbars and shifting sands off the African coast in the Mediterranean Sea that posed a hazard for ships (Acts 27:17). *Syrtis:* NRSV.

QUIRINIUS.

See *Cyrenius.*

QUIVER.

A sheath for arrows carried by foot soldiers or hung on the sides of chariots (Lam. 3:13). The word is also used figuratively for God's protection (Isa. 49:2) and the blessing of children (Ps. 127:5).

QUMRAN, KHIRBET.

A site near the Dead Sea where the Dead Sea Scrolls were discovered. See also *Dead Sea Scrolls; Essenes.*

Q

RAAMSES. See *Rameses*.

RABBAH/RABBATH. The capital city of the Ammonites (Deut. 3:11) captured by David's army under Joab. The city's destruction was prophesied by Amos (Amos 1:14). *Rabbath:* Ezek. 21:20.

RABBI/RABBONI (RABBOUNI). A title of great respect, meaning "master" or "teacher," used by Nicodemus in addressing Jesus (John 3:2). Its Aramaic form is *rabboni* (John 20:16). *Rabbouni:* NRSV.

RABBIT. See *Hare*.

RAB-SHAKEH. The chief cupbearer or aide for King Sennacherib of Assyria who demanded the surrender of Jerusalem from King Hezekiah (2 Kings 18:17; Isa. 36:13–22).

RACA. A term of insult, meaning "worthless" or "good for nothing," that was forbidden by Christ. Expressing such contempt for a fellow human being will lead to God's judgment and condemnation (Matt. 5:21–22).

RACE. This word in the N.T. refers to popular Grecian contests, such as races by foot, horseback, or chariot (1 Cor. 9:24). It is also used figuratively of the Christian's call to pursue the goal of Christlikeness (Heb. 12:1).

RACHAB. See *Rahab*.

RACHEL/RAHEL. Jacob's favorite wife (Gen. 29:28–30) and the mother of his sons Joseph and Benjamin (Gen. 30:22–24; 35:16–18). She died giving birth to Benjamin and was buried near Bethlehem (Gen. 35:16–20). Jeremiah referred to Rachel weeping for her children carried into the Babylonian Exile (Jer. 31:15; *Rahel*). See also *Jacob*.

RAHAB/RACHAB. A harlot in Jericho who hid the spies sent by Joshua to scout the city (Josh. 2:1–6). Later she and her family were spared when Jericho fell to the invading Israelites (Josh. 6:22–25). In the N.T., Rahab was commended for her faith (Heb. 11:31). *Rachab:* Jesus' ancestry (Matt. 1:5).

RAHEL. See *Rachel*.

RAID. See *Road*.

RAIN. God's life-giving moisture from the sky was sometimes withheld because of the sin of His people (Deut. 11:17). Excessive rain produced the great flood in Noah's time as an instrument of God's judgment (Gen. 7:4). See also *Former Rain; Latter Rain*.

RAINBOW. A colored arch in the clouds after the great flood, given by God as a promise that He would never again destroy the world with water (Gen. 9:9–17).

RAISE [D, TH]

Ps. 113:7 He [God] r'*th* up the poor
Matt. 10:8 Heal the sick...r the dead
Matt. 16:21 he [Jesus] must...be killed...be r'*d* again
Acts 10:40 Him [Jesus] God r'*d* up the third day
Rom. 6:4 Christ was r'*d*...we...walk in newness of life
Rom. 10:9 believe...God hath r'*d* him [Jesus] from the dead
1 Cor. 6:14 God...will also r up us by his...power
1 Cor. 15:16 dead rise not, then is not Christ r'*d*
2 Tim. 2:8 Christ...was r'*d* from the dead
Heb. 11:19 God was able to r him

[Jesus] up

RAISINS. Dried grapes
that were preserved in
clusters (1 Sam. 25:18)
and used in cakes known
as flagons (Song 2:5). See
also *Flagon*, No. 1.

RAM
1. A long beam used
to batter down the gates
of walled cities (Ezek.
4:2).
2. A male sheep used
for food (Gen. 31:38)
and favored as a sacrifi-
cial animal (Num. 15:6).

RAMA (RAMAH). A
Benjamite city near Je-
rusalem and the proba-
ble site of Rachel's tomb
(Matt. 2:18). *Ramah:* NIV,
NRSV.

RAMAH. See *Ramoth-gilead.*

RAMESES/RAAM-
SES. A fertile district of
Egypt where Jacob and
his descendants settled

(Gen. 47:11). This name may have been given
later to a royal treasure city built by the Hebrew
slaves (Exod. 1:11; *Raamses*).

RAMOTH-GILEAD/RAMAH/RA-
MOTH. An ancient Amorite stronghold east
of the Jordan River that became one of the
six cities of refuge after its conquest by the

*RAM. This gold statue of a ram eating from a bush is reminiscent of the ram that
got caught in a bush for Abraham. The statue is from Abraham's era and from his
hometown, Ur, in what is now Iraq. God provided a ram for Abraham as
a substitute sacrifice for Isaac.*

Israelites (Deut. 4:43). *Ramah:* 2 Kings 8:29; *Ramoth:* 1 Kings 22:3. See also *Cities of Refuge.*

RAMPART. A low wall around a military trench or embankment that served as the first line of defense for a walled city (Lam. 2:8; Nah. 3:8). See also *Bulwark.*

RAM'S HORN. The curved horn of a ram that was blown like a trumpet as a signal to worshipers and warriors (Josh. 6:4–13). See also *Trumpet.*

RANSOM. To redeem or buy by making a payment. Because of His atoning death, Christ is described as a "ransom for all" (1 Tim. 2:6).

Prov. 13:8 The *r* of a man's life are his riches
Hosea 13:14 I [God] will *r* them from…the grave
Mark 10:45 Son of man came…to give his life a *r*

RAPTURE, THE. A doctrine held by some that deals with the transformation of the redeemed into a glorified state at Christ's return (Phil. 3:20–21). The dead in Christ will be raised at Christ's return and given an incorruptible body (1 Cor. 15:51–53). They will be caught up into the air, along with living saints, to meet the Lord (1 Thess. 4:16–17). See also *Second Coming.*

RAVEN. A bird of prey considered unclean under the Mosaic Law (Lev. 11:15). God used ravens to sustain the prophet Elijah (1 Kings 17:4–6).

RAZOR. A sharp instrument made of flint, bronze, or steel and used for cutting hair (Ezek. 5:1).

READY
Exod. 17:4 they be almost *r* to stone me [Moses]
Ps. 86:5 thou, Lord, art good, and *r* to forgive
Mark 14:38 spirit truly is *r*…flesh is weak

Luke 22:33 Lord, I [Peter] am *r* to go with thee
Rom. 1:15 I [Paul] am *r* to preach…at Rome also
2 Tim. 4:6 I [Paul] am now *r* to be offered
1 Pet. 3:15 be *r* always to give an answer to every man

REAP. To harvest grain (Ruth 2:3, 14). The spiritual law of the harvest declares that we reap what we sow (Gal. 6:7–8). See also *Harvest.*

REAP [ETH]
Lev. 19:9 not wholly *r* the corners of thy field
Ps. 126:5 They that sow in tears shall *r* in joy
Hosea 8:7 they have sown the wind…*r* the whirlwind
Luke 12:24 they [ravens] neither sow nor *r*
John 4:37 One soweth, and another *r'eth*
Gal. 6:9 shall *r*, if we faint not

REASON
Ps. 90:10 by *r* of strength they [days of our years] be fourscore years
Isa. 1:18 let us *r* together, saith the Lord
1 Pet. 3:15 asketh you a *r* of the hope that is in you

REBEKAH/REBECCA. The wife of Isaac and the mother of his twin sons, Jacob and Esau. She encouraged her favorite son, Jacob, to obtain Esau's birthright by deceiving the aging Isaac. Then she encouraged Jacob to flee to her relatives in Mesopotamia to escape Esau's wrath (Gen. 27). *Rebecca:* Greek form (Rom. 9:10). See also *Isaac.*

REBUKE [D]
Ps. 6:1 Lord, *r* me not in thine anger
Eccles. 7:5 It is better to hear the *r* of the wise
Matt. 16:22 Peter took him [Jesus], and began to *r* him
Mark 8:33 he [Jesus] *r'd* Peter…behind me, Satan
Luke 8:24 he [Jesus] arose, and *r'd* the wind
Rev. 3:19 As many as I [Jesus] love, I *r*

RECEIVE [D, TH]
Mal. 3:10 not be room enough to *r* it [God's blessing]
Matt. 7:8 every one that asketh *r'th*
Matt. 10:8 freely ye have *r'd*, freely give
Matt. 21:22 ask in prayer, believing, ye shall *r*
Acts 1:8 ye [the apostles] shall *r* power

Acts 20:35 It is more blessed to give than to *r*
Rom. 8:15 ye have *r'd* the Spirit of adoption
1 Cor. 3:14 any man's work abide...*r* a reward
James 4:3 ask, and *r* not, because ye ask amiss
1 Pet. 5:4 shall *r* a crown of glory that fadeth not
Rev. 4:11 Thou art worthy, O Lord, to *r* glory

RECENT CONVERT. See *Novice.*

RECHAB. The father of Jehonadab and founder of the Rechabites, a tribe committed to abstain from wine and to live in tents. Because of their faithfulness, the prophet Jeremiah promised they would not cease to exist (Jer. 35:8–19). The descendants of this tribe still live in Iraq and Yemen.

RECOMPENSE. To pay back in kind (Prov. 12:14). Believers are assured their courage and faith will be rewarded (Heb. 10:35–36). See also *Reward.*

RECONCILIATION. The process of bringing opposing parties or people together (Matt. 5:24). Believers, who are justified by faith and reconciled to God by Christ's victory over sin and death (Rom. 5:1, 10; 2 Cor. 5:20), are to be ambassadors of reconciliation for others (2 Cor. 5:18–20). See also *Atonement; Mediator, Christ the; Propitiation.*

RECORD (TESTIMONY). A witness or testimony to one's faithfulness. Jesus told His enemies, "My record is true" (John 8:14). Paul defended his record of faithfulness to God (Acts 20:26–27). *Testimony:* NIV, NRSV. See also *Testimony; Witness.*

RECORDER. An aide to a king who kept official records and served as a counselor or adviser (2 Kings 18:18, 37).

RED DRAGON. A name for Satan. After being cast out of heaven, Satan turned his fury on God's people (Rev. 12:3–17). See also *Satan.*

RED HEIFER. An unblemished cow or ox that had never been yoked. It was used as a sacrifice in a sin offering (Num. 19:1–9).

RED KITE. See *Glede; Vulture.*

RED SEA. The sea between Egypt and Arabia that the Israelites crossed miraculously through God's intervention when fleeing from the Egyptian army (Exod. 14:16; 15:4, 22). This body of water is also called the Sea of Reeds because of its reed-filled marshes at the head of the Gulf of Suez.

RED SEA. *The Red Sea is alive with coral the color of the sea's name. Moses and the Israelites miraculously crossed the sea while fleeing from an Egyptian chariot unit.*

REDEEM. To buy back property that had been forfeited because of indebtedness or to buy back a person who had been sold into slavery (Exod. 6:6). This idea describes perfectly the work of Christ, who "bought us back" from sin and death through His atonement on the cross as our Redeemer (Matt. 20:28). See also *Atonement; Lamb of God.*

REDEEM [ED, ETH, ING]

Ps. 34:22 Lord *r'eth* the soul of his servants
Ps. 107:2 Let the *r'ed* of the Lord say so
Isa. 43:1 I [God] have *r'ed* thee [Israel]
Isa. 52:9 Lord...hath *r'ed* Jerusalem
Luke 1:68 Lord...hath visited and *r'ed* his people
Gal. 3:13 Christ hath *r'ed* us...curse of the law
Gal. 4:5 To *r* them that were under the law
Eph. 5:16 *R'ing* the time...the days are evil
Col. 4:5 Walk in wisdom...*r'ing* the time

REDEMPTION

Ps. 130:7 with the Lord there is...*r*
Rom. 3:24 justified...through the *r*...in Christ
Eph. 1:7 we have *r* through his [Jesus'] blood
Heb. 9:12 by his [Jesus'] own blood he...obtained...*r*

REED. A tall grass, common in marshes and swamps, used to make paper, musical instruments, and writing pens. The word is also used figuratively for weakness and fragility (Matt. 11:7). See also *Bulrush; Paper.*

REFINER. A craftsman who removed impurities from precious metals by melting the ore (Jer. 6:29)—an apt description of God, who purifies His people through affliction and chastisement (Isa. 48:10). See also *Finer.*

REFUGE, CITIES OF. See *Cities of Refuge.*

REFUSE (RUBBISH). Waste or worthless matter (Amos 8:6). Paul declared his accomplishments were as garbage compared to the riches of knowing Christ (Phil. 3:8). *Rubbish:* NIV, NRSV. See also *Dung.*

REGENERATION. New birth; spiritual change brought about by the Holy Spirit in those who trust in Christ (2 Cor. 5:17–21). See also *New Birth; Salvation.*

REGISTER (FAMILY RECORDS, GENEALOGICAL RECORDS). A tablet on which census records or genealogical lists were inscribed, with the names of the living on one side and the dead on the other (Ezra 2:62). *Family records:* NIV; *genealogical records:* NRSV. See also *Genealogy.*

REHOBOAM/ROBOAM. The son and successor of Solomon as king of Judah (reigned about 931–913 B.C.). He refused to implement the reform measures called for by northern leaders after Solomon's death—a foolish act that resulted in the split of the ten northern tribes into the Northern Kingdom (1 Kings 12:1–24). *Roboam:* Jesus' ancestry (Matt. 1:7).

REIGN [ED]

Gen. 37:8 Shalt thou [Joseph] indeed *r* over us
Judg. 9:8 trees...said unto the olive tree, *R*...over us
2 Sam. 5:4 David was thirty years old...began to *r*
Ps. 146:10 Lord shall *r* for ever
Luke 1:33 he [Jesus] shall *r* over the house of Jacob
Rom. 5:14 death *r'ed* from Adam to Moses
Rom. 6:12 let not sin...*r* in your mortal body
Rev. 11:15 Christ...shall *r* for ever and ever

REINS. KJV word for the kidneys, a vital body organ in humans and animals. The reins of an animal were considered a special ceremonial sacrifice (Lev. 3:4–5). In humans, the kidneys were regarded as the seat of conscience and affection (Prov. 23:16).

REJECT [ED]

1 Sam. 15:26 thou [Saul] hast *r'ed* the...Lord
Isa. 53:3 he [God's servant] is despised...*r'ed* of men
Mark 7:9 ye [Pharisees] *r* the commandment of God
Mark 12:10 The stone which the builders *r'ed*
Luke 17:25 must he [Jesus] suffer...be *r'ed* of this generation

REJOICE. To be glad or to express one's joy. Joy may result from God's blessings (Exod. 18:9) or assurance of salvation (Acts 8:39). See also *Joy*.

REJOICE [D]

Ps. 97:1 Lord reigneth; let the earth *r*
Ps. 118:24 the day...Lord hath made; we will *r*
Joel 2:21 glad and *r*...Lord will do great things
Matt. 2:10 they [the wise men] *r'd* with...great joy
Matt. 5:12 *R*...great is your reward
Luke 15:6 *R* with me; for I have found my sheep
Rom. 12:15 *R* with them that do *r*

REMEMBER [ED]

Exod. 2:24 God heard their [Israel's] groaning...*r'ed* his covenant
Exod. 20:8 *R* the sabbath day, to keep it holy
Deut. 8:18 thou shalt *r* the Lord thy God
Ps. 20:7 we will *r* the name of the Lord
Ps. 137:1 we [Israelites] wept, when we *r'ed* Zion
Eccles. 12:1 *R* now thy Creator in...thy youth
Jer. 31:34 I [God] will *r* their sin no more

Luke 22:61 Peter *r'ed* the word of the Lord
Luke 24:8 they [the disciples] *r'ed* his [Jesus'] words
2 Tim. 2:8 *R* that Jesus Christ...raised from the dead
Heb. 10:17 their sins...will I [God] *r* no more

REMEMBRANCE

Ps. 30:4 give thanks at the *r* of his [God's] holiness
Luke 22:19 this is my [Jesus'] body...this do in *r* of me
John 14:26 Comforter...bring all things to your *r*

REMISSION. God's forgiveness or pardon of our sins. This forgiveness is based on Christ's atoning death (Matt. 26:28; Heb. 9:22) and our repentance (Mark 1:4; Acts 2:38) and faith in Christ (Acts 10:43). See also *Forgiveness*; *Pardon*.

REMNANT (SURVIVORS). A small group of God's people who remained loyal to Him in the midst of widespread sin and idolatry. The prophet Isaiah declared that Israel would be

REMNANT. Jewish prisoners are marched into exile as their nation falls to invaders. But God promised he would save a remnant of his people and bring them back to rebuild their country.

punished for its unfaithfulness (Isa. 1:9). However, a righteous remnant of His people would be preserved (Isa. 10:20–22). God continues to work through His righteous remnant, the Church (Rom. 11:5). *Survivors:* NIV, NRSV. See also *Outcasts.*

REMPHAN (REPHAN). A star god of the Babylonians worshiped secretly by the Israelites—an act for which they were taken into exile by the Babylonians (Acts 7:41–43). *Rephan:* NIV, NRSV.

REND (TEAR). To tear apart by force. Rending one's clothes was a sign of great sorrow or repentance (Esther 4:1). *Tear:* NIV, NRSV.

RENDER [ED]
Ps. 116:12 *r* unto the Lord for all his benefits
1 Cor. 7:3 husband *r* unto the wife due benevolence
1 Thess. 5:15 See that none *r* evil for evil

RENEW [ED, ING]
Ps. 51:10 *r* a right spirit within me
Isa. 40:31 they that wait upon the Lord...*r* their strength
Rom. 12:2 transformed by the *r'ing* of your mind
2 Cor. 4:16 inward man is *r'ed* day by day

REPENT. The act of turning from sin and changing one's orientation from rebellion against God to acceptance of God's will and lordship. A patient God commands all persons to repent (Matt. 9:13; Acts 17:30). Christ came to call sinners to repentance (Luke 5:32), and He also counsels believers to forgive a brother who repents (Luke 17:3). See also *Contrite; Conviction; Penitence.*

REPENT [ED, ETH]
Gen. 6:6 it *r'ed* the Lord that he had made man
Job 42:6 I [Job] abhor myself...*r* in dust and ashes
Matt. 4:17 Jesus began to preach, and to say, *R*
Luke 15:7 joy...in heaven over one sinner that *r'eth*
Acts 2:38 Peter said...*R*, and be baptized

REPHAIM
    1. A race of giants in Palestine defeated by Chedorlaomer, a king of Elam, and allied kings (Gen. 14:5). *Rephaites:* NIV.
    2. A fertile valley near Jerusalem where David defeated the Philistines (2 Sam. 5:18–25).

REPHAN. See *Remphan.*

REPHIDIM. A camping site of the Israelites between the wilderness of Sin and Mount Sinai where Moses struck the rock and where Amalek was defeated (Exod. 17:1).

REPROACH. Shame, blame, or scorn. Jesus the Messiah suffered reproach for our sake (Isa. 53:3–6; Rom. 15:3).

REPROACH [ED]
Ps. 31:11 I was a *r* among all mine enemies
Prov. 14:34 sin is a *r* to any people
Heb. 11:26 of Christ greater riches than...treasures in Egypt
Heb. 13:13 go...unto him [Jesus]...bearing his *r*
1 Pet. 4:14 ye be *r'ed* for the name of Christ, happy are ye

REPROBATE (DEPRAVED, DEBASED). A person who is depraved, corrupt, or worthless—a term applied to those who reject God (Rom. 1:28; 2 Tim. 3:8). *Depraved:* NIV; *debased:* NRSV.

REPROOF. A sharp rebuke for misconduct. John the Baptist reproved Herod for his incestuous marriage (Luke 3:19–20).

REPROVE
Ps. 50:8 I [God] will not *r* thee for thy sacrifices
John 16:8 he [the Holy Spirit] will *r* the world of sin
2 Tim. 4:2 *r*, rebuke, exhort with all longsuffering

RESIN. See *Myrrh.*

RESIST [ED]

Matt. 5:39 I [Jesus] say…That ye *r* not evil
Acts 7:51 ye do always *r* the Holy Ghost
Heb. 12:4 Ye have not yet *r'ed* unto blood
James 4:7 *R* the devil, and he will flee from you

RESPECT [ETH]

Gen. 4:4 Lᴏʀᴅ had *r* unto Abel and to his offering
Ps. 40:4 Blessed is that man that…*r'eth* not the proud
Ps. 119:15 I will…have *r* unto thy [God's] ways

RESTITUTION. To make a fair settlement with a person for property lost or wrong done. Restitution was strictly required by the Mosaic Law (Exod. 22:1). Zacchaeus promised to make fourfold restitution of what he had taken unlawfully as a tax collector (Luke 19:8).

RESTORE [TH]

Ps. 23:3 He [God] *r'th* my soul
Ps. 51:12 *R*…the joy of thy [God's] salvation
Acts 1:6 Lord, wilt thou…*r*…the kingdom to Israel?
Gal. 6:1 *r* such an one in the spirit of meekness

RESURRECTION. A raising to life beyond physical death that leads to eternal life for believers. This truth was taught by Jesus (John 6:40, 44) and demonstrated by His miracles (Matt. 9:24–25) as well as His own resurrection (Acts 2:32). Paul taught that Christians will have a glorified body like that of Christ (Phil. 3:20–21) and that it will last through eternity (Rom. 2:7).

Matt. 27:53 [the saints] came out of the graves after his [Jesus'] *r*
Luke 20:33 in the *r* whose wife of them is she
John 11:25 I [Jesus] am the *r*, and the life
Acts 4:33 gave the apostles witness of the *r* of…Jesus
Acts 17:32 they [philosophers] heard of the *r*…mocked
1 Cor. 15:13 no *r* of the dead, then is Christ not risen
1 Pet. 1:3 a lively hope by the *r* of Jesus Christ
Rev. 20:6 Blessed…is he that hath part in the first *r*

RESURRECTION OF CHRIST. The return of Jesus to physical life following His death.

His resurrection was foretold in the Psalms (Ps. 16:10–11) and prophecy (Isa. 53:10–12), announced by Christ Himself (Mark 9:9–10), and proclaimed by the apostles (Acts 2:32; 3:15). It validates our faith and witness (1 Cor. 15:14–15), assures believers of resurrection (1 Cor. 15:19–20), emphasizes our final victory over sin and death (1 Cor. 15:17, 26, 54, 57), and inspires faithfulness in Christian service (1 Cor. 15:58).

APPEARANCES OF JESUS AFTER HIS RESURRECTION

1. To Mary Magdalene at the empty tomb (Mark 16:9; John 20:11–18)
2. To other women at the empty tomb (Matt. 28:1–10)
3. To two followers on their way to Emmaus (Mark 16:12–13; Luke 24:13–32)
4. To Peter, apparently in Jerusalem (Luke 24:33–35)
5. To ten of His disciples in Jerusalem, Thomas absent (Luke 24:36–43; John 20:19–25)
6. To the eleven disciples in Jerusalem, Thomas present (John 20:26–29)
7. To His disciples at the Sea of Galilee (John 21:1–14)
8. To His disciples at His ascension near Jerusalem (Mark 16:19–20; Luke 24:44–53)
9. To 500 followers (1 Cor. 15:6)
10. To James and all the apostles (1 Cor. 15:7)
11. To the apostle Paul (1 Cor. 15:8)

RETRIBUTION. A repayment for wrong done; God's wrath and punishment against man's rebellion and unbelief (Rom. 1:18). Only trust in Jesus and His atoning death can deliver us from God's retribution (1 Thess. 1:10). See also *Judgment, Last; Punishment; Tribulation, Great.*

REUBEN. The oldest son of Jacob and Leah and founder of one of the twelve tribes of Israel (Gen. 29:32). He lost his birthright by committing adultery with his father's concubines (Gen. 35:22; 49:3–4). Reuben likely saved Joseph's life when his brothers proposed to kill him (Gen. 37:21–22). The tribe of Reuben settled east of the Jordan River, along with Gad and Manasseh (Num. 32:1–25). See also *Tribes of Israel.*

REUEL. See *Jethro.*

REVEAL [ED]

Job 20:27 heaven shall *r* his [man's] iniquity
Isa. 40:5 glory of the LORD shall be *r*'ed
Matt. 16:17 flesh and blood...not *r*'ed it unto thee [Peter]
Luke 10:21 hid...from the wise...*r*'eth them unto babes
Rom. 1:17 righteousness of God *r*'ed...faith to faith
1 Cor. 3:13 it [man's work] shall be *r*'ed by fire
1 Pet. 4:13 when his [Jesus'] glory shall be *r*'ed

REVELATION. The uncovering or presentation of truth at God's initiative (2 Cor. 12:1–7). Christ, the only begotten Son, reveals the Father (John 1:18). God's searching Spirit (1 Cor. 2:10) interprets the divine purpose through the prophets (1 Pet. 1:10–12) and the apostles (Gal. 1:16).

Gal. 1:12 was I [Paul] taught it...by the *r* of Jesus Christ
Eph. 3:3 by *r* he [God] made known...the mystery
Rev. 1:1 *R* of Jesus Christ, which God gave

REVELATION OF JOHN. The last book of the N.T. consisting of a series of seven visions revealed directly by the Lord to the apostle John. Through symbols such as angels, horsemen, and plagues, these visions are considered

by some to portray the end of the present age and the coming of God's kingdom.

The seven visions serve as a convenient outline of the book: (1) Christ encouraging His church against attacks (1:9–3:22); (2) Christ the Lamb with a sealed scroll (chaps. 4–7); (3) seven angels blowing trumpets (chaps. 8–11); (4) Satan and the beast persecuting the church (chaps. 12–14); (5) seven bowls pouring out the wrath of Christ (chaps. 15–16); (6) the judgment of Babylonia, or Rome (17:1–19:3); and (7) the final victory of God and His final judgment (19:11–21).

The book ends on a triumphant note with God's promise of a new heaven and a new earth (chaps. 21–22). See also *Apocalypse; John the Apostle; Seven Churches of Asia.*

REVENGE. Retaliation against another, or "getting even." Jesus rebuked His disciples for a vengeful spirit (Luke 9:54–56) and commanded forbearance (Matt. 5:38–44). He commanded us to love our enemies and show mercy toward others (Luke 6:35–38). The Bible declares that vengeance should be exacted only by God (Prov. 20:22; Heb. 10:30).

REVERENCE. A feeling of deep respect and awe that believers are to show toward God and the sanctuary devoted to worship (Lev. 19:30; Ps. 89:7). Reverence should also be shown to kings (1 Kings 1:31), parents (Heb. 12:9), and family members (Eph. 5:33).

REVILE [D]

Matt. 5:11 Blessed are ye, when men shall *r* you
Mark 15:32 [two thieves]...crucified with him [Jesus] *r*'d him
1 Pet. 2:23 Who [Jesus], when he was *r*'d, *r*'d not

REVILER (SLANDERER). A mocker. Revilers will not inherit God's kingdom (1 Cor. 6:10). Those reviled for Christ's sake will be blessed and rewarded (Matt. 5:11–12). *Slanderer:* NIV.

REWARD. A return or payment for service. God rewards those who diligently seek Him (Heb. 11:6). See also *Recompense*.

REWARD [ED]
Gen. 15:1 I [God] am thy [Abraham's]...great *r*
Ps. 18:20 Lord *r'ed* me according to my righteousness
Ps. 103:10 He [God]...not...*r'ed* us...our iniquities
Matt. 5:12 great is your *r*...so persecuted they the prophets
Matt. 5:46 love them which love you, what *r* have ye
Luke 23:41 we [two thieves] receive...due *r* of our deeds
1 Cor. 3:8 every man shall receive his own *r*
Col. 3:24 ye shall receive the *r* of the inheritance
1 Tim. 5:18 labourer is worthy of his *r*

RHODA. A servant girl in the home of Mary, mother of John Mark, who answered the door for Peter after his miraculous release from prison (Acts 12:13–16).

RHODES. A Greek island in the Aegean Sea that Paul's ship passed when sailing from Assos to Palestine (Acts 21:1). This was the site of the ancient lighthouse known as the Colossus of Rhodes, one of the seven wonders of the ancient world.

RICHES. Material goods and earthly treasures, which are portrayed as deceitful (Matt. 13:22), fleeting (Prov. 23:5), and uncertain (1 Tim. 6:17). Jesus urged believers to lay up spiritual treasures in heaven rather than earthly possessions (Matt. 6:19–20).

RICH ROBE. See *Stomacher*.

RIDDLE. A story with a hidden meaning. Samson posed a riddle to the Philistines (Judg. 14:12–19).

RIE (SPELT). A common Egyptian grain plant that thrived in poor soil under hot, dry conditions (Exod. 9:32). *Spelt:* NIV, NRSV. See also *Fitch*.

RIGHT HAND. A symbol of power and strength (Ps. 77:10). Jesus is exalted in power at God's right hand (Eph. 1:20). See also *Hand of God*.

RIGHTEOUS, RIGHTEOUSNESS. An attribute of God that signifies His holiness, sinlessness, and justice (Ps. 35:24). Through faith in Christ, God's righteousness is imputed or granted to believers (Titus 3:5). Christians are encouraged to pursue the interests of God's righteous kingdom (Matt. 6:33). See also *Godliness; Goodness*.

RIGHTEOUS [NESS]
Gen. 15:6 Lord...counted it [Abraham's faith]...for *r'ness*
Ps. 1:6 Lord knoweth the way of the *r*
Ps. 19:9 judgments of the Lord are true and *r*
Ps. 97:6 heavens declare his [God's] *r'ness*
Prov. 15:29 Lord...heareth the prayer of the *r*
Amos 5:24 judgment run down...*r'ness* as a mighty stream
Matt. 5:6 Blessed are they...thirst after *r'ness*
Matt. 6:33 seek...first...kingdom of God...his *r'ness*
Rom. 3:10 There is none *r*, no, not one
Rom. 4:3 Abraham believed God...counted...for *r'ness*
Rom. 10:10 with the heart man believeth unto *r'ness*
Eph. 6:14 having on the breastplate of *r'ness*
2 Tim. 4:8 laid up for me [Paul] a crown of *r'ness*
James 5:16 fervent prayer of a *r* man availeth much

RIM. See *Nave*.

RIMMON. A Syrian god worshiped by Naaman the leper (2 Kings 5:18), possibly a god of the sun or rain.

RING. A circular band worn as an ornament on fingers, wrists, ankles, and in ears and nostrils. The pharaoh of Egypt presented a ring to Joseph as a symbol of authority as his aide or adviser (Gen. 41:42).

RIVER. A freshwater stream. The largest rivers mentioned in the Bible are the Abana (2 Kings 5:12), Euphrates (Gen. 2:14), Jordan

R

(Matt. 3:6), Pharpar (2 Kings 5:12), and Tigris, or Hiddekel (Gen. 2:14). The river mentioned in Exod. 7:21 is probably the Nile.

RIVER OF EGYPT (WADI OF EGYPT). A small stream flowing into the Mediterranean Sea that marked the old boundary between Egypt and Palestine (Num. 34:5). *Wadi of Egypt:* NIV, NRSV.

RIZPAH. The concubine of King Saul who was taken by Abner after Saul's death (2 Sam. 3:6–8). Her two sons were hanged by the Gibeonites during David's reign (2 Sam. 21:8–11).

ROAD (RAID). A path or trail for public travel, also called a highway or way (Mark 10:46). The word is also used as a figure of speech for a raid by robbers or invaders (1 Sam. 27:10). *Raid:* NRSV. See also *Highway*.

ROBE. A long outer garment similar to a tunic or mantle. The soldiers mocked Jesus at His crucifixion by dressing him in a scarlet robe (Matt. 27:28). See also *Mantle*.

ROBOAM. See *Rehoboam*.

ROCK. A stone. The word is used metaphorically for God to show His strength and stability (Ps. 18:31). Jesus changed Peter's name to "rock" or "rocklike" (Greek: *petras*) when He called him as His disciple (John 1:42).

ROCK BADGER. See *Coney*.

ROD (SHOOT). A staff or stick (Ps. 23:4). The word is used figuratively for a branch or offshoot of a tribe or family; for example, in reference to Christ (Isa. 11:1). *Shoot:* NIV, NRSV.

ROE/ROEBUCK (GAZELLE). A graceful deer noted for its swiftness (2 Sam. 2:18).

It was considered a clean animal by the Jews (Deut. 12:15, 22). *Roebuck:* 1 Kings 4:23. *Gazelle:* NIV, NRSV. See also *Deer; Hart; Hind*.

ROLL (SCROLL). A strip of parchment that was written on, then rolled on a stick (Jer. 36:2). It was unrolled for reading, just as a modern reader turns the pages of a book. *Scroll:* NIV, NRSV. See also *Scroll*.

ROMAN EMPIRE. The powerful pagan empire that dominated the known world during N.T. times (Rom. 1:7). Founded on the Tiber River in 735 B.C. by Romulus, the nation was governed by kings until 509 B.C., when it became a republic. Rome extended its borders greatly during the republic period, eventually annexing Palestine and Syria in 63 B.C.

Augustus Caesar became emperor of the far-reaching empire in 27 B.C. and was reigning at Jesus' birth (Luke 2:1–7). Jesus was crucified by Roman soldiers under sentence from Pilate, the Roman governor of Judea (Matt. 27:24–26).

ROMANS, EPISTLE TO THE. An epistle of the N.T. on the themes of righteousness and salvation, written by the apostle Paul to the Christians at Rome. The most systematic and theological of all of Paul's epistles, Romans expresses his conviction that the gospel is the power of salvation to all who believe (1:16–17).

Other themes discussed in the epistle include (1) the truth that all people, both Jews and Gentiles, are unworthy of God's grace (1:18–3:20); (2) God's imputed righteousness, through which He justifies and sanctifies believers (3:21–8:39); (3) Israel in God's plan of redemption (chaps. 9–11); and (4) the practical application of faith in the life of believers (12:1–15:13). See also *Righteousness; Salvation*.

R

ROME. The capital city of the Roman Empire (Rom. 1:7) and the place where Paul was imprisoned during his final days and where he likely died as a martyr (Phil. 1:12–13; 4:22; 2 Tim. 4:6–8). His epistle to the Romans was addressed to the Christians in this city (Rom. 1:1–7). In the N.T., Rome is figuratively portrayed as Babylon (1 Pet. 5:13).

ROOT. The life-sustaining part of a plant. The word is also used figuratively to describe Christ's humiliation (Isa. 53:2) and exaltation (Isa. 11:10) and the believer's foundation in Christ (Col. 2:7).

ROPE/CORD. A heavy cord. Ropes on the head or neck signified distress (1 Kings 20:31–32) and perhaps submission, since cords were used to bind prisoners. *Cord:* Judg. 15:13. See also *Line.*

ROSE (CROCUS). A flowering plant, perhaps the narcissus—a fragrant flower that grew in the plain of Sharon (Isa. 35:1). *Crocus:* NIV, NRSV.

ROYAL DEPUTY. See *Chancellor.*

ROYAL OFFICIAL. See *Nobleman.*

RUBBISH. See *Dung; Refuse.*

RUBY (CORAL). A precious stone, perhaps coral or pearl (Prov. 3:15; Lam. 4:7). *Coral:* NRSV. See also *Coral.*

RUDDY. Having a reddish or fair complexion, in contrast to the dark skin of most people of the Middle East (1 Sam. 16:12).

RUE. An herb with a strong odor and bitter taste. Jesus denounced the Pharisees who were careful to tithe this insignificant plant while neglecting more important matters (Luke 11:42).

RUFUS. A fellow believer at Rome greeted and commended by Paul (Rom. 16:13). He was perhaps the son of Simon of Cyrene, who carried the cross of Jesus (Mark 15:21).

RUHAMAH. A symbolic name for Israel, meaning "having obtained favor," given by Hosea to his daughter to show that Israel would be forgiven after their repentance (Hosea 2:1).

RULE [ING, TH]
Gen. 1:16 the greater light to *r* the day
2 Sam. 23:3 He that *r'th* over men must be just
Matt. 2:6 a Governor...shall *r* my people Israel
Col. 3:15 let the peace of God *r* in your hearts
1 Tim. 3:5 a man know not how to *r* his own house
1 Tim. 3:12 deacons...*r'ing*...their own houses well

RULER. See *Governor; Prince.*

RUN [NETH]
Ps. 23:5 my cup *r'neth* over
Isa. 40:31 they shall *r*, and not be weary
Amos 5:24 let judgment *r* down as waters

Hab. 2:2 Write the vision...may *r* that readeth it
1 Cor. 9:24 *r* all, but one receiveth the prize
Gal. 5:7 Ye did *r* well; who did hinder you
Heb. 12:1 us *r* with patience the race...before us

RUSH. A plant that grew in marshes, perhaps the same as the bulrush (Job 8:11). See also *Bulrush; Flag.*

RUST. A substance that corrodes metal. Jesus used this word to warn against the instability and uncertainty of earthly treasures (Matt. 6:19–20).

RUTH. A Moabite woman who remained loyal to her Jewish mother-in-law, Naomi, after the death of their husbands. Ruth moved with Naomi to Bethlehem (Ruth 1:16–19), where she gleaned grain in the fields of Boaz. She eventually married Boaz and became an ancestor of David and Christ (Ruth 4:9–22). See also *Boaz; Naomi.*

RUTH, BOOK OF. A short book of the O.T. that reads almost like a short story on the power of love in dismal circumstances. Love bound Ruth and her mother-in-law, Naomi, together in spite of the death of their husbands (chaps. 1–2). And Ruth found happiness and security again through her marriage to Boaz, a kinsman of Naomi's family (chaps. 3–4). See also *Levirate Marriage.*

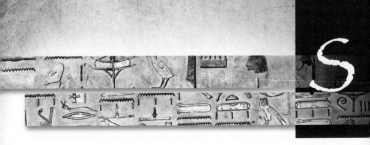

SABAOTH. A Hebrew word for "hosts." See *Hosts, Lord of.*

SABBATH. The Jewish day of worship and rest, established when God rested after the six days of creation (Gen. 2:1–3). The fourth of the Ten Commandments calls for the Sabbath to be observed and "kept holy" (Exod. 20:8). The Pharisees placed restrictions on Sabbath observance that prohibited acts of mercy or necessity (Mark 2:23–24). But Jesus declared that "the sabbath was made for man and not man for the sabbath" (Mark 2:27).

The O.T. Sabbath fell on the seventh day of the week, or our Saturday. Most Christian groups observe Sunday as the day of worship because of Christ's resurrection on the first day of the week (1 Cor. 16:2).

SABBATH DAY'S JOURNEY. The distance under law by which a person was permitted to travel on the Sabbath—2,000 paces outside the city wall, or about 3,000 feet (Exod. 16:29–30; Acts 1:12).

SABBATICAL YEAR. Every seventh year—or a Sabbath year—considered sacred to the Lord, when the land went uncultivated and debtors were released from their obligations (Lev. 25:20–21).

SABEANS. Natives or inhabitants of ancient Sheba in southwest Arabia, a country now known as Yemen. Job's livestock was stolen by Sabeans (Job 1:13–15). The wealthy queen of Sheba visited King Solomon (1 Kings 10).

SACKBUT (LYRE, TRIGON). A triangular-shaped stringed musical instrument similar to a harp (Dan. 3:5). *Lyre:* NIV; *trigon:* NRSV.

SACKCLOTH. A coarse fabric made of goat hair that was worn to express grief, sorrow, and repentance (Joel 1:8, 13). Jacob wore sackcloth in anguish when he thought his son Joseph was dead (Gen. 37:34). See also *Mourn.*

SACRAMENT. A ritual or religious act that serves as a channel of God's grace. While Roman Catholics and most orthodox churches observe seven sacraments, most Protestants admit only two—baptism and the Lord's Supper—and even these are called "ordinances" by most evangelical groups.

SACRIFICE. An offering made to God or to false gods for the purpose of gaining favor or showing respect. In O.T. times, animals were sacrificed on the altar to atone for transgression against God and His law (Deut. 18:3). Christ offered Himself as the final and perfect sacrifice for our sins (Heb. 9:11–14). See also *Atonement; Burnt Offering; Redeem.*

SACRIFICE [S]
1 Sam. 15:22 to obey is better than **s**
Hosea 6:6 I [God] desired mercy…not **s**
Jon. 2:9 I will **s** unto thee [God] with…thanksgiving
Rom. 12:1 present your bodies a living **s**

Heb. 7:27 Who [Jesus] needeth not daily…to offer up **s**
Heb. 11:4 Abel offered…more excellent **s** than Cain
Heb. 13:15 offer the **s** of praise to God
1 Pet. 2:5 offer up spiritual **s's**, acceptable to God

SACRILEGE. See *Blaspheme*.

SADDUCEES. A priestly aristocratic party of N.T. times that—in contrast to the Pharisees—rejected the oral traditions of the Jewish faith and accepted only the original teachings of Moses as authoritative. They did not believe in a bodily resurrection (Matt. 22:23) or angels and spirits (Acts 23:8). They often opposed Jesus and His teachings (Matt. 16:6, 12). See also *Pharisees*.

SAFFRON. A plant used in perfume, dyes, and medicines and for flavoring food and drinks (Song 4:13–14).

SAINT. A N.T. word for a Christian believer set apart for God's service (Rom. 1:7; Heb. 6:10). In the O.T., the word refers to a pious Jew (Ps. 16:3). Spiritual blessings are reserved for the saints of God's kingdom (Col. 1:12). See also *Church; Congregation; People of God*.

SAINTS
2 Chron. 6:41 let thy [God's] **s** rejoice in goodness
Ps. 30:4 Sing unto the Lord, O ye **s**
Ps. 116:15 Precious in the sight of the Lord is the death of his **s**
Matt. 27:52 bodies of the **s** which slept arose
Rom. 12:13 Distributing to the necessity of **s**
1 Cor. 1:2 sanctified in Christ Jesus, called to be **s**
Eph. 3:8 Unto me [Paul]…less than the least of all **s**
Eph. 4:12 perfecting of the **s**…work of the ministry

SAKE [S]
Ps. 23:3 paths of righteousness for his [God's] name's **s**
Matt. 5:10 Blessed…those…persecuted for righteousness' **s**
Luke 21:17 ye shall be hated…for my [Jesus'] name's **s**
Acts 9:16 he [Paul] must suffer for my [Jesus'] name's **s**
1 Cor. 4:10 We are fools for Christ's **s**
2 Cor. 8:9 for your **s's** he [Jesus] became poor
1 Pet. 3:14 suffer for righteousness' **s**, happy are ye

SALAMIS. A town on the island of Cyprus where Paul and Barnabas preached during the first missionary journey (Acts 13:4–5).

SALEM. See *Jerusalem*.

SALIM. A place near Aenon west of the Jordan River where John the Baptist baptized (John 3:23).

SALOME. A woman who witnessed the Crucifixion and visited Jesus' tomb after His resurrection (Mark 15:40; 16:1). She may have been the mother of Jesus' disciples James and John.

SALT. A mineral used to season and preserve food. Jesus called His followers the "salt of the earth" but warned that compromise would diminish their witness (Matt. 5:13; Luke 14:34–35).

SALT, CITY OF. A city in the wilderness of Judah near the Dead Sea, or "Salt Sea" (Josh. 15:62).

SALT SEA. See *Dead Sea*.

SALT, VALLEY OF. A valley with heavy salt deposits near the Dead Sea where King David and King Amaziah were victorious in battle (2 Sam. 8:13; 2 Kings 14:7–8).

SALUTATION. An elaborate greeting, usually involving repeated bowing and embracing (Luke 15:20). Perhaps because of the urgency of their message, Jesus advised His disciples whom He sent out to "salute no man by the way" (Luke 10:4).

SALVATION. The total work of God in delivering us from sin and reconciling us to Himself. The apostle Peter declared that salvation is found in Christ alone (Acts 4:12). See also *New Birth; Regeneration.*

SAMARIA. The capital city of Israel, or the Northern Kingdom, and a name often applied to the surrounding region. The city was built by Omri, king of Israel, about 900 B.C. It was destroyed about 722 B.C. when the Assyrians overran the Northern Kingdom (2 Kings 17:3–24). See also *Omri.*

SAMARITAN. An inhabitant of the district of Samaria between Judea and Galilee. These people were considered inferior by the Jews because of their mixed-blood ancestry going back to their intermarriage with foreign colonists placed there by the Assyrians (2 Kings 17:3–24). Jesus, however, associated with Samaritans (Luke 9:51–52; John 4:4–30) and even used a kindhearted Samaritan as an example of a good neighbor (Luke 10:29–37).

SAMGAR-NEBO. A prince of the family of Nebuchadnezzar of Babylonia who sat in the middle gate of Jerusalem while the city was being captured (Jer. 39:3).

SAMOS. An island of Greece off the coast of Lydia visited by the apostle Paul (Acts 20:15).

SAMOTHRACIA (SAMOTHRACE). An island in the Aegean Sea visited by Paul on his way to Macedonia (Acts 16:11). *Samothrace:* NIV, NRSV.

SAMSON. A judge of Israel set apart as a Nazarite before his birth. Samson had great physical strength, which he used effectively

SAMARITAN. Samaritans in the early 1900s gather to celebrate Passover on Mount Gerizim, a mountain sacred to them. It was from this hilltop that Joshua ordered the blessings of God read to the Israelites after they conquered the Promised Land.

against the Philistines, as long as he was faithful to his vows. But his strength failed when he revealed his secret to Delilah, who cut his hair and turned him over to his enemies. Samson died, along with his captors, when he destroyed the pagan Philistine temple at Gaza (see Judg. 14–16). See also *Nazarite*.

SAMSON THE NAZARITE

Nazarite was a person who made a vow to dedicate himself exclusively to God for some special service (Num. 6:1–21). While under such a vow, he was not to shave, cut his hair, drink wine, or defile himself by touching a dead body.

Most people made such a vow for a limited time, but it was also possible to become a Nazarite for life. Samson was a lifelong

SAMUEL/SHEMUEL. A prophet and the last judge of Israel who anointed the first two kings of Judah—Saul (1 Sam. 10:1) and David (1 Sam. 16:1–13). Samuel was dedicated to God's service by his mother, Hannah, even before his birth (1 Sam. 1:11–22), and he grew up under the tutelage of Eli the priest to prepare for priestly service (1 Sam. 3:1–20). A popular leader, he was mourned by the entire nation at his death (1 Sam. 25:1). *Shemuel:* 1 Chron. 6:33. See also *Hannah*.

SAMUEL, BOOKS OF. Two historical books of the O.T. named for the prophet Samuel, who anointed Saul and David as the first two kings of Israel. Their anointing marked the transition of the nation from a loose confederacy of tribes to a united kingdom under the leadership of a king.

Major events covered by these books include (1) Samuel's rule as the last judge of Israel (1 Sam. 1–7); (2) King Saul's reign (1 Sam. 8:1–15:9); (3) the rivalry between Saul and David (1 Sam. 15:10–31:13); and (4) the accession of David to the throne and his military triumphs, shortcomings, and troubles (2 Samuel). Some of the information about David's administration in 2 Samuel is repeated in the book of 1 Chronicles. See also *Chronicles, Books of; David; Samuel; Saul.*

SANBALLAT. An influential Samaritan who plotted to kill Nehemiah to stop his rebuilding projects and reform projects in Jerusalem (Neh. 4:7–8; 6:1–4). See also *Tobiah*.

SANCTIFICATION. The process of consecrating or setting something apart for holy purposes. In the O.T., priests, Levites, and each family's firstborn child were consecrated to the Lord. In the N.T., sanctification was regarded as a work of grace following conversion (Phil. 1:6). God calls all believers to holiness and sanctification (1 Thess. 4:3, 7; 2 Thess. 2:13). Those sanctified are committed to God's truth and serve as witnesses to His power and grace in the world (Rom. 6:11–13). See also *Consecration.*

SANCTIFY [IED]

Gen. 2:3 God blessed the seventh day…*s'ied* it
Lev. 20:7 *S* yourselves…and be ye holy
Josh. 3:5 Joshua said unto the people, *S* yourselves
1 Cor. 6:11 ye are *s'ied*…ye are justified
1 Tim. 4:5 it is *s'ied* by the word of God and prayer
1 Pet. 3:15 But *s* the Lord God in your hearts

SANCTUARY. A holy place (Lev. 4:6), a place of public worship (Ps. 73:17), or a place of refuge where a person is safe under God's protection (Ezek. 11:16).

SAND. Fine, granular soil that is seldom found in Palestine except along the seashore. The word is used figuratively for countless numbers or multitudes (Gen. 32:12).

SANDALS. Footwear consisting of leather or wood bound to the feet with straps (Acts 12:8). They were removed before entering a house or holy place (Josh. 5:15). See also *Latchet*.

SANHEDRIN. See *Council*.

SAPPHIRA. An early believer at Jerusalem who was struck dead for lying and withholding money she had pledged to the church's common treasury (Acts 5:1–11). See also *Ananias*.

SAPPHIRE. A light blue gem or precious stone used in the breastplate of the high priest (Exod. 28:18) and in the foundation of New Jerusalem (Rev. 21:19).

SARAH/SARA/SARAI. A wife of Abraham and the mother of Isaac (Gen. 11:29; Rom. 9:9), also called *Sarai*. Although she was barren for many years, Sarah received God's promise that she would be "a mother of nations" (Gen. 17:15–16), and she bore Isaac past the age of ninety (Gen. 17:17–21; 21:2–3). She is commended in the N.T. for her faith and obedience (Heb. 11:11; *Sara:* Greek form). See also *Abraham*.

SARDINE (CARNELIAN). A precious stone (Rev. 4:3). Probably the same as the sardius. *Carnelian:* NIV, NRSV. See *Sardius*.

SARDIUS (CARNELIAN). A precious stone of blood-red color used in the high priest's breastplate (Exod. 28:17) and in the foundation of New Jerusalem (Rev. 21:20). *Carnelian:* NIV, NRSV.

SARDONYX (ONYX). A precious stone that combines the qualities of sardius and onyx, thus its name *sardonyx*. It is used in the foundation of New Jerusalem (Rev. 21:20). *Onyx:* NRSV. See also *Onyx; Sardius*.

SARDIS. The chief city of Lydia in Asia Minor and site of one of the seven churches of Asia Minor. This church was characterized as "dead" (Rev. 3:1–5).

SAREPTA. See *Zarephath*.

SARGON. The king of Assyria (reigned about 722–705 B.C.) who completed the siege of Samaria and carried the Northern Kingdom into captivity (Isa. 20:1). See also *Assyria*.

SARON. See *Sharon*.

SATAN. An evil being who opposes God; the devil. In the Garden of Eden, Satan was represented as a serpent who tempted Eve (Gen. 3:1–6). He falsely accused and harassed Job (Job 1:6–12). Jesus regarded Satan as a person (Matt. 4:1–10) whom He described as a murderer and the father of lies (John 8:44). While he is called "the prince of this world" (John 16:11), Satan is subject to God's greater power (1 John 4:4) and will be cast into the bottomless pit (Rev. 20:1–3). See also *Belial; Lucifer*.

SATRAP. NIV, NRSV word for the governor of a province in the ancient Persian Empire (Dan. 6:1). *Prince:* KJV. See also *Governor; Lieutenant*.

SATYR (GOAT-DEMON). A word used by Isaiah for a wild animal that would dance among the ruins of Babylon (Isa. 13:21). *Goat-demon:* NRSV. A satyr was a mythological creature with the features of a man and a goat.

SAUL AND THE PHILISTINES

Saul had the misfortune of serving as king of Israel when the Philistines were the nation's most formidable enemy. Their monopoly on making and sharpening iron weapons put Saul and his army at a distinct disadvantage (1 Sam. 13:15–23). His sons were eventually killed in a battle with the Philistines, and he was mortally wounded (1 Sam. 31:1–13). Not until the time of David, Israel's popular warrior-king, were the Philistines finally defeated.

SAUL

1. The first king of Israel who displeased God by his disobedience and his insane jealousy against David. Anointed privately by Samuel (1 Sam. 10:1) and publicly proclaimed king at Gilgal (1 Sam. 11:15), he waged war against the Philistines during his administration (1 Sam. 17–18). He kept the spoils of war from at least one battle, assumed duties of the priestly office, and murdered Ahimelech and eighty-four other priests (1 Sam. 22:11–19)—acts that brought God's judgment. After his sons were killed, Saul committed suicide rather than be captured by the Philistines (1 Sam. 31:1–6).

2. The original name of Paul the apostle. See *Paul*.

SAVE [D]

Isa. 45:22 be ye **s'd**, all the ends of the earth
Matt. 1:21 he [Jesus] shall **s** his people from their sins
Matt. 10:22 he that endureth to the end shall be **s'd**
Mark 8:35 will **s** his life shall lose it
Luke 19:10 Son of man...seek and to **s** that which was lost
John 3:17 world through him [Jesus] might be **s'd**
John 12:47 I [Jesus] came not to judge...but to **s** the world
Acts 4:12 none other name...whereby we must be **s'd**
Rom. 5:10 we shall be **s'd** by his [Jesus'] life

1 Cor. 1:21 foolishness of preaching to **s** them that believe
Eph. 2:8 by grace are ye **s'd** through faith
1 Tim. 1:15 Christ Jesus came into the world to **s** sinners
James 2:14 though a man...have not works? can faith **s** him

SAVIOR. A title for Christ that emphasizes His work of salvation (Matt. 1:21)—a ministry foretold by the prophet Isaiah (Isa. 61:1–3).

SAVIOUR

Isa. 43:11 beside me [God] there is no **s**
Luke 2:11 unto you is born...a **S**
1 John 4:14 Father sent the Son...**S** of the world

SAW. A tool with sharp teeth used in building the temple in Jerusalem and sometimes used to execute prisoners of war (2 Sam. 12:31).

SCAB. A sore on the skin or a hardened, scaly spot left by a skin disease (Lev. 13:2, 6–8).

SCABBARD. See *Sheath*.

SCALES. See *Balance, Balances*.

SCALL (ITCH). An inflammation of the scalp (Lev. 13:30–37). *Itch:* NIV, NRSV.

SCAPEGOAT (AZAZEL). A goat symbolically bearing the sins of the people and sent into the wilderness by the high priest on the Day of Atonement (Lev. 16:8–22). This goat is a symbol of Christ, our sin bearer (see Isa. 53:6). *Azazel:* NRSV.

SCARF. See *Muffler*.

SCARLET (CRIMSON). A red color highly prized as a symbol of wealth and position (2 Sam. 1:24). Its brilliance symbolized Israel's glaring sin against God (Isa. 1:18). *Crimson:* NRSV.

SCENTED WOOD. See *Thyine Wood.*

SCEPTRE. A staff or baton carried by a king or other high official as an emblem of authority (Esther 4:11).

SCEVA. A Jewish priest at Ephesus whose sons tried in vain to cast out evil spirits in imitation of Paul (Acts 19:11–16).

SCHOOLMASTER (DISCIPLINARIAN). A household servant who accompanied children to school but did not function as a teacher. Paul used the word to show the shortcomings of the law. It could make a person aware of sin, but it fell short of providing salvation (Gal. 3:24–25). *Disciplinarian:* NRSV.

SCORPION. An eight-legged insect with a poisonous tail (Deut. 8:15). The word is also used symbolically of a whip for scourging (2 Chron. 10:11). See also *Scourging.*

SCOURGING (FLOGGING). A severe beating with a leather strap containing bits of sharp metal. This punishment was limited to forty lashes (Deut. 25:3). Jesus was scourged before His crucifixion (Matt. 27:26). *Flogging:* NIV, NRSV.

SCREECH OWL. A bird noted for its strange cries at night (Isa. 34:14). See also *Bittern; Night Hawk.*

SCRIBE (TEACHER OF THE LAW). A public secretary who specialized in copying the law, in the days when documents had to be laboriously reproduced by hand. Many scribes became interpreters and teachers, and in N.T. times they were committed to preserving the law. Their burdensome technicalities brought Jesus' condemnation (Matt. 5:20). *Teacher of the law:* NIV. See also *Lawyer.*

SCRIBE'S KNIFE. See *Penknife.*

SCRIP (BAG). A small bag or satchel (Matt. 10:10) used for carrying food or other provisions on a journey (Luke 9:3). *Bag:* NIV, NRSV.

SCRIPTURE. See *Bible.*

SCROLL. A piece of papyrus or leather written on and then rolled on a stick. It was unrolled for reading (Rev. 6:14). See also *Roll.*

SCUM. See *Offscouring.*

SCURVY. A skin disease caused by extended exposure and an unbalanced diet, characterized by dry, scaly skin with bright spots (Lev. 21:20; 22:22).

SCYTHIANS. Members of the nomadic tribes north of the Black Sea and the Caspian Sea. Paul used the word as a general term for barbaric persons (Col. 3:11).

SEA. A large body of salt water. In the O.T., the word is used for any large expanse of water, including rivers and lakes (Gen. 1:10; Isa. 19:5).

SEA GULL. See *Cuckow.*

SEA MONSTER. A giant sea creature of uncertain identity, perhaps a whale or large fish (Lam. 4:3).

SEA OF CHINNEROTH. See *Galilee, Sea of.*

SEA OF GLASS. A clear, crystal sea or lake that appeared to John in a vision, indicating

S

SCOURGING. *A Louisiana slave in 1863 shows the lingering effects of a scourging. (Inset) Romans often beat prisoners with a whip made of several loose strips of leather, sometimes lashed with sharp bits of metal.*

God's purity and holiness and the victory of His redeemed people (Rev. 4:6).

SEA OF THE PLAIN. See *Dead Sea.*

SEA OF TIBERIAS. See *Galilee, Sea of.*

SEAL. See *Signet.*

SEBA. A son of Cush and grandson of Ham (Gen. 10:6–7); the nation made up of Seba's descendants (Ps. 72:10; Isa. 43:3).

SEBAT (SHEBAT). The eleventh month of the Hebrew year (Zech. 1:7). *Shebat:* NIV, NRSV.

SECOND COMING. Christ's return to earth to punish the wicked and unbelieving and to receive glory from believers (2 Thess. 1:7–10). This event will happen suddenly, and Jesus will be "revealed from heaven with his mighty angels" (2 Thess. 1:7). He will raise the dead (1 Thess. 4:13–17), destroy death (1 Cor. 15:25–26), gather the redeemed (Matt. 24:31), judge the world (Matt. 25:32), and reward God's people (Matt. 16:27).

Christians should be prepared for the Lord's coming (Matt. 24:42) and remain faithful in Christian service (1 Cor. 15:58). See also *Maranatha; Rapture.*

SECRET. See *Mystery.*

SECT. A religious movement in Judaism (Pharisees, Sadducees, Essenes) as well as a political party (Herodians, zealots). Early Christians were regarded as "the sect of the Nazarenes" (Acts 24:5). The word also relates to early perversions of Christian truth (Gal. 5:20).

SECUNDUS. A Christian who accompanied Paul on his third missionary journey (Acts 20:4).

SEED (OFFSPRING). A person's descendants and thus the means of transmitting life from one generation to another (Gen. 21:12). Believers in Christ were said to be born of "incorruptible seed" (1 Pet. 1:23) and true heirs of the promise made by God to Abraham (Gal. 3:29). *Offspring:* NIV, NRSV. See also *Offspring; Posterity.*

SEEK [ETH]

2 Chron. 7:14 If my [God's] people...pray...**s** my face
Ps. 63:1 thou art my God; early will I **s** thee
Ps. 105:4 **S** the LORD, and his strength
Isa. 55:6 **S** ye the LORD while he may be found
Matt. 7:7 **s**, and ye shall find
Mark 8:12 doth this generation **s** after a sign
Luke 12:31 rather **s** ye the kingdom of God
Luke 17:33 shall **s** to save his life shall lose it
Luke 19:10 Son of man is come to **s** and to save...lost
Rom. 3:11 none that **s'eth** after God
1 Cor. 1:22 Greeks **s** after wisdom
Col. 3:1 **s** those things...above

SEER. See *Prophet.*

SEIR, MOUNT. See *Edom,* No. 2.

SELA. See *Petra.*

SELAH. A musical term in the Psalms, possibly calling for a pause or a sudden outburst of voices or instruments (Ps. 44:8).

SELEUCIA. A seaport in Syria from which Paul and Barnabas set sail on the first missionary journey (Acts 13:4).

SELF-CONTROL. See *Sober; Temperance.*

SEPULCHRE. The Garden Tomb in Jerusalem is one of the most famous sepulchers, or tombs, on earth. Though most experts agree it probably wasn't the tomb in which Jesus was buried, the garden setting helps Christian worshipers visualize the kind of place where Jesus was buried.

SELF-DENIAL. Voluntary limitation of one's desires, a requirement of Jesus for His followers (Matt. 16:24). Paul also urged Christians to make an offering of themselves to God (Rom. 12:1). Sacrifices for Christ's sake will be rewarded (Luke 18:29–30).

SEM. See *Shem.*

SENIR. See *Hermon, Mount.*

SENNACHERIB. The king of Assyria (reigned about 705–681 B.C.) who captured all fortified cities of Judah except Jerusalem and then demanded tribute from King Hezekiah (2 Kings 18:13–16). Sennacherib was eventually assassinated by his own sons as he worshiped a pagan god (2 Kings 19:36–37). See also *Assyria.*

SENSIBLE. See *Sober.*

SENTINEL. See *Watchman.*

SEPARATE [D]

Isa. 59:2 iniquities have *s'd* between you and…God
Matt. 25:32 he [Jesus] shall *s* them one from another
Acts 13:2 *S* me Barnabas and Saul for the work
Rom. 8:39 Nor height…shall…*s* us from the love of God
2 Cor. 6:17 come out…and be ye *s*, saith the Lord

SEPHARVAIM. A city whose residents, the Sepharvaites, were sent to colonize the Northern Kingdom after Samaria was captured by the Assyrians (2 Kings 17:24–31). See also *Samaritan.*

SEPTUAGINT. The translation of the O.T. from Hebrew into the Greek language about 250 to 150 B.C.—a work accomplished by Jewish scholars who were brought to Alexandria, Egypt, especially for this purpose.

Seven

SEPULCHRE (TOMB). A natural cave or a place carved out of rock where bodies were buried (Gen. 23:6–9). Some sepulchers were whitened for easy visibility (Matt. 23:27), since contact with a body made a person ceremonially unclean (Num. 19:16). Jesus was buried in a sepulcher or tomb prepared by Joseph of Arimathea (Matt. 27:57–60). *Tomb:* NIV. See also *Cave; Grave.*

SERAIAH

1. David's secretary or recorder who served also in Solomon's administration (2 Sam. 8:17). Also called *Sheva* (2 Sam. 20:25), *Shisha* (1 Kings 4:3), and *Shavsha* (1 Chron. 18:16).

2. A prince of Judah who carried Jeremiah's prophecy of doom to the city of Babylon (Jer. 51:59–64).

SERAPHIM (SERAPHS). Six-winged creatures that sang God's praises and also purified Isaiah's lips in his vision in the temple (Isa. 6:1–7). *Seraphs:* NIV, NRSV.

SERGIUS. See *Paulus Sergius.*

SERMON ON THE MOUNT. Jesus' ethical teachings in Matt. 5–7, delivered to His followers on a hillside near Capernaum. Subjects covered include true happiness (5:3–12); Christian influence (5:13–16); relation of the law and Christian conduct (5:17–48); the practice of charity, prayer, and fasting (6:1–18); God and possessions (6:19–24); freedom from anxiety (6:25–34); judging others (7:1–6); the key to God's blessings (7:7–12); warnings about deception (7:13–23); and building life on a secure foundation (7:24–27). See also *Beatitudes.*

SERPENT. A snake. Satan in the form of a serpent tempted Adam and Eve to sin (Gen. 3:1–5). Poisonous serpents were sent to punish the Israelites for complaining in the wilderness (Num. 21:6). Moses' upraised serpent symbolized Jesus' future sacrificial death (John 3:14).

SERVANT. One who serves others; any person under the authority of another (Matt. 8:9). Isaiah depicted the coming Messiah as a Suffering Servant (Isa. 53:3–12). Jesus declared His mission was to serve and save (Matt. 20:28; Luke 22:27). See also *Maidservant; Manservant.*

SERVANT [S]
Ps. 34:22 LORD redeemeth the soul of his *s's*
Ps. 119:125 I am thy [God's] *s*; give me understanding
Prov. 14:35 king's favour is toward a wise *s*
Isa. 42:1 Behold my [God's] *s*, whom I uphold
Mal. 1:6 son honoureth his father, and a *s* his master
Matt. 23:11 he that is greatest…shall be your *s*
Matt. 25:21 Well done…good and faithful *s*
Mark 9:35 same shall be last of all, and *s* of all
Luke 15:19 make me [the prodigal son] as one of thy hired *s's*
John 8:34 Whosoever committeth sin is the *s* of sin
1 Cor. 9:19 I [Paul] made myself *s* unto all
Gal. 4:7 Wherefore thou art no more a *s*, but a son
Phil. 2:7 took upon him [Jesus] the form of a *s*

SERVANT GIRL. See *Handmaid.*

SERVE [ING]
Gen. 27:29 Let people *s* thee [God]…nations bow down
Deut. 6:13 fear the LORD thy God, and *s* him
Ps. 72:11 all nations shall *s* him [God]
Matt. 4:10 worship the LORD…him only shalt thou *s*
Luke 16:13 No servant can *s* two masters
John 12:26 any man *s* me [Jesus], let him follow me
Rom. 12:11 fervent in spirit; *s'ing* the Lord
Gal. 5:13 by love *s* one another

SETH/SHETH. The third son of Adam and the father of Enoch (Gen. 4:25–26). *Sheth:* 1 Chron. 1:1.

SEVEN. A number often used symbolically because it was considered a round or perfect number. God's creation established an order of seven days (Gen. 2:2). Seven times or sevenfold suggested abundance (Matt. 18:21–22).

SEVEN CHURCHES OF ASIA. The seven churches in Asia Minor addressed by John in Revelation. The messages to these churches ranged from warnings and rebukes to commendations for their faithfulness (see Rev. 2–3).

> **MESSAGE TO THE SEVEN CHURCHES**
>
> 1. To Ephesus: Recover your lost love (Rev. 2:1–7).
> 2. To Smyrna: Hold steady under persecution (Rev. 2:8–11).
> 3. To Pergamos: Shun idolatry and immorality (Rev. 2:12–17).
> 4. To Thyatira: Watch out for false teachings (Rev. 2:18–29).
> 5. To Sardis: Renew your dead faith (Rev. 3:1–6).
> 6. To Philadelphia: Keep on being loyal to Christ (Rev. 3:7–13).
> 7. To Laodicea: Move beyond spiritual apathy (Rev. 3:14–22).

SEVEN SAYINGS FROM THE CROSS. The seven separate utterances that Jesus made as He suffered on the cross: (1) "Father, forgive them" (Luke 23:34); (2) "To day shalt thou be with me in paradise" (Luke 23:43); (3) "Woman, behold thy son!" (John 19:26); (4) "My God, my God, why hast thou forsaken me?" (Matt. 27:46); (5) "I thirst" (John 19:28); (6) "It is finished" (John 19:30); and (7) "Father, into thy hands I commend my spirit" (Luke 23:46).

SEVEN STARS (PLEIADES). A brilliant cluster of stars named for the seven daughters of Atlas and Pleione in Greek mythology (Amos 5:8). *Pleiades:* NIV, NRSV. See also *Pleiades.*

SEVENTH MONTH FESTIVAL. See *Trumpets, Feast of.*

SEVENTY WEEKS. See *Daniel, Book of.*

SEXUAL IMMORALITY. See *Fornication.*

SHACKLES. See *Fetters; Stocks.*

SHADRACH. The Babylonian name of Hananiah, one of Daniel's friends, who was cast into the fiery furnace but miraculously delivered at God's hand (Dan. 3). See also *Daniel.*

SHALLUM. See *Jehoahaz, No. 2.*

SHALMANESER. An Assyrian king (reigned about 730–720 B.C.) who defeated Israel, or the Northern Kingdom, and carried its leading citizens into captivity (2 Kings 17:3–6.) See also *Assyria.*

SHAME. Disgrace or disrepute that produces a feeling of guilt. It may be caused by idleness (Prov. 10:5), excessive pride (Prov. 11:2), or evil companions (Prov. 28:7).

SHAME [D]
Ps. 4:2 will ye turn my [God's] glory into *s*
Ps. 14:6 Ye have *s'd* the counsel of the poor
Ps. 119:31 O LORD, put me not to *s*
Prov. 29:15 a child left to himself bringeth his mother to *s*
1 Cor. 14:35 a *s* for women to speak in the church
Heb. 12:2 Jesus…endured the cross, despising the *s*

SHAMGAR. A judge who delivered Israel from oppression by killing 600 Philistines with an ox goad (Judg. 3:31). See also *Judges of Israel.*

SHAMMUA. See *Shimea.*

SHAPHAN. A scribe who helped King Josiah carry out his religious reforms by recording temple contributions and proclaiming the law (2 Kings 22:3–13).

SHARON/SARON. A fertile coastal plain between Joppa and Mount Carmel along the Mediterranean Sea (1 Chron. 27:29). *Saron:* Acts 9:35.

SHAVEH. See *King's Dale.*

SHAVSHA. See *Seraiah,* No. 1.

SHEARING HOUSE. A place between Jezreel and Samaria where Jehu assassinated the family of King Ahaziah of Judah in order to become king (2 Kings 10:12–14).

SHEAR-JASHUB. A symbolic name meaning "a remnant shall return" given by Isaiah to his son to show God's promise to His people after their period of exile (Isa. 7:3).

SHEATH (SCABBARD). A carrying case for a dagger or sword (1 Sam. 17:51). *Scabbard:* NIV (John 18:11).

SHEBA. See *Sabeans.*

SHEBAT. See *Sebat.*

SHEBNA. A treasurer under King Hezekiah who made a sepulchre for himself. Isaiah predicted Shebna would die in exile (Isa. 22:15–19).

SHECHEM
1. A tribal prince who was killed by Simeon and Levi for seducing their sister, Dinah (Gen. 34).
2. A city of refuge on a trade route in the territory of Ephraim (Josh. 20:7). *Sichem:*

Gen. 12:6. *Sychem:* Acts 7:16. See also *Cities of Refuge.*

SHECHINAH. See *Shekinah.*

SHEEP. A domesticated animal prized for the food and fleece that it provided, and also used as a sacrificial offering (Lev. 9:2–4; 12:6). Large flocks of sheep were a sign of wealth (Job 1:3). Jesus spoke of straying sheep as a symbol of lost or sinful persons (Luke 15:4–6). See also *Fleece; Lamb; Wool.*

Ps. 44:22 we are counted as **s** for the slaughter
Ps. 119:176 I have gone astray like a lost **s**
Isa. 53:6 All we like **s** have gone astray
Matt. 10:16 send you forth as **s** in the midst of wolves
Matt. 15:24 I [Jesus] am...sent...unto the lost **s** of...Israel
Mark 6:34 Jesus...saw...people...as **s** not having a shepherd
John 10:7 I [Jesus] am the door of the **s**
John 10:11 good shepherd [Jesus] giveth his life for the **s**
John 21:16 He [Jesus] saith to him [Peter]...Feed my **s**
1 Pet. 2:25 ye were as **s** going astray

SHEEP GATE. A gate in the wall of Jerusalem repaired under Nehemiah's leadership (Neh. 3:1, 32).

SHEEPFOLD. A strong enclosure that provided protection for sheep. Jesus is the Good Shepherd who protects His sheep (John 10:1–11).

SHEKEL. A Jewish coin or unit of measure. The silver shekel was worth about sixty cents; the gold shekel about eight dollars (Gen. 23:15; Neh. 10:32; Jer. 32:9).

SHEKELS OF SILVER. See *Silverlings.*

SHEKINAH. A visible manifestation of God's glory, usually as a bright light, fire, or cloud (Exod. 13:21; Matt. 17:5).

SHELTER. See *Pavilion.*

S

SHEPHERD. A young shepherd keeps an eye on his family's sheep near Jericho.

SHEM/SEM. The oldest son of Noah who was preserved in the ark (Gen. 5:32). Shem was the father of Elam, Asshur, Arphaxad, Lud, and Aram—ancestors of the Semitic nations known as the Jews, Arameans, Persians, Assyrians, and Arabians (Gen. 10:22). *Sem:* Greek form (Luke 3:36).

SHEMA, THE. The noted confession of faith quoted by faithful Jews each day: "Hear, O Israel: The LORD our God is one LORD" (Deut. 6:4–9). The complete Shema also includes Num. 15:37–41 and Deut. 11:13–21.

SHEMAIAH. A prophet of Judah who warned King Rehoboam not to attack Israel (1 Kings 12:22–24). He revealed that Pharaoh Shishak of Egypt was being used by the Lord to punish Judah for its sins (2 Chron. 12:5–9).

SHEMER. The landowner who sold King Omri of the Northern Kingdom a hill on which the capital city of Samaria was built (1 Kings 16:24). His name is reflected in the city's name.

SHEMINITH. A musical term appearing in the titles of Pss. 6 and 12 and in 1 Chron. 15:21. It may designate the manner of singing or the instrument to be used.

SHEMUEL. See *Samuel.*

SHENIR. See *Hermon, Mount.*

SHEOL. See *Hell.*

SHEPHERD. A person who tends sheep, an honorable but dangerous vocation among the Jews (Gen. 31:38–40). The word is also used of ministers and of Christ, who referred to Himself as the "good shepherd" (John 10:11, 14). See also *Minister; Pastor.*

SHEPHERD [S]
Gen. 47:3 Thy servants [the Hebrews] are **s's**
Ps. 23:1 Lᴏʀᴅ is my **s**; I shall not want
Isa. 40:11 He [God] shall feed his flock like a **s**
Matt. 9:36 were scattered abroad, as sheep having no **s**
Luke 2:8 in the same country **s's** abiding in the field
Heb. 13:20 that great **s** [Jesus] of the sheep
1 Pet. 5:4 when the chief **S** [Jesus] shall appear

SHESHACH. See *Babylonia.*

SHESH-BAZZAR. See *Zerubbabel.*

SHETH. See *Seth.*

SHEVA. See *Seraiah,* No. 1.

SHEWBREAD (BREAD OF THE PRESENCE). Unleavened bread kept in the temple or tabernacle for ceremonial purposes. Its name indicated it was exhibited in the presence of the Lord (Num. 4:7). *Bread of the Presence:* NRSV.

SHIBBOLETH. A password used to distinguish Ephraimites from Gileadites in battle. Unable to pronounce the first *h* in *shibboleth,* 42,000 Ephraimites were killed by the Gileadites (Judg. 12:5–6).

SHIELD. A piece of armor made of wood and covered with hide or metal and carried in battle for protection (1 Chron. 18:7). See also *Buckler.*

Gen. 15:1 Fear not, Abram: I [God] am thy **s**
2 Sam. 22:3 in him will I trust: he [God] is my **s**
Ps. 33:20 the Lᴏʀᴅ is...our **s**
Ps. 84:11 the Lᴏʀᴅ God is a sun and **s**
Eph. 6:16 Above all, taking the **s** of faith

SHIGGAION. A musical term in the title of Ps. 7, possibly referring to an increased tempo for singing.

SHILOAH. See *Siloam.*

SHILOH

1. A town in the territory of Ephraim where the Philistines defeated the Israelites and captured the ark of the covenant (1 Sam. 4:3–11).

2. A title of the coming Messiah that identified Him as a descendant of Judah (Gen. 49:10).

SHIMEI. A Benjamite who insulted David when he was fleeing from Absalom (2 Sam. 16:5–13). Pardoned by David, he was later executed by Solomon (1 Kings 2:36–46).

SHINAR. See *Babylonia*.

SHINE [D, ING, TH]

Num. 6:25 LORD make his face *s* upon thee
Prov. 4:18 path of the just is as the *s'ing* light
Eccles. 8:1 man's wisdom maketh his face to *s*
Isa. 9:2 upon them [people in darkness] hath the light *s'd*
Isa. 60:1 Arise, *s*; for thy light is come
Matt. 5:16 Let your light so *s* before men
Matt. 17:2 his [Jesus'] face did *s* as the sun
John 1:5 light *s'th* in darkness
2 Cor. 4:6 God...hath *s'd* in our hearts
Rev. 21:23 city had no need of the sun...to *s*

SHIP. A seagoing vessel propelled by oars or sails (Jon. 1:4–5). The Jews were not mariners,

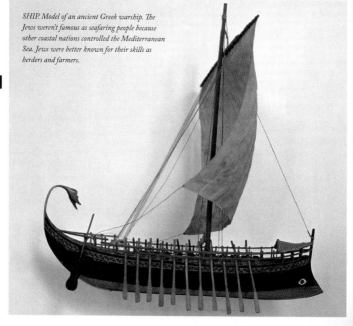

SHIP. Model of an ancient Greek warship. The Jews weren't famous as seafaring people because other coastal nations controlled the Mediterranean Sea. Jews were better known for their skills as herders and farmers.

since most of the Mediterranean coast was controlled by the Phoenicians and Philistines. Solomon's fleet was manned by Phoenicians (1 Kings 9:26–28). See also *Mariner*.

SHISHA. See *Seraiah*, No. 1.

SHISHAK. See *Pharaoh*, No. 1.

SHITTAH (ACACIA). A tree that produced lumber used in building the ark of the covenant and furnishing the tabernacle (Exod. 25:10–16; 30:1; Isa. 41:19). *Acacia:* NIV, NRSV.

SHITTIM
    1. The last campsite of the Israelites before they entered the land of Canaan. It was located across from Jericho in Moab on the eastern side of the Jordan River (Num. 25:1).
    2. The wood or lumber produced from the shittah tree. See *Shittah*.

SHOA. A tribal enemy of the Jews. The prophet Ezekiel predicted these people would invade Judah (Ezek. 23:23–25).

SHOBI. An Ammonite who brought provisions to David at Mahanaim when he fled from Absalom (2 Sam. 17:27–29).

SHOE. See *Sandals*.

SHOOT. See *Rod*.

SHOSHANNIM. A musical term meaning "lilies" in the titles of Pss. 45, 69, and 80, possibly indicating the pitch or tune to which these psalms were to be sung.

SHOULDER. To drop the shoulder signified servitude (Gen. 49:15); to withdraw it denoted rebellion (Neh. 9:29); to put a responsibility on

a person's shoulder was to entrust it to his or her keeping (Isa. 9:6).

SHOVEL. A tool used by priests to remove ashes from the altar (Exod. 27:3). The word sometimes refers to a winnowing fork or fan (Isa. 30:24). See also *Fan*.

SHRINE. A miniature replica of the temple where the pagan goddess Diana was worshiped, placed in homes as an object of devotion. The silversmiths of Ephesus earned their livelihood by making and selling these trinkets (Acts 19:24). See also *Demetrius*, No. 1.

SHUHITE. A member of an Arabic tribe that descended from Shuah, son of Abraham and Keturah. Job's friend Bildad was a Shuhite (Job 2:11).

SHULAMITE (SHULAMMITE). A native of Shulam; the beloved or cherished one in Solomon's song (Song 6:13). *Shulammite:* NIV, NRSV.

SHUNAMMITE. A native of Shunem; a woman from Shunem who provided food and lodging for Elisha. The prophet restored her son to life (2 Kings 4:8–37).

SHUR. A wilderness in southern Palestine (Gen. 16:7) where the Hebrew people wandered for three days after passing through the Red Sea (Exod. 15:22).

SHUSHAN/SUSA. A wealthy and powerful city where Persian kings lived and where Esther interceded for her people (Esther 1:2). *Susa:* NIV, NRSV.

SHUTTLE. A weaving device that shoots the thread rapidly from one side of the cloth to the

S

other between threads of the warp. The word is used as a symbol of fleeting time (Job 7:6). See also *Warp; Weaver.*

SIBBOLETH. See *Shibboleth.*

SICHEM. See *Shechem,* No. 2.

SICKLE. A tool for cutting or harvesting grain (Deut. 16:9). The word is also used as a symbol of God's coming judgment (Rev. 14:14–19).

601 SIDON/ZIDON. A Canaanite city about twenty miles north of Tyre founded by Sidon, the oldest son of Canaan (Gen. 10:15). Noted for its shipbuilding (Ezek. 27:8), silverware, and dyed fabrics, the city was often rebuked by the prophets for its idolatry (Isa. 23:4; Ezek. 28:21). Jesus ministered in this city (Matt. 15:21). *Zidon:* Josh. 11:8.

SIEGE. An extended military assault and blockade against a walled city. King Sennacherib of Assyria besieged Jerusalem and other fortified cities of Judah (Isa. 36:1). See also *City; Fenced City.*

SIEVE. A cooking utensil for sifting flour or meal. Early sieves were made of bulrushes, horsehair, or papyrus (Amos 9:9).

SICKLE. Restored bronze tools from the time of King David include a sickle, far right, used to cut grain in the field.

SIGN. An event foretelling future happenings or a miracle confirming a person's faith (John 4:48). Jesus warned the wicked to heed the sign of Jonah's deliverance from the stomach of the great fish (Matt. 16:1–4). Jesus foretold signs of His return (Matt. 24:3, 29–31). See also *Miracle; Token.*

SIGN [S]
Gen. 1:14 let them [lights] be for *s's*
Deut. 6:8 bind them [Scriptures] for a *s* upon thine hand
Isa. 7:14 Lord himself shall give you a *s*

Dan. 4:3 How great are his [God's] *s's*
Matt. 12:39 evil…generation seeketh after a *s*
Luke 2:12 this shall be a *s* unto you
1 Cor. 1:22 the Jews require a *s*

SIGNS AND WONDERS

Deut. 6:22 LORD showed *s-a-w*…upon Egypt
Mark 13:22 false prophets shall rise…show *s-a-w*
John 4:48 Except ye see *s-a-w*, ye will not believe
Acts 5:12 by the…apostles were many *s-a-w* wrought

SIGNET. An official or royal seal, used like a signature to legalize documents (Jer. 22:24).

SIHON. An Amorite king who refused to allow the Israelites to pass through his territory on their way to Canaan. He was defeated by Moses (Num. 21:21–30).

SILAS/SILVANUS. A leader in the Jerusalem church who accompanied Paul on the second missionary journey and who was imprisoned with him at Philippi (Acts 15:40–41; 16:19–23). He was also with Paul at Corinth and Thessalonica (2 Cor. 1:19). *Silvanus:* 2 Thess. 1:1.

SILENCE

Ps. 39:2 I was dumb with *s*, I held my peace
Eccles. 3:7 a time to keep *s*…a time to speak
Hab. 2:20 all the earth keep *s* before him [God]
1 Cor. 14:28 no interpreter, let him keep *s*
1 Cor. 14:34 your women keep *s* in the churches

SILK. A cloth derived from the silkworm (Rev. 18:12).

SILOAM/SHILOAH/SILOAH. A reservoir in Jerusalem supplied with water through King Hezekiah's underground tunnel from a spring outside the city (2 Kings 20:20). Jesus commanded a blind man to wash in the Pool of Siloam for healing (John 9:6–7). *Shiloah:* Isa. 8:6; *Siloah:* Neh. 3:15. See also *Hezekiah; Pool.*

SILVER. A precious metal used in utensils and jewelry (Gen. 44:2). First mentioned in the days of Abraham (Gen. 13:2), silver was used as a medium of exchange and was valued by weight (Ezek. 27:12).

SILVERLINGS (SILVER SHEKELS, SHEKELS OF SILVER). Bits of silver used like money as a medium of exchange (Isa. 7:23). *Silver shekels:* NIV; *shekels of silver:* NRSV.

SILVERSMITH. A craftsman who formed silver into valuable objects. The Ephesian silversmiths made models of the temple of Diana (Acts 19:24–29). See also *Finer.*

SIMEON

1. A son of Jacob by Leah (Gen. 29:33) and ancestor of one of the twelve tribes of Israel (Gen. 46:10). He was held hostage by Joseph to assure Benjamin's safe arrival in Egypt (Gen. 42:24, 36). See also *Tribes of Israel.*

2. A righteous man who blessed the child Jesus in the temple at Jerusalem (Luke 2:25–35).

3. A Christian prophet at Antioch associated with Paul and Barnabas (Acts 13:1). He was also called *Niger.*

SIMON

1. Simon Peter, one of the twelve apostles or disciples of Christ and the leader of the church in Jerusalem after the resurrection and ascension of Jesus. A fisherman from Galilee, Peter followed Jesus after he was encouraged to do so by his brother Andrew (John 1:40–41). He was called *Cephas* by Jesus, a name meaning "stone" (John 1:42), perhaps indicating the promise that Jesus saw in him in spite of his reckless temperament and impetuous personality.

Peter swore he would never forsake Christ,

but he denied Him three times on the night before His crucifixion (Matt. 26:69–75). He went on to become a bold spokesman for Christ in the early years of the Christian movement (Acts 2:14–40). Peter's surname was *Bar-jona* (Matt. 16:17). *Son of Jonah:* NIV, NRSV. See also *Twelve, The.*

2. Another of the twelve apostles or disciples of Jesus, called Simon Zelotes (Luke 6:15) or Simon the Canaanite (Matt. 10:4) to distinguish him from Simon Peter. He may have been a zealot, a Jew fanatically opposed to Roman rule. See also *Canaanites, No. 2; Twelve, The; Zelotes.*

3. A magician or sorcerer condemned by the apostle Peter because he tried to buy the power of the Holy Spirit (Acts 8:18–24).

4. A tanner at Joppa and apparently a friend with whom the apostle Peter lodged (Acts 9:43; 10:6, 17, 32).

SIN. Rebellion against God. Adam and Eve's disobedience in the Garden of Eden resulted in the introduction of sin into the human race (Rom. 5:12–14). Sin is committed against three parties: ourselves (Prov. 8:36), others (Rom. 5:12), and God (Ps. 51:4; 1 Cor. 8:12). Sin is described as transgression (Matt. 15:3), perversion of the right (1 John 5:17), disobedience (Rom. 5:19), rebellion (Isa. 1:2), and lawlessness (1 John 3:4).

The consequence of unforgiven sin is spiritual death, but God's gift to the believer is eternal life through Jesus Christ (Rom. 6:23). See also *Evil; Iniquity; Transgression.*

SIN [NED, S]
Ps. 32:1 Blessed is he…whose *s* is covered
Prov. 14:34 but *s* is a reproach to any people
Isa. 1:18 though your *s*'s be as scarlet…white as snow
Jer. 31:34 I [God] will remember their *s* no more
Matt. 1:21 he [Jesus] shall save his people from their *s*'s
Matt. 18:21 how oft shall my brother *s* against me

John 1:29 Lamb of God…taketh away the *s* of the world
John 8:7 without *s*…let him first cast a stone
John 9:2 who did *s*, this man, or his parents
Rom. 3:23 all…*s*'ned…come short of the glory of God
Rom. 6:1 continue in *s*, that grace may abound
2 Cor. 5:21 he [God] hath made him [Jesus]…*s* for us
Heb. 9:28 Christ was…offered to bear the *s*'s of many
1 John 1:7 blood of Jesus…cleanseth us from all *s*
1 John 1:8 say that we have no *s*, we deceive ourselves
1 John 1:9 he [Jesus] is faithful…to forgive us our *s*'s
1 John 2:2 he [Jesus] is the propitiation for our *s*'s

SIN OFFERING. An offering of a sacrificial animal presented to God to gain forgiveness for sins, particularly those committed unintentionally or in ignorance (Lev. 4:2–3). A sin offering for all the people was made once a year by the high priest on the Day of Atonement (Lev. 16:6, 15). See also *Atonement, Day of; Sacrifice.*

SIN AND SUFFERING

In Bible times, many of the Jewish people believed that suffering was a direct result of sin in one's life. While Jesus was on earth, His disciples asked about a blind man, "Master, who did sin, this man, or his parents, that he was born blind?" (John 9:2).

Jesus replied that this man's suffering could not be explained by such a neat theory. Then He healed the man in a demonstration of His power and compassion.

SIN, WILDERNESS OF. A wilderness region between the Red Sea and Sinai where manna and quail were miraculously provided by the Lord for the Israelites (Exod. 16).

SINAI/SINA (HOREB). A mountain peak more than one mile high in the wilderness of

SISERA. Sisera, a Canaanite commander on the run from a lost battle, stops for a little rest in the tent of a stranger. What he gets is a tent peg hammered into his head while he's sleeping.

Sinai where Moses tended sheep and saw the burning bush with God's call to deliver His people (Exod. 3:1–10). *Sina:* Greek form (Acts 7:30). *Horeb:* KJV, NIV, NRSV.

SINEW. A muscle along the thigh by which muscles are attached to bones (Job 10:11). Because of Jacob's thigh injury, Israelites avoided eating the sinew of the thigh (Gen. 32:24–32). See also *Thigh.*

SING [ING]
Exod. 15:21 **S** ye to the LORD…he hath triumphed
Ps. 67:4 let the nations be glad and **s** for joy
Ps. 100:2 come before his [God's] presence with **s'ing**
Ps. 137:4 How shall we **s** the Lord's song in a strange land?
Isa. 49:13 break forth into **s'ing**, O mountains
Col. 3:16 **s'ing** with grace in your hearts to the Lord
James 5:13 Is any merry? let him **s** psalms

SINIM (ASWAN, SYENE). An unidentified country or region—perhaps China, Egypt, or the wilderness of Sin—from which Jewish exiles would return (Isa. 49:12). *Aswan:* NIV; *Syene:* NRSV.

SINITES. Members of a tribe descended from Canaan who settled in northern Phoenicia (Gen. 10:17; 1 Chron. 1:15). They were perhaps inhabitants of Sin, a city near Mount Lebanon.

SINNER [S]
Ps. 1:1 Blessed is the man that walketh not…way of **s's**
Eccles. 9:18 one **s** destroyeth much good

Mark 2:17 I [Jesus] came…to call…*s's* to repentance
Luke 5:30 Why do ye [Jesus] eat…with…*s's*
Luke 15:10 joy…over one *s* that repenteth
Luke 18:13 God be merciful to me [publican] a *s*
Rom. 5:8 we were yet *s's*, Christ died for us
1 Tim. 1:15 Christ…came into the world to save *s's*

SION. See *Zion.*

SIPHMOTH. A place in southern Judah where David hid from King Saul during his days as a fugitive (1 Sam. 30:26–28).

SIRION. See *Hermon, Mount.*

SISERA. A Canaanite commander killed by Jael, who drove a tent peg through his head while he slept (Judg. 4:2–22). See also *Deborah; Jael.*

SISTER. A general term for any near female relative, including a stepsister or half sister (2 Sam. 13:2; Matt. 13:56). The word is also used to denote members of the same spiritual family (Rom. 16:1).

SIVAN. The third month of the Hebrew year (Esther 8:9), corresponding closely to our June.

SKULL, THE. See *Calvary.*

SLANDER. A deceitful and destructive statement against another (Ps. 52:2). Such statements are uttered by the wicked against the righteous (Job 1:9–11) and believers (1 Pet. 2:12).

SLANDERER. See *Reviler.*

SLAVE. A person bought as a piece of property and pressed into service by his or her owners. Slavery was common in Bible times, but Christian teachings brought some

moderation of the practice (Eph. 6:5–9). Paul appealed to Philemon to receive his runaway slave Onesimus as a brother in the faith (Philem. 10–18).

SLAVEMASTER. See *Taskmaster.*

SLAYER. See *Manslayer.*

SLEEP [ETH, ING]
Ps. 13:3 lighten mine eyes, lest I *s* the *s* of death
Prov. 6:9 How long wilt thou *s*, O sluggard?
Mark 5:39 damsel is not dead, but *s'eth*
Mark 13:36 suddenly he [Jesus] find you *s'ing*
Mark 14:41 *S* on…take your [the disciples'] rest
John 11:11 he [Jesus] saith…Lazarus *s'eth*
1 Cor. 15:51 shall not all *s…shall* all be changed

SLIME (TAR, BITUMEN). A tarlike substance, possibly bitumen or mortar, used in building the tower of Babel (Gen. 11:3). It was used as mortar for bricks and waterproofing (Exod. 2:3). *Tar:* NIV; *bitumen:* NRSV. See also *Pitch.*

SLING. A weapon made of leather thongs and used to throw stones (Judg. 20:16). The shepherd boy David killed Goliath with a sling (1 Sam. 17:50).

SLUG. See *Snail.*

SLUGGARD. A lazy, inactive person. Habitual idleness leads to poverty (Prov. 13:4; 20:4). Paul declared that those who won't work shouldn't eat (2 Thess. 3:10). See also *Idleness.*

SMITH. A metalworker who fabricated tools, weapons, and ornamental objects. Tubal-cain is the first smith mentioned in the Bible (Gen. 4:22). See also *Finer.*

SMYRNA. A city of Ionia about sixty miles north of Ephesus where one of the

SNOW. *Snow rarely accumulates in Israel and is mentioned only once in the Bible. Here, a blanket of snow shrouds the cold tombs overlooking Jerusalem from the Mount of Olives.*

seven churches of Asia Minor was located (Rev. 1:11). The Lord encouraged this church, which was being persecuted by the "synagogue of Satan" (Rev. 2:8–11).

SNAIL (SLUG). A creature with a spiral shell that leaves a trail of slime. The psalmist expressed hope that his enemies would "melt away" even as a snail shrinks after depositing its slime (Ps. 58:7–8). *Slug:* NIV.

SNARE (NOOSE). A trap or net for catching animals. The word is used figuratively for the pitfalls of the wicked (Job 18:10). It also represents calamity or death (2 Sam. 22:6). *Noose:* NIV.

SNOW. Frozen precipitation. One snowfall is recorded in the Bible (2 Sam. 23:20). The word is used figuratively of winter (Prov. 31:21) and moral purity (Matt. 28:3).

SNUFFER, SNUFF DISH. Two separate tools for ceremonial use, one for trimming the wicks of lamps in the tabernacle and the other for carrying away the trimmings (Exod. 25:38). See also *Tongs.*

SO. See *Pharaoh,* No. 2.

SOAP. See *Sope.*

SOBER (SENSIBLE, TEMPERATE, SELF-CONTROLLED). Moderation or seriousness, a quality desired in church leaders (1 Tim. 3:2). This is an appropriate attitude for believers as we await the Lord's return (1 Thess. 5:5–6). *Sensible:* NRSV (1 Tim. 3:11). *Temperate:* NIV, NRSV. *Self-controlled:* NIV.

SOBER [LY, NESS]
Acts 26:25 I [Paul]…speak…words of *s'ness*
1 Thess. 5:6 let us not sleep…watch and be *s*

1 Tim. 3:2 bishop…must be blameless…vigilant, *s*
Titus 2:12 should live *s'ly,* righteously, and godly

SODA. See *Nitre.*

SODOM/SODOMA. One of five cities destroyed by God because of its wickedness (Gen. 19:1–28). It is often mentioned in the Bible as a symbol of evil and as a warning to sinners (Isa. 1:9; Rev. 11:8). *Sodoma:* Greek form (Rom. 9:29). See also *Cities of the Plain; Gomorrah.*

SODOMITE (TEMPLE PROSTITUTE). A man who engaged in sexual activities with other men—a perversion condemned by God (Deut. 23:17–18). *Temple prostitute:* NRSV.

SOJOURNER. A person who lived temporarily in a foreign country (Heb. 11:9). Abraham sojourned in Egypt (Gen. 12:10) as did the Jews in captivity and exile (Ezra 1:4). The word is also used symbolically of Christians in the world (1 Pet. 1:17). See also *Alien; Foreigner.*

SOLDIER. A person engaged in military service (Num. 1:3). The word is also used figuratively of Christian workers (Eph. 6:11–18).

SOLEMN ASSEMBLY. A religious gathering, usually occurring during a major Jewish festival, that was devoted to repentance, confession, and prayer (Lev. 23:36; Deut. 16:8).

SOLOMON. David's son and successor as king of Israel (reigned about 970–930 B.C.). Solomon got off to a good start by praying for divine wisdom and insight (1 Kings 3), and he developed fame as a wise and efficient king of great wealth (1 Kings 4).

At God's command, Solomon completed the building of the temple in Jerusalem (1 Kings 5–8). But he drifted away from commitment to the one true God through his marriages with pagan wives (1 Kings 11:1–8). He also oppressed his people with burdensome taxes to support his ambitious kingdom-building projects (1 Kings 12:4).

After Solomon's death, the ten northern tribes rebelled under Jeroboam and formed their own nation known as Israel, or the Northern Kingdom (1 Kings 12:1–19).

SOLOMON, POOLS OF. Water reservoirs built by King Solomon near Bethlehem to supply water for Jerusalem through a system of underground passages (Eccles. 2:6).

SOLOMON'S PORCH (SOLOMON'S COLONNADE, SOLOMON'S PORTICO). A porch on the eastern side of the temple in Jerusalem that featured a double row of elaborate columns about forty feet high (Acts 3:11). Jesus entered the temple by Solomon's porch (John 10:23). *Solomon's Colonnade:* NIV; *Solomon's Portico:* NRSV).

SOLOMON'S SERVANTS. Canaanites enslaved by Solomon and forced to work on the temple and other building projects (1 Kings 5:17–18).

SON. A male descendant. The birth of a son brought joy and celebration, since a family's heritage and traditions were passed on through its sons (Gen. 21:2).

SON OF GOD. A title of Christ that emphasizes His deity. An angel revealed to Mary that she would give birth to the "Son of God" (Luke 1:35). After Jesus was baptized, a voice from heaven declared, "This is my beloved Son" (Matt. 3:17). John's Gospel was written specifically to encourage belief in the Son of God (John 20:31). See also *Emmanuel; Jesus Christ; Messiah.*

SON OF MAN. A title of Christ, used often by Jesus Himself, that emphasized His humanity and messiahship. This title was probably inspired by Daniel's prophecy of God's messenger who would come on a mission of redemption (Dan. 7:13–14). See also *Messiah.*

"SON OF MAN" IN EZEKIEL

The title "son of man" was also used for the prophet Ezekiel (Ezek. 2:1; 34:2). It set him apart as a representative member of the human race who was on a special mission for God. Like Ezekiel, Jesus was also a representative sent by God, but His mission was to provide salvation for sinful humanity.

SONG OF SOLOMON. A short book of the O.T. filled with expressions of affection between two lovers (see 1:13; 4:1–11; 7:1–10). These words have been interpreted both symbolically and literally. Some insist the song symbolizes God's love for His people Israel, while others believe the book is a healthy affirmation of the joys of physical love between husband and wife. Most scholars believe Solomon wrote the book, since he is mentioned several times in the poems (1:1, 5; 3:7, 9, 11; 8:11–12). See also *Solomon.*

SOOTHSAYER (DIVINER). A fortune-teller who claimed to have the power to foretell future events (Josh. 13:22), reveal secrets (Dan. 2:27), and interpret dreams (Dan. 4:7). Paul and Silas healed a soothsayer in Philippi who was being exploited. *Diviner:* NIV, NRSV. See also *Enchanter; Medium.*

SOP. A small portion of food or bread held in the hand in accordance with Palestinian dining customs and used to soak up liquid foods, such as soup (John 13:26–30).

SOPATER. A Christian who accompanied Paul on the third missionary journey (Acts 20:4). This may be the same person as Sosipater (Rom. 16:21). See *Sosipater*.

SOPE (SOAP). An alkaline substance used for bathing and for purifying metals. Jeremiah indicated soap would clean externally but could not remove sin or iniquity (Jer. 2:22). *Soap:* NIV, NRSV.

SORCERY (MAGIC). The exercise of power received from evil or departed spirits to gain hidden knowledge (Exod. 7:11; Acts 8:9–24). The practice of sorcery and witchcraft was specifically prohibited by God (Lev. 19:31). *Magic:* NRSV. See also *Magic; Witchcraft*.

SORROW. Grief or sadness, which may be caused by sin (Gen. 3:16–17), the death of a loved one (John 11:33–35), or persecution (Esther 9:22). The Christian's eternal hope is a source of comfort in times of sorrow (1 Thess. 4:13, 18). See also *Mourn*.

SORROW [FUL, S]

Ps. 38:17 my *s* is continually before me
Isa. 53:3 man of *s's*...acquainted with grief
Jer. 45:3 LORD hath added grief to my *s*
Matt. 19:22 he [rich young ruler] went away *s'ful*
Matt. 24:8 these are the beginning of *s's*
Matt. 26:38 My [Jesus'] soul is exceeding *s'ful*
John 16:20 your *s* shall be turned into joy

SOSIPATER. A kinsman of Paul whose greetings were sent to the church at Rome (Rom. 16:21). This may be the same person as Sopater (Acts 20:4). See *Sopater*.

SOSTHENES. A ruler of the synagogue at Corinth who was beaten by a mob when Paul was arrested for preaching there (Acts 18:17). This may be the same person as the believer greeted by Paul in 1 Cor. 1:1.

SOUL. The part of humans' inner nature that is the seat of our appetites, passions, and sensations. Sometimes the word *soul* means "person" (Rom. 13:1). See also *Spirit*.

SOUL [S]

Gen. 2:7 man became a living *s*
Deut. 6:5 love the LORD...with all thy *s*
Ps. 25:1 Unto thee, O LORD, do I lift up my *s*
Ps. 35:9 my *s* shall be joyful in the LORD
Ps. 84:2 My *s*...fainteth...courts of the LORD
Prov. 11:30 he that winneth *s's* is wise
Ezek. 18:20 The *s* that sinneth, it shall die
Matt. 11:29 find rest unto your *s's*
Matt. 16:26 man give in exchange for his *s*
Mark 14:34 My [Jesus'] *s* is...sorrowful unto death

SOUND [ING]

John 3:8 wind bloweth...hearest the *s*
Acts 2:2 *s* from heaven...mighty wind
1 Cor. 13:1 I [Paul] am become as *s'ing* brass
1 Cor. 14:8 the trumpet give an uncertain *s*
1 Cor. 15:52 trumpet shall *s*, and the dead...raised
2 Tim. 4:3 they will not endure *s* doctrine

SOUR WINE. See *Vinegar*.

SOUTH COUNTRY (NEGEV, NEGEB). A hilly, wilderness region in southern Palestine around the Dead Sea. This region is also called "the South" and "the land of the South" (Judg. 1:16). *Negev:* NIV; *Negeb:* NRSV.

SOUTH RAMOTH. A place bordering the desert in southern Judah where David hid when fleeing from King Saul (1 Sam. 30:26–27).

SOVEREIGN. See *Potentate*.

SOVEREIGNTY OF GOD. A theological phrase that expresses the truth that God is in control of the universe. God's creation of humans and the world implies His continuing rule and sovereignty (Gen. 1:1; Ps. 8:1–5). His supreme authority is also expressed by the title "Almighty" (Rev. 1:8). In His holy character, the Sovereign must punish sin, but He has graciously provided salvation for all who trust Christ (Rom. 9:22–24). See also *Almighty; Omnipotence.*

SOW [ED, ETH]
Prov. 22:8 He that *s'eth* iniquity shall reap vanity
Luke 8:5 he [a sower] *s'ed*, some fell by the way side
Luke 12:24 Consider the ravens…neither *s* nor reap
John 4:37 One *s'eth*, and another reapeth
2 Cor. 9:6 *s'eth* bountifully…also reap also bountifully
Gal. 6:7 a man *s'eth*, that shall he also reap

SOWER. One who plants seeds, as in Jesus' parable of the sower (Matt. 13:3–23). Sowing was done mostly by hand.

SOWN
Hosea 8:7 have *s* the wind…reap the whirlwind
Hag. 1:6 Ye have *s* much, and bring in little
1 Cor. 15:42 It [the body]…*s* in corruption…raised in incorruption

SPAIN. A country in southwestern Europe that Paul expressed a desire to visit (Rom. 15:24, 28). It was known to ancient Greeks as Iberia and to Romans as Hispania. Jonah's ship was headed for Tarshish, Spain, when he was thrown overboard by the superstitious sailors (Jon. 1:3, 15).

SPAN. A measure of length equal to about nine inches (Exod. 28:16). The word was also used to indicate a small amount of space or time (1 Sam. 17:4; Isa. 40:12).

SOWER. Egyptian farmers sow their seed, in a collection of paintings that portrays the cycle of planting and harvest.

SPARROW. A small bird, common in Palestine, that was sold as food for the poor (Matt. 10:29, 31).

SPEAR. A weapon of war (2 Sam. 2:23) consisting of a metal point on the end of a long shaft (1 Sam. 13:22). It was similar to but bigger than a dart or javelin. See also *Dart; Javelin.*

SPEARMEN. Soldiers with light arms, such as spears (Acts 23:23).

SPECK. See *Mote.*

SPECKLED BIRD (BIRD OF PREY). A phrase of uncertain meaning. Jeremiah compared the nation of Israel to a speckled bird (Jer. 12:9). *Bird of prey:* NRSV.

SPEECH
Gen. 11:1 the whole earth was...of one *s*
Exod. 4:10 I [Moses] am slow of *s*
1 Cor. 2:1 I [Paul]...came not with excellency of *s*
Col. 4:6 Let your *s* be...seasoned with salt

SPELT. See *Fitch; Rie.*

SPICE. An aromatic vegetable compound used in perfumes and ointments (Exod. 30:22–38) and also used to prepare bodies for burial (Mark 16:1).

SPIDER. An insect whose frail web provided a lesson on the fleeting schemes of the wicked (Job 8:14; Isa. 59:5).

SPIES. The twelve scouts, one from each of the twelve tribes of Israel, sent to investigate Canaan and report on their findings (Num.13:1–3, 30–33).

SPIKENARD (NARD). An expensive and highly prized perfume or ointment (Song 4:13–14) that was used to anoint Jesus' hands and feet (John 12:3). *Nard:* NIV, NRSV.

SPINNING. The process of making yarn into cloth by hand on a rotating loom or wheel (Prov. 31:19). See also *Warp; Weaver.*

SPIRIT. A word that denotes our reason, conscience, and nobler affections (2 Cor. 7:1; Eph. 4:23)—in contrast to the soul—our appetites, passions, and sensations. The root meaning of the word is "wind" (John 3:8). See also *Ghost; Soul.*

Ps. 31:5 Into thine hand I [Jesus] commit my *s*
Ps. 51:10 O God...renew a right *s* within me
Ezek. 11:19 I [God] will put a new *s* within you
Dan. 6:3 an excellent *s* was in him [Daniel]
Joel 2:28 I [God] will pour out my *s* upon all flesh
Matt. 5:3 Blessed are the poor in *s*
Matt. 26:41 the *s*...is willing...flesh is weak
John 3:5 a man be born of water and of the *S*
John 4:23 worship the Father in *s* and in truth
John 16:13 the *S* of truth [Holy Spirit], is come
Gal. 5:22 fruit of the *S* is love, joy, peace
Eph. 4:3 unity of the *S* in the bond of peace
Eph. 6:17 sword of the *S*...the word of God
Rev. 2:7 hear what the *S* saith unto the churches

SPIRIT OF GOD/SPIRIT OF THE LORD
Gen. 1:2 *S-o-G* moved upon the face of the waters
Judg. 6:34 the *s-o-t-L* came upon Gideon
1 Sam. 11:6 the *S-o-G* came upon Saul
1 Sam. 16:13 the *s-o-t-L* came upon David
Job 33:4 The *S-o-G* hath made me [Job]
Isa. 11:2 the *s-o-t-L* shall rest upon him [God's servant]
Isa. 61:1 the *s-o-t-L* GOD is upon me [God's servant]
Matt. 3:16 Jesus...saw the *S-o-G* descending like a dove
Luke 4:18 The *s-o-t-L* is upon me [Jesus]
Acts 8:39 the *S-o-t-L* caught away Philip
Rom. 8:14 led by the *S-o-G*, they are the sons of God
1 Cor. 3:16 Know ye not...the *S-o-G* dwelleth in you?
2 Cor. 3:17 where the *S-o-t-L* is, there is liberty
Eph. 4:30 And grieve not the holy *S-o-G*

SPIRITIST. See *Wizard*.

SPIRITS IN PRISON. A much-debated phrase from 1 Pet. 3:18–20 that seems to indicate that Christ, in His spiritual existence, preached to the "spirits in prison" who disobeyed God during the days of Noah. Some scholars claim that Christ did not descend into hell but that His eternal spirit (which later was made alive in His resurrection) preached to the spirits at the time of their disobedience.

SPIRITUAL [LY]

Rom. 8:6 to be *s'ly* minded is life and peace
1 Cor. 14:1 Follow after charity…desire *s* gifts
1 Cor. 15:44 sown a natural body…raised a *s* body
Eph. 6:12 we wrestle…against *s* wickedness

SPIRITUAL GIFTS. Gifts bestowed freely by the Holy Spirit upon believers (James 1:17) for the edification of fellow believers and the church (Rom. 1:11; 1 Cor. 12:28). Gifts listed in Romans are preaching, serving, teaching, encouraging, giving, leading, and helping others (Rom. 12:6–8). Gifts listed in 1 Corinthians are wisdom, knowledge, faith, healing, miracles, prophecy, discernment of spirits, tongues, and interpretation of tongues (1 Cor. 12:8–11). Love is the supreme spiritual gift (1 Cor. 12:31; 13:13).

SPIT. To spit was a gesture of extreme contempt (Num. 12:14), but Jesus used saliva to cure a man's blindness (Mark 8:23).

SPOIL (PLUNDER, BOOTY). Plunder taken in war or seized by bandits (Num. 31:9). David established strict regulations for division of the spoils of war among his soldiers (1 Sam. 30:20–25). *Plunder:* NIV; *booty:* NRSV. See also *Booty*.

SPOON (PITCHER, FLAGON). A shallow dish or pan used as a censer for burning incense in the tabernacle and temple (Exod. 25:29). *Pitcher:* NIV; *flagon:* NRSV. See also *Pitcher; Flagon*, No. 2.

SPRING RAIN. See *Latter Rain*.

STABLE. A shelter for animals. Ezekiel denounced the Ammonites by prophesying the city of Rabbah would become a stable for livestock (Ezek. 25:2, 5).

STACTE (GUM RESIN). An ingredient used in the sacred incense burned in temple ceremonies, possibly a gum or spice from the styrax tree (Exod. 30:34). *Gum resin:* NIV.

STAFF. A long stick or rod used to goad animals, to remove fruit from trees (Isa. 28:27), and as support or defense for the old and infirm (Exod. 21:19).

STALL. A stable and storage area. King Solomon had at least 4,000 stalls "for horses and chariots" (2 Chron. 9:25).

STAND [ETH]

Exod. 14:13 *s* still…see…salvation of the LORD
Ps. 24:3 who shall *s* in his [God's] holy place
Isa. 40:8 word of our God shall *s* for ever
Matt. 12:25 house divided…shall not *s*
Rom. 14:10 all *s* before the judgment seat of Christ
1 Cor. 10:12 thinketh he *s'eth* take heed lest he fall
1 Cor. 16:13 Watch ye, *s* fast in the faith
Gal. 5:1 *S* fast…in the liberty…Christ hath made us free
Eph. 6:11 able to *s* against the wiles of the devil
2 Thess. 2:15 Therefore, brethren, *s* fast
Rev. 3:20 I [Jesus] *s* at the door, and knock

STANDARD (ENSIGN). A banner, flag, or streamer to identify groups of troops or warriors. In the wilderness, each tribe of Israel marched under its own unique banner (Num. 2:2, 34). *Ensign:* NRSV. See also *Ensign*.

STANDARD BEARER. A person who carried the flag or standard of his army or his people—a highly regarded position (Isa. 10:18).

STAR. A luminous body visible in the sky at night. The Hebrews regarded all heavenly bodies as stars, except the sun and moon (Gen. 1:16). The stars were considered a noble mark of God's creative power (Ps. 19:1). Stars were used symbolically for rulers, princes, angels, and ministers (Job 38:7; Dan. 8:10; Rev. 1:16–20). Christ was called "the bright and morning star" (Rev. 22:16).

STARGAZERS. Astrologers; persons who predicted the future by the movement of the stars. The Babylonians were noted for their reliance on astrology (Isa. 47:1, 13). See also *Astrologer; Wise Men.*

STATUTE (DECREE). A law, commandment, or official pronouncement that regulates behavior and conduct (Exod. 18:16). *Decree:* NIV. See also *Commandment; Decree.*

STATUTE [S]
Exod. 27:21 a *s* for ever unto their generations
Lev. 16:34 this shall be an everlasting *s*
Ps. 19:8 The *s's* of the LORD are right
Ps. 119:12 O LORD: teach me thy *s's*

STEADFAST. Persistent and patient in one's faith and activities (Heb. 3:6, 14). Believers are encouraged to endure chastening (Heb. 12:7) and persecution (Rom. 8:35–37). See also *Patience; Perseverance.*

STEDFAST [LY, NESS]
Luke 9:51 he [Jesus] *s'ly* set his face to go to Jerusalem
1 Cor. 15:58 Therefore…be ye *s*, unmoveable
Col. 2:5 the *s'ness* of your faith in Christ

STAR. Pleiades star cluster, known since ancient times as the Seven Sisters. The books of Job and Amos each mention this cluster.

STEEL. KJV word for copper or brass (Jer. 15:12). See also *Brass*.

STEP. See *Pace*.

STEPHEN. A zealous believer who became the first martyr of the Christian cause. A Jewish believer of Greek background, Stephen was among the seven "deacons" selected by the early church to provide relief for other Greek-speaking Christians (Acts 6:5–8). His criticism of O.T. laws and traditions brought him into conflict with Jewish leaders, and he was stoned to death on a charge of blasphemy (Acts 7:55–60).

STEW. See *Pottage*.

STEWARD. A person employed as a custodian, manager, or administrator, usually of a large household (Gen. 43:19). Christians are urged to be faithful stewards of God's gifts (1 Cor. 4:1–2). See also *Treasurer*.

Matt. 20:8 said unto his **s**…give them their hire
Luke 16:8 lord commended the unjust **s**
Titus 1:7 bishop must be blameless, as the **s** of God

STEWARDSHIP. Wise and responsible use of one's God-given resources. Christian stewardship is based on God's ownership of all things (Gen. 1:1; Ps. 24:1–2) and man's assigned dominion of God's creation (Gen. 1:26; 2:15). Good stewardship involves faithfulness in use of one's time (Eph. 5:16), talents (2 Tim. 1:6; 2:15), and money (Mal. 3:10). See also *Tithe*.

STIFFNECKED. See *Neck*.

STOCKS (SHACKLES). A wooden frame for public punishment of offenders, containing holes for confining hands, feet, and sometimes the neck (Job 33:11). *Shackles:* NIV (Job 13:27). See also *Fetters*.

STOICKS (STOICS). A group of philosophers encountered by Paul in his visit to Athens (Acts 17:18). Highly independent moralists, the Stoics were fatalistic in their outlook on life. *Stoics:* NIV, NRSV. See also *Epicureans*.

STOMACH. See *Maw*.

STOMACHER (RICH ROBE). An expensive, festive robe worn by women (Isa. 3:24). *Rich robe:* NRSV.

STONE. See *Rock*.

STONECUTTER. See *Hewer*.

STONING. The Jewish mode of capital punishment, specified in the law for these offenses: sacrificing of children to idols (Lev. 20:2–5), breaking of the Sabbath (Num. 15:32–36), idolatry (Deut. 17:2–7), rebellion of children against parents (Deut. 21:18–21), and adultery (Deut. 22:23–24). Godly men who were stoned for their faith included the prophets (Heb. 11:37), Stephen (Acts 7:59), and Paul, who was presumed dead from stoning (Acts 14:19–20).

STORE CITY (STORAGE TOWN). A city or a supply depot in a city for the storage of food, equipment, and weapons of war (2 Chron. 8:4). *Storage town:* NRSV. See also *Treasure City*.

STOREHOUSE. A building for storing food. Joseph built grain storehouses in Egypt to get ready for the years of famine (Gen. 41:48–49).

STORK. A long-necked migratory bird similar to the crane (Ps. 104:17); an unclean animal to the Jews (Lev. 11:19).

STORM. See *Tempest; Whirlwind*.

STRAIGHT
Isa. 40:3 make s...a highway for our God
Luke 3:4 Prepare ye the way of the Lord, make his paths s
Acts 9:11 go into the street which is called S

STRANGER. See *Foreigner.*

STRAW. A food for livestock. Straw was also used as a strengthening and binding ingredient in bricks (Exod. 5:7, 16).

STREET. A traffic lane in a city. Streets of Bible times were mostly crude, crooked, and narrow, much like a dirty alley (Jer. 37:21). The street in Damascus called Straight was exceptionally wide (Acts 9:11).

STRENGTH
Exod. 15:2 LORD is my s and song
Job 12:13 With him [God] is wisdom and s
Ps. 27:1 the LORD is the s of my life
Ps. 46:1 God is our refuge and s
Ps. 71:9 forsake me not when my s faileth
Isa. 12:2 LORD...is my s and my song
Isa. 30:15 quietness and in confidence shall be your s
Isa. 40:31 that wait upon the LORD...renew their s
Mark 12:30 love the Lord thy God...with all thy s

STRENGTHEN [ETH, ING]
Ps. 27:14 he [God] shall s thine heart
Luke 22:43 appeared an angel...s'ing him [Jesus]
Phil. 4:13 all things through Christ which s'eth me [Paul]

STRIFE. Bitter conflict caused by self-seeking (Luke 22:24) or a worldly spirit (1 Cor. 3:3). Strife may be avoided by unselfishness and a brotherly spirit (Gen. 13:7–8; Phil. 2:3). See also *Contention.*

STRIPES
Isa. 53:5 with his [God's servant's] s we are healed
2 Cor. 11:24 five times received I [Paul] forty s
1 Pet. 2:24 by whose [Jesus'] s ye were healed

STRIVE [D, ING]
Luke 13:24 S to enter in at the strait gate
Rom. 15:20 so have I [Paul] s'd to preach the gospel
Phil. 1:27 one mind s'ing together for...the gospel

STRONG [ER]
Deut. 31:6 Be s and of a good courage
Ps. 24:8 The LORD s and mighty
Ps. 71:7 thou [God] art my s refuge
Prov. 18:10 name of the LORD is a s tower
Eccles. 9:11 race is not to the swift, nor the battle to the s
Luke 2:40 child [Jesus] grew, and waxed s in spirit
Rom. 15:1 ought to bear the infirmities of the weak
1 Cor. 1:25 weakness of God is s'er than men
2 Cor. 12:10 when I [Paul] am weak, then am I s

STRONG DRINK. See *Wine.*

STRUTTING ROOSTER. See *Greyhound.*

STUBBLE. The short stumps of grain stalks left in the ground after harvesting (Exod. 5:12). Regarded as worthless, stubble symbolized instability and impermanence (Isa. 33:11).

STUMBLINGBLOCK. A hindrance to belief or understanding. Israel's iniquity and idolatry were a stumblingblock (Jer. 6:21; 18:15). Paul urged Christians not to offend or serve as a hindrance to a weak brother (Rom. 14:13; 1 Cor. 8:9). The preaching of "Christ crucified" was a stumblingblock to the Jews (1 Cor. 1:23).

SUBMIT [TING]
Eph. 5:21 S'ting yourselves one to another...fear of God
Eph. 5:22 Wives, s yourselves unto your own husbands
James 4:7 S yourselves therefore to God
1 Pet. 5:5 younger, s yourselves unto the elder

SUBURBS (PASTURE LANDS). The open country around a city used for grazing livestock or other purposes (Josh. 21:11). *Pasture lands:* NIV, NRSV.

S

SUPPER. At a supper in the village of Emmaus, after His resurrection, Jesus blesses the bread. Only then do those with Him recognize who He is. Then suddenly He disappears.

SUCCOTH-BENOTH. An idol set up in Samaria by the pagan peoples who colonized the area after Israel (Northern Kingdom) fell to the Assyrians (2 Kings 17:29–30).

SUCKLING. An infant or young animal not yet weaned from its mother's milk. As judge, Samuel offered a suckling lamb as a burnt offering to the Lord (1 Sam. 7:9).

SUFFER [ED, ETH, INGS]

Ps. 55:22 he [God]...never *s* the righteous to be moved
Matt. 16:21 Jesus...must go...*s* many things
Matt. 19:14 *S* little children...forbid them not
Luke 24:26 Ought not Christ to have *s'ed* these things
Luke 24:46 thus it behoved Christ to *s*

Acts 9:16 he [Paul] must *s* for my [Jesus'] name's sake
1 Cor. 10:13 not *s* you to be tempted above that ye are able
1 Cor. 13:4 Charity *s'eth* long, and is kind
2 Tim. 2:12 we *s*, we shall also reign with him [Jesus]
Heb. 5:8 learned he [Jesus] obedience by the things...he *s'ed*
1 Pet. 4:13 ye are partakers of Christ's *s'ings*

SUFFERING. Pain or distress. Suffering for Jesus' sake may be regarded as fellowship with Christ (Phil. 3:10) and as a stewardship (Phil. 1:29). See also *Affliction; Anguish.*

SUICIDE. To take one's own life. Suicide may be brought on by hopelessness (Judg. 16:28–30), sin (1 Kings 16:18–19), disappointment (2 Sam. 17:23), and betrayal (Matt. 27:3–5).

This act violates the principles of life's sacredness (Gen. 9:5–6; 1 Cor. 6:19) and God's sovereign rule (Rom. 9:20–21).

SUKKIIM (SUKKITES). An African or Ethiopian tribe allied with Pharaoh Shishak of Egypt when he invaded Judah (2 Chron. 12:3). *Sukkites:* NIV.

SULFUR. See *Brimstone.*

SUMER. The southern division of ancient Babylonia (now southern Iraq), consisting largely of the fertile plain between the Tigris and Euphrates rivers. In the O.T., it was called Shinar (Gen. 10:10) or Chaldea (Jer. 50:10). See also *Babylonia.*

SUN. The luminous solar body that provides light and heat to Earth. Some of the ancient civilizations surrounding Israel worshiped the sun, and even the Israelites burned incense to the sun on occasion (2 Kings 23:5). God is spoken of figuratively as a sun and shield (Ps. 84:11).

SUPERSCRIPTION (INSCRIPTION). Words engraved on coins or other surfaces. The superscription "King of the Jews" was placed above Jesus on the cross (Mark 15:26). *Inscription:* NRSV.

SUPPER. The main daily meal of ancient times, usually the evening meal (Luke 14:6) as observed by Jews, Greeks, and Romans. In the N.T. the word is used of the Passover (John 13:1–2) and the Lord's Supper (1 Cor. 11:20).

SUPPLICATION (PETITION). An earnest prayer or request. Paul urged supplication with thanksgiving as an antidote to anxiety (Phil. 4:6). *Petition:* NIV. See also *Petition.*

SUPPLY CITY. See *Store City; Treasure City.*

SUPREME COMMANDER. See *Tartan.*

SURETY (GUARANTEE). One who guarantees payment of another person's debt or obligation. Jesus' perfect priesthood was a surety or guarantee of a better covenant (Heb. 7:22). *Guarantee:* NIV, NRSV.

SURVIVORS. See *Remnant.*

SUSA. See *Shushan.*

SUSANNA. A female follower of Jesus who apparently provided food and lodging for Him and perhaps His disciples (Luke 8:2–3).

SWADDLING CLOTHES, SWADDLING BANDS. A square cloth like a quilt or a blanket that was wrapped around a newborn baby (Luke 2:7, 12). This cloth was held in place by swaddling bands—narrow strips of cloth (Job 38:9).

SWALLOW. A swift bird that nests in buildings and makes a mournful sound (Ps. 84:3; Prov. 26:2).

SWAN (WHITE OWL, WATER HEN). An unclean water bird, perhaps the ibis or water hen (Lev. 11:18). *White owl:* NIV; *water hen:* NRSV.

SWEAR
Lev. 19:12 not *s* by my [God's] name falsely
Matt. 5:34 I [Jesus] say unto you, *S* not at all
Mark 14:71 he [Peter] began to curse and to *s*

SWEARING. See *Oath.*

SWINE (PIGS). Pigs or hogs. The flesh of swine was forbidden as food (Lev. 11:7). Swine were regarded as offensive to the Lord (Isa. 65:2–4). *Pigs:* NIV, NRSV.

SWORD. A sharp blade carried by soldiers as a weapon of war. Simeon and Levi used swords in the massacre at Shechem (Gen. 34:25).

SYCAMINE (MULBERRY). A tree or shrub that bore a fruit similar to blackberries (Luke 17:6). *Mulberry:* NIV, NRSV. See also *Mulberry.*

SYCHAR. A city of Samaria where Jesus talked to the woman at Jacob's well (John 4:5–40).

SYCHEM. See *Shechem.*

SYCOMORE (SYCAMORE). A fig-bearing tree valued for its fruit and soft, durable wood (Luke 19:4). *Sycamore:* NIV, NRSV.

SYENE. See *Sinim.*

SYMBOL. A word, action, or object that stands for truths or spiritual realities. Circumcision was a symbol of God's covenant with Israel (Rom. 4:11). The rainbow signified God's promise not to destroy the world by water again (Gen. 9:12–13). The tearing of the temple curtain at Christ's death represented the believer's direct access to God through Christ (Matt. 27:50–51).

SYNAGOGUE. A house of worship for the Jews that developed during their period of exile in Babylonia and Persia. Synagogues shifted the emphasis of the Jews from animal sacrifices to worship and teaching of the law. Paul regularly proclaimed the message of Christ in Jewish synagogues on his missionary journeys outside Palestine (Acts 18:4).

SYNOPTIC GOSPELS. A phrase used for the Gospels of Matthew, Mark, and Luke to set them apart from the Gospel of John. The Synoptic Gospels are similar in their straightforward and factual treatment of the life of Jesus, while John gives the theological meaning of these facts and events.

SYRIA/ARAM. A nation northeast of Israel that was a persistent enemy of the Jews across several centuries (1 Kings 15:18–20), particularly from David's administration until Syria fell to the Assyrians about 700 B.C. This nation was allied with Babylonia and Assyria at one point in its history; thus its name *Syria.* When Jesus was born, Syria was a province under Roman control (Luke 2:2). This nation was also known as *Aram* (Num. 23:7). See also *Damascus.*

> **DAMASCUS, SYRIA**
>
> Syria's capital was Damascus, a city that still exists today. It is one of the oldest continually inhabited cities in the world. The apostle Paul was converted to Christianity while traveling to Damascus to persecute Christian believers in that city (Acts 9:1–9).

SYRIA-DAMASCUS. See *Damascus.*

SYRO-PHOENICIAN. An inhabitant of Phoenicia during the time when Phoenicia was part of the Roman province of Syria. Jesus ministered in this area (Mark 7:25–31).

SYRTIS. See *Quicksands.*

TAANACH/TANACH. A Canaanite city west of the Jordan River conquered by Joshua and assigned to the Levites (Josh. 12:21). *Tanach:* Josh. 21:25.

TABERNACLE/TENT OF MEETING. A tent or portable sanctuary built in the wilderness at God's command as a place of worship for the Israelites (Exod. 40:1–8). It was also called the *Tent of Meeting* because it was considered a place of encounter between God and His people. The tabernacle foreshadowed Christ's incarnation when "the Word was made flesh, and dwelt among us" (John 1:14). See also *Holy Place; Holy of Holies.*

TABERNACLES, FEAST OF/FEAST OF BOOTHS. A festival, also known as the Feast of Booths and the Feast of Ingathering (Exod. 23:16; Num. 29:12), observed annually during the harvest season to commemorate Israel's wilderness wandering experience. The people lived in tents or booths in remembrance of their days as tent dwellers while waiting to enter Canaan (Lev. 23:39–43).

TABERNACLE. The Tabernacle—a tent worship center—is where Israelites offered sacrifices to God during the Exodus. Priests carried the animal remains to the horned altar, in the foreground, and burned them as fragrant offerings to God.

TABITHA/DORCAS. A Christian widow at Joppa whom Peter restored to life (Acts 9:36–40). Her Greek name was *Dorcas*.

TABLET. A flat piece of stone on which the Ten Commandments were engraved by the finger of God (Exod. 24:12).

TABOR, MOUNT. A mountain on the border of the territories of Zebulun and Issachar about six miles from Nazareth in Galilee. From this mountain the judge Deborah sent Barak to defeat Sisera and the Canaanites (Judg. 4:6–14).

TABRET (TAMBOURINE). A musical instrument that was probably similar to the tambourine (Gen. 31:27). *Tambourine:* NIV, NRSV.

TADMOR (TAMAR). A trading center between the city of Damascus in Syria and the Euphrates River that was rebuilt by King Solomon about 1000 B.C. (1 Kings 9:17–18). *Tamar:* NRSV.

TAHPANHES/TAHAPANES/TEHAPH- NEHES. An Egyptian city on the Nile River to which citizens of Judah fled after the fall of Jerusalem to the Babylonians (Jer. 43:7–10). *Tahapanes:* Jer. 2:16; *Tehaphnehes:* Ezek. 30:18.

TALEBEARER (GOSSIP). A person who gossips about or slanders another with destructive words (Prov. 18:8). *Gossip:* NIV. See also *Busybody; Gossip*.

TALENT. A common unit of weight or measure of monetary value used by the Hebrews, Greeks, and Romans (Matt. 25:14–30).

TAMAR

1. The widow of Er and Onan, sons of Judah, who eventually bore Judah's twin sons, Perez and Zerah (Gen. 38:6–30). *Thamar:* Jesus' ancestry (Matt. 1:3).

2. Absalom's sister who was sexually assaulted by her half brother Amnon. Absalom avenged the crime by killing Amnon (2 Sam. 13:1–32).

3. NRSV word for Tadmor (1 Kings 9:17–18). See *Tadmor*.

TAMARISK. A small tree or shrub. King Saul and his sons were buried under a tamarisk (1 Sam. 22:6).

TAMBOURINE. See *Tabret; Timbrel*.

TANNER. A person who cured animal skins. This probably was not a reputable vocation among the Jews because of the problem of defilement by touching unclean animals. Peter lodged with a tanner at Joppa (Acts 10:5–6). See also *Leather*.

TAPESTRY. An expensive curtain or cloth embroidered with artwork and owned generally by the wealthy (Prov. 7:16; 31:22).

TAR. See *Slime*.

TARE. A weed, now known as the darnel plant, that resembles wheat. In Jesus' parable, tares represent wicked seed sown by Satan that will ultimately be separated and destroyed (Matt. 13:25–30, 36–43).

TARPELITES. A tribe that colonized Samaria after the citizens of the Northern Kingdom were carried to Assyria as captives about 722 B.C. (Ezra 4:9). See also *Samaritan*.

T

8 F 3

TARSHISH/THARSHISH. A coastal city, probably in Spain, that was the destination of the ship boarded by the prophet Jonah (Jon. 1:3). *Tharshish:* 1 Kings 10:22.

TARSUS. Capital city of the Roman province of Silicia and the place where Paul was born (Acts 9:11). Once an important center of learning, Tarsus was on the Cydnus River about ten miles north of the Mediterranean Sea.

TARTAK. A false god worshiped by the Avites, a people who colonized Samaria after the Northern Kingdom fell to the Assyrians (2 Kings 17:31).

TARTAN (SUPREME COMMANDER). The title of the commander of the Assyrian army who demanded the surrender of Jerusalem from King Hezekiah (2 Kings 18:17). *Supreme commander:* NIV.

TASKMASTERS (SLAVEMASTERS). Egyptian overseers or supervisors who forced the Hebrew slaves to do hard labor at the command of the pharaoh (Exod. 1:11–14). *Slavemasters:* NIV.

TASSEL. See *Fringe.*

TATNAI (TATTENAI). A Persian official who appealed to King Darius of Persia to stop the Jews from rebuilding the temple in Jerusalem (Ezra 5:3–9). *Tattenai:* NIV, NRSV.

TAUGHT
Isa. 54:13 thy children shall be *t* of the LORD
Mark 1:22 he [Jesus] *t* them as one...authority
2 Thess. 2:15 hold the traditions...ye have been *t*

TAVERNS, THE THREE. A station on the Roman road known as the Appian Way about thirty miles south of Rome where believers met the apostle Paul (Acts 28:15).

TAX COLLECTOR. See *Publican.*

TAXES. Money, goods, or labor paid by citizens to a government. The Hebrews originally paid taxes known as tithes or firstfruits to support priests and Levites. The tax burden grew heavier under kings, particularly Solomon, and rebellion against his son and successor Rehoboam eventually split the kingdom (1 Kings 12:4, 8). The Romans sold the privilege of collecting taxes to independent contractors, resulting in great extortion (Luke 19:2, 8). See also *Toll.*

TEACH [ING]
Job 21:22 Shall any *t* God knowledge?
Ps. 25:4 Show me thy [Lord's] ways...*t* me thy paths
Ps. 90:12 So *t* us to number our days
Jer. 31:34 shall *t* no more every man his neighbour
Matt. 28:20 *T'ing* them to observe all things
Mark 8:31 he [Jesus] began to *t*...Son of man must suffer
Luke 11:1 Lord, *t* us [the disciples] to pray
Luke 12:12 Holy Ghost shall *t* you...what ye ought to say
John 14:26 the Comforter...shall *t* you all things
1 Tim. 3:2 A bishop...given to hospitality, apt to *t*

TEACHER. A person who communicates knowledge or religious truth to others. Teachers are mentioned along with pastors as persons whose skill and ministry are needed in the church (Eph. 4:11–12). See also *Master.*

TEACHER OF THE LAW. See *Scribe.*

TEAR. See *Rend.*

TEARS. Visible signs of sorrow. Jesus shed tears over the unbelief of Jerusalem (Luke 13:34) and wept at the grave of his friend Lazarus (John 11:35).

TEMPLE. The Jewish temple dominated the Jerusalem landscape, as seen in this model of the city in Jesus' time. The large building is the sanctuary, which only priests could enter.

Ps. 126:5 They that sow in *t* shall reap in joy
Jer. 9:1 my [Jeremiah's]...eyes [were] a fountain of *t*
Rev. 21:4 God shall wipe away all *t* from their eyes

TEBETH. The tenth month of the Hebrew year (Esther 2:16).

TEETH. See *Tooth*.

TEHAPHNEHES. See *Tahpanhes*.

TEIL (TEREBINTH). A common tree in Palestine that resembled the elm or oak (Isa. 6:13). *Terebinth:* NIV, NRSV.

TEKOA/TEKOAH. A fortress city of Judah near Bethlehem; home of Amos the prophet (Amos 1:1). *Tekoah:* 2 Sam. 14:4.

TEL, TELL. An Arabic word for "mound," or a hill marking the site of an ancient city that has been built up over centuries of occupation. See also *Archaeology of the Bible*.

TEL-ABIB. A Babylonian city on the Chebar River where Ezekiel lived with the other Jewish captives (Ezek. 3:15).

TEMPERANCE (SELF-CONTROL). Moderation, restraint, or self-discipline—

behavior that should characterize believers (Gal 5:23; 2 Pet. 1:6). *Self-control:* NIV, NRSV. See also *Moderation; Sober.*

TEMPEST (STORM). A furious storm. Jesus calmed a tempest on the Sea of Galilee to save His disciples (Matt. 8:24–26). *Storm:* NIV.

TEMPLE. The central place of worship for the Jewish people. Three separate temples were built on the same site in Jerusalem.

The first was Solomon's temple, built about 961–954 B.C. A partition divided the Holy Place from the Holy of Holies (1 Kings 6:2; 20, 31). Ten golden candlesticks, the table of shewbread, and the ark of the covenant were housed in this temple. Solomon's temple was destroyed by the Babylonian army in 587 B.C.

Zerubbabel's temple was completed in 515 B.C. by Jews who returned to Jerusalem after a period of exile among the Babylonians and Persians. The partition was replaced by a veil or curtain. The ark, which had been destroyed by the Babylonians, was not replaced.

About 10 B.C. Herod the Great began reconstruction of Zerubbabel's temple. The third temple was more ornate and larger than its predecessors, with outer courts added. The infant Jesus was brought to this temple for dedication, and here Jesus taught and drove out the moneychangers (Mark 11:15; John 2:14–15). This temple was destroyed by the Romans in A.D. 70. A Moslem mosque known as the Dome of the Rock stands on the site today. See also *Herod,* No. 1; *Zerubbabel.*

TEMPLE PROSTITUTE. See *Sodomite.*

TEMPLE SERVANTS. See *Nethinim.*

TEMPORARY RESIDENT. See *Foreigner.*

TEMPT [ED, ING]

Deut. 6:16 Ye shall not *t* the LORD your God

Ps. 78:41 they [Israelites] turned back and *t'ed* God

Matt. 4:1 was Jesus led into the wilderness to be *t'ed*

Matt. 4:7 Thou shalt not *t* the Lord thy God

John 8:6 *t'ing* him [Jesus]…to accuse him

1 Cor. 10:13 not suffer you to be *t'ed* above that ye are able

Heb. 4:15 high priest [Jesus]…was…*t'ed* like as we are

James 1:13 Let no man say…I am *t'ed* of God

TEMPTATION. Testing, or enticement to sin (Matt. 4:1–10). Jesus' temptation experiences provide a guide to help believers resist Satan the tempter (Matt. 4:10; Heb. 2:18). God promises a means of escape for every temptation (1 Cor. 10:13).

TEMPTATION [S]

Matt. 6:13 lead us not into *t*

James 1:2 count it all joy…fall into divers *t's*

James 1:12 Blessed is the man that endureth *t*

2 Pet. 2:9 Lord knoweth how to deliver…out of *t's*

TEN COMMANDMENTS. The ethical commands given by God to Moses on Mount Sinai. Also called the Decalogue, the Ten Commandments summarize the basic moral laws of the O.T. Four of these commandments enjoin duties to God (Exod. 20:1–11), while six deal with obligations to other people (Exod. 20:12–17). Jesus summed up these commandments in two great principles—loving God above all else and loving our neighbors as ourselves (Matt. 22:37–40).

TENT. The house or dwelling place of nomadic peoples (Gen. 12:8). Tents were made of goat hair and supported by poles and ropes tied to stakes. See also *House.*

TENT OF MEETING. See *Tabernacle.*

TENTH DEAL. A dry measure equaling one-tenth of an ephah (Exod. 29:40). See also *Ephah.*

TENT. A Bedouin couple at the turn of the 1900s poses in front of their mobile home, a tent they take with them as they follow their herds from one pasture to the next.

TENTMAKER. A skilled workman who made tents, a lucrative trade in Bible times. Paul supported himself as a tentmaker (Acts 18:3).

TERAH/THARA. The father of Abraham and a native of Ur in Chaldea or ancient Babylonia. Through his sons Abraham, Nahor, and Haran, he was an ancestor of the Israelites, Ishmaelites, Midianites, Moabites, and Ammonites (Gen. 11:26–32). *Thara:* Jesus' ancestry (Luke 3:34).

TERAPHIM. Small images representing human figures that were venerated in households as guardians of good fortune (Judg. 17:5). Rachel stole her father's teraphim when Jacob left for Canaan (Gen. 31:19, 35). See also *Household Idols.*

TEREBINTH. See *Teil.*

TERTULLUS. A lawyer who accused Paul of desecrating the temple in a hearing before Felix at Caesarea (Acts 24:1–8).

TESTAMENT. A covenant or agreement with legal standing. The Old and New Testaments are covenants ratified first by the blood of sacrificial animals and then by the blood of Christ (Exod. 24:8; Matt. 26:28). See also *Covenant.*

TESTIFY [IED]
Isa. 59:12 our sins *t* against us
Acts 23:11 Paul...hast *t'ied* of me [Jesus] in Jerusalem
1 John 4:14 we...do *t* that the Father sent the Son

TESTIMONY. A declaration of truth based on personal experience (Acts 4:20). The testimony of Paul and Barnabas at Iconium was confirmed by their performance of miracles (Acts 14:3). See also *Record; Witness.*

TESTIMONY [IES]
Ps. 19:7 *t* of...Lord is sure, making wise the simple
Ps. 119:24 Thy [God's] *t'ies* also are my delight
Mark 6:11 shake off the dust...for a *t* against them
John 21:24 we know that his [God's] *t* is true

TETRARCH. The governor or ruler of a Roman province (Luke 3:1). See also *Governor.*

THADDAEUS. See *Judas, Brother of James.*

THAMAR. See *Tamar, No. 1.*

THANK OFFERING. A sacrificial animal presented to God as an expression of thanks for an unexpected special blessing (2 Chron. 29:31). See also *Sacrifice.*

THANKS
1 Chron. 16:34 give *t* unto the Lord; for he is good
Ps. 92:1 good thing to give *t* unto the Lord
Luke 22:19 he [Jesus] took bread, and gave *t*
1 Cor. 15:57 *t* be to God, which giveth us the victory
1 Thess. 5:18 in every thing give *t*...this is the will of God

THANKSGIVING. The act of expressing one's gratitude. The psalmist praised the Lord for His goodness and blessings (Ps. 116:12–19). Our Christian inheritance of salvation and eternal life should inspire our thanksgiving to God (Col. 1:12). See also *Praise.*

THARA. See *Terah.*

THARSHISH. See *Tarshish.*

THEATER. An outdoor meeting place, similar to a stadium, where dramatic performances and sporting events were held. The theater at Ephesus was an impressive Roman structure made of stone and marble that seated thousands (Acts 19:29–31).

THEBES. See *No.*

THEOCRACY. A government in which God is the ruler. Israel was an imperfect example of this form of rule, beginning with their deliverance from Egypt (Exod. 15:13) and the giving of the law at Mount Sinai (Exod. 19:5–8), until Samuel agreed to the people's demand for a king (1 Sam. 8:5).

THEOPHANY. A visible appearance of God. Examples are the burning bush (Exod. 3:1–6), the pillar of cloud and fire (Exod. 13:21–22), and the cloud and fire at Mount Sinai (Exod. 24:16–18). Some scholars believe theophanies before the incarnation of Jesus were visible manifestations of the preincarnate Son of God (John 1:1, 18).

THEOPHILUS. A friend of Luke to whom he addressed his writings—the Gospel of Luke and the book of Acts (Luke 1:3; Acts 1:1). See also *Luke*.

THESSALONIANS, EPISTLES TO THE. Two N.T. epistles written by the apostle Paul to the believers in the church at Thessalonica. The theme of both letters is the second coming of Christ, although Paul also included instructions on sexual morality (1 Thess. 4:1–8) and the need for diligent labor rather than idle speculation (1 Thess. 4:9–12; 2 Thess. 3:6–15).

Paul declared that believers' assurance of Christ's return should motivate them to righteous living (1 Thess. 3:13; 5:23) but that uncertainty about the exact time of His return should make them watchful and alert (1 Thess. 5:1–11).

THESSALONICA. A city on the Macedonian coast where Paul preached and founded a church. It was also the scene of a riot incited by Jews who opposed the preaching of Paul and Silas (Acts 17:1–9).

THEUDAS. The leader of an unsuccessful revolt mentioned by Gamaliel before the Sanhedrin. Gamaliel probably named this person to discourage premature action that might result in bloodshed (Acts 5:34–36).

THIEF [VES]

Matt. 6:20 where *t'ves* do not break through nor steal
Mark 15:27 with him [Jesus] they crucify two *t'ves*
Luke 10:30 A certain man…fell among *t'ves*
Luke 19:46 ye have made it [God's house] a den of *t'ves*
John 12:6 This he [Judas] said…because he was a *t*
2 Pet. 3:10 day of the Lord will come as a *t* in the night

THIGH. The part of the leg between the hip and the knee. Placing the hand under the thigh signified obedience or subjection. Abraham's servant swore by this method that a Canaanite wife would not be chosen for Abraham's son Isaac (Gen. 24:2–9). See also *Sinew*.

THINK [ETH]

Prov. 23:7 as he *t'eth* in his heart, so is he
Jer. 29:11 [God] know the thoughts…I *t* toward you
John 16:2 killeth you will *t*…doeth God service
Rom. 12:3 *t* of himself…highly than he ought to *t*
1 Cor. 10:12 *t'eth* he standeth take heed lest he fall
1 Cor. 13:5 [charity]…*t'eth* no evil
Gal. 6:3 man *t* himself to be something, when he is nothing
Eph. 3:20 [Jesus]…able to do…above all that we ask or *t*

THIRTY PIECES OF SILVER. The blood money given to Judas to betray Christ—the usual price for a slave. A remorseful Judas threw his silver on the temple floor and hanged himself (Matt. 27:3–8).

THISTLE. A briar or thorn that was used for hedges and burned for fuel (Isa. 33:12; Hosea 2:6). The word was also used figuratively of neglect and desolation (Prov. 24:30–31).

THOMAS. One of the twelve apostles or disciples of Jesus, also called *Didymus* or "twin"

(Luke 6:15), who refused to believe that Christ was alive until he could actually see and feel the wounds on Christ's resurrected body (John 20:25–28). See also *Twelve, The.*

THONG. A strip of leather. Paul was bound with thongs at Jerusalem (Acts 22:25–29). See also *Latchet.*

THORN. A plant with heavy briars or thistles. A crown of thorns was placed on Jesus' head in mockery as He hung on the cross (Matt. 27:29).

THORN IN THE FLESH. An unknown affliction from which the apostle Paul prayed to be delivered (2 Cor. 12:7–8). Some scholars believe it was an eye ailment, since he normally dictated his epistles and apologized for his own large handwriting (Gal. 6:11).

THORNBUSH. See *Bramble.*

THOUGHT [S]
Job 21:27 I [God] know your *t's*
Ps. 92:5 O Lord...thy *t's* are very deep
Isa. 55:8 my [God's] *t's* are not your *t's*
Matt. 6:27 you by taking *t* can add one cubit
Mark 7:21 out of the heart of men, proceed evil *t's*
1 Cor. 3:20 Lord knoweth the *t's* of the wise
1 Cor. 13:11 I [Paul]...*t* as a child

THRESHINGFLOOR. A place where grain was threshed, or separated from the stalk and husk after harvesting (2 Sam. 6:6). See also *Fan; Winnowing.*

THROAT. The throat was compared to an "open sepulchre" because of the deadly falsehoods that it could utter through the mouth (Ps. 5:9; Rom. 3:13). See also *Lips; Mouth; Tongue.*

THRONE. An ornate chair occupied by kings (1 Kings 2:9) and sometimes priests and judges (1 Sam. 1:9; Jer. 1:15) as a symbol of their power and authority. The word is also used to designate the Lord's supreme authority (Isa. 6:1).

Ps. 45:6 Thy *t*, O God, is for ever
Isa. 66:1 The heaven is my [God's] *t*
Lam. 5:19 thy [God's] *t* from generation to generation
Matt. 19:28 Son of man shall sit...*t* of his glory
Luke 1:32 God shall give unto him [Jesus] the *t* of...David
Heb. 4:16 Let us...come boldly unto the *t* of grace
Rev. 4:2 one [Jesus] sat on the *t*

THUMB. The thumb was involved in the ceremony consecrating Aaron and his sons to the priesthood. The blood of rams was smeared on their thumbs as well as their ears and feet (Exod. 29:19–20).

THUMMIN. See *Urim* and *Thummin.*

THUNDER. Since thunder was rare in Palestine, it was considered a form of speaking by the Lord (Job 40:9) and often regarded as a sign of His displeasure (Exod. 9:23; 1 Sam. 12:7).

THYATIRA. A city in the Roman province of Asia and home of Lydia, a convert under Paul's ministry (Acts 16:14). Noted for its dye industry, Thyatira was also the site of one of the seven churches of Asia Minor addressed by the apostle John. This church was commended for its faith and good works but condemned for its tolerance toward the false prophetess Jezebel and her heretical teachings (Rev. 2:18–29).

THYINE WOOD (CITRON WOOD, SCENTED WOOD). A valuable wood resembling cedar used for fine cabinet work (Rev. 18:12). It was also burned as incense because of its fragrance. *Citron wood:* NIV; *scented wood:* NRSV.

TIBERIAS. Tiberias, a village along the Sea of Galilee, as painted in 1839 by David Roberts.

TIBERIAS. A city on the western shore of the Sea of Galilee (John 6:1, 23) built by Herod Antipas and named for the Roman emperor Tiberius. It was shunned by many Jews because it was built on a cemetery site. Tiberias became a center of learning after the fall of Jerusalem in A.D. 70.

TIBERIUS. See *Caesar,* No. 2.

TIBNI. A king of Israel (reigned about 885– 880 B.C.) who ruled at the same time as Omri. Upon Tibni's death, Omri became the sole claimant to the throne (1 Kings 16:21–22).

TIGLATH-PILESER III/TILGATH PILNESER III/PUL. A powerful Assyrian king (reigned about 745–727 B.C.) who defeated the Northern Kingdom and carried Jewish captives to Assyria (2 Kings 15:29). *Tilgath-pilneser:* 2 Chron. 28:20. *Pul:* 1 Chron. 5:26.

TIGRIS. A major river of southwest Asia that is possibly the same as the *Hiddekel* of the Garden of Eden (Gen. 2:14). Beginning in the Armenian mountains, the Tigris flows southeastward for more than 1,100 miles until it joins the Euphrates River. Mesopotamia, or "the land between the rivers," lies between these two streams. See also *Euphrates.*

TILE (CLAY TABLET, BRICK). A slab of baked clay used as roofing on houses (Ezek. 4:1). The tiles were removed from a roof to give a paralyzed man access to Jesus for healing (Luke 5:18–19). *Clay tablet:* NIV; *brick:* NRSV. See also *Brick.*

TIGRIS. *Photographed from a space shuttle, the Tigris and Euphrates rivers merge just north of the Persian Gulf, where they empty into the sea. The fertile land in the center was once called Mesopotamia, meaning "land between the rivers." The Tigris flows on the east side of that land, with the Euphrates on the west.*

TILGATH-PILNESER. See *Tiglath-pileser.*

TIMBREL (TAMBOURINE). A small hand drum or percussion instrument believed to resemble the tambourine (Exod. 15:20). *Tambourine:* NIV, NRSV. See also *Tabret.*

TIMNATH-SERAH/TIMNATH-HERES. A town in the territory of Ephraim given to Joshua as an inheritance and the place where he was buried (Josh. 24:29–30). *Timnath-heres:* Judg. 2:9.

TIMOTHY/TIMOTHEUS. A young missionary friend of Paul, also called *Timotheus* (see Rom. 16:21), who accompanied the apostle on some of his travels and briefly shared his imprisonment at Rome (Heb. 13:23). Born to a Greek father and a Jewish mother (Acts 16:1), Timothy was reared by his mother, Eunice, and grandmother, Lois, in a godly home (2 Tim. 1:5). He was converted during Paul's first visit to Lystra (Acts 16:1) and served for a time as leader of the church at Ephesus (1 Tim. 1:3; 4:12). Paul addressed two of his pastoral epistles to Timothy. See also *Eunice.*

TIMOTHY, EPISTLES TO. Two short epistles of the apostle Paul to his young friend and fellow missionary, Timothy. The first epistle is practical in scope, instructing Timothy to teach sound doctrine (chap. 1), organize the church appropriately (chaps. 2–3), beware of false teachers (chap. 4), administer church discipline (chap. 5), and exercise his pastoral gifts with love and restraint (chap. 6).

Second Timothy is perhaps Paul's most personal epistle, in which he expresses tender affection for the young minister (chaps. 1–2) and speaks of approaching days of persecution for the church (3:1–4:5) as well as the possibility of his own execution (4:6–22). See also *Pastoral Epistles; Timothy.*

TIN. A well-known and malleable metal (Num. 31:22) brought by ship from Tarshish and used in making bronze (Ezek. 27:12).

TINDER. See *Tow*.

TIRE. A headdress, such as a turban, or an ornament worn in the hair by a high priest, a bridegroom, or women (2 Kings 9:30; Isa. 3:18).

TIRHAKAH. See *Pharaoh*, No. 3.

TIRSHATHA (GOVERNOR). The title of the governor of Judea under Persian rule. Both Zerubbabel and Nehemiah were appointed by Persian kings to this position (Ezra 2:63; Neh. 7:65). *Governor:* NIV, NRSV. See also *Governor; Lieutenant*.

TIRZAH. A Canaanite town captured by Joshua (Josh. 12:24). In later years it served as a capital of the Northern Kingdom until Samaria was built (1 Kings 14:17).

TISHBITE. An inhabitant of Tishbeh, a city of Gilead. The prophet Elijah was called a Tishbite (1 Kings 17:1).

TITHE. One-tenth of a person's income presented as an offering to God. Abraham paid tithes to Melchizedek (Gen. 14:18–20), and Jacob vowed to give tithes in accordance with God's blessings (Gen. 28:20–22). In N.T. times, the Pharisees were scrupulous tithers (Matt. 23:23). Jesus encouraged generosity and promised to bless sacrificial giving (Luke 6:38). Paul endorsed the principle of proportionate giving (1 Cor. 16:2). See also *Stewardship*.

TITHE [S]
Lev. 27:30 the *t* of the land...is the LORD'S
Deut. 14:22 shalt...*t* all the increase of thy seed

Neh. 13:12 brought all Judah the *t* of the corn
Mal. 3:8 robbed thee [God]? In *t*'s and offerings
Mal. 3:10 Bring ye all the *t*'s into the storehouse
Luke 11:42 ye [Pharisees] *t* mint...and...herbs
Heb. 7:6 he [Melchisedec]...received *t*'s of Abraham

TITTLE. A dot or other small mark that distinguished similar letters of the alphabet. Jesus used the word to emphasize the enduring quality of the law's most minute requirement (Matt. 5:18).

TITUS. A Greek Christian and traveling companion of Paul who was sent by the apostle to correct problems in the church at Corinth (2 Cor. 7:6; 8:6, 23). Titus also served as a church leader in Crete (Titus 1:4–5). See also *Crete*.

TITUS THE DEPENDABLE

Titus was one of Paul's most dedicated and dependable missionary associates. The apostle sent messages to the Corinthian church by Titus (2 Cor. 7:5–16). He also assigned Titus the task of collecting an offering for the impoverished believers of Jerusalem (2 Cor. 8:6, 16–24; 12:18).

TITUS, EPISTLE TO. A short epistle written by the apostle Paul to his helper and companion Titus, who apparently was serving as a leader of the church on the island of Crete (1:5). Paul dealt with several practical church matters, including the qualifications of elders (1:5–9), ways to deal with false teachers (1:10–16), and the behavior of Christians in an immoral world (3:1–11). See also *Pastoral Epistles*.

TOB/ISH-TOB. A place in Syria east of the Jordan River where the judge Jephthah took

333

refuge (Judg. 11:3, 5). The soldiers of Tob sided with the Ammonites against David (2 Sam. 10:6, 8). *Ish-tob:* 2 Sam. 10:8.

TOBIAH. An Ammonite servant of Sanballat who ridiculed the Jews and opposed Nehemiah's reconstruction of Jerusalem's wall (Neh. 2:10, 19; 4:3, 7). See also *Sanballat.*

TOKEN (SIGN). A sign or signal. Circumcision was a token of God's covenant with Abraham (Gen. 17:11). The blood on the Israelites' doorposts was a sign for the death angel to "pass over" these houses (Exod. 12:13). *Sign:* NIV, NRSV. See also *Miracle; Sign.*

TOLA. A minor judge of Israel who succeeded Abimelech and ruled for twenty-three years (Judg. 10:1–2). See also *Judges of Israel.*

TOLERANCE. See *Forbearance.*

TOLL (TAX). A tax or fee levied against the citizens of a conquered nation (Ezra 4:13). *Tax:* NIV. See also *Taxes; Tribute.*

TOMB. See *Sepulchre.*

TONGS. A tool for handling hot coals or trimming burning lamps (Exod. 25:38; Num. 4:9); probably the same as a *snuffer.* See also *Snuffer.*

TONGUE. The organ of the body associated with speech. The tongue may be used as an instrument of punishment (Gen. 11:1–9) or blessing (Acts 2:1–12) and for good or evil (James 3:5–10). See also *Lips; Mouth; Throat.*

TONGUES, SPEAKING IN. Glossolalia or ecstatic utterances; a spiritual gift exercised by some believers in the N.T. church. This gift apparently first occurred on the day of Pentecost

with the outpouring of God's Spirit on believers (Acts 2:1–13). Paul also mentioned this gift in 1 Cor. 14:2–28, although it is unclear whether this is the same as the phenomenon described in Acts.

TOOTH. The gnashing or grinding of one's teeth symbolized frustration or despair (Matt. 8:12).

TOPAZ (CHRYSOLITE). A precious stone, thought to resemble modern chrysolite, used in the high priest's breastplate (Exod. 28:17). It is also used in the foundation of New Jerusalem (Rev. 21:20). *Chrysolite:* NRSV. See also *Chrysolyte.*

TOPHET (TOPHETH). A place of human sacrifice in the Valley of Hinnom near Jerusalem (Jer. 7:31–32). *Topheth:* NIV, NRSV. See also *Hell; Hinnom, Valley of.*

TORAH. A Hebrew word meaning "teaching" or "instruction" and used for the Pentateuch or the Law, the first five books of the O.T. See also *Law, Law of Moses; Pentateuch.*

TAMING THE TONGUE

James compared the tongue to a fire that rages out of control, leaving destruction in its wake (James 3:6). All of us have learned through personal experience that careless, thoughtless words can cause great damage—to ourselves as well as others. The book of Proverbs also has some wise words on this subject: "Whoso keepeth his mouth and his tongue keepeth his soul from troubles" (Prov. 21:23).

TORCH. A burning brand made of resinous wood or twisted flax and used to light one's path at night (John 18:3). See also *Lantern*.

TORTOISE (GREAT LIZARD). A reptile regarded as unclean by the Jews (Lev. 11:29). *Great lizard:* NIV, NRSV.

TOW (TINDER). The waste or refuse produced from flax when spinning thread. Isaiah used the word figuratively of the weakness of sinful people when facing God's punishment (Isa. 1:31). *Tinder:* NIV, NRSV.

TOWER (STRONGHOLD). A defensive turret in a city wall or a tall structure used as a watchtower. The word is also used figuratively of God's protection (2 Sam. 22:3). *Stronghold:* NIV, NRSV.

TOWNCLERK (CITY CLERK). An official of the city of Ephesus who restored order after a riot against Paul (Acts 19:29–41). *City clerk:* NIV.

TRADITION. An unwritten code or interpretation of the law that the Pharisees considered as binding as the written law itself (Matt. 15:2, 6; Mark 7:5).

TRANCE. A state of semiconsciousness, often accompanied by visions. Peter's trance at Joppa prepared him for a ministry to Cornelius the Gentile. See also *Dreams and Visions*.

TRANSFIGURATION OF JESUS. A radical transformation in the Savior's appearance through which God was glorified. Accompanied by His disciples Peter, James, and John, Jesus went to a mountain at night to pray. Moses and Elijah appeared and discussed Jesus' death, emphasizing Jesus as the fulfillment of the Law and the Prophets (Matt. 17:1–8). This

experience attested Christ's divinity and mission and helped prepare Jesus and His disciples for the events leading to His death.

TRANSGRESS [ED, ETH]
Deut. 26:13 I have not *t'ed* thy [God's] commandments
Jer. 2:29 all have *t'ed* against me, saith the LORD
1 John 3:4 Whosoever committeth sin *t'eth* also the law

TRANSGRESSION. A violation of God's law that may be personal (1 Tim. 2:14), public (Rom. 5:14), or premeditated (Josh. 7:19–25). Transgression produces death (1 Chron. 10:13) and destruction (Ps. 37:38), but it may be forgiven by confession (Ps. 32:1, 5) through the atoning death of Christ (Isa. 53:5–6). See also *Sin*.

TRANSGRESSION [S]
Job 13:23 make me [Job] to know my *t*
Ps. 32:1 Blessed is he whose *t* is forgiven
Ps. 51:3 I acknowledge my *t's*
Prov. 12:13 wicked is snared by the *t* of his lips
Prov. 29:6 In the *t* of an evil man there is a snare
Isa. 53:5 he [God's servant] was wounded for our *t's*

TRANSGRESSOR [S]
Ps. 51:13 Then will I teach *t's* thy [God's] ways
Prov. 22:12 he [God] overthroweth the words of the *t*
Mark 15:28 he [Jesus] was numbered with the *t's*

TRANSJORDAN. A large mountainous plateau or tableland east of the Jordan River, generally referred to in the KJV as the land "beyond Jordan" (Gen. 50:10; Matt. 4:15). This is the area from which Moses viewed the Promised Land (Deut. 34:1–4). After the conquest of Canaan, it was occupied by the tribes of Reuben, Gad, and East Manasseh.

TRAVAIL. The labor pains associated with childbirth (Gen. 38:27). The word is also used figuratively of the birth of God's new creation (Rom. 8:22–23).

TREASURE [S]

Ps. 135:4 Lord hath chosen…Israel for his peculiar *t*

Matt. 2:11 they [the wise men] opened their *t's*

Matt. 6:20 lay up for yourselves *t's* in heaven

Matt. 13:44 kingdom of heaven is like unto *t* hid in a field

Luke 12:34 where your *t* is…will your heart be also

2 Cor. 4:7 we have this *t* in earthen vessels

TREASURE CITY (STORE CITY, SUPPLY CITY). A fortified city in which a king stored his valuables. The Hebrew slaves built treasure cities at Pithom and Raamses for the Egyptian pharaoh (Exod. 1:11). *Store city:* NIV; *supply city:* NRSV. See also *Store City.*

TREASURE OF ALL NATIONS. See *Desire of All Nations.*

TREASURER (STEWARD). An important financial officer in a king's court, charged with accounting for receipts and disbursements (Isa. 22:15). *Steward:* NIV, NRSV. See also *Steward.*

TREASURY. The place in the temple where offerings were received (Mark 12:41–44). Thirteen trumpet-shaped receptacles for offerings were placed in the outer court.

TREATY. See *League.*

TREE OF KNOWLEDGE OF GOOD AND EVIL. A specific tree placed in the Garden of Eden to test the obedience of Adam and Eve. Eating of the fruit of this tree was specifically prohibited by the Lord (Gen. 2:9, 17). After they ate the forbidden fruit, Adam and Eve were banished from the garden and became subject to hard labor and death (Gen. 3).

TREE OF LIFE. A tree in the Garden of Eden with fruit that would bring eternal life

if eaten (Gen. 3:22). In the heavenly Jerusalem, there will also be a tree of life, with leaves for the healing of the nations (Rev. 22:2).

TRESPASS [ES]

Ezra 9:15 we are before thee [God] in our *t's*

Mark 11:25 your Father…may forgive you your *t's*

Luke 17:3 thy brother *t* against thee, rebuke him

2 Cor. 5:19 God was…not imputing their *t's* unto them

TRESPASS OFFERING. A sacrificial animal offering presented for lesser sins or offenses after full restitution to persons wronged had been made (Lev. 5:6–7, 15–19). See also *Sacrifice.*

TRIALS OF JESUS. A series of trials or appearances of Jesus before Jewish and Roman authorities that ended with His death. Jesus appeared before Annas, the former high priest (John 18:12–23); Caiphas, the current high priest, and the full Jewish Sanhedrin (Matt. 26:57–68); Pilate, the Roman governor (John 18:28–38); and Herod Antipas, ruler of Galilee (Luke 23:6–12) before finally being sentenced to death by Pilate (Mark 15:6–15).

TRIBES OF ISRAEL. The tribes that descended from the sons of Jacob—Asher, Benjamin, Dan, Gad, Issachar, Judah, Levi, Naphtali, Reuben, Simeon, and Zebulon (Gen. 49:1–28)—plus the two sons of Joseph (Ephraim and Manasseh; Gen. 48:5). After the conquest of Canaan, these tribes were assigned specific territories in the land, with the exception of Levi, the priestly tribe. The Levites were assigned to forty-eight different towns and scattered among all the other tribal territories to perform ceremonial duties. See also *Levites.*

TRIBULATION. Affliction and trouble caused by persecution (1 Thess. 3:4) and severe testing (Rev. 2:10, 22). The tribulation of believers may be overcome by patience (Rom.

T

8:35–37; 12:12) and a joyful spirit (2 Cor. 7:4). See also *Affliction; Persecution.*

TRIBULATION

Matt. 24:21 then shall be great *t*
John 16:33 in the world ye shall have *t*
Rom. 5:3 *t* worketh patience
2 Cor. 1:4 Who [Jesus] comforteth us in all our *t*

TRIBULATION, GREAT. A time of great suffering and affliction in the end-time, sent upon the earth by the Lord to accomplish His purposes (Dan. 12:1; Rev. 7:14). Students of the Bible disagree on whether this event will precede or follow Christ's millennial reign or come before the ushering in of the new heavens and new earth. See also *Millennium; Persecution.*

TRIBUTE. A toll or tax imposed on citizens by a government. Every Hebrew male over age twenty paid an annual tribute of a half-shekel to support temple services (Exod. 30:13; Matt. 17:24–27). See also *Half-Shekel Tax; Taxes; Toll.*

TRIGON. See *Sackbut.*

TRINITY, THE. God as expressed through the Father, the Son, and the Holy Spirit. The word *Trinity* does not appear in the Bible, but the reality of the triune God was revealed in the O.T. at the creation of the world (Gen. 1:1–3, 26). In the N.T., the Trinity was revealed at Christ's baptism (Matt. 3:16–17) and in His teachings (John 14:26; 15:26) as well as His Great Commission (Matt. 28:19).

The Holy Spirit, whom Christ sent, convicts of sin, inspires believers, and empowers them for service (John 16:8, 13). The Father gives converts to Christ, and they hear His voice and follow Him (John 10:27, 29).

TRIUMPHAL ENTRY OF JESUS. Jesus' entry into Jerusalem on the Sunday before His crucifixion the following Friday. He was greeted by shouts of joy from the crowds, who were looking for an earthly king. With His entry, Jesus acknowledged He was the promised Messiah—but a spiritual deliverer rather than a conquering military hero (Matt. 21:1–11).

TROAS. An important city on the coast of Mysia where Paul received a vision. A man across from Troas in Macedonia pleaded, "Come . . . and help us" (Acts 16:8–10).

TROPHIMUS. A Christian who accompanied Paul on the third missionary journey (Acts 20:4).

TROUBLE [D]

Job 14:1 Man. . . is of few days, and full of *t*
Ps. 9:9 The Lord. . . a refuge. . . in times of *t*
Ps. 46:1 God is. . . a very present help in *t*
Ps. 90:7 by thy [God's] wrath are we *t'd*
Luke 1:29 she [Mary] was *t'd* at his [the angel's] saying
John 12:27 Now is my [Jesus'] soul *t'd*
John 14:1 Let not your heart be *t'd*. . . believe. . . in me [Jesus]
2 Cor. 4:8 We are *t'd* on every side
Gal. 1:7 some that *t* you, and would pervert the gospel

TROUSERS. See *Hosen.*

TRUE

Ps. 19:9 judgments of the Lord are *t*
John 1:9 the *t* Light [Jesus]. . . lighteth every man
John 6:32 my [Jesus'] Father giveth you the *t* bread
John 15:1 I [Jesus] am the *t* vine
John 21:24 his [John's] testimony is *t*
Rom. 3:4 let God be *t*, but every man a liar

TRUMPET. A wind musical instrument made of animal horn or metal. Trumpets were used in temple ceremonies (1 Chron. 16:6). See also *Ram's Horn.*

TRUMPET. Blowing a shofar, a trumpet made from a ram's horn, an Orthodox Jew calls worshipers to the synagogue for Sabbath.

TRUMPETS, FEAST OF. A Jewish religious festival, also called the *Seventh Month Festival* (Lev. 16:29). It was ushered in by the blowing of trumpets and observed by reading the law and presenting burnt offerings (Lev. 23:24–25; Neh. 8:2–3, 8–12). The exact reason for its observance is not clear.

TRUST. To put one's confidence in a person or thing. God's name and His Word are worthy of our trust (Ps. 33:21; 119:42). Christ warned that humans may deceive and be unworthy of trust (Matt. 10:17–21), but we may place

ultimate trust and confidence in Him (John 6:35–37). See also *Faith.*

TRUST [ED, ETH]

Deut. 32:37 Where are their gods…in whom they *t*'ed
2 Sam. 22:3 God of my rock; in him will I *t*
Job 13:15 he [God] slay me [Job]…I *t* in him
Ps. 56:3 What time I am afraid, I will *t* in a thee [God]
Prov. 3:5 *T* in the Lord with all thine heart
Prov. 11:28 He that *t*'eth in his riches shall fall
Mark 10:24 hard…for them…*t* in riches to enter…the kingdom

TRUTH. That which is reliable and consistent with God's revelation. Truth is established by God's law (Ps. 119:142–144) and personified by Jesus Christ (John 14:6). Believers are purified by obedience to the truth (1 Pet. 1:22) and worshiping God in spirit and truth (John 4:23–24).

Ps. 100:5 his [God's] *t* endureth to all generations
Ps. 119:30 I have chosen the way of *t*
John 1:17 grace and *t* came by Jesus Christ
John 8:32 the *t* shall make you free
John 16:13 Spirit of *t*…will guide you into all *t*
John 18:38 Pilate saith unto him [Jesus], What is *t* ?
1 Cor. 13:6 [charity] rejoiceth in the *t*
Eph. 4:15 speaking the *t* in love
2 Tim. 2:15 rightly dividing the word of *t*
1 John 1:8 say that we have no sin…*t* is not in us

TUBAL. The fifth son of Japheth (Gen. 10:2) and ancestor of a tribe descended from Tubal and Japheth. Isaiah mentioned Tubal as a people who would declare God's glory among the Gentiles (Isa. 66:19).

TUMORS. See *Emerods.*

KING HIRAM OF TYRE

King Hiram, also known as Huram, entered a trade agreement with Solomon (1 Kings 5:1–18). He was the king of Tyre, a city on the coast of the Mediterranean Sea about 100 miles north of Jerusalem. The Tyrians were known for their ambitious trade ventures, especially by sea.

Judah was not a seafaring nation. When Solomon established a port on the Red Sea for trading with other countries, he used ships and sailors from Hiram's fleet (2 Chron. 8:17–18).

TURBAN. See *Mitre.*

TURTLEDOVE (DOVE). A migratory bird noted for its plaintive cooing and affection for its mate (Song 2:12). A turtledove was an acceptable sacrificial offering for the poor (Lev. 12:6–8). *Dove:* NIV. See also *Pigeon.*

TWELVE, THE. The twelve apostles or disciples chosen by Jesus. They were Andrew; Bartholomew (Nathanael); James, son of Alphaeus; James, son of Zebedee; John; Judas; Lebbaeus (Thaddaeus); Matthew; Philip; Simon the Canaanite; Simon Peter; and Thomas (Matt. 10:1–4; Mark 3:13–19; Luke 6:12–16).

TWIN BROTHERS. See *Castor and Pollux.*

TYCHICUS. A Christian who accompanied Paul on his third missionary journey (Acts 20:4).

TYPE. A person or thing that foreshadows something else. For example, the brass serpent placed upon a pole by Moses in the wilderness (Num. 21:4–9) pointed to the atoning death of Jesus on the cross (John 3:14–15).

TYRANNUS. A man of Ephesus who allowed Paul to use his lecture hall. Paul taught here for two years after he was banned from the local synagogue (Acts 19:8–10).

TYRE/TYRUS. An ancient coastal city of Phoenicia north of Palestine. Hiram, Tyre's ruler, helped David and Solomon with their building projects (1 Kings 5:1–10). In the prophet Ezekiel's day, the city was a thriving trade center. He predicted Tyre's destruction because of its sin and idolatry (Ezek. 28:1–10). Jesus visited the city (Mark 7:24), and Paul landed here (Acts 21:3, 7). *Tyrus:* Amos 1:10.

582

T

UCAL. An unknown person to whom proverbs in the book of Proverbs are addressed (Prov. 30:1).

ULAI. A river of Persia beside which Daniel was standing when he saw the vision of the ram and goat (Dan. 8:2–16).

ULCERS. See *Emerods*.

UMPIRE. See *Daysman*.

UNBELIEF. Refusal to believe in God and to acknowledge His works (John 16:9). Unbelief is caused by Satan's power (John 8:43–47), an evil heart (Heb. 3:12), and self-glorification and pride (John 5:44). Those who refuse to believe and reject the gospel are in turn rejected by God (John 3:18–20; 8:24). See also *Atheism; Infidel*.

Mark 9:24 Lord, I believe; help thou mine *u*
Heb. 3:12 lest there be in…you an evil heart of *u*
Heb. 4:11 lest any man fall after…the…example of *u*

UNBELIEVER. See *Infidel*.

UNBELIEVING

Acts 14:2 the *u* Jews stirred up the Gentiles
1 Cor. 7:14 the *u* husband is sanctified by the wife
Titus 1:15 unto them that are…*u* is nothing pure

UNCIRCUMCISED. A Jewish term for impurity or wickedness of any kind (Jer. 6:10) as well as a general reference to Gentiles (Rom. 2:25–29). See also *Circumcision*.

1 Sam. 17:26 this *u* Philistine [Goliath]
Ezek. 44:9 No stranger, *u* in heart…shall enter…[God's] sanctuary
Acts 7:51 stiffnecked and *u* in heart and ears

UNCIRCUMCISION

1 Cor. 7:19 Circumcision is nothing…*u* is nothing
Gal. 5:6 neither circumcision availeth any thing, nor *u*
Col. 3:11 neither Greek nor Jew, circumcision nor *u*

UNCLEAN. A term for physical, spiritual, or ritual impurity—a condition for which rituals of purification were prescribed (Lev. 11–15). See also *Clean*.

UNCLEAN [NESS]

Isa. 6:5 I [Isaiah] am a man of *u* lips
Isa. 64:6 we are all as an *u* thing
Mark 6:7 he [Jesus]…gave them [the disciples] power over *u* spirits
Acts 10:14 I [Peter] have never eaten any thing…*u*
Rom. 1:24 God also gave them up to *u'ness*
Gal. 5:19 works of the flesh…Adultery…*u'ness*
1 Thess. 4:7 God hath not called us unto *u'ness*

UNCLEAN ANIMALS. Under Mosaic Law, only animals that chewed the cud and were cloven-footed were considered "clean" and suitable for eating (Lev. 11:2–3). Even touching the flesh of an "unclean" animal made a person unclean (Lev. 11:8).

UNDEFILED

Ps. 119:1 Blessed are the *u*…walk in the law of the LORD
Heb. 7:26 high priest [Jesus]…who is holy…*u*
James 1:27 Pure religion and *u* before God and the Father

UNDERGARMENT. See *Breeches*.

UNDERSTAND [ETH, ING]

Kings 4:29 God gave Solomon wisdom and *u'ing*

ob 28:28 to depart from evil is *u'ing*

Ps. 119:27 to *u* the way of thy [God's] precepts

Prov. 2:2 apply thine heart to *u'ing*

Prov. 3:5 lean not unto thine own *u'ing*

Mark 8:21 How is it that ye [the disciples] do not *u*?

Rom. 3:11 none that *u'eth*...that seeketh after God

Cor. 13:2 though I [Paul]...*u* all mysteries

Phil. 4:7 peace of God, which passeth all *u'ing*

UNDERSTANDING. See *Knowledge; Wisdom.*

UNDERSTOOD

Job 13:1 mine [Job's] ear hath heard and *u* it

Job 42:3 I [Job] uttered that I *u* not

John 12:16 These things *u* not his [Jesus'] disciples

1 Cor. 13:11 When I [Paul] was a child...I *u* as a child

UNGODLY [INESS]

Ps. 1:1 man that walketh not in the counsel of the *u*

Prov. 16:27 An *u* man diggeth up evil

Rom. 1:18 wrath of God is revealed...against all *u'iness*

Rom. 5:6 in due time Christ died for the *u*

Titus 2:12 denying *u'iness*...we should live soberly

Jude 18 mockers...walk after their own *u* lusts

UNICORN (WILD OX). A large animal of great strength, probably the wild ox (Num. 23:22). Yoking it and harnessing its power was considered impossible (Job 39:9–11). *Wild ox:* NIV, NRSV.

UNJUST

Matt. 5:45 he [God]...sendeth rain on the just and...*u*

Luke 16:8 the lord commended the *u* steward

1 Pet. 3:18 Christ...suffered for sins...just for the *u*

UNKNOWN

Acts 17:23 altar with this inscription, TO THE *U* GOD

1 Cor. 14:4 speaketh in an *u* tongue edifieth himself

1 Cor. 14:19 speak...with...understanding...than...in an *u* tongue

UNLEAVENED BREAD, FEAST OF. See *Passover* and *Feast of Unleavened Bread.*

UNPARDONABLE SIN. Blasphemy against the Holy Spirit, or attributing the work of Christ to Satan, as the critics of Jesus did (Mark 3:22–30). Many interpreters believe this sin consists of rejecting the testimony of the Holy Spirit about Christ's person and work.

UNPLOWED GROUND. See *Fallow Ground.*

UNRIGHTEOUS [NESS]

Ps. 92:15 there is no *u'ness* in him [God]

Isa. 55:7 Let the wicked forsake his way...*u* man his thoughts

Rom. 1:18 wrath of God is revealed...against all...*u'ness*

1 Cor. 6:9 the *u* shall not inherit the kingdom of God

2 Cor. 6:14 what fellowship...righteousness with *u'ness*

1 John 1:9 he [Jesus] is faithful...to cleanse us from all *u'ness*

UNSEARCHABLE

Ps. 145:3 Great is the LORD...his greatness is *u*

Rom. 11:33 how *u* are his [God's] judgments

Eph. 3:8 I [Paul] should preach...the *u* riches of Christ

UNTEMPERED MORTER (WHITE-WASH). A thin layer of clay used as a protective coating on the exterior walls of buildings. The term is used figuratively of the futile promises of false prophets (Ezek. 13:10–15; 22:28). *Whitewash:* NIV, NRSV.

UPHAZ. A place in Arabia where gold was obtained, perhaps the same place as Ophir (Jer. 10:9).

UPPER EGYPT. See *Pathros.*

UPPER ROOM. A chamber or room usually built on the roof of a house and used in the summer because it was cooler than the regular living quarters (Mark 14:15). Such a room was the site of Jesus' last meal with His disciples (Luke 22:12). See also *Loft.*

U

UR OF THE CHALDEES (UR OF THE CHALDEANS). A city in Mesopotamia where Abraham spent his early life with his father, Terah, and his wife, Sarah, before he was called by the Lord to go to Canaan (Gen. 11:28, 31). Excavation has revealed that Ur was a thriving city and center of moon worship. *Ur of the Chaldeans:* NIV, NRSV. See also *Mesopotamia*.

URIAH

1. A Hittite warrior in David's army whose wife, Bath-sheba, was taken by David after the king plotted to have Uriah killed in battle (2 Sam. 11:15, 24–27). *Urias:* Greek form (Matt. 1:6).

2. NIV, NRSV name for the prophet Urijah. See *Urijah*.

URIJAH (URIAH). A faithful prophet in Jeremiah's time who was killed by King Jehoiakim for predicting God's judgment on Judah (Jer. 26:20). *Uriah:* NIV, NRSV.

URIM AND THUMMIN. Two objects in the breastplate of the high priest (Exod. 28:30), possibly colored stones cast as lots to help determine God's will (Num. 27:21). See also *Lots, Casting of.*

USURY (INTEREST). Interest on mone loaned. Under the Mosaic Law, Jews coul exact interest only from non-Jews, not from their own countrymen (Lev. 25:36–37). Nehe miah denounced those who were breaking thi law (Neh. 5:7, 10). *Interest:* NIV, NRSV. See als *Debt; Loan.*

UZ. A place in southern Edom west of the Arabian desert where Job lived (Job 1:1 Jer. 25:20).

UZZA (UZZAH). An Israelite who was struck dead for touching the ark of the covenant while carting it to Jerusalem (1 Chron. 13:7–11) *Uzzah:* NIV, NRSV.

UZZIAH/AZARIAH/OZIAS. The son and successor of Amaziah as king of Judah (reigned about 767–740 B.C.). A godly king, excellent general, and noted city builder (2 Chron. 26:1–15), he contracted leprosy as a divine punishment for assuming duties that belonged to the priesthood (2 Chron. 26:16–21). *Azariah:* 2 Kings 14:21; *Ozias:* Jesus' ancestry (Matt. 1:8).

VAGABOND (WANDERER). A wanderer or fugitive. Life as a fugitive was part of the curse against Cain for murdering his brother Abel (Gen. 4:12). *Wanderer:* NIV, NRSV. The "vagabond Jews" of Acts 19:13 were professional exorcists.

VAIN

Exod. 20:7 not take the name of the LORD…in **v**
Ps. 2:1 Why do…the people imagine a **v** thing?
Prov. 31:30 Favour is deceitful…beauty is **v**
Matt. 6:7 when ye pray, use not **v** repetitions
Cor. 3:20 Lord knoweth…thoughts of the wise…**v**
Cor. 15:14 if Christ be not risen…our preaching **v**
Tim. 2:16 shun profane and **v** babblings

VALE OF SIDDIM. A valley of tar pits near the Dead Sea where Sodom and Gomorrah were located (Gen. 14:1–10).

VALLEY OF DRY BONES. A vision of the prophet Ezekiel. When Ezekiel addressed the bones, representing Israel's exile in a foreign land, they came to life by God's Spirit. This served as God's assurance that His people would return one day to their native land (Ezek. 37:1–14). See also *Ezekiel, Book of.*

VANITY. Emptiness and futility. Life is vain and empty unless it is lived in obedience to God and His will (Eccles. 12:13).

VANITY [IES]

Job 35:13 God will not hear **v**
Ps. 39:5 every man…is altogether **v**
Eccles. 1:2 **v** of **v'ies**; all is **v**
Isa. 41:29 they are all **v**; their works are nothing
Eph. 4:17 walk not…in the **v** of their mind

VASHTI. The queen of Ahasuerus of Persia who refused the king's command to appear with the royal court and was replaced by Esther (Esther 1:10–12; 2:2, 15–17).

VEGETABLES. See *Pulse.*

VEIL

1. A screen or curtain that separated the Holy Place and the Holy of Holies in the tabernacle and temple. This veil was torn at Christ's death to symbolize direct access of all people to God's salvation through Jesus Christ (Matt. 27:51). *Curtain:* NIV, NRSV (Heb. 4:14–16). See also *Court of the Gentiles; Middle Wall of Partition.*

2. NIV word for *muffler.* See *Muffler.*

VENGEANCE. See *Revenge.*

VENISON (GAME). The flesh of any wild animal used for food. Isaac loved his son Esau because he was a "cunning hunter" who cooked venison (Gen. 25:27–28). *Game:* NIV, NRSV. See also *Hunter.*

VENOM (POISON). A poisonous fluid secreted by animals such as snakes and scorpions. The word is used figuratively of the destructive power of wine (Deut. 32:33). *Poison:* NRSV. See also *Poison.*

VENOMOUS SNAKES. See *Fiery Serpents*.

VERMILION. A bright red substance used for ornamentation and painting of houses and images (Ezek. 23:14).

VESTIBULE. See *Porch*.

VIA DOLOROSA. The name, meaning "way of sorrow," for the traditional route that Jesus took from Pilate's judgment hall to Calvary for His crucifixion. It is impossible to determine the precise route, since Jerusalem was destroyed by the Romans in A.D. 70 and then rebuilt. This name does not appear in the Bible.

VIAL (FLASK). A bottle or flask that held oil or other liquids (1 Sam. 10:1). *Flask:* NIV.

VICTORY
Isa. 25:8 He [God] will swallow up death in *v*
1 Cor. 15:55 O grave, where is thy *v*?
1 Cor. 15:57 God...giveth us the *v* through...Jesus Christ
1 John 5:4 the *v* that overcometh the world

VILLAGE. A collection of houses or a small town not protected by a defensive wall (Ezek. 38:11).

VINE. A plant that bore grapes. Jesus referred to Himself as the "true vine" (John 15:1).

VINE [S]
Judg. 9:12 said the trees unto the *v*...reign over us
Song 2:15 little foxes, that spoil the *v's*
Mic. 4:4 sit every man under his *v* and...fig tree
Luke 22:18 I [Jesus] will not drink...fruit of the *v*
John 15:5 I [Jesus] am the *v*, ye are the branches

VINE OF SODOM. A plant that grew near the Dead Sea and produced a beautiful fruit that was unfit to eat—a fitting description of Israel's idolatry (Deut. 32:32).

VINEGAR (SOUR WINE). A beverage consisting of wine or strong drink that was excessively fermented until it turned sour. This drink was offered to Jesus on the cross (Matt. 27:34, 48). *Sour wine:* NRSV.

VINEYARD. A field or orchard of grapevines. The word is used symbolically for Israel (Ps. 80:8, 15–16).

VINTAGE. The time of year for making wine. Grapes were gathered with shouts of joy (Jer. 25:30), then put in baskets and carried to the winepress (Jer. 6:9). See also *Wine*.

VIOL (LYRE). A stringed musical instrument, probably similar to the psaltery (Isa. 5:12). *Lyre:* NIV. See also *Harp; Psaltery*.

VIPER. See *Asp*.

VIRGIN. A general term for a young unmarried woman (Gen. 24:16).

VIRGIN BIRTH. The miraculous conception of Jesus by the Holy Spirit and His birth to the Virgin Mary. This event was foretold by the

ISRAEL AS A VINE

The image of the nation of Israel as a vine (Ps. 80:8–11) appears throughout the Bible. The prophet Isaiah declared that the nation yielded the "wild grapes" of idolatry (Isa. 5:1–7). Hosea the prophet called Israel an "empty vine" (Hosea 10:1).

Perhaps Jesus had this image in mind when He identified Himself as the "true vine" (John 15:1). As the perfectly obedient Son, He fulfilled the purpose to which God the Father had called His chosen people.

prophet Isaiah (Isa. 7:14) and revealed to Mary by an angel (Luke 1:26–33). The Messiah's supernatural conception in a human mother corresponds to His unique role as God-man. See also *Advent of Christ, The First; Incarnation of Christ.*

VIRTUE.

Moral excellence in association with power and ability—a characteristic of Jesus (Luke 6:19).

Mark 5:30 Jesus...knowing that *v* had gone out of him
Phil. 4:8 if there be any *v*...think on these things
2 Pet. 1:5 add to your faith *v*; and to virtue knowledge

VIRTUOUS

Ruth 3:11 all the city...doth know...thou art a *v* woman
Prov. 12:4 A *v* woman is a crown to her husband
Prov. 31:10 Who can find a *v* woman?...price...above rubies

VISION [S]

Prov. 29:18 Where there is no *v*, the people perish
Joel 2:28 your young men shall see *v's*
Hab. 2:2 Write the *v*...make it plain upon tables
Luke 1:22 he [Zacharias] had seen a *v* in the temple
Acts 16:9 a *v* appeared to Paul in the night
Acts 26:19 I [Paul] was not disobedient...heavenly *v*

VOCATION (CALLING).

A calling based on God's purpose and grace (2 Tim. 1:9). Paul urged believers to "walk worthy" of their Christian vocation (Eph. 4:1). *Calling:* NIV, NRSV. See also *Calling.*

VOICE [S]

Gen. 22:18 thou [Abraham] hast obeyed my [God's] *v*
Exod. 5:2 is the LORD, that I [Pharaoh]...obey his *v*
1 Kings 19:12 and after the fire a still small *v*
Isa. 40:3 The *v* of him that crieth in the wilderness
Matt. 3:3 The *v* of one crying in the wilderness
Matt. 3:17 a *v* from heaven...my [God's] beloved Son
John 10:27 My [Jesus'] sheep hear my *v*
Acts 9:4 a *v*...Saul, why persecutest...me [Jesus]
1 Cor. 14:10 There are...many...*v's* in the world
Heb. 3:15 To day if ye will hear his [God's] *v*
Rev. 1:10 I [John]...heard behind me a great *v*

VULTURE. Figurines of a vulture and a hawk, from ancient Egypt. Scavengers, vultures feed mostly on abandoned carcasses.

VOID (EMPTY).

Containing nothing; empty. The earth was formless and void before God shaped it and filled it with life through His creative power (Gen. 1:2). *Empty:* NIV.

VOW.

A pledge or agreement to perform a service for God in return for some expected benefit (Gen. 28:20–22).

VOW [ED, EST, S]

Ps. 50:14 pay thy *v's* unto the most High
Eccles. 5:4 *v'est a v* unto God, defer not to pay it
Jon. 2:9 I will pay that that I have *v'ed*

VOW OFFERING.

A gift or freewill offering that accompanied a vow to the Lord (Deut. 23:23).

VULTURE (RED KITE, BUZZARD).

A large bird that fed mostly on dead animals or other wastes and was thus considered unclean (Lev. 11:14). *Red kite:* NIV; *buzzard:* NRSV. See also *Ossifrage.*

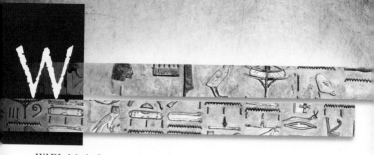

W

WADI. A bed of a stream that is dry except during the rainy season (Gen. 26:19). This word does not occur in the Bible, but Palestine has hundreds of these wadis.

WADI OF EGYPT. See *River of Egypt.*

WAFER. A thin cake made of fine, unleavened flour and anointed with oil for meal offerings (Exod. 29:2). Wafers were sometimes sweetened with honey (Exod. 16:31).

WAGES. Payment for work rendered by field hands or common laborers. Wages were paid daily, at the end of the workday (Lev. 19:13). Paul declared that the wages, or payoff, of sin is death (Rom. 6:23).

WAR. In a war with the Jews, Roman General Titus leads his troops in the battle for Jerusalem. Rome overran and destroyed Jerusalem and the temple in A.D. 70.

WAGON. A crude wooden cart pulled by oxen (Gen. 45:19). See also *Cart*.

WALL. A massive fence of stone or brick around a city for protection against enemy attack (2 Sam. 18:24). Defense towers and even houses were often built on these walls (Isa. 2:15). See also *Fenced City; Siege*.

WALL OF PARTITION. See *Middle Wall of Partition*.

WANDERER. See *Vagabond*.

WAR. Armed conflict between nations or tribes. The Hebrews considered their conflicts with enemy nations as the Lord's battles (Num. 10:9). Early skirmishes were fought by spearmen, archers, and slingers; horses and chariots were a later development in Israel's history. The prophets envisioned an age without war (Mic. 4:3).

WARD. A prison cell or lockup room. This word is also used for a detachment of soldiers on guard duty (Acts 12:10). See also *Prison*.

WARDROBE. A place where royal robes or priestly vestments were kept (2 Kings 22:14).

WARP. The long threads in hand-spun cloth. These threads are extended lengthwise in the loom and crossed by the *woof*, or threads running in the opposite direction. See also *Weaver*.

WARRIORS. See *Mighty Men*.

WASH. To cleanse (Matt. 27:24). The Hebrews emphasized cleanliness and ceremonial purity. Washing the hands before meals or the feet after a journey was considered a religious duty (Matt. 15:2). See also *Clean; Purification*.

WASHERMAN'S FIELD. See *Fuller's Field*.

WATCH
Job 14:16 dost thou [God] not *w* over my sin
Matt. 24:42 *W* therefore…ye know not what hour
Mark 14:37 couldest not thou [Peter] *w* one hour
Luke 2:8 shepherds…keeping *w* over their flock
1 Pet. 4:7 be ye…sober, and *w* unto prayer

WATCHMAN (SENTINEL). A guard or sentry stationed at a city gate. These watchmen also patrolled the streets and called out the hours of the night (2 Sam. 18:24–27). *Sentinel:* NRSV.

WATCHTOWER. A tall guard station or lookout post that provided early warning of approaching dangers (Isa. 21:5).

WATER. In Palestine's arid climate, water was a precious commodity. People were dependent on wells or cisterns during the dry summer and fall. Public wells or reservoirs were provided for travelers (Gen. 26:19). Jesus promised the "water of life" to a sinful Samaritan woman (John 4:10–14). See also *Well*.

WATER [S]
Gen. 1:2 Spirit of God moved upon…*w's*
Num. 20:11 Moses…smote the rock…*w* came out
Ps. 1:3 tree planted by the rivers of *w*
Prov. 5:15 Drink *w's* out of thine own cistern
Eccles. 11:1 Cast thy bread upon the *w's*
Song 8:7 Many *w's* cannot quench love
Isa. 55:1 every one that thirsteth, come ye to the *w's*
Jer. 2:13 forsaken me [God] the fountain of living *w's*
Amos 5:24 let judgment run down as *w's*
Mark 1:8 I [John the Baptist]…have baptized you with *w*
John 3:5 Except a man be born of *w* and of the Spirit
Acts 1:5 John…baptized with *w*; but ye…with the Holy Ghost
Rev. 22:17 let him take the *w* of life freely

WATER CARRIER. See *Drawer of Water*.

WATER HEN. See *Swan*.

W

WATER OF JEALOUSY. A mixture of water with dust prescribed as a test for a woman accused of adultery by her husband (Num. 5:11–31).

WATER OF SEPARATION (WATER OF CLEANSING). Water mixed with ashes to purify a person after defilement through contact with the dead (Num. 19:13–22). *Water of cleansing:* NIV. See also *Bitter Water.*

WATERING TROUGH. See *Gutter.*

WATERPOT. A large clay vessel in which water for the household was stored (John 2:6–7).

WATERS OF MEROM. A lake ten miles north of the Sea of Galilee through which the Jordan River flows on its southward passage (Josh. 11:5–7).

WAVE OFFERING (ELEVATION OFFERING). A sacrificial animal presented to God to celebrate restoration of a right relationship with God. The sacrifice was "waved" before the Lord to gain acceptance (Exod. 29:24). *Elevation offering:* NRSV. See also *Sacrifice.*

WAX. A substance formed by bees while making honey. The word is also used figuratively for the punishment of the wicked in God's presence (Ps. 68:2).

WAY OF THE SEA. A road that ran from Sidon in Phoenicia to Egypt, passing through Palestine (Isa. 9:1). See also *Highway; Road.*

WAY, THE. A term of contempt for the Christian faith used by the enemies of the early church (Acts 9:2; 24:14, 22).

WAYS

1 Sam. 18:14 David behaved…wisely in all his **w**
2 Chron. 7:14 If my [God's] people…turn from their wicked **w**
Ps. 25:4 Show me thy **w**, O Lord
Prov. 3:6 In all thy **w** acknowledge him [God]
Prov. 14:12 the end thereof are the **w** of death
Prov. 28:18 he that is perverse in his **w** shall fall
Isa. 55:8 neither are your **w** my **w**, saith the Lord
James 1:8 A double minded man is unstable in all his **w**

WEAK [NESS]

Ps. 6:2 Have mercy upon me, O Lord; for I am **w**
Matt. 26:41 spirit…is willing…flesh is **w**
Acts 20:35 ye ought to support the **w**
1 Cor. 1:27 **w** things of the world to confound the…mighty
1 Cor. 9:22 became…**w**, that I [Paul] might gain the **w**
1 Cor. 15:43 it [the body] is sown in **w'ness**…raised in power
2 Cor. 12:9 my [Jesus'] strength is made perfect in **w'ness**

WEALTH. See *Mammon; Money.*

WEASEL. An unclean animal, possibly the mole or polecat (Lev. 11:29).

WEAVER. A craftsman who made cloth from several different raw materials, including wool and camel hair (Exod. 35:35; Lev. 13:47). The Hebrews may have learned the art of weaving in Egypt.

WEDDING. A marriage ceremony. A Jewish wedding was a festive occasion with the entire community participating. The bride wore jewels and an ornamented white robe with a veil. The bridegroom, accompanied by friends and musicians, proceeded to the bride's home to conduct her to the wedding hall. Festivities continued for seven days (Matt. 25:6–10; Luke 12:36; 14:8). See also *Betrothal; Dowry; Marriage.*

WEED. See *Cockle.*

WEEKS, FEAST OF. See *Pentecost.*

WELL. A deep hole dug in the ground to reach groundwater. Wells were usually covered with stone slabs or surrounded by low stone walls (John 4:6). The word is also used figuratively of salvation (Isa. 12:3) and wisdom (Prov. 16:22). The phrase "wells without water" shows the futility of wickedness (2 Pet. 2:17). See also *Water.*

WHALE. A large sea-dwelling fish (Gen. 1:21). The "great fish" that swallowed Jonah is thought to be an enormous white shark, common in the Mediterranean Sea (Jon. 1:17).

WHEAT. A grain that was ground and baked into bread (1 Kings 5:11). The wheat harvest was observed as a festival and time of celebration (Exod. 34:22). See also *Corn.*

WHIRLWIND (GALE, STORM). A great storm or tempest (Job 37:9). Elijah was transported to heaven by a whirlwind (2 Kings 2:1, 11). The word was also used figuratively for swift and sudden destruction (Isa. 17:13). *Gale:* NIV; *storm:* NRSV. See also *Tempest.*

WHITE OWL. See *Swan.*

WHITED SEPULCHRE. See *Sepulchre.*

WHITEWASH. See *Untempered Mortar.*

WICKED [NESS]
Gen. 6:5 God saw that the *w'ness* of man was great
Job 4:8 they that…sow *w'ness*, reap the same
Ps. 10:2 *w* in his pride doth persecute the poor
Ps. 71:4 Deliver me…out of the hand of the *w*
Ps. 94:3 LORD…how long shall the *w* triumph?
Prov. 4:17 they [evil men] eat the bread of *w'ness*
Prov. 15:29 The LORD is far from the *w*
Isa. 53:9 he [God's servant] made his grave with the *w*
Jer. 4:14 O Jerusalem, wash thine heart from *w'ness*
Jer. 17:9 The heart is…desperately *w*
Matt. 16:4 A *w*…generation seeketh after a sign

Eph. 6:12 we wrestle…against spiritual *w'ness*
Eph. 6:16 quench all the fiery darts of the *w*

WICKEDNESS. Evil, malice, and wrongdoing. See *Evil; Iniquity; Sin.*

WICKED ONE
Matt. 13:19 the *w-o*…catcheth…which was sown
Matt. 13:38 tares are the children of the *w-o*
1 John 2:14 and ye have overcome the *w-o*
1 John 3:12 Cain…was of that *w-o*…slew his brother

WIDOW. A woman whose husband has died. Fair and just treatment of widows was enjoined under Mosaic Law (Exod. 22:22). In the N.T., visiting the fatherless and widows was cited as evidence of true religion (James 1:27). See also *Levirate Marriage.*

MINISTRY TO WIDOWS

Paul's admonition to his missionary associate, Timothy, was that the church should "relieve them that are widows indeed" (1 Tim. 5:16)—those without any means of support who were in dire financial need. In Bible times, women whose husbands died did not have public assistance or life insurance to fall back on. The early church provided a measure of support for widows within its fellowship (Acts 6:1).

WIFE. A married woman. Wives are urged to love and respect their husbands and to be faithful to them (Eph. 5:33; Prov. 31:11–12). Husbands and wives are to be mutually committed to each other and to fulfill each other's needs (1 Cor. 7:2–5). See also *Family; Husband.*

WILD OX. See *Unicorn.*

WILDERNESS. A dry, desolate, uncultivated region where little vegetation grew. John the Baptist preached in the Judean wilderness (Matt. 3:1). See also *Desert*.

WILDERNESS WANDERINGS. The aimless course taken by the Hebrew people in the Sinai Peninsula for forty years after they left Egypt—God's punishment for their sin of disobedience (Deut. 1:1; Josh. 5:6). God provided food and guidance through Moses until they arrived in Canaan (Exod. 16:35; Neh. 9:24).

WILL OF GOD. God's desire and wish for His people. The Father's will is that those who believe on the Son will have eternal life and that none will be lost (John 6:39–40). The disciples of Jesus were taught to pray for God's will to be done on earth as it is in heaven (Matt. 6:10). Paul urged the Christians at Rome to allow God to transform their minds to know the perfect will of God (Rom. 12:2).

Mark 3:35 do the *w-o-G*...same is my brother
1 Thess. 4:3 the *w-o-G*...abstain from fornication
1 Thess. 5:18 give thanks...the *w-o-G* in Christ Jesus
1 John 2:17 doeth the *w-o-G* abideth for ever

WILLOW (POPLAR). A tree that grew by streams; perhaps the weeping willow (Ps. 137:1–2). Its branches were used for booths at the Feast of Tabernacles (Lev. 23:40). *Poplar:* NIV. See also *Poplar*.

WIMPLE (CLOAK). A mantle, scarf, or shawl worn around the neck by women (Isa. 3:22). *Cloak:* NIV, NRSV.

WIND. The movement of the air. The Bible speaks of the "four winds" (Jer. 49:36): the north wind (Job 37:22), the warm south wind (Luke 12:55), the cool west wind bringing rain (Luke 12:54), and the scorching east wind from the desert (Job 27:21). Jesus illustrated the freedom of the Holy Spirit with the mysteries of the wind (John 3:8).

WINDOW. A small opening in a house or public building that let in light and cool breezes (1 Chron. 15:29). These openings were probably covered with shutters or latticework.

WINE/STRONG DRINK. The juice of grapes, fermented to produce a strong beverage that was very popular among the Jews (Gen. 40:11). Commonly referred to as *strong drink* (Prov. 31:6), wine was prohibited to Nazarites (Num. 6:3) as well as to priests before they officiated at the altar (Lev. 10:9). Excessive consumption of wine was denounced (Prov. 20:1; Eph. 5:18). See also *Grape*.

WINE

Prov. 4:17 they...drink the *w* of violence
Isa. 5:22 Woe unto them that are mighty to drink *w*
Mark 2:22 no man putteth new *w* into old bottles
John 2:3 mother of Jesus saith...They have no *w*
Acts 2:13 men (believers at Pentecost) are full of new *w*
1 Tim. 3:8 deacons be grave...not given to much *w*
1 Tim. 5:23 use a little *w* for thy stomach's sake

WINEBIBBER (DRUNKARD). A person addicted to wine (Prov. 23:20–21). Jesus was accused of being a winebibber because He befriended sinners (Matt. 11:19). *Drunkard:* NIV, NRSV.

WINEPRESS. A vat or tank where juice was squeezed from grapes in the wine-making process. Usually hewn out of rock, the winepress had an upper vat where the grapes were crushed and a lower vat that received the juice (Judg. 6:11; Isa. 63:2–3). See also *Grape*.

WINESKIN. See *Bottle*.

W

valuable than riches (Prov. 8:11), and it produces good fruit (James 3:17). Christ is the key that opens the hidden treasures of God's wisdom (Col. 2:3).

Job 28:28 the fear of the Lord, that is **w**
Job 34:35 his [Job's] words were without **w**
Ps. 90:12 number our days…apply our hearts unto **w**
Prov. 4:7 **W** is the principal thing; therefore get **w**
Eccles. 1:18 in much **w** is much grief
Jer. 9:23 Let not the wise man glory in his **w**
Luke 2:52 Jesus increased in **w** and stature
Acts 6:3 seven men…full of the Holy Ghost and **w**
1 Cor. 1:20 God made foolish the **w** of this world
1 Cor. 1:22 Jews require a sign…Greeks seek after **w**
1 Cor. 3:19 **w** of this world is foolishness with God
Col. 3:16 word of Christ dwell in you…in all **w**
James 1:5 any of you lack **w**, let him ask of God

WISDOM LITERATURE. A distinct category of literature in the Bible, including Job, Proverbs, Ecclesiastes, and some of the psalms, so named because they deal with some of the most important ethical and philosophical issues of life—the meaning of suffering, the nature and purpose of God, human relationships, and so on.

WISE

Prov. 6:6 consider her [the ant's] ways…be **w**
Isa. 5:21 Woe unto them that are **w** in their own eyes
Jer. 9:23 Let not the **w** man glory in his wisdom
Matt. 2:1 when Jesus was born…came **w** men from the east
Matt. 7:24 a **w** man…built his house upon a rock
Matt. 10:16 **w** as serpents…harmless as doves
Matt. 11:25 thou [God] hast hid these things from the **w**
Matt. 25:8 foolish said unto the **w**, Give us of your oil
Rom. 12:16 Be not **w** in your own conceits
1 Cor. 1:26 not many **w** men after the flesh…are called

WISE MEN. Astrologers from Mesopotamia or Persia, often referred to as the *magi*, who brought gifts to the young child Jesus in Bethlehem (Matt. 2:10–11). See also *Astrologer*.

VINEPRESS. In this ancient mosaic, Roman vineyard workers walk on grapes to squeeze out the juice for wine. The juice flows out of the stone vat and into small containers below.

WING. A symbolic expression for God's protection. He delivers His people on the wings of eagles (Exod. 19:4).

WINNOWING. The process of separating chaff or straw from the grains of wheat by beating the stalks and throwing them into the air; symbolically, to rid oneself of sin or worldly desires (Matt. 3:12). See also *Fan; Threshingfloor.*

WINTERHOUSE (WINTER APARTMENT). A dwelling used by kings in the winter months (Jer. 36:22). *Winter apartment:* NIV, NRSV.

WISDOM. Knowledge guided by insight and understanding. Reverence for God is the source of wisdom (Prov. 9:10). Wisdom is more

W

WITCHCRAFT. The practice of sorcery or black magic by witches and wizards—an activity denounced by God (Deut. 18:10; Mic. 5:12). King Saul displeased God by asking the witch of Endor to summon the spirit of Samuel from the dead (1 Sam. 28:3–25). See also *Magic; Sorcery.*

WITNESS. One who gives testimony about an event or another person's character. Under Mosaic Law, the testimony of at least two persons was required to convict a person of a capital offense (Deut. 17:6). False witnesses were punished severely (Deut. 19:18–19). Believers are empowered to serve as witnesses for Christ (Acts 1:8). See also *Record; Testimony.*

WITNESS [ES]
Exod. 20:16 not bear false *w* against thy neighbour
Ps. 35:11 False *w's* did rise up
Prov. 19:9 false *w* shall not be unpunished
Mark 14:56 many bare false *w* against him [Jesus]
Rom. 8:16 Spirit itself beareth *w* with our spirit
Heb. 12:1 compassed about with…a cloud of *w's*

WIVES
Matt. 19:8 Moses…suffered you to put away your *w*
Eph. 5:22 *W,* submit…unto your own husbands
Eph. 5:25 Husbands, love your *w*…as Christ…loved the church
Col. 3:18 *W,* submit…unto your own husbands
Col. 3:19 Husbands, love your *w*…be not bitter
1 Tim. 4:7 But refuse profane and old *w'* fables
1 Pet. 3:1 *w,* be in subjection to your own husbands

WIZARD (SPIRITIST). A male witch, or practitioner of black magic, who claimed to have secret knowledge given by a spirit from the dead (2 Kings 21:6). Under Mosaic Law, wizards were to be put to death by stoning (Lev. 20:27). *Spiritist:* NIV. See also *Familiar Spirit.*

WOE. An expression of extreme grief or distress (Matt. 24:19). The word also expressed the threat of future punishment (Jer. 48:46).

WOLF. A fierce wild animal of the dog family that posed a threat to sheep (Isa. 11:6). Jesus also used the word figuratively of false prophets (Matt. 7:15).

WOMB. Barren women regarded themselves as cursed by the Lord (1 Sam. 1:5–10). Children were described as "fruit of the womb" and a blessing from God (Ps. 127:3–5). See also *Barren; Children.*

WONDERS
Ps. 77:14 Thou art the God that doest *w*
Ps. 96:3 declare his [God's]…*w* among all people
John 4:48 Except ye see signs and *w,* ye will not believe
Acts 2:43 *w* and signs were done by the apostles
Acts 6:8 Stephen, full of faith…did great *w*

WOODCUTTER. See *Hewer.*

WOOF. See *Warp.*

WOOL. The furlike coat of sheep that was highly prized by the Jews for making clothes (Prov. 31:13). Its vulnerability to moths was a problem (Matt. 6:19). See also *Fleece; Sheep.*

WORD [S]
Ps. 12:6 The *w's* of the LORD are pure *w's*
Ps. 19:14 *w's*…be acceptable in thy [God's] sight
Ps. 119:11 Thy [God's] *w* have I hid in mine heart
Ps. 119:105 Thy [God's] *w* is a lamp unto my feet
Isa. 40:8 the *w* of our God shall stand for ever
Mal. 2:17 have wearied the LORD with your *w's*
Luke 4:32 his [Jesus'] *w* was with power
John 1:1 In the beginning was the *W*
John 6:68 thou [Jesus] hast the *w's* of eternal life
Acts 8:4 they…went every where preaching the *w*
2 Cor. 5:19 committed unto us the *w* of reconciliation
2 Tim. 2:15 workman…rightly dividing the *w* of truth
James 1:22 doers of the *w*…not hearers only
1 John 3:18 let us not love in *w*…but in deed

WORD OF GOD. God's revelation of Himself to humans, especially through Jesus and the

W

Bible (Heb. 4:12). The written Scriptures, which Christians accept as the Word of God, testify to Jesus as the eternal and living Word of God (John 1:1; 5:39). See also *Bible; Logos.*

Prov. 30:5 Every **w-o-G** is pure
Luke 4:4 not live by bread alone but by every **w-o-G**
Rom. 10:17 faith...by hearing...hearing by the **w-o-G**
Eph. 6:17 sword of the Spirit, which is the **w-o-G**
Heb. 11:3 the worlds were framed by the **w-o-G**

WORK. Labor in a worthwhile cause; fruitful activity. A Christian's work should be performed as service to the Lord (Eph. 6:6–8).

WORK [ETH]

Exod. 23:12 Six days thou shalt do thy **w**
Neh. 4:6 people had a mind to **w**
Ps. 115:4 idols are...the **w** of men's hands
John 4:34 My [Jesus'] meat is...to finish his [God's] **w**
John 9:4 night cometh, when no man can **w**
Acts 13:2 Separate...Barnabas and Saul for the **w**
Rom. 8:28 all things **w** together for good
Rom. 13:10 Love **w'eth** no ill to his neighbour
Eph. 4:12 perfecting of the saints...**w** of the ministry
1 Tim. 3:1 office of a bishop, he desireth a good **w**

WORKERS

Ps. 6:8 Depart from me...ye **w** of iniquity
1 Cor. 12:29 are all teachers? are all **w** of miracles?
Phil. 3:2 Beware of dogs, beware of evil **w**

WORKS. Good deeds performed as an expression of a believer's commitment to Christ. Works cannot save or justify (Eph. 2:9), but they do fulfill God's purpose for His people. We are created in Jesus Christ in order to perform good works for the building of God's kingdom (Eph. 2:10).

1 Chron. 16:9 talk ye of all his [God's] wondrous **w**
Job 37:14 consider the wondrous **w** of God
Ps. 40:5 Many, O Lord...are thy wonderful **w**
Matt. 5:16 see your good **w**, and glorify your Father
Matt. 13:58 he [Jesus] did not many mighty **w** there
John 6:28 that we might work the **w** of God
John 14:12 greater **w** than these shall he do

Gal. 2:16 man is not justified by the **w** of the law
Titus 3:5 Not by **w** of righteousness...we have done
James 2:17 faith, if it hath not **w**, is dead

WORK [S] OF GOD/WORK [S] OF THE LORD

Ps. 64:9 all men...shall declare the **w-o-G**
Ps. 66:5 Come and see the **w's-o-G**
Ps. 77:11 I will remember the **w's-o-t-L**
Ps. 78:7 not forget the **w's-o-t-L**
Ps. 118:17 I shall...declare the **w's-o-t-L**
Eccles. 7:13 Consider the **w-o-G**
Eccles. 8:17 Then I beheld all the **w-o-G**
Jer. 51:10 declare in Zion the **w-o-t-L** our God
John 6:28 that we might work the **w-o-G**
Acts 2:11 hear them speak...wonderful **w's-o-G**
1 Cor. 15:58 stedfast...abounding in the **w-o-t-L**

WORK. Working his way up a Jerusalem street, a broom vendor sells his wares to anyone willing to buy. The Bible praises hard work and condemns laziness.

W

WORLDLY. See *Carnal.*

WORM. An insect that destroyed plants and consumed dead flesh (Job 7:5). The word is also used symbolically of human helplessness or insignificance (Isa. 41:14) and frailty (Ps. 22:6).

WORMWOOD. A plant noted for its bitter taste (Jer. 9:15). The phrase "gall and wormwood" describes something offensive or sorrowful (Deut. 29:18). See also *Hemlock.*

WORSHIP. The praise and adoration of God expressed both publicly and privately (Deut. 6; 1 Chron. 16:29). The Jews worshiped in the tabernacle until the temple became their worship center. After their period of exile among the Babylonians and Persians, they worshiped in neighborhood synagogues. The book known as Psalms contains many spiritual songs and hymns chanted or sung in public worship. See also *Hymn; Praise; Psalms, Book of.*

WORSHIP [PED]

Ps. 95:6 **w** and bow down [before God]
Ps. 99:5 **w** at his [God's] footstool…he is holy
Jer. 25:6 go not after other gods…to **w** them
Matt. 2:2 we [the wise men]…are come to **w** him [Jesus]
John 4:24 they…must **w** him [God] in spirit and in truth
Acts 17:25 Neither is [God] **w'ped** with men's hands
Rev. 7:11 angels…fell…on their faces…**w'ped** God

WORTHY. Of value or merit. The Lamb of God is worthy of praise because He redeemed us, made us kings and priests, and will share His reign with us (Rev. 5:9–14).

WRATH. Strong anger or indignation. Human wrath may be kindled by false accusation (Gen. 31:36) or disobedience (Num. 31:14–18), but God's wrath is exercised against ungodliness (Rom. 1:18), idolatry (Ps. 78:58–59), and unbelief (John 3:36). See also *Judgment; Punishment.*

Exod. 32:11 why doth thy [God's] **w** wax hot
Ps. 21:9 Lord shall swallow them up in his **w**
Ps. 90:7 by thy [God's] **w** are we troubled
Matt. 3:7 warned you [Pharisee] to flee from the **w**
Eph. 4:26 let not the sun go down upon your **w**
Eph. 6:4 fathers, provoke not your children to **w**
Rev. 6:17 great day of his [God's] **w** is come

WRATH OF GOD

Ps. 78:31 The **w-o-G**…slew the fattest of them
John 3:36 believeth not the Son…**w-o-G** abideth on him
Rom. 1:18 **w-o-G** is revealed…against all ungodliness
Rev. 16:1 pour out the vials of the **w-o-G** upon the earth

WREATH. See *Garland.*

WRITING. The Hebrews probably learned writing from the Egyptians. Earliest writing was done on stone, clay tablets, papyrus, and animal skins. See also *Ink; Paper.*

W

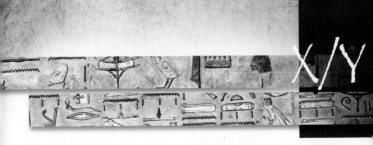

XERXES. See *Ahasuerus.*

YAHWEH. The Hebrew spelling of the major name for God in the O.T., translated in most English Bibles as "Lord" or "Jehovah." See *Jehovah.*

YARN. Thread used in weaving cloth. Yarn was produced from linen and wool fiber as well as the hair of camels and goats (Exod. 35:25–26). See also *Warp; Weaver.*

YEAR OF JUBILEE. See *Jubile.*

YEAST. See *Leaven.*

YIELD [ED, ING]
Gen. 1:11 earth bring forth grass, the herb **y'ing** seed
Ps. 67:6 Then shall the earth **y** her increase
Matt. 27:50 Jesus...**y'ed** up the ghost
Rom. 6:13 but **y** yourselves unto God

YIRON. See *Iron,* No. 1.

YOKE. A wooden collar or harness placed on the neck of draft animals and attached to plows and other agricultural tools (Jer. 31:18). The word was also used to denote servitude or oppression (1 Kings 12:1–4). Jesus declared His yoke is not burdensome (Matt. 11:29–30).

YOKEFELLOW (COMPANION). A fellow worker or comrade in a common cause. Paul appealed to an unknown "yokefellow" in Philippi to help two women resolve their differences (Phil. 4:3). *Companion:* NRSV.

YOUTH
Ps. 25:7 Remember not the sins of my **y**
Prov. 5:18 rejoice with the wife of thy **y**
Eccles. 12:1 Remember now thy Creator in the days of thy **y**
Matt. 19:20 All these things have I kept from my **y** up
1 Tim. 4:12 Let no man despise thy **y**

ZABULON. See *Zebulun*.

ZACCHAEUS. A wealthy tax collector who, after a conversation with Jesus at Jericho, vowed to give half of his wealth to the poor and make fourfold restitution to those whom he had cheated. Jesus declared that salvation had come to Zacchaeus (Luke 19:1–10). See also *Publican*.

ZACHARIAH. The son and successor of Jeroboam II as king of Israel. Zachariah ruled only about three months (about 753–752 B.C.) before being assassinated by Shallum (2 Kings 14:29; 15:8–12).

ZACHARIAS (ZECHARIAH). A godly priest and the father of John the Baptist. Zacharias was stricken speechless for his reluctance to believe a son would be born to him in his old age (Luke 1:18–22). *Zechariah:* NIV, NRSV.

ZADOK. The priest who anointed Solomon king. He served as high priest for a time under both David and Solomon (2 Sam. 8:17; 1 Kings 1:39; 2:35).

ZAMZUMMIMS (ZANZUMMITES, ZAMZUMMIM). A race of giants who lived in the region later occupied by the Ammonites (Deut. 2:20–21). *Zanzummites:* NIV; *Zamzummin:* NRSV. See also *Zuzim*.

ZAPHNATH-PAANEAH. See *Joseph*, No. 1.

ZAREPHATH/SAREPTA. A coastal town of Phoenicia where Elijah restored a widow's son to life. Elijah lodged with her during a drought (1 Kings 17:10–24). *Sarepta:* Luke 4:26.

ZEAL. Ardent desire and determination (Ps. 69:9; Phil. 3:6). Isaiah predicted the "zeal of the Lord" would establish the Messiah's kingdom (Isa. 9:7).

ZEALOTS. See *Zelotes*.

ZEALOUS
Acts 21:20 Jews...which believe...**z** of the law
Acts 22:3 I [Paul]...was **z** toward God
Titus 2:14 a peculiar people, **z** of good works

ZEBEDEE. A Galilean fisherman and father of two of Jesus' disciples, James and John (Matt. 4:21–22).

ZEBOIM/ZEBOIIM. One of the five cities near the Dead Sea destroyed along with Sodom and Gomorrah because of its sin (Deut. 29:23). *Zeboiim:* Gen. 14:8. See also *Cities of the Plain*.

ZEBULUN/ZABULON. The sixth son of Jacob and Leah (Gen. 30:19–20) and the tribe descended from Zebulun's three sons (Num. 26:26). This tribe settled in the fertile hill country of Galilee (Josh. 19:10–16). *Zabulon:* Greek form (Matt. 4:13). See also *Tribes of Israel*.

ZECHARIAH'S VISIONS

God revealed His messages for the people to the prophet Zechariah in a series of visions, including the vision of four chariots in Zechariah 6:1–8. Other prophets who had visionary experiences were Jeremiah (Jer. 1:4–19), Ezekiel (Ezek. 1), and Daniel (Dan. 7). Visions left no doubt that the message of these prophets came directly from the Lord.

ZECHARIAH

1. A prophet after the Babylonian conquest of Judah who probably helped rebuild the temple in Jerusalem (Ezra 5:1), and author of the O.T. book that bears his name.

2. NIV, NRSV name for *Zacharias*. See *Zacharias*.

ZECHARIAH, BOOK OF.

A prophetic book of the O.T. written to encourage the Jewish people during the difficult years back in their homeland following their period of exile among the Babylonians and Persians. Zechariah, through a series of eight visions (1:7–6:8) and four specific messages from God (7:4–8:23), encouraged the people to complete the task of rebuilding the temple in Jerusalem.

The prophet also presented God's promises for the future, including the coming of the Messiah (9:9–10:12), the restoration of the nation of Israel (chap. 10), and the universal reign of God (chap. 14). See also *Messiah*.

ZEDEKIAH/MATTANIAH.

The last king of Judah (reigned about 597–587 B.C.), who was renamed and placed on the throne as a puppet ruler by King Nebuchadnezzar of Babylonia (2 Kings 24:15, 17). Ignoring Jeremiah's advice, he rebelled against the Babylonians, only to be blinded and taken to Babylon in chains after seeing his sons put to death (2 Kings 25:6–7). His original name was *Mattaniah* (2 Kings 24:17).

ZELAH (ZELA).

The place where King Saul and his son Jonathan were buried in the territory of Benjamin (2 Sam. 21:14). *Zela:* NIV, NRSV.

ZELOPHEHAD.

A member of the tribe of Manasseh whose five daughters petitioned for the right to inherit his property because he had no sons. Their request was granted on the condition that they not marry outside the tribe (Num. 26:33; 27:1–8).

ZELOTES (ZEALOT).

A member of a political-religious party of zealous Jews in N.T. times whose aim was to overthrow Roman rule and establish a Jewish theocracy. Jesus' disciple known as Simon the Canaanite may have been a member of this party or sympathetic with its views (Luke 6:15). *Zealot:* NIV, NRSV. See also *Canaanites*, No. 2.

ZEPHANIAH.

A priest and friend of Jeremiah and author of the O.T. book that bears his name. Zephaniah often served as a messenger between Jeremiah and King Zedekiah of Judah (Jer. 21:1–2). After Jerusalem fell, Zephaniah was killed by the Babylonians (Jer. 52:24–27).

ZEPHANIAH, BOOK OF.

A short prophetic book of the O.T. known for its vivid portrayal of the certainty of God's judgment against the nation of Judah (chaps. 1–2). The prophet also declared that God would spare a faithful remnant (3:13), through which His promise of a future Messiah would be accomplished.

Z

ZERUBBABEL/ZOROBABEL/SHESH-BAZZAR. A leader of the second group of Jews who returned to Jerusalem about 520 B.C. after their period of exile in Babylonia and Persia (Ezra 2:2). He supervised the rebuilding of the temple and helped restore religious practices among his people (Zech. 4; Ezra 5:2). He apparently was appointed governor of Judah by King Cyrus of Persia (Hag. 2:21). *Zorobabel:* Jesus' ancestry (Matt. 1:12). *Sheshbazzar:* Ezra 5:14.

ZEUS. See *Jupiter.*

ZIBA. A former servant of King Saul who helped David locate Jonathan's son Mephibosheth. He became Mephibosheth's servant on the land restored by the king (2 Sam. 9:2–11).

ZIDON. See *Sidon.*

ZIF (ZIV). The second month of the Hebrew year, corresponding to *Iyyar* in the later Jewish calendar (1 Kings 6:1, 37). *Ziv:* NIV, NRSV.

ZIGGURAT. A tall Mesopotamian temple tower, built like a pyramid with staircases outside and a shrine for pagan worship on top. The tower of Babel was a ziggurat (Gen. 11:1–9). See also *Babel, Tower of.*

ZIKLAG. A city on the border of Judah assigned to David by King Achish of Gath as a place of refuge from King Saul (1 Sam. 27:5–6).

ZILPAH. Leah's maid who became a concubine of Jacob and bore two of his twelve sons, Gad and Asher (Gen. 30:9–13). See also *Jacob; Leah.*

ZIMRI. A chariot commander under King Elah of Israel who killed the king and assumed the throne (about 885 B.C.), only to commit suicide seven days later to escape the wrath of Omri's army (1 Kings 16:8–18).

ZIN. A desert wilderness near the Dead Sea through which the Hebrews passed. Moses' sister, Miriam, died and was buried here (Num. 20:1).

ZION/SION. One of the hills on which Jerusalem was built and the site of an ancient Jebusite fortress before the city was captured by David. In Solomon's time this section of Jerusalem was extended to include the temple area. Sometimes all of Jerusalem is referred to as "Zion" (1 Kings 8:1). *Sion:* Rev. 14:1. See also *Jerusalem.*

ZIPPORAH. A daughter of Jethro the Midianite priest, the wife of Moses, and mother of Moses' sons Gershom and Eliezer (Exod. 2:21–22).

ZIV. See *Zif.*

ZOAR/BELA. An ancient city of Canaan destroyed, along with Sodom and Gomorrah, because of its sin (Gen. 19:20–25). This city was also known as *Bela* (Gen. 14:2). See also *Cities of the Plain.*

ZOPHAR. One of Job's friends or "comforters" (Job 2:11).

ZOROBABEL. See *Zerubbabel.*

ZUZIM (ZUZITES). A race of giants in the land east of the Jordan River (Gen. 14:5). This is probably the same tribe as the *Zamzummins. Zuzites:* NIV. See also *Zamzummins.*

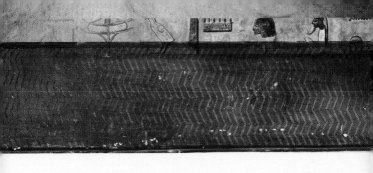

Maps

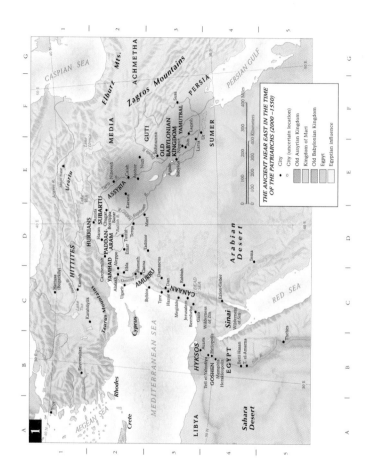

THE ANCIENT NEAR EAST IN THE TIME
OF THE PATRIARCHS (2000–1550)

- City
- City (uncertain location)
- Old Assyrian Kingdom
- Kingdom of Mari
- Old Babylonian Kingdom
- Egypt
- Egyptian influence

Adapted from *The Holman Bible Atlas* © 1998. Used by permission.

THE TRIBAL ALLOTMENTS
OF ISRAEL
JOSH. 13:8–19:49

• City
○ City (uncertain location)
▲ Mountain peak

MEDITERRANEAN
SEA

TYRE
Sidon
Damascus
ARAM
Abana River
Ijon
Mt. Hermon
Tyre
Dan
Beth-anath
Pharpar River
Kedesh
Yiron
Hazor
Lake Huleh
Bashan
ASHER
NAPHTALI
EAST
MANASSEH
Acco
Mishal
Cabul
Gotan
Ashtaroth
Aphek
Nahalal
Hannathon
Capernaum
Sea of Galilee
Achshaph
Rakkath
Rimmon
Hammath
Mt. Carmel
Helkath
ZEBULUN
Sariddoth
Daberath
Jabneel
Edrei
Yokneam
Bethlehem
Sarid
Mt. Tabor
Mt. Tabor
Forbiddah
Lo-debar
Dor
Megiddo
Shunem
Endor
Jarmuth
Ramoth-gilead
Taanach
Jezreel
ISSACHAR
Beth-shan
Plain of Sharon
En-gannim
Jabesh-gilead
Dothan
Ibleam
WEST
MANASSEH
Socoh
Tirzah
Zaphon
Gerasa
AMMON
Joppa
Pirathon
Mt. Ebal
Shechem
Succoth
Peniel
Mahanaim
Aphek
Mt. Gerizim
Tappuah
GAD
Gath-rimmon
Shiloh
Jebud
Ophrah
Inzer
Lod
EPHRAIM
Amman
Ono
Upper
Bethel
Mizpah
Nadan
Beth-nimrah
Gloizim
Beth-horon
Shaalbim
Ramah
Gilgal
Abel-
Jabneel
DAN
Chephirah
Gibeon
Jericho
Shittim
Baalath
Aijalon
Manza
Kirjath-
Adumm
Heshbon
Ashdod
Ekron
Chesalon
jearim
Jerusalem
Beth-hoglah
Timnah
Zorah
Eshtaol
Mt. Nebo
Bezer
Gath
Beth-
BENJAMIN
Medeba
shemesh
Bethlehem
Ashkelon
Beth-zur
Tekoa
REUBEN
Kedemoth
Lachish
Mareshah
Hebron
Jahaz
Gaza
Eglon
Juttah
En-gedi
Dibon
Gerar
Ziklag
JUDAH
Aroer
Bethul
Jattir
Arad
Sharuhen
Ashan
Kabzeel
Hormah
MOAB
Beersheba
Baalah
Kir-hareseth
Hazar-shual
SIMEON
Eltolad
Ezem
Sodom and
Gomorrah (?)
DEAD
SEA
Tamar
EDOM
Arabah
Negev

0   10   20   30   40 Miles
0 10 20 30 40 Kilometers

33°N
32°N
32 N
31°N
30 E

A   B   C   D   E   F

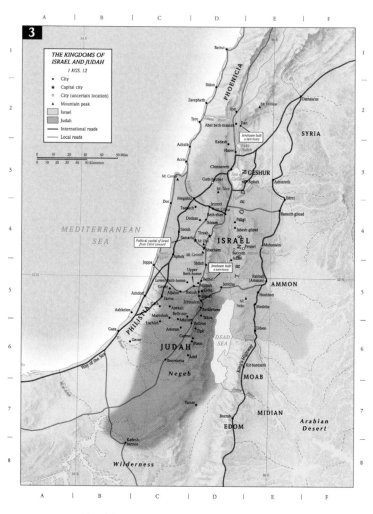

3

THE KINGDOMS OF ISRAEL AND JUDAH
1 KGS. 12

- • City
- ★ Capital city
- ○ City (uncertain location)
- ▲ Mountain peak

Israel
Judah

International roads
Local roads

0   10   20   30   40   50 Miles
0 10 20 30 40 50 Kilometers

MEDITERRANEAN SEA

Beirut

Sidon

Zarepheth

Tyre

Abel beth-maacah

Ijon

PHOENICIA

Damascus

SYRIA

Mt. Hermon

Dan

Jeroboam built a sanctuary

Kedesh

Hazor

Achzib

Lake Hulah

Acco

Chinnereth

Gath-hepher

Aphek

GESHUR

Sea of Galilee

Ashtaroth

Mt. Carmel

Mt. Tabor

Edrei

Dor

Megiddo

Jezreel

Taanach

En-Gedi

Ramoth-gilead

Dothan

Beth-shan

Ibleam

Jabesh-gilead

Political capital of Israel from Omri onward

Samaria

Tirzah

ISRAEL

Penuel

Socoh

Mt. Gerizim

Shechem

Mt. Ebal

Succoth

Mahanaim

Adam

Joppa

Aphek

Shiloh

Jeroboam built a sanctuary

Lower Beth-horon

Upper Beth-horon

Bethel

Jericho

Rabbah (Amman)

AMMON

Gezer

Ekron

Ramah

Geba

Gibeon

Mizpah

Heshbon

Ashdod

Aljalon

Jerusalem

Mt. Nebo

Medeba

Ashkelon

Azekah

Bethlehem

Mareshah

Beth-zur

Tekoa

Dibon

Lachish

Adullam

Hebron

Gaza

Adoram

Carmel

Ziph

Maon

DEAD SEA

Gerar

JUDAH

Arad

King's Highway

Kir-hareseth

Beersheba

Negeb

MOAB

Way of the Sea

Tamar

MIDIAN

Arabian Desert

Bozrah

EDOM

Kadesh-barnea

Wilderness

Adapted from *The Holman Bible Atlas* © 1998. Used by permission.

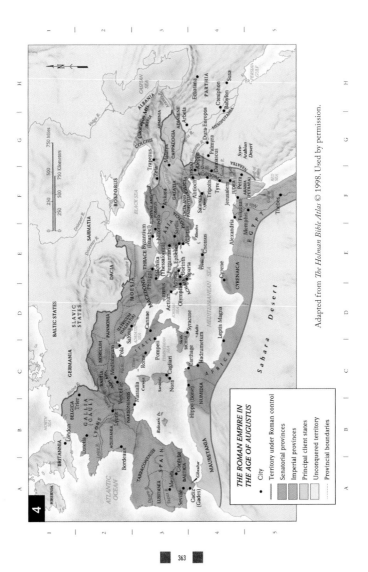

THE ROMAN EMPIRE IN THE AGE OF AUGUSTUS

• City

— Territory under Roman control
Senatorial provinces
Imperial provinces
Principal client states
Unconquered territory
.... Provincial boundaries

Adapted from *The Holman Bible Atlas* © 1998. Used by permission.

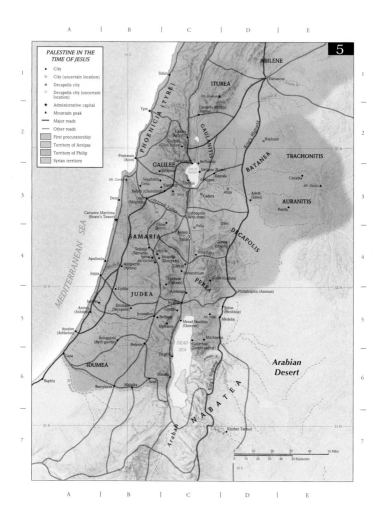

Adapted from *The Holman Bible Atlas* © 1998. Used by permission.

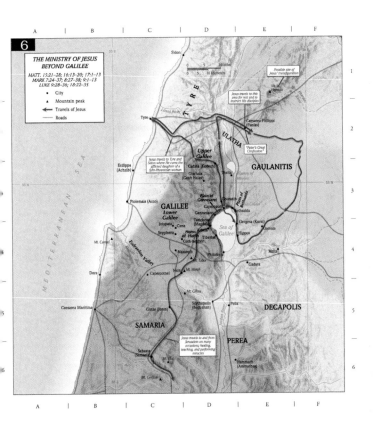

THE MINISTRY OF JESUS BEYOND GALILEE

MATT. 15:21–28; 16:13–20; 17:1–13
MARK 7:24–37; 8:27–38; 9:1–13
LUKE 9:28–36; 18:22–35

- • City
- ▲ Mountain peak
- ← Travels of Jesus
- — Roads

6

Sidon

Possible site of Jesus' transfiguration
Mt. Hermon

Jesus travels to this area for rest and to instruct His disciples

Tyre

Caesarea Philippi (Panias)

ULATHA

"Peter's Great Confession"

GAULANITIS

Jesus travels to Tyre and Sidon where he cures the afflicted daughter of a Syro-Phoenician woman

Upper Galilee

Ecdippa (Achzib)

Gabra (Kedesh)
Gischala (Gush Halav)

Pella

Waters of Merom

Ptolemais (Acco)

Plain of Gennesaret

Chorazin
Capernaum

GALILEE
Lower Galilee

Gennesaret
Tabgha

Bethsaida

Jotapata
Cana
Sepphoris
Gath-hepher

Tabgha (Magdala)

Sea of Galilee

Gergesa (Kursi)

Mt. Carmel

Horns of Hattin
Tiberias

Hippos
Gamala

Nazareth

Philoteria

Abila

Dora

Mt. Tabor

Gadara

Capercotnei

Nain
Mt. Moreh

DECAPOLIS

Mt. Gilboa

Caesarea Maritima

Ginae (Jenin)

Scythopolis (Beth-shan)

Pella

SAMARIA

PEREA

Jesus travels to and from Jerusalem on many occasions, healing, teaching, and performing miracles

Sebaste (Samaria)

Mt. Ebal

Hammath (Amathus)

Mt. Gerizim

MEDITERRANEAN SEA

TYRE

Litani River

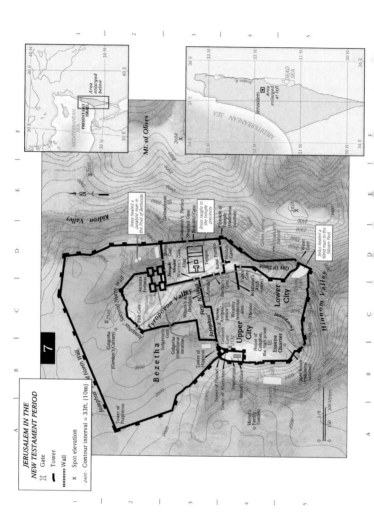

JERUSALEM IN THE
NEW TESTAMENT PERIOD

Gate
Tower
x   Spot elevation
2400 Contour interval = 33ft. (10m)

7

Mt. of Olives

Kidron Valley

Jesus healed a
paralytic man in
the Pool of Bethesda

Jesus taught in
the temple
precincts

Jesus healed a
blind man at the
Pool of Siloam

Bezetha

Tyropoeon Valley

Upper City

Lower City

Hinnom Valley

City Of David

Temple

Antonia
Fortress

Golgotha
(Gordon's Calvary)

Tower of Psephinus

Tower of Mariamne

Herod's Palace

Upper Room
(traditional location)

Essene Quarter

House of Caiaphas,
the high priest

Herod's Family
Tombs

Adapted from *The Holman Bible Atlas* © 1998. Used by permission.

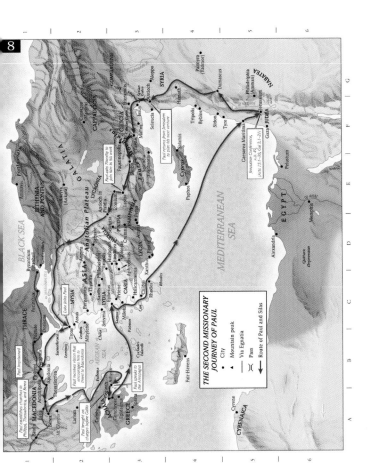

THE SECOND MISSIONARY
JOURNEY OF PAUL

- City
- ▲ Mountain peak
-)(Pass
- → Route of Paul and Silas

Adapted from *The Holman Bible Atlas* © 1998. Used by permission.

ART CREDITS

Alinari/SEAT/Art Resource, NY: Page 9
Art Resource, NY: Pages 27, 47
Bildarchiv Preussischer Kulturbesitz/Art Resource, NY: Page 91
Bill Aron: Page 52
Borromeo/Art Resource, NY: Page 167
Brynn Bruijn/Saudi Aramco World/PADIA: Page 239
Cameraphoto Arte, Venice/Art Resource, NY: Pages 18, 28, 177, 249
Corbis Images: Pages 233, 235, 309
David Malin: Page 233
Dick Doughty/Saudi Aramco World/PADIA: Pages 21, 122
Dorothy Miller/Saudi Aramco World/PADIA: Page 186
Erich Lessing/Art Resource, NY: Pages 110, 124, 133, 165, 184, 219, 275, 279, 325, 345, 351
Greg Schneider: Pages 21, 35, 45, 60, 65, 129, 135, 136, 147, 149, 161, 171, 199, 221, 227, 228, 262, 267, 300, 353
HIP/Art Resource, NY: Pages 56, 66, 68, 223
Images Works, The: Pages 272, 277, 294, 304
The Jewish Museum, NY/Art Resource, NY: Pages 108, 142, 212, 307
John Fenney/Saudi Aramco World/PADIA: Page 253
Khalil Abou El-Nasr/Saudi Aramco World/PADIA: Page 120
Library of Congress: Pages 96, 119, 146, 154, 196, 209, 209, 289, 327, 331, 338
Model Maker R Walsh@www.noahs-ark.net: Page 33
The New York Public Library/Art Resource, NY: Page 104
Nimatallah/Art Resource, NY: Page 346
ORBIMAGE, Inc. Processing by NASA Goddard Space Flight Center: Pages 31, 88, 113, 126, 332
Peter Sanders/Saudi Aramco World/PADIA: Page 216
The Pierpont Morgan Library/Art Resource, NY: Page 83
Réunion des Musées Nationaux/Art Resource, NY: Page 192
A. M. Rosati/Art Resource, NY: Page 163
Scala/Art Resource, NY: Pages 173, 182, 188, 231, 261, 302, 319
SEF/Art Resource, NY: Page 255
Smithsonian American Art Museum, Washington DC/Art Resource, NY: Page 204
Stephen M. Miller: Pages 17, 23, 42, 101
Vanni/Art Resource, NY: Page 37
Victoria & Albert Museum, London/Art Resource, NY: Page 99
Werner Forman/Art Resource, NY: Page 62
Werner Forman; Dr. Eugen Strouhal/Art Resource, NY: Page 233
Zev Radovan: Pages 24, 51, 73, 76, 80, 103, 152, 179, 242, 245, 247, 258, 265, 294, 296, 313, 322

ALSO BY ZACHARY KARABELL

PARTING THE DESERT
The Creation of the Suez Canal

The dream was a waterway that would unite East and West, and ambitious French diplomat and entrepreneur Ferdinand de Lesseps was the mastermind behind the project. Lesseps saw the project through fifteen years of financial challenges, technical obstacles, and political intrigues. He convinced ordinary French citizens to invest their money and won the backing of Napoleon III and of Egypt's Prince Muhammad Said. But the triumph was far from perfect: the construction relied heavily on forced labor, and both technical and diplomatic obstacles constantly threatened completion. The Suez Canal was heralded as a symbol of progress that would unite nations, but its legacy is mixed. *Parting the Desert* is both a transporting narrative and a meditation on the origins of the modern Middle East.

History/978-0-375-70812-1

THE LAST CAMPAIGN
How Harry Truman Won the 1948 Election

In 1948, Harry Truman was one of the most unpopular presidents the country had every known: his Republican rival, Thomas Dewey, was widely thought to be a shoe-in. These two major party candidates were flanked on the far left by the Progressive Henry Wallace, who espoused racial equality, economic justice, and accommodation with the Soviets, and on the far right by white supremacist Dixiecrat Strom Thurmond. In Karabell's masterful analysis we see all aspects of the campaign, from high-minded rhetoric to politics as usual. We also see how radio and print media allowed these disparate views to be brought to the American people, in contrast to the way television has turned politics into prime-time entertainment in recent years. And, of course, we see how Truman scored the greatest comeback victory in the history of American politics.

History/978-0-375-70077-4

VINTAGE BOOKS
Available at your local bookstore, or visit
www.randomhouse.com

Peace Be upon You

Introduction

THERE IS KNOWN history and forgotten history, history that supports our sense of present and history that suggests other pathways. Here is the known: in A.D. 632, the Prophet Muhammad died in
Mecca. He left a vibrant set of teachings, nine wives, a number of children, and several thousand Arab followers who called themselves Muslims. Less than two decades after his death, the adherents of this new
faith had destroyed one empire and crippled another: the Persian shah
was hunted down and killed on the banks of the Oxus River after a
thousand-mile chase; Heraclius, the Byzantine emperor, who had only a
few years before retaken Jerusalem, saw his realm cut in half as the heirs
of Muhammad occupied Damascus, Antioch, Alexandria, and Jerusalem. The emperor collapsed and died when he learned that the city of
Christ had fallen, even though the Muslims had spared the inhabitants
the depredations normally inflicted by conquering armies.

With the Persians annihilated and the Byzantines crippled, the victorious Muslim armies were limited only by numbers and their own internal divisions. Had they stayed united, they might have continued on to
India in the east and Europe in the west. As it was, they paused to fight
two civil wars. Then the conquests began again, and Arab navies reached
the walls of Constantinople before they were halted by a mysterious
substance called Greek fire that set ships ablaze. Thousands of miles to
the west, the general Tariq ibn Ziyad crossed from North Africa into the
Iberian Peninsula and advanced to the Pyrenees. His armies might have
continued all the way to the English Channel had he not been recalled
by the caliph. He returned across the strait that now bears his name—

Jebel Tariq, the Mountain of Tariq, Gibraltar. Some years later, his vanguard met the stiff resistance of Charles Martel at the battle of Tours, in what would later become southern France, and the conquerors retreated from Europe, content with their new kingdom, al-Andalus, where they would remain for nearly a thousand years.

The sudden eruption of Islam left an indelible mark on Europe and established a template of conflict between Islam and the West. But conflict is not the only story: after the Muslims consolidated their gains, the Abbasid caliphate came to power in Baghdad in the middle of the eighth century. At its height, the Abbasid Empire stretched from present-day Morocco to the mountains of Afghanistan. The greatest of its caliphs was Harun al-Rashid, who ruled from Baghdad in a palace as ornate and romantic as subsequent imagination described it. He gathered the greatest musicians, poets, dancers, and, above all, theologians. Poets would appear at court and sing praises to the wonders of wine, while pious scholars, many of whom took the Quranic injunction against alcohol seriously, listened politely. A winning poem or a delightful song could earn a poet gold, or horses groomed in the caliph's stables, or a slave girl for the night.

On countless evenings, the court was transformed into an arena for theological debate. Muslim men of learning, schooled in sharia, the law derived from the Quran, offered their wisdom and drew on the philosophical tradition of the ancient Greeks. The works of Aristotle and Plato were translated into Arabic and used not only to enrich Islam but to create new science and new philosophy. And the caliph was not content simply to take the word of his learned men. He wanted to see how their ideas met opposing theologies, and he invited scholars and preachers of other faiths to his court. Jews, Christians, Buddhists, and Muslims engaged in spiritual and spirited jousts, and each tradition was enriched by knowledge of the others.

From the beginning of Islam, Muslims viewed Jews and Christians as distant, slightly errant, relatives. In honor of the fact that they worshiped the same God and had been given the same revelation as Muhammad, they were called *ahl al-kitab*, the People of the Book. Muslims were expected to treat them honorably. Though Harun al-Rashid went further than most to embrace different faiths, he was fully within the Islamic tradition.

But Harun al-Rashid soon passed into myth, known in the West and

in the Muslim world mostly as a character in *A Thousand and One Nights,* along with Ali Baba, Sinbad the Sailor, and Scheherazade. Today, the notion that a Muslim ruler and a Muslim state might tolerate and even welcome other faiths is alien, not only to people in the Judeo-Christian West but to hundreds of millions of Muslims as well. The early-twenty-first-century world is polarized by the conflict between Muslims, Christians, and Jews. Many Americans and Europeans see Islam as a religion of violence, especially toward those who do not share the faith, and millions of Muslims understand the history of Islam to be one of conquest and victory over nonbelievers, followed by defeat and setbacks. On all sides, this lens distorts the past, constricts our present, and endangers our future.

In truth, each of the three traditions has a core of peace. In churches throughout the world, worshipers turn to one another and say, "Peace be upon you." Walk into any store, home, or mosque anywhere in the Muslim world, and you will be greeted with *salaam alaykum,* "Peace be upon you." And the response is always the same: "And upon you, peace." Jews in Israel will begin and end a conversation with the simple salutation *shalom,* "peace." Each of the faiths teaches its followers to greet friends and strangers with the warm open arms of acceptance. Peace comes first and last.

That is not the common view. Scholars have rarely lost sight of the legacy of coexistence, and a student at almost any university can take courses or read one of the thousands of books and articles that illuminate it. Yet somehow that awareness has remained locked away in university libraries or confined to college courses. As a result, in America and in Europe, all that most people hear is the echo of the Arab conquests that followed Muhammad's death. And in the Muslim world, the memory of imperialism and Western aggression obscures memories of cooperation.

I have spent much of my life asking why this is. The reason may be simple: perhaps times of death and war leave a more lasting impression than periods of peace and calm. Maybe turmoil and confrontation sear the memory more deeply. But there are consequences to our selective readings of the past, in both the Muslim world and the Western world. As much as we want history to say something definitive about the present, it does not. History is a vast canvas, where it is possible to find support for nearly every belief, every statement about human nature, and

every possible outcome of the present. That doesn't make history any less important, but it is up to each of us to use it well.

My first political memories were shaped by growing up in the 1970s, when the Arab-Israeli conflict was a focus of American foreign policy and the cause of unending international tension. With the exception of the Cold War between the United States and the Soviet Union, the Arab-Israeli conflict seemed to be the most likely candidate for plunging the world into chaos, and the phrase "peace in the Middle East" was always met by a derisive laugh. But while the Israeli side of the story was well represented in the media and in classrooms, the Arab side was not. That was the side I wanted to learn about.

That led to more than a decade of study, first as an undergraduate in New York and then as a graduate student in England and in Boston. I studied Arabic, traveled throughout the Middle East, and began to teach the history of the region and the history of Islam. I found that my students usually viewed Islam through a dark prism of Muslim hordes threatening to deluge Christendom. The actual stories might have been blurry in their minds, but each time they saw a picture of a mosque or of an imam leading prayer, it struck a deep negative chord: Islam is a religion of war and violence, and Muslims have clashed with Christians and Jews forever. Those beliefs were hardly limited to my students. They are part of our culture.

Throughout the Middle East and North Africa, I encountered a similar prejudice toward the West. Well before the events of September 11, 2001, there was an entrenched belief that the West is the enemy of Islam. That has only intensified in recent years. Images of an aggressive, imperialist West from the time of the Crusades through the twentieth century animate angry Pakistani preachers in Peshawar, indignant Saudi clerics in Medina, and of course Osama bin Laden. Not only is the court of Harun al-Rashid forgotten, but so too is medieval Iberia, where the Jewish polymath Maimonides, the Sufi mystic Ibn 'Arabi, and a phalanx of Christian monks helped one another unravel the meaning of God and the universe; so too is the twelfth-century Levant, where the inhabitants of Crusader city-states and Muslim emirates traded, bartered, and intermarried; so is the Ottoman Empire, where each religious community, whether Greek Orthodox, Jewish, or Maronite Christian, was allowed almost complete autonomy save for the payment of annual taxes. The

Ottoman system, in fact, was a form of religious freedom nearly as expansive as what existed in the early United States.

But while anti-Western prejudice was part of the culture of the Middle East, it was only one part. The Islam I encountered barely resembled the images I grew up with and that continue to surround us today. The Islam of a cabdriver who helped me navigate Cairo, who stopped to pray and then played his bootleg Madonna cassette, who wanted to know about New York and looked at me as a good way to get a week's worth of pay to feed his family, didn't fit the narrow images that surround us in the West. The Islam of village mosques in Egypt or of a Saudi truck driver who gave me a lift in Jordan and then took an hour-long detour just so I could gaze over the Sea of Galilee; the Islam of Ahmed the hairdresser on a bus to Syria, who did his best to convince a twenty-something me to go to his salon in Damascus; and the Islam of the Kurdish family that sold me a kilim near Lake Van, in eastern Turkey—none of that was familiar.

But what was perhaps most unexpected was how infrequently I encountered Islam in the Muslim world. We have heard so often that there is no separation of church and state in Islam, and that religion is at the heart of everyday life. It is for some, but it shares space with the ebb and flow of daily existence. A man might pray at a mosque, spend a quiet moment submitting to God, and then be plunged into his workaday world, squabbling with neighbors, speaking with friends, watching the soccer game on television, going home to his children. The uneventful reality of everyday life should be obvious, so obvious that it shouldn't even bear mentioning. But what is so startling is that it isn't obvious to us, nor is the prosaic quality of our daily lives obvious to them.

That is true not just for our present but for the past. Today more than ever, bringing the panoply of the past into sharper focus is vital. That means clearing away the cobwebs and paying attention to the long periods where coexistence was more prominent, and also examining the reasons for war and violence that had little to do with religion, even when it was Muslims fighting Christians or Muslims fighting Jews.

Like any prejudice, the mutual animosity between Islam and the West is fueled by ignorance and selective memory. If we emphasize hate, scorn, war, and conquest, we are unlikely to perceive that any other path is viable. If we assume that religion is the primary source of conflict, we

are unlikely to address factors that have nothing to do with religion. Unaware of the history of coexistence between Islam and the West, Americans tend to believe, though perhaps not say, that until the Muslim world becomes less Muslim and more Western, terrorism, nuclear proliferation, and war are inevitable. The same myopia about the past inclines Muslims from Rabat to Jakarta to dismiss talk of democracy and freedom as simply the latest Western, not to mention Christian and Jewish, assault on their independence and dignity.

Reclaiming the legacy of coexistence may not make the world whole, but it does show that Islam and the West need not be locked in a death dance. To the degree that each creed holds that it alone has the key to truth and salvation, there will always be a degree of tension. But rivalry and competition do not lead inexorably to war and violence. Christians, Jews, and Muslims have lived constructively with one another. They have taught one another and they have learned from one another. Judaism was central to the formation of Islam, and for a millennium and a half, until the end of World War II, Jews under Muslim rule enjoyed more safety, freedom, and autonomy than they ever did under Christian rule. Muslim states over the course of fourteen centuries have allowed for religious diversity and not insisted on trying to convert those who follow a different creed. From the beginning of Islam, Christian and Muslim states traded with one another. For fourteen centuries, Christians fought as soldiers in Muslim armies, and in the twentieth century, Arab Christians were instrumental in creating the states of the modern Middle East.

Focusing only on conflict is like skipping every other page while reading a book. It isn't just incomplete; it is misleading to the point of incoherence. At the same time, it is important to avoid the opposite temptation and not replace one distorted reading of the past with another. Too often, those who attempt to rectify the imbalance provide the missing pages but delete the others. The result is just as skewed. The tolerance of Muslim society is praised and moments of concord are highlighted, but the violence and animosity are downplayed. Coexistence is treated as the norm and conflict as the anomaly, when in truth, both are threaded through the past and our present. Also overlooked is the fact that not all cooperation is good cooperation. Alliances between Muslim and Christian states were often the result of "the enemy of my

enemy is my friend," concluded for the purposes of war, not peace. That should temper any optimism that we can all just get along.

So as not to substitute one skewed version of the past with another, the pages that follow present stories of both conflict and cooperation. This book is not meant to be a comprehensive history of the past fourteen hundred years, and most of the stories have been told elsewhere by others in more depth. However, because the periods of concord are less known to most people, the lesson for the present and the future naturally seems optimistic: there is a possibility of peace and constructive coexistence between Muslims, Christians, and Jews—and more to the point, between believing Muslims, Christians, and Jews who, in their heart of hearts, think that their creed and their creed alone reflects God's will. Given today's realities, that is a hopeful message.

This book is, of course, framed by the events of the early twenty-first century. Muslim societies have been their most tolerant when they have been secure. That is hardly unusual in human affairs, but for most of the past century, few Muslim communities have felt secure. One of the results of September 11 is that Western societies have also become insecure, rationally or not. The result is a rise of intolerance on all sides. Increasingly, more people throughout the world believe that Muslim and Western societies are destined to clash and that they will always clash until one or the other triumphs. That belief is poisonous, and one antidote is the rich historical tradition that says other paths are not only possible but have been taken time and again.

By historical standards, today's fissure between Islam and the West is not exceptional, but because of the technologies of death and because of weapons of mass destruction, that fissure has the potential to undo us. That is reason enough to take a look back and recognize that while the relationship between Islam and the West can be fratricidal, it can also be fraternal. Retrieving the forgotten history of relations between Islam and the West isn't a panacea, but it is a vital ingredient to a more stable, secure world. The story begins in the seventh century, on the western coast of the Arabian Peninsula, in the city of Mecca, where a man named Muhammad, born of the tribe of Quraysh, heard the voice of God. "Recite!" he was told, and he did. And the world changed forever.

꙳꙳꙳ ꙳꙳꙳

Iᴎ ᴛʜᴇ Ναмᴇ ᴏꜰ ᴛʜᴇ Lᴏʀᴅ

Sᴏᴍᴇᴛɪᴍᴇ ᴀʀᴏᴜɴᴅ the year 570 in the Western calendar, Muhammad ibn Abdullah was born in the oasis town of Mecca, just off the western coast of the Arabian Peninsula. The town was separated from the Red Sea by a narrow, steep mountain range, and it sat at the edge of the vast desert that defined the Arabian Peninsula. The oasis was dominated by the Quraysh tribe, who controlled the camel trade that passed through Mecca. The trade route linked Yemen, in the south, to the settled agrarian regions hundreds of miles north, which were then divided between the Byzantine emperor and the Sasanian monarch of Persia.

Though Muhammad was a member of the ruling tribe, his clan was not particularly prominent. His father died when Muhammad was a boy, and his uncle Abu Talib became his protector. For most of the next forty years, Muhammad lived an anonymous life like that of many others in Mecca; he established himself as a merchant and married an older widow named Khadija. Had he died before the age of forty, his would have been one of the countless lives invisible to history, and Mecca itself would have remained a small provincial town no more important than thousands of others throughout the world. But around the year 610, Muhammad began to hear the voice of God, and for the first time, God spoke in Arabic.

Muhammad did not share these revelations with anyone other than his wife. Prophets were rarely welcome, and Muhammad did not have sufficient standing in the community to defend himself against adversaries who might not welcome the message he was being given. While the experience of receiving the revelations was physically wrenching for

Muhammad, the substance was socially wrenching for the Meccans. Rather than a system anchored by tribe, clan, and family, Muhammad announced a new order, anchored by God's will and human submission to it—hence the words *islam*, the Arabic word for "submit," and *muslim*, the Arabic word for one who does.

Muhammad began to share the content of what he was being told with a small circle of friends and family, and slowly the message spread. At first, the more powerful members of the Quraysh dismissed the sermons as irrelevant, but as more people started to listen, the Quraysh became concerned. From what they could glean, Muhammad's call represented a challenge to the social order that they dominated.

They were right to be concerned. In their Mecca of tribe and clan, they were supreme. Obeisance was given to the various gods and spirits known as jinn (the kindred English word is "genie"), but one's tribe was more consequential than any god. At the time, there was a nascent sense of monotheism, though not much more developed than a vague notion that there was one god more powerful than the others. But the Quraysh of Mecca were not prepared to embrace Him alone, because that would have upended the status quo. In their world, the tribe, not any god, determined social standing and marriage, and it was up to the tribe and the clan to avenge wrongs committed by others. Tribal authority was absolute—until Muhammad announced that it was not.

The core message was simple: there is one God, one messenger, and a choice. The God is Allah, who is the same as the God of Abraham, the God of the Hebrew prophets, the God of Jesus, and the God of the Christians. The messenger is Muhammad, a man like any other until he was chosen to convey God's word in Arabic. And the choice is to surrender to God's will and to the truth of Muhammad's recitations and thus be saved for eternity.

The initial revelations emphasized the extent of God's power and the degree of human powerlessness in the face of it. Later assembled in the Quran, these verses paint a vivid picture of a world destined to end in a final judgment, and they warn that only those who embrace the message conveyed by Muhammad will be blessed. Because the revelations unfolded over the course of many years, it took some time before they congealed into a coherent belief system. Within a decade, however, Muhammad began to challenge the system of the Quraysh directly.

The most prominent symbol of that confrontation involved the so-called Satanic Verses, which were an earlier version of a portion of the Quran that seemed to allow for the dual worship of Allah and of three of the gods of the Quraysh: al-Lat, al-Uzza, and Manat. The Satanic Verses may have been an attempt to strike a compromise with the increasingly hostile Quraysh, but the Quraysh were not placated. Instructed by the archangel Gabriel, Muhammad recanted the verses. He claimed that they had been a trick of the devil and issued an unequivocal condemnation of al-Lat, al-Uzza, and Manat. They were not gods, he declared, only mere names.

This assault on the prevailing religious system marked a dramatic turn away from conciliation with the rulers of Mecca. Initially, Muhammad had emphasized social justice, the mystery of life, and Allah's supreme power, and had hoped that the Quraysh would accept him. When it became clear that they would not, he indicted not just the religion of the Meccans but the Quraysh who upheld it.

As long as his uncle Abu Talib was alive, Muhammad could be criticized and marginalized but he could not be silenced or physically harmed. When Abu Talib died, in 619, however, Muhammad was placed in a precarious position. Faced with an antagonistic tribe and few options, he was responsible for the security and well-being of a community of followers, most of whom occupied the fringes of Meccan society, and he was beginning to attract adherents beyond the city.

As the position of the Muslims in Mecca deteriorated, it was not simply a problem of discrimination and intimidation. Without the protection that his uncle provided, Muhammad and his followers were in physical danger, and he began looking for a new home. He could not, however, simply pick up and leave. He had to find a tribe in another town willing to offer him protection and acceptance. In a world where resources were scarce and water, date palms, and trade were tightly controlled, there was no such thing as moving to another town to start a new life, and certainly not with eighty followers in tow.

After several false starts, Muhammad through his intermediaries negotiated an arrangement with several tribes in the oasis of Yathrib, later known as Medina, two hundred miles north of Mecca. They wanted Muhammad to become their chief. The tribes of Medina were at an impasse, and they were willing to turn to Muhammad because he could

act as a neutral arbiter. Having secured a home in Medina, Muhammad and his followers then began to leave Mecca, quietly, in small groups, so that the Quraysh would not notice.

The move from Mecca to Medina in 622, known as the Hijra, was one of the defining moments in Islamic history. It led to the establishment of an independent and increasingly powerful Muslim community. It also put this community in direct contact with three Jewish tribes. Muhammad expected that they would embrace him as the last in a long line of prophets. They did not.

THE PEOPLE OF THE BOOK

THE WORLD of early-seventh-century Arabia was sparsely populated. Settlements centered on water sources, and these attracted traders and tribes. Some worshiped local deities; others not at all. But there were also a substantial number of Jews and Christians. The Christians were from several different sects, and few followed the doctrines established by the patriarchs in Constantinople. The Monophysite Christians of Egypt, believing that Christ's human nature had been absorbed by his divine nature, were deeply disenchanted with the Byzantine emperor and the official interpretation of the Trinity; the Christians of Syria and Palestine were only slightly less disaffected; and the Assyrian (Nestorian) Christians of what is now Iraq, who had their own view of the nature of Christ, had long been seen as heretics by the church fathers further west. But even though the Christians of Arabia were disparate, Muhammad and the Meccans would have been familiar with the outlines of their faith, including the life of Christ and the basic precepts of the New Testament.

The Jews had been in Arabia for centuries. Before Muhammad's birth, the Arabian king Dhu Nuwas had converted to Judaism and then launched what appears to have been a mini pogrom against the Christians. In many respects, Arabian Jews were indistinguishable from other tribes. The harsh realities of desert life and the way that people adapted and survived did not know from clan or creed. Jews dressed in the way everyone else dressed, and confronted the same challenges posed by nature. They traded with the Quraysh and other leading Arab tribes, and spoke a dialect of Arabic. Because of their God and certain aspects of

diet, marriage, and law, they were culturally distinct. On the whole, however, they were more familiar than alien to Muhammad, and that may explain his initial hope that they would welcome him and his message. The Quran is quite clear that there is an unbroken line from the Hebrew prophets through Jesus Christ leading ultimately to Muhammad. When the Jews of Medina refused to acknowledge that, Muhammad and his increasingly powerful followers began to treat them as enemies.

Initially, when Muhammad arrived in Medina, an agreement was reached between the two non-Jewish tribes, the three Jewish tribes, and the new community of Muhammad and his followers. Whether this was a written document or a verbal understanding, it became known as the Constitution of Medina, and it was a model of ecumenism. It was also a necessity. Given the circumstances of Muhammad's arrival in Medina, it was essential that the various parties agree on how this new confederation would be governed. Without that, there would be no way to settle the conflicts that would inevitably arise.

Many of the constitution's clauses dealt with relations between the newly arrived Muslims and the major tribes of Medina. "The believers and their dependents constitute a single community [*umma*]" was the first clause, and in terms of later Islamic history, one of the most important. In that simple statement, the unity of Muslims everywhere was established. To this day, there is a deep sense in the Muslim world that all believers constitute one community. That means that state boundaries and doctrinal differences that separate Muslims are false and wrong.

Having established the principle of unity, the constitution laid out the responsibilities of the tribes: they would each police themselves and administer justice to their own members, and murder was forbidden. No individual Muslim was to act in a manner contrary to the will or needs of other Muslims, and believers were enjoined to take care of their dependents. And as for the Jews, they "belong to the community and are to retain their own religion; they and the Muslims are to render help to one another when it is needed." Intertribal alliances were hardly unknown in pre-Islamic Arabia, and tribes did not need to share a religious system in order to act in concert. In that sense, Muhammad and the other interested parties could draw on past precedent in drawing up the Constitution of Medina.[1]

For a brief moment, Medina became a unified Jewish-Muslim community. In the words of the constitution, "The Jews have their religion, and the Muslims have their religion," and yet the two lived side by side as equals and supported each other when and where support was needed. Muhammad saw himself as the last in a series of Jewish prophets, and he instructed his followers to face Jerusalem when they prayed. In this hybrid community, Muhammad had the role of first among equals and the arbiter of disputes. The Constitution of Medina created a precedent for peaceful and cordial coexistence. Unfortunately, it did not last long.

There were three powerful Jewish tribes, and the first that Muhammad confronted was the Banu Qaynuqa. The precise reason for the fissure isn't clear. The ninth-century chronicler al-Baladhuri reported only that "the Jews of Qaynuqa were the first to violate the covenant and the Prophet expelled them from Medina."[2] Al-Bukhari, also writing in the ninth century, mentioned that as the Muslim community grew, the Muslim immigrants needed more land and more date groves, and the reluctance of the Jews to accede to Muhammad's authority made them a legitimate target. Another aggravating factor was the refusal of the Jewish tribes to come to Muhammad's aid during the battle of Badr, when the Muslims of Medina, to the astonishment of the Quraysh, defeated a small army sent from Mecca. Still others claim that hostilities erupted because an Arab woman was the victim of a practical joke that resulted in her skirt riding up too high, which led a Muslim man to kill the perpetrator, who happened to be Jewish. Whatever the proximate cause, the Jews of the Banu Qaynuqa refused to validate Muhammad's claims to prophethood. After a standoff, they were expelled, and that led to a symbolic shift in how Muslims prayed. Instead of facing Jerusalem, they now turned toward Mecca. Jerusalem would remain a holy city for Muslims, but after the banishment of the Banu Qaynuqa, Mecca became the focal point.

Over the next three years, the Muslims of Medina gained converts, including some Jews. Events alternated between skirmishes with the Quraysh and confrontation with the remaining Jewish tribes. After Muhammad led his followers to a battlefield victory against the Meccans, he broke with the second Jewish tribe, the Banu Nadir. They were expelled after a two-week siege, but unlike their predecessors, they were not allowed to take their weapons.

The final tribe, the Banu Qurayza, having watched as Muhammad

consolidated his power, made a fateful choice: they cast their lot with the Meccans, who were preparing a final assault on Medina. The Muslims had taken control of the trade caravans, and had cut Mecca off from the source of its wealth and strength. While the Banu Qurayza did not actually consummate an alliance with the Meccans, they did not support Muhammad, and may well have been in negotiations with his enemies. Either way, they were in a difficult position. A victory for the Meccans would reduce the autonomy and influence of Medina, and lessen the power of the remaining Jewish tribe even if it removed the threat of Muhammad. A victory for the Muslims was hardly much better, and indeed turned out to be much worse. After the Meccans failed to take Medina in 627 and were forced to retreat, Muhammad ordered an attack on the Qurayza, who succumbed after a siege that lasted nearly a month. This time, the penalty wasn't expulsion; it was execution.

The fate of Medina's Jews did not establish a good precedent for future relations, but subsequent history has magnified the conflict. Some of the animosity between the Muslims and Jews of Medina was about God and prophecy, but just as much was about power and who had it. After their flight to Medina, Muhammad and the Muslims struggled to build a viable state, and the Jews of Medina as well as the Meccans represented real threats. In seventh century Arabia, when tribes fought, expulsion was the typical consequence of defeat, and the execution of all adult males, while extreme, was not beyond the pale. In truth, it would not have been beyond the pale anywhere in the world at that time, and much greater acts of brutality were commonplace.

The Jews may have been a threat to Muhammad, but Muhammad was also a threat to the Jews. He offered a vision of the world that was at once similar to the Torah and yet not. Many of the stories in the Quran were part of the Jewish tradition and familiar to the Jews. But Muhammad's telling of those stories was different, in both subtle and significant ways. For instance, in the Quran, Joseph is imprisoned for refusing the advances of a powerful woman, but that woman is not Pharaoh's wife but rather a governor's wife, and in a scene not in the Bible she is then made to recant her accusations when Joseph is brought into Pharaoh's court. The theological consequences of these discrepancies may be minor, but the problem for both Jews and Muslims was the fact they existed at all. Moses, Noah, Jacob, and other biblical heroes figure prominently in the Quran, and while their stories are largely the same as in the Torah, they

are not precisely the same. And that in itself opened a fissure between Muhammad and the Jews.

The reaction of the Jewish tribes was a mixture of bemusement and derision. They viewed Muhammad as a bumpkin, and assumed that he couldn't get the Bible right. At least that is the impression given by later sources. It's difficult to be sure of any of what happened in Muhammad's lifetime, given the long remove between the written record of what transpired and the actual events. While the gospels, for instance, were composed within decades after the death of Jesus, the most authoritative written biographies of Muhammad date from more than two centuries after his death. Even so, it is hard to imagine that the Jews of Arabia, believing themselves to be the heirs of two thousand years of tradition, would have rushed to embrace a man from Mecca claiming to wear the mantle of a prophet. Initially, they could stand apart from Muhammad, and still hope to use him to keep the peace in Medina. As his political and military power increased, and as he began to attract more converts, he became a threat. The Jewish tribes did what they could to undermine Muhammad. They failed, but the way they were then treated had little to do with their Jewishness.

To a considerable degree, how Muhammad confronted the Jews was little different from how his immediate successors dealt with Arabian tribes who refused to bow to the Muslim caliphs. In fact, it was little different from the way the warring tribes of Israel dealt with one another during the rise and fall of the kingdom of David and Solomon, recounted in the Bible. What was distilled and preserved in historical memory, however, was that from its founding days, Islam did not tolerate Judaism. That memory seeped into Muslim cultures and into Western culture, while the context evaporated.

THE PASSAGES from the Quran that speak about the Jews are often linked to passages that speak about Christians. Muhammad encountered fewer Christians than Jews, but Christians were also part of the theological landscape. To the north and across the Red Sea to the west, the Byzantine Empire was ruled by a Christian emperor, and while Muhammad and the other inhabitants of the west coast of Arabia were not immersed in the issues that troubled the Byzantines, bits and pieces of news made their way along the trade routes. So did bits and pieces of

Christian theology, which was lumped with Jewish traditions to form from Muhammad's perspective (and that of other Arabs as well) a single continuum, from Noah to Abraham to Joseph, leading inexorably to Jesus.

In the Quran, Jews and Christians are often treated as one people, related to each other but distinct from the new community of Muslims. Together, Jews and Christians were called the *ahl al-kitab,* the People of the Book; the "Book" is the Bible. The Quran is ambivalent about the People of the Book, and the verses that discuss them alternate between respect and scorn. On the one hand, the People of the Book, like the Muslims, had been chosen by Allah to receive his message. That entitled them to recognition and honor. According to Quran 28:63, "Those to whom we gave the Book before this believe in it, and when it is recited to them, they say, 'We believe in it; surely it is the truth from our Lord. Indeed even before we had surrendered.' These shall be given their wage twice over for what they patiently endured." Or 29:46: "Dispute not with the People of the Book, save in the fairer manner . . . and say, 'We believe in what has been sent down to us, and what has been sent down to you; our God and your God is One, and to him we have surrendered.' " These are two of many passages where Muslims are ordered to treat Christians and Jews with the utmost respect, because they answered God's call earlier and stayed true to their faith.

But other passages adopt a different tone and criticize the People of the Book for losing their way. "We sent Noah, and Abraham, and We appointed the Prophecy and the Book to be among their seed; and some of them are guided, and many of them are ungodly. Then We sent, following in their footsteps, Our Messengers; and We sent, following, Jesus son of Mary, and gave unto him the Gospel. And we set in the hearts of those who followed him tenderness and mercy . . . but many of them are ungodly" (57:26–27). Other passages drip with antagonism. "The Jews say, 'Ezra is the son of God'; the Christians say, 'The Messiah is the Son of God.' That is the utterance of their mouths, conforming with the unbelievers before them. God assail them. How they are perverted!" (9:30).[3]

It would have been much simpler for the early Muslim community to make a clean, harsh break from the Jews and the Christians. Rather than wrestle over whether they were entitled to special treatment, Muhammad and his immediate successors could have dismissed them as apostates and adversaries and presented them with the choice to convert or

be eliminated. But that was not an option. Just as Christian societies, no matter how violently and harshly they persecuted Jews, were unable to arrive at a justification for ending Judaism, Muslim societies had to make room for the People of the Book.

The result was ambivalence. Jews and Christians were neither warmly embraced nor unequivocally condemned. The Quran frequently acknowledges that they were, in their time, chosen by God, and that initially they heeded his call. The message that Allah delivered to the Hebrew prophets and then to Jesus was pure, but according to the Quran and Muslim tradition, in the process of transcribing what God had said, Jews got the stories and the morals wrong, and Christians erred in thinking of Jesus as the Son of God rather than as a prophet and the son of Mary. The mistakes committed by the People of the Book made the revelations to Muhammad necessary. Just as God repeatedly sent messengers to the tribes of Israel when they strayed from the path, he sent Muhammad to the Arabs. The new revelations were addressed to the People of the Book as well, and the fact that most of them did not rush to follow Muhammad was taken as proof of how far they had strayed. The more they resisted, the more the later verses of the Quran railed against their ungodliness.

For Muslims, the great failing of the People of the Book was that they had distorted the message. That created anger and indignation, but rarely hatred. The Quran condemns the People of the Book for perversion but also commands Muslims to treat them differently than other nonbelievers. Jews and Christians were not the only ones to merit special treatment; Zoroastrians were later added to the mix. But Jews and Christians were the only ones linked so intimately to Islam. In fact, because of a shared tradition, Jews, Muslims, and Christians could all be considered People of the Book. They were all members of a family, a family created by God. And just as a brother cannot kill his brother no matter how misguided that brother is, Muslims had to find a way to tolerate Christians and Jews, no matter how lost, foolish, and sinful they were.

In looking for the foundation of relations between the faiths, it makes sense to focus primarily on how Muslims dealt with Jews and Christians rather than on how Jews and Christians dealt with Muslims. Judaism evolved over centuries before the emergence of Christianity, and early Christianity had to grapple with Judaism but not with Islam. Muslim identity, however, was tied to the People of the Book. There was never a

time when Muslims did not have to grapple with Jewish and Christian arguments against Islam. From the start, they had to figure out how to deal with Jews and Christians living next to them and under them as conquered people. As a result, Muslims had to think through relations between the faiths far more than Christians and Jews ever did. The subsequent history of relations between the three, therefore, begins with how Muslims treated Jews and Christians. Only after the first wave of Muslim conquests were Jews and Christians forced to invent theologically acceptable compromises that would allow them to acquiesce to Muslim rule.

THE CONQUESTS

MUHAMMAD'S political achievements were impressive. What happened shortly after his death was astonishing. Between 627 and 632, Muhammad removed the Jews from Medina, defeated the last of the Meccan resistance, and extended the reach of Islam throughout the Arabian Peninsula and north toward the fringes of the Byzantine and Sasanian Empires. When Muhammad died, in 632, his father-in-law and one of the earliest and oldest converts to Islam, Abu Bakr, was chosen as his successor and given the title *khalif rasul Allah*. The title literally translates as "successor to the messenger of God," but what that meant in practice was anyone's guess. It clearly did not suggest that Abu Bakr was also a messenger of God, because Muhammad was heralded as "the seal of the prophets," and therefore the final emissary to be sent by Allah before the end of days. It also did not mean that Abu Bakr or any subsequent caliph had the same moral or religious authority that Muhammad had possessed.

The issue of religious authority raises a freighted question: what is the connection between church and state in Islam? Because of Muhammad's role as both prophet and leader, it is sometimes said that Islam was born as a theocracy. In some respects, that is true. The community of Medina was both a religious community of the faithful and a political community composed of Muslim emigrants, the Arab tribes of Medina, and for a time Jews, with Muhammad as the first among equals. But while Muhammad was blessed as a prophet and revered, he was not seen as infallible, at least not during his lifetime. His was, therefore, a theoc-

racy that understood that distinction between an all-powerful God and an honored leader.

Though Medina under Muhammad is revered by Muslims as an ideal, it has never been a viable model for Muslim society. When Muhammad was alive, there was no church-state dichotomy. However, as the Muslim community took on a military character after his death, there was a clear sense that the political and military realms were separate from the spiritual and personal. That was supported by the Quran, which drew an unambiguous distinction between the spirit and the flesh, and between the earthly world and the world beyond. Some verses in the Quran speak to human history and worldly affairs; others speak to the mysterious power of God and man's insignificance in the face of that. Muhammad was both prophet and political leader, but while those roles were united in him, they were distinct.

The questions surrounding the parameters of the caliph's authority demonstrate that most Muslims understood the distinction. No one questioned that Abu Bakr, as caliph, would lead the armies. But most rejected the notion that he had inherited the doctrinal authority of Muhammad. Respected for his wisdom and acclaimed for his piety, Abu Bakr ordered his soldiers to attack the tribes who had used Muhammad's death as an excuse to break away from the community of Islam. The fragmentation of the community after Muhammad's death was a crucial test: if Abu Bakr had not been able to maintain the coalition that Muhammad had assembled, it is more than likely that Islam would have wilted before it had even bloomed and that the message would never have made its way out of the desert. The brief, bloody wars waged by Abu Bakr to reestablish the federation may have been couched in the religious terms of apostasy, but the political dimension was just as important.

These wars not only cemented the legacy of Muhammad, but also established a hierarchy of priorities that remain until today. Many of the Arab tribes that Abu Bakr defeated had only recently become Muslims; others had never truly converted in the first place. All were treated as enemies of the faith who deserved (and were given) no mercy. Ever since, apostasy has been the most severe offense against the Muslim community, greater by several orders of magnitude than anything that a non-Muslim can do. Only a Muslim can be a Muslim apostate, and only apostates are marked as unforgivable. Neither Christians nor Jews

roused that level of animosity, not in Muhammad's lifetime and not for most of the next fourteen hundred years.

Within two years of Muhammad's death, most of the Arabian Peninsula was under the control of the caliph. In a few instances, there was slaughter, but Abu Bakr's greater aim was to subjugate and unite the tribes, not annihilate them. One of the best ways to ensure loyalty for the future was to reward the faithful in this world with material riches. Usually, tribal chieftains consolidated their authority by leading their followers on successful raids. But with Arabia more or less unified, and intertribal raiding no longer permissible, the caliph had to look elsewhere for booty, and the most promising targets were the rich empires of the Persians and the Byzantines to the north.

In the space of less than a decade, Arabs conquered the area now covered by Egypt, Israel, Syria, Lebanon, Jordan, Iraq, southern Turkey, western Iran, and the Arabian Peninsula. At the time, Iran and Iraq were controlled by the Persian Sasanian Empire, and the regions to the west of the Euphrates River were ruled by the Byzantine emperor in Constantinople. Both were elaborate, centralized states, with monotheistic state religions—Zoroastrianism in Persia and Christianity in Byzantium. Both had existed for centuries, and had inherited state structures, armies, and imperial traditions that stretched back centuries more. The Sasanians were the latest in a long line of dynastic potentates that had governed Persia, part of a heritage that included Darius and Xerxes and the armies that had nearly overwhelmed classical Greece five hundred years before the birth of Christ. For their part, the Byzantines were the direct offshoot of the Roman Empire, and Christianity had become the state religion after the conversion of Emperor Constantine in the first decades of the fourth century.

On the face of it, the fact that Arab nomads swept out of the desert and crushed these dynasties is difficult to fathom. But in history as in life, timing is everything. The Sasanians and Byzantines had just concluded an especially bitter and taxing war against each other. The Sasanians had taken Jerusalem and Damascus and penetrated deep into Asia Minor, cutting off Egypt and North Africa and jeopardizing the integrity of the Byzantine Empire. The emperor Heraclius had simultaneously been confronted with an invasion of Slavic tribes that threatened Constantinople from the Balkans. Only by virtue of his great skill as both a leader and a general did he manage to withstand these dual

onslaughts. While the war between the Persians and the Byzantines wasn't a religious conflict per se, the Persian king treated Heraclius with contempt, and Jerusalem was singled out for humiliation. In turn, as Heraclius began to reverse the tide, he destroyed Zoroastrian fire temples in revenge.

Heraclius proved his mettle as a leader and a commander when he repelled both the Slavs and the Sasanians. The culmination was the liberation of Jerusalem. Having achieved an improbable victory, Heraclius made a point of going to the holy city in 630. To great fanfare, he personally restored the True Cross to its place in the Anastasis (later called the Church of the Holy Sepulchre) and proclaimed the recent triumph of the empire as a victory for Christ. "There was much joy at his entrance to Jerusalem," said a contemporary account, "sounds of weeping and sighs and abundant tears...extreme exaltation of the emperor, of the princes, of all the soldiers and inhabitants of the city; and nobody could sing the hymns of our Lord on account of the great and poignant emotion of the emperor and the whole multitude."[4]

But the war had taken a toll on both regimes, on their treasuries and their soldiers, and neither had recovered its full strength four years later when the successor to Abu Bakr, the caliph Umar ibn al-Khattab, ordered his forces to attack. The Persian Empire had descended into a brief but ruinous civil war, and Heraclius had withdawn in exhaustion from an active role in leading the Byzantine armies. In contrast to an emperor whose power was waning, the new caliph was a physical and military dynamo, an early convert known for his passionate, bristling persona and his unbridled allegiance to Muhammad. At some point during his rule, Umar acquired the title *amir al-mumin*, Commander of the Faithful, which became part of the moniker of all subsequent caliphs. Umar took the military dimension of his role seriously, and he executed it brilliantly.

Three battles essentially decided the fate of both empires. In 634, at Ajnadin, south of Jerusalem, and in 636, at Yarmuk, in Syria, the main Byzantine divisions in the region were wiped out by smaller, more mobile Arab forces. In 637, at the battle of Qadisiya, near the Euphrates, the Persian army led by General Rustam was annihilated. The Persian capital of Ctesiphon was occupied, and for the next decade and a half, the Sasanian emperor was pursued by Arab detachments across Persia until he was cornered and killed. To the west, in 639, the Muslim com-

mander Amr ibn al-As invaded Egypt. The cities of Alexandria and Heliopolis (north of modern Cairo) quickly fell, and by 641, all of Egypt was under the control of the caliph.

As Arab armies fanned out across the Near East and North Africa, they were faced with a problem: how were they going to govern the conquered people? Would there be a mass exodus of Arabs from the peninsula into the major urban centers? Would they raid and then retreat with the spoils? Would they isolate themselves from the Christians, Jews, and Zoroastrians that comprised the population of the conquered lands? And how would they handle societies that were primarily agricultural, that required a different social organization to keep irrigation works intact, to ensure harvests? Some Arabs had settled in cities like Mecca, but others were primarily nomadic, and not accustomed to living in one location year-round. There was nothing in the Quran to provide an easy answer to these new and urgent questions, and the breathtaking speed of the victories meant that there was no luxury to sit back and deliberate over options.

Because the Quran had been so explicit about the People of the Book, however, there was some guidance about how to treat the Christian populations of Syria, Palestine, and Egypt. Zoroastrians, who made up a considerable portion of the Persian Empire, were also granted protections. Like the Quran, the Zoroastrian holy text, the Avesta, had initially been an oral revelation, but parts of it were eventually put in writing. That made it possible for the Arab conquerors to include the Zoroastrians as a People of the Book, simply because they had a book. But alongside *ahl al-kitab,* another category developed, the *ahl al-dhimma* (People of the Pact), which encompassed not only the Zoroastrians but a whole range of sects and local religions that were alien to the Arabs of Mecca and Medina.

The line between People of the Book and People of the Pact is hard to discern. The first "pact" was supposedly between the defeated Jews of Medina and Muhammad, but it's unclear whether such a pact existed or whether it was an invention of later theologians. Over the centuries, the legal distinctions between People of the Book and People of the Pact were the subject of countless treatises and debates. Muslim jurists, like jurists everywhere, parsed every conceivable angle, and probed every hypothetical issue they could imagine. By the middle to late seventh century, however, the idea of *dhimmis* (the term for someone who is enti-

tled to the protections guaranteed to the People of the Pact) was ensconced in the Arab-Muslim empire.[5]

The People of the Book who lived under Muslim rule were *dhimmis*. They were set apart, favorably, by their possession of holy scripture inspired by revelations from God (Allah). That entitled them to a modicum of respect by Muslims. But to earn favored status, the People of the Book had to acknowledge the authority of their Muslim rulers, and they had to pay a poll tax. In return, they were allowed to govern themselves. They could worship freely in churches or synagogues or fire temples. They could eat pork and drink alcohol. They picked their own local leaders who had wide latitude over most aspects of daily life, from marriage to inheritance and estates, from petty crimes to crimes of passion. The People of the Book had no armies; they did not control any city or province; but most of the time, they were left alone.

This didn't mean that they were treated well, only that they were not treated as badly as conquered peoples usually were. Later traditions suggest that both Muhammad and Umar, for instance, were not willing to extend this tolerance to those Jews and Christians living in Arabia itself, and Umar is said to have carried out the last major expulsion of the Jews of Arabia when he removed the Jewish tribes from the Khaybar oasis. Outside the Arabian Peninsula, however, the treatment was more benign.

The Arab-Muslim invasions were significantly less violent and disruptive than the Persian-Byzantine wars that immediately preceded them, or than many of the previous wars of conquest undertaken by the likes of Alexander the Great and the Roman legions. Though there were a fair number of pitched battles, many cities fell without bloodshed. Damascus in the seventh century was a key part of the Byzantine Empire, but its inhabitants were disenchanted with the emperor and with the church leaders in Constantinople. The key issue was a long-simmering doctrinal dispute over the nature of Christ, and the bishops in Constantinople had little patience with the intransigence of churches in Damascus and throughout the Near East. As a result, when faced with an Arab army near its walls, Damascus put up only token resistance.

Besieged by five thousand horsemen commanded by Khalid ibn al-Walid, the citizens of Damascus were faced with a quandary: they had little enthusiasm for laying down their lives to defend the empire, but they did not want to surrender the city only to face slaughter. The bish-

ops of the city's various sects entered into talks with Khalid to discuss a peaceful surrender. To assuage their concerns, Khalid wrote out a promise on a piece of parchment, stating,

> In the name of Allah, the compassionate, the merciful. This is what Khalid would grant the inhabitants of Damascus, if he enters therein: he promises to give them security for their lives, property and churches. Their city-wall shall not be demolished; neither shall any Muslim be quartered in their houses. Thereunto we give them the pact of Allah and the protection of his Prophet, the caliphs, and the Believers. So long as they pay the poll-tax, nothing but good shall befall them.

Having secured these promises from Khalid, the bishops unlocked the gates, let the Muslims enter the city, and doomed the Byzantine garrison to defeat.

Similar scenes were repeated throughout the Near East. The Christian inhabitants of the city of Hims, north of Damascus, were so infuriated with Heraclius that they chose to join the Arabs in order to fight against the Byzantines. The Arab commanders promised the people of Hims that they would be protected if they surrendered. Instead, they volunteered to help. "We like your rule and justice far better than the state of oppression and tyranny in which we were. The army of Heraclius we shall indeed repulse from the city." The Jews also joined the cause. "We swear by the Torah," they told the Muslim commanders, "no governor of Heraclius shall enter the city of Hims unless we are first vanquished and exhausted."[6]

In a similar vein, the Arab general who led the invasion of Egypt, Amr ibn al-As, went out of his way to assuage the fears of Egyptian Christians. Legend has it that before he became a Muslim, Amr had saved the life of a Christian deacon from Alexandria. In gratitude, the deacon purchased Amr's entire stock of goods, and Amr then began to do regular business in Egypt. The Nile Delta was the breadbasket of the Mediterranean, and Alexandria was a commercial hub. It was Amr ibn al-As who purportedly convinced the caliph Umar to authorize an invasion, and one of the reasons he gave was that the Christian population, like the Christians of Syria, was disaffected with the rule of Constantinople.

The rift between the Egyptian church and Constantinople had been

growing for decades, and it was based on both politics and theology. The Coptic Church of Egypt adhered to the doctrine of Monophysitism, which stated that Christ had one nature, and that nature was divine. (Hence the term "Monophysite," from the Greek meaning "one nature.") This was in direct contradiction to the creed that had been established by the Council of Chalcedon almost two hundred years before, which held that Christ had both a human nature and a divine nature. Though these debates hardly seem worth fighting and dying for, in the early centuries of Christianity the exact nature of Christ was the most divisive issue. Wars were waged over whether Christ was equally divine and human, more human than divine, or more divine than human. The division between Egypt and Constantinople also had a political dimension. The bishop who had been sent by the emperor to keep the Copts in line succeeded only in intimidating the Egyptians with pogroms and inquisitions. By the time of the Arab conquests, the alienated populace was deeply resentful of Byzantine rule.

Amr ibn al-As took advantage of these strains in order to gain the allegiance of the Egyptians, and that may explain why Egypt fell so quickly to an army of less than five thousand soldiers. Later Arab chroniclers even claimed that the Coptic Church actively aided the Arabs and helped them defeat the Byzantine garrisons in the Delta, having been promised by Amr that their churches would be undisturbed and their tax burden manageable. For the Copts and their bishops, it was a tolerable trade-off. They knew they had to pay taxes to someone, and at least the Muslims would allow them to practice their faith the way they wished, free from the repressive, arrogant authority of Constantinople.[7]

In many respects, the conquests were swift and largely bloodless. Instead of the usual scenes of wanton death and destruction, the cities and towns occupied by the Arabs were treated almost gently, and seem to have welcomed the exchange of rulers. Given the disarray of both the Persian and the Byzantine armies in the region, and the absence of strong organized resistance, that makes sense. There was, in essence, no need for substantial violence. Yet that has not prevented other conquerors at other times from committing nauseating atrocities. Why, then, were the Muslim conquerors relatively benign? The paucity of sources makes it difficult to answer that question, but one thing is undeniable: the Quran instructed Muslims to respect the People of the Book, and that is precisely what they did. The early history of Islam, there-

fore, unfolded against the backdrop of toleration for the religions of the conquered.

There were also pragmatic reasons. Compared to the number of people spread across thousands of miles of territory, the percentage of Arabs and Muslims was tiny. The early caliphs grasped that there was no way for them to rule without the active cooperation of the conquered. In fact, unless the local administrative systems were left intact, the caliph would not be able to gather taxes; without the local officials, who would physically collect them? And while there was pressure on the caliph to allow his commanders to raid and pillage the occupied cities, that would have created further complications. Once that was done, what then? Many of the tribal leaders who led these armies also wanted the caliph to allow their troops to take land and replace the Byzantine or Persian administrators. But then the armies would have disbanded, leaving the newly acquired regions in a vulnerable and potentially chaotic state.

The solution was to create garrison cities, at Basra and Kufa in what is now southern Iraq, and to leave only a minimal number of troops in the older, established urban centers. The garrison settlements in southern Iraq, and later one at Fustat (Cairo), on the Nile, were a way to keep the armies intact, but that in turn meant that there were precious few soldiers to maintain control of formerly Byzantine cities such as Damascus, Jerusalem, and Antioch, or of Persian centers like Rayy and Merv. That made it imperative for the Muslims to do as little as possible to disrupt the status quo in the newly acquired lands. They removed the top layer of Byzantine and Persian administration, but initially they left the other layers untouched. In that sense, religious toleration was a pragmatic component of an overall strategy of staying separate from the conquered peoples.

Later accounts portray Muslim armies sweeping across the region. But while they did inflict crushing defeats on the legions of two different empires, and then occupied a large number of cities, many people in the lands now controlled by the Arabs were only vaguely aware of what had happened. In fact, for years, many had only sketchy details about the conquests. They knew that the Byzantine rule had evaporated, and that people dressing and speaking differently had appeared demanding tax payments. They learned that these were Arabs calling themselves Muslims, and slowly, they gleaned the basic precepts of Islam. But as late as 680, a Christian named John from the city of Fenek in the region of

Mosul wrote an account that was remarkably uninformed about Islam and about the Muslim conquests, although he praised the Arabs for respecting both ordinary Christians and Christian monks. Other Christians from different regions were similarly confused. This was partly a function of the isolation of most people and the time it took for news to spread from the metropolises to the provinces. But it was also the result of the particular nature of the conquests. As one scholar has noted, the Muslims left such a light footprint on the parts of the world they occupied that it took more than a century before many of the people under their rule began to adjust their lives significantly and figure out what had taken place between 630 and 640.[8]

The simple fact is that if you weren't in Damascus or central parts of Iraq, if you weren't in the Nile Delta or the old centers of Sasanian power, your life didn't change dramatically after the conquests. Once every year or so, a group of soldiers and a local governor might appear to demand payment, but that had also been the case under the prior regime. In time, a few soldiers settled in your town, and they might have been Muslim. Gradually, local governors appointed by the caliph set up their own commercial and cultural networks, which were tied to the larger world of Islam, but this happened so slowly that it would have been almost imperceptible to any one person living during these years.

Much of this is contrary to the imagined history of Arab warriors carrying the Quran in one hand and a scimitar in the other. Yes, they were driven by religion, and yes, they were magnificent fighters, mobile, unconventional, and fearless. They combined a pre-Islamic tradition of raiding with the solidarity and certainty of true believers. But they were also tribal, and tribes rarely admit converts. The message of Islam had been given to Muhammad in Arabic for an Arab audience, and while Arabs believed that the message was universally true, they did not go out of their way to convince non-Arabs. They sought to rule and to tax the peoples of the Near East and beyond, but they did not try to save their souls or show them the true light. If non-Arabs wanted to hear the message, it was there to be heard, but they were not embraced if they did. Non-Arab converts were initially treated not much better than the People of the Book, and in some circumstances they may have been treated worse. There were reports, shaded by later animosity no doubt, that the governor of Iraq in the late seventh century, Hajjaj ibn Yusuf, known as a brutal but effective administrator, rounded up all the non-Arab converts

from Basra and Kufa, tattooed their foreheads, and sent them back to their villages and towns.

Eventually, the shabby treatment of converts would lead to a revolution, but for the first hundred years after the conquests, the empire was ruled by an Arab elite that only gradually became absorbed into the societies that they had conquered. While in Egypt and the Tigris-Euphrates region garrison cities were created, even in the far-flung corners of the empire, in Andalus to the west or in the remote corners of what is now northeast Iran and Afghanistan, the Arabs stood apart and separate, secure in their faith, uninterested in missionary work.

Scholars have long since disposed of the image of Islam being spread by the sword, but that has not altered popular imagination. The belief that the Arab conquests were wars of conversion has been stubbornly immune to the facts. Forced conversion would have been directly at odds with the Quran, which states in one of its least ambiguous verses, "No compulsion is there in religion" (2:256). This clear scriptural injunction was obeyed by the early conquerors.

In only one tenuous respect is the image of Islam as welded to the sword legitimate. Eventually, the vast lands that came under Muslim domination did become Muslim societies. The process of conversion took centuries, and happened peacefully and organically. But conversion did happen, and only because of those initial military victories followed by strong Muslim dynasties that managed, with some difficulty, to retain control. That was no small accomplishment. History is littered with victories that did not lead to new empires. Insofar as the sword and the Quran together removed Christianity as the dominant religion in North Africa, Egypt, the Near East, and, much later, Turkey, they did go hand in hand. But only by conflating centuries can it be said that Islam was spread by force, and it simply cannot be said that the initial conquests imposed Islam on the conquered.[9]

While there is ample documentation of these facts, not all accounts of the conquests convey an impression of Muslim tolerance, and the gap between what happened and what people think happened is partly the result of Christian chroniclers. At the time of the fall of Jerusalem, the patriarch, Sophronius, led the resistance to the Arabs and negotiated the surrender of the city. He also acted as Umar's tour guide in 638 when the caliph made a pilgrimage to receive the city personally. Though Jerusalem had been demoted by Muslims in favor of Mecca, it was still

considered a holy site, and Umar understood the significance of its passing into Muslim hands. Entering the walls, he rode his usual white camel and wore his usual unpretentious bedouin garb. Umar was met by the resplendent patriarch, wearing the rich robes of his office, and surrounded by his equally resplendent retinue. The caliph was taken on a tour of the holy sites, after which he promised that he would leave the Anastasis (Holy Sepulchre) untouched. He then ordered that a mosque be built on the Temple Mount, which less than a century later was replaced with Al-Aqsa.

The occupation of Jerusalem was among the least tumultuous that it has ever known, and for a city that has been raided, sacked, and destroyed so many times, that is saying something. Even so, that did not endear the Arabs to the vanquished. The construction of a mosque on the site of Solomon's Temple was seen by Jews and Christians as a sign of God's severe displeasure. The patriarch interpreted the victory of the Arabs as a punishment for the sins of Christians. "If we were to live as is dear and pleasing to God," he told his congregation, "we would rejoice over the fall of the Saracen enemy and observe their near ruin and witness their final demise. For their blood-loving blade will enter their hearts, their bow will be broken and their arrows will be fixed in them."

Sophronius was a staunch defender of the two-nature creed enshrined by the Council of Chalcedon, and he used the triumph of the Arabs as an excuse to berate dissident sects throughout the Near East, especially the Egyptian Copts, for rejecting that formula. In retribution, God had sent the Arabs to "plunder cities, devastate fields, burn down villages, set on fire the holy churches, overturn the sacred monasteries, oppose the Byzantine armies arrayed against them." Though acting as an agent of God's wrath, Muhammad, continued the patriarch, was a "devil," and his message a blasphemy. But the Christians had only themselves to blame for straying, and that had led to their utter defeat.[10]

The patriarch viewed the Muslim occupation as a tragedy on a cosmic scale. So did his master, the emperor Heraclius. For both men, the defeat was mortally crushing. Having spent long years wresting control of Jerusalem from the Sasanians, Heraclius had assumed that he had found favor in the eyes of God, and when he replaced the True Cross in the Church of the Anastasis in 630, he must have believed himself blessed. When he heard that a desert chieftain with the strange title of "caliph" had entered the holy city as a conqueror, he was stricken, emo-

tionally and physically. He had been in Antioch at the time, and as the Arabs advanced, he retreated to the coast of Asia Minor. In Constantinople, adversaries took advantage of the setbacks and began to plot. Ailing and despondent, Heraclius returned to a capital and a family conspiring against him. He died within months.

While the emperor and his patriarch in Jerusalem saw Muslim success as the result of Christian sin, some went even further and claimed that Islam was nothing more than a Christian heresy. So said John of Damascus, one of the last great Christian theologians of the Muslim Near East. Though he grew up in Damascus, he left the city sometime in the late seventh century and spent significant portions of his life penning angry rebuttals of Muslim theology. In contrast to the ecumenical portrait of the early Arab commanders left by medieval Muslim historians, John of Damascus condemned Islam as

> a people-deceiving cult of the Ishmaelites, the forerunner of the Antichrist.... It derives from Ishmael, who was born to Abraham of Hagar, wherefore they are called Hagarenes and Ishmaelites. And they call them Saracens, inasmuch as they were sent away empty-handed by Sarah.... These were idolaters and worshipers of the morning-star ... and until the time of Heraclius they were plain idolaters. From that time till now a false prophet appeared among them, surnamed Muhammad, who, having happened upon the Old and the New Testament and apparently having conversed with an Arian monk, put together his own heresy.

According to John, Muhammad then "composed frivolous tales," which were cobbled together by his followers to form the bare bones of a sect.[11]

In essence, John treated Islam as no different from the dozens of other heresies that had contaminated early Christianity. While his interpretation was harsh, his denunciation of Islam as Christian heresy is a powerful testament to the close connection between the two faiths. Christian polemicists never described Zoroastrianism as a bastardization of Christianity, nor did later Europeans link Hindus and Buddhists to Christianity. The schisms of the early Christian church represented alternate and opposed interpretations of the scripture. These schisms could last decades or even centuries, but eventually one side lost or was marginalized and was then labeled a "heresy" by the "orthodox." John of

Damascus, writing during a time when the strength of the church in the Near East was waning, was dismayed and angered by the success of Islam. He believed that Muslims had distorted the true word of God by denying the divinity of Christ, just as earlier heretics had. Unlike those earlier heresies, however, Islam had resisted efforts to quash it and now was a direct challenge to the legitimacy and survival of the Byzantine Church.

THE COMMUNITY DIVIDES

MUSLIM ATTITUDES toward the People of the Book were hardly the focus in these early years. Instead, the first generation of Muslims were occupied with defining a new political order. The initial wave of conquests paused in the middle of the seventh century because of internal divisions. The succession to Muhammad had been a problem even with the choice of Abu Bakr, but after Umar ibn al-Khattab, the issue became more acute. The third caliph, Uthman, was assassinated, and Ali ibn Abu Talib, who had married Muhammad's daughter Fatima and was also the Prophet's cousin, then became the fourth caliph. During Ali's brief reign, the tenuous unity of the Arab tribes collapsed. The central debate was over who should be the rightful heirs to Muhammad. Different clans of the Quraysh staked their claim. The Meccan aristocracy tried to seize the upper hand and were in turn challenged by the Medinese, who asserted that because they had joined Muhammad first, they should be preeminent. But even amongst the Medinese and Muhammad's immediate family, there were divisions.

If these political and tribal fissures weren't sufficient to create chaos, there was an added doctrinal dimension: did the caliph have to be connected to and descended from Muhammad by blood, or was piety the most important factor? In short, the question was whether the caliph would be a hereditary monarch, who would pass on his rule to his children, or a first among equals who would earn his authority through the respect of the community.

Ali was the most controversial of the first four caliphs. His elevation to the caliphate triggered a civil war. He had fiercely loyal followers who believed he had been Muhammad's favorite and was then unjustly denied the caliphate for more than two decades. At the same time, he

was attacked not only by rival clans and other claimants but by groups who believed that the caliphate should be reserved for the pure of faith regardless of blood ties to Muhammad. The civil war that ended with Ali's assassination in 661 was a kaleidoscope of warring factions, and the partisan nature of subsequent sources makes it even harder to sort out what happened. Ali seems to have tried to negotiate with his enemies in order to keep the Muslim community intact, but that only alienated some of his followers. The purists who assassinated him felt that he had betrayed them and abdicated his responsibility by not vigorously campaigning against his adversaries. While the specifics are clouded, the outcome is not: the caliphate of Ali opened a religious chasm within the Muslim community. The *shi'a Ali,* or "party of Ali," became known as the Shi'a, and the rest became known as Sunni, or "traditionalists." Each of these in turn fragmented into multiple factions and sects, but the Sunni-Shi'a division has lasted to this day.

To subsequent generations of Muslims, Ali's death marked the end of the "Rightly Guided Caliphate." The first four caliphs had all been personally connected to Muhammad, by blood, friendship, or marriage. The caliph who replaced Ali, Muawiya, was one of the Quraysh and related to Uthman. He had been a superb general during the initial conquests, and then governor of Syria. But even with formidable backing of the garrison cities and of Cairo, only when Ali's eldest son, Hasan, agreed not to contest Muawiya's leadership was his hold on the caliphate secure.

The Umayyad dynasty founded by Muawiya lasted for nearly a century. The Muslim empire shifted from loosely organized, dynamic confederacies of tribes into a more structured state spanning thousands of miles and ruled from Damascus. Initially, the Umayyads tended more to internal affairs than to continuing the wars of expansion, but skirmishes with the Byzantines continued, especially given the proximity of Damascus to the heartland of the Byzantine Empire. The Umayyads built a navy, and seized Crete and Rhodes, but these were minor acquisitions compared with the territory conquered only a few years before. Muawiya's death and the ineptitude of his son triggered another civil war, which again featured the partisans of Ali and rebellion in Mecca and Medina. After, the victorious Umayyads initiated a new wave of conquests and more substantial attacks on Constantinople.

The Umayyads led the first Muslim empire that directly impacted the Christians of Europe. Advancing from Egypt, Arab armies took

Carthage (Tunis) toward the end of the seventh century, and then proceeded west along the Mediterranean coast. At the beginning of the eighth century, Tariq ibn Ziyad, a freed Berber slave of the Muslim governor of North Africa, invaded Spain with an army that he led across the narrow strait that would be named after him, Jebel Tariq, known in the West as Gibraltar. The Iberian Peninsula at the time was ruled by the Visigoths, a Germanic tribe that had seized the region during the last days of the Roman Empire. As in Egypt, relations between rulers and the ruled were tense and hostile, and the local populace did not go out of their way to halt Tariq's advance. Cities such as Córdoba and Toledo fell without a fight, and while the Goths did mount some resistance, the entire peninsula, called by the Arabs al-Andalus, was soon under Tariq's control. Only the Pyrenees stood between him and Europe. He might have continued his advance had he not been recalled by the caliph, who, it would appear, had never actually given his consent to the invasion of Spain and was not clear what value it added to his empire.

The conquest of Spain had an incalculable impact on Europe and on the evolution of Western civilization, but initially, it was a footnote for the Umayyads. More important to the Muslims at the time was that the success of the Umayyads was a defeat for those who believed the community should be ruled not by the most powerful dynasty, but by the most pious and pure.

The relocation of the capital to Damascus cemented the new order, and reduced the influence of Medina and Mecca. The result was that the Umayyad Empire evolved like other empires. Its ruling class, and a small but growing percentage of its subjects, were Muslim, but the state was governed and organized much like the Byzantines, the Persians, or medieval states in Christian Europe were. The caliph retained the title Commander of the Faithful, and he was the ultimate arbiter of religious disputes, but the same was true of the Byzantine emperor. The caliph had supreme authority and a court, governors, and an army, but so too did the Han emperor in China. And in matters of faith, law, and doctrine, the Umayyads began to defer to religious scholars and judges.

For the caliph in Damascus, what mattered was control, order, and income. Control was maintained by placing strong governors in each province and making them responsible for collecting revenue. The garrison settlements evolved into thriving cities, and the armies of the caliph were the ultimate keepers of the peace. But day to day, the

decentralized nature of the empire meant that its inhabitants enjoyed substantial autonomy. The overwhelming majority of those inhabitants were People of the Book, and autonomy meant toleration for their religious beliefs and institutions. While the conquerors were not above inflicting humiliations on the conquered, that was not the predominant experience. For the Copts of Egypt, for the peoples of Andalusia, and for the Christians of the Near East, the reign of the Umayyads was more benign and less intrusive than what had come before the arrival of Arabs and Islam. Communities were left to organize themselves, with minimal intrusion from the state. While the Copts, for instance, were second-class citizens relative to the ruling Arab elite, they had also been second-class citizens relative to the ruling Byzantine elite. At least under the Arabs they did not face religious persecution. They had to pay a poll tax, and were sometimes subjected to restrictions on travel, especially between villages and cities, but it wasn't as if most Egyptians had enjoyed personal freedoms under the Byzantines that were then denied by the Muslims.

Today, millions of people—especially in the Muslim world—still believe the myth that the caliph ruled the spirit as well as the flesh of his subjects and that the early Muslim empires represented a unique and potent synthesis of faith and power. This has troubling implications for how Islam has been defined in the modern world. Most people living under Muslim rule in the seventh and eighth centuries would not have recognized this picture of their world. Unless they directly and explicitly challenged the authority of the caliph and his deputies, they were allowed an extraordinary degree of latitude. No doubt there were examples to the contrary. People with power usually abuse that power, and governors overstepped. But those abuses were not systematic. Instead, the system was designed to maintain much of the status quo, and that meant a small Muslim ruling class that impinged as little as possible on a large Christian-Jewish populace.

By the early decades of the eighth century, the initial conquests were mostly complete. The Umayyads staged several more assaults on Constantinople, and one, led by the caliph's brother in 717, nearly succeeded. The Umayyads attacked from both land and sea and laid siege to the metropolis. A combination of famine, Bulgarian mercenaries, and Greek fire annihilated the Arab fleet and debilitated the army. It was the last time that the Umayyads came close to toppling Constantinople, and

soon, the Byzantine emperor had reclaimed most of Asia Minor and pushed the Umayyads over the mountains and back into the river valleys and deserts of Syria and Iraq.

Within the Muslim world, Christians began converting to Islam, but in trickles rather than droves. As they moved out of the garrison cities, Arabs were slowly integrated into the societies that the first caliphs had tried to keep them separate from. They married, and their wives and children became Muslim. Arab soldiers found ways to settle and acquire land; Arab merchants began to trade; and men of religion started to carve out a special sphere of influence. Christians who hoped to advance found work with local governors or mayors or even at the court in Damascus, as scribes, translators, and advisers. And slowly, born of contact in both the cities and the surrounding countryside, a new, hybrid culture evolved that combined elements of Islam, Christianity, Judaism, and Zoroastrianism, and of Persian, Byzantine, Egyptian, Greek, and Arab society. In North Africa and Spain, Berber and Visigoth were added to the mix. Had the phrase existed, it would have been called a multicultural world.

The tolerance of Muslims toward the People of the Book unfolded in the context of unquestioned Muslim dominance. The conquerors could afford to be tolerant because the People of the Book posed little threat. During Muhammad's lifetime, that was not the case. The Jews of Medina could have jeopardized Muhammad's status as both Prophet and leader of the community, and the result was harsh treatment. But once the conquests began, and it became clear that the Christians of the Near East would not and could not resist Muslim domination, the Muslims adopted a policy of tolerance that was both sublime and mundane, sublime because it was grounded in the Quran and mundane because it allowed them to rule an empire with minimal manpower.

Muhammad's life and the subsequent conquests established a framework for the next millennium and a half. The seeds of both conflict and peaceful coexistence were sown, and however fascinating subsequent history has been, most of what followed has differed only in specifics. The same notes have been endlessly replayed, with variations on the theme, but no radical departures from the score.

For centuries after the initial conquests, coexistence was the norm, but not one whose echo can be heard today. The fall of Jerusalem, the expulsion and execution of the Jews of Medina, and the wars between

the Umayyads and the Byzantines—those are remembered. What came after, in Damascus, in Iraq, Iran, and Andalusia, has become a mirage—glimpses of it appear in the modern world, flickering on the periphery of our collective vision, and then evaporate and disappear. Unlike a mirage, however, that past is real, and nowhere was it more real than on the banks of the Tigris at the court of the caliph in Baghdad.

CHAPTER TWO

⟫⟫ ⟪⟪

At the Court of the Caliph

During the reign of the caliph al-Mahdi, around A.D. 780, the Nestorian patriarch, Timothy I, was summoned to the palace in Baghdad to debate theology with the caliph himself. Al-Mahdi was a devout man, who spent most of his brief decade as Commander of the Faithful consolidating the realm recently taken over by his family, the Abbasids. Baghdad was a new city in an ancient land, but already it was bustling with the wealth, commerce, and knowledge that came with its status as the epicenter of an empire.

The Nestorian Christians of Iraq had long since broken with the bishops of Constantinople over those fraught questions of Christ's true nature and whether Mary should be thought of as the mother of God or instead as the mother of Christ. The Nestorians, like the Copts in Egypt, had been deeply disenchanted with Constantinople and had almost welcomed the Muslim conquest. But slowly, they came to see Islam as a threat to Christianity in the Near East, especially because it was the creed of the ruling class. With each passing year, more Christians defected to Islam. As Islam matured, its scholars developed more coherent arguments against Christianity. In an attempt to stem the tide, the Nestorians had to formulate an equally compelling defense.

Timothy was a learned man, befitting his station and status. He was schooled in Greek and in Arabic, and at the time of his audience with the caliph, he had overseen the translation of numerous works of Greek philosophy into Arabic, including scientific tracts by Ptolemy and political treatises by Aristotle. These had been commissioned by the caliph to enhance the wisdom of the Muslim community, and they had been pre-

served by the Nestorians because the tools of argument and philosophy were useful to them as well. Those deadly debates about the nature of Christ had been fought not just with swords but with the weapons of rhetoric and logic honed by the ancient Greeks.

It was Timothy's status as a translator of Aristotle's *Topics* that drew the attention of the caliph. Al-Mahdi was a man ripe for a challenge, especially a theological one. He had been ruthless in his pursuit of Persian Manichaeans and instituted a pogrom against them. Unlike Christians and Jews, and distinct from Zoroastrians, Manichaeans preached what Muslims took as a godless world defined by a war between Good and Evil. They also were accused of trying to prevent people from converting to Islam, and thereby undermining the legitimacy of the caliph. That made them anathema to the Abbasids, and evicted them from the protective shield that covered the People of the Book.

The brutal suppression of the Manichaeans casts Muslim tolerance for the People of the Book into even sharper relief. The Abbasids were capable of suppressing religious expression if they perceived a clear and present danger. Coexistence with Jews and Christians was therefore a deliberate choice. Unlike the Manichaeans, the Nestorian Christians did not explicitly challenge the legitimacy of Abbasid rule; they simply rejected the message of the Quran, as they had from the beginning of Islam. That was a challenge that al-Mahdi and his court enjoyed.

It was not the first time that the court was the scene of an elaborate debate pitting one faith against another, but it was the first time that the caliph had been one of the debaters. Al-Mahdi's motivations are lost to us. Perhaps he invited Timothy for a friendly joust simply for sport. After all, the court was the scene of revolving nightly entertainment, with ribald poetry one evening, love songs the next, and scholarly disquisition the evening after. Perhaps the reasons were more serious and sober. Al-Mahdi had a reputation for devotion, and he showered holy sites from Mecca to Jerusalem with his largesse. He was also a reader, and by the time Timothy was summoned, the caliph had studied the works of Aristotle and other philosophers. Just as al-Mahdi would not have gone into battle without a sword and the training to use it, he was not about to invite a Christian scholar to a debate without learning the arts of rhetorical war.

After more than a century of living in a predominantly Christian world, Muslims had analyzed Christian doctrine and found what they

considered to be several glaring issues. Once Timothy had been ushered into the audience chamber, al-Mahdi confronted him with questions about the virgin birth and the nature of Christ, which were two of the hardest questions a Christian theologian could face. If Timothy had been wise, and we have every reason to suppose that he was, he would have anticipated these, but it must have been intimidating nonetheless to stand in front of the Commander of the Faithful and be told the following: "O Catholicus, it does not benefit someone like you, a man of learning and experience, to say about God Almighty that He took himself a wife and bore her a son." Timothy responded, reasonably enough, that God did not have a wife, and that anyone who said so was a blasphemer. The caliph, wearing the black garments of the Abbasids, sitting on an elevated, richly cushioned platform surrounded by retainers, then asked the patriarch to describe Christ and to explain how it was that God could have had a son. The debate continued in this vein for several hours, the tone courteous and the dialogue elevated.

Both men acknowledged the kinship of Islam and Christianity, though their perspectives could not have been more different. The caliph argued that the Muhammad's arrival was actually prefigured in the gospel of Saint John. John referred to the "Paraclete," to the guide or counselor who would come after the death of Jesus to lead his followers, and Muslims argued that the Paraclete was, in fact, Muhammad. The failure of the Christians to flock to the Quran was, said the caliph to Timothy, a failure to heed the prophecy of their own scripture. Timothy, naturally, disagreed. "If I found in the Gospel a prophecy concerning the coming of Muhammad, I would have left the Gospel for the Quran, as I have left the Torah and the [Hebrew] Prophets for the Gospel."

The caliph then asked Timothy whether he believed that the Quran was the word of God. This was, to say the least, a dangerous question. Timothy could not explicitly say no, because that would have crossed a perilous and possibly fatal line. Even in the court of the caliph, with the understanding that there would be freewheeling and open debate, a Christian could not attack one of the central tenets of Islam. Timothy adeptly sidestepped a direct answer but left no ambiguity about what he thought. "It is not my business to decide whether it is from God or not ... but all the words of God found in the Torah and the Prophets, and those of them found in the Gospel and the writings of the Apostles have been confirmed by signs and miracles; as to the words of your book [the

Quran] they have not been corroborated by signs and miracles. Since signs and miracles are proof of the will of God, the conclusions drawn from their absence in your Book is well known to your majesty."[1]

THE GOLDEN AGE OF BAGHDAD

TIMOTHY'S MEETING with the caliph was one of many similar encounters between Muslim scholars and Christians in Baghdad and elsewhere. It is easy to overlook how astonishing these exchanges were, and how unusual. The previous centuries had been marked by acrimonious controversies between different Christian sects, which rarely ended with a cordial meal and usually resulted in the imprisonment, death, or excommunication of one or more of the parties. The internecine fighting among Christians, and between Christians and the pagans of Rome, stood in stark contrast to the relative comity between Muslims, Christians, and Jews under the first Muslim empires.

The exchange between al-Mahdi and Timothy took place at the height of the Abbasid power. Only thirty years before, the family of al-Mahdi had led a revolt against the Umayyads. The victory of the Abbasids shifted the locus away from Syria and Damascus and toward Iraq and Iran. The Abbasid revolution had been organized in distant Khurasan, in northeast Iran. It was a disparate coalition of non-Arab Muslims, followers of the party of Ali (Shi'ites), and provincial governors. The revolution had been planned for years, and was launched as a coordinate assault on the Umayyad state. Part of the appeal was the suggestion that the end of days was near, and that the Umayyads had betrayed the message of the Quran. Like the followers of Ali, the Abbasids also claimed that the Umayyads were not the rightful heirs to Muhammad and had unjustly seized the mantle of the prophet.

Buoyed by the eschatological fervor of their followers, the victorious Abbasids (who traced their lineage to al-Abbas, an uncle of Muhammad) soon distanced themselves from many of the allies that had helped them overthrow the Umayyads. Radical ideologies have a way of spinning out of control, and the Abbasids had no intention of relinquishing what they had fought so hard to obtain. If that meant executing erstwhile friends who were more motivated by the hereafter than the now, that was a price the first Abbasid rulers were willing to pay.

In later years, the early Abbasid Empire would be romanticized as the golden age of Islam, and for good reason. At their apex in the late eighth and early ninth centuries, the Abbasids controlled a vast realm. They faced few external threats, possessed immense wealth, exercised astute judgment in administering the empire, and exuded confidence. Their erudition, intellectual sophistication, and artistic creativity easily surpassed the Umayyads. Histories were written, poems composed, works translated, and cities built with graceful architecture and planning. Islamic jurisprudence caught up with the more established corpus of Jewish law, and Islamic mysticism borrowed from Christian monasticism and then flowered on its own. Successive caliphs relentlessly pressured the Byzantines and conspired with the Slavs and other enemies of Constantinople to undermine the power of the emperor. The island of Sicily fell to Muslim control at the beginning of the ninth century, and the Mediterranean became a Muslim lake. To the far east, only the mountains of Afghanistan and the Hindu Kush stood between the Abbasids and China.

Yet because of its sheer size, the empire was rarely stable and faced constant threats from within. The revolutionary genii unleashed against the Umayyads could not be so easily rebottled, and each one of the Abbasid caliphs was confronted with internal revolts and ideological challenges. Rarely did a year pass without some uprising in some town or province. These hardly jeopardized the regime, but they still required dispatching troops, fighting battles, and bringing the perpetrators to justice, usually be executing them in dramatic fashion. Dismemberment, gibbeting disfigured corpses, and other forms of ritual humiliation were common, in the hope that future rebels would think twice about mounting a challenge. Judging from how frequently the caliph and his representatives had to resort to such punishments, that hope was in vain.

These uprisings could be dealt with easily when they were within a few hundred miles of Iraq or Iran, but the farther away they were, the harder they were to suppress. The journey from the central regions to distant North Africa took months, and already the Abbasids had failed to retain Andalusia, which remained under the control of the last of the Umayyad princes. Even Khurasan, the seat of Abbasid power, was susceptible to rebellion, especially after the Abbasids turned their back on the more fervent believers in the end of days. But while the loss of Spain could be managed, the loss of Khurasan and the central lands could not.

The Abbasids understood this from the start. Having staged a revolution from Khurasan, they knew that distant provinces needed to be tethered to the center. But they also realized that the empire was too large and that it would be nearly impossible to govern both North Africa and Central Asia. The choice to tilt toward Iran and Central Asia was automatic. Sometime after 760, the caliph al-Mansur decided to build a new capital on the banks of the Tigris, which would become Baghdad. He needed to be closer to Khurasan but still near the heart of the Near East, and he wanted his base to be a city without entrenched factions that might undermine his authority. The location he chose was not far from the ancient Persian capital of Ctesiphon, and it was in the middle of the major agricultural provinces of the Fertile Crescent, connected by a canal to the Euphrates River to the west, and along the trade routes linking Egypt to Central Asia and China. By building a new capital, the caliph could also determine who would live there, further enhancing his power.

Baghdad was conceived as a round, walled city with four gates and circles emanating from the caliph's palace at the center. Markets, schools, and mansions filled the districts beyond the walls, and in the suburban outskirts, troops and retainers were rewarded with tracts of land irrigated by canals extending from the river. Baghdad was an artificial creation that soon became the only island of stability in a tumultuous, ever-disintegrating imperium, a place that the caliph and courtiers would retire to as a respite, to ponder the impenetrables of God, poetry, wine, and women.[2]

The move to Baghdad was more than geographic. With it, the empire shifted toward Persia and away from Arabia, toward an Islam that was more diverse and less Arab, and toward a culture that celebrated the divine right of kings and sybaritic pleasures. It was also a more urban and cosmopolitan society—which shaped the evolution of Muslim theology. Creativity, reason, and openness to new ideas were embedded in early Abbasid culture. "A city without peer in the world was Baghdad then," said one medieval historian, and for a time, Baghdad thrived as few cities ever have or ever will.

One of the hallmarks of that openness was the easy toleration of Christians and Jews, who still made up a majority of the population ruled by the Abbasids. That toleration ran the gamut from cool coexistence to fruitful dialogue and active collaboration. Muslim scholars

studied the wisdom of the societies they had conquered and liberally borrowed and incorporated ideas and practices. In the two centuries after the Abbasids gained power, Islam took on most of the characteristics that were to define it for the next thousand years, and a fair number of those characteristics drew on the pre-Islamic traditions of Christians, Jews, and Persians. In those two centuries, the four major Muslim schools of law emerged, and judges and scholars placed their stamp on thousands of questions about how a Muslim should act and behave.

This openness to the wisdom of the pre-Islamic past stemmed in part from the regime's focus on maintaining power. Having overthrown one dynasty, the Abbasids were acutely aware that they too might be overthrown, and they were determined not to be. Any tool, technique, or philosophy that might help them govern was welcome, regardless of its provenance. In addition to studying the legacy of the Christian states that they had supplanted, they examined classical Greece and the imperial legacy of the Persian shahs. They were also utilitarian about people, and the Abbasid caliphs invited Christians, Jews, and Zoroastrians to serve the state.

As a result, non-Muslims held high administrative posts in the government bureaucracies (*diwans*). From the treasury to the department of public works to the department of war, the People of the Book and *dhimmis* were employed as tax collectors, guards, and scribes. One of the most influential tax collectors under Caliph al-Mansur was a Jew, and many of the ninth-century viziers of the Abbasids were Nestorians or Nestorian converts, who had replaced the first family of viziers, the Barmakids, who were Buddhist converts from what would now be Afghanistan. These non-Arabs and non-Muslims had crucial skills that the caliphs needed. They were often multilingual, and knew Greek, Persian, and Arabic, as well as Syriac. The Byzantine administration of Syria and the Near East had been conducted in Syriac and Greek, and the Abbasids were able to maintain continuity and stability by drawing on individuals who knew those languages and were in some way connected to that legacy. Al-Mansur was aware, however, that he could not simply rely on their knowledge. That would give the People of the Book too much influence over the court and the empire. In order to build up a Muslim alternative, he ordered the translation of Syriac, Greek, and Persian texts.

The consequences of this state-sponsored translation movement were tectonic. The impetus may have been banal—how to govern an

empire using a predecessor's tools. But the translation of Greek knowledge into Arabic eventually paved the way for the transmission of classical knowledge into Western Europe. It is not a stretch to say that the West as we know it could not have emerged had it not been for the translations commissioned by the Abbasids in Baghdad as well as in Basra. Similar efforts occurred in Egypt and later in Andalusia, but the movement began in the late eighth century under the caliph al-Mansur, his children, grandchildren, and great-grandchildren.

The range of translated works stretched from classical Greece through the early years of the Roman Empire. There was a particular focus on the Neoplatonists, who, beginning in the third century B.C., had combined the philosophy of Plato and Aristotle with the science of Hellenistic geniuses such as Ptolemy and the mysticism of later thinkers such as Plotinus. The subjects covered by these writers were eclectic and sometimes obscure, but the net effect for the Abbasids was a burst of theological discourse as complicated, arcane, and divisive as the debates over the nature of Christ had been in early Christianity.

Among the central concerns of the Neoplatonists was the divide between the material and the spiritual, between the body and the soul. That in part accounts for the almost obsessive concern in early Christianity over whether Christ was fully divine, fully human, or an alchemical combination of the two. It also explains the evolution of Muslim theology under the Abbasids, and the emergence of three distinct approaches to Islam.

Encouraged by successive caliphs, philosophers debated whether the Quran was the "uncreated" word of God or created by God. Those who believed that the Quran was created came to be known as the rationalists, as opposed to traditionalists, who believed that the Quran was the pure emanation of God. The traditionalists were not open to using Greek philosophy to illuminate the Quran, and they did not approve of debates with the People of the Book. For them, the Quran was part of God, and hence unquestionable, unalterable, and not subject to human interpretation. The rationalists (or *mu'tazali* in Arabic) disagreed. They felt that the idea of an uncreated Quran came perilously close to the Christian idea of the Trinity, which to their thinking meant worshiping more than one God. That was heresy. Not only was the Quran created by God, and hence separate from him, but it could, as one of God's creations, be examined by human reason in order to understand it better. It

could be "interpreted," and humans were entitled to use their minds in order to become better acquainted with God's will.

This split between rationalists and traditionalists has continued in one form or another to the present day. At various points, rationalists, by whatever name, have had the upper hand. At other points, the traditionalists have. In the modern era, the rationalists have been the reformers, those who have argued for change and modernization in the Muslim world. The traditionalists have resisted science and innovation as contrary to God's will, and the most extreme have turned toward forms of radical fundamentalism. Over the course of centuries, however, the rationalists have been just as central, perhaps more so, and they were the guiding force in the heyday of Baghdad.

There was another group, loosely defined but still part of the warp and woof of society, that distanced itself from both factions and refused to enter the debate or serve as judges and officials. They were men, and not a few women, of quiet piety. At some point, they began to call themselves Sufis, named for the wool cloth they wore. They preferred to stay clear of the court and worship God as simply and purely as they could. They too borrowed from Christianity, but from the tradition of hermits and ascetics. Like the Desert Fathers and Saint Antony, they embraced physical extremes and practiced self-denial, isolated themselves in remote and unforgiving regions, and engaged in constant prayer.

These ninth-century divisions—between rationalists and traditionalists, between those who believed that reason, science, and philosophy were tools meant to be used for God's glory and those who looked to a literal reading of the scripture with minimal human innovation, along with the emerging Sufis and the ever-present Shi'ites—not only deepened over time, but became hydraheaded. Each one produced its own sects and splinter groups, until centuries later, Islam was as fragmented and varied as Christianity with its many sects and offshoots. The early fissures within the Muslim community are a guide to how Islam evolved in much the same way as the debates among the Founding Fathers in the United States are crucial to understanding the American soul.

These divides also shaped how Muslims related to the People of the Book. The rationalist approach that found favor at the Abbasid court welcomed discourse with Christians, Jews, Zoroastrians, Buddhists, and many others. The dialogue between Timothy and al-Mahdi was repeated nearly fifty years later, when the caliph al-Ma'mun invited

Theodore Abu Qurra, a Greek Orthodox bishop from Syria, to the court. Much like Timothy years before, Abu Qurra stood before the caliph to defend Christian theology. Al-Ma'mun, in turn, tried to expose what he saw as the inconsistencies of the Christian faith. Abu Qurra had written extensively about the competing religions of the Near East, and he had concluded that only Christians could lay claim to possessing the one true religion.

Rather than simply asserting the truth of the gospel, Abu Qurra used analogies, hypotheticals, and parables to prove his point. "Let's say that I grew up on a mountain ignorant of the nature of people," he wrote in one treatise, "and one day...I went down to the cities and to the society of people, and I perceived them to be of different religions." He would have noticed that most religions forbid some things and permitted others, and most "claimed to have a god." How then could he tell which was true? Well, God, in his wisdom, would have sent a messenger to inform people of the truth. But that person who came down from the mountain would also notice that different people had claimed to be messengers and put forth a set of teachings. How then to separate the wheat from the chaff? By studying each tradition, Abu Qurra claimed that he could identify inconsistencies and weaknesses in all of them except for the gospel.

Like Abu Qurra, Muslim scholars dissected competing scriptures, and the rationalists delighted in analyzing the Torah and the gospel to find errors of logic. Both sides could be mean-spirited. Abu Qurra frequently disparaged Muslims in subtle ways, calling them "those who claim to have a book sent down to them by God." Muslims responded by ridiculing the inconsistencies in the New Testament. They also excoriated the idea of virgin birth and the Trinity as inherently illogical and hence proof that Christianity was not the true religion. From the vantage point of the early twenty-first century, what is most striking about these debates is not just that they took place, but that such a premium was placed on logic rather than faith. An elite group of Muslims and Christians in the Abbasid ninth century relied on reason and philosophy, not personal piety or the strength of belief, in order to demonstrate the truth of their religions.[3]

What also stands out is how much common ground there was, not just between the philosophers, caliphs, and theologians, but between Sufis and Christian and Jewish hermits and monks. Those ascetics who recoiled from the imperial opulence that accompanied empire looked at

the life of Muhammad and saw a man and a society characterized by piety uncluttered by materialism. Like the Jewish Essenes at the time of Christ and the Desert Fathers of Egypt in the fourth century, they were disgusted by the finery of the court, and they viewed the elaborate theological debates and the exquisite complexity of Greek philosophy as signs of decadence. Rather than fight to change the system, they retreated from the material world. These early ascetics were the precursors to the more organized Sufi movements of later centuries. They believed that the greatest good was unity with God, and that only with strict and arduous spiritual discipline could that unity be achieved.

The Sufi ascetics were a thorn for the ruling class, a reminder of how removed those rulers were from Muhammad's life. Though the Abbasid caliphs were diligent about leading the annual pilgrimage to Mecca as often as feasible, the frequency diminished. By the late ninth century, most caliphs went on the pilgrimage once or at most twice during their reign. That was only one example of the untethering from the early roots of Islam, and that disturbed the ascetics. They urged more attention to personal faith and less to the affairs of the world. They borrowed techniques from Christian monks, and from the Buddhists of Khurasan, and emulated their rituals. Often, communities would form around one holy individual, usually but not always male. That person would dictate how the group prayed, what verses of the Quran would be recited and when. In time, as Sufi movements proliferated, Sufis split into different camps, some stressing silent prayer and self-restraint, others emphasizing dancing and ecstatic rituals that would send the practitioner into a frenzy of faith.

What made Baghdad and much of Abbasid culture so vibrant, however, was that these opposed elements lived together in relative peace. Sometimes, that meant distinct and separate groups. But it was also true that individuals could seamlessly fit into different, and seemingly contradictory, categories. A caliph might be pious on Friday and deliver a sermon from the mosque pulpit and then be drunk Saturday night while listening to erotic poetry. A merchant attached to his material possessions might take two months for the pilgrimage, or spend one day a week praying under the leadership of a holy man or ascetic. A soldier might be a farmer when he wasn't fighting, and a government official could both serve a Muslim caliph and belong to one of several religions.

Even the line between Muslims and Christians blurred. Prayer and

ritual were often a mix of Muslim customs and Christian. In Baghdad, Christians lived in the eastern districts, near a large Jacobite monastery that had been built on the banks of the Tigris. But Muslims took part in Christian celebrations like Palm Sunday, and Christians honored Muslim festivals such as Eid al-Fitr, which is the ritual breaking of the fast at the end of the month of Ramadan. According to a medieval Egyptian historian, this mixing and matching of festivals "was a sign of mutual respect and brotherhood between the religions.... Moreover, some of the converts to Islam, as Muslims, continued their old practices even after accepting Islam."[4]

Slowly, Muslim converts gained more acceptance, especially in the eastern parts of the empire, where Arabs were few and far between. Where some Umayyad governors had humiliated the converts, the Abbasids began to welcome them. The spread of Islam was facilitated by urbanization. As more people moved to urban centers, they left their old lives behind for new opportunities. In order to participate fully in society and in order to have more social mobility, many of these immigrants to the cities converted, especially as the stigma attached to conversion waned. The act of conversion, however, did not mean that all aspects of one's older identity suddenly disappeared. That took several generations, and even then, non-Muslim rituals, habits, and attitudes survived in different guise. Whether it was the way Sufis prayed or the way Abbasid judges approached questions of law and philosophy, elements of Byzantine, Christian, Jewish, and Persian culture were incorporated into Abbasid society.[5] In North Africa and Spain, there was even more of a synthesis, and Muslim culture took on attributes of the Berber and Roman culture that the Arabs had conquered.

Open religious debate was simply one facet of the Abbasid court. Until late in the ninth century, Muslim society was a messy mélange of philosophy, piety, politics, and passion. The caliph Harun al-Rashid, who succeeded his father, al-Mahdi, after the brief rule of his brother, is one of the few caliphs whose name in known in the West. That is because he figures prominently in *A Thousand and One Nights*, but his centrality in those fables in no accident. To later generations, his reign and those of his second son and grandsons were seen as the apex of Muslim greatness. Harun may have fostered learning, but he seems to have celebrated poetry and indulged in wine and women with at least as much enthusiasm.

It is too easy, in the harsh light of the modern world, to forget the com-

plexity of these centuries. In the West, there is only the vaguest sense that Arabs, Persians, and Islamic society in general were once at the cutting edge of innovation, science, and creativity. The prevailing image is that Muslim history has been the story of stern orthodoxy, hostile to other creeds and foreign influences. Even within the Muslim world, the memory of the age of the great caliphs has been distorted and sanitized to fit the mold of today's traditionalists. It is remembered as a golden age, after which there was a slow, steady decline. But for many in the contemporary Muslim world, who equate power with moral and spiritual purity, the decadence of the Abbasid court might be hard to reconcile. The Abbasids were powerful, but they were not pure. In their daily lives, they were like other rulers from time immemorial. Islam was a distinguishing characteristic, but the caliphs shared more with Chinese emperors and Byzantine rulers than they did with the companions of Muhammad. They were cosmopolitan, erudite, and attached to the pleasures of wealth.

Even al-Mahdi, known for his piety, had a court full of eunuchs and female slaves. According to the ninth-century historian al-Tabari, "al-Mahdi had a profligate streak and was passionately fond of talking about women and sexual relations." He could also be cruel in his punishments, and was not above taunting his concubines, one of whom, a Christian slave girl, cried when he snatched a cross from her neck. Rather than giving it back to her, he ordered a poet to compose a song about her distress.

Poets and singers loomed large at the court. That was an artifact from pre-Islamic Arabia as well as a legacy of Persian culture. Songs were often paeans to the virtues of the ruler, occasionally parables about the right way to live and rule, and sometimes odes to sex and wine. One of the most celebrated poets was Abu Nuwas, who was a fixture at the court of Harun al-Rashid. Part jester, part comic, and part philosopher, Abu Nuwas regaled the caliph with the high and the low. Once, when Harun al-Rashid was overcome with one of his periodic bouts of melancholy, Abu Nuwas greeted him, "By God, I never saw a man so unfair to himself as the Prince of True Believers is. The pleasures of this world and the Other are in your hand; why not enjoy them both? The pleasures of the world to come are yours for the sake of your charity to the poor and the orphans, your performance of the Pilgrimage, your repairing of mosques.... As for the pleasures of this world, what are they but these: delicious food, delicious drink, delicious girls."[6]

The line between the holy and the profane was not as sharp as

it became in later centuries. The poetic style of Abu Nuwas—who employed it for profane purposes—was also used by Sufis to describe the experience of approaching unity with God. Sufis appropriated the language of passion and wine to describe God as a lover, much as Christian monks and Jewish mystics did. Instead of that love culminating in sex, the apex was the union of the devout believer with God. Not all mystics approved of this approach, and some pious-minded found it as distasteful and immoral as they found the court. But at the height of its power, the Abbasid Empire was a mélange of contradictory elements, and thrived accordingly.

While there are considerable differences between now and then, the similarity to the contemporary West is hard to deny. In Europe and America of the twenty-first century, the language of pop culture makes its way into churches, rock music is appropriated by evangelicals to spread the word, and material extravagance is part and parcel of the lives of the rich and famous. Western society has been a mix of the holy and the profane for some time. Materialism and the pleasures of the flesh don't negate faith and piety. It may even be that the friction has been a source of creativity and dynamism, and that Abbasid culture flourished because of, not in spite of, this delicious stew of piety, intellectual curiosity, and decadence.

While Harun al-Rashid may be the most famous of the Abbasid caliphs, his son al-Ma'mun presided over an equally magnificent court, which surpassed his predecessors in both hedonism and erudition. Al-Ma'mun not only continued the translation movement begun by his grandfather; he expanded it. He funded an extensive group of scholars, physicians, and astronomers, and their works were assembled in a state-funded library known as the *bayt al-hikma*, the House of Wisdom. The library was a center for translations from Greek to Arabic, and it was said to be the intellectual hub of the empire. It is difficult to untangle the myth from reality, and it may be that the actual House of Wisdom was little more than an administrative office that coordinated the translation not of Greek works of philosophy, but of Persian works into Arabic.[7] But even if the actual, physical place were less than the legend, it is still a powerful symbol.

Al-Ma'mun was a man of contradictions. He initiated a theological inquisition over the createdness of the Quran, yet he also sent envoys to the Byzantine emperor asking for as many manuscripts as the emperor

cared to share. The Abbasids and the Byzantines were in a constant state of war, with regular campaigns and frequent skirmishes. Yet that did not stop al-Ma'mun from politely requesting treatises ranging from Euclid the mathematician to the physicians Hippocrates and Galen. It's not known what the emperor said in response, but the manuscripts were obtained and added to the already considerable trove being assembled in Baghdad.

Al-Ma'mun's encounter with Theodore Abu Qurra was one of many similar debates staged between Christians and Muslims at the court. According to one account, the caliph held a salon every Tuesday afternoon where questions of theology and law were explored. Food and drink were served first. When everyone had relaxed at the end of a meal, the discussions began and lasted well into the evening. On one occasion, the chamberlain interrupted a debate to inform the caliph that a Sufi was at the gate, wearing a "coarse white frock," who asked to be admitted. Addressing the caliph, the Sufi did not mince words. "This throne here, on which thou sittest—dost thou sit thereon by common agreement and consent of the body of True Believers, or by abuse of power and the violent forcing of thy sovereignty upon them?" Few rulers in any century allow their legitimacy to be questioned. The usual response would have been to throw anyone who spoke in this fashion into a dark dungeon and then execute him. Instead, al-Ma'mun answered the challenger and replied that he had been chosen by his father, Harun al-Rashid, and that he held power only in order to protect all true believers and maintain order. If those believers found some other man more worthy, the caliph concluded, he would happily resign his position and bow to the new caliph's authority.[8]

This willingness to engage controversial issues created an environment where ideas could flourish. The historian al-Tabari described another incident, when al-Ma'mun hosted a debate on Shi'ism at the court. One of the debaters, who was hostile to the party of Ali, lost his temper and began shouting at his opponent, calling him "an ignorant peasant." The caliph admonished him, "Hurling insults is unseemly, and unpleasant language is reprehensible. We have allowed theological disputation to take place and have staged the open presentation of religious viewpoints. Now upon whoever speaks the truth, we bestow praise; for whoever does not know the truth, we provide instruction." Al-Ma'mun understood that only in an atmosphere where divergent views were wel-

come could knowledge advance, and that such advancement was to the greater glory of God. The Abbasids in their prime reaped the rewards of this openness.

For example, during al-Ma'mun's reign, a young man came to court looking for patronage. His name was Abu Yusuf Yaqub ibn Ishaq al-Kindi, and he became one of the great minds of his age. Al-Kindi was credited with more than 260 works on subjects ranging from philosophy to logic, music to astronomy, geometry to medicine, astronomy to the natural sciences. He believed that the only way to live as a true Muslim was to understand the meaning of the Quran and the life of the Prophet, and that the only way to understand either of those was to use the power of the mind to interpret what the Quran said. His defense of philosophy was simple and timeless: God gave man the power to think, and only by using that power could humans submit to God fully. Al-Kindi also believed, like the Neoplatonists before him, that the material world often prevented people from seeing the true nature of God and his creation. With reason and intellect, the truth could be discerned.[9]

The glories of his court may have sparkled, but al-Ma'mun had another, less noble side. Though he fostered debate and translations, he also conducted an inquisition against the traditionalists. He was, in short, tolerant of all except those who were intolerant of him. Granted, the traditionalists tended to be enemies of inquiry, reason, and philosophy, but al-Ma'mun was willing to violate his own principles of open disputation when that suited his interests. Abbasid culture was tolerant, but there were limits. As much as Christians, Jews, and others who did not share the faith were accepted, there were times when they were not.

For instance, in 806, during the height of Harun al-Rashid's power, violence erupted between Christians, Jews, and Muslims. This may have been triggered by a Byzantine attack on an Abbasid outpost, but the result was not good for the People of the Book. In retaliation, the caliph ordered his soldiers to destroy a number of churches. Rumors then spread that the churches had actually been burned down by Jews looking to stoke animosity between Christians and Muslims. Somewhat later, the writer, philosopher, poet, and jester al-Jahiz penned a lengthy exposition in which he mocked Christians and excoriated the Jews. He made a special point of ridiculing the Christians as unappealing to look at, and the Jews as downright ugly—which is ironic, given that al-Jahiz himself had a reputation as one of the most physically hideous, albeit intellectually

luminous, men of his time. Also during Harun al-Rashid's reign, the chief judge of Baghdad issued an opinion that "no *dhimmi* should be beaten in order to extract payment of the poll tax, nor made to stand in the hot sun, nor should hateful things be inflicted upon their bodies, or anything of the sort. Rather they should be treated with leniency." However, according to the judge, they should be imprisoned for failure to pay the tax, and held in prison until they did.[10]

Discrimination increased later in the ninth century as the Abbasid Empire began to fray. Laws were passed that limited the ability of Christians and Jews to serve as officials, and edicts forbade the ringing of church bells and made it illegal for non-Muslims to ride horses. They were to ride donkeys or mules only. Both Jews and Christians were told to wear "honey-colored turbans" and their women were instructed to don "honey-colored scarfs." They were also ordered to wear wooden symbols around their necks that marked them as non-Muslims, and to nail wooden images of the devil to their doors.

Seen through a modern filter disposed to assume religious hatred, those actions are easily interpreted as signs of Muslim animosity toward other faiths. The Abbasids, much like the Umayyads before them, alternated between the noblesse oblige of tolerance and contemptuous indifference, with much more of the former than the later. The mid-ninth-century edicts against the People of the Book need to be placed in the context of an overall strategy to retrench and regain lost ground. The impetus was not animosity toward the People of the Book per se but rather the growing power of Turkish mercenaries, who had become the shock troops for the Abbasids and were becoming a threat to the caliph's authority. The persecution of the People of the Book was only one small element of a major effort to establish a new power base. That effort relied on traditionalists who would not question the caliph and on troops who would serve only him. Marginalizing the People of the Book and suppressing dissent were necessary, albeit cold-blooded, tactics.

The swing from tolerance in secure times toward intolerance in times of threat would be repeated for the next thirteen hundred years. At their apex, the Abbasids invited questioning, dialogue, and debate. They looked for knowledge wherever they could find it. As their power waned, as provinces started to break away and armies began to mutiny, toleration yielded to us versus them. Feeling that their authority and control were in jeopardy, the Abbasids resorted to predictable paranoid behav-

ior by turning toward the conservative traditionalists, who were willing to rubber-stamp royal absolutism. Afterward, in the intermittent decades of calm, the court would again embrace philosophy and debate. But the pattern had been established: security and coexistence on the one hand, and insecurity and intolerance on the other.

THE CLASH OF CIVILIZATIONS?

THROUGHOUT THIS PERIOD, the Abbasids contended with a still powerful Christian empire emanating from Constantinople. After the failed sea assaults of the Umayyads, the war between the Byzantines and Abbasids reverted to the land. Just as the caliphs often led the annual pilgrimage to Mecca as a symbol of their authority, they also led armies to the frontier with the Byzantines to demonstrate their mettle. Young princes were sent to the front for their first taste of battle. In parts of what is now southeastern Turkey, there was a continuous state of war for more than a century, as cities like Malatya were seized and then retaken, seized and then retaken, until the inhabitants learned not to become too attached to one regime or the other. On both sides, there were instances of forced deportation and relocation, but these were not the norm. Rarely did the conquerors take revenge on the local populace, recognizing them for the pawns that they were. In the case of Malatya, famous for its delicious, sweet apricots, it was far wiser for both sides to keep production going and enjoy, in this case literally, the fruits of war.

Ever since Edward Gibbon penned his magisterial *Decline and Fall of the Roman Empire,* in the eighteenth century, the historical reputation of Byzantium has suffered in the West. Gibbon's literary skills are indisputable, but his choice of title is a bit odd. Constantinople was founded at the beginning of the fourth century, and the Byzantine Empire did not end until the fifteenth century, when the Ottoman Turks finally occupied the once-great city. It took more than one thousand years, an entire millennium, for the empire to "fall." Either this was the slowest, most drawn out collapse in human history or there was much more to that millennium than decline. Elsewhere in the world, entire civilizations rose, flourished, and evaporated while the Byzantines were supposedly falling apart.

Until well after the year 1000, Byzantium was *the* great Christian

power, and the one that the Muslim world, with the possible exception of Andalusia, used to define Christianity. It was also a constant adversary, and relations between Muslim dynasties and the Byzantines shaped how later Muslims understood the relationship between Christian states and Muslim ones.

The Muslims called the Byzantines "Romans," which they were and were not. They were the heirs to the eastern part of the Roman Empire, but they spoke Greek. They represented a fusion of Greek and Roman society. They also developed a form of Christianity different from what evolved in the West. The Byzantine emperor was both a political and a religious authority, and he had the last word in matters of both doctrine and law. There was no division between church and state, though there were bitter disputes over theology that pitted the emperor against different factions.

The lack of separation between religion and state in Christian Byzantium helps explain why the war between the Abbasids and the Byzantines always had a religious component. Faced with an adversary that fused the church and the state, the Abbasids relied on the caliph as the defender of his faith. When the two empires fought each other, therefore, it became a war between Islam and Christianity.

The concept of holy war, jihad, is embedded in the Quran, but it is and always has been a word fraught with multiple meanings. Muslims speak of jihad as both a struggle to submit to God's will and a battle against unbelievers. It was not true, historically, that Muslims were obligated to wage war against those who refused to bow to Allah. As we have seen, Muslims were content to rule over a large population of non-Muslims without expending the slightest bit of effort to convert them or to challenge their beliefs. But when Muslims did face war with non-Muslims, they could draw on the concept of jihad as a source of strength and justification.

The modern West is uncomfortable with the notion that war might be sanctified by God, but the idea that war is something separate from God and faith would have been alien to Muslims, Christians, and Jews for most of recorded history. In the Old Testament, when the Israelites wage war, God is almost always a factor, either urging them on or admonishing them. From Constantine the Great through Justinian and Heraclius, the Byzantine emperor viewed war as a holy errand. Victory was a sign of God's pleasure, defeat indicative of moral weakness. And the Byzantines

framed their wars against the Persians and then the Muslims as Christian struggles against those who had not seen the light of Christ.

The early Abbasid caliphs believed that war with the Byzantines was a religious obligation. Not all of them pursued it with equal vigor, but Harun al-Rashid relished the task. He got his first taste of battle as a teenage prince, and when he became caliph in his early twenties, he was so eager to fight against the Greeks that he often moved his court out of Baghdad and relocated to the garrison city of Raqqa, more than a hundred miles to the northwest on the Euphrates, so that he could be closer to the Byzantine front. When poets lauded his achievements, as court poets were supposed to do, they spoke of his victories over the "polytheists." One way that Muslims denigrated Christians was to accuse them of polytheism because of the worship of the Holy Trinity. It was easy enough for Muslim propagandists to portray the Trinity not as the three emanations of one God but as three separate Gods. That made the war against the Byzantines much more satisfying.

For Harun the outcome was also satisfying, because he was able to force the Byzantines to pay tribute in return for an end to hostilities. This was celebrated as proof that Islam was the true faith, but the triumph may have had less to do with his strength than with the disarray of his enemy. At the time, the Byzantine Empire was in the midst of a grave theological crisis that led to a near collapse of the state. The Iconoclast Controversy pitted those who believed that images of Christ were no better than idols against those who believed that icons were essential aids. During Harun's reign, power in Constantinople was seized by the icon-friendly Empress Irene, who had fought a war with her son and had secured the throne after she had him dragged in chains before her and ordered his eyes plucked out. But the victory had taken years, and she was wise enough to fight one fight at a time, even if that meant paying the Abbasid caliph to leave her alone.

She, in turn, was overthrown and exiled by her finance minister, Nicephorus, who discontinued the payments to Harun al-Rashid, saying, "the Queen who was my predecessor put you in the Knight's square and herself in the square of the pawn and sent you the sort of wealth that you should really have been sending her, but that was because of the weakness of women and their foolishness." Harun was not pleased. "In the name of God, the Compassionate, the Merciful. From Harun, Commander of the Faithful, to Nicephorus the dog of the Byzantines: I have

read your letter, son of an infidel woman. You shall see my answer, and it will not be in words." True to his threat, in 806, Harun marched into central Anatolia and captured the city of Heraclea. Though that was still hundreds of miles from Constantinople, it was on the other side of the Taurus Mountains that separated the two realms and on the edge of an unguardable plateau that stretched nearly to the Byzantine capital. Nicephorus was forced to ask for peace and once again pay tribute.[11]

Not surprisingly, the campaign against Byzantium coincided with the harsh measures Harun took against Christians in 806. In the tense atmosphere of war, tolerance gave way to something akin to Abbasid nationalism, and the brief, intense persecution of Christians in Iraq was one manifestation of holy war. Once the battle was over and Nicephorus had sued for peace, the restrictions disappeared.

However, just because Harun al-Rashid was fighting a jihad against one Christian power did not mean that he was waging jihad against all Christians. During these years, he made multiple overtures to the Carolingian, and very Christian, Charlemagne, who had been crowned by the pope as Holy Roman Emperor in Rome on Christmas Day in the year 800. Charlemagne was just as much a Christian monarch as the Byzantine emperor, and had in fact set himself up as the Western alternative to the Byzantines. Members of his court even referred to him as "King David" as a way of linking him to the biblical tradition of rulers who owed their throne to God's will. But because Charlemagne was a rival of the Byzantines, and a sworn enemy of the remaining Umayyads in Spain, he was seen as a potential ally by Harun al-Rashid. The caliph wooed him with emissaries bearing fulsome praise and lavish gifts, including an elephant transported at great expense from North Africa.[12]

Harun's son al-Ma'mun was equally inconsistent. One moment he was dispatching envoys to Constantinople asking for original works of Aristotle; the next he was sending armies into Turkey looking to inflict as much harm on the Byzantines as possible. Toward the end of his life, al-Ma'mun seems to have become more ardent about waging jihad, and in 833, he too captured Heraclea, just as his father had. The emperor at the time was Theophilus, who was forced to ask for terms and wrote a conciliatory letter to the caliph:

It seems more sensible that the two opposing sides should come together over their respective shares of good fortune than adopt

courses injurious to themselves.... I have written you inviting you to make a peace agreement...so that you may remove the burdens of war from upon us and so that we may be to each other friends and a band of associates, in addition to accruing the benefits and widened scope for trading through commercial outlets.... If you reject this offer...I shall penetrate into the innermost recesses of your land.

Al-Ma'mun responded in kind. He told Theophilus that he would not be fooled by a letter that combined honeyed words with threats. Instead, he would send his own armies forth. "They are more eager to go forward to the watering-places of death than you are to preserve yourself from the fearful threat of their onslaught.... They have the promise of one of the two best things: a speedy victory or a glorious return" to God as martyrs in battle. He offered the emperor a choice: pay a tribute, or be made to understand Islam by watching the caliph's armies eradicate his.[13] Not surprisingly, neither man was swayed, but al-Ma'mun died before he could carry out his retaliation.

These battles continued on and off for the next few centuries, but soon enough, both empires were more absorbed in fending off the Turks than in fighting each other. The Abbasids, by the end of the ninth century, had only nominal control over North Africa, and by the middle of the tenth century had lost Egypt. Powerful generals, backed by Turkish soldiers recruited or enslaved from Central Asian steppes and the regions surrounding the Caspian Sea, swore allegiance to the caliph but functioned as autonomous viceroys in distant provinces. Turkish tribes also began to pose a serious problem for the Byzantines, but like the Germanic tribes that had slowly sapped the energies of the Roman Empire, the Turks were anything but unified, and shared little in common except common linguistic roots. Their lack of cohesiveness made life even more difficult for the Abbasids and the Byzantines. Even when one tribe was defeated, others sprang up. And both empires tried, sometimes successfully but usually not, to use the Turks as a weapon against the other.

The Abbasids sank more quickly. Although the caliphate remained intact in Baghdad until the thirteenth century, after the mid-tenth century, the caliph's reach did not extend much beyond Iraq. At times, the irrelevancy of Iraq and the caliphate meant that the region was calm and stable. Central and southern Iraq were often the only places of peace in

a thousand-mile radius. As a result, Baghdad remained a cultural hub where philosophy, science, and art survived. Throughout much of the tenth century, Baghdad was a center for inquiry, where Arab scholars probed ever more deeply into metaphysical questions that had once been the purview of the Greeks. Philosophers built on the work of al-Kindi and fused mysticism and rationalism. Yet, in relative terms, Baghdad did decline, and the creative flame relocated far to the west, to al-Andalus.

It is true that the glory of Baghdad was never quite as glorious as it looked through the misty eyes of later generations. By modern standards, it was hardly a model of law and order. The caliphs were men of their age, and that age did not know from the legal and moral niceties that the modern world demands. But during the height of the Abbasids, there was an eruption of intellectual and philosophical creativity that has rarely been exceeded. Wealth certainly played a part, but many societies have generated wealth without fostering thought. Simple curiosity was also a factor. One thing, however, is undeniable: this flowering of inquiry, this preservation of the knowledge of ancient Greece and the advancement of math, science, and philosophy took place in an environment where Muslim rulers welcomed and invited interaction with the People of the Book. They used Christian scholars and administrators as foils to hone their own arguments about Islam, and the interaction between the faiths—sometimes friendly, often competitive, occasionally contemptuous, and now and then violent—ignited a cultural renaissance.

The heated, passionate embrace of coexistence was central to a golden age whose prerequisite was a powerful Muslim state secure in its legitimacy. That was true when Harun al-Rashid ruled, and it was true when Abd al-Rahman, the last of the Umayyads, retreated to the Iberian Peninsula after most of his family had been massacred by the first Abbasid caliph. Insulated by the Pyrenees to the north and by the Strait of Gibraltar to the south, Spain was the last redoubt of the Umayyads, and it became a cultural mecca. Even after the Umayyads fell to dynasties from North Africa, Spain continued to be a place where Muslims ruled but the People of the Book thrived. Between them they created a jewel that shone every bit as bright as the golden light that emanated from the caliph's court in Baghdad.

CHAPTER THREE

THE SACRIFICE OF ISAAC

THE CITY OF CÓRDOBA in the middle of the ninth century was blossoming. The Umayyads, exiled from Damascus, had carved out a kingdom, and Córdoba was their jewel. Though Spain had prospered under the Romans, under the Muslims it thrived even more. By the mid-ninth century, Andalusia was entering a period of nearly unrivaled prosperity. For a brief period, in fact, Muslim Spain was the most vibrant spot on earth, a place that saw a magical fusion of commerce, learning, and power that put it in the rarefied company of classical Greece, imperial Rome, Han China, and Renaissance Italy. But in 851, something happened that nearly ended its golden age before it had barely begun.

Except for the extreme north and west of Iberia, the whole peninsula was ruled from Córdoba, and the city matched Baghdad as a seat of culture, wealth, commerce, and learning. As in the eastern regions of the Islamic world, Muslims were significantly outnumbered by Christians. Spain was also home to a large Jewish population that had migrated there in the second century. While the rate of conversion to Islam in Spain may have been faster than in Iraq or Egypt, in the middle of the ninth century, Muslims were nowhere near a majority of the population. Both Christians and Jews occupied prominent positions in society, and they shared the rewards of Córdoba's increasing power and wealth.

One day in 851, a monk named Isaac, who had left the city three years before in despair as more Christians converted to Islam, returned. He entered the palace of the prince and was admitted to the chambers of one of the city's leading Muslim judges. Isaac was no stranger to the

court, and he was no ordinary monk. He had been trained in both Latin and Arabic and had occupied an important position in the government before he resigned his office and retreated to a self-imposed exile. Having worked in the palace until his abrupt resignation, he was known there, and the judge received him warmly.

Claiming that he wished to learn more about Islam, he questioned the judge about Islamic law and theology. Happy to engage in the conversation, and perhaps hoping that Isaac had returned because he was contemplating converting, the judge began to speak. But before he could finish his answers, Isaac cut him off and denounced Islam as an evil religion, and Muhammad as a false prophet who had been consigned to hell for deceiving the Arabs. Now, there were things you could say about Islam as a Christian, and things you could not. You could have a heated dialogue with a Muslim about the finer points of theology. You could profess that you believed that Jesus was the Christ and the Son of God, and you could politely refrain from praising Muhammad and the Quran. But you could not, under any circumstances, say what Isaac said that day, and you certainly could not say it to one of the most prominent judges in the city.

Hearing Isaac's sudden outburst, the judge was both confused and outraged, confused because Christians had been living peacefully and prosperously under Muslim rule for more than a century, and outraged to hear Muhammad and the holy Quran spoken of in such vile terms. He struck Isaac across the face, and was about to do so again when one of his advisers reminded him that until guilt could be established beyond a reasonable doubt, religious law demanded that Isaac not be physically harmed. The judge offered Isaac a chance to recant what he had just said, and suggested that he must be drunk or in a temporary state of insanity. Isaac answered that he was of sound mind, knew exactly what he was saying, and meant every word of it. He was, he announced, "on fire with a zeal for righteousness." He had lived for too long amid the Muslims, and stayed silent. He had retreated from the world, but he could not shut it out. He had come to Córdoba to speak, and to die a martyr.

That gave the judge no alternative but to have Isaac arrested and brought before the ruler. Isaac then repeated his denunciation of Muhammad and of Islam. The sentence was automatic: death. He was decapitated, and his body was hung upside down across the river from the palace for public humiliation. After that, his corpse was cremated

and his ashes scattered in the Guadalquivir River to deny him the consecration of a Christian burial and prevent others from using the body as a holy relic.

If the prince hoped he could keep the contagion from spreading, he was mistaken. Isaac's martyrdom set off a chain reaction that lasted for the next eight years. Within weeks, another half dozen Christians sought death by publicly condemning Islam as a false faith. Said one who appeared before the judge who had sentenced Isaac, "We abide by the same confession, O judge, that our most holy brother Isaac professed. Now hand down the sentence, multiply your cruelty, be kindled with complete fury in vengeance for your prophet. We profess Christ to be truly God and your prophet to be a precursor of the antichrist and an author of profane doctrine." Hearing this, the judge had little choice, and probably little hesitation, in granting their wish and sentencing them to death.

While there were lulls that lasted as much as six months, these outbursts continued on and off until 859. Some of the martyrs were women. Some were recent converts to Islam who repudiated their new faith, and thereby commited the dual capital crimes of blasphemy and apostasy. Some were married; some young; some old; but all met the same end.

The main chronicler of the Córdoba martyrs was the monk Eulogius, who after describing the fate of his fellow Christians, emulated their example and was himself executed in 859 in the same gruesome fashion. It was said by one contemporary that Eulogius presented his neck to the executioner's blade while making the sign of the cross and that when "his body was thrown from the upper level [of the palace] onto the riverbank, a dove of snowy whiteness, gliding through the air, in the sight of all flew down and sat on the martyr's body." It was also said that he told the executioner that he welcomed death. "Sharpen your sword, so that you can return my soul, freed from the chains of the body, to Him who gave it." His followers were so overcome by his death that the guards of the city took mercy and allowed them to retrieve his body so that they could give Eulogius a proper burial.

By the time the last of the Córdoba martyrs had been executed, more than fifty people had sacrificed themselves on the altar of their faith. They courted capital punishment, and they received precisely what they yearned for. Later generations embellished their stories, and added the poetic touches about doves and other symbols of sanctification. A num-

ber of them, including Eulogius, were canonized. They became for generations of Catholic Spaniards heroic symbols of resistance against Islam and against the Arab encroachment. The story of the martyrs was used by later Christian princes to rouse passions in their war to expel the Muslims from Spain. That feat was finally accomplished when the last Muslim kingdom fell to Ferdinand and Isabella in 1492, the same year that a Genoese merchant named Christopher Columbus sailed across the Atlantic, and in their moment of victory the victorious monarchs carried with them the memory of the martyrs who had perished more than six hundred years before.

CHRISTIANS AND CÓRDOBA

THE ACTIONS OF the martyrs were especially startling given the status of Christians in Muslim Spain. While the rapid spread of Muslim rule in the eighth century had hardly been a welcome development, it also was not as disruptive as early invasions had been. Before the Arab conquest, the peninsula had been wracked by wars. After, though Christians lost prestige and power, they were left to govern themselves. Some cities suffered during the wave of conquests after 711, but many others surrendered without violence when the Visigoth state disintegrated. As in Syria, Palestine, and Egypt in the seventh century, the Arabs promised the local inhabitants that their homes and land would not be seized and that their religious customs would not be curtailed.

For instance, in 713, one of Tariq's generals signed a treaty of capitulation with the notables of the city of Murcia. Under its terms, the Christians of the city and the surrounding towns would "not be killed or taken prisoner, nor ... separated from their women and children. They will not be coerced in matters of religion, will not be burned, nor will sacred objects be taken from their realm." In return for this leniency, the Christians vowed not to resist the conquerors, and not to assist their enemies. They also agreed to pay taxes on livestock and harvests, as well as a poll tax of one dinar per year. The Arab and Berber armies occupied the city, a handful settled down, and life for the local population continued with only minimal disruption.[1]

Córdoba became the seat of Muslim power in Andalusia after Abd al-Rahman, the last of the Umayyads, seized control in 756. His reign ushered

in a long period of stability, and while there was often tension between the various Muslim principalities, Córdoba itself remained relatively calm and unscathed. The battle of Tours, near Poitiers, France, may have halted the Muslim advance into Europe, but it did nothing to undermine Arab control over the lands south of the Pyrenees. By the time that Isaac made his fateful visit to the palace in 851, Christians had been living side by side with Muslims for longer than anyone then living could remember.

However, as was happening thousands of miles away in the Abbasid heartland, Christians in Spain were gradually being coopted into mainstream Muslim society. Year by year, more of them were abandoning the faith and converting. The advantages were undeniable. Though a Christian could rise high, there was a limit. A Muslim lord might employ a Christian or a Jew as a minister, and the People of the Book could become rich and powerful, but they were never allowed to forget that their freedoms were at the mercy of the Muslims who controlled the armies and the treasuries. Marriage was one of the primary bonds that cemented alliances between rulers and elites, but the People of the Book could not marry Muslims. Even as they adopted Arabic as their primary language, Christians could not avoid the fact that they were second-class citizens in their own country.

In order to integrate themselves, young, ambitious Christian men began to emulate the manners and mores of the ruling Muslims. Paul Alvarus, who recorded the last days of Eulogius, lamented that

> the Christians love to read the poems and romance of the Arabs; they study Arab theologians and philosophers, not to refute them but to form a correct and elegant Arabic. Where is the layman who now reads the Latin commentaries on the Holy Scriptures, or who studies the Gospels, prophets or apostles? Alas! All the talented young Christians read and study with enthusiasm the Arab books...they despise the Christian literature as unworthy of attention.

Like so many conquered peoples throughout history, the Christians of Andalusia were drawn to the power and culture of those that had conquered them.

Though many resisted the urge to convert and lived quiet yet secure lives, they still benefited, even with their second-class status, from the success of Córdoba. That was why they were appalled when Isaac set off

a chain reaction of martyrdom—not at the decision of the Muslim authorities to execute the Christians, but at the decision of the martyrs to provoke a response. In courting execution, the martyrs were jeopardizing the delicate balance that had evolved between Christians and Muslims, and most Christians sided with the Muslim authorities and denounced the martyrs as deluded fanatics.

While Paul Alvarus and Eulogius lauded Isaac and the others as saints equal to those who had suffered persecution at the hands of Roman emperors in the third century, other Christians vehemently disagreed. Where the Romans were pagans who had murdered Christian saints in order to prevent the spread of monotheism, the Muslims were believers. In fact, some Christians denied that Isaac and his followers even qualified as martyrs, because they had been killed not by pagans but by "men who worship God and acknowledge heavenly laws."

At the same time, that made Muslims a greater threat than the pagans ever were. Because they identified themselves as part of the heritage that began with Abraham, they were unlike previous adversaries. As some Syrian Christians had noted in the eighth century, Muslims posed the same challenge to mainstream Christianity that Christian "heretics" did. A Christian who would never be tempted by paganism might see Islam as a viable alternative. Not only did Muhammad place himself within the prophetic traditions that spanned the Old and New Testaments, but he carved out a special sphere for Christians and Jews as People of the Book. While that established a degree of tolerance, it also made it harder for Spanish Christians to resist the relentless pressure to assimilate.

In short, the real fight for Eulogius and the other martyrs of Córdoba wasn't between Christians and Muslims, but between Christians who were trying to stay true to the church and those who were falling away. It was an archetypal struggle that conquered peoples face: resist or assimilate. With each passing decade of Muslim rule, the pull of assimilation grew stronger. Whether or not they converted, Christians were adapting to a world governed by Muslims. They were learning Arabic, forgetting the scripture, and looking for ways to ingratiate themselves with the ruling class. Eulogius railed against Christians who collected taxes from other Christians on behalf of Muslim lords. Before his martyrdom, Isaac had been a classic case of the Christian who curried favor at the court of the prince. Like nineteenth-century Indians who donned English accents and morning coats in an effort to make themselves more accept-

able to the British ruling class, many Christians took great pains to mimic the Muslim elites.

The martyrs stirred the pot, but their efforts backfired. The bishop of Seville condemned them, and after the death of Eulogius, the movement came to a halt. Spanish Christians were not prepared to rise up en masse, and if they had tried, they would have failed. They had numbers on their side, but no army and no organization. Besides, well into modern times, popular uprisings rarely took place and almost never succeeded. Rather than causing Christians to remain steadfast and resist Muslim rule, the martyrs may have had the opposite effect. By showing the futility of active defiance, they cemented the case for coexistence. Christian rulers in the northwest of Spain continued to fight against the kingdom of Córdoba, but the Christians who lived under Muslim rule became progressively more "Arabized." There was no repeat of the Córdoba martyrs.

THIS LAST GASP of defiance on the part of Spanish Christians was followed by a dazzling 150 years. Constructive relations between Muslims, Christians, and Jews was part of Córdoba's genius. The city grew to nearly a hundred thousand inhabitants, larger than Paris, London, and Rome combined, and nearly the size of Constantinople and Baghdad. The rulers of Córdoba adopted the title of caliph in the tenth century, after the Abbasids in Baghdad came under the domination of Turkish generals who had once served them. The caliphs of Córdoba, like their brethren in Baghdad, turned their city into a capital of commerce, learning, and architectural brilliance. They ruled with the certainty of power and wealth, and with the calm haughtiness that comes with knowing that you are blessed by God.

Córdoba became a cultural jewel, so beautiful and refined that it was dubbed by one Christian visitor "the ornament of the world." It was filled with wonders, crowned by the Mesquite, the Great Mosque, whose rows of seemingly endless columns—graceful, curved, perfectly geometrical—created a space at once huge and intimate. Drawing on the architectural legacy of Rome and Byzantium, it was in its day as awe-inspiring as any ancient wonder. The marvels extended beyond the metropolis itself. Near Córdoba, the caliph built a retreat of palace complexes, a symbol of wealth and power that crested only for a moment before the caliphate began a rapid decline in the eleventh century. The

complex was constructed on the orders of Abd al-Rahman III; ten thousand laborers and artisans worked for decades crafting the inlaid buildings and courtyards replete with fountains and airy domes.[2]

With this opulence came arrogance. John of Gorze, the delegate of a German prince, was kept waiting for three years before he was at last ushered into the caliph's presence. He was awestruck by the rows of soldiers outside the complex, and he had never in his life seen what appeared before his eyes when he was actually admitted to the caliph's audience chamber. According to a contemporary account, when John "arrived at the dais where the caliph was seated alone —almost like a godhead accessible to none or very few—he saw everything draped with rare covering, and floor-tiles stretched evenly to the walls. The caliph himself reclined upon a most richly ornate couch, and as John came into his presence, the caliph stretched out his hand to be kissed." The contrast between the world John knew and the one he now witnessed could hardly have been greater. Germany in the tenth century was a jumbled mess of warring fiefdoms, and princelings were fortunate if they had a roof that didn't leak, a castle at least partly fortified with stone, and enough wood for heat. There was almost as much cultural distance between John and Abd al-Rahman as there was between Marco Polo and the court of Kublai Khan in the thirteenth century and between the tribes of the Amazon and the Spanish and Portuguese conquistadors in the sixteenth.[3]

John must have imagined that he was in the presence of a kingdom that would last centuries, but it would barely survive the new millennium. In retrospect, the eleventh-century collapse of the caliphate is less surprising than the fact that it endured for more than 250 years. There were sharp divisions among the Muslims who ruled Andalusia. The conquest of Spain had been accomplished by an uneasy alliance between Arabs from Syria and Arabia and Berbers from what is now Morocco. The Arabs treated the Berbers as second-class clients, and for the first centuries of Muslim rule in Spain, the Arab elites were able to control the fertile lands and prosperous cities and relegate the Berbers to less desirable and less profitable areas of the Iberian Peninsula. Although the princes of Córdoba were dominant, smaller cities frequently tried to escape the control of the Umayyads, and they often established alliances with Christian lords. Rarely was there a period without at least one active minor war. For a time, this constant state of war increased the power of the caliphate. The need to maintain a significant army was

a spur for technical innovation and more effective administration. It also made commerce essential. Trade was a vital source of revenue. In essence, low-level warfare was part and parcel of Córdoba's success, and its undoing.

THE JEWS OF SPAIN

THE RELENTLESS DEMAND for more revenue benefited both Christians in the countryside and Jews in the cities. The Arabs who settled in Iberia shunned farming, and they needed the Christian peasantry to remain on the land. Agriculture was not only a source of food; it was also a source of income. The best way to maintain production was to cause as few interruptions as possible, and that meant leaving the Christians alone except for collecting taxes. Even here, Christians were often delegated to be the tax collectors on behalf of the Muslims, much to the chagrin of zealots like Eulogius but to the satisfaction of almost everyone else.

But while Christians often saw their relative status decline, Jews tended to benefit, both in Spain and throughout the Mediterranean world. In the towns and cities, Jews found themselves in a unique position as intermediaries between Muslim-dominated Spain and the rest of the world. Having suffered severe discrimination at the hands of the Visigoths, Jewish communities under the Muslims enjoyed more freedom, affluence, and social standing than any Jewish community would until the nineteenth century.

Jewish merchants established international networks. In the ninth and tenth centuries, no one Muslim state controlled the Mediterranean, but though there were pirates and raiders, the region was a much safer place and more open to trade than any part of Europe at the time. Because commerce was in everyone's interest, and because no ruler had the ability to control it, the Mediterranean evolved into a de facto free trade zone. Spain was its western anchor, and it produced textiles, paper, and leather, as well as spices, olive oil, and countless other products.

Jews acted as agents for Muslim rulers who wanted either to import luxury goods or to export for profit. Because of their close networks and international contacts, they were able to overcome the limitations that faced merchants everywhere: how to ensure that goods were paid for.

Without an international banking system, payment depended on a high level of trust, and such trust was usually a function of personal and family bonds, often cemented by marriage. Jews in Cairo married Jews from Spain; Jews from Spain married Jews from the Levant. The result was that there were Jewish merchants and moneymen in most major commercial centers in the Mediterranean, and they had counterparts throughout the Muslim world whom they trusted and were eager to do business with. While there were also powerful Muslim merchant families, who had their own networks and were more numerous than the Jews, it was easier for a Jew to trade with Christians in Europe than it was for Muslims, and it was far easier for Jews to trade with the independent Christian kingdoms in northern Spain.[4]

Because of a rare and precious discovery of a trove of documents buried in the basement of a Cairo synagogue, there is an unusual amount of information about the links between Jewish merchant families during these centuries. These merchants ventured well beyond the Mediterranean. They crossed the Turkish steppe and sailed the Indian Ocean. However, in those areas, they were simply one group among many, whereas in the northern Mediterranean and in northern Spain they alone were capable of acting as go-betweens. The independent Spanish Christian kingdoms were locked in constant battle with the Muslims, but Jews lived on both sides of the divide. North of the Pyrenees, Western Europe was an economic and cultural wasteland, with a few centers of commercial activity where Jewish merchants led the way. Graced with their connections to the rich and sophisticated Muslim cities of Spain and of the eastern Mediterranean, Jews were a bridge between the Muslim world and the Christian hamlets of Europe.

Two names stand out in these centuries: Hasdai ibn Shaprut and Samuel the Nagid. Born early in the tenth century, Hasdai served two of the Cordoban caliphs as a physician and counselor. Muslims had long debated whether Jews and Christians could act as doctors for Muslim patients, but in the end, pragmatism trumped theological concerns. The caliph expected the best medical treatment available, and he didn't particularly care what scripture his doctors read as long as they kept him and his family alive and healthy. Hasdai ibn Shaprut was born into a wealthy family and trained not just in Hebrew but in Latin and Greek. He was given Christian tutors, studied ancient physicians such as Galen and Hippocrates, and learned Arabic. As legend has it, he gained the

notice of the caliph because of his studies of poisons and their antidotes. No ruler was secure enough not to need a skilled physician who might save him from the murderous inclinations of a courtier or rival, and antidotes for poison were coveted.

Having demonstrated his utility, Hasdai was rewarded with a position at the court. He flourished, and he became a patron not just of other Jews, but of anyone who could write an appealing poem or make a compelling argument. As the highest-ranking Jew in the caliph's court, he was treated as the leader of the Jewish community of Córdoba, and they seem to have embraced him as such. Within a short time, he had cemented both his position as a trusted adviser to the caliph and as the representative of the Jews. The caliph then turned to Hasdai for two delicate and unusual negotiations, one with the Byzantine Empire and the other with a distant tribe of Jews living in the land of the Khazars on the southern reaches of the Russian steppe.

The diplomatic exchanges between the Byzantine emperor and the Cordoban caliph were motivated by the same political calculations that had led Harun al-Rashid to reach out to Charlemagne more than a century before. Córdoba was competing not just with Baghdad, but with a new empire in Egypt that claimed leadership over the Muslim world. Very little of this competition was military, although as the new rulers of Egypt grew in power, they moved across North Africa and approached closer to the center of Cordoban power. But there was a competition over who could legitimately claim to be the successors to Muhammad as true rulers of the Muslim community. For their part, the Byzantines, who were enjoying something of a revival, had never accepted the presence of Muslim kingdoms in the Near East, and they took advantage of the bitter animosity between the Umayyads of Spain and the Abbasids of Iraq. Given that the caliph in Córdoba and the emperor in Constantinople both wanted to eliminate the Abbasids, they had a common cause.

The emperor, Constantine, sent a delegation to the caliph, which included not just the usual pleasantries, gifts, and fulsome words of praise, but also several manuscripts. One of these, by the Greek physician Dioscorides, was an encyclopedia of rare and valuable remedies, ointments, and other treatments for ailments. It had been partially translated in Baghdad, but from a corrupt and fragmentary manuscript. The one sent by the emperor Constantine was much closer to the original. One of the few people in Córdoba capable of translating it was Hasdai.

The manuscript was in Greek, and Hasdai worked closely with a Greek monk to make sense of its more arcane passages and translate them into Latin. Hasdai then used both the Latin and the Greek texts to create a complete version in Arabic.

Muslim Spain never did cement an alliance with Christian Byzantium, but relations remained cordial, and intermittent trade, facilitated by Jewish merchants, continued. So did the transmission of knowledge and learning. Spain remained a crucial conduit for Western Europe, and in pursuit of translations and manuscripts, creed took a backseat to expertise. No Muslim ruler cared whether the people translating works by the likes of Dioscorides were Jewish, Christian, or Muslim. The only relevant consideration was skill. All who possessed the linguistic tools and intellectual capacity to render these texts into Latin and Arabic were welcome to participate, and they were rewarded for speediness and success. Hasdai may have been charming and politically adept, but what made him stand out was his knowledge of multiple languages.

Throughout this period, the Jewish community of Córdoba was left to itself. Courts were not composed of layers of bureaucracy, at least not by modern standards, and rather than micromanage the affairs of Jews or other religious minorities, Muslim rulers preferred not to get involved with marriage, inheritance, or the social relations of their subjects. While there were laws governing the interaction between Muslims and other People of the Book, there were hardly any for relations between Jews and other Jews, or Christians and other Christians. Jews and Christians were subject to the poll tax, but it was left to each community to collect it. They could not build churches or synagogues outside of their quarter, but within the quarter, they lived in their own world governed by their own laws and traditions.

However, it was necessary for at least a few members of the community to interact regularly with the court. These intermediaries lived in both worlds, and they had to to navigate both. Men like Hasdai formed a bridge between the cultures, and by all accounts, the most adroit of them garnered universal respect.

Hasdai's position at the court led to at least one odd and unexpected encounter. When Hasdai met with the Byzantine delegates, he was told of a Turkish tribe on the borders of the Byzantine Empire that had, to the surprise and evident fascination of everyone who heard the story, converted to Judaism. The Khazar Turks lived north of the Caspian Sea,

and in time would migrate and become the dominant tribe of the Crimean Peninsula. For reasons that are shrouded in the mists of time, one of their rulers decided that he and his people would become Jews. The Jews of Spain were in the habit of making contact with Jewish communities throughout the world, to explore opportunities for trade and to reinforce the solidarity of the Jews in exile from the Holy Land. So it was natural for Hasdai to write a letter to Joseph, the king of the Khazars, when he learned of the conversion.

"I, Hasdai, son of Isaac, son of Ezra, belonging to the exiled Jews of Jerusalem in Spain, a servant of my lord the King, bow to the earth before him and prostrate myself towards the abode of your Majesty from a distant land. I rejoice in your tranquillity and magnificence and stretch forth my hands to God in heaven that He may prolong your reign in Israel." Hasdai expressed the hope that regular relations could be established between them, and he asked Joseph to describe how it was that the Khazars had adopted Judaism and if they had any insight into when, if ever, the long exile of the Jews from Jerusalem might come to an end.

It was several years before Hasdai received a response from Joseph explaining the complicated history that had led to the conversion of his people. Apparently, sometime in the middle of the eighth century, the Khazars were visited by envoys from both the Byzantines and the Arabs, each of whom hoped to convert them and make them allies. The king at the time was a cautious man, not easily convinced, and he sent for a Jewish scholar to test the strength of their arguments.

According to Joseph in his letter to Hasdai,

The King searched, inquired, and investigated carefully and brought the sages together that they might argue about their respective religions. Each of them refuted, however, the arguments of his opponent so that they could not agree. When the King saw this he said to them: Go home, but return to me on the third day. On the third day he called all the sages together and said to them, "Speak and argue with one another and make clear to me which is the best religion."

They began to dispute with one another without arriving at any results until the King said to the Christian priest, "What do you think? Of the religion of the Jews and the Muslims, which is to be preferred?" The priest answered: "The religion of the Israelites is better than that of the Muslims." The King then asked the qadi [a

Muslim judge and scholar]: "What do you say? Is the religion of the Israelites, or that of the Christians, preferable?" The qadi answered: "The religion of the Israelites is preferable." Upon this the King said: "If this is so, you both have admitted with your own mouths that the religion of the Israelites is better. Wherefore, trusting in the mercies of God and the power of the Almighty, I choose the religion of Israel, that is, the religion of Abraham. If that God in whom I trust, and in the shadow of whose wings I find refuge, will aid me, He can give me without labor the money, the gold, and the silver which you have promised me. As for you all, go now in peace to your land."[5]

This world—of Jewish doctors, Muslim princes, and Khazar kings—is very different from the remembered history of Islam and the interaction between the faiths. Think of it: a Turkish kingdom on the banks of the Volga River in modern-day Russia adopts Judaism after its king listens to representatives from each faith debating the merits of their system. Later, a Jewish official serving at the court of the Muslim ruler of Córdoba writes a letter in Hebrew to the Jewish ruler of the Turkish tribe after learning of their existence from Christian emissaries, sent by the Byzantine emperor, who were hoping to establish an alliance with the Muslims of Spain against the Abbasid Empire in Iraq.

None of this would have struck any of the people involved as strange. While religion was central to their identity, faith did not create absolute barriers to interaction. Even in the realm of marriage, the walls were porous. Muslims, Christians, and Jews weren't supposed to intermarry, but in places like Spain where the populations lived side by side, they inevitably did, and people found ways to deal with it. Usually, the woman adopted the religion of her husband, but if the woman was Muslim, then the husband would usually convert. These marriages weren't common, but they weren't unheard of either.

The historian William McNeill once wrote that vibrant societies are often the product of unexpected and jarring interactions with strangers. His point was that unless people are forced to confront alien groups, different habits, and unfamiliar customs, they become rigid, brittle, and complacent. Spain was a place where such meetings were unavoidable. Muslims, Christians, and Jews lived side by side, and they in turn were connected to international communities of other Muslims, Christians,

and Jews, whom they visited and traded with and who visited and traded with them. There was also war, which though deadly and violent was also a form of jarring interaction, and it forced rulers to be alert and creative in order to defeat their enemies and remain in power.

The competition between the faiths was one reason for the rapid spread of monotheism beyond the Mediterranean. The Khazar king, if the story is to be believed, would never have converted to Judaism had it not been for Christian and Muslim delegates trying to win his allegiance. The interaction between the faiths also fed intellectual creativity. The Muslims of Córdoba would not have gained the valuable medical wisdom of the ancients if there had not been Spanish Christians and Jews with linguistic skills that no Muslim possessed. And the Jews would not have thrived as merchants throughout the Mediterranean world without the Pax Islamica that extended to Jews the protections granted to the People of the Book.

Trade was the primary focus of most Jews living in the Muslim world, but in Spain, and especially in Córdoba before the eleventh century, they became prominent not just as merchants but as scholars, courtiers, generals, and poets. War and poetry marked opposite ends of the culture spectrum, one devoted to destruction, the other to creativity. Muslim Spain, and indeed much of the Muslim world, celebrated the poet and the warrior in equal measure. Few people were great poets or great warriors. Samuel ibn Nagrela, known as the Nagid, was that rare person who was both. That in itself was extraordinary; the fact that he was a Jew who commanded Muslim armies was even more so.

In the eleventh century, the power of the caliph in Córdoba began to wane, and the political unity of Andalusia disintegrated. The chaos and flux were both a boon and a bane to Jews and Christians. Where most things had revolved around the court in Córdoba, now multiple cities and rulers competed for power. Each of these required not just armies but also translators and administrators, and Jews possessed many of the skills needed to fill these positions. They were literate, multilingual, and loyal to their patrons.

Samuel was the son of a merchant. He learned both Arabic and Hebrew, and prepared for a quiet, prosperous life. Instead, he found his world plunged into turmoil as the caliphate collapsed. Political tumult took a toll on business, and when the situation became so dire in Cór-

doba that Samuel could no longer be assured of personal safety, he, along with thousands of Christians, Muslims, and other Jews, fled. He went to Málaga and eked out a living as a shopkeeper near the palace of the vizier of Granada. Word of his skill as a letter writer reached the court, or so later legend claimed, and he soon found himself employed as a counselor to the Berber ruler of Granada. After several timely deaths and various palace intrigues, he became the second-most-powerful person in the city and the general of its armies for more than twenty years, until he died in 1056.

With his rise to power, Samuel earned the title Nagid, which is a Hebrew term for "governor" or "worthy." As such, he was a central figure in the public life of Granada during a chaotic time. Protected by mountains and situated high above a fertile plain in southeastern Iberia, Granada, an isolated fortress demesne, would eventually be the last redoubt of Islam and the only surviving Muslim state after the peninsula was reconquered by Christian armies in the thirteenth century. During Samuel's life, however, Granada was simply one of many competing principalities, known as *taifa*s. Whether it would survive was very much in question, and had it not been for the Nagid's skill, it might not have.

Samuel led campaigns against other city-states, both Muslim and Christian. He oversaw public works and buildings, and tried to imbue the fortress of Granada with the glory of Cordoban architecture. Córdoba had been a city of mosques, fountains, courtyards, and palaces, and during Samuel's time; Granada acquired these as well. He also built a library that housed the greatest texts of Hebrew, Arabic, and Latin. These included Hebrew commentaries on the Torah, Latin works of medicine and philosophy, and Arabic works of poetry, astronomy, and material science. As one later hagiographer wrote, in Samuel's time, "the kingdom of science was raised from its lowliness, and the star of knowledge once more shone forth. God gave unto him a great mind which reached to the spheres and touched the heavens; so that he might love Knowledge and those that pursued her, and that he might glorify Religion and her followers."

Samuel did not just collect knowledge; he added to it. He was a grammarian who wrote extensively on Hebrew and its various dialects. He believed in the power of knowledge to transform a man and his society. As he wrote in one of his many poems,

Man's wisdom is at the tip of his pen,
His intelligence is in his writing.
His pen can raise a man to the rank
That the scepter accords to a king.

He was a scholar of the Torah and of Talmudic commentary. He wrote ballads in Arabic and Hebrew, including one celebrating a recent victory in which he dubbed himself "the David of his age." Self-aggrandizing, yes, but it was an apt comparison. Like David, Samuel was an unlikely hero who rose higher than many would have believed possible given his origins. He was not only a military leader but a protector and sponsor of Judaism and Jews. He sent money to Jerusalem to help the small Jewish community maintain its synagogues. And he worked to support trade as well as the familial networks that had been so assiduously created over the previous centuries and that were now threatened by the breakdown of the political order in Andalusia.

Yet, Samuel was like David in less flattering ways as well. "And David slew twenty-two thousand men of the Syrians," says 1 Chronicles, in the Old Testament. Just as David massacred adversaries and showed little mercy for those who opposed the kingdom of Israel, Samuel was an avid warrior. As he wrote triumphantly after one of his many successes on the field,

> The slain we left for the jackals, for the leopards and wild boars; their flesh we gave as a gift to the wolves of the field and the birds of heaven. And great was the banquet, all were satiated. Over thorns and thistles were their limbs dragged; the lionesses stilled their young with them…. Great and rich was the banquet prepared, and all were filled, drunk on blood without measure. The hyenas made their rounds, and the night was deafened with the cries of the ostriches.

A David for his age he may have been, but that meant not just power, fame, and culture. It meant reveling in the art of death and pursuing his enemies until they were utterly broken.[6]

The world inhabited by Samuel was nasty and brutish. One day of the week, a courtier might compose an ode to the beauty of a fountain, or to the serenity of courtyard lit by the moon. If he was Muslim, he

might have chanted with Sufis the next evening and praised the unity of God. If he was Jewish, he might have prayed with the rabbis. He might even have felt himself stirred by the joy that came with glimpsing the love of the creator. And the next day, that same courtier might have marched out at the head of an army of several thousand men and butchered his adversaries.

Samuel was succeeded by his son Joseph, who tried to maintain the legacy of the father but could not. The Berber princes of Granada were never secure for long. Rivals from within and marauders from outside were a constant challenge, and court life was precarious. Joseph attracted enemies not just because he was a Jew, but because he had influence. He was targeted, just as the prince he served was targeted. Factions that were on the out used whatever weapons they could find, and the fact that Joseph was Jewish was adroitly exploited by his enemies. If he had not been Jewish, his rivals would have tried to defame him in other ways. They would have whispered to the prince that he had a secret agenda, or ill-gotten gains, or designs on one of the prince's wives. Instead, they seized on the fact that he was Jewish and used it to their advantage.

The most effective and vicious of his enemies was Abu Ishaq, who had fallen out of favor and got his revenge by bringing Joseph down. According to Abu Ishaq, the prince had made a mistake because he had

> chosen an infidel as his secretary, when he could, had he wished, have chosen a Believer. Through him the Jews have become great and proud and arrogant—they, who were among the most abject.... And how many a worthy Muslim humbly obeys the vilest ape among these miscreants. And this did not happen through their own efforts but through one of our own people who rose as their accomplice. Oh why did he not deal with them, following the example set by worthy and pious leaders? Put them back where they belong and reduce them to the lowest of the low, roaming among us, with their little bags, with contempt, degradation and scorn as their lot, scrabbling in the dunghills for colored rags to shroud their dead for burial.

As for Joseph, Abu Ishaq concluded,

> He laughs at us and at our religion and we return to our God. Hasten to slaughter him as an offering, sacrifice him, for he is a fat ram and

do not spare his people for they have amassed every precious thing. Break loose their grip and take their money.... They have violated our covenant with them so how can you be held guilty against violators. How can they have any pact when we are obscure and they are prominent?[7]

The result of this campaign was disastrous. Joseph's palace was raided by a mob. He was dragged out, beaten, and crucified. Hundreds of other Jews in positions of prominence in Granada were then subject to days of terror and death.

It is almost impossible to revisit the massacre of the Jews of Granada in 1066 without seeing it as evidence of the inherent animosity between Muslims and Jews. It sorely tests the idea that there is any substance to the Quranic injunction about fair and tolerant treatment of the People of the Book, and for later generations, it has been easy enough to draw a line from Muhammad and the destruction of the three Jewish tribes of Medina through Granada in 1066 to the conflict between Muslims and Jews in the twentieth century.

Doing this, however, distorts the past. It is a lens formed by the bitterness and hatred of our present. It is easy to scour the past and find examples of conflict—if that is what one wants to find. Granada happened in 1066; the massacre of the Banu Qurayza happened in 627. But many other things also happened, and those episodes of extreme violence perpetrated by Muslims against Jews were few and far between. Four hundred years separated Muhammad and the massacre of Granada, and it would be hundreds of years more before another such event. There was nothing common about this type of treatment, not when compared to the routine persecution of Jews in Europe during these centuries and not when contrasted with the centuries during which Jews flourished commercially and culturally, often working with Muslims and for Muslims, and in the case of Samuel the Nagid, even ruling Muslims.

THE SHIFTING SANDS

RELATIONS between the People of the Book in general, and between Muslims and Jews in particular, comprised a matrix. One quadrant was defined by violence and yes, hatred. But there were others, ranging from

disdain to grudging respect to active cooperation for a common goal. Usually, that common goal involved the pursuit of knowledge and the task of translating the philosophy and wisdom of the ancient world. But there was also pedestrian cooperation between Christian and Muslim farmers in Andalusia, who often celebrated each other's holidays and prayed side by side. Everyone needed to have good harvests, and a Christian saying the prayers of a Muslim or a Muslim intoning the liturgy of the Christians would help guarantee that the rain would fall, the lands would be irrigated, and the grain would be reaped.

To identify moments of violence and call those more true and more representative warps the past beyond recognition. History becomes polemic. It would be just as egregious to portray the golden age of Córdoba as typical of how Muslims and the People of the Book interacted, but that distortion is less common, either in the contemporary West or in the Muslim world.

Isolating and highlighting moments of interfaith violence also distorts in other ways. Relations between *all* adversaries—regardless of religion—were ugly and violent. Muslims fighting other Muslims were no less brutal with one another than Muslims such as Abu Ishaq were toward the Jews of Granada. The warring states of Andalusia in the eleventh century were frequently ruled by Berbers who had built up centuries of resentment against the Arab elites. Their armies, in turn, were often staffed by a mix of Arabs, Berbers, and Christian mercenaries, and when they took a rival city, especially after a long siege or difficult fighting, they could be merciless and wanton. The Muslim Berber prince who sacked Córdoba at the beginning of the eleventh century allowed his troops to expiate the rage and shame of having been treated as uncivilized men of limited intelligence by an arrogant Arab aristocracy. They burnt the palace; they destroyed the library; and they massacred the city's inhabitants. Such treatment of conquered peoples did not happen frequently. It was more typical to terrorize, loot, and rape. But the behavior of the Berbers was not beyond the pale.

Muslims and Christians were rarely more charitable with each other. While massacre was atypical, it did happen. The shifting border between the Christian kingdoms of León and Aragon in the north and the Muslim city-states of Andalusia in the central and southern portions of the peninsula meant that at any given time after the tenth century, some Christian king was fighting some Muslim prince. The reason that mas-

sacre was the exception and not the norm had little to do with morality. Massacre as a policy was impractical and would have been the medieval equivalent of nuclear war. Soon enough, each side would have decimated the other. There would have been no one left to conduct trade or grow crops. Instead, Christians and Muslims in Spain worked out a system of organized slavery and equally organized ransom procedures. This was one way of making the loser pay, literally, while avoiding the depopulating effects of killing one another in large numbers.

At times, these conflicts were cast in religious terms, but that doesn't mean that they were fought because of religious differences. A Muslim prince would occasionally declare that his struggle against the Christians was akin to the early conquests of the companions of Muhammad, and that the cause was a holy war. For their part, Christians sometimes framed the reconquest of Spain and Portugal as a war spurred by the church and demanded by fealty to the cross. But because alliances often transcended religion, and because the political landscape shifted so frequently, it was more common for wars to be fought without clear religious ideology. Berbers from North Africa competed with Berbers who had lived in Spain for centuries, who in turn fought with Arabs, and in their efforts to unseat one another, they allied with Christian rulers who could provide money and soldiers. No one seems to have thought that such alliances violated an unwritten boundary between the faiths.

The kaleidoscope of coalitions could be dizzying. In the middle of the eleventh century, for instance, the Muslim ruler of Toledo signed a treaty with the Christian prince of Navarre for help against the Muslim city of Guadalajara. The price was steep, and included a large payment of gold. In turn, the Navarre Christians were given the right to harvest a portion of the crop of Guadalajara, if the city was captured. In response, the Muslim elites of Guadalajara concluded a treaty with the Christian king of León-Castile, and those soldiers then sacked Toledo. The Muslims of Toledo responded by sending emissaries of their own to the king of León, who demanded a large sum of gold from them in return for breaking his initial treaty and switching sides.[8]

During these battles, both Christians and Muslims prayed to God for aid. The irony that they were praying to the same God surely escaped them. However, the cosmopolitan Muslims of Andalusia, as opposed to their Berber allies in North Africa, were usually uncomfortable describing conflict with Christians as a holy war. That must have been a deliber-

ate choice. In the other parts of the Muslim world, the Shi'ite conquerors of Egypt and Tunisia claimed that their wars against the Sunni Abbasids were a manifestation of God's will, and the Berber tribes of North Africa and Morocco united behind the banner of Islam. In contrast, the Muslims of Andalusia rarely used doctrinal differences to justify war against Christian enemies. Aggressive Christian princes wanted to remove Muslims from Spain and annihilate them; that was reason enough to fight.

In addition, for both Christians and Muslims passions could dissipate as quickly as they formed. At the end of the eleventh century, the Muslims of Toledo might have described their war against Christian León as a holy one, but then they might have been attacked from the south by another Muslim principality, looked to León for help, and quickly dropped the holy war concept. It has always taken some effort to get men to kill one another, and shouting holy war was one way to motivate soldiers; ordering them to bang their shields with their swords was another. The goal in either case was pre-battle frenzy. Holy war was more often a tactic rather than a strategy, and it would be a mistake to apply to the Muslims and Christians of eleventh-century Spain the ideological passions we associate with the early twenty-first century.

It wasn't long, however, before something happened that shifted the balance in Spain and led Christians to think in terms of holy war. The principalities of what would later become France and Germany had regular contact with the Christian kingdoms of northern Spain, and as the eleventh century progressed, they became more involved in the contest between the Christian north and the Muslim south of the peninsula. As Andalusia fragmented, the Christian states of Aragon and of León and Castile became more powerful, winning battle after battle and acquiring territory. They developed closer relations with princes in southern France, and in the process, fell under the influence of a monastic order centered in Cluny.

The Benedictine order of Cluny was founded early in the tenth century. At a time when the organization of the church could be charitably described as anarchic, the monks of Cluny were disciplined, focused, and intent on imposing order. The array of fiefdoms in France, northern Italy, and Christian Spain had always been chaotic, but with the breakdown of the Carolingian system, established by Charlemagne, the situation became much worse. It may be a cliché that nature abhors a

vacuum, but it is also true. And in that wilderness of the late tenth and eleventh centuries, the Cluniacs filled the void.

Acting as a mini state, Cluny sent envoys to the kings of León and Castile and funded the establishment of satellite monasteries in northern Spain. As the wealth of the Cluniacs grew, so did their power. Bishops were appointed from their ranks, and these bishops looked to the order for guidance. The order, in turn, favored rulers who at least gave lip service to the church. That meant framing battles and campaigns against the Muslims as divine acts, sanctioned not just by the church but by God. Alfonso VI, king of León, was particularly adept at fusing his family's dynastic ambitions to expand into Muslim Iberia with the rhetoric of a holy warrior, and he established close relations with the Cluniacs.

The rise of Christian power in Spain corresponded with the decline of Muslim unity, but victors rarely credit their foes' weaknesses as a reason for success. Both the church and the state interpreted their hard-won victories as a sign of divine favor, and as a testament to their skill as warriors and rulers.

Had it been left to the inhabitants of the peninsula alone, the Christian reconquest probably would have been completed by the end of the eleventh century rather than dragging on until 1492. But the vigor and zeal of the combined kingdom of León-Castile provoked a counterreaction. Since the Muslim conquest, Berbers who had settled in Spain had maintained close contact with their brethren across the Strait of Gibraltar. At the same time that Cordoban power disintegrated, a dynasty emerged in the Atlas Mountains of present-day Morocco. Called the Almoravids, they established a base at the new city of Marrakesh, and fanned out north and west until they reached Ceuta on the Mediterranean. Then, sometime after 1085, they crossed into Spain and confronted not just the forces of León's Alfonso VI, but also Muslim rulers in cities such as Seville. Though the Almoravids suffered the occasional setback, challenged not just by the tenacity of Alfonso but by the quirky brilliance of the mercenary warrior known as El Cid, before the end of the century they had created a new dynasty stretching from Marrakesh to the middle of Spain.

The only problem, at least for those Muslims, Christians, and Jews that fell under their rule, was that the Almoravids abhorred the cosmo-

politan live-and-let-live attitudes that had characterized much of Cordoban history. They were puritans intent on restoring what they believed was the lost piety of early Islam. They roused their followers to fight against injustice and for righteousness in the path of Islam, and they viewed the decline and collapse of the Muslims of Spain as a sign of divine displeasure. Muslims had strayed, and God had punished them by giving the Christians the upper hand. It was the duty of the Almoravids, and of all Muslims in Spain, to cleanse the community, rid it of impurities, and reverse the tide.[9]

The Almoravids succeeded in stemming the Christian advance and then ruled what remained of Muslim al-Andalus with far less tolerance for the People of the Book. Under the Almoravids, Christians and Jews were subject to heavier taxation and more restrictions. Had the dynasty lasted, the noose of cultural chauvinism might have tightened even more. As it turned out, once ensconced in the palaces of their predecessors, the Almoravids began to feud with one another. The glue of holy war could form only an initial bond, and once the object was attained, it weakened.

As for the Christians, the success of the war against the Muslims of Iberia did not escape the notice of the church in Rome. Western and Central Europe may have been fragmented, but across the small world of elites, news traveled. Monks traded manuscripts and ideas, and princes and barons intermarried. At the very end of the eleventh century, the former prior of Cluny was elected pope, and he took the name of Urban II. He had lived most of his life in the region now called Burgundy, and he had played a central role in the rise of the Cluniacs to such prominence. His selection as pope in 1088 was a triumph for the order, and it raised the hope that he would be able to magnify the power of the papacy throughout Christendom. Those hopes were not disappointed. In 1095, in the town of Clermont, closer to Cluny than to Rome, Pope Urban dramatically shifted the focus of Christian holy war away from Spain. He called on all good Christians to turn their efforts to retaking Jerusalem. And so they did.

≫≫ ≪≪

THE CRUSADES

IN PURELY MILITARY TERMS, the Crusades were negligible. At least seven times over the course of two centuries, armies from France, Germany, Italy, and England invaded the Near East. Initially, these armies were led mostly, though not entirely, by second-tier nobles and third sons who faced dead-end lives as retainers. Later, they were led by kings and princes who sought both temporal and spiritual glory in campaigns against the Muslims. At their height, the Crusader states of the Near East comprised a narrow band that barely included present-day Israel, Lebanon, and slivers of Jordan, Turkey, and Syria. While the crusading urge took centuries to dissipate, by the beginning of the fourteenth century the Crusades as a mass movement were over, and the Crusader states were eradicated. The movement began in a burst of religious fury, but in the end it probably did more harm to the Christian Byzantine Empire than it did to the Muslim states of the Near East.

In purely symbolic terms, however, the Crusades became the perfect metaphor for conflict between Islam and the West. Out of the sorry, often pathetic history of the Crusades, the myth of endless conflict was forged.

The Crusades were launched by Pope Urban to liberate the holy city of Jerusalem from the grip of Muslims, who were described as uncouth infidels defiling the holiest of holies and as "a race alien to God" who had desecrated ground sanctified by the blood of Christ.[1] It would take thick rose-colored lenses to transform the Crusades into a symbol of harmony. The blood-soaked streets of Jerusalem, taken after a long siege in 1099, and the armies of Christendom indulging in what even later Western

propagandists admit was a wild orgy of death, make that impossible. But the killing fields of Jerusalem lasted days. Crusader states were enmeshed in the Near East for more than two hundred years. In between the intermittent battles, there were long periods of calm and poignant moments of amity.

Even with the Crusades, therefore, the memory that has survived is incomplete. It is a memory framed by prejudice, and whatever doesn't fit the history of conflict has been elided, forgotten, and buried. In the long years that separated the actual Crusades, Muslims lived uneventfully under Christian rule in the Near East. While there was far less of the cultural interaction that made Muslim Spain so dynamic, there was also little animosity. Indifference may not be the stuff of legend, but it more accurately describes the decades of live-and-let-live that separated the brief but exciting episodes of armies mustering, sieges laid, and battles fought.

While the Muslims of Egypt and the Near East were accustomed to clashes with Christian Byzantium, the arrival of the first Crusaders from Western Europe took them by surprise. The ferocity of the Crusaders stunned them, as did the simple intensity of their faith. By the end of the eleventh century, Muslims of the Near East had only the faintest connection to the early fervor of Muhammad and the Arab conquests. They were used to war, but not to war inspired by religious passion.

The exception, perhaps, was the animosity between Sunnis and Shi'ites, which seemed to worsen with each passing century. The sudden rise of the Shi'ite Fatimid empire in Egypt in the tenth century was seen by the Sunni majority of the Near East as a grave threat, and for good reason. The Fatimids forged an unlikely coalition of North African tribes, and then swept across the desert from Tunisia and into Egypt. Their leader proclaimed himself caliph, which meant that in the middle of the tenth century no fewer than three people simultaneously donned that mantle, one in Baghdad, one in Córdoba, and one in Cairo. Then Hakim, the Fatimid caliph of the early eleventh century, declared that he was also the messiah, and began to persecute those who did not bow to him. Instead of showing tolerance, he stripped the People of the Book of their rights. Like a Muslim Caligula or Nero, his behavior was erratic, confusing, and often cruel. He demanded that shops in Cairo stay open all night on the off chance that he decided to stop by, and he instituted a lottery where some were rewarded with gold, others with death.[2]

Hakim meted out draconian punishments to everyone—Sunni, Shi'a, Christian, black, brown, or fair-skinned—who might challenge his legitimacy. The persecution of Christians, however, had consequences that he neither foresaw nor lived to see. In 1009 his soldiers desecrated and then partly destroyed the Church of the Holy Sepulchre in Jerusalem to punish Christians for their refusal to embrace his new revelation. Word of that deed spread to the West, and though the pope and the royals of Europe could do little more than rail against the Fatimids, the memory did not fade. Instead, it festered over the next decades, until it sparked what became the First Crusade.

By then, however, Hakim was long dead. He had made far too many enemies, and he finally alienated one too many faction. His end was suitably bizarre. He rode out of Cairo on a donkey and disappeared. He had been in the habit of leaving the palace with only a small retinue of guards, and that was his undoing. But the absence of a body provided one group of followers with a sliver of hope. Various Shi'ite factions over the years had declared that their imam had not died but had instead removed himself from visible society to wait until the time was right for him to appear again. When Hakim vanished, a few steadfast followers refused to believe that he had been assassinated and claimed instead that he had gone into hiding to await the end of times. Hounded out of Egypt, these followers became known as the Druze, a secretive, close-knit community that survived in the mountains of Lebanon, Syria, and Palestine.

When the Sunnis were not fighting the Fatimid Shi'ites, they were fighting one another. The tenth and eleventh centuries saw the rise of Turkish power. The Turks had filtered into the Near East and Anatolia from Central Asia and had slowly converted to Islam after they were hired as mercenaries by both the Abbasid caliph and other Arab rulers. The emergence of the Turkish Seljuk dynasty in the eleventh century threatened all of the established powers in the region, especially the Byzantines and the Fatimid Shi'ites.

Because the Near East of the eleventh century was wracked by internecine conflicts between Muslim sects and Muslim states, it was ripe for a foreign invasion. Even so, no one expected a war with Christians from Europe, and few of the inhabitants of the Near East had any dealings with the West. Spain was far removed from the daily world of Damascus, Antioch, Jerusalem, or any of the other city-states of the

Near East. Though Jewish clans kept in touch with one another across the thousands of miles spanned by the Mediterranean, most Muslims were more provincial. Merchants traveled widely, and men of learning did as well, but even these had little contact with the backward states of Europe. As a result, the sudden appearance of thousands of European knights claiming a divine mandate to liberate Jerusalem was not something Muslims in the Near East had ever imagined.

It was unexpected for Western European Christians as well. They had never launched a campaign against so distant a goal. They had, however, fought "crusades" against non-Christians and heretics. While scholars have analyzed the various strands that led to the First Crusade, there are heated academic debates about how new the Crusades actually were. There had been campaigns against pagans in northern Europe and against Muslims in Spain and in Italy. Christian rulers routinely whipped up the passions of their soldiers by linking sacrifice in battle to Christ's sacrifice on the cross. But there was a difference between evoking Christ in pre-battle speeches and calling for a military holy pilgrimage thousands of miles away.[3]

Regardless of how novel the idea was, the result of Pope Urban's call was unprecedented. Never before had an army of Christians from the West been raised against the Muslims of the Near East.

THE CALL IS ANSWERED

THE GIST of Urban's speech at Clermont in late 1095 was simple: Christians had a sacred duty to liberate Jerusalem from Muslim rule. No official version of the speech has survived, and the various contemporary accounts differ considerably in detail and in tone. But they all suggest that Urban urged the bishops and princes of Christendom to assemble an army for the sole purpose of taking Jerusalem. In some accounts, Urban dwelt on the purported atrocities being committed by Muslims against pious Christians and pilgrims. In classic demagogic fashion, he listed the tortures that Christians were supposedly suffering, ranging from disembowelment and intestines twirled around filthy metal instruments to unfathomable acts committed within the Church of the Holy Sepulchre, including the forced circumcision of monks on the bloodstained altar. Other accounts of the speech stressed the

redemptive power of liberating the city. Urban admonished the princes that they had been living lives of sin and had themselves committed atrocities in their petty wars with one another. For that, Urban declared, they would be held responsible on judgment day, unless they dedicated themselves to the noble cause of Jerusalem.

"Let therefore hatred depart from among you," Urban announced; "let your quarrels end, let wars cease, and let all dissensions and controversies slumber. Enter upon the road to the Holy Sepulchre; wrest that land from the wicked race, and subject it to yourselves." The Holy Land itself, Urban continued, was crying out for help.

That land which as the Scripture says floweth with milk and honey, was given by God into the possession of the children of Israel. Jerusalem is the navel of the world; the land is fruitful above others, like another paradise of delights. This the Redeemer of the human race has made illustrious by His advent, has beautified by residence, has consecrated by suffering, has redeemed by death, has glorified by burial. This royal city, therefore, situated at the center of the world, is now held captive by His enemies, and is in subjection to those who do not know God, to the worship of the heathens. She seeks therefore and desires to be liberated, and does not cease to implore you to come to her aid.

And those who answered the call, Urban promised, would be rewarded. "All who die by the way, whether by land or by sea, or in battle against the pagans, shall have immediate remission of sins. This I grant them through the power of God with which I am invested." The task at hand was one that every believer had a duty to undertake, provided they had the means. The alternative, Urban declared, was unacceptable.

O what a disgrace if such a despised and base race, which worships demons, should conquer a people which has the faith of omnipotent God and is made glorious with the name of Christ! With what reproaches will the Lord overwhelm us if you do not aid those who, with us, profess the Christian religion! Let those who have been accustomed unjustly to wage private warfare against the faithful now go against the infidels and end with victory this war which should have been begun long ago. Let those who for a long time, have been

robbers, now become knights. Let those who have been fighting against their brothers and relatives now fight in a proper way against the barbarians. Let those who have been serving as mercenaries for small pay now obtain the eternal reward.... Let those who go not put off the journey, but rent their lands and collect money for their expenses; and as soon as winter is over and spring comes, let them eagerly set out on the way with God as their guide.[4]

Those listening to Urban could have been forgiven for thinking that Jerusalem had only recently been captured by Muslim hordes. In fact, Jerusalem had been under the rule of one Muslim prince or another since the seventh century, and Christian pilgrims had rarely been denied access. Even the brief, albeit shocking, depredations of the mad caliph Hakim had taken place nearly a century before Urban stood in Clermont and made his history-altering speech. But the motivation for launching the Crusade had less to do with goings-on in Jerusalem than with the situation in Western and Central Europe.

As many have noted, the Crusades proved to be a brilliant solution for the anarchy and chaos of Europe. The princes of France in the eleventh century, aside from the successful Norman invasion of England in 1066, were engaged in constant battle with one another, and the situation wasn't much better to the east, in Germany. The church, aside from centers like Cluny, functioned at the whim of nobles. By calling for the liberation of Jerusalem, Urban hoped to focus the energies of the princes on something other than infighting and thereby increase the prestige and influence of the church. He enjoined the knights to wear the symbol of the cross in order to mark themselves as soldiers of Christ, and he instructed his bishops to spread the word. They did, and the response was immediate. The Normans were especially keen. So were the peasants of central Germany, led by an enigmatic figure known as Peter the Hermit, whose rough-shod, ill-clad army assembled around the Danube and followed it south and east

The road to Jerusalem went through Constantinople. While some of the Italian cities had ships, there was no fleet in Europe capable of transporting an army of fifty thousand and its retainers across the Mediterranean. The legions of the West had to go overland, and that meant a journey of thousands of miles to Constantinople and from there across Turkey and into Syria and Palestine.

The First Crusade was blessed with extraordinary, perhaps even divine, luck. The timing could not have been better. Much as the early Muslim conquests took place at a nearly perfect juncture just after the Byzantines and the Sasanians had exhausted each other after decades of war, the Crusaders arrived in Constantinople just as both the Byzantines and the Seljuk Turks were struggling to retain their empires. By the eleventh century, the Seljuks had replaced the Abbasids as the primary threat to the Byzantines. In 1071, at the battle of Manzikert, the Byzantine army was annihilated by the Turkish sultan, and the emperor was captured. As a result of this decisive and humiliating defeat, all of Asia Minor except for the ancient imperial city of Nicaea, a scant few hundred miles from Constantinople, fell under the control of the Seljuk federation.

After Manzikert, however, the Seljuks fragmented. They had never been a centralized federation, and each Seljuk prince commanded the loyalty of his own small army. With multiple marriages, the number of princes tended to balloon. Corralling them into a unified force was the exception, not the rule, and in perfect illustration of the law of entropy, the Seljuk state disintegrated into dozens of small units almost as soon as it had formed. These units then dissolved into even smaller units, until many of the cities that ringed Jerusalem, including Antioch and Damascus, were ruled by different and often antagonistic Seljuk factions, none of whom were willing or prepared to come to the aid of the others. Quite the contrary. As long as they themselves were not the object of a Crusader assault, they were perfectly content to let the Christians eliminate rival city-states on their way to Jerusalem.

Not only were the Seljuks disunited and the Byzantines hobbled, but the Fatimids of Egypt, who still nominally controlled Jerusalem and much of the territory of Palestine, were also a shadow of their former selves. Unable to mount an effective challenge to the splintered Seljuk emirs in Syria, the Fatimids welcomed the Crusaders as an effective deterrent. When the Fatimid caliph in Cairo learned that Christian armies from Europe were advancing toward Syria from Constantinople, he sent envoys offering them assistance. The enmity between the Sunni Seljuks and Shi'a Fatimids could hardly have been greater, but neither of them had strong feelings about the princes of Europe. The Crusaders were unfamiliar, and their motives were a mystery. The Fatimid caliph unfortunately overlooked the most trenchant detail, which was that the

ultimate goal of the Crusaders was not Syria but Jerusalem, which was then ruled by the Fatimids themselves.[5]

In short, when the Crusaders set out for Jerusalem, not a single strong state stood in their way. Had the movement begun only a decade earlier, the Seljuk sultan who orchestrated the victory at Manzikert would still have been alive, and the Crusaders would not have stood a chance against him. At any other time in the eleventh century, they would have faced a powerful and hostile Byzantine emperor in Constantinople, as well as a cohesive Fatimid empire, had they somehow managed to make it to southern Syria.

Not only were the Crusades blessed with good timing, but they were also graced with adversaries who had scant knowledge of their tactics, ambitions, and ideology. In retrospect, the First Crusade was clearly a holy war waged by Christians against Muslims, but it is striking how unaware of that fact Muslims at the time were. The Seljuks and then the Fatimids viewed the initial forays by the knights of Europe as a nuisance and then as a military challenge, yet even after the fall of Jerusalem, there was no sense in the Muslim world that this was a religious war or a clash of civilizations.

In fact, it is stretching matters to even speak of a "Muslim world." There was no unity among Muslims even when faced with a Christian invasion of the Levant. As we will see, after the success of the First Crusade, some Muslims tried—and failed—to create a pan-Muslim alliance against the Christians. Even when, nearly a century later, Saladin united the disparate city-states and led them to retake Jerusalem, he succeeded primarily because of his abilities as a military commander, not because of people rallied to a pan-Islamic banner. In the years after the First Crusade, while there was no shortage of platitudes about Muslim solidarity in the face of a Christian challenge, few in a position of authority did more than give lip service to the idea of a unified Muslim community.

In short, religion mattered, except when it didn't, and it didn't matter, except when it did. The link between faith and action is blurry. The call of Urban spurring armies to march on Jerusalem in the name of God is often treated as proof that men will fight and die for their religion. The reaction of Muslims almost a hundred years later, when Jerusalem was retaken in 1187, is treated the same way. But what about the times when Muslims or Christians called on their brethren to rise up in the name of God and no one listened? What about the periods in between the

fighting, after the fall of Jerusalem? Where was religion when Christian knights formed alliances with Sunni Muslims to fight Shi'a Muslims or when one Christian lord looked for help from a Muslim Kurd in order to subdue another Christian lord? If religion mattered more than anything, how do we explain those times when it mattered hardly at all?

Though the Crusades eventually became synonymous with conflict between Christianity and Islam, at the time the picture was decidedly more ambiguous. It's not that the war to take Jerusalem and the subsequent efforts of various Muslim rulers to retake it were not colored by religion. It's that religion was one of several reasons for fighting. Omitting these other factors reduces the Crusades to one dimension. Yes, faith was vital—at least for the Christian knights. From what we can tell at many centuries' remove, they were driven by piety, which Pope Urban tapped but did not create. They believed that the struggle to liberate Jerusalem would serve as a penance for their sins and lead to rewards in the hereafter. They were drawn by a potent promise of material and spiritual rewards, and they were moved by the image of the city where Christ played out his passion being occupied by people who had little regard for that blessed legacy. But even here, the fury of the Crusaders was easily channeled not just against Muslims, but also against Jews or other Christians who did not see the universe in quite the same way. Conflict between faiths was one of many conflicts, and not always the one that mattered most.

The intra-Muslim rivalries and antagonisms were mirrored by similar divisions among the Crusaders themselves and between the Catholic Crusaders, who at least nominally followed the edicts of the pope in Rome, and the Eastern Rite Byzantines, who had their own clerical establishment and refused to recognize the pope's supreme authority. Arriving at the borders of the Byzantine Empire, the Crusaders expected to be greeted warmly by the emperor Alexius Comnenus, and to be welcomed as allies in the war against the infidel. This was in spite of the fact that the Eastern and Western Churches had split in 1054 when the papal legate in Constantinople excommunicated the patriarch for heresy, in the Church of Hagia Sophia, which was the Eastern equivalent of Saint Peter's Basilica in Rome. The Byzantines did not appreciate the public insult to their church father, and had someone loudly insulted the pope in Saint Peter's, the reaction would have been much the same. Among the reasons for the schism, the Byzantine church refused to accept

Rome's addition to the Nicene Creed of the word *filioque*, which signified that the Holy Spirit flowed from both the Father and the Son, and not, as the Eastern Church believed, from God the Father alone. There was also the delicate and inflammatory matter of the use of unleavened versus leavened bread in the Eucharist. These issues were enough to cause a rupture.

In the decades before the First Crusade, both churches had attempted to heal the wound. As a result, by the end of the eleventh century, the princes of Europe viewed Byzantium as a natural friend in the war against the infidels, and they tended to overlook the chasm that had opened between the Catholic and Orthodox religious establishments.

The Byzantines were skeptical. Alexius, the heir to a rich and sophisticated tradition, understood that Jerusalem was not cause enough to align his interests with the Crusaders. He was a shrewd man, erudite and hard-nosed, who was also graced with a favorable biographer in his daughter. When he ascended to the throne, the empire was in disarray and in need of leadership. The Turks were only one of several threats, and Alexius had to repel Slavic and Serbian tribes invading from the northern Balkans as well as the vulturous Venetians and Normans. The tax system was in shambles; the army was undermanned and fragmented; and while the court and the palaces of Constantinople remained as magnificent as ever, there was a dispiriting sense that the end might be near.

Alexius reversed the tide. He rallied the army, appointed skilled governors, replenished the treasury, and looked to the West for mercenaries, especially Normans. He had fought Norman princes in Sicily and in the Balkans, so he knew that they excelled at combat and chafed at being ruled, but he was willing to take the risk of hiring them in return for the reward of using them. In a similar vein, he intended to use the Crusaders to loosen the grip of the Seljuks on Asia Minor, but he had to make sure that they did not keep what they conquered. In addition, their armies were not under his command, and when they needed food and supplies, they tended to loot. Alexius was faced with a challenge that a man of lesser abilities could not have met. He wanted to exploit the Crusaders for his purposes without allowing them to jeopardize his lands. As the price of his assistance, he demanded that the princes swear an oath that if they captured any territory that had previously been ruled by Constantinople, they would return it to him.

The cultural gulf between the Byzantines and the Crusaders could hardly have been wider. Byzantine splendor had faded, but it still shone brighter than anything in Europe. The proud Byzantines saw the Crusaders as ignorant peasants, albeit well armed and pious. While some chroniclers called the Byzantines "Greek" because of the language they spoke, the Byzantines called themselves "Romans," because they saw themselves, with justification, as the heirs of the empire that had been founded a millennium before by Augustus. While the Crusaders were also descendants of the Romans, they had long since lost touch with Roman learning and culture, so much so that they were dependent on the Muslims of Spain for the wisdom of antiquity. The Muslims referred to the Crusaders as the "Franks," because most of them, including the Normans, were from Frankish lands once ruled by Charlemagne. The Byzantines, however, referred to the Crusaders as "barbarians," which was what the ancient Greeks had called the uncultured, uncivilized tribesmen of Central Europe.

The Crusaders were a curiosity to the Byzantines, and the emperor's daughter Anna Comnena recorded her impressions of them with the critical, bemused eye of an anthropologist writing about a primitive tribe. She was particularly struck by the character and physique of the Norman prince Bohemond of Taranto. According to Anna, he "was so tall in body that he exceeded even the tallest men by almost fifty centimeters.... The flesh on his body was very white.... His hair was light brown and did not hang on his back as it did on other barbarians.... Some charm also manifested itself in this man, but it was obscured by the fear he inspired all around him." Anna's account, penned years after the fact, was undoubtedly colored by the fact that Bohemond went on to become ruler of Antioch and an uneasy, often antagonistic vassal of the emperor. Other Crusaders, such as Godfrey of Bouillon and Baldwin of Boulogne, later of Edessa and later still king of Jerusalem, also merited description, but Bohemond stood out as the archetype—the faithful, barely civilized knight heading to Holy Land as a warrior for God.[6]

And at the time, that is all they were. The term "Crusader" was not invented until the thirteenth century, although the absence of the word does not mean the absence of the concept. Scholarly debates notwithstanding, the men who set off for Jerusalem in 1096 thought of themselves as what one French historian called "armed pilgrims."[7] There was a long and established history of pilgrimage to Jerusalem, especially as

penance for sins, and Pope Urban and his messengers had dangled the promise of spiritual reward for taking up arms to restore the Holy Land to Christian control. These armed pilgrims may have exhibited behavior that our contemporary morality would condemn as brutal and barbaric, but however greedy and rapacious they may have been, they lived in a world of deep and simple faith, one that not only coexisted with the sins of the flesh but was often fueled by them. The Crusaders knew that they had committed petty and not-so-petty sins, and that made the act of pilgrimage far more significant.

While the shifting sands of Near East politics were ultimately a gift to the Crusaders, the fate of Peter the Hermit and his followers, who had set off first, provided them with additional unexpected help. Peter's farce of an army had, by virtue of sheer size, managed to massacre the Jews of several towns along the Danube, but it was no match for the Seljuks. Alexius and his court were appalled at the filth and chaos of Peter's rabble, and the emperor made sure that the peasant "army" was quickly transported across the Bosphorus and away from the city. Once on the Asian side, they were cut to pieces by the local sultan, who naturally took them as representative of what the Franks could offer. When the far better disciplined and outfitted armies of the Normans and the other knights arrived soon after, the Seljuk emir mistakenly assumed that they were more of the same.

The local Seljuks may not have taken the Crusaders seriously, but Alexius did. Having persuaded most of them to swear allegiance, he had them escorted out of the city and across the Bosphorus into Asia. They took Nicaea (known as Iznik in Turkish) in May 1097 and then advanced south to the same pass that had welcomed Xerxes and Alexander in centuries past. The narrow Cilician pass between the mountains of southern Anatolia separated Asia Minor from Syria, and once through, the Crusaders laid siege to the ancient city of Antioch. Until its capture by the Seljuks in 1085, Antioch had been one of the most important Christian cities in the world, along with Jerusalem, Constantinople, and Rome.

After an arduous eight-month siege, Antioch fell to the Crusaders in June 1098. The task had been made easier by the squabbling that divided the Arab and Turkish factions trying to defend the city's formidable walls. Antioch was also home to a large Christian population that had lived there since the first century, and when the Crusaders arrived at the

gates, the Turkish governor expelled them. "Antioch is yours," he told them, "but you will have to leave it to me until I see what happens between us and the Franks." He promised to look after their wives and children, but he did not allow them to return. These exiles received a cool reception from the Franks. Primarily Greek Orthodox and Armenian, they spoke different languages and worshiped with different rites, and the Franks treated them with suspicion and disdain. The feelings were mutual, and the proud Christians of Antioch, who traced their lineage to Saint Paul, felt less allegiance to the Crusaders than to the Arabs and Turks whom they had lived with, largely in peace, for the previous centuries. Though they served as useful intelligence agents for Bohemond and the other commanders, they did not trust the motives of the invaders.

Antioch finally succumbed after the Crusaders gained the aid of a Turkish general disenchanted with the local faction. Bohemond then allowed his soldiers, who had suffered through long months, to ravage the once-great city. And as in other cities on the road to Jerusalem, the Crusaders did not stop to ask whether the home they looted was owned by Christians, or whether the women they raped could recite the Nicene Creed or the opening verse of the Quran.[8]

After several days of indiscriminate pillaging, the princes reined in their army. The treatment meted out to Antioch seemed extreme at that time, but it was hardly out of the norm for Frankish and German warfare, nor did it compare to what was in store for Jerusalem. The duplicity of Bohemond shocked both the Muslims and the Byzantines but would not have raised eyebrows in Europe. He did not honor his commitment to Alexius to return Antioch to Byzantine control and instead set himself up as its king. That alienated not only the emperor but Bohemond's fellow knights as well. One of them, Baldwin, veered east with his army in a fit of jealousy and took the city of Edessa. The remaining forces, now significantly depleted, continued south.

The siege and capture of Antioch roused the Seljuk princes, as well as the Fatimid caliph in Cairo, to take serious notice. One twelfth-century Muslim chronicler later described the Christian victory at Antioch as the culmination of years of aggression against Islam that had begun with the fall of Toledo in Spain to the Christians in 1071, and then continued with the Norman invasion of Sicily, led by kinsmen of Baldwin of Edessa. The pattern, at least to one Muslim historian, was clear: Christians had

been waging an international battle to turn back Muslim advances, and the assaults on Antioch, Edessa, and Syria were only the latest in a series.[9]

But even after Antioch, not all Arab and Turkish elites of the Near East took the Crusaders seriously. That would change forever when Jerusalem fell in 1099. Compared to the eight-month siege of Antioch, Jerusalem was taken easily, in less than two months. But while the Crusaders had camped under the walls of Antioch mostly during winter and spring, the contest for Jerusalem was waged during the scorching heat of summer. After more than three years of nearly continuous warfare in unfamiliar territory, the Crusaders were exhausted and anxious for the end of their mission. Perhaps that explains what happened when the walls were finally breached.

As it had been for centuries, Jerusalem was then inhabited by a mix of Jews, Christians, and Muslims. The Jewish quarter had existed since before the time of Christ, and the major Christian sects each had a sliver of the city and some responsibility for maintaining the holy stations along the Via Dolorosa. But the city's defenses were under the control of the Fatimid governor, and he viewed the local Christian and Jewish population as a potential fifth column. He made a Solomonic decision; the Christians he ordered out of the city, and the Jews he allowed to stay. Most Christians left, with the exception of the guardians of the Holy Sepulchre, which was still not fully reconstructed since Hakim's desecrations.

The siege was straightforward, and in mid-July 1099, the soldiers of Godfrey of Bouillon, by dint of formidable towers, heavy battering rams, and brute force, breached the walls. Some of the city's Christians aided the attackers, as the Fatimid governor had feared. They probably hoped that the victorious armies would reward them for their aid. Had they known what would actually happen, they would have fought to the last man to keep the Crusaders from occupying the city.

The Muslim accounts of the fall of Jerusalem described the usual outrages, but what sets Jerusalem apart in the annals of cold-blooded conquest is that the Christian chroniclers were equally shocked at what happened. The Crusaders had journeyed for an elusive goal, and once they had achieved it, their rage exploded. Whatever the reason, the city wasn't just sacked; it was desecrated and its inhabitants were massacred.

In spite of the paltry efforts of Godfrey and the other Christian general, Tancred, to exercise restraint, their soldiers swept through the city and killed every single soul they found. The massacre was not limited to Arab and Turkish Muslims. The Jews of the city took refuge in their synagogues only to be locked inside and burned alive. Eastern Orthodox monks tried to keep the shrine of the Holy Sepulchre from being looted by soldiers more interested in booty than in blessings, but they were cut down where they stood. There were stories of infants dashed against stones, of torture that lasted for days to amuse the troops, of beheadings, impalings, flayings, dismemberment, and corpses everywhere; and now and then, neat piles of heads surrounded, almost artistically, by pools of blood.[10]

LIVE AND LET LIVE

THE SACK of Jerusalem deeply disturbed the Muslim world. Muslims venerated the city, and the brutality of its conquest by the Christians was a wound that never quite healed. It's not that the treatment meted out to the unfortunate inhabitants was extraordinary by the standards of the day. But the fact that it happened in Jerusalem, a city so revered, was unsettling, and not only to Muslims. The proverbial morning after, even the Crusaders were shamed by what had transpired, judging from the Christian accounts of the city's capture. The massacre of Muslims who had taken refuge in Al-Aqsa Mosque may have been marginally acceptable, but the slaying of Eastern Rite Christians in the sanctuary of the Holy Sepulchre was not.

In time, the fall of Jerusalem became a rallying cry for the Muslims of the Near East, but in the immediate aftermath, the outrage was not met by action. Poets wrote laments about what had occurred, and some called for a campaign to repulse the Christian invasion. These had no effect. The Turkish emirs of Damascus and Aleppo were too weak, too antagonistic to the Fatimids, too suspicious of the rulers of Mosul and Iraq, and too competitive with each other to form an alliance capable of challenging the Franks. Calls for Muslim unity in the face of a foreign incursion were not persuasive enough to overcome the political, cultural, and theological divisions between the various factions that con-

trolled the Near East. "The sultans did not agree among themselves," wrote the Arab historian Ibn al-Athir, "and it was for this reason that the Franks were able to seize control of the country."[11]

It is tempting to identify the Crusades as dramatic chapters in the war between Islam and the West, especially given the way Jerusalem fell in 1099. And that temptation is bolstered by some of what took place after the First Crusade. As the twelfth century progressed, it became common to view the Crusades as one prong of an international campaign conducted by Western Christians against Muslims. Both Christian and Muslim scholars of the Crusades, beginning centuries ago and resuming in the nineteenth century, lumped the various battles, waged by very different factions thousands of miles apart, under the banner of religious war. Polemicists at the time, again both Muslim and Christian, also had good reason to create this framework.

Yet the fact remains that *at the time,* holy war did not hold enough appeal to the rulers or to the people of the Near East to function as an effective rallying cry. The later tendency in both the West and the Muslim world to focus on the Crusades as war between religions makes it seem as if religion were the only factor, but in truth, it was only one factor, whose importance waxed and waned unpredictably. Put simply: if wars between religions had been of such overriding importance, then Christians throughout Europe would have rushed to fight side by side with their Byzantine brothers, and Muslims would have overcome their divisions and joined hands to fight a common adversary. That did not happen.

Instead, the First Crusade was led mostly by Frankish knights, and then the Franks—rather than fighting a perpetual war against Muslims—became part of the political fabric of the Near East. The victory in 1099 led to a dramatic increase in the number of pilgrims to Jerusalem, as well as a mini migration of settlers. Though exact numbers are impossible to come by, it seems that tens of thousands of people from Western and Central Europe immigrated to the new kingdoms of Jerusalem and Edessa. Some of these were petty nobility looking for a new start; others were artisans, soldiers, or peasants brought by their lords or drawn by a new frontier. Still others were merchants from Genoa, Pisa, Venice, or Amalfi who settled in the coastal ports such as Acre, Tyre, and Jaffa. The Italians, with their superior ships and vibrant

commercial networks in the Mediterranean, took control of what they hoped would be lucrative trade routes stretching into Central Asia, India, and beyond.

Popular histories of the Crusades in both the West and the Muslim world focus exclusively on the conflict. Even the contemporary chroniclers, writing in the twelfth and thirteenth centuries, rarely devoted attention to daily life. There was little drama in that, and no heroism. The relentless focus on war has been a problem of history writing in general, and not confined to the subject of Muslims and Christians in the Near East. Until the second half of the twentieth century, few who wrote history—whether they were Muslim, Christian, Jew, or Hindu—wasted time on farming, trade, immigration, domestic life, and the humdrum aspects of getting through the day. History writing has thus exaggerated the frequency and centrality of war, revolution, mayhem, and changes in government. The consequence for the Crusades is that we remember the fighting, but not the peace. For two centuries, however, Western Europeans lived in the Near East, and while a year rarely passed without some skirmish against some adversary, there were long periods of quiet.

Recent historians have made concerted efforts to fill in the blanks of daily life in Europe at the time, but far less effort has gone into painting a complete picture of Near Eastern societies under the Franks. Since the middle of the twentieth century, and with very few original threads, scholars of medieval societies have expertly pieced together a tapestry of the so-called Dark Ages. Yet that skill has barely been employed to flesh out the contours of everyday life in the Crusader states.

As a result, for most of the past nine hundred years, histories of the Crusades—both in the West and in the Muslim world—have told a simple narrative of religious clash, begun by the papacy, fought by the knights of Europe, and then continued at the end of the twelfth century with equal fervor by the Muslims of the Near East and their savior, Saladin. That story has become part of the collective memory of both Westerners and Muslims. In the West, within a few years of the creation of the kingdom of Jerusalem, it was already being told in Europe, especially by those who used the First Crusade to create a more centralized church and more powerful states in Europe. Then the story made its way into ballads and epic poems, meant to inspire and entertain. Over the

centuries, long after the last of the Franks had been evicted from the Near East, the memory seeped into popular culture through novels, plays, and eventually, in the twentieth century, movies.

In the English-speaking world, the nineteenth-century novels of Sir Walter Scott did more than anything to establish the popular image of the Crusades. Borrowing liberally from Edward Gibbon, Scott celebrated Saladin and Richard the Lionheart as icons of the contest between Islam and Christianity, and his books were later taken by Hollywood as the source material for films. In novels such as *The Talisman* and *Ivanhoe*, Scott portrayed Saladin as an aristocratic adversary, a Muslim warrior who respected the code of honor held so dear by Christian noblemen and knights. But Saladin was the exception to the rule that portrayed "Saracens" as heretical brutes.

Central to the popular story were the orders of religious knights: the Templars and the Hospitallers. The Templars, with their chain mail girded with white linen emblazoned with a red cross, became archetypes of the Christian warrior. Named after the Temple of Solomon in Jerusalem, where they lived, the Templars received the official sanction of the church early in the twelfth century. Not only was the temple the purported center of the first Israelite kingdom in the Holy Land, it was also where later Muslims had built Al-Aqsa Mosque. As a religious order blessed by the pope and sponsored by Bernard of Clairvaux, the Templars represented the fusion of the soldier and the priest, and their fame and wealth survived long after they departed the Holy Land. They and the Hospitallers eventually retreated to Mediterranean islands such as Malta and Rhodes, until the Ottomans supplanted them. As the order disappeared, however, the legend grew until the image of the Templars was permanently imprinted on Western consciousness. They became Crusader icons. They have graced forgettable Victorian novels, French romances, Hollywood films, and international best sellers, and have been cast as sinister characters pulling the levers of history, a dark, hidden force along with the Masons and the Illuminati.

But while the religious orders were prominent in Frankish society in the Near East, they were a small, albeit powerful, minority of all European settlers in the Orient and arguably less important than the Italian merchants who controlled trade but did not fight wars. Even generous estimates suggest that the Templars and Hospitallers never had more than a thousand armed knights at any one time. Yet a quick glance at a

library catalog will yield thousands of entries on the crusading orders, which dwarfs the literature on trade. Merchants may have mattered more in the greater scheme of things, but what they did was less compelling to writers and polemicists, either at the time or centuries later. What would a romantic novelist do with a dull Genoese merchant in Acre? Much better to focus on knights, castles, war, and men in shiny chain mail. For Arab and Turkish court chroniclers, the Templars made a perfect foil, proof of the greed and rapaciousness of the Christians. A spice merchant from Pisa arranging shipments in Sidon was of far less interest.

In the workaday world of the Crusader kingdoms of the twelfth century, however, those merchants, artisans, and peasants outnumbered the Templars and Hospitallers, who were important as vassals of Rome but did little to shape everyday society in Syria, Lebanon, or Palestine. The orders were integral to the ambitions of the pope, but they were only one element of the balance of power in the Near East.[12] The actual history of daily life during the age of the Crusades is more mundane and lacks dynamic characters and dominant leaders. The names of the people who lived and died are obscure, if recorded at all. The princes and kings of the Frankish states in the Near East are kept alive by scholars, and most battles of consequence were recorded by either Muslims or Christians. The long lulls in between were not.

Part of the explanation is prosaic: lulls make for boring reading. Until the late twentieth century, no one wrote a novel about a hum-drum life, or filmed a movie with no plot. And it is not only that periods between the wars are less dynamic. They also make history more complicated and ambiguous, and thereby undermine the black-and-white story of conflict. Neither Western cultures nor Muslim cultures have wanted to focus on coexistence. Yet, for much of the twelfth-century in the Near East, daily life was shaped not by heroic warriors but by small Western Christian city-states ruled by a few nobles and bureaucrats who were surrounded by Muslim Arabs and Turks and by Eastern Christian peasants and elites who had never converted to Islam. Their history, largely forgotten, is neither glorious nor ignominious.

The conquest of Jerusalem was followed by the creation of the Frankish kingdom of Jerusalem and the crowning of its first king, Godfrey. He soon died and was succeeded by Baldwin of Edessa, who became King Baldwin I of Jerusalem and remained so until his death in 1118. Frankish armies pushed to the coast of Palestine, attacked Tripoli,

and battled both the Fatimids and the Seljuks. As the new Christian states established themselves, they re-created Western Europe feudalism. The kingdom of Jerusalem nominally ruled many of the city-states in what is now Israel and the Palestinian West Bank; the lords of Antioch claimed sovereignty over large parts of present-day Lebanon; and the kingdom of Edessa carved out several thousand square miles inhabited mostly by Armenian Christians.

The Frankish princes ruled over a sparsely settled countryside dotted with towns. Many Muslims had fled just before and after 1099 as word of Christian barbarity spread. Jerusalem was nearly emptied of its inhabitants through the combined effects of flight and massacre, and even a decade later, the population of the city was only in the low thousands. Outside of Jerusalem, the areas controlled by the Crusaders were populated by a mix of Christians and Muslims. Most scholars agree that the Near East even at this point, nearly five hundred years after the first Arab conquests, was still home to a large Christian population, which in many regions was in the majority. That meant that Crusaders found themselves ruling states with substantial numbers of Christians. The conquerors, however, looked down on them because they spoke an incomprehensible language, had alien ways of celebrating mass, and held theological positions that had long ago been declared heretical in the West.

At first, the Franks treated the local Christians as conquered peoples. Though there was some loosening of social constraints, the locals remained second-class citizens. The Franks did not even lift the unpleasant poll tax that Muslims had imposed on the People of the Book. Instead, they maintained the tax, added Muslims to the lists, and continued to assess native Christians and Jews. In essence, most of the population, whether Christian or Muslim, found their lives little changed.

Eastern Christians neither rose up against the Crusaders nor fully embraced them. They served their new masters, just as they had served their old, but they at least shared a basic belief in the centrality of Christ to their lives. The Franks may not have respected the local Christians, but the local Christians found new opportunities for social advancement, primarily as intermediaries between the Muslims of the Near East and the new Crusader kingdoms.

In addition, Eastern Christians had an easier time getting hired as

mercenaries by the Crusader states than they had by the Seljuks or the Fatimids. Unlike the Templars and the Hospitallers, who answered mostly to themselves and nominally to the pope, Eastern Christian mercenaries did the bidding of the prince or king who hired them. It was a good arrangement for both the Frankish rulers and the local population. The Maronite Christians of Mount Lebanon, who had been moving ever closer to Rome, benefited enormously from the establishment of trading posts along the coast, and they found lucrative employment as soldiers for the princes of Acre, Sidon, and Tripoli. They also served as translators and intermediaries for Italian merchants who wanted to access the Seljuk-controlled trade routes east of Damascus and Aleppo. The legacy of close relations between the Maronites and the Franks (French) lasted well into the twentieth century and culminated in the creation of the modern state of Lebanon.

Gradually, however, the Franks began to assimilate. They changed how they dressed, the language they spoke, and even who they married. The majority of intermarriages occurred between Franks and local Christians; marriages between Christians and Muslims were frowned upon by both sides. But men and women have a way of circumventing social controls. Knights who had come to fight and then stayed needed women. Sex was easy enough to obtain, for a price or from a slave, but marriage was a bit more challenging. The aristocrats could arrange marriages to cement alliances between crusading states, between ruling Frankish families in the Near East and Byzantine royals, or with nobility in Europe. But for the rest, the most promising avenue was the easiest one—women from the local population. Often these were Christian, but not always.

The increase in intermarriage drew the notice of the chronicler Fulcher of Chartres. Writing around the year 1127, he observed that the Crusader states had become as corrupt, petty, and divisive as their counterparts in Europe. "Occidentals have now been made Orientals. He who was a Roman or a Frank is now a Galilean or an inhabitant of Palestine.... We have now forgotten the places of our birth.... Some already possess here homes or servants which they have received through inheritance. Some have taken wives not merely of their own people but Syrians, or Armenians, or even Saracens who have received the grace of baptism."[13]

As part of the process of assimilation, Western Christians in the Near

East became more tolerant of religious diversity than they had been in Europe. While they disdained the rites of Eastern Christians and treated Muslims (and Jews) as lost souls, they neither proselytized nor went out of their way to make life untenable for these subjects. In part, that was out of necessity. They were vastly outnumbered by Christians of different sects and by Muslims whose aid and support they often needed. Once the goal of retaking Jerusalem had been accomplished, the Franks confronted the daunting task of creating viable states, without a master plan for governing. They were forced to improvise, and faced with the more sophisticated societies that they had conquered and now ruled, they borrowed liberally.

The Crusader states emulated not just the dress and mores of local Christians but also the policies of the Muslim rulers they had supplanted. The result was a grudging culture of toleration. As long as taxes were paid, most of the local populace was left alone, free to enforce their own social and religious mores. One Muslim chronicler, who was unstinting in his hostility to the Franks, nonetheless acknowledged that they did not interfere with the right of Muslims to worship God as they pleased and "did not change a single law or cult practice." The courts set up by the Franks, while privileging the testimony of Christians, provided protections to Muslims as human beings "like the Franks."

The new rulers of Jerusalem did convert Al-Aqsa Mosque into a church, with a monastery for the Templars. They also set aside space for Muslims to worship there. It was understood that when major centers were occupied by Christians or by Muslims, the main church or mosque would be symbolically switched over to reflect the religion of the rulers. As a result, there was no Muslim outcry when Al-Aqsa was transformed into a church. Given the image of the Crusades as a period of unmitigated holy war, the lack of outrage is difficult to reconcile. A similar event in Jerusalem today would plunge the region into chaos.

In the first half of the twelfth century, however, there was no ingrained culture of religious war in the Near East. It was as common for Franks to fight Franks or Byzantium as it was for Franks to fight Muslims. Most Muslim states expended more energy scheming and plotting against one another than they did against the Christian invaders. That seems to have dismayed few inhabitants of Damascus, Aleppo, Mosul, or Cairo. Although the occasional cry for war against the infidel was not unheard of, later polemicists—in the interest of giving muscle to the

clash-of-civilizations perspective—have excavated those and emphasized them out of all proportion to their frequency. Muslim calls for holy war in the twelfth century were much like calls to end poverty in the twentieth—no one could disagree with the noble ambitions, but few were interested in actually doing anything.

In fact, Muslims who found themselves under Christian rule, rather than resisting their new overlords, began to emulate them. Much as Christians in Andalusia learned Arabic and tried to ingratiate themselves with the Muslim ruling class, Muslims of the Crusader states did what they could to win the favor of the new lords. Some found that Christian rulers were more equitable than the Muslims they had replaced. In a refrain remarkably like that of the Córdoba martyrs of the ninth century who despaired when they saw Christians embracing Muslim culture, the chronicler Ibn Jubayr moaned that Muslim peasants preferred Christian landlords. "Their hearts have been seduced.... This is one of the misfortunes afflicting the Muslims. The Muslim community bewails the injustice of a landlord of its own faith, and applauds the conduct of its opponent and enemy, the Frankish landlord, and is accustomed to justice from him." And it wasn't just Muslims under Christian rule who accepted coexistence. Local sultans signed treaties and established fruitful trade alliances with the Crusader states. According to the chronicler Ibn al-Qalanisi, the Muslim governor of Ascalon sent emissaries to King Baldwin of Jerusalem to arrange a treaty because "he was more desirous of trading than fighting, and inclined to peaceful and friendly relation and securing the safety of travellers."[14]

It is a truism that most people, most of the time, follow the path of least resistance. Faced with a new political order, people tend to adapt rather than resist. That was true of Christians in Muslim-ruled Spain, and it was true of Muslims in the Christian-ruled Crusader states of the twelfth century. Until recently, most scholars assumed that the few Franks and Italians who immigrated to the Near East lived only in the coastal cities, in Jerusalem or Edessa, or in the fortified castles that lined the north-south corridor from Krak des Chevaliers, between Beirut and Damascus, to Kerak, south of present-day Amman in Jordan. In part, these assumptions were based on the absence of records listing land ownership, but they were also fueled by a long-standing belief that the Crusaders would never have settled in the midst of a hostile and alien rural population. But they did, and the local populace accommodated them.

While many Westerners did settle in cities, others carved out rural estates comparable to what might have been found in France or the Rhine Valley. These estates were tended by Christian and Muslim peasants whose particular creed mattered less to their masters than their ability to tend to crops, herds, and other agricultural business. For the better part of a century, Christian rule over those peasants generated no more, though perhaps no less, tension and animosity than what would have been found in feudal Western Europe at the time. Peasants resented their lords; barons disdained the peasantry. People gossiped, occasionally dreamt of a different world, and almost never did anything about it. The one thing everyone—high and low, Christian, Jew, or Muslim—abhorred was chaos. Injustice was hardly desirable, but it was preferable to revolution. In the world of the Crusader states, what mattered most was class and economic status, not religion.[15]

Though there are few surviving accounts of relations between Westerners and Muslims, one Muslim aristocrat did leave a vivid memoir of his life and times. Usama ibn Munqidh grew up in the city of Shayzar in northern Syria. He was, in the words of his translator and master scholar Philip Hitti, "a warrior, a hunter, a gentleman, a poet, and a man of letters. His life was the epitome of Arab civilization as it flourished during the early crusading period." As a young man, Usama received the typical education of a genteel urban aristocrat and learned classical poetry, grammar, calligraphy, and of course, the Quran. As an adult, he dabbled in rhetoric, philosophy, mysticism, and the arts of war, but to the end, he had a fatalistic view that God determined all moments of all lives and that all anyone could do is live out his allotted days. Toward the end of his life, after the entire region had been unified under the rule of Saladin the Kurd, Usama sat down and recorded his memories.

Usama delighted in the human condition and loved the absurdity of human existence. He recorded the story of a man named Ali Abd ibn abi al-Rayda who had made a name for himself as a soldier and a marauder raiding caravans. He served a local Muslim prince who was killed, and then was hired by a Frankish noble. With his knowledge of the region and his experience intercepting Muslim caravans, Ali helped his new Christian master become rich at the expense of local Muslim traders. Not only did that not please his former companions, it also deeply offended his wife. One night, she hid her brother in her home, and when her hus-

band returned, they attacked and killed him. She claimed that she was "angered on behalf of the Muslims because of what this infidel perpetrated against them." But she also took all of her murdered husband's belongings and relocated to the city of Shayzar, where Usama lived. He reported that she was treated with great respect by the neighbors. In another story, Usama told of a Frankish maid taken captive during a battle who caught the eye of the local Muslim emir. She bore him a son, who became the prince when his father died. Rather than living in luxury as the esteemed mother, however, she left the castle and married a Frankish shoemaker.

Usama was fascinated with the Franks. Much like the Byzantines, he was alternately bemused and appalled by how crude they could be. "Mysterious are the works of the Creator, the author of all things," he wrote. "When one comes to recount cases regarding the Franks, he cannot but glorify Allah and sanctify him, for he sees them as animals possessing the virtues of courage and fighting but nothing else; just as animals have only virtues of courage and fighting." Usama was particularly amazed at Frankish medical practices, which were so rudimentary that they tended to kill the patient. He wrote of an Eastern Christian physician who healed a Frankish knight with an abscess on his leg and saved a woman suffering from a mysterious affliction. The physician applied a poultice to the leg that absorbed the infection, and he altered the woman's diet until she showed signs of renewed health. The Franks, however, did not trust the remedies and sent their own physician, who scoffed at the treatments. The Frankish physician, refusing to believe that the knight's leg was getting better, said to him, "Which wouldst thou prefer, living with one leg or dying with two?" Faced with this choice, the knight said he'd rather have one leg than no life. So the physician called for an ax and had a few strong men hold the knight down while another chopped off his leg. The blow wasn't accurate. It cut the patient's bone and artery, and he promptly bled to death. As for the woman, the Frankish physician took one look at her and declared that she was possessed by the devil. He had her head shaved, fed her nothing but garlic and mustard, watched as she became weaker, carved a crucifix in her skull, peeled off the skin, rubbed the exposed bone with salt, exorcised the demon, and killed the patient.

To be fair, Usama also described instances when Frankish medicine succeeded in healing patients with treatments unknown in Syria at the

time, such as a concoction of ashes, vinegar, burnt lead, and clarified butter applied as a balm for a neck wound. But on the whole, he was both appalled and amused by the raw ignorance of the Franks.

Their sexual mores also astonished him. Usama was hardly the first or last person titillated by lurid tales. He recalled the time he was staying at an inn that served both Muslim and Christian travelers, and the innkeeper told him that a Christian man had come back to his room only to find another man sleeping with his wife. Naturally, he was a bit perturbed and woke the fellow up. "What are you doing here with my wife?" he asked the man. "Well, I was tired," the man replied. The wife was already in the bed, and it would, he told the irate husband, have been rude to wake her.

Usama also recounts a story told to him by the Muslim owner of a public bathhouse. One day, the owner went to the bath accompanied by a Frankish noble, and he was surprised at how immodest the Franks could be. He put a towel on before entering the bath, but found that the Franks didn't cover themselves. One of them came up to him and yanked off his towel, which promptly revealed another cultural difference. The owner, like most cultured gentlemen of the Near East, kept his hair trim—*everywhere!* The Frank looked and demanded that the Muslim trim him accordingly. The Frank liked the outcome so much that he called for his wife to be brought. He told her to lie on her back and then asked the owner to do the same for her and offered to pay for it!

The only editorial comment Usama made in telling the story was that the Franks seemed immune from both jealousy and modesty. The fact that the bathhouse owner had shaved the pubic hair of both a Frankish knight and his wife in public was apparently unremarkable to Usama. The only oddity from Usama's perspective was that the knight had asked. Presumably, the fact that the owner obliged was simply good manners.

Usama was also struck by the rough justice of the Franks. Muslim jurisprudence was well advanced by the twelfth century. Judges could call on centuries of legal precedent as well as volume upon volume of law books in order to apply the principles of the Quran to the case at hand. There was no equivalent among the Franks, who had forgotten most of the Roman legal system and long since abandoned the careful deliberations that had characterized Roman law at its best. In one episode relayed by Usama, a local Frankish blacksmith was accused of aiding sev-

eral thieves, and he in turn challenged his accuser to a duel. Rather than trying the case in a court, the local lord agreed, and the blacksmith and the accuser then beat each other to a pulp. The blacksmith won, dragged the corpse away, and then hanged it in an act of ritual humiliation. Usama also described an "ordeal by water" trial. The accused was bound and then dropped in a cask of water. If he sank, he would be presumed innocent, but if he floated, he would be declared guilty. Given that human bodies do not tend to sink immediately, he bobbed a bit, and as a result he was found guilty and punished by having red-hot rods inserted in his eyes.[16]

Usama was a Muslim aristocrat who served the emir of Aleppo and Damascus and frequently fought against Frankish armies. But he also had warm relations with Christian knights. On several occasions, he went to Jerusalem to pray in Al-Aqsa Mosque and then shared a meal with the Templars who occupied the grounds. He referred to the Templars as "my friends," and seems to have spent considerable time in their company. He may have been alternately amused and repelled by the Franks, but his world was not so different. It too was punctuated by routine acts of violence, and by casual attitudes toward life, death, and slavery. In his memoirs, people live, people die, they kill and they get killed, and little of it shocks him.

Today's notions of religious conflict would have made no sense to Usama. Unlike Osama bin Laden, Usama ibn Munqidh did not see religious identity as all-encompassing. His faith was vital, and Allah's will was paramount. The Franks were infidels—and risked damnation—but so were the Shi'ites and the Fatimids. One month, he might be at war with them; the next, he might be the guest of the Templars at Al-Aqsa Mosque.

Though he was an unusually astute observer of human nature, Usama was also a man of his times. The way he related to his Christian and Frankish neighbors was typical for a person of his class and occupation. Traders and soldiers traveled frequently and freely throughout Syria and Palestine, in spite of dangerous roads and shifting political landscapes. Alliances were fleeting and made and broken promiscuously. When it was convenient, Franks signed peace treaties with the Seljuks or the Fatimids, and when it was advantageous they fought alongside Muslims against mutual enemies. Frankish nobles were as prone to wars with other Franks as they were to waging campaigns against Muslims. Just as

Spain had seen shifting coalitions depending on who was fighting whom, Frankish soldiers fought alongside Turks one year and against them the next. Sometimes religion was the fault line; often it was not.

Until the middle of the twelfth century, the Crusader states had the upper hand in the Near East. Then the tide shifted. Several talented Turkish emirs unified Syria and eventually Egypt. While their motive was to build powerful dynasties, they used the rhetoric of holy war, and when possible, they defined the politics of the Near East in terms of Muslims versus Franks. Whether or not they believed their rhetoric, in what was otherwise a divided region, it united Arabs and Turks, Syrians, Egyptians, and above all, Kurds and transformed them into a potent force capable of expelling the Crusaders from the Near East. The first to urge all Muslims to fight the Franks was a Turkish emir named Zengi, but the most famous was a Kurdish prince, born in the town of Tikrit along the Tigris, named Yusuf, son of Ayyub, later known by his surname, Honor of the Faith, Salah ad-Din.

Saladin's Jihad?

THE SOLDIERS APPEARED on the outskirts of Jerusalem in late September, just before the autumn solstice in 1187. It had been nearly a century since the Franks had occupied the city, and no Muslim army had come close to retaking it. After the massacre of its former inhabitants in 1099, the kingdom of Jerusalem entered a long period of calm and prosperity. Pilgrims from Europe came and went freely, and the king enjoyed the tribute of towns and estates up and down the coast of Palestine.

Over the decades, however, the Franks failed to extend their initial victories. By the fall of 1187, though the rulers in Jerusalem were aware of the looming threat, they were still ill prepared when it finally arrived at their walls. The military backbone of the kingdom had been shattered just months before, when Saladin, the sultan of Egypt and lord of Damascus and Aleppo, decimated the armies of the Templars and the Franks at the battle of Hattin. The king of Jerusalem was captured and held hostage, and the administration of the city was left to the queen, Sibylla, and the patriarch. Word of Saladin's advance on Jerusalem, after an attack on Ascalon, preceded his arrival, but the queen could do little but watch as the city came under siege.

For his part, Saladin was overcome with the magnitude of what he was to accomplish. He had, over the prior fifteen years, changed the political landscape of the Near East and created a new dynasty that united Egypt and Syria for the first time in centuries. During years of tactical battles against both Christians and Muslims, he had one goal in mind: the expulsion of the Franks and the creation of a new empire with

himself as sultan in the service of God. Now, with his armies arrayed and prepared to capture Jerusalem, he remembered why he was there in the first place.

Just weeks before, outside of Ascalon, a delegation of Jerusalem merchants had approached him with an offer of peace. Their proposal was that Jerusalem proper would remain independent and intact, but Saladin would become master of its environs. Saladin, whose reputation for fairness was even then legend, took their suggestion seriously. He knew what had happened the last time the city had changed hands, when it had been emptied and its holy places turned into scenes of carnage, and he wanted no replay. "I believe," he told the delegation, "that Jerusalem is the House of God, as you also believe, and I will not willingly lay siege to the House of God or put it to assault." He said that in exchange for the surrender, he would permit the Christians to retain their possessions and some of the land. It was as good an offer as they could have hoped for, yet they refused.

At any other point during the previous century, that would have spelled the end of the city and its inhabitants. But Saladin was of a different mold. Determined to honor Jerusalem, he forced Balian, a nobleman charged with the hopeless task of defending the city, to come to terms. After the Muslims breached the walls, Balian, on the urging of the patriarch, went under the flag of truce to Saladin's tent. The only weapons he had left were words, and he warned Saladin that the knights of Jerusalem, and the Templars and the Hospitallers above all, were prepared to die as martyrs defending the city. They might lose in the end, he said, but they would make it costly. Saladin dismissed the warning as the bluff of a defeated man, and he reminded Balian what had happened when the Christians had taken the city decades before. Did Balian want to be responsible for an even greater slaughter? It was not an idle threat. Saladin had a reputation for tolerance, but he had also shown flashes of rage and ruthlessness. Like any successful ruler of that time and place, he was capable of violence. Faced with the reality of defeat, the Franks surrendered.

On Friday, October 2, 1187, Saladin's troops took control of Jerusalem. They were scrupulously fair toward the conquered. Discipline held, and the city changed hands quickly and bloodlessly. Saladin's men repossessed the Dome of the Rock and Al-Aqsa Mosque, and they did so

on a day full of symbolism. By the Muslim calendar, it was the anniversary of Muhammad's night journey, when, in honor of Christ's passion, he had been transported on a magical horse-like creature, the Buraq, to the Dome of the Rock and from there to heaven.

Saladin was humbled by the enormity of what he had achieved. He interpreted the recapture of Jerusalem as a sign of God's pleasure, and he was determined to show his respect. Later court chroniclers tripped over themselves to describe what happened. After securing the city, Saladin focused on the purification of Al-Aqsa Mosque. Because it had been occupied by the Templars for so many years, that was no easy task. But with men working around the clock, it was soon restored. Then, according to the chronicler Imad ad-Din,

> The Quranic readers arrived, the official prayers were read, the ascetics and pious men congregated.... They joined in groups to pray and prostrate themselves, humbling themselves and beating their breasts, dignitaries and ascetics, judges and witnesses, zealots and combatants in the Holy War, standing and sitting, keeping vigil and committed to prayer by night.... The traditionists recited, the holy orators comforted men's souls, the scholars disputed, the lawyers discussed, the narrators narrated.

Though a fair number of the Christians of the city were held for ransom, they were treated honorably. Given Saladin's commitment to the basic tenets of Islam, that made sense. He took the Quranic injunctions about the People of the Book seriously, and that may have guided his choice of the preacher who gave the first sermon in the resanctified Al-Aqsa Mosque: the chief judge of Aleppo, known for his eloquence and learning, who delivered an impassioned lecture about the significance of Jerusalem to Muslims everywhere.

"O Men," he cried,

> rejoice at good tidings. God is well-pleased with what you have done, and this is the summit of man's desire; he has helped you bring back this strayed camel from misguided hands and to restore it to the fold of Islam, after the infidels had mishandled it for nearly a hundred years. Rejoice at the purifying of this House.... It was the dwelling

place of your father Abraham, the spot where the Prophet Muhammad, God bless him, ascended to Heaven, the *qibla* to which you turned to pray in the early time of Islam, the abode of prophets, the resort of the saints, the grave of the saints, the place where God's revelation came down, and where all mankind must gather on the Day of Resurrection and the Day of Judgement.... It is the city to which God sent his servant and apostle, the Word which entered into Mary and Jesus.[1]

The retaking of Jerusalem was the culmination of a dream for Saladin. Early in his life, he had dedicated himself to the unification of Syria and Egypt as a necessary prelude for a coordinated assault on the Crusader states and their jewel, the kingdom of Jerusalem. Donning the mantle of holy war, he had achieved his life's ambition and evicted the Christians from the Dome of the Rock. And yet, in that moment of glory, his chosen preacher gave a triumphant sermon that linked Jerusalem to the biblical tradition of Abraham and Jesus.

Jerusalem was holy to Islam precisely because it had been holy to the Jews and to the Christians. It later became sacred to Muhammad and to the Muslim community, but only because it was the city of apostles. In short, Jerusalem was sanctified in Muslim eyes not in spite of but because it had been the holiest of holies for the People of the Book. For Saladin, Jerusalem was the glue binding the People of the Book to Islam. His holy war had been fought against both Muslim and Christian states that stood in the way of the unification of the entire community of believers—Christian, Jew, and Muslim—under the banner of Islam and the house of Saladin.

This is a far cry from how this period is commonly viewed. The simple black-and-white of us versus them, Muslims versus Christians, doesn't come close to explaining why Saladin did what he did, and the modern understanding of holy war doesn't help. Though Saladin is one of the few historical Muslims who enjoys a favorable image in the West, that does not mean he is understood. He may have been a noble soul in comparison with his contemporaries, but he was also a man of his era. He waged a jihad against the Christian invaders from Europe as part of a grand strategy to build a dynasty and restore the Near East to the glory of the seventh and eighth centuries.

HOLY WAR

SALADIN WAS NOT the first to use the language of holy war, but before him, it had been ineffective. Even with the failure of the Second Crusade in 1147 and the inability of the Christian princes to capture Damascus, Jerusalem remained untouched and unchallenged. The Turkish and Arab emirs of Syria and Egypt remained at least as committed to fighting one other as they did to fighting the Franks or the Byzantines. Sometime in the middle of the twelfth century, however, the landscape began to change. A succession of strong Turkish and Kurdish princes cobbled together a formidable state to rival Jerusalem. The first crack to appear in the Frankish façade was the fall of Edessa, and the next was the Christian debacle at the gates of Damascus during the Second Crusade. Stepping into this breach was the ruler of Aleppo, Nur al-Din.

The political balance in the Near East was defined by two rivalries: one between Aleppo and Damascus, the other between the kingdom of Jerusalem and the surrounding Muslim states. In Aleppo, Nur al-Din, known as "the Saint King," succeeded his father, Zengi, in 1146. His father cast a long a shadow, so feared that the rival emir of Damascus had entered into an alliance with the king of Jerusalem solely to contain him. It was a classic case of "the enemy of my enemy is my friend." It was also business as usual in the Near East at the time. One month, armies were arrayed on the side of faith, and Christians squared off against Muslims. Then, as one set of princes died, or were killed, old alliances melted away and new ones formed, based not on creed but on who wanted what. In the shifting political sands of the region, the Byzantines, transplanted Franks, intermittent Crusaders from Europe, the Fatimids of Egypt, Seljuk sultans, and Arab emirs jockeyed for preeminence. Strategically placed on central trade routes and standing between the Frankish states of the Mediterranean coast and the Turks inland, Damascus was the prime prize.

The ruler of Damascus, pinned between a cold alliance with the Franks to the west and the threat of Aleppo and Nur al-Din to the north and east, tried to have it both ways. While technically maintaining his pact with Jerusalem, he aggressively wooed Nur al-Din, who eventually agreed to a partnership. That upset the balance between Damascus and the kingdom of Jerusalem, and helped trigger the Second Crusade. Nur

al-Din then seized the opportunity created by the departure of the failed Crusader armies after 1147 to extend his reach. Seven years later, he did what the armies of the Second Crusade could not and captured Damascus.

The annexation of Damascus not only transformed Nur al-Din into one of the most powerful players in the region; because of his unusual character, it also set in motion a shift in tone. Nur al-Din was less inclined to accommodate the Franks. Instead, he wanted to remove the transplanted Westerners. Unlike most Muslim warlords, who were feared for their ferocity or ridiculed for their timidity but rarely, if ever, praised for their character, Nur al-Din was lauded for humility and devoutness. And unlike so many before him, he was driven not just by ambition but by faith.

The image of the Muslim warrior riding into battle with the Quran in one hand may be familiar, but to Muslims of the Near East in the twelfth century, it would have been alien. Nur al-Din was remarkable not because he was an archetype but because he was so different. Ambition was commonplace, but piety was a rare quality in a prince. Muslim jurists, recognizing that rulers used the Quran mostly when it was convenient and did what they wanted when it was not, had come to the conclusion that it was better to suffer the cruelties of a mercurial, even unjust ruler than risk the chaos that might come with trying to overthrow him.

The result was a political philosophy of accommodation. Muslim theologians were hesitant to challenge the legitimacy of a ruler, whether or not that ruler honored the laws of Islam, which rulers rarely did. With the decline in the power and prestige of the Baghdad caliphate, Muslim scholars adopted a pragmatic approach to the warlords and draped it with religious justification. That was not overly difficult, given that Islam, at heart, involved submission to the ultimate authority, God. Faced with political fragmentation, the *ulama* emphasized the duty of Muslims to submit obediently to the ruler. If the ruler was unjust, he would ultimately answer to God, and in the interim, it was the responsibility of the individual Muslim to submit to the ruler's authority. The *ulama,* for their part, had a duty to ensure that religious law, the sharia, was preserved and honored, if not by the ruler, then at least by judges and scholars.

The ethos of accommodation and obedience was often challenged by individuals, but without a unified church, the *ulama* were less able to

resist the will of any particular ruler than bishops, cardinals, and popes were in Europe at the time. Occasionally, some scholar would denounce a ruler for his actions, but usually from a distance. A judge living in Baghdad could safely inveigh against an emir in Syria, but he would risk his life if he said the same things in Damascus. It was the rare individual who took a stand against a perceived violation of religious law by a ruler, and it was the even rarer individual who did not then have to flee to escape that ruler's rage.

By contrast, Europe at the time was in the midst of a centuries-long struggle between church and state. The Crusades were a means to an end for the Catholic Church, which used the rallying call of war against unbelievers as a way to gain influence and power. Crusades were waged not just against Muslims in the Near East but also against pagan tribes in the Baltics, against heretics in Europe, and of course against Muslims in Spain. Most of these Crusades were spurred by a church and a papacy that were competing with political leaders for a dominant position in society.

But in the Muslim world, the political class was preeminent. In Baghdad, the Abbasid caliphate continued to exert a pull on the collective heartstrings of parts of the Muslim world, primarily because it was a reminder of an ideal of unity. The fact that such unity had rarely existed was less important than the fact that the ideal had always been central. No one could dispute that the Muslim world had been fractured for centuries, but the yearning for a unified community (*umma*) never faded. If anything, it grew stronger the more the reality of the Muslim world underscored its absence. As a result, while the invasion of the Crusaders did not initially lead to a counterreaction, the seeds were there. The inability of the Muslim states of the Near East to repel the Franks was a stark reminder of their divisions. After a tepid, shell-shocked response during the first part of the twelfth century, the political and military leaders of the Near East began to channel the unease and use it to craft a new balance of power capable of challenging the invaders.

It is impossible to understand the rise of Nur al-Din, and of his successor Salah ad-Din, without this context. Muslims were not only divided in the face of Western Christians, but they suffered from a debilitating legacy of doctrinal schisms that had afflicted the *umma* since the time of Ali and the formation of Shi'a. For the Sunnis, the Shi'ite Fatimid state in Egypt was just as disturbing as the Crusader states in Palestine.

Both represented the dire consequences of disunity. Both demonstrated what would happen to the *umma* if it fragmented.

When Nur al-Din died in 1174, he was praised throughout the Near East as a ruler of wisdom, maturity, and piety. But it was not immediately clear who would succeed him. The most likely candidate was his deputy, Saladin, the governor of Egypt who had spent more than a decade dealing with Frankish invasions and the intrigues of the rapidly decaying Fatimid state. Year by year, Saladin had acquired more influence, aided by the fortuitous death of assorted rivals. His battlefield victories were impressive, but his political instincts were also remarkably keen. After years of delicate maneuvering, he finally ended the life of the feeble Fatimid empire and ordered that the name of the Fatimid caliph be omitted from the Friday prayer and the name of the Sunni Abbasid caliph be included instead. Then, when he learned of the death of Nur al-Din, he moved with alacrity.

It was natural for Saladin to believe that he was the rightful heir to Nur al-Din. Like his former master, he professed a deep commitment to bringing the Near East under one Sunni overlord. At least that is the impression that has survived the centuries. Judging from the few contemporary histories that survive, it is hard to believe that Saladin was a man of flesh and blood. Either he was a master of propaganda or he was truly blessed with grace and nobility and motivated by a genuine passion to make the Muslim community whole. In truth, he may have been both.

It is ironic that Saladin is so celebrated in the West. In his day, he was the greatest defender of the concept of jihad in the Muslim world. In the words of one his biographers,

> Saladin was extremely diligent in waging this holy war, and it was constantly on his mind. One could swear by one's right hand without fear of contradiction that, from the time he first set out, intent on jihad, until he died, he did not spend a single gold or silver coin except on jihad and pious works. His heart and mind were so taken over by this burning zeal for jihad that he could speak of nothing else. Out of his desire to fight for God's cause, he left behind him his family, children, country, home.

In addition to being a dedicated holy warrior and man of God, he was "sociable, well mannered and entertaining.... The purity of his charac-

ter was always evident: when in company he would allow no one to be spoken ill of in his presence, preferring to hear only their good traits; when he himself spoke, [he was] never disposed to insult anyone."[2]

If that were not enough, he was also—apparently—handsome, with kind, clear eyes and a finely trimmed beard. He was prone to acts of generosity and gentle in his interactions with women and children. It was said that he would share his food with supplicants and visitors, in honor of the old custom of the Arabs, rather than hide behind the elaborate rituals of later monarchs. He prayed regularly and publicly and delighted in listening to the verses of the Quran recited by expert readers. He was distrustful of philosophers and mystics who went beyond what the Quran and the tradition dictated. It was said after his death that one of his only regrets was that he had never been able to make the pilgrimage to Mecca. At the end of an expansive list of Saladin's remarkable traits, which stretched to many pages and thousands of words, one of his biographers explained that those were "simply a few examples of his soul's lofty and noble qualities. I have limited myself... in order not to extend this book unduly and bore the reader."

By the time Saladin encountered the armies of the Third Crusade, his image had been burnished to perfection. But in the years immediately after Nur al-Din's death, there were some who disagreed with the haloed portrait. Where most surviving accounts are unabashed hagiographies, not everything written about Saladin was so flattering. One satirist described drunken orgies, stupid scribes, humpbacked ministers, and cowardly generals who fought only when victory was certain. Like the court jester in Europe, satirists were allowed to poke fun at the powerful, to a point. The dark side of Saladin's piety may well have been a lack of humor about himself, and he was so offended by one description that he had the author banished. The poor soul was hurt and surprised, and wrote a bitter letter asking what he had done to deserve such treatment. "Why have you sent away a trustworthy man who has committed no crime and no theft? Banish the muezzins [who call the faithful to pray] from your lands if you are sending away all those who speak the truth."[3]

These sour notes, however, were drowned out by the chorus of praise, not just in his own time but in later generations. Western historians were particularly impressed. One of the premier twentieth-century scholars of Near Eastern history, H. A. R. Gibb, summarized Saladin's

legacy in language that would have done a court historian proud. "For a brief but decisive moment, by sheer goodness and firmness of character, he raised Islam out of the rut of political demoralization." High praise from a sober English don, but nothing compared to the fulsome portrait left by Edward Gibbon in the eighteenth century. Gibbon, who rarely hesitated to use his pen to commit character assassinations, elevated Saladin high above the rank and file of humanity. He wrote that Saladin, having been fond of wine and women as a youth, saw the error of his ways and transformed himself.

> The garment of Saladin was of coarse woollen; water was his only drink; and while he emulated the temperance, he surpassed the chastity, of his Arabian prophet [Muhammad].... The justice of his divan was accessible to the meanest supplicant against himself and his ministers.... So boundless was his liberality that he distributed twelve thousand horses at the siege of Acre... and in a martial reign, the tributes were diminished, and the wealthy citizens enjoyed, without fear or danger, the fruits of their industry.

Yet Gibbon was not blind to Saladin's core. "In a fanatic age, himself a fanatic, the genuine virtues of Saladin commanded the esteem of the Christians; the emperor of Germany gloried in his friendship; the Greek [Byzantine] emperor solicited his alliance; and the conquest of Jerusalem diffused, and perhaps magnified, his fame both in the East and West."[4]

Gibbon, who embodied the swirl of contradictions that flowed through English society of the eighteenth century, which was still attached to the church yet testing the limits of that allegiance, recognized that Saladin was both a believer to the core and an empire builder. Which took priority in Saladin's soul is impossible to determine. But it is safe to assume that resurrecting an imperial Arab state and serving God were one and the same for him. His political ambitions were fully compatible with his religious passions, and his religious fervor gave him a strength and determination that most of his rivals lacked.

Some Western historians have argued that Saladin was primarily a dynast who manipulated religious imagery and language to justify his actions and craft his image. They note, correctly, that between 1174, when Nur al-Din died, and 1187, when Jerusalem was taken, Saladin spent nearly three years actively fighting other Muslim rulers, and little

more than a year fighting Christians. Yet even when battling other Muslims, Saladin used the justification of holy war. Against the Shi'ite Fatimids, that was easy: wars between competing Muslims sects were every bit as vicious and ideological as wars between Christian sects could be. And judging from the Old Testament, battles between different Israelite tribes were hardly civilized affairs. But Saladin also relied on the language of holy war to validate his campaigns against other Sunni Muslim states.

Throughout his career, Saladin wrote letters to the Abbasid caliph in Baghdad, hoping to receive a blessing. Even in its absence, he claimed that he was acting as a loyal servant of the Commander of the Faithful and as the caliph's sword. As such, he would sweep away heretics and bring the errant Muslim city-states of the region once more into the fold of the community of believers. Those cities that resisted his entreaties he attacked because they were standing in the way of God's will. When the emir of Mosul refused to bow, Saladin claimed that the city was a key element in a master plan. With Mosul safely in Saladin's camp, the rest of the region would follow as surely as night follows day. Every other holdout would succumb, and then Jerusalem and finally Constantinople, "until the word of God is supreme and the Abbasid caliphate has wiped the world clean, turning the churches into mosques." Later, face-to-face with the leaders of Mosul, Saladin stated that he had only one reason for wanting the city, and it had nothing to do with his Kurdish roots. "We have come," he declared, "to unite the word of Islam and restore things by removing differences."[5]

For Saladin, the ends ultimately justified the means. Though he didn't seem to take any pleasure in war, he saw it as a necessary instrument. At each stage in his career, he was able to identify what was required to get to the next stage. After he had solidified his position in Egypt, he knew he still could not mount a credible challenge to the kingdom of Jerusalem. To do so would require the combined resources of the various states of the Near East. Unless they voluntarily submitted to him, he would force them to join him. If that meant war, then he would fight.

Yet Saladin's jihad was not the jihad of the twenty-first century. It was not a holy war of hate. It was a war of restoration, a struggle *for* orthodox Islam rather than *against* Christians or against Muslims who deviated from the Sunni path. There was a reason that Saladin spent more time

fighting against other Muslims—including the fierce, fanatical, and at times suicidal cult of the Assassins, who were the al-Qaeda of their day—than he did against Christians. But that reason had nothing to do with doctrine. It was tactical. Only a unified Muslim Near East could defeat the Christian kingdom of Jerusalem.

If holy war is understood primarily as a struggle against non-Muslims and Muslims who have strayed, Saladin doesn't make much sense. But the problem here is not Saladin's jihad; it is how jihad has come to be defined by both Westerners and Muslims in the modern world.

As Islam evolved, so did the idea of jihad. Traditionally, there are two types of jihad in Islam: the greater jihad, which is an individual struggle for purity, and the lesser jihad, which is a campaign against those who dishonor or defeat the community of the faithful. The greater jihad is something all devout individuals must wage against their desires, especially those desires that contradict the central teachings of the Quran. The mystics of Islam often spoke of jihad as a dark night of the soul, where the striver is faced with his demons and must confront them in order to stay on the path toward God. The lesser jihad can take the form of a war against unbelievers, but it can also be any focused effort to restore Muslim society. War is one tool; political reform might be another; and economic policies could be as well.[6]

When Saladin spoke of jihad, he meant the remaking of Muslim society in the Near East, both because that was the right thing to do and because only then could Muslims once again rule Jerusalem. Not once was he accused of hypocritically using the language of jihad to advance selfish ambitions, in large measure because he first tended to his own spiritual house. In short, he seems to have embraced the greater jihad before he embarked on the lesser. And there lies the explanation why Saladin, the holy warrior par excellence, is nonetheless admired in the West and remains an icon in the Near East and in many parts of the Muslim world.

THE THIRD CRUSADE

BUT AS LAUDED as he was and still is, Saladin was also a flesh-and-blood warrior. The Saladin admired by most Westerners is so good and

pure that he is almost a caricature. The real Saladin, however, was not always disposed to forgive his enemies or treat them with leniency. He had little tolerance for mystics who refused to fight and instead retreated from society to probe the inner meaning of the Quran, and he developed an obsessive hatred for at least one Christian adversary, named Reynald of Châtillon. This Saladin, the angry general, the stubborn commander who was neither curious about theology nor kind to those who were, has been safely tucked away in the past.

That said, it was not as though Reynald was undeserving of contempt. He had a checkered career, as an adventurer, knight, and political prisoner who married well in 1176 and thereby became lord of one of the most imposing fortresses in Jordan, the castle of Kerak. Its ruins still inspire awe, perched high above the Dead Sea in the biblical land of Moab. Before Reynald became a castellan, he was known for his brutalities, one of which entailed beating the patriarch of Antioch, then smothering the wounds on his face with honey and leaving him out in the middle of the summer in the Syrian desert to be tormented by flies and assorted carrion fowl until he agreed to pay an exorbitant ransom. Once in control of his own fortress, Reynald apparently took unseemly pleasure in casting enemies off its ramparts.

Saladin could not have cared less about what Reynald did to the patriarch of Antioch or other Christians who crossed him, but he took offense at Reynald's attacks on pilgrimage caravans headed to Mecca. Not only was the north-south route through Syria a central artery for pilgrims, it was—as it had been for centuries—a primary trade route. Disrupting the caravans, harming the pilgrims, and stealing their goods posed a serious challenge to Saladin. So did Reynald's successful raids along the Red Sea. Any ruler who had aspirations of being accepted as a viable sultan had to be able to protect access to the holiest place of Islam. If Saladin could not guarantee the safety of pilgrims making the annual hajj to Mecca and Medina, he could not claim the respect of the Muslim world. Reynald's attacks also jeopardized Saladin's revenue. Protecting the caravans meant not just respect, but the right to collect moderate payments for the service.

The raids staged by Reynald provoked a lethal response. Saladin declared war, raised an army of more than twelve thousand cavalry, and invaded the kingdom of Jerusalem. The Franks, recognizing the magnitude of the threat, patched over their differences. The count of Antioch,

who had been flirting with Saladin and had even entered into a preliminary alliance with him, fell into line and made peace with the Templars and Hospitallers. The Crusader states assembled a formidable army, but that only made their subsequent defeat worse. Their military strategy was poorly conceived and proved to be no match for their adversary. They were gulled into meeting Saladin at a place of his choosing, on terrain that he desired, and at the hour he elected. The result in 1187 was a devastating battle at the Horns of Hattin, a labyrinth of barren hills just west of the Sea of Galilee.

On the morning of July 3, 1187, the Frankish armies woke to no dawn. Instead, the skies were filled with burning smoke. They had spent the previous day in the arid vale of Hattin, and though they knew that Saladin was near, they did not know precisely where. That morning, engulfed by the smoke generated by the brushwood and dry grass fires set by Saladin's forces, the disoriented Franks were surrounded and annihilated. The king of Jerusalem and the masters of both the Templars and the Hospitallers were captured. So was the hated Reynald and a precious, irreplaceable relic: a piece of the True Cross.

With the dead still on the battlefield, the captives were brought to Saladin's tent. According to one Frankish account of what happened, Saladin

ordered that a syrup diluted with water in a cup of gold be brought. He tasted it, then gave it to the king to drink, saying: "Drink deeply." The king drank, like a man who was extremely thirsty, then handed the cup on to Prince Reynald. Prince Reynald would not drink. Saladin was irritated and told him: "Drink, for you will never drink again!" The prince replied that if it pleased God, he would never drink or eat anything of his. Saladin asked him: "Prince Reynald, if you held me in your prison as I now hold you in mine, what, by your law, would you do to me?" "So help me God," he replied, "I would cut off your head." Saladin was greatly enraged at this most insolent reply, and said: "Pig! You are my prisoner, yet you answer me so arrogantly?" He took a sword in his hand and thrust it right through his body. The mamluks who were standing by rushed at him and cut off his head. Saladin took some of the blood and sprinkled it on his head in recognition that he had taken vengeance on him. Then he ordered that they carry the head to Damascus, and it was dragged along the

ground to show the Saracens whom the prince had wronged what vengeance he had had.

Muslim accounts differ only in slight details. In one, Saladin denounced Reynald for attacking pilgrims on the way to the holy places of Islam. But all agree that Saladin himself executed Reynald, and then spared the life of the king of Jerusalem and the others.[7]

The victory at Hattin opened the way for the subsequent fall of Jerusalem, which in turn aroused another wave of European Crusader armies determined to reclaim the city. Neither the occupation of Jerusalem not the vengeful killing of Reynald sullied Saladin's reputation. Instead, Reynald received the brunt of history's ire. Though some contemporary Christian polemicists denounced Saladin and described him as the devil incarnate, in time the picture born of wartime propaganda faded and a softer version emerged.

In the nineteenth century, Sir Walter Scott turned the execution of Reynald into a metaphor for Saladin's nobility. In *The Talisman,* Reynald is the grand master of the Templars and a duplicitous schemer loyal only to his own twisted greed. His death is presented not as an act of vengeance but as a heroic deed. The scene begins with Saladin entertaining Richard the Lionheart and his retinue in a battlefield tent replete with "carpets of the richest stuffs with cushions laid for the guests," along with whole roasted lambs, sweetmeats, "and other niceties of Eastern cookery." Then, as the guests are enjoying their iced sherbet, Saladin suddenly unsheathes his scimitar and slices off the head of the grand master of the Templars. Before his horrified guests can draw their swords, Saladin explains that the dead man has been plotting against Richard's life. In this telling, therefore, Scott recast the execution as the selfless act of a prince who treasured honor and chivalry.

Noble character notwithstanding, in taking Jerusalem, Saladin had seized the jewel of the Crusader crown. The kings of Europe, urged on by the pope, responded with the Third Crusade. Richard the Lionheart of England, Philip Augustus of France, and Frederick Barbarossa of Germany prepared for war. By now, the crusading idea had been woven into the fabric of Western and Central Europe. No longer a movement attractive primarily to younger sons, crusading became a central focus of both the church and the nobility. The armies of the Third Crusade were the elite of Germany, France, and England, and they might have succeeded

but for the misfortune of Frederick Barbarossa drowning in a river after a convincing victory over the Seljuks of Anatolia. The rivalry between Richard and Philip hardly helped, and Richard's bullheadedness, while an advantage on the battlefield, did not make him an easy ally.

The Third Crusade is remembered, if remembered at all, for the epic struggle between Richard and Saladin. Militarily, the two were evenly matched, but Saladin, aging, with his acute skill as a general in decline, still outmaneuvered Richard. The only thing worse than defeat and stalemate on the battlefield is reputational defeat off it. Here Richard lost. Though each had court historians and partisans, Saladin emerged the undisputed champion in the propaganda war.

Except for a glowing aura in the story of Robin Hood, King Richard survives as a fearless and crude ruler driven by avarice, lust, and rage. Though we will never know what he was truly like, there is probably more than a grain of truth in the image that survives. The child of Henry II and the even-then-legendary Eleanor of Aquitaine, Richard developed an early and lasting reputation as a leader for whom subtlety and statecraft were alien concepts. This was not a question of wartime ethics, though here too, Richard managed to offend even the callous sensibilities of his day. It was a question of culture. England was barely removed from illiterate tribal confederations, and English society had only the slightest overlay of Christianity with a smattering of literacy confined to the monasteries. Saladin's Egypt and Syria, on the other hand, had experienced six centuries of Muslim rule and had benefited from the high culture of Damascus and Baghdad. That culture, which prized literature, art, science, medicine, astronomy, engineering, law, and agriculture, had been built on the foundations of Greece, Rome and Byzantium, and then blended with the courtly tradition of ancient Persia. The Crusaders did surpass the Muslims in certain areas—especially in the building of castles and, not coincidentally, the construction of siege engines to capture them. But in most respects, the contest between Richard and Saladin, much like the initial fighting between the Crusader armies and the Muslims of the Near East a century before, pitted brawn against brain.

Brawn sometimes had a distinct advantage. Richard, a physically imposing redhead who would sooner rush into the fray than command from the heights, stormed the Near East by sea, captured Cyprus as an advance post, and then took Acre after a tortuous siege. The commander of the Acre garrison surrendered before receiving Saladin's orders not

to, and Richard found himself in control of a large number of captives. The rules governing prisoners of war were straightforward: a ransom would be set, high enough to be profitable for the victors and punitive for the losers but not so high that it couldn't be paid. Richard, however, was anxious to maintain momentum and wanted to advance inland. He could go nowhere until the fate of his prisoners was resolved. The negotiations bogged down, and Richard decided he didn't need the money or the hassle. He ordered his soldiers to kill the three thousand men, women, and children of Acre who had been so unfortunate as to be captured. Said one Christian apologist, the soldiers—looking to avenge the Christians who had died at Saladin's hands—happily carried out the task of beheading the captives.[8]

Massacre was juxtaposed with camaraderie. For many months, Richard's armies and Saladin's fought to a standstill. Camped near each other, the knights and commoners of each side fraternized during the long periods of inactivity. According to some accounts, the combatants would even stop fighting in the midst of a battle if they perceived that neither side had the upper hand. Arms would be laid down; there would be conversation and storytelling; one side would extend an invitation to dinner. At other times, contests were held to see who had more prowess in the arts of war, and then all would celebrate the winners.[9]

These scenes hardly square with the image of fierce warriors of God confronting one another with the fervor of true believers. Rather than generating rage and hatred, Saladin's faith often produced compassion. He respected the Christian willingness to fight and die for Jerusalem, and simultaneously deployed armies to kill as many of them as possible. And with the exception of Reynald, he could do all of this without hate. His faith, if we are to believe that it was as genuine as the chroniclers claim, was grounded in humility. His Islam was the Islam of submission, based on the recognition that all humans are fallible and all are sinners. God is the path, and only God is the judge. Saladin waged a jihad for the glory of God and for Islam, not a jihad against his enemies. They were obstacles, but they were not the object.

The Christians also defy easy characterization. They could speak of the evils of the infidels and glory in their slaughter. They could travel thousands of miles to restore the Holy Sepulchre to Christian control and to cleanse the Holy Land of the impurity of Muslim rule. Yet not only were they willing to fraternize with these infidels on slow days dur-

ing a hot summer war, but by the fall of 1191, they were also willing to call the whole thing off and get married.

It wasn't the most obvious solution, but after less than two years, Richard's armies were stretched, and the Frankish advance was stalled. Saladin had absorbed the most intense blows without crumbling, and other than his bloody victory at Acre, Richard had done little more than secure the coast that had until recently been firmly under the control of the kingdom of Jerusalem. With Frederick Barbarossa dead, the Germans in disarray, and Philip Augustus having fallen ill and returned to France, it was left to Richard to challenge Saladin alone. But word reached him that back in England, his brother John was attempting to usurp his throne, and Richard needed to make an exit. He had no wish to win in Palestine only to lose his throne in England.

What Richard did made perfect sense to him, though it surprised his contemporaries. He wrote to Saladin, "I am to salute you, and tell you that the Muslims and Franks are bleeding to death, the country is utterly ruined and goods and lives have been sacrificed on both sides. The time has come to stop this. The points at issue are Jerusalem, the Cross, and the land." Richard declared that he could not leave without securing the right of Christians to worship freely in Jerusalem, nor could he depart without the True Cross that had been taken by Saladin at the battle of Hattin. Saladin responded quickly, "Jerusalem is ours as much as yours; indeed it is even more sacred to us than to you, for it is the place from which our Prophet accomplished his nocturnal journey and the place which our community will gather on the Day of Judgment. Do not imagine that we can renounce it.... The land was originally ours, whereas you have only just arrived and have taken it over only because of the weakness of the Muslims living there at the time." As for Richard's other demands, Saladin did not say yes and he did not say no.

The negotiations then took an interesting turn. It's not clear who proposed what, but the proposal was simple: Richard's sister Joanna of Sicily would marry Saladin's brother Sayf ad-Din, and the two would become joint monarchs ruling from Jerusalem. All prisoners held by both sides would be freed; the True Cross would be restored to the Holy Sepulchre; and Richard would sail home to England.

When Saladin heard the terms, he instructed his delegates to say no, apparently because he thought it was either a trap or a joke. His brother took the idea more seriously, and tentatively agreed. Unbeknownst to

Richard, one of his erstwhile allies was also negotiating terms with Saladin, and Saladin, therefore, knew he had the luxury to bargain from a position of strength. But Richard's offer of his sister's hand was genuine, and to him at least, made good strategic sense. Wars between princes in Europe often ended with intermarriage between rival families. Having campaigned vigorously against a worthy enemy, he decided it was time to stop and move on. Marriage seemed a natural, and necessary, component to secure a lasting peace.

Other Crusaders were less ecumenical. Richard found that not only was his sister opposed to the idea, but she had rallied others to her side. He was pressured to retract the offer. Instead, he wrote to Saladin to amend the initial proposal. "The Christian people disapprove of my giving my sister in marriage without consulting the Pope," Richard wrote. "If he authorizes the wedding, so much the better. If not, I will give you the hand of my niece, for whom I shall not need Papal consent."

Saladin, for his part, may have been reluctant to sign a truce, given that the struggle to which he had dedicated his life was still short of its ultimate aim of evicting the Franks from Palestine. But he saw the ravages that the wars were causing, and with Jerusalem secure in the Muslim fold, he agreed to end hostilities. He was reminded by one learned judge that even the Quran advised making peace when it was advantageous. "If they incline to peace, you too should incline to it." According to Imad ad-Din, Saladin had to be convinced by his commanders that peace was needed, even though he had committed his life to jihad. It was a convenient portrayal, whether it was strictly true or not, because it allowed him to preserve his reputation as a warrior but not one so blinded by fervor that he could not do what was best for his subjects.

The result of these negotiations was a truce leaving the Franks in control of Antioch, Tripoli, and much of the coast. Merchants—regardless of their creed or country of origin—were permitted to keep trading without being subject to onerous duties. And most important of all, Saladin promised that any Christian who wished to make the pilgrimage to the Holy Sepulchre in Jerusalem would be granted safe passage and unhindered access.[10] With that, the Third Crusade came to an end.

And so, what are we to make of a jihad waged by a devout Muslim against a Crusade prosecuted by Christians that included massacres and beheadings but nearly ended with a wedding between the families of the two leading adversaries? How are we to interpret Saladin, who was at

once the holy warrior par excellence and the noble adversary of Western imagination for centuries thereafter? And most perplexing of all, how do we square contemporary ideas about war, religion, and Islam with the world of the twelfth century?

Today's image of the jihadist as an individual whose entire identity is subsumed to an ideology bears only passing resemblance to Saladin. Indeed, the very notion of an ideology that dominates all aspects of life has been alien to most cultures throughout history. In the twelfth century, the daily realities of farming, transportation, shelter, surviving disease, and fighting arduous, labor-intensive wars usually trumped ideas.

Religion and beliefs were one part of a kaleidoscope. At times, the words of the Quran and the hadith (traditions) drove men like Saladin to act as they did. At times, the words of the Bible and the pope spurred men like Richard to fight, or not to fight. But at other times, family issues, dynastic challenges, health problems, and political rivalries mattered more. Sometimes men fought with the words of a holy text ringing in their ears; and sometimes they met on the battlefield, slapped each other on the back, and played games.

Before the fall of Jerusalem in 1187, the Crusader states governed over and coexisted with a large local Christian population and with an even larger Muslim population. The result was hardly equivalent to Córdoba, but neither was it a period of conflict defined by faith. The war between Saladin and Richard had the markings of a religious conflict, but in the end, it was just a struggle between rulers that ended in a stalemate and nearly in a peace secured by marriage. The root of conflict in the modern world can be found in the Crusades, but only by forgetting much of what actually happened.

While the crusading movement continued to flourish for more than a century in Europe, Jerusalem was not threatened again by Western Christians. In 1204, the armies of the Fourth Crusade, transported by the Venetian fleet, took a detour and landed at Constantinople. The city was ransacked and terrorized by Western armies whose purported goal had been the liberation of the Holy Land. The fury with which the Fourth Crusaders, a combination of Frankish and German nobles, attacked the bastion of Eastern Christianity had been building for many years. Ever since Alexius Comnenus sent the First Crusade on its way, resentment of Byzantium had grown. The Venetians also coveted Byzantine wealth and influence over the commercial sea lanes of the Mediterranean.[11]

Saladin died soon after Richard's departure, and his sons set up a dynasty that dissipated in a remarkably short amount of time. His heirs were everything he was not: despotic, hedonistic, undisciplined. The subsequent Mongol invasion that destroyed the Abbasid caliphate in 1258 would have continued on to Cairo and perhaps across North Africa had it not been for the slave army of Mamelukes who had first supported and then overthrown the sybaritic sons and grandsons of Saladin in their palaces in Cairo. The Mameluke army stopped the Mongols at the battle of Ain Jalut near Nazareth in 1260, and the horsemen never again threatened the Near East.

The Egypt of the Mamelukes was a stable, prosperous state, linked by trade to the West and the East thanks to a thriving merchant class of Jews, Christians, and Muslims of all denominations. The Franks and Germans understood the importance of Egypt, and the later Crusades of the thirteenth century targeted Egypt in the belief that it was the strategic key to Jerusalem. These attempts failed. Egypt easily repelled the armies of Europe, and Cairo was untouched.

The relative safety of Cairo was a magnet, and among the many it attracted was a Spanish Jew from Córdoba who arrived with little more than his clothes and a few books after fleeing from the violence and chaos that was then engulfing Andalusia. Having seen his homeland overrun by Berber armies from Morocco and his city, Córdoba, once again consumed by flames, he made his way across the Mediterranean to Egypt. Had he remained in Córdoba, he may never have written what he did, or learned what he learned. But because he was welcomed at the court of Saladin, he thrived, burdened with a deep sadness but driven by an intellectual hunger. Saladin's most significant legacy for Islam is the capture of Jerusalem. Without intending to, he also shaped the evolution of modern Judaism, when his chamberlain in Cairo hired a Jewish refugee, Moses Maimonides, to be a court physician.

THE PHILOSOPHER'S DREAM

MOSES MAIMONIDES was not a shy man. He knew his own heart, and he minced few words. He was not modest, and he did not suffer fools. His goal was at once lofty and simple: he wanted to illuminate the darkness and banish doubt and ignorance in order to help the enlightened seeker. "I am the man," he stated, "who when concern pressed him and...he could find no other device by which to teach a demonstrated truth other than by giving satisfaction to a single virtuous man while displeasing ten thousand ignoramuses—I am he who prefers to address that single man by himself... I shall guide him in his perplexity until he becomes perfect and he finds rest."

Maimonides wrote these words in the preface to his magnum opus, *Guide for the Perplexed*. He was by then an old man who had seen more of the world than he had ever intended or ever wished. He had been born in 1135 in Córdoba, a city that may have been a shadow of its former greatness but remained a beacon of culture. He was the child of a judge and descended from scholars and rabbis, and from the time he could talk, he was initiated into the family business. But when he was barely a teenager, Andalusia fell under the control of yet another puritan dynasty from Morocco, the Almohads, who like their Almoravid predecessors emerged from Marrakesh and expanded in wave after wave until they inundated southern Spain.

The Almohads considered themselves reformers who would use the Quran as the foundation for law and justice, but like many puritans, they conveniently ignored passages of scripture that did not fit their world-

view. Though the Quran insists on respect and tolerance for the People of the Book, the Almohads were openly hostile to the Christians and Jews who populated the cities of southern Iberia. They placed restrictions on them, many of which were purely symbolic but nonetheless humiliating. In some areas, Jews and Christians were punished for wearing certain types of clothing, and unlike the Muslim rulers whom they supplanted, the Almohads did not welcome Jews or Christians into their courts.

Finding life uncomfortable and pathways to advancement closed, the family of Moses Maimonides left Córdoba and moved to Fez, in the heart of Almohad Morocco. At first glance that looks like a dubious decision, but Almohad rule in the Moroccan heartland may have been less restrictive than it was in the newly conquered and still insecure cities of Andalusia. The Almohads were not blessed with friendly chroniclers, and they were denigrated as narrow-minded tribesmen with no ear for music and no eye for culture. Later Jewish sources depicted the Almohads as fanatics bent on exterminating Iberian Judaism. When they conquered Morocco, they dealt harshly with anyone who did not embrace their brand of religion, including other Muslims and Jews. But Jewish accounts may also have been colored by "a narrative of persecution,"[1] which inclined Jewish writers to portray diaspora Judaism as a series of tests and trials similar to the tribulations suffered by the Jews in the Old Testament after the destruction of Solomon's Temple.

Maimonides rejected the cataclysmic, melodramatic interpretation of the Jewish experience. After a period in Fez, he traveled across North Africa, often by ship, and settled briefly in Palestine. But Palestine, divided between warring Christian and Muslim princes, was inhospitable, and Maimonides and his family relocated to Cairo, where he would spend the rest of his life. His family's commercial enterprises blossomed in Egypt, and his brother proved to be an adept and flexible merchant who increased the family's fortunes. Maimonides, fluent in Arabic, Hebrew, and Latin, absorbed the learning and culture of the Mediterranean world and evolved into a philosopher whose advice was sought by Jews, Christians, and Muslims alike. He was a voluminous writer, a voracious reader, and a generous teacher, and he had only scorn for those who preferred to play the victim. The world was not kind, and it was foolish, he believed, to expect otherwise. Equally foolish, in his

view, was to bow one's head and accept punishment and oppression. God had given man ingenuity and choice, and thus the tools to survive and thrive.

In fact, one reason that Maimonides and his family may have been able to relocate to Fez was that they converted to Islam. In the long history of relations between the faiths in Spain, false conversion was common. The Almohads were unusually harsh toward nonbelievers, and the advantages of converting were obvious. No one can see into the heart of another, and recognizing that simple truth, persecuted religious minorities developed a practice known in Arabic as *taqiyya*. Translated literally as "dissimulation" or even "diplomacy," *taqiyya* was in essence a prudent form of faking it. Early Shi'ites had done the same thing under hostile Sunni rule, and some Jews and Christians in Spain decided that, faced with hostile Muslim rulers, the pragmatic thing was to pretend to be Muslim and practice their own faith in private and in secret.

Maimonides had no patience for those who took a purist line and advocated martyrdom and death rather than survival. Defending martyrdom, he said, was "long winded foolish babbling and nonsense." In his view, temporary conversion was acceptable, though it was best if those who did so eventually moved somewhere that would allow them to practice their rites openly.

Though he was certain that no one can know God's will, the goal, for Maimonides, was to live a philosophical life, dedicated to understanding God's wisdom and helping others do the same. He had grown up in an environment that nurtured philosophy. The rabbinical tradition handed down to him by his father encouraged questioning and demanded intellectual rigor, and twelfth-century Andalusia teamed with singular minds who continued to fuse the legacy of the Greeks with the theology of Islam. Though it was a Muslim society, Jews and Christians were supporting characters who played vital roles in translating and interpreting the texts of the ancients. While Jewish scholars had distinguished themselves as astronomers and as commentators on the Old Testament, Maimonides evolved into much more than a brilliant Jewish philosopher and became one of the great synthesizers of Christian, Muslim, and Jewish wisdom.

For much of his life, he was acutely aware that he was an exile. Wandering defined him, and wandering taught him. "Every righteous and intelligent person will realize that the task I undertook was not

simple.... In addition, I was agitated by the distress of our time, the exile which God decreed upon us, the fact that we are being driven from one end of the world to the other. Perhaps we have received reward for this, inasmuch as exile atones for sin." He feared that the fact that he was an exile might lower his status and lead others to take him less seriously. But rather than accept that fate, he turned the fear into fuel. He was an exile from his home; Jews had been exiled from their Holy Land; and mankind was in exile from God. Instead of passively accepting his fate, he used his exile, and it became his spark.

His output was extraordinary, even in an age of thinkers and philosophers who routinely wrote thousands of pages on all aspects of human existence. Maimonides composed lengthy treatises on the Torah, Talmud, and the Mishnah; he carried on correspondence with Jews and learned men throughout the Muslim world; he delved into mathematics, astronomy, and medicine; and he crowned his career with his magisterial synthesis of philosophy and theology, *Guide for the Perplexed*.

THE MYSTICS AND THE LAW

As a DOCTOR at the court of Saladin, Maimonides won the trust of the ruling class. Like Hasdai ibn Shaprut, Maimonides' erudition and meticulous approach to diagnosing and treating the ills of the human body made him an invaluable servant to Muslim rulers. Medicine was not yet a distinct branch of knowledge. It was instead an amalgam of philosophy, science, mysticism, and theology. Anyone who wanted to be counted among the learned needed to have working familiarity with each of those, as well as fluency in Arabic and Latin, at the very least. A physician's study began with the ancients: Hippocrates, Galen, and Aristotle. It may seem odd that Maimonides, who began his formal study of medicine only late in his life, became a court physician with such a flimsy medical background. But in that day and age, he was qualified to be a doctor for one unimpeachable reason: he knew about as much as any man could know.

Though many of his treatises focused on Jewish law and scripture, he frequently wrote in Arabic. That was one of the languages he learned as a child, and it was the language of scholarship throughout the Muslim world and much of the Mediterranean. His fluency allowed him to

absorb the works of the most prominent philosophers in the Arab-speaking world, and he built on what they had created.

Maimonides was not the first Jewish scholar to use the methods of Greek and Arab thinkers to unlock the keys to Jewish scriptures, but he was surely among the most masterful. He moved easily between the rabbinical tradition and the writing of Muslim scholars. The eleventh and twelfth centuries in Persia and the Near East saw a flourishing philosophical tradition that continued what had begun in Baghdad and Iraq centuries earlier. Over time, however, the arguments became more arcane, to the point where only those immersed in the corpus could understand the references and relate to the questions. Andalusian thinkers also contributed to the debates, especially Ibn Rushd, who was known in the West as Averroës and who like Maimonides had been born in Córdoba but unlike him carved out a niche as a court intellectual under the puritanical Almohads.

While this fraternity of Arabic-speaking philosophers differed greatly in their actual answers, they shared common questions: What was the role of human reason in explaining the world? To what degree could men rely on their intellect to unveil God's plan, and how much should they look to faith and belief instead? Could the intellect act as a conduit to the truth, or was it a distraction that would keep man from God? Maimonides lived at a crucial juncture when the balance shifted decisively in the direction of faith over reason, belief rather than philosophy, and heart over mind.

Philosophers such as Averroës and the Persian Ibn Sina (known in the West as Avicenna) were themselves suspicious of pure philosophy. They believed that reason had a place in explaining God's wisdom but only in conjunction with theology and faith. Much of what they wrote was esoteric. Thousands of pages were consumed by questions such as: How eternal is eternity? Was the universe created by God "in time" or before time itself was created? Does God have foreknowledge of all details of human history and action, or simply access to all details but no advance knowledge? Unless one had spent long years steeped in these issues, the references and the logic were difficult if not impossible to follow. But threading through the esoterica was a portentous debate about the proper relationship between reason, free will, and faith.

Standing in the way of the philosophers were the jurists. The philosophers emphasized the role of reason and looked to Aristotle and Plato

for guidance on how to interpret the Quran. The jurists ranged from those who accepted only the most literal understanding of holy texts to those who embraced a limited amount of interpretation based on the early schools of law. The philosophers and the jurists disliked each other, and their disputes occasionally turned lethal. By the eleventh century, the traditions were deadlocked; neither side had managed to eliminate the other, much to their mutual frustration.

Just before Maimonides was born, Abu Hamid al-Ghazali of Baghdad attempted to resolve the apparent split between philosophy and theology. He embraced the methods of the philosophers in order to prove the supremacy of faith. Al-Ghazali was as essential to the evolution of Muslim theology as Thomas Aquinas was to the development of Catholicism. His brilliance was to synthesize science, philosophy, mysticism, and law. He had drunk deeply at the well of each. He became a scholar of Aristotle and sat at the feet of Sufi masters learning the mystical traditions. He then delved into the arcana of Muslim law, analyzed how the traditional schools interpreted the Quran, and absorbed dense and lengthy canons of jurisprudence.

After years of study, al-Ghazali composed a series of treatises that marked the apex and the end of a certain type of Muslim scholarship. In his quest to answer unresolved questions, al-Ghazali drew definitive conclusions, and among them was that both philosophy and mysticism were flawed. Only submission, the Quran, love of God, and respect for the law could lead a believer to live a proper life. While philosophy, science, reason, and mysticism each had something to offer, none was sufficient as a path to the truth. According to al-Ghazali, the philosopher risked turning the human intellect into a god, while the mystic often came close to worshiping his own soul rather than submitting to God's will. Al-Ghazali was urbane and sophisticated, but he was also, in the end, a conservative. Worried that Muslim societies had lost direction and purpose, he tried to find a new formula that would restore the pure, powerful faith of the Prophet and the companions.

Using the tools of the philosopher in order to discredit many of the claims of philosophy, and embracing the path of the mystic while rejecting many of the beliefs of mystics, al-Ghazali developed a complex system with a simple core: God is all-powerful, and Islam is the true path. He made mysticism respectable, but at a price. He insisted that all Muslims, mystic or not, were bound by the Quran. The path of

the Sufis did not give them the right to live outside the law. The same principle applied to philosophy. Reason and intellect could never take priority over the Quran and the tradition of the Prophet.

In his own time, al-Ghazali was respected, but after his death, he was sanctified. The questions that he asked ceased to be asked, and Islamic philosophy began to ossify. It was said that after al-Ghazali, the door of interpretation (*ijtihad*) closed. For centuries after Muhammad, there had been active debates about the true meaning of the Quran and the hadith, about the proper tools of interpretation and the way one could approach God. But after al-Ghazali, debate was discouraged. Islamic law and theology became more rigid, and schools became repositories of received wisdom rather than generators of new ideas.

Men like Maimonides, who lived more than a generation removed from al-Ghazali, still probed, but whether as a direct result of al-Ghazali's influence or not, they began to recede from the world. They did not reject philosophy, but they narrowed their audience. They divided reality into outer truth and hidden truth. The outer truths could be learned by the masses, but the inner truths were for the select. These attitudes transcended religious differences. Maimonides was Jewish, but he had more in common with Muslim and Christian scholars than he did with most Jews. Regardless of creed, scholars and mystics shared a sensibility; they asked similar questions and employed similar methods to find answers.

Where Maimonides probed the gulf between man and God, others attempted to close the gap, and no one did so more poignantly than the Andalusian philosopher Ibn Arabi. In a world replete with brilliant minds and passionate seekers, Ibn Arabi was among the most brilliant and the most passionate. He confronted the ancient human dilemma of loneliness. Why, he wanted to know, was there such a distance between God and his creation? Was mankind forever doomed to the excruciating pain of separation from God? That plaintive question had been asked by Jewish scholars ever since they had begun to interpret the story of Adam and Eve's expulsion from Eden, and it had been a central concern of early Christian monks and mendicants. Ibn Arabi, however, drew on centuries of Jewish, Greek, Christian, and Muslim learning to arrive at a unique conclusion: man's separation from God was a product not of God but of man's limited ability to perceive the truth. A more aware mankind

would realize that the gulf was an illusion, and that God and man were as close as two could be without being one.

Ibn Arabi wrote almost as extensively as Maimonides. Like the Jewish sage, he was born in Spain but then traveled for years before finally settling in the Near East, in Damascus. In his work, he touched on most major areas of human knowledge, but unlike so many others, he expressed a new idea. The distance between man and God was not real, he claimed. Duality was not real. Instead, creation is defined by unity, and by the unity of man and God above all. God created man as a mirror in which to view himself and his creation. Throughout history, there had been a "Perfect Man," who embodied that unity. All of the prophets and the great Sufi saints had been emanations of the Perfect Man, and the path of the mystic was to emulate them.

Ibn Arabi's style was metaphorical, elliptical, esoteric, and challenging. He fused the Greek concept of Logos, which was at the center of the New Testament gospel of John, with Muslim-Greek philosophy. He added to the mix Sufi wisdom, which sometimes used words as guides and sometimes used language to mislead the uninitiated. Embedded in his work was a bare, unadorned statement about every believer: "God is the mirror in which you see yourself, as you are His mirror in which he contemplates His names." In the primordial unity of being, man is God's way of seeing himself and God's way of knowing himself.

How ironic that twelfth-century Andalusia, ruled as it was by a dynasty with a numbingly narrow ideology, nurtured some of history's most profound thinkers about man and God. Even more ironic that a dynasty that tried to cleanse Islam produced thinkers who were the product not just of Muslim diversity but of multiple cultures. Ibn Arabi, Ibn Rushd, and Maimonides stood at the apex of more than fifteen hundred years of human civilization, some of which was Muslim, much of which was not. We will never know if they could have thought what they thought and written what they wrote had they been steeped only in their own traditions. We do know that they were immersed in Greek, Latin, and Arabic scholarship and that they drew on that accumulated wisdom not to write polemics but to explain the meaning of life. And we know that they deployed their intellect and channeled their passion not to attack but to illuminate. They walked the path of love and compassion, and served as guides to seekers trying to find their way to God.

And none more than Maimonides. With his days filled by his medical duties, he lived a busy life, and his descriptions of his routine as doctor to the royal family in Cairo do not convey the sense that he loved his day job. "My duties to the Sultan are very heavy," he wrote. "I am obliged to visit him every day, early in the morning; and when he or any of his children, or any of the inmates of his harem, are indisposed, I do not quit Cairo, but stay during the greater part of the day in the palace." Then, when he returned home late in the day, he usually found his house full of Jews, Christians, and Muslims seeking his counsel for ailments both physical and spiritual. At the close of the day, he was so spent that he barely had time for his writing and his studies.

Yet this was the same man, weary from his long hours, who was able to write *Guide for the Perplexed*. In it, he divided the world into those who can learn the inner truths and those who cannot. "It is not the purpose of this treatise to make its totality understandable to the vulgar or the beginner in speculation," he announced in the introduction, "nor to teach those who have not engaged in any study other than the study of the Law—I mean the legalistic study of the Law." It was a treatise for philosophers and for seekers. It was a guide for those who were advanced in learning yet still had unanswered questions. It was a map drawn by a master for those who had glimpsed behind the curtain separating the learned from the vulgar, who had started on the path but found themselves confused and uncertain.

Maimonides believed that there were truths that the masses could grasp and messages that any common man could hear and that there were truths accessible only to the learned, the wise, and the religious. In time, hidden truth became the foundation of the Jewish mystical tradition. The study of the kabbalah, which probed the inner meanings of the Torah and the Jewish holy texts, flourished in late medieval Spain and owed a considerable debt to the legacy of Maimonides. Though he would have been uncomfortable with the degree to which later kabbalists turned away from the world, he too believed in a hierarchy of truth and in the notion that only a select few are qualified to see God's plan in all of its glory.

Maimonides was a seeker who rejected the notion that all are created equal. The democratic side of Islamic and Jewish mysticism said that all believers could establish a personal, intimate relationship with God—provided they were willing to walk the long and arduous road. But as

articulated by Maimonides and men like Ibn Arabi, there was also an elitism, which said that the world is inherently corrupt and that the true path is open only to those pure and wise enough to take it.

The consequence of these attitudes for Judaism was an increasing disengagement from society. The consequence for Islam was a growing unwillingness to engage new ideas. While the Jews of Spain may not have been able to prevent their marginalization by Muslim and Christian rulers, the Muslims of North Africa and the Near East suffered from the shift away from creative thought and away from grappling with the contentious questions that had been part and parcel of the Mediterranean world since the days of Plato and Aristotle. As the majority turned to orthodoxy and a minority turned toward a dynamic but secretive mysticism, Muslim culture in the Arab world slowly began to wither.

As for Maimonides, he died as he had lived: a pious man, who in spite of his erudition and willingness to learn what there was to learn, identified himself as simply a child of Abraham in long exile from his home. He believed that the Jews of Spain and the Near East had brought their fate upon themselves, because of the sins of their forefathers, and that their subjugation to the Arabs had been foretold by the scripture. He prayed throughout his life that God would allow the Jews one day to return and enter the Temple in Jerusalem once again, and until that day, he prayed that Jews would learn from their exile and, through love of God, be forgiven.

Had he been asked if his life demonstrated the possibility of coexistence between Islam and Judaism, Maimonides would almost certainly have said no. From his vantage, Jews under Muslim rule were constrained in what they could do and dependent on the sufferance of their rulers. Identified as he was with his tribe, he could hardly have felt otherwise. But even a wise individual is not always the best guide to his own life. As we have seen, Maimonides was not just a Jew. He was steeped in multiple cultures and a product of all of them. In much the same way, Ibn Arabi believed himself to be a Sufi seeker, but he too was the product of diverse cultural streams. The beauty, intensity, and sophistication of their visions were the result of that diversity. They represented the juxtaposition of religious traditions, whether they realized it or not. They were and are a testament to what is possible.

The intellectual and spiritual creativity of these men appeared to be in vivid contrast to the Almohad dynasty that ruled southern Spain. But

on closer examination, even the Almohads were less rigid than history has made them. Their creed called for a return to the unadorned piety of Muhammad, yet they looked to logic and reason to defend their vision. "It is by necessity of reason that the existence of God, Praise to Him, is known," went one line of the Almohad *Doctrine of Divine Unity*. They took a hard line against the philosophical tendency to interpret the Quran in terms of analogies and had contempt for the notion that God had human characteristics. "Minds have a limit at which they stop and which they do not exceed," and when people attempt to explain the inexplicable, they tend to latch on to "anthropomorphism," which was, according to the Almohads, "absurd."[2]

In essence, the simple piety of the Almohads was not so simplistic. They drew on the same philosophical tradition that supported Maimonides and Ibn Arabi, even though they arrived at radically different conclusions. Both the Almohads and the Almoravids are rightly seen as early versions of what would later evolve into "Islamic fundamentalism." But their history shows that there was nothing unsophisticated about them. They were not ignorant country rubes. They knew the intellectual and spiritual terrain just as well as their adversaries, and they proffered a vision of Islam that relegated interpretation and human reason to small supporting roles and elevated the literal text of the Quran above everything. They saw the intellectual fancies of the elite as decadence, and they saw decadence as weak. But in spite of themselves, they shared more with those elites than they wished to acknowledge, and their success was not a function of military prowess alone. Only a few thousand Almohads and Almoravids settled in Andalusia, yet they managed to rule. They tapped a dormant chord of unease, a belief among the Muslims of Spain that the growing power of the Christians was a reflection of God's displeasure. It was the same alarm that Jewish prophets had sounded from time immemorial—that the strength of the enemy was God's punishment for communal sins.

Twelfth- and thirteenth-century Spain is one of the crucibles of history. The philosophical glories of Ibn Arabi confronted the puritan Almohad reaction, and the puritans won. The multicultural Islam of Andalusia confronted the renaissance of Christian power and lost. While the philosophical tradition never disappeared, it became less significant, and while the puritan tradition never fully triumphed, it became more dominant. Throughout the Muslim world, similar developments took

place. There had always been considerable pockets of intolerance and animosity, whether toward the People of the Book or toward new ideas, but these had only occasionally had the upper hand. If the balance had been in favor of openness and inquiry before the twelfth century, it shifted the other way after. The inclusiveness of medieval Baghdad and Andalusia gave way to exclusivity. Flexibility was replaced by rigidity. And champions of orthodoxy, who had never had much success in the Muslim world, were increasingly able to silence dissent.

THE CYCLES OF HISTORY AND THE CHRISTIAN RECONQUEST

TO A CONSIDERABLE DEGREE, these reactions went hand in hand with a change of political fortunes. In Iberia, the Christian kings of Castile, Aragon, and Portugal were becoming more powerful at the expense of Muslims. In the Near East, the Crusaders had shown just how easy it would be to conquer weak and divided Muslim city-states. Then, in the thirteenth century, wide swaths of Iran and Iraq were conquered by the Mongols. The Abbasid caliphate was swept away, and the last caliph was executed. In Turkey, the Seljuk Turks were decimated by another central Asian invader, Timur the Lame, more commonly known in the west as Tamerlane.

For the first five centuries of Muslim history, the story had been one of military, political, and cultural dominance. Suddenly, the tide was reversing, and Muslims suffered defeat upon defeat. Before, the only time Muslim states were overthrown was by other Muslims. Now, pagans, animists, and Christians seemed to be crushing one Muslim dynasty after another.

One response was to close ranks and try to recapture the formula that had brought Muslims their success. This was not nearly as self-conscious or systematic as the reaction to Western power that gave rise to the fundamentalist movements of the twentieth century. But the pattern is similar: Muslims responded to the challenges by looking back and turning inward, hoping against hope to reclaim the early glories of Islam's past.

This pattern did not go unnoticed by at least one astute contemporary observer. Writing in the fourteenth century, Ibn Khaldun was a North African version of Gibbon and Herodotus who attempted to

describe the forces of history that had resulted in the world as he knew it. His theory of Muslim history was that success had always been the product of a tight-knit tribal culture. The first example was the Arab tribes of Mecca and Medina, led by Muhammad. They were bound by strong ties that created what Ibn Khaldun called *asabiyya*, which translates as "group cohesion" or "communal spirit." The cohesion of the Arab tribes was the product of ethnicity and ideology. The rigors of desert life hardened them, and the intense faith of early Islam bound them. As a result, they were able to erupt from the desert and obliterate what should have been two formidable adversaries—the Byzantines and the Persians. By the second and third generation, the piety and discipline that had generated such strength began to dissipate. The new conquerors moved to cities. The Umayyads became a dynasty and built palaces in Damascus. They took on the airs of royalty. No longer hardened by the desert, they became soft and corrupt. By the third generation, they were ripe for defeat, and were in turn supplanted by another group whose *asabiyya* was strong, the Abbasids. And then the cycle started again.

Ibn Khaldun believed that this pattern explained Muslim history. A tribe bound by ties of family and faith is forged on a desert anvil and then sweeps away an established empire. That tribe then creates a state, and decay sets in. Soon, cohesion gives way to selfishness, greed, and hierarchy, which leads to decadence and makes the group weak. Ibn Khaldun saw the emergence of the Almohads and Almoravids as the latest example of a pattern that had been occurring for centuries, and they did indeed fit his thesis. But later critics of Ibn Khaldun noted that they may have fit it too well. Reared in what is now Tunisia, Ibn Khaldun was acutely aware of the tension between desert tribes like the Berbers and the more settled cities along the Mediterranean coast. He knew how frequently tribes had emerged either from the mountains or the fringe of the Sahara to overthrow the established dynasties centered in cities such as Marrakesh and Tunis. But however well that described the history of North Africa, it was less true of the Near East and beyond. For Ibn Khaldun, however, the theory explained not just Muslim North Africa, but the entire history of Islam.[3]

The strength of his analysis far outweighed the weaknesses. He did what all great historians have done: he identified a pattern that shed light

on why things happened as they did. The tribal element fused with a strong faith did give groups such as the Mecca-Medina Arabs, the Seljuk Turks, the Almohads, and others a unique strength. It also characterized a new force then emerging in the Muslim world, a Turkish tribe named after its putative founder, Osman, that became known as the Ottomans.

Much as Ibn Khaldun would have predicted, the zealous North African dynasties who conquered Andalusia began to run out of steam. Challenged in Morocco by Berber tribes and in Andalusia by the Christian kings of Aragon and Castile, they at first held their ground and then rapidly lost it. Córdoba fell to King Fernando III in 1236; Valencia (which had once seen Muslims and Christians serving together in its army) fell in 1238; and Seville surrendered after a siege that lasted from the end of 1247 until November 1248. By the middle of the thirteenth century, all that remained of the once-powerful Muslim kingdoms of Spain was the small enclave of Granada in the southeast, guarded by a ring of mountains on one side and the sea on the other. The kingdom of Granada would survive for two centuries, the last, lonely bastion of Andalusian Islam. In return for a hefty annual tribute to the Christians, Granada remained a Muslim state, but it was isolated. Its rulers turned their palace complex into a monument to past glories, and just before it fell at the end of the fifteenth century, the Alhambra was completed. It was a testament to what Muslim Spain had been—an architectural marvel combining the most sophisticated elements of Christian and Muslim art and engineering, its walls a mass of inlay, its courtyards hushed and cool even in the heat of summer, with only the soft melody of fountains breaking the stillness.

Where Ibn Khaldun dispassionately wrote of the natural rise and fall of dynasties, the capture of Seville and Córdoba in the thirteenth century was interpreted by the Christians of Spain as a validation of their faith. The crusading spirit animated the royalty of Castile, León, and Aragon, and the resounding defeat of the Muslim kingdoms ushered in a new era of Christian triumphalism on the Iberian Peninsula. The Muslims recognized that the shift was significant, and the capture of Seville, in particular, was seen as a catastrophe. Assessing the change in fortunes, one Muslim poet described the collapse as the inevitable decay of all human endeavors, and though he may have strived for detachment, his pain was all too evident. "Everything declines after reaching perfection,"

he wrote, "therefore let no man be beguiled by the sweetness of a pleasant life." All past empires had fallen, and the fate of Seville was no different, except that for him, it was.

> *Where is Cordoba, the home of the sciences?*
> *Where is Seville and the pleasures it contains, as well as its sweet river*
> *overflowing and brimming full?*
> *They are capitals which were pillars of the land, yet when the pillars are*
> *gone, it may no longer endure!*
> *[We] ... weep in despair, like a passionate lover weeping at the departure*
> *of the beloved, over dwellings emptied of Islam that were first vacated*
> *and are now inhabited by unbelief;*
> *In which mosques have become churches wherein only the bells and*
> *crosses may be found.*
> *O you who remain heedless though you have warning in Fate; if you are*
> *asleep, Fate is always awake.*[4]

Outside of Spain, the conquest of Andalusia save for Granada did not shake the Muslim world in the same way that the fall of Jerusalem had. The Iberian Peninsula had always been at the outermost edge of the community of believers, and had been the scene of back-and-forth wars for almost half a millennium. But to the Muslims of Spain, the reversal of the thirteenth century was a calamity from which they never recovered. Unlike the fall of Jerusalem, the surrender of Seville and Córdoba did not spur other Muslim states to organize and launch a counterattack. The Christian triumph was not only decisive; it was permanent.

The Christian victories changed the nature of Muslim, Christian, and Jewish coexistence. For hundreds of years, the three had lived in Spain, but mostly under Muslim rule. The conditions of coexistence had been determined by Muslims, first by the Cordoban caliphate and then by different city-states. While Christians had ruled Muslims and Jews in the north of the peninsula, they had not made much of an effort to develop a governing philosophy. After the fall of Seville and Córdoba, that changed. Christians found themselves in the position of administering a large population of Muslims and a small but economically important community of Jews. In time, the demographics changed, but for most of the thirteenth and early fourteenth centuries, Christian over-

lords depended on a passive and productive Muslim population for revenue, farming, trade, soldiers, and stability.

At first, the governments of Castile and Aragon treated the conquered Muslims and Jews much as the Muslims had treated the People of the Book. When the coastal port of Valencia fell to the soldiers of Aragon in 1238, its Muslim inhabitants were forced to leave the city with only those possessions they could carry. They had committed the unforgivable sin of resisting, and they paid a steep price—but not the steepest. They were granted safe passage, which was one indication that the Christians were not secure enough or strong enough to depopulate and resettle all of Andalusia.

More common were treaties with the local population guaranteeing the same freedoms of movement and worship that the Muslims had granted the People of the Book. For instance, the king of Aragon promised the Muslims in the vicinity of Valencia that they would be able "to make use of waters just as was custom in the time of the Saracens. And they may pasture their stock in all their districts as was customary in the time of the pagans [Muslims].... Christians may not forbid preaching in their mosques or prayer being made on Friday ... but the Muslims are to carry on according to their religion." Muslims could still determine local laws, and their own judges could decide all issues of marriage, estates, and contracts. In addition, Muslims were given the right of free passage by land or by sea and were not to be forced to pay extra tariffs or taxes.[5]

With the change of regimes, there was a considerable amount of land redistribution and new settlement of Christian knights on formerly Muslim estates. Most of that came at the expense of the defeated Muslim nobility and did not take the form of outright seizures from local farmers or peasants. Instead, Christian lords replaced Muslim lords as the recipients of taxes and tithes.

Initially, Christians were humbled by the victory they had achieved. They recognized the Muslims of Andalusia as a worthy adversary, and they shared with them the peculiar intimacy that comes with years of war. Christian writers simultaneously condemned Islam and praised Muslims. "If we wish to consider the nobility of the Muslims," wrote one, "who can be unaware of the many kings, princes, and noblemen who have arisen from among them?"[6] Crusading fervor had helped turn the

tide, but once the goal of reconquest had been achieved, Christian rulers appropriated the system that the Andalusian Muslims had created, and their culture as well.

The first Christian king to rule in peace over this new world was Alfonso X of Castile. Unlike his warrior father, Fernando, who had brought the great cities of Muslim Spain to their knees, Alfonso inherited a stable kingdom that had recently vanquished its enemies. War had defined Castile, but now an administrator was needed. On that score, Alfonso's record was mixed. He was not a meticulous soul, and he had little enthusiasm for administration. That may be one reason that so much of the existing order was maintained. To do anything different would have required energy and innovation. Alfonso possessed both, but no interest in applying them to either war or bureaucracy. To the joy of scholars and poets, Alfonso had one obsession. He loved literature, music, and history, and he dedicated his court and its considerable resources to their preservation. Over the course of a thirty-two-year reign, beginning in 1252 and ending in 1284, he did his best to rival the cultural output of Baghdad and Córdoba. And his best was very, very good.

An early sign of Alfonso's predilection was the tomb he erected for his father. Though he had fought by Fernando's side during the siege of Seville, Alfonso's design for his father's sepulcher was more literary than martial. It included inscriptions in Latin, Arabic, Castilian, and Hebrew in honor of the four cultural streams that had converged because of Fernando's efforts.[7]

Soon after Alfonso was crowned, he gathered the greatest minds of Spain to his court to work on a plan of breathtaking scope. He wanted to create a written monument to Spanish culture—its history, literature, poetry, astronomy, music, philosophy, law, mathematics, and of course, religion. His intent was to leave a compendium of human knowledge that could be read in Castilian and that would include the seminal texts of Muslims, Jews, and Christians. It was not only an ambitious undertaking; it was an expensive one as well, and not everyone shared his conviction that it was worth the price.

During the three decades of his reign, Alfonso was rarely popular, but he achieved his cultural goals. The teams he assembled produced a comprehensive history of Spain, illuminated manuscripts charting the stars, complicated musical scores, love poems, legal codes, and even a book dedicated to games, their rules, origins, and the best strategy for playing

them. These achievements earned Alfonso the sobriquet *el Sabio,* the Learned. His lust for learning won him the lasting admiration of scholars and academics, and they have repaid him with a favorable historical verdict. He cherished the arts, and his dedication to culture was extraordinary even compared with the later patrons of Renaissance Italy. But it was not just personal passion that motivated him. He was certain that the success of the new kingdom that his father had cemented depended on its unique fusion of Muslim, Christian, and Jewish history. If no effort were made to preserve and record that legacy, it would inevitably be forgotten. Alfonso believed that this would be more than a cultural loss. He feared that unless these elements were purposely woven into the fabric of Castile and Spain, the kingdom would decay. Detached from its history, it would wither and fade.

Alfonso turned the city of Toledo into the hub of his kingdom. In addition to being his birthplace, the town was blessed with an old and established intellectual community, including a considerable number of Jews. Like many of his predecessors, Alfonso employed Jews as his court physicians, and they also served as translators for a number of the works compiled at his behest. Jewish doctors tended to know the major languages needed to complete the project, and they were able to render Hebrew and Arabic into either Latin or Castilian. Usually, they worked as leaders of translation teams. That in itself had been standard practice in Spain for centuries, but the scale of Alfonso's enterprise was much larger and required both more people and more organization.

Among the translations were a catalog of the known stars, Arabic books on the construction of clocks and on the proper manufacturing of measuring devices like the astrolabe, and a description of Muhammad's night journey to heaven. No one seems to have objected that the man appointed to render the Arabic version of this sacred Muslim story into Spanish happened to be a Jew named Abraham of Toledo. Nor was it seen as odd that Abraham oversaw several other translations, including one in Latin and one in Castilian. Muslims, Christians, and Jews in Spain were both separate from one another and entwined with one another. They shared a common heritage, and no one, the Castilian king least of all, would have denied that.

Alfonso was intent on translating both Jewish and Muslim religious texts in addition to scientific treatises. Though he was not the first Christian in Europe to create a Latin version of the Quran—Peter the Vener-

able, the twelfth-century abbot of Cluny, had already accomplished that—he was almost certainly the only one to insist on translations of the Talmud as well. His motives here were decidedly mixed. He wanted to preserve the heritage of the Iberian Peninsula, but he also wanted to establish the superiority of Christianity. According to his nephew, he "ordered the translation of the whole law of the Jews, and even their Talmud, and other knowledge which is called the *qabbalah* and which the Jews keep closely secret. And he did this so it might be manifest that it is a mere representation of that Law which we Christians have, and that they, like the Moors, are in grave error and in peril of losing their souls."[8]

This ecumenical translation project was a prime example of cooperation, but there was competition and hostility as well. An implicit recognition of common roots and the undeniable reality of a shared culture was offset by animosity that occasionally flared into outright aggression. Jews served as advisers to Christian and Muslim rulers, and as their physicians were entrusted with their lives and bodies, yet laws limited how intimate contact could be. Each community had strict prohibitions against intermarriage, as well as harsh penalties for sexual contact. It is a truism that no community ever passes laws designed to prevent something that isn't happening, and the intensity of these prohibitions is a sign of just how easy and how tempting it was to transgress. Even though each group lived in its own quarter, towns like Toledo or even cities like Seville had a small number of inhabitants by modern standards and people could not avoid interaction. The fact that so many people from each major group knew the languages of the others is itself an indication of how close relations actually were, even if sex was a line that was crossed only at great personal peril.

Alfonso's reign, unfortunately, did not herald a new era of cooperation in Spain. Instead, it marked the apex of Spanish Christian tolerance. Religious freedoms and coexistence gradually gave way to intolerance. Laws restricting the activities of both Muslims and Jews became more common, even though they were erratically enforced. Jews were permitted to worship, provided that they did so quietly and without "speaking ill of the faith of Our Lord Jesus Christ" and without attempting to preach to Christians or challenge their beliefs. That presented a problem for Jews when they were summoned to local courts to engage in theological debates designed to show the superiority of Christianity. These debates were a cultural pastime, much as they had been in Baghdad cen-

turies before. The Jewish invitee, often a rabbi, had to tread the line between capitulating, which might anger the audience, and winning the argument, which might not only displease the audience but lead to legal jeopardy. Jews were rarely compelled to convert, because they were supposed to recognize their errors and come to God of their own free will. Until then, however, they were to be constrained in what they could do and how openly they could worship.

Muslims were treated in much the same way, but unlike the Jews, they were a majority of the population in the south, and remained so into the early fifteenth century. Converting the Moors became a preoccupation of the Spanish church, and as more land was redistributed and more Christians settled in what used to be Muslim Spain, Muslims began to convert or depart. Some Muslims, as well as Jews, hid their religion and after public conversion celebrated their old rites in secret. Scholars have long debated just how many Muslims and Jews went underground and practiced their religion in private even as they acted as Christians in public. But one result was widespread suspicion, even paranoia, in the Spanish church that Muslim and Jewish conversions were false. Beginning in the fourteenth century and gaining force in the fifteenth, this paranoia was enflamed by the office of the Spanish Inquisition.

The achievements of Alfonso notwithstanding, the contrast between Muslim and Christian Spain is startling. Muslim Spain saw long centuries of coexistence, interrupted by sporadic episodes of violence and brief periods of discrimination, much of which was not the result of tensions between Muslims, Christians, and Jews per se, but was simply an unremarkable aspect of medieval society. That Muslims sometimes punished or attacked the People of the Book is less significant than the fact that eruptions of violence between groups or between rival states were common and were as likely to occur within religious communities as they were between them. Christian violence toward other Christians and Muslim aggression against Muslims was ubiquitous. True, Jewish violence against Jews, except at an individual level, was rare, as was Jewish retaliation against Muslims or Christians—but that was because Spanish Jews never controlled the state and were always a small proportion of the population.

Christian Spain, however, did not cherish tolerance and coexistence. Instead, there was a culture of discrimination against Muslims and Jews, with only intermittent periods of harmony and cooperation. Under the

rule of Castile, Muslims were marginalized, disdained, and then targeted as aliens and enemies. Within a few generations after the fall of Córdoba and Seville in the thirteenth century, the tolerance that marked Alfonso's realm and that had been a central element of Muslim Andalusia evaporated and was replaced by a zealous intolerance that demanded conversion and was often not satisfied even with that.

The hostility of Christian Spain to the Muslims and Jews grew even as the power of Castile increased. It cannot be explained as reaction born of insecurity. It wasn't as though Castile and Christian Spain was attacked by a foreign power or was disintegrating within. Quite the opposite. The contrast with Islam is stark. Muslim society, from the outset, had been forced to think about the balance between Muslims and the People of the Book. Christian Spain followed a different path, as did Western Europe. Crusades against Muslims had gone hand in hand with the consolidation of Christian power. The success of Spanish Christianity, at least in the political sense, cannot be separated from war with Muslims.

The stronger Christian Spain became, the more intolerant it grew. Muslim Granada had been allowed to remain independent and then proved difficult to eliminate. Its conquest became a national fixation, and the monarchs of Castile and Aragon launched a crusade to capture it once and for all. By the time Granada finally fell in 1492, antagonism toward Muslims and Jews had reached a new peak. Secure in the reconquest, the king and queen of Castile and Aragon, Ferdinand and Isabella, ordered the Moors and the Jews of Spain to convert or depart. While it took many decades to fulfill the edict, Spain became almost entirely Christian. Only the art and architecture that graced its cities remained as reminders of what once was.

What we are left with, then, is two very different histories. One is of a Muslim Spain that with notable exceptions rested on a foundation of coexistence and cooperation between the three faiths. The other is a Christian Spain that with few exceptions thrived because of a crusading ideology that rejected Muslims and Jews. The Spanish monarchs of the fifteenth century were convinced that both were a threat, and the campaign against them was given added urgency by what was happening on the other side of the Mediterranean.

In 1453, with a suddenness that shook Christian Europe, the last Christian empire in the Near East, the once great city of Constantinople, fell. Just as the Christian monarchs of Spain were achieving their

goal of cleansing the peninsula of Jews and Christians, a new Muslim empire emerged that had the will and the power to threaten the very existence of Christian Europe. Had that not occurred, the subsequent relationship between Muslims, Christians, and Jews might have taken a different path. Instead, it reinforced a belief, already prevalent in the Christian West, that Muslims were the enemy.

The Lord of Two Lands

WHEN THE END finally came, it was a calamity. It was also meaningless. After more than a thousand years, the city of Constantine, the seat of the greatest empire Christendom had ever known, was occupied by a Muslim army. But by the time that Sultan Mehmed II, ever after known as the Conqueror, marched into the Church of Hagia Sophia, in the heart of Constantinople, Byzantium had long since ceased to be an empire in anything but name.

Mehmed came to power burdened with a substantial Oedipal complex. His father, Murad, had significantly enlarged the scope of Ottoman rule, and when Murad died in 1451, Mehmed succeeded him—for a second time. After victories over the Hungarians and the Serbs, Murad had abdicated in 1444, only to be recalled by the court when the teenage Mehmed, obstinate and disdainful of his father's advisers, proved unable to govern effectively and unwilling to work with the vizier appointed by Murad to guide the young prince. Though there are no records recording what Mehmed felt at being installed and then abruptly shunted aside by his commanding father, it's unlikely that he took it in stride. In portraits, his face defined by the long, sharp nose and the classic beard of an Ottoman prince, it is difficult to discern his character. But his later behavior suggests that he never forgave or forgot what his father had done, and Constantinople paid the steep and fatal price.

His father had won almost every confrontation with almost every adversary that the Ottomans faced, but one prize eluded him. Constantinople had been taken exactly once, in 1204, but not by Muslims. The Venetians had done what no other power had accomplished—not the

Slavs, not the Huns, not the first wave of Arab armies to emerge in the seventh and eighth centuries, and not the Seljuk Turks in the eleventh. For fifty years after the brutal sack of Constantinople in 1204, the Latins ruled the imperial city, and the Byzantine emperor sat in exile. In the middle of the thirteenth century, the imperial family returned, but hardly in triumph. For the next two hundred years, Byzantium was more a name and a legend than a real power capable of determining what went on in the eastern Mediterranean or the Balkans. Controlling only a few thousand square miles of land, the latter-day rulers of a once-mighty empire watched helplessly as the Ottomans sealed them in their city.

Though Byzantium had shrunk and its emperor was reduced to a man in robes barely able to raise five thousand men to defend the city's ramparts, it remained a potent symbol as the last relic of Rome. For that reason alone, it was a target worthy of young Mehmed's ambitions. And even with a handful of defenders, the walls of the city and its strategic placement between the waters of the Golden Horn and the Bosphorus represented a formidable challenge to any adversary that wanted to take it. Siege technology was not advanced enough to breach the ramparts. From the heights along the water's edge, a few defenders could destroy ships that attempted a landing. Some of Mehmed's predecessors had tried to take the city and had failed, even with numbers on their side. Constantinople was weak, but it could still defend itself.

Mehmed was impetuous, arrogant, and seething with resentment, but even at the age of twenty-one, he knew better than to attack the city unprepared. He marshaled a large army, built a fleet, and commissioned the construction of an immense cannon before he began the attack on Constantinople in the spring of 1453.

The Byzantines did the best they could. Some Genoese and Venetian ships and mercenaries came to their aid, though most of Europe refused Emperor Constantine's request for help. Some Western Christians suggested that if the emperor were willing to bow to the pope, more active support might be forthcoming, but that was not a price he was willing to pay. While the Roman Church had established itself as the supreme doctrinal authority in the West, the Eastern Orthodox Church had never acknowledged that the pope was anything more than the bishop of Rome, worthy of respect but not obeisance. Given the choice between capitulating to the pope and surrendering to the Ottomans, Constantinople preferred the infidel. "Better the turban of the Muslim in the

midst of Constantinople," the saying went, "than the miter of the Latin."
The emperor Constantine was left with his guile, intimate knowledge of
the walls that had been built by the emperor Theodosius a millennium
before, and prayer. Those were not enough.

Though Constantine shared the name of the city's founder, he did
not share the same luck. The Ottoman generals did what had been considered impossible and breached the iron gate that protected the Golden
Horn from enemy ships. Mehmed had numbers on his side, and he
exploited the thinness of the defenses and weaknesses in the fortifications. Tens of thousands of his soldiers poured into the city and overwhelmed it. Constantine ripped off his imperial insignia, charged into
the onslaught, and died. He declared that he would not be remembered
as the emperor who fled the greatest city in the world in the hour of its
greatest need.

RELIGIOUS FREEDOM AND "THE CONQUEROR"

THE OTTOMAN ARMY entered the city on May 29, 1453. Because the
Byzantines had refused to surrender, Mehmed gave his troops license to
loot and pillage; they would have rebelled if he had not. But the city was
already depopulated and all but a handful of churches and palaces were
deserted. Some later Western accounts describe a horrific sacking, but
there is little evidence of that. No matter how psychologically devastating, the physical damage was relatively mild, both to property and to
people.

Mehmed made directly for Hagia Sophia. For a millennium, the
church had stood as a monument to the empire, the center of Eastern
Christianity. At the end of May 1453, an alien language was heard under
its domes, and a conquering people replaced the old rites with theirs.
The church echoed with the sound of the *shahada*, and with the Muslim
call to prayer. Thereafter, Hagia Sophia would be a mosque, with the
names of the first four caliphs surrounding its main dome. When
Mehmed first entered, so legend has it, a soldier was attempting to pry
loose the tiles in the floor. The sultan struck him with the flat of his
sword, and said, "For you the treasures and the prisoners are enough.
The buildings of the city fall to me."

The sultan soon halted the pillaging. The city was to be the capital of

his empire, and he did not want to be burdened with unnecessary renovations. The place was in sorry enough shape as it was and in need of repair. In the ensuing months, the Ottomans refashioned the city, both physically and culturally. Some Byzantine nobles had escaped; others were taken captive; some were ransomed; and a few were executed. But Mehmed could not afford to have the entire city emptied of its Greek inhabitants. In order to keep it functioning, he did what he could to assure the population that their rights would be respected. He even tried to entice those who had left to return and offered to pay them restitution if their property had been damaged or destroyed.

As an added incentive, Mehmed promised that he would not interfere with religion. The Byzantine emperor had stood at the head of the Orthodox Church, and with him gone, the patriarch was the logical replacement. But at the time of the city's fall, the reigning patriarch was abroad, and in his place, Mehmed turned to Gennadius—one of the most respected monks in the city, who was known to be fiercely independent and equally fierce in his opposition to Rome—and announced that he would be the leader of the church.

It was later said that Mehmed ordered his officials to scour Constantinople for someone worthy of the appointment. In the words of one contemporary Greek chronicler, "Gennadius was a very wise and remarkable man.... When the Sultan saw him, and had in a short time had proofs of his wisdom and prudence and virtue and also of his power as a speaker and his religious character, he was greatly impressed, and held him in great honor and respect, and gave him the right to come to him at any time, and honored him with liberty and conversation." In January 1454, the sultan installed the new patriarch and granted him authority over the daily lives of the city's Christian populace, "no less than that enjoyed previously under the emperors."

The extent of the patriarch's power was spelled out in a charter drawn up by the sultan's vizier. Gennadius was more than the spiritual guide of the Greek Orthodox who had fallen under Ottoman rule. He was in many ways their king, with power to tax and judge and the authority to appoint local representatives throughout the empire. Much like the Byzantine emperor, he had more influence than the heads of other Christian churches in the East. While he ultimately answered to the sultan and to the Ottoman state, on issues ranging from birth to marriage to death, including estates, taxes, and intracommunal trade, he had

wide latitude. The Ottomans may have ruled, but Mehmed II had no interest in micromanaging the daily lives of Christian subjects. That would have required more bureaucracy and more effort. Better to find a partner and delegate the dirty work of administration to him.[1]

It did not seem remarkable to anyone at the time that Mehmed could be simultaneously so merciless with the nobles and the ruling class and so merciful toward most of the people and their religious leaders. But it runs contrary to the modern notion that there is no separation between church and state in Islam. That lack of separation is said to be in contrast to the wall dividing secular and religious power in the West. Yet until at least the nineteenth century, those walls did not exist in the Western world, and the entire framework has never made much sense when applied to the Muslim world.

For instance, the Byzantine Empire, which the Ottomans ended, never had separate spheres for religion and politics. The emperor was simultaneously the head of the state and the head of the church—and that formula was replicated in other parts of the Christian world, including Reformation England, where the king demanded the obedience of the archbishop of Canterbury. Throughout Byzantine history, the emperor enforced doctrine, led military campaigns, and convened tribunals to punish those who dissented from the imperial orthodoxy. As we saw, the refusal of Egyptian Coptic Christians to bow to the authority of both emperor and the patriarch in Constantinople in the sixth and seventh centuries was one reason for the ease of the Arab conquest of Egypt soon after Muhammad's death.

In contrast, while there were occasions when Muslim rulers attempted to dictate doctrine, those times were the exception, and not the rule. In one sense, the Ottoman sultan had unlimited power over his subjects. He had power over life and death. But in other ways, he was as constrained by, and in theory just as subject to, religious law as any other Muslim. Like earlier rulers, he deferred to the scholars and judges who comprised the *ulama*. Even when the Ottoman sultan added the title of caliph in later centuries, he did not exercise total doctrinal authority. True, he could issue laws of his own whether or not those agreed with sharia (religious) law. But he still needed, and cultivated, the support of the *ulama*. The only sense in which it can be said that there is no separation between church and state in Islam is that there is no church. The possible exception is Iran. After the sixteenth century, Iran's Shi'a mul-

lahs gradually coalesced into an institution that in its hierarchy and coherence resembled the Catholic Church, but without the ability to coerce errant believers. Almost everywhere else, Islam had no central, governing religious body. Throughout the history of Muslim societies, from the emergence of a clerical establishment in Baghdad during the Abbasid caliphate through the evolution of Sufism and other forms of individual piety, the political and doctrinal spheres were distinct and governed by different people.

The de facto separation helps explain why Mehmed could be so indifferent to the religion of his subjects. Like most imperial rulers, the Ottomans drew a distinction between the state and the people. Neither Mehmed nor any of the Ottomans evinced an interest in converting the Greek Christian population of Constantinople. To the contrary. The Ottomans provided incentives to encourage the Greeks to work with the new regime to revive the city and restore it to greatness. For their part, the Christians of Constantinople, their religious rights intact, seem to have accepted the new rulers. Greek Christian architects drew up plans to reinforce and reconstruct the decaying walls and fortifications that had in the end failed to protect the city. They designed mosques and helped Mehmed transform Hagia Sophia into a Muslim house of worship. They also built a vast new covered market, which would become the famed Grand Bazaar of Istanbul, and manned many of its stalls and shops.

Had Mehmed stopped with the capture of Constantinople, he would have earned his sobriquet "the Conqueror." But he was still very young, and his ambitions were not sated. He took on his father's old adversaries in Hungary and Serbia, and he solidified Ottoman control over much of the Balkans and the southern coast of the Black Sea. More often than not, cities surrendered, opening their gates to the sultan rather than suffer death and destruction. The Ottomans honored the flag of truce. When they promised to protect the rights of the local populace, they did.

Inevitably, after decades of leading his armies, Mehmed grew tired and ill. He did not age gracefully, and his accomplishments had not made him happy. He drank too much and became ever-more distrustful of those around him. At the risk of unfairly psychoanalyzing him from a distance of many centuries, it might be said that he did everything he could to banish the memory of his father, and he failed. Had he consulted a Sufi master, he might have learned that he could go to the ends of the earth, win every battle, and become rich beyond imagination, but

unless he bared his soul to God, he would remain restless and unfulfilled. And so he was, until he died in 1481, fat, gout-ridden, surrounded by Jewish and Persian physicians helpless to heal him, an old man at the age of forty-nine.

Though the Europeans were dismayed at the loss of the city they had done so little to help and so much to undermine, whatever affinity they felt was an illusion. In truth, the Christians of Western Europe were more alien and more hostile to Orthodox Byzantium than the Ottomans. The Ottomans and the Byzantines had been fighting for more than a hundred years, and they had also lived side by side while each attended to other enemies. Mehmed's father had married a Byzantine-Serbian princess, which was neither the first and nor the last time that a Muslim Ottoman married a Christian woman for reasons of state. The two empires had been bound not only by marital ties, but by financial ones. For many years, before Mehmed, the Ottoman sultan paid an annual fee to the Byzantine emperor, because the Ottomans preferred a toothless Byzantium to a rival power in Constantinople guarding the vital crossroads. Later, in the nineteenth century, the powers of Europe were to make the same calculations about the Ottomans, and the empire would survive not because it was strong but because it was weak.

EUROPE AND THE OTTOMANS

THE OTTOMAN EMPIRE lasted nearly five hundred years, longer than all but a handful of dynasties the world has known. Byzantium, and Rome before that, each survived more than a thousand years, but only the Ottomans could claim that the same family ruled in succession from the beginning until the end. Though there may have been some convenient rewriting of the family tree, there was an unbroken chain stretching from Osman in the fourteenth century through the last sultan, Mehmed VI, in the first decade of the twentieth. By way of comparison, European dynasties have rarely lasted more than a few hundred years and have usually ruled an area no larger than an Ottoman province. For the better part of five centuries, however, the Ottoman Empire encompassed the entire eastern Mediterranean. From the early sixteenth century until the early twentieth, it also ruled North Africa and Egypt; the Caucasus between the Black and Caspian Seas; the Crimean Peninsula and the

surrounding regions; all of the Near East from present-day Israel to the borders of Iran; and the Balkans, including Greece, Serbia, Croatia, Bulgaria, Romania, and parts of modern Hungary.

In the collective memory of the West, the Ottomans loom large. More than the first wave of Arab conquests, more than the Muslims of Spain or Saladin and his armies, the Ottomans were woven into the consciousness of modern Europe. At the very time that the centralized monarchies of Western and Central Europe were emerging, they faced an adversary whose size, organization, wealth, and power dwarfed anything they could muster. The lords of Spain, France, England, the German lands, and the Holy Roman Empire may have thought of themselves as titans, but against the Ottomans, they barely rated as pygmies. Acting in concert, the fleets of the Italians, the knights of Spain and France, and the foot soldiers of Hungary, Poland, Austria, and Prussia were able to stave off total defeat, but until the eighteenth century, the shadow of what they called "the perfidious Turk" clouded even the brightest of their days.

Gradually, the Ottomans lost their comparative advantage, and in the late eighteenth century, the monarchs of Europe and Russia reversed the tide. Even then, the empire shrank but did not collapse. Unlike many other regions of the globe, the core of the Ottoman Empire was never occupied or ruled by the Europeans. The empire contracted, but the central lands of Turkey and large parts of the Middle East, including Iraq and Arabia, remained under Ottoman rule until the end of World War I.

Close in proximity, the Ottomans and the Europeans were separated by a wide cultural gulf. Religion, however, was perhaps the least important dividing line. The Ottomans were ruled by a Turkish family, whose origins were, as many scholars have noted, shrouded in obscurity. There is as little known about Osman, the dynasty's founder, as there is about Romulus and Remus, the mythic progenitors of Rome. There are almost no written records about the Ottomans for the first century of their existence, and their primary adversaries—Serbs, Hungarians, Byzantines, and the Turkish emirs in Anatolia, did not leave many accounts of the defeats that they suffered at Ottoman hands.

In time, Europe became familiar with the Ottoman state, but well until the nineteenth century, its inner workings remained opaque. The sultan and his harem became legendary, but few Westerners understood

how the Ottomans governed, fought, or lived. Western ambassadors in Istanbul wrote accounts of the imperial capital, but they had limited contact with the elite and were shown only those aspects of courtly life they were allowed to see. Not until the nineteenth century, when the Ottomans were forced to open up more of their society to foreign scrutiny, was the veil pulled aside, and even then, only partway.

One result of ignorance was imagination. In fanciful, often salacious accounts, Westerners conjured a picture of a sultan serviced by a harem of willing women guarded by eunuchs from sub-Saharan Africa and defended by a slave army of men taken as captives while still young boys and trained to a hard life as warriors who would just as soon die at the sultan's command as breathe. In his throne room, surrounded by viziers plotting the next campaign against the West, the Ottoman sultan sat, shrouded in mystery. Like the Eastern potentates that he emulated, he seldom allowed visitors to gaze upon him, which only enhanced the aura of mystery. Westerners filled the gaps in their knowledge with fears and transformed the sultan into a holy warrior bent on extinguishing Christian power in order to fulfill what Muhammad had started and to avenge the Muslim world for the loss of Spain.

This mixture of half-truths and legends fed Western anxiety. Feared, loathed, and grudgingly admired, the sultan ruled a formidable empire on the borders of Europe. Though the Turks were only one of many different groups in the empire, the word "Turk" became a proxy for all things Ottoman, and not a positive one. For the English, as for most Europeans, "Turk" meant barbarism and savagery.[2]

In the absence of evidence to the contrary, caricature was taken as fact. Even after the Ottoman Empire was exposed as a state like any other, with its own strengths and more than its share of weaknesses, the image never fully faded. In fact, it outlasted the empire itself. The memory of Turkish warriors fighting in the name of a Muslim God against the armies of Christendom survived the fall of the Ottomans and lodged itself in Western culture. When Turkey applied for membership in the European Union at the start of the twenty-first century, French, German, and Dutch voices murmured uncomfortably that Turkey was still too alien, too other, and perhaps too Muslim. Laced through these concerns were hints that having fought the Ottomans for centuries and finally triumphed, Europe was not about to allow the Turks to enjoy the fruits of that hard-won victory.

The reputation of the Ottomans also suffered from the nationalist movements that swept the Balkans and the Near East in the nineteenth and twentieth centuries. First the Greeks in the 1820s and then the Hungarians, Serbs, Bulgarians, Romanians, and, finally, the Arabs of the Near East defined themselves as nations that had been conquered, brutalized, and silenced by Ottoman autocrats. For the Greeks and other Balkan peoples, there was an added religious element: the Muslim Ottomans, they claimed, had oppressed Christian peoples. Even the Arabs, who caught the infectious bug of nationalism just before World War I, distanced themselves from the Ottomans, though their main bone of contention was more ethnic than religious.

Here as elsewhere, conflict has received the most attention, and in the West the religious undertones have been emphasized. Without question, the early Ottoman rulers considered themselves Muslim warriors. They called themselves *ghazi*s, which in Arabic meant "holy raiders," in order to link themselves to the companions of Muhammad and to the Arab dynasties that had ruled after his death. In their relations with the Christian West, the Ottomans were anything but peaceful. Once they had defeated Christian Byzantium and taken control of the Balkans, they turned to the last fortresses of the Frankish Crusaders on the islands of Rhodes, Crete, and Malta, and to the cities along the Danube, including Buda, Pest, and above all, Vienna.

But what is usually overlooked and forgotten is that the title of *ghazi* was only one of a long line of titles, which included not only Lord of Two Lands, but also Lord of Two Seas; Sultan of the Arabs, Persians, and Romans; Distributor of Crowns to the Rulers of the Surface of the Earth; Sovereign of the White Sea, Black Sea, Rumelia, Anatolia; Overlord of Rum and Karama, of Dulkadir and Diyarbakir, Azerbaijan, Syria, Aleppo, Egypt, Noble Jerusalem, Venerated Mecca and Sacred Medina, Jidda, Yemen, and Many Other Lands; and Thunderbolt of War, the World Conqueror. The Ottomans were proud of their victories, proud to style themselves as the heirs not just to the early caliphs but to Caesar and Rome and to the Persian monarchs of antiquity, proud to rule both Europe and Asia, both Jerusalem and the holy cities of Arabia, and proud that the monarchs of Europe feared and reviled them. The fact that the Ottomans were also Muslims who had won victories rivaled only by the caliphs of the seventh and eighth centuries was one laurel, but hardly the only one.

What is also forgotten is that for most of those five hundred years, the Ottomans were indifferent to the religion of their subjects. The empire was ruled by a small number of governors and judges and a formidable army barracked in the capitals of each major province. Except for the sultan and his family, membership in the ruling class was not based on race or religion. It was based on a system of organized enslavement of young boys. Taken from their villages, they were sent to schools in Istanbul, and in the imperial capital of Adrianople, and trained as soldiers or as bureaucrats. The soldiers were known as Janissaries, and many of them began life as Christian peasants, who then converted to Islam. Theirs was not, however, an orthodox Islam, but one suffused with the mysticism of a Sufi order known as the Bektashis that seems to have preserved many Christian rites.

Every year, Janissary corps would sweep through the villages of the Balkans and the Caucasus and collect a quota of children. Few aspects of Ottoman rule have generated as much controversy and ill will. By the nineteenth century, the practice had largely come to an end, but the memory was enough to rouse the Balkan peoples against their overlords. The Janissaries were slaves in the sense that their rights and their wealth, property, and status were at the whim of the sultan. But in many other respects, they were a privileged elite. Unlike the Africans enslaved in the Americas, the Janissaries were the ruling class of an empire and enjoyed the concomitant benefits. Though later generations of Westerners decried the forced recruitment, the opportunity to have sons rise high in the ranks of the empire was not seen as a grave injustice by many families. Besides, in the fifteenth, sixteenth, and seventeenth centuries, no peasants—whether Christian or Muslim—had expectations of Jeffersonian democracy. The Ottoman ruling class was harsh and unsentimental, but they differed from the rulers of Europe only in efficiency. When the kings of France or Spain needed to raise an army, their troops also entered villages and violently drafted eligible young men without asking permission. The recruitment of the Janissary corps in the Balkans and Greece was, in that sense, no different.[3]

While the Ottoman ruling class was Muslim, the empire was not, and Islam did not act as a glue holding together the disparate parts of the state. A majority of the population of the European lands controlled by the Ottomans was Christian and remained that way until the end. Even

in regions such as Egypt and Iraq where Muslims were in the majority, the Sunni Islam of the Ottoman ruling class was somewhat different than the Islam of many Arabs. On the whole, while the sultan proclaimed himself caliph and protector of the holy cities of Mecca and Medina, he seems to have cared not one whit about the religion of his subjects. No efforts were made to convert Christians and Jews, nor did the Ottomans try to enforce one version of Muslim law. Being a Muslim was no guarantee of better treatment by local governors, and being Christian or Jewish was not necessarily a burden to overcome.

While the Ottomans fought against the Christian states of Europe, they fought against the Shi'ite shahs of Iran with just as much intensity. In neither case was the propagation of Islam a primary motivation. The Ottomans were a dynasty bent on expanding and perpetuating their own rule. As with the Romans, the Mongols, the Han, and other empires, power was primary, and all else was secondary. Religion was at best an instrument of control. If the mantle of religion could be used to justify expansion, all the better. If religious toleration helped pacify subject peoples and maintain stability, so be it.

JEWS UNDER OTTOMAN RULE

THE OTTOMAN FORMULA that stressed obedience to the sultan and indifference to the religion of subject peoples was developed before the fall of Constantinople, but it only became vital to the empire's success after. By leaving the religion of his subjects alone, the sultan was able to use them to enhance the power of the state. For instance, in his effort to restore the glory of Constantinople, Mehmed ordered thousands of people throughout the empire to relocate. Some of these were Turks and Muslims, but many more were not. Greek Orthodox from Anatolian cities with needed skills were told to move, and though they were given assistance and guaranteed an income and jobs, they were not given a choice. Nor were the soldiers of the sultan's armies, of course. And nor were thousands of Jews, many of whom lived in the Balkans. Their ability to act as intermediaries between the Muslim eastern Mediterranean and the Christian West meant that they could, and soon did, play a pivotal role in the commercial and economic success of the Ottoman state.

Under the Byzantines, Jews had been tolerated but hardly embraced. In Christian Constantinople, an affluent Jewish community performed the same function as economic intermediaries that they did in numerous other cities in the Mediterranean world. They were represented at the emperor's court by a chief rabbi who was both a leader and an advocate. In the Byzantine system, his authority was narrow. Under the Ottomans, however, the Jews gained more autonomy and in time became active supporters of the sultan's rule. After the conquest, Mehmed allowed the chief rabbi who had served the Byzantines to retain his position. This rabbi was not, as some have suggested, the head of all Jews in the Ottoman Empire, though in time the position would become the chief rabbi of Jewish lore. Initially, he was responsible only for the Jewish community of Constantinople, which was fairly small in 1453, but which soon swelled by thousands because of Mehmed's resettlement policies.

Faced with an underpopulated capital and insufficient numbers of people capable of carrying out complicated tasks, Mehmed ordered thousands of Jews to move to Constantinople. They were singled out not because of their beliefs, but because they were a close-knit group that possessed skills that the Ottoman state dearly needed. The forced relocation of Jews from various parts of the Balkans and Anatolia could not have been pleasant for those made to move their homes, and there have been heated debates among scholars about how to characterize Mehmed's edicts. Some have likened the removals to the pogroms and persecutions of the late nineteenth and twentieth centuries. Others, including the fifteenth-century Jewish poet Elijah Capsali, had little to say about the relocations and saw the Ottomans as a significant improvement over both the Western Christian regimes in Europe and the Eastern Christian rulers of Byzantium. Capsali, in fact, took the fall of Constantinople as a divine punishment against those who had abused the Jews and a sign of God's favor for those who showed tolerance.

In short, there was nothing about Mehmed's policies that discriminated against the Jews as Jews, or against any Christian denomination as Christian per se. The Ottoman bureaucracy treated all subjects as instruments of the state and servants of the sultan, to be used and disposed of as he saw fit. In that sense, all citizens of the empire were discriminated against by the sultan and the ruling elite, and had few rights separate from what the sultan permitted. In no part of the world in the fifteenth

century was the situation dramatically different. While the Jews who were forced to relocate to the new capital may have suffered, only through a very particular contemporary prism can it be said that they suffered because of their religion.

And by the end of the fifteenth century, the Jews of Constantinople were thriving, and Jewish communities in other parts of the empire were living secure, prosperous lives. Skepticism and fear during the first years of Mehmed's reign gave way to acceptance and then outright enthusiasm. While Jews and Christians had to pay a head tax, these were offset by the tax benefits they received for setting up business first in Istanbul and then in other major cities. Jews dominated what primitive forms of banking there were, as well as trade in jewels, pearls, and satin. The Jewish community of Egypt remained intact, and when Egypt was finally conquered by the Ottomans early in the sixteenth century, they reaped economic benefits. And one foreign community of Jews found a home in the empire and were met with a warm embrace that contrasted sharply with what they had left behind.

In 1492, after the defeat of the Muslim kingdom of Granada, the triumphant monarchs of Spain fulfilled a long-standing ambition of the Spanish Catholic Church and ordered the expulsion of the Jews. With little time to prepare and in danger for their lives, thousands packed what they could and left the country. The cities of Western Europe shunned them, and North Africa was divided into petty principalities with little economic vitality. But the Ottomans announced that the exiled Jews of Spain were welcome and would receive aid and support, including transportation from Spain to the heart of the empire on the other side of the Mediterranean. Jews were allowed to move to Istanbul, but the sultan proclaimed that he would be particularly pleased if they settled in one of the oldest cities in the Balkans, Thessaloniki, also known as Salonica.

Not all who made the trip survived. Said one taciturn contemporary account, "A part of the exiled Spaniards went overseas to Turkey. Some of them were thrown into the sea and drowned, but those who arrived there the king of Turkey received kindly, as they were artisans." These transplanted Jews willingly shared their wisdom and learning with their new overlords, including knowledge about the arts of war. Jewish engineers and artisans helped the Ottomans manufacture advanced artillery

and complicated siege engines, which the sultan put to good use against the Europeans in the sixteenth and seventeenth centuries. The outcasts of Spain thus became an asset for the Ottomans.[4]

Some of the exiles moved to Istanbul, but the bulk settled in Salonica. By the middle of the sixteenth century, the city had a substantial Jewish population and had established itself as a metropolis that could stand proudly in the shadow of Istanbul. The Jews of Salonica were self-governing, answerable to the Ottoman governor and ultimately to the sultan but not to the chief rabbi in Istanbul. That began to change in later centuries, as the sultan ceded more authority to religious leaders in the imperial capital, which meant enhanced powers not only for the chief rabbi, but for the patriarchs of the Greek and Armenian churches as well. Initially, however, the Jews of Spain who settled in Salonica competed not with the Jews of Istanbul but with the older population of Greek Jews who had lived in the city for fifteen hundred years and had hosted Saint Paul on his travels through the Roman world spreading the gospel. These rivalries faded, though never completely, and with each passing century, the Jews of Salonica became richer, more powerful, and more central to the commercial life of the empire.

The illustrious history of the Jews of the Ottoman Empire stands in sharp relief to the treatment of their brethren in Christian Europe until the mid-eighteenth century and of course during the Holocaust of the twentieth. The kingdoms of Europe cared greatly about the religion of their subjects and fought destructive wars in order to coerce belief and stifle heresy. The Ottomans were ruthless as conquerors but once they had achieved military victory, they preferred a lean and tranquil administrative system.

This tolerance may explain why few Christians and Jews converted to Islam during the Ottoman centuries, especially compared with the earlier rates of conversion in Andalusia or in the Near East, Egypt, and Persia after the coming of Islam in the seventh century. The presence of increasingly powerful Christian states in Europe, who represented the possibility, however unlikely, of a different order and a different regime may also have dissuaded Christians from converting. Other factors notwithstanding, the benign neglect of the Ottoman state allowed Jews, Greek Orthodox, Armenians, Catholics, Copts, and others to live in peace and security and to practice their beliefs unmolested. There are many reasons why the Ottomans were so successful and so resilient, but

perhaps the most important was that they gave people just enough autonomy to keep them content, loyal, and uninterested in change.

SULEYMAN AND THE APEX OF EMPIRE

MANY OF TODAY'S inhabitants of the Balkans would dismiss the characterization of the Ottoman Empire as tolerant and relatively benign. Bulgarians, Serbians, and Greeks bear no affection for the Ottomans or for the Turks, and they recall an empire notable for its brutality and its ill treatment of them. The issue here is not whether the Ottomans were cruel; like most imperial powers, they could be. It is not whether individual governors took advantage of their power to steal, rape, and otherwise abuse their subjects. In their treatment of the peasants of the Balkans, however, the Ottomans were neither more nor less cruel than feudal lords in Europe were toward their peons. Some Ottoman governors were tyrants, others were not, and the ones who were tend to get the attention. There are many chronicles written by peoples that the Ottomans ruled that depict their masters in a very unkind light. Some of these highlight religion as the dividing line, but that does not mean that it was. The dividing line for the Ottomans was power, who had it and who did not.

The Ottomans did what was expedient. In today's terms, they were realists, not idealists. Sultans from Mehmed on may have described themselves as holy warriors when they took the field against enemies, but when it came to governing, they were pragmatists to the core. The unspoken formula was beautiful and elegant: the empire was ruled by a sultan with nearly unlimited powers, answerable only to God and in theory to the *ulama*, who almost always validated what he wanted to do. That included marrying Christians, employing Jews, and forging alliances with Catholic states—none of which were held to be incompatible with orthodox Islam as then understood.

The Ottoman bureaucracy, in turn, did not discriminate on the basis of religion or race. From the Janissary corps to the civil service to the palace eunuchs, the government was run by a motley collection of races. While becoming a Janissary did entail converting, there was often more form than substance to the Islam of the foot soldiers who fought the sultan's battles so ably.

Tartars, Serbs, Greeks, Arabs, Berbers, Copts, Armenians, Jews, Sun-

nis, Shi'ites, Druze, Nubians, Slavs, Bulgars, Hungarians, Georgians, and of course Turks combined to form a crazy quilt of languages, traditions, and rites. The Ottoman court in Istanbul and various provincial administrators also made use of Venetians, Genoese, Florentines, and Romans, as well as merchants and translators from France, Austria, Spain, and England. Not until the ruling class seized on the notion of "Turkishness" in the late nineteenth century was there anything particularly Turkish about the Ottoman state.

The sultans also viewed marriage through the lens of politics rather than race, religion, or love. Wives and the concubines of the harem came from a wide range of ethnic groups and multiple faiths. The goal was to bind the disparate groups of the empire to the sultan, and so he could hardly sleep with only Muslim women or only Turks. That in turn meant that most sultans—as the children of such unions—were of mixed ethnicity. The empire not only had a multicultural administration; it had a multicultural sultan.

The reality of the harem itself is at odds with the myth. The seductive mysteries of the harem became an obsession of Westerners who fantasized about lascivious nights, willing women, lots of silk, a surfeit of pillows, and black eunuchs with gold earrings and scimitar-laden cummerbunds. There was that, perhaps, though as the Western women who penetrated the harem later reported, there was much less sex and much more tea drinking and sewing. While one purpose of the harem may have been to gratify the sultan's desires, the primary aim was to make sure that there was at least one male heir and that the pool of possible mothers reflected the diversity of the empire. It was, in that sense, a version of sexual democracy unburdened by concerns of race, class, or religion.

The willingness to ignore religion in order to focus on realpolitik defined the reign of the empire's greatest sultan—Suleyman. Though he was known as "the Magnificent" in the West, his primary sobriquet in the Ottoman world was different, and telling. To his subjects, he was "the Lawgiver." During his reign of more than forty years, the empire reached its apex. His conquests brought the Ottomans to the gates of Vienna in the West and deep into Persia in the East. All of North Africa came under his nominal control, and the last of the Crusader principalities, the demesne of the Hospitallers on the island of Rhodes, which had

resisted all challengers for more than two hundred years, fell after a long and gritty battle in 1526.

But while Suleyman led his armies to victory on the periphery, the core of the empire was peaceful, prosperous, and stable. After centuries of struggle, the Ottomans were able to consolidate their rule. Suleyman's forty-six years in power were dramatic, but less because of external pressures than because of familial squabbles that turned deadly, as they often did among Ottoman princes. In most other respects, it was a placid and stable time. Suleyman formalized and codified the administrative practices that he had inherited from his father and grandfather, and for nearly three hundred years thereafter, his laws governed the state. During his reign, revenue flowed into the coffers in Istanbul; the Janissaries recruited their own version of the best and the brightest; provincial governors were dispatched from the capital to rule comfortably in the sultan's name; and only the Safavid shahs of Iran to the east and the Habsburgs of Austria to the west prevented the Ottomans from extending their reach from China to the English Channel.

Every apex is also the beginning of decline. Suleyman's armies achieved such rapid victories against the Hungarians in 1529 that they unexpectedly were able to advance up the Danube to Vienna. The army had not prepared for a long siege of the city, and was not equipped for winter. After weeks of stalemate, Suleyman, ensconced in a tent more opulent than many of the palaces of Europe, decided that it was more prudent to withdraw than submit his Janissaries to a winter campaign. The march on Vienna had been so easy that he imagined he could return again the following spring. Instead, it was a lost opportunity, and Ottoman forces would not seriously threaten the city again until 1683, when they would fail once more.

During these years, European diplomats and merchants had more contact with the Ottomans. Suleyman was an imposing, enigmatic figure, but he did grant audiences, and a number of diplomats wrote their impressions. Much of what they said reinforced the sense that the Ottomans, with Suleyman at their head, were utterly alien and brutally effective.

Regular diplomacy and occasional interaction did begin to peel away the mystique. In 1520, a Venetian envoy described a young Suleyman as "tall and slender, with a thin and bony face. The sultan appears friendly

and in good humor. Rumor has it that he...enjoys reading, is knowledgeable and shows good judgment."[5] He had the same aquiline nose as his great-grandfather Mehmed, and an even narrower face adorned with the sparse Ottoman beard favored by his family. That look did not change over the decades, though he grew paler and more sallow with the passing years. Toward the end of his life, the sultan received a perspicacious emissary named Ghiselin de Busbecq while "seated on a rather low sofa, not more than a foot from the ground and spread with many coverlets and cushions embroidered with exquisite work.... His expression...was anything but smiling, and had a sternness which though sad was full of majesty." Suffering from gangrene, heavily made up, and deathly pale, Suleyman exuded a potent and painful combination of grandeur and tragedy.

He had every reason to be sad. His victories notwithstanding, his personal life was a shambles. He had broken the cardinal rule of the Ottoman ruling class and married one of his concubines. Sultans were not supposed to love the mothers of their children, but Suleyman did. She, in turn, used her position to champion her sons and turn her husband against the children of his other mistresses. The result was death all around. Suleyman ordered the execution of two of his sons, and another's life ended under questionable circumstances. When his wife died, his two remaining sons by her turned on each other, and on him. He had yet another executed, along with several grandchildren, leaving only Selim, who would succeed him.

These dramas were duly recorded by the European envoys in the city. Much as the Roman emperors had combined an exquisite ability to rule the known world with dark and depraved family dramas, Suleyman and his heirs led lives rent by passions, intrigue, sex, and murder. While some of these stories fed the European imagination about the lascivious Turk, more to our point is that religion never entered the equation.

To wit: Suleyman commissioned the construction of a major mosque in Istanbul, the Suleymaniye. It was the most important Muslim monument of its day, but over half of the workers and artisans who built it were Christian. In addition, the sultan may have believed himself to be a devout servant of God, but as was true of the clergy in Rome at the time, such devotion didn't preclude sin. The Medici and Borgia popes commissioned works of art, kept mistresses, and tried to ensure the well-

being of their many illegitimate children. The Ottoman sultans conducted themselves in a similar manner.

The absence of a rigid, doctrinal Islam was in stark contrast to the role of religion in the West. As the Ottomans drew closer to Europe, they held up the mirror to Western Christians who were descending into a long period of intolerance. Disgusted with the corruption of the Catholic Church, the German monk Martin Luther set in motion a chain of events that produced both the Reformation and decades of war in Europe. Luther viewed the Ottoman Empire under Suleyman as an exemplar of religious toleration. Though he did decry the Ottomans as "servants of the devil," for Luther that was a mild critique compared to what he said about the pope and about Jews. Luther hoped that a reformed and purified church could one day emulate the Ottoman model.

Several decades later, the French philosopher Jean Bodin, committed though he was to his Catholic faith, wrote favorably of the Ottomans, "The great emperor of the Turks doth with as great devotion as any prince in the world honor and observe the religion by him received from his ancestors and yet detests he not the strange religions of others; but to the contrary permits every man to live according to his conscience… and suffers four diverse religions: that of the Jews, that of the Christians, that of the Greeks, and that of the Mohametans." Having lived through the wars of religion that were sundering Europe in general and France in particular, Bodin had witnessed the costs of intolerance. Protestants and Catholics regarded each other with contempt, hurling invective and promising punishment in this life and damnation in the next. The Ottoman Empire presented an alternative that Bodin could not help but admire.

The Islam of the Ottomans did not create obstacles to allying with Christian states, and Suleyman became enmeshed in the politics of Europe, not just as an adversary but as a strategic partner. Europe was cross-hatched with divisions, especially between Protestants and Catholics and between two royal families, the Habsburgs and the Valois, whose feud was acrimonious and intense. The Habsburgs ruled Spain, and under Charles V they governed the central European lands of the Holy Roman Empire as well. The Valois controlled France and posed a challenge to Habsburg hegemony. Under Francis I, the animosity

between the two families became personal. The two monarchs developed an abiding hatred for each other, which was based less on direct experience than on dynastic aims. But that did not make the hatred any less intense, and it led Francis I to court the enemies of the Habsburgs, no matter where they were or what God they worshiped.

The Habsburgs had more territory and more wealth (especially given the flow of silver from the new lands of South America), but they also confronted more enemies. Not only was Charles V faced with Francis, but he also had to contend with Protestant German princes, rebellious Dutch burghers, an increasingly unpredictable England, and of course, a restive and expansionist Ottoman Empire led by a sultan who could draw on seemingly inexhaustible resources to outfit his army. Having conquered the Hungarians, Suleyman came face-to-face with the Habsburgs. Watching from Paris, Francis decided in the early 1520s that the enemy of his enemy was a friend, and he reached out to Suleyman for an alliance. Suleyman, recognizing the strategic advantage, agreed.

For the remainder of Suleyman's life, the French and the Ottomans worked together to humble the Habsburgs. The pincer alliance was a constant irritant to Charles V and his heirs, but they never succumbed, in part because of skilled leadership and in part because Central Europe was never a prime objective for Suleyman. Persia presented a more immediate threat to the Ottomans, as did Venetian raiders interrupting trade in the Mediterranean. But as one historian has written, "The French alliance was the cornerstone of the Ottomans' European diplomacy." Suleyman knew that his partnership with France kept the Habsburgs on the defensive, and that freed him to pursue other ambitions. He also undermined Habsburg power by stirring the pot inside the Holy Roman Empire. He reached out to Protestant princes and offered his protection, claiming that the Protestants, because they had risen up against the idolatry of the Catholic Church, were in their way much like the first Muslims who had rejected the idolatry of the Meccans.[6]

These snapshots from Suleyman's life barely do justice to his reign of more than forty years, but they reveal an Ottoman state that was no more, and no less, defined by creed than the Habsburgs were defined by Christianity or the Romans by whatever pagan cult was in vogue. Islam was part of the governing creed, but it shared space with the imperatives of maintaining order, propagating the dynasty, and jockeying for position in foreign affairs. The sultans at times used Islam as a spur and jus-

tification for war, but they drew on the legacy of Muhammad and the warrior culture of the early Arab conquests only when it suited them. When they wished to do things that might be seen as problematic in light of Islamic law and jurisprudence, they did so without hesitation, knowing that even in the unlikely event that one of the *ulama* objected, others would support whatever the sultan did. Many of their actions should have raised such flags, if Islam had been the vital force keeping the empire together. There was no way to justify fratricide and rebellion using the Quran or the hadith, nor was the harem or the system of eunuchs easy to reconcile with Islamic law.

The Ottoman legacy also forces us to reconsider what we mean when we say "Islam." The alliances that Suleyman cemented with the Catholic French did not lead anyone to question his bona fides as a Muslim. The autonomy that Mehmed granted to the Jews, Greek Orthodox, and Armenians did not trigger challenges to his standing as a devout believer. Islam, like any great religion, is an umbrella that encompasses a wide range of virtues and a multitude of sins. Scholars and judges may have retained a right to criticize the sultan, but they almost never exercised it. Rulers were seen as a necessary element because they held back the chaos that would inevitably ensue if the state collapsed.

Suleyman's death did not immediately remove the Ottomans as a threat to Europe. A century later, in 1683, another sultan again menaced Vienna, and he came very close to taking the city. But even had he succeeded, it is unlikely that the Ottomans would have overrun Europe. The Russians had become a formidable foe, as had the French and the English. And while its rivals had evolved, within the empire, little had changed. The Ottomans were slowly losing their competitive edge. After 1683, Europe began to push back, and the balance tipped. For centuries, the Ottomans had stood as monument to equilibrium. Then the empire began to fray, and when it finally collapsed in the early years of the twentieth century, relations between Muslims, Christians, and Jews took a turn for the worse.

CHAPTER EIGHT

THE TIDE BEGINS TO TURN

FOR THE FIRST thousand years after the death of Muhammad and the initial Arab conquests, the world of Islam expanded. There were setbacks, of course, some major and some not. The Crusades were a brief interregnum of Christian rule in the Near Eastern heartland, and the fall of Spain represented a significant loss. The Mongol invasion that decimated Baghdad and came close to overrunning North Africa was a severe test, but one that was ultimately met. The coming of the Ottomans in the fifteenth century revitalized the Muslim world, and thousands of miles away, the Moghuls, another Muslim dynasty, expanded south from what is now Pakistan into northern India. At the same time, Muslim merchants, fanning out from these centers, carried Islam across the Sahara into Western Africa and across the Indian Ocean to Indonesia. By the end of the sixteenth century, the reach of Islam was greater than it ever had been, and the call to prayer could be heard five times a day from Morocco to Java.

But while millions across continents identified themselves as Muslim, they did not form a cohesive community. In the second half of the twentieth century, as travel became safer, faster, and accessible to the masses, unprecedented numbers of Muslims became hajjis and journeyed to Mecca. There, they were thrust into contact with Muslims from around the globe, and that experience connected them as few things did to a sense of an international Muslim community. But before the innovations of the industrial age, before the telegraph, radio, television, airplanes, and automobiles, few Muslims made the pilgrimage to Mecca, and few had contact with anyone outside their family and vil-

lage. Some trading centers bustled with merchants from far-off places, and cosmopolitan cities like Alexandria in Egypt, Istanbul and Salonica in the eastern Mediterranean, and Zanzibar on the coast of East Africa were crazy quilts of languages, foreign dress, and multiple currencies. On the whole, however, while Islam spanned the globe, most Muslims had little in common.

That meant that, save for a shared knowledge of the opening verses of the Quran and a few Arabic words memorized for daily prayers, a camel merchant in Khartoum was almost as alien to a fisherman in Java or a mason in Konya as each was to a tailor in London or a count in Versailles. Even within the Ottoman Empire, there was no one Islam. There was a religious establishment in Istanbul, with the *sheikh ul-Islam* nominally at the head of the religious class. He was appointed by the sultan, and like the chief rabbi or the Orthodox patriarch, he had the authority to issue edicts on questions of religious law that were binding on the *ulama* and on judges (*mufti*) throughout the empire. As often as not, however, the *sheikh ul-Islam* was either silent or his decrees were quietly ignored and trumped by local mores. The result was that hundreds of variants of law and traditions characterized Islam in the Ottoman world.

Complicating matters even further was the amorphous nature of Sufism. While Sufism first emerged as a mystical tradition, it also evolved into folk religion. Some Sufi lodges retained their mystical focus, and nurtured monasticism and meditation. Others, however, combined Muslim practices with whatever pre-Muslim traditions had existed before Islam took root. North Africa was home to Sufi "saints" who practiced magic, charmed snakes, and read auguries, and whose shrines became pilgrimage sites after they died. In the heart of Anatolia in the city of Konya, dervishes spun themselves into ecstasy chanting the words of their great master Rumi. In Indonesia, the bare-bones Islam of Muslim merchants fused with local variants of Hinduism and animism to form a religion that bore some of the trappings of traditional Islam but would have been as strange to the camel nomads of Arabia as it was to the Calvinist burghers of Amsterdam. In its many forms, Sufism became a grab bag of Islam and pre-Islamic traditions.

It is both familiar and convenient to talk of a "Muslim world" stretching from Morocco to Indonesia, but that has led to a widespread tendency to assume that Muslims historically had one cultural identity. Yes, there was a notion of an *umma*, of a Muslim community united in faith,

just as there were vague notions of a Christendom united under the banner of Christ. But like Christianity, Islam splintered into hundreds of rival sects, and whatever cohesion it might initially have promised evaporated. In both "Christendom" and the "house of Islam" (as Muslims have called their world), religion was one identity among many. And what that identity meant to the political, social, or cultural life of any particular village, town, state, or society is beyond generalization.

Of the three religions, Judaism was perhaps the most cohesive, though Jews from northern Europe bore little resemblance to Jews from Yemen. Few in numbers and scattered across the Ottoman and European worlds, Jews during thousands of diaspora years had come to identify themselves as a scattered people divided into hundreds of villages, towns, and cities. As merchants, artisans, and bankers, they had developed international networks that survived different regimes, multiple dynasties, war, plague, and revolution. While the more agrarian Jewish peasants of Russia and the northern steppe slowly lost contact with the more urban, educated Jews of Western Europe and the Mediterranean, most Jews in the Ottoman Empire perceived themselves as one community. For Christians and Muslims, the picture was more ambiguous.

THE MILLET SYSTEM AND THE RISE OF THE WEST

OVER TIME, the semiautonomous religious communities of the Ottoman Empire became known as *millet*s and each had a leader appointed by the sultan. Each *millet* was self-governing, and its leader was responsible for assisting the Ottoman state in collecting taxes. The Jews had a chief rabbi, and the major Christian groups had a patriarch or bishop. There were also groups within groups. The Christian sects included the Greek Orthodox and the Armenians. There were also Maronites in Lebanon, Copts in Egypt, and Assyrians (also known as Nestorians) in Iraq. Even the Jews were divided into several millet communities.

The *millet* system did not resolve all conflicts. When issues arose between different *millet*s or between a member of a *millet* and a Muslim, the matter was referred to an Ottoman court. Sometimes, Christians or Jews tried to have internal disputes decided in an Ottoman court when

they believed that Islamic law would render a more favorable verdict. Christians occasionally attempted to have their divorces validated in a Muslim court because the provisions for divorce under the sharia were less onerous. Catholics in particular were antagonistic to the idea of divorce, while Muslims, in general, were more flexible. Both Christian men and women looked to Muslim courts for assistance, and there were cases when a husband or wife, desperate to escape a bad marriage, converted to Islam for the sole purpose of ridding themselves of a troublesome spouse. And different Christian groups, who had been fighting one another for more than a thousand years, often took their disputes to Muslim courts because mutual animosity prevented either from respecting the other's laws and traditions.

Limitations aside, the *millet* system enjoyed the active support of its members. Jews in the Ottoman world were well aware of how much better it was to live in Salonica, Istanbul, or Izmir (Smyrna) than almost anywhere in Europe. The Ottoman ruling class continued the tradition begun by earlier Arab dynasties of employing Jews as physicians, and for most of his reign, Suleyman himself was attended to by a Jewish doctor in Istanbul. Prominent Jews had the ear of court officials, and used the Ottoman system to discredit or undermine rivals. On occasion, Jews served as intermediaries to European powers, especially during periods when diplomatic relations between the Ottomans and the princes of Western Europe were strained or severed.

The diverse Christian communities, though rarely satisfied with their status, understood that the autonomy they enjoyed under the Ottoman system was an improvement over what had come before. That didn't stop them from competing for influence, and throughout the seventeenth, eighteenth, and nineteenth centuries, Christian *millet*s waged quiet campaigns against one another in provincial courts and in palace chambers in Istanbul. But these internecine conflicts existed under the watchful eye of the Ottoman state, which kept ancient rivalries from spinning out of control and into outright violence. Hatred and resentment festered, but actual fighting was kept to a minimum.

That fact did not go unnoticed or unappreciated. In the eighteenth century, the Greek patriarch in Jerusalem, who was well acquainted with the struggles between different Christian groups, lauded the Ottomans for all that they had done to keep the peace.

> God raised out of nothing this powerful empire of the Ottomans, in place of our Roman [Byzantine] Empire which had begun ... to deviate from the beliefs of the Orthodox faith.... The all-mighty Lord has placed over us this high kingdom, for there is no power but of God, so as to be to the people of the West a bridle, to us the people of the East a means of salvation. For this reason he puts into the heart of the Sultan of these Ottomans an inclination to keep free the religious beliefs of our Orthodox faith and ... to protect them, even to the point of occasionally chastising Christians who deviate from the faith.[1]

For centuries under the Byzantines, a sizable minority of Christians had nurtured grievances and built up resentments against the Greek Orthodox, who dominated political and religious life. While the Orthodox were able to retain a measure of influence under the Ottomans, their story was one of relative decline. Other Christian communities took the defeat of the Byzantines as an opportunity to make up lost ground. The Armenians initially thrived under the *millet* system, and were able to carve out a sphere of autonomy and prosperity. Armenian merchants captured a monopoly on the trade of valuable items such as silk, and in provincial Anatolian towns such as Diyarbakir they had nearly as much power as at any point in their storied history.

Later, in the nineteenth and early twentieth centuries, the Armenians suffered from the emergence of Turkish nationalism, and more than a million were killed as a result of Turkish policies during World War I. But the treatment of the Armenians at the hands of early-twentieth-century Turks is in sharp relief to their success earlier in the empire's history. Only in the late nineteenth century, in its attempts at reform, did the Ottoman Empire move away from the decentralized *millet* system and begin to emulate the European model of centralization and modernization. With that came a more explosive and destructive force, nationalism, which was hostile to religion, rested on a secular view of the world, and would prove far more lethal to groups like the Armenians than the Ottoman ruling class ever was.

Until then, in many corners of the empire, Christians lived peacefully and securely. The island of Cyprus and much of the Peloponnesian Peninsula of Greece, for instance, were predominantly Christian when they fell under the control of the Ottomans, and they remained that way

until the empire disintegrated. Conversion was less typical than it had been under the Umayyads and Abbasids. The Ottoman authorities did not encourage it, and at times actively discouraged it. Being Muslim was not a requirement for playing a meaningful role in the life of the empire.

True, non-Muslims never occupied the innermost sanctums of power in Istanbul. Politics, however, have always been local, and the Ottoman Empire was no exception. Christians tended to focus on their local community and region. The Orthodox Christians of Crete wanted dominion over the island, and so long as the Ottoman authorities were willing to abet those ambitions, they were content. Though Crete saw a higher rate of conversion than other parts of the empire, that was more a function of Cretan peasants looking to join the Janissaries than any active attempt by the Ottomans to evangelize. On the contrary, Ottoman governors and elites worked with the heads of the *millet*s to prevent non-Muslims from converting. Given that the primary goal of the Ottoman state was to keep the family of Osman in power and the sultan's treasury full, conversion served no purpose. To the contrary, it threatened the delicate status quo. Conversion was change, and if there was one thing the Ottomans did not welcome after the sixteenth century, it was change.[2]

Unfortunately, change was forced on them. Uncurious about their enemies, the Ottomans after Suleyman complacently rested in the knowledge that they were the most powerful state in the world. The navies of Venice and the Habsburgs triumphed at the battle of Lepanto in 1571, but the Ottomans shrugged off the defeat the way an elephant shrugs off a gnat. They rebuilt their fleet within a year, and the balance in the eastern Mediterranean shifted hardly at all. But their enemies learned a crucial lesson from the victory: the Ottomans, formidable and feared, were not invincible.

It is hard to imagine a world frozen for more than two hundred years, but from the middle of the sixteenth century until late in the eighteenth, the Ottoman state was rarely as innovative as its European rivals. Some laws were rewritten, administrative districts were redrawn, and titles were changed. Sultans lived and died; inconclusive battles were fought against the Persians to the east; somewhat more conclusive ones were waged against the Hungarians, Austrians, and Russians to the north and west. But through it all, the core of the empire was untouched and undisturbed. The recruitment of the Janissaries, once so dramatic and disrup-

tive, became routinized. The Janissaries were supposed to be celibate and loyal only to the sultan, but over time, they devolved into an interest group bent on their own self-perpetuation. They turned to commerce and industry to augment their income. Their officers took wives, and with that came familial ambitions. As the children of Janissaries themselves became Janissaries, the need for fresh blood decreased. The Janissaries lost the edge born of a harsh system of recruitment and training; they became less effective and less feared. Soon, they were simply one group—albeit a heavily armed one—competing for influence and prestige in Istanbul. They were the subject of endless gossip, the butt of countless jokes, a dangerous, independent force still living in barracks near the imperial palace, immersed in networks of graft and marriage with the elites of the capital, and a bulwark against any who might even think about reforming a system that was becoming a shadow of its former self.

Meanwhile, the states of Europe began to fight one another less and turned instead to conquering the world. After the Thirty Years' War nearly destroyed Central Europe, the princes and premiers gathered in Westphalia in 1648 and agreed not to wage wars over religion. The strength of the "Westphalian system" has been lauded and overstated, but it did lead to fewer pitched battles in the heart of Europe for the next century and a half, until the twin earthquakes of the French Revolution and the rise of Napoleon. For much of the seventeenth and eighteenth centuries, Europeans focused less on the Ottomans than on expanding across the seas. The Mediterranean remained a vital link in world trade, but the Venetian stranglehold on commerce in what was otherwise an Ottoman lake spurred the Spanish, Portuguese, Dutch, and English voyages of exploration that led to the discovery of the New World and the extension of European influence throughout the globe.

The Venetians and the Ottomans continued to skirmish over Crete, Malta, and other strategic islands. At the same time, Venice was the European gateway for trade with the Ottoman world, conducted through intermediaries such as Jews, Greek Orthodox, and Armenians who resided in cities such as Salonica, Alexandria, Smyrna, Istanbul, and Beirut. The regular flow of foreign goods was an important source of revenue for the Ottomans, and the state welcomed European merchants even as the sultan retained designs on conquering Europe itself.

Until 1683, the Ottomans had good reason to believe that they might

achieve what Suleyman had not. In that year, a new army was raised for the sole purpose of taking Vienna. The other cities of the Danube had succumbed to Ottoman rule, and Vienna was all that remained between the sultan and the fertile lands of Germany and Poland. The sultan's armies, led by the grand vizier Kara Mustafa, seemed on the verge of victory when an unexpected ally came to the rescue. The Polish king, Jan Sobieski, at the head of a substantial force, injected new life into the defenders, inflicted severe casualties on the Janissaries, and caused the Ottomans to withdraw in confusion. The defeat led Sultan Mehmed IV to order the gruesome execution of Kara Mustafa. It also permanently shifted the momentum from the Ottomans to the West. The war between the Ottomans and the Habsburgs technically ended in a stalemate, but in truth, it was a defeat for the sultan.

For the next century, the empire drifted. While the ruling class hardly noticed, others did. Slowly, quietly, almost imperceptibly, the non-Muslims of the empire became less content with the status quo. At times, that triggered a reaction. Local *ulama* would issue edicts designed to put the People of the Book in their place. These included restrictions on dress and attempts to make it more difficult for Jews or Christians to build churches or synagogues. But these were isolated incidents, short-lived and usually ineffective. Ottoman Jews found themselves less secure, but the reason had less to do with the Ottomans than it did with the influence of Europeans. As the states of Europe started to expand internationally, they looked to the Christians—and not the Jews—of the Ottoman lands as natural allies. Those Ottoman Christians welcomed the support, and they began to supplant Jewish merchants and businessmen.

But there was one other reason for the shifting fortunes of the Jews of the Ottoman Empire, which spoke to both the strength and the weakness of the Ottoman order. In 1665, a Jew from Smyrna proclaimed himself the messiah. It was not the first time such claims had been made, nor was it to be the last. But it was certainly one of the most divisive and disruptive, as much for its ending as for its beginning.

SABBATAI SEVI

SABBATAI SEVI was born to a prosperous merchant family. His father, Mordecai, had been a successful chicken merchant who was not content

with the life of a poulterer. In Smyrna, on the Aegean coast of Anatolia, he switched careers and became an intermediary for European merchants. It was common for European businessmen to hire locals who could serve as translators and as representatives who would ensure that goods were delivered and paid for on time. Mordecai Sevi helped make at least one English merchant quite wealthy, and that merchant in turn enriched him. Unfortunately for Mordecai, his successful life and what might have been a decent legacy were obliterated by his son.

Sabbatai had not lived long when people began to notice that there was something strange about him. Few records of his life are unbiased; his chroniclers were either defenders or prosecutors. But friends and foes agreed that Sabbatai, from a young age, was not like others. Manic at times, sullen at others, he entered an altered state while praying, and at synagogue he was a powerful, disturbing presence. To his acolytes, he was a teenager who showed signs of divinity, including miraculous and inexplicable actions. It was said that he glowed when he prayed, that he was given to loud and disturbing outbursts, that his body emitted a faint yet unmistakable perfume that marked him as an anointed one. To his detractors, he bore all the marks of a madman, and that was why, barely into his twenties, he was asked to leave his home city and forced into an exile that would eventually take him to the Holy Land. His community could have tolerated his odd behavior. His obsessive interest in the kabbalah, uncomfortable though it was for the rabbinical establishment, could also have been accepted. But his very sudden and very public declaration that he was the messiah—that was going too far.

Expelled by the rabbis of Smyrna, he made his way across the Aegean to Salonica, which then had a Jewish majority. He was welcomed and honored as a scholar of the Lurianic kabbalah. The mystic rabbi Isaac Luria had lived and died in Safed, in Palestine, in the sixteenth century and had developed a secretive reading of the Torah that explicated the relationship between God and man. By design, the complexity of Luria's system defies easy explanation. It was a stew that combined the major religious and philosophical traditions of the Near East. Luria held that the Genesis stories of creation and the expulsion from the Garden of Eden were metaphors for the fragmentation of the divine. Centuries earlier, Ibn Arabi of Spain had spoken of the unity of God and man, a unity that was continually obscured by human inability to see the truth. Luria went a step further, and suggested that the divine had been splin-

tered and that the point of human life was to help it reassemble. At some point, an intermediary would appear who would enable both God and man to become whole once again. Sabbatai Sevi claimed to be that someone.

Once it became clear to the rabbis of Salonica who Sabbatai Sevi thought he was, they expelled him. Sabbatai had enthralled many of those who came to listen to his interpretation of the Torah, and that disturbed the conservative rabbis, who saw him as both mentally unstable and a threat to their status. He did little to assuage their concerns, and in fact seems to have taken delight in flouting their authority. They responded predictably, and sent him on his way. This pattern was repeated in city after city as Sevi moved from Salonica to Athens to Cairo to Jerusalem and finally to Gaza, where in 1665 he proclaimed his mission—to lead an army of followers to Istanbul, announce the coming of a new age, and supplant the Ottoman sultan.

News of this new messiah spread quickly throughout the Jewish world. Sabbatai provided ample grist for the international gossip mill. He violated one of the cardinal rules of Judaism and spoke the name of God; he allowed women to recite the Torah in public; he declared that the laws of the Hebrew Scriptures were null until a new testament could be written; he appointed deputies as kings (and queens) of various parts of the Ottoman Empire and Europe; and he claimed that his disciples were the reincarnated souls of long-dead prophets.

From Poland, Germany, and Italy to the metropolises of the Ottoman Empire, Sabbatai Sevi gained adherents. Steeped in the mystical end-of-times prophecies of the kabbalah, Jewish communities throughout the Near East and Europe were receptive to the message that a new messiah had finally arrived, one who would overturn the old laws, announce a new covenant, and restore the kingdom of the Jews. Sevi interpreted the international euphoria as a favorable sign. He marched to Istanbul convinced that the waters would part, the sultan would bow, and a new age would begin. As for his followers, thousands left their homes and converged on Istanbul, certain of "the imminent establishment of the kingdom of Israel, the fall of the Crescent and of all the royal crowns in Christendom."[3]

The sultan and his vizier, who were occupied with a war against the Venetians over the island of Crete, viewed Sevi as a minor threat. In the greater scheme of the empire, he was insignificant, but even the insignif-

icant can irritate. As long as he remained in the provinces, he could be ignored. He may have been important to his followers, but he was a nonentity to the Ottomans—until he marched on Istanbul proclaiming the end of the empire and the coming of a new kingdom. Then he aroused a response.

Soon after arriving in Istanbul, Sevi was arrested. He might have been left in jail indefinitely, but the influx of pilgrims who had come to greet the new messiah was not something that the sultan was prepared to tolerate. On the orders of the vizier, who astutely used the movement to solidify his status as the sultan's most humble servant, Sevi was taken to the summer palace a hundred miles from Istanbul in Edirne (Adrianople), and offered a choice: he could suffer execution for inciting rebellion, or he could renounce his faith and convert. To the horror and astonishment of his followers, he decided to convert. According to most accounts, he did so willingly, even cheerfully, and required little coaxing before he denounced the religion of the Torah, recited the Muslim profession of faith—"There is no God but God, and Muhammad is his Prophet"—in Arabic, in front of the sultan, and took a new name, Aziz Mehmet Effendi.

The story, however, does not end there. Sevi was released from prison, and most of his followers drifted away, shocked that their messiah had committed an act of apostasy and embraced Islam rather than dying for his faith. A few, however, did not quite see it that way. Rather than interpreting what had happened as a repudiation, they claimed that Sevi's actions were part of a master plan revealed in the kabbalah. His supposed conversion was a test of his followers. Jewish communities became sharply divided between those who remained faithful to Sevi's vision and those who renounced him for having renounced them.

As for Sabbatai himself, he remained in Istanbul and Edirne, supported by a smaller group of acolytes. Some of them converted; some did not. Surrounded by an unlikely community composed of Jews, Muslims, and Jews who had converted to Islam, Sevi was once again at the center of his world, looked to for leadership and guidance. Soon after his release from prison, he proclaimed that he and his Muslim disciples were not really Muslims but were indeed fulfilling a mysterious kabbalistic prophecy. In 1672, the Ottoman authorities reacted to the provocation and exiled Sabbatai and his group to a remote part of the Albanian coast on the Adriatic, where he died in 1676.

For the sultan and his court, Sabbatai Sevi's movement was a sideshow that for a brief moment looked as if it might lead to an uprising of the empire's Jewish population. Revolts by disaffected groups were not uncommon but neither were they frequent. They happened, and they required attention. When the issue could not be resolved by suasion and money, it was handled with swift and brutal efficiency by the Janissaries. Sabbatai Sevi spared his followers certain death by his act of conversion, though whether that was part of his motivation we will never know. His memory survived in Jewish communities, and his life gave rise to legends and kabbalistic prophecies about the end of days. For the Ottomans, however, the movement barely registered.

That is itself a testament to the supreme capacity of the Ottomans to maintain order. Faced with an uprising led by a man who loudly announced his intention to overthrow the sultan, the government reacted calmly, deliberately, and effectively. The fact that the man was a Jew who claimed to be the messiah, as well as the fact that he proclaimed that his revelation would supersede not just the Old Testament but also any subsequent messages in the New Testament and the Quran, did not in and of itself agitate the Ottoman authorities. They were secure enough to tolerate outrageous claims. When Sevi crossed the line from rabble-rouser to rebel and marched on the imperial capital, only then was he arrested, imprisoned, and sentenced to death. His crime had less to do with creed than with law and order.

Sevi's movement tells us a good deal about the nature of the Ottoman state and about the status of non-Muslims within it. One of the most striking things was how quickly Sevi's message spread throughout the empire and into Europe. Within months of announcing his mission and marching on Istanbul, word had reached every Jewish community in Europe and the Near East. The seventeenth century was hardly notable for the ease of travel and communication, yet knowledge of Sabbatai Sevi penetrated the farthest corners of Poland, Russia, Greece, and the Near East with remarkable speed. That shows how connected the Jewish community was, even though it was spread out among different states. Jews were international conduits not just of commerce but of information as well. Sevi's story also highlights that one way the Ottomans were able to remain in control of their vast territory was through well-developed and equally well-maintained networks of both communication and transportation.

The movement also demonstrates just how indifferent to religion the Ottomans could be. As long as Sevi didn't challenge the state, his actions were permitted. He could travel freely and unencumbered from one part of the empire to another, say what he wished, and never be required to answer to any Ottoman authority outside of Istanbul. He was forced out of different places not by the Ottomans, but by conservative rabbis who were concerned about their own positions and his potential to unseat them. Sabbatai Sevi lived his entire life in the Ottoman Empire, but even as a rebel, his contact with the state was limited. Once he had converted, he was left alone, and only after repudiating his conversion and hinting that his movement would again challenge the sultan did the state once again take action against him.

STRENGTH BECOMES WEAKNESS

THE WAY that the Ottomans handled Sevi is emblematic of the way they managed an imperium of different races, religions, and peoples. They took Occam's Razor to heart, and believed that the simplest solution was usually the best. They understood that in matters of state, less was often more, and that to maintain the equilibrium, they would take action only when it was forced upon them.

That allowed communities as diverse as Jews, Armenians, Greek Orthodox, Moroccans, Egyptians, Bulgars, Serbs, and Turks to thrive. The tolerance that permitted communities to go about their lives and pursue their own particular ambitions was a strength. The fact that Istanbul contained Janissaries, Ottoman princes, Armenian and Greek merchants and craftsmen, and Jewish doctors, to name a few, contributed to its greatness. Some of the world's most vital urban centers have been the product of different groups living next to one another, if not actually with one another. Rome in its imperial grandeur teemed with peoples from every corner of Europe and the Mediterranean, and New York in the nineteenth century flourished with a population that consisted mostly of immigrants.

Ottoman diversity amazed the elites of Europe. In the early 1700s, Lady Mary Wortley Montagu, the colorful, erudite wife of the British ambassador to the Ottoman court, wrote an astute account of Ottoman

life. In addition to deflating some of the cherished English myths of the lascivious harem, Lady Montagu described an Istanbul defined by variety. "My grooms," she wrote, "are Arabs, my footmen, French, English and German, my nurse an Armenian, my housemaids Russian, half a dozen other servants Greeks; my steward an Italian; my Janissaries Turks, [and] I live in the perpetual hearing of this medley of sounds." There was nothing unusual about the Montagu household retinue. It was a microcosm of a cosmopolitan society. Little did Lady Montagu realize that the empire was slowly decaying.

When the empire finally crumbled in the late nineteenth and early twentieth centuries, one of the first casualties was tolerance. Armenians suffered near annihilation, and Christians in the Balkans were brutalized. But these events should not stand as an indictment of earlier centuries, or be used as a proxy for five centuries of Ottoman history. Tolerance and coexistence were real, even if they dissipated at the end.

If tolerance was an Ottoman strength, lack of curiosity about the wider world was a weakness. The states of Europe, locked in deadly competition with one another, could not afford to be insular. As they jockeyed for advantage, they spread throughout the known and the unknown world. That meant not just voyaging to the Americas and beyond, but also paying more attention to the Ottomans.

Lucrative trade was reason enough to attract the revenue-hungry European states. Given that the Ottomans were less interested in coming to them (at least not until the eighteenth century), they came to the Ottomans. The empire accommodated them with the same level of indifference that it accorded to protected minorities, but Ottoman officials did make it clear that European merchants and official representatives were to limit their activities to trade. That was fine with the Europeans, who proceeded to open consulates and offices in the major ports and trading centers. The only condition they demanded was the right to be tried in their own courts. The Ottomans, accustomed to allowing the *millets* to govern themselves, agreed. They also permitted select nations to pay lower tariffs on the goods they imported and exported, which was a boon to trade but ultimately a bane to the Ottoman treasury. Known as "capitulations," the self-governance that foreigners in the empire enjoyed became a wedge that helped the states of Europe undermine the Ottomans. Though the system initially

spurred economic activity to the mutual benefit of European merchants and the Ottoman state, as European power grew and Ottoman influence waned, the Ottomans came to regret the concessions they had made.

By the middle of the eighteenth century, it was clear to the major European powers that the Ottomans were becoming weaker. The Janissaries were no longer a premier fighting force, and instead were corrupt, undisciplined, and unable to compete with the more technologically advanced armies of the West. While the Ottomans suffered significant defeats on their borders north of the Balkans and in the Caucasus, these were not yet severe enough to shake the complacency. Said one wise European envoy,

> The Ottomans will probably persist in their errors for some time, and submit to be repeatedly defeated for years, before they will be reconciled to such a change; so reluctant are all nations, whether it proceeds from self-love, laziness, or folly, to relinquish old customs: even good institutions make their progress but slowly among us.... The Turks are now an instance of the same; for it is neither in courage, numbers nor riches, but in discipline and order that they are defective.[4]

The end of the eighteenth century brought more military setbacks. The Russians, flush from the reforms of Peter the Great decades earlier, expanded their reach. As the tsar's armies advanced south, the Ottomans were swept aside. The Russian victories signaled to the other states of Europe that the Ottomans were now an easy mark, and had it not been for the French Revolution and the subsequent wars that racked the continent, the empire might have faced even greater pressures. Instead it was given a respite, and successive sultans used the opportunity to make the first tentative steps toward change.

For too long, the Ottoman ruling class, not to mention most of the empire's inhabitants, mistook internal stability for strength. At the end of the eighteenth century, the court still treated foreigners with disdain, and still demanded obeisance from European envoys. Ottoman emissaries to foreign states expected the sort of deference that the Romans had demanded from the Gauls and were shocked and appalled when that was not forthcoming. Many Europeans saw through the veil of vanity

and observed an arrogant, decrepit state. In the words of one English envoy:

It is undeniable that the power of the Turks was once formidable to their neighbors not by their numbers only, but by their military and civil institutions, far surpassing those of their opponents. And they all trembled at the name of the Turks, who with a confidence procured by their constant successes, held the Christians in no less contempt as warriors than they did on account of their religion. Proud and vainglorious, conquest was to them a passion, a gratification, and even a means of salvation, a sure way of immediately attaining a delicious paradise. Hence their zeal for the extension of their empire; hence their profound respect for the military profession, and their glory even in being obedient and submissive to discipline.

Besides that the Turks refuse all reform, they are seditious and mutinous; their armies are encumbered with immense baggage, and their camp has all the conveniences of a town, with shops etc. for such was their ancient custom when they wandered with their hordes. When their sudden fury is abated, which is at the least obstinate resistance, they are seized with a panic, and have no rallying as formerly. The cavalry is as much afraid of their own infantry as of the enemy; for in a defeat they fire at them to get their horses to escape more quickly. In short, it is a mob assembled rather than an army levied. None of those numerous details of a well-organized body, necessary to give quickness, strength, and regularity to its actions, to avoid confusion, to repair damages, to apply to every part to some use; no systematic attack, defense, or retreat; no accident foreseen, nor provided for....

The artillery they have, and which is chiefly brass, comprehends many fine pieces of cannon; but notwithstanding the reiterated instruction of so many French engineers, they are ignorant of its management. Their musket-barrels are much esteemed but they are too heavy; nor do they possess any quality superior to common iron barrels which have been much hammered, and are very soft Swedish iron. The art of tempering their sabers is now lost, and all the blades of great value are ancient. The naval force of the Turks is by no means considerable. Their grand fleet consisted of not more than

seventeen or eighteen sail of the line in the last war, and those not in very good condition; at present their number is lessened.[5]

By the early nineteenth century, even the sultan, who would have been the last to be informed that he was not wearing any clothes, noticed that the comparative position of the empire was becoming untenable. It was one thing to observe that fact, but it was quite another to know what to do about it. Not surprisingly, successive sultans and their advisers tackled that portion of the problem that seemed amenable to a solution: the military. If the deficiencies of the empire were most apparent in battles with the powers of Europe, then it made sense to remake the military. If European guns and ships were overwhelming Ottoman forces, then it was obvious that the sultan needed new guns, new ships, and soldiers capable of using them. But no matter how much the Ottomans tried to revamp the army, they kept losing battles. Having suffered a series of humiliating defeats, the Ottoman elite in Istanbul finally recognized that the changes required were more extensive than buying new guns.

The pivotal figure was Mahmud II, who came to power in 1808 after Sultan Selim III had been overthrown in a plot concocted by enraged Janissaries who feared (rightly) that Selim meant to build a new army and make them obsolete. Having survived a tumultuous two years during which the Janissaries attempted to rule the empire through a puppet sultan, Mahmud vowed that he would respect the status quo, but he lied, and lied brilliantly. He had no intention of allowing the Janissaries to retain a monopoly on military affairs. The Balkans were beginning to exhibit disturbing signs of unrest. The Arabian Peninsula had recently seen the emergence of the religious puritan Muhammad ibn Abd al-Wahhab, who in alliance with the Saudi tribe called for a return to the simple faith of Muhammad and was willing to eradicate anyone who did not agree. And Egypt and Palestine had fallen under the control of an Albanian mercenary appointed by Istanbul, who managed to fend off the Europeans while signaling to Istanbul that he would no longer heed the sultan's orders.

Until the nineteenth century, most of the millions who lived under the Ottoman state would have been unaware of these large trends. The wars of Europe, the military innovations of the French, Germans, and English, and the changing patterns of world trade were so distant as to

be nonexistent. Before the sudden, unanticipated French invasion of Egypt in 1798, daily life in Cairo in the eighteenth century wasn't markedly different from daily life in the sixteenth or seventeenth centuries. The same could be said of Morocco and Syria and central Anatolia. The *millet* system continued much as it had, becoming more refined and more tightly organized as part of the modest reforms of Ottoman administrative system in the late seventeenth century, but not in ways that would have made a Christian in the Peloponnesus or a Jew in Smyrna perceive any radical shift in status.

What did change, inexorably, was the place of the Ottomans in the world, and that had much to do with events beyond their control. The reason for the sudden and dramatic rise of the West at the expense of the rest remains one of the great unsolved riddles of the modern world. There is no lack of theories, but there is no one settled answer. The countries of Europe had fought one another to a standstill for so long that they had been forced to innovate, and to find new sources of revenue and better technology. European nations were forged in a cauldron of war and hatred, and emerged on the world stage uniquely capable of fighting. They combined the ruthlessness of all great powers past and present with the means to enforce their will. The Ottoman Empire was only one of the many obstacles that stood between them and the world, and it withstood the onslaught better than most.

For the first time in the history of Muslim societies, however, the trajectory shifted from offense to defense. As we have seen, there had been earlier setbacks, during the Crusades, in Spain, and for the brief but devastating Mongol interregnum. But then the Ottomans had appeared and restored the narrative to its proper form, with Sunni Muslims ruling and the People of the Book ruled or on the defensive. Early in the nineteenth century, it became clear to both the Ottoman elite and to the Europeans that the empire could no longer resist the expansion of the West. The thousand-year history of Muslim dominance had come to an end.

Muslim societies spent more than a millennium accustomed to power. They have spent the past two hundred years dealing with the loss of it. They met the challenges of dominance; they are still struggling with the challenges of defeat.

꜒ ꜒

Brave New Worlds

T HE SHIFT FROM dominance to decline occurred gradually. There was no one pivotal military loss that marked the end, but the reversal was shocking all the same. From the early decades of the seventh century until the nineteenth century, states ruled by Muslims had validated the promise of the Quran and the early Arab conquests. They had vanquished or outlasted all rivals; they had carefully constructed social orders based on the preeminence of Islam relative to other religions; and for the most part, they had enjoyed the rewards of success. The ascendency of the West in the nineteenth century, therefore, was as revolutionary and disruptive as the rise of Islam had been twelve centuries before.

To reiterate, until the nineteenth century, relations between Muslims, Christians, and Jews had unfolded in the context of Muslim dominance. Even in those periods and places where that wasn't the case, such as the twelfth-century Crusader states and Spain after the thirteenth century, the patterns that had been established under Muslim rule conditioned how the three different faiths interacted. Religion, as we have seen, was only one of many factors shaping these societies, but it did define boundaries and it did set limits. At no point was it a simple matter for a Christian to marry a Muslim, or a Jew to marry either, and that in itself guaranteed a degree of separateness. But over the centuries, under Muslim rule, Christians and Jews had been able to lead their lives and contribute in meaningful ways to the shape and success of their societies.

Beginning in the nineteenth century, the states of Europe came to dominate the Muslim world. This included the Ottoman Empire, as well

as Persia, India, and Indonesia, each of which had substantial Muslim populations—and in the case of India, a Muslim emperor. The expansion of Europe was, as political scientists might say, "overdetermined." There was no one reason; there were many, ranging from economic to political to religious and ideological. But insofar as most inhabitants of these European nations were Christian, it is fair to call them "Christian states." Just as Islam was a central part of the identity of the Muslim world, Christianity was woven into European manners, mores, and attitudes. Granted, European nations had an ambivalent relationship to Christianity, at times bringing the gospel to the unconverted masses around the globe, at other time abjuring religion in the name of secular progress. But while it has been common to overstate the place of religion in both the Muslim world and in Europe, it would be a mistake to go too far in the other direction. Especially at times of head-to-head competition between states whose rulers were Muslim and states whose leaders were Christian, religion could be central. Just as Muslims had both implicitly and explicitly taken their worldly success as a sign of divine favor, Christian states in the nineteenth century attributed their strength not only to country but to God as well.

With few exceptions, the nineteenth century has gained a bad historical reputation. American historians may glory in the history of the United States during these years, and historians of science can point to discovery after discovery. On the whole, however, the century has been seen as the placid middle child between the revolutions of the eighteenth century and the transformations of the twentieth. Generations of writers and scholars in the second half of the twentieth century heaped scorn on the nineteenth century as a period of harsh industrialization marked by a rapacious West sweeping across the globe in a fit of nationalist, capitalist imperialism that despoiled the riches of countless societies and left them hobbled. That remains the prevailing thesis, and it is fair to say that the nineteenth century has a dowdy image in comparison to the Enlightenment, the Renaissance, or (thankfully) the horrific drama of the first half of the twentieth century.

The rise of the West and its effects on the rest of the world also have their known history and their forgotten. A vocal minority defensively celebrate the civilizing mission of the West in spreading liberalism and democracy throughout the world, and they trumpet the Industrial Revolution as a vital step in the march of modern progress. But more preva-

lent today is history that treats the West as a malign force and emphasizes the destructive effects of imperialism on the non-Western world.
This perspective holds that Muslim societies suffered acutely from the
rise of Europe, and that the roots of the present problems confronting
states from Morocco to Afghanistan were planted in the 1800s.[1] This
vision of the nineteenth century and of relations between the West and
the rest paints a dark picture of Western power and its effects on the
globe.

To be fair, these debates are more active in academia than in popular
culture, especially in the United States. In England, there is an audience
for popular books about the Victorians and what they wrought, but few
nonacademics in the United States pay attention to what happened in
the mid-nineteenth century outside America. While textbooks in England try to give a sense of the pros and cons of empire, the tendency in
the past decades on both sides of the Atlantic has been to decry the negative effects of empire. As for the Middle East and other parts of the
world, the nineteenth century is seen as a sorry, sad period of setbacks
and decline punctuated by Western imperialism. It is said that the
humiliation of Muslim societies at the hands of Western states, and of
the Arabs, Persians, and Turks in particular, produced a legacy of hatred
and animosity that eventually led to the fundamentalism, violence, and
terrorism of the late twentieth and early twenty-first centuries. The
nineteenth century, therefore, carries a heavy burden—even without
including the forces of nationalism that originated in the later part of the
1800s and have been held responsible for the wars that not only eviscer-
ated Europe but wreaked havoc on much of the world between 1914 and
1945.

The problem, once again, is not that this history is wrong, but that
it is incomplete. Side by side with military defeats and Western expansion was a spectrum of coexistence and cooperation. While nationalism
eventually proved to be a destructive force in the wars of the twentieth
century, in its early forms it was closely linked to liberal, progressive
ideals. While the imperial experiment ultimately left a sour aftertaste, it
had redeeming features. Fueled by the Enlightenment and by the forces
unleashed by the French Revolution, Europeans spread across the globe
and exported a hodgepodge of ideals that included an unshakable belief
in human progress. And while there was ever and always a racial component to European attitudes toward everyone else, there was also a will-

ingness to view all human beings as capable and able to attain the highest levels of civilization.

In the Muslim world, nineteenth-century European expansion triggered both resistance and accommodation. Unable to defeat the states of Europe on the battlefield, Muslim rulers from Istanbul to Cairo to Persia and India did what they could to adapt. It was more than a simple tale of European aggression. The notion of progress was appealing and infectious. It held out the possibility that with reform, any state and any society could join the ranks of the elite, and that the gap between Europe and the rest would be a temporary phenomenon.

The belief in progress was dealt a severe blow by the wars of the twentieth century, but on the whole, it remains deeply entrenched in both the United States and Western Europe. Even Communism was a utopian system based on the notion that a better world was within reach if only society could be reorganized. The American creed that everything is possible embraces progress as an essential component to life, liberty, and the pursuit of happiness. It is difficult, therefore, to remember that the notion of progress is a recent phenomenon, a product mostly of the past few hundred years. Medieval Europe at best promised a better world in the hereafter. The idea that the future could and would be better than the present was alien. Few embraced change for its own sake, and most resisted it. In the nineteenth century, as Europeans distanced themselves from both organized religion and the divine rule of kings, the belief in progress filled the void.

There was something naive yet seductively universal about the cult of progress. It was critical of the old systems that had purportedly kept mankind from realizing its full potential. That meant disdain for established religion and for political systems that had governed people from time immemorial. The guiding spirit of the cult of progress was the French Revolution, which enshrined the notion that any state could reform and thereby unleash the full potential of its citizens. Imbued with the spirit of innovation, people could transform the material world using technology and remake society using the tools of philosophy and science.

The belief in progress shaped how Muslim societies and Western Christian states interacted. Just as the American Revolution cannot be understood without looking at the ideas of liberty and freedom that fueled it, the interaction between Muslims, Christians, and Jews in the

nineteenth century was framed not just by Western expansion but by a potent set of ideas about the untapped potential of human beings and the promise of a future better than anyone had ever known.

Here, as throughout this complicated story of relations between Muslims, Christians, and Jews, it is not a question of either-or. There are ample episodes of rapacious greed, racism, and abuse meted out by the imperial powers of the West on the rest. There are numerous times when they found surrogates to do their bidding. None of that negates the other history, of coexistence and cooperation.

So while it is true that Western states used raw power to dominate the world, it is also true that they found willing and avid partners who were devoted to the progress of their societies. Unfortunately, most of those who joined hands with Western states to work for progress, many of whom were heroes at the time, became scapegoats in the twentieth century, denigrated as fools and collaborators in their own subjugation by the West. Some were fools, no doubt, but not all, or even most. A closer look reveals that they often understood the ways of the world better than those who caricatured and lampooned them a century later. They recognized the weakness of their societies, confronted their limitations, and partnered with Western states in order to reform. They were willing to undertake the hard work of change. They were Muslims who decided to cooperate with Christian states, who did not look first to religion for answers, and often not even for guidance. And at times they were met not by Europeans who wanted to subjugate them but by Westerners who looked to them as allies in a common, human cause.

THE SICK MAN OF EUROPE

THROUGHOUT the nineteenth century, the fate of the Ottoman Empire was inextricably entwined with European politics. From Napoleon's invasion of Egypt in 1798 through World War I, the states of Europe fought over who would claim which Ottoman lands. As the century wore on, the empire shrank, and province after province either was absorbed into Europe's orbit or became an independent state in its own right.

After the Congress of Vienna in 1815, which ended the long period of war that had wracked the continent since the French Revolution, the

countries of Europe competed with one another, not by fighting directly but by carving up the globe. The balance of power in Europe was maintained at the expense of anything but a stable balance of power globally. The Ottoman Empire, sitting directly on the frontiers of Europe, was both more vulnerable to European encroachment and more able to ward off annihilation.

By midcentury, the Ottomans became a crucial player in European politics. The empire was treated as a hobbled but important component of the diplomatic system that kept peace on the continent. Too weak to defend themselves on the battlefield, the Ottomans survived because no European state wanted another European state to occupy Istanbul and thereby gain control of the sea lanes connecting the Black Sea to the Mediterranean. The empire was kept on life support, but the sultan understood that in order to keep Europe at bay, his diplomats would have to become master manipulators—and they did. Astute at survival but never strong enough to compete militarily, the empire became known as the "Sick Man of Europe."

For much of the nineteenth century, European ministers jockeyed for influence in Istanbul, and the armies of Europe nibbled at the empire's edges. Every foreign ministry had a department dedicated to the "eastern question," and more than once during the century, the system established at the Congress of Vienna threatened to disintegrate in the face of a crisis involving the Ottomans.[2] This was usually the result of a European state attacking an Ottoman province or demanding unreasonable concessions from the sultan and his vizier. But some of the challenges came from within the empire, and one of them nearly ended its life.

In 1798, Napoleon Bonaparte invaded Egypt. His career in Paris was at a standstill, and his plans for a cross-channel assault on England were not going well. Convinced that if he stayed in Paris he would become lost in the political labyrinth, and even more convinced that it was his destiny to reshape the world, he decided to undermine England by striking at its empire. By taking Egypt, which was then under Ottoman control, Napoleon hoped to disrupt England's plans in India and beyond. The choice of Egypt was strategically questionable, and Napoleon remained in the desert land for only two years, until Admiral Nelson destroyed the French fleet off Alexandria. But while Napoleon's invasion was a sideshow to the larger continental conflict between France and everyone else, it set in motion a chain of events that fundamentally

altered not just the Ottoman Empire but the future history of Muslim societies and their interaction with the West.

Since its conquest by Suleyman at the beginning of the sixteenth century, Egypt had been left alone by Istanbul. The old Mameluke elite still dominated the country, and though the Ottoman governor was in theory the most powerful official, the appointees sent by Istanbul depended on the Mamelukes to make sure taxes were collected and order was maintained. Egypt was also home to a large and prosperous Coptic Christian population, and Cairo and Alexandria sheltered an affluent and established Jewish community. Napoleon shattered that calm. The Mamelukes, who had not fought a battle of consequence for centuries, were comically overmatched. The French, even in the dead of summer, even after a scorching, debilitating march across the desert from Alexandria to Cairo, destroyed the Mameluke army in an afternoon.

The ease of the victory did not surprise Napoleon. He knew how weak his adversary was, and he had planned for the occupation of the country by bringing administrators and civil servants on the expedition. He also gathered a group of scholars, known as the *savants,* who were tasked with the study of Egyptian life and history. These mathematicians, engineers, geographers, linguists, and historians were given the responsibility of classifying and cataloging Egyptian culture. They had the eye of clinicians and they were acolytes of the religion of progress, which had triumphed when the French king was humbled, deposed, and finally executed. The French Revolution represented the demise of a social order based on God and king, and the intellectuals who accompanied Napoleon, as well as Napoleon himself, looked to a new world where reason and science would trump faith. Trained at the Polytechnic School in Paris, the *savants* treated Egypt as a canvas primed for a new tableau.

The French Revolution, whose radical leaders renamed 1793 as "Year 1," embodied the spirit of an era when men (and they were mostly men) believed that society could be purged of past impurities. Organized religion was perceived as one of those impurities. The revolutionaries treated religion, and Catholicism in particular, as a primitive force, hostile to inquiry and reason, and inimical to science and progress. The *savants* were scarcely more forgiving of Islam, but Napoleon at least was

sensitive to the vital role of religious authorities in maintaining the status quo in Egypt. With less than fifty thousand troops, he intended to govern a large, mostly desert country, and he needed the tacit cooperation of the *ulama* to achieve that. In both Alexandria and Cairo, he issued proclamations declaring that he had no fight with Islam, only with the Mamelukes. Earlier, in Italy, Napoleon had ordered his troops not to interfere with religious leaders, including rabbis. He reiterated those commands in Egypt: "Deal with them as you dealt with Jews and with Italians," he commanded. "Respect their *muftis* and their *imans*, as you respected rabbis and bishops. Show the same tolerance towards the ceremonies prescribed by the Koran that you showed towards convents and synagogues."

Not since the fall of Granada in 1492 had a Christian power occupied a major Muslim metropolis. Though Napoleon and many of the revolutionary soldiers did not think of themselves as Christian armies, the inhabitants of Cairo did. They were shocked at what they took to be the barbarity of the French. Napoleon had scarcely begun to establish himself in the city when a revolt broke out. As he had demonstrated in suppressing rebellions in Italy, Napoleon was ruthless when challenged. His artillery shelled densely populated areas, and his soldiers occupied the precincts of Al-Azhar Mosque. The behavior of the French, both during these weeks and after, fueled the anger of at least one notable Azhar sheikh, al-Jabarti. In his meticulous multivolume history of the French occupation, al-Jabarti was scathing in his denunciations of the French and was appalled at how filthy, rude, and uncultured they were. He expressed the outrage of many of Cairo's leading citizens about the disrespectful way French troops behaved in Al-Azhar, alleging that "they treated the books and Koranic volumes as trash, throwing them on the ground, stamping on them with their feet and shoes.... They soiled the mosque, blowing their snot in it, pissing and defecating in it. They guzzled wine and smashed their bottles in the central court."[3]

What al-Jabarti interpreted as disrespect for Islam, however, was something rather different for the French army. At that time, flush with the spirit of the French Revolution and imbued with the fervor of their charismatic but somewhat amoral general, the French were at best indifferent and at worst acutely hostile to religion in general. They had no particular animus toward Islam as Islam. In fact, they almost certainly

had more rage toward Catholicism, which they saw as an impediment to the evolution of humanity. They scorned Islam, not because of its particular attributes but simply because it was a religion.

The French expedition survived barely two years, long enough to give Egypt a taste of the West but not long enough to reshape Egyptian society. After Nelson destroyed his fleet, Napoleon escaped to France. With the Mamelukes scattered but still dangerous, Egypt was left in a vacuum, which both the Ottomans and local factions attempted to fill. Though the country was hardly a priority for the sultan, who was then engaged in a power struggle in Istanbul with the Janissaries, it was important. The grand vizier looked for a governor who would be loyal to the sultan, and in 1805 he chose a rising young star. The new governor saved Egypt, but he almost destroyed the empire.

MUHAMMAD ALI

BORN IN ALBANIA, Muhammad Ali served the Ottoman armies as a loyal mercenary. Given the state of the empire at the turn of the century, that was not such an oxymoron. The Janissaries had ceased to be an effective fighting force outside of Istanbul, and the sultan and his cabinet relied on a motley assortment of paid soldiers and officers to keep the peace within the empire's borders. Muhammad Ali was an unusually capable soldier of fortune who went to Egypt in 1801 precisely because he perceived an opportunity in the turmoil. By the time officials in Istanbul appointed him governor in 1805, it was largely a formality. In his four years in the country, he had consolidated his hold through an adroit combination of guile and force.

Muhammad Ali Pasha ruled Egypt for more than forty years, and under his stewardship, the country went from a quiet province of the Ottoman Empire to a pivotal actor in world affairs. Alexandria blossomed as a commercial center, home to merchants and bankers from every major country in Europe, and Egypt emerged as a vital link between Europe and India, which had become the fulcrum of the British Empire. The pasha himself became a legendary figure, known throughout the world as the man who modernized his country and nearly brought down the sultan.

As gifted as he was, Muhammad Ali made one major miscalculation.

Earlier than most in the Ottoman world, he recognized the superiority of Western armies. Unlike the officials in Istanbul, he had seen close up what the French army could do and watched as Napoleon had easily overrun Egypt. He also witnessed the unparalleled skill of the British navy, and the discipline of both the infantry and sailors in battle. He recognized that armies and navies like these were the product of more than good training. They were the result of a radically different society, with an education system designed to foster both independence and loyalty, and state bureaucracies capable of extracting considerably more revenue than the Ottomans.

After becoming governor, Muhammad Ali plotted for nearly six years to end the threat of the Mamelukes. Finally, in 1811, he invited them to a banquet in the Citadel in Cairo, sealed the doors, and had his soldiers massacre them as they ate. All but one of the Mamelukes were killed, and the pasha emerged as the sole power in Egypt, answerable only to the sultan.

He then embarked on a campaign to modernize the country. He sent promising young men to school in Europe. Some were dispatched to Italy; Italian merchants were well represented in Egypt, and closer relations would be a financial boon. Others went to Paris, which inaugurated more than a century of Egyptian Francophilia. There, they encountered Turkish civil servants who had been sent by the sultan, Mahmud II, with a similar goal. Among the young Egyptians in Paris in the 1820s was an Al-Azhar scholar named Rifa'a al-Tahtawi. Though he had been studying at the most established Muslim university in the world, a bastion of tradition, Tahtawi embraced the new and the foreign. The pasha himself had commissioned translations (into Turkish, not Arabic, which the pasha never learned to read) of Voltaire, Montesquieu, and Machiavelli, and he wanted the students he sent to Europe to exhibit the same curiosity. Even more, he expected them to learn engineering and science. But he did not approve of them fraternizing with the local population. Like the Russians who sent students to the West during the Cold War, Muhammad Ali had an intuitive sense of the dangers of "going native." The students were to take what they could from Europe and apply it to the betterment of Egypt.

Tahtawi quietly disregarded the pasha's orders. He went out and about in Paris, made friends, attended dinner parties, and took in the social scene. But there was never any danger of him being seduced by

what he saw. In fact, the experience left him, as it left many subsequent generations of students from the Middle East, unsettled. To his eyes, the French were too liberal, too decadent, and too disorderly in their social lives. While he agreed that they had much to teach Egypt and the Ottomans about running a state and fielding an army, he returned to Egypt more loyal to the autocracy of Muhammad Ali than he had been before he had left.

Over the next decades, Tahtawi articulated a vision of a modern Egypt that was one part autocracy, one part Islam, and two parts Industrial Revolution. The result was a society that combined the unchallenged authority of a ruler like Muhammad Ali with cutting-edge techniques of farming, efficient organization of the state bureaucracy, and advanced technologies for communication and transportation. As for the place of religion, Tahtawi did not agree with the French example. The French believed that "national welfare and human progress [could] take the place of religion and that the intelligence of learned men is greater than that of the prophets," and they had banished Christianity from the public sphere and affairs of state. That was unacceptable to Tahtawi, who insisted that Egypt could modernize without antagonism toward Islam, a religion that he believed was firmly compatible with science, technology, and progress.[4]

As Albert Hourani noted in his studies of this period, Tahtawi "lived and worked in a happy interlude of history, when the religious tension between Islam and Christianity was being relaxed and had not yet been replaced by the new political tension of east and west." That meant that forward-looking Egyptians could pick and choose those aspects of the West that fit their model of an emerging Egypt and reject the rest. Unburdened by a sense of civilizational clash, they looked on France and on Europe as challengers and competitors who had distinct strengths. They understood that it was important to learn from those strengths, and they dedicated their lives to modernizing Egypt using the European model as a guide. Muhammad Ali and much of the Egyptian ruling class took an à la carte approach, selecting those aspects that they liked while rejecting those they did not. Educational reform they approved of; democracy and secularism held little appeal. The same process was unfolding in Istanbul under the sultan, though the entrenched interests there made reform far more difficult. And that was why Muhammad Ali nearly replaced the sultan, not once but twice, in 1833 and again in 1839.

It wasn't that the pasha intended to challenge the sultan, at least not at first. In fact, he had repeatedly come to the sultan's aid, notably in Greece when the powers of Europe intervened to support the independence movement, and on the Arabian Peninsula when the followers of Ibn Abd-al-Wahhab captured Mecca and Medina and massacred pilgrims making the hajj. But by the late 1820s, having nearly suppressed the Greek revolt before the English fleet sank Egypt's navy in Navarino Bay, Muhammad Ali came to the conclusion that the real danger to his future and that of Egypt and the Near East wasn't Europe. It was the ineffectual Ottoman sultan, who ruled in Istanbul while the empire disintegrated around him.

Convinced that the Europeans would destroy the empire if he did not prevent them, Muhammad Ali sent his son to invade Syria and Turkey. Between 1830 and 1833, Egyptian armies inflicted defeat after defeat on Ottoman garrisons and detachments. By the middle of 1833, the pasha's forces had advanced to within 150 miles of Istanbul, and his recently rebuilt fleet was moored near the Bosphorus. Panicked, the sultan asked the Russians for help. The tsar had long nurtured a desire to establish Russian dominance in Istanbul, and he decided to save the sultan and thereby become the protector of the empire. In order to keep Russian influence in check, the English and the French then closed ranks and issued communiqués informing Muhammad Ali that they would not permit him to occupy the capital. Faced with the combined might of the European powers, Muhammad Ali negotiated terms. His armies departed, but he was now lord not just of Egypt but of Syria, Arabia, and the Sudan as well. Having suffered no setbacks on the field, he remained a formidable threat.

The sultan, Mahmud II, knew that, and it was intolerable. He had spent most of his decades in power one step behind Muhammad Ali, and the humiliation of 1833 made him determined to established his authority over the Egyptian upstart. However, he needed European support to succeed. By the end of the decade, Ottoman diplomats had successfully convinced the English that Muhammad Ali had to be humbled. The pasha himself had made no moves against the sultan, and had sought only to make his family hereditary rulers of Egypt and Syria. But in the summer of 1839, assured of English backing, Mahmud sent his new army to challenge Muhammad Ali in Syria, and the result was a disastrous defeat for the sultan. Soon after, the Ottoman fleet, whose commanders had been seduced by the promise of titles and gold, deserted to

the Egyptian side. Mahmud, suffering from tuberculosis, died before he learned of these disasters. In great pain and weary after thirty years in power, he drank himself into a fatal stupor just before messengers arrived in the capital bearing the grim news.

Once again, however, the states of Europe defended the sultanate against the Egyptian vassal. This time, Muhammad Ali did not blink. He refused to withdraw. But in his age and pride, he had forgotten just how strong the English were, and his fleet was destroyed in the harbors of Acre and Beirut. The pasha was forced to withdraw his army from Turkey and Syria, and while he was allowed the face-saving gesture of a decree establishing his sons and heirs as rulers of Egypt, the damage had been done. Egypt never again threatened the integrity of the Ottoman Empire. Unfortunately, the Ottomans had to confront the fact that their continued existence now depended on the European countries that had rescued them.

THE OTTOMANS REFORM

THE CHALLENGE posed by Muhammad Ali and the humiliation of needing to turn to Europe for survival precipitated the next wave of Ottoman reforms. While the Ottomans never ceased to identify themselves as a Muslim dynasty that was part of a long and noble tradition stretching back to the first four caliphs, religion was all but invisible as a factor during these decades of reform. The Ottomans wore their Islam lightly, especially when it came to governing. Their lack of dogmatism made them flexible and resilient, and even though the state had stagnated, that underlying strength remained. With Europe a critical threat to their power, the Ottomans tried to adapt, and their version of Islam did not stand in the way of change. As a result, the reforms of the nineteenth century owed more to Europe than to the Quran, and the Ottoman state became barely distinguishable from that of its European rivals.

Mahmud had wanted to modernize the army but tried to keep the traditional structure of the empire unchanged. Though the Ottoman elites dabbled with the ideas unleashed by the French Revolution, they had no appetite for liberal reform. But with the death of Mahmud and the near death of the Ottoman state, a new generation came to power.

Many of these young men had spent a few years in Paris along with the Egyptian students sent by Muhammad Ali. They had studied the success not just of European armies but of European bureaucracies. With the passing of Mahmud, they engineered a stunning new wave of reform.

The *Hatt-i Serif of Gulhane* (Noble Edict of the Rose Chamber) was issued on November 4, 1839. It was read out loud by the dynamic foreign minister, Mustafa Reshid Pasha, in front of the assembled nobles of the court, including the sultan and the grand vizier, in a formal garden beneath the Topkapi Palace. No one who listened that day failed to appreciate its significance. Along with the 1856 *Hatt-i Humayun*, these edicts were to the Ottoman state what the Declaration of Independence and the Constitution were to the American republic. These decrees set the empire on a path of reform that simultaneously centralized the state and granted specific and unalienable rights to its citizens.

The Rose Chamber decree began with the simple, uncontroversial statement that all law in the empire flowed from the Quran and the sharia, and that those two pillars were the foundation of the state. "But in the last 150 years," it continued, "former power and welfare turned into weakness and poverty. It is absolutely impossible for a country not ruled by shariah rules to survive.... [As a result], we decided to issue some new laws to govern our sublime state and our country through the mercy of God and guidance of our Prophet." Having established the reasons for the decree, Mustafa Reshid then described the new laws. First, the life and property of all citizens of the empire, whether they were Muslims, Christians, or Jews, were to be treated with the utmost respect and no punishment was to be meted out without due process in courts of law. The old system of tax farming, often abused by capricious officials, was abolished and replaced with a new tax code; and military conscription was ended.

The subsequent edict of 1856 built on these foundations The sultan, basking in his semi-victory over the Russians during the Crimean War, declared that all subjects of the empire, Muslim and non-Muslim, were equal, and that henceforth the *millet*s would be integrated into the bureaucracy. In essence, each religious community would retain its self-government for certain matters and also become part of a centralized system based in Istanbul. In addition, every inhabitant of the empire, regardless of religion or ethnicity, was considered a citizen, and all citi-

zens had rights and obligations. Some of these would be protected and enforced by the *millet*, while others would be guaranteed by the government in Istanbul.

Collectively, these reforms were known as *Tanzimat*, the reordering of Ottoman society. For most of its history, the empire had been, as one English writer cleverly put it, "less like a country than a block of flats inhabited by a number of families that met only on the stairs." The families were the various religious and ethnic communities, and the flats were the *millet*s. As a result of the decrees of 1839 and 1856, however, some of the walls separating the families came down, and the sultan became a more active presence. Having lived semiautonomously for centuries, the citizens of the empire were now told they were members of a single political community with the sultan at the top and Istanbul at the center. While this change temporarily strengthened the Ottoman state, it also led to its demise.[5]

The *Tanzimat* was nothing if not contradictory. The reforms were initiated by a ruler who had rarely been answerable to anyone but God and by ministers who borrowed from the secular French Revolution to enshrine notions of individual rights and civil law. While increasing the power of the *millet*s, the reforms were designed to strengthen the central bureaucracy and allow the government in Istanbul to collect more revenue so that it could outfit a larger, more modern army and navy. And while the movement declared its respect for ethnic and religious diversity, it unleashed the same forces of nationalism that ultimately pushed both the empire and the states of Europe away from inclusiveness and toward arrogant intolerance.

The official language of the Rose Chamber decree invoked God, the sharia, and the Quran, yet the actual reforms steered the state away from its traditional pillars. In fact, the entire history of these decades highlights just how minimal a role religion played in the evolution of the Ottoman Empire and the Near East in the nineteenth and early twentieth centuries. The ruling elites of the empire were culturally Muslim, yet there was nothing about their Islam that precluded turning to the Russian tsar, who was the head of the Russian Orthodox Church, for help against an Albanian Muslim ruler of the mostly Muslim but partly Coptic province of Egypt. Nothing in their Islam precluded alliances with the thoroughly Protestant England or with the adamantly secular

French state. And their Islam fluidly accommodated the melting-pot nationalism in vogue in Europe.

On the borders of the Ottoman Empire, the Austro-Hungarian Empire, ruled by a Catholic monarch, was a mix of Catholics, Orthodox, Protestants, Jews, and Muslims. The Catholicism of the ruling class was the top layer of a multiconfessional society, and while the emperor demanded the loyalty of his subjects, he did not insist that they worship as he did. That was the model that the sultan emulated.

It was an easy shift. Centuries of Ottoman jurisprudence and practice supported the live-and-let-live approach that the decrees of 1839 and 1856 enshrined. The ancient Quranic prescription that the People of the Book should be allowed to practice their religion and should not be subject to coercion was in harmony with liberal notions of freedom and equality. And the *dhimmi* framework that had been established in the early centuries of Islam, which required Christians and Jews to pay the state a tax in return for living peacefully under Muslim rule, fit neatly with the nineteenth-century efforts by the Ottomans to rationalize and modernize the tax collection system.

In essence, the reforms of the *Tanzimat* era were less of a departure than they seemed; they made explicit what had been implicit. The decrees announced that all religions would be tolerated and that the *millet*s would form the basis of administrative units, but this was more a change in form than substance. The goal of the reformers was to replace the traditional hidebound Ottoman bureaucracy with a modern state apparatus capable of raising revenue and defending the borders in the face of aggressive European competitors. But in doing so, the reformers built on a framework that had divided the empire into ethnic and religious communities for centuries.

The contradictions should have been apparent. Rather than forcing the inhabitants of the empire to see themselves as "Ottomans," the reforms instead led each group to become more conscious of its religious and ethnic distinctiveness. Greeks, Armenians, Arabs, Turks, and Jews became more attuned to their own identities, and in short order began to resent the attempts of the government in Istanbul to forge them into one Ottoman nation.

And yet, here as elsewhere, the picture is complicated. In the end, the Ottoman state did not successfully transform itself, but large numbers of

people within the empire found the notion of progress, equality, tolerance, and citizenship appealing. In cities such as Smyrna and Istanbul, the second half of the nineteenth century was a heady, exciting time. Greek, Jewish, and Armenian merchants were at the forefront of substantial social and political changes. Not only did they serve as economic and social middlemen connecting Europe and the empire, but they also saw a possible future when the last vestiges of discrimination against them would dissolve. In Egypt, Alexandria (which was staunchly independent but still part of the Ottoman ecosystem) grew into a cosmopolitan city that prized its diversity and prospered in a way it had not since the days of Cleopatra. In the Balkans, the city of Salonica continued to be a trading hub, and in the eastern Mediterranean the sleepy ports of Acre, Beirut, and Tripoli, which in the twelfth and thirteenth centuries had bridged Europe and the Near East, once again became centers of trade and culture.

Throughout the Muslim world, there was a concerted effort to move closer to Europe. The sultans who succeeded Mahmud II worked tirelessly to establish themselves as respectable monarchs who would be welcome in the halls of Europe. The family of Muhammad Ali devoted themselves to transforming Egypt into a nation worthy of European respect. "Egypt," said Khedive Ismail, Muhammad Ali's grandson and ruler during the building of the Suez Canal, "must become part of Europe." In order to show just how European he was and could be, Ismail built rail lines, palaces, military barracks, and roads. Not only did he underwrite the construction of the Suez Canal, but he also spent lavish sums of money to turn Cairo into the Paris of the Near East, complete with an opera house, a museum, wide tree-lined boulevards, and hulking overdecorated edifices to house the new bureaucracy he created. Unfortunately, in order to pay for these endeavors, he went heavily into debt to European banks, and soon found that his reach had exceeded his grasp.

In Istanbul, the sultans and their ministers did the same. A new imperial residence, the 250-room Dolmabahce Palace, was built along the water in the modern section of the city, at an extraordinary cost for what amounted to a knockoff of Versailles. Crystal chandeliers lit overly large formal dining halls and ballrooms, and almost every piece of furniture was imported from Europe. The Ottoman ruling class exchanged its traditional robes for the latest fashions from Paris and Vienna, and traded

divans and pillows for stiff-backed couches and armoires. They drank wine from German crystal goblets, dined with imported cutlery and imported ceramic plates, and dabbed their mouths with imported linens. They held balls where string quartets played the latest waltzes by Schumann, where the ladies danced in gowns that the empress Eugénie of France might have worn, and the men wore frock coats that would have suited any masquerade in Prague or Berlin.

In order to show the world that they were not the warriors of old, Sultan Abdul Aziz and Khedive Ismail of Egypt both went to Paris for the Exposition of 1867. To their delight and surprise, they were feted as celebrities. Prior to their arrival, they had underwritten the construction of sumptuous pavilions for the exposition in order to demonstrate the progress their societies had made, and to show that they belonged among the leading nations of the world. Though Ismail was still theoretically the sultan's vassal, the two were in competition, and they eyed each other warily. They were not the only Muslim rulers to jockey for favor in Europe. Several years later, the shah of Iran, annoyed that the sultan had been so well received in Paris, set out on an official tour of his own, by way of Russia. He was also feted, but he insisted that his wives return early after he discovered that the Europeans allowed the sexes to mingle in public.

Had a poll been conducted surveying Muslim attitudes toward the West in the second half of the nineteenth century, with samples drawn from Morocco, Algeria (which was then mostly under French control), Egypt, Syria, Turkey, Persia, and northern India, the response would have been overwhelmingly positive. By and large, European nations were admired for the rigor and efficiency of their armies and for the way they organized their societies in support of the state. While a strong undercurrent of rivalry and distrust remained, many believed that the future would see less war, more commerce, and more peaceful coexistence.

As always, there were exceptions: the Balkan provinces were anything but placid. The Serbs and the Bulgarians were seized with nationalist ambitions, supported by selective historical memory and overlaid with religious and ethnic grievances. The governing Turks viewed the Balkans with suspicion and disdain, and relations deteriorated as the century progressed, thanks in no small measure to the meddling of the Austro-Hungarians, the Russians, and the English. The Balkans eventually became the most contentious and unstable point of contact between

Muslims and Christians, which led to multiple small wars and eventually set off the conflagration of World War I.

Hindsight allows us to see what worked and what didn't in the nineteenth century, but at the time, the Ottomans seemed to be succeeding in wrenching a moribund bureaucracy out of its stupor and making the empire competitive. The army was retrained and acquitted itself respectably alongside the French and the English in the Crimean War against the Russians. The administration of the empire was rationalized, and the new taxation regime made it possible for the treasury to collect a steady stream of income. Roads, railways, and irrigation systems boosted economic and agrarian activity. Istanbul joined London, Paris, Saint Petersburg, Berlin, and Vienna as a leading European capital, and whenever the sultan toured Europe, he was greeted not just as a visiting dignitary but as a charismatic visionary responsible for bringing the empire into the concert of nations.

In private, European leaders were less respectful and scorned the empire for its weakness, but little was said about its religious makeup. Christianity and Judaism were in retreat from public life on the continent. There were exceptions, of course, Catholic Ireland being just one, but in general, religion in nineteenth-century Europe was less important than nationalism. The French and English looked down on the Ottomans as a backward race mired in ossified customs and traditions, and they certainly identified Islam as a factor contributing to the decadence of the empire. But they felt the same about the Indians and the Chinese and their religions and customs. In short, Western powers regarded all non-Western peoples as less civilized, and they tended to view traditional organized religion, including Christianity, as a source of weakness. Even with the missionary impulses of English and Scottish imperialists, religion as a spur to global expansion was never as potent as economic interests, political rivalries, and nationalist imperatives.

European expansion combined a passion for progress with pure power politics. The utopian impulse to create a better world, where human reason and ingenuity would invent technologies to make hunger, war, and disease obsolete, walked hand in hand with the ancient human desire to conquer and control. Until early in the twentieth century, the gloss on the nineteenth century was that it was a period of human progress, defined by the spread of liberalism emanating from Europe

and by the scientific advances of the age. Later it became fashionable to excoriate the Victorians and the French of the many republics as hypocrites barely more civilized than the people they conquered. But reality is never quite so binary, and the nineteenth century was no exception.

For most of the century, however, religion was rarely a primary cause of either conflict or concord between Muslims, Christians, and Jews. The Ottoman Empire, along with other Muslim communities in Persia, India, and Indonesia, emulated the European powers, and that meant that Islam receded from public and political life. Though historians and polemicists have looked back at the nineteenth century and found the seeds of modern religious conflicts, at the time, few people thought of religious identity as an important factor propelling their societies. European expansion, science, technology, and ideas such as nationalism would have come to mind more readily, while religion would, more often than not, have been seen as a quaint anachronism.

Of course, religion as a source of tension had not been completely eliminated, but it was the supposedly secular Europeans who aggravated matters. While the French and the English, and in their own way the Russians, all moved away from the religious fervor of the Middle Ages and the Reformation, they still felt an affinity for their coreligionists. As a result, they developed bonds with those communities within the Ottoman Empire that shared their faith. French merchants needed partners in Lebanon and Syria, and found them in Catholics and Maronite Arabs. Russian diplomats and traders looked for bankers and translators and found them in Slavic communities in the Balkans that were still part of the Ottoman state.

The links between these groups and the European powers then became an excuse for intervention in the internal affairs of the Ottoman state. The old system of capitulations mutated into a series of laws that allowed Europeans to act with near impunity within the empire, untouchable by the Ottoman authorities, and European diplomats and merchants extended their protection to those who had helped them. That created tension between the Christians and Jews who worked for and with the Europeans and the Muslims who did not. What began as convenient relationships grounded in religious affinity became an irritant and then a wedge that jeopardized not only the Ottoman effort at reform but the internal stability and integrity of the entire state.

THE DARKEST HOUR AND THEN A NEW DAWN

DAMASCUS IN 1860 was a mélange of Christian sects, Muslims, Druze, and Jews, along with a powerful group of European merchants and envoys. The city had become a conduit for Mediterranean trade with the inland regions of central Anatolia and Iraq. As Lebanon was drawn into the orbit of France and its ambitious emperor, Napoleon III, the Maronite Christians grew not only wealthier but more independent. They formed tight networks with Catholics in Damascus, who also benefited from the increased economic activity.

These developments did not go unnoticed, especially by those who did not have the same advantages. In 1856, the *Hatt-i Humayun* granted the Christians in the Ottoman Empire full legal equality with Muslims. While theoretically this made Christian subjects eligible for military service, it was relatively easy for them to pay a fee instead of actually serving in the army. Furthermore, in Syria and in Lebanon especially, Christians enjoyed the protection of European consuls. Each of the major European powers in effect sponsored one of the Christian denominations. In addition to the French interest in the Catholics and the Maronites, the Russians became patrons of the Greek Orthodox, and the English extended their hand to Protestant communities as well as to the non-Christian Druze.

It was one thing not to have to serve in the army; even most Muslims did not begrudge that. But under the capitulations, Europeans and their clients were exempt from taxation and were outside the Ottoman legal system. Local businessmen took advantage of the capitulations by becoming affiliated with a consulate and thereby making their ventures essentially tax-free. That struck established Muslim merchants as cheating, because it gave the Christians a distinct advantage. The new relationships with the Western powers also disrupted the delicate equilibrium that had existed in the region for centuries. The average Muslim had no recourse to consular protection; he had no easy way of avoiding taxes; and it was only with great difficulty that he could avoid conscription. And as in any situation where the status quo changes dramatically and rapidly, there was resentment, and there was a backlash.

It began in 1858 in Lebanon. The Druze had been losing ground to the Maronites, and they struck back. The local civil war led to refugees, most of them Christians, fleeing over the mountains to what they

thought was the safety of Damascus and Aleppo. But the influx proved to be a fatal spark for the simmering animosities of the Muslims of Damascus. Bitter after years of watching their relative status slip and that of the Christians, with their European protectors, increase, they retaliated. On July 9, 1860, Muslims massacred five thousand Christians in Damascus. There were also riots in Aleppo and nearby towns, and there might have been further violence but for the efforts of both Muslims and Christians to contain it. Hearing the news, Napoleon III of France threatened to send an army to restore order.

For their part, the Ottoman authorities responded forcefully. They understood the stakes. The Francophone foreign minister, Fu'ad Pasha, was dispatched to settle matters in both Syria and Lebanon. Druze and Muslim leaders who had incited the murderous mobs were sentenced to exile or execution. The government and the administrative districts of Lebanon were reorganized along denominational lines in order to give the Maronite Christian community more buffers. These measures placated the Europeans, and also reassured the Christians of Syria and Lebanon. Justice had been done, and life returned to normal.[6]

Much like the violence in Andalusia that culminated in the massacre of Cordoban Jews in 1066, the civil war between Muslims, Christians, and Druze from 1858 to 1860 has been taken as another exhibit in the case against Islam. But to indict Islam for this violence is the equivalent of condemning Anglicanism for the occasional depredations of the British army in its many wars of conquest in the nineteenth century, or to excoriate Catholicism because of French massacres of Algerians during the same period, or to charge American Protestantism for the slaughter of Native Americans at Wounded Knee in 1890. Religious identity and affiliation in all of these cases did contribute to "group cohesion," as Ibn Khaldun might have said. And religion was one way that groups differentiated themselves and distinguished "us" from "them." But in none of these cases, including what happened in Damascus, was religion the cause of the violence.

The year 1860 in Damascus was an anomaly that had more to do with the encroaching West than with relations between Christians and Muslims. We know that it was an anomaly because Muslims and Christians had lived side by side in Damascus for centuries without violence. Even during the time of the Crusades, when Muslims of Syria looked on native Christians and Jews as a possible fifth column who would open the

gates (literally) to Western Christian armies, there were no comparable acts of retribution. What changed in 1860 was that the centuries-old balance between Muslims and Christians in Syria and Lebanon was disrupted by the presence of the West. After the Anglo-French intervention against Muhammad Ali, there was increased European involvement in the internal affairs of the Near East, which meant both more trade and a shift in the status quo. The eruption of violence in 1860 was one consequence.

Remarkably, within months after the riots, not only was order restored, but so too was something resembling the old harmony. Christians once again went about their lives as a flourishing minority in the midst of a Muslim majority. The *Tanzimat* reforms emanating from Istanbul promised equal rights and special privileges for religious communities in the empire, and the Christian sects of Syria and Lebanon were among the beneficiaries. Aided by Europe, Christians in the Near East enjoyed more rights and freedoms than they had before the deadly riots.

A casual observer in the years after 1860 would have been struck by the relative harmony that prevailed, and by the energy and hum of commercial and intellectual activity. But there were problems beneath the surface. The Ottoman reform movement established clear and nearly equal rights for religious minorities. That was supposed to make all citizens of the empire legally the same, but by building on the *millet* system, the *Tanzimat* created inadvertent problems. Loyalty to the *millet* community was almost always stronger than loyalty to the sultan or to the empire, and the concept of "Ottoman" citizenship was still unfamiliar. Though the *Tanzimat* reforms were designed to preserve, strengthen, and modernize the empire, they had the unintended consequence of sharpening religious and ethnic differences.[7]

As the nineteenth century neared its end, ethnic nationalism became more evident. The Turks began to imagine a new, smaller empire defined by its Turkishness. There was a parallel development among the Arabs of the Near East, who contemplated a future separate from the Ottoman Empire. They started to think of themselves as Arabs first, Muslims or Christian second, and distinct and different from the Turks who ruled them. They turned to the distant memory of the early Arab dynasties, and to their days of past glory. Interestingly, Arab Christians were forceful proponents of the ideas and programs that evolved into

Arab nationalism, and they unequivocally asserted that Arab national-ism could not be detached from Islam.

In the second half of the nineteenth century, these ideas were in their infancy, and were part of a mix that included Ottoman nationalism, European notions of a global community of peoples and nations freed by technology from the cycles of the past, and a belief in religious coex-istence that would lead to a dwindling of old traditions in the face of that strange force known as modernity. Many Arabs and Turks viewed the mosque as a quaint institution, prone to superstition and backwardness. Some educated Syrians or Egyptians, like their counterparts in England or Germany, believed that religion was retreating from the public sphere and would eventually be relegated to the home and family. The *ulama* were seen as ignorant, though earnest, individuals who could not grasp the demands of the modern world but could make it more difficult for the Arabs to become part of it. Others, however, were not so quick to dis-miss religion and tried to blend it with reform. They recognized that their societies needed to evolve and modernize but believed that it was possible both to "Westernize" the "Muslim" world and to keep Islam central.

As in any period when the old order is breaking down, there was no lack of ideas. These decades were tumultuous and chaotic, swirling with conflicting visions. The Ottoman Empire in the nineteenth century was in profound flux. The only constant was that the old was evaporating. Uncertain but hopeful, Arabs, Turks, Christians, Muslims, and Jews looked to a future of working with the West to construct a new order.

The Age of Reform

In the last decades of the nineteenth century and the early years of the twentieth, European pressure intensified on all parts of the Muslim world, and more territory was conquered. Morocco, the rest of Algeria, and Tunisia fell under the direct rule of France. In 1882, Egypt was invaded and then governed by England. France became the de facto protector of Lebanon, and England extended its influence over both Persia and parts of the Balkans. Russia became more aggressive in its support for Bulgarian independence and came into conflict with the British in remote parts of Central Asia. Successive generations of British politicians jockeyed with the Russians for influence in Afghanistan and Persia because of Russian desires to expand south and England's desire to provide an ever larger buffer for its prize possession, India. While Russia was England's primary rival in Asia and the Balkans, France was its main rival in Africa. As the French moved south into the Sahara and toward West Africa, the British tried to create an unbroken line of control stretching from Egypt to South Africa. That led to friction with the French, which at several points in the late 1800s nearly escalated into war.

The societies of the Muslim world reacted to these developments with more reforms and more soul searching. What began as a trickle of changes in the early nineteenth century became a roaring current in the final decades. While Algeria was as different from Persia and India as England was from Argentina, the way these societies reacted to Western expansion was similar. In almost every part of the Muslim world, there were some who enthusiastically embraced the mores and manners of the

West, and others who resisted at all costs. There were some who ventured abroad, studied the fundamentals of Western science and philosophy, and returned home to lead a new wave of reform; and there were others who retreated more deeply into the comfortable lassitude of the past, clinging to dreams that the West would retreat as surely as the Crusaders had left Palestine centuries before.

Almost everywhere, however, reform movements became the driving force. Some looked to remake the Muslim world along Western lines, with constitutions that mimicked those of France and, to a lesser extent, the United States. In Istanbul in 1876 and Tehran in 1905, constitutionalists inaugurated a new era of government that limited the power of the sultan, shah, or khedive and granted judges and legislatures a measure of autonomy and independence. The constitutionalist movements were careful to incorporate the ancient Quranic protection of the rights of the People of the Book, and they were models of multicultural toleration for religious and ethnic minorities.

Even as many leading voices argued for reform, attitudes toward the West remained ambivalent. It wasn't as if millions in the Muslim world suddenly decided that it was time to change. Change was forced on them—not all at once, but with each passing decade, it became impossible for societies ruled by Muslim leaders to deny that the balance had shifted decidedly against them and in favor of the West. The challenge at the beginning of the century and at the end was similar—how to compete with the West and remain independent—but the stakes seemed higher as the century wore on. The heirs of Muhammad Ali in Egypt and the second generation of reformers in the Ottoman Empire asked the same question, but with the added knowledge that France, England, and Great Britain were more likely to invade and rule directly than they had been before.

As the nineteenth century ended, the idea of progress became more deeply embedded. Reformers have to believe that the future can be better, and that the right choices made by the right people will create a stable, prosperous, and successful society. The late nineteenth and early twentieth centuries were the golden age of Muslim reform movements, and the outcome of these movements in turn shaped how Muslims, Christians, and Jews would interact in the twentieth century and into the twenty-first.

ΛΩ ΕϚΥΡΤΙΛΩ ΛϜϜΛΙℜ

THE DIPLOMATS of the Ottoman Empire continued to hone their skills of playing one European power against another. Internally, Ottoman identity fought what was ultimately a losing battle against Turkish identity, but for a time, that made for a vibrant intellectual life in Istanbul. Poets, playwrights, philosophers, and writers debated the virtues of "Ottomanness" and "Turkishness" with the same vitality that French intellectuals argued socialism, democracy, and class in the Third Republic. But the brief success of the constitutional movement was ended by a coup from above. Sultan Abdul Hamid II abrogated the newly passed document and used the reforms of the previous decades to create a harsh autocratic government interested primarily in collecting revenue to fund armies and railroads.

The Ottomans were able to keep the Europeans at bay, but the Egyptians were not. The building of the Suez Canal ensured that Egypt would be drawn more closely into the orbit of Europe. At first, that had been one of the selling points that convinced Khedive Said and then Ismail to join with the French entrepreneur Ferdinand de Lesseps to fund the construction of the massive hundred-mile-long trench connecting the Mediterranean to the Red Sea. With the completion of the canal in 1869, however, Ismail found himself heavily in debt to French and English bankers, who continued to extend his line of credit in the 1870s as he scrambled to remake his country. Soon, he was personally insolvent, as was the Egyptian treasury.

Forced by his creditors to hand control of Egypt's finances to a consortium of European banks, Ismail was then deposed, and his ramshackle treasury and tottering government were left to his young, untested son. English and French officials installed themselves as advisers in the major ministries. This takeover of the government did not go unnoticed, and a resistance movement formed. It was led by a native Egyptian army officer, and its aims were straightforward: to restore sanity to Egypt's finances, to make the government of Egypt less Turkish and more Egyptian, and to decrease the influence of England. It was, in short, the first major eruption of Egyptian nationalism.

Muhammad Ali and his heirs may have wanted to transform Egypt into a power to be respected, but they were an Albanian family surrounded by a Turkish elite governing an Arab-speaking populace. When

the country's finances cracked under the weight of Ismail's ambitions, some Egyptians began to consider an alternate Arab Egypt that would be independent of both Europe and of the Ottoman elite. The sultan in Istanbul disapproved, but he was consumed with unrest in the Balkans. The British, however, with the newly opened Suez Canal linking Europe to Asia, were not prepared to let a popular Egyptian army officer take control of the government. When riots broke out in Alexandria in the summer of 1882, the British fleet bombarded the port, and a British army quelled the uprising with its customary, not to mention lethal, efficiency.

British control of Egypt lasted, in one form or another, until the end of World War II. Though Egypt was declared independent by Great Britain in 1922, British troops remained in control of the Suez Canal zone, and British influence over Egypt's foreign policy was close to total. In time, Egypt developed a robust nationalist movement that worked to end British rule, but in the immediate aftermath of the 1882 occupation, most Egyptian nationalists resigned themselves to the changed reality and looked for ways to reform the country. The soul searching produced at least one reformer who not only fused Islam with Western modernity but offered a template for dozens of other movements throughout the Muslim world in the twentieth century.

Muhammad Abduh was born in 1849 in a village in the Nile Delta. Life in that lush, fecund land was beginning to change, but it was still a world determined by the waxing and waning of the Nile floods, by peasants planting crops, by festivals full of music and noise and Sufi masters walking on coals and charming snakes, and by the village mosque with its imam preaching sermons that could have been heard a thousand years before. As a bright, precocious child, Abduh was sent to study at Al-Azhar, which was the oldest university in the Muslim world and still among the most prestigious. It was not, however, known for being forward-looking. Unlike most of his contemporaries, Abduh took his formal education, which would have included immersion in the Quran, the sharia, the hadith, and jurisprudence, and applied it to the pressing question of his day: what to do about the West?

The events of 1882 sharpened his answers, but even before, he had been intent on synthesizing the traditions of Islam with the philosophical and scientific innovations introduced by the West. While he excelled as a student and then as a teacher of the traditional curriculum of Al-

Azhar, he had been drawn into the orbit of progressive thinkers who congregated in Cairo in the 1870s. One of the leading lights of that circle was an itinerant teacher named Jamal al-Din al-Afghani. An Iranian who claimed to have been born in Afghanistan, he was in fact a Shi'ite who pretended to be a Sunni in order to broaden his appeal. Afghani spent most of his adult life in a peripatetic whirl. He was a decade older than Abduh, and by the time they met in the 1870s, he had become a minor celebrity, known for his lectures and his writings on science, Islam, and the West. He was charismatic and eccentric, and maintained an aura of mystery. He was part Pied Piper, part academic philosopher, and part agitator who gravitated toward the innermost circles of power and influence in both Europe and the Muslim world. At various points in his career, he was a confidant of the Ottoman sultan, a fixture at the court of the Qajar shah in Persia, a gadfly to the salon intellectuals of Paris, and a dinner guest of the Churchills in London. Like Socrates, he was known as much for the fame of his pupils as he was for his own teachings, and Abduh was his Plato.

Afghani had one creed: Muslim societies had fallen behind the West because they had strayed from the core strength of Islam. Unlike all other world religions, Afghani claimed, Islam celebrated science and reason. That was what had allowed the Abbasids and other dynasties to flourish, and it was why Muslim societies had been successful in the past. Over the centuries, Muslims had lost sight of that. They had closed the door to innovation and become antagonistic to change, with the result that the West had raced ahead. The so-called traditionalists who opposed Western science were, Afghani believed, forsaking the Islamic tradition. True Muslims should embrace the science, technology, and social advancements of the Western states and build on them. Then the community would be whole and strong once again, and a new golden age would begin.

These ideas were not only radical in the Muslim world; they were a direct challenge to the prevailing winds in Europe. In France especially, increasing numbers of the bourgeoisie were indifferent and often hostile to religion, and to organized religions such as Catholicism most of all. The intellectuals of the day, epitomized by the brilliant, arrogant scholar Ernest Renan, believed that all religions were antithetical to innovation, and that religion stood in the way of human progress.

In 1883, a series of electric debates took place between Renan and Afghani. The two men engaged in a multiround duel over the question

of whether Islam was compatible with science. In many ways, their dialogue was a latter-day re-creation of the tense rhetorical battles that Christians, Jews, and Muslims had fought in front of courtiers in Córdoba and Baghdad centuries earlier. But there was one crucial difference: Renan did not defend Christianity; he denounced it, and he denounced Islam. Renan was an avatar for the modern age, an ardent acolyte of reason, a devotee of logic, and an enemy of what he thought was cant and superstition in the guise of religion and faith. A onetime seminary student, he was fluent in Hebrew, versed in the Quran and had devoted years to the study of the Orient. He admired the Persians, but had little respect for what Arabs had wrought over the centuries, and that added to his antipathy for the deleterious effects of organized religion. In his view, the philosophical achievements of the Muslim world during the Middle Ages were in spite of, not because of, Islam. The Persians had done better than the Arabs, he believed, because they were less in thrall to orthodox Islam. Renan held that no religion nurtured the scientific spirit. No religion could afford to, because science was based on the limitless capacity of human reason and intellect while religion rested on the infinite power of God the creator.

Afghani had a different perspective. While he acknowledged that in all religions there was tension between science and faith, he saw Islam as unique in its embrace of reason and its warmth toward science. Drawing on a corpus of works from eighth-century Baghdad through the flowering of medieval Andalusia, Afghani's argument was buttressed by evidence. He stressed that the great philosophers of Islam—Ibn Sina, Ibn Rushd, Ibn Arabi—were often mystics as well. They used reason, and they were also men of faith, who submitted to the mystery and power of God even as they employed logic to probe the meaning of his creation. If Muslims were to meet the challenge of the West, Afghani declared, they would have to reclaim their lost inheritance.

Afghani had many disciples, but none more skilled than Muhammad Abduh. While Afghani roamed restlessly throughout the Muslim world, Abduh dedicated himself to the cause of Egypt. Afghani, wise in so many ways, allowed himself to be used as an ornament by rulers such as the Ottoman sultan, who pointed to his presence at their courts as proof of how forward-looking they were yet had little intention of putting his more radically democratic ideas into practice. Afghani believed that the most important ingredient for change was education, and that only by

taking the curriculum out of the hands of the hidebound *ulama* and putting progressives like him in charge could a new generation be trained to grapple with the West and implement real reform. Abduh took up that mantle in Egypt. By the end of his life he had some success in turning those ideas into a reality, but not without considerable anguish at the failure of the nationalist movement in the early 1880s, and not before being exiled by the British for five years.

When Abduh returned to Egypt, he reestablished himself at Al-Azhar, and then emerged as one of the most serious, and influential, reformers during the long years of British rule. Like Afghani, Abduh took as his starting point Quran 13:11, which states, "Verily God does not change what is in a people, until they change what is in themselves." Generations of exegesis had taken the verse to mean that mankind has free will. With free will comes reason, and reason is integral to progress. Abduh, who had witnessed the absence of progress firsthand when he was taught a curriculum at Al-Azhar that had been frozen for centuries, believed that ignorance was a greater threat to Egypt and the Arab and Muslim world than the West was. "If we continue to follow the method of blind acceptance," he wrote, "no one will be left who holds this religion. But if we return to that reason to which God directs us in this verse and other verses like it, there is hope that we can revive our religion." And that religion, Abduh continued in other writings, "may be counted a true friend of science, a stimulus into the secrets of the universe, and an appeal to respected established truths, and we may rely upon it in cultivating our spirits and reforming our actions."

Like his teacher Afghani, Abduh did not limit his aspirations to one country. Afghani has been called, rightly or not, one of the creators of pan-Islam, a movement that has been tainted as an early-twentieth-century version of Islamic fundamentalism. But where Afghani tried to spark a reformation everywhere, Abduh diligently pursued reform in Egypt as an incubator for the rest of the Muslim world. His faith in reason, as it were, led him to excoriate the structure of the Egyptian state that had evolved under both the Ottomans and Muhammad Ali and his heirs. Law had been based on the whim of the ruler, supported by a placid religious and judicial establishment. If Egypt was to change, Abduh believed, it would need not only a better education system, but a legal system that was more powerful than any one man.

Abduh's dedication and erudition impressed the British administra-

tion, and late in his life, in 1899, he was made grand mufti of Egypt, in charge of all religious law and jurisprudence. In that position, he revised the curriculum for training civil servants and imams alike. He attempted to reorient Egypt away from blind adherence to tradition and toward a reborn society that fused reason, science, and the Quran. Though he did not fulfill his own high ambitions, he did create a new way, one that demanded internal reform based on laws that honored the Islamic tradition but were in harmony with the modern world. That in turn was to be the foundation of a modern Egypt led by men trained to think, to question, and to learn, who not only accepted but fostered innovation, and who nurtured the spirit of scientific inquiry that had always been part of the glory and strength of Islam.

Though Abduh saw Egypt as an important test case, his ultimate goal was the renaissance of all Muslim societies. Unlike Afghani, he was less focused on active resistance to the West than he was on awakening the dormant spirit of Islam. In his reading of history, the past success of Islam was the product not just of fearless inquiry but of toleration for religious minorities. Abduh's vision embraced Christians and Jews as equal partners who had been vital to Muslim success in the past, and would be essential to success in the future. In short, his Islam not only was compatible with the modern ethos articulated by the West; it also predated it.

Science, military prowess, respect for law, and liberalism were among the cornerstones of Western culture in the nineteenth century, which along with more than a dollop of greed and rapaciousness led to the dominance of Europe relative to the rest of the world. But Europe's great weakness, Abduh believed, was that it had created a false tension between religion and modernity. According to Abduh's reading of the past, Muslim societies had once surpassed the West because that tension did not exist in the centuries after Muhammad. Unlike post-Enlightenment Europeans, the *Salaf* (the elders of the early community of Muslim believers) had prospered because they combined reason with faith. That meant that modern Egyptians, as the vanguard of Muslim states, had the potential not only to hold its own, but to set an example by adding religion to the mix instead of banishing it from the public sphere.

That, at least, was Abduh's dream. But he knew that until Egypt and other Muslim states did the hard work of wrenching themselves out of their stupor, they would follow the West and not lead the world. And as

long as Muslim societies remained mired in ossified traditions, they would invite scorn and condescension. Abduh felt the sting of British disdain, but he understood that it was a natural and appropriate reaction to Egyptian backwardness. He reserved his most stringent criticisms not for the conquerors but for the failings in his own society that made it unable to resist Western encroachment.

Centuries earlier, with the passing of al-Ghazali and others, the Muslims of the Near East and North Africa had gradually retreated from interpreting the Quran and the traditions of the Prophet. Abduh represented a break from that unfortunate legacy. He claimed the right to interpret Islam and adapt it to the circumstances of his time, and he did so believing that this was the birthright of every Muslim and every human being. The fact that interpretation had been discouraged was the failing of Muslims and Muslim societies, but not indicative of the true Islam of Muhammad, his companions, and those who immediately followed them. Understanding that human beings were weak and prone to error, Abduh treated his countrymen with compassion rather than contempt, and regarded the Christians and Jews in his midst as people worthy of the respect that he believed the Quran demanded. In spite of the ossified culture of Egypt and of much of the Arab world, he rarely doubted that progress was possible, and that a new era of peace and prosperity was within reach so long as the Arab world in general and Egypt in particular recognized that they had lost their way and began the process of rebirth.

Abduh set the tone for a generation of activists and intellectuals who helped define Arab nationalism in the first part of the twentieth century. Slowly, however, his legacy was distorted by followers who were less convinced that the modern trappings of science and European liberalism were compatible with Islam and Arab independence. Other Muslim countries, Turkey and Iran among them, grappled with similar issues and experienced similar fissures between those who envisioned a future of peaceful rivalry with the West and those who resisted the changes that the rise of Europe had forced on the world. Some became bitter and angry that reforms did not yield immediate benefits, and as the West continued to dominate the economic, political, and military destiny of much of the Muslim world in the first decades of the twentieth century, that bitterness generated darker versions of Abduh's teachings. Abduh believed that the *Salaf* had been ecumenical and tolerant, but others saw

them instead as a tight-knit community of believers whose strength lay in the rejection of the message given to the People of the Book and in their willingness to silence any who challenged the words of the Quran and the hadith. In fact, within Muslim communities, people known in the West as "fundamentalist" are often referred to as *salafiyya*, because they look to the founders of Islam for answers about how to confront the challenges of the present.[1]

Abduh would have been dismayed by the twentieth-century evolution of the *salafiyya*. He vigorously opposed what the British government had done in Egypt and elsewhere, but he warmly embraced the English and French friends he made in Cairo and in the capitals of Europe. One of his closest companions was Wilfrid Scawen Blunt, an Englishman who devoted his life to fighting against imperialism and to defending Islam to a skeptical English public. Blunt was a full-fledged member of the British ruling class, yet he was outside the mainstream. Having married the granddaughter of Lord Byron, he was drawn to the mysteries of the desert and the esoteric, and he shared with his wife an insatiable yearning for something other than what England had to offer. Seeking adventure, they shunned London society and spent nearly a decade riding their horses through the most desolate tracts of the African Sahara and the Arabian Najd, where they were guests of Ibn Rashid, whose family was then locked in a struggle with the Saudis and their Wahhabi followers. The Blunts also lived with the bedouin of the Euphrates in central Iraq, and they wrote a book about their experiences that was avidly read by the English public.

Among the bedouin, Wilfrid Blunt found what he had been looking for. Disillusioned by imperial Britain, he romanticized the moral code of the bedouin, their purity of faith, and their lack of hypocrisy. The bedouin were a society of merit, who through Blunt's rose-tinted vision offered "the purest example of democracy to be found in the world—perhaps the only one in which the watchwords of liberty, equality, and fraternity are more than a name." Their Islam had not been sullied by the ostentatious displays that marked the High Anglicanism of Blunt's England. While most of his contemporaries compared the Arabs to Europe and found them culturally deficient, Blunt concluded that it was the Europeans who were deficient. The Arabs may have temporarily fallen behind the West, but for that Blunt blamed the Ottomans. He believed that once the empire finally collapsed, the Arabs could restore

their caliphate and rise again as a beacon of freedom and creativity that would put the West to shame.

In 1880, Blunt visited Egypt and met Abduh. Through Abduh, he was drawn into the nationalist movement that ultimately culminated in the British occupation, an event that Blunt did everything he could to prevent and that devastated him when it finally took place. The scorn that most of his countrymen felt toward Arabs and Islam was a disgrace, Blunt wrote on the eve of the invasion. Islam, he said, "must be treated as no vain superstition but a true religion, true inasmuch as it is a form of the worship of the one true God in whom Europe, in spite of her modern reason, still believes. As such it is entitled to whatever credit we may give true religions of prolonged vitality and while admitting the eternal truth of Christianity for ourselves, we may believe that in the Arabian mind... Islam too will prove eternal." He tried to persuade the British prime minister William Gladstone that Egypt should be allowed to manage its own destiny and that it was contrary to Gladstone's liberal creed and against the true tenets of the Christian faith to sanction an occupation of a country undertaken solely to appease European creditors. But Gladstone, anxious about any potential threat to the sea lanes from Suez to India, did not agree.[2]

The searing events that culminated in the British invasion cemented a bond between Abduh and Blunt that would span decades. Blunt continued to pound at successive British governments for the follies of imperialism, while Abduh worked within the system established by the British protectorate in Egypt and campaigned tirelessly for educational and legal reform. Both were critics of their respective societies, and in many ways, they were mirror images: Blunt the Englishman who rejected the bombastic self-assurance of imperialism and railed against the hypocrisy of a liberal society ruling an illiberal empire; Abduh the esteemed shaikh who rejected the moribund tradition handed down to him and demanded that his society remember what it had forgotten.

MERCHANTS, MISSIONARIES, AND MISFITS

DURING THE LAST decades of the nineteenth century, Blunt watched with dismay as the British Empire grew in scope and in arrogance. The old policy of intervention only when absolutely essential gave to way to

intervention everywhere. The reason for the shift was the competition between the states of Europe. An emerging Germany after 1870 had altered the balance cultivated by the Congress of Vienna, and the major powers—England, France, Russia, Germany, Holland, and Italy—rushed to plant their flags on the remaining unclaimed parts of the globe, from sub-Saharan Africa to Southeast Asia and the Near East.

The Ottoman Empire continued to play one European state off the next, manipulating the hopes and fears of each of the contenders, but by the early part of the twentieth century, the Balkan provinces had declared their independence, North Africa was directly controlled by either France or England, Arabia was largely autonomous, the Caucasus was under the sway of Russia, and French influence in Syria and Lebanon made even collecting taxes difficult at best. In Africa, France and England nearly came to blows in the Saharan hinterland, while in southern Africa, the Germans tried to gain a symbolic foothold to demonstrate to the world that they too were a global empire. Even the United States, which had traditionally confined its expansionist ambitions to the Western Hemisphere, acquired its own colony in the Philippines at the expense of Spain in 1898.

Blunt was part of a vocal minority who believed that imperialism was not just wreaking havoc on the globe but destroying England and its cherished liberalism. In his eyes, the mores of imperialism were incompatible with the ethics of liberalism, and any country that used brute force to control the destiny of others would soon be incapable of nurturing the values of democracy and liberty in its own citizens. His ideal of mutual respect between cultures clashed with the views of many of his countrymen that Britain was superior not just militarily and economically but morally as well. Because he moved in elite circles, his words were listened to, but rarely heeded. He was the conscience of his class, a reminder to an increasingly self-satisfied imperial elite that power can corrupt.

Blunt was also a member of a select club of Europeans who were drawn to the Arab world and to Islam. The pull of the desert was lost on most of his contemporaries, but not all. The known history of the nineteenth century paints a stark picture of European conquest and disdain for the conquered, but the forgotten history includes a panoply of other reactions and interactions. It may have been the case that few Europeans traveled far from home, that even fewer traveled beyond the continent to

the other shores of the Mediterranean, and that those who did by and large looked down on foreign cultures. But some fell in love, others felt complete, and still others were swept away with awe and respect for the alien societies they encountered. Blunt was one of them; Sir Richard Burton was another.

Burton's relationship to the Arabs was fraught, but so was his relationship with everyone else. He not only managed to pass as a Muslim in Mecca but provided the romantics back home with a tingling erotic translation of the *Arabian Nights*. Blunt and Burton's fraternity included not only eccentrics but also members of the elite such as the young Benjamin Disraeli. Descended from a Jewish family and struggling to find his place in English society, Disraeli looked on the Near East and Palestine as a realm of wonder, danger, and promise. Before entering politics, he penned several novels where East met West, and he might have merited a footnote as an author had he not risen to the heights as Queen Victoria's prime minister. In addition to Disraeli and Burton, the cohort included intrepid travelers such as Gifford Palgrave, Charles Doughty, Lucy Duff-Gordon, and anonymous seekers and misfits who were never comfortable in the parlors of London or Paris but were at home in the souks and oases of the Arab world.

Similar souls could be found in France, though their focus was not just the Near East but also the North African coast stretching from Morocco to Tunisia. Germans and Italians came late to the imperial party, but German universities excelled at producing scholars who could read and translate the classics of Arabic and Persian literature. They studied what Muslim societies had produced during their heyday and parsed the Quran as well as the rich philosophical and cultural heritage that had defined medieval Baghdad and Spain and that, as Abduh so acutely recognized, had begun to fade from memory in the contemporary Muslim world. Often, these "Orientalists," as they were called, took a condescending attitude toward their subject. The nineteenth-century imbalance between Muslim societies and the West was taken as proof of a fatal flaw in Islam. By carefully analyzing the central texts of Islam, the Orientalists hoped to solve the puzzle of why the Muslim world had fallen so far behind the West.[3]

The question was perfectly reasonable. It was the same question that reformers in Istanbul, Cairo, and Tehran asked. And for the most part, the answers suggested by both Westerners and reformers in the Muslim

world were the same: Muslim states, at their height, had encouraged interpretation as well as adaptation of the Quran and hadith to the circumstances of the present. When those societies turned away from inquiry and shunned science in favor of unquestioned acceptance of the authority of the past, they lost touch with the spark that had made them so successful. The result was stagnation. Some Orientalists, like Renan, indicted Islam as a whole, but others drew a distinction between vibrant, classical Islam and what came later. These scholars focused on the conundrum of what went wrong in the Muslim world. While their immediate influence was on a relatively small group of like-minded students, their views were adopted by statesmen and diplomats, who had a more direct impact on the interaction between Western states and the Muslim world. In fact, one of the indirect consequences of Orientalism was the Arab Revolt in 1916, whose celebrated protagonist was T. E. Lawrence, made famous by the American journalist Lowell Thomas as "Lawrence of Arabia."

The "Orientalist" legacy was more than one of patronizing attitudes and flawed policies. Some scholars went native, and like Blunt became ardent critics of the West and avid defenders of the virtues of Islam and of Muslims. One of the strangest and most colorful of these was the improbably named William Marmaduke Pickthall. He was born in Suffolk, England, in 1875, and attended the famed Harrow school, which he hated. The only consolation of his wretched experience there was the beginning of a lifelong friendship with another student who suffered through its Darwinian rigors, Winston Churchill. Pickthall lost himself in languages but couldn't find an adequate Arabic teacher, so as soon as he reached eighteen and the end of Harrow, he set off for Port Said on the northern end of the Suez Canal. As it had been for Blunt, it was love at first sight.

Pickthall found a tutor and began reading the *Arabian Nights* in the original. He was enthralled. Recounting how he felt when he read the stories of Harun al-Rashid, he wrote that the old Arabic revealed to him "the daily life of Damascus, Jerusalem, Aleppo, Cairo, and the other cities as I found it in the nineteenth century. What struck me, even in its decay and poverty, was the joyousness of that life compared with anything that I had seen in Europe. The people seemed quite independent of our cares of life, our anxious clutching after wealth, our fear of death." As he traveled through the Near East, he confronted a society that

seemed to him a perfect mix of community and individualism, and that practiced a truer form of democracy than what passed for it in Europe. Where most of his contemporaries saw decadence and decay, he saw personal liberties, freedom from the ominous hand of the state, and genuine piety. After a near-conversion experience in Damascus, he returned to England just as the century was ending, wrote a novel, and became a literary celebrity with his tales of the Orient.

Events in the Ottoman Empire drew Pickthall back. He was appalled when he heard his countrymen railing against the "infidel Turks" during successive wars that were fought between the Ottomans and the newly independent Balkan states before World War I. He was equally disillusioned by the Gallipoli campaign waged by his old schoolmate Churchill against the Ottomans during the war. In 1917, he renounced Christianity and very publicly converted to Islam. He went to India to support Mahatma Gandhi, and then began work on a translation of the Quran, which he published in 1930, a few years before his death. By then, he had become well known in India and throughout the Muslim world as a convert who spoke out against the injustices of European rule and who defended Islam against its many Western critics. Pickthall applauded the honesty and moral purity that he observed in Muslim communities, and was angered by the hypocrisy of the British. The West, he believed, claimed a moral high ground based on the principles of liberty, but then flagrantly violated those principles in the way it governed its empires and treated their people. For Pickthall, it wasn't Islam that needed reform; it was the West.[4]

Disenchanted souls like Blunt and Pickthall were not the only ones drawn to the Muslim world. There were also merchants who saw the Near East as a land of opportunity to make a fortune. Many of them were undoubtedly adjuncts to imperialism, interested in exerting control and extracting what they could. Businessmen, however, tended to be indifferent to ethnicity and religion and sought only to cement contracts. Europeans often relied on Christians in the Near East to act as intermediaries, but in other parts of the Muslim world—Algeria and Persia for instance, or northern Nigeria—they partnered with Muslims. Religion almost never intruded on these commercial interactions, and local Muslim merchants did not hesitate to work with European Christian businessmen. If an English aristocrat wanted to buy horses in Egypt, he could find a dozen Egyptian horse traders; if a French concern

wanted carpets from Isfahan, Tabriz, or Van, it had only to demonstrate its willingness to buy in order to find many who wanted to sell.

As Europe became more involved in the Arab and Ottoman world, those regions became more tightly tied to the continental economy. In Lebanon and Syria, the increased influence of France in the second half of the nineteenth century was an economic boon. Textile and silk merchants and manufacturers enjoyed a burst of demand for their products. Beirut became an international center for the cultivation of silk pods and the production of fine silk thread, and the riots of 1860 only hastened the economic integration of the Levant with Europe. The British occupation of Egypt in 1882 also led to a long period of economic development. The rewards were unevenly distributed, but the country nonetheless saw the influx of considerable foreign capital. A similar process occurred in the still-independent Ottoman Empire, which late in the century under the autocratic and crafty Sultan Abdul Hamid II courted a rising Germany as a counterweight to France, England, and Russia. German banks worked closely with Ottoman officials to build the Baghdad Railway connecting the provinces of Iraq to central Turkey and Istanbul.[5]

It wasn't just Western merchants who ventured forth. In Beirut and in Cairo, American missionaries opened schools that shaped educational life for decades. The school that became the American University in Beirut was founded as the Syrian Protestant College in the 1870s by a group of Presbyterians and Congregationalists under the aegis of the aptly named Daniel Bliss. His missionary impulse was augmented by his zeal to educate. "We do not aim," Bliss said at the end of his career in 1904, "to make Maronites, or Greeks, or Catholics, or Protestants, or Jews, or Muslims, but we do aim to make perfect men, ideal men, God-like men, after the model of Jesus against whose moral character no man ever has said or can say aught." His creed was a liberal Christianity that championed religious freedom, and while he was adamant about the necessity of belief in a higher power, he was indifferent about what form the worship of that higher power took. "We wish every student to be religious," he proclaimed, but he did not force his students to be religious in any particular way.

The spirit of religious tolerance governed not only the curriculum but the choice of the school's name. When members of the board of trustees proposed that the name be changed to Beirut Christian Univer-

sity, Bliss's successors vetoed the suggestion, on the grounds that using the term "Christian" in the title "seemed to provide unnecessary emphasis on religious differences which might prove unfortunate." While the school never lost touch with its missionary roots, it always attracted a mix of Jews, Muslims, and Christians to study on the campus. There was occasional friction between them, but the only major complaint of the Jewish and Muslim students was that university officials were less than accommodating about respecting dietary restrictions in the choice of food served at the cafeteria. Even as sectarian tensions increased in the early twentieth century, the American University remained a haven. It set an example for toleration and coexistence that resisted successive waves of conflict in Lebanon but could not withstand the 1975 civil war that engulfed the entire country.[6]

Beirut was one melting pot, but perhaps the most extraordinary crossroads was Alexandria. This ancient capital of Egypt, founded by Alexander the Great and ruled by the Greek Ptolemies until their last descendant, Cleopatra, cuddled up with an asp and died, had dwindled to a cultural and economic backwater by the early nineteenth century. Then it began to stir under Muhammad Ali. As he looked to the West to reinvigorate his country, Alexandria connected Egypt to the ports of Europe. Foreigners flooded the districts just off the quays, and the city became a bustling hodgepodge of languages and cultures, home to a diverse assortment of Muslims, Christians, and Jews united by their common interest in lucre. Under the ambitious Khedive Ismail, Alexandria became even more central to the financial and economic life of the eastern Mediterranean, though its bombardment by the English navy in 1882 destroyed some of the gracious mansions lining the shore. The economy soon recovered, and Alexandria attracted bankers, merchants, artisans, archeologists, and wanderers who were drawn by the chaotic rhythms of a city planted partly in Europe, partly in Egypt, and fully in neither.

For a brief few decades, Alexandria was home to a permissive culture that winked and nodded at the offbeat sexual proclivities of many of its expatriate denizens. At the old century's end and the new century's beginning, it attracted a literary crowd that included most famously the Greek Constantine Cavafy, the American Lawrence Durrell, and the very British E. M. Forster. Like other cosmopolitan port cities, it was

both part of and separate from its hinterland. Arabic was spoken, but so were Greek, French, Armenian, English, Italian, and Turkish. The call to prayer could be heard from the mosques along the shore and inland, but so could the ringing of bells from the churches, and the blowing the ram's horn on the Jewish holiday of Rosh Hashanah from one or more of the city's synagogues.

The locals were no more homogeneous than the expatriates and themselves formed a crazy quilt of ethnicity and religion. The Muslims were mostly Sunni, but the Christians represented almost every denomination. There were Greek Orthodox, Syrian Orthodox, Copts, Armenians, Latin Uniates, Greek Catholics, Maronites, Armenian Catholics, Presbyterians, Anglicans, and even a few members of the Church of Scotland. These Christian sects were usually friendly or indifferent to Muslims and Jews but could be quite antagonistic toward one another. The Copts said—correctly—that they had been there the longest and so deserved some sort of respect and primacy, but few of the other sects cared about tenure. Meanwhile, there was also a wealthy Jewish community that could trace its roots back to the Hellenistic period and claimed, with some justification, to be one of the oldest continuous Jewish settlements in the world. And though the Jews, Christians, and Muslims of Alexandria were aware of their sects and subsects, they all worked to extract what they could from a world dominated by Europeans. They were intrepid and entrepreneurial, and looked to a future where people and nations would be judged on what they did and how much they earned rather than on what they believed or the god they worshiped.[7]

ΠΑΤΙΟΠΑL HOPEꟅ ΑΠD DREΑϻꟅ

AS THE NINETEENTH century came to a close, Europeans had exported not only technology but ideas, and the belief in progress had taken root almost everywhere. At times, it was an awkward graft, especially in Eastern societies that had a less linear sense of time and history. But in many parts of the Muslim world, it was an attractive formula. As Abduh understood, one of the strengths of classical Muslim states was their ability to evolve. The notion of "progress," if not the word itself, was embedded in their culture. And so when most of the Muslim world

fell under the direct or indirect sway of Europe in the nineteenth century, there was no shortage of people who believed that change was possible.

When the reformers looked ahead, they envisioned a day when their countries would be able to stand with Europe when they wished, and against Europe if they had to. In the interim, they recognized that the playing field wasn't level, and they sought European financial, intellectual, and military advice and assistance. But even as they learned from the West, they knew that there might be conflict before there could be genuine coexistence. Until Europe ceased to rule, there could be no meeting of independent equals. Preferably, conflict would be minimal or nonexistent. In the face of pressure, protests, and resistance movements, the British and French would do what was prudent and withdraw. After that, there would still be competition, of course, but it would not need to take the form of war. Instead, the Ottoman elite, the rulers of Egypt who worked with the English occupation, and others looked to a time when the Muslim world and the West would trade and exchange ideas as equals. The first step was internal reform; the next would be to reclaim full independence.

The dream of progress, therefore, did not mean a passive acceptance of European rule. Quite the opposite. Progress for the reformers meant the end of European hegemony and the restoration of full independence. The humiliations of imperial rule were real. Lord Cromer, who almost single-handedly controlled what went on in Egypt from 1882 until early in the twentieth century, was undisguised in his contempt for the country. He treated its inhabitants as wayward children in need of instruction. "What Egypt required most of all," he said in 1883, "was order and good government. Perhaps... liberty would follow afterwards. No one but a dreamy theorist could imagine that the natural order of things could be reversed and that liberty could first be accorded to the poor ignorant representatives of the Egyptian people, and that the latter would then be able to evolve order out of chaos."[8]

Even those who agonized about the problems in their societies were repelled by these patronizing attitudes. Educated, cultivated Egyptians chafed at being treated like errant children. Who were the British, they mused, to lecture us about religious tolerance and liberty when Copts, Muslims, and Jews had lived side by side for fourteen hundred years "in the greatest unity and harmony"? Who were they to tell Egypt about

civilization when the inhabitants of the Nile Valley had created a society thousands of years before the English had even learned to write? Admiration for what Europe could offer sat side by side with indignation about what Europeans often did offer.

These were the dominant themes, but, of course, some followed their own muses and approached these encounters from a different perspective. There were the voices crying in the wilderness like Blunt and Pickthall who believed that the hypocrisy of the West was a more damning weakness than any of the problems in the Muslim world. There were merchants on both sides who had no interest in these larger ideas. And there were missionaries who worked not to convert Muslims but to improve relations between faiths and cultures and who spent decades trying to build bridges.

In the final decades of the nineteenth century, however, nationalism complicated matters even further. In his book *Imagined Communities*, Benedict Anderson defines nationalism as a collective act of imagination. A nation "is imagined because the members of even the smallest nation will never know most of their fellow members, meet them or even hear of them, yet in the minds of each lives the image of their communion." The concept of nation is a product of European history. With the development of mass printing in the sixteenth century, individuals slowly began to imagine nations that were distinct from the religious community and the ruling dynasty.[9] As nationalism gathered momentum in the nineteenth century, organized religion in Europe declined. As God and the church faded, or were banished, from public life in Europe, the cult of the nation took their place.

Nationalism became a pivotal force in Europe and throughout the world. Bulgarian and Serbian nationalism led to independence from the Ottoman Empire in the final decades of the nineteenth century, and in turn helped launch a wave of Turkish nationalism that resulted in a cycle of violence in the Balkans. Inside the Ottoman Empire, Turkish nationalism became increasingly prominent at the end of the reign of Sultan Abdul Hamid II. As the Ottoman reforms failed to make the empire an equal competitor, and as North Africa, Egypt, and Lebanon became provinces of the West, a new generation of Turks distinguished Turkishness from Ottomanness. Disillusioned by Abdul Hamid, a group calling themselves the "Young Turks," many of whom were in exile in Paris, dedicated themselves to the cause of the Turkish nation. In their

reading, Ottoman greatness was Turkish greatness, and the Arab provinces were simply areas that had been ruled and acquired by Turkish rulers. This revision of the Ottoman past, though it erased the rich legacy of multiethnic and multireligious cooperation, took root in Istanbul and in Turkey itself. The Turkish nationalists did what all nationalists do: they defined an "us" based on language, ethnicity, a shared past, and a common religion. And they defined a "them" who spoke different languages, had a different past, and were not only distinct but lesser and even inferior.

Nationalism accelerated the breakup of the Ottoman Empire. The old *millet*s began to think of themselves as independent nations, as did many of the provinces. Armenians demanded Armenian autonomy; Egyptians fought for Egyptian independence; and the Arabs of Syria agitated for an Arab nation. These ideas did not develop simultaneously. Egyptian nationalism emerged before the Arab nationalism of the early twentieth century. Nonetheless, the concept of nationalism took root almost everywhere, from Morocco and Algeria in the west to Iran in the east.

The process was not linear, and for many years, nationalism was a phenomenon confined to the elite. A fellah working the fields in Upper Egypt would not have spoken of an Egyptian nation any more than a Turkish farmer in central Anatolia would have thought of himself as a citizen of a place called Turkey. To confuse matters further, there were competing nationalisms. There were Ottoman nationalists, who argued that the empire, with its shared history, actually constituted a nation-state. They had limited success convincing others of that, but their campaign was no more or less futile than that of elites in the Austro-Hungarian Empire trying to do the same. There was also a group of Islamic nationalists who combined the modern European idea of a nation-state with the Islamic ideal of the *umma* to argue that there was a transnational Muslim community that had been fragmented for centuries but that should be reconstituted under the leadership of a new caliph.

Later on, nationalism would reveal its darker side, of ethnic purity and state control of what citizens said and thought. At first, however, nationalism was allied to the ideals of progress and linked to the sense that Muslim societies were changing for the better. An independent, sovereign nation was hailed as the fulfillment of Muslim hopes and dreams,

and independent states would be the reward for the arduous work of reform. The beginning of the twentieth century was heralded in Europe as the dawn of a better age of mankind, and that sentiment permeated the Muslim world. Just as the prevailing attitude in Europe was that war and disease would disappear in the twentieth century, it was widely believed in the Muslim world that the twentieth century would see an end to imperialism and the revival of Muslim societies. That would require effort and would not come about without a struggle, but there was optimism that everything would eventually work out.

The dream of a renaissance after reform was secular. Educated, elite Muslims did not see a prominent role for religion in public life. Nonetheless, their dreams were grounded in a past that had demonstrated the power of a covenant and the promise that if the word of God was heeded, earthly rewards would follow. The promise of the new century was similar, except that the terms were different. Instead of listening to the word of God, Muslims had to embrace the tenets of the modern world—science, innovation, education—in order to reap earthly rewards. The first decades of the century seemed to offer proof that with reform would come a rebirth. For a while, the vision of the reformers was vindicated—but only for a while.

Hope and Despair

A T THE BEGINNING of the twentieth century, religion as a central force in the fate of nations was almost nonexistent. It was commonly believed, at least by the educated and the elite, that religion would soon fade away, to survive perhaps as a quaint tradition kept alive out of sentimentality and habit but no more part of the modern world than magic and witchcraft. Insofar as Muslims embraced the attitudes and manners of the West, they shared similar sentiments.

As we now know, the death of religion was prematurely announced, and the story of the twentieth century is one of retreat followed by a regrouping and an advance, not so much in Europe, but in many parts of the world. Just as the rise of nationalism went hand in hand with the decline in organized religion, the failures of nationalism contributed to a new religious revival.

Failure is, of course, always defined in relation to expectations. Had the expectations been more modest, the story of the twentieth century would have been different. But nationalism and modernity embodied utopian dreams of a world without physical or spiritual want. They held out the promise that nations would be able to satisfy both the material needs of their citizens and the intangible ones as well. The nation would provide not just security but meaning and purpose. That was a tall order, and even if it was not bound to fail, it did.

A millennium of success, punctuated by challenges such as the Crusades and the Mongol invasions, had conditioned much of the Muslim world to believe that those who embraced Islam would in return be

given power relative to those who rejected it. The tolerance that Muslim communities exhibited toward the People of the Book went hand in hand with that power, and it stood in sharp contrast to the intolerance that Christian societies displayed toward Jews and Muslims during the same centuries. Given that Christian societies were rarely secure in their power until a few hundred years ago, it's hard not to conclude that security is a precondition for tolerance. There are exceptions, including the early Muslims in Medina in relation to their non-Muslim neighbors. Theirs was tolerance born of expediency and weakness. But in general, tolerance is often a by-product of strength and an expression of confidence.

Throughout the nineteenth and early twentieth centuries, Muslim societies were anything but secure in the face of Western encroachments and expansion. Yet with the exception of Damascus in 1860, that didn't lead to intolerance. In fact, the reform movements trumpeted coexistence and protected religious diversity. Not only the *Tanzimat* reforms of the Ottoman Empire but the various constitutions written throughout the Muslim world all enshrined religious toleration as a cornerstone of the modern state.

This nineteenth- and early-twentieth-century spirit of tolerance is another overlooked chapter of history. In the West, the prevailing image of Muslim societies is that, at best, they discriminated against non-Muslims and at worst they treated other religions with outright hatred.[1] The forgetting of the past is just as acute within Muslim countries. In the late twentieth and early twenty-first centuries, the principle of tolerance for Christians and Jews has been denounced by extremists, and Muslim defenders of coexistence have had a difficult time being heard. That is in contrast to centuries of Islamic history, when respect had been so woven into the moral framework that no one thought to challenge it.

But however much the ideologies of intolerance have come to dominate the public realm, that does not mean that most people are intolerant. Societies have public faces that do not necessarily reflect what the people who inhabit them think and feel. Even in the contentious modern age, the quiet norm in the Muslim world has been a tacit acceptance of religious minorities and a continued willingness to work with the West when that is perceived as beneficial. That reality, less dramatic than angry sermons meant to stoke passions, has been almost completely

obscured by fundamentalists who see the reforms of the nineteenth and twentieth century as a long march away from Islam and away from everything that had once made Muslims powerful.

There was nothing inevitable about public abandonment of tolerance and coexistence. Even as the West invaded and occupied parts of the Muslim world, the initial response was to find ways to accommodate and cooperate. There was no widespread call for jihad against the West in the early twentieth century. There were calls for a restored caliphate and for reforms that would generate an Arab or Muslim renaissance, but not for war against the West. And as long as the promise of independence and revival stayed alive, most Muslim societies distinguished between illegitimate Western domination, which was to be resisted, and continued coexistence between Muslims, Christians and Jews, which was to be preserved.

THE ARAB REVOLT AND
THE BALFOUR DECLARATION

TWO EVENTS profoundly shaped how Muslims, Christians, and Jews interacted in the twentieth century. One was the Arab Revolt against the Ottomans, which was supported and encouraged by the British. The other was the creation of a Jewish state in Palestine, also supported and encouraged (at least initially) by the British. Both had their origins in World War I.[2]

In many ways, World War I was the direct result of the erosion of the Ottoman Empire and the outbreak of more virulent strains of nationalism. In the decades leading up to the assassination of the Archduke Franz Ferdinand in Sarajevo on June 28, 1914, the Balkans were a cauldron of nationalist zeal. The balance between the new Balkan states was continually disrupted by the powers of Europe, which treated them as pawns to be used and sacrificed. The Ottoman Empire was roiled by a struggle between Turkish nationalists who wanted to retrench and redefine the empire as a Turkish state and Ottoman nationalists who wanted to regroup and recapture lost territories. In the Balkans, the Russians aggressively asserted their claim to be the protector of Slavic states such as Bulgaria and Serbia, and thereby came into direct conflict with the Habsburg-ruled Austro-Hungarian Empire, which was itself wrestling

to maintain its control in the face of nationalist movements. When Franz Ferdinand, the heir to the Austrian throne, was killed by a Serbian nationalist, a chain reaction led to war between the major European states. Soon after, the Ottoman Empire joined the fray on the side of Germany against the French, Russians, and English.

In the Near East, the war became a contest between England and the Ottomans. The British Empire depended on the Suez Canal to link Britain to its colonies in India and Asia. With the outbreak of hostilities, the British treated Egypt as a strategic center that could serve as a launching point for attacks on the Ottomans. They also viewed Egypt as potentially vulnerable, and redoubled their military presence in the canal zone. The other source of British concern was the three Ottoman provinces of Mosul, Baghdad, and Basra (which would eventually form the modern state of Iraq).

Within the Ottoman Empire, the war provided the government with a rationale for suppressing dissent. Given that most dissent came from ethnic and religious minorities who wanted independence, the result was predictable. Turkish governors dispatched by the cabal then ruling in the sultan's name showed no mercy in the Armenian provinces in eastern Anatolia and in the Arab provinces of Syria and Lebanon. The Ottoman Turks were so concerned about Armenian nationalism that they engineered the forced removal of millions of Armenians, many of whom died or were killed in the process. In the Near East, anyone who had spoken for Arab nationalism or for an independent Arab state faced imprisonment or execution. The empire, which had for centuries epitomized tolerance, became a police state.

In Cairo, a group of British officials set up an Arab Bureau in order to coordinate efforts to support Arabs who wanted to work with the Allies against the Ottomans. One of the junior officers assigned to the bureau was T. E. Lawrence, a young but preternaturally old and already eccentric student of classical Islamic castle architecture who had fallen for the desert. He idolized the bedouins as warriors pure of heart, humble in their faith, and still connected to the natural world. But though he celebrated their culture, his attitudes toward the Arabs he actually encountered were paternalistic and condescending. He saw them as lost souls, who had forgotten what had made them great centuries ago. Condescension aside, his interpretation was not much different than that of Muhammad Abduh or the Arab reformers, but unlike them, he was an

Englishman who didn't believe that the Arabs were capable of claiming their own destiny. Instead, he was convinced that they could move forward to a better future only if the more civilized and advanced England assisted them.

The Arab Revolt of 1916 had several triggers. One was the British struggle against the Ottomans. By sponsoring a revolt of the Arab provinces, the British High Command hoped to distract the Ottoman military and force the empire to direct precious resources to fight in what was otherwise the strategic backwater of Syria and the Arabian Peninsula. Another spark was the dream of national awakening that had been fostered in equal measure by sympathetic Europeans like Wilfrid Blunt and by hardheaded reformers like Afghani, Abduh, and their successors. Though Lawrence was at the outset only a staff officer responsible for implementing policy rather than making it, he fused the contradictory aspirations of the British Empire. As his influence grew, he then embodied the inevitable disillusionment that ensued once those visions ran up against great-power politics. Sent by the Arab Bureau to support Sharif Husayn of Mecca, Lawrence set in motion events that would remake the Near East.

"All men dream," he wrote in later years,

> but not equally. Those who dream by night in the dusty recesses of their minds wake in the day to find that it was vanity: but the dreamers of the day are dangerous men, for they may act their dream with open eyes, to make it possible. This I did. I meant to make a new nation, to restore lost influence, to give twenty millions of Semites the foundations on which to build an inspired dream palace of the national thoughts, and made them play a generous part in events: but when we won, it was charged against me that the British petrol royalties in Mesopotamia were become dubious, and French Colonial policy ruined the Levant.[3]

Lawrence, with his florid prose and profound sense of destiny, became a key player in the Arab Revolt as the liaison between the Arabs and the British. He was also a capable military commander, who favored the hit-and-run tactics that had been perfected over the course of centuries by bedouin raiders. In the eyes of the West, he was the public face

of the Arab Revolt. Lionized as Lawrence of Arabia, he was pictured in bedouin garb and credited with organizing the tribal Arabs, mounted on camels and on horseback, against the stolid and better armed Turkish occupiers.

Yet the Arabs that Lawrence worked with were hardly passive pawns. They had their own plans and their own vision. They treated him as a partner, and in the end they used him just as he used them. By the time he wrote his memoirs, he had become an international celebrity, and the dreams of the Arab Revolt had collided with the postwar realities of the Paris peace conference and the refusal of the European powers to honor their wartime pledges. But in 1916 Lawrence still believed, with a naive, compelling fervor, that he was fighting for the restoration of Arab glory.

The movement was led, at least initially, by Sharif Husayn ibn Ali, who was the head of the Hashemite clan that traced its lineage back to the Prophet Muhammad. Though his family had governed the holy cities of Mecca and Medina for generations, he answered to the Ottomans and paid tribute to the sultan, and he had begun to chafe under the control of Istanbul. He was also facing a challenge from Ibn Saud, who controlled the central part of the Arabian Peninsula and could call on the formidable support of the puritanical Wahhabis. Even before the war, Husayn entered into a dialogue with the British authorities in Cairo, and the letters between him and the British high commissioner, Sir Henry McMahon, set forth the conditions under which he would agree to declare independence.

Husayn wanted more than to rule Arabia. He intended to create an Arab state stretching from Syria to Yemen that would potentially include parts of Iraq as well. Though he needed British military and economic aid in order to mount a credible campaign against the Ottomans, he was a proud, stubborn man with several ambitious sons, and he correctly perceived that he was in a position to make demands. As a result, the British guaranteed that his family would have the right to rule the lands "lying to the west of the districts of Damascus, Homs, Hama, and Aleppo." The terms would come back to haunt not just the British and Husayn, but the Hashemite clan, the Arab world, and the future state of Israel. The text of the letters excluded Lebanon but did not address who would control Palestine. Jerusalem and its environs were symbolically important both to the Ottomans and the British, and

it isn't surprising that their status was left out of discussions between Husayn and McMahon. Yet the omission proved costly to the future of coexistence between the Arab world and the West.

With the parameters established, Husayn announced the Arab Revolt in June 1916. Soon after, he proclaimed himself king of the Arabs. Lawrence later claimed that he designed the military and political strategy adopted by Husayn and his sons, and while he almost certainly overstated his role, he did act as a trusted adviser. Husayn's sons Abdullah, later the first king of Jordan, and Faysal, soon to be the first king of Iraq, both relied on Lawrence's counsel, Faysal most of all. They knew he wanted the same thing for them that they wanted for themselves: an independent Arab nation allied with Great Britain. They saw themselves as walking in the footsteps of the first Arab conquerors, destined to inherit the legacy of Muhammad and the caliphs, their great-grandfathers many times removed. And in their most optimistic moments, preparing for an ambush on a Turkish outpost or readying an assault on the port city of Aqaba, they saw their dreams coming true and believed that the English, represented by Lawrence, were on their side, working for a common goal.

What Lawrence didn't know, or chose not to acknowledge, was that the British had no intention of honoring their promises to Husayn and his family. All may be fair in love and war, but that does not mean that there are no hurt feelings. Husayn, Faysal, and Abdullah led a revolt against the Ottomans at great personal peril, and they expected the British to keep their word. But the British were trying to win a war, and they were willing to make empty promises to gain allies. As important as the Arab Revolt was, it was a minor affair in the greater scheme of things, and less important than the Anglo-French alliance.

The French had their own designs on Lebanon and Syria, having worked tirelessly for much of the nineteenth century to secure their influence in those regions. Just as McMahon was promising Syria and more to Husayn, a British diplomat named Mark Sykes concluded a secret compact with a French diplomat named Charles François Georges-Picot. The Sykes-Picot agreement established a template for the postwar division of the Arab provinces of the Ottoman Empire: France would get Syria, Lebanon, and parts of oil-rich northern Iraq; Britain would get Palestine and southern and central Iraq.

To complicate matters further still, the British government made another wartime promise. This one had little to do with the war and did

nothing to advance the campaign against the Ottomans. It was, instead, the culmination of years of effort by a nationalist group that had blossomed in the late nineteenth century. Like so many others, this group traced its origins to a distant point in the past and claimed the right of self-determination. But unlike so many others—unlike the Serbs or the Turks or the Arabs—this movement looked to a land that its people had not occupied in any great numbers in nearly two thousand years. That was what made Zionism different, and what made the declaration of the British foreign secretary in 1917 all that more unusual.

The idea that Jews were an ethnic group that had the right to self-determination and their own state was no more or less unusual than any other nationalist movement of the time. But the homeland claimed by the Jews was Palestine, and the ones claiming it were European Jews. Graced with well-connected and extremely disciplined leaders, the Zionists found a sympathetic audience in the inner circles of the British government. Just as there is a long and complicated history between Muslims and the People of the Book, there is also another history, of relations between Jews and Christians. Rarely had Jews fared well in Christian states. They had been barely tolerated, but with a lingering threat of violence that compared poorly to the climate of benign neglect in the Muslim world. In the nineteenth century, as most Western European states distanced themselves from organized religion, the position of Jews improved, especially in countries such as England, France, and Germany. But leading families like the Rothschilds were aware that the security of the present was not something to rely on. Only if the Jews had their own country could their survival be assured.

In England, support for Zionism stemmed from the same source as support for Arab independence. Most of the men who governed the British Empire had gone to schools whose curriculum was heavily influenced by both the Bible and the classics of Rome and Greece. The result was a deep affinity for the Holy Land, which in turn led to an ambivalent and troubled relationship to Judaism. There was shame and guilt over the ill treatment that Jews had suffered throughout most of the medieval and early modern period—and there was also anti-Semitism, which led members of the British ruling class to prefer the idea of Jews living somewhere else. Leaders of the Zionist movement toiled for years to gain the support of the British government (and the American government of Woodrow Wilson as well) for a homeland in Palestine, but as

long as the Ottoman Empire was still intact, there was little the British were willing or able to do. With the war, however, the aspirations of the Zionists received an unexpected boost, and in 1917, the British foreign secretary, Sir Arthur Balfour, issued a stunning declaration.

"His Majesty's Government," Balfour wrote in a letter to the Lord Rothschild,

> view with favor the establishment in Palestine of a national home-land for the Jewish people, and will use their best endeavors to facil-itate the achievement of this object, it being clearly understood that nothing shall be done which may prejudice the civil and religious rights of existing non-Jewish communities in Palestine, or the rights and political status enjoyed by Jews in any other country.

The British government later claimed that it had informed Husayn before issuing the statement, as well as at least one of his sons, Faysal. Husayn, according to British accounts, had no objections, as he did not see Palestine as essential to the national aspirations of the Arabs. He also did not believe that the declaration precluded an Arab state governing the territory, as long as the rights of local Jews and any Jewish immi-grants from Europe were protected. In Britain, a number of prominent Jewish leaders, including a member of the cabinet, Sir Edwin Montagu, were less warm to the idea of the British endorsing Zionism. They were concerned that doing so would undermine the hard-won status of the Jews in England and in other countries in Europe. Hence the final words of the declaration, and hence, as well, why Balfour spoke only of a "national homeland" rather than a state, which left open a variety of possibilities short of actually nationhood.[4]

This triad of documents—the Husayn-McMahon correspondence, the Sykes-Picot agreement, and the Balfour Declaration—determined the shape of the modern Middle East. Even more, the hopes and expec-tations raised by these promises were the source of many of the conflicts both within the Arab world and between the Arab world and the West for the remainder of the twentieth century. After the Russian Revolution in 1917, the Bolsheviks, in order to embarrass and undermine the Allied war effort, made public a variety of secret documents, one of which was the Sykes-Picot agreement. Its revelation had the desired effect. British duplicity was exposed. The British had told Husayn that Syria would be

his and then secretly assured the French that it would be theirs. Had Britain known how much bitterness these conflicting promises would generate, it may have thought twice, but in the heat of war, lies seemed a small price to pay for victory.

Few were more disillusioned by what happened in the aftermath of the war than Lawrence himself. He had been used and misled by his government no less than Husayn and his sons. After the war, he went to Paris, as did Faysal, to plead the case for Arab independence. Woodrow Wilson had opened the floodgates of nationalism when he announced before the peace conference that the postwar world would honor the self-determination of all peoples. Faysal was one of many supplicants who asked the victorious powers to grant his people a state, and he was one of many whose requests were politely, but firmly and perhaps cynically, rejected.

Faysal appeared at the conference not just as the representative of his father, but as the ruler of Damascus. In the final days of the war, the forces of the Arab Revolt occupied the city and Faysal was proclaimed king. Lawrence both reveled in the success and dreaded what he knew, or at least feared, would come after. The French coveted Syria, and they had no intention of ceding it to Faysal or the Arabs. In a similar fashion, the British wanted Iraq. In fact, with the exception of the unclear status of oil-rich Mosul, the map of the Near East had been drawn long before Faysal or Lawrence arrived in Paris.

But with American president Woodrow Wilson having unleashed the genie of self-determination, the powers of Europe could not simply brush aside Faysal's claims and those of others who were in a similar position. The result was a compromise between imperialism, nationalism, and Wilson's idealism: the Mandate System. Under its terms, various European nations were given control of specified territory under the condition that they established a timeline for eventual independence. Syria and Lebanon were declared French mandates; Iraq, Transjordan, and Palestine were awarded to the British. Faysal returned to Damascus, only to be forcibly removed by the French. The British, who needed someone to govern the new state of Iraq, decided to install the now-stateless Faysal as its new king in 1921. His brother Abdullah became the first ruler of the new state of Transjordan, and their father, Husayn, was left in control of the western part of Arabia.[5]

The subsequent fate of the Hashemites was mixed. Sharif Husayn,

having been a hero to the Allied war effort, alienated the British because of his refusal to kowtow after the war. He soon found himself without sufficient aid and unable to resist the onslaught of Ibn Saud, who evicted Husayn from Arabia in 1924. Faysal remained king when Iraq became independent in 1932, and ruled until his death the following year. His heirs controlled the country, under the watchful eye of the British, until his grandson Faysal II was overthrown and assassinated in a coup in 1958. Only Abdullah's family survived much past midcentury as rulers of Jordan, though Abdullah himself was gunned down for the unforgivable sin of allowing an independent state of Israel to come into existence in 1948 and planning to make a separate peace with the Israelis. His legacy was continued by his grandson Hussein, who in turn was succeeded by his son Abdullah II, the current ruler of Jordan.

Outside of Jordan, it is rare today for those who remember these events to portray Husayn, Faysal, and their family as anything but puppets in an imperial game.[6] The regimes that replaced them in both Saudi Arabia and Iraq reviled their legacy and labeled them collaborators. They were viewed, at best, as benighted fools who had legitimate goals but who failed utterly in implementing them, and, at worst, as corrupt and venal manipulators who sold out the Arabs to the West. As for the British, the French, and the West in general, they were indicted for cloaking their greed for oil and for land in the noble language of the League of Nations and self-determination.

Without question, Western motives were ambiguous. Many genuinely respected the Arabs, admired the bedouin, and supported the right to self-determination. The contradictory promises that the British made were largely the product of incompatible goals. Men like Balfour and Prime Minister Lloyd George were both idealistic romantics and hardheaded practitioners of realpolitik. They genuinely supported a homeland for the Jews and a new Arab nation, and also wanted to make sure that the balance of power in the postwar Near East did not favor the French. They did not believe that either the Arabs or the Jews were ready for self-government without a period of tutelage, and they were willing and eager to be the tutors.

On the other side, men like Faysal and Husayn made their compromises knowingly. They were prepared to do what was necessary to achieve their ultimate goal. For Faysal, that meant accepting the loss of Syria in order to get Iraq. His aim was an independent Arab nation, and

he was pragmatic enough to change tactics as the situation demanded. After the war, the British in Iraq were desperate for a credible ruler who could unite a country on the verge of revolt. In 1920, Iraq had been racked by a bloody insurgency, and though the British army and air force quelled the uprising, there was still no viable Arab ruler. Faysal was offered the throne of Iraq, provided he was willing to work under the terms of the British Mandate until the League of Nations determined that Iraq was ready for full independence. Winston Churchill, then colonial secretary, wired the British high commissioner in Iraq about British expectations: "You should explain to Faysal that ... we must expect to be consulted so long as we are meeting heavy financial charges in Mesopotamia [Iraq]. He must show that he is capable of maintaining peace and order unaided ... then he can become sovereign.... This will certainly take some time."[7] Faysal, who was almost as much a stranger to Iraq as the British were, agreed, and in 1921 he arrived in Basra. He soon won a rigged election that the British made sure he could not lose, and was acclaimed king by 96 percent of the population. Eleven years later, Iraq gained full independence.

Here as well, what is most remarkable in light of subsequent history is the almost complete absence of religion from the debates. In Iraq, the same divisions that define the country in the early twenty-first century defined the political landscape under Britain and Faysal. The Shi'ites were predominant in the south, the Sunnis in the central regions, and the Kurds in the north. But while the British played on regional and religious rivalries as part of their tactics of divide-and-rule, no one demanded a Muslim state or called for a government controlled by the *ulama*. Religious differences were secondary to tribal, ethnic, and regional divisions, and Iraqi elites argued not over the role of religion in public life but over the merits of the British, the virtues or faults of Faysal, and the shape of the nascent "Arab nation" emerging from the shadow of the Ottomans in the Near East.

Although the Hashemites became synonymous with collaboration with the West, they were architects of their own destiny and made strategic choices that involved collaboration with the British in order to achieve independence. As Faysal said in 1921, "The British and I are in the same boat and must sink or swim. Having, so to speak, chosen me, the British must treat me as one of themselves and I must be trusted." Stripped of the baleful context of later interpretations, the relationship

between Britain and Faysal in Iraq was a marriage of convenience, but a marriage it was. It was an example of cooperation and coexistence, and it created a new state.

Similar relationships existed between the British and Abdullah in Jordan, between the French and nascent political parties in Syria and Lebanon, and between the British and nationalist leaders in Egypt. Throughout the Near East, and in Turkey under the charismatic leadership of Kemal Atatürk, elites made common cause with Western powers, who in turn looked to them as partners who would facilitate their access to oil. It was not a union of equals, as the West retained military and economic dominance. But neither was it a black-and-white case of an oppressive, rapacious West and passive Muslim states with puppet leaders. The West was ascendant, and presented a still unsolvable puzzle to Muslim societies, but within that framework there was a wide scope of cooperation, coexistence, and common ground.

Nationalism was the most fertile common ground. It was understood that Muslim societies would achieve full independence from the West only when they became modern nations. Politicians and intellectuals throughout the Muslim world ingested the history and ideas that had led to the emergence of the Western nation-state, and they then applied those to their own societies. That process had begun in the late nineteenth century, but truly blossomed after World War I, especially in the Arab world. While Arab nationalism aimed to remove the onerous presence of the Western powers, Arab states in the first half of the twentieth century was still dependent on and subservient to the West. The relationship was laced with tension, competition, and animosity, but there was also respect, shared goals, and similar world views.

EGYPT, SYRIA, AND ARAB NATIONALISM

AFTER WORLD WAR I, France remained in direct control of North Africa from Morocco to Tunisia, but in the Near East, the situation was more varied. Egypt was declared independent in 1922 after a popular uprising against the British, although Britain retained wide latitude to intervene in Egypt's internal affairs and had almost complete control over its foreign policy and its major source of revenue, the Suez Canal. Though Transjordan, Palestine, and Iraq had been awarded to the British,

and Iraq became independent in 1932, Palestine remained under British rule until after World War II, and in Transjordan Abdullah depended on London's military support in order to rule an arid territory inhabited by a few hundred thousand bedouin. The French retained Syria and Lebanon and refused to allow either to emerge from mandate status. Saudi Arabia thrived as an independent country under the autocratic Ibn Saud, in part because he was so amenable to Western oil companies investing in the infrastructure necessary to transform the desert kingdom into a petro powerhouse. Non-Arab Iran and Turkey avoided direct European control, and were ruled by modernizing strongmen. Atatürk in Turkey and Reza Shah Pahlavi in Iran instituted a European-style education system, which meant removing the curriculum from the hands of the clerics and the *ulama*. They also stepped up the pace of economic and agricultural reform. They enacted laws to enforce a more modern dress code, especially for women, and the veil—a potent symbol of the old order—was outlawed.

Both Syria and Egypt were centers of Arab nationalism. In Syria, one movement was led by a Christian named Michel Aflaq, who was a founder of the Ba'ath Party. Aflaq had attended French schools, lived in Paris, and studied at the Sorbonne. Though initially more socialist, he later flirted with extreme forms of nationalism modeled on the fascism of Mussolini and Hitler. Aflaq lived a long life, and he witnessed first the victory and then the perversion of his legacy when the 1958 Ba'athist coup in Iraq eventually led to the dictatorship of Saddam Hussein. Though Aflaq wanted to create a modern state, he believed that Islam was a vital component of Arab unity. The irony of a Christian intellectual creating the framework for a nationalist movement that embraced Islam was lost on most at the time (and since), but Arab Christians in Lebanon, Syria, and Palestine were at the forefront of the development of Arab nationalism. Aflaq called Islam "the most precious element of Arabism," and he enjoined all Arabs, whether Christian or Muslim, to revere Muhammad as a hero.

The West was perceived as an obstacle and an adversary, yet in emulating European nationalism, socialism, and even fascism, Arabs were in some respect cooperating with the West. That may not be a legacy to remember fondly. Ba'athism was only one of many Arab nationalisms, of course, and in Syria alone, there were mainstream nationalist parties that rejected the philosophy of Aflaq. But while many of the principles

of Ba'athism were distasteful and many of its subsequent leaders were corrupt, it was nonetheless a movement born of integration between Muslims and Christians, between the Middle East and the West. Aflaq wasn't shy about crediting French and German intellectuals for his inspiration, and the Ba'ath Party that he helped create borrowed heavily from both communism and the national socialism that burgeoned in Europe between the wars. Aflaq also defended the rights of the poor and the universal right to free speech, and he called for secular government in the Arab world. He had, at least, a moral compass, compromised though it may have been. Though he lived to see the Ba'ath Party come to power in both Syria and Iraq, and was appointed to a ceremonial ministerial post in Iraq, Aflaq was never comfortable with the politicians who led the party, including Saddam Hussein. In the 1960s and 1970s, Hussein used Aflaq and the Ba'athist label when he thought it convenient and ignored them when they were not.[8]

Aflaq and Ba'athism were one form of synchronicity with the West. The constitutional nationalist movement in Egypt was another. After World War I, Egypt was still directly governed by the British, but unlike Iraq, it was not part of the Mandate System. Egyptian opposition to the British coalesced around the Wafd Party and its grand old man, Sa'd Zaghlul. Zaghlul succeeded Muhammad Abduh as the leading reformer in Egypt at the turn of the twentieth century, and he was the driving force behind Egyptian independence. After his arrest by the British for organizing protests in 1919, he was deported to Malta. That triggered an uprising, which shook British resolve and led to Egyptian independence in 1922. Zaghlul, promising to decrease the influence of Britain over Egyptian affairs, became prime minister in 1924. While he did not succeed in diminishing the presence of the British in the Suez Canal zone, Egypt was admitted as a full member of the League of Nations in 1937.

The Wafd Party remained the dominant force in Egyptian politics for more than three decades. The party was infused with the dignity, probity, and pride of Zaghlul, but it was led by several equally formidable men in the 1930s and 1940s, who were faced with the same challenge of a Britain that was unwilling to yield its control of the canal or Egypt's foreign policy to a domestic, elected government. Some Egyptian nationalists then turned to Germany as a natural ally in the struggle against the British. It was a classic example of "the enemy of my enemy

is my friend." The Germans challenged British hegemony in Egypt, especially during the early years of World War II, when the North Africa campaigns of the "Desert Fox," General Erwin Rommel, threatened to evict Britain from Egypt and the Suez Canal. The Wafd Party, however, resisted an explicit break with the British, and a Wafd prime minister was in fact forced on King Farouk in 1942 when British tanks broke down the gates of Abdin palace and ordered the king to change his government. But while supportive of the British war effort, the Wafd continued to work for full independence. One product of its struggle was the creation of the League of Arab States in 1945, which remained a prominent vehicle for pan-Arab nationalism into the twenty-first century.[9]

The Syrian Ba'ath and the Egyptian Wafd represented two different forms of nationalism. One veered toward socialism, the other emulated English liberalism. The Ba'ath saw nationalism as a force that transcended the artificial borders that separated the Arab world into states. The dream, in fact, was that one day there would be a unified nation—or *umma*—stretching from North Africa to Iraq, encompassing the entire Arabic-speaking world.

Arab nationalism had an uneasy relationship with religion. While Islam was supposed to bind Arabs together, it was neither the only nor the dominant force. It shared space with language, history, and vague notions of race. Christians like Aflaq were often more comfortable with placing Islam at the center of Arab nationalism than Muslims were. Almost all of the leaders of the nationalist independence movements had gone to school in Europe or were educated in schools with a European curriculum. They had been inculcated with the virtues of secular society and the scientific method, and they had been taught to treat traditional religions as bastions of backwardness. Many of them had also studied Islam at a local mosque, and their experiences with neighborhood preachers often reinforced their skepticism. Christians like Aflaq, however, could adopt a more utilitarian attitude. Unburdened by personal ambivalence about Islam, they articulated a vision of an Arab nation that was at once Islamic and tolerant of the People of the Book.

The promise of Arab nationalism, like the promise of the nineteenth-century reform movement, was simple: if the Arabs could find a way to erase the false divisions that separated them, if they could throw off the yoke of European dominance, and if they could demonstrate that they

were capable of governing their own affairs, then there would be an Arab renaissance to rival the court at Baghdad and the glories of Saladin. Turkish nationalism under Atatürk and Iranian nationalism under the shah held out similar promises, though the Turks looked to restore the glories of past Turkish dynasties, and the Iranians the power of Persian monarchs both before and after the advent of Islam.

What happened in the Middle East in the twentieth century helped determine the framework for how Muslims, Christians, and Jews interacted throughout the globe. Even though most of the Muslim world lay outside the Middle East—including hundreds of millions of Muslims in India and Indonesia who had little or no contact with Christians or Jews—the Middle East in the twentieth century was a crucible, as it had been when this story began in the seventh century, nearly fourteen hundred years ago, and as it continues to be today.

THE BIRTH OF ISRAEL AND ITS CONSEQUENCES

THIRTY YEARS stood between the Balfour Declaration and the birth of the independent state of Israel. For most of those three decades, it seemed unlikely that the outcome would be a Jewish state. Jews in Palestine were a minority living amid Arabs, some of whom were Muslim and some of whom were Christian. In the end, because of a series of decisions made by both Palestinian and Zionist leaders, as well as because of events in Europe and in the world well beyond the control of either, what materialized was a Jewish state vehemently opposed by almost every Arab nation. The creation of Israel in 1948 is one of those rare before-and-after moments, one that disrupted a tenuous balance that had existed between Muslims and Jews from time immemorial and that has yet to be restored.

It is almost impossible to write about the creation of Israel without offending someone. The history has become so politicized and so partisan that there is simply no agreement about the facts. Emotion trumps all else when the subject of Israel is raised, especially in the contemporary Middle East. Israel has become a third rail for rational, sober discourse. If the Holocaust stands as a never-ending rebuke to relations between Christians and Jews, then the intractable conflict between the

Palestinians and the Israelis has come to color not just discussions about Judaism in the Muslim world but discussions about Islam and the West in general.

The creation of Israel is a historical Rubicon. On one side is a dynamic past of coexistence and cooperation along with episodes of antagonism and cruelty. On the other is an increasingly simplistic picture of hostile relations between the parties. In short, the creation of Israel led to disturbing revisions of the past in light of the present. Muslims, Christians, and Jews are all guilty of revisionism. Most books about "Muslim intolerance" use the lens of the Arab-Israeli conflict to categorize the entire history of Islam. The vehement anti-Israeli attitudes of the Arab world since the middle of the twentieth century have been beamed backward a millennium and a half into the past, the presumption being that if many present-day Arabs who are also Muslim hate or oppose the Jewish state of Israel, then it must be because of some essential component of Islam. In a similar vein, Muslims tend to collapse Judaism and the state of Israel into one. Detesting the existence of Israel, they implicate Judaism, and thereby forget the coexistence with Jews that marked so much of their shared history.

Increasingly, Muslims and Jews, as well as Western Christians who span the spectrum from the most secular in Europe to the most fundamentalist in the United States, treat the Arab-Israeli conflict as the latest episode in a long war between the faiths. The assumption in the Western world is that Muslims have always opposed the existence of Judaism, and nurtured an animosity toward Christians and the West as well. In the Arab world, the existence of Israel has become a symbol of Arab weakness, proof that the reformers and the nationalists failed in their goal of resurrecting Arab greatness.

Complicating matters even further is the loose use of words and confusion about who is fighting whom and why. There is an Arab-Israeli conflict, which includes Arab Christians who have opposed or fought the state of Israel. Arab Christians in Lebanon, in Israel itself, and in Egypt have at times been the most adamant opponents of Israel, and Christians have been prominent in the leadership of the Palestine Liberation Organization. With each passing decade in the twentieth century, the Arab-Israeli conflict was exported throughout the Muslim world, first as a symbol of the injustice of the West, then as a symbol of

Muslim failure, and finally as a vindication of the Muslim fundamentalist argument about the clash between Islam and the People of the Book.

Muslims thousands of miles from the conflict, in corners of Nigeria, India, Afghanistan, Indonesia, and the Philippines, identified with the Palestinians and came to view the conflict with Israel as the prime example of how far the Muslim world had fallen behind the West. The Palestinians became doppelgängers for all Muslims, and their fate was taken as a painful reminder of the wrong turn that the Arabs had taken. Muslims who had never met a Jew, and who may never have met a Christian, began to view both from the perspective of being an oppressed minority. It didn't matter whether they were living in a predominantly Muslim society. What mattered was an emerging transnational Muslim identity.

The creation of Israel alone cannot and does not explain the climate of animosity and distrust that has disfigured relations between Muslims, Christians, and Jews since the middle of the twentieth century. The legacy of European intervention and colonialism is at least as important, and the inability of numerous Muslim states to achieve the dreams of both the nineteenth-century reformers and the twentieth-century nationalists is perhaps the crucial element. Had Muslim societies in general, and Arab societies most of all, been able to transform themselves, maintain their sense of identity, and become competitive with the West, then Israel may never have become a lightning rod.

Until 1948, the creation of a state of Israel with a Jewish majority was itself in doubt. The Balfour Declaration had promised a "national homeland," but that did not necessarily mean a state. The British Mandate for Palestine was supposed to provide not just for the settlement of Jews in Palestine, but for the self-governance of the half-million Palestinian Arabs who lived in the region. In 1922, the British tried to allay Arab concerns and issued a disingenuous statement that His Majesty's Government had not "at any time contemplated, as appears to be feared by the Arab Delegation, the disappearance or subordination of the Arab population, language or culture in Palestine."[10] But unrestricted Jewish emigration from Europe sparked a violent Arab backlash, which led the British government to restrict the influx of Jews in 1939. British restrictions coincided with the rise of virulent anti-Semitism in Europe, especially in Nazi Germany. That caused more European Jews to emigrate, but they found the British government in Palestine hostile to Jewish set-

tlement. By the end of the 1930s, the British had managed to alienate both the Arab and Jewish populations of Palestine, and were seen as an adversary by both.

The hope that a combined Arab-Jewish polity could be created under the benign and watchful tutelage of the British took time to die completely, but the Arab revolt in 1936, this time against both the Jewish community and the British authorities, shattered whatever illusions anyone may have had that such a state was feasible. Hajj Amin al-Husayni, the mufti of Jerusalem and one of the most prominent Palestinian leaders, disdained compromise with the Jewish immigrants and turned against the British for refusing to support Palestinian dominance. After the outbreak of war between England and Germany, Hajj Amin tilted toward Germany and the Nazis in order to gain leverage against Britain. He spent the war years in Berlin, where he was warmly received by Hitler and the Nazi leadership.

At the same time, the Jewish Agency, which was the Zionist organization responsible for governing Palestine's Jews, also increased its pressure on the British. Several splinter groups (most notably the Irgun Zvai Leumi, led in part by future Israeli prime minister Menachem Begin) used terrorist tactics—roadside bombs, assassinations, and targeting civilians—against the Palestinian Arabs and later against the British in order to force a change in British immigration policy, an end to the mandate, and the creation of a Jewish state.

In 1939, the British government issued a white paper that appeared to abandon the promises of the Balfour Delcaration. They were in no mood to placate the Zionists. Instead, needing stability in Palestine, they did their best to satisfy the Palestinians. The white paper promised an end to Jewish immigration within five years and an eventual Palestinian Arab state rather than a Jewish one. It also struck down the idea of a partition that would result in a two-state solution. The Jewish leadership was horrified, but war in Europe changed the landscape once again. Violence in Palestine escalated, and the British cracked down on Jewish resistance groups. The Jewish Agency, recognizing that the war and the Holocaust had raised the stakes, started to mend fences with the British, and the Palestinian leadership became even more disillusioned. The end of the war, with Britain victorious but exhausted and financially spent, signaled the end of the mandate, and the British government looked for a way out.

The end of the war also saw the fateful beginning of American

involvement in the politics of the Middle East. U.S. oil companies had been active since the 1920s, and had assiduously courted the rulers of Saudi Arabia. But the scope of that involvement was minor compared to the years after World War II. As the British receded, the Americans stepped in to fill the void. In the case of Palestine, American interests were nebulous. Though Zionist leaders lobbied the Truman administration to support the establishment of a Jewish state, at the United Nations, they had to compete with Arab leaders who lobbied just as strongly against one. The postwar path from the mandate to the creation of Israel was chaotic and uncertain. The British asked the United Nations to take charge of the situation, and Palestine became one of the first issues that the U.N. attempted to solve.

In November 1947, after substantial back-and-forth, the U.N. General Assembly accepted a partition plan that would have transformed Palestine into an unwieldy checkerboard of Jewish and Palestinian areas. The problem, and a glaring one, was that the eleven Muslim members of the United Nations (including non-Arab states such as Turkey, Afghanistan, and Pakistan) voted against the plan. Denouncing it as "absurd, impracticable, and unjust," they vowed to prevent its implementation by any means necessary. True to their word, when Israel declared its independence on May 15, 1948, the armies of five Arab states (Egypt, Lebanon, Jordan, Iraq, and Syria) mobilized for war. The Israel Defense Forces raised thousands more men than the combined Arab armies and Palestinian militias, and proved to be far superior to their disorganized adversaries. By the fall, not only was the partition plan null and void, but 750,000 Palestinians had been turned into refugees, and Israel controlled large portions of territory that had at least nominally been promised to the Palestinians.[11]

Defeat was not followed by reconciliation. After long and painful months of U.N.-mediated negotiations, Israel signed armistice pacts with each of the Arab states individually. Not only was there no universal peace agreement, there was no peace agreement, period. Armed hostilities ceased, but Israel remained in a state of war with its neighbors. Internationally, the United Nations and its constituents were divided. The United States had, at the last minute, recognized Israel, but only after heated debate within the Truman administration. Most of official Washington was opposed to recognition, largely out of concern that the gesture would weaken the United States in its global campaign against

the Soviet Union and undermine its ability to function diplomatically and economically in the Arab world. The Europeans were somewhat more favorable, largely because of guilt over the horrors of the Holocaust. On the whole, however, the new Israeli state found itself intact but isolated and ostracized. Its ability to buy weapons or seal economic agreements was hampered, and it was surrounded by hostile states whose lack of coordination made them ineffectual but whose daily animosity made them unpleasant and dangerous neighbors.

In the Arab world, the establishment of Israel became known as the *naqbah*, the catastrophe. All of the members of the Arab League, including those of North Africa and the Arabian Peninsula, vowed never to recognize Israel and refused to negotiate until there was a return of the refugees and a Palestinian state, with Jerusalem as its capital. The creation of a Jewish state was widely perceived in the Arab world as the ultimate indignity, a glaring example of the strength of the West and the feebleness of the Arabs. After more than a century of reform efforts, the Arab states—or their leadership at their very least—were becoming frustrated. The liberal, constitutional reforms of the nineteenth century and the nationalism of the twentieth century had led to a degree of independence from Europe, but by all measures, the Arab world still could not compete with the West. Algeria, Tunisia, and Morocco remained colonies of France, although the latter two were on the road to independence. Jordan, Iraq, and Egypt could not make foreign policy decisions without the approval of the British Foreign Office. Saudi Arabia was independent, but ringed by British protectorates in Kuwait and the emirates on the Persian Gulf coast and dependent on European and American oil companies for income.

The sense of humiliation grew, as Israel proved impossible to dislodge. In the late 1940s and 1950s, however, the Arab-Israeli conflict was confined to the Middle East. Many, but not all, Muslim countries outside the Middle East voted in sympathy with the Arab states if and when the subject of Israel came up at the United Nations, but Israel was not yet a central concern for their people or their governments. A century of pan-Islamic movements had succeeded only in creating a general sense of shared interests. The result was empathy with the political aims of the Arabs but not virulent opposition to Israel or to Jews. Outside the Middle East, the creation of Israel was taken as one more instance of selfish Western imperialism, but hardly the worst episode. On the other hand,

for the central Arab states, and of course for the displaced Palestinians, it was seen as a tragedy that ended, once and for all, the dreams of reform and progress. For them, and soon for many parts of the Muslim world, 1948 was not a beginning but an end. From the ashes of the failed promise, a new set of ideas emerged—virulent, dark, and despairing—that ran counter to centuries of history.

The most immediate and destructive consequence was that hundreds of thousands of Jews were forced to leave their homes and emigrate to Israel. Iraq had one of the oldest Jewish communities in the world, with families that could trace their lineage to the time of the Babylonians, centuries before the birth of Christ. By the 1940s, there were nearly 150,000 Iraqi Jews, many of whom were prominent as financiers, businessmen, and doctors. Iraqi Jews had also played a behind-the-scenes role in bolstering the Hashemite monarchy, especially with loans. Yet after 1948, they came under extraordinary pressure from the Iraqi government, which passed laws limiting their property rights and restricting their freedom of movement, and which ultimately coerced them to leave with only a fraction of their property. By the early 1950s, barely four thousand Jews remained in Iraq; the bulk had left for Israel, with the rest scattered to England, the United States, and other parts of the world.

It was not just Iraq. Of the approximately 1.7 million Jews in Arab lands, hundreds of thousands emigrated to Israel, and hundreds of thousands more left for Europe, Latin America, or the United States. The emigration to Israel included a massive airlift of nearly fifty thousand Yemeni Jews, and the involuntary departure of tens of thousands of Jews from Egypt, Syria, Morocco, and Iran. For nearly two thousand years, Jewish communities had been rooted in these countries, and for most of that time, they had lived peacefully under the rule of Muslim governments. They enjoyed a level of autonomy greater than what they had known under the Babylonians, the Romans, or the Christian states of Europe. Muslim tolerance of Jews was often laced with contempt, but that did not prevent coexistence and occasional cooperation. Here too, it is important to remember that at very few moments in human history have ruling majorities treated minorities with respect, and they have rarely allowed them access to power, privilege, and prosperity. Within those parameters, Jews under Muslim rule lived about as well as any minority under any majority at any point in history.

That made the forced emigration in the late 1940s all the more startling. After 1492, Jews expelled from Spain were welcomed into the Ottoman Empire. Four hundred and fifty years later, that welcome came to an end. In light of nearly a millennium and a half of coexistence, what happened after 1948, and indeed what has happened between Muslims, Christians, and Jews since then, is an exception to the historical pattern of coexistence. It is tempting to ascribe these events to a deep dislike of Jews that began in Medina, when Muhammad turned on the Jewish tribes. But in order to draw that unbroken line, centuries of other history, of Hasdai ibn Shaprut, of Maimonides, and of their countless descendants, must be forgotten and ignored.

The events of the nineteenth and early twentieth centuries, and the inability of the Arab and Muslim world to compete with the West, led to an increasing level of bitterness and insecurity. Before the nineteenth century, Muslim states were rarely threatened by the People of the Book. Christians and Jews lived as protected minorities, and Christian states were more often than not on the defensive in the face of Muslim dynasties beginning with the Umayyads and continuing with the Ottoman Empire. The Crusades were an exception, but the Crusader states were quickly contained and, in the greater scheme, quickly defeated. Only in the nineteenth century were Muslim societies put on the defensive, and it took the establishment of Israel—and Jewish military victories over the Arabs—to unleash the waves of intolerance that led to the exodus of the ancient Jewish communities of the Near East.

The Arab-Israeli conflict has focused attention on conflict between Muslims and Jews, and between Muslims and the West. But here too, the narrative that has become so familiar is incomplete. The relentless focus on conflict and its continuance in the present has left little room for other stories. The result is a numbing, never-ending litany of war, hatred, animosity, and death. The history of coexistence has been lost in that fog.

⫸ ⫷

In an Otherwise Turbulent World

O VER THE PAST DECADE, and particularly after September 11, 2001, more people have become familiar with the story of how Arab and Muslim disillusionment provided the impetus for the evolution of a virulent strain of fundamentalism. Since September 11, there is a common understanding of why some fundamentalists embraced terrorism. "Common understanding" doesn't mean wide and deep awareness, of course, but many in Europe, the United States, and the rest of the world now have a basic sense that the creation of Israel and the inability of Arabs and Palestinians to prevent that produced widespread disenchantment with modernization and Westernization. The subsequent rise of extreme forms of fundamentalism epitomized by al-Qaeda has been dissected, studied, and debated. And after the U.S. invasion of Iraq in 2003, and bombings in Bali, Madrid, and London, the citizens of many nations have been forced to grapple with the rise of radical groups in Iraq, Europe, and Asia.

The picture is still unclear, but its outlines are straightforward. At some point in the middle of the twentieth century, a critical mass of despair was reached in the Muslim world. Both the reforms of the nineteenth century and the nationalism of the twentieth were judged as failures. At first, the reaction against Arab nationalism was muted. The Egyptian Muslim Brotherhood was an early proponent of a return to a purer Islam, and though its vision of the golden age of the caliphs was more fiction than fact, the Brotherhood did tend to the poor and to the newly urbanized and gave them a sense of place and belonging in a cold impersonal world. The Brotherhood was vigorously suppressed and its

leader was killed in 1949. Egyptian fundamentalism then went underground, and the torch was passed to Sayyid Qutb, who turned his attention to the corruption of Arab regimes and the pernicious influence of the Western world. In his eyes, the bankruptcy of reform was the inevitable result of the turning away from Islam and toward the false gods of progress and modernization. In 1966 Qutb was executed, and became a sanctified martyr to generations of fundamentalists.

While the foundations for radical fundamentalism were laid in the Arab world, there were related movements in India, Pakistan, and Indonesia. Each shared a basic conviction that contemporary Muslim states were ruled by godless governments and that society had been corrupted and weakened by the influence of the West. They wove a vision of the past that glorified the first four caliphs and the early Muslim community, but their reading of history was highly selective. The ecumenical spirit of the Abbasid court, the medieval philosophical tradition that celebrated interpretation and reason, the mystical traditions that emphasized God's love, and the relaxed attitudes toward People of the Book were absent from their version of the past. Instead, they imagined a time when Islam was the alpha and the omega, when everyone from the caliph to the slave imbibed the piety of the Quran and the tradition of the Prophet, and then in return, God graced his believers with power, fortune, and security.

Muslim fundamentalist movements shared certain characteristics, but they were also deeply divided. Much like American Protestantism, Muslim fundamentalism of the twentieth century was decentralized and constantly changing shape. Groups would form, and then splinter. There was little agreement about tactics, and more to the point, no consensus about goals. Was the adversary the corrupt governments of Muslim states? Was it Israel? Was the goal the creation of new Muslim societies through revolution, through reform, through education, or through violence and chaos? Which enemy should be targeted—the so-called near enemy, such as secular Arab nationalists, Nasserists, local governments, and neighboring states? Or should it be the far enemy, such as the West in general or the United States as the most powerful Western country? Was the most pressing issue the plight of the Palestinians? Or was it the mass of disenfranchised Muslims who were forced to suffer under decadent monarchs like King Muhammad in Morocco, King Idris in Libya, the shah in Iran, the Hashemites in Jordan and Iraq (until 1958), and

under atheistic nationalists like Nasser in Egypt and the heirs to Atatürk in Turkey? Decade by decade, the appeal of fundamentalism grew, but so did the divisions. In the 1970s, the most violent took to calling themselves jihadis, because they believed that armed jihad against unbelievers— apostates and secular governments, Jews and Christians, "Zionists and Crusaders"—was incumbent on all good Muslims and that the means, no matter how violent, justified the end of reestablishing a moral society.[1]

Even the jihadis were not united, however. They came from different regions with different historical experiences. There were Afghan jihadis whose worldview was informed by the 1979 Soviet invasion and the subsequent U.S. aid for the mujahideen (the "freedom fighters"), and who turned Afghanistan into a Soviet Vietnam War. There were disaffected Saudis who were disgusted by the rampant materialism of the Saudi royal family and their unholy alliance with Western oil companies. There were Algerians who rejected the socialist Algerian revolutionaries who had fought a bitter independence war against France. There were Pakistanis who followed the teachings of an early-twentieth-century preacher named Maulana Maududi (who influenced Sayyid Qutb) and who wanted to establish the sharia as the sole legal code for Pakistan and for Muslims living in India. And there were Palestinian Islamic radicals who organized Hamas in order to contest both the state of Israel and the leadership of Yasser Arafat and the PLO. To add to the confusion, there were also Shi'ite jihadis, who looked to Iran and Ayatollah Khomeini rather than to Sayyid Qutb for inspiration and who created parties like Hezbollah ("The Party of God") in Lebanon.

In short, while fundamentalism has been a significant force in the modern Muslim world, the notion that there is a single fundamentalist movement whose leader is Osama bin Laden is utterly incorrect. Even more troubling is the tendency of both jihadis and Western observers to read history through a fundamentalist lens. The result is a vision of the Islamic past where there is no separation between church and state, where reason is subservient to orthodox acceptance of revealed truths, and where there is no mention of the wild creativity of Córdoba and Baghdad, the eccentric individualism of Ibn Arabi and the philosophers, the piety of the Sufis or the modernist, Islamic synthesis of Abduh. This narrow version of the past is widely accepted by Muslims and non-Muslims alike, but that does not mean it is accurate.

The other unfortunate result of the contemporary obsession with

radicals and jihadis is that history is read backward in order to find the roots of the present. Of course, no matter how much we might try to look at the past neutrally, some "presentism" always creeps in. But in seeking to explain the origin of the current struggles over Israel or the clash between Muslim extremists and the West, people have magnified the role of fundamentalism and the prevalence of historical conflict and minimized those aspects of the past that don't fit the mold of the present.[2]

In addition to misreading history, too many of us also misread the present and the recent past. Certainly, the creation of Israel ushered in a new and troubling period of relations between Muslims, Christians, and Jews, and contemporary Islamic fundamentalism and its most violent offshoots did emerge from disgust with nationalism and Western-style modernization. But fundamentalism, violence, and the Arab-Israeli conflict are hardly the whole story of the modern world. Conflict is only part of the picture. Even the creation of Israel has a hidden history. If the main plot was war, the subplots were accommodation, coexistence, and cooperation.

JORDAN AND ISRAEL

UNTIL THE END of the mandate period, and throughout the 1920s and 1930s, the daily interactions between Palestinians and Jewish settlers were often cordial and sometimes quite friendly. In fact, relations between Jewish settlers and Christian and Muslim Palestinians were warmer and more intimate than relations between the Crusader states and the local populace had been centuries before. There were joint business endeavors and shared agricultural projects. One early Jewish settler thought that the tension between Jews and Arabs could be decreased by marriage between the bedouin and the settlers. Chaim Weizmann, one of the leaders of the Zionist movement, met often with Arab leaders and tried to convince them to support an Arab-Jewish polity based on common interests rather than divided by different creeds. The socialist philosophy of the early Zionists tended to be hostile to organized religion. Judaism for them was an identity that owed more to ethnicity and history than religion. The Jewish immigrants were by and large agrarian laborers, who worked on farms bought from the Arabs, and tilled the soil alongside Arab farmers. Some Zionists, therefore, took the logical step of

imagining a state designed to serve the needs of laborers, Arab and Jew alike. Of course, these attempts at concord gave way to successive waves of violence, caused by dispossessed Palestinians who hoped to halt Jewish immigration and then by Zionists determined to establish a national home. Moderation always has a difficult time in the face of extremism, and is usually trumped by it. Palestine was no different.

Relations between the Jewish Agency and the neighboring states were marked by animosity, especially on the part of the Arabs, but here as well there were periods of calm and concord. The Christian Maronite leadership of Lebanon welcomed a Jewish state as a possible counterbalance to a Middle East dominated by Muslims. More than a few Maronite leaders in the 1930s and 1940s made overtures to the Zionists and discussed the possibility of future alliances should a Jewish state come into being. At the time, the Maronites were struggling for the termination of the French Mandate, much as the Zionists were fighting to end British rule. In light of their parallel goals, the Maronite patriarch even signed a treaty with the Jewish community of Palestine, promising support and economic aid, as well as diplomatic backing for unlimited Jewish immigration. In return, the Jewish signatories promised to abet the establishment of an independent Maronite-controlled Lebanon.[3]

The most extensive collaboration between the Jews of Palestine and their neighbors occurred with Jordan and King Abdullah. Transjordan had been formed at the Cairo Conference of 1921 when British diplomats, including most notably an imperious Winston Churchill, literally drew lines on a map to determine the states of the modern Middle East. There was almost nothing organic about the boundaries of Jordan, except for part of its western border, which ran along the Sea of Galilee and the Jordan Valley, from which the state gets its name. Having received his crown as a consolation prize after losing Arabia, Abdullah worked diligently to make Jordan into a viable state.

The separation of Jordan from Palestine and Syria had little grounding in history, and the region was inhabited largely by bedouin tribes who respected Abdullah's Hashemite lineage but questioned his legitimacy as their ruler. His army was a British creation and was answerable to Sir John Glubb. While Glubb never shed his English identity, he became a loyal partisan of Abdullah. It was a particular sort of loyalty, tinged as it was with a patronizing attitude toward the Arabs and their capacity for self-government, but like T. E. Lawrence, Glubb felt at

home in the desert among the bedouin. He and his wife adopted bedouin and Palestinian children, and he saw no contradiction in serving both Abdullah and the British government. By 1948, Glubb could look back at his years in the desert with pride, and he led an army that was by far the most professional in the region.

Faced with the establishment of a Jewish state, Abdullah took a less adversarial stance than the other Arab leaders. Though he publicly sided with the Arab League in the months before Israel declared independence in May 1948, he secretly negotiated with the Israelis to arrange an equitable division of Palestine that would leave Jordan in control of what became the West Bank. There was even hope that he would not have to use his army. A young Golda Meir, who would later become Israel's first and only female prime minister, disguised herself as an Arab woman and sneaked into Amman four days before Israel declared independence to try to conclude an agreement with Abdullah. But the king was unwilling to risk ostracism by the other Arab states. He told Meir that he "firmly believed that Divine Providence had restored you, a Semite people who were banished to Europe and have benefited by its progress, to the Semite East, which needs your knowledge and initiative.... But the situation is grave.... I am sorry. I deplore the coming bloodshed and destruction. Let us hope we shall meet again."

There was some cynicism at work here. Abdullah recognized that Israel was not going to be pushed into the sea, and that sooner or later, the Arabs would have to come to terms with its presence. Confident in his army and in Glubb as a general, Abdullah believed that he could put pressure on the Israeli defense forces in the West Bank, and even threaten west Jerusalem. Abdullah described his strategy to a friend: "I will not begin the attack on the Jews and will only attack them if they first attack my forces. I will not allow massacres in Palestine. Only after order and quiet have been established will it be possible to reach an understanding with the Jews." Throughout the summer of 1948, the Jordanian army hovered but, perhaps realizing it would lose if it confronted the Israelis too aggressively, never attempted to advance into the territory that had been assigned to Israel under the 1947 U.N. Partition Plan. The Jordanians kept civilian casualties to a minimum, and Israel regarded Abdullah as a respected adversary. It was an odd sort of war, and an odd relationship, which led one Israeli diplomat at the time to refer to Israel and Jordan as "the best of enemies."

As a result, the government of Prime Minister David Ben-Gurion embraced Abdullah's willingness to talk. In the fall of 1948 and into 1949, there were multiple clandestine meetings between Israelis and Abdullah and his court. One of the negotiators was Moshe Dayan, who would later become Israel's most famous general and whose rakish, one-eyed visage came to epitomize both the energy and the determination of the Israeli military. At the time, he was a junior member of a delegation led by Moshe Sharett, Ben-Gurion's foreign minister and later prime minister himself. The meetings were cordial but often awkward. At dinner one evening, Sharett managed to offend Abdullah by correcting him about whether China had been a member of the League of Nations. As Dayan wryly remarked in his memoirs, "A king never errs, and Abdullah stood by the statement." Other visits were laden with ceremony and formality, which tried the patience of the rough-and-tumble Dayan. "We would dine with the king prior to getting down to business and for an hour or so before the meal there would be political gossip of what was happening in the capitals of the world, an occasional game of chess, and poetry readings. In chess, it was obligatory not only to lose to the king but also to show surprise at his unexpected moves. And when he read his poems, in epigrammatic Arabic, one had to express wonder by sighing from the depths of one's soul."

As close as the Jordanians and the Israelis came to a formal peace treaty, in the end Abdullah would not break ranks with the rest of the Arab states. He could not afford to become isolated. The result was an entente with Israel but not an explicit peace. Though the king tried his best to keep the negotiations secret, too many high-level players were involved, and it was widely known that discussions had taken place.

Abdullah paid a high price. In 1951, while visiting Al-Aqsa Mosque in Jerusalem, he was gunned down by a Palestinian Arab. His young grandson Hussein was walking just behind him and watched in horror. He soon succeeded Abdullah, and as King Hussein, continued the delicate balancing act that his grandfather had begun.

For nearly fifty years, King Hussein—who could use his mellifluous baritone to recite classical Arabic to his subjects and then speak in a beautiful English accent for an address at the United Nations—maintained respectful relations with the Israelis, even as his goals and theirs were often diametrically opposed. He was a voice of moderation in the Arab world, at times accused, like his grandfather Abdullah, of being a

pawn of the Western powers, and of the United States especially. He had to contend with a restive Palestinian population, and he lost the West Bank to Israel during the 1967 war. Yet Israel only reluctantly went to war with Jordan in 1967, and at no point did either Hussein or Prime Minister Golda Meir cease to describe each other as friends. To his dying day, through the most perilous times, during the extremism of the Palestinian Liberation Organization in the 1960s and 1970s and the Palestinian uprising known as the *intifadah* in the 1980s, he remained true to his vision of a Middle East governed by peace. In 1994, that vision was at least partly vindicated, and Jordan and Israel signed a peace treaty that led to formal diplomatic relations and agreements on everything from boundaries to water rights. Even as the accords between Israel and the Palestinian leadership disintegrated, the interaction between Israel and Jordan—ruled after 1999 by Hussein's son Abdullah II—was marked by an unusual level of mutual respect.[4]

The relationship between Israel and Jordan doesn't fit the familiar template of the Arab-Israeli conflict. While it is certainly possible to write a history of Israeli-Jordanian interaction as a series of wars separated by periods of cold peace, that requires ignoring far too much of the past, and the present. In his later years, King Hussein frequently remarked on the peculiar intimacy of Israel and its Arab neighbors. The bulk of Jordan's people live on the highlands above the Jordan River Valley, scant miles from the most inhabited areas of Israel, and they can literally gaze out over Israel and the West Bank when they watch the setting sun. In turn, many in Israel can look at the Jordanians every morning, stare at them from the beach resorts of the Dead Sea and from the Red Sea city of Eilat, which is separated from the Jordanian city of Aqaba by nothing more than a heavily fortified fence. Hussein took the ancient notion of the People of the Book very seriously. The kinship of race, history, and a shared God infused his sense of the region, as it still does for his son Abdullah.[5]

Even at its worst moments, the Jordanian-Israeli relationship has rarely been colored by *religious* animosity. The Hashemites take great pride in their lineage as descendants of Muhammad, but they have never supported the agenda of the fundamentalists. They have a conservative, hierarchical approach to government, which is more in the mold of classical Muslim states. Islam is central to their personal identity much as Christianity is central to British monarchs and politicians, and to Amer-

ican presidents. But Islam is not a political force per se, and the Jordanians have resisted calls to turn their country into a polity where the *ulama*
have ultimate authority.

As for Israel and Judaism, some of the post-1967 Israeli settlers were
motivated by zealous notions of a biblical re-creation of greater Israel.
But the Israeli state has remained, in spite of the rise of Jewish fundamentalism, more secular than not. Some of the Palestinians who became
Jordanian citizens turned toward Islamic fundamentalism in their opposition to Israeli policies on the West Bank. But the leaders of both countries have never used religion as an excuse to fight one another. To the
contrary. The Jordanian royal family's sense of kinship with Israel
derives from a basic belief that Jews and Arabs and Jews and Muslims are
woven from the same cloth and are children of the same creator.

But because of the fraught nature of the larger Arab-Israeli conflict,
the positive aspects of the Jordanian-Israeli entente have been downplayed by Israelis and Jordanians alike. Instead, war and extremism have
dominated the Arab-Israeli agenda, and the nuance and moderation that
have marked relations between Jordan and Israel have been pushed aside
and neglected as a model for the present and the future.

LEBANON

LEBANON IS ANOTHER ambiguous story that can serve almost any
vision of relations between Muslims, Christians, and Jews. Though its
history is indelibly colored by the disastrous civil war that rent the country from 1975 until the mid-1990s (not to mention the more recent
Israeli-Hezbollah war in the summer of 2006), for more than a century
Lebanon seemed to be a shining example of Muslim-Christian coexistence. The Maronites occupied a central place in the political and economic life of the region, and they had been crucial in the independence
struggle against France. They were not the only Christian sect, but
they outnumbered the Greek Orthodox, the Greek Catholics, and the
Armenian Orthodox. The Muslims were themselves sectarian, with a
large group of Sunnis, a growing population of Shi'a, and a concentrated
Druze community. Beirut was a cosmopolitan city, with a powerful
Maronite contingent but with other groups well represented. It was also

a commercial hub that looked more toward Europe than to the Arab world.

Outside of Beirut, each major group dominated a particular region, with the Maronites in the mountainous center, the Shi'ites mostly in the south, and the Sunnis along the coast and in the urban areas. Each of these communities was in turn led by a few powerful clans who could trace their lineage back centuries. The clan lords had fought one another in the past, but under the auspices of the Ottomans and the French, they had come to a modus vivendi. That balance was occasionally disrupted, as in 1858–60 and in 1958, usually after one group or another sought to change the status quo. These civil wars, lethal while they lasted, were always inconclusive, and were resolved by only slight changes to a system that gave each group sufficient autonomy and security.

The modern cornerstone of that system was an accord known as the "National Pact." In 1943, recognizing that no one group was powerful enough to dominate the whole country, the leading Maronite family and one of the influential Sunni clans made a deal. They agreed that the president of Lebanon would be Maronite, the prime minister would be Sunni, and the head of the chamber of deputies would be a Shi'ite. It was, according to one of its architects, "the fusion of two tendencies into one ideology: complete and final independence without resorting to the protection of the West or to a unity or federation with the East."

In the 1950s, the rise of Egypt's Gamal Abd al-Nasser and the pan-Arab ideology of Nasserism put pressure on conservative regimes throughout the Arab world. Nasser had led a military coup that overthrew the Egyptian king, and that put the other Arab monarchies on notice. The Hashemites reacted by looking to the United States for support. Jordan and Iraq also made common cause with the aloof Saudis, who gravitated toward their onetime Hashemite adversaries in the face of the anti-royalist threat of Nasserism. Lebanon and Syria became pawns in this struggle, and when Syria tilted toward Egypt, the Maronites of Lebanon appealed to the United States. The balance between the sects in Lebanon was stable but susceptible to external disruptions. After the king of Iraq was overthrown and killed in 1958, and after King Hussein in Jordan narrowly avoided a coup, the Maronite president of Lebanon asked the United States to send troops to prevent incursions of Nasserist forces from Syria. Concerned that another pro-Western

regime was in jeopardy, President Eisenhower agreed. Within weeks, in the summer of 1958, more than ten thousand U.S. marines landed on the beaches of Beirut, where they found surprised sunbathers who were not aware that the country was in danger.

After this brief interruption, balance was restored, and Lebanon prospered in the 1960s. Beirut enjoyed halcyon days as a global entrepôt, filled with wealthy bankers and traders, and blessed with an enviable night life that welcomed the jet set no less than the French Riviera. The American University in Beirut attracted students from around the world and established itself as a premier research college. As Nasserism crested and then diminished, Lebanon looked forward to a period of calm, but that was not to be. The influx of Palestinian refugees after both the 1948 and 1967 Arab-Israeli wars was one factor; changing demographics were another. The Shi'ites were becoming a larger portion of the population, yet their share of influence was still limited by the National Pact, which had been drawn up when they were a distant third in numbers. The civil war that erupted in 1975 was in fact multiple wars between ever-shifting factions who made and broke alliances at a dizzying pace. By the 1980s, Israel, Syria, and Iran intervened, and the influence of each remained pronounced even after the fighting ceased in the 1990s. Israeli presence in the south, Syrian control of the interior and the Bekaa Valley, and Iran's support for Hezbollah hobbled the country and precluded any lasting stability.

Before 1975, the peace in Lebanon had been maintained through a combination of clan politics and a free-market economy in Beirut. The traditional leaders had managed the affairs of their own community, much as the *millet*s under the Ottoman Empire had, and the national government served as a town square for the notables to air disputes. But the country never developed a cohesive national identity, or a strong military, and when groups of Palestinian refugees began to use parts of Lebanon to stage operations against Israel and against various parties in Lebanon that they disliked, the equilibrium disintegrated into the civil war that lasted in one form or another for more than two decades.

Which of these stories best captures Lebanon? The decades of peace and harmony between Christians and Muslims, or the civil war that saw not only Christians fighting Muslims, but Sunnis fighting Shi'ites, pro-Syrian groups fighting Palestinians, and the Druze fighting just about

everyone and Maronites most of all. Which is the "real" Lebanon—a failed experiment of what was known as "confessional democracy," which honored the rights of each religious community, or a successful example of coexistence and toleration destroyed not by problems from within but by troubles in the surrounding region? And which of these stories will be seen in the future as the "real Lebanon"? A history of the United States in 1862 might have displayed skepticism about the American experiment and how it had finally foundered on the shoals of slavery. In the 1960s, Lebanon was celebrated as a beacon of toleration and openness. After 1975, it was the subject of eulogies for shattered dreams and lost generations. But as the civil war recedes into the distance, the memory of a stable past comes back into focus. Even with the Israeli bombardment of Hezbollah in the summer of 2006, whether Lebanon will once again be taken as a model for how different religious communities can coexist will depend not on what has happened in the past but on what happens now and in the future.[6]

ΛΛOTHER ЅTORY

WE ARE ALL, to varying degrees, captives of our culture. With few exceptions, the current image of relations between Muslims, Christians, and Jews is negative, and the belief that conflict has been ever present is deeply entrenched. Yet if the stories told in these pages say anything, it is that there is another perspective. Throughout history, there has been active cooperation. There has been tolerance, and there has been indifference. The only way to describe the arc of fourteen hundred years as primarily a history of conflict is to forget and ignore not only the stories told here, but countless others that have been lost to history because no one thought that they merited recording.

This is not just a problem of how we see the past. When future generations look back at the second half of the twentieth century and the early decades of the twenty-first, they will have at their disposal an unparalleled amount of information. Yet unless they try to find other stories, they too will be left with the impression that these years—our present— were defined by a war between civilizations and by ever-increasing hostility between Muslims, Christians, and Jews. They will say that our time

was marked by escalating violence, acts of terrorism, suicide bombings, and by fear that some group would obtain and use a weapon of mass destruction in the name of God. These future generations will be forgiven if they too look to the distant past and retell the familiar tales of hatred between the faiths that began with Muhammad and the Jews and continued episodically over the centuries.

Today, Muslims, Christians, and Jews are equal offenders in their relentless focus on conflict. Each tends to paint the past as a series of indignities suffered at the hands of the other two. Westerners, whether or not they adhere to an organized religion, are disposed to view Muslim societies as backward and intent on war and violence. And most inhabitants of the Muslim world tend to believe that the West bears ill will toward Islam and Muslims and wants not peace or coexistence but economic and cultural domination.

Indeed, in the past few decades, polemics about the coming war between Islam and the West have proliferated, as have what one clever critic dubbed "travel narratives from Hell." These are primarily penned by Western writers addressing a Western audience who explore the Muslim world and come back with reports of gloom and doom. We are told of new madrassas (schools) from Nigeria to Pakistan to Indonesia being funded by Saudi extremists preaching hate. We are told of generations that celebrate violence against Israel, against corrupt governments, against Europe and the United States. We are told of Muslim rage on every street, and of angry young men and women who watch helplessly as the modern world passes them by, their faces pressed to the glass gazing on possibilities that they can never obtain, while their own worlds decay and their traditions succumb to Coca-Cola and McDonald's.[7] There are, of course, books and articles that reject this framework and posit a different reading of Islam and of the past, that suggest the compatibility of Islam and democracy and Islam and the West, but it is fair to say that these have not gained the same level of influence as their more shrill counterparts.[8]

The history of conflict is not untrue. It is incomplete. By the same token, the reality of religious extremism in the modern world cannot and should not be downplayed. There are radicals who will dedicate their lives to inflicting pain and death on those who do not agree with their vision. And there is a still-simmering Arab-Israeli conflict that remains a source of pain and anger for all involved. Nonetheless, there

are other stories that garner less attention but are no less part of the tapestry.

Take the Arabian American Oil Company, known as Aramco. It began as an arrangement between Standard Oil of California (which in time became Chevron), Texaco, and King Ibn Saud. The Saudi monarch had been wooed by both Europeans and Americans, but he ultimately felt most comfortable with the Americans, either because they charmed him or because they weren't the British. Aramco, with the involvement of Standard Oil of New Jersey (later called Exxon) and of New York (later called Mobil), remained the dominant Western oil company in Saudi Arabia for decades. In the 1970s, the Saudis began to purchase it, and within a few years, Saudi Aramco controlled not only half of Texaco and more than a thousand gas stations in the United States and Europe, but as much as one-quarter of all the proven oil reserves in the world.

The issue of oil and the Middle East has been peripheral to most of the history in this book. Oil did not become central for Saudi Arabia and Iraq until the 1920s, and only during World War II did the region take on global significance as a source of petroleum. By the end of the twentieth century, however, it was widely understood, both in popular culture in Europe and the United States and "on the Arab street," that American involvement in the Middle East has been motivated by three things: Israel, Christianity, and oil.

And yet, Aramco is an Arab oil company. Specifically, it is a Saudi company with close ties to the global petroleum industry. The Saudi state rests on two foundations: an alliance between the royal family and the puritanical Wahhabis, and a symbiotic relationship with the major economies of the world as the dominant producer of oil. The Saudi oil barons own land, businesses, and investments throughout Europe, Japan, and the United States. Many of them have been educated in American schools, and live a double life as tribal potentates and Western billionaires. Today, Aramco executives and workers inhabit the peculiar twilight zone of Dhahran, as they have for decades, with fathers often passing their positions to their sons, and in their walled and heavily guarded compounds, they live a life that is not quite Western and very definitely not Saudi.

Whether one views this relationship as symbiotic or parasitic, a testament to free-market capitalism or a sign of Western imperialism; whether there is a genuine partnership between the Saudi oilmen and

American executives and engineers or a cynical compact, the existence of Aramco is a product of cooperation between an austere Muslim state and an unabashedly Christian country, the United States.[9]

Then there is the saga of Turkey's struggle to gain full membership in the European Union. After World War I, Atatürk remade his country as a secular state, and it has stayed on that path. Throughout the Cold War, Turkey was an ally of the United States and a member of NATO. In the 1980s and 1990s, Turkey's government and its business class made a concerted effort to join the European Union, and after considerable debate, the EU decided to commence the official talks that could lead to Turkey's membership after 2010.

In both Turkey and Europe, there is unease and ambivalence. After decades of staunch secularism, Turkey in 2003 elected a prime minster, Recep Erdogan, who supported a more prominent role for Islam. That alarmed not only the Turkish military and the loyal inheritors of the Atatürk's legacy, but also the Europeans. The European Union says nothing per se about the religion of its members, but one of its official criteria is the vague category of "Europeanness." Suffice it to say that Islam has never been embraced as an aspect of European identity. To the contrary, Europe thinks of itself as having been forged in opposition to Islam, and to organized religion.

Erdogan, however, has consistently resisted attempts of Turkish Islamists to force traditional religion into the public sphere. He has refused, for example, to reconsider the ban on head scarves for women in public classrooms. Atatürk used reforms of traditional dress, including bans on head scarves for women and the fez cap for men, as a symbol that Turkey would be part of, and not distinct from, the modern world. That world was, he realized, governed by Western values and rules, and he wanted Turkey to become part of it. Erdogan belongs to a generation who, on the whole, accept that basic principle and yet also wish to integrate elements of traditional Turkish culture, including Islam. He personally is devout, yet that is no more antithetical to the "modern world" than the devoutness of American presidents.

The European Union, however, has been apprehensive about Turkey. Some Austrian opponents have explicitly raised the specter of the Ottomans at the gates of Vienna. Germans have also been suspicious. Millions of Turks live and work in Germany, but Germans, who outside of Bavaria have become increasingly less religious, express discom-

fort with the Muslim nature of the Turkish government—just as they have been uncomfortable with the evangelical Christian character of George W. Bush's administration. They have also questioned Turkey's economic development and its commitment to human rights, but the core arguments have all, in one way or another, circled around the issue of religion, identity, and politics.

The irony, of course, is that it is the avowedly secular Europeans who have been equivocal, whereas the Muslim party leading the governing coalition in Turkey expressed no reservations about relinquishing sovereignty to the European Union in return for closer economic ties. Turkey has also cultivated a cordial, though not exactly warm, relationship with Israel and maintained close relations with the United States, even through the highly charged atmosphere after September 11 and especially after the U.S. invasion of Iraq in the spring of 2003.[10]

Turkey's path challenges most generalizations about Islam and the West, but that is only because these generalizations are so incomplete. Few people imagine that it is possible for a state to be Muslim in cultural and religious identity and also be a full participant in the global economy. Even fewer believe that it can prize the rule of law, have a healthy interest in constructive ties with Europe and the United States, and simultaneously cherish Islam. That type of state does not fit the either-or template that says a society has to put religion into a confined box in order to be a full-fledged participant in the modern world, nor is it easily reconciled with the notion that the relationship between Muslims, Christians, and Jews is inherently unstable.

The status of Muslim immigrants in Europe often seems to support that notion. Riots in Parisian suburbs; the killing of the prominent, provocative Dutch filmmaker Theo van Gogh by a disaffected young Dutch Muslim; the increase of jihadi sympathy in the anonymous apartment blocks of English cities; and the bombings in Madrid in 2003 and London in 2005 have led to considerable anxiety in Europe about whether Islam and secular Christianity can coexist. Yet here as well, the daily lives of millions of immigrants who live and work in their adopted societies willingly and ardently is given scant attention. It is not just a problem of the "squeaky wheel" syndrome, where angry voices of protest get more notice. It is that other lives and other stories are actively ignored because they don't fit.

The result is that the cultural and economic cooperation that occurs

so regularly and so effortlessly that it should be considered common-place is unmentioned or lost in the fray. In Jordan, King Abdullah II, heir to his father, Hussein, in so many ways, has tried to honor the tradition of intellectual openness, tribal solidarity, independence, and progress that marked the most vibrant days of the caliphs and the Ottomans. Jordan today is a hybrid of bedouin, Palestinian Christians and Muslims, a Muslim Brotherhood that participates (albeit grudgingly) in the politi-cal process, and a Western-educated and Western-leaning elite. That doesn't mean that all is well, simply that the country and its monarchs have tried to steer a course of moderation and international integration, working assiduously with governments and businesses abroad, from the United States to the European Union to Iraq, Iran, China, and Japan.

And then there is Morocco, which under both King Muhammad VI and his father, King Hassan, has tilted toward France. Cities like Mar-rakesh, Fez, and Tangier are cosmopolitan. Having once ruled Iberia, Moroccans never ceased to feel that they are as much a part of Europe as they are of North Africa and the Arab world. In the last decades of the twentieth century and into the twenty-first, Marrakesh for one has become increasingly entwined with Europe in general and France espe-cially. The French expatriate community has blossomed, and yet the city has maintained its eccentric Muslim culture. The call to prayer still blankets the old city at dawn and dusk, even as people drink alcohol in the Djemaa al-Fna, the airy open space that fills with crowds, food, and acrobats each night and that guards the entrance to the labyrinthine markets and to an old city whose tendrils extend from the twenty-first century back to the fifteenth.

And there are the 200 million Muslims of India, who live and prosper amid a billion Hindus, with flashes of conflict and long periods of indif-ference and communion. There are the young of Iran, an oil-rich coun-try that is ruled by a brittle mullocracy spending the dwindling political capital of the 1979 revolution but that now has a majority of population under the age of twenty-five who cannot remember the shah and who have little but scorn for the clerics. While the mullahs may yearn for nuclear weapons, the young dream vibrant dreams of the United States, and Hollywood, and of men and women being able to walk hand in hand without being confronted by thugs claiming the mantle of the Prophet. And there are the five million Muslims in the United States, a few of whom are African-American converts and many more who are immi-

grants and the children of immigrants from Pakistan, Bangladesh, and elsewhere, who go to neighborhood mosques and are appalled at the violence of distant men and women claiming to be the only true Muslims. And there are other stories, of people consumed not by religious fervor but by the daily, universal concerns of money, work, and family.

In a world where technology will make it easier for the angry few to do great harm, the perpetuation of a model of conflict is dangerous. Remembering that each of the three traditions carries the seeds of peace will not by itself heal the world. A more complete picture will not convert today's jihadis from war to love, and it will not alone force the Western world to reconsider Islam. But if these stories are integrated into our sense of the past and the present, it will be more difficult to treat religion as destiny. Religion is a force coursing through the past, but hardly the only force. Muslims, Christians, and Jews are entwined, but their history is as varied as the story of the human race. It points in no one direction, or in all directions. If conflict is what we want to see, there is conflict. But if peace is what we are looking for, then peace is there to be found.

❦❦ ❦❦

I⸱ Dubai the Future?

W<small>E READ EVERY DAY</small> news of death and violence in Iraq. The stories include Sunni Iraqis killing Shi'ite Iraqis, al-Qaeda assassinating rivals, Shi'ite factions in the southern part of the country skirmishing with one another, Iranian-funded groups fighting against Saudi-funded groups, and everyone fighting the Americans. Many people throughout the world no doubt long ago ceased to pay these reports much attention, but in Europe, the United States, and the Middle East, it is nearly impossible to avoid the news. The daily litany creates an indelible impression that Islam and violence keep close company.

Iraq has been only one element of that toxic brew. The continued struggle between Israel and the Palestinians is another, albeit familiar, ingredient. The presidency of Mahmoud Ahmadinejad in Iran has added a new dimension. The president has rarely lost an opportunity to inflame passions, which he seems to stoke with glee, calling one moment for the eradication of Israel and the next for a united Muslim front against the American-led West. Flush with an unexpected injection of petrodollars, thanks to China's increased demand for oil, Iran's government and its populist president have pursued a path of confrontation with the United States and with any who question Iran's right to a nuclear power program that might or might not go hand in hand with the capacity to produce a nuclear weapon.

And with the eruption of armed hostilities between Israel and the Iranian-backed Hezbollah in Lebanon in July 2006, it looked as if, once again, Muslims, Christians, and Jews were locked in a death dance, and

that with the prospect of nuclear weapons in the hands of Iran and Israel, the conflict could one day have an Armageddon potential.

But five hundred miles south of Iran and Iraq, on the western shore of the Persian Gulf, lies the emirate of Dubai. Until 2006, few Americans—though a somewhat higher percentage of British and Europeans—knew where Dubai was, but that changed when Dubai Ports World, one of the largest companies of its kind, concluded a $6.8 billion agreement to purchase Britain's Peninsular and Oriental Steam Navigation Company, which operated a number of ports in the United States, including Newark, Miami, and New Orleans. The transfer of ownership seemed destined to be a quiet, uneventful event until Congress proceeded to bludgeon the Bush administration for gross negligence and dereliction of duty. The crime was allowing the sale of vital national security to an Arab state.

The criticism was not limited to Democratic opponents of the Bush administration. It was, in fact, a rare moment of bipartisan dudgeon, with heated rhetoric erupting throughout the country against the proposed deal. There were allegations that the government of Dubai was linked to terrorism, based on the fact that several of the participants in the 9/11 attacks had availed themselves of Dubai's banking system. While similar logic could have been used to denounce the government of Germany for abetting the 9/11 attacks, the fact that Dubai is a family-ruled Arab principality and that Dubai Ports World is controlled by the government was translated into proof that American national security would be endangered if the deal were allowed to go through. Said one outraged Republican congressional representative, "In regards to selling American ports to Dubai, not just *no*—but *hell no!*"

After a flurry of hearings and a wave of uproar, Dubai Ports World agreed to alter the arrangement so that the American ports would not be included. The emir of Dubai, in public, was tight-lipped, but in private he was apparently furious. More than almost any state in the Arab world, Dubai had embraced the logic of global capitalism, and yet it was still treated as a pariah by the American public and lumped together with al-Qaeda.

It was easy enough to read what happened as the latest chapter in the history of conflict. Yet here as well, all was not as it seemed. For while the ports deal was scuttled, other arms of the Dubai government were wrap-

ping up the purchase of several luxury hotels and office buildings in Manhattan, including the Essex House on Central Park South and the W Hotel in Union Square. Two of the Park Avenue buildings bought by the Dubai company Istithmar were acquired from Boston Properties, which is controlled by Mortimer Zuckerman, who is not only a prominent New York developer but a publisher and an outspoken American Jewish financial backer of Israel. Another investment arm of Dubai purchased the second-largest private homebuilder in the United States, John Laing Homes, for $1.05 billion in the late spring of 2006, after the ports imbroglio. Around the same time, the international hotel and casino operator Kerzner International announced its intention to become a private company in a management buyout. Among other things, Kerzner owns the Atlantis complex in the Bahamas and is working on a Dubai project that will include a lavish resort on an artificial island, which may have the first casino in the Persian Gulf. The company's primary owners are the Kerzners, a South African Jewish family, and the royal family of Dubai.

Dubai was the beneficiary of the spectacular rise in the price of oil between 2004 and 2006, but unlike the other Gulf states, the country itself has few oil reserves. While it receives a share of the oil revenues of Abu Dhabi and the other states that comprise the United Arab Emirates, Dubai's wealth and power is a product of a purposeful decision by Sheikh Rashid al-Maktoum in the 1970s to align his strip of desert with the West. That policy was continued by his sons, who turned a weakness— the absence of oil—into a strength. Unable to rely on petrodollars, the royal family was forced instead to become entrepreneurial. The results have far exceeded Sheikh Rashid's ambitions.

With fewer than a hundred thousand citizens, Dubai in the early years of the twenty-first century became one of the largest construction zones in the world and home to more than 1 million people, almost all of whom were citizens of other countries drawn to Dubai by low taxes, loose credit, unintrusive banking, easy-to-obtain menial jobs, and countless opportunities to get rich. An odd amalgam of Las Vegas, Singapore, and Miami, Dubai is the only city in the conservative Gulf region to allow consumption of alcohol and to welcome Western and global tourists unconditionally. It is a free-trade and duty-free zone that built on its earlier foundation as a port and used the national airline to attract visitors to the dozens of malls that the city has to offer. Tourists from

Europe and Asia flock to Dubai for shopping holidays, as do Arabs from oil states. The Emirates Mall, opened in late 2005, includes a Ralph Lauren boutique, a Carrefour hypermarket, and a Harvey Nichols department store. It also has hundreds of boutiques, one of which offers custom-made burqas to cover upper-class women from Saudi Arabia; two shops over, La Perla displays nearly naked mannequins. A hundred yards farther on, there is Ski Dubai, a four-hundred-meter snow-packed ski slope fully enclosed and air-conditioned, with a Chili's restaurant providing a view of the surreal sight of people skiing in the middle of a desert where temperatures often exceed 110 degrees.

In spite of the furor over the ports deal in the United States, Dubai simply doesn't fit the images of a Middle East defined by conflict with the West, or images of Christians and Jews locked in a battle with Muslims. What are we to make of a Muslim ruling family doing business with a gambling and leisure company run by Jews? Or of a company owned by the royal family concluding real estate deals with an American Jewish real estate mogul who makes no secret of his ardent support for Israel? Or of a city-state that borders a puritanical Saudi Arabia and acts as an escape valve for the same Saudis who accept the stricture of Wahhabi dogma at home? Or of a burgeoning state that annually draws half a million British tourists, who are lured by the prospect of cheap shopping and beaches? What are we to make of Dubai, a city-state that epitomizes the excesses and successes of capitalism in a globalized age?

Contrary to predictions that the scuttling of the ports deal would imperil relations between the United States and Western-leaning regimes in the Middle East, within weeks it was business as usual. The virulent reactions of the United States did leave a bitter residue, but at the beginning of the twenty-first century—as in most of the prior fourteen hundred years—conflict and cooperation do not cancel each other out; they exist simultaneously.

Dubai is no longer ignored. It has too much glitz. It makes great copy for travel magazines and media outlets looking to observe the lifestyles of the rich and famous. It has a hotel shaped like a traditional fishing boat that rises a thousand feet above the water with rooms that start at $1,000 a night. It has sports tournaments and nightclubs that draw global sponsors and international celebrities, and it has resorts and condominiums that spring out of the dunes, along with a booming (and occasionally busting) stock market that piques the interest of international investors.

But Dubai as a counterpoint to the relentless drumbeat of civilizational war is unappreciated. It may be a shrine to greed and decadence, and it may be but a beneficiary of high oil prices and so will face hard times if those prices head south, but none of that makes it any less than a testament to the ability of Muslims, Christians, and Jews to find common cause.

And it is hardly the only one. In Egypt, a business dynasty led by the Coptic Christian Sawiris family has been trying to break out of the parochial backwater that has been the Egyptian economy. Perhaps in response to the petrodollars flooding the region and anxious to offset the rise in the fundamentalist movement, the Egyptian government of Hosni Mubarak finally realized that you can have political reform, you can have economic reform, but you cannot have neither. The loosening of state control over the economy—overseen by another Copt, the finance minister, Yousef Boutros-Ghali—proved to be a boon to the Sawiris clan, and especially to Naguib Sawiris, the fifty-year-old head of Orascom, the largest telecom company in the region. He seized the opportunity to create a new mobile phone network in American-occupied Iraq, and then negotiated a multibillion-dollar purchase of Wind, a subsidiary of one of the largest telecom operators in Italy.

Sawiris is strongly pro-American yet works assiduously to improve the lot of Gaza Palestinians by opening businesses in the impoverished region. He has been openly critical of Mubarak for the slowness of economic reform, and is unapologetically secular in his demeanor and outlook. He is, in short, a global capitalist who happens to be an Egyptian. He is a Coptic Christian who has created a company that employs tens of thousands of Muslims and offers its shares on international stock exchanges to Americans, Asians, Middle Easterners, and Europeans. And like any successful businessman, he is more likely to speak of the world becoming flat than he is to think in terms of any inherent antagonism between Muslims, Christians, and Jews.

And therein lies a final lesson and a real danger. Muslims, Christians, and Jews have been so enmeshed in a framework of conflict and so determined to view not only history but the present through that lens that they risk missing the next wave of history. Many parts of the world that are emerging in the twenty-first century have not been party to that history, and are neither interested in nor constrained by it, China most of all.

In no small measure, the rulers of Dubai and the Sawiris family have

been able to turn their aspirations into reality because they are unencumbered by the history of conflict. They have shed the burdens of the past, and have instead taken advantage of the opportunities that cooperation and coexistence create and have always created. They are not trying to restore a golden age. They are not driven by a sense of grievance. They are simply working with the world around them. But whether or not they greet strangers with the word of peace, they are emissaries of it just the same. And so are the millions who go about their daily lives seeking only the betterment of themselves and their families, uninterested in dogma, theology, and hatred. That has been true for the entire history of Muslims, Christians, and Jews, even though that part of the story has been neglected, even though discord makes for better drama and more passion. It remains true today. Peace is woven into our collective past; it is there to be seen in our messy present; and it will be there in our shared future.

The Early Muslim Conquests
and Abbasid Empire, ca. 800

*CAROLINGIAN
EMPIRE*

× Battle of Tours
732

Rhône River

Danube River

PYRENEES
MOUNTAINS

Rome

Constantinople

BYZANTINE EMPIRE

TAU

Tagus River

UMAYYAD SPAIN
Córdoba

Gibraltar

Tunis

ATLAS MOUNTAINS

MEDITERRANEAN SEA

Alexandr

Cairo/Fust

EGYPT

NORTH AFRICA

S A H A R A

☐ *Abbasid Empire*
▨ *Byzantine Empire*
▦ *Carolingian Empire*
▥ *Umayyad Spain*

0   500   1,000 Miles

0   500   1,000 Kilometers

N

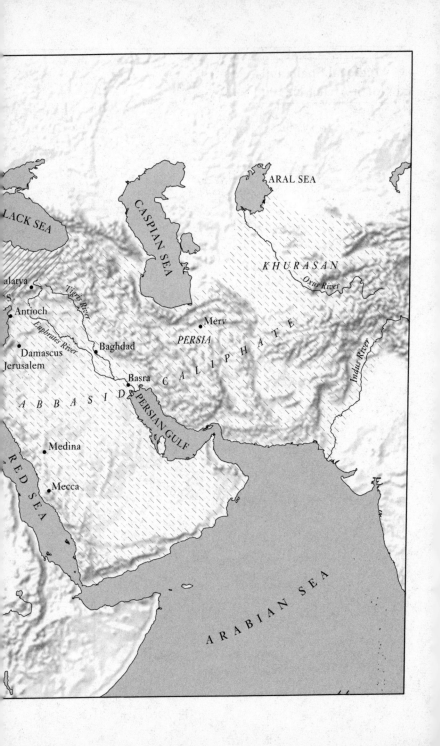

Medieval Spain and North Africa, ca. 1000

PYRENEES MOUNTAINS

KINGDOM OF LEÓN

Douro River

Ebro River

KINGDOM OF CASTILLE

KINGDOM OF ARAGON

• Madrid

Tagus River

• Toledo

• Valencia

IBERIAN PENINSULA

Guadiana River

CALIPHATE OF CORDOBA

KINGDOM OF PORTUGAL

• Lisbon

Córdoba

Seville •

Guadalquivir River

• Granada

Cadiz •

• Gibraltar

• Ceuta

ATLANTIC OCEAN

MEDITERRANEAN SEA

ALMORAVID EMPIRE

ATLAS MOUNTAINS

• Féz

MOROCCO

• Marrakesh

S A H A R A

N

| 0 | 100 | 200 Miles |
| 0 | 100 | 200 Kilometers |

	Almoravid Empire
	Kingdom of Aragon
	Kingdom of Castille
	Kingdom of León
	Kingdom of Portugal

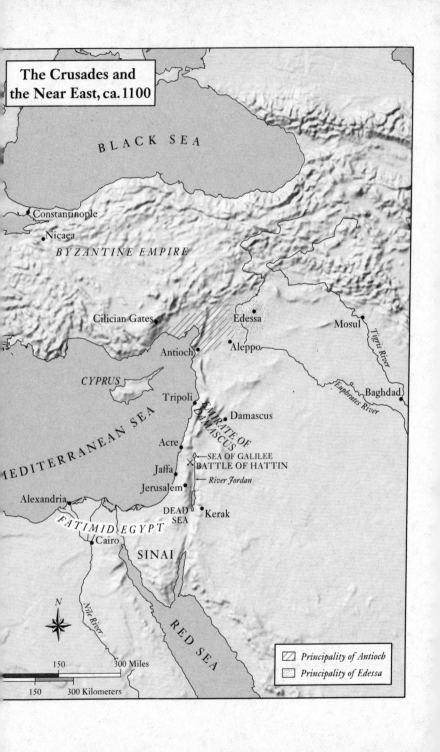

The Crusades and
the Near East, ca.1100

BLACK SEA

Constantinople

Nicaea

BYZANTINE EMPIRE

Cilician Gates

Edessa

Mosul

Antioch

Aleppo

Tigris River

CYPRUS

Tripoli

Baghdad

Euphrates River

EMIRATE OF DAMASCUS

Damascus

MEDITERRANEAN SEA

Acre

SEA OF GALILEE
BATTLE OF HATTIN

Jaffa

River Jordan

Jerusalem

Alexandria

DEAD
SEA

Kerak

FATIMID EGYPT

Cairo

SINAI

N

Nile River

RED
SEA

150   300 Miles

150   300 Kilometers

▨ *Principality of Antioch*

▦ *Principality of Edessa*

The Ottoman Empire, ca.1600

ATLANTIC OCEAN

Paris

FRANCE

Danube River

Vienna

Buda Pest

AUSTRO-HUNGARIAN EMPIRE

Venice

Belgrade

BALKAN

Salonica

PYRENEES MOUNTAINS

Rome

PORTUGAL

Madrid

SPAIN

Marrakesh

CRE

MEDITERRANEA

S A H A R A

N

Ottoman Empire, 1492

Ottoman conquests by 1566

| 0 | 500 | 1,000 Miles |

| 0 | 500 | 1,000 Kilometers |

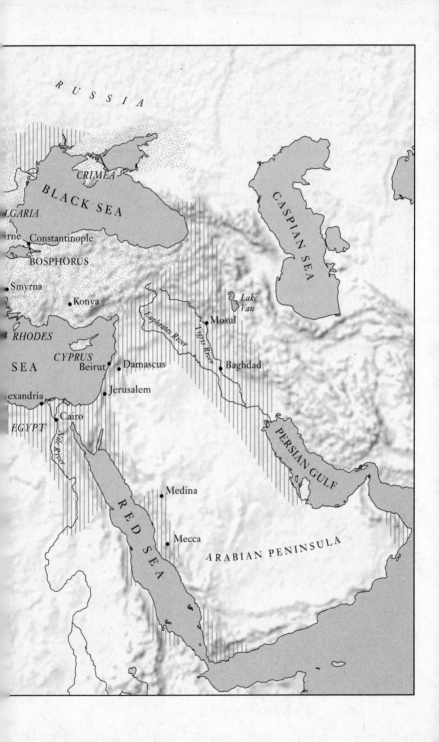

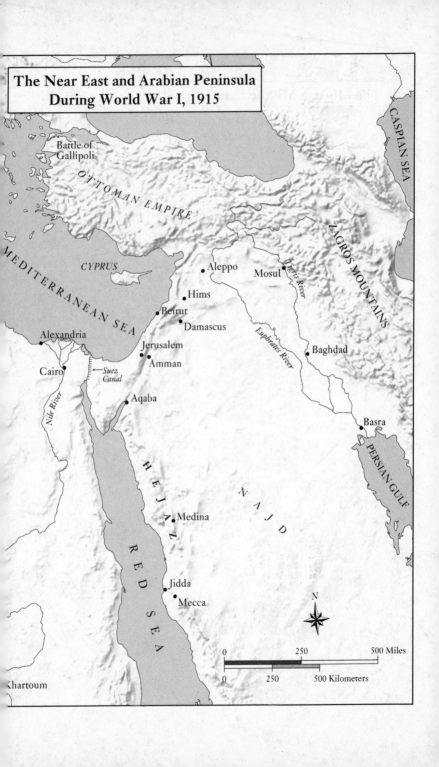

The Near East and Arabian Peninsula During World War I, 1915

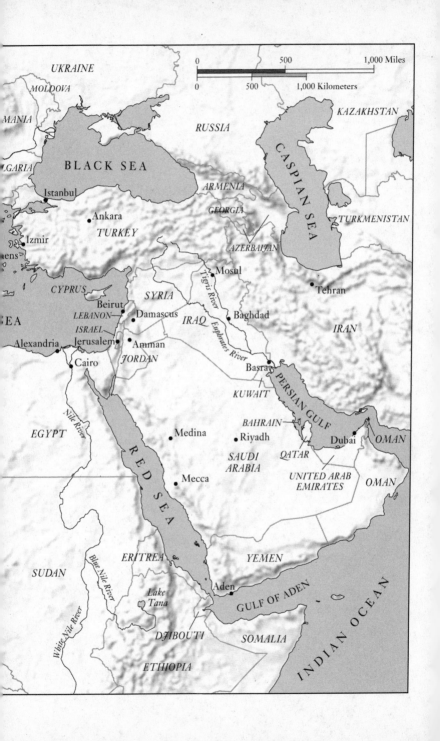

NOTES

CHAPTER ONE: IN THE NAME OF THE LORD

1. This description relies on Stephen Humphries, *Islamic History: A Framework for Inquiry* (Princeton, N.J.: Princeton University Press, 1991), 92–98, and W. Montgomery Watt, *Islamic Political Thought* (Edinburgh: University of Edinburgh Press, 1968), 4–9 and appendix. Watt relies on the account of Ibn Ishaq, one of the canonical biographers of the Prophet, who wrote in the eighth century. For pre-Islamic alliances, see Michael Cook, *Forbidding Wrong in Islam* (Cambridge: Cambridge University Press, 2003), 150ff. Some scholars question whether this agreement actually existed and believe that it was invented by chroniclers writing several hundred years after the fact. But to dismiss the notion entirely seems foolish. See John Wansbrough, *Quranic Studies: Sources and Methods of Scriptural Interpretation* (New York: Oxford University Press, 1977), and Patricia Crone and Michael Cook, *Hagarism: The Making of the Islamic World* (Cambridge: Cambridge University Press, 1976).

2. Abu-l Abbas Ahmad ibn Jabir al-Baladhuri, *The Origins of the Islamic State*, trans. Philip Khuri Hitti (Piscataway, N.J.: Gorgias Press, 2002), 33. This is a reprint of the original 1916 edition, published by Columbia University Press.

3. Passages from the Quran are taken from A. J. Arberry, *The Koran Interpreted* (New York: Touchstone, 1955, 1996).

4. The account was written by the Armenian historian Sebeos and is quoted in A. A. Vasiliev, *History of the Byzantine Empire*, vol. I (Madison: University of Wisconsin Press, 1952), 199. See also George Ostrogorsky, *History of the Byzantine State* (London: Blackwell, 1956), 110ff. For a unique take on the origin of the caliphate, see Patricia Crone, *God's Rule: Government and Islam* (New York: Columbia University Press, 2004).

5. See Claude Cahen, "Dhimma," in *The Encyclopedia of Islam* (Leiden: E. J. Brill, 1991); Bat Ye'or, *The Decline of Eastern Christianity: From Jihad to Dhimmitude* (London, 1996), 121ff.; Suhayl Qasha, *Al-Masihiyan fi al-Dawlah al-Islamiya* [Christians in the Muslim State] (Beirut: Dar al-Malak, 2002), 54ff.; C. E. Bosworth, "The Concept of Dhimma in Early Islam," in Bosworth, *The Arab, Byzantium, and Iran* (Burlington, Vt.: Ashgate Publishing, 1996), 285ff.

6. Quoted Khalid ibn al-Walid, and the inhabitants of Hims all quoted in al-Baladhuri, *The Origins of the Islamic State,* 187, 211. Though some of the depiction of Christians and Jews rushing to the side of the Arabs may be exaggerated by al-Baladhuri, he is far from the only early historian to record the widespread discontent with Byzantine rule.

7. See for instance Ibn Abd al-Hakam, *History of the Conquests of Egypt, North Africa, and Spain,* ed. Charles Torrey (Piscataway, N.J.: Gorgias Press, 2002), and Jamal al-Din Shayyal, *Tarikh Misr al-Islamiya* [The Islamic History of Egypt] (Alexandria: Dar al-Ma'arif, 1967).

8. Chase F. Robinson, *Empire and Elites After the Muslim Conquest: The Transformation of Northern Mesopotamia* (Cambridge: Cambridge University Press, 2000), 28ff.

9. For the best analysis of conversion to Islam, see Richard Bulliet, *Conversion to Islam in the Medieval Period* (Cambridge: Harvard University Press, 1979). For a detailed analysis of Quran 2:256, see Yohanan Friedmann, *Tolerance and Coercion in Islam: Interfaith Relations in Muslim Tradition* (New York: Cambridge University Press, 2003), 100ff.

10. A good account of the fall of Jerusalem and Umar's visit can be found in Karen Armstrong, *Jerusalem: One City, Three Faiths* (New York: Knopf, 1996), 226–34. For Sophronius, see Robert Hoyland, *Seeing Islam as Others Saw It: A Survey and Evaluation of Christian, Jewish and Zoroastrian Writings on Early Islam* (Princeton, N.J.: Darwin Press, 1997), 66–74.

11. Hoyland, *Seeing Islam as Others Saw It,* 480ff.; Hugh Goddard, *A History of Muslim-Christian Relations* (Chicago: New Amsterdam Books, 2000), 38–41.

CHAPTER TWO: AT THE COURT OF THE CALIPH

1. Dimitri Gutas, *Greek Thought, Arabic Culture: The Graeco-Arabic Translation Movement in Baghdad and Early Abbasid Society* (New York: Routledge, 1998), 28ff. Timothy quotation from Sydney Griffith, *Arabic Christianity in the Monasteries of Ninth-Century Palestine* (Burlington, Vt.: Ashgate Publishing, 1992), 140–45. See also Hugh Kennedy, *The Early Abbasid Caliphate* (London: Croom & Helm, 1981); Jacob Lassner, *The Shaping of Abbasid Rule* (Princeton, N.J.: Princeton University Press, 1980); al-Tabari, *The Early Abbasid Empire,* vol. 2, trans. John Alden Williams (New York: Cambridge University Press, 1989).

2. For the building of Baghdad, see Hugh Kennedy, *The Court of the Caliphs: The Rise and Fall of Islam's Greatest Dynasty* (London: Weidenfeld & Nicholson, 2005), 132ff.

3. Sydney Griffith, *The Beginnings of Christian Theology in Arabic: Muslim-Christian Encounters in the Early Islamic Period* (Burlington, Vt.: Ashgate, 2002), 155ff.; Majid Fakhry, *Islamic Philosophy, Theology, and Mysticism* (Oxford, England: Oneworld, 1997); Ignaz Goldziher, *Introduction to Islamic Theology and Law* (Princeton, N.J.: Princeton University Press, 1991); Hoyland, 454–56; Goddard, 52–54; Louis Cheikho, *Ulama' al-Nasraniyah fi al-Islam, 622–1300* [Christian Scholars Under Islam] (Juniyah, Lebanon: al-Maktabah al-Bulusiyah, 1983).

4. Qasha, 110; G. Stange, *Baghdad During the Abbasid Caliphate* (London: Oxford University Press, 1924), 202ff.

5. The best study, bar none, of this process is Richard Bulliet, *Conversion to Islam in the Medieval Period* (Cambridge: Harvard University Press, 1979).

6. Abu Nuwas quoted in Eric Schroeder, *Muhammad's People: An Anthology of Muslim Civilization* (Mineola, N.Y.: Dover Publications, 1955, 2002), 315. Also see Marshall C. S. Hodgson, *The Venture of Islam,* vol. 1 (Chicago: University of Chicago Press, 1974), 462–63.

7. See Dimitri Gutas, 58–60, for the argument that the *bayt al-hikma* was little more than a simple library.

8. Quoted in Schroeder, 366–67.

9. Al-Ma'mun quoted in al-Tabari, *The History of al-Tabari,* vol. 32, trans. C. E. Bosworth (Albany: State University of New York Press, 1987), 100–101. For al-Kindi, see Fakhry, 21–29, and Felix Klein-Franke, "Al-Kindi," in Seyyed Hossein Nasr and Oliver Leaman, eds., *History of Islamic Philosophy: Part 1* (London: Routledge, 1996), 165ff.

10. Both al-Jahiz and the chief judge quoted in Bernard Lewis, *The Jews of Islam* (Princeton, N.J.: Princeton University Press, 1984), 15, 59–60.

11. This exchange is frequently cited, and the translation here is from Hugh Kennedy, 80–81. See also J. J. Saunders, *A History of Medieval Islam* (London: Routledge and Kegan Paul, 1965), 114; C. E. Bosworth, *The Arab, Byzantium and Iran* (Burlington, Vt.: Ashgate Publishing, 1996).

12. See Alessandro Barbero, *Charlemagne: Father of a Continent* (Berkeley: University of California Press, 2004), 90–91; Richard Fletcher, *The Cross and the Crescent: Christianity and Islam from Muhammad to the Reformation* (New York: Viking, 2004), 50ff.

13. Al-Tabari, *The History of al-Tabari,* vol. 32, 195–97.

CHAPTER THREE: THE SACRIFICE OF ISAAC

1. There have been many accounts of the Córdoban martyrs. See Jessica Coope, *The Martyrs of Córdoba: Community and Family Conflict in an Age of Mass Conversion* (Lincoln: University of Nebraska Press, 1995); Norman Daniel, *The Arabs and Mediaeval Europe* (London: Longman, 1975), 230–48; Kenneth Baxter Wolf, *Christian Martyrs in Muslim Spain* (New York: Cambridge University Press, 1987). Also, Paul Alvarus, "The Life of Eulogius," in Olivia Remie Constable, ed., *Medieval Iberia: Readings from Christian, Muslim, and Jewish Sources* (Philadelphia: University of Pennsylvania Press, 1997), 48–51. For the text of the surrender of Murcia, see Constable, 37.

2. The phrase "ornament of the world" comes from the Saxon writer Hroswitha in the tenth century and is used as the title of Maria Rosa Menocal's superb study, *The Ornament of the World: How Muslims, Jews and Christians Created a Culture of Tolerance in Medieval Spain* (New York: Little Brown, 2002). Earlier Paul Alvarus quotation from Menocal, 66. The phrase "men who worship God and acknowl-

edge heavenly laws" is from John McManners, *The Oxford Illustrated History of Christianity.* (New York: Oxford University Press, 2001).

3. The excerpt from the life of John of Gorze and descriptions of tenth-century Córdoba come from Richard Fletcher, *Moorish Spain* (Berkeley: University of California Press, 1992), 66–70; see also Richard Reilly, *The Medieval Spains* (Cambridge: Cambridge University Press, 1993).

4. See S. D. Goitein, *A Mediterranean Society: An Abridgement in One Volume* (Berkeley: University of California Press, 1999). This is a condensed version of Goitein's lifetime study of the documents of the Cairo Geniza, charting the intricate commercial ties between Jews throughout the Mediterranean. See also Olivia Remie Constable, *Trade and Traders in Muslim Spain: The Commercial Realignment of the Iberian Peninsula* (New York: Cambridge University Press, 1994).

5. Translations of these letters can be found at the Web site www.fordham.edu/halsall/source/khazars1.html, which is part of the Internet Medieval Sourcebook compiled by the Fordham Center for Medieval Studies and edited by Paul Halsall. See also Douglas M. Dunlop, *A History of the Jewish Khazars* (Princeton, N.J.: Princeton University Press, 1954); Jane Gerber, *The Jews of Spain: A History of the Sephardic Experience* (New York: Free Press, 1992), 46–61; Vivian Mann et al., eds., *Convivencia: Jews, Muslims, and Christians in Medieval Spain* (New York: Braziller and the Jewish Museum, 1992), 40–44.

6. The description of Samuel as a lover of knowledge comes from Moses ibn Ezra, "Kitab al-Muarah," from Joseph Jacobs, "Samuel Ha-Nagid," in www.jewish encyclopedia.com. See also Jefim Schirmann, "Samuel Hannagid, the Man, the Soldier, the Politician," *Jewish Social Studies* 2 (April 1951), 107. The excerpted poem that begins "Man's wisdom…" is from David Goldstein, *Hebrew Poems from Spain* (New York: Schocken Books, 1996). For the Nagid's poem in which he calls himself "the David of his age," see Menocal, 102. For the poem describing the carnage of the battlefield, see Israel Zinberg, *History of Jewish Literature: Arabic-Spanish Period,* trans. Bernard Martin (Cleveland: Case Western Reserve University Press, 1972).

7. From Constable, ed., *Medieval Iberia,* 97–99.

8. Hugh Kennedy, *Muslim Spain and Portugal: A Political History of al-Andalus* (New York: Longman, 1996), 146.

9. Kennedy, 154ff.; Richard Fletcher, *Moorish Spain,* 105ff.; Bernard Reilly, 90–128; Andrew Wheatcroft, *Infidel: A History of the Conflict Between Christendom and Islam* (New York: Random House, 2003), 85ff.

CHAPTER FOUR: THE CRUSADES

1. Pope Urban II quoted in Thomas Asbridge, *The First Crusade: A New History: The Roots of Conflict Between Christianity and Islam* (New York: Oxford University Press, 2005), 32–33. Some scholars have questioned whether Jerusalem was indeed the stated goal of the First Crusade, but most have concluded that it was.

For these historiographical debates, see Andrew Jotischky, *Crusading and the Crusader States* (New York: Longman, 2004), chap. 1.

2. Al-Hakim's eccentricities are described in Marshall Hodgson, *The Venture of Islam*, vol. 2, 26–28. Some have said that Hakim was the victim of later polemicists and that he was not at all addled.

3. The literature on the origins of Christian holy war is immense. See Asbridge, *The First Crusades*, chap. 1; Christopher Tyerman, *Fighting for Christendom: Holy War and the Crusades* (New York: Oxford University Press, 2004); Jotischky, *Crusading and the Crusader States*; Claude Cahen, *Orient et Occident au temps des Croisades* (Paris: Editions Aubier, 1983), 54–80.

4. The first Urban quote is from the account written by Fulcher of Chartres, the second by Robert the Monk, both of which can be found in the Internet Medieval Sourcebook at www.fordham.edu/halsall/sbook1k.html.

5. The story about a possible alliance between the Fatimids and the Crusaders comes from a thirteenth-century chronicler named Ibn al-Athir, quoted in Carole Hillenbrand, *The Crusades: Islamic Perspectives* (New York: Routledge, 2000), 46.

6. Anna Comnena is the primary source on Alexius. Good secondary sources include John Julius Norwich, *Byzantium: The Decline and Fall* (New York: Knopf, 1995), 31–35; Ostrogorsky, *History of the Byzantine State*, 349–70. Anna Comnena on Bohemond quoted in Elizabeth Hallam, ed., *Chronicles of the Crusades: Eye-Witness Accounts of the Wars Between Christianity and Islam* (New York: Welcome Rain, 2000), 69–70.

7. For the phrase "armed pilgrims," see Georges Bordonove, *Les Croisades et le royaume de Jerusalem* (Paris: Editions Pygmalion, 2002).

8. See the accounts of Ibn al-Athir, quoted in Francesco Gabrielli, *Arab Historians of the Crusades* (Berkeley: University of California Press, 1969), 3–9; Ibn al-Qalanisi, *The Damascus Chronicle of the Crusades*, ed. and trans. H. A. R. Gibb (New York: Dover Publications, 1932, 2002), 43–46. See also the magisterial history of Steven Runciman: *A History of the Crusades*, vol. 1, *The First Crusades and the Foundation of the Kingdom of Jerusalem* (Cambridge: Cambridge University Press, 1951), 213ff.

9. The historian, Ibn al-Athir, is quoted at length in P. M. Holt, *The Crusader States and Their Neighbors* (New York: Longman, 2004), 18.

10. See Runciman, 279ff.; Hallam, *Chronicles of the Crusades*, 88–94; Hans Eberhard Meyer, *The Crusades* (New York: Oxford University Press, 1965, 1988), 54–57; Asbridge, *The First Crusaders*, 316–19; Amin Maalouf, *The Crusades Through Arab Eyes* (New York: Schocken Books, 1983, 1987), 48–52.

11. Ibn al-Athir quoted in Maalouf, 55.

12. Piers Paul Read, *The Templars* (London: Weidenfeld & Nicholson, 1999); Edith Clementine Bramhall, "The Origins of the Temporal Privileges of Crusaders," *American Journal of Theology* (April 1901), 279–92.

13. Quoted in Holt, 45.

14. The first quotation, about Frankish religious toleration, is from Imad al-Din

and is quoted in Benjamin Kedar, "The Subjected Muslims of Frankish Levant," in James M. Powell, ed., *Muslims Under Latin Rule, 1100–1300* (Princeton, N.J.: Princeton University Press, 1990), 161. The second, from Ibn Jubayr, is quoted in Kedar, 167. Ibn al-Qalanisi quoted in Hillenbrand, 396.

15. See Ronnie Ellenblum, *Frankish Settlement in the Latin Kingdom of Jerusalem* (Cambridge: Cambridge University Press, 1998).

16. Usama ibn Munqidh, *An Arab-Syrian Gentleman and Warrior in the Period of the Crusades,* trans. Philip Hitti (New York: Columbia University Press, 1929, 2000), 161–70.

CHAPTER FIVE: SALADIN'S JIHAD?

1. Imad ad-Din quoted in Gabrielli, *Arab Historians of the Crusades,* 160ff.; Saladin's response to the delegation from Jerusalem and the speech of the *qadi* of Aleppo in Al-Aqsa Mosque both quoted in Stanley Lane-Poole, *Saladin: All Powerful Sultan and the Uniter of Islam* (New York: Cooper Square Press, 1898, 2002), 224–25, 236ff., which in turn translates from Ibn Khallikan. Also see Runciman, *A History of the Crusades,* vol. 2, *The Kingdom of Jerusalem and the Frankish East, 1100–1187.*

2. The account of Saladin's character comes from Baha al-Din ibn Shaddad, quoted in Hallam, 155–56.

3. Quoted in Malcolm Cameron Lyons and D. E. P. Jackson, *Saladin: The Politics of Holy War* (New York: Cambridge University Press, 1982), 119–20.

4. Gibbon quoted in Hillenbrand, 185. See also Edward Gibbon, *The Decline and Fall of the Roman Empire,* vol. 3 (New York: Heritage Press, 1946), 2084–85.

5. Both quotations in Lyons and Jackson, 194 and 228, as are statistics about time spent fighting Christians versus time spent campaigning against Muslims. Also, for a skeptical portrait of Saladin, see Andrew Ehrenkreutz, *Saladin* (Albany: State University of New York Press, 1972).

6. See David Cook, *Understanding Jihad* (Berkeley: University of California Press, 2005); Sayyid Hossein Nasr, *Islam: Religion, History and Civilization* (San Francisco: HarperSanFrancisco, 2003), 91ff.

7. Frankish account by Ernoul, written c. 1197, trans. Peter Edbury and Paul Hayams, in Fordham's Medieval Sourcebook, www.fordham.edu/halsall/source/1187.ernoul.html. See also the account of Ibn al-Athir in Gabrielli, 122–25.

8. Runciman, *A History of the Crusades,* vol. 3, *The Kingdom of Acre and the Later Crusades,* 53. For the Christian chronicler see *Itinerarium Peregrinorum et Gesta Regis Ricardi,* ed. William Stubbs, Rolls Series (London: Longmans, 1864), IV, 2, 4 (pp. 240–41, 243), translated by James Brundage in *The Crusades: A Documentary History* (Milwaukee: Marquette University Press, 1962), 183–84.

9. Runciman, vol. 3, 27.

10. Most of this account of the marriage proposal is taken from Baha ad-Din, in Gabrielli, 225–31. Saladin's reluctance to agree to truce is in Imad ad-Din, also in Gabrielli, 236–37.

11. For an excellent recent account, see Jonathan Phillips, *The Fourth Crusade and the Sack of Constantinople* (New York: Penguin Group, 2004).

CHAPTER SIX: THE PHILOSOPHER'S DREAM

1. See for instance Mark Myerson, *A Jewish Renaissance in Fifteenth-Century Spain* (Princeton, N.J.: Princeton University Press, 2004), 12. Derogatory quotation about those who favored martyrdom from Jane Gerber, *The Jews of Spain*, 81. All Maimonides quotations from Isadore Twersky, ed., *A Maimonides Reader* (Springfield, N.J.: Behrman House, 1972). On Maimonides and philosophy, see Joel Kraemer, "Maimonides and the Spanish Aristotelian School," in Mark Myerson and Edward English, eds., *Christians, Muslims, and Jews in Medieval and Early Modern Spain* (Notre Dame, Ind.: University of Notre Dame Press, 2000). For al-Ghazali, see Fakhry, *Islamic Philosophy*, 69–106, as well as Marshall Hodgson, *The Venture of Islam*, vol. 2, 180–92. For Ibn Arabi, see Seyyid Hossein Nasr, *Three Muslim Sages* (Cambridge: Harvard University Press, 1964), chap. 3 (the Ibn Arabi quotation is on p. 116). Also on Ibn Arabi, al-Ghazali, and mysticism in general, see Annemarie Schimmel, *Mystical Dimensions of Islam* (Chapel Hill: University of North Carolina Press, 1975), and John Renard, *Seven Doors to Islam: Spirituality and the Religious Life* (Berkeley: University of California Press, 1996).

2. Almohad "Doctrine of Divine Unity" in Olivia Remie Constable, *Medieval Iberia*, 190ff.

3. Ibn Khaldun, *The Muqaddimah*, trans. Franz Rosenthal (Princeton, N.J.: Princeton University Press, 1967).

4. Abu al-Baqa al-Rundi, "Lament for the Fall of Seville," in Constable, 120–23.

5. Charter issued by King Jaime of Aragon in Constable, 214–15.

6. Mosen Diego de Valera quoted in Vivian Mann et al., *Convivencia*, 75.

7. The description of Fernando's tomb, as well as the relevant details about Alfonso's life, are taken from Robert Burns, ed., *Emperor of Culture: Alfonso X the Learned of Castile and His Thirteenth-Century Renaissance* (Philadelphia: University of Pennsylvania Press, 1990).

8. See Menocal, *Ornament of the World*, 225–226; quotation of Alfonso's nephew in Norman Roth, "Jewish Collaborators in Alfonso's Scientific Work," in Burns, *Emperor of Culture*, 59ff.

CHAPTER SEVEN: THE LORD OF TWO LANDS

1. The story of Mehmed and the soldier in Hagia Sophia is told in countless narratives. This version is from Lord Kinross, *The Ottoman Centuries: The Rise and Fall of the Turkish Empire* (New York: Morrow, 1977), 109. For the fall of the city, see David Nicol, *The Last Centuries of Byzantium, 1261–1453* (New York: Cambridge University Press, 1993), chap. 18; John Freely, *Istanbul: The Imperial City* (New York: Penguin Books, 1996), chap. 15. For the quotation "better the turban

of the Muslim," see David Talbot Rice, *The Byzantines* (New York: Praeger, 1962), 74. For a primary source on Mehmed, see the work of the fifteenth-century Ottoman chronicler Tursun Beg, *The History of Mehmed the Conqueror*, trans. Halil Inalcik and Rhoads Murphy (Minneapolis: Bibliotheca Islamica, 1978). On the appointment of Gennadius, see for instance Daniel Goffman, *The Ottoman Empire and Early Modern Europe* (New York: Cambridge University Press, 2002), 171–73; the contemporary chronicler was Kritovoulus and is quoted in Benjamin Braude, "Foundation Myths of the Miller System," in Benjamin Braude and Bernard Lewis, eds., *Christians and Jews in the Ottoman Empire: The Functioning of a Plural Society*, vol. 1 (New York: Holmes & Meier, 1982), 78; Kritovoulus, *History of Mehmed the Conqueror*, trans. Charles Riggs (Princeton, N.J.: Princeton University Press, 1954).

2. That is exactly what *The Oxford English Dictionary* suggests the word meant in the sixteenth and seventeenth centuries. See Roger Crowley, *1453: The Holy War for Constantinople and the Clash of Islam and the West* (New York: Hyperion, 2005), 243.

3. For good primers on the Ottomans, see Kinross, *The Ottoman Centuries*; Jason Goodwin, *Lords of the Horizon* (New York: 20004); Colin Imber, *The Ottoman Empire, 1300–1650: The Structure of Power* (New York: Palgrave, 2002). For skepticism on the so-called *ghazi* thesis, see Cemal Kafadar, *Between Two Worlds: The Construction of the Ottoman State* (Berkeley: University of California Press, 1995). On relations between the West and the Ottomans and the legacy of negative images, see Goffman, *The Ottoman Empire and Early Modern Europe*. See also Bruce Masters, *Christians and Jews in the Ottoman Arab World: The Roots of Secularism* (New York: Cambridge University Press, 2001). The best survey on the Mediterranean world in this period and into the seventeenth century is Ferdinand Braudel, *The Mediterranean World*.

4. Joseph Hacker, "Ottoman Policy Toward the Jews and Jewish Attitudes Toward the Ottomans During the Fifteenth Century," in Braude and Lewis, eds., *Christians and Jews in the Ottoman Empire*, 117–26; quotation about the Turks welcoming the Jews from Mark Mazower, *Salonica, City of Ghosts* (New York: Knopf, 2005), 48.

5. Bartolomeo Contarini quoted in Alan Fisher, "The Life and Family of Suleyman I," in Halil Inalcik and Cemal Kafadar, eds., *Suleyman the Second and His Time* (Istanbul: Isis Press, 1993), 2. Also, Antony Bridge, *Suleiman the Magnificent* (New York: Dorset Press, 1966). Busbecq quoted in Kinross, 202. Luther quotations and Bodin quotations (which I have put in contemporary English) both from Goffman, 109–111. The primary Turkish source is Sinan Chavush, *Suleymanname* (Istanbul: Historical Research Foundation, 1987).

6. For Suleyman and European Protestants, see Halil Inalcik, *The Ottoman Empire: The Classical Age, 1300–1600*, trans. Norman Itzkowitz and Colin Imber (New York: Praeger, 1973), 30–38. Also, Stephen Fischer-Galati, *Ottoman Imperialism and German Protestantism* (Cambridge: Harvard University Press, 1959); Eugene Rice and Anthony Grafton, *The Foundations of Early Modern Europe, 1460–1559* (New York: Norton, 1994), 135–45.

CHAPTER EIGHT: THE TIDE BEGINS TO TURN

1. On the *millet* system, see Bruce Masters, *Christians and Jews in the Ottoman Arab World*, 34ff. One of the best Turkish sources is Gulnihal Bozkurt, *Alman-Ingiliz ve siyasi gelismelerin isigi altinda gayriMuslim Osmanli vatandaslarinin hukuki durumu* (Ankara: Turk Tarik Kuruma Basimevi, 1989). Also, Carter Findley, *Ottoman Civil Officialdom* (Princeton, N.J.: Princeton University Press, 1989); Mark Epstein, "The Leadership of the Ottoman Jews in the Fifteenth and Sixteenth Centuries," and Joseph Hacker, "Ottoman Policy Toward the Jews and Jewish Attitudes Towards the Ottoman During the Fifteenth Century," in Braude and Lewis, 100–126. Quotation of the patriarch of Jerusalem from Benjamin Braude and Bernard Lewis, Introduction, in Braude and Lewis, 17. See also Caroline Finkel, *Osman's Dream: The Story of the Ottoman Empire* (London: John Murray, 2005).

2. For Ottoman rule on Crete, see Molly Greene, *A Shared World: Christians and Muslims in the Early Modern Mediterranean* (Princeton, N.J.: Princeton University Press, 2000).

3. Quotation from a Catholic chronicler in 1667, cited in John Freely, *The Lost Messiah: In Search of the Mystical Rabbi Sabbatai Sevi* (New York: Overlook Press, 2001), 99. The magisterial work in the field remains Gershom Scholem, *Sabbatai Sevi: The Mystical Messiah* (Princeton, N.J.: Princeton University Press, 1973).

4. Lady Montagu quotation from Goffman, 169; the French general was Count Maurice de Saxe, quoted in Bernard Lewis, ed., *A Middle East Mosaic*, 290–91.

5. Sir William Eaton, *A Survey of the Ottoman Empire* (London, 1799), excerpted in the Internet Modern History Sourcebook at www.fordham.edu/halsall. On the capitulations, see Caglor Keydar, Y. Eyup Ozverum, and Donald Quataert, "Port-Cities in the Ottoman Empire," *Fernand Braudel Center Review* 16 (fall 1995), 519–58.

CHAPTER NINE: BRAVE NEW WORLDS

1. Examples of trumpeting the period are Niall Ferguson, *Empire* (New York: Basic Books, 2004), and Paul Johnson, *The Birth of the Modern* (New York: HarperCollins, 1991). The negative stereotypes are too numerous to list, though one pure example might be the works of the English historian Eric Hobsbawm, or earlier in the century, J. A. Hobson, *Imperialism* (London: Allen & Unwin, 1948), originally published in 1902, which set the tone for much of what has been written subsequently.

2. See M. S. Anderson, *The Eastern Question* (London: Macmillan, 1966).

3. Napoleon quoted in J. M. Thompson, *Napoleon Bonaparte* (Oxford, England: Blackwell, 1952), 109. Al-Jabarti's observations found in Abd al-Rahman al-Jabarti, *Journal d'un notable du Cairo durant l'expédition française, 1798–1801*, trans. and annotated by Joseph Cuoq (Paris: Albin Michel, 1979), 90–95.

4. On Tahtawi, see Albert Hourani, *Arabic Thought in the Liberal Age, 1798–1939* (Cambridge: Cambridge University Press, 1983), 67–84. The quotation about

national welfare and human progress comes from Tahtawi himself, in Hourani, 82. Also, Lisa Pollard, "The Habits and Customs of Modernity: Egyptians in Europe and the Geography of Nineteenth-Century Nationalism," *Arab Studies Journal* (fall 1999), 51–60. On Muhammad Ali, see Afaf Lutfi al-Sayyid Marsot, *Egypt in the Reign of Muhammad Ali* (Cambridge, England: Cambridge University Press, 1984); Henry Dodwell, *The Founder of Modern Egypt* (1931; repr., New York: AMS Press, 1977); P. J. Vatikiotis, *The History of Egypt*, 3rd ed. (Baltimore: Johns Hopkins University Press, 1985); Khaled Fahmy, "The Era of Muhammad Ali Pasha," in *The Cambridge History of Egypt*, vol. 2, 139–180; Alain Silvera, "The First Egyptian Student Mission to France Under Muhammad Ali," *Middle Eastern Studies* 16 (May 1980), 1–19. I have also drawn on my own descriptions of Muhammad Ali in *Parting the Desert: The Creation of the Suez Canal* (New York: Knopf, 2003).

5. On the Ottoman reforms, see Roderic Davison, *Reform in the Ottoman Empire, 1856–1876* (New York: Gordian Press, 1973). Quotation about the Ottoman state being like a "block of flats" found in Kemal Karpat, "Millets and Nationality," in Braude and Lewis, eds., 141–69. See also Alan Palmer, *The Decline and Fall of the Ottoman Empire* (New York: Barnes & Noble, 1992), 105–43; Stanford Shaw and Ezel Kural Shaw, *History of the Ottoman Empire and Modern Turkey*, vol. 2, *Reform, Revolution and Republic* (New York: Cambridge University Press, 1977), 55ff.; Carter Findley, *Bureaucratic Reform in the Ottoman Empire: The Sublime Porte, 1789–1922* (Princeton, N.J.: Princeton University Press, 1980); Bernard Lewis, *The Emergence of Modern Turkey* (New York: Oxford University Press, 1961).

6. A. L. Tibawi, *A Modern History of Syria* (London, 1969), 138–40; Kamal Salibi, *The Modern History of Lebanon* (London: Weidenfeld and Nicholson, 1965), 139; Meir Zamir, *The Formation of Modern Lebanon* (Ithaca, N.Y.: Cornell University Press, 1985), chap. 1; Samir Khalaf, "Communal Conflict in Nineteenth-Century Lebanon," in Braude and Lewis, eds., *Christians and Jews in the Ottoman Empire*, vol. 2, *The Arabic-Speaking Lands* (New York: Holmes & Meier, 1982), 107–33.

7. For the failures of the *Tanzimat*, see Kemal Karpat, "Millets and Nationality," in Braude and Lewis, vol. 1, 141–69; Fatme Muge Goçek, "Ethnic Segmentation, Western Education, and Political Outcomes: Nineteenth Century Ottoman Society," *Politics Today* (1993); and Fatma Müge Göçek, *Rise of the Bourgeoisie, Demise of Empire: Ottoman Westernization and Social Change* (New York: Oxford University Press, 2002).

CHAPTER TEN: THE AGE OF REFORM

1. Abduh quotations come from Charles Adams, *Islam and Modernism in Egypt* (New York: Russell & Russell, 1933, 1968), 130, and from Malcolm Kerr, *Islamic Reformers* (Los Angeles: University of California Press, 1966), 149. On Abduh, also see Hourani, *Arabic Thought in the Liberal Age*, 131–60. On Afghani, see Hourani as well; also, Nikki Keddi, *An Islamic Response to Imperialism: The Writings*

and Teachings of Sayyid Jamal ad-Din Afghani (Berkeley: University of California Press, 1983). On the legacy of the *salafiyya*, see Nazib Ayubi, *Political Islam: Religion and Politics in the Arab World* (New York: Routledge, 1991); also, Olivier Roy, *The Failure of Political Islam*, trans. Carol Volk (Cambridge: Harvard University Press, 1994). For a look at how the ideas of Abduh and Afghani evolved in the twentieth century, see Jacob Landau, *The Politics of Pan-Islam* (New York: Oxford University Press, 1990).

2. Anne Blunt, *Bedouin Tribes of the Euphrates* (London: Frank Cass, 1968; originally published in 1879). The quotation about the eternal truth of Islam is from Wilfrid Scawen Blunt, *The Future of Islam* (London, 1882), 142. Also, see Elizabeth Longford, *A Pilgrimage of Passion* (London: Weidenfeld & Nicholson, 1979). On Egypt, see Jacques Berque, *Egypt: Imperialism and Revolution*, trans. Jean Stewart (New York: Praeger, 1972).

3. The seminal, and controversial, work describing this group is Edward Said, *Orientalism* (New York: Random House, 1978). The book also contains extensive references to Renan.

4. William Marmaduke Pickthall, *Meaning of the Glorious Koran: An Explanatory Translation* (New York: Knopf, 1930), and *Islam and Progress* (London: Muslim Book Society, 1920).

5. For a general survey of economic trends, see Roger Owen, *The Middle East in the World Economy 1800–1914* (London: I. B. Tauris, 1981). Also, Charles Issawi, *An Economic History of the Middle East and North Africa* (New York: Columbia University Press, 1982).

6. Elie Kedourie, "The American University in Beirut," *Middle Eastern Studies* (October 1966), 74–90; "The American University of Beirut," *Journal of World History* (fall 1967); Daniel Bliss, *The Reminiscence of Daniel Bliss* (New York: Revell, 1920).

7. See E. M. Forster, *Alexandria: A History and a Guide* (New York: Oxford University Press, 1922).

8. Lord Cromer, *Modern Egypt* (New York, 1908), 343; Roger Owen, *Lord Cromer* (New York: Oxford University Press, 2004); Afaf Lutfi al-Sayyid Marsot, *Egypt Under Cromer* (London: John Murray, 1968).

9. Benedict Anderson, *Imagined Communities* (New York: Verso, 1983), 15.

CHAPTER ELEVEN: HOPE AND DESPAIR

1. See, for instance, Robert Spencer, ed., *The Myth of Islamic Tolerance: How Islamic Law Treats Non-Muslims* (New York: Prometheus Books, 2005).

2. See David Fromkin, *A Peace to End All Peace: Creating the Modern Middle East* (New York: Holt, 1989); John Marlowe, *The Seat of Pilate: An Account of the Palestine Mandate* (London: Cresset, 1959)

3. T. E. Lawrence, *Seven Pillars of Wisdom* (New York: Penguin, 1935), 23; Jeremy Wilson, *Lawrence of Arabia: The Authorized Biography of T. E. Lawrence* (New York: Atheneum, 1989).

4. See Fromkin, *A Peace to End All Peace,* 273–300. For the complete text of the Husayn-McMahon correspondence, see George Antonius, *The Arab Awakening;* also, Marlowe, *The Seat of Pilate,* and Christopher Sykes, *Crossroads to Israel* (Bloomington: Indiana University Press, 1973).

5. Quincy Wright, *Mandates Under the League of Nations* (New York: Greenwood Press, 1930, 1968).

6. One of the more prominent of those who portray them as puppets is Elie Kedourie, *England and the Middle East, 1914–1921* (London: Bowes & Bowes, 1956). More nuanced is Elizabeth Monroe, *Britain's Moment in the Middle East, 1914–1956* (Baltimore: Johns Hopkins University Press, 1963).

7. Churchill to Sir Percy Cox, August 15, 1921, in Colonial Office records 730/4/40704, Public Records Office, Kew Gardens, England. On Iraq, see Peter Sluglett, *Britain in Iraq, 1914–1932* (London: Ithaca Press, 1976).

8. Quoted in Sylvia Haim, *Arab Nationalism* (Berkeley: University of California Press, 1976), 64. Also, Fred Lawson, "Westphalian Sovereignty and the Emergence of the Arab State System: The Case of Syria," *International History Review* (September 2000), 529–56.

9. Janice Terry, *The Wafd, 1919–1952: Cornerstone of Egyptian Political Power* (London: Third World Centre, 1982); Marius Deeb, *Party Politics in Egypt: The Wafd and Its Rivals, 1919–1939* (Oxford, England: Ithaca Press for St. Antony's College, 1979).

10. From the White Paper of 1922, quoted in Bernard Wasserstein, *The British in Palestine* (London: Royal Historical Society, 1978), 118.

11. The literature on the creation of Israel is vast. Here are a few select titles: Conor Cruise O'Brien, *The Siege: The Story of Israel and Zionism* (London: George Weidenfeld & Nicolson, 1986); Avi Shlaim, *The Iron Wall: Israel and the Arab World* (New York: Norton, 1999); Benny Morris, *1948 and After: Israel and the Palestinians* (New York: Oxford University Press, 1990); Philip Mattar, *The Mufti of Jerusalem* (New York: Columbia University Press, 1988); Tom Segev, *One Palestine, Complete: Jews and Arabs Under the British Mandate* (New York: Metropolitan Books, 2000); Charles Smith, *Palestine and the Arab-Israeli Conflict,* 3rd ed. (New York: St. Martin's Press, 1996); Howard Sachar, *A History of Israel: From the Rise of Zionism to Our Time* (New York: Knopf, 1996).

CHAPTER TWELVE: IN AN OTHERWISE TURBULENT WORLD

1. See for instance, Fawaz Gerges, *The Far Enemy: Why Jihad Went Global* (New York: Cambridge University Press, 2005); Malise Ruthven, *A Fury for God: The Islamist Attack on America* (London: Granta, 2002); Cook, *Understanding Jihad;* Mark Juergensmeyer, *Terror in the Mind of God: The Rise of Global Religious Violence* (Berkeley: University of California Press, 2003); Nazih Ayubi, *Political Islam* (New York: Routledge, 1993).

2. Here, too, there are of course notable exceptions, one of the most stunning of

which is Richard Bulliet, *The Case for Islamo-Christian Civilization* (New York: Columbia University Press, 2004).

3. Amos Elon, *The Israelis: Founders and Sons* (New York: Penguin, 1971), 106–76; Eyal Zisser, "The Maronites, Lebanon, and the State of Israel: Early Contacts," *Middle Eastern Studies* (October 1995), 889ff.

4. Abdullah quotations from Sachar, *A History of Israel*, 322–23. The "best of enemies" quotation is in Shlaim, *The Iron Wall*, 38. Also see Avi Shlaim, *Collusion Across the Jordan: King Abdullah, the Zionist Movement and the Partition of Palestine* (New York: Columbia University Press, 1988). The Moshe Dayan quotations are from his memoirs, and quoted in Conor Cruise O'Brien, *The Siege*, 368. On Hussein, see for instance Douglas Little, "A Puppet in Search of a Puppeteer: The United Sates, King Hussein, and Jordan," *International History Review* (August 1995), 512–44; Robert Satloff, *From Abdullah to Hussein: Jordan in Transition* (New York: Oxford University Press, 1994); Mary Wilson, ed., *King Abdullah, Britain, and the Making of Jordan* (New York: Cambridge University Press, 1988). See also King Abdullah, *Memoirs*, ed. Philip P. Graves (London: Cape, 1950); and Nadav Safran, *Israel: The Embattled Ally* (Cambridge: Belknap Press, 1981).

5. This was brought home to me most clearly in a speech that King Hussein gave at Oxford University in May 1990, and at a series of conversations I was part of at a World Economic Forum conference at one of Jordan's Dead Sea resorts, hosted by Abdullah and his wife, Queen Rania, in May 2004.

6. The quotation on the National Pact is from Bisharra al-Khuri, in Raghid Solh, *Lebanon and Arab Nationalism, 1936–1945* (unpublished Ph.D. dissertation, St. Antony's College, Oxford University, 1986), 289. On Lebanon and faded dreams, see Fouad Ajami, *The Dream Palace of the Arabs* (New York: Pantheon, 1998); Kamil Salibi, *A House of Many Mansions: The History of Lebanon Reconsidered* (Berkeley: University of California Press, 1989).

7. And the literature here is endless, beginning with V. S. Naipaul, *Among the Believers: An Islamic Journey* (New York: Knopf, 1981), and *Beyond Belief: Islamic Excursions Among the Converted Peoples* (New York: Random House, 1998); Robert Kaplan, *To the Ends of the Earth: A Journey at the Dawn of the 21th Century* (New York: Random House, 1996); Benjamin Barber, *Jihad v. McWorld* (New York: Times Books, 1995); Samuel Huntington, *The Clash of Civilizations and the Remaking of World Order* (New York: Simon & Schuster, 1996); Jeffrey Taylor, *Angry Wind: Through Muslim Black Africa by Truck, Bus, Boat, and Camel* (New York: Houghton Mifflin, 2005); Yaroslav Trofimov, *Faith at War: A Journey on the Frontlines of Islam from Baghdad to Timbuktu* (New York: Henry Holt, 2005); Andrew Wheatcroft, *Infidels: A History of the Conflict Between Christendom and Islam* (New York: Random House, 2004); Bernard Lewis, *What Went Wrong: The Clash Between Islam and Modernity in the Middle East* (New York: Oxford University Press, 2001), and *The Crisis in Islam: Holy War and Unholy Terror* (New York: Modern Library, 2003). There is also the highly regarded and sober work of Giles Kepel, most recently his *The War for Muslim Minds: Islam and the West* (Cambridge: Belknap Press of Harvard University Press, 2004). Then the polemics from the right

and from the left: Robert Spencer, *Islam Unveiled* (New York: Encounter Books, 2002); Tony Blankley, *The West's Last Chance: Will We Win the Clash of Civilizations?* (New York: Regnery, 2005); Irshad Manji, *The Trouble with Islam Today: A Muslim's Call for Reform in Her Faith* (New York: St. Martin's Press, 2004).

8. See once again Richard Bulliet, *The Case for Islamo-Christian Civilization;* also, Noah Feldman, *After Jihad: America and the Struggle for Islamic Democracy* (New York: FSG, 2003); Imam Faisal Abul Rauf, *What's Right with Islam: A New Vision for Muslims and the West* (New York, 2004); Reza Aslan, *No God but God* (New York: Random House, 2005); the many works of John Esposito, including *The Islamic Threat: Myth or Reality?* (New York: Oxford University Press, 1999).

9. Daniel Yergin, *The Prize: The Epic Quest for Oil, Money, and Power* (New York: Simon & Schuster, 1991); David Lamb, "Oil Company Is Heart of Confrontation," *Los Angeles Times,* December 16, 1990; "Discovery! The Story of Aramco Then," *Aramco World* (this multipart series ran in all six issues in 1968). Rachel Bronson, *Thicker Than Oil: America's Uneasy Partnership with Saudi Arabia* (New York: Oxford University Press, 2006).

10. Behcet Yesilbursa, "Turkey's Participation in the Middle East Command and Its Admission to NATO," *Middle Eastern Studies* (October 1999), 70–101; Birol Yesilada, "Turkey's Candidacy for EU Membership," *Middle East Journal* (winter 2002), 94–111; Andrew Mango, "Turkey and the Enlargement of the European Mind," *Middle Eastern Studies* (April 1998), 171–91.

BIBLIOGRAPHY

Abd Allah ibn Hussein. *Memoirs of King Abdullah of Transjordan.* New York: Philosophical Library, 1950.

Adams, Charles. *Islam and Modernism in Egypt.* New York: Russell & Russell, 1933, 1968.

Ajami, Fouad. *The Dream Palace of the Arabs.* New York: Pantheon, 1998.

Anderson, Benedict. *Imagined Communities.* New York: Verso, 1983.

Anderson, M. S. *The Eastern Question.* London: Macmillan, 1966.

Antonius, George. *The Arab Awakening: The Story of the Arab National Movement.* London: Kegan Paul, 2000.

Arberry, A. J. *The Koran Interpreted.* New York: Touchstone, 1955, 1996.

Armstrong, Karen. *Jerusalem: One City, Three Faiths.* New York: Knopf, 1996.

————. *The Battle for God.* New York: Knopf, 2000.

Asbridge, Thomas. *The First Crusade: A New History: The Roots of Conflict Between Christianity and Islam.* New York: Oxford University Press, 2005.

Aslan, Reza. *No God but God: The Origins, Evolution, and Future of Islam.* New York: Random House, 2005.

Ayubi, Nazih. *Political Islam: Religion and Politics in the Arab World.* New York: Routledge, 1991.

al-Baladhuri, Abu-l Abbas Ahmad ibn Jabir. *The Origins of the Islamic State.* Trans. Philip Khuri Hitti. Piscataway, N.J.: Gorgias Press, 2002. Reprint of original 1916 edition, Columbia University Press.

Barber, Benjamin. *Jihad v. McWorld.* New York: Times Books, 1995.

Barbero, Alessandro. *Charlemagne: Father of a Continent.* Berkeley: University of California Press, 2004.

Beg, Tursun. *The History of Mehmed the Conqueror.* Trans. by Halil Inalcik and Rhoads Murphy. Minneapolis: Bibliotheca Islamica, 1978.

Berque, Jacques. *Egypt: Imperialism and Revolution.* Trans. Jean Stewart. New York: Praeger, 1972.

Blankley, Tony. *The West's Last Chance: Will We Win the Clash of Civilizations?* New York: Regnery, 2005.

317

Bliss, Daniel. *The Reminiscence of Daniel Bliss.* New York: Revell, 1920.

Blunt, Anne. *Bedouin Tribes of the Euphrates.* London: Frank Cass, 1968; originally published 1879.

Blunt, Wilfrid Scawen. *The Future of Islam.* London, 1882.

Bordonove, Georges. *Les Croisades et le royaume de Jerusalem.* Paris: Editions Pygmalion, 2002.

Bosworth, C. E. *The Arabs, Byzantium, and Iran.* Burlington, Vt.: Ashgate Publishing, 1996.

Bozkurt, Gulnihal. *Alman-Ingiliz ve siyasi gelismelerin isigi altinda gayriMuslim Osmanli vatandaslarinin hukuki durumu.* Ankara: Turk Tarik Kuruma Basimevi, 1989.

Bramhall, Edith Clementine. "The Origins of the Temporal Privileges of Crusaders." *American Journal of Theology* (April 1901): 279–92.

Braude, Benjamin and Bernard Lewis, eds. *Christians and Jews in the Ottoman Empire.* Vol. 1, *The Central Lands.* New York: Holmes & Meier, 1982.

———. *Christians and Jews in the Ottoman Empire.* Vol. 2, *The Arabic-Speaking Lands.* New York: Holmes & Meier, 1982.

Braudel, Fernand. *The Mediterranean and the Mediterranean World in the Age of Philip II.* Vol. 1. Berkeley: University of California Press, 1996 (reprint edition).

Bridge, Antony. *Suleiman the Magnificent.* New York: Dorset Press, 1966.

Bronson, Rachel. *Thicker than Oil: America's Uneasy Partnership with Saudi Arabia.* New York: Oxford University Press, 2006.

Brundage, James *The Crusades: A Documentary History.* Milwaukee: Marquette University Press, 1962

Bulliet, Richard. *The Case for Islamo-Christian Civilization.* New York: Columbia University Press, 2004.

———. *Conversion to Islam in the Medieval Period.* Cambridge: Harvard University Press, 1979.

Burns, Robert, ed. *Emperor of Culture: Alfonso X the Learned of Castile and His Thirteenth-Century Renaissance.* Philadelphia: University of Pennsylvania Press, 1990.

Cahen, Claude. "Dhimma." In *The Encyclopedia of Islam.* Leiden: E. J. Brill, 1991.

———. *Orient et Occident au temps des Croisades.* Paris: Editions Aubier, 1983.

Chavush, Sinan. *Suleymanname.* Istanbul: Historical Research Foundation, 1987.

Cheikho, Louis. *Ulama' al-Nasraniyah fi al-Islam, 622–1300* [Christian Scholars Under Islam, 622–1300]. Juniyah, Lebanon: al-Maktabah al-Bulusiyah, 1983.

Constable, Olivia Remie. *Trade and Traders in Muslim Spain: The Commercial Realignment of the Iberian Peninsula.* Cambridge: Cambridge University Press, 1994.

Constable, Olivia Remie, ed. *Medieval Iberia: Readings from Christian, Muslim, and Jewish Sources.* Philadelphia: University of Pennsylvania Press, 1997.

Cook, David. *Understanding Jihad.* Berkeley: University of California Press, 2005.

Cook, Michael. *Forbidding Wrong in Islam.* Cambridge: Cambridge University Press, 2003.

Coope, Jessica A. *The Martyrs of Córdoba: Community and Family Conflict in an Age of Mass Conversion.* Lincoln: University of Nebraska Press, 1995.

Cromer, Lord. *Modern Egypt.* London: Macmillan, 1908.

Crone, Patricia. *God's Rule: Government and Islam.* New York: Columbia University Press, 2004.

Crone, Patricia, and Michael Cook. *Hagarism: The Making of the Islamic World.* Cambridge: Cambridge University Press, 1976.

Crowley, Roger. *1453: The Holy War for Constantinople and the Clash of Islam and the West.* New York: Hyperion, 2005.

Daniel, Norman. *The Arabs and Mediaeval Europe.* London: Longman, 1975.

Davison, Roderic. *Reform in the Ottoman Empire, 1856–1876.* New York: Gordian Press, 1973.

Deeb, Marius. *Party Politics in Egypt: The Wafd and Its Rivals, 1919–1939.* Oxford: Ithaca Press for St. Antony's College, 1979.

al-Din Shayyal, Jamal. *Tarikh Misr al-Islamiya* [The Islamic History of Egypt]. Alexandria: Dar al-Ma'arif, 1967.

Dodwell, Henry. *The Founder of Modern Egypt.* 1931. Reprint, New York: AMS Press, 1977.

Dunlop, Douglas M. *A History of the Jewish Khazars.* Princeton, N.J.: Princeton University Press, 1954.

Eaton, Sir William. *A Survey of the Ottoman Empire.* London, 1799. In Fordham Internet Modern History Sourcebook at www.fordham.edu/halsall.

Ehrenkreutz, Andrew. *Saladin.* Albany: State University of New York Press, 1972.

Ellenblum, Ronnie. *Frankish Settlement in the Latin Kingdom of Jerusalem.* Cambridge: Cambridge University Press, 1998.

Elon, Amos. *The Israelis: Founders and Sons.* New York: Penguin, 1971.

Esposito, John. *The Islamic Threat: Myth or Reality?* New York: Oxford University Press, 1999.

Fahmy, Khaled. "The Era of Muhammad Ali Pasha." Edited by M. W. Daly. Vol. 2 of *The Cambridge History of Egypt.* Cambridge, England: Cambridge University Press, 1998.

Fakhry, Majid. *Islamic Philosophy, Theology, and Mysticism.* Oxford, England: Oneworld, 1997.

Feldman, Noah. *After Jihad: America and the Struggle for Islamic Democracy.* New York: Farrar, Straus and Groux, 2003.

Ferguson, Niall. *Empire.* New York: Basic Books, 2004.

Findley, Carter. *Bureaucratic Reform in the Ottoman Empire: The Sublime Porte, 1789–1922.* Princeton, N.J.: Princeton University Press, 1980.

———. *Ottoman Civil Officialdom.* Princeton, N.J.: Princeton University Press, 1989.

Finkel, Caroline. *Osman's Dream: The Story of the Ottoman Empire.* London: John Murray, 2005.

Fischer-Galati, Stephen. *Ottoman Imperialism and German Protestantism.* Cambridge: Harvard University Press, 1959.

Fletcher, Richard. *The Cross and the Crescent: Christianity and Islam from Muhammad to the Reformation.* New York: Viking, 2004.

———. *Moorish Spain.* Berkeley: University of California Press, 1992.

Fordham Center for Medieval Studies. Internet Medieval Sourcebook, compiled by and edited by Paul Halsall. www.fordham.edu/halsall/source.

Forster, E. M. *Alexandria: A History and a Guide*. New York: Oxford University Press, 1922.

Freely, John. *Istanbul: The Imperial City*. New York: Penguin Books, 1996.

———. *The Lost Messiah: In Search of the Mystical Rabbi Sabbatai Sevi*. New York: Overlook Press, 2001.

Friedmann, Yohanan. *Tolerance and Coercion in Islam: Interfaith Relations in Muslim Tradition*. New York: Cambridge University Press, 2003.

Fromkin, David. *A Peace to End All Peace: Creating the Modern Middle East*. New York: Holt, 1989.

Gabrielli, Francesco. *Arab Historians of the Crusades*. Berkeley: University of California Press, 1969.

Gerber, Jane. *The Jews of Spain: A History of the Sephardic Experience*. New York: Free Press, 1992.

Gerges, Fawaz. *The Far Enemy: Why Jihad Went Global*. New York: Cambridge University Press, 2005.

Gibbon, Edward. *The Decline and Fall of the Roman Empire*, vol. 3. New York: Heritage Press, 1946.

Göçek, Fatma Müge. "Ethnic Segmentation, Western Education, and Political Outcomes: Nineteenth Century Ottoman Society." *Politics Today* (1993).

———. *Rise of the Bourgeoisie, Demise of Empire: Ottoman Westernization and Social Change*. New York: Oxford University Press, 2002.

Goddard, Hugh. *A History of Muslim-Christian Relations*. Chicago: New Amsterdam Books, 2000.

Goffman, Daniel. *The Ottoman Empire and Early Modern Europe*. New York: Cambridge University Press, 2002.

Goitein, S. D. *A Mediterranean Society: An Abridgement in One Volume*. Berkeley: University of California Press, 1999.

Goldstein, David. *Hebrew Poems from Spain*. New York: Schocken Books, 1996.

Goldziher, Ignaz. *Introduction to Islamic Theology and Law*. Princeton, N.J.: Princeton University Press, 1991.

Goodwin, Jason. *Lords of the Horizon: A History of the Ottoman Empire*. New York: Picador, 2003.

Greene, Molly. *A Shared World: Christians and Muslims in the Early Modern Mediterranean*. Princeton, N.J.: Princeton University Press, 2000.

Griffith, Sydney. *Arabic Christianity in the Monasteries of Ninth-Century Palestine*. Burlington, Vt.: Ashgate Publishing, 1992.

———. *The Beginnings of Christian Theology in Arabic: Muslim-Christian Encounters in the Early Islamic Period*. Burlington, Vt.: Ashgate Publishing, 2002.

Gutas, Dimitri. *Greek Thought, Arabic Culture: The Graeco-Arabic Translation Movement in Baghdad and Early Abbasid Society*. New York: Routledge, 1998.

Haim, Sylvia. *Arab Nationalism*. Berkeley: University of California Press, 1976.

Hallam, Elizabeth, ed. *Chronicles of the Crusades: Eye-Witness Accounts of the Wars Between Christianity and Islam*. New York: Welcome Rain, 2000.

Hillenbrand, Carole. *The Crusades: Islamic Perspectives.* New York: Routledge, 2000.

Hobson, J. A. *Imperialism.* London: Allen & Unwin, 1948; originally published 1902.

Hodgson, Marshall C. S. *The Venture of Islam,* vols. 1 and 2. Chicago: University of Chicago Press, 1974.

Holt, P. M. *The Crusader States and Their Neighbors.* New York: Longman, 2004.

Hourani, Albert. *Arabic Thought in the Liberal Age, 1798–1939.* Cambridge: Cambridge University Press, 1983.

Hoyland, Robert. *Seeing Islam as Others Saw It: A Survey and Evaluation of Christian, Jewish and Zoroastrian Writings on Early Islam.* Princeton: Darwin Press, 1997.

Humphries, Stephen. *Islamic History: A Framework for Inquiry.* Princeton, N.J.: Princeton University Press, 1991.

Huntington, Samuel. *The Clash of Civilizations and the Remaking of World Order.* New York: Simon & Schuster, 1996.

Ibn Abd al-Hakam. *History of the Conquests of Egypt, North Africa, and Spain.* Edited by Charles Torrey. Piscataway, N.J.: Gorgias Press, 2002.

Ibn Khaldun. *The Muqaddimah.* Trans. Franz Rosenthal. Princeton, N.J.: Princeton University Press, 1967.

Ibn Munqidh, Usama. *An Arab-Syrian Gentleman and Warrior in the Period of the Crusades.* Trans. Philip Hitti. New York: Columbia University Press, 1929, 2000.

Ibn al-Qalansi. *The Damascus Chronicle of the Crusades.* Ed. and trans. H. A. R. Gibb. New York: Dover Publications, 1932, 2002.

Imber, Colin. *The Ottoman Empire, 1300–1650: The Structure of Power.* New York: Palgrave, 2002.

Inalcik, Halil. *The Ottoman Empire: The Classical Age, 1300–1600.* Trans. Norman Itzkowitz and Colin Imber. New York: Praeger, 1973.

Inalcik, Halil and Cemal Kafadar, eds., *Suleyman the Second and His Time.* Istanbul: Isis Press, 1993.

Irwin, Robert. *For Lust of Knowing: The Orientalists and Their Enemies.* London: Allen Lane, 2006.

Issawi, Charles. *An Economic History of the Middle East and North Africa.* New York: Columbia University Press, 1982.

al-Jabarti, Abd al-Rahman. *Journal d'un notable du Cairo durant l'expédition française, 1798–1801.* Trans. and annotated by Joseph Cuoq. Paris: Albin Michel, 1979.

Jacobs, Joseph. "Samuel Ha-Nagid." www.jewishencyclopedia.com.

Johnson, Paul. *The Birth of the Modern.* New York: HarperCollins, 1991.

Jotischky, Andrew. *Crusading and the Crusader States.* New York: Longman, 2004.

Juergensmeyer, Mark. *Terror in the Mind of God: The Rise of Global Religious Violence.* Berkeley: University of California Press, 2003.

Kafadar, Cemal. *Between Two Worlds: The Construction of the Ottoman State.* Berkeley: University of California Press, 1995.

Kaplan, Robert. *To the Ends of the Earth: A Journey at the Dawn of the 21th Century.* New York: Random House, 1996.

Karabell, Zachary. *Parting the Desert: The Creation of the Suez Canal.* New York: Knopf, 2003.

Keddi, Nikki. *An Islamic Response to Imperialism: The Writings and Teachings of Sayyid Jamal ad-Din Afghani.* Berkeley: University of California Press, 1983.

Kedourie, Elie. "The American University in Beirut." *Middle Eastern Studies* (October 1966): 74–90.

———. *England and the Middle East, 1914–1921.* London: Bowes & Bowes, 1956.

Kennedy, Hugh. *The Court of the Caliphs: The Rise and Fall of Islam's Greatest Dynasty.* London: Weidenfeld & Nicholson, 2005.

———. *The Early Abbasid Caliphate.* London: Croom & Helm, 1981.

———. *Muslim Spain and Portugal: A Political History of al-Andalus.* New York: Longman, 1996.

Kepel, Giles. *The War for Muslim Minds: Islam and the West.* Cambridge: Belknap Press of Harvard University Press, 2004.

Kerr, Malcolm. *Islamic Reformers.* Los Angeles: University of California Press, 1966.

Keydar, Caglor, Y. Eyup Ozverum, and Donald Quataert. "Port-Cities in the Ottoman Empire." *Fernand Braudel Center Review* 16 (Fall 1995): 519–58.

Kinross, Lord. *The Ottoman Centuries: The Rise and Fall of the Turkish Empire.* New York: Morrow, 1977.

Kritovoulus. *History of Mehmed the Conqueror.* Trans. Charles Riggs. Princeton, N.J.: Princeton University Press, 1954.

Landau, Jacob. *The Politics of Pan-Islam.* New York: Oxford University Press, 1990.

Lane-Poole, Stanley. *Saladin: All Powerful Sultan and the Uniter of Islam.* 1898. Reprint, New York: Cooper Square Press, 2002.

Lassner, Jacob. *The Shaping of Abbasid Rule.* Princeton, N.J.: Princeton University Press, 1980.

Lawrence, T. E. *Seven Pillars of Wisdom.* New York: Penguin, 1935.

Lawson, Fred. "Westphalian Sovereignty and the Emergence of the Arab State System: The Case of Syria." *International History Review* (September 2000): 529–56.

Lewis, Bernard. *The Crisis in Islam: Holy War and Unholy Terror.* New York: Modern Library, 2003.

———. *The Emergence of Modern Turkey.* New York: Oxford University Press, 1961.

———. *The Jews of Islam.* Princeton, N.J.: Princeton University Press, 1984.

———. *What Went Wrong: The Clash Between Islam and Modernity in the Middle East.* New York: Oxford University Press, 2001.

———, ed. *A Middle East Mosaic: Fragments of Life, Letters, and History.* New York: Random House, 2000.

Little, Douglas. "A Puppet in Search of a Puppeteer: The United States, King Hussein, and Jordan." *International History Review* (August 1995): 512–44.

Lockman, Zachary. *Contending Visions of the Middle East: The History and Politics of Orientalism.* Cambridge: Cambridge University Press, 2004.

Longford, Elizabeth. *A Pilgrimage of Passion.* London: Weidenfeld & Nicholson, 1979.

Lyons, Malcolm Cameron, and D. E. P. Jackson. *Saladin: The Politics of Holy War.* New York: Cambridge University Press, 1982.

Maalouf, Amin. *The Crusades Through Arab Eyes.* New York: Schocken Books, 1983, 1987.

Mango, Andrew. "Turkey and the Enlargement of the European Mind." *Middle Eastern Studies* (April 1998): 171–91.

Manji, Irshad. *The Trouble with Islam Today: A Muslim's Call for Reform in Her Faith.* New York: St. Martin's Press, 2004.

Mann, Vivian B., Thomas F. Glick, and Jerrilynn D. Dodds, eds. *Convivencia: Jews, Muslims, and Christians in Medieval Spain.* New York: Braziller and the Jewish Museum, 1992.

Marlowe, John. *The Seat of Pilate: An Account of the Palestine Mandate.* London: Cresset, 1959.

Masters, Bruce. *Christians and Jews in Ottoman Arab World: The Roots of Secularism.* New York: Cambridge University Press, 2001.

Mattar, Philip. *The Mufti of Jerusalem.* New York: Columbia University Press, 1988.

Mazower, Mark. *Salonica, City of Ghosts: Christians, Muslims and Jews, 1430–1950.* New York: Knopf, 2005.

McManners, John. *The Oxford Illustrated History of Christianity.* New York: Oxford University Press, 2001.

Menocal, Maria Rosa. *The Ornament of the World: How Muslims, Jews and Christians Created a Culture of Tolerance in Medieval Spain.* New York: Little Brown, 2002.

Meyer, Hans Eberhard. *The Crusades.* New York: Oxford University Press, 1965, 1988.

Monroe, Elizabeth. *Britain's Moment in the Middle East, 1914–1956.* Baltimore: Johns Hopkins University Press, 1963.

Morris, Benny. *1948 and After: Israel and the Palestinians.* New York: Oxford University Press, 1990.

Myerson, Mark. *A Jewish Renaissance in Fifteenth-Century Spain.* Princeton, N.J.: Princeton University Press, 2004.

Myerson, Mark and Edward English, eds., *Christians, Muslims, and Jews in Medieval and Early Modern Spain.* Notre Dame, Ind.: University of Notre Dame Press, 2000.

Naipaul, V. S. *Among the Believers: An Islamic Journey.* New York: Knopf, 1981.

———. *Beyond Belief: Islamic Excursions Among the Converted Peoples.* New York: Random House, 1998.

Nasr, Seyyed Hossein. *Islam: Religion, History, and Civilization.* San Francisco: HarperSanFrancisco, 2002.

———. *Three Muslim Sages.* Cambridge: Harvard University Press, 1964.

Nasr, Seyyed Hossein, and Oliver Leaman, eds., *History of Islamic Philosophy: Part 1.* London: Routledge, 1996.

Nicol, David. *The Last Centuries of Byzantium, 1261–1453.* New York: Cambridge University Press, 1993.

Norwich, John Julius. *Byzantium: The Decline and Fall.* New York: Knopf, 1995.

O'Brien, Conor Cruise. *The Siege: The Story of Israel and Zionism.* London: George Weidenfeld & Nicolson, 1986.

Ostrogorsky, George. *History of the Byzantine State.* London: Blackwell, 1956.

Owen, Roger. *Lord Cromer.* New York: Oxford University Press, 2004.

————. *The Middle East in the World Economy, 1800–1914*. London: I. B. Tauris, 1981.

Palmer, Alan. *The Decline and Fall of the Ottoman Empire*. New York: Barnes & Noble, 1992.

Phillips, Jonathan. *The Fourth Crusade and the Sack of Constantinople*. New York: Penguin Group, 2004.

Pickthall, William Marmeduke. *Islam and Progress*. London: Muslim Book Society, 1920.

————. *Meaning of the Glorious Koran: An Explanatory Translation*. New York: Knopf, 1930.

Pollard, Lisa. "The Habits and Customs of Modernity: Egyptians in Europe and the Geography of Nineteenth-Century Nationalism." *Arab Studies Journal* (Fall 1999): 51–60.

Powell, James M., ed., *Muslims Under Latin Rule, 1100–1300*. Princeton, N.J.: Princeton University Press, 1990.

Qasha, Suhayl. *Al-Masihiyan fi al-Dawlah al-Islamiya* [Christians in the Muslim State]. Beirut: Dar al-Malak, 2002.

Rauf, Imam Feisal Abdul. *What's Right with Islam: A New Vision for Muslims and the West*. San Francisco: HarperSanFrancisco, 2004.

Read, Piers Paul. *The Templars*. London: Weidenfeld & Nicholson, 1999.

Reilly, Richard. *The Medieval Spains*. Cambridge: Cambridge University Press, 1993.

Renard, John. *Seven Doors to Islam: Spirituality and the Religious Life*. Berkeley: University of California Press, 1996.

Rice, David Talbot. *The Byzantines*. New York: Praeger, 1962.

Rice, Eugene, and Anthony Grafton. *The Foundations of Early Modern Europe, 1460–1559*. New York: Norton, 1994.

Robinson, Chase F. *Empire and Elites After the Muslim Conquest: The Transformation of Northern Mesopotamia*. Cambridge: Cambridge University Press, 2000.

Roy, Olivier. *The Failure of Political Islam*. Trans. Carol Volk. Cambridge: Harvard University Press, 1994.

Runciman, Steven. *A History of the Crusades*. 3 vols. Cambridge: Cambridge University Press, 1951–54.

Ruthven, Malise. *A Fury for God: The Islamist Attack on America*. London: Granta, 2002.

Sachar, Howard. *A History of Israel: From the Rise of Zionism to Our Time*. New York: Knopf, 1996.

Safran, Nadav. *Israel: The Embattled Ally*. Cambridge, Mass.: Belknap Press, 1981.

Said, Edward. *Orientalism*. New York: Random House, 1978.

Salibi, Kamil. *A House of Many Mansions: The History of Lebanon Reconsidered*. Berkeley: University of California Press, 1989.

————. *The Modern History of Lebanon*. London: Weidenfeld and Nicholson, 1965.

Satloff, Robert. *From Abdullah to Hussein: Jordan in Transition*. New York: Oxford University Press, 1994.

Saunders, J. J. *A History of Medieval Islam*. London: Routledge and Kegan Paul, 1965.

al-Sayyid Marsot, Afaf Lutfi. *Egypt in the Reign of Muhammad Ali*. Cambridge: Cambridge University Press, 1984.

————. *Egypt Under Cromer.* London: John Murray, 1968.

Schimmel, Annemarie. *Mystical Dimensions of Islam.* Chapel Hill: University of North Carolina Press, 1975.

Schirmann, Jefim. "Samuel Hannagid, the Man, the Soldier, the Politician." *Jewish Social Studies* 2 (April 1951).

Scholem, Gershom. *Sabbatai Sevi: The Mystical Messiah.* Princeton, N.J.: Princeton University Press, 1973.

Schroeder, Eric. *Muhammad's People: An Anthology of Muslim Civilization.* Mineola, N.Y.: Dover Publications, 1955, 2002.

Segev, Tom. *One Palestine, Complete: Jews and Arabs Under the British Mandate.* New York: Metropolitan Books, 2000.

Shaw, Stanford, and Ezel Kural Shaw. *History of the Ottoman Empire and Modern Turkey.* Vol. 2, *Reform, Revolution, and Republic.* New York: Cambridge University Press, 1977.

Shlaim, Avi. *Collusion Across the Jordan: King Abdullah, the Zionist Movement, and the Partition of Palestine.* New York: Columbia University Press, 1988.

————. *The Iron Wall: Israel and the Arab World.* New York: Norton, 1999.

Sluglett, Peter. *Britain in Iraq, 1914–1932.* London: Ithaca Press, 1976.

Silvera, Alain. "The First Egyptian Student Mission to France Under Muhammad Ali." *Middle Eastern Studies* 16 (May 1980): 1–19.

Smith, Charles. *Palestine and the Arab-Israeli Conflict.* 3rd ed. New York: St. Martin's Press, 1996.

Spencer, Robert. *Islam Unveiled.* New York: Encounter Books, 2002.

————, ed. *The Myth of Islamic Tolerance: How Islamic Law Treats Non-Muslims.* New York: Prometheus Books, 2005.

Stange, G. *Baghdad During the Abbasid Caliphate.* London: Oxford University Press, 1924.

Sykes, Christopher. *Crossroads to Israel.* Bloomington: Indiana University Press, 1973.

al-Tabari. *The Early Abbasid Empire,* vol. 2. Trans. John Alden Williams. New York: Cambridge University Press, 1989.

————. *The History of al-Tabari,* vol. 32. Trans. C. E. Bosworth. Albany: State University of New York Press, 1987.

Taylor, Jeffrey. *Angry Wind: Through Muslim Black Africa by Truck, Bus, Boat, and Camel.* New York: Houghton Mifflin, 2005.

Terry, Janice. *The Wafd, 1919–1952: Cornerstone of Egyptian Political Power.* London: Third World Centre, 1982.

Thompson, J. M. *Napoleon Bonaparte.* Oxford, England: Blackwell, 1952.

Tibawi, A. L. *A Modern History of Syria.* London, 1969.

Trofimov, Yaroslav. *Faith at War: A Journey on the Frontlines of Islam from Baghdad to Timbuktu.* New York: Henry Holt, 2005.

Twersky, Isadore, ed. *A Maimonides Reader.* Springfield, N.J.: Behrman House, 1972.

Tyerman, Christopher. *Fighting for Christendom: Holy War and the Crusades.* New York: Oxford University Press, 2004.

Vasiliev, A. A. *History of the Byzantine Empire,* vol. 1. Madison: University of Wisconsin Press, 1952.

Vatikiotis, J. *The History of Egypt.* 3rd ed. Baltimore: Johns Hopkins University Press, 1985.

Wansbrough, John. *Quranic Studies: Sources and Methods of Scriptural Interpretation.* New York: Oxford University Press, 1977.

Wasserstein, Bernard. *The British in Palestine: The Mandatory Government and the Arab-Jewish Conflict 1917–1929.* London: Royal Historical Society, 1978.

Watt, W. Montgomery. *Islamic Political Thought.* Edinburgh: University of Edinburgh, 1968.

Wheatcroft, Andrew. *Infidels: A History of the Conflict Between Christendom and Islam.* New York: Random House, 2004.

Wilson, Jeremy. *Lawrence of Arabia: The Authorized Biography of T. E. Lawrence.* New York: Atheneum, 1989.

Wilson, Mary, ed. *King Abdullah, Britain, and the Making of Jordan.* New York: Cambridge University Press, 1988.

Wolf, Kenneth Baxter. *Christian Martyrs in Muslim Spain.* Cambridge: Cambridge University Press, 1987.

Wright, Quincy. *Mandates Under the League of Nations.* New York: Greenwood Press, 1930, 1968.

Ye'or, Bat. *The Decline of Eastern Christianity Under Islam: From Jihad to Dhimmitude: 7th–20th Century.* Trans. Miriam Kochan and David Littman. Cranbury, N.J.: Fairleigh Dickinson University Press, 1996.

Yergin, Daniel. *The Prize: The Epic Quest for Oil, Money, and Power.* New York: Simon & Schuster, 1991.

Yesilada, Birol. "Turkey's Candidacy for EU Membership." *Middle East Journal* (Winter 2002): 94–111.

Yesilbursa, Behcet. "Turkey's Participation in the Middle East Command and Its Admission to NATO." *Middle Eastern Studies* (October 1999): 70–101.

Zamir, Meir. *The Formation of Modern Lebanon.* Ithaca, N.Y.: Cornell University Press, 1985.

Zinberg, Israel. *History of Jewish Literature: Arabic-Spanish Period.* Trans. Bernard Martin. Cleveland: Case Western Reserve University Press, 1972.

Zisser, Eyal. "The Maronites, Lebanon, and the State of Israel: Early Contacts." *Middle Eastern Studies* (October 1995): 889ff.

ACKNOWLEDGMENTS

Like all books, this one would not have existed without the help and support of friends, colleagues, spouses, and children (though in this particular case, the children in question were either preverbal or not yet born). I also benefitted enormously from that newfangled creation, the Internet and its attendant features, such as the comprehensive used-book network created by Amazon.com and B&N.com that allowed me to assemble a considerable library delivered to my door overnight.

My passion for this subject goes back almost as long as I can remember, but not until my freshman year in college was I introduced to the early history of Islam and the West, in a class taught by Richard Bulliet of Columbia. Not only was he an astonishing lecturer with acute and quirky insights into a long and complex history, but he became a friend and mentor for the next decade and a half, and he has remained a central inspiration. He also offered invaluable advice on the manuscript for this book. Subsequent teachers and colleagues were equally vital, especially the late Albert Hourani of St. Antony's College, Oxford, who guided me gently but firmly toward a more rigorous approach to the past. I owe a debt as well to Derek Hopwood, Rashid Khalidi, Roy Mottahedeh, Roger Owen, and Avi Shlaim.

Though I once knew Arabic, working knowledge has faded, and I benefitted from the assistance of Ja'far Muhibullah in tracking down both old and new Arabic texts and translating select passages. In a related vein, Koray Caliskan provided Ottoman-era documents and contemporary Turkish scholarship to broaden my perspective of the empire and its governance. And LeeAnna Keith once again came to the rescue and did the arduous work of culling through twentieth-century articles on the contemporary Middle East.

Perspective on one's own writing is always difficult, and a number of people generously spent time critiquing and correcting my prose, my interpretations, and my facts. Though I doubt the final text is free from problems in any of these areas, their input can only have improved it. Bruce Feiler, Fareed Zakaria, Gideon Rose, Steven Cook, and Timothy Naftali, dear friends all, and my father, David Karabell (who remains my Platonic ideal of the perfect reader), made me rethink the framework and the tone. Both Zachary Lockman and Rashid Khalidi then went through

the later sections line-by-line and forced me to hone my earlier drafts. I cannot thank all of them enough.

It has been more than ten years since John Hawkins agreed to represent me, and I do not know what I would have done without him. As an agent, he has done what any great agent does, but as a friend, he has been more supportive and generous with his time than I ever could have asked. And along with John, Moses Cardona has again made sure that the trains ran on time.

For this work as for others, I have been blessed with an editor whose acumen and pitch-perfect sense for what works and what doesn't makes all of his authors better writers. Ash Green has taught me more about books and writing than I could have imagined, and has done so with fewer words than I might have thought possible. His assistants Luba Ostashevsky and Sara Sherbill have also been invaluable. In England, I owe thanks to Caroline Knox, Gordon Wise, and Eleanor Birne of John Murray in its several incarnations, and each has also added to the manuscript and made possible its final publication.

At Knopf, I have once again been in the capable and astute hands of a marketing and publicity team that includes Sarah Gelman, Nicholas Latimer, and Kathy Zuckerman, all of whom have done their utmost to see that the book gets heard in a noisy, busy world; at John Murray in London, the effervescent Lucy Dixon has done the same. And to Sonny Mehta, thank you for once again gracing this book with your support.

Finally, my wife and companion Nicole Alger read and reread and through it all (and it was a long haul for this one) made her adamant, unwavering support unequivocally clear—even with a toddler in tow and one on the way, with Griffin and then Jasper filling the house with tumult and love. I hope this book makes a contribution to our sometimes-wrenching present, but they are what matters.

INDEX

CONTENTS

FIRST VINTAGE BOOKS EDITION, MARCH 2008

The Library of Congress has cataloged the Knopf edition as follows:
Karabell, Zachary.
Peace be upon you / by Zachary Karabell.
p. cm.
Includes bibliographical references and index.
1. Religions—Relations. I. Title.
BL410.K37 2007
201'5—dc22
2006031501

Vintage ISBN: 978-1-4000-7921-6

Author photograph © Joanne Chan
Book design by Robert C. Olsson
Maps by Mapping Specialists

www.vintagebooks.com

Printed in the United States of America
10 9 8 7 6 5 4 3

Peace Be upon You

FOURTEEN CENTURIES OF MUSLIM,
CHRISTIAN, AND JEWISH CONFLICT
AND COOPERATION

Zachary Karabell

Vintage Books
A Division of Random House, Inc.
New York

Peace Be upon You

Zachary Karabell

Peace Be upon You

Zachary Karabell was educated at Columbia; at Oxford,
where he received a master's degree in modern Middle
Eastern studies; and at Harvard, where he earned his
Ph.D. in 1996. He has taught at Harvard, the University
of Massachusetts at Boston, and Dartmouth. He is the
author of several books, including *The Last Campaign*,
which won the *Chicago Tribune*'s Heartland Prize for best
nonfiction book of the year. His essays and reviews have
appeared in various publications, including *The New
York Times*, *The Wall Street Journal*, the *Los Angeles Times*,
Newsweek, and *Foreign Affairs*. He lives in New York City.

◈

The notion of spiritual rebirth has been taken over in recent years by Pentecostalists and "born-again Christians," as I will discuss later in my chapter on the gift of the Holy Spirit. For the present, I want to ask you to consider a late nineteenth-century example of spiritual rebirth that has nothing to do with the Holy Spirit—on the surface, that is.

Did you ever see *The Miracle Worker* on stage or screen? It retells the story of Anne Sullivan, a teacher who helped a blind and deaf child, Helen Keller, to discover the relationship between words and things. Helen became blind and deaf after she had scarlet fever when she was nineteen months old. When she was seven, her parents hired Anne Sullivan as her teacher and companion. With what must have been almost infinite patience, Sullivan worked the miracle. Because of the gift of water, Helen Keller was reborn into a world of language.

Keller herself gives a powerful account of the event in her book, *The Story of My Life*, which she wrote at the age of twenty-three, near the time of her graduation with honors from Radcliffe College:

> We walked down the path to the well-house, attracted by the fragrance of the honeysuckle with which it was covered. Someone was drawing water and my teacher placed my hand under the spout. As the cool stream gushed over one hand, she spelled into the other *water*, first slowly, then rapidly....
>
> Suddenly I felt a misty consciousness as of something forgotten—a thrill of returning thought; and somehow the mystery of language was revealed to me. I knew then that "W-A-T-E-R" meant that wonderful cool something that

was flowing over my hand. That living word awakened my soul, gave it light, hope, joy, set it free![3]

To me this passage illustrates what it means to be reborn by water and the word. Helen Keller came newly alive because of water pouring over her and a word being pronounced.

So it is in the service of baptism. In the prayer immediately beforehand, the celebrant prays "for those that are here born again." The candidate, supported by the loving presence of sponsors, feels the sensation of running water and hears the word, "I baptize you in the Name of the Father, and of the Son, and of the Holy Spirit."

No single person has left a more indelible mark on the theology of baptism than that great figure, Augustine, bishop of Hippo, who himself experienced baptism as a rebirth. Augustine was baptized in April 387 at the hand of Ambrose, bishop of Milan, who had himself been chosen as bishop when he was still a catechumen—he was baptized and consecrated all within one week. Augustine, then a young teacher of rhetoric, went to hear Ambrose preach. Shortly thereafter he applied to be accepted as a candidate for baptism, which required a course of instruction by the clergy in the essentials of the faith that could take as long as three years, with more intensive preparation (fasting, exorcism, blessing) in the weeks of Lent preceding the baptism. Together with his illegitimate son Adeodatus and his friend Alypius, Augustine was baptized during the Easter Vigil, and as he put it in his *Confessions*, "all anxiety as to our past life fled away." He wept at the beauty of the hymns and canticles, he tells us, "and the truth streamed into my heart."[4]

Augustine has left us many sermons that he preached on Easter Eve, Easter Day, and throughout Easter week. In light of his own experience, it is not surprising that the metaphor of rebirth was one of his favorites. In one sermon, addressed to the newly baptized on Easter Eve during the early years of the fifth century, for example, Augustine speaks of the spotless white robes the neophytes were wearing. He calls them "newborn infants" who have been made inwardly clean. They have been "purified in the layer of forgiveness, washed in the fountain, and suffused with the light of justice."[5]

Over and over in these paschal sermons, Augustine addresses the new Christians as "reborn to a new life." They are "new offshoots of grace, reborn of water and the Holy Spirit," planted and watered in the garden of God. On the Octave of Easter, which marked the eighth day after Easter, when the newly baptized took off their white robes and resumed ordinary street wear, he is virtually carried away by his own rhetoric, heaping up metaphor upon metaphor:

> I must speak to you, the newborn infants, little children in Christ, new offspring of the Church, the gift of the Father, the fruitfulness of the Mother, God-fearing offshoots, the new colony, flower of our priesthood, fruit of our labor, my joy and my crown, all who stand fast in the Lord.[6]

Over the course of his long episcopate Augustine fought two theological battles that decisively affected his baptismal theology. The first was against the schismatic Donatists. The complicated details of this schism in the North African church need not worry us here, but we need to know the heart of the matter.

Like Augustine, Donatus was a North African bishop. During persecution of Christians under the Roman Emperor Diocletian in the year 303, an imperial edict decreed that all copies of Scripture be delivered to the magistrates for destruction. Those bishops who obeyed the edict were considered traitors by those who resisted, which led to a dilemma: were the official actions of those who betrayed the church effective or not? Donatus said no. Accordingly, he and his followers rebaptized anyone who had originally been baptized by the traitors who no longer belonged to "the true church."

Augustine disagreed, remaining adamant throughout the quarrel that even heretical baptism was still baptism if it had been administered with water in the name of the triune God. The bishop of Rome, on the contrary, sided with Donatus and insisted that heretics rejoining the church must be rebaptized since the heretical baptism was ineffectual. Augustine's view prevailed over time, and that is why the prayer book today says firmly that the bond established through baptism using the proper form and matter is "indissoluble" and must under no circumstances be repeated. Once is enough.

The second controversy was more protracted and of a more serious kind because it concerned a proper understanding of human nature—a nature made, we are told, in the image of God. The infamous Pelagian controversy, which lasted from 412 to 430, provoked Augustine to develop a rigorist doctrine of predestination and original sin. Earlier, Augustine had affirmed free will; eventually he denied it altogether. I think he simply tired of the whole controversy in his later years.

From the Pelagian point of view, a just God would not command certain behaviors unless human beings were able to obey God's commandments. Human beings are free and responsible. Since an infant cannot be held responsible for its behavior, the Pelagians argued, why is it baptized "for the forgiveness of sins," that is, for not obeying God's will? Furthermore, they said, Adam's sin injured no one but himself.

"Original sin" is a misnomer. It is not that the disobedience of the first human beings is inherited biologically by everyone, but rather that everyone chooses to disobey God. In what I think are his best discussions of the subject of sin, Augustine argues ontologically that human being has slipped, fallen back, in the order of being. We have "lost being"—that is, we have lost the full power of being human.

That is where rebirth comes in. Human creatures made in the image of God are free to sin or not to sin. When they choose to sin, they lose that freedom. Unbaptized human beings are *not* able *not* to sin. Augustine uses a double negative: *non posse non peccare.* He argued that we cannot simply flex our spiritual muscles and live a moral life; without Christ's help, we are *unable* to do so. What happens at baptism is the restoration of the fullness of created humanity in Christ Jesus, so that we are, with the grace of God, again able to sin or not to sin. In other words, we are reborn in the full image of God, with the full freedom we were created to have.

This summary of Augustinian thought on the subject of sin, grace, and free will in the best of the theologian's controversial writings against Pelagius may be oversimplified, but I think it is a legitimate interpretation of that state of sin for which even an infant is forgiven in baptism. Here Augustine is sounding somewhat like Paul, albeit with the Platonic overtones he never entirely lost. In baptism, we are given new being. Baptism is a new birth.

Theologian James F. White has aptly pointed out that the idea of new birth is the most explicitly feminine of the biblical images. As newborns, human beings are "passive, completely dependent upon God's love and nurture," he writes. "Perhaps this is why we have been so uncomfortable with birth images and tended to suppress them." White adds that at various times in history baptismal fonts have been designed to resemble pregnant women. At the Easter Vigil the font can be seen as a womb from which those born through water enter a new body, the church.[7] Just as Christians have God as their Father, through baptism the church becomes their Mother.

At the beginning of this chapter on the image of rebirth I noted the close connection between that metaphor and the metaphor of washing. I want to go back to that connection in concluding this chapter with a story about a recent Easter baptism in East London.

In 1995, in the multicultural parish of St. Andrew's, a white British laborer, a woman from Zaire, and a man from India—John, Martha, and Simon—were baptized. The baptism began with the lusty singing of "Jesus Christ is Risen Today" by the congregation of two hundred people. Beside the baptismal pool children with black, brown, and white faces watched and smiled with delight and wonder. The reporter who wrote this account for *Christian Century* admitted she climbed up on her chair in her stocking feet in order to see better, as did many others. She watched "rough-hewn John, stately Martha, and sober, resolute Simon" go down under the water and rise up to a new life. In her article describing the event she observes that each of the three was

> washed by Christ's blood in the cleansing, holy water at a church that is trying to wash away the stench of prejudice and cruelty that hovers like a London fog outside St. Andrew's stone walls.[8]

Such a rebirth, such a washing, has all the marks of God the Holy Spirit stirring up and shaking the church of God. To that Spirit we turn next.

PART TWO

Holy Spirit

CHAPTER FOUR

Gift

─────────────────────────────

Give them a love of your commandments,
and courage to live always by your Gospel,
and so prepare them to receive your Spirit.
(Prayers for Catechumens, BOS 119)

What was the most exciting Christmas present you received as a child? What gift do you remember best? I
am torn between choosing my first two-wheeled bicycle and a
boy doll that a remarkable bachelor uncle once gave me. The
doll came with an entire wardrobe, including a ski suit, zip-
pered galoshes, and mittens on a string. The excitement of
Christmas, already enormous for many a child, is sharpened
by anticipation. What will Santa bring this year?

Before the Risen Lord was taken up to heaven, according
to Luke, he instructed his apostles to wait in Jerusalem for
the promise of the Father. Jesus said to them, "You will be
baptized with the Holy Spirit not many days from now."
How keen do you suppose their sense of anticipation was?
What do you suppose they expected?

You remember the story of that first Pentecost. It is a
richly amazing tale of the gift of the Holy Spirit. The apostles
were all together in one place when they heard the mighty
rushing wind, saw the tongues of fire resting on the heads of
their friends, and began to speak in other languages "as the

Spirit gave them ability" (Acts 2:4). The event was witnessed
by pilgrims from all over the Roman Empire who had come
from east and west for the festival in Jerusalem. Certainly one
of the reasons why the Christian movement spread so rapidly
is the fact that these crowds went home and told the story of
hearing Jews speak in the languages of Mesopotamia, Phrygia, and other far-flung places.

The story of the first Pentecost culminates in the baptism
of three thousand people who "receive the gift of the Holy
Spirit" (Acts 2:38). Later we will discuss the different gifts of
the Spirit enumerated in the Bible, but first we must recognize that when we receive the gift of the Spirit at baptism, we
are receiving a gift to grow into. Particularly in the case of infant baptism, it is a gift to grow up with. Baptism is not
magic; it is not an injection of spiritual or mystical juice. The
"gift of the Spirit" is a gift of relationship and companionship.

The theme of companionship is underlined in this prayer
that accompanies the laying on of hands during the service of
baptism in the Episcopal Church:

> Defend, O Lord, your servant *N.* with your heavenly
> grace, that *he* may continue yours for ever, and daily in-
> crease in your Holy Spirit more and more, until *he* comes
> to your everlasting kingdom. (BCP 309)

This theme of companionship comes from the gospels, where
it is most strongly emphasized in John's use of the word
paraclete, literally, "one called alongside." *Paraclete* occurs just
four times in the New Testament, all in Jesus' farewell discourse in the fourth gospel.

No English word is really an adequate translation for
paraclete. The *Revised Standard Version* uses "counselor"; the
NRSV has chosen "advocate," although a footnote offers
"helper" as an alternative. The Jerusalem Bible translators
also chose "advocate," but they indicate in a footnote that
the term could also mean intercessor, protector, support, or
counselor. In any case, as Jesus makes clear, this gift will ful-

fill his promise not to leave his friends alone, orphaned, or bereft of companionship. This gift is the presence of the Holy Spirit, who will be with them always.

What is the role of the Spirit as counselor and companion? The Spirit is the one who sustains and gives comfort in the root sense of *with strength.* The current baptismal rite asks God the Father to give the new Christian "an inquiring and discerning heart, the courage to will and to persevere, a spirit to know and to love you, and the gift of joy and wonder" in all the works of creation (BCP 308). If you look closely at this prayer of thanksgiving after the baptismal washing, it answers the question of how the Holy Spirit is related to the human spirit. The Spirit does not annihilate the human spirit; rather, it sharpens our spirit, helps us to become all that we are created to be. In a fine phrase from *The Gifts of God,* the authors call the gift of the Spirit "a new gift of ourselves from God."[1]

In the light of that phrase, think about the kind of person the baptismal prayer of thanksgiving envisions. What is a person like who has "an inquiring and discerning heart"? That suggests to me someone with intellectual curiosity and good judgment. "The courage to will and to persevere"? The phrase that immediately leaps to my mind is—someone with guts. Paul Tillich might have said someone with the *courage to be.* How about "a spirit to know and to love" God? That is a person who knows about a life of prayer—including, of course, the prayer of listening.

Finally, we ask for "the gift of joy and wonder in all God's works." What are we praying for? Remember the petition in the eucharistic prayers of the people, where we ask that God would open our eyes to behold God's gracious hand in all God's works? We need to become open-eyed.

John V. Taylor, in a magnificent series of lectures to Oxford University students, tells the story of a young father taking his eighteen-month-old son to a public toilet while he and his family were at the seaside for a picnic. The trip took half an hour because the child had to squat to examine every pebble, every bit of shell, and every dry twig on the surface of the road. Taylor asks where that intensity of response, that gift of seeing the ordinary as extraordinary, goes when we become adults. He observes, "This is why Jesus Christ said that the Kingdom of God is for the childlike, for it is the kingdom of the fully alive."[2]

If you are about to present a child for baptism, either your own or someone for whom you are serving as a sponsor, can you think of anything you'd rather ask for than that child be fully alive? The child is received into "the household of God," the community where he or she may experience the love of God. The Spirit can be communicated on noncognitive levels. The Spirit can undoubtedly begin to refashion and reshape the whole being of a child long before the child is aware of it. One does not need to have reached the "years of discretion," as the older prayer book used to call them, to have the full benefit of the Spirit's companionship.

Holy Baptism is *full* initiation by water and the Holy Spirit into Christ's body, the church. It is important to emphasize that completeness because our understanding of "full initiation" conflicts with some of the older ideas on baptism and how it is related to the sacrament of confirmation.

Confirmation is the laying on of hands by the bishop during a ceremony at which individual believers reaffirm their baptismal vows; it is regarded as a mature profession of the Christian faith. When I was growing up, however, I was given the idea that in baptism you received only your "first installment" of the gift of the Holy Spirit, as it were. Then you needed to be "ready and desirous" of being confirmed by a bishop in order to get the second installment after reaching those "years of discretion." You needed the second installment before you could receive Holy Communion. I am sure I was not alone in that understanding.

The New Testament does afford some support for the separation of baptism from the gift of the Holy Spirit. One of the critical texts is Acts 8:14-18, which was one of the texts read aloud in the service of confirmation in the 1928 *Book of Common Prayer:*

> Now when the apostles at Jerusalem heard that Samaria had accepted the word of God, they sent Peter and John to them. The two went down and prayed for them that they might receive the Holy Spirit (for as yet the Spirit had not come upon any of them; they had only been baptized in the name of the Lord Jesus). Then Peter and John laid their hands on them, and they received the Holy Spirit.

The key words are: "they had only been baptized in the name of the Lord Jesus," implying that the sacrament was only half-completed.

Two other passages that seem to support the older idea of baptism as a two-stage process are the story of the conversion of Cornelius the centurion in Acts 10 and that of twelve baptized Ephesians who had never even heard of the Holy Spirit, told in Acts 19:1-7. Cornelius was a Roman centurion who, as a result of a vision, sent for Peter to come to tell him the good news of Jesus. During Peter's address, the Holy Spirit fell on all who heard the word, astounding Peter's companions that even Gentiles received the Holy Spirit. So Peter ordered that all those present be baptized "in the name of Jesus Christ."

In Acts 19:1-7, we find the situation is reversed. Paul arrives in Ephesus and encounters those who have been baptized but have no experience of the Holy Spirit. They did not even know of any such being; their baptism, the text makes clear, had been that of John. So Paul baptizes them in the name of the Lord Jesus and they receive the Holy Spirit, evidenced by an outbreak of *glossolalia*, or speaking in tongues, and of prophecy. Both of these incidents come from an early period in Christian history when the trinitarian formula of baptism "in the name of the Father, and of the Son, and of the Holy Spirit" (as prescribed in Matthew 28:19) was still fluid and evolving.

During the first centuries of the life of the church, baptism and confirmation were all one rite, and the reasons for the eventual split between them are complex. Through the fourth century, while the Christian church was still small, the officiant at a baptism was the bishop himself. Until the time of Constantine, moreover, the usual candidate for baptism was an adult; Christians put off baptism as long as possible, since at that time many believed that sins committed after baptism could not be forgiven. Furthermore, during the times of persecution, being a Christian was a dangerous affiliation. One did not lightly risk the lives of children.

With the rapid growth of the church under Constantine's policy of religious toleration, however, and the move toward infant baptism as the norm, priests and deacons became the most frequent officiants. In most places they were permitted by the bishop not only to baptize with water but also to lay on hands and anoint, though in the city of Rome the bishop kept this function for himself.

Within a few days of their baptism, therefore, catechumens went to the bishop for the final part of the rite. As the church grew and its organization became more complex, however, the amount of time it took for the completion of the rite was so protracted that eventually baptism and confirmation evolved into two separate rites.[3]

In this century, with strong encouragement from the liturgical revival of the past forty years, however, the earlier integrity of the baptismal rite has been restored. For a time during
the long and painful process of prayer book revision in the
Episcopal Church, there was even talk of eliminating confirmation altogether and some people joked that soon all bishops would be unemployed. Of course no such drastic step was
ever taken, since the relationship between the bishop and the
people of the diocese is essential. A bishop needs to visit
every parish and lay hands on all baptized people, but confirming and renewing them in their baptismal promises is not
the same as adding another injection of God's Spirit.

Although so far in this chapter I have emphasized the gift of
the Holy Spirit given in baptism as the gift of relationship, of
companionship with God, we also need to consider the fact
that the Bible has a great deal to say about gifts of the Spirit,
in the plural. So do present-day charismatic Christians, based
on their reading of Scripture.

The term "charismatic" comes from the Greek word for
gift, *charisma*. From the Hebrew scriptures comes one traditional list of spiritual gifts: the list from Isaiah 11 of the gifts
of the Spirit that will rest upon the Lord's anointed, the Messiah—wisdom and understanding, counsel and might, knowledge and the fear of the Lord (v. 2). This list was
incorporated into the old prayer for one being confirmed:

> Daily increase in them thy manifold gifts of grace: the
> spirit of wisdom and understanding, the spirit of counsel
> and ghostly strength, the spirit of knowledge and true god-
> liness. (1928 BCP, 297)

New Testament lists of spiritual gifts come to us from St.
Paul's letters, and they have helped to cause some of the
church's confusion about what constitute true manifestations

of the gifts of the Spirit. In fact, Paul gives us four different lists of the gifts of the Spirit. In his letter to the Romans, he commends prophecy, ministry, teaching, exhortation, generosity, diligence, and cheerfulness (12:7-8). The list in 1 Corinthians adds knowledge and wisdom, faith, healing, miracle-working, discernment of spirits, speaking in tongues, and the interpretation of tongues (12:7-10). Although there is some overlap, all of these lists of gifts are different in their details. It seems to me that Paul makes out his lists much the way I make out my list for grocery shopping, not systematically but writing down items as they occur to him.

In his discussion of spiritual gifts Paul makes three claims that all baptized Christians would do well to ponder. First, everyone has a gift. To be given the Holy Spirit in baptism is also to be given some kind of spiritual gift, be it a special ability to listen to another, a sunny disposition, or any number of other such gifts that Paul never thought to mention. Perhaps you are especially good with children, or are an especially gracious host. I think such attributes are spiritual gifts, gifts of God to the human spirit, and I have always taken comfort in the fact that Paul mentions teaching as a spiritual gift more than once on these lists.

Second—and Paul certainly emphasizes this—your special gift doesn't make you any better than anyone else in the church. Take a look at his amusing discussion of the many members of the body in 1 Corinthians 12. The body, he reminds them, can't very well get along without any of its parts, even those we don't undress in public. All are needed. Some members of the charismatic movements have tended to stress the more spectacular gifts of the Spirit that Paul mentions, especially speaking in tongues, prophecy, and the working of miracles. But Paul himself insists that each is given a gift of the Spirit for the common good. Indeed, he actually disparages speaking in tongues: "I thank God that I speak in tongues more than all of you," he tells the Corinthian Christians. "Nevertheless, in church I would rather speak five words with my mind, in order to instruct others also, than ten thousand words in a tongue" (1 Cor. 14:18-19).

Thus although there is no formal hierarchy among members of Christ's body because of their differing gifts, Paul does speak of a hierarchy of gifts of the Spirit. When he writes to the Corinthians about these gifts, he ends with the injunction, "But strive for the greater gifts." What are these? These greater gifts are faith, hope, and love—"but the greatest of these is love." The supreme gift of God's Spirit to our human spirit is the gift of love.

$\mathcal{P}ower$

Spirit of God, unleashed on earth
with rush of wind and roar of flame!
With tongues of fire saints spread good news;
earth, kindling, blazed her loud acclaim.
(*The Hymnal 1982*, 299)

On the day he ascended into heaven, according to Luke's account in the book of Acts, Jesus instructed his disciples to stay in Jerusalem until they experienced what God the Father had promised. "You will receive power when the Holy Spirit has come upon you," Jesus promised his followers, "and you will be my witnesses in Jerusalem, in all Judea and Samaria, and to the ends of the earth" (Acts 1:8).

The word translated here as "power" is *dynamis*, the same Greek word from which we get "dynamite." Few of us will ever forget those devastating pictures of the bombed-out Federal Building in Oklahoma City, or the precision with which the demolition experts made the remaining shell come tumbling down in a few seconds weeks later. There on the television news we witnessed the explosive power of dynamite.

The power of the Holy Spirit, which was such a conspicuous part of Jesus' promise, is further revealed to his apostles on the day of Pentecost. The roar of a violent wind filled the entire house where the apostles were gathered. If you have ever experienced even the fringes of a hurricane you know what violence and power is unleashed in that wind. Or just think of a heavy winter storm, the kind where the wind howls around your house and loudly rattles the windows in the night.

Consider this prayer for catechumens to be said during the Sundays of Lent preceding their baptism:

> Come, O Holy Spirit, come; come as the wind and cleanse; come as the fire and burn; convict, convert, and consecrate the minds and hearts of *these* your *servants,* to *their* great good and to your great glory. (BOS 125)

God the Spirit comes with that sort of power. We try to domesticate the Spirit to our peril.

One of the best books on the Holy Spirit I have ever read is John V. Taylor's *The Go-Between God.* It includes a chapter explicitly on the power of the Spirit—what Taylor refers to as the "violence" of mission—but the language of power pervades the whole work. What this former missionary bishop means by the violence of mission becomes clear in the following paragraph:

> Mission is often described as if it were the planned extension of an old building. But in fact it has usually been more like an unexpected explosion. By recording the growth of the church in mainly institutional terms, we have suggested a slow, even expansion and maturing, whereas the great leap forward and the equally sudden collapse have been such common features of the story that we should have had the modesty to recognize that the Breath of God has always played a far more decisive part than our human strategy.[1]

Taylor uses other Spirit language that is even more vehement. Jesus immerses himself in the "flood tide" of the Holy Spirit. An experience of the Spirit has a "higher voltage than a flash of lightning," "an elemental energy," the energy of communion itself. The Holy Spirit is "the power which opens eyes that are closed, hearts that are unaware, and minds that shrink from too much reality." It is life-giving energy.

Most of us are looking for a God who is too small and too tame. When he speaks of the power of the Spirit, Taylor urges us to discover the "many splendoured glory of God" within everything. We live in a world charged with the grandeur of God, but this grandeur is not a soft nimbus around the commonplace. Rather, our discovery of the power of God is more like "suddenly catching sight of the volcanic inferno beneath the earth's familiar crust."[2] Yes, it is the force of love, but love's fervor exceeds our expectations.

What does this tell us about the power of baptism? The awesome dynamism of God the Spirit should lead us to ask ourselves: with what kind of expectation and anticipation do we prepare for baptism, either our own or that of someone we love? Do we really expect to be shaken to our foundations? Do we really expect to change? Are we willing to discover that volcanic inferno beneath everydayness? Most often, I suspect, we are not. Ours is more like the infamous and probably apocryphal prayer of St. Augustine, "O Lord, make me chaste, but not yet."

Countless Christians, however, have been shaken up, changed, and renewed by the Spirit through the centuries, although often it takes a while for the Spirit to accomplish the job. Think of John Wesley, that eighteenth-century Anglican priest who when still a young man went out to Georgia as a missionary and was a dismal failure. During a storm while crossing the Atlantic, he was greatly impressed by the calm faith of some fellow voyagers who were Moravian missionaries. He subsequently visited them in their community in Saxony called *Hernhutt.*

God the Spirit undoubtedly was at work in Wesley through all of this, but it was not until May 1738, at a meeting in Aldersgate Street in London, that he was converted and felt his heart "strangely warmed." After that he caught fire, becoming a powerful preacher and attracting hundreds of followers who were eager to escape the cold rationalism of established religion.

In a thoughtful discussion of what it means to be a person, to "be yourself," theologian Charles Price makes a helpful distinction about the human spirit. He reflects on the fact that we can and do talk about a spirited horse, but we are not at all likely to speak of a spirited mosquito, no matter how loudly it buzzes just above our ear as we cower under the sheet on a summer night. Price attributes the difference to intelligence, or mind.

A spirited horse, a Triple Crown winner restrained at the starting gate, is intentional and controlled power. It is ready to burst forth and break out and reach a goal. So is a spirited person. The spirited person has life, purpose, intelligence, and controlled power ready to be unleashed. It is important to say that the human spirit is awakened by the coming of the Holy Spirit, but never overwhelmed or extinguished.

A biblical paradigm of this relationship might well be the Annunciation. The angel Gabriel, a messenger of God, is sent to Nazareth to visit Mary when she is already betrothed to Joseph. The angel tells Mary that the Holy Spirit will come upon her, and the power of the Most High will overshadow her. But it is the spirited young woman, Mary herself, who replies, "Here am I, the servant of the Lord; let it be to me according to your word" (Luke 1:38). To put it baldly, without the power of Mary's "yes," I think the power of the Holy Spirit would have been thwarted.

A more recent example is Martin Luther King, Jr., surely a spirited person. I haven't any doubt that he was literally a prophet, a spokesman for God, with the Spirit of the Lord upon him. Anyone who has listened to his powerful "I Have a Dream" speech on the steps of the Lincoln Memorial has felt some tingle of anticipation and power. King's courage and ability to provide leadership in the civil rights movement came from his spirit saying "yes" to God's Spirit.

Go back in your mind and consider the long period of preparation that catechumens were expected to undergo in the early church, sometimes up to three years. It was a period of intense training in Christian faith and life, culminating in a shorter time of even more rigorous preparation with prayer and fasting just before the final event of baptism. Imagine what level of expectation had developed over those months, what eager anticipation of the coming of the Spirit, as each candidate came from the darkness of the presbytery, went down into the water, and emerged to be wrapped in white robes. But the decisive moment, as in any baptism today, is when the candidate agrees to be washed in the waters of baptism and receive the Spirit. The celebrant asks, "Do you desire to be baptized?" The candidate replies, "I do." Human spirit opens itself to Holy Spirit.

It would be a major mistake, however, to speak as though the power of the Holy Spirit is a matter experienced only by the individual Christian. Baptism is and remains a community affair. Listen to St. John Chrysostom's description of baptism in fourth-century Antioch:

> As soon as the newly baptized comes forth from the sacred waters, all who are present embrace them, rejoice with them, and congratulate them, because those who were heretofore slaves and captives have suddenly become free

men and women and sons and daughters and have been invited to the royal table.[3]

The baptismal service today invites the congregation to welcome the new Christian with a similarly enthusiastic reception, when the officiant invites everyone present to welcome the newly baptized. The exchange of the peace follows and in many parishes it is as exuberant a display of community affection and cohesion as could be imagined.

A rector in suburban Houston links the idea of power to the power of water. To illustrate this he took some of the catechumens in his parish on a field trip to a great cascade of water that flowed down from a tower in the city. Sitting on the grass together, with the power of water most visible and audible, the group explored the question that the Samaritan woman asked of Jesus at the well in the gospel of John: "Where do you get that living water?" (John 4:11). Jesus replies, "The water I will give will become in them a spring of water gushing up to eternal life" (John 4:14). Water power is one of the oldest forms of energy human beings have harnessed for their own use. Those Texans must have been profoundly affected by that fountain of living water springing up even as they watched a Niagara of water pouring down the Houston tower.

In an essay on the loss of baptismal discipline, theologian Richard Norris speaks of both the power and the cost of baptism, which marks a fundamental change in our way of standing before God. It is a transition from one state to another: the baptized "are fresh from the hands of God, remade."[4] With these words Norris evokes the memory of the octagon, the eight-sided form of many fonts and of many baptisteries in early and medieval churches. These octagonal baptisteries symbolize creation. The Lord's day, the first day of the week, is the eighth day, the first day of a new creation: "If anyone is in Christ, there is a new creation" (2 Cor. 5:17).

✂

For the last ten years, biblical scholar Walter Wink has been studying biblical ideas of power. In *Naming the Powers* Wink examines the language of power he finds in the texts of the New Testament, such as that in Colossians:

> For in [Christ] all things in heaven and on earth were created, things visible and invisible, whether thrones or dominions or rulers or powers—all things have been created through him and for him. (Col. 1:16)

In this letter Paul is warning the Colossians against placing their hope in angels and spirits rather than the lordship of Christ, in whom all power dwells.

The language of power, however, pervades the whole New Testament, and the most unique and essential element, Wink discovers, is that power always has a spiritual dimension. Quoting Romans 8:26-27, where Paul speaks of the travail of creation and the groaning of the Holy Spirit within us, Wink reminds us that the Holy Spirit helps us in our weakness, helps us to pray. This is how he expresses it:

> If we are sharply attentive to what God wants of us, we can then very modestly, in the strength of God, anticipate the impossible, can expect miracles within that delimited sector in which we have been given to work. We must expect miracles, because the God who has called us to act at this precise time and place is also at work within us. The groaning of the Holy Spirit inside us is the hum of a great dynamo producing the power to envision and act. Without being so borne up, we could not bear to engage the powers.[5]

In the hymnal called *Lift Every Voice and Sing* is a spiritual that is a curious variation on "Swing Low, Sweet Chariot." The refrain is "Wade in the water." This is a baptismal song as well as the title-song of a Sunday afternoon program of gospel music on National Public Radio. The third stanza of the hymn echoes the idea of looking over Jordan:

Look over yonder, what do I see?
The Holy Ghost a-coming on me,
God's gonna trouble the water.

I find something a little ominous here. The juxtaposition of the Holy Ghost "a-coming on me" and the promise that God will "trouble the water" sounds to me like the threat of an assault. Yet the troubling of the water is an allusion to the fifth chapter of John, where we are told of the pool by the Sheep Gate in Jerusalem in which invalids were healed whenever the water was stirred up. The troubled waters of this spiritual become the healing waters of baptism. They become the waters through which God the Spirit claims you "in power and beginning," claims you for Christ's ministry in the world.

CHAPTER SIX

Seal

You are sealed by the Holy Spirit in Baptism
and marked as Christ's own for ever.
(BCP 308)

If you have a dollar bill in your wallet, take it out and look closely at the reverse side. Reproduced there is the Great Seal of the United States. It is so familiar that few of us have ever looked at it closely. On July 4, 1776, the Continental Congress appointed a committee consisting of Benjamin Franklin, John Adams, and Thomas Jefferson to bring in a design for a seal. The one adopted bears a bald eagle with a ribbon in its mouth and arrows of war and an olive branch of peace in his talons. The seal represents the authority of government.

Most institutions have a seal, often bearing a motto, even as the seal of the United States bears the motto *E pluribus unum*, "one out of many." I once was a visiting professor at a small liberal arts college in Kentucky that featured a cross on its seal. Almost everything belonging to the college was stamped with this seal, and the students joked that it was even on the cans of cleansing powder in the bathrooms.

In the baptismal rite, "sealing" takes place when the bishop or priest places a hand on the head of the newly baptized and marks the forehead with the sign of the cross, using chrism, or consecrated holy oil, if desired. That is the point in the service at which the celebrant proclaims, "You are sealed by the Holy Spirit in Baptism and marked as Christ's own for ever."

The custom of making a sign on the forehead may have come from early Jewish baptismal rituals, where proselytes were marked with the letter T for *Taw*, the last letter of the Hebrew alphabet. It was meant to signify God's ownership of the new convert. The making of this mark may have evolved into the sign of the cross used in Christian baptism. In the early church and throughout the middle ages, individual Christians made the sign of the cross in personal devotions as a way of recollecting their own baptism, and many still do to-day.[1]

The idea of sealing with the Holy Spirit is found in letters from the New Testament, especially in 2 Corinthians, where in the opening greeting of his letter Paul tells his readers that God has set the seal of ownership upon them and given them the Holy Spirit in their hearts (2 Cor. 1:22). The letter to the Ephesians begins in a similar way; the Christians at Ephesus are said to be "marked with the seal of the promised Holy Spirit" (Eph. 1:13).

The imagery in these letters is that of marking or branding in order to establish ownership. The word "seal" refers not only to the impress of a signet ring in wax in order to seal a letter but, even more drastically, to the branding of a slave with the mark of the slave's owner. In the same way, the newly baptized is marked as belonging only to Christ.

Archaeologists have found hundreds of seals in Israel dating as far back as the eighth century B.C.E., each bearing the owner's name. They are made either to be worn as a ring or to be hung around the neck. One very old story in the Elijah cycle of legends gives a sinister place to the seal of King Ahab. This story concerns Ahab's desire to possess the vineyard of a man named Naboth, a vineyard located near Ahab's house (1 Kings 21). Ahab planned to use it for a vegetable garden. Naboth refused because his property was his ancestral heritage, and his refusal so distressed the king that he lost his appetite.

Enter the infamous Queen Jezebel, who promised to get her husband what he so badly wanted. She forged letters to the elders and nobles in Jezreel, where Naboth lived, in Ahab's name, and she "sealed them with his seal" so that they bore the authority of the king himself. As a result of the power of that seal, Naboth was stoned to death on Jezebel's trumped-up charges.

One New Testament book says more about seals and sealing than all the others put together. That is the enigmatic Apocalypse, the Revelation to John that occurred while he was "in the Spirit" on the Lord's Day. John had a vision of seven seals or seven woes which were sealed in a book only the Lamb of God was worthy to open. The first four woes introduce the four horsemen of the Apocalypse, including the pale horse ridden by Death. Before the seventh seal can be opened there is an interlude, a chapter packed with allusions to baptism and to worship in general.

At its beginning an angel is heard to say, "Do not damage the earth or the sea or the trees, until we have marked the servants of our God with a seal on their foreheads" (7:3). One hundred forty-four thousand were sealed: twelve thousand from each of the tribes of Israel.

Then, with the abrupt shift of focus that is characteristic of apocalyptic literature, John sees a great multitude from every nation standing before the throne of God, robed in white. They fall on their faces in worship. These are the martyrs who "have washed their robes and made them white in the blood of the Lamb" (7:14). They worship God night and day within his temple. The chapter ends with the promise that the Lamb at the center of the throne will "guide them to springs of the water of life, and God will wipe away every tear from their eyes" (7:17).

In the early church St. Augustine, among others, stressed the sealing aspect of the sacrament of baptism; he saw the seal as akin to a tattoo. The imprint made an abiding mark, a *character indelibilis* on the soul. Earlier, Clement of Alexandria had used the phrase "the Lord's seal" for baptism.

The use of the sign of the cross in baptism, including the use of blessed oil or chrism, goes back to the *Apostolic Rite of Hippolytus.* There the baptized person is anointed several times, twice by the presbyter and once by the bishop, at the laying on of hands. It is called the "oil of exorcism" and the "oil of thanksgiving" and goes back to the anointing of kings and priests. Even as Christ is the Anointed One, the Messiah, so too the one anointed in baptism belongs to Christ.

The sign of the cross in anointing was probably already in use when Ephesians was written in the first century, and by the beginning of the third century Tertullian mentions it in *De Resurrectione Carnis* as part of a complex series of baptismal actions:

The flesh is washed
   that the soul may be made spotless:
the flesh is anointed
   that the soul may be consecrated:
the flesh is signed
   that the soul too may be protected:
the flesh is overshadowed by the imposition
   of the hand
   that the soul may be illumined by the Spirit.

In Puritan England, the use of the sign of the cross in baptismal rites became a serious bone of contention. The Puritans charged that the 1549 prayer book "smelt of popery." In their 1572 "Admonition to Parliament" the prayer book was called "an imperfect book, culled and picked out of the popish dung hill."[2] Although Cranmer had changed the position of the sealing or signing in the 1552 book, he had retained the use of the sign of the cross.

The great Anglican theologian Richard Hooker includes a long defense of the baptismal use of the sign of the cross in his great work, *Laws of Ecclesiastical Polity*. He argued in favor of making the sign of the cross as an ancient practice in the church, one which urges believers to glory in the service of Jesus Christ. Rather than being a superstitious and scandalous practice as the Puritans charge, it is the seal of God's care. "Arm your foreheads with all boldness," Hooker writes, "that the sign of God may be kept safe."[3] It is amusing to note in passing, moreover, that the judicious Hooker's spirited defense of the sign of the cross in baptism is preceded by a long chapter with the heading, "Baptism by Women Not Invalid."

In 1604 the Church of England adopted a canon citing the reasons for the continued use of the sign of the cross in baptism, but it also stressed the fact that use of the sign was not part of the substance of the sacrament. The substance was simply water and the trinitarian formula. The church ruled, however, that making the sign of the cross was "a lawful outward ceremony and honorable badge."[4] The canon ruled that the use of the sign of the cross was not a popish superstition but among "the things indifferent" that believers did not have to worry about, and that it should be retained in the Church of England. Nevertheless, this decision did not eliminate prejudice against making the sign of the cross, and in American prayer books down to 1928 its use could be eliminated if the sponsors objected to it.

Sealing with the Spirit and signing with the cross go together in the baptismal service. The metaphor of sealing is present also in the Easter Vigil, the traditional occasion for baptisms, which includes this collect following one of the lessons:

> Almighty God, by the Passover of your Son you have brought us out of sin into righteousness and out of death into life: Grant to those who are sealed by your Holy Spirit the will and the power to proclaim you to all the world; through Jesus Christ our Lord. (BCP 291)

The image of sealing is especially important to the doxological baptismal hymn 294, where the first line of all three verses begins "Baptized in water, sealed by the Spirit." The hymn was written in 1977 at Ealing Vicarage in West London by an Anglican priest named Michael Saward, while he was giving a course of lectures on the doctrine and practice of baptism for his parish. He wrote several such hymns to be sung at Ealing with each lecture. The music to "Baptized in water, sealed by the Spirit" was written by a priest-musician in San Diego expressly for use with the Saward text, a nice example of the Anglican Communion in action.

Once you have been baptized in water and sealed by the Holy Spirit, you are a full member of Christ's body, the church, the community of all those who have received the Spirit and been born again into new life. To the topic of community we now turn.

PART THREE

Church

$\mathcal{B}ody$

*For in the one Spirit we were all baptized into one
body—Jews or Greeks, slaves or free—and
we were all made to drink of one Spirit.*
(1 Cor. 12:13)

In a huge yellow and white circus tent on the campus of the
University of British Columbia one summer night in 1984,
a large body of Christians, some three thousand, gathered for
an ecumenical vigil for peace and justice. They came from all
over the world. Archbishop Desmond Tutu was to have been
among them but the government of South Africa at that time
refused to grant him an exit visa. The word spread that evening, however, that the government had relented at the last
minute and Tutu was on his way.

Almost precisely at midnight the back flap of the worship
tent opened and there he was—a Christian giant in a small
body. He was escorted to the podium amidst thunderous ap-
plause. I remember his brief address almost verbatim. He
said, "When I look at the state of the world today, I say,
'Thank God, I'm not God.' But when I come into a body of
Christians like this, I say, 'Thank you, God, that you are
God.'"

All of the people at that World Council of Churches' assembly had been baptized. All of us were members of one

body. I was fortunate to serve on a committee to plan the worship for that circus tent. Committee membership reflected the diversity in Christ's body. We were from six denominations and five continents: we had a Methodist from Argentina, a Presbyterian from the Cameroon, a Lutheran from Germany, a member of the Church of South India in her sari, a Greek Orthodox bishop from Toronto, and me, an American Anglican. That group gave me a powerful and lasting experience of Christ's body, the church, in today's world.

Think for a minute about the Greek and Latin words for body. The Greek is *soma*, familiar to us from such terms as "psychosomatic." The Latin is *corpus*, from which we get a number of English words such as corporation, corps of marines, and corpse. It is said that the phrase "hocus pocus" derives from a corruption of the words said at the administration of the elements in the Latin Mass: *Hoc est corpus meum*, "This is my Body." The English word "body" has an equal variety of referents. We speak of a student body, a body politic, a body of water. It is not surprising, then, to find that the image of the "body of Christ" offers a rich metaphor for speaking of the Christian church.

In addition to the body, there are many other metaphors for the fellowship of Christians in all times and places. In the New Testament there are as many as ten principal ways of speaking of the *ecclesia*. Along with "one body in Christ," we have the saints and the sanctified, believers, those who are faithful, slaves and servants, the people of God, kingdom and temple, household and family, the new Exodus, vineyard and flock, and the new humanity.

Along with those well-known metaphors, there are other, less prominent images such as salt, leaven, and the Way. In commenting on this diversity of images, New Testament scholar Paul Minear suggests that the New Testament idea of the church "is not so much a technical doctrine as a gallery of pictures."[1] Nevertheless, I think it is fair to say that among members of the liturgical churches, the phrase "body of Christ" is a favorite way of designating the church. Perhaps the reason for this preference is that we are in the habit of regularly thanking God for assuring us in the eucharist that we are living members of the body of his Son.

The idea of the church as the body of Christ is found chiefly—although not exclusively—in the letters of St. Paul. With the help of another New Testament scholar, John A. T. Robinson, we will look at the principal passages in which Paul develops that motif. In fact, Robinson also considers to be equally important in Pauline theology the phrases "the body of the flesh," "the body of the Cross," and "the body of the resurrection." He claims it can be said without exaggeration that the concept of the body forms the keystone of Paul's theology:

> To trace the subtle links and interaction between the different senses of the word *soma* is to grasp the thread that leads through the maze of Paul's thought.[2]

We will, however, try to focus just on the church as the body of Christ.

Paul's longest discussion of the body of Christ is found in 1 Corinthians 12, the discussion of spiritual gifts that immediately precedes the renowned hymn on love in chapter 13. The body passage begins:

> For as the body is one and has many members, and all the members of the body, though many, are one body, so it is with Christ. For in the one Spirit we were all baptized into one body—Jews or Greeks, slave or free—and we were all made to drink of one Spirit. (1 Cor. 12:12-13)

There follows Paul's amusing discussion among the ear and the eye and the head and the feet, which concludes:

> The eye cannot say to the hand, "I have no need of you," nor again the head to the feet, "I have no need of you." (1 Cor. 12:21)

His point is that there must be many members if there is to be any body at all. The problem that Paul is addressing in Corinth is disunity. The diverse gifts among members of the community were creating jealousy and rivalry in the church. Paul is describing the body of Christ by means of an analogy with the human body in an effort to call for harmony and co-operation.

Paul's argument here echoes another important reflection on the body of Christ that he wrote to the Christians in Rome:

> For as in one body we have many members, and not all the members have the same function, so we, who are many, are one body in Christ, and individually we are members one of another. (Rom. 12:4-5)

Again, Paul is calling on baptized Christians to live in harmony with one another: the fact that they have different gifts does not make anyone better than anyone else. He urges them to outdo one another in honoring the gifts of others. Paul does not say so explicitly, but underlying his argument is the conviction that by virtue of their baptism Christians are intimately interconnected. God has knit us together.

The conviction that we are members of one another always reminds me of a children's book I cherish, illustrated by Maurice Sendak and bearing the title *I'll Be You and You Be Me*. It is also a favorite theme of Charles Williams, the Anglican novelist, poet, theologian, and contemporary of C. S. Lewis, who called this interconnection of believers in Christ "co-inherence." As a postscript to his *Descent of the Dove*, which is a history of the Holy Spirit in the church, Williams wrote about co-inherence in the natural order:

> A man can have no child unless his seed is received and carried by a woman; a woman can have no child unless she receives and carries the seed of a man—literally bearing the burden....The child itself for nine months literally co-inheres in its mother....It has been the habit of the Church to baptize it, by the formula of the Trinity-in-Unity. As it passes from the most material co-inherence it is received into the supernatural.[3]

In other words, after birth the child is "incorporated" into the church.

At the beginning of this chapter I called the phrase "the body of Christ" a metaphor, but John A. T. Robinson cautions against this. He claims that to call the church the body of Christ is no more a metaphor than to say that the flesh of the incarnate Jesus or the bread of the eucharist is the body of Christ. "It is almost impossible," Robinson writes, "to exaggerate the materialism and crudity of Paul's doctrine of the church as literally now the resurrection body of Christ."[4] An awesome thought, isn't it? Christians really are the hands and feet of the post-Easter Jesus. To stress this organic thrust, the theologian suggests paraphrasing 1 Corinthians 12:27 as, "You are one body of Christ and severally *membranes* thereof." You and I are the soft connective tissue which holds Christ's body together.

Other New Testament authors have other ways of speaking of the body of Christ, but they do so with a difference. In the letters that are undoubtedly written by Paul he has in mind the church as the whole body, what Augustine used to call the *totus Christus.* In the letters to the Ephesians and Colossians, however, individual Christians are the body and Christ is the head. This difference is one of the reasons that some scholars have suggested that Ephesians and Colossians may not be genuine letters of Paul, even though their theology is similar to his. In any case, between them these two short letters use the body of Christ language frequently.

Ephesians has one characteristic reference in its opening section that emphasizes the distinction between the body and the head. God has put all things under Christ's feet, making him "the head over all things for the church, which is his body, the fullness of him who fills all in all" (Eph. 1:22-23). This is a different view of the community from that set forth in Paul, where all the members depend equally on one another. Here, every part of the body depends on the head, which is Christ. Later, in Ephesians 4, we meet that well-known affirmation of Christian unity:

> There is one body and one Spirit, just as you were called to the one hope of your calling, one Lord, one faith, one baptism, one God and Father of all, who is above all and through all and in all. (Eph. 4:4-6)

The letter goes on to speak in a striking way of the growth and spiritual maturing of Christians, who must "grow up" into their relationship with Christ and one another:

> We must grow up in every way into him who is the head, into Christ, from whom the whole body, joined and knit together by every ligament with which it is equipped, as each part is working properly, promotes the body's growth in building itself up in love. (Eph. 4:15-16)

Colossians also begins by calling Christ "the head of the body, the church" (1:18). Later on, its author warns the Colossian Christians that they must hold fast "to the head, from whom the whole body, nourished and held together by its ligaments and sinews, grows with a growth that is from God"

(Col. 2:19). As in Ephesians, the author uses the language of organic growth, intimacy, and dependence to speak of the building up of the Christian community.

One good explanation for these different ways of talking about the body of Christ is offered by John Shea, a theologian at the University of Notre Dame and a marvelous storyteller. He thinks the situation in Colossae was different from that in Corinth. Instead of quarreling among themselves, the Christians at Colossae were worshiping elemental cosmic spirits—a whole galaxy of mediators between God and humankind. These are the thrones, dominions, principalities, and authorities of Colossians 1:16, forces which Walter Wink sums up under the name of "powers." In this different situation, the body of Christ image is developed differently. As head of the body, Shea says, Christ has full authority to protect his body the church and guarantee its freedom from cosmic spirits. There is no need to grovel before the powers.[5]

In his study of the church as the body of Christ, Roman Catholic theologian Hans Küng points out that Paul himself is thinking of the local community as the body of Christ—the concrete historical life of Christian communities in Corinth or Rome or Philippi. His aim is to help people live their real lives in a bodily way in the light of Christ. The authors of Colossians and Ephesians, on the other hand, are thinking of the entire church as the body of Christ, not merely a particular community. In both letters Christ is the ruler of the cosmos, but he is head of the church. Now the body grows through its mission to all people, and through its service to the world. It must show its unity in love, especially the unity between Jews and Greeks. Christ broke down the dividing wall between them by his death on the cross.[6]

Another way of understanding the body of Christ is through the idea of *koinonia*, which can mean fellowship, partakers, and communion. It occurs most notably in the familiar doxology at the end of 2 Corinthians:

> The grace of the Lord Jesus Christ, the love of God, and the *koinonia* [communion] of the Holy Spirit be with all of you. (2 Cor. 13:13)

An Anglican theologian who has made a significant contribution to the understanding of baptism as initiation into a community is Lionel Thornton, and he is particularly clear about both the individual and corporate aspects of the initiation rite. In his book, *The Common Life in the Body of Christ,* Thornton writes, "The initiation of the Christian neophyte is highly personal," and almost immediately he adds, "Yet it is equally true that there is...the social aspect of our entrance into the Christian life. We are received into the community of Christ's people."[7]

The baptismal service as we have it today achieves a fine balance between the individual and communal, the personal and social dimensions of this event. On the one hand, each candidate is addressed by name at least twice, and often in the homily as well. Each candidate is supported by a group of sponsors—good friends or relatives who promise to remain in close and prayerful relationship. In the case of a child, the parents themselves are among the sponsors.

On the other hand, this baptism is a public event. No longer can you have a child baptized in your living room, perhaps as a prelude to a private "christening" party. Baptism is normally to be administered within the eucharist as the chief service on a Sunday or other feast day. Four days are designated in the prayer book as especially suited to baptisms—the Easter Vigil, Pentecost, All Saints' Day, and the Feast of the Baptism of our Lord.

Baptism is a corporate celebration: together with the sponsors, the whole congregation is called upon to pledge its continuing support of the new Christians. On occasion, when the initial response is not fervent enough, I have heard the officiant repeat the question, "Will you who witness these vows do all in your power to support these persons in their life in Christ?" The result has been a hearty, "We will!" In the church nowadays, the newly baptized can echo St. Paul's words in his defense before King Agrippa, "This was not done in a corner" (Acts 26:26).

Lionel Thornton also highlights another tension in the baptismal event, that between present and future. Baptism is an eschatological event, expressive of the already/not yet dimension of Christian experience. Thornton points out that the whole work of our salvation was accomplished in Christ's death and resurrection, and that by baptism we are made partakers of the fullness of this salvation. Yet again he quickly adds, "The full fruits of this saving work, for us and in us, still lie in the future."[8]

The "great transformation" exists only in germ in each of us. Its fruition lies ahead. That insight is a healthy corrective to any theology that sees baptism as an instant or overnight accomplishment, for baptism is the starting point of a process. Growing into our baptism is a life-long adventure.

CHAPTER EIGHT

Covenant

Look upon these catechumens whom you have called to enter your
covenant, free them from the power of the Prince of darkness, and
number them among the children of promise.
(BOS 120)

WOULD YOU BAPTIZE AN EXTRATERRESTRIAL? This arresting headline in the *New York Times* magazine in late May, 1994, brought me up short. What a strange question. Why would you? On the other hand, why not?

The headline was on an interview article with a Jesuit astrophysicist, the director of the Vatican Observatory, who works in rural Arizona near a place called Turkey Flat. The interviewer never posed this question directly to the priest, but the fact that it was raised at all seems significant as we turn to consider the church under one of its most popular designations, the covenant people of God. Just who does the term "people" include? Could ET become part of the people of God?

A turning point in the service of baptism comes at a time following the candidates' vows, or in the case of babies and children, those promises made in their names. At that time everyone present in the congregation is invited to reaffirm their promises with the words, "Let us join with those who are committing themselves to Christ and renew our own baptismal covenant" (BCP 303).

This renewal of covenant is expressed primarily in the words of the Apostles' Creed. The people are asked the three questions:

> Do you believe in God the Father?
> Do you believe in Jesus Christ, the Son of God?
> Do you believe in God the Holy Spirit? (BCP 304)

In reply, the people recite portions of the creed. Five additional questions follow, namely:

> Will you continue in the apostles' teaching and fellowship, in the breaking of bread, and in the prayers?
> Will you persevere in resisting evil, and, whenever you fall into sin, repent and return to the Lord?
> Will you proclaim by word and example the Good News of God in Christ?
> Will you seek and serve Christ in all persons, loving your neighbor as yourself?
> Will you strive for justice and peace among all people, and respect the dignity of every human being? (BCP 304-305)

The answer in each case is, "I will, with God's help."

What exactly *is* a covenant? What does it mean? The Hebrew word for covenant is *berith*, and it occurs often in the Hebrew scriptures. Its precise derivation is unknown, but it probably comes from an ancient Akkadian word meaning "bond" or "fetter," signifying a relationship that is binding.

All biblical dictionaries point to the difference between a parity covenant, which is a covenant pledge between equals, and the kind of covenant that exists between God and Israel—a covenant between a stronger and a weaker party. The Israelite covenant is similar to the "suzerainty" treaties found among the Hittites, an ancient people of Asia Minor and Syria, in which a strong conqueror makes a treaty with a vassal state. He pledges them protection, in return for which they promise obedience.

Typically these treaties contained six elements: a preamble; an historical prologue; some stipulations setting forth the obligations to which the vassal state bound itself; a provision calling for public reading of the treaty at regular intervals; a list of witnesses, including the gods of both states; and a series of blessings and curses. The whole treaty was sealed with an oath by the vassal.

All of these elements appear in one or another of the biblical covenants, whether with Abraham, Moses, or David. In addition to reminding us of the strong intercultural influences in Israel from tribes like the Hittites, this form of treaty reflects the profound recognition among the Israelites that their covenant with Yahweh was quite different from a contract between equals. The Lord who brought Israel out of slavery in Egypt evoked responses like the Song of Moses, one of the canticles read or sung at the Easter Vigil:

> The Lord is my strength and my refuge;
>   the Lord has become my Savior....
> Who can be compared with you, O Lord,
>   among the gods?
> Who is like you, glorious in holiness,
>   awesome in renown, and worker of wonders?
>   (BCP 85)

Their sense of obligation to obey the Lord was a response to his prior action of delivering them into freedom. The same root experience is voiced in the Song of Zechariah, who was the father of John the Baptist, that we know as Canticle 4 in the service of Morning Prayer:

> Blessed be the Lord God of Israel,
>   for he hath visited and redeemed his people;...

That we should be saved from our enemies,
  and from the hand of all that hate us;
To perform the mercy promised to our forefathers,
  and to remember his holy covenant.
    (BCP 50-51)

The relationship between Yahweh and Israel, therefore, is one based on the kind of commitment that a covenant implies: long-lasting and entered into with promises and obligations on both sides.

A classic account of the formation of Israel's covenant with Yahweh occurs in the book of Genesis in the story of the covenant made with Abraham and his descendants. When Abraham was ninety-nine years old, the account tells us, the Lord appeared to him and announced that he was making a covenant with him whereby Abraham would become the ancestor of a multitude of nations. The Lord says to Abraham:

> I will establish my covenant between me and you, and your offspring after you throughout their generations, for an everlasting covenant, to be God to you and to your offspring after you. And I will give to you, and to your offspring after you, the land where you are now an alien, all the land of Canaan, for a perpetual holding; and I will be their God. (Gen. 17:7-8)

As a sign of this covenant, the Lord decrees that every male baby is to be circumcised when he is eight days old. This story culminates with God's promise that Sarah, Abraham's wife, who is ninety years old, will become pregnant and bear a son.

To my mind, however, an even clearer and more eloquent expression of the covenant is found in Exodus 19. The Israelites finally reach Mount Sinai "on the third new moon" after leaving Egypt. Moses goes up the mountain and God says to him:

> You have seen what I did to the Egyptians, and how I bore
> you on eagles' wings and brought you to myself. Now
> therefore, if you obey my voice and keep my covenant,
> you shall be my treasured possession out of all the peo-
> ples. Indeed, the whole earth is mine, but you shall be for
> me a priestly kingdom and a holy nation. (Exod. 19:4-6)

When Moses summons the elders and reports the words of
the Lord, the people answer in one voice, "Everything that
the Lord has spoken we will do" (19:8).

In his commentary on this passage, Martin Buber claims
that the "eagles' wings" are more than just a happy metaphor.
He thinks, on the contrary, it is based on the actual behavior
of a male eagle who "stirs up his nest and flies hither and
thither above it in order to teach his young to fly." Buber becomes almost lyrical about the parenting ability of the eagle,
who "spreads out his wings over the nestlings; he takes up
one of them, a shy or weary one, and bears it upon his pin-
ions, until it can at length dare the flight and follows the father on his mounting gyrations."[1] In Buber's mind all of this
adds up to a theology of election, deliverance, and education.
God has chosen the people of Israel. They have been freed
from slavery. They have been brought to God, into God's
presence at Mount Sinai, where God will give them the ten
commandments.

The poetry of Israel being borne on eagles' wings into
God's very presence is surely powerful, but Israeli eagles must
be different from the American bald eagle. In one of my
books on bird behavior there is an extensive entry on the
bald eagle with no mention of these flying lessons from the
father; instead, it is explicit that both male and female parents share equally in the care of the young eaglets.

These two covenants—one with Abraham and Israel and
one with Moses and Israel—are part of the oldest stratum of
the Torah, or Five Books of Moses, but the Easter Vigil of the
Christian church highlights another important covenant, that

with Noah following the forty-day flood. The designated readings at the vigil are selections from chapters 7 through 9 of Genesis, where we hear that when the waters recede God establishes a covenant with Noah and all creatures after him. Never again shall God destroy the earth. The rainbow is to be the sign of this everlasting covenant.

Following the reading of the flood comes this collect, using familiar baptismal language:

> Almighty God, you have placed in the skies the sign of your covenant with all living things: Grant that we, who are saved through water and the Spirit, may worthily offer to you our sacrifice of thanksgiving; through Jesus Christ our Lord. (BCP 289)

❧

Two other instances of covenant-making in Hebrew scripture help to shed further light on the baptismal covenant. One is a covenant-renewal ceremony described in Joshua 24; the other is the promise of a new covenant in Jeremiah 31.

In Joshua the occasion is a gathering of the leaders of the tribal confederacy at Shechem, a walled city forty miles from Jerusalem, early in Israel's history before the tribes were united under a monarch. Joshua, who is Moses' successor as leader of all Israel, is growing old. Knowing he is about to die, he becomes deeply concerned about his people straying away from Yahweh. At this ceremony he calls upon them to give up the worship of the gods of the Canaanites among whom they live and rehearses their holy history from Abraham through to the entry of the Promised Land, reminding them of everything God has done for them. Joshua finishes by giving them a challenge and a command: "Choose this day whom you will serve" (Josh. 24:15).

The Christian congregation's renewal of the baptismal covenant, with its promises to resist evil, repent, serve God, and strive for peace, is reminiscent of this ceremony at Shechem. As Joshua realized, people need to be constantly reminded of all that God has done for them. Christians need similar rehearsals of their own holy history. They need to be called upon to renew their own promises, to choose again this day whom they will serve.

The promise of a new and different covenant in Jeremiah is interpreted by Christians as one basis for the church's claim to be the New Israel. In Jeremiah's prophecy he proclaims:

> The days are surely coming, says the Lord, when I will make a new covenant with the house of Israel and the house of Judah. (Jer. 31:31)

This new covenant will not be written on tablets of stone, but directly on the human heart. It is an amazing word of comfort from a prophet who was the sole voice in Israel during the years before the fall of Jerusalem to Babylon in 587 and the sending of her citizens into exile.

Like the other great Hebrew prophets, Jeremiah was in the thick of public affairs. He did not always speak words of comfort, but called Israel to repentance. "Run to and fro through the streets of Jerusalem," he cried out, "look around and take note! Search its squares and see if you can find one person who acts justly and seeks truth" (5:1). Jeremiah continued:

> This people has a stubborn and rebellious heart; they have turned aside and gone away....They have grown fat and sleek. They know no limits in deeds of wickedness; they do not judge with justice the cause of the orphan, to make it prosper, and they do not defend the rights of the needy. (Jer. 5:23, 28)

The old covenant is broken, Jeremiah tells them. The new covenant is a vision of the future in which Israel will be transformed, the words of the promise written not on stone but on the hearts of the people.

✤

In the New Testament (or "new covenant"), the word translated "covenant" appears relatively few times. Most familiar
to us is its use in the "words of institution" Jesus speaks when
he shares the cup at the Last Supper. We hear it, therefore, at
every eucharist:

> Drink this, all of you: This is my Blood of the new Cove-
> nant, which is shed for you and for many for the forgive-
> ness of sins. (BCP 363)

Ancient covenants were sometimes sealed with the blood
of sacrificial animals, as is the case in the story about establishing the Mosaic covenant:

> Then [Moses] took the book of the covenant, and read it
> in the hearing of the people; and they said, "All that the
> Lord has spoken we will do, and we will be obedient."
> Moses took the blood and dashed it on the people, and
> said, "See the blood of the covenant that the Lord has
> made with you in accordance with all these words. (Exod.
> 24:7-8)

Such a phrase as "the blood of the covenant" would therefore
be familiar to Jesus' disciples from hearing the Torah read in
the synagogues.

One of the earliest bits of evidence (outside the New Testament) that the early Christians thought of themselves as a
covenant community comes to us from an exchange of letters
between two non-Christian officials in the early second century. Pliny, a governor in Bithynia, which was a province in
western Asia Minor, wrote to the emperor, Trajan, asking how
he should handle the people called Christians. He reports
that it was their habit to "assemble before daylight to recite a
form of words to Christ as a god; and that they bound themselves with an oath." In context, it appears that these early

Christians recited the ten commandments. The word translated "oath" is *sacramentum*. Trajan replies, "They are not to
be sought out; but if they are accused and convicted, they
must be punished."[2]

Within the New Testament writings, it is the letter to the
Hebrews that has the most to say about covenant. Hebrews
contrasts the old and new covenants, as well as the old and
new priesthoods, an idea from the baptismal service we will
examine in the final chapter.

Although it was once attributed to St. Paul, the letter to
the Hebrews is by an unknown author writing to an unknown
congregation of Jewish Christians, possibly in Rome, to whom
the theology of the covenant would have been very familiar.
The author warns these Christians against returning to the
Mosaic system of priesthood and sacrifice. He holds up the
new order over against the old: Christ's sacrificial death need
not be repeated, because it has opened the way to God once
and for all. This is the context in which he insists on the superiority of the new covenant over the old, quoting the "new
covenant" passage from Jeremiah:

> This is the covenant that I will make with the house of Is-
> rael after those days, says the Lord: I will put my laws in
> their minds, and write them on their hearts, and I will be
> their God, and they shall be my people. (Heb. 8:10)

The thought-world of Hebrews is somewhat obscure to us
today, but the contrast of the old and new covenants is fairly
straightforward. If the first covenant had been faithfully kept,
there would have been no need to look for a second one
(8:7). In speaking of a new covenant, the old becomes obsolete. Jesus is the mediator of a new covenant (9:15).

The letter also contains a clear reference to baptism, inviting its readers with these words:

Let us approach with a true heart in full assurance of faith, with our hearts sprinkled clean from an evil conscience and our bodies washed with pure water. (Heb. 10:22)

We are back to the image of baptism as a bath, but the drawing near with faith is quickly followed by parallel mentions of hope and love (vv. 23-25).

Throughout his letter, the author of Hebrews describes the covenant life of the people of God, the *laos tou theou*. According to Paul Minear, the phrase "the people of God" is "more frequent, more ubiquitous, more evocative of the sense of identity and mission" in the New Testament than the term church, *ecclesia*.[3] It should always be remembered that "laity" means people, and that the laity do not have an inferior status in the Christian church. Bishops, for example, even archbishops, are still lay people, members of the people of God. That is the status conferred in baptism and it is indelible.

The reintroduction of regular opportunities for adult Christians to renew their baptismal covenant is to some extent a compromise between those who baptize infants and those who favor a "believer's baptism." The latter is the baptism of adults who take responsibility to claim for themselves, or rather to accept consciously and gratefully, membership in Christ's body the church, the covenant people of God. Such occasions meet a widespread pastoral need in churches today.

Baptismal vows have historically been commemorated or renewed in the Roman Catholic Church by the "*asperges*," the sprinkling of holy water on the altar and the congregation during the principal mass on Sundays. The custom goes back to the ninth century, when the ceremony was accompanied by chanting the portion of Psalm 51 which begins "*Asperges me*": "Purge me from my sin, and I shall be pure; wash me, and I shall be clean indeed." During Eastertide, furthermore, an anthem called *Vidi Aquam* is sung; it combines verses from Ezekiel 47 in which the prophet sees water flowing out of the temple.

As for the Protestant churches, the Methodist Church in Britain has introduced an annual service of covenant renewal in which the believer vows, "I am no longer my own, but Thine."[4] The 1978 *Lutheran Book of Worship* also includes confirmation, reception into membership from other denominations, and restoration of membership all under the title "Affirmation of Baptism." The Renewal of Baptismal Vows in the liturgy for the Easter Vigil in the Episcopal Church's *Book of Common Prayer* concludes with this grace:

> May Almighty God, the Father of our Lord Jesus Christ, who has given us new birth by water and the Holy Spirit, and bestowed upon us the forgiveness of sins, keep us in eternal life by his grace, in Christ Jesus our Lord. (BCP 294)

All of these ways of renewing our baptismal vows are much-needed pastoral resources in the church, allowing believers to remember and reflect upon the vows they have made and to continue growing into their promises. As in the days of Joshua and the covenant-renewal ceremony at Shechem, today's Christians are given an opportunity to choose yet again the One whom they will serve.

CHAPTER NINE

Web

Our natural life begins by being borne in another; our mothers have to carry us. This is not (so far as we know) by our own will. The Christian church demands that we shall carry out that principle everywhere by our will—with our friends and with our neighbors, whether we like our neighbors or not.

(Charles Williams[1])

Baptism is not only the beginning of a covenant relationship with God, as we discussed in the last chapter, but a sacrament that gives us a new set of family relationships as well. The newly baptized acquire a large number of new sisters and brothers in Christ. Not only are they all members of the particular congregation into which they have been baptized, they are also members of the body of Christ (incredible as it may sound) in all places and at all times. You are not baptized into St. Peter's or St. Swithin's, but into the church of God. You are now a member of the communion of saints, invited to sing God's praises with angels, archangels, and all the company of heaven.

No one has written more powerfully of the communion of saints—that "web of glory," as he was fond of calling it—than Charles Williams, Anglican novelist, poet, theologian, and friend of Lewis and Tolkien. Williams earned his living as an editor at Oxford University Press, and during the bombing of

London in the Second World War he was evacuated from London to the city of Oxford. There he became a member of the Inklings, a circle of writers and friends gathered around C. S. Lewis who met twice a week to read their works-in-progress to one another and drink beer in the local pub. Williams is perhaps less well-known than Lewis because he died at the end of the war, in 1945.

His phrase "web of glory" always reminds me of the glory of the perfect cobweb I am sometimes lucky enough to see on an early morning in Vermont, a web still bejeweled with dew, sparkling in the morning sunshine. Such a web is a marvel of engineering exactitude. That was one essential of the "pattern of glory" Williams saw all around him. At the center of Williams's web, however, was no hungry spider, but the cross of Christ.

For Williams's theology, the doctrine on which the Christian church depends is the doctrine of substitution: Christ's substitution for us on the cross and our substitution for one another. We are to love others as Christ loved us, laying down our lives for one another. Williams took with utter seriousness—indeed, literally—St. Paul's injunction, "Bear one another's burdens, and in this way you will fulfill the law of Christ" (Gal. 6:2). He made the act of carrying a friend's burden of anguish or fear sound as simple and everyday as saying to a friend, "May I carry your suitcase for you?"

Williams's theology of substitution and exchange has implications for baptism, too. Substitution could also mean the making of promises on behalf of another, which is why he saw infant baptism as an act of substitution on the part of the baby's sponsors. An infant cannot have intentions or make promises for itself; the godparents take on this responsibility instead. "It is simpler sometimes and easier," Williams wrote in *He Came Down from Heaven*, "and no less fatal and blessed, to do it so; to surrender and be offered to destiny by another rather than by oneself; it is already a little denial of the self."[2]

         ☙

The novels of Charles Williams have frequently been called "supernatural thrillers," although T. S. Eliot, a longtime friend, said in his introduction to *All Hallows' Eve* that Williams wanted his novels to be read in the first place simply as entertainment—something to hold your attention for two or three hours on a train trip. *All Hallows' Eve* certainly does that, yet I have read it now at least five times and discovered new spiritual insights at every reading, especially about the theology of interdependence and substitution as they relate to baptism.

    Williams's novel focuses on two young women, Lester and Betty, who are old friends. At the beginning of the novel Lester is killed in a plane crash over London, and one of the supernatural elements of the novel is the fact that even though she is dead, she is able to help Betty escape from the forces of sorcery and evil in the person of a magician called Simon the Clerk. Williams, who saw *All Hallows' Eve* as the story of a cosmic battle between good and evil, was interested in witchcraft and once wrote a book on it (librarians at the seminary where I taught had to keep it locked up along with all the other books on the occult because they kept disappearing from the open stacks). Perhaps it was from that research that he encountered the extra-biblical legends he recounts in *All Hallows' Eve.*

    The themes of baptism and interdependence come together in a chapter entitled "Wise Water," which is Betty's account of her earliest memory. The memory is that of a lake filled with fish:

> None of them took any notice of me, except one with a kind of great horned head which was swimming round me and diving under me....Presently the fish dived again and went below me, and I felt him lifting me up with his back,

and then the water plunged under me and lifted me, and I came out on the surface. And there I lay; it was sunny and bright, and I drifted in the sun—it was almost as if I was lying on the sunlight itself—and presently I saw the shore—a few steps in a low cliff, and a woman standing there....It was a nurse I once had, but not for very long. She bent down and lifted me out of the water. I didn't want to leave it. But I liked her, it was almost as if she was my real mother, and she said, "There, dearie, no one can undo that; bless God for it."[3]

Later in the story, Betty goes to visit the old nurse of her memory, Mrs. Plumstead. The nurse is delighted to see her, but has something on her mind that she needs to confess:

"Well, my dear," the old nurse went on and ever so faintly blushed, "as I say, I was younger then, and in a way I was in charge of you, and I was a little too fond of my own way and very obstinate in some things. And now I do not think it was right. But you were such a dear little thing and I did once mention it to my lady, but she was very putting-off and only said, 'Pray, nurse, do not interfere'—her ladyship and I never suited—and I ought to have left it at that, I do think now, but I was obstinate, and then you were such a dear little thing, and it did seem such a shame, and so"—the old nurse said, unaware of the intensity of the silence in the room—"well, I christened you myself."

Betty's voice, like the rush of some waterfall in a river answered, "It was sweet of you, nurse."

"No, it wasn't right." Mrs. Plumstead said. "But there it is. For I thought then that harm it couldn't do you and good it might—besides getting back on her ladyship: Oh I was a wicked woman—and one afternoon in the nursery, I got the water and I prayed God to bless it, though I don't know now how I dared, and I marked you with it, and said the Holy Name, and I thought, "Well, I can't get the poor dear godfathers and godmothers, but the Holy Ghost'll be her godfather, and I'll do what I can."[4]

Williams comments that Betty, a child of magic, had been "saved from magic by a mystery, beyond magic."

The phrase "saved from magic by a mystery, beyond magic" is tremendously important. It is imperative to distinguish between the sacraments, "these holy mysteries," and the exercise of magic. Magic is a human effort to manipulate ultimate reality. A mystery beyond magic is God's gift to human beings. That distinction, which Williams makes so freshly, is another protection from mistaken notions that the rite of baptism results in an instant and total change. A little water sprinkled on the infant's head, along with the correct words, does not produce a fully mature Christian, any more than the laying on of a bishop's hands at ordination produces a mature priest. It is only the beginning of a process of growth.

Elsewhere in his novel Williams illustrates the theology of substitution even more dramatically than this account of a child's baptism. For example, at one critical point in *All Hallows' Eve*, Lester, still newly dead, offers herself to help Betty, who is becoming steadily weaker under the domination of Simon the magician and her mother, Lady Wallingford, Simon's disciple. Standing at the foot of Betty's bed, Lester says and means with all her heart, "Betty, if you want me, I'm here." With these words, she puts herself at Betty's disposal.

As Betty relaxes and goes to sleep, Lester is suddenly racked with pain. She becomes aware that at first she had been standing, but now she is leaning back on a frame of some sort that supports her from buttocks to head. Her arms are thrust out, one to each side, holding onto a part of the frame. She does not guess what is happening, but Williams leaves us in no doubt—we know that there is a cross at the heart of the web. We know that we are to bear one another's burdens and so fulfill the law of Christ.

Because the power of good is baptismal and life-giving, Williams closes the episode with a transformation of the cross. For Lester the hard, painful frame becomes "marvelously spring-livened; spring of the world, spring of the heart; joy of spring water, joy."[5]

These acts of substitution, of bearing our neighbors' burdens, also take place across time and space. One of the characters in another of Williams's novels, *Descent into Hell*, has been haunted by a terrifying vision of herself—her "double"—who at any time can appear in the distance and walk toward her. When she admits her paralyzing fear to Peter Stanhope, a poet and playwrite, he offers to take the fear from her and carry it himself, just as he would carry a bag of groceries.

> "It's so easy," he went on, "easy for both of us. It needs only the act. For what can be simpler than for you to think to yourself that since I am there to be troubled instead of you, therefore you needn't be troubled? And what can be easier than for me to carry a little while a burden that isn't mine?"[6]

Pauline accepts his offer, if only to humor him, but walks home that night free of fear for the first time since the apparition first began to appear. Peter Stanhope, sitting in his armchair in a state of intense concentration, experiences the terror and dread in her place.

Furthermore, because he has led the way for her, Pauline can now take her own place in the great web of human interchange and bear the burden of someone else. In a climactic scene that dramatizes the familiar phrase in the liturgy "at all times and in all places," she is able to receive the burden of her martyred ancestor John Struther's fear as he waits in prison to be burned at the stake. Here is how Williams describes her vision of John Struther, which cuts across past, present, and future:

> In front of her, alone in his foul Marian prison, unaware of the secret means the Lord he worshipped was working swiftly for his peace, believing and unbelieving, her ancestor stood centuries off in his spiritual desolation and agony of sweat. He could not see beyond the years the child of his house who strove with herself behind and before him. The morning was coming; his heart was drained. Another spasm shook him; even now he might recant. Pauline could not see the prison, but she saw him. She tried to choose and to speak....
>
> "Give it to me, give it to me, John Struther." He stretched out his arms again: he called, "Lord, Lord!" It was a devotion and an adoration; it accepted and thanked....He fell on his knees, and in a great roar of triumph he called out: "I have seen the salvation of my God!"[7]

Afterward, Pauline feels herself at peace. She has taken her place "at the table of exchange" and her act of reconciliation reaches across four centuries.

In writing about the web of glory Williams has challenged us to see that everyone baptized into that web is given a special call to ministry. It may be a call to minister to someone in trouble, as Lester was called to minister to Betty, or a call to carry someone else's fear, as Stanhope did for Pauline. It may come in some different way entirely. Yet Williams knew full well that all the baptized are called, anointed for some special ministry. To the topic of ministry we now turn in our final chapter.

A Royal Priesthood

You are a chosen race, a royal priesthood, a holy nation, God's own people, in order that you may proclaim the mighty acts of him who called you out of darkness into his marvelous light.
(1 Peter 2:9)

In the previous chapters we have focused on nine images for baptism. We looked at the topic of water with the images of river, bath, and birth. For the work of the Holy Spirit we explored the images of gift, power, and seal; and for the church, the body of Christ, covenant, and web. All but the last image are both biblical and baptismal. That is, both the words and the ideas come from the Bible and from the service of baptism. You won't find the word "web" in the Bible or the prayer book, but the ideas it signifies—coinherence, mutuality, and interdependence—certainly are.

Throughout I have tried to suggest that Christian baptism is at once an extremely simple rite of Christian initiation and also a "holy mystery" of great profundity, a mystery beyond magic. As we have seen, baptism knows no single setting. It can be administered in a racially diverse parish in East London, a ravine in El Salvador, a river in Israel. Similarly, baptism is not limited to a short, ten-minute liturgical event on a Sunday morning. It begins a life-long process of Christian growth, no matter what the age of the one being baptized. Part of this maturation process involves the baptized person in active ministry and mission.

At the conclusion of a baptism, the congregation welcomes the one who is newly baptized. In the prayer book of the Episcopal Church, the people use these words of greeting:

> We receive you into the household of God. Confess the faith of Christ crucified, proclaim his resurrection, and share with us in his eternal priesthood. (BCP 308)

These are puzzling words. They clearly charge the new members of God's church to do three things: they are to confess the faith and proclaim the good news of the resurrection, but they are also to share in Christ's eternal priesthood. What does that mean?

The idea that Christ is a high priest lies at the heart of the argument in the letter to the Hebrews, that New Testament document by an unknown author to an unidentified Christian church that we discussed in the chapter on covenant. Hebrews is not very familiar to most of us, beyond a few passages at least, because the thought-world that produced it remains alien to us.

At the beginning of chapter 3, the writer calls upon these Jewish Christians to consider Jesus "the apostle and high priest of [their] confession." Evidently the author fears that the people to whom he is writing are backsliding, neglecting to meet together, falling away from the living Lord. He urges them to recognize that Jesus is able to sympathize with all their temptations because he was tempted as they were, but that he is also the source of eternal salvation, our anchor in the holy of holies. The crux of the matter is worship. To share in Christ's eternal priesthood means, from the point of view of the writer of Hebrews, to share in "drawing near" to God.

The New Testament elaborates on Christ's priesthood only in Hebrews, but other writers were also familiar with the idea that Christians are a priestly people. You will recall that earlier I cited 1 Peter as a likely baptismal homily in which the newborn Christians are to "long for the pure, spiritual milk" (2:2). They are to let themselves "be built into a spiritual house, to be a holy priesthood" (2:5) because they are "a chosen race, a royal priesthood, a holy nation, God's own people" (2:9).

These verses echo God's words through Moses to Israel, "You shall be for me a priestly kingdom and a holy nation" (Exod. 19:6). Similarly, the author of the Revelation to John tells the seven churches to which he is writing that Jesus Christ has made them to be "a kingdom, priests serving his God and Father" (Rev. 1:6). Christians who share in the resurrection "will be priests of God and of Christ, and they will reign with him a thousand years" (Rev. 20:6).

Later Christian writers did not dwell much on Christ's priesthood or ours, as far as I know, until the Reformation, when it became an important theme to both John Calvin and Martin Luther. In his monumental *Institutes of the Christian Religion*, Calvin elaborated on the three offices of Christ—prophet, priest, and king. All three offices involve anointing with holy oil, or chrism, as new Christians are anointed in baptism. His priestly office is that of mediator. By the sacrifice of his death, Christ wiped away guilt and made satisfaction for sin, Calvin argues, and we ourselves are priests in him. We are "clothed with his holiness."[1]

In the 1545 *Catechism* of Calvin's Geneva church, children were taught the meaning of Christ's offices of prophet, priest, and king through a series of question posed by the "master" to the "scholar":

M. What of the priesthood?

S. It is the office and prerogative of appearing in the presence of God to obtain grace and of appeasing his wrath by the offering of a sacrifice which is acceptable to him.

M. To what is the office of priest conducive?

S. First by means of it he is the mediator who reconciles us to the Father; and secondly, access is given to us to the Father, so that we can come with boldness into his presence, and offer him the sacrifice of ourselves, our all. In this way he makes us, as it were, his colleagues in the priesthood.[2]

Martin Luther is a more congenial thinker for most of us in his teaching on the priesthood of all believers. In the community of the church, he believed, all people are priests to each other as occasions for and messengers of grace and support. In his 1520 treatise on Christian liberty, Luther spelled out two seemingly contradictory theses:

A Christian is a perfectly free lord of all, subject to none.

A Christian is a perfectly dutiful servant, subject to all.[3]

In the course of developing these theses Luther talks of Christ's priesthood, which does not consist "in the splendor of robes and postures like those of the human priesthood of Aaron and our present-day church." It consists of spiritual things, by which Christ intercedes for us in heaven. Furthermore, he teaches us inwardly through "the living instruction of his spirit." Thus, Luther sums up, Christ performs the two real functions of a priest, those of prayer and preaching.[4] For Luther all Christians are priests because they are free to ap-

pear before God to pray for others and to teach one another
spiritual things.

In contemporary theology, the priesthood of all believers is
stressed by Hans Küng, who rightly insists that Christ is the
only high priest and mediator. Playing with the etymology of
the word "priest," he demonstrates that the proper meaning
of the term refers to someone who offers sacrifices. Like
Calvin and Luther, Küng too focuses on the argument in the
letter to the Hebrews where Christ is the mediator of a new
and far superior covenant. Küng's exposition of Hebrews
speaks of our sacrifices of praise and thanksgiving. Through
Christ we have immediate access to God. We offer him ourselves.

The royal priesthood of all believers through baptism is a
priesthood set apart for worship and service. Küng gives a
five-fold content to this assertion. It means direct access to
God without the need of any holy go-between. It means sacrifices that are made in the middle of everyday life, the loving
service of God. It involves the preaching of the word to "proclaim the mighty acts of him who called you out of darkness
into his marvelous light," as 1 Peter puts it. It also involves
the administration of baptism, the Lord's supper, and absolu-
tion as functions given to the whole church. And, finally, it
impels us to mission. Priesthood must become effective in the
world, in service of one's fellow human beings in the church
and the world.[5]

Not all baptized persons recognize the fact that by virtue
of their baptism they are the chief ministers of the church.
The catechism of the Episcopal Church explicitly asks, "Who
are the ministers of the Church?" The answer begins, "The
ministers of the Church are lay persons" and goes on to describe what that ministry entails:

> The ministry of lay persons is to represent Christ and his
> Church; to bear witness to him wherever they may be; and,
> according to the gifts given them, to carry on Christ's work
> of reconciliation in the world; and to take their place in the
> life, worship, and governance of the Church. (BCP 855)

That description is broad in scope, reminding the baptized of
the last three questions in the baptismal covenant when they
pledged themselves to proclaim by word and example the
Good News of God in Christ, to seek and serve Christ in all
persons, and to strive for justice and peace among all people,
respecting the dignity of every human being.

The mission of the members of Christ's body is a mission to
the world. It finds expression in how you vote as well as how
you pray. And let it be remembered that it includes *all* the
baptized, even infants. Have you ever thought much about
the ministry of the very young? Or the very old, for that matter?

I was privileged to know a very senior citizen who carried
on an active phone ministry from her bed. I also know a very
small Christian, the great-granddaughter of a friend of mine,
who ministers (most of the time) to everyone through a
charming, sparkling smile. It is necessary to emphasize this:
once you have been baptized, you are never too young to be
ministering to others, nor can you ever retire from this role.
My bedridden friend must have run up a hefty long-distance
phone bill each month, but her calls were an outward and visible sign of her practice of intercessory prayer. The little girl
simply had the gift of cheering people up.

Do you find it troubling, as I do, that a specified number
of hours of community service is now considered part of a
sentence for breaking the law? That distorts the meaning of
the term "service," which is virtually synonymous with the

word "ministry." Think of the dozens of kinds of ministry going on right now in your own parish or community.

In the little north country village where I live half the year, some citizens have banded together to form a care-ring, described in their flyer as a neighbor-to-neighbor caring and sharing telephone network. If you live alone or are ill or otherwise have a need, a volunteer will telephone you every day to make sure that everything is all right. If you need a ride to a doctor, they will arrange that. During a time when I needed the service my volunteer called every afternoon right after she got home from school, where she was a cook. Her cheerful voice was a ministry even if she was not consciously a Christian.

One parish where I was a member kept a kitchen refrigerator full of frozen casseroles to take to people who had a death in the family or an illness that incapacitated the cook. A growing number of parishes participate in Meals-on-Wheels programs, taking hot meals to shut-ins. Another group shares in giving shelter to the homeless, especially in the winter months. These and similar activities are frequently done ecumenically.

All of these examples of ministry come straight out of Matthew's gospel and its description of the Last Judgment:

> I was hungry and you gave me food, I was thirsty and you gave me something to drink, I was a stranger and you welcomed me, I was naked and you gave me clothing, I was sick and you took care of me, I was in prison and you visited me. (Matt. 25:35-36)

There are an enormous number of ways to enact the baptismal promise "to seek and serve Christ in all persons, loving your neighbor as yourself," as well as of working for justice and peace. In the latter category, no matter what your politics may be, former President Jimmy Carter offers a splendid example. His mission to Haiti, to cite one instance, did not win universal approval, but it did unquestionably further the peace process.

☙

I would like to consider just two additional examples of the ministry of baptized Christians because they are so closely related to sharing in Christ's eternal priesthood; that is, they are directly connected with worship. It is fashionable these days to insist that ministry is not all churchy activity, and of course it isn't. But some of it is.

One such ministry helps to create the beauty of holiness. Service on the altar guild is a ministry too seldom recognized as such in any parish. Quietly, behind the scenes, week after week, someone washes and irons the linens. Someone orders and arranges flowers. Someone buys wine and bakes or provides the bread for use at the eucharist. Mysteriously, the brass and silver seem always freshly polished as they gleam in the candlelight.

The second is the ministry of music. Many an organist and choir director now carries the title Minister of Music, but all those in a congregation who help make a joyful noise unto the Lord are engaged in a ministry of music, whether or not they are members of the choir or even able to sing a tune. A young college student I know often plays his guitar in church. A young trumpeter adds enormously to the worship at a festive service. It always reminds me of Psalm 150:

> Praise him with the blast of the ram's-horn;
>   praise him with lyre and harp.
> Praise him with timbrel and dance;
>   praise him with strings and pipe.
> Praise him with resounding cymbals;
>   praise him with loud-clanging cymbals.
> Let everything that has breath
>   praise the Lord.
>   Hallelujah! (BCP 808)

Without question, those who have been fully initiated into
Christ's body the church through baptism and the Spirit are
also called to ministry and to a mission far beyond the walls
of any church building. They are Christ's ambassadors to the
world. They are agents of the good. Liturgist Daniel B.
Stevick has expressed this aspect of our baptism well:

> It is not just the redemptive meanings—forgiveness,
> Christ, Church, the Spirit—that are included in Baptism;
> it is also the commitments of Christian life. Baptism is—or
> ought to be understood as being—a commissioning for
> ministry; it is strength for spiritual combat; it is the ordi-
> nation of the laity; it is the sacrament of childhood and
> maturity. It sets one within the people of God, the holy
> priesthood; it brings one into the eucharistic fellowship.
> There is nothing left over that must be said at a later stage
> because it was not said at Baptism.[6]

Even so, baptism is just the beginning of a long process of
response for both infants and adults. It is the beginning of a
life-long adventure. And it is an invitation to joy as well as to
service. All of this is implicit in the prayer book definition we
have been following from the outset:

> Holy Baptism is full initiation by water and the Holy
> Spirit into Christ's Body the Church. The bond which
> God establishes in Baptism is indissoluble. (BCP 298)

Chapter Notes

Notes to Chapter 1

1. Flannery O'Connor, *The Complete Stories* (New York: Farrar, Straus and Giroux, 1972), 157-174.
2. Sally Fitzgerald, ed., *The Habit of Being: Letters of Flannery O'Connor* (New York: Vintage Books, 1980), 171.
3. Cyril of Jerusalem, *Mystagogical Catecheses*, II, 4.
4. *Didache*, ch. 7, in Cyril C. Richardson, ed., *Early Christian Fathers*, Library of Christian Classics, vol. 1 (Philadelphia: The Westminster Press, 1953), 174.
5. John J. Putnam, "Down the Teeming Ganges, Holy River of India," in Merle Severy, ed., *Great Religions of the World* (Washington, D.C.: National Geographic Society, 1971), 51-76.
6. Barbara Grizzuti Harrison, "Shiva's Holy City," in *The New York Times Magazine* (May 16, 1993), 85.
7. "Sonia's Baptism," in *El Salvador: A Spring Whose Waters Never Run Dry*, Scott Wright, Minor Sinclair, Margaret Lyle, David Scott, eds. (Washington, D.C.: Ecumenical Program on Central America and the Caribbean, 1990), 52-53.

Notes to Chapter 2

1. Tom F. Driver, *Patterns of Grace: Human Experience as Word of God* (San Francisco: Harper & Row, 1977), 1.
2. F. Van Der Meer, *Augustine the Bishop*, trans. Brian Battershaw and G. R. Lamb (London: Sheed & Ward, 1961), 361.
3. Charles P. Price and Louis Weil, *Liturgy for Living* (New York: The Seabury Press, 1979), 98.
4. *The First and Second Prayer Books of Edward VI* (London: J. M. Dent & Sons, Everyman Library, 1952), 237.
5. *Faith and Order Paper No. 111* (Geneva: World Council of Churches, 1982), 6.
6. James F. White, *Sacraments as God's Self Giving* (Nashville: Abingdon Press, 1983), 40.
7. Walter Brueggemann, *Living Toward a Vision* (Philadelphia: United Church Press, 1976), 137.

Notes to Chapter 3

1. George Macdonald, *The Princess and the Goblin* (London: Puffin Books, 1964), 154. First published in 1872.
2. Quoted in *The Hymnal 1982 Companion*, ed. Ray Glover, vol. 3A (New York: Church Hymnal Corporation, 1994), 295.
3. Helen Keller, *The Story of My Life* (New York: Bantam Books, 1990), 16. Originally published in installments in *Ladies' Home Journal* in 1902.
4. Augustine of Hippo, *Confessions*, book 9, chp. 6.
5. Philip T. Weller, *Selected Easter Sermons of Saint Augustine* (St. Louis: B. Herder Book Co., 1954), 96.
6. *Ibid.*, 173.
7. James F. White, *Sacraments as God's Self Giving: Sacramental Practice and Faith* (Nashville: Abingdon Press, 1983), 41.
8. Amy L. Sherman, "Easter Life in East London," *Christian Century* (May 17, 1995), 532-533.

Notes to Chapter 4

1. Eugene Goetchius and Charles Price, *The Gifts of God* (Wilton, Conn.: Morehouse Barlow, 1984), 70.
2. John V. Taylor, *A Matter of Life and Death* (London: SCM Press, 1986), 20.
3. Charles P. Price and Louis Weil, *Liturgy for Living* (New York: The Seabury Press, 1979), 113, 119ff.

Notes to Chapter 5

1. John V. Taylor, *The Go-Between God: The Holy Spirit and the Christian Mission* (New York: Oxford University Press, 1979), 53.
2. *Ibid.*, 45.
3. Quoted in Michael W. Merriman, *The Baptismal Mystery and the Catechumenate* (New York: Church Hymnal Corporation, 1990), 95.
4. Richard Norris, "The Result of the Loss of Baptismal Discipline," in Merriman, *Baptismal Mystery*, 27.
5. Walter Wink, *Naming the Powers: The Language of Power in the New Testament* (Philadelphia: Fortress Press, 1984), 104.

Notes to Chapter 6

1. Marion Hatchett, *Commentary on the American Prayer Book* (New York: The Seabury Press, 1980), 279-280.
2. J. R. H. Moorman, *A History of the Church in England* (Wilton, Conn.: Morehouse-Barlow, 1973), 208.
3. Richard Hooker, *Laws*, Book V, as excerpted in Paul Elmer More and Frank Leslie Cross, *Anglicanism* (London: SPCK, 1935), 434.
4. "The Canons of 1604" in More and Cross, *Anglicanism*, 432.

Notes to Chapter 7

1. *Interpreter's Dictionary of the Bible*, vol. 1, 607-617.
2. John A. T. Robinson, *The Body: A Study in Pauline Theology*, Studies in Biblical Theology No. 1 (London: SCM Press, 1952), 9.

3. Charles Williams, *The Descent of the Dove* (New York: Pellegrini and Cudahy, 1939), 234.

4. Robinson, *The Body*, 51.

5. John Shea, *An Experience Named Spirit* (Chicago: The Thomas More Press, 1983), 40.

6. Hans Küng, *The Church* (New York: Sheed and Ward, 1967), 227-233.

7. Lionel Thornton, *The Common Life in the Body of Christ* (London: Dacre Press, 1950), 91-92.

8. *Ibid.*, 61.

Notes to Chapter 8

1. Martin Buber, *Moses, the Revelation and the Covenant* (New York: Harper & Row, 1958), 102.

2. J. Stevenson, *A New Eusebius: Documents Illustrating the History of the Church to A.D. 337*, revised edition, ed. W. H. C. Frend (Cambridge: SPCK, 1989), 18-21.

3. Paul S. Minear, "Church, Idea of," *Interpreter's Dictionary of the Bible*, vol. 1 (Nashville: Abingdon Press, 1962), 611.

4. Geoffrey Wainwright, *Doxology: The Praise of God in Worship, Doctrine, and Life* (New York: Oxford University Press, 1980), passim.

Notes to Chapter 9

1. Charles Williams, "The Way of Exchange," in *Charles Williams: Essential Writings in Spirituality and Theology*, ed. Charles Hefling (Cambridge, Mass.: Cowley Publications, 1993), 212.

2. Charles Williams, from *He Came Down from Heaven*, in Hefling, *Charles Williams*, 222.

3. Charles Williams, *All Hallows' Eve* (New York: Pellegrini & Cudahy, 1949), 134-135.

4. *Ibid.*, 207-208.

5. *Ibid.*, 164.

6. Charles Williams, *Descent into Hell* (London: Faber and Faber, 1937), 98.

7. *Ibid.*, 169-170.

Notes to the Conclusion

1. John Calvin, *Institutes of the Christian Religion*, tr. Henry Beveridge (London: James Clarke & Co., 1957), Vol. I, Book II, 425-432.

2. John Dillenberger, ed., *John Calvin: Selections from his Writings* (Garden City, N.Y.: Doubleday Anchor Books, 1971), 253-254.

3. John Dillenberger, ed., *Martin Luther: Selections from his Writings* (Garden City, N.Y.: Doubleday Anchor Books, 1961), xxxiii.

4. *Ibid.*, 63.

5. Hans Küng, *The Church* (New York: Sheed and Ward, 1967), 363-387.

6. Daniel B. Stevick, "Holy Baptism," Supplement to *Prayer Book Studies 26* (New York: Church Hymnal Corporation, 1973), 88-89.

Questions for Discussion

PART ONE
Water

CHAPTER ONE
✐ River

1. In Flannery O'Connor's short story "The River," the preacher baptizes new converts by submerging them and holding them underwater. What connections can you see between this vivid description of baptism and the polite rituals experienced in most churches?

2. Harry's death by drowning is a powerful and ironic statement about the symbolic death of baptism. What do you think are some of the ways in which people "die" when they are baptized?

3. In Romans 6:3-4 St. Paul makes a connection between our baptism and Christ's death on the cross: we are "buried" with

Christ by virtue of our baptism. What do you think Paul means? Can you think of other places in the New Testament where we are told that we must die in order to live?

4. In a letter Flannery O'Connor jokingly asked, "How can you document the sacrament of baptism?" How would you?

5. Reread the final story in this chapter about the community in El Salvador. What does it mean to say, "In a liberated community, all of us are the child's godparents"? How has this been true of the communities where you have worshiped?

CHAPTER TWO

✥ *Bath*

1.The dominant image for baptism in this chapter is being washed clean. Do you think that is an apt image?

2. In this chapter water appears in a very different way from in the chapter on the river; here water is restorative and life-giving instead of death-dealing. Micks tells the story of Namaan the Syrian and his cure from leprosy in the river. What are other places in Scripture where water is a source of life and healing?

3. When a child or an adult is baptized in your congregation, do you have the opportunity to renew your baptismal vows as part of the service? If so, how does your renewal change the way you participate in the baptism?

4.The desire to feel "clean" is a deep part of all religious yearnings. Can you think of circumstances or situations where someone might feel in need of baptismal cleansing as a way of starting over?

5. Walter Brueggemann speaks of the tools of his trade being "hardware." When you look around your home or office, what tools do you see? Are they hard or soft? Do they bear the imprint of your ministry?

CHAPTER THREE
❧ *Birth*

1. Reread the Nicodemus story in John 3:1-21. Can you think of someone you know who has been "born again" in the middle of his or her life?

2. St. Augustine called the newly baptized "newborn infants." What do you think he meant?

3. Birth brings pain as well as rejoicing. What would be some painful or difficult aspects of being reborn as a Christian?

4. In this chapter the idea of rebirth is linked to freedom and the ability to make choices, rather than bondage and confusion. How does that fit in with your experience?

5. Institutions can be reborn as well as individuals. Have you witnessed the rebirth of an institution that was in the process of dying?

PART TWO

Holy Spirit

CHAPTER FOUR

✍ *Gift*

1. What is the most exciting or meaningful present you have ever received?

2. Those of us baptized as babies cannot remember the event. Are you aware of a time, however, when you first began to have the sense of "growing into" the gift of your baptism?

3. What is your understanding of the gift of companionship? What do you look for in a good companion?

4. Sometimes the gifts we receive are troublesome or unwelcome: they force us to go out on a limb, or undertake something we don't want to do, or make us stand out in some way. Can you think of gifts you have received that were unwelcome?

5. Each age of the church needs to have the spiritual gifts that are right for its time and opportunities. What do you think are the spiritual gifts needed in your generation of Christians?

CHAPTER FIVE

❧ *Power*

1. The author describes a priest in Houston who takes his adult class to a waterfall in order to convey the reality of baptismal power. Where would you take someone to teach about baptism?

2. John Taylor, the author of *The Go-Between God*, speaks of the Holy Spirit and the "violence of mission." What do you think he means?

3. Have you ever been in a situation where it seemed clear that the Holy Spirit was "troubling the waters"? Was it exhilarating? Terrifying? How did you know it was the Spirit?

4. What are some of the ways you see the Spirit troubling the churches today?

5. Walter Wink speaks of the spiritual dimensions of power. What do you think he means by this? Is he talking about power, force, or coercion?

CHAPTER SIX

❧ *Seal*

1. In the baptismal liturgy of the Episcopal Church, candidates are "sealed" by the Holy Spirit and "marked as Christ's own for ever." Is it possible to change your mind about baptism?

2. In its original context, a seal signified ownership, slavery, or possession—whether an object, person, or animal. How does this idea fit in with the notion that we are baptized into

freedom? Is Christian freedom different from other kinds of freedom?

3. In baptism, believers are marked with the sign of the cross, meaning ownership, but also anointed with oil as are royalty. Does this seem like a contradiction?

4. Sealing has a protective function. In Ezekiel 9:4-6 the foreheads of all the faithful are marked with a seal so that they will be spared the great tribulation. In Revelation the visionary scrolls are sealed; they are kept unalterable and secret. What does this say about baptism?

PART THREE

Church

CHAPTER SEVEN
❧ *Body*

1. Why is it important that a baptism not be a private affair, but instead be conducted with the whole congregation present?

2. The bodies of athletes have to be not only strong, but also well-coordinated. Is this a metaphor you can apply to the body of Christ?

3. When you think of the body of Christ, do you think primarily of your local parish church, your diocese or region, your denomination, or the whole of Christendom?

4. What does the notion of the body of Christ suggest about the presence of pain, suffering, and intercession in the congregation?

5. Which sort of church do you prefer—the churches of Paul's letters to the Corinthians, in which all are mutually interdependent, or the churches of Ephesians, which stresses the headship of Christ over all? How are both these views of the church valuable?

CHAPTER EIGHT

❧ *Covenant*

1. What kinds of covenants have you have made in your life? Have they been public or private, written or spoken? Have they been contracts, commitments, promises, or intentions?

2. What words or pictures come to mind when you think about being part of a "covenant people"? Is it an idea that makes sense to us today as citizens of a democratic society?

3. Some churches form prayer or covenant groups that promise to meet regularly. What do these covenants require on the part of those who make them?

4. One aspect of covenant renewal emphasizes the recalling of "holy history," the story of God's mighty works on behalf of the people. If you were to renew your baptismal covenant, what "mighty works" of God on your behalf would you want to remember?

5. In what ways do you feel you have a personal covenant with God, as well as the more public commitment of being part of the people of God?

CHAPTER NINE

✍ *Web*

1. What do you think of Charles Williams's idea that we can carry a friend's burden as easily and simply as we could lend a hand with the groceries?

2. We tend to think of emotions as purely personal, belonging only to us. What would it mean to carry someone else's burden of anxiety, sorrow, or rage? Does this suggest that in Christ nothing is personal or private?

3. Can you think of some simple exchanges or substitutions Christians could make for one another in order to carry out Paul's injunction to "bear one another's burdens and so fulfill the law of Christ"?

CONCLUSION

✍ *A Royal Priesthood*

1. Micks notes that the words of greeting to the newly baptized, "share with us in his eternal priesthood," are puzzling words. What do you think sharing in Christ's priesthood means?

2. Do you think of yourself as a minister of the church? In what ways do you see yourself as a minister?

3. Ministry can be offered by every baptized Christian, even the very young and very old. Can you remember times when you witnessed or received the ministry of those you did not expect to be ministers?

4. What ministries connected to worship do you see happening in your church?

5. Daniel B. Stevick describes baptism as including "the commitments of Christian life." In what ways has your baptism been a "commissioning for ministry"? Provided "strength for spiritual combat"? Been "a sacrament of childhood and maturity"? Set you "within the people of God, the holy priesthood"?

6. What do you think it means that "the bond which God establishes in Baptism is indissoluble"? Can you think of times or ways in which the bond would dissolve? Are there other bonds in our lives that are indissoluble?

Cowley Publications is a ministry of the Society of St. John the Evangelist, a religious community for men in the Episcopal Church. Emerging from the Society's tradition of prayer, theological reflection, and diversity of mission, the press is centered in the rich heritage of the Anglican Communion.

Cowley Publications seeks to provide books, audio cassettes, and other resources for the ongoing theological exploration and spiritual development of the Episcopal Church and others in the body of Christ. To this end, it is dedicated to developing a new generation of theological writers, encouraging them to produce timely, creative, and stimulating publications of excellence, and making these publications available widely, reaching both clergy and lay persons.